7-31-51

A TREASURY OF
WESTERN FOLKLORE

BOOKS BY B. A. BOTKIN

THE AMERICAN PLAY-PARTY SONG *(Out of print)*

Edited:

FOLK-SAY: A REGIONAL MISCELLANY, 1929 *(Out of print)*, 1930, 1931, 1932 *(University of Oklahoma Press)*

LAY MY BURDEN DOWN: A FOLK HISTORY OF SLAVERY *(University of Chicago Press)*

A TREASURY OF AMERICAN FOLKLORE

A TREASURY OF NEW ENGLAND FOLKLORE

A TREASURY OF SOUTHERN FOLKLORE

THE POCKET TREASURY OF AMERICAN FOLKLORE

A TREASURY OF WESTERN FOLKLORE

In Preparation:

A TREASURY OF MIDWEST FOLKLORE

A TREASURY OF WESTERN FOLKLORE

EDITED BY B. A. BOTKIN

Foreword by

BERNARD DEVOTO

For these States tend inland and toward the Western sea, and I will also.

—Walt Whitman

CROWN PUBLISHERS, INC. · NEW YORK

LIBRARY OF CONGRESS CATALOG CARD NUMBER 51-12013

PRINTED IN THE UNITED STATES OF AMERICA

ACKNOWLEDGMENTS

The editor and publishers wish to thank the following authors or their representatives, folklore societies, publishers, and publications for their kind permission to use material in this book. Full copyright notices are given on the pages on which the material appears.

J. Cecil Alter; American Book Co.; American Folklore Society, Inc.; *The American Magazine;* Appleton-Century-Crofts, Inc.; *Arizona Highways;* Automobile Club of Southern California; R. G. Bailey Printing Co.; Mody C. Boatright; The Bobbs-Merrill Co., Inc.; Rudolf Bretz; Verne Bright; Arthur L. Campa; W. S. Campbell; Pete Cantos; The Caxton Printers, Ltd.; The Arthur H. Clark Co.; Neil McCullough Clark; Columbia University Press; Mrs. Courtney R. Cooper; Robert G. Cowan; Sidney Robertson Cowell; Kyle Crichton; Thomas Y. Crowell Co.; John H. Culley; Current Books, Inc.; Curtis Publishing Co.; Levette J. Davidson; Everett Dick; Oliver Ditson Co.; J. Frank Dobie; Dodd, Mead & Co., Inc.; Edward Arthur Dolph; Dorrance & Co., Inc.; Doubleday & Co., Inc.; Duell, Sloan & Pearce, Inc.; E. P. Dutton & Co., Inc.; Duncan Emrich; Sam Eskin; Joe M. Evans; Alta M. and Austin E. Fife; Samuel French; Lemuel A. Garrison; Archer B. Gilfillan; John Gross; Grossett & Dunlap, Inc.; Alice S. Gunter; Woody Guthrie; LeRoy R. Hafen; Harcourt, Brace & Co., Inc.; Harper & Brothers; Harvard University Press; Hastings House Publishers, Inc.; Adelaide Hawes; Stewart H. Holbrook; Henry Holt & Co., Inc.; Houghton Mifflin Co.; Frank M. King; Alfred A. Knopf, Inc.; Winifred Kupper; Stuart N. Lake; J. B. Lippincott Co.; Little, Brown & Co.; Mrs. Frank C. Lockwood; Ruby Terrill Lomax; Michael Loring; The Macmillan Co.; Meador Publishing Co.; H. G. Merriam; George R. Miller; William Morrow & Co., Inc.; Nolie Mumey; Debs Myers; Native Sons of the Golden West, Arrowhead Parlor No. 110; The Naylor Co.; New York *Herald Tribune;* W. W. Norton & Co., Inc.; Oklahoma Historical Society; Oxford University Press, Inc.; Paull-Pioneer Music Corp.; G. P. Putnam's Sons; William MacLeod Raine; Random House, Inc.; Rinehart & Co., Inc.; Roy Rogers Enterprises; Will Rogers, Jr.; *The Saturday Review of Literature;* Charles Scribner's Sons; Charles Seegar; Clara R. Skinner; William Sloan Associates, Inc.; *Southwest Review;* Stanford University Press; James Stevens; Texas Folk-Lore Society; *Time,* The Weekly Newsmagazine; *Times-Mirror Press;* Trail's End Publishing Co.; Trendle-Campbell Enterprises, Inc.; University of Arizona Press; University of California Press; University of Chicago Press; University of Minnesota Press; University of New Mexico Press; University of Oklahoma Press; University of Pennsylvania Press; Vanguard Press, Inc.; The Viking Press, Inc.; The Westerners (Chicago Corral and Denver Posse); Mrs. Rufus Rockwell Wilson; World Book Co., Publishers; Yale University Press.

An exhaustive effort has been made to locate all persons having any rights or interests in material, and to clear reprint permissions. If any required acknowledgments have been omitted or any rights overlooked, it is by accident and forgiveness is desired.

The title page illustration is from Frederic Remington's *Pony Tracks,* Harper & Brothers, 1895, reprinted by Long's College Book Co., 1951.

Foreword

We devoutly believe many things about the American sections and the people who live in them that mean nothing in particular. What is "a real Southerner" or "a typical Middle Westerner"? Everybody knows, everybody specifies eagerly and in detail, and for the most part everybody is just talking. There must be differences or at least differentiations, but they are hard to isolate and harder to define. An old cliché, not often heard any more, held that Boston was a state of mind. It was probably true: the differences are to be found, if anywhere, in the habit or the pattern of thought. But they must originate in exceedingly faint shadings or colorations, and probably they exist rather below thought than in its conscious processes. Though minute, they must be complex, for they are the products of many forces.

A good place to look for them may be the stories people tell about themselves. We must, however, be exceedingly careful if we decide to follow that lead, for the obvious thing may be deceptive and indeed formal literature may be less reliable than the underlying strata of sub-literature. If you travel across rural Wisconsin, for instance, you will be constantly struck by the beauty of the land, the rich plenty of the farms, the multiform evidence of ease and comfort and security. Here is probably the freest, most vigorous, most rewarding rural life in all the United States. Here the wilderness has been made the Land of Canaan. Allowing for all the failure, bitterness, and defeat which necessarily accompanied that transformation, the countryside itself constantly proclaims human achievement. Surely, one thinks, surely the basic story to which the Wisconsin novelist grows up, the story to which he was born and in the midst of which he spent his formative years, is one of triumph. And yet from the Grangerite Hamlin Garland, through Zona Gale, down to the latest young man out of Madison desperately trying to appear more decadent than the smudge of barnyard manure on his rope-soled sandals will permit, the Wisconsin story of our fiction has been frustration.

Now travel across the vast emptiness of Wyoming and Montana. All about you is the unmistakable evidence of frustration—of the defeat to which hope and labor came. Surely the basic story here, the story instinctive to the Western novelist, one must decide, is human failure. Surely. And yet the Western writer for the most part produces the sun-god story, with an all-conquering hero riding the open range in a freedom and with a triumph enjoyed by no lesser myths, pistol-whipping sheriffs by the half-dozen, shooting rustlers by the score, and overcoming the merely formal reluctance of all women whenever there may be no chairs to hurl at suborned second heavies. . . . Yes, we had better pick our way carefully through the evidence fiction offers us.

Well, everybody knows that the West is the Land of Little Rain, the arid country, where land will not grow crops unless it is irrigated, where water has exactly the value of blood. So the West begins where the annual rainfall drops below twenty inches, roughly the hundredth meridian. East of 100° is something else but west of it is assuredly West. Glance therefore at North Platte, Nebraska, and Pierre, South Dakota. They are both west of that line, they get about the same amount of rain, they ship about the same number of steers. But Pierre is West and North Platte isn't. A large area of Washington gets eighty inches of rain, some of it gets one hundred and twenty inches, but it would be injudicious to tell the people who live there that they are not Westerners. What about the western slope of California, that fascinating state of mind which tries so diligently to be an improved Texas? San Francisco gets thirty inches of rain: are its people Westerners? All Montana, whose people certainly are, shouts "No!" in concert. But, aware that many signal though deserved favors of providence set it apart from other towns, San Francisco nevertheless counts as foremost among them the fact that it is West. It is thinking accurately. For, stranger, San Francisco is West as all hell.

The West is the largest and the youngest of the sections—and the most paradoxical. Like this: Mount Whitney is the highest place in the United States and from its tip you can look into Death Valley, the lowest place. Or take that adjective "youngest." To any candid mind New Mexico is not only younger than, say, Pennsylvania, it is younger than Oregon or Colorado. Yet it has a continuity of more than three hundred years; it was traversed by white men long before Cape Ann was, it was both massacring and Christianizing Indians long before the Plymouth Company ever saw one, and it was producing scholars and old families long before Virginia ever bred up a single one. Or this: the South is not the section most imprisoned in its own history, the West is, and yet it has less history than any other section.

Such as it has is pretty violent. History is a social expression of geography and Western geography is violent. The West has all the deserts in the United States and most of the mountain ranges, all the big ones. They are all mixed together. Snowcapped peaks rise from alkali or greasewood plains, an hour's climb will take you from lizards to lichens, an hour's drive from sunstroke to a blizzard. Or look at it the other way: an irrigation canal runs along a hillside and fifty feet above it you are in cactus and fifty feet below it in an orchard growing better peaches than Georgia ever knew. It follows that the climate is violent. All the places in the United States where temperatures below –60° have been recorded are in Montana, all those where temperatures above 120° have been recorded are in Arizona. It is a country of blizzards, cloudbursts, northers, chinooks, every kind of sudden storm, of floods, landslides, mudflows, even earthquakes, and the U. S. volcano is Western. Watch out when you cross a dry gulch. You may be fifty miles from a spring and the sun may be drying the marrow from your bones, but also the arroyo may be about to bury you under an advancing wall of water thirty feet high, from a storm so far away you didn't hear any thunder. On the north side of this valley, carefully inspect your body for ticks; on the south side never mind, the ticks don't carry Rocky Mountain Fever. The camas with the blue flower will save you from starvation; the one with the white flower will poison you.

From the beginning the American pioneer was an adaptable person—he had to be—but till he reached the West he had never had to meet such contrasts and intensities as these. "Hardship" is a subjective word, and it had not been fun to die of starvation at Roanoke or of "the milk sick" at New Salem. But the West was the hardest country to bring it. It was actively, not merely passively, hostile to men. To trust it was always foolish and usually fatal. Beauty could be treacherous and cruel, majesty could be murderous, and a fixed condition of life was the threat of destruction by natural cataclysm. You could love such a country but you were bound to hate it, too—and the splits in the Western soul begin right here. With finding water before we can camp tonight. With a blizzard getting the herd and a freeze getting the apples. With corn ceasing to grow at twelve inches because there has been no rain since April 28. With billions of crickets coming down out of the foothills and settling on the wheat.

Moreover, it was a long time before anyone got into the West who intended to stay there. If it was a violent country, it was treated violently. It was raped more brutally than any other section. Clean out the beaver and go back to the States. Clear-cut the timber and move on. When the grass is gone, there'll be plenty somewhere else. Beaver, timber, grass were all wealth and seemed inexhaustible. So it was a bonanza country, so it was a boom country, so it was always a country going broke. The true Western stampede is not the thundering herd but the placer miners—frenzied, dreambound and nightmare-led, herd-minded, violent, and at the end of the grubstake. You might make a strike—so take a chance, back your hunch, shoot the moon. . . . Hell will be more beautiful and more productive than the valley of a stream that has been placer-mined. So a dredge comes in and makes it worse.

The boom-or-bust psychology is not specifically the miner's, it is Western. Beef is down and you're in hock to the bank (till a few years ago twelve percent was the usual interest on loans, twenty percent not uncommon) but next year beef will be up, so slap on another mortgage and buy yearlings. This drought can't last forever, so raise a loan somehow and plant more wheat, and next year we'll be riding in Cadillacs. Back your hunch, you'll be able to get out before the bust—and a Western proverb remarks that it takes three bankruptcies to make a farm. A drought makes the Dust Bowl out of wheat farms that should have been cattle ranges and everybody goes broke. The East bails out the West, the Soil Conservation Service teaches the farmers how to stay solvent through the next drought, everybody gets religion—and when the wet half of the cycle coincides with the war boom in farm produce, the Soil Conservation Districts get voted out of existence and everybody backslides and plants wheat. That's Western, pardner, but not so Western as the satchel-farmer who under the same stimulus plowed ranges that never had been plowed, knowing that the unstable soil thus loosened would soon blow away but counting on getting out before another Dust Bowl formed.

All men find out they are fools. In the West, necessarily, they made that discovery with the dramatic violence inherent in the country. The by now tired symbol is the covered wagon that heads west lettered "Pike's Peak or Bust" and comes back lettered "Busted, by God." But make the whitetop an emigrant wagon and see it stalled in some stretch of red-rock desert, the wheels buckled, the tongue snapped off, and two of the three ox teams bloated and dying from alkali water. Or transpose it into the crumbling shacks of a ghost town where the last dust has been washed from Bonanza Bar and a few veterans too broke to move on are panning the worthless gravel once more. Or think of Pete, Jens, or Emil with nothing but a foreclosure-notice in his wallet, watching one more set of false rain clouds pile high above the peak before loading the kids in a borrowed wagon and driving off down the road. An indigenous Western expletive runs, "Well, I'll be go to hell!" We arrive at one of those faint colorations: part of the Western consciousness is the self-derision of a man who has shot the moon and missed.

Presently that exasperation got a second edge, for the West turned out to belong to the East. The Westerner had been so intent on chasing his mirage, on filling his straight and cashing in, that more realistic people had jumped his claim. Westerners were just hired hands, principals in a gaudy drama that might be called "The Rapers Raped." They were in hock not only to the bank but to the railroad, the grain elevator, the water company, and a lot of shrewd gents who borrowed Eastern money at three or four percent, lent it to them at twelve or fifteen, and took over. They were cutting a corporation's timber, running a corporation's herd, mining a corporation's ore, harvesting a corporation's wheat. Eastern corporations, which piped the West's wealth east and thereby got their directors the nation's applause as Empire Builders. Already aware that he had missed the moon, the Westerner now understood that the cartridges he had been shooting with were blanks. What recourse has a doubly self-exposed sucker got? He can make himself the butt of his own sardonic joke, and he can seek compensation in splendid dramas that confer the hero's role on him. With the first he can immunize himself against the laughter of others, and though the second will not take in many of the home folks maybe strangers will fall for it.

The story of the cowboy-culture-hero, in fact, is hardly even compensation; it is mainly the blue-sky ad of a wildcat mining company. The West knows well enough that New Mexico or Montana novelists alone kill off more sheriffs every year than the Cattle Kingdom managed to kill during its whole history, that badmen were always scarcer than white buffalo in the historic West, that neither the rancher nor the drug clerk of today has got a six-gun on his hip even spiritually. But the cowpoke story is nevertheless true to the West in one respect: gunfire *is* violent. And in the stories which the West has always told itself, the shading or coloration that makes them Western is usually twofold. Usually there is an element of violence, which may be not overt but latent or perhaps only conceptual, and usually there is an element of fantasy, which may be apparent at first glance but is just as likely to be hidden deep down at the roots. The Western story tends to depersonalize man, and why not?—drought, blizzards, scalping do, the vast and empty landscape does. Or it tends to cut him down to size, quite a way down. It tends to be a joke on the protagonist, though there is no requirement that the joke be funny. The Westerner lives in the West, and a man seen making his way across a sagebrush desert rimmed at the horizon by mile-high peaks lacks stature. If he can't see himself in scale the story-teller can and has been there himself. A tragic figure, this thirsty, sun-baked wanderer in barren space? No, not tragic; on so small a scale there can't be tragedy.

Humor is a good index. In the humor of all other sections one basic situation is the sly yokel outwitting the city slicker who had taken him for a simpleton. For generations this fable has caressed the self-esteem of rural populations, but it does not often turn up in the West. There are no Western yokels—I should have said earlier that it is the most cosmopolitan section and probably the most sophisticated—and if there were yokels they would still be Westerners. That is, men who have found out that both nature and the United States sold them a salted claim. Western humor is thus self-depreciatory. It is also extreme, bizarre, grotesque, thunderous—or understated, oblique, ironical, paradoxical. But violent and out of fantasy. The liquor that was called forty-rod farther east is tarantula juice or Taos lightning here—extreme, from nature's hostility, with a tinge of remorselessness. Or take the judge's sentence at the end of a traditional yarn that is four-sevenths historical fact: "Alfred Packer, you black-hearted Republican cannibal, stand up. I sentence you to be hanged by the neck until you are dead. Why, you conscienceless and debased enemy of society, there was only six Democrats in Hinsdale County and, by God, you've et five of them." It has impact and it ought to, for it pivots on murder and cannibalism. But observe that the punishment is for political activity.

Both strains were strengthened by the inheritance from the Indians. They were the earliest Westerners, and the firstcomers from the East, setting the pattern, treated them in precisely the way they themselves were to be treated by the East when their time came. They took the country away from the people who thought they owned it, with more bloodshed than the East was to inflict on them but hardly with greater violence, and felt superior to the suckers they had thus displaced. There is much cruelty in the Indian's stories, cruelty as a force of nature and the condition of life. And an Indian story is always fantasy: dream and reality are the same substance, no distinction can be made between them, for no difference exists. That is perfectly harmonious with the Western setting—vindictive toward mankind and, if beautiful, so fantastic, so improbable, that it may well be dream. The Western bestiary, too, has a strong Indian coloration, very fashionable on the upper levels of Western literature just now, for Greenwich Village has been erected on the West's campuses after a forty-year hiatus elsewhere, and the extremity of advanced art is to find hawks and cougars more admirable than men, though the Indian only found them interchangeable. The involved, rather clumsy mechanism of metaphor which was the Indian's medium of abstract thought has provided the white brother with a few symbols. Indian humor, which is on a wave length that seldom wakes laughter in white men and is unbelievably obscene, has made little communication, and the Indian comic hero has made none.

We may see the bulk of Western literature, and especially of the sub-literature that is more instinctive and nearer the heart, as the discharge or resolution of strains so great that they can only just be borne. Feeling his personality shrunk to miniature size by the enormousness in which he lives, surviving his country's hostility only in a battle that may be a tie to date but goes on under constant threat of his annihilation, aware that all the con-men in the United States have sold him gold bricks and all the note-shavers have defrauded him, aware that he will never lick his inborn compulsion to pursue mirages which he knows are false but just this once may lead to the real bonanza—the Westerner has shaped his literature to a therapeutic purpose. In outline it is confession by avoidance, and usually it is self-derisive. If any of it appears to be simple, do not be deceived. The consciousness it expresses is complex, the basic pattern is intricate, the symbols are convoluted. The violence cannot be separated out from the fantasy, nor either of them from the inner derision. No doubt it is an admission of defeat but what literature is not? And the self-scorn with which the admission is made is at the opposite pole from self-pity. A man who is laughing at himself is secure against the cruder indecencies of fate, and if he is not a tragic figure, he has dignity.

And there remains something very solacing to Westerners, who have paid high to become connoisseurs of the double-cross. Presumably the Texans would not consider it ridiculous but only their just due if the United States at large were to accept at par their insistent advertising of their own, alleged, virility. They miss something the West greatly relishes, the second and more subtle point of a joke. Of the symbols of American experience that are heavily charged with emotion and capable of instantly arousing it, a disproportionate number are Western. List a few of them: the trapper (the West's variant of the man in buckskin), the Forty-Niner, the prospector, and always and especially the cowboy. That Hollywood has sentimentalized these images is unimportant; what matters is that serious literature has romanticized them. It has deputized them to stand for magnificences which the West knows all too sardonically never existed. They do not fail to rouse emotion in the Western soul, but it is a realistic emotion associated with desperately hard ways of making a living. Take the batwing chaps, which are seldom worn now, since we don't often run steers and when we do, use a Ford. Originally and functionally they were work clothes, a fairly good way of protecting your legs from brush. The Westerner wears them as a holiday costume nowadays—but if the dudes want to take them as symbolic of the gallant caballero's adventurous life, well I'll be go to hell!

It reverses the joke. In addition it creates an opportunity to cash in, to get back some of the money that the system so efficiently funnels eastward. (Irrigating is desperately hard work, too, but if a half-billion-dollar dam will symbolize American Achievement to dudes willing to pay high for Achievement out of their own pockets, we can readily Work Miracles out West.) But most of all, the dude's eagerness to romanticize Western trades and business is emancipating. It sanctions the Westerner to act out his magnificent fantasy not only artfully, not only derisively, but with the heady knowledge that he is getting away with it. He can put on his picturesque costume, get out in front of his spectacularly improbable backdrop, and be admired as the gallant caballero though he knows in his heart that he is just a hired man and underpaid at that. For the duration of the drama, or at least of the dude's illusion, he can carry Sam Colt's equalizer on his hip, swagger as one ready to spit in any man's eye, and bid you smile, stranger, when you say that. As a rule you can't talk that way to a stranger who owns your horse and batwing chaps and holds a chattel mortgage on the equalizer, but if he succumbs to your private fantasy, shoot the moon.

BERNARD DEVOTO

Cambridge, Massachusetts

Contents

Part Two: The West Begins

I. QUEER COUNTRY

II. WESTWARD JOURNEY

Part Three: Taming the West

I. Red Men and White

II. "Law and Order, Ltd."

Part Four: The Changing West

II. Cowboys

III. Herders

IV. Settlers

Introduction

This book is the third in a series of regional folklore collections of the United States. It deals with the traditions and folkways, the songs and stories, both in and out of print, of the people of the Great Plains and the Far West—the meeting place and melting pot of North, East, South, and West. In general conception and design, the book follows the pattern of its predecessors. It treats folklore as an imaginative expression that is a part of, not apart from, the main stream of culture in a given time and place. By thus relating the lore to ways of living, ways of making a living, and ways of looking at life, the book aims to give a folk's eye view of the region—the land, the people, and their history.

From this point of view, the folk is as important as the lore, and no sharp distinction is drawn between literature *of* and *about* the folk. The criterion of selection is a dual one: Does the material contain traditional elements of theme, motif, symbol, character, idiom, and style? Does it tell us something interesting and important about the character of the people involved?

The present volume differs somewhat from earlier volumes in the series. Instead of separate sections of "Beliefs and Customs" and "Word Lore," as in *A Treasury of New England Folklore* and *A Treasury of Southern Folklore,* the reader will find folkways and folksay interspersed throughout, especially as embodied in songs and stories. Reflecting the nature of Western expansion, migration, and settlement, the material follows roughly the history of the West and, within the historical framework, a loosely geographical order. This flow is inherent in the dynamic view of folklore as the stuff that travels and the stuff that sticks, nowhere better demonstrated than in the West, with its interplay of the desire to keep moving and the desire to stay put.

As in previous volumes, the emphasis (for reasons of space and scope) is on the Anglo-American and English-speaking tradition, but not to the exclusion of the Indian and Spanish-speaking folk. Here the Indian appears chiefly in connection with Indian-white relations, and the Spanish-American and Mexican in their contributions to regional food and occupational lore and folksay. Indian myth and Spanish-American folk literature as such do not fall within the scope of the book. However, a sampling of Indian and Spanish-American tales and legends and a handful of Spanish-American songs have been included.

Throughout, preference is given to Western lore that has entered into the tradition of the region and the nation as a whole. As a result, purely local items of place and place-name lore have been kept to a minimum.

Three kinds of printed sources have been used to supplement oral sources. (The latter are particularly prominent in the songs, the majority of which have been transcribed from recordings.) These are the literature of folklore collection and research, regular literature, and subliterature, such as guidebooks, dime novels, and diaries. Wherever I have drawn upon professional story-tellers and humorists, from Mark Twain to Will Rogers, I have done so because they are good story-tellers as well as folk artists. Although no systematic coverage of the rich regional literature and native humor of the West has been attempted, local-color and dialect writings have been sampled.

In point of time the Westerner is closer to his historical past than other Americans. As a result, history and folklore often overlap. If a sharp line between the two is not drawn, it is for the reason given by J. Frank Dobie in "The Line That Travis Drew": "What makes history, whether authenticated or legendary, live is that part of it that appeals to the imagination. . . . Not everything orally transmitted is *mere* legend; there is traditional history as well as traditional folklore."

The "West" of this book is the trans-Missouri West of the Northern and Southern Great Plains, the Rocky Mountains, the Great Basin or intermountain region, and the Pacific Coast (including both the Oregon-Washington North and the California South). Covering as it does both Southwest and Northwest, the book is actually two volumes in one and has the advantage of an over-all view of the region. If the Southwest (including parts of Colorado and California) bulks larger in the total picture, it is because the Southwest, with its strong infusion of Southern and Spanish traditions, bulks large in the American folk imagination.

The structure of the book has been made as simple and logical as possible. Part One, "The Western Brand," attempts to answer the first two questions that occur to any one approaching the region: What is the Westerner like ("As Big as All Outdoors") and how did he get that way ("A Fresh Deal All Round")? Part Two, "The West Begins," attempts to show how Easterners got to the West ("Westward Journey") and what they found there ("Queer Country"). Part Three, "Taming the West," deals with the subduing of the Wild West of wild Indians ("Red Men and White") and wild men ("Law and Order, Ltd."). Part Four, "The Changing West," covers approximately a hundred years of Western development, in the course of which the Old West became the New West and the Easterner was Westernized and then partially Easternized again. In Parts Five and Six, the land, the people, and the experience flower in "Western Story-Tellers" and "Western Songs and Ballads," respectively.

In a complex collection of this size and nature, the reader is bound to miss certain favorites. If he does not find them where he expects to find them, he is urged to look elsewhere in the text, in the sectional introductions, or, failing both, in the footnotes, with their cross references to other Western material (not duplicated here) in *A Treasury of American Folklore*. Many pieces, alas, originally scheduled for inclusion, had later to be omitted to make room for others.

I spent the summer of 1950 traveling in eight Western states, interviewing librarians, historians, and folklorists, making recordings, and sampling the rich folklore resources of Western libraries, historical societies, and universities. As a former Oklahoman by adoption, I felt that I had come home again. But as a Bostonian by birth and a Yorker by present residence, I felt that I was still pretty much of a dude. And if the book succeeds in communicating some of the excitement and humanity of Western folk and folklore that have inspired me ever since I first went to Oklahoma in 1921, I have some expert dude-wranglers among my Western friends to thank.

For assistance of one kind and degree or another, I want to thank the following hospitable and helpful Westerners: in Denver—Caroline Bancroft, Don and Marie Bloch, Arthur L. Campa, Louis Carter, Levette J. and Mary Davidson, Tom and Helen Ferril, LeRoy R. and Ann W. Hafen, Tom Harvey, Marjorie Kimmerle, Paula Mechau and her children, Vanni, Dorik, Duna, and Mike; in Salt Lake City—Kate B. Carter; Brewster Ghiselin; in Portland—Arthur Boose, Verne Bright, Howard McKinley Corning, John Gross, Nelson Hazeltine, Stewart H. Holbrook, Ben Hur Lampman, Michael Loring; in Seattle—Byron Fish, Ivar Haglund, James Stevens, Guy Williams; in Willows, California—Arlene Piper Clements and A. D. Piper; in Sacramento—Michael and Margaret Harrison, Agnes Wright Spring; in Berkeley—Woodrow Wilson Borah, Herbert O. Brayer, C. Grant Loomis, Carl Sauer; in San Francisco—Joseph Henry Jackson, Oscar Lewis; in Los Angeles—Joseph A. Brandt, Valentine Davies, Wayland D. Hand, John Storm, Elliot and Mildred Sweet, Carey McWilliams, Matt Weinstock, Arthur Woodward, Jake Zeitlin; in Phoenix—Bert Fireman, Al and Clarice Lehman, Joseph Miller; in Albuquerque—F. W. Baughman, Powell Boyd, Mr. and Mrs. Bill Brophy, Rubén Cobos, Erna Fergusson, F. M. Kercheville, T. M. Pearce, James Threlkeld; in Santa Fe—Ina Sizer Cassidy, Haniel and Helen Long, Mr. and Mrs. Robert McKinney; in Taos—John Candelario, Edward Donahoe, Willard Johnson, Doughbelly Price, Frank Waters.

Thanks are also due to Mody C. Boatright, the University of Texas; Mamie Meredith, the University of Nebraska; Desmond Powell, the University of Arizona; J. D. Robb, the University of New Mexico; to the English departments of the University of Denver and the University of Colorado; to singers Pete Cantos, Altadena, California, and Rudolf Bretz, Croton-on-Hudson, New York.

For valuable services and kind favors I am indebted to the following libraries and organizations: the Western Folklore Conference of the University of Denver; the Library of the State Historical Society of Colorado; the Western History Collection, Denver Public Library, and Alys Freeze; the Wyoming State Library and Mary Elizabeth Cody, Cheyenne; the Utah State Historical Society, the Church of the Latter Day Saints and A. W. Lund, the Daughters of Utah Pioneers, and the Utah Humanities Foundation, all of Salt Lake City; the Salt Lake City Public Library; the Portland Public Library; the Oregon Historical Society and Elise Beeh and Inez Haskell, Portland; the Seattle Public Library; the Library of the Seattle *Post Intelligencer;* the Pacific Northwest Collection of the University of Washington Library and Harry C. Bauer; the California State Library and Caroline Wenzel, Sacramento; the Sacramento Public Library; the Bancroft Library, University of California, and John Barr Tompkins; the San Francisco Public Library and Dolores Caddell; the Henry E. Huntington Library and Art Gallery, San Marino; the Los Angeles Public Library; the Library of the University of California in Los Angeles and Neal Harlow and Ed Carpenter, Jr., together with its William Andrews Clark Memorial Library and Richard H. Archer; the Libraries of the Los Angeles County Museum and the Southwest Museum and Ella Robinson, both of Los Angeles; the Arizona State Library, Phoenix; the Library of the Museum of New Mexico, Santa Fe.

Here at home I am under heavy obligations to the New York Public Library and its expert and accommodating Information and American History staffs, especially F. Ivor D. Avellino, Shirley Barker, and Sylvester Vigilante (to the last of whom I am grateful for bibliographical suggestions and the loan of material from his private library); the Columbia University Libraries; the Library of the New York Historical Society; the Library of Congress and its Archive of American Folk Song and Duncan Emrich and Rae Korson; the Library of the Department of the Interior and Paul Howard; the Croton Free Library; the Ossining Public Library.

I am also grateful to Ruth Crawford Seeger for serving as music consultant and for her excellent transcriptions; to Charles Seeger and Peggy Seeger for helping with the music; to Sam Eskin, for opening his folk song collection to me; to Evan Esar, for many helpful suggestions; to the Pageant Book Store, New York City, for locating and loaning material; to the editorial and production staff of Crown Publishers, especially Bertha Krantz for a bang-up job on copy, permissions, proofs, and indexing; to my daughter, Dorothy, for help; and, most important of all, to my wife, Gertrude F. Botkin, for the infinite pains and patience required by the laborious task of preparing the typescript and reading proof.

B. A. Botkin

Croton-on-Hudson, New York
October 9, 1951

PART ONE

The Western Brand

All America must have been much like this not so long ago when all this soil was new, and every one was led to hold himself as good as the next, or better.

—Russell Lord

On the Plains, history was telescoped. Indians now live who hunted with and even manufactured stone arrow-points. White men still breathe who began as buffalo hunters, turned cowboy when the bison vanished, plowed and reaped on farms with the first settlers, freighted goods to the new towns and made fortunes as frontier merchants, drilled oil-wells, dug mines, built factories as industrialists, and ended as financiers sitting behind mahogany desks in skyscrapers.

—Stanley Vestal

Introduction

IN the American folk imagination the West has come to stand for all the virtues (and some of their defects) of a free, adventurous, generous, rugged outdoor life in a new country. A young man's country, where he can grow up with it, without the past getting in the way of the present or the future. A big, open country, with room for all sorts and conditions of men, each of whom regards himself as good as (but seldom better than) the next man. Where folks can be good friends and neighbors with or without fences and in spite of distance. From neighborliness sprang democracy, which was "inevitable on the Plains, first because no one could be sure of making a go of it without the help of his neighbors, and secondly, because nobody could be compelled to help. It was too easy to pull out, skip, vamoose."[1]

The frontier—a civilization in the making and on the make—put a premium on mobility and versatility, of the kind illustrated by the Nebraska barber of the Seventies who could not be found at the saloon where he was sought because he had gone south of town to plaster a house.[2] A corollary of mobility was nomadism. "I was looking for a job when I got this one," said the oilfield worker. "I always keep one foot in the road." Another corollary is the feeling that, things being transient and conditions changing, it is the *man* that counts, judged not by what he says but by what he is and does. In adapting himself to change, a man had to make do or do without, and had to be able to "tough it through." He had to be ready for any emergency, equal to the occasion, and superior to circumstance—in other words, independent, and *big*, as big as all outdoors.

Because the open range, with its free grass and the "freedom of the great out-of-doors," most nearly approached a Western paradise on earth, and because the cowboy on his horse seemed the most self-sufficient and biggest-hearted being in the world, the cattle country and the ranch have put their brand on the character and code of the trans-Missouri West more clearly and permanently than any other of the several historical and geographical Wests.

If the West, as has been said of Texas, was "a good country for men and dogs but an awful hard place for oxen and women," then the cattle country was a man's (a he-man's and a bachelor's) country par excellence. The cowboy may have been only a "hired man on horseback," but all that he needed to become a cowman (in the days when there was plenty of unbranded cattle) was "a stout rope and a running iron." As a "man with guts and a horse," the cowboy was sure of himself and afraid of nothing and no one. His uncomplaining "cheerfulness," according to Philip Ashton Rollins, was probably the "mother

---

[1] Stanley Vestal, *Short Grass Country* (New York, 1941), p. 260.

[2] Everett Dick, *The Sod-House Frontier* (New York, 1937), p. 504.

of that quality sometimes known as 'Western breeziness,' "[3] which is compounded of casualness and "orneriness"—the latter in the sense not of "cultivated meanness" but of a refusal to admit discouragement or defeat.

One day at a rodeo, a bucker fell on his rider, pinning the cowboy to the earth. His friends ran out to save him, calling, "Take it easy. We'll help you up."

"Hell," the bronc-buster replied indignantly, "help the *horse* up. I'm still in the saddle."[4]

It was an inflexible rule of the cow camp that whoever complained about the "chuck" must do the cooking. Thus a fine sense of diplomacy dictated the cowboy's comment on the biscuits: "They are burnt on the bottom and top and raw in the middle, and salty as hell, but shore fine, just the way I like 'em."

Far better than chuck-wagon fare was range hospitality. "Howdy, partner, get down. Been to chuck?" was a traditional ranch salutation to the visitor. On the roundup, the "ranch that sent out the chuck-wagon fed all men free, as their men were fed by other chuck-wagons free."[5] A "grub-line rider" became the name for a "stray man" or "drifter" visiting, and eating, from ranch to ranch, exchanging sociability for hospitality, or a "starve-out" nester (perhaps a widower or a bachelor) who arrived just in time for a meal. Acceptance of hospitality carried with it the obligation of reciprocating or of cleaning up or of filling up the wood box. Hence the ranch house kitchen warnings:

If you can't wash dishes, don't eat.

If you are hungry, grab a plate;
You have my best wishes.
But jest before you pull your freight,
Be shore to wash the dishes.[6]

If the cattle country was democratic, it was also semi-feudal, and every man who wasn't a "pardner" was a "stranger" until he proved himself a friend. According to the code of cowboy chivalry, this meant making his intentions known on approaching another on the trail. Or, as in the case of the Virginian, he might have to prove to the local bully that he could "dish it out" as well as "take it." After that a man was accepted at his face value, and no questions asked ("You ought to get a job as a detective," an inquisitive stranger was rebuked; "then you could get *paid* for asking questions"[7]), and generally given the benefit of the doubt.

The friendliness of the West is part of its hospitality. In Oklahoma,

[3] *The Cowboy* (New York, 1922), p. 66.

[4] Stanley Vestal, *op. cit.*, p. 43.

[5] Evan G. Barnard, *A Rider of the Cherokee Strip* (Boston and New York, 1936), p. 49.

[6] "Montana Folkways," *Frontier and Midland*, Vol. 18 (Autumn, 1937), No. 1, p. 17.

[7] Stanley Vestal, *op. cit.* p. 256.

"one of the friendliest states in the Union" (according to Ernie Pyle) the taxi driver opens the front door for a single passenger so that they can sit together and talk.[8] In Kansas City, he asks: "You won't mind, friend, if we give the lady a lift on the way to the hotel, will you?"[9]

Traditionally a man of action—the strong, silent type—the Westerner makes every word, like every shot, count. If he prefers "violent assertion" to "calm statement," encouraged by a country where nature itself is apt to be exaggerated, he tends to boast when he has too little and to exaggerate downward or underestimate when he has too much. This dualism, plus the democratic love of puncturing affectation and taking pretense down a peg, holds the key to Western humor, from Mark Twain to Will Rogers.

If much of this humor is at the expense of the Easterner, that is because every tenderfoot has to be initiated or because every tourist is a natural sucker in the West, no matter how smart he may be back home.

> The people of the West are not particularly looking for some one to impose upon and tell silly fables to; but they are kind-hearted, and when they see that the tourist is disappointed unless he is "filled"—as is generally the case—they try to accommodate him.[10]

The same goes for selling the Easterner the myth of the West. In spite of increasing standardization and Easternizing, the West will always remain "different" and "typical" to the Easterner. And the Westerner will want to keep it so, not merely from sectional pride and loyalty but also to put back into circulation some of the money that Easterners have taken out of the West.[11] Since the Westerner is, after all, only a transplanted Easterner (as most of his social and political institutions are transplanted Eastern institutions—even his hospitality and chivalry being Southern and backwoods in origin), he remains a dude at heart, still clinging to the big hat and the cowboy boots; and the Eastern dude merely follows in a great tradition. Together the Eastern dudes and the Western dude-wranglers will keep alive the professional, commercial, and synthetic West—the "one West," according to Thomas Hornsby Ferril, "that refuses to end."[12]

In 1851 J. L. B. Soule wrote an editorial in the Terre Haute (Indiana) *Express* entitled "Go West, Young Man, Go West." Fourteen years later, Horace Greeley reprinted the editorial in the New York *Tribune* with the addition—"and grow up with the country." Greeley's enthusiasm for the West was doubtless stimulated by his "luck" in finding gold in a "salted mine" in Gregory Gulch. But long before the Soule-Greeley slogan, "Going West" has been a magnet for all people seeking new

---

[8] *Home Country* (New York, 1947), p. 88.
[9] See Ladd Haystead, below, p. 81.
[10] Charles F. Lummis, *A Tramp across the Continent* (New York, 1892), p. 108.
[11] Cf. Philip Ashton Rollins, *op. cit.*, pp. 86–88.
[12] *I Hate Thursday* (New York, 1946), p. 181.

opportunities and escape from the conventions and taboos of older, established societies—as far back as the Romantic movement and even the Renaissance in Europe, or, still earlier, if we may trust Vachel Lindsay, "since the hordes and their caravans stampeded across Asia in the days which are almost before history."[13] The refreshing, liberating, relaxing effect—spiritual as well as physical—of the Western country has its psychological and social counterpart in Western culture; and one of the most widespread and deep-rooted of Western cults and panaceas is the faith in the miracle-working "cure" effected by the social "climate," with its relative absence of artificial distinctions of caste and class. " 'Mister,' " wrote James W. Steele in 1882, "is the designation of a stranger; but if a borderer calls an individual 'Mister' after he has known him a week, it means that he does not particularly like him, to say the least."[14] "Sooner or later," laments Ladd Haystead in 1945, "the West will probably have all the evils of the rest of the country, including calling people 'Mister' instead of by their first names."[15]

Historical upsets settled and unsettled the West. "It takes three moves to settle a country," and history was telescoped by the superimposition upon one another of three distinct cultures—Indian, Spanish-American, and Anglo-American—as well as by the succession of a whole string of frontiers, including those of furs, gold, lumber, cattle, sheep, transportation, oil, and agriculture. The history and geography of these ethnic and occupational cultures has been a force for the diversification and distribution of the West's human and natural resources, resulting sometimes in a blend (as in the Spanish conquest of the Indian), sometimes in exploitation and extermination (as in the Anglo-American conquest of both) but always in a fascinating kaleidoscope of cultural contacts, conflicts, and interchanges.

The type and symbol of the frontier melting pot and kaleidoscope of the West is the mining camp, with its violent cataclysms and its chaotic mixture of ethnic groups and all sorts and conditions of men from North, East, South, and West. "A fresh deal all round" calls for drastic shifts and expedients rather than mere versatility. Bret Harte tells of the newly arrived emigrant who said to his friend, "If there isn't any gold, what are you going to do with these sluice-boxes?" "They will make first-class coffins," answered the friend, with the simple directness of a man who has calculated all his chances.[16] "Fertile in expedients," Harte comments, the Argonauts "twisted their failures into a certain sort of success." The newly arrived Reverend William Taylor, inquiring whether there were any ministers of the gospel or churches in San Francisco, was told: "Yes, we have one preacher, but preaching won't pay here, so he quit preaching and went

---

[13] Stephen Graham, *Tramping with a Poet in the Rockies* (London, 1922), p. 78.

[14] *Frontier Army Sketches* (Chicago, 1882), p. 50.

[15] *If the Prospect Pleases* (Norman, 1945), p. 182.

[16] *The Writings of Bret Harte,* Standard Library Edition (Boston and New York, 1896), Vol. II, p. xii.

to gambling. There is but one church in town, and that has been converted into a jail."[17]

The prospector has also put his stamp on the West—the mark of the luck-hunter, the boom-chaser, and the horizon-seeker. Where the passion is for the seeking rather than the mere finding, and where the dream of wealth is more important than the wealth itself, "mining camp psychology" has endowed the West with an "off again, on again, gone again, Finnegan" cycle of poor today, rich tomorrow, and broke again the next day. After the boom, the bust; and after the boom town and the mushroom town, the ghost town and the shack town. The luck of the mines and the gambling fever have enriched our language with luck-phrases that run the gamut of the gold rush itself—"Gold is where you find it," "Gold in them hills," down to bedrock, strike it rich, strike pay dirt, pan out, peter out.

After the pay streak has petered out and the gold fever subsided, land hunger still drives men west, in the vicious cycle of "raise more wheat and buy more land" and make more land to make more wheat. A new form of land-grabbing and land-skinning succeeds the miner's land-stripping. And a new gamble—"the United States government is betting you 160 acres of land that you can't live on it eight months."

Today the old-timer, who has lived to see the West pass through all stages of its development, seen the grass plowed up and turn to dust and the "black gold" flow where the dust blows, is less apt to think in terms of space and elbow room, like the homesteader who thought it was time to move when he saw the smoke of his neighbor's chimney. He thinks rather in terms of time and change, endings and new beginnings, like the frail, ailing pioneer looking at Oklahoma City for the last time and musing: "Big and pretty, but, hot damn, wouldn't it be fun to tear her down and start all over again!"

B. A. B.

---

[17] *California Life Illustrated* (New York, 1861), p. 16.

I. AS BIG AS ALL OUTDOORS

Wherever one found informality, unconventionality, a firm handclasp, an open door, a breezy rhetoric, an unrestrained manner, there was the West.

—CAREY MCWILLIAMS

A Man of Very Few Words

It seems that the cowboy had . . . worked for a very arrogant and very famous old ranchman . . . very arrogant . . . but as the cowboy told my friend, he "worked only half a day."

The morning after he had signed on, he happened to be near the ranch house when out came the arrogant old ranchman, his hair sticking up straight with the frost of dawn.

"Hey! Come over here, Bill!" he called.

Bill came.

"Bill, I want to explain something to you."

"Yes, sir—Mr. Trompee." We'll call the ancient ranchman Mr. Trompee.

"Bill, you're new around here, and I've got my own system, and anybody who wants to work for me has to learn that system. The point is, I'm a man of very few words, and I don't like to waste 'em, see?—A man of very few words. Now, any time you're around and I whistle, you come running, and I'll tell you what I want. Understand? Don't call, and don't just stand and look at me. When I whistle, you come running. I'm a man of very few words, and I don't like to waste 'em."

"And what did you say, Bill?" my friend inquired.

"Well, sir, I looked at him, and I said, 'Mr. Trompee, that's mighty interesting! Yes, sir, mighty interesting! I got exactly the same nature as you, Mr. Trompee. I'm a man of very few words, and I don't like to waste 'em. And when you whistle, Mr. Trompee, and I shake my head thisaway . . . why, that means, Mr. Trompee, I'm not coming.' "

From *Powder River, Let 'er Buck,* by Struthers Burt, p. 370. *The Rivers of America,* Editor, Constance Lindsay Skinner. Copyright, 1938, by Struthers Burt. New York and Toronto: Farrar & Rinehart, Inc.

Clothes and the Man

. . . [A] man . . . accosted [Old Man Shannon] on the streets of San Angelo [Texas,] one day and reproved him for his careless appearance.

"Look here, Mr. Shannon," he said, "you're a millionaire now. Why do you still go around looking like a sheepherder? Look at you, no socks, sloppy old pants, greasy hat. Why don't you *dress* like a man that owns two banks?"

"Aw," replied Old Man Shannon, "don't have to. Everybody knows who I am here. Don't have to dress to show what I've got."

A few months after this encounter, the same man met Old Man Shannon on the streets of St. Louis—same sockless state, same sloppy pants and greasy hat.

"Now, see here," he expostulated, "you're in a big city now, Mr. Shannon. You ought not to be seen like that."

"Aw," said Old Man Shannon, "nobody knows who I am here. Why not?"

"A Man Afoot Is No Man at All"

. . . In New Mexico . . . three or four young punchers rode their horses into a saloon when one of those overdressed Eastern drummers happened to be at the bar partaking of his after-dinner refreshment. Being considerably jostled by one of the horses, he complained bitterly to the bar-tender.

This bar-dog, an old stove-up former cowpuncher, glared at him a minute and came back in characteristic style with,

"What the hell y'u doin' in here afoot anyhow?"

From "Folk Characters of the Sheep Industry," by Winifred Kupper, *In the Shadow of History,* Texas Folk-Lore Society Publications No. XV, J. Frank Dobie, Mody C. Boatright, Harry H. Ransom, editors, pp. 99–100. Copyright, 1930, by the Texas Folk-Lore Society. Austin.

Often the legends of the early sheepman center on this theme of disreputable appearance. Wherever sheepmen of those days are talked of, the name of John M. Shannon of San Angelo crops up sooner or later. Old Man Shannon he is called, and legends have fallen thick around his name.—W. K.

From *Western Words: A Dictionary of the Range, Cow Camp and Trail,* by Ramon F. Adams, pp. 46–47. Copyright, 1944, by the University of Oklahoma Press. Norman.

Colt on Revolvers

Judge Williamson, or "Three-legged Willie," as he was familiarly called, was one of the early judges of Texas. In his court a lawyer by the name of Charlton started a point of law, and the court refused to admit the counsel's statement as sufficient proof.

"Your law, sir," said the judge; "give us the book and page, sir."

"This is my law, sir," said Charlton, pulling out a pistol, "and this, sir, is my book," drawing a bowie knife, "and that is the page," pointing the pistol toward the court.

"Your law is not good, sir," said the unruffled judge; "the proper authority is *Colt on Revolvers,*" and he brought a six-shooter instantly to bear on the head of the counsel, who dodged the point of the argument and turned to the jury.

When You Need a Gun

. . . [An] eminent divine from New England . . . traveling in Colorado for his health, one day went in search of a barber shop in a Western city, and on entering the establishment observed, it is said, a big double-barreled gun leaning against the wall. Having a constitutional awe of firearms, he hastily asked the barber if the gun was loaded. A half-shaved native, who occupied the chair, turned around his lather-beaten face and exclaimed,

"Stranger, ef you're in an all-fired hurry, you'll find a six-shooter what *is* loaded in my coat-tail pocket."

. . . An English tourist . . . proposed to visit Arkansas, and asked a citizen if he ought to provide himself with a revolver.

"Well," replied the citizen, "you mout not want one for a month, and you mout not want one for three months; but ef ever you did want one, you kin bet you'd want it almighty sudden!"

From *Bench and Bar,* A Complete Digest of the Wit, Humor, Asperities, and Amenities of the Law, by L. J. Bigelow, p. 280. New Edition, Greatly Enlarged. Entered according to Act of Congress, in the year 1871, by Harper & Brothers in the Office of the Librarian of Congress, at Washington. New York.

From *Camps in the Rockies,* Being a Narrative of Life on the Frontier, and Sport in the Rocky Mountains, with an Account of the Cattle Ranches of the West, by William A. Baillie-Grohman, p. 4. Copyright, 1882, by W. A. Baillie-Grohman. New York: Charles Scribner's Sons.

Everybody, or nearly everybody, has heard of these two old Western revolver stories of the divine and the English tourist.—W. A. B-G.

Old Cattleman

[Tom O'Connor] had deeds to scores of sections of lands and he owned ten thousand cattle on the prairies and in the brush, and now Old Tom O'Connor could no longer ride across the seas of grass and watch his cattle thrive. One day he told his boss, Pat Lambert, to take all hands out early next morning and bring in the biggest herd they could gather. To Pat Lambert, early morning always meant by four o'clock. After he and his hands had ridden out a ways, they stopped to wait for daylight. They rode hard and they rode far, and about an hour before sundown they drove a vast herd of mixed cattle to the holding and cutting grounds not far from the O'Connor ranch house. Bulls were challenging, cows were bawling, steers and stags were bellowing, calves were bleating. Heifers, yearlings, old moss-horned steers, all ages of cattle of both sexes, were milling about, their blended voices rising above the dust from their hoofs.

While some of the hands held the herd and others changed horses, Pat Lambert went into the room where Tom O'Connor lay on his bed.

"We made a big drag, Mr. Tom," he said.

"I hear them," Tom O'Connor replied. His voice was thin.

"What do you want me to do with them, Mr. Tom?"

"Nothing. Just hold them there. I'm dying, Pat, and I want to go out with natural music in my ears."

"Boss of the Plains"

There are thousands of cattle brands, many of them famous in the history of the cattle industry and in literature, but there is only one all-inclusive symbol of the West—the ten-gallon hat. There are famous boots, of course, but many brands and types; there are distinctive leather britches, saddles and horses of many varieties. But there's only one hat. In the West, throughout the whole cattle country, it's the "Stetson."

No other commercial article has had such a lasting effect on the habits and taste of the Westerner. And no other specific trade brand, with the possible exception of the Colt's six-shooter, has been so much a character in the literature of the region. The John B. Stetson hat is the Westerner's trade mark, his crowning glory.

From "The Writer and His Region," by J. Frank Dobie, *Southwest Review,* Spring, 1950, p. 7. Copyright, 1950, by the Southwest Review. Dallas, Texas: University Press in Dallas, Southern Methodist University.

By Lewis T. Nordyke. From *The Saturday Review of Literature,* Vol. XXV (May 16, 1942), No. 20, pp. 18–19. Copyright, 1942, by The Saturday Review Associates, Inc. New York.

The notion for a distinctive Western hat started struggling in the mind of John B. Stetson one day on a Colorado prairie. Stetson, son of a Philadelphia hatter, was going West in the 1860's to seek a cure for tuberculosis, the plague of hatters. He and a small group of companions, in a trek from St. Joseph, Missouri, to the Pike's Peak region, camped in the cold. Talk naturally turned to the subject of shelter, particularly the immediate need of a tent. Tents made of untanned animal skins were exceptionally unpleasant, and Stetson, being a hatter, happened to mention that a fur could be processed without tanning and that cloth could be made without weaving. His companions contested the statement and challenged Stetson to prove it.

With hatchet and improvised tools, Stetson used an age-old process of felting and converted fur from a rabbit skin into felt. The little square of soft fur felt amazed Stetson's companions. For amusement, he fashioned a hat which he considered the best head protector for the rigors of Western weather. It was a big hat, one that would protect a man from rain, sun, cold, wind, and even hail.

Stetson wore the hat and was the talk of the mining camps. Most of the talk was good-natured ridicule—but Stetson had his moment. A rough but handsome horseman rode about the camps one day. He saw the hat and wanted to try it on. Stetson handed over the hat and the horseman placed it on his head. The ex-hatter surveyed the picture. Here was a giant of a man—the Western type—in a silver-ornamented saddle on a spirited horse. Stetson liked the effect. The horseman did, too. He gave Stetson five dollars.

About a year later, after Stetson regained his health, he returned to Philadelphia and started making hats—just ordinary hats—which he peddled to the dealers. But the hatted horseman kept riding in Stetson's mind, and he groped for the reason. He looked at the horseman from stirrup to the big hat. For months the hatter fought poverty and worried about the hatted horseman. One night the whip cracked. The horseman looked like a cattle king, the boss of the plains.

Stetson knew the cattle business was gaining headway; he knew, too, that cattlemen didn't wear hats, at least any one particular kind of hat. The cattlemen were from every walk of life. Captain Richard King, founder of the King Ranch, which is still the nation's greatest land and cattle empire, was a steamboat captain and had spent his time during the Civil War running the federal blockade. There were no born cattlemen; the industry wasn't old enough. So Stetson reasoned that the cattle kings might be receptive to something new.

The hatter sat in his dark little upstairs shop at Seventh and Callowhill Street, and mulled over the idea of a hat for the cattle kings. He determined to gamble everything, including his credit and health, on the notion.

Stetson fashioned a big, natural-colored felt hat. The new hat pleased him, and he made a number of them. He named the hat "The Boss of the Plains." Then he sent out the hats as samples to dealers in the Southwest and West and invited orders.

Within three weeks the orders poured in; Stetson's big job became that of making enough hats. The Boss of the Plains caught the eye of the cattlemen; they needed in a hat the very things Stetson had needed when he made the hat for Colorado weather. Besides that, the hat looked good; it had a distinctive appearance. The Texas Rangers quickly adopted it. Dealers rushed orders and repeat orders, some of them sending cash and requesting preference. Within a year Stetson abandoned his Eastern trade and made only the Western hat. He built a 30 by 100 foot, three-story factory. And the big hats rolled out of Philadelphia.

About the time Stetson got his business going, the long-horns were plodding over the trail to the Northern markets, and within a short time the big hat was the one distinguishing thing about the cowman's dress. Moreover, it was the utility piece of the cowboy's wearing apparel. In case of emergency the cowboy carried oats or corn in the crown for his horse; many a cowboy climbed into almost inaccessible places, dipped up water in his hat, and carried it out to his horse; or cupped the brim and used it as his own drinking vessel. A prospector caught in the desert with a leaky canteen conserved his water by pouring it in his Stetson; a ranger caught in a forest fire buried himself in the ground, leaving only his face exposed. He covered his face with his Stetson; when rescuers found him, he was uninjured, but his hat was badly charred.

The Stetson was handy for fanning campfire into life, for blindfolding or whipping stubborn horses, for slapping ornery steers in the face, for fighting grass fires, for replacing broken window panes, for dummy, or actual, targets in gun fights. Then the cowboy brushed it with his elbow and wore it to town or to the Saturday night dance. A Stetson with a bullet hole in it has always been a prize possession with Westerners, and there's a common expression: "You can put a dozen bullet holes in a Stetson and it won't ravel." When you own a big Stetson you don't brag about how new it is but about how old it is. Many a Stetson has been in service twenty to thirty years and a hat that old is a prized family heirloom. A Stetson will take on weight and it will get to the point where you can smell it across the room, but you can't wear it out.

When he died at the age of 76 in 1906, Stetson was making hundreds of thousands of hats each year. Since that time the big 30-acre factory in Philadelphia has increased production to almost 4,000,000 John B. Stetsons annually, but the Boss of the Plains remains much the same as the first one. Saddles have changed. Methods of ranching have changed. Cowmen got out of the saddle and stepped into automobiles; now many a ranch has at least one airplane. Everything in the West of the 1870's and 1880's has changed—that is, except the J.B. and perhaps a few cuss-words.

The Stetson is perhaps the most popular character of Western fiction, and has appeared by trade name alone in much of the general literature of the country. A Western story would not be complete, or even plausible, without a few Stetsons every several pages. Will James rarely mentioned the hats of his cowboy characters because, he explained, he figured that everyone interested in reading a Western story knew that a big Stetson was just part of the cowboy.

"When You Call Me That, Smile!"

I left that company growing confidential over their leering stories, and I sought the saloon. It was very quiet and orderly. Beer in quart bottles at a dollar I had never met before; but saving its price, I found no complaint to make of it. Through folding doors I passed from the bar proper with its bottles and elk head back to the wall with its various tables. I saw a man sliding cards from a case, and across the table from him another man laying counters down. Near by was a second dealer pulling cards from the bottom of a pack, and opposite him a solemn old rustic piling and changing coins upon the cards which lay already exposed.

But now I heard a voice that drew my eyes to the far corner of the room.

"Why didn't you stay in Arizona?"

Harmless looking words as I write them down here. Yet at the sound of them I noticed the eyes of the others directed to that corner. What answer was given to them I did not hear, nor did I see who spoke. Then came another remark.

"Well, Arizona's no place for amatures."

This time the two card dealers that I stood near began to give a part of their attention to the group that sat in the corner. There was in me a desire to leave this room. So far my hours at Medicine Bow had seemed to glide beneath a sunshine of merriment, of easy-going jocularity. This was suddenly gone, like the wind changing to north in the middle of a warm day. But I stayed, being ashamed to go.

Five or six players sat over in the corner at a round table where counters were piled. Their eyes were close upon their cards, and one seemed to be dealing a card at a time to each, with pauses and betting between. Steve was there and the Virginian; the others were new faces.

"No place for amatures," repeated the voice; and now I saw that it was the dealer's. There was in his countenance the same ugliness that his words conveyed.

"Who's that talkin'?" said one of the men near me, in a low voice.

"Trampas."

"What's he?"

From *The Virginian*, by Owen Wister, pp. 26–30. Copyright, 1902, by The Macmillan Company. New York and London.

"Cow-puncher, bronco-buster, tin-horn, most anything."

"Who's he talkin' at?"

"Think it's the black-headed guy he's talkin' at."

"That ain't supposed to be safe, is it?"

"Guess we're all goin' to find out in a few minutes."

"Been trouble between 'em?"

"They've not met before. Trampas don't enjoy losin' to a stranger."

"Fello's from Arizona, y'u say?"

"No. Virginia. He's recently back from havin' a look at Arizona. Went down there last year for a change. Works for the Sunk Creek outfit." And then the dealer lowered his voice still further and said something in the other man's ear, causing him to grin. After which both of them looked at me.

There had been silence over in the corner; but now the man Trampas spoke again.

"*And* ten," said he, sliding out some chips from before him. Very strange it was to hear him, how he contrived to make those words a personal taunt. The Virginian was looking at his cards. He might have been deaf.

"*And* twenty," said the next player, easily.

The next threw his cards down.

It was now the Virginian's turn to bet, or leave the game, and he did not speak at once.

Therefore Trampas spoke. "Your bet, you son-of-a——."

The Virginian's pistol came out, and his hand lay on the table, holding it unaimed. And with a voice as gentle as ever, the voice that sounded almost like a caress, but drawling a very little more than usual, so that there was almost a space between each word, he issued his orders to the man Trampas:—

"When you call me that, *smile*." And he looked at Trampas across the table.

Yes, the voice was gentle. But in my ears it seemed as if somewhere the bell of death was ringing; and silence, like a stroke, fell on the large room. All men present, as if by some magnetic current, had become aware of this crisis. In my ignorance, and the total stoppage of my thoughts, I stood stock-still, and noticed various people crouching, or shifting their positions.

"Sit quiet," said the dealer, scornfully to the man near me. "Can't you see he don't want to push trouble? He has handed Trampas the choice to back down or draw his steel."

Then, with equal suddenness and ease, the room came out of its strangeness. Voices and cards, the click of chips, the puff of tobacco, glasses lifted to drink,—this level of smooth relaxation hinted no more plainly of what lay beneath than does the surface tell the depth of the sea.

For Trampas had made his choice. And that choice was not to "draw his steel." If it was knowledge that he sought, he had found it, and no mistake! We heard no further reference to what he had been pleased to style "amatures." In no company would the black-headed man who had visited Arizona be rated a novice at the cool art of self-preservation.

Cow Camp Rule

I[1]

You know the rules in a cow camp when they have no regular cook. When anybody complains about the chuck they have to do the cooking. One cowboy broke a biscuit open and he says, "They are burnt on the bottom and top and raw in the middle and salty as hell, but shore fine, just the way I like 'em."

II[2]

Uncle Ike Hubbard was once eating supper at the roundup wagon and at the same time complaining about the grub. Finally the cook got so sore that he became quite sarcastic.

"Do you think you kin manage to eat the biscuits, Uncle Ike," said he with strained sweetness, "or shall I throw 'em out and try makin' up another batch?"

"They hain't so bad," answered Uncle Ike. "If you put a lot o' this butter on 'em you can't taste 'em quite so much. Course you kin taste the butter, but then I'm purty strong myself, as the feller said, and anyhow your coffee's weak enough to bring up th' general average."

The Best He Had

Western hospitality prevails; it is reminiscent of the kind displayed earlier here by a host who said to an unexpected guest, "Stranger, you take the wolf skin and the chaw o' sowbelly— I'll rough it."

Drunkard's Rights

In the early days it was really remarkable how much common sense if not common law was expressed by the Western courts with prac-

---

1 From *A Corral Full of Stories*, rounded up by Joe M. Evans, page 48. Copyright, 1939, by Joe M. Evans. El Paso, Texas: Printed by the McMath Company, Inc.

2 From *Cow Country*, by Edward Everett Dale, p. 144. Copyright, 1942, by the University of Oklahoma Press. Norman. 1945.

From *Texas, A Guide to the Lone Star State*, Compiled by Workers of the Writers' Program of the Work Projects Administration in the State of Texas, p. 485. Sponsored and copyright, 1940, by Texas State Highway Commission. New York: Hastings House, Publishers.

From "Justice in Montana," by former Chief Justice Howard A. Johnson, *The Westerners Brand Book*, Vol. V (May, 1948), No. 3, p. 20. Chicago, Illinois: Issued monthly as the official publication of the Chicago Corral of Westerners.

tically no statutes or decisions to guide them. Back in 1855 the territorial supreme court of California reversed the case of Robinson v. Pioche by a decision found in Volume 5 of the California Decisions at page 460. The trial court had instructed the jury that the plaintiff, who had fallen into a hole in the sidewalk, was guilty of contributory negligence by being drunk at the time. It took the court just fifty words to reverse the case. It said: "If the defendants were at fault in leaving an uncovered hole in the sidewalk of a public street, the intoxication of the plaintiff cannot excuse such gross negligence. A drunken man is as much entitled to a safe street as a sober one, and much more in need of it."

In Quest of Elbow Room

One day, out in Sioux County, the extreme northwestern county of Nebraska, I met one of these professional homesteaders. He stood by a prairie schooner, out of which came a stovepipe. Behind was a cow and calf and two dogs.

"Where is your home?" I asked.

"H'n't got no house," he said, as he kicked one of the dogs and took a chew of tobacco.

"Where do you live?"

"Where d' I live!" he exclaimed, with the grandeur of a king. "Where d' I live? I don't have to live anywhere. I'm marchin' ahed of civ'lization, sir. I'm homesteadin'."

"Well, where do you sleep?"

"Sleep? I sleep over on the government land, drink out of the North Platte, eat jack rabbits and raw wolf. But it's gettin' too thickly settled round here for me. I saw a land agent up at Buffalo Gap to-day, and they say a whole family is comin' up the North Platte fifty miles below here. It's gettin' too crowded for me here, stranger. I leave for the Powder River country to-morrow. I can't stand the rush!"

Boom Town

[At Ranger, Texas,] barns were made into habitations and rich men from Eastern centers paid two dollars a night for shelter—and gladly. The owner of an eight-room house made from twenty to thirty dollars a night renting cots.

From "Wild West Exaggerations," *Eli Perkins Thirty Years of Wit, and Reminiscences of Witty, Wise and Eloquent Men,* by Melville D. Landon (Eli Perkins), p. 93. Copyright, 1891, by Cassell Publishing Company. New York City.

From *Were You in Ranger?* by Boyce House, pp. 29–30. Copyright, 1935, by the Tardy Publishing Co., Inc. Dallas, Texas.

A stranger went into a hotel that was still under construction and was shown to a room. There were no panes in the windows and there was no door.

"But I want to stay here tonight," he protested.

"It will be ready by then," he was assured. "We are completing the hotel a room at a time so we can rent each one as rapidly as possible. Three dollars in advance, please."

The Booster Spirit

. . . A Los Angeles man took a trip East. Arriving at a little town he got off the train, and was among strangers. Seeing a good many people entering a house, he concluded to investigate. Going near, he saw that it was a church, and concluded to go in and hear a sermon. But it was funeral services. The corpse of a man was in a coffin, and the minister was telling of the many virtues of the deceased, and of the great loss that the community suffered in his death. When he concluded his laudatory remarks, he asked if any one there wished to say anything. Our Los Angeles friend jumped to his feet, and said:

"I am a stranger in this place, and unfortunately was not acquainted with the deceased, but after listening to the story of his great worth I am convinced that he was a noble citizen. I can add nothing more regarding him, but I will tell you about Los Angeles. It is the greatest . . ."

O Pioneers

In Oklahoma City, born overnight out of the red dust, the past meets the future head-on. To-day, where there was once only Indian pasture land, a city is coming of age with spires that reach higher than the smoke signals of the nomadic tribes who roamed there long ago.

There are factories and mansions and spidery derricks pumping oil where once there were tents and shacks and prairie grass rutted deep with wagon tracks. The old men and old women look at this, and they are proud; this is something that has happened in their lifetime.

. . . A pioneer, frail and ailing, . . . went on an automobile ride with his grandson for a final look at the city he had helped build. He looked at the broad streets, the rows of homes, the domeless capitol, the

---

From *Pioneer Days and Kebo Club Nights,* by George W. Wear, p. 131. Boston: Meador Publishing Co.

. . . The main thing that has made a great city of Los Angeles is the manner in which the people of that place stand together, with the single intention of advancing their town, of which they have a right to be proud.—G.W.W.

From "Oklahoma City," by Debs Myers, *Holiday,* Vol. 7 (May, 1950), No. 5, p. 129.

glittering stores, and was silent. "Well, grandpop," said the youth, "she sure is big and pretty, isn't she?" The old man nodded. "Yep," he said, "big and pretty, but, hot damn, wouldn't it be fun to tear her down and start all over again!"

More Sheep

. . . These hardy pioneers enjoyed life, notwithstanding its many privations. Everything was open and free, and nature stimulated hope and ambition. When prices were fair and grass good, they were prodigal in their prosperity. When winters were hard and grass short and prices low, they accepted their losses without grumbling. On one occasion when the price of sheep had reached a low point, Rose and Dickenson shipped a car of sheep to St. Louis. The commission house sent a statement showing a balance against Rose and Dickenson, claiming the sheep did not bring enough to pay freight, and calling for a remittance to cover this balance. After reading the statement, Dickenson returned it with this notation on the bottom: "Go to thunder; I've got no money; I'll ship you more sheep."

All in the Day's Work

On a lower street of Olympia stands a grey, slender-spired church, the building of which was the occasion of the most famous pioneer story of the southern Sound. The Judge of the Municipal Court, if you find him in chambers, will recall it for you, while his clerk will sometimes add a detail, for he too is a pioneer and knew at least one of the principals.

"My father," the Judge will tell you, "was Captain Crosby, retired from sea. He kept a little store at Tumwater in the fifties and owned the sawmill there. One morning De Vore came in. Everybody knew De Vore. He was a six-foot Methodist preacher, the greatest money raiser in the country. Father looked up, 'Well, De Vore, what are you wanting now?' 'Captain,' said he, 'we've got to have a church for our people in Olympia and,' rubbing his hands, 'seeing, Captain, that you, well, that you have the mill'—'Look here, De Vore,' my father turned on him, 'I've never seen you or any of you damned preachers, for that matter, do a hard day's work in my life. I'll tell you what I'll do—I'll let you have for your church as much lumber as you can tote over to the River and raft with your own hands in a day!' 'Thank you, thank

---

From "Early Days in Haskell County, West Texas," by R. E. Sherrill, *West Texas Historical Association Year Book,* Volume III, June, 1927, p. 28.

From *On Puget Sound,* by Robert Walkinshaw, pp. 36–37. Copyright, 1929, by G. P. Putnam's Sons. New York and London.

you, Captain,' said the preacher as he walked out. Father didn't think anything about it till a few mornings after, when he went down to the mill, as he always did before breakfast. There he saw some fellow in a white shirt working like a beaver. If it wasn't De Vore! He kept at it all morning. About eleven o'clock, Father said, 'De Vore, better come up to the house and have a bite with us.' 'Thanks, Captain, I can't stop. I have a snack in my coat.' He quit at sundown for he had figured it so as to catch the ebb."

"When he got his raft together," the Clerk may add, "and climbed aboard, the tide carried him past Olympia and beached him down the Inlet. He had to wait for the turn before he could get back."

"That's right," the Judge will rejoin. "And do you know, sir, De Vore rafted enough of my father's lumber in one day to build his church from the ground to the steeple!"

Beauty and the Cowboy

. . . Two city men I knew had come to a cow ranch on business and had an old-time cowboy taking them around. One day they were discussing the beauties of nature, and when each one decided what he thought was the most beautiful thing he ever saw one of them asked the cowboy his idea of beauty. He promptly answered: "The prettiest thing I ever saw was a four-year-old fat steer. . . ."

Jim Baker and the Cuspidor

On one of Baker's visits to Denver, while seated in one of the hotels chewing tobacco, he spat on the carpet. A Negro porter who happened to see him moved the cuspidor to the spot where he had expectorated, whereupon Jim turned his head and spat in the opposite direction. The porter again moved the cuspidor to that side. Jim, not heeding this, spat again on the carpet.

Finally the porter made several attempts to place it within the range of his amber spray, and having been unsuccessful, he placed the brass receptacle directly in front of him. Old Jim looked down and replied . . ., "You know, by G—, if you keep movin' that thing around I'm li'ble to spit in it."

From *Memories of Old Montana,* by Con Price (Masachele Opa Barusha), p. 140. Copyright, 1945, by Con Price. Pasadena, California: Trail's End Publishing Co., Inc.

From *The Life of Jim Baker, 1818–1898, Trapper, Scout, Guide, and Indian Fighter,* by Nolie Mumey, pp. 172–173. Copyright, 1931, by Nolie Mumey. Denver, Colorado: The World Press, Inc.

Cabin Fever

"Cabin fever" is a term well known in the Rockies, also in Alaska, and is duly dreaded. By cabin fever is meant the state of mind of two people isolated for a long time, often all winter, together. After a time, even though they be husband and wife, or twin brothers, or father and son, even mother and son, they begin to wear on each other, "get on each other's nerves," and soon become dire, though unreasonable, enemies, usually for life thereafter. Cabin fever is illustrated by a story well known in the Rockies.

Two old cronies prospected together all summer and, thus becoming bosom friends, naturally decided to "hole up" together for the winter on their claim, far from the nearest neighbor. As they built their cabin, the loneliness slowly began to work on them; and the first night in the newly roofed place they sat silent before the fire. There was a noise outside; one got up and went out. When he came back, he said, "Cow," and the other nodded silently.

Without another word they sat there till bedtime, when the other went out for more wood to last till morning. When he came back, he said, "Bull." Then he blew out the light and they went to sleep.

Next morning, after a wordless breakfast, the first man rolled his blankets, shouldered his rifle, and started for the door. His partner asked, "Why?"

The man in the door turned, and growled back: "Too damn much argument here," and went down the trail for good.

Just Ornery

. . . "Orneriness" is [an] excellent, commonly used far Western word that has several definitions, directly opposed. Orneriness is a good old American expression now, unfortunately, mostly lost east of the Mississippi. In the case of orneriness, the diversity of implication is more a question of intonation and facial expression than of anything else. In its primary sense orneriness means distinguished meanness. Not just plain meanness, but inherent and cultivated meanness; meanness indulged in for meanness' sake. If you say a man is "ornery," and frown about it, you describe him as an artist in meanness; if you say he's an "ornery sort of cuss" and smile, you mean he's a hard man to keep down. Used in this sense, orneriness is about as high a compliment as you can pay. It means a refusal to go under; a refusal to stay down; it

---

By Chauncey Thomas, Denver, Colorado, 1930, in a letter to the editor.

From *Powder River, Let 'er Buck,* by Struthers Burt, pp. 333–335. Copyright, 1938, by Struthers Burt. New York and Toronto: Farrar & Rinehart, Inc.

means the little spark at the back of a man's spirit that the winds of Fate can never quite blow out.

The phoenix, arising from its ashes, is an "ornery bird." John Colter's flight from the Blackfeet was an epic example of orneriness.

The badmen and women of the Powder had plenty of orneriness in its primary meaning; the good men and women of the Powder were equally distinguished by orneriness in its secondary usage. Neither Indians, nor badmen, nor range wars, nor bonanzas, nor winters of '87, nor anything else could drive the best of them out. They knew why they were there, and they stayed.

Two summers ago Powder River and all of eastern Wyoming suffered from the worst drought in their history. Old Colonel Jones—I'll call him that—smiled when I asked him what he was going to do. This was the seventh time he had been wiped out.

"I'm getting together quite a nice little bunch of yearlings," he said. "I'll get along."

Colonel Jones was eighty-two.

I suppose the big difference is that the Far West lives by the weather, and the Northeast by the stock market. The Far Westerner gets up in the morning and looks at the sky and not the market reports. That's why the Far West is constantly fooling the East, politically and otherwise. To the Far Westerner a cloud is more important than a headline. The Far Westerner is all the time smelling earth, and he is interested in it. And he wouldn't be half as interested in his earth if it was soft, easy earth. When the Far West is up it can wear evening clothes, when it's down it can go back to overalls and sowbelly. Neither overalls nor sowbelly depresses nor mortifies it.

There is another meaning to orneriness . . . a sort of halfway meaning. Every far Western country cherishes the sagas of certain local bad goodmen who seem to have been bad merely because they were too healthy, in the manner of cowboys who come into town once a month and drink too much simply because they can't stand being in such splendid condition.

Powder River, like every other far Western country, has had its quota of these harmless, if at times annoying, trolls. Such a bad goodman was George W. Pike, a gay and careless young man who flourished in Converse County, just south of the Powder, in the 1890's and early 1900's, and who was often in the Powder River country. Everybody loved George, even those he stole from, which was the entire community. He was generous. Having been accused one day by a neighbor of stealing his horses, George waved an indulgent hand and said, "All right! Go on down to my corral and pick out any horses you like—they're all stolen!" . . .

Comeback

Some friends were consoling one of the old pioneer cowmen who had been a big operator and had lost everything he had, including his home. He said to them, "You don't need to sympathize with me, I'm all right. I'll come back. I came here fifty years ago with only sixty-five cents and asthma, and I still got the asthma."

A Rancher on Railroads

Some years ago an investigation was under way relative to a most destructive train wreck that had occurred out in the Southwest range country. Two trains had crashed together in a frightful head-on collision at a blind curve where the railway swept around the point of a long, high ridge. Most of the members of both train crews had been killed or injured, but the investigators at last found an old ranchman who had witnessed the disaster.

"Tell us exactly what you saw," demanded the chairman of the investigating committee. "Well, I was ridin' along the backbone of that ridge lookin' for mavericks when I saw off down to the south a train comin' north about fifty miles an hour. Then I looked north an' saw another 'un comin' south at about the same speed and I saw they uz goin' to smash into one another right at that curve."

"What did you do?" asked the chairman.

"Do? I didn't do nothin'."

"Didn't you ride down there and try to stop 'em?"

"No."

"Didn't you even *think* anything?"

"Yes, I thought a little."

"What did you think?"

"Well, I thought to myself that's a helluva way to run a railroad."

The Joke's on Us

. . . It is recorded that in one California community a mob hanged a man for supposed horse-stealing, but afterward discovered that he was innocent. The mob's messenger broke the news to the victim's widow in this manner: "We hanged Jim for stealing a horse, but come to find out he didn't do it, so I guess the joke's on us."

From *A Corral Full of Stories*, rounded up by Joe M. Evans, p. 64. Copyright, 1939, by Joe M. Evans. El Paso, Texas: Printed by the McMath Company, Inc.

From *Cow Country*, by Edward Everett Dale, pp. 145–146. Copyright, 1942, by the University of Oklahoma Press. Norman.

From *Outposts of Civilization*, by W. A. Chalfant, pp. 13–14. Copyright, 1928, by the Christopher Publishing House. Boston.

Pete Kitchen and the Horse Thief

Some bandits from Sonora once stole two or three of Kitchen's favorite horses. He took up their trail while it was still hot, followed them across the line, and, pursuing them day and night for about three days, at last came up with them. He killed one, I believe; one fled; and he captured the third and recovered the horses. As soon as he recrossed the Arizona line and could safely do so, he made camp so that he could get some sleep, being almost dead for want of it.

The prisoner, tied hand and foot, and with a rope around his neck, was left on horseback under the limb of a tree to which the other end of the rope was attached. In telling this story, Pete was wont to punch his listener in the ribs with his thumb and say with a chuckle:

"You know, while I was asleep that damned horse walked off and left that fellow hanging there."

Mormon Swearing

. . . What swearing there is among Mormons in general is likely to be fairly tame, and this in spite of the fact that both Brother Brigham and Heber C. Kimball, his right-hand man, were notable swearers and threateners from the pulpit. They were always offering to send their enemies to hell across lots, or give them a dose that would puke them worse than lobelia. A little of that fresh and vigorous tradition remains, though in the staider communities it is likely to be buried under a layer of piety like sausages put up in lard, and to emerge only on great occasions. The story is told of a pious brother in one of the rural settlements who forgot for some reason to milk his cow before he got dressed for Sunday meeting. Rather than change to overalls, he tucked up his coat tails, folded back the lapels of his Prince Albert, and sat down gingerly on the stool. The cow was "ringy." She kept looking around suspiciously and switching her matted tail across the elder's Sunday shirt. He compressed his lips and tied the tail to her leg. For a while he milked steadily, and then in one disastrous motion the cow kicked the bucket into his lap and upset him on the dirty stable floor. The elder, legend says, rose slowly to his feet. His stature grew from second to second, until he stood on tiptoe with the pressure of wrath in him. His hands made futile clawing motions down the stained lapels of his coat. Finally he found words. "If I wasn't a man of God . . . If I

From *Arizona Characters,* by Frank C. Lockwood, p. 52. Copyright, 1928, by Frank C. Lockwood. Los Angeles: The *Times-Mirror* Press.

From *Mormon Country,* by Wallace Stegner, pp. 143–144. American Folkways Series, edited by Erskine Caldwell. Copyright, 1942, by Wallace Stegner. New York: Duell, Sloan & Pearce.

wasn't the Bishop of this Ward . . . If I wasn't a member of the Quorum of the Priesthood in this State . . . If I didn't have duties and obligations to live up to . . . If I wasn't called upon to put away wrath and bind the evil passions . . ., *I'd break your God-damned neck*!"

The Biggest Raise in Poker History

Probably the most noted of the hundreds of gamblers who operated in the old Southwest were Doc Holliday and John Dougherty, both of whom were prominent figures in Tombstone. . . . John Dougherty followed the well-nigh universal custom of carrying a revolver, but he was no gun-fighter; he attended strictly to his own business, which was gambling, and as far as the record shows he died without a single notch on his pistol butt. He was an expert at all games from Faro to Craps, but in Tombstone and the Southwest he was renowned for two things—the smallness of his feet, of which he was inordinately proud, and the bigness of his stakes in his Poker games. He commonly carried a roll of $100,000, played only no limit games, and refused to join a session unless the other players could show at least $10,000. When he bought a drink, he paid for it with a five dollar bill, and was insulted if change were offered him. If Southwestern tradition is to be credited, Dougherty in one of his games made the biggest raise ever risked on a Poker hand anywhere.

This historic event occurred in 1889, when Dougherty and Ike Jackson, a rich cattle owner of Colorado City, Texas, met in Bowen's Saloon in Santa Fe and agreed to play a square, no limit game for the Poker championship of the West. A hundred prominent citizens of Santa Fe, including L. Bradford Prince, Governor of New Mexico, crowded into the saloon to watch the battle. For a few hands the play was desultory, but soon both men drew good hands at the same time, and the betting immediately became heavy. In a few minutes $100,000 in coin and currency was piled on the table between the players. Jackson was then short of cash, so he wrote out a deed to his ranch and 10,000 head of cattle, and with this document raised Dougherty a hundred thousand. Dougherty hadn't money enough either to call or to raise, but he was equal to the emergency. He called for paper and pen, wrote rapidly for a moment or two, and then handed the paper to Governor Prince, at the same time drawing a revolver.

"Now, Governor," he said, "you sign this or I will kill you. I like you and would fight for you, but I love my reputation as a Poker player better than I do you or any one else."

Without reading what Dougherty had written, Governor Prince

From *Sucker's Progress,* An Informal History of Gambling in America from the Colonies to Canfield, by Herbert Asbury, pp. 347–349. Copyright, 1938, By Dodd, Mead and Company, Inc. New York.

hastily signed, and with a smile of triumph Dougherty flung the paper into the pot, saying impressively:

"I raise you the Territory of New Mexico! There's the deed!"

The Texan threw down his cards with a mighty curse.

"All right," he said, "take the pot. But it's a damned good thing for you that the Governor of Texas isn't here!"

The Only Ways to Die in the High Border Country

A citizen of Fargo (or Butte, or Bismarck, or Wallace, or Sheridan) returned home after an absence of some days and found a corpse in front of his house.

"He get shot?" he demanded of a stranger who was taking in the sight.

"Nope!"

"Too much whisky?"

"No."

"Then I reckon he must be alive, because that's the only way they die in Fargo (or Butte, or Bismarck, or Wallace, or Sheridan)!"

Kit Carson to the Rescue

. . . How true it now seems to me, as the recollections of my boyish days, when I read of the exploits of Kit Carson, crowd upon my memory! I firmly believed him to be at least ten feet tall, carrying a rifle so heavy that, like Bruce's sword, it required two men to lift it. I imagined he drank out of nothing smaller than a river, and picked the carcass of a whole buffalo as easily as a lady does the wing of a quail. Ten years later I made the acquaintance of the foremost frontiersman, and found him a delicate, reticent, undersized, wiry man, as perfectly the opposite of the type my childish brain had created as it is possible to conceive.

At Fort Union, our mail arrived every morning by coach over the Trail, generally pulling up at the sutler's store, whose proprietor was postmaster, about daylight. While Maxwell and Kit were my guests, I sauntered down after breakfast one morning to get my mail, and while waiting for the letters to be distributed, happened to glance at some papers lying on the counter, among which I saw a new periodical—the

---

From *High Border Country,* by Eric Thane, pp. 17–18. American Folkways Series, edited by Erskine Caldwell. Copyright, 1942, by Eric Thane. New York: Duell, Sloan & Pearce.

From *The Old Santa Fe Trail,* the Story of a Great Highway, by Colonel Henry Inman, p. 381. Copyright, 1897, by The Macmillan Company. New York and London.

Day's Doings, I think it was—that had a full-page illustration of a scene in a forest. In the foreground stood a gigantic figure dressed in the traditional buckskin; on one arm rested an immense rifle; his other arm was around the waist of the conventional female of such sensational journals, while in front, lying prone upon the ground, were half a dozen Indians, evidently slain by the singular hero in defending the impossibly attired female. The legend related how all this had been effected by the famous Kit Carson. I purchased the paper, returned with it to my room, and after showing it to several officers who had called upon Maxwell, I handed it to Kit. He wiped his spectacles, studied the picture intently for a few seconds, turned round, and said: "Gentlemen, that thar may be true, but I hain't got no recollection of it."

Crazy Quartz

. . . [This] is about the one time, in his youth that [Crazy Quartz Davis] did strike a good pocket, and made money enough to go to New York—or so he always said.

Davis used to love to tell about that trip.

"Made up our minds all at once, we did," he used to say. "Picked up and went, straight from the mines, just as we stood. Mud on our boots, mud in our hair, mud in our beards.

"But we got to New York all right and we set out to get the best there was. Gold? We had plenty of it. Nuggets all through our clothes, and every man had a good-sized sack of dust, too.

"We went to the best hotel we could find, left our gold with the manager and sat down to eat. Would you believe it? They brought us corned beef and cabbage! I told 'em what we thought of 'em and what we wanted. 'Bring the best in the house,' I said to 'em. 'Chicken and apple pie is none too good for us!' They called the manager. 'Give these boys anything they want,' he said. 'They're as rich as anybody in New York!' "

But old Crazy Quartz always saved the best of his yarn to the last.

"After that," he used to go on, "we had to get shaved. Full beards like ours were no style in New York then.

"When we went into the barber shop I told the feller, 'Look here,' I said, 'I'll make a deal with you. Will you shave me for what you can get out of my beard?' He looked at me as though I was crazy. 'Certainly not!' he says. 'Very well,' says I, 'bring me a basin!' When he brought it I told him to see that every hair of my beard when he shaved it, and every hair he clipped off my head, fell into that basin. He didn't know what was up, but he was careful. It all got in. Then I says, 'All right, now get me some water and watch me!'

From *Anybody's Gold,* The Story of California's Mining Towns, by Joseph Henry Jackson, pp. 354–356. Copyright, 1941, by D. Appleton-Century Company, Inc. New York and London.

"He got me the water, and I sloshed all that mess of hair up and down, up and down in the water until every speck of dirt was out of it. Then I scooped it out and settled down to pan out the gravel that was left. Boys, I got five dollars and twenty cents in gold out of my beard, and that barber was the sorriest critter you ever did see!"

Crazy Quartz Davis died years ago, but that story of his lives on in Calaveras County, along with many another one of the old days. . . .

Haynie and the Bear

"One year when I started out in the fall early to get my winter's meat," said Haynie, when in one of his reminiscent moods, "I had a great deal of trouble with bears stealing the meat after I would make the kill. It was one of those falls when snow was late in coming, and the bears were slow in holing up.

"I had killed several fat bucks, hung them up, and gone back to camp for my horses. On each occasion, when I would return for the meat the bears had beat me to it and eaten all the choice morsels. The next kill I made I had a bright idea and one I felt sure would fool Mr. Bear. I killed the animal near a high ledge of rock. Near the foot of this bluff was a tree, with a limb paralleling the bluff and on a level with the top of the rocks. I dragged the deer to the edge of the bluff, tied a lash rope to the carcass, and then threw the other end of the rope over the limb of the tree. When all was secure, I shoved the animal off and let it swing in the air twenty feet above the ground.

"But imagine my surprise when I returned in the morning and found half the meat gone. 'How did the bear get it?' you ask? Well, sir, that bear had patiently carried sticks, logs, and stones to the spot until he had built up a mound high enough so he could reach the meat and had then leisurely eaten his fill."

Out Where the Jest Begins

A dude wrangler who had also been cowboy, miner and scout, and who was otherwise distinguished by the most extraordinary mustachios ever seen on a human face, was entertaining his customers after a hard

---

From *River of No Return (The Great Salmon River of Idaho)*, A Century of Central Idaho and Eastern Washington History and Development, Together with the Wars, Customs, Myths and Legends of the Nez Perce Indians, by Robert G. Bailey, pp. 490–491. Copyright, 1935, by Robert G. Bailey. Lewiston, Idaho: Bailey-Blake Printing Co.

From "Out Where the Jest Begins," by Eric Howard, *Esquire, The Magazine for Men,* Vol. XIII (February, 1940), No. 2, pp. 73, 144–145. Copyright, 1940, by Esquire, Inc. Chicago.

day. He was telling the thrilling story of the time he had been swept off a raft into the swirling waters of the muddy Colorado. He mounted the ladder of suspense to the top rung. The silt was weighing him down, taking him under. Then he paused. An Eastern lady, his unconscious stooge, gasped: "But how did you escape?"

"Ma'am," he assured her with true Western solemnity, "I didn't."

There you have the basic formula for Western humor of exaggeration. There are countless variations of the same yarn. There is also the familiar classic of the man who claimed that he dug the Grand Canyon. When some one expressed doubt, another old-timer spoke up and swore it was the solemn truth—he knew, because he himself had wheeled the dirt away and had made the San Francisco Peaks!

Exaggeration, in the humor that is uniquely of the West, sometimes runs to such wild and fantastic extremes that it is breath-taking; imagination can go no further. Yet such tall tales are usually related solemnly, slowly, in a way that makes them seem like everyday occurrences.

It has often been pointed out that exaggeration is the basis of most American humor, notably the humor of the frontier. Understatement, however, is perhaps even more often the foundation of the Westerner's special brand of comedy—as unique an expression of regional character as remains in this country.

I drove into a small Western city recently. On the main street I saw a sign over a restaurant: The World's Finest Steak. I called it to the attention of my companion, a cowman. He looked at it skeptically for a moment, then drawled: "Ought to be a fair piece o' meat."

The instinctive tendency of the slow-spoken, humor-loving Westerner is to take everybody and everything down a peg.

A man who owned, leased or controlled an area twenty by forty miles, in New Mexico, was asked about his ranch by a Californian he was visiting. He said of it, "Oh, it's just a little-bitty old cow outfit up in the mountains—country not even the Injuns wanted." When I told the Californian, who took this literally, that the rancher owned thousands of head of cattle, hundreds of horses, employed scores of men, permitted a dozen Mexican families to squat on his land, and had his own little tribe of Indians living on his bounty, the Californian was incredulous. The Californian, during the past few decades, has become known as a boaster and a booster; the Westerner of the still wide-open spaces is more given to disparagement and understatement, except where his fancy runs wild in tall tales, which are supposed to be enjoyed but not believed.

Westerners seldom play tricks on visitors—such as giving a man a bad horse to ride—unless their guests are boastful. If a man claims he can ride anything, they may give him a horse no one can ride. If he rides well but, in the Western tradition of understatement, says, "I'm the sorriest rider that ever forked a bronc," he'll draw a decent mount.

I heard a world's champion cowboy and rodeo star say, "That horse is dynamite. You couldn't get me on him for seven hundred dollars!"

Seven hundred dollars is a significant sum, for what reason I have never been able to learn. One hears it everywhere in such phrases as: "Drunker than seven hundred dollars," "Crazier than seven hundred dollars," "Madder than seven hundred dollars."

Westerners habitually and humorously make light of their possessions.

"Poor?" one man drawled. "I'm so poor a coyote would pass me up." He then proceeded to build a new house, buy a new car, and send his two children to college.

"Nothin' to eat but beans," a rancher said earnestly, "but you're welcome to them."

Whereupon we sat down to a groaning board that held two kinds of roast meat in unlimited quantity, several vegetables including the inevitable beans, relishes, pickles, bread, biscuits, coffee, and pie. Eating heartily and enjoying it is in the tradition: Western women delight in feeding their men; Western men are usually excellent cooks. A lot of Western humor has food for its subject.

Sex, the *sine qua non* of sophisticated humor, is seldom discussed or joked about. In a relatively womanless country, men are still woman-shy. There are still only two kinds, good and bad, and the good are pedestaled. . . .

Indians, on the other hand, are very frank in their talk, in their own languages, and often jest about the relations of men and women. Among the Pueblos, the clown dancers often amuse the crowds by simulating sexual pursuit and relations. Navajo women, so modest in dress that their ankles are seldom seen, say things that would go big at a party of sophisticates.

The humor of the Spanish-American or Mexican in the Southwest is another thing. They are a rather sad people, except when engaged in the business of making fiesta. Often, their humor is merely an amusing twist given an unfamiliar language. . . .

Much genuine Western humor has its origin in the impulse to bring the high and mighty, the uppity, down to a common, human level. The instinct of these real individualists is to democratize everything. The dude, the dandy, the show-off, the person who puts on airs in any way, except in fun, becomes the butt of the jest. Comments are usually slow, cynical, realistic, but deadly.

* * * * *

A pompous little man, in shorts, carrying a knapsack, turned up at a trading post. He announced that he was a psychiatrist from an Eastern college.

"Do you know what a psychiatrist is?" he inquired condescendingly.

"Why, let me see," the trader said, looking at him with blue-eyed innocence. "Why, that there is an escaped lunatic, ain't it, mister?"

There is often a literal logic in Western humor; the Indians, especially the Navajos, have this mental directness, too. For example, a trader, selling a rifle to a Navajo, said: "Why, sure it has power. You could kill a cow with that gun!" The Navajo bought it, went out, and tried it on the first cow he saw. The cow belonged to the trader; the Navajo assured him he had told the truth.

* * * * *

. . . A young artist and his wife did the wilds in white shorts. Said a cowboy, "I wear 'em, too, but I'm scared to take off my Levis."

* * * * *

The typical Westerner of the cow country is astonishingly observant. A stranger, riding through the country, paused for a few minutes at a chuck-wagon, then went on. A few days later an officer came through.

"Did you see a stranger around?"

"Yeah. Uh-huh."

"What did he look like?"

"Well, sir," the chuck-wagon cook drawled, "he was ridin' a dun horse with a white stockin' on its left hind foot, a loose shoe on the right, an' a X-Bar brand. Horse was a four-year-old. Had a mangy saddle, red an' white Navajo saddle blanket, two Navajo conchas on his bridle. The man was right around five eight, had on Levis an' a blue shirt, corduroy vest. Scar on his right cheek, runnin' down his neck inside his collar. Two-three days beard. A sharp-eyed man; eyes kind o' blue. Long nose, with the tip twisted to the left, like he was smellin' somethin' bad over there. Had on a J. B. Stetson hat, kind o' wore out, with a woven hair band. I didn't take a close look at him, but that's about how he stacked up."

* * * * *

The humorous effect often depends upon the poker face, the slow, casual speech, the calm acceptance of things that would excite others.

A rancher, angry at being overcharged and dunned, strode into a big store in a Western town. He headed for the manager's office at the rear, ignoring the sleepy-eyed clerk.

"Where you goin'?" the clerk lazily inquired.

"I'm going to kill Pat O'Malley!" the rancher said.

O'Malley was the store manager.

The clerk didn't change his restful pose. He called out casually, "If you need any help, let me know."

An Indian trader solemnly explained why a can of peaches cost ten cents more at his place than in the railroad town sixty miles away with one word, "Freight." When it was pointed out that the freight was only a few cents on a case of canned goods, he said blandly, "I've thought a lot about that. But the only way I can explain it is freight. If you can do any better, you go right ahead."

There may be something in the country itself that makes for calm nerves and slow speech. One typical man of the country, driving on a washed-out mountain road, said with no acceleration of speech, "We're going to turn over." By the time he got to the first syllable of the last word, the car had overturned.

Once a motion picture company, on location in the Navajo country, picked up a man of the region to play a small part. He was slow-moving, slow-talking. The director was nervous, cocky, hard-boiled. The line of dialogue was: "Where do you want those machine guns put?"

The director instructed the amateur actor to utter the words quickly, like this: "Whered'youwantthosemachinegunsput?" "Snap it up! Snap it up!" he said. "You're excited, see?"

After ten rehearsals, the slow-spoken Westerner was still drawling: "Wheah — do you — want — them — machine guns — *put?"* The final word came out like a noise from a backfiring motor; that was his attempt to speed up. The director worked hard to get the man to talk like a city gangster, or a movie version of one; he did not realize that he had a chance to capture the authentic essence of Western speech and timing.

Much of the effectiveness of Will Rogers depended on his timing; most Westerners have the same thing and the Rogers drawl and the Rogers knack of poking good-humored fun at the high and mighty.

Charles Laughton reports that when he first worked in pictures, he envied the timing of Gary Cooper. An engaging trouper, if no great shakes of an actor, Cooper probably acquired it in his Montana days. Once a cowboy, once a Westerner, always. The stamp remains. Gary Cooper can dress like Marco Polo or a rich young man loose in Paris; he still belongs on a bronc.

By the same token, dudes can—and often do—rig themselves up in all the trappings of the West, from boots to sombreros, and nobody who knows the real article will mistake them for cow-persons. Let a cowman put on any garb—even, as I caught one doing, golf knickers!—and no one with savvy will take him for a retired banker.

A business man who punched cows in Texas, many years ago, and has lived in cities since then, was talking in his office to a visitor. He hadn't said more than a few words when the other man asked, "What part of Texas you from?"

The indelible stamp is as plain as that.

Quite a lot of Western humor, in these days, is conscious. The Westerner is living up to his tradition and his literary character. He reads Western writers, some of whom have developed an outlandish lingo never heard on mesa or in canyon. Life is at its old business of copying art. Western clothing, always colorful and expensive, has also become somewhat influenced by the movie cowboys and the magazine illustrations. But Western humor has always been intentional. There seems to be something in the atmosphere, the landscape, the way of life that develops this special brand of dry, laconic wit, this slow, pointed speech.

A man who had grown up in a remote part of New Mexico went East to college, became a famous football star, later a football coach. Returned to the ranch, he gradually shucked most of the traces of Eastern influence and became again a man of the range, in clothes, speech and habits. He told tall tales, added to the extraordinary legend of the Lost Adams Diggings, and was proud of his reputation as a champion liar.

* * * * *

An old-timer was once telling me something about a notorious bad man of other days. He spoke at some length of what the man had done—bank and train robberies, killings, escapes. But he didn't reveal the man himself.

"You knew him well," I urged. "What was he really like?"

"Well, sir," he said, "he was the politest man ever I knew. Had to be. If he wasn't all-fired polite, somebody might take exception to something he said and there'd be trouble. Natchally, he always tried to avoid trouble."

* * * * *

Whether it takes the form of fanciful exaggeration or depends for its effect upon drawling understatement and slow timing, Western humor is a native growth, unique, flavorsome. To the connoisseur of humor who can drift into the lazy rhythm of Western ways, its study will be rich and engaging.

Almost always it contains a mild acid that corrodes pretense and cracks the shell of arrogance.

There is little that the Westerner takes too seriously. He is easygoing, tolerant, and regards even his own misfortunes with something of detached amusement. Consciously or unconsciously, he still aims to live so that he can get up every morning, look the world in the face, and tell everybody to go to hell—in a quiet, good-humored way.

It was a Westerner—it had to be—who, when asked what he had done during the Depression, replied, with an engaging combination of frankness and earnestness, "Mister, I et!"

He who drinks the waters of the Hassayampa is never again able to tell the unvarnished truth. Many Westerners seem to have sipped these waters, for tellers of tall tales—proud liars of the purple sage—are everywhere. When not engaged in fanciful exaggeration, they are equally adept at understatement; or in a combination of the two.

A Westerner recently said of a Senator from his State: "Why, I've knowed him all his life. The poor feller couldn't make a livin'—all he had was a gift o' gab—so some of us boys got together an' said, 'Let's send him to Washington, so's we won't have to listen to him.' We did, an', by gravy, he's been there ever since."

There is an oft-told tale that accurately suggests the spirit of Western humor. The mayor of a Texas town called on the Rangers to quell a riot. A lone, undersized Ranger got off the first train. "Only one

Ranger?" the mayor yelled. The Ranger spat. "Only one riot, ain't they?" he shot back.

No such story, I think, has been told of the Royal Mounted, the F.B.I., or any force of policemen. It's amusing, yes; but it's more than that. One mild, soft-spoken, undersized Ranger often proved himself equal to such a situation; he was not speaking with bravado; he was merely expressing the quiet confidence of a man whose nerves are in good shape.

Humor of that type still rides the range, in the vast cow country that follows the Continental Divide from Mexico to Canada. Quite unlike urban, sophisticated wit, it is earthy, full of savor, masculine and meaty. It contains surprise and mockery.

Best of all, it is funny. So much humor is not.

II. "A FRESH DEAL ALL ROUND"

> *"The boys seem to have taken a fresh deal all round," said Mr. John Oakhurst . . ., "and there is no knowing whether a man will turn up knave or king."*
>
> —Bret Harte

Go West, Young Man

In May, 1859, a lone prospector pushed his way into the mountains and made a trail to the now famous Central City region. . . .

Gregory Gulch was the name given to the new find. It continues to be a great treasure-house of precious metals. This discovery gave the country another boom.

Horace Greeley, of the New York *Tribune,* had been making a trip through California and Nevada, and was on his return to the States when he heard of the gold strike in Colorado. He determined to feast his eyes on some of the "paltry stuff" that was creating such a furor throughout the land.

From *Tales of the Colorado Pioneers,* by Alice Polk Hill, pp. 29–31. Denver: Pierson & Gardner. 1884.

When he arrived in Denver he was received with all the honor that the infant city could command. He said he didn't intend to be deceived in this matter, that seeing was believing, and he wanted to wash out some of the dirt himself. So the men put their heads together to see how they could "come it" over the old gentleman. They themselves were satisfied as to the richness of Gregory Gulch, it was no intention to deceive, but Solomon says "there is a time for all things," and they wanted a "good one" on Horace Greeley. So they sent a message to the camp that Horace was coming, and to salt a mine.

The boys took down an old shotgun and fired gold dust into a hole for all it was worth.

Bright and early the next morning a spanking team was rigged up, and the distinguished gentleman started for the gulch, accompanied by some of the most plausible, entertaining and versatile talkers of the country. They escorted him over the diggings, related all the interesting events in the history of its discovery, showed him specimens of the dirt and the pure gold that had been washed out. Mr. Greeley's soul was in arms, and, eager for the task, he called for a shovel and pan, rolled up his sleeves, and went down into the pit. They gave him all the necessary instructions as to the process of panning, and looked on with palpitating anxiety.

Mr. Greeley was an apt scholar, and put his dirt through like an adept in the art. It panned out big. All the bottom of the pan was covered with bright gold particles. They slapped him on the shoulders in regular Western style, and told him to try it again—which he did—with the same success. Then he gathered up his gold dust in a bag, and said:

"Gentlemen, I have worked with my own hands and seen with my own eyes, and the news of your rich discovery shall go all over the world, as far as my paper can waft it."

Mr. Greeley left, believing he had made a thorough test. As soon as he reached New York he devoted a whole side of the *Tribune* to an ecstatic description of the camp, headed with large, glaring type, such as "bill-stickers" use. The report was read all over the country, and caused a great rush to the land of promise. Those who had the fever took a relapse, and they had it bad. It was a raging epidemic, and spread faster than the cholera in Egypt.

He shouted into the ears of the over-crowded East until the welkin rang, "Young man, go West!" It was his glowing articles and earnest advice about "going West" that caused the first great boom in Colorado. The honest old man went down to his grave ignorant of the joke that was played upon him.

Going to California

. . . I reckon you don't remember the big excitement. No? Well, it swept all Tennessee like a fire in prairie grass. I first heard it one day at Manchester, when the Whigs had a pole-raisin' along o' the election o' old Zach Taylor, an' a man jist from Noo York spoke, and said old Zach had conquered for us a country with more gold in it than any nation on earth had. Pretty soon the news come thick. They said men just dug gold out o' the rocks—thousands in a day. You ought to heard the stories that was told for solemn facts. One man said a feller dug out one lump worth eight hundred thousand dollars, an' as he set on it, a feller come by with a plate o' pork an' beans, an' he offered him fifty thousand for it, an' the feller stood him off for seventy-five thousand. It was in the Nashville paper, an' so every body in our parts believed it.

Then every loose-footed man wanted to go. Some jist throwed down their tools an' started; an' some men that was tied with families actually set down an' cried 'cause they couldn't go. My boys was as crazy as the rest. But they was only sixteen an' eighteen, an' I seed it wouldn't do. So I said: "Boys, let me go, an' I'll let you know in time," an' then I bound 'em to take care o' their mother till I sent for 'em. It woulda been ruination for them young innocent boys to go off with such a lot o' men. Jest as soon as the Tennessee was up so boats could run over Muscle Shoals, a company of forty of us shipped teams an' started, an' landed at Independence, Missouri, the last o' March. The whole country was under water, but our fellers was crazy to git on; so they hitched up and started right across the Kaw an' into the Delawares' country. But it was all foolishness to start so early. Accident after accident we had. The mud was thicker an' stickier every day, an' all the creeks was up; but the men kept up a-hoopin' an' swearin', an' often had to double teams, an' sometimes we'd stick an' pull out two or three wagon tongues 'fore we'd get through. I never seed men so crazy to git on. They whipped an' yelled, an' wouldn't listen to reason. They was plenty started three weeks after us, an' passed us on the road. An' what was strange, the trains that laid by an' kept Sunday got to Californy first. You wouldn't believe it, but I've heard hundreds say the same thing.

Bimeby we got righted up an' on drier ground, an' went on after

---

From *Western Wilds and the Men Who Redeem Them,* An Authentic Narrative, Embracing an Account of Seven Years Travel and Adventure in the Far West; Wild Life in Arizona; Perils of the Plains; Life in the Cañon and Death on the Desert; Thrilling Scenes and Romantic Incidents in the Lives of Western Pioneers; Adventures among the Red and White Savages of the West; A Full Account of the Mountain Meadow Massacre; the Custer Defeat; Life and Death of Brigham Young, etc., by J. H. Beadle, pp. 38–42. Copyright, 1877, by John T. Jones. Cincinnati, Philadelphia, Chicago: Jones Brothers & Co.

killin' two or three hosses an' leavin' one wagon. The trains got strung out all along the trail, so we had grass an' game plenty along up the Blue River an' over to the Platte. There we struck the Mormon emigration an' all the Californy trains that went that way. The whole country was et out, an' the Injins threatened, an' the men got to quarrelin'. I tell you it takes a mighty good set o' men to travel together three thousand miles an' not fuss. Sometimes it was Whig and Democrat, an' then it was Tennessee agin Geawgey. I tell you when men are tired an' dirty they'll quarrel about anything. About half a dozen swore Californy was all humbug an' turned back, an' at Laramie Forks the company split into two. At South Pass our half split agin, an' ten of us went off with a company to go the new route, south of the Salt Lake. We got to the Mormon City all beat out, an' more'n half a mind not to go a mile further. Plenty got there in worse humor than us. Some had split up till it was each man for himself, an' some actually divided wagons, an' made two carts out o' one, or finished the trip on hosses. We took a rest, an' traded every thing with the Mormons, givin' two of our hosses for one fresh one, an' finally got off in pretty good shape agin.

But all we'd seed was nothin' to the country from there on. Rocks an' mountains an' sand; an' sand, an' rocks an' mountains—miles on miles of it. Sometimes the water was white as soapsuds with alkali, an' sometimes as red as brick-dust, not one time in five sweet an' clean. I reckon I swore a thousand times if I ever got home agin nothin' stronger 'n cold water should pass my lips. I've drove all day 'thout seein' a spear o' green, or a speck of anything but sand; an' if we got grass once a day, we was in luck. Every day the men swore nothin' could beat this, an' the next day it was always worse. I reckon God knows what he made that country for—he hain't told anybody, though.

At last we got into a region that was the hind end o' creation—seventy miles 'thout a drop o' water or a spear o' grass! Nothin' but hot sand an' beds of alkali as white as your shirt. The trains used to start in one afternoon an' drive two nights an' a day, an' get to water the second mornin'. The whole way was lined with boxes an' beds an' clothes, an' pieces of wagons, one thing an' another the trains ahead had left, an' the last ten miles you mighta stepped from one carcass to another on the dead hosses an' mules an' oxen. Two o' our men got crazy as loons —you can see such strange things on them deserts. My head was clear as a bell, an' yet half the time I could see off to one side of us a train jest like our'n, only the men an' hosses ten times as big, an' jest as like as not they'd raise in the air an' move off upside down. It was sort o' skeery, an' no mistake. We left four or five dead hosses on that tract, but when we got to Carson River, it was too pretty a sight to tell about. There was sweet, clean water an' grass an' trees an' trains strung along for miles a-restin' their stock. Some of our men run right into the water an' swallowed an' swallowed till they staggered like drunk men. All the rest of the way was in the mountains, but grass and water was plenty, an' the trees—how I did admire to see 'em! Hundreds o' miles I hadn't seen a bush as thick as my thumb.

Well, we was into Californy at last, an' it looked like heaven to me. There was big trees, an' the wind blowin' soft away up in their tops; an' the pretty clear streams down the mountain side an' through the gulches made music all day. In some places the air was jist sweet that blowed out o' the pine woods, an' week after week the sky was so blue, an' the air so soft, it seemed like a man could stand anything. An' no matter how hard you worked in the day, or how hot it was, it was always so cool an' nice at night; you could sleep anywheres—on the ground or on a pile o' limbs, in the house or out o' doors, an' never catch cold.

But if the country was like heaven, the folks was like the other place, I reckon. Such sights—such doins'! I'd never-a believed men would carry on so. I went to minin' in the Amador, an' first they wasn't a woman in a hundred miles. And when one did come in one day on a wagon, the men all run to look at her as if she was a show. Better she'da stayed away, an' twenty more like her that come in when the diggins begun to pan out rich. I believe every woman was the cause o' fifty fights an' one or two deaths. It made me mad to see men fight about 'em, when they knowed jest what they was—men that had mothers an' sisters back in the States, an' some of 'em sweethearts an' wives. They was mostly Mexican women, an' some Chilaynos an' South Spainers; an' somehow it was a sort o' comfort to me that there was hardly ever an American woman among the lot.

Bimeby these diggins sort o' worked out, an' I went down on Tuolumne, an' then mined about Angells an' Murphy's Camp, an' finally to Sonora. Then all sorts o' new ways o' minin' come in, but they took capital, an' I let 'em alone. Men was all the time runnin' about from camp to camp—so many new excitements—no matter how rich the ground where we was, some feller would come in with a big story about a new gulch, an' away they'd go. I've seen a thousand men at work along one creek, an' a big excitement break out, an' before night they wouldn't be twenty left. Sometimes a man would get title to big ground, an' hold it at a thousand dollars, an' when the rush come you could buy him out with two mules an' a pair o' blankets. Many an' many a time I've seen a man go off that way with a little money an' never be seen alive. Like enough his body was found away down the river an' like enough it was never found. It got so they was men there that would cut a throat for ten dollars. It wasn't all one way, though. More'n once the robbers would tackle some gritty man that was handy with his "barkers," an' he'd get away with two or three of 'em. Everybody carried the irons with him, ready to pop at a minute's notice, an' if a man traveled alone, he took his life in his hand.

It wasn't long though till we got some kind o' government. Californy was made a State the year after I got there, but that didn't signify in the mountains; an' at Angell's Camp we chipped in together and hired regular guards to look after every suspicious man. The worst thing was to get down from the mines to Frisco; for if it was known that a man was goin' to leave, it was 'sposed he'd made his pile, an' had it with him. At last I made a little raise—that was in the spring of '52—an' concluded to come home. Me an' my partner jest laid down our tools one night right where we worked, an' packed up, an' when the camp was asleep lit out over the hills 'thout sayin' a word to any human bein'. Got home round by Panama all right, an' found every thing chipper, an' when I figured up, I was just three hundred ahead on the three year's trip. Better stayed at home *for gold*—but it saved the boys.

Society in the Mining Camp

It is a country unlike any other. Nature here is as rude, as inchoate, as unfinished, as the life. The people seem to have come here a thousand years too soon, and before the great hostess was ready to receive them. The forests, vast, silent, damp with their undergrowth of gigantic ferns, recall a remote carboniferous epoch. The trees are monstrous, somber, and monotonously alike. Everything is new, crude, and strange. The grass blades are enormous and far apart, there is no carpet to the soil; even the few Alpine flowers are odorless and bizarre. There is nothing soft, tender, or pastoral in the landscape. Nature affects the heroics rather than the bucolics. Theocritus himself could scarcely have given melody to the utterance of these Aetnean herdsmen, with their brierwood pipes, and their revolvers slung at their backs. There are vast spaces of rock and cliff, long intervals of ravine and cañon, and sudden and awful lapses of precipice. The lights and shadows are Rembrandtish, and against this background the faintest outline of a human figure stands out starkly.

[The Argonauts] lived at first in tents, and then in cabins. The climate was gracious, and except for the rudest purposes of shelter from the winter rains, they could have slept out of doors the year round, as many preferred to do. As they grew more ambitious, perhaps a small plot of ground was inclosed and cultivated; but for the first few years they looked upon themselves as tenants at will, and were afraid of putting down anything they could not take away. Chimneys to their cabins were for a long time avoided as having this objectionable feature. Even at this day, deserted mining camps are marked by the solitary adobe chimneys still left standing where the frame of the original cabin was moved to some newer location. Their housekeeping was of the rudest kind. For many months the frying pan formed their only available cooking utensil. It was lashed to the

From *The Writings of Bret Harte*, Standard Library Edition, Volume II, pp. xx–xxx. Copyright, 1872, 1875, by James R. Osgood & Co.; 1878, 1879, by Houghton, Osgood & Co.; 1896, by Houghton, Mifflin & Co. Boston and New York.

wandering miner's back, like the troubadour's guitar. He fried his bread, his beans, his bacon, and occasionally stewed his coffee, in this single vessel. But that Nature worked for him with a balsamic air and breezy tonics, he would have succumbed. Happily his meals were few and infrequent; happily the inventions of his mother East were equal to his needs. His progressive track through these mountain solitudes was marked with tin cans bearing the inscriptions: "Cove Oysters," "Shaker Sweet Corn," "Yeast Powder," "Boston Crackers," and the like. But in the hour of adversity and the moment of perplexity, his main reliance was beans! It was the sole legacy of the Spanish California. The conqueror and the conquered fraternized over their *frijoles.*

The Argonaut's dress was peculiar. He was ready if not skillful with his needle, and was fond of patching his clothes until the original material disappeared beneath a cloud of amendments. The flour-sack was his main dependence. When its contents had sustained and comforted the inner man, the husk clothed the outer one. Two gentlemen of respectability in earlier days lost their identity in the labels somewhat conspicuously borne on the seats of their trousers, and were known to the camp in all seriousness as "Genesee Mills" and "Eagle Brand." In the Southern mines a quantity of seamen's clothing, condemned by the Navy Department and sold at auction, was bought up, and for a year afterwards the somber woodland shades of Stanislaus and Merced were lightened by the white ducks and blue and white shirts of sailor landsmen. It was odd that the only picturesque bit of color in their dress was accidental, and owing to a careless, lazy custom. Their handkerchiefs of coarse blue, green, or yellow bandana were for greater convenience in hot weather knotted at the ends and thrown shawlwise around the shoulders. Against a background of olive foliage, the effect was always striking and kaleidoscopic. The soft felt, broad-brimmed hat, since known as the California hat, was their only head-covering. A tall hat on anybody but a clergyman or a gambler would have justified a blow.

They were singularly handsome, to a man. Not solely in the muscular development and antique grace acquired through open-air exercise and unrestrained freedom of limb, but often in color, expression, and even softness of outline. They were mainly young men, whose beards were virgin, soft, silken, and curling. They had not always time to cut their hair, and this often swept their shoulders with the lovelocks of Charles II. There were faces that made one think of Delaroche's Saviour. There were dashing figures, bold-eyed, jauntily insolent, and cavalierly reckless, that would have delighted Meissonier. Add to this the foreign element of Chilian and Mexican, and you have a combination of form and light and color unknown to any other modern English-speaking community. At sunset on the red mountain road, a Mexican pack-train perhaps slowly winds its way toward the plain. Each animal wears a gayly colored blanket beneath its pack saddle; the leading mule is musical with bells, and brightly caparisoned; the muleteers wear the national dress, with striped *serape* of red and black, deerskin trousers open from the knee, and fringes with bullion buttons, and have on each heel a silver spur with rowels three inches in diameter.

If they were thus picturesque in external magnificence, no less romantic were they in expression and character. Their hospitality was barbaric, their generosity spontaneous. Their appreciation of merit always took the form of pecuniary testimonials, whether it was a church and parsonage given to a favorite preacher, or the Danaë-like shower of gold they rained upon the pretty person of a popular actress. No mendicant had to beg; a sympathizing bystander took up a subscription in his hat. Their generosity was emulative and cumulative. During the great War of the Rebellion, the millions gathered in the Treasury of the Sanitary Commission had their source in a San Francisco bar-room. "It's mighty rough on those chaps who are wounded," said a casual drinker, "and I'm sorry for them." "How much are you sorry?" asked a gambler. "Five hundred dollars," said the first speaker aggressively. "I'll see that five hundred dollars, and go a thousand better," said the gambler, putting down the money. In half an hour fifteen thousand dollars was telegraphed to Washington from San Francisco, and this great national charity—open to North and South alike, afterwards reinforced by three millions of California gold—sprang into life.

In their apparently thoughtless free-handedness there was often a vein of practical sagacity. It is a well-known fact that after the great fire in Sacramento, the first subscription to the rebuilding of the Methodist Church came from the hands of a noted gambler. The good pastor, while accepting the gift, could not help asking the giver why he did not keep the money to build another gambling house. "It would be making things a little *monotonous* out yer, ole man," responded the gambler gravely, "and it's variety that's wanted for a big town."

They were splendidly loyal in their friendships. Perhaps the absence of female society and domestic ties turned the current of their tenderness and sentiment towards each other. To be a man's "partner" signified something more than a common pecuniary or business interest; it was to be his friend through good or ill report, in adversity or fortune, to cleave to him and none other—to be ever jealous of him! There were Argonauts who were more faithful to their partners than, I fear, they had ever been to their wives; there were partners whom even the grave could not divide—who remained solitary and loyal to a dead man's memory. To insult a man's partner was to insult him; to step between two partners in a quarrel was attended with the same danger and uncertainty that involves the peacemaker in a conjugal dispute. The heroic possibilities of a Damon and Pythias were always present; there were men who had fulfilled all those conditions, and better still without a knowledge or belief that they were classical, with no mythology to lean their backs against, and hardly a conscious appreciation of a later faith that is symbolized by sacrifice. In these unions there were the same odd combinations often seen in the marital relations: a tall and a short man, a delicate sickly youth and a middle-aged man of powerful frame, a grave reticent nature and a spontaneous exuberant one. Yet in spite of these incongruities there was always the same blind unreasoning fidelity to each other. It is true that their zeal sometimes outran their discretion. There is a story extant that a San Francisco stranger, indulging in some free criticism of religious denominations, suddenly found himself sprawling upon the floor with an irate Kentuckian, revolver in hand, standing over him. When an explanation was demanded by the crowd, the Kentuckian pensively returned his revolver to his belt. "Well, *I* ain't got anythin' agin the stranger, but he said somethin' a minit ago agin Quakers, and I want him to understand that my *pardner* is a Quaker, and—a *peaceful man!*"

I should like to give some pictures of their domestic life, but the women were few and the family hearthstones and domestic altars still fewer. Of housewifely virtues the utmost was made; the model spouse invariably kept a boarding-house, and served her husband's guests. In rare cases, the woman who was a crown to her husband took in washing also.

There was a woman of this class who lived in a little mining camp in the Sierras. Her husband was a Texan—a good-humored giant, who had won the respect of the camp probably quite as much by his amiable weakness as by his great physical power. She was an Eastern woman; had been, I think, a schoolmistress, and had lived in cities up to the time of her marriage and emigration. She was not, perhaps, personally attractive; she was plain and worn beyond her years, and her few personal accomplishments—a slight knowledge of French and Italian, music, the Latin classification of plants, natural philosophy and Blair's Rhetoric—did not tell upon the masculine inhabitants of Ringtail Cañon. Yet she was universally loved, and Aunt Ruth, as she was called, or "Old Ma'am Richards," was lifted into an idealization of the aunt, mother, or sister of every miner in the camp. She reciprocated in a thousand kindly ways, mending the clothes, ministering to the sick, and even answering the long home letters of the men.

Presently she fell ill. Nobody knew exactly what was the matter with her, but she pined slowly away. When the burden of her household tasks was lifted from her shoulders, she took to long walks, wandering over the hills, and was often seen upon the highest ridge at sunset, looking toward the east. Here at last she was found senseless—the result, it was said, of overexertion, and she was warned to keep her house. So she kept her house, and even went so far as to keep her bed. One day, to everybody's astonishment, she died. "Do you know what they say Ma'am Richards died of?" said Yuba Bill to his partner. "The doctor says she died of *nostalgia*," said Bill. "What blank thing is nostalgia?"

asked the other. "Well, it's a kind of longin' to go to heaven!" Perhaps he was right.

As a general thing the Argonauts were not burdened with sentiment, and were utterly free from its more dangerous ally, sentimentalism. They took a sardonic delight in stripping all meretricious finery from their speech; they had a sarcastic fashion of eliminating everything but the facts from poetic or imaginative narrative. With all that terrible directness of statement which was habitual to them, when they indulged in innuendo it was significantly cruel and striking. In the early days, Lynch law punished horse-stealing with death. A man one day was arrested and tried for this offense. After hearing the evidence, the jury duly retired to consult upon their verdict. For some reason—perhaps from an insufficiency of proof, perhaps from motives of humanity, perhaps because the census was already showing an alarming decrease in the male population—the jury showed signs of hesitation. The crowd outside became impatient. After waiting an hour, the ringleader put his head into the room and asked if the jury had settled upon a verdict. "No," said the foreman. "Well," answered the leader, "take your own time, gentlemen; only remember that we're waitin' for this yer room to lay out the corpse in!"

Their humor was frequent, although never exuberant or spontaneous, and always contained a certain percentage of rude justice or morality under its sardonic exterior. The only ethical teaching of those days was through a joke or a sarcasm. While camps were moved by an epigram, the rude equity of Judge Lynch was swayed by a witticism. Even their pathos, which was more or less dramatic, partook of this quality. The odd expression, the quaint fancy, or even the grotesque gesture that rippled the surface consciousness with a smile, a moment later touched the depths of the heart with a sense of infinite sadness. They indulged sparingly in poetry and illustration, using only its rude, inchoate form of slang. Unlike the meaningless cues and catch-words of an older civilization, their slang was the condensed epigrammatic illustration of some fact, fancy, or perception. Generally it had some significant local derivation. The half-yearly drought brought forward the popular adjuration "dry up" to express the natural climax of evaporated fluency. "Played out" was a reminiscence of the gambling-table, and expressed that hopeless condition of affairs when even the operations of chance are suspended. To "take stock" in any statement, theory, or suggestion indicates a pecuniary degree of trustful credulity. One can hardly call that slang, even though it came from a gambler's lips, which gives such a vivid condensation of death and the reckoning hereafter as was conveyed in the expression, "handing in your checks." In those days the slang was universal; there was no occasion to which it seemed inconsistent. Thomas Starr King once told me that, after delivering a certain controversial sermon, he overheard the following dialogue between a parishioner and his friend. "Well," said the enthusiastic parishioner, referring to the sermon, "what do you think of

King now?" "Think of him?" responded the friend. "Why he took every trick!"

Sometimes, through the national habit of amusing exaggeration or equally grotesque understatement, certain words acquired a new significance. I remember the first night I spent in Virginia City was at a new hotel which had been but recently opened. After I had got comfortably to bed, I was aroused by the noise of scuffling and shouting below, punctuated by occasional pistol shots. In the morning I made my way to the bar-room, and found the landlord behind his counter with a bruised eye, a piece of court plaster extending from his cheek to his forehead, yet withal a pleasant smile upon his face. Taking my cue from this I said to him: "Well, landlord, you had rather a lively time here last night." "Yes," he replied, pleasantly. "It *was* rather a lively time!" "Do you often have such lively times in Virginia City?" I added, emboldened by his cheerfulness. "Well, no," he said, reflectively; "the fact is we've only just opened yer, and last night was about the first time that the boys seemed to be gettin' really *acquainted!*"

The man who objected to join in a bear hunt because "he hadn't lost any bears lately," and the man who replied to the tourist's question "if they grew any corn in that locality" by saying "not a d——d bit, in fact scarcely any," offered easy examples of this characteristic anticlimax and exaggeration. Often a flavor of gentle philosophy mingled with it. "In course I'd rather not drive a mule team," said a teamster to me. "In course I'd rather run a bank or be President; but when you've lived as long as I have, stranger, you'll find that in this yer world a man don't always get his 'drathers.' "

Often a man's trade or occupation lent a graphic power to his speech. On one occasion an engineer was relating to me the particulars of a fellow workman's death by consumption. "Poor Jim," he said, "he got to running slower and slower, until one day—he stopped on his center!" What a picture of the helpless hitch in this weary human machine! Sometimes the expression was borrowed from another's profession. At one time there was a difficulty in a surveyor's camp between the surveyor and a Chinaman. "If I was you," said a sympathizing teamster to the surveyor, "I'd jest take that chap and theodolite him out o' camp." Sometimes the slang was a mere echo of the formulas of some popular excitement or movement. During a camp-meeting in the mountains, a teamster who had been swearing at his cattle was rebuked for his impiety by a young woman who had just returned from the meeting. "Why, Miss," said the astonished teamster, "you don't call that swearing, do you? Why, you ought to hear Bill Jones exhort the impenitent mule!"

But can we entirely forgive the Argonaut for making his slang gratuitously permanent, for foisting upon posterity, who may forget these extenuating circumstances, such titles as "One Horse Gulch," "Poker Flat," "Greaser Cañon," "Fiddletown," "Murderer's Bar," and "Dead Broke"? The map of California is still ghastly with this unhallowed christening. A tourist may well hesitate to write "Dead Broke" at the top of his letter, and any stranger would be justified in declining an invitation to "Murderer's Bar." It seemed as if the early Californian took a sardonic delight in the contrast which these names offered to the euphony of the old Spanish titles. It is fortunate that with few exceptions the counties of the State still bear the soft Castilian labials and gentle vowels. Tuolumne, Tulare, Yolo, Calaveras, Sonoma, Tehema, Siskyou, and Mendocino, to say nothing of the glorious company of the Apostles who perpetually praise California through the Spanish Catholic calendar. Yet wherever a saint dropped a blessing, some sinner afterwards squatted with an epithet. Extremes often meet. The omnibuses in San Francisco used to run from Happy Valley to the Mission Dolores. You had to go to Blaises first before you could get to Purissima. Yet I think the ferocious directness of these titles was preferable to the pinchbeck elegance of "Copperopolis," "Argentinia," the polyglot monstrosities of "Oroville," of "Placerville," or the remarkable sentiment of "Romeosburgh" and "Julietstown." Sometimes the national tendency to abbreviation was singularly shown. "Jamestown," near Sonora, was always known as "Jimtown," and "Moquelumne Hill," after first suffering phonetic torture by being spelt with a "k," was finally drawn and quartered and now appears on the stagecoach as "Mok Hill." There were some names that defied all conjecture. The Pioneer coaches changed horses at a place called "Paradox." Why Paradox? No one could tell.

The Englishman on the Range

I[1]

[A] friend of mine [on the Powder River] told me that when he was working as a young cowpuncher there came to the ranch house on foot a tall, dusty Englishman, under his arm a little sewing machine. He asked for work.

"Ranch work?" asked the owner.

"No," said the Englishman. "I'm tired of that. Sewing is what I want. I'm rather good at sewing. I'll keep all your clothes, and saddles and things, and everybody else's in order."

And he did, with contentment, for five years—mending bridles and saddles, and torn overalls, and shirts, and towels.

At the end of five years he turned up for supper one night and said, "Sorry! I got a letter this afternoon, and I'm afraid I'll have to be going. My father's dead, and I suppose I'm in for a title or something."

---

[1] From *Powder River, Let 'er Buck,* by Struthers Burt, pp. 247–248. Copyright, 1938, by Struthers Burt. New York and Toronto: Farrar & Rinehart, Inc.

II[2]

While on Powder River I was told lots of funny stories about the English colony that I should not have learned otherwise. There was the gag on Whallop (or Wachoup, as it should be), recalled a year or so ago to be a member of the House of Lords. Whenever he was in an awkward situation, and some were racy, he would say, "I wonder what my mother, the Duchess, would say if she could see me now." All the cowboys in the country would get that gag off every once in a while. Sidney Padget was asked one time by a curious puncher called Billy, "Say, Sid, is it true that in the old country you are the son of a lord?" "Billy," says Sid, "in the old country they call me a son of a lord, and in this country they call me a son of a b——, but it's the same old Sid all the time."

Then there was the horseman whose ranch was on Pumpkin Creek—I forget his name—but his brother, the Major, came out one summer with his valet. The valet got sick one day, or something happened to him, and the Major called on one of the boys to shine up his riding boots. "Sure," said the puncher, "I'll do 'em," and he did a good job. Then the puncher told the Major to do just as good a job on his (the puncher's) boots. The Major put up something of a kick, and tried to work the single eyeglass trick, but "cowboy" would not stand for it—was not quite satisfied, even after the Major *had* shined his shoes, that it was as good a job.

Young Carrillo Forgets Spanish

There was another Carrillo—we will call him the Judge. The Judge was a highly educated gentleman, in fact he was educated in Boston. A hide drogher carried him from Santa Bárbara around the Horn to Boston to college when he was about twelve years old, and brought him home again some four years later. That was, of course, when California was a province of Mexico.

The homecoming was somewhat startling. The young graduate presented himself at the parental mansion, a delightful old adobe in the town that was the seat of old Spanish aristocracy in California, dressed in high Boston style and feeling himself to be a very important Yankee-wise cosmopolitan. The Señora, his mother, was overjoyed to see her boy, and, after tears, laughter, and caresses, she sat him down in the

[2] From "Blue Blood—Horse and Man—on the Mizpah, 1887," by H. C. B. Colvill, *The Frontier,* A Magazine of the Northwest, edited by Harold G. Merriam, Vol. X (May, 1930), No. 4, pp. 333–334. Copyright, 1930, by H. G. Merriam. Missoula, Montana.

From *On the Old West Coast,* Being Further Reminiscences of a Ranger, Major Horace Bell, edited by Lanier Bartlett, pp. 118–119. Copyright, 1930, by William Morrow & Co., Inc. New York.

sala to have a talk with him in dignified Castilian. But the boy seemed to have forgotten his mother tongue; his replies were couched in the Yankee idiom.

With amazement which grew to indignation, the Señora de Carrillo rebuked her son, but he continued to show off his superior education. Whereupon the Señora stalked out of doors, armed herself with a length of rawhide rope, swept into the *sala* again like an avenging goddess and sailed into the embryo judge with such expletives as: "Thou canst no longer speak Spanish, hey? Well, *I'll* teach thee Spanish!" Rap! Whack! Slap!

"Por Dios, mama—mamacita—por Dios, no, no!" yelled the previously arrogant cosmopolite. Swish! Snap! continued the rawhide until the youth poured forth a torrent of Spanish, imploring and promising without the least trace of Boston accent. At that moment he reverted to his racial heritage and remained thenceforth quite typical, as some of the incidents of his distinguished career may suggest; although the fact that he had enjoyed a Boston education he stressed with great success in advancing himself under the American régime. He was a member of the first State Constitutional Convention that framed the Constitution of the State of California in 1849, became a state senator and a member of the judiciary.

General Carrillo Apologizes to the Mormon Captain

A great family were these Carrillos. Some of them were mighty men and the women were all beautiful to look upon. The most noted of the men was General José Antonio. He commanded the Californians at the battle of Los Cuerbos, commonly called the Battle of Domínguez, when the American marines under Captain Mervine of the frigate *Savannah* were marching on Los Angeles from San Pedro during the Mexican War. It occurred near where Compton now stands. He had previously represented California in the Mexican Congress. A remarkable fellow he was, standing six feet four inches tall, weighing about two hundred and forty pounds, and bearing a perfect resemblance to the statues of some of the old Roman senators.

General Carrillo was full of humor and boiling over with sarcasm. He came very near getting into a duel with a captain in the Mormon Battalion in Los Angeles in 1847. Doña Luisa Avila was married to a Mexican officer, Lieut. Col. Manuel Gárfias, who was a nephew of Porfírio Díaz, later ruler of Mexico for so many years. Gárfias had been a member of the famous Micheltorena Battalion which had been expelled by the revolting Californians. He had resigned his commission in the army and returned to Los Angeles to marry the daughter of Doña Concepción de Avila. Doña Concepción was owner of the San

---

Ibid., 116–118.

Pascual grant, where Pasadena now stands and which later passed into the possession of Colonel Gárfias.

A great fiesta followed the nuptials, and the party developed into an occasion of reconciliation between the American army officers and those of the late Californian army. The generals were all there and the captains and lieutenants. General Carrillo was there, grim and sarcastic. He was far from being reconciled. There was a certain Mormon captain there, too, who thought himself a great dancer. Carrillo stared with pointed disapproval at his awkward performances and finally remarked to some dignitary of the American faction: "That officer of yours dances like a bear."

The Mormon captain was informed of the remark and on the following day sent a challenge to General Carrillo to meet him in mortal combat. The Californian at once accepted the challenge and appointed his seconds, and excitement ran high on both sides. General Kearny, the commander-in-chief of the American forces of occupation, decided there must be no bloodshed and offered his services as mediator.

In the course of these peace negotiations the whole crowd, principals and all, brought up at the hospitable home of Nathaniel Pryor. The Pryor house was famous for good cheer; it was a fine house, backed up by a fine vineyard that supplied a fine cellar with fine wines. The vineyard was bounded on the east by Alameda Street and extended from Aliso Street south to Wolfskill's line. The place had a high whitewashed adobe wall around it and was altogether quite grand.

Going into conference again here, in the midst of these congenial surroundings, General Kearny, aided by Major Emory, brought such diplomacy to bear on General Carrillo as to persuade him that he owed an apology to the Mormon. But the friends of the Mormon stubbornly insisted that the apology must be in writing. To the pleased surprise of the sticklers for the written word Carrillo immediately agreed; whereupon it is to be presumed that the cheery stock in Nathaniel Pryor's famed cellar suffered further depletion.

General Carrillo's only stipulation was that he was to be given until the next day to write and deliver the apology, delivery to be made here at this same pleasant gathering place.

At the appointed time the principals, mediators, seconds, and friends were present; indeed, the crowd was considerably larger than it had been the day before. The Americans were on tip-toe to see what sort of an apology a haughty Californian ex-general and high dignitary would make to an American volunteer captain.

After the wine had circulated a translator was selected to read aloud the apology, which was as follows:

> I am a native of California; I love my country and stick up for it, the bear is my countryman so I love the bear. I now apologize to the bear for suggesting that the redheaded captain danced like a bear. The injury is to the bear, because the captain could not dance half so well.
>
> José Antonio Carrillo

The Mormon captain was more wroth than ever and insisted on a fight then and there. But the droll apology had struck everybody's funny-bone. Both factions turned on the aggrieved redhead with so much ridicule that he was laughed off the place, and the crisis was averted for good and all.

New Mexico Folksay

. . . Since we live in a multilingual state (Spanish is widely spoken, as well as half a dozen or more Indian tongues), we expect some linguistic exchanges in proverbial sayings. For instance, one hears a saying in English in New Mexico: "Wherever the ox goes, he plows." It is Spanish: "El buey, donde que irá, ará." Another English saying with a debt to Spanish is: "Always sweep where your mother-in-law looks." This is likely to persist in English for it has no rival saying, to my knowledge. "A crooked tree will never straighten its branches," say English-speaking Spanish Americans.[1] "As the twig is bent, so is the tree inclined" is the form most Americans have heard, but the expression of Spanish origin is simpler and quite as effective. The Spanish *dichos* come slowly into English, but they are an important contribution nevertheless, adding the quiet wit and sagacity of the Spanish outlook to the gustier metaphor and epithet of the Anglo.[2]

In New Mexico there are two veins of Anglo-American life from which proverbial sayings may be drawn. One is the pioneer vein which runs deep and back to the fourth and fifth generation, the talk of New Mexicans whose forbears came into the territory in the mid-nineteenth century after annexation from Mexico in 1848. The other is the recent deposit of settlers drawn from every state in the Union, colonizers of the region since statehood in 1912, whose talk carries the proverbs of Kentucky or Pennsylvania or Maine. . . . Such sayings as "There she goes, hud [head] up and tail over the dashboard" could be as much Missourian as New Mexican, and "Be a man or a mouse or a long-tailed rat" is known to have Kentucky as a source (if no other place).[3]

From "The English Proverb in New Mexico," by T. M. Pearce, *California Folklore Quarterly,* Vol. V (October, 1946), No. 4, pp. 351–353, 354. Copyright, 1946, by the California Folklore Society.

[1] *Arbol que crece torcido nunca sus ramos enderese.*—T.M.P.

[2] A proverbial saying which combines English and Spanish is "to be on the *cuidado,*" which means "to be on the lookout" or "on the dodge." At the May, 1946, meeting of the New Mexico Folklore Society, a member presented the following proverb as of Indian origin: "One shot meat; two shots maybe; three shots no good." But in Miss Hardie's collection (Jente, "The American Proverb," *American Speech,* VII, June, 1932, pp. 345–347) appears "One cook's a cook, two cooks are half a cook and three cooks are no cooks at all." The New Mexico files also have: "One boy—all boy; two boys—one half a boy; three boys—no boys at all." Professor Jente was not able to find any information as to the provenience of this proverb.—T.M.P.

[3] Professor Jente, University of North Carolina, has compiled "A Checklist of 1250 Proverbs" for use of collectors contributing toward a dictionary of American Proverbs. One of his proverbs is "To-day a man, tomorrow a mouse."—T.M.P.

But "This little nester[4] gal was so pore she made a five-toed track on her way to Sunday School" couldn't spring from any locality east of Kansas. In this case, the speaker came from Tecolotenos, New Mexico, and was born on a mountain ranch at Beulah in this state. His father was a pioneer settler at Moran, Texas, who moved to the mountains of New Mexico about 1890. The speaker also sent in such sayings as "He looked as harassed as a stump-tailed bull in fly-time" and "No man can ride a bronco if he ain't split up the middle."

In a state where 90 per cent of the total area is range land, proverbs and sayings flavored by ranch life should be extremely common. Many of these are picturesque and humorous, expressing a universal truth in homely metaphor. Such are:

High-powered saddles ain't half as hard to find as high-powered hombres in 'em.
He hit the ground in the high places (meaning "he rode fast").
The toughest broncs is them you've rode some other place.
A windy is a feller huntin' grizzly bears in camp.
Riggin' ain't ridin'.

A large group of local sayings deal with the weather, always a source of annoyance or satisfaction in dealing with "cow critters."

You get so dry you have to be primed to spit.
Nothin' to stop the wind but a bob-wire fence, and that blew down in the last norther.
It sure is hell when it's this way, and it's this way now.
I hope it rains hard enough so we have to dive down to grease the windmill.

Common to mountain men, river men, and plainsmen, as they moved west on the frontier, are similes and metaphors describing physical prowess. To localize these may be difficult, for they could have picked up the mark of the wilderness almost anywhere between the Atlantic and the Pacific.

I'm a curly wolf and it's my night to howl.
I told them I was from Bitter Creek and the higher up the worse they got, and I was from the head.
I can boast a little wildcat blood my own self.

Only one of the proverbs or sayings quoted so far in this paper can be found in Professor Jente's Checklist or in Apperson's *English Proverbs and Proverbial Phrases* (London, 1929). However, there are many Western sayings that are recognizable adaptations of familiar sayings known in England and in the eastern United States.

---

[4] The term *nester* was applied by cattlemen in the Southwest to the first homesteaders, supposedly because their cleared patches with brush stacked around them to protect the crops from roving cattle resembled nests. (See article by John M. Hendrix in *West Texas Today,* March, 1936, p. 6.) Later, cowboys used the word in gibing at other cowboys who married and settled down to farming.—T.M.P.

Between a rock and a hard place.—Between the devil and the deep blue sea.
Down to chili and beans.—Down to their last penny.
To kick a hog barefooted.—To kick against the pricks.
To feed someone Mexican oats.—To feed someone "baloney" or to feed (hand out) a line.

Sayings stressing independence of spirit and love of freedom are conspicuous in our State collections. Some of these are:

I'm thankful this is a country where a man can switch his tail.
Let's keep this a country where every man is entitled to scratch his own itch.
I've got the world by the tail on a downhill drag.
That kind of man ain't got to ask nobody when he wants an egg to suck.

In conclusion, I want to quote a proverb spoken by an old cowpuncher living in the Sandia Mountains near Albuquerque. I don't know whether it appears in other collections or not, but it has the right ring for a native American proverb, East or West.

Give some people everything you have and they still want the moon for a cow pasture.

Ba'tiste's Story of the Medicine-Bag (in "American")

"Bien, excusez—now Monsieur Bogard, you must know first place, de *'Medicine-Bags'* is mere humbug, he is no *medicine* in him—no pills; he is someting mysterieux. Some witchcraft, súppose. You must know que tous les sauvages have such tings about him, pour for good luck. Ce n'est que (pardón) it is only *hocus pocus,* to keep off witch, súppose. You must know, ces articles can nevare be sold, of course, you see dey cannot be buy. So my friend here, Monsieur Cataline, who have collect all de curiosités des pays sauvages, avait made strong applique to me for to get one of dese *medicine-bags* for his Collection curieux, et I had, pour moimeme, le curiosité extreme pour for to see des quelques choses ces étranges looking tings was composi.

"I had learn much of dese strange custom, and I know wen de Ingin die, his *medicine-bags* is buried wis him.

"Oui, Monsieur, so it never can be got by any boday. Bien. I hap to tink one day wen we was live in de mous of Yellowstone, now is time, and I avait said to Monsieur Cataline, que pensez vous! *Kon-te-wonda* (un des chefs du) (pardón, one of de chiefs of de Knisteneux) has die tó-day. Il avait une *medicine-bag* magnifique, et extrement curieux; il est composé d'un, it is made (pardón, si vous plait) of de wite wolf skin,

---

From *The Manners, Customs, and Conditions of the North American Indians,* by George Catlin, Written during Eight Years' Travel amongst the Wildest Tribes of Indians in North America, 1832–39, with Four Hundred Illustrations, Carefully Engraved from the Original Paintings, and Colored after Nature, in Two Volumes, Volume the Second, pp. 178–180. London: Published by the Author, at the Egyptian Hall, Piccadilly. 1841.

ornement et stuff wid tousand tings wich we shall see, ha? Good luck! Súppose Monsieur Cataline, I have seen him just now. I av see de *medicine-bag* laid on his breast avec his hands crossed ovare it. Que pensez-vous? I can get him to-night, ha? If you will keep him, if you shall not tell, ha? 'Tis no harm—'tis no steal—he is dead, ha? Well, you shall see. 'But, would you not be afraid, Ba'tiste, (said Monsieur Cataline), to take from dis poor fellow his medicines (or mysteries) on which he has rest all his hopes in dis world, and de world to come?' Pardón, je n'ai peur; non, Monsieur, ne rien de peur. I nevare saw ghost—I have not fear, mais, súppose, it is not right, éxact; but I have grand disposition pour for to obligé my friend, et le curiosité moimeme pour to see wat it is made of; súppose tó-night I shall go, ha? 'Well, Ba'tiste, I have no objection (said Monsieur Cataline) if your heart does not fail you, for I will be very glad to get him, and will make you a handsome present for it, but I think it will be a cold and gloomy kind of business.' Nevare mind, Monsieur Cataline (I said) provide he is well dead, *perfect dead!* Well, I had see les Knisteneux when dey ave bury de chap—I ave watch close, and I ave see how de medicine-bags was put. It was fix pretty tight by some cord around his bellay, and den some skins was wrap many times áround him—he was put down in de hole dug for him, and some flat stones and some little dirt was laid on him, only till next day, wen some grand ceremonays was to be pérform ovare him, and den de hole was to be fill up; now was de only times possibe for de *medicine-bag,* ha? I ave very pretty little wife at dat times, Assineboin squaw, and we sleep in one of de stores inside of de Fort, de Trade-house, you know, ha?

"So you may súppose I was all de day perplex to know how I should go, somebody may watch—súppose he may not be dead! not quite dead, ha? nevare mind—le jour was bien long, et le nuit dismal, *dismal!* oh by gar *it was dismal!* plein, plein (pardon) full of apprehension, mais sans *peur, je n'avais pas peur!* So some time aftere midnights, wen it was bout right time pour go, I made start, very light, so my wife must not wake. Oh diable l'imagination! quel solitude! well, I have go very well yet, I am pass de door, and I am pass de gate, and I am at lengts arrive at de grave! súppose 'now Ba'tiste, courage, courage! now is de times come.' Well, súppose, I am not fraid of *dead man,* mais, perhaps, dese *medicine-bag* is give by de Grand Esprit to de Ingin for someting? possibe! I will let him keep it. I shall go back! No, Monsieur Cataline will laughs at me. I must have him, ma foi, mon courage! so I climb down very careful into de grave, mais, as I descend, my heart rise up into my mouse! Oh mon Dieu! courage, Ba'tiste, courage! ce n'est pas *l'homme* dat I fear, mais le *medicine,* le *medicine.* So den I ave lift out de large stones, I ave put out my head in de dark, and I ave look all de contré round; ne personne, ne personne—no bodé in sight! Well, I ave got softly down on my knees ovare him, (oh, courage! courage! oui) and wen I ave unwrap de robe, I ave all de time say, 'pardón, courage! pardón, courage!' until I ad got de skins all off de bodé; I ave den take hold de cord to untie, mais!! (dans l'instant) two cold hands seize me by de wrists and I was just dead—I was petrifact in one instant. Oh, St. Esprit! I could just see in de dark two eyes glaring like fire sur upon me! and den, (oh, eugh!) it spoke to me, 'Who are you?' (Sacré, vengeance! it will not do to deceive him, no,) 'I am Ba'tiste, *poor* Ba'tiste!' 'Then thou art surely mine, (as he clenched both arms tight around my boday) lie still Ba'tiste.' Oh, holy Vierge! St. Esprit! O mon Dieu! I could not breathe! miserable! je suis perdu! oh pourquoi have I been such a fool to get into dese cold, cold arms! 'Ba'tiste? (drawing me some tighter and tighter) do you not belong to me, Ba'tiste?' Yes, súppose! oh diable! belong? Oui, oui, je suis certainment perdu, lost, lost, for evare! *Oh! can you not possibe let me go?* 'No, Ba'tiste, we must never part.' Grand Dieu. c'est finis, finis, finis avec moi! 'Then you do not love me any more, Ba'tiste?' Quel! quoi! what!! est-ce vous, *Wee-ne-on-ka?* 'Yes, Ba'tiste, it is the *Bending Willow* who holds you, she that loves you and will not let you go? Are you dreaming, Ba'tiste?' Oui, diable——"

Laforey's Lament for Coffee

The fare in Laforey's house was what might be expected in a hunter's establishment: venison, antelope, and the meat of the *carnero cimarrón,* the Rocky Mountain sheep, furnished his larder; and such meat (poor and tough at this season of the year), with cakes of Indian meal, either *tortillas* or *gorditas,*[1] furnished the daily bill of fare. The absence of coffee he made the theme of regret at every meal, bewailing his misfortune in not having at that particular moment a supply of this article, which he never before was without, and which I may here observe, amongst the hunters and trappers when in camp or rendezvous, is considered as an indispensable necessary. Coffee, being very cheap in the States, is the universal beverage of the Western people, and finds its way to the mountains in the packs of the Indian traders, who retail it to the mountain men at the moderate price of from two to six dollars the half-pint cup. However, my friend Laforey was never known to possess any, and his lamentations were only intended to soften my heart, as he thought (erroneously) that I must certainly carry a supply with me.

"Sacré enfant de Gârce," he would exclaim, mixing English, French, and Spanish into a puchero-like jumble, *"voyez-vous* dat I vas nevare tan pauvre as dis time; mais before I vas siempre avec plenty café,

---

From *Ruxton of the Rockies,* collected by Clyde and Mae Reed Porter, edited by LeRoy R. Hafen, pp. 197–198. Copyright, 1950, by the University of Oklahoma Press. Norman.

[1] The *tortilla* is a round flat pancake, made of Indian corn meal; the *gordita* is of the same material, but thicker.—G.A.F.R.

plenty sucre; mais now, God dam, I not go à Santa Fe, God dam, and mountain men dey come aquí from autre côté, drink all my café. Sacré enfant de Gârce, nevare I vas tan pauvre as dis time, God dam. I not care comer meat, ni frijole, ni corn, mais widout café I no live. I hunt may be two, three day, may be one week, mais I eat nothin; mais sin café, enfant de Gârce, I no live, parceque me not sacré Espagnol, mais one Frenchman."

English Words in Southwest Spanish

I asked a professor of Spanish how many English words are now in common use in our daily Spanish. His answer was: "Three or four hundred certainly—I could not tell you exactly without knowing how many have been invented today." Then he quoted this speech: "No parquea su carro allí, porque se escratchea." "Don't park your car there, because it will get scratched." "Park" is not Spanish, and "carro" does not mean automobile, but wagon. And the corruption of *scratch* is probably the most barbarous hybridization yet recorded!

Sooners

I[1]

. . . Much of western Oklahoma was opened to settlement by the so-called "Runs." In these it was literally true that "the race was to the swift, the battle to the strong." The first of these, that of the "Unassigned Lands," was at high noon, April 22, 1889. When the President's proclamation, issued thirty days earlier, fixed the date of this opening, it also provided that anyone entering upon these lands prior to that date should forfeit all claim to any part of them as a homestead.

Before the day fixed for the opening many thousand eager young men had gathered along the border of this new Promised Land impatiently waiting for the hour when they would be free to cross the line and choose a claim. Some of these had for years been urging, or "booming," the opening of these lands to settlement and were, in consequence, known as "Boomers."

It is not surprising that some of them should grow weary of waiting and under the cover of darkness cross into the forbidden area too soon. Here they chose their tracts and either occupied them or lay in con-

---

From *Our Southwest*, by Erna Fergusson, p. 353. Copyright, 1940, by Alfred A. Knopf, Inc. New York.

---

[1] By Edward Everett Dale. From *Oklahoma, A Guide to the Sooner State,* compiled by Workers of the Writers' Program of the Work Projects Administration in the State of Oklahoma, pp. 4–5. American Guide Series. Sponsored and copyright, 1941, by the University of Oklahoma. Norman: University of Oklahoma Press.

cealment near by ready to dash out and assert their claims when the hour of opening had come.

These men, known as "Sooners" because they had entered the territory too soon, had not technically committed any crime for which they could be punished by law. Yet they could not legally secure any of these lands by homestead or acquire a right to any part of them. In the language of sport, they were merely put out of the game for a violation of the rules.

For a long time the term "Sooner" was one of reproach, but with the passing of the years the word began to lose its original connotation. As its origin was gradually forgotten, it eventually came to mean merely one who is alert, ambitious, and enterprising, or one who gets up earlier than others, always takes the lead, and strives to triumph over obstacles.

II[2]

. . . We cowpunchers were blamed for almost everything that happened around the neighborhood, and during these times the United States Marshals were very busy.

As a matter of fact we cowpunchers were all looked upon as sooners. But who had a better chance of getting the best claims in Oklahoma? Men who had worked in the country for years, or people who had never been there before? Why, the girl I married even got a splendid claim, and she ran for it.

However, no stranger could work his way into our confidence. As time went on many of the cowpunchers improved their claims, and settled down to be real nesters, building good homes and raising fine livestock.

I never knew of any cowpunchers who were proved guilty of being sooners. They loved a race too well, and were among the best riders in the world. Too, the race was run in their own stamping-ground, where they had worked for years.

Of course, there were sooners in Oklahoma. One man with a team of oxen was on a claim forty miles from the line when the fastest horses reached his claim, and he had a garden up and young chickens hatched out. Some sooners lathered their horses with soap to make them look as if they had been ridden hard. I knew of two men who were in the country on foot ten miles from the line, and they claimed that their horses got away. These men did not stay long. A sooner was like some politicians—anything to beat the other fellow.

Anyway, we cowpunchers were soon enough to get many of the best claims in Oklahoma, but we were not as fast as the men who had good gardens and onions six inches high that had been raised in fifty min-

---

[2] From *A Rider of the Cherokee Strip,* by Evan G. Barnard, pp. 154–155. Copyright, 1936, by Evan G. Barnard. Boston and New York: Houghton Mifflin Company.

utes. A man on a claim a mile south of us had a good garden all up when we arrived.

"Say, Partner, where did you get that kind of seed?" asked Ranicky. "I want some of it."

"Oh," he replied, "I just transplanted these."

"Seems like you'd do well in any country," Ranicky opined.

The Rawhiders

The rawhiders got their name from the many uses they had for cowhide. Cattle were plentiful and cheap in those days. When about to emigrate and even before setting out on a long hunting trip, the rawhiders usually killed three or four large steers, not for food, but for hides. The dried hides were stored in their wagon beds and supplied a hundred and one needs. If they had a breakdown they soaked the hide and cut it into long strips, called whangs, which they wrapped around the broken hub, wheel, or tongue. As the whang dried the edges of the break drew together. I have seen chairs, camp stools, wheelbarrows, and buckets made from hides. Since nails were hard to get, the upright poles around their corrals were fastened by strips of rawhide. Their oxen were shod with it and the *zapatas,* or shoes they wore, were usually made from left-over pieces. I'll venture to say that most of the old timers' corrals in West Texas are still held together by thongs of rawhide.

All rawhiders came from West Texas years before farming and drilling for oil became common there. They were on the move nearly all the time, driving their horses and cattle with them, also numerous large cur, or mongrel dogs. The families traveled in covered wagons, which overflowed with women and children. They were all kinsfolk, continually marrying and intermarrying. Race suicide was unknown. Grandpas and grandmas and babies at the breast were huddled together in almost every wagon. They never carried tents, but there were always a few extra wagon sheets. Everyone over ten used snuff. The rawhider generally looked as if he had a billiard ball under his jaw, and his roll of Pigtail was never long out of sight. This was dry, twisted roll of natural leaf. When they ran out of tobacco the wagon wheels stopped turning. All waited until a John Wesley or a Thomas Jefferson got back with a fresh supply. Sometimes this meant a hundred-mile trip to the nearest government sutler.

Rawhide outfits were usually made up of ten or fifteen wagons strung out for miles. They made it a point, however, to drift together before sun-down. One saw pinto horses, scraggly cattle, and white-haired youngsters, whose heads looked as if they had not been washed or

---

From *Black Range Tales,* Chronicling Sixty Years of Life and Adventure in the Southwest, by James A. McKenna, pp. 159–162. Copyright, 1936, by Wilson-Erickson, Inc. New York.

combed for months. All the wagons were either Bain's or Shuttler's, and many a child was born in them. Sometimes a widow joined the caravan with a brood of children, but as a rule she did not stay single long, as it was against the rawhider's creed. "Increase and multiply" was their maxim. Popular wedding gifts were heifers, sows, fillies, and pullets. Divorces were common. The cast-off wife or husband often stayed in the same outfit with the ex-spouse, perhaps marrying the former husband's brother, or his first wife's sister.

Like gypsies they were ever on the move, sometimes halting but never staying long anywhere, even if they found plenty of water or a fine range with good grass. They were genuine squatters, and if some pilgrim came along and offered them a few cattle or a little cash, they pulled up stakes and migrated the next day, without a thought for the future.

Their food was mostly beef, no matter whose. They never ate their own, claiming that J X T or X L C's had a sweeter taste. I lived amongst them for years and I never saw a piece of roast beef except at a barbecue or a big feast. All meat was boiled or fried. Sometimes they cooked wild greens with the boiled meat. They used suet for frying and cooked everything to a frazzle. Coffee was drunk as black as soot and so strong it could float a bottle. Biscuits, raised with soda or cream of tartar, were apt to be the color of an orange. Some of the old women could cook very well when settled in a shack or a cabin, but the younger element, who never took a bath nor combed their hair, did not know how to boil water.

Who were these people and where did they come from? This has always been a mystery to the other Texans. It is believed they came from the mountain districts of Tennessee or North Carolina. Their Scotch-Irish names suggest this. In the mountain cabins of these states, one may still find chairs, buckets, hoops, and rugs made of rawhide. They lived there by fishing, hunting, and trapping. Pelts and roots were traded off for flour, sugar, and tobacco. Slavery was unknown among them, and they were looked upon by slave-holders as white trash. When the Civil War started, and the South tried to conscript them, they either joined the northern troops or came west to the new lands. Cotton raising did not appeal to them and they drifted to farther western lands. There they found abundant game, plenty of wild horses, and thousands of unbranded cattle. Soon they were joined in this land of milk and honey by many of their kinsfolk.

When the Civil War ended many former slave-owners also came out to these Western lands. They were a wide-awake set of people. Good houses and corrals appeared here and there in the wilderness. Immense herds of wild cattle were branded. The fat ones were driven to the railroad and sold to eastern markets. The rawhiders woke up, and many of them also took up ranges and branded wild mavericks, but the roving fever was still there. Selling often and always moving farther west, they at last reached the banks of the Rio Grande. A spring or a water seepage often invited settlement, but they never built and went on cooking outside. Never in a hurry, they sometimes stayed for months in a wild, grassy valley. No one knew who was President; in fact, they never voted. Without schools or newspapers, there was nothing to interest them except cattle, tobacco, and horse or pony racing. Most of them could neither read nor write, but they could beat the devil himself at swapping. Owners were always trading wagons.

The women even blamed certain makes of wagons for carrying certain diseases. One mother said, "My Georgia Anne is much healthier than Ollie. You know, Mrs. Allison, my Georgia Anne was born in a *Shuttler*. My Zeke traded it for a *Studebaker* to Ike Johnson, and that wagon is sure great for every epidemic or itch, or measles that comes along. Then Zeke traded the *Studebaker* for a *Bain,* and my kids got the mumps in that wagon. Give me a *Shuttler* any day for healthy kids, Arabella."

As soon as the boys could walk they were roping old Lije, the dog, or grandpa. As for roping or branding cattle the rawhider or border Mexican cowboy could do more with the lariat than any other roper in the world. Most of the boys' legs were so bowed you could throw a barrel between them. In fact, if they went to the spring for some water or chopped a little wood they did it on horseback. Some of them could hardly walk. Their highest ambition was to own a bronco, a riding saddle, a pair of spurs and a quirt. Oh, what Biblical names they had! Ike, Zeke, and Luke among the boys while the girls had such names as Patience, Prudence, Ruth, or Martha. But in every family, if they had only one or two children, would be found a John Wesley or an Arabella, or both. They married very young, and before they reached the age of twenty-five they were often the fathers and mothers of five or six children.

A few became rich, taking up ranges and settling down. The later generations who went to school were smart and rather good-looking. Probably, it was having to wash and comb their hair that made the difference. There certainly was a crowd of them with hair of fiery red. A marriage among them was a great event, the dancing and other festivities sometimes lasting for a week.

They were experts at getting around the law. No rawhider was ever found guilty of cattle stealing in a Texas court. They could name every brand from Del Rio to Tucson, and most of them knew the owners and the number of head they had on the range. Some of the women were as handy as the men folk with the rope and branding irons. One and all had a marvelous gift for sighting a maverick or an unbranded calf. They were born cattlemen, but God help the pilgrim who was located near them!

The rawhider, like the buffalo and the Indian, belongs to the past. Wire fences, autos, nesters, and cattle associations put an end to his wanderings.

Texas and California Cowboys

On the California coast the cowboys were called vaqueros (buckaroos, the Northwesterners soon translated it). They used rawhide ropes of dainty size and paid fabulous amounts for silver-mounted bridles, spurs, and bits. Their saddles were masterpieces of the saddler's art, with great high horns on the pommels, fancy stamping all over the skirting, and solid silver plates on the corners of the skirts. Their dainty toes slipped into four-inch-wide wooden stirrups with huge "eagle bill" tapaderos, the wings of which were often ten inches long. Their saddles had but one cinch, a horsehair affair, six to eight inches wide, generally with a long fancy-colored horsehair tassel hung from its center under the horse's belly. These saddles the Texans dubbed "center fires" from the rifle and pistol cartridges just then coming into general use.

The California vaqueros were undoubtedly the most expert horsemen and ropers the world has ever seen. Their skill with the lasso was marvelous. They worked almost entirely on horses. No unnecessary footwork for them. No bulldogging of husky steers or flanking of calves at branding time in their days. Roping was a fine art, and they were artists in their line.

To throw a two-day-old calf called for two men, both mounted, one to rope it by the neck, the other to "pick up its hind feet" with his reata. Very cleverly they did it. With the calf stretched out between the two horses, the broncos "sat back" on the ropes. A man on foot would jerk the calf on his side and do the branding with the ropes held taut. There was a maximum of horseback work with a minimum of footwork, the last done by the new men on the ranch.

Then came the Texans over the line. They overflowed the whole range country, showing new tricks in handling cattle and riding and roping that completely revolutionized the business. With them cowpunching was straight work without any fancy artistic attachments.

Along in 1883 or '84, the first double-rigged Texas saddle found its way into northern Arizona. A long keen cowboy from the Pecos country drifted along one day looking for work (a Texas ranger drifted after him a couple of months later and coaxed him to go back to the Lone Star State with him to talk over some matters with a grand jury). He rode one of those low-horned, clumsy-looking Texas saddles. It had two cinches—two, count 'em—the rear one a piece of stiff leather, the front one of horsehair. Neither was more than three inches wide. To add to Arizona's disgust, instead of the long flexible latigos of soft whang leather he merely had a heavy leather strap—"like a damned trunk strap," one old fellow put it, "with holes punched in it and a

---

From *Cattle,* by William MacLeod Raine and Will C. Barnes, pp. 290–293. Copyright, 1930, by William MacLeod Raine and Will C. Barnes. Garden City, New York: Doubleday, Doran & Company, Inc.

buckle instead of a ring on the cinch." Also, he used a narrow iron stirrup into which he stuck his feet clear to the heels.

On the saddle he carried a common sisal rope, not more than thirty feet long. One end of it was tied hard and fast to the saddle horn. His bit was the commonest of affairs, without fancy ornamentation of any kind, and with a "U" in the center of the bar not more than an inch high. No long dangling chains were on the end of his reins next to the bit, and the reins, unlike the expensive fancy plaited reins in use in Arizona and California, were merely long, heavy, inch-wide straps, not tied together but each independent of the other, "open reins," the Texans called them.

The Texan did not tie his mount with a hair rope, but merely dropped the two strap reins on the ground. Instead of heavy silver inlaid spurs with clanking chains and jingling steel ornaments, he wore a pair of steel "Petmaker" spurs set close to the heel of his boots with a solid rowel two inches wide, more like a circular saw than a spur—an affair that cut the horse terribly unless used with care. "Sure makes them git a wiggle on theirselves, though," said the Texan.

They were cowmen, those Texans. Their double-cinch saddles "stayed put" once they were cinched up, and that without cutting a poor horse half in two. When his saddle needed tightening, he did not have to get down and work on the latigos with their fancy loops. He simply leaned over, grabbed his "trunk strap," pulled it up a hole or two, caught the tongue of the buckle in the hole, and [it] was done.

When he went into a herd to rope, he "dabbed his loop" onto the animal he was after, swung his horse round, and started calmly for the branding fire, paying very little attention to the lively object dancing and bawling at the end of the rope. The men on the ground were expected to flank or bulldog anything up to an eighteen-months "long yearling." Only in cases of larger cattle was a second roper called in to catch the hind feet and help throw the animal. The Texas system was rough on stock, but it delivered the goods when it came to handling cattle.

The rollicking, hard-working Texans showed the rest of Cattleland a lot of new wrinkles in working range cattle. The North and the West died hard, but eventually accepted the inevitable, tied their ropes to the saddle horn, rode "rim-fire" saddles, gave up the fancy ornaments, headstalls, hair ropes, and other beloved equipment, and got down to real work.

Texas also taught some new tricks about roping saddle horses. The Californian always swung the largest loops to rope a saddle horse. The Lone Star State man, on the contrary, would slip up to the remuda like a darkey to a chicken coop and, with his loop lying flat on the ground give it a clever underhanded throw and drop it over the neck of the horse, without stirring up the whole bunch into a rioting, milling mob as those with the huge whirling loops always did. "Ay de mi," but those Texans did knock the romance out of the cow business.

The Bad Man from Bodie

The man who swears and shoots turned up in San Jose the other day and created a sensation. He was a Bad Man from Bodie and as such had been duly honored by the civilized press of the State. Having made a close study of the peculiar class of "bad men" generally known as Bad Men from Bodie I am prepared to add my plethora of wisdom in this respect to that already extant in the world at the present time. One of the peculiarities of a Bad Man from Bodie is his profanity. A Bad Man from Bodie who never used an oath is as impossible as perpetual motion or an honest election in Nevada. This trait is especially noticeable whenever he kills a man or endeavors to kill one. Whenever you hear of a man from Bodie who did not swear when he "pulled his gun" you may depend upon it that he is base metal, a tenderfoot, a man from Pioche, or Cheyenne, or Leadville. The oath of the Bad Man from Bodie is like the cheerful warning of the rattlesnake, and like that warning the blow follows close upon its heels. This brings us to another peculiarity of the Bad Man from Bodie, namely, his excessive prudence. Ill-natured critics have designated this morbid caution of the Bad Man from Bodie to cowardice, but every true bad man knows this to be wholly false, and will resent the imputation as a personal insult. Whenever a Bad Man from Bodie dons his war paint and strikes the bloody trail of carnage he is prepared for every contingency. His little gun nestles cosily in his right hand coat pocket, the latter generally being lined with velvety buckskin to prevent the hammer from catching and frustrating his purpose of converting his enemies into full fledged angels. Meeting an eligible candidate for a place in his graveyard he emits his stereotyped oath and "blazes away." This mode of procedure is termed in the elegant vocabulary of the Bodie classics "getting the drop on his Injun"—the vulgar bad man of other and inferior localities term it "getting the bulge on the bloke," a highly reprehensible and slangy way of expressing the idea. Sometimes the bad man from Bodie entertains his victim with a short oration before butchering him. He is very deliberate in his speech and always prefaces his remarks by stating that he "means bizness" which is Bodie for an intention to open up a little business for the Coroner, the undertaker, the tombstone sculptor and the sexton. This oration is replete with eloquence, its well rounded periods do not languish in the couch of verbosity and its metaphors abound in gigantic figures. Like the sublime grandeur of his own mighty hills and limitless deserts, his language reaches out and grasps the irresistible and terrible in nature, lifting it as the Titans lifted the mountains and flinging it with awful force against those who listen to him. I have seen him leap

---

By E. H. Clough, Sonora, California, October 10th, 1880. From *The Daily Bee*, Sacramento, California, October 12, 1880, Vol. XLVIII, No. 7,335, p. 1.

upon a billiard table and shout his defiance in the following stirring manner: "Here I am again, a mile wide and all wool. I weigh a ton and when I walk the earth shakes. Give me room and I'll whip an army. I'm a blizzard from Bitter Creek. I can dive deeper and come up drier than any man in forty counties. I'm a sand storm mixed with a whirlwind, and when I hump myself I tear. I'm a wild hog from Texas and it's about my time to bristle. I was born in a powder house and raised in a gun factory. I'm bad from the bottom up and clear grit plumb through. The wild grizzly screams with scare when I crawl into his den, and the bloodthirsty panther jumps the woods when I choke her kittens. I'm old Gash from Bloody Run and Deadman's Bar; I'm chief of Murdertown, and I'm dry. Whose treat is it? Don't all speak at once, or I'll turn loose and scatter death and destruction full bent for the next election. Your treat, is it? Well, stand in, boys, the red-headed woodpecker from Cow Creek is going to liquidate. Come up, everybody. Pass over the rot old poison." If the "red-headed woodpecker from Cow Creek" does not resent the appellation his case is attended to after the "treat" is over, the auburn-haired gentleman oftentimes rusticating a few weeks in the County Hospital for the benefit of his health. Occasionally, however, the Bad Man from Bodie does not fare as well as his talents, his courtesy and his chivalrous conduct should warrant. Last summer a bad man sprang through the screen of a Mammoth City saloon and declared himself as "the wild horse of the Pogonip, just in from his pasture on the Tioga range—" The dash which I have employed symbolizes silence. It is also a clumsy device whereby is sought to be conveyed the fact that the "wild horse of the Pogonip" didn't know, to use another Bodie figure of speech, "what struck him." If the heavy barroom chair had been hurled with a single pound more force the gentleman from Pagonip would have been inventoried by the Public Administrator (if such an official existed at that time). On another occasion a Bad Man from Bodie, being abroad without his gun, was stared at by a stranger, and as a matter of course resented the insult in true Bodie fashion by challenging the stranger to pugilistic combat. The challenge was readily accepted by the tenderfoot and resulted in the complete defeat of the Bad Man. Had he been caressed by a steam threshing machine he would scarcely have fared worse. His astonishment at the result was even greater than the injuries he had received. "Who am I, anyhow!" he wailed. "What'm I browsin' round these diggins fur, I'd like to know. Licked by a pilgrim! Whaled by a tenderfoot!"

"If you hadn't been drunk you wouldn't-a got into this row, dad," remarked his son, who had witnessed the row from a distance.

"I know it, son, I know it," groaned the father, "an' ef I hadn't bin tight I'd-a jumped down his throat an' worried him to death. Thar was a time, boy, w'en a hundred an' eighty couldn't tech yer dad, but I reckon ol' age an' bug juice is gittin' a leetle the best o' the ol' man." Then he limped home for repairs.

The Bad Man from Bodie is drifting down into the valleys. He is locating in the metropolitan centers where he may enjoy life without the inconvenience of always dreading a vigilance committee, that mushroom tribunal of justice from which there is no appeal save at the bar of Eternity. Besides, the Winters in Bodie are very severe and it is hard to "spar" a meal wherewith to sustain a useful as well as an ornamental existence. The Bad Man from Bodie, if not too cautious occasionally, dies with his boots on, but never, within the memory of man, has one been hung by a civilized hangman. He may, accidentally, drop down into oblivion through the instrumentality of an eighteen-inch Bowie, but he has not yet dropped through a legal deathtrap, and it is not likely he ever will. When the warm weather beguiles the flitting swallow back to its last year's nests the Bad Men from Bodie will return to his stamping grounds in the high Sierras, or again breathe alkali and desert sand in the wilds of southwestern Nevada. His lungs will once more expand with oath-burdened wind, his cheery voice will ring out defiance to trembling auditors, the short, sharp yelp of his derringer or "whistler," will send the echoes flying, and the people of the camp where he takes up his abode will smile grimly and rub their palms as they remark in a *sotto voce* tone: "Reckon it's goin' to liven up this Spring—I see the Bonebreaker's got in." And the undertaker dusts out his gorgeous dead-wagon and unrolls the oilcloth containing his assortment of hearse plumes; the Coroner gets ready his jury lists and makes a bargain with a particular physician in regard to the holding of autopsies; the grave-digger buys a new spade, and the man who epitaphs the dead on imperishable marble lays in a stock of new chisels. The bad man has arrived and there is joy in Bodie.

The Temperance Lecturer and the Methodist Preacher

. . . Hastings . . . went about lecturing on temperance in Ohio where he became intimate with a fellow named McDonald, who was acting the Methodist preacher and pretending, with considerable success, to raise funds for missionary purposes. At last they separated, McDonald preceding Hastings to California, where he became bartender for a man named Vioget, who owned a saloon and billiard table, the first, I think, on the Pacific Coast. Hastings returned later, and, reaching San Francisco in a cold rain, went up to Vioget's and called for brandy. He poured out a glassful and was about to drink it when McDonald, recognizing him, leaned over the bar, extended his hand, and said, "My good temperance friend, how are you?" Hastings, in great surprise, looked him in the eyes, recognized him, and said, "My dear Methodist brother, how do you do?"

From "Echoes of the Past about California," in *Echoes of the Past about California*, by General John Bidwell, and *In Camp and Cabin*, by Rev. John Steele, edited by Milo Milton Quaife, pp. 93–94. Chicago: The Lakeside Press, R. R. Donnelly & Sons Co. 1928.

The Preacher and the Gambler

There is a story told by Californians which is illustrative of early miner times. It is said that a certain preacher found his way to a mining camp, and began to labor for the salvation of immortal souls. But mammon, women, wine, and gaming held control over the minds of men in those wicked parts, and the unfortunate minister not only failed to reap any spiritual harvest of his labors, but carnal things also began soon to be sadly lacking. In short, he got entirely out of money. Then the miners, with true Californian generosity, made him up a purse of $600, to enable him to reach some more favorable region.

But alas! for human nature, the unfortunate minister had departed from the ways that are right, through the force of bad example, and in an evil hour he yielded to the seduction of the monte bank, and staked his money. As a matter of course, in about an hour and a half, he saw the last dollar of it slide from his hands.

At this stage of the proceedings, the heart of the monte-dealer relented within him. He proposed to the unhappy man of God that he should offer up prayers in his behalf, to the value of $600. He consented, a bargain was forthwith struck, the first installment of the money was promptly deposited, and the minister engaged in prayer. . . . The prayer was so protracted, earnest, and, doubtless, so thoroughly repentant that the monte-dealer said he would consider it an equivalent for the entire sum, which he at once turned over to the contrite minister.

The Coroner Story

In the West *good stories* are rife, and to the stranger nothing is more puzzling than to tell their real age. In the phenomenal complexity of social organism in frontier country, a genuinely healthy *good story* never dies, and even such unwholesome ones as, for instance, Greeley's coaching horror,[1] will evince in the naturally salubrious atmosphere of the Plains and mountains an amazing tenacity of life.

You hear a *good story,* and as it is the first time, you enjoy it. You

---

From *Afoot and Alone,* A Walk from Sea to Sea by the Southern Route, Adventures and Observations in Southern California, New Mexico, Arizona, Texas, etc., by Stephen Powers, pp. 262–263. Entered according to Act of Congress, in the year 1871, by Columbian Book Co., in the office of the Librarian of Congress at Washington, D.C. Hartford, Conn.

From *Camps in the Rockies,* Being a Narrative of Life on the Frontier, and Sport in the Rocky Mountains, with an Account of the Cattle Ranches of the West, by William A. Baillie-Grohman, pp. 369–373. Copyright, 1882, by William A. Baillie-Grohman. New York: Charles Scribner's Sons.

[1] See "Horace Greeley's Ride to Placerville," Part Two, below.

go your way, and, if you are lucky, you travel from Kansas to San Francisco, and fate permits you to grow one week older before you hear it for a second time; but hear it again you shall, let you wander whither you will. It will be told you perhaps while sitting at your camp-fire on the arid Plains of New Mexico or while cantering along at the side of an Oregon "Webfoot"; you possibly have to lend your ear to it in the depth of a Nevada silver-mine, half a mile under the earth, or on the top of the Great Divide of the Rocky Mountains, three or four miles over the earth. The first six words suffice to put you on the track of it, let it be ever so cleverly adapted to entirely different circumstances, let the narrator make ever so "personally conducted" a story of it; you immediately recognize the good old tale you heard the first time in Chicago, San Antonio, or Sacramento, till finally sheer practice enables you to *point* them as easily as were their trails marked in the fashion of the Miook Indians in California, who used to drag the carcass of a defunct "fragrance pedlar," *i.e.,* skunk, along the intricate paths through the forests, so as to enable their friends to follow them guided by their noses.

Some *good stories* take their origin in the Eastern Cities, but by the time they reach the Territories they are Westernized. The Coroner's *good story* is an instructive instance of the adaptability of some of the Eastern tales to Western life. I have traced its origin to facts which occurred in New York A.D. 1879. In that year, as I see from a leading New York daily paper now lying before me, reporting the proceedings,[2] a famous case of bogus inquests was unearthed. Coroner D—— was the ingenious official, and in the course of the law proceedings it was proved that this gentleman, whose domain was Staten Island, near New York, where numerous cases of *found drowned* are the rule, had hit upon the ingenious plan of anchoring a corpse in a quiet cove of the sea, and holding inquest at will on him. When discovered, nine Coroner's inquests had sat on this one SPECIALLY RESERVED corpse, each putting a shabby nine dollars into his pocket. The idea was one that "took." Cases of anchored corpses were heard of all over the Union. Inland cities, that had no rivers or lakes handy, had always town-water reservoirs to fall back on. Everything gets old very quickly in America, and by the time California had gripped the idea, it had assumed very mature form, though only a few short weeks had elapsed since Coroner D—'s preliminary examination in New York, a fact which the following conversation between a Californian official and a San Francisco Judge, as reported by a 'Frisco paper, will prove:—

" 'The fact of it is,' said old Dr. Potts, the Los Angeles Coroner, the other day, as he strolled through the morgue with Judge Van Snyder, 'the fact of it is, that these San Francisco coroners don't really understand how to work up their business for all its worth, and make it boom as it were.'

---

2 The *World,* June, 1879.–W.A.B-G.

" 'What do you mean?' said the Judge, somewhat horrified.

" 'Why, they don't know how to really run a corpse for all the coin that is in it. They don't handle 'em scientifically, so to speak. Now we do that sort of thing better down our way.'

" 'Do, eh?'

" 'Yes. For instance, there was a Chinaman killed by smoking opium a few months ago, out in the suburbs of our town, and of course I was around there and had sworn in a jury before the cadaver got cold, and what with summoning witnesses, taking testimony, &c., before night I had a bill against the county for $96.50.'

" 'More than the Chinaman was worth, I should think," said the Judge.

" 'But wait. I opened the grave in the county burial-ground the same night, rushed the corpse down to the laboratory and had it embalmed, and all ready for emergencies. Well, about three nights after that they had a free fight out at the Digger Indian encampment, and so I had the Celestial pigtail cut short, a few feathers twisted in it, and hid him in a bush out that way. Of course it was discovered pretty soon, and reported; and as the jury couldn't agree as to the particular tribe of Indians the deceased belonged to, I impaneled another one—nearly double the fees, don't you see?—and gave the papers a rousing good item. It's a way-up plan to keep in with the reporters, by the way.'

" 'How much did that make?'

" 'Well, I was about $240 ahead on the speculation then, so I waited until a lot of Dago emigrants passed through the town, and the next day one of 'em was found dropped dead on the road of heart-disease—don't you see? Same old corpse, with a big felt hat and rawhide boots, and his pocket full of macaroni. I think I squeezed about $175 more out of the taxpayers that time. Well, I kinder let up for about a week after that, and then had the remains doubled up in a packing-box and found among the unclaimed freight down at the railroad station. The papers wrote it up as a "Mysterious Murder Case," and we had a ten days' examination. Lemme see, I think it was $445.50 the whole thing panned out before we were through that time. What do you think of that?'

" 'Why, it's the most extraordinary—'

" 'Why, that's nothing, my dear sir, nothing. I haven't got half through with that Chinaman yet. When I left home I just kinder wedged him in among the top branches of a tree in the woods just out of town, dressed in a suit of complete black with an old telescope in his coat-tail pocket, and a pair of big green spectacles on his nose. Catch the idea, don't you?'

" 'Can't say I do.'

" 'Why, that's the aeronaut dodge, don't you see? Unknown scientific party, fallen out of a balloon. My own design entirely. Splendid, isn't it? The corpse is a little worn by this time, I know; but what are you going to do with such an infernally unhealthy climate as Los Angeles?

I expect to send the old lady and the girls to Paris on those remains yet, if I have to wire 'em together to do it. No, my dear sir, depend upon it what those metropolitan coroners lack is push, enterprise, sir, and ingenuity.'

"And the doctor reluctantly stopped poking a defunct stock speculator with his cane, and permitted the Judge to take him out for a drink."

Buck Fanshaw's Funeral

There was a grand time over Buck Fanshaw when he died. He was a representative citizen. He had "killed his man"—not in his own quarrel, it is true, but in defence of a stranger unfairly beset by numbers. He had kept a sumptuous saloon. He had been the proprietor of a dashing help-meet whom he could have discarded without the formality of a divorce. He had held a high position in the fire department and been a very Warwick in politics. When he died there was great lamentation throughout the town, but especially in the vast bottom-stratum of society.

On the inquest it was shown that Buck Fanshaw, in the delirium of a wasting typhoid fever, had taken arsenic, shot himself through the body, cut his throat, and jumped out of a four-story window and broken his neck—and after due deliberation, the jury, sad and tearful, but with intelligence unblinded by its sorrow, brought in a verdict of death "by the visitation of God." What could the world do without juries?

Prodigious preparations were made for the funeral. All the vehicles in town were hired, all the saloons put in mourning, all the municipal and fire-company flags hung at half-mast, and all the firemen ordered to muster in uniform and bring their machines duly draped in black. Now—let us remark in parenthesis—as all the peoples of the earth had representative adventurers in the Silverland, and as each adventurer had brought the slang of his nation or his locality with him, the combination made the slang of Nevada the richest and the most infinitely varied and copious that had ever existed anywhere in the world, perhaps, except in the mines of California in the "early days." Slang was the language of Nevada. It was hard to preach a sermon without it, and be understood. Such phrases as "You bet!" "Oh, no, I reckon not!" "No Irish need apply," and a hundred others, became so common as to fall from the lips of a speaker unconsciously—and very often when

---

From *Roughing It,* by Mark Twain, Vol. II, pp. 59–70. Entered According to Act of Congress, in the year 1871, by The American Publishing Company, in the Office of the Librarian of Congress, at Washington; copyright, 1899, by The American Publishing Company; 1899, by Samuel L. Clemens. New York and London: Harper & Brothers. 1903.

they did not touch the subject under discussion and consequently failed to mean anything.

After Buck Fanshaw's inquest, a meeting of the short-haired brotherhood was held, for nothing can be done on the Pacific coast without a public meeting and an expression of sentiment. Regretful resolutions were passed and various committees appointed; among others, a committee of one was deputed to call on the minister, a fragile, gentle, spiritual new fledgling from an Eastern theological seminary, and as yet unacquainted with the ways of the mines. The committeeman, "Scotty" Briggs, made his visit; and in after days it was worth something to hear the minister tell about it. Scotty was a stalwart rough, whose customary suit, when on weighty official business, like committee work, was a fire helmet, flaming red flannel shirt, patent leather belt with spanner and revolver attached, coat hung over arm, and pants stuffed into boot tops. He formed something of a contrast to the pale theological student. It is fair to say of Scotty, however, in passing, that he had a warm heart, and a strong love for his friends, and never entered into a quarrel when he could reasonably keep out of it. Indeed, it was commonly said that whenever one of Scotty's fights was investigated, it always turned out that it had originally been no affair of his, but that out of native goodheartedness he had dropped in of his own accord to help the man who was getting the worst of it. He and Buck Fanshaw were bosom friends, for years, and had often taken adventurous "potluck" together. On one occasion, they had thrown off their coats and taken the weaker side in a fight among strangers, and after gaining a hard-earned victory, turned and found that the men they were helping had deserted early, and not only that, but had stolen their coats and made off with them!

But to return to Scotty's visit to the minister. He was on a sorrowful mission, now, and his face was the picture of woe. Being admitted to the presence he sat down before the clergyman, placed his firehat on an unfinished manuscript sermon under the minister's nose, took from it a red silk handkerchief, wiped his brow and heaved a sigh of dismal impressiveness, explanatory of his business. He choked, and even shed tears; but with an effort he mastered his voice and said in lugubrious tones:

"Are you the duck that runs the gospel-mill next door?"

"Am I the—pardon me, I believe I do not understand?"

With another sigh and a half-sob, Scotty rejoined;

"Why you see we are in a bit of trouble, and the boys thought maybe you would give us a lift, if we'd tackle you—that is, if I've got the rights of it and you are the head clerk of the doxology-works next door."

"I am the shepherd in charge of the flock whose fold is next door."

"The which?"

"The spiritual adviser of the little company of believers whose sanctuary adjoins these premises."

Scotty scratched his head, reflected a moment, and then said:

"You ruther hold over me, pard. I reckon I can't call that hand. Ante and pass the buck."

"How? I beg pardon. What did I understand you to say?"

"Well, you've ruther got the bulge on me. Or maybe we've both got the bulge, somehow. You don't smoke me and I don't smoke you. You see, one of the boys has passed in his checks, and we want to give him a good send-off, and so the thing I'm on now is to roust out somebody to jerk a little chin-music for us and waltz him through handsome."

"My friend, I seem to grow more and more bewildered. Your observations are wholly incomprehensible to me. Cannot you simplify them in some way? At first I thought perhaps I understood you, but I grope now. Would it not expedite matters if you restricted yourself to categorical statements of fact unencumbered with obstructing accumulations of metaphor and allegory?"

Another pause, and more reflection. Then, said Scotty:

"I'll have to pass, I judge."

"How?"

"You've raised me out, pard."

"I still fail to catch your meaning."

"Why, that last lead of yours is too many for me—that's the idea. I can't neither trump nor follow suit."

The clergyman sank back in his chair perplexed. Scotty leaned his head on his hand and gave himself up to thought. Presently his face came up, sorrowful but confident.

"I've got it now, so's you can savvy," he said. "What we want is a gospel-sharp. See?"

"A what?"

"Gospel-sharp. Parson."

"Oh! Why did you not say so before? I am a clergyman—a parson."

"Now you talk! You see my blind and straddle it like a man. Put it there!"—extending a brawny paw, which closed over the minister's small hand and gave it a shake indicative of fraternal sympathy and fervant gratification.

"Now we're all right, pard. Let's start fresh. Don't you mind my snuffling a little—becuz we're in a power of trouble. You see, one of the boys has gone up the flume—"

"Gone where?"

"Up the flume—throwed up the sponge, you understand."

"Thrown up the sponge?"

"Yes—kicked the bucket—"

"Ah—has departed to that mysterious country from whose bourne no traveler returns."

"Return! I reckon not. Why, pard, he's *dead*!"

"Yes, I understand."

"Oh, you do? Well I thought maybe you might be getting tangled some more. Yes, you see he's dead again—"

"Again! Why, has he ever been dead before?"

"Dead before? No! Do you reckon a man has got as many lives as a cat? But you bet you he's awful dead now, poor old boy, and I wish I'd never seen this day. I don't want no better friend than Buck Fanshaw. I knowed him by the back; and when I know a man and like him, I freeze to him—you hear *me*. Take him all round, pard, there never was a bullier man in the mines. No man ever knowed Buck Fanshaw to go back on a friend. But it's all up, you know, it's all up. It ain't no use. They've scooped him."

"Scooped him?"

"Yes—death has. Well, well, well, we've got to give him up. Yes, indeed. It's a kind of a hard world, after all, *ain't* it? But pard, he was a rustler! You ought to seen him get started once. He was a bully boy with a glass eye! Just spit in his face and give him room according to his strength, and it was just beautiful to see him peel and go in. He was the worst son of a thief that ever drawed breath. Pard, he was *on* it! He was on it bigger than an Injun!

"On it? On what?"

"On the shoot. On the shoulder. On the fight, you understand. *He* didn't give a continental for *any*body. *Beg* your pardon, friend, for coming so near saying a cuss-word—but you see I'm on an awful strain, in this palaver, on account of having to cramp down and draw everything so mild. But we've got to give him up. There ain't any getting around that, I don't reckon. Now if we can get you to help plant him—"

"Preach the funeral discourse? Assist at the obsequies?"

"Obs'quies is good. Yes. That's it—that's our little game. We are going to get the thing up regardless, you know. He was always nifty himself, and so you bet you his funeral ain't going to be no slouch—solid silver door-plate on his coffin, six plumes on the hearse, and a nigger on the box in a biled shirt and a plug hat—how's that for high? And we'll take care of *you*, pard. We'll fix you right. There'll be a kerridge for you; and whatever you want, you just 'scape out and we'll 'tend to it. We've got a she-bang fixed up for you to stand behind, in No. I's house, and don't you be afraid. Just go in and toot your horn, if you don't sell a clam. Put Buck through as bully as you can, pard, for anybody that knowed him will tell you that he was one of the whitest men that was ever in the mines. You can't draw it too strong. He never could stand it to see things going wrong. He's done more to make this town quiet and peaceable than any man in it. I've seen him lick four Greasers in eleven minutes, myself. If a thing wanted regulating, *he* warn't a man to go browsing around after somebody to do it, but he would prance in and regulate it himself. He warn't a Catholic. Scasely. He was down on 'em. His word was, 'No Irish need apply!' But it didn't make no difference about that when it came down to what a man's rights was—and so, when some roughs jumped the Catholic boneyard and started in to stake out town-lots in it he *went* for 'em! And he *cleaned* 'em, too! I was there, pard, and I seen it myself."

"That was very well indeed—at least the impulse was—whether the act was strictly defensible or not. Had deceased any religious convictions? That is to say, did he feel a dependence upon, or acknowledge allegiance to a higher power?"

More reflection.

"I reckon you've stumped me again, pard. Could you say it over once more, and say it slow?"

"Well, to simplify it somewhat, was he, or rather had he ever been connected with any organization sequestered from secular concerns and devoted to self-sacrifice in the interests of morality?"

"All down but nine—set 'em up on the other alley, pard."

"What did I understand you to say?"

"Why, you're most too many for me, you know. When you get in with your left I hunt grass every time. Every time you draw, you fill; but I don't seem to have any luck. Let's have a new deal."

"How? Begin again?"

"That's it."

"Very well. Was he a good man, and—"

"There—I see that; don't put up another chip till I look at my hand. A good man, says you? Pard, it ain't no name for it. He was the best man that ever—pard, you would have doted on that man. He could lam any galoot of his inches in America. It was him that put down the riot last election before it got a start; and everybody said he was the only man that could have done it. He waltzed in with a spanner in one hand and a trumpet in the other, and sent fourteen men home on a shutter in less than three minutes. He had that riot all broke up and prevented nice before anybody ever got a chance to strike a blow. He was always for peace, and he would *have* peace—he could not stand disturbances. Pard, he was a great loss to this town. It would please the boys if you could chip in something like that and do him justice. Here once when the Micks got to throwing stones through the Methodis' Sunday-school windows, Buck Fanshaw, all of his own notion, shut up his saloon and took a couple of six-shooters and mounted guard over the Sunday-school. Says he, 'No Irish need apply!' And they didn't. He was the bulliest man in the mountains, pard! He could run faster, jump higher, hit harder, and hold more tanglefoot whisky without spilling it than any man in seventeen counties. Put that in, pard—it'll please the boys more than anything you could say. And you can say, pard, that he never shook his mother."

"Never shook his mother?"

"That's it—any of the boys will tell you so."

"Well, but why *should* he shake her?"

"That's what *I* say—but some people does."

"Not people of any repute?"

"Well, some that averages pretty so-so."

"In my opinion the man that would offer personal violence to his own mother, ought to–"

"Cheese it, pard; you've banked your ball clean outside the string. What I was a-drivin' at, was, that he never *throwed* off on his mother—don't you see? No indeedy. He give her a house to live in, and town lots, and plenty of money; and he looked after her and took care of her all the time; and when she was down with the smallpox I'm d–d if he didn't set up nights and nuss her himself! Beg your pardon for saying it, but it hopped out too quick for yours truly. You've treated me like a gentleman, pard, and I ain't the man to hurt your feelings intentional. I think you're white. I think you're a square man, pard. I like you, and I'll lick any man that don't. I'll lick him till he can't tell himself from a last year's corpse! Put it *there*!" [Another fraternal hand-shake–and exit.]

The obsequies were all that "the boys" could desire. Such a marvel of funeral pomp had never been seen in Virginia. The plumed hearse, the dirge-breathing brass bands, the closed marts of business, the flags drooping at half mast, the long, plodding procession of uniformed secret societies, military battalions and fire companies, draped engines, carriages of officials, and citizens in vehicles and on foot, attracted multitudes of spectators to the sidewalks, roofs, and windows; and for years afterward, the degree of grandeur attained by any civic display in Virginia was determined by comparison with Buck Fanshaw's funeral.

Scotty Briggs, as a pall-bearer and a mourner, occupied a prominent place at the funeral, and when the sermon was finished and the last sentence of the prayer for the dead man's soul ascended, he responded, in a low voice, but with feeling.

"AMEN. No Irish need apply."

The Vanishing Frontier

I have stated that the majority of the residents of California, at least in the mining regions, had now become well satisfied with their adopted home, and intended to remain; but there were a few, nevertheless, who pined for their Eastern home, for various reasons. For instance:

I chanced to meet a family one day upon the emigrant road, evidently upon their return journey. It was during the spring of '57. The family was composed of an old man and his wife, the former driving a

From *The Argonauts of California,* Being the Reminiscences of Scenes and Incidents That Occurred in California in Early Mining Days, by a Pioneer, Text and Illustrations Drawn from Life by C. W. Haskins, pp. 201–203. Entered according to Act of Congress, in the year 1889, by C. W. Haskins, in the Office of the Librarian of Congress at Washington, D.C. New York: Published for the Author by Fords, Howard, and Hulbert. 1890.

yoke of cattle attached to a regular immigrant wagon covered, and with all the trimmings usually found in connection with an emigrant team. It was so unusual to see a team of this description headed for the East that, from curiosity, I enquired of them whither they were bound.

"Wall, stranger," the old man replied, "me an' the ole woman air a-gwine away from hyar. We air on the homestretch to ole Missouri again whar we cum frum nigh on ter ten years ago."

He explained further that many years before he and his wife had become imbued with a desire to retire to some secluded place, to live in solitude away from the noise and confusion of the city, and, where, as he said:

"We can jest enj'y oursel's, an' raise lots o' chickens without interferin' with anybody.

So they moved away out west and made their home in solitude upon the frontier.

"Wall, stranger, that was a rale quiet place out thar fur a spell, but jest as soon as they diskivered gold out'n California, the jig were up, fur all them chaps who was a-goin' thar, came right along my way, and just shoved that air frontier of ourn right along ahead of 'em t'ords the west.—So one mornin' Nancy ses to me, ses she, 'Hiram! Hiram! ef we air a-gwine to enj'y solitude along with a frontier we mus' git away from hyer t'ords the west, and git a leetle ahead of all them fellers.' 'That's so, Nancy,' ses I, 'an' ef you pack up ther chickens, hitch up ther team, an' load ther wagon, we'll get ahead on 'em and diskiver another frontier somewhar.' But durn my buttons, stranger, we've been tryin' to git a leetle ahead on' em ever sence. But 'taint no use. We thot we had struck a frontier in Californy agin fur sartin, when we fust git thar, but one mornin' arter we hed hed a long wet spell, the fust thing I seen when I got up wus a steamboat right in ther back yard. So ses I, 'Nancy, Nancy, hyer they air jest a-comin' agin.' So we loaded our traps in the wagon, and went over them mountains whar the ocean is, an' we jest thot that we hed got it now fur shure, fur hyer was a sort o' a nat'ral frontier that couldn't stan' any pushin'. So we ontied the chickens an' got ready, kind o' hum like, when one mornin' we heered the awflest n'ise, and wen we went out, durned if thar wern't a sawmill right back of our chicken house, an' they were just buildin' 'nother one 'cross the creek, and some ships was a-sailin' in frum ther ocean to load up ther lumber. Now Nancy never did like sawmills. Sed she'd ruther hear it thunder enny day 'cause the sawin' n'ise sets her teeth on aidge so. On'y she ain't got a nat'ral tooth in her hed ennyhow."

"Well," said I, "where did you go next?"

"Wall," the old lady replied, "we thot we mought try it further north fur a spell, so we moseyed 'long up through Oregin, an' 'way off up inter Idyho, whar we foun' a frontier at las', fur sartin. An' I reckon 't will stay thar fur a spell, too. We stayed on 't a hull year, but hed to git off on't agin on 'count of ther chickens."

I asked her the reason.

"Oh, shucks," she replied, "a sawmill was nothin' t' ther racket up thar, an' I'll tell ye how it wuz. Yer see, in ther winter 't is tarnal cold, an' ther roosters couldn't crow, fur yer see jest as they 'gun to crow it all fruz harder'n a icicle, so jest soon's spring thaw cum on, why all their crowin's thet was fruz in ther winter 'gun t' chirp, an' sich a crowin' time ye never heerd in all yer born days. An' fur more'n two weeks, me nur Hiram didn't sleep blessed wink. Wall, stranger, we just packed up agin, an' thot we'd try the southern kintry, 'mong the cactuses an' th' sandy desert down in Aryzony. Frum ther looks o' things down thar, we thot mebbe we'd be 'way frum 'em all an' hev the frontier all to ourselves, but we wus hasty though. One mornin' Hi run an' ses he, 'Nancy, Nancy! 'tain't no use.' They wus comin' agin sure 'nuff, fur 'way up in ther valley we cud see th' dus a-risin' an' we knowed what that mean; an' now yer see we air jest a-moseyin' back to ole Missouri agin."

"Yass," says Hiram, "the kintry's gittin' to be no 'count, an' purty soon thar won't be a mite o' frontier lef', fur they air just a-crowdin' 't 'way down inter Mex'co, an' 't won't be long 'fore they'll be a-tryin' ter chuck it 'way up over inter Kennady. Yer can't fin' enny solertude now anywhar."

"Nary a solertude," says Nancy. "Fur 't is jest fizz! buzz! buzz! geerat! whang! slang! kerbang! All over ther hull blessed kintry. Now we'll go back ter ole Missoury agin, whar we kin git suthin' fit ter eat, anyhow, an' we'll try an' stub through ther rest o' our days 'thout enny frontier in our'n."

PART TWO

The West Begins

Among the few likenesses which do cover fairly large numbers of Westerners is, first, the Awareness of Distance. . . . Another thing that seems to make a community of interest among large numbers of Westerners in contradistinction to Easterners is the truly dominant size of the area that is subhumid to downright arid.

—Ladd Haystead

"Dis yer's a quar country, stranger, you bet! All sorts of quar things out yer. Folks chop wood with a sledge-hammer and mow grass with a hoe. Every bush bears a thorn and every insect has a sting. The trees is pretty nigh all cactuses. The streams hain't no water, except big freshets. The rivers get littler, the furder they run down. No game but rabbits, and them's big as jackasses. Some quails, but all topknotted, and wild as jackasses. No frost, no dew. Nobody kums yer, unless he's runnin away. Nobody stays, unless he has to."

—James F. Rusling

Introduction

WHETHER one thinks of the West as beginning with a stronger handclasp or the hundredth meridian depends upon whether one thinks of the West as a "state of mind" or a region. Perhaps, as has been suggested, the difficulty of drawing the geographical boundaries of the West, or any of the several "Wests" that compose it, has resulted in the practice of defining "region from character rather than character from region."[1] "Where the West begins" depends partly on where one starts, since the question implies "West of what?"

The history of Western expansion has been marked by the shifting of the dividing line from the Hudson (anything west of which is still "West" for many New Yorkers) to the Alleghenies to the Mississippi to the Missouri and 98 (or between 97 and 98) degrees west longitude. By the time one has reached a town like Pierre, the capital of South Dakota, "at approximately the geographical center of the state and North America," one is pretty sure one is in the West. For here is a no-man's land between the Middle West (which is no longer really West) and West (which is really Far West). Here the East-River farmer rubs elbows with the West-River rancher, and here "To the east gentle rolling fields of grain swell to the rich farming region and to the west a long, flat prairie stretches for miles into the cowboy realm."[2]

The first "Great West" to be encountered by the westward traveler or emigrant is the prairie. Almost everyone seeing the treeless "level land" for the first time is bound to be struck by its resemblance to the sea. For the pioneers and traders, crossing the plains had something of the mood and discipline of a voyage, from the names given to the "jumping-off places"—Westport in Missouri and the "coast of Nebraska" (for the Platte River Valley), to the favorite name for the covered wagon—Josiah Gregg's "prairie schooner"—and the use of "pilots" to guide the great wagon trains or caravans.

When travelers meet upon the plains, it reminds one of ships meeting at sea. The first question is, "Where are you from and where bound?" and then follows, "How many days out? What kind of weather have you had, and what Indians have you met on the way?" If either party is short of provisions, the other supplies him if he has them to spare, and in all such things there is a comity between travelers upon the plains.[3]

Once arrived on the Great Plains, the traveler learned that this "sea of grass" was a sea with little or no water. West of the Mississippi, according to Webb's formula, two of the three legs of civilization—land, water, and timber—were withdrawn and only one leg—land—was left for the West and the Westerner to stand on.[4] "Dry land" be-

[1] Carey McWilliams, "Myths of the West," *North American Review,* Vol. 232 (November, 1931), p. 427.

[2] *Guide to Pierre, South Dakota, and Vicinity* (Pierre, 1937), p. 2.

[3] W. W. H. Davis, *El Gringo* (New York, 1857), pp. 24–25.

[4] Walter Prescott Webb, *The Great Plains* (Boston, 1931), p. 9.

came a unifying bond if at times a terrifying experience, for most Westerners east of the Cascades and the Siskiyous. Rainlessness, drouth, the preciousness of water, fights over water-holes, water rights, and irrigation, the destructiveness of torrential rains, floods, hail, prairie fires, northers, blizzards, twisters, dust storms, insects, varmints, predators—all these penetrated and irritated the consciousness of the plainsman like the "fine, thin soil that packed like mortar, swirled into dust clouds, or washed down the creek leaving great gullies in the eroded fields."[5]

Where dry farming was a form of gambling and farm life a nightmare of "wind nerves" and "dust nerves," new techniques and inventions, as well as mental adjustments, were mothered by necessity. Barbed wire, windmills, the short-lived wind wagon, the chuck-wagon (invented by Charles Goodnight); sod houses, dugouts, hay-burning stoves, sour-dough biscuits or bread; rain makers and rain making, prayers for rain;[6] the purely fanciful crowbar or log-chain test of wind velocity; the scientific control of erosion and the devastation of drifting, blowing, gullying, and washing soil, through the use of cover crops like Bermuda grass, contour plowing, tree windbreaks and shelter belts. Along with these went the painful breaking in, the breaking down of the "tenderfoot" into a "mosshorn."

A "moss horn" . . . is a scraggly old steer which has been wintering in the breaks of some crick, plowing up the dirt along the banks to get at the reed sprouts and the fresh green stuff. Moss gets onto his horns, and like as not some of it takes root and grows there till summer is half over. Us Westerners call ourselves "moss horns," because we have to rustle to live. A "tenderfoot" also has to do with cattle. Immigrants or freighters coming in here from some ways East are sure to have oxen with feet sore from the long pull. We call the whole outfit of them "tenderfeet" because they are just fresh from the East. You see, every country makes its own language on account of what the people have to put up with.[7]

By the time the "pilgrim" had reached the "Great American Desert" (the old name for the region between the Missouri and the Rockies, the Platte and the Arkansas river valleys), he had acquired a whole new store of folk-say as well as a new vocabulary.

The "boomer" bound for the "Territory" had scrawled on his wagon sheet:

White-capped in Indiany,
Chintz-bugged in Illinoy,
Cicloned in Nebraska,
Oklahoma or bust.[8]

---

[5] Angie Debo, *Prairie City* (New York, 1944), p. 104.

[6] Cf. Louise Pound, "Nebraska Rain Lore and Rain Making," *California Folklore Quarterly*, Vol. V (April, 1946), No. 2, pp. 129–142.

[7] Charles C. Lowther, *Dodge City, Kansas* (Philadelphia, 1940), pp. 48–49.

[8] H. H. McConnell, "Five Years a Cavalryman, *Frontier Times* (Bandera, Texas), Vol. II (February, 1934), No. 5, p. 213.

And the Panhandle had him singing:

> Pickin' up bones [buffalo bones] to keep from starving,
> Pickin' up chips [dried buffalo or cow chips] to keep from freezing,
> Pickin' up courage to keep from leaving,
> Way out West in No Man's Land.[9]

From the short grass country (with its bunch grass and buffalo grass and innumerable other varieties), the traveler soon passed into cactus country—land of the prickly pear, sahuaro, bisnaga or barrel cactus, cholla, yucca, and Joshua tree—the "land of journey's ending" of Western New Mexico and Arizona.

Any one asking directions in the Southwest is apt to be told to "keep right along this road, here, until you come to an *arroyo*—not one of these little *arroyos,* but a regular *hondo*—then you keep up along the foot of the *barranca* until you come to a *cienaga,* then you go up along the *loma* until you come to a *cienaguilla,* and you find a *placita.* . . ."

For, Mary Austin continues,

> the topography of the country between the Colorado and the Rio Grande cannot be expressed in terms invented for such purpose in a low green island by the North Sea. A *barranca* is terrifyingly more than an English bank on which the wild thyme grows; an *arroyo* resembles a gully only in being likewise a water gouge in the earth's surface, and we have no word at all for *cañada,* halfway between an *arroyo* and a *cañon,* which–though, naturally, you have been accenting the syllable that best expresses the trail of the white man across the Southwest–is really pronounced can-*yon.*[10]

In the West the word "desert" (originally an uninhabited place) took on a new meaning from the fact that these deserted places were dry places.[11] Because of the importance of water-holes (pools of standing and often dirty and stagnant water that passed for springs), the Spanish word *jornada* (a day's journey) came to mean both a dry stretch and a day's ride between water-holes. John C. Van Tramp paints a vivid picture of the most famous of these *jornadas,* the *Jornada del Muerto* (Journey of the Dead), between El Paso and Socorro, the eighty miles between water-holes being covered from three o'clock of one afternoon to late morning of the following day:

> Sometimes the trail led us over large basins of deep sand, where the trampling of the mules' feet gave forth no sound; this, added to the almost terrible silence, which ever reigns in the solitudes of the desert, rendered our transit more like the passages of some airy spectacle, where the actors were shadows instead of men. Nor is this comparison a constrained one, for our way-worn voyagers with their tangled locks and unshorn beards (rendered white as snow by the fine sand with which the air in these regions is often filled) had a weird and ghost-like look, which the gloomy scene around, with its frowning rocks and moonlit sands, tended to enhance and heighten. There

---

9 *Oklahoma* (Norman, 1941), p. 249.
10 *The Land of Journeys' Ending* (New York, 1924), pp. VIII–IX.
11 George R. Stewart, *Names on the Land* (New York, 1945), pp. 219–220.

were other matters, too, to render the view impressive; scattered along our route we found numerous skeletons of horses, who at some former period had dropped down and died by the wayside. . . .[12]

On emerging from the Eastern hills and woodlands, the emigrant was to find not only his agricultural tools and techniques but his firearms inadequate. To accommodate himself to the longer range and larger game—buffalo, elk, antelope, mountain lion, grizzly—he learned to make the plains rifle out of his old squirrel rifle by shortening the barrel and increasing the caliber and weight of the bullet. He also found new species of small game—prairie chickens and jackrabbits—besides a host of little creatures to entertain or torment him—trade rats, lizards, horned toads, road runners, Mormon crickets, chiggers, gophers, ground squirrels, scorpions, tarantulas, and Gila monsters. Every traveler felt an obligation to describe the antics of prairie dogs and coyotes; and the scouts taught the emigrants to imitate coyote yelp and howl as signals. Captain William F. Drannan found still another ingenious use for howling coyotes, as a dance band to dance to.[13]

The West also taught the Easterner to be weather-wise (although he knows that "All signs fail in dry weather"), weather conscious and weather humorous. Where the land dominates and the sky determines, a certain grim fatalism creeps into humor.

The Oregonian learned that California's heat was a "dry" heat; that Montana's cold was a "dry" cold; and was immediately inspired to prove to any one that Oregon's rain was, after all, only a "dry" rain. . . .[14]

"Hello, there, Bill. What do you know for certain?"

"Nothin'."

"Well, I know it's windy and dusty. It's got so we get a half a day between the Spring Dust Storm and the Summer Dust Storm, and then we get a day and a half between the Summer Dusts and the Fall Dusts." (Cimarron County, Oklahoma, August 14, 1938.) [15]

. . . the northern panhandle of Texas . . . 'way up on the wild and windy plains, 3600 feet high, flat as a floor, bald as an eight ball, with nothin' in the world to stop that North Wind but a barb wire fence about a hundred mile north, and all of them barbs is turned the same way . . . where the oil flows, the wheat grows, the dust blows, and the farmer owes.[16]

A whole literature of Western travel—by Eastern and European visitors, explorers, old-timers—has grown up about Western climate

---

[12] *Prairie and Rocky Mountain Adventures* (Columbus, Ohio, 1866), p. 183.

[13] *Capt. W. F. Drannan, Chief of Scouts,* as Told by Himself (Chicago, 1910), pp. 123–125.

[14] Archer Butler Hulbert, *Frontiers* (Boston, 1929), p. 47.

[15] Dorothea Lange and Paul Schuster Taylor, *An American Exodus* (New York, 1939), p. 103.

[16] Woody Guthrie, "Woody, 'The Dustiest of the Dust Bowlers,' The Tale of His Travels, Making of his Songs," Leaflet for *Dust Bowl Ballads,* Victor Album P–28, 1940.

and landscape; and the guidebooks, the "sweet singers," and the tourist bureaus have followed in the tradition of booming and boosting that differs from the boasting of pioneer days mainly in that it is "civic" rather than personal.

Part of the [Arizona] atmosphere . . . is a common tendency to speak of the state in superlatives. . . . As stoutly and as loudly as any [the tenderfoot] will maintain that Arizona has the most spectacular scenery, the finest climate, the most fertile soil, the deepest canyons, the biggest dams, the richest mines. He can prove it about the canyons and the dams, feel no less positive about other points which are necessarily matters of opinion.[17]

And so we return to the "firm handclasp," which by now has grown into a boosting slap on the back, and which, with the aid of a "breezy rhetoric," converts the West as a region into the West as a state of mind.

In the West Nature exacts subtle penalties from those who live amidst its glories and comforts. The Southern Californian pays for his pleasures (the "cult of the out-of-doors" and the "cult of the body") with an enervating state of *mañana* approaching nirvana. In the Rockies the realization that "it is physically impossible for men to change materially the appearance of their surroundings . . . perpetuates the pioneer legend."[18]

The whole nonsense is summed up in the inscription on the California State Capitol Building: "Bring me men to match my mountains!" A mountain-matcher is the most disagreeable person in the world, having glorified, therefore lost, whatever traits might once have made him interesting. He's just too big and noble to have around.[19]

B. A. B.

[17] *Arizona* (New York, 1940), p. 5–6.

[18] Thomas Hornsby Ferril, "Rocky Mountain Metaphysics," *Folk-Say, A Regional Miscellany: 1930,* edited by B. A. Botkin (Norman, 1930), p. 315.

[19] Thomas Hornsby Ferril, *I Hate Thursday* (New York, 1946), p. 181.

I. QUEER COUNTRY

The rabbits have somehow gotten the body of the hare and the ears of the ass; the frogs, the body of the toad, the horns of the stag-beetle, and the tail of the lizard; the trees fall uphill, and the lightning comes out of the ground.—"SOCRATES HYACINTH"

Where the West Begins

I. FOR THE EASTERNER[1]

All travelers from inland know the moment when they have the authentic sense of the sea. It may yet be miles away; but there comes an instant when one is aware of its influence—on the soil, the atmosphere, and no less on the human spirit. There is a point on the Union Pacific Railroad where you pass with equal definiteness from the Middle to the Far West. A boundary, a sort of Mizpah stone of warning, might be set up at North Platte, Nebraska, without belying the fact. All North Platte actually does is to advertise itself engagingly as "Buffalo Bill's town." Perhaps, set in that vast plain, that is all it can do. Yet when you pass westward from North Platte, you realize that something is happening: the air changes, the land seems to be gathering itself for its long and slow approach to the Great Divide; these are different winds upon your face, these are horizons that will presently become Wyoming and the high plains; not yet do you see mountains, but for the first time since you left home you feel them imminent. You have reached the real West, and there are confirmations all about you as subtle and strong as a perfume in your nostrils. Western Nebraska belongs as definitely to the Far West as eastern Nebraska to the Middle West. You cannot demonstrate it any more than you can demonstrate the inward and spiritual grace of a sacrament: you merely know.

---

1 From *The Aristocratic West,* by Katharine Fullerton Gerould, pp. 5–6. Copyright, 1925, by Harper & Brothers. New York and London.

II. To a Westerner's Ear[2]

To the New Yorker, anything west of Hoboken is The West. The average Easterner starts the West some place on the far slope of the Alleghenies, while the people in that region extend the beginning point to West Chicago, or perhaps Elgin. Chicagoans start The West any place from Cheyenne on. A Westerner, on the other hand, bounds his territory by the beginning of "back East." It, too, varies for a Californian is likely to feel that Denver is "back East," while a Washingtonian may not begin The East until he hits the South St. Paul stockyards. This confusion of geographical definitions gives some little validity to the well-known verses of "Out Where the West Begins," which delimit the area by sensory stimuli and psychological reactions as well as locational items. However, the West *is* an area.

* * * * *

Now I am quite sure where the West begins. . . . [It is where] the first people I meet when I step from a train or stop at a gas station . . . seem to talk my language. They have the same ridiculous hyperbole I use in describing anything from a crop to a coyote. They will probably speak to me on the street even though I have never seen them before in my life, and are remarkably generous with misinformation, matches, whisky, food, and county treasurers who are forever getting mixed up on what is personal finance and what belongs to the political subdivision they represent. . . .

I believe that I could be taken blindfolded into Kansas City and know that it was home by hearing the taxi driver say, "You won't mind, friend, if we give the lady a lift on the way to the hotel, will you?" Whereupon a lady, two children, a dog, and six assorted bags, baskets, crates, and box lunches will spill across my lap and some part of them remain nervously balanced thereon while the taximan drives a mile or so out of his way to deliver the good woman and brood to their destination.

Only recently I was reminded forcefully that I was home again by a 'teen-aged young lady waiting on tables at Mr. Fred Harvey's La Fonda Hotel. Harvey girls, before the war, usually were capable, reserved persons of post-debutante age who came from anywhere east of Stephens College. Not a few of them were college girls working for a semester or a year to get funds to carry on their education. But war shortages have brought Mr. Harvey a good many less experienced girls. The youngster mentioned was probably not quite old enough for college, but whether she was or not, she certainly was a part of the West.

Her opening remark to my wife and me as she cleared away the

---

[2] From *If the Prospect Pleases: The West the Guidebooks Never Mention,* by Ladd Haystead, pp. 3, 4–7. Copyright, 1945, by the University of Oklahoma Press. Norman.

debris of the last customers' meal was, "Now, you kids just be patient and I'll be with you in a jiffy." The "kids" will never see forty again, and it's probable their social status is somewhat different from that the coeducational greeting would suggest. (To be sure, the male "kid" slung many a plate of hash in years gone by.) The point is that the Western proletariat haven't yet discovered they are proletariat, have little sense of caste, and probably know by their first names at least one or two millionaires who yesterday were schoolmates without shoes, or drove a tractor for a couple of dollars a day while they waited for oil wells, mines, or some other fairy story to come true.

Again, to the Westerner there are certain locutions and pronunciations that are as typical of his country as the baked-bean accent is typical of New England, or the "sho-nuff" is typical of the South. The character in the roadside diner who asks the cashier, "Please, ma'am, have you got a match?" is probably Western, as is his mate who tells the waitress, "I'll thank ya, ma'am, for the salt." The fellow telling a story and referring to the hero as "That little ol' boy" is probably from Oklahoma or West Texas. The man who agrees with another by saying *"bueno hay"* is likely a New Mexican. The chap who, as Mr. H. L. Mencken has noted, so acutely, speaks with a complete lack of accent, pronouncing all syllables distinctly, is a Californian. Any one who slides over jawbreaking Indian names with no hesitation and great familiarity is apt to be an Oregonian or a Washingtonian. Of course, these observations are not rules, are not infallible or even half-certain to be true, but to a Westerner's ear these and the general manner of speaking will give more than a hint from whence a man came. . . .

Across the Wide Missouri

I[1]

The Missouri River is the dividing line between East and West. All of South Dakota on the Chamberlain side is called East-river and beyond is West-river. A man with a chunk of land on the east side is a farmer; on the west he is a rancher. A cow on one side is milked; on the other punched.

II[2]

"One of the greatest differences between the east and west," says a veteran conductor, "is in regard to talking with strangers. The Mis-

[1] From *We Went Thataway,* by H. Allen Smith, p. 73. Copyright, 1949, by H. Allen Smith and Nelle Smith. Garden City, New York: Doubleday & Company, Inc.

[2] By "Tourist." From the *Omaha Bee,* cited in *American Notes and Queries,* A Medium of Intercommunication for Literary Men, General Readers, Etc., Vol. VIII, No. 3 (November 21, 1891), p. 35. Copyright, 1891, by the Westminster Publishing Co. Philadelphia, Pa.

souri river is the dividing line in regard to talk. The very minute passengers get east of Omaha and Council Bluffs they freeze each other.

"Strangers are strangers, and they grow more so until they reach the East coast. The difference is just as marked the other way. Passengers who would not dare to speak or be spoken to, quit playing clams as soon as they reach the west end of the Union Pacific bridge. From that point on, clear to the setting sun, the tongues get nimbler and nimbler. Yes, the Missouri river is the line of loquacity."

That Vivifying Western Air

I[1]

You seem to be growing younger, not older; and you begin to understand the plainsman's opinion of it [the climate] when he told you that out West men take twice as much killing and horse-thieves have to hang five minutes longer than anywhere else.

II[2]

The undulating prairies and high hills of the great stock-raising counties of Western Texas are the most healthy part of the earth's crust I have ever seen, or ever expect to see. It is asserted that there the inhabitants never die of disease or age. They either shuffle off the coil through the instrumentality of a six-shooter, or grow old, dry up, and blow away. Tradition tells of a misguided young doctor who went West hoping to make a living out of the sufferings of his fellows, but he soon found that his pills were literally a drug on the market. People refused his twenty-drops-in-a-teaspoonful-of-water, and would have nothing to do with his mustard-plasters; so he went from bad to worse, and from worse to whisky; and the last heard from him he had stolen a grindstone and was rolling around trying to make a living sharpening bowies, scissors, and razors.

There is a legend to the effect that once upon a time some immigrants, entering Texas at Red River, met a very old man, with beard as white as snow, and features seared and shrunken by the hand of time—a mere shadow of antiquity, a human wrinkle, an allegory of age. This antique petrification was hurrying with all speed to the boundary of the State. On being interrogated as to his reasons for such

---

[1] From *Camps in the Rockies,* Being a Narrative of Life on the Frontier, and Sport in the Rocky Mountains, with an Account of the Cattle Ranches of the West, by William A. Baillie-Grohman, p. 4. Copyright, 1882, by W. A. Baillie-Grohman. New York: Charles Scribner's Sons.

[2] From *On a Mexican Mustang, through Texas, from the Gulf to the Rio Grande,* by Alex. E. Sweet and J. Armoy Knox, p. 184. Copyright, 1883, by Sweet and Knox. Hartford: S. S. Scranton & Co.; Marshalltown, Iowa: The Barnes & Ballou Publishing Co. 1884.

haste, he stopped not, neither did he pause; but, as his weird form disappeared in the distance, the murmuring winds brought back the mournful reply: "I am tired of life and of the monotony of the ages, I am weary of the slow steps of time and the dragging march of the centuries, and I am hurrying out of Texas that I may find some place where people can die."

III[3]

. . . A man "Back East," lying at the point of death, wires his friend in Albuquerque to come and receive his last messages. The Westerner is on his bicycle when the message is handed him. He rides hastily to the station just in time to catch his train, upon which he checks his wheel.

Arriving "Back East," our hero peddles madly to his chum's house, and is so excited he trundles his bicycle directly into the dying man's room. In so doing, just as he enters the chamber, he runs over a tack and the air, direct from the Rio Grande, hisses through the puncture. Laden with healing in every breath, it reaches the stricken patient's lips. The effect is instantaneous; the man sits up half well already.

The New Mexican, on the moment realizing what has happened, jabs a pen knife into the other tire and holding the aperture to his friend's mouth, completes the cure. Selah!

Dry Farming in a Wagon

. . . One day a waddy out on the range incredulously squirted some tobacco juice at the nearest clump of sage. Sure enough, he saw a wagon drawn by a couple of browbeaten horses. On the wagon box sat a gray-bearded stranger and in the wagon was a gleaming steel plow.

The waddy rode up and pointed to the plow. "Beggin' yore pardon, dad, what in hell is that?"

"Why, my boy," the old man said genially, "that's a plow."

"A plow. . . . What's it for? What do yuh do with it?"

The old man snorted. "Do with it? Why, you break up the earth with it. I'm agoin' to stop right here, pre-empt myself about eighty acres, fence it and plow it and raise corn, garden sass, mebbe a little wheat."

The waddy scratched his ear. "But look here, don't yuh hafta have a little moisture to raise that stuff—rain, for instance?"

The old man chuckled at his innocence. "Son, you've got behind

[3] From *Yarns of the Desert,* by Will H. Robinson, Copyright, 1921, by William Henry Robinson. Phoenix, Arizona: The Berryhill Company.

From *The Humboldt,* Highroad of the West, by Dale L. Morgan, pp. 320–322. The Rivers of America Series, edited by Stephen Vincent Benét and Carl Carmer. Copyright, 1943, by Dale L. Morgan. New York and Toronto: Rinehart & Co., Inc.

times. Ain't you heard about this new dry farmin'? You can farm without rain." He filled his pipe and between puffs explained about the new way of using half the land and summer-fallowing the other half to store moisture.

"But yuh can't do that here," the cowboy objected. He thought up half a dozen reasons why. But the old man was stubborn; he cal'lated to have him a farm right here. At last the waddy sighed, pushing back his Stetson and mopping his brow with his sleeve. "Dad, I'll tell yuh a story.

"A while back an Eastern dude inherited a lot of money. He'd heard about the West and he come out here, right out here, and he started to have him a farm. The first year he spent quite a lot of money, gettin' the land plowed, fenced, and planted. Well, dad, there wasn't no rain, and nothin' came up. He was a stubborn galoot, and he tried again the next year, and there wasn't no rain that year neither. He still had a lot of money left, though, and the third year he got a bright idee.

"He went into town and bought hisself a wagon, a big, strong wagon, yuh know, with four-inch tires. He put fourteen-inch sideboards on the wagon, and got a load of good soil—yuh gotta say that for him, dad, he got a load of good soil some'eres around. Nobody couldn't never figger out where he got that there good soil. Then he got a good team of horses, big, fast horses, and he hired a chore boy. Then he planted hisself another garden in that wagon, and he says to the boy, he says, 'Nick, I want yuh to keep yore eye skinned all the time, day and night. And if yuh see a cloud, no matter where it is, no matter anything, I want yuh to hitch up this-yere team and drive like hell till yuh get under the cloud. And if the cloud does percipitate, then the rain'll germinate the seed in the good earth on this-yere wagon, and damn if I won't have me a garden!'

"But the fack is, dad," the waddy said sorrowfully, "that rich dude, he went plumb, flat broke, buyin' oats for the horses and axle grease for the wagon."

"All Signs Fail in Dry Weather"

Dry weather is the common handicap of both farmer and stockman in Northwestern Oklahoma, where farming and stock raising are the most important industries. Rain, the lack of it, or the possibility of it enters into nearly every person's daily thoughts and forms a topic of discussion and conversation. Rarely is there too much rain; generally

---

From "You Can't Tell about the Weather," by Walter R. Smith, *Folk-Say, A Regional Miscellany: 1930,* edited by B. A. Botkin, pp. 178–182, 184. Copyright, 1930, by B. A. Botkin. Norman: University of Oklahoma Press.

it is wished for, hoped for, prayed for. Quite naturally most of the weather lore is concerned with rainfall. Texas and Kansas have been the heaviest contributors to the imported lore of rainfall, while the rain lore of the Cheyenne Indians seems to be the most nearly native to the region. Of all the weather lore of this section it seems to me that the most interesting and significant is that touching upon rainfall.

Among the memories of the first summer I spent in Oklahoma there stands out quite clearly the remembrance of the great swarms of "buffalo gnats" which were found almost everywhere whenever the sun shone. I recall riding many a mile in a wagon behind a team of slow horses while those gnats settled upon me or buzzed about my face so thickly that I could hardly breathe. Where the idea originated I could never learn, but we believed that the gnats were a sign of showers. The presence of gnats in large numbers is to-day interpreted in the same way, and the swarming of flies about doors or windows of a house indicates their attempt to find shelter from an approaching rain. The biting of flies or the extraordinary activity of ants, both large and small, indicates rain.

Domestic animals are credited with knowing when rain is approaching. When a cat moves her kittens under shelter of a roof or from low ground to higher ground, it is taken as a certain indication of rain. When a dog moves her puppies into a sheltered location, especially if she persists against difficulty in her efforts, rain is accepted as a certainty. Chickens also "know" when rain is coming. One afternoon while playing with a boy friend I learned of the way chickens show their knowledge of, and preparation for, the approach of rain. Our play was interrupted by the boy's mother who called, "Come on, Jim-my, an' git in the wood for the night. Better git in extry kindlin'. Jest look at them chickens oilin' their feathers! It sure must be goin' to pour down to-night." And it did. When cats or dogs eat grass, rain may be expected.

Prairie dogs prepare for rain by banking up earth about the entrance of their burrows, and ants prevent the entrance of water by the same means. Popular belief is that neither uses much forethought; and their being engaged in this engineering work forecasts the near approach of rain. Just before a rain toads travel into low places where water will stand, while most snakes, especially rattlesnakes, migrate to higher and drier ground. A high school student at Supply told me that he had seen a "rise" of Beaver drive the snakes out of bottom land and up into a hay meadow where he was working. Snakes were found in every shock of hay, and the percentage of rattlesnakes was too great for his peace of mind. The trails of the snakes from the lower land to the meadow were easily seen, and the snakes began coming into the meadow before the rain started or the stream began to rise!

Rattlesnakes are lazy during dry weather, but they become more active and even so vicious before the approach of a rain that they will go out of their way looking for trouble. The first instance of such behavior of rattlesnakes that I ever saw was one spring when I was working on the I S Ranch northwest of Supply. I was driving a team of six mules, four abreast and two in the lead, to a "cake" wagon, when a rattlesnake came rapidly toward the road from considerable distance, rattling as it came and seemingly bent on doing battle. After I had killed the snake and coaxed "Red," the most tricky of the lead mules, from under the wagon tongue where he went when he heard the rattler, I started down the trail and met Old Joe, the oldest man on the ranch and an old timer who rode the same range long before the "Run." I asked what it all meant, and he told me that it was a sure sign that the dry weather was going to "break."

But animals do not always show by dumb actions only that rain is coming. Frequently they give vocal utterance to their warning. The howling of coyotes at nightfall indicates a change of weather. The change is more certain if the howling takes place just after sunrise or just before sunset; but the energetic howling of coyotes after dark, or in fact any time through the night, is regarded as a "good sign." The hooting of an owl in daylight is considered a certain sign of rain, but the hooting of owls at the time a new moon appears is given almost the same consideration even if it occurs at night. The presence of the new moon, however, may be the chief element in this sign. When roosters crow at sunset or at midnight, rain may be expected; and the name "raincrow" is given to the yellow-billed cuckoo because its cry is thought to presage rain.

Although animals are the source of most Northwestern Oklahoma weather lore, there are abundant other signs of the weather. Many signs are there regarded which elsewhere might have no meaning. When pumps or water pipes "sweat," an old resident will nine times out of ten look for rain. Or if he notices that his smoking tobacco is damp, he believes rain is near. The same importance is attached to a heavy dew. It seems that proof of moisture in the air is taken as evidence that moisture is going to fall from the air. During the summer, whirlwinds, or dust devils, as they are sometimes called, are taken as an indication of continued dry weather; and if the whirlwinds are numerous, the expectation of dry weather is accordingly stronger. The rise of water in the sand of a creek bed which has dried up in a dry time is, I believe, the most common accepted rain sign. Few who observe weather signs at all do not know it, and many who disregard nearly all others accept it religiously. I know that such rises in the water level do occur, and that rain does follow—after more or less time. An illiterate old woman in Harper County told me of her faith in this sign which she insisted she had never seen fail. I asked her how long she had lived in that country.

"Well, sir, mister, I can't tell you," she replied. "First we filed a claim north of the line (in Western Kansas) and then we filed one out northwest (Old Beaver County); but I've been here since before the sojers took the canyons off of the River. I guess I've been here fifteen or thirty-five years." (Beaver Creek is in local parlance called the "River," and she referred to the time before the artillery was moved away when Old Fort Supply was abandoned as a military post.) According to her, a rise of water which wets what has been dry sand always "brings" rain.

* * * * *

. . . But the most definite rain signs Northwestern Oklahoma ever had were safeguarded by the saying which every one knew and all believed: "All signs fail in dry weather." (Or, less frequently: "All signs fail in Oklahoma.")

Testing the Lord

A certain very fine Christian man owned a ranch in West Texas during [the drouth of] 1934. He had faith to believe the Lord would provide if he only did his part. His cattle were dying around the headquarters and he and his cowboys were kept so busy they hadn't had a chance to look over all the range. One particular part he hadn't heard from in some time, so he sent one of his cowboys to look it over and report back to him. This old boy was gone all day; it was long after dark before he returned. The boss waited up for him to learn the news. While the cowboy ate his supper at the bunk house, this anxious owner of the big ranch and cattle sat there on one end of the bench, and asked questions. "Well, Jim, how does it look where you were today?"

"It looks bad. I never saw enough grass all day to build a bird's nest; the water's dried up and there's dead cattle everywhere. If it don't rain purty soon I don't know what we'll do."

The good Christian cattleman replied by saying, "I guess the Lord will send us rain when we need it bad enough."

The cowboy poured out another cup of coffee and said, "Well, if he don't know we need rain now, he's a darn poor cow man."

Decline in Land Values

A good story is told of an Irishman, passing through Dodge City, from Morton County in the southwest part of Kansas on his way to

---

From *A Corral Full of Stories,* rounded up by Joe M. Evans, pp. 55–56. Copyright, 1939, by Joe M. Evans. El Paso, Texas: Printed by the McMath Company, Inc.

From *Dodge City,* The Cowboy Capital and the Great Southwest in the Days of the Wild Indian, the Buffalo, the Cowboy, Dance Halls, Gambling Halls, and Bad Men, by Robert M. Wright, pp. 328–329. [Copyright, 1913, by Robert M. Wright.]

his wife's folks in the East, with a little old team of horses, a wagon, and a small cow tied behind the wagon. He stopped to water his team, and, when some one asked him where he was from and what were the conditions out there, he said, "It is a beautiful country for prospects, bless your soul!"

"Why did you leave?" he was asked.

"Got tired, and my wife wanted to see her folks," he replied.

"What is the price of land out there?"

He said: "Come here! You see that little cow behind my wagon? I traded a quarter section of land for her, and by gobs! before I made the deed, I found the critter I sold to couldn't read, so I just slipped in the other quarter section I had into the deed, and the fellow didn't know it."

Oklahoma Norther

On Monday evening, April 15 [,1895], we camped on the north side of Black Bear Creek, just north of Perry. Will rode to town for provisions and left me to watch the cattle grazing in the creek bottom. The weather was balmy, but soon after he left there came up a "norther." The cattle became so restless I could not leave them to go to the wagon for my coat. Was most frozen when Will came back and brought me my coat and helped round in the cattle.

A Pawnee paper telling of this storm said a citizen driving out in the afternoon saw a man skinning an ox. He stopped and asked the trouble, learned the ox had died of sunstroke. Returning in the evening, he saw the same man skinning an ox, again asked the trouble and was told this one had frozen to death. Another wise guy said that frogs froze up with their heads sticking out of the ice, not having time to draw them in.

The Crowbar Hole

On the [Oklahoma] farms, where there is leisure for "codding," almost every dwelling will have some opening that can be pointed out

---

From "Reminiscences of Pioneer Days in the Cherokee Strip," by G. E. Lemon, *The Chronicles of Oklahoma,* Vol. XXII (Winter, 1944–45), No. 4, p. 448. Oklahoma City: Published quarterly by the Oklahoma Historical Society.

From *Oklahoma, A Guide to the Sooner State,* compiled by Workers of the Writers' Program of the Work Projects Administration in the State of Oklahoma, p. 115. American Guide Series. Sponsored and copyright, 1941, by the University of Oklahoma. Norman: University of Oklahoma Press.

as a "crowbar hole." The town innocent, inquiring into the purpose of the opening, will learn that it is to test the wind velocity. If the crowbar merely bends when thrust through the hole, it is safe to go out. However, if the bar is broken off, it is better to stay in the house.

A Texas Sandstorm

I came to El Paso in 1879, and they were having sandstorms then and have been ever since. I remember one time we were coming in off of an Indian scout. The wind had been blowing for three days and nights and the sand had covered up the grass and mesquite bushes. As we rode along through the sand hills between El Paso and Alamorgordo, we discovered a man's hat lying there on a sand dome. We got down to pick it up and found there was a man's head in it. We scratched the sand out of his eyes and ears and mouth with our fingers. He said, "Get a shovel, I'm horseback."

Trouble in Heaven

A terrible roaring and ear-splitting noise, they say, was disturbing the angels so much that the Lord called on Saint Peter for explanation. "It's just those Texans," Saint Peter said. "What's the trouble with them this time?" "They are howling and praying for rain," Saint Peter said. "Turn on the spigot," the Lord told him. Saint Peter turned it on. A week later the noise was worse than before. "It's those Texans again," the official explainer said. "And what's the trouble this time?" "They're howling for dry weather." "Well, let nature take its course."

As told by Captain Gillett of the Texas Rangers. From *A Corral Full of Stories*, rounded up by Joe M. Evans, p. 43. Copyright, 1939, by Joe M. Evans. El Paso, Texas: Printed by the McMath Company, Inc.

From "Texas," by J. Frank Dobie, *Holiday*, Vol. 4 (October, 1948), No. 4, p. 94. Copyright, 1948, by the Curtis Publishing Company. Philadelphia.

Hell and the Southwest

I[1]

"A man named Cousins [Samuel W. Cozzens] from Boston had been West into Arizona. On his return he wrote a book called *The Marvelous Country,* and gave lectures about it. In one of his lectures he was quoted as saying that Arizona was one of the finest lands in the world, and all they lacked there was plenty of water and good society. Some one in his audience replied, 'That's all they lack in Hell.' "[2]

. . . General Sherman . . . is often credited with saying that if he owned both Hell and Texas, he would rent out Texas and live in the other place.

"That's right, every man for his own country," a Texan is said to have retorted.

II[3]

The summers of the Southwestern deserts are hot. The native doesn't deny it; he boasts of it. It is summer sunshine that gives him five or six crops of alfalfa, that improves his cotton, that makes his grapefruit so sweet it needs no added sugar, that adds tonnage to his raisins and flavor to his crop of figs.

Still one must confess that it does wilt collars, make coats superfluous and waistcoats actual objects of suspicion. In the real pioneer times when shade trees were non-existent, and ice was something one oc-

---

[1] From "A Postscript by the Editor," by J. Frank Dobie, to "Hell in Texas," by George E. Hastings, in *Southwestern Lore,* Publications of the Texas Folk-Lore Society No. IX, edited by J. Frank Dobie, pp. 180, 182. Copyright, 1931, by the Texas Folk-Lore Society. Dallas: Published for the Texas Folk-Lore Society, Austin, Texas, by the Southwest Press.

For a Nevada version, see Richard G. Lillard, *Desert Challenge* (New York, 1949), p. 130: Someone in a railroad party showed the new, mellower attitude toward Nevada: "With water to settle the dust and congenial companions, Nevada would be all right." But ex-Senator Ben Wade of Ohio, no whit lenient, replied, "With plenty of water and good society, Hell would not be a bad place to live in."

Cf. Joseph Kinsey Howard, *Montana: High, Wide, and Handsome* (New Haven, 1943), p. 201: That month, too [July, 1919], was chosen by a party of Eastern industrialists as the one during which they would look Montana over. An embarrassed Great Falls businessman told them it was unfortunate that they had come at such a lean time; but, he said loyally, "all Montana needs is rain." A Grand Rapids capitalist looked up Great Falls' blistered Central Avenue, closed his aching eyes against the sun, and thought of the hundreds of miles of parched prairie over which he had come in an oven-hot train. "Yes," he said quietly; "and that's all hell needs!"

[2] Quoted from William M. Breakenridge, *Helldorado: Bringing the Law to the Mesquite* (Boston, 1928), pp. 73–74.

[3] From *Yarns of the Southwest,* by Will H. Robinson, pp. 17–20. Copyright, 1921, by William Henry Robinson. Phoenix, Arizona: The Berryhill Company.

casionally read about in eastern newspapers but never saw, it must in truth have been a thirsty and a tropic land. No wonder so many of the old time stories have scenes laid in that orthodox post mortem abiding place of the unregenerate sinful, which the Hassayamper believed could easily be compared to the burning air on summer desert trails.

The earliest of these yarns, as everybody knows, had to do with the soldier from Fort Yuma who found hell so much cooler than what he had been used to that he sent back for his blankets. (Our apology for mentioning this hoary tale is, that like the story of Eve and the apple, its very antiquity gives it a certain prestige.) Equally honored by long and hardy handling is the saying regarding the alleged necessity of shipping in cracked ice from California to feed the hens to keep them from laying hardboiled eggs.

Along the same line is the story about the corpse from Parker who, after the fire in the crematory was going nicely, sat up and politely asked the attendant to close the crack in the door as the draft made him shiver.

To offset these, however, there is the tale related by a returned visitor to heaven; how, noticing that all the people from Prescott were kept in gilded cages, he was given the explanation that even the delights of the celestial abode could not make these folk forget the beauties of the Yavapai hills, and if they didn't keep them locked up they'd all go back.

This is a kindlier story than the one told about the hooks in the lower regions where they had to hang the arrivals from B— up to dry for a week, as they came too green to burn.

There is a persistent tradition that if a tenderfoot is caught looking askance at thermometer maximums for July there is always a real estate agent hard by who will say: "But, my dear sir, you must remember that owing to the extreme dryness of the atmosphere, 110 degrees in the Southwest is really no hotter than eighty in New York."

The worm finally turned and we have the following story:

Once there was a real estate agent from (here insert not your town but the other fellow's) who died and went to his proper reward, and when he got there the devil was very glad to see him and asked him if he would like to inspect his quarters.

The real estate man yawned delicately, said "Yes," and remarked that he wanted a private bath and a pitcher of ice water.

At this an imp of a bell boy, with little horns sticking out under his cap, grinned openly and his majesty started leading the way down a very long hall. The further they went, the hotter it grew, until the pitch began to ooze out of the woodwork.

"Aren't we almost there?" asked the real estate man, who finally was beginning to get nervous.

"It's the last room!" said the devil.

After a half hour of going they reached an apartment where they found the furniture all of iron and glowing a nice warm pink. Through an open door they could see the bath tub full of bubbling pitch.

The devil picked up a red-hot shingle nail from an ash receiver and lighted his cigaret. "How do you like your quarters?" he asked easily.

The real estate man looked at the smoking sulphuric acid in the imp's water pitcher and wiped the sweat from his forehead. "It's a little hot, isn't it?"

"Not the *sensible* heat," smiled the devil pleasantly. "Some times our thermometer registers pretty high, but owing to the extreme dryness of the atmosphere 110 here is no hotter than eighty in New York."

"Seems to me," sneered the real estate man, "I have heard that chestnut before."

"Yes," replied the devil cheerfully. "You've told it. That's why you're here!"

However, no one ever summarized the climate of the Southwestern desert country more happily, perhaps, than did the minister at a Yuma banquet who stated that while the people were most hospitable and the town beautiful, the local field presented unusual difficulties to the spiritual shepherd. In ministering to his flock he found the winters were so delightful that heaven could offer no further charms, while in summer the weather was so hot that hell had no terrors!

Death Valley Heat

"Well, you know in Death Valley it ain't the humidity; it's the heat. I figured this out my own self the summer of nineteen and ten when I was layin' over a day at Furnace Creek Ranch. . . .

"Well, I was layin' there in the shade o' the house, watchin' the flies crawl up the doorjamb. 'Bout that time o' year the flies quit flyin' in the valley, and start crawlin'. Their wings is burned off. And the chickens start to wadin' in the creek. They hold out their wings to let the air under, and wade in clear up to the wish-bones, and stand there with their beaks open, gaspin'. Well, I was watchin' phe-nom-e-na like that, and I noticed the olla full o' water, hangin' there in the porch smokin' away like it was on fire. I says to myself, 'It must be a hot day. I disremember when I ever saw water burn before.' That made me kinda thirsty, and I got up to get a drink. I dip the gourd in the olla, and do you know that water was right cool. It stimulated my mental processes.

"I figured it out. It ain't the humidity, it's the heat. There ain't no humidity at all. It's plumb dry. So when you hang water up in a jar like one o' them ollas, and let the dry air get at it all around, the air

From *Here's Death Valley,* By C. B. Glasscock, pp. 51–53. Copyright, 1940, by C. B. Glasscock. Indianapolis and New York: The Bobbs-Merrill Company.

just naturally sucks out the water at every pore of the jar, and evaporates it, and that's what looks like smoke. And some way I can't figure out, that's what makes the water cool. I figure you ought to be able to cool it a lot more by fixin' it so it would do the same thing faster.

"So when night come on, and the temperature dropped down to a reasonable hundred and twenty, I made me a waterbag out of some canvas, and filled it up and packed by boorows, and said good-by to Oscar, and started for Beatty. Makin' the bag, and explainin' it all to Oscar took time, and I got a late start. I was only half way to Stovepipe Well when the sun came up and it begun to get warm. Pretty soon I wanted a drink. So I got the waterbag off a boorow, and tipped it up to get a nice, cool drink, and what do you think?"

"I can't think."

"Well, nothin' come out. That's the funny part of it. My figurin' was too good. The evaporatin' had been so fast that it froze what was left in the bag. I ripped it open and there was a chunk of ice inside. By that time I need a drink of water terrible bad. I still had four-five miles to go to Stovepipe Well, and the temperature was up to a hundred and fifty in that sun."

"Oh, you carried a thermometer too, as well as an ice plant."

"Everybody carries a thermometer in the valley, only most of 'em don't know how to read it. All you do is hold out your hand in the sun, back up, and when the fingernails bust loose at the back end it's a hundred and fifty."

"Well, what did you do about it? Five miles to go in the sun at one hundred and fifty; no water, and the relative humidity at zero. It must have been pretty tough."

"Yeh, it must of. But I made it. I was unconscious of course, but I must have made it, because that's where they found me. It was several years later."

"Who found you? How did you manage to live all that time?"

"I didn't. A feller named Brownie found my skeleton in that old dugout that used to be at Stovepipe Well."

"Oh yes; I know Brownie. His name is W. H. Brown. He's a deputy. He told me about finding that skeleton. He said there wasn't any skull."

"Yes; that's right. That was me."

"High Fog"

After a particularly violent rainstorm [in Los Angeles], which was described in the papers as having originated in the Northwest, a Seattle paper retaliated beautifully. It told of the arrest of an itinerant who

From *My L. A.,* by Matt Weinstock, pp. 35–36. Copyright, 1947, by Matt Weinstock. New York: Current Books, Inc. A. A. Wyn, Publisher.

had fled there to escape the Los Angeles rains and who had a strange type of thermometer in his pocket. Police were baffled by the instrument. Put on a radiator, the mercury went up only a few degrees. Dipped into a pitcher of ice water, it fell only two or three degrees. Finally the itinerant confessed. It was a Los Angeles Chamber of Commerce thermometer. The temperature was fixed to register a low of seventy-six, a high of eighty.

Another apocryphal story deals with an old timer's explanation of a siege of surplus dew.

"Those rain clouds," he said, "were heading for Florida and got off the track."

A newcomer, pointing skyward, said: "Is that so? Then what are those up there?"

"Oh," countered the defender, "those are just the empties coming back."

California Earthquake Lore

The persistent failure of the press to report the findings of modern seismologists has resulted in an immense amount of folklore about earthquakes in Southern California. Most Southern California residents are thoroughly convinced that tall buildings are peculiarly perilous in a quake area, that earthquakes are caused by the drainage of oil from the bowels of the earth, and that earthquakes are invariably preceded by a period of what is called "earthquake weather." Despite the fact that earthquakes have occurred in summer and winter, spring and fall, the belief in earthquake weather persists. In the sense in which most residents understand the expression "earthquake weather" refers to a close, stifling, sunless, muggy day. The belief in the oil-drainage superstition is of equal tenacity and antiquity. As a matter of fact, there is a slightly melodramatic quality, a hint of the sinister, about an oil field. The great shining storage tanks, the forest of derricks that assume fantastic shapes in mist and cloud, light and darkness, and the ceaseless idiotic thumping of the pumps does make for an atmosphere of doubt and misgiving.

When a major quake jars Southern California, popular fancy is immediately quickened. After the Long Beach quake of 1933, I culled the following items from the local press: a hen laid three eggs a few moments after the first shock was felt; a woman who had been suffering from paralysis for years was immediately cured by the vibrations of the quake and walked forth from an invalid's room without assistance; the quake was "predicted" by "scientists" weeks before it happened,

From *Southern California Country,* by Carey McWilliams, pp. 202–204. American Folkways Series, edited by Erskine Caldwell. Copyright, 1946, by Carey McWilliams. New York: Duell, Sloan & Pearce.

but the information was "suppressed"; a woman, taking a bath in Long Beach when the first shock came, was compelled to remain in the bathroom without clothes for three days and nights when a section of the wall fell in and blocked the doorway (she was eventually rescued by a squad of legionnaires); sixteen boys were killed in the Polytechnic High School in Long Beach, but were never reported as missing and their parents were promptly "hushed up." It also seems that, while gazing at the Los Angeles City Hall, a group of people saw the hall sway out of sight, come back into sight, sway out of sight in the opposite direction, and then come to rest "with an awful jar"; that a worker in a chemical plant in Long Beach was thrown thirty feet in the air after the first shock and that, on hitting the ground, he bounced skyward, and was thus bounced up and down "for three times in rapid succession"; that the earthquake was really caused by a moving mountain near Durango, Colorado; that an automobile on a Long Beach boulevard shook so hard during the quake that it lost all four tires; that the undertaker in Long Beach did not charge "a single penny" for the sixty or more interments following the quake; that the quake was the first manifestation of an awful curse which the Rev. Robert P. Shuler had placed on Southern California, after he failed to be elected to the United States Senate; that sailors on a vessel a mile or more offshore saw Long Beach's Signal Hill disappear from sight; that the bootleggers of Long Beach saved hundreds of lives by their public-spirited donation of large quantities of alcohol; that women showed more courage than men; that men, for some reason, simply cannot stand up to an earthquake; that the shock of the quake caused a dozen or more miscarriages in Long Beach and that an earthquake will often cause permanent menstrual irregularities; that every building not damaged by the quake was "earthquake proof"; that a cross on a Long Beach church was not damaged although the rest of the building was destroyed; that an earthquake is much more terrifying than a cyclone, but not quite so frightful as a tornado, and just slightly less ghastly than a hurricane; that Californians should construct "earthquake cellars"; that "the first temblor is always the hardest"; that, in fact, there is only one real quake, the subsequent temblors being merely "echoes" of the first; that it is extremely dangerous to rush out of doors during an earthquake; that the best place to be during an earthquake is in a doorway; that the reason the government never built a fort in California was because of the earthquake hazard; that every community which escaped serious damage was "not in the path of the fault" and was, therefore, a safe and good place to live; and that the earthquake, followed as it was by the appearance of a mighty meteor on March 24, presaged the beginning of the end.

How deeply the experience of living in an earthquake country has impressed the residents of the region is clearly shown in the novels that have been written about California. In many of these novels, one will find the climax of the tale invariably is reached at precisely the moment when the dishes begin to rattle, the stove to bounce, and the chairs to dance. According to the novelist Lawrence Rising, there is a stillness and expectancy in California "found only in earthquake countries." Myron Brinig closed a novel about Southern California with a fantastic, perhaps prophetic, vision: "Los Angeles tobogganed with almost one continuous movement into the water, the shoreline going first, followed by the inland communities . . . the small pink and white, blue and orange houses of the shore were blown like colored sands into the tempest. All of California, from the Siskiyous to Mexico, from the eastern border to the coast, started sliding swiftly, relentlessly, into the Pacific Ocean." (See also Frank Fenton's novel, *A Place in the Sun,* pp. 182-183, where a somewhat similar impression is recorded,) As a matter of fact, the German geographer, Alfred Wegener, in a treatise written in 1924, hinted that something of this sort might actually happen. Studying his theory of the origin of continents and islands, one can readily imagine that this island-on-the-land that is Southern California, this sub-tropical paradise, might someday be severed from a continent to which it has always been capriciously attached and float gently westward into the Pacific to become, as it has always been destined to be, a charming Tahiti in some glazed and azure sea.

"Webfoot"

The term "webfoot" became current during the early mining days of Southern Oregon, and it is said to have originated through a sarcastic remark of a commercial traveler who had spent the night at the house of a farmer located on the marshy banks of the Long Tom, Lane County. It had been raining quite hard, and in consequence water stood everywhere, which caused him to say: "The children living around here ought to be webfooted." The farmer's wife replied: "We have thought of that," at the same time showing the astonished visitor her baby's feet, which had webs between the toes. The story lost nothing in telling, and webfoot became the pseudonym for Oregonians.

Sudden Cold

The [Montana] cold is right sudden, too. . . . Cowboy artist Charley Russell used to tell about his friend who left the poker game

---

From *Oregon Native Son,* Vol. I (July, 1899), No. 3. p. 132. Portland, Oregon: Native Son Publishing Co.

From *Montana: High, Wide, and Handsome,* by Joseph Kinsey Howard, pp. 148–149. Copyright, 1943, by Yale University Press. New Haven.

downtown in Great Falls and started home afoot one winter night. He froze plumb to death, instant, said Charley, on a corner about a block from the poker game.

At that point in the story, Charley's interlocutor would remark that that was a terrible thing.

"Hell, no!" contradicted Charley. "He come in handy. We hung a lantern on him an' used him for a lamppost all winter."

The Wind in Dakota

The wind in Dakota has been in a very robust condition this spring and has exercised right along. It has blown steady from the south with a velocity only equaled by electricity, and then for the next week has backed up and got in position to come again. That is the worst thing about the wind in this country; if it would blow from one direction for a while and then go around somewhere and so keep away for a few days and not insist on backing up to get ready for a fresh start it wouldn't be so bad. Dakota wind is a double-ender, and backs up just as fast as it goes ahead. In either case it goes as if it must get there in about five minutes. It is the next fastest thing to a jack-rabbit. When it says "Come on" to a dry goods box or a barrel or a high board fence they mosey right along. These things all come back, however, when the wind does. In early days in the territory, when there was prairie everywhere, we have seen the wind get started under a corner of a county and keep working in until pretty soon it peeled the whole thing off and rolled it away.

The Big Muddy

At Jefferson—dreariest and dismalest of State capitals—I took steamer up "the great yellow river of the Massorites," as La Hontan named it two centuries ago. Later travelers called it "the Messourie." It is still dense as then with the crumbling prairies which it cuts away to deposit along the lower Mississippi, or add to the new land at its

---

From The *Cheyenne* (Wyoming) *Daily Sun*. May 15, 1887, p. 2, col. 2.

There are people in Wyoming who complain because there is an occasional gentle zephyr from the mountains, but what would they say if they encountered the breezes of a sister territory. The Dakota *Bell,* published at Sioux Falls, gives the following neat bit of description.—Ed.

From *Beyond the Mississippi:* from the Great River to the Great Ocean, Life and Adventure on the Prairies, Mountains, and Pacific Coast . . . 1857–1867, by Albert D. Richardson, pp. 19–20. Entered according to Act of Congress, in the year 1867, by Albert D. Richardson, in the Clerk's Office of the District Court of the Southern District of New York. Hartford, Connecticut: American Publishing Company . . .

mouth, rising from the gulf, as rose the primeval earth from the face of the deep.

John Randolph exaggerated in declaring that the Ohio was frozen over one half the year and dry the other half. But Benton told almost the exact truth when he described the Missouri as a little too thick to swim in, and not quite thick enough to walk on. By daylight the broad current is unpoetic and repulsive—a stream of liquid brick-dust or flowing mud, studded with dead tree-trunks, broken by bars and islands of dreary sand, and inclosed by crumbling shores of naked soil. Its water will deposit a sediment an eighth of an inch thick upon the bottom of a tumbler in five minutes. Though at first unpalatable and medicinal, one soon finds it a pleasant, healthful beverage. I have seen errant Missourians so partial to it as to urge that the pure waters of the Rocky Mountains were unfit to drink because of their clearness!

One of our eastern passengers, pouring out half a pitcher-full for ablution, was utterly disgusted with its color in the white porcelain basin.

"Here waiter," he exclaimed, "bring me *clean* water; somebody has washed in this."

Its aspect quite justifies the Indian appellation of "strong water," and possibly accounts for the tendency of whites to the manner born to weaken it with whisky. A novice fancies bathing in it must sadly soil any one not very dirty to begin with; but it proves soft and cleansing.

Why Kansas Is God's Country

"What do you think of Kansas?" Father asked, eager to get the conversation launched upon constructive lines.

"It is God's own country," was the reply.

A look of pride came over the questioner's face, as much as to say, "Did I not tell you so?" Father wanted to like Kansas.

"Yes, sir," resumed Mr. Johnston, "it says: 'Them the Lord loveth, he chasteneth.' Well, He ain't done very much for us Kansas fellers but chasten us with sand storms, chinch bugs, cyclones, dry weather, blizzards, and grasshoppers. He must love us a turrible sight."

"You should learn to adjust to conditions," Father admonished.

"I take it you are a parson."

"I am a minister," admitted Father.

"Which denomination?" he was asked.

"Methodist."

"Well, that is something like it," answered Johnston. "You see, the last feller we had down on Crooked Creek was a Baptist and he had to

---

From *Dodge City, Kansas,* by Charles C. Lowther, pp. 41–43, 48–49. Copyright, 1940, by Dorrance & Co., Inc. Philadelphia.

leave because there was no use to convert anybody. The creek was too shallow to baptize them in, and before it would rain they would plumb backslide again. It was like running down a maverick, and then not having any rope to hogtie him with. Now Methodists can save a sinner on mighty little water. They sprinkle them and let it go at that. I have preached some myself, only I can't say I am any top hand at it. I am too apt to jaw the members for being as narrow as a Scotchman's dime looked at edgewise. Some of 'em take a heap of comfort a-meditating on how hot it is going to be for the sinners and then forget that they might make a misreckon themselves and stumble into the hot place by accident. To tell the facts, I ain't never give as much attention to savin' my soul as I have to savin' my hide. A feller has to be kind of single-minded when he is running from a cyclone or getting in out of a blizzard. That is why I say this is God's country. There ain't much out here for anybody to be wicked on."

* * * * *

"Now give me your honest opinion of western Kansas," Father asked.

"Well, sir, Parson," began Johnston, "this here country is the 'short grass country.' From the one hundredth meridian, which we are now a-settin' on, clean through to the foot hills and on south and west, it is a desert and will not raise nothing but grass, unless you irrigate. It is a land of sand burrs, soap weeds, cacti, badgers, owls, and coyotes—everything out here needs thorns, claws, or some kind of stickers. Sometimes I think we need fish hooks to help hang on with when the wind blows. This here country is the 'American Desert.' "

"What do you stay here for then?" asked Father.

"That is a fair question," admitted the other. "I reckon I am like the coyotes, rattlesnakes, and prairie dogs," said he. "I have always been a triflin' sort of a cuss and maybe living out here in this place is good enough for me—serves me right, good place to do penance. Maybe when I die, it will kind o' hurry the devil to find some punishment for me that I ain't already been used to from livin' in Kansas."

What a Drink of Red River Water Will Do

. . . One time, a story goes, a young fellow from Missouri whom Colbert was ferrying over confessed that he was timid about going to Texas, he had heard so much concerning the desperate men there. "But," the ferryman assured him, "don't bother any more about that. As soon as we butt against the other bank, get down off your horse, drink yourself full of this Red River water, and you'll be able to hold your own with any of them." The youngster took the advice literally

From "Stories in Texas Place Names," by J. Frank Dobie, *Straight Texas,* Publications of the Texas Folk-Lore Society, No. XIII, J. Frank Dobie, editor, Mody C. Boatright, associate editor, p. 58. Copyright, 1937, by the Texas Folk-Lore Society. Austin.

and drank until he was swelled up like a poisoned pup. Then he bounded into the saddle and started off. "Hold on!" Colbert cried. "You did not pay your ferriage." "Now see here," the youth answered back, "I'm not a-going to pay it. I've done tanked up on Red River water." All Colbert could say was, "Well, it has taken effect remarkably soon."

An Iowa Farmer Learns about Oklahoma Rivers

The streams of the Plains are very different in their behavior from ordinary streams. Most streams constantly tend to cut their channels deeper, and are therefore called degrading streams. The streams of the Plains, on the other hand, are building up their channels. The cause is twofold: first, the immense amounts of sand which the streams carry; and second, relatively small amounts of water carried by the streams. In other words, the rainfall along the various rivers is not sufficient to furnish water enough to scour the stream channel, and so the streams are aggrading, or building up their channel.

This in turn means that these streams are constantly changing their courses. They have low, sandy banks, and with every freshet the channel shifts back and forth. This causes destruction of farms, and it is no uncommon thing for a stream that has been bridged to abandon its channel under the bridge and leave the structure high and dry.

People coming to this Western country do not always understand the behavior of our rivers and, until they learn better, attempt to treat them as they did the streams in the East. This method of treatment is not always successful.

Some twenty years ago I happened to be down on the South Canadian, near Norman [,Oklahoma], and found an Iowa farmer, who had bought a river-bottom farm, building a dike along the river bank. He had three teams at work with scrapers throwing up a wall of loose sand between his field and the water in the river.

His neighbor, a former cowboy who had lived in Indian Territory all his life and who owned the adjoining farm, came sauntering up to see what was going on. He wore the regulation cattleman's outfit, high-heeled boots and broad-brimmed white hat. He stood for a time watching the teams at work moving dirt.

"Well, neighbor," he said, "what do you reckon you're doing?"

"Building me a dike," said the Iowa farmer.

"Dike? What's it for?" inquired the cowboy.

"Why, to keep out the water, of course."

"Do you reckon it'll do it?" asked the cowboy.

From "Tales of an Oklahoma Geologist," by Charles N. Gould, *Folk-Say, A Regional Miscellany: 1930,* edited by B. A. Botkin, pp. 62–64. Copyright, 1930, by B. A. Botkin. Norman: University of Oklahoma Press.

"Don't see why not," replied the farmer. "I built just such a dike back in Iowa and it did the work."

The cowboy said nothing for quite a while. He walked over to the bank, looked up the river, and down the river, spit into the water, and turned to the Iowa man.

"Did you ask the river?" he said.

The very next rise not only took out the dike but washed away half the farmer's field.

Deceiving Distances and Narrow Rivers

From this point we started towards Cheyenne, and on the way we passed a number of streams dignified by the name of rivers. One of them, called Spring River, was about three feet deep, and here I accomplished the impossible feat of crossing a river three feet deep without any kind of a bridge and without wetting any part of the wheels of the wagon or the horses' feet. The banks of this narrow river were overgrown with a very thick, coarse grass which bent over the stream and which had probably, in the course of growing, accumulated and held quite a lot of loose soil blown there by the wind. At any rate, this dirt-laden grass formed a firm bridge which bent over the stream with a gap at the top of not more than eight inches, and although there was a rushing stream two feet below it, all the driver had to do was to induce the horses to step over this narrow gap, and the trick was done.

It was this river that inspired the making of a little story to use in illustrating how deceptive the distances are in the clear air of this country. The now nearly worn-out joke runs something like this:

A stranger to the country was visitor for a few days in a sheep camp, and seeing a mountain which appeared to him not more than a mile or two away, he told his host that he would walk to it and back again to gain an appetite for breakfast. The sheepman let him go without undeceiving him; so the man started and steadily walked till noon, but he found himself very little nearer the mountain. He had by this time reached the banks of one of these deep but narrow streams and paused in his walk. It looked too deep to wade, so he began to strip off his clothing. A native of the place happened to see him and asked what he was stripping for.

From "Folk-Characters of the Sheep Industry," by Winifred Kupper. *In the Shadow of History,* Texas Folk-Lore Society Publications No. XV, J. Frank Dobie, Mody C. Boatright, Harry H. Ransom, Editors, pp. 104–105. Copyright, 1939, by the Texas Folk-Lore Society. Austin.

One tale that grew out of a sheep drive became widespread into various versions. Robert Maudslay [in the unpublished chronicle of his life on the open range] claims to have made it up out of an idle mind from experiences with deceitful distances and narrow rivers he encountered on his long drives. When this story was last seen in print, it was in the book *Sheep,* by Archer B. Gilfillan, published in 1929 [p. 18].—W.K.

"To swim across the river, of course," he answered.

"Lord, you don't need to strip for that; you can just step across it."

"You can't fool me with any such talk as that. You see that hill over there? Well, I've been walking toward it for five hours and I haven't got any nearer; so I'm sure that on the same basis this river is at least twenty miles wide, and I'm going to swim it."

It was I who originated this poor joke. I conceived it at the time I crossed that strange river, and I told it to my men at the time, but after several years the story was told to me more than once, and with little variation, and I felt as I imagine the father of the prodigal son felt.

Powder River! Let 'er Buck!

The night we camped on the divide between the head of Poison Creek, near where the town of Hiland now stands, and the headwaters of dry Powder River, I told the boys we would water the herd in Powder River at about 10 o'clock the next morning.

None of them had ever seen Powder River, and they were all excited. In the morning when they were catching horses for the day, I called out to them to get their swimming horses as we were going to cross Powder River several times before night. Missouri Bill Shultz, who had already roped his horse, turned him loose, muttering that "this damn buckskin couldn't even wade a river."

About 10 o'clock the lead of the herd reached the river and it was almost dry, the water standing in holes and barely running from one hole to the other. The herd followed down stream for a distance of about two miles before they were watered, and we crossed it many times.

When Missouri Bill saw it he looked at it very seriously for some time and then said, "So this is Powder River," and that night in camp he told us he had heard of Powder River and now he had seen Powder River, and he kept referring to Powder River nearly every day until we reached Caspar, which we did in twenty-eight days' trailing.

From *Western Words,* A Dictionary of the Range, Cow Camp and Trail, by Ramon F. Adams, pp. 118–119. Copyright, 1944, by the University of Oklahoma Press. Norman.

A shout of encouragement, a password, a cry of derision. This is a very familiar cry throughout the cattle country of the Northwest. During World War I, in the Argonne, it was the battle cry of the Ninety-first Division, and it might be said that it has been heard around the world.

While in Cheyenne, Wyoming, I met Agnes Wright Spring, a member of the editorial staff of the *Wyoming Stockman-Farmer,* who gave me a story of the origin of this famous phrase, originally told by E. J. Farlow, a former cowman mayor of Lander. According to Mr. Farlow the saying originated in the fall of 1893, when a herd of cattle was being driven to Caspar.—R.F.A.

In the evening before we were going to load for shipping and [when] the cattle were all bedded down near the stockyards, the boys all adjourned to the saloon for a social drink, and Missouri Bill said, "Boys, come and have a drink on me. I've crossed Powder River." They had the drinks, then a few more, and were getting pretty sociable.

When Missouri Bill again ordered, he said to the boys, "Have another drink on me. I've swum Powder River," this time with a distinct emphasis on the words *Powder River*. "Yes, sir, by God, Powder River," with a little stronger emphasis. When the drinks were all set up, he said, "Well, here's to Powder River, let 'er buck!"

Soon he grew louder and was heard to say, "Powder River is comin' up—eeyeeep! Yes sir, Powder River is risin'," and soon after with a yip and a yell, he pulls out his old six-gun and throwed a few shots through the ceiling and yelled, "Powder River is up, come an' have 'nother drink." Bang! Bang! "Yeow, I'm a wolf and it's my night to howl. Powder River is out of 'er banks. I'm wild and woolly and full o' fleas, and never been curried below the knees."

Bill was loaded for bear, and that is the first time I ever heard the slogan, and from there it went around the world.

Many a cowboy, exuberant with whisky, brought to light his own version, such as: "Powder River, let 'er buck—she's a mile wide—an inch deep—full o' dust and flat fish—swimmin' holes for grasshoppers —cross 'er anywhere—yeou—uhh—yippee—she rolls up hill from Texas."

The "Sinks" of Nevada

The rivers of Nevada are none of them of great size. They all pour their waters into lakes that have no outlets, where they sink into the earth or are dissipated by the active evaporation that goes on in all this region during the greater part of the year. Each river empties into its lake, or what in that country is called its "sink." Not a river of them all gets out of the state or through any other river reaches the sea.

This condition of the rivers of Nevada was once thus curiously accounted for by an old mountaineer and prospector. Said he:

From *History of the Big Bonanza:* An Authentic Account of the Discovery, History, and Working of the World Renowned Comstock Silver Lode of Nevada, including the Present Condition of the Various Mines Situated Thereon; Sketches of the Most Prominent Men Interested in Them; Incidents and Adventures connected with Mining, the Indians, and the Country; Amusing Stories, Experiences, Anecdotes, &c., &c., and a Full Exposition of the Production of Pure Silver, by Dan De Quille (William Wright), pp. 19–20. Entered according to Act of Congress in the year 1876, by the American Publishing Company, in the office of the Librarian of Congress at Washington, D.C. Hartford, Connecticut.

The way it came about was in this wise: The Almighty, at the time he was creatin' and fashionin' of this here yearth, got along to this section late on Saturday evening. He had finished all of the great lakes, like Superior, Michigan, Huron, Erie, and them—had made the Ohio, Missouri, and Mississippi rivers, and, as a sort of wind-up, was about to make a river that would be far ahead of anything he had yet done in that line. So he started in and traced out Humboldt River, and Truckee River, and Walker River, and Reese River, and all the other rivers, and he was leadin' of them along, calkerlatin' to bring 'em all together into one big boss river and then lead that off and let it empty into the Gulf of Mexico or the Gulf of California, as might be most convenient; but as he was bringin' down and leadin' along the several branches—the Truckee, Humboldt, Carson, Walker, and them—it came on dark and instead to carry out the original plan, he jist tucked the lower ends of the several streams into the ground, whar they have remained from that day to this.

Directions in the Southwest

Ask a direction in Arizona, or western New Mexico, and the answer may be like this: "Well, you go on up this wash until you get to the second tank. Then follow the caprock till you pass a couple of Texas gates and one cattle-guard. There's a doby there. Then bear right, pass a chindi hogan, and keep on up the potrero and you'll drop right over that saddle onto Horse Thief Mesa. You can't miss it."

Oh, can't you? To translate: a wash has nothing to do with laundry, but is a stream-bed temporarily unoccupied by a stream. A tank is a dip in the ground which, in good seasons, holds a little water, where stock may drink. Etymologically, it is a descendant of the Spanish *tanque,* pond. A Texas gate is a section of a barbed-wire fence swinging loose on a pole, which fits into loops of wire at top and bottom of the gatepost. Open, it lies on the ground, looking innocent enough, but it is capable of going into a hideous snarl of tangled wires and vicious barbs; and even after you get the butt of the pole into the bottom loop, its top will enter the upper loop only under such strains as may spring the whole contraption back into your face. Still, all gates, even Texas gates, must be closed, if you do not wish to rate as the worst sort of dude. A doby is an adobe house. A potrero is a narrow ridge between canyons, and a saddle is a sag between peaks.

From *Our Southwest,* by Erna Fergusson, pp. 353–354. Copyright, 1940, by Alfred A. Knopf, Inc. New York.

Colorado Road Hazards

. . . On account of the heavy and continuous snow, the stage had ceased to run between Silverton and Ouray. But in order to catch a train we were compelled to make the trip by sleigh, over the pass of Red Mountain.

"Is it very dangerous?" I inquired of a citizen, and he answered:

"Well, the livery stable man is willing to risk his horses, ain't he? And you don't pretend to say you are worth as much as a horse, do you?"

This was encouraging, and at 4 o'clock in the morning, wrapped in wolfskins, we set out. The dogs barked a farewell and a gambling house winked its red eye. The moon was full and the mountain tops gleamed, a silver range in the distant heavens.

"Is this the road where the stage tumbled off the other day?" I inquired of the driver.

"Yes, but not in a very bad place."

"Is it customary to topple over in the best places?"

"Well, generally."

"What do you think of this trip?"

"Didn't see me takin' it before I had to, did you?"

"How high is Red mountain?"

"It is 13,000 feet."

"Can you fall all the way down?"

"Well, not very easy. You hit a crag down about a thousand feet."

"Do people fall very often?"

"Only once."

With me were Eugene Banks, the poet, and Wallace Bruce Amsbery, whose French-Canadian dialect poems in the *Century* are attracting attention. Banks was gazing at the moonlight. Amsbery was watching the horses floundering in the snow. I was taking my chances. Up toward the timber line, terrific beauty above, majestic shudder below, one was almost forced to cry aloud? "Oh, poverty-stricken pen! Oh, mendicant brush!" There was so much of tremendous magnificence that fear summoned a thousand eyes and gazed in wonder.

Coming day and the moon were blending their lights, a silvery struggle for supremacy, and then came the whirling charge of the snowstorm. On the top of the mountain the sleigh poised for a moment, so sharply defined was the crest, and the horses, shoulder deep, floundered in the snow.

"Have we passed the worst of it?" I inquired of the driver.

"Worst of what? The danger? You haven't got halfway to it."

By Opie Read. From the Chicago *American*, under the dateline of Ouray, Colorado, November 20, 1902. Cited in the Denver (Colorado) *Times*, November 25, 1902. Clipping files of the Western History Collection, Denver Public Library, Denver, Colorado.

I knew that this was not true, but it was. The storm was left behind and ghastly daylight conquered the moon. We passed through a dead mining town. Not a soul lived in the place. There were the windows through which the eyes of hope and longing had gazed toward the east, the broken fireplaces where love had gathered in the evening. All was desolation, and through it rang the faraway tones of a howling wolf.

A few turns and we were upon the narrow ledge of Uncompangre cañon. And now we knew that the driver had told the truth.

"Here," said the poet, "we believe you to be the best driver in the world, and that you can make quicker turns than any other man, but please don't prove it. Take your time."

"I ain't cutting no scollops," the driver replied.

Slipping and sliding along a shelf, and with the runners at a sharp turn shoving snow over the cliff, was not pleasant to contemplate. Far below there was a stream, but the rush of its waters made no noise. Out of that awful abyss came naught but silence.

"You told me the truth," I said to the driver. "We had not begun to see the most dangerous places."

"Yes, but you tried mighty hard to make me lie."

Perhaps in the supremest of joy there must be an element of danger, but if it be really true I'd rather not enjoy myself so well. I knew that I was coming down off that hill, but I didn't know how.

A Long Night

Avalanches also put in an appearance, and in March a man who was cutting wood on a hill just north of Virginia was buried by one, and his body was not recovered till the snow had melted away. Avalanches are still of occasional occurrence, and several lives have been lost and a number of buildings demolished in the southern part of Virginia City by heavy slides of snow rushing down the side of Mount Davidson into the western suburbs of the town.

In the spring of 1860 an avalanche that fell near Silver City covered the mouth of a tunnel in which half a dozen miners were living. It came down in the night when they were all asleep. At the usual hour in the morning some of the men awoke, but, finding it still dark, turned over and went to sleep again. Others of the party did the same. After a time all were tired of sleeping and began talking about what a long night it seemed. However, they concluded it was all right, and each again addressed himself to the task of trying to sleep the

---

From *History of the Big Bonanza:* An Authentic Account of the Discovery, History, and Working of the World Renowned Comstock Silver Lode of Nevada . . ., by Dan De Quille (William Wright), pp. 106–107. Entered according to Act of Congress in the year 1876, by the American Publishing Company, in the office of the Librarian of Congress at Washington, D.C. Hartford Connecticut.

night through. All would not do, and in an hour or two they were again discussing the apparent great length of the night, wondering, also, whether or not all hands might not be unusually wakeful.

At length one of the party said he would go out to the mouth of the tunnel and see if he could perceive any sign of the approach of daylight. On reaching the mouth of the tunnel, he ran his nose into a solid bank of snow. The exclamation of surprise he uttered brought all to their feet. They soon comprehended the situation. Luckily they had several shovels in the tunnel. Lighting a candle, they set to work, and in half an hour had dug their way out, when they found that it was almost sundown.

The Great Landslide Case

The mountains are very high and steep about Carson, Eagle, and Washoe valleys—very high and very steep, and so when the snow gets to melting off fast in the spring and the warm surface-earth begins to moisten and soften, the disastrous landslides commence. The reader cannot know what a landslide is, unless he has lived in that country and seen the whole side of a mountain taken off some fine morning and deposited down in the valley, leaving a vast, treeless, unsightly scar upon the mountain's front to keep the circumstances fresh in his memory all the years that he may go on living within seventy miles of that place.

General Buncombe was shipped out to Nevada in the invoice of Territorial officers, to be United States Attorney. He considered himself a lawyer of parts, and he very much wanted an opportunity to manifest it—partly for the pure gratification of it and partly because his salary was Territorially meagre (which is a strong expression). Now the older citizens of a new Territory look down upon the rest of the world with a calm, benevolent compassion, as long as it keeps out of the way—when it gets in the way they snub it. Sometimes this latter takes the shape of a practical joke.

One morning Dick Hyde rode furiously up to General Buncombe's door in Carson City and rushed into his presence without stopping to tie his horse. He seemed much excited. He told the General that he

---

From *Roughing It,* by Mark Twain, Vol. I, pp. 265–272. New York and London: Harper & Brothers, Publishers.

Cf. Effie Mona Mack, *Mark Twain in Nevada* (New York and London, 1947), pp. 143, 364: This joke, as old as the very hills of Nevada, has been told and retold, sometimes in one way, sometimes in another. The Sam Clemens version of it will live longest. To-day it goes by the title of "The Story of Slide Mountain." . . . The ranch belonged to Dick Sides (Dick Hyde in *Roughing It*), an early settler in Washoe Valley.

wanted him to conduct a suit for him and would pay him five hundred dollars if he achieved a victory. And then, with violent gestures and a world of profanity, he poured out his griefs. He said it was pretty well known that for some years he had been farming (or ranching, as the more customary term is) in Washoe District, and making a successful thing of it, and furthermore it was known that his ranch was situated just in the edge of the valley, and that Tom Morgan owned a ranch immediately above it on the mountain side. And now the trouble was, that one of those hated and dreaded landslides had come and slid Morgan's ranch, fences, cabins, cattle, barns, and everything down on top of *his* ranch and exactly covered up every single vestige of his property, to a depth of about thirty-eight feet. Morgan was in possession and refused to vacate the premises—said he was occupying his own cabin and not interfering with anybody's else's—and said the cabin was standing on the same dirt and same ranch it had always stood on, and he would like to see anybody make him vacate.

"And when I reminded him," said Hyde, weeping, "that it was on top of my ranch and that he was trespassing, he had the infernal meanness to ask me why I didn't stay on my ranch and hold possession when I see him a-coming! Why didn't I *stay* on it, the blathering lunatic—by George, when I heard that racket and looked up that hill it was just like the whole world was a-ripping and a-tearing down that mountainside—splinters and cord-wood, thunder and lightning, hail and snow, odds and ends of haystacks, and awful clouds of dust! trees going end over end in the air, rocks as big as a house jumping 'bout a thousand feet high and busting into ten million pieces, cattle turned inside out and a-coming head on with their tails hanging out between their teeth! —and in the midst of all that wrack and destruction sot that cussed Morgan on his gatepost a-wondering why I didn't *stay and hold possession!* Laws bless me, I just took one glimpse, General, and lit out'n the county in three jumps exactly.

"But what grinds me is that Morgan hangs on there and won't move off'n that ranch—says it's his'n and he's going to keep it—likes it better'n he did when it was higher up the hill. Mad! Well, I've been so mad for two days I couldn't find my way to town—been wandering around in the brush in a starving condition—got anything here to drink, General? But I'm here *now,* and I'm a-going to law. You hear *me!*"

Never in all the world, perhaps, were a man's feelings so outraged as were the General's. He said he had never heard of such high-handed conduct in all his life as this Morgan's. And he said there was no use in going to law—Morgan had no shadow of right to remain where he was —nobody in the wide world would uphold him in it, and no lawyer would take his case and no judge listen to it. Hyde said that right there was where he was mistaken—everybody in town sustained Morgan; Hal Brayton, a very smart lawyer, had taken his case; the courts being in vacation, it was to be tried before a referee, and ex-Governor Roop had already been appointed to that office and would open his court in a large public hall near the hotel at two that afternoon.

The General was amazed. He said he had suspected before that the people of that Territory were fools, and now he knew it. But he said rest easy, rest easy and collect the witnesses, for the victory was just as certain as if the conflict were already over. Hyde wiped away his tears and left.

At two in the afternoon Referee Roop's court opened, and Roop appeared throned among his sheriffs, the witnesses, and spectators, and wearing upon his face a solemnity so awe-inspiring that some of his fellow-conspirators had misgivings that maybe he had not comprehended, after all, that this was merely a joke. An unearthly stillness prevailed, for at the slightest noise the judge uttered sternly the command:

"Order in the court!"

And the sheriffs promptly echoed it. Presently the General elbowed his way through the crowd of spectators, with his arms full of law-books, and on his ears fell an order from the judge which was the first respectful recognition of his high official dignity that had ever saluted them, and it trickled pleasantly through his whole system:

"Way for the United State Attorney!"

The witnesses were called—legislators, high government officers, ranchmen, miners, Indians, Chinamen, Negroes. Three-fourths of them were called by the defendant Morgan, but no matter, their testimony invariably went in favor of the plaintiff Hyde. Each new witness only added new testimony to the absurdity of a man's claiming to own another man's property because his farm had slid down on top of it. Then the Morgan lawyer made his speech, and seemed to make a singularly weak one—he did really nothing to help the Morgan cause. And now the General, with exultation in his face, got up and made an impassioned effort; he pounded the table, he banged the law-books, he shouted, and roared and howled, he quoted from everything and everybody, poetry, sarcasm, statistics, history, pathos, bathos, blasphemy, and wound up with a grand war-whoop for free speech, freedom of the press, free schools, the Glorious Bird of America and the principles of eternal justice! [Applause.]

When the General sat down, he did it with the conviction that if there was anything in good, strong testimony, a great speech and believing and admiring countenances all around, Mr. Morgan's case was killed. Ex-Governor Roop leant his head upon his hand for some minutes, thinking, and the still audience waited for his decision. And then he got up and stood erect, with bended head, and thought again. Then he walked the floor with long, deliberate strides, his chin in his hand, and still the audience waited. At last he returned to his throne, seated himself, and began impressively:

"Gentlemen, I feel the great responsibility that rests upon me this day. This is no ordinary case. On the contrary, it is plain that it is the most solemn and awful that ever man was called upon to decide. Gentlemen, I have listened attentively to the evidence, and have perceived that the weight of it, the overwhelming weight of it, is in favor of the plaintiff Hyde. I have listened also to the remarks of counsel, with high interest—and especially will I commend the masterly and irrefutable logic of the distinguished gentleman who represents the plaintiff. But gentlemen, let us beware how we allow mere human testimony, human ingenuity in argument and human ideas of equity, to influence us at a moment so solemn as this. Gentlemen, it ill becomes us, worms as we are, to meddle with the decrees of Heaven. It is plain to me that Heaven, in its inscrutable wisdom, has seen fit to move this defendant's ranch for a purpose. We are but creatures, and we must submit. If Heaven has chosen to favor the defendant Morgan in this marked and wonderful manner; and if Heaven, dissatisfied with the position of the Morgan ranch upon the mountainside, has chosen to remove it to a position more eligible and more advantageous for its owner, it ill becomes us, insects as we are, to question the legality of the act, or inquire into the reasons that prompted it. No—Heaven created the ranches, and it is Heaven's prerogative to rearrange them, to experiment with them, to shift them around at its pleasure. It is for us to submit, without repining. I warn you that this thing which has happened is a thing with which the sacrilegious hands and brains and tongues of men must not meddle. Gentlemen, it is the verdict of this court that the plaintiff, Richard Hyde, has been deprived of his ranch by the visitation of God! And from this decision there is no appeal."

Buncombe seized his cargo of law-books and plunged out of the court-room frantic with indignation. He pronounced Roop to be a miraculous fool, an inspired idiot. In all good faith he returned at night and remonstrated with Roop upon his extravagant decision, and implored him to walk the floor and think for half an hour, and see if he could not figure out some sort of modification of the verdict. Roop yielded at last and got up to walk. He walked two hours and a half, and at last his face lit up happily and he told Buncombe it had occurred to him that the ranch underneath the new Morgan ranch still belonged to Hyde, that his title to the ground was just as good as it had ever been, and therefore he was of opinion that Hyde had a right to dig it out from under there and—

The General never waited to hear the end of it. He was always an impatient and irascible man, that way. At the end of two months the fact that he had been played upon with a joke had managed to bore itself, like another Hoosac Tunnel, through the solid adamant of his understanding.

Mirage

Bill Sanger was known to have ridden the rods all over the map. In his time he had seen all there was to see. One day he was talking with Jim Craig about mirages. Mirages are common sights. You see a lot of them, millions of them, in the dry lake bed out there at Amboy.

"Bill," said Jim, "did you ever see the city that gleams out there on the lake in hot weather?"

"Yeah," Bill replied.

"What d'ye make of it?" said Jim.

"Nothing," Bill answered. "I don't hold with those dude scientists that try to explain ghosts by saying the light rays pick up a picture hundreds of miles away and then bend it back and drop that same picture out there on the lake. It don't make sense. They're ghosts, that's what they are. Just plain ghosts. One time," Bill went on, "I nearly killed myself trying to hop a ghost train pulling out across Bristol Lake. I was walking out toward the salt works when along came a freight, not going very fast. I forgot where I was, and made a run for it. It started to pick up speed, so I gave a leap and grabbed on—to nothing! I sprawled out flat on that dry lake bed. I looked up and saw the ghost train running along as nice as you please—forty-two cars and one caboose I counted. They rode right smack over me and never even mussed my shirt. They're ghosts, I tell you. Ghosts!"

Buffalo Wallows and Alkali Mud

When we'd first got there and the snow melted, we seen that the whole valley was covered with buffalo wallows. . . .

In the dry summers the buffalo had kicked up soft dirt with their hooves and throwed it on their backs to get rid of the flies. Then when it rained the holes would fill up with water, and them buffalo had wallowed around in them places just like an old hog does in a mud hole. I suppose at first they was just little puddles, but buffaloes is big, and after a number of them rolled in the same place, they left considerable of a hole. I never figgered that buffaloes wanted to go around with all them chunks of dirt hanging on their sides. They must of rolled in them wallows to get rid of the flies or maybe just to scratch theirselves.

From *The Old West,* Pioneer Tales of San Bernardino County, Compiled by Workers of the WPA Writers' Program of the Work Projects Administration in Southern California, p. 47. Sponsored by Arrowhead Parlor No. 110, Native Sons of the Golden West. Copyright, 1940, by Native Sons of the Golden West. San Bernardino: The Sun Company.

From *Them Was the Days,* Another Mont Hawthorne Story, by Martha Ferguson McKeown, pp. 109, 110–111. Copyright, 1950, by Martha Ferguson McKeown. New York: The Macmillan Company.

But having them do that turned out to be a blamed nuisance for us because the water couldn't run out of them places, and it just evaporated after they went off wearing some of the best topsoil, and down in the bottom of each of them wallows was a thick alkali deposit that we gathered up, mixed with water, and smeared on our roof like plaster.

Excepting for using that stuff out of the bottom of them buffalo wallows on our roof, they turned out to be about the worst nuisance we had. Us children had all helped pick up bones so that Father could plow some sod under for corn and for our house. He told me to go ahead and plow while him and Aaron worked on the house. Why, sure, I was nine years old by then and that team was more broke than it had been to start with.

Father wanted the plowing to go along because it's lots easier to do when the ground ain't dried out, unless you've got buffalo wallows. But the stuff in them wallows, even the ones only eight inches or a foot deep, sticks to your feet when it's wet. It was bad enough for the oxen, but all that bothered them was carrying around that extra weight. But I was barefoot and that moist alkali mud would stick to my feet and they would crack, and the blood would run out. I tell you it was bad. When I went in at night, Mama rubbed linseed oil on them and the next morning I put more on before I went back to plowing again. That's where I made my mistake. That linseed oil that was dried on my feet just seemed to make that mud stick harder than ever. I never knowed nothing could stick and burn like that. Finally I went clumping over to the house with my feet in them big balls of alkali mud, and Mama chiseled them off and fixed me up the best she could, and that's what made Father see how good that stuff would be to put on top of a roof, because I couldn't have been no worse off if I'd put my feet in concrete and then let them dry.

The only way Father could handle them wallows when it come to farming was to haul in wagon loads of sand and dump them in to sort of loosen that ground up and work it. Of course manure would of been better, but we didn't have none. But he figgered on getting a herd of cows just as soon as he could, and when him and Aaron throwed up a shelter of poles, with a brush and a straw roof, for the oxen, they made it big enough for some cows, too.

A Rolling Stone

. . . Hathaway Jones, veteran pack-mule man of Curry County, gave the following account of what he personally saw along a wild, canyoned

---

From *Redwood Country,* The Lava Region and the Redwoods, by Alfred Powers, pp. 280–282. American Folkways Series, edited by Erskine Caldwell. Copyright, 1949,

Cf. *A Treasury of Southern Folklore* (New York, 1949), pp. 465–466, for an Ozark variant, "The Rolling Log."

tributary of the Rogue River where it dashes through the Coast range:

"I was out huntin'. About twenty years ago, I guess it was. In October. Was comin' down a long ridge, it was gettin' along late in the day, and I was about tuckered out from all the up-hill walkin'. I come to a big boulder, shady and cool on the side away from the sun. I set down to rest, with my gun across my knees, and then leaned back—and, instead of the dern thing being solid, I thought it moved with my weight, big as it was.

"I turned around and pushed on it with my hand. I could move it as easy as anythin'. It was about twelve feet through itself, but it was balanced on a little rock not a foot through.

"I thought to myself, it would sure be fun to roll it down into the canyon. Its size would sure make it go a-tearin'.

"I give it a good hard push and it kind of rocked a little. Pretty soon I got it teeterin' good and then away she went. The canyon was about two thousand feet to the bottom and it was awful steep.

"Well, you know, it just plowed a furrow right down through the trees, and you could look down and see it tearin' along. It went down to the bottom, and—get me—instead of stoppin' it went right up the other side, pretty near to the top. Fact I thought it was goin' right over.

"It got just about to the top, like I say, and then back down it come, right down the same track. And—get me—when it got to the bottom, it didn't stop either, but come right back up toward me. It was comin' fast, too.

"I got scared, thinkin' it might knock a tree down on me. So I got a good long ways off. But it didn't. It got right near to the place I'd pushed it off from, and stopped, and down she went again.

"I had all the rock-rollin' I wanted that day. So I went on home.

"Well, it was near two years later, about the same time of the year, too, in another October, I come walkin' up this same canyon. But I just didn't think about it bein' the same one right then.

"I come along, not thinkin' about the year before, and then I looked and there seemed to be quite an open spot, a kind of cleared right-of-way, in the trees just ahead. Then I heard the queerest rattlin' sound, like no animal ever made. I got up to the open place, and—get me—there was a strip of bare ground kind of like a ditch and fifteen feet wide, runnin' way up to near the top on both sides of that canyon.

"And, you know, about that time I heard the queer rattlin' sound again, and here, down in the bottom of the ditch, come a little rock about the size of a little marble, rollin' like everything. It kept a-comin' and a-comin' till it got near to where I was and then got slower and stopped. Right away it went down again, and went way out of sight in the bottom of the canyon and up the other side. Pretty soon it come back again, and that went on all the time I stood there and watched it.

"And—get me—that big rock I pushed over two years before must have been a-rollin' all that time, till it was wore down, as I say, no bigger'n a marble, and was still a-rollin' and I reckon' gettin' smaller. Anyhow, when I come along there the next year I couldn't see nothin' or hear that rattlin' sound in the faintest way, and bushes was growin' up in the bare strip."

How Paul Bunyan Dug Puget Sound

That year Paul was loggin' down at Astoria and he was just finishin' up his work there the next summer when one Saturday night he lost a couple of rafts of logs on the Columbia River bar; and that was about the time Mr. Rainier come down to see him, about the first part of August that year. Paul'd knowed Mr. Rainier when he first come out West at the time he was gettin' ready to scrip his land that he had to have, but he'd just about forgot all about him. But I guess Mr. Rainier thought the acquaintance was strong enough for him to ask a favor of Paul and anyway that's what he come down to see him for.

Paul went up and got out a raft of logs first and got it down in the river to take the place of the ones he'd lost on Saturday, and then he come in and sat down and started in to talk to Mr. Rainier, who'd been sittin' there in the office waitin' for him most of the afternoon. But Paul thought it was kind of funny, I guess, for he wasn't used to havin' any visitors come to see him that way. But anyway they talked about the weather for a couple of hours, and then about old times what they could remember, and then they didn't have nothin' more to talk about for a while, and so finally Mr. Rainier come out with what he wanted.

"And so we'd like to have you come up and help us dig the Sound," he says.

And Paul says: "I guess I can do that. Loggin's kind of slow anyway this time of the year. Though it ain't hardly in my line," he says.

The way that was: Mr. Rainier and Mr. Puget of the Puget Construction Company, and Old Dad Hood and Mr. Elliott was associated together under a contract to dig a Sound for Seattle so's Seattle would have a harbor, and they'd been given just two years by the government to finish the job, and now already twenty-two months was up and they seen they wasn't goin' to get it done, and so that's why they sent down for Paul to come and help 'em. The Republicans in Congress was askin' the contractors to report progress and the contractors naturally didn't have no progress to report and they figgered they'd have to hurry up and do somethin' about it, and I guess they was pretty near up a stump.

"We ain't gettin' this Sound dug," says Old Man Puget.

"No, we ain't" says Dad Hood.

"Except of course I pretty near got the Bay dug though, with my badgers and catapults," says Mr. Elliott.

From *Paul Bunyan,* by Esther Shephard, pp. 191–201. Copyright, 1924, by Esther Shephard. New York: Harcourt, Brace, and Co.

"The bay ain't half finished," says Old Man Puget, "and besides what good's a bay goin' to do without a Sound behind it, I'd like to know. We got to do somethin' different than that, I reckon."

And so then Mr. Rainer suggested havin' met Paul Bunyan one time and the Blue Ox, and Old Man Puget says, "As chairman, that's just the point I was comin' to."

And so then he made his proposition in the legal and proper form.

What they proposed to do was that they should send down for Paul to come up and dig the Sound for 'em and they'd give him part of the money that they was goin' to get, because they'd have to, but keep a good big margin for themselves, because they was the ones that was lettin' the contract and so was entitled to it. And they didn't need to say anythin' to him about the mountain they was goin' to make of course.

When they'd took the contract to dig the Sound they knowed they was goin' to have to have some place to dump the dirt, and so they'd got their Congressman from Seattle to introduce a bill in Congress that they should make somethin' for Tacoma too at the same time and a mountain would be just the thing, that they could name after their city. And so that way the contractors could get paid twice for doin' the one job of course. But now they wouldn't have to say nothin' to Paul about that, but could just tell him where to dump the dirt.

And so then they sent Mr. Rainier, the secretary, down to see Paul about it, and like I said, Paul promised he'd help 'em out.

"I think I can do it for you all right," he says. "I'll be up tomorrow and look over the job."

But when Paul come up and see what a haywire outfit they was tryin' to do the excavatin' with he was sure pretty near plum disgusted.

"Ain't you got a plow and a scraper?" he says.

"No. Elliott's badgers and catapults is all we got," they says. "Exceptin' some mules and single harness—and we got a six-tooth harrow."

"I got the Bay pretty near dug with my catapults, though," says Mr. Elliott.

"The Bay ain't but just big enough for you to put your name on it," says Old Man Puget.

"I'll send to my friend, Andrew Carnegie, for a plow and a scraper for your job," says Paul. "He can probably make one back there in Pittsburgh."

It took Carnegie's whole output of steel for the last year and six months to make them implements Paul ordered for the company and it took sixteen Mogul engines to ship 'em across the country.

But even after all that bother and after pretty near a perfectly good whole week of waitin' they wasn't half or even quarter big enough, and Paul couldn't use 'em. The plow went down only forty foot or so the deepest it could be set, and the scraper couldn't only carry about 408 ton at a time.

Paul was thinkin' for a minute and then, like always, he got an idea.

"What's the matter with me?" he says. "Why ain't I thought of it before? There's glaciers up in Alaska that can dig lakes and rivers and sounds and valleys and anything else you've a mind to. I'll go up and get one of them."

And so he gets Babe and goes up there to Alaska and hitches onto one of the biggest of them glaciers up there and brings it down, and then he goes ahead to plow out the Sound.

Naturally he didn't need no scraper, because that glacier hadn't been used to havin' a scraper workin' behind it anyhow and could do the whole process in one swipe by itself, the way it'd always done up in Alaska all them thousands of years. And so it didn't take Paul long to dig the Sound.

One day when Paul was plowin', Babe shied at a school teacher with a pink parasol, and started to run away. Paul dug his heel into the ground to stop the Ox, and that's how Hood's Canal happened to be made. But he got him stopped before he got quite through, and he never bothered to go back there again, and so it's never been quite finished.

Babe shouldn't of scared that way—it wasn't nothin' to be afraid of—only Old Dad Hood's daughter on her way home from school—but that was the first umbrella he'd ever seen, and he never could abide pink anyhow.

I should of mentioned before now, I guess, that Babe'd growed kind of ornery and queer since he'd come out to the Coast. It was the feed that didn't agree with him, I know. That was the principal reason, except the hotcakes, of course. But Douglas fir tops ain't exactly the right kind of fare and not as good as what he'd always been used to havin' back in Dakota and Wisconsin—clover hay, and baled timothy, and redtop.

The alfalfa that Paul tried to raise for him had all been drowned out the fall before by the yellow rain that had come up from China—between the two of 'em, the dry Washington rain comin' down from on top and the yellow Chinese rain comin' up from below, it was too much for alfalfa hay, and soaked the roots all out and killed it dead.

I never understood about that Chinese rain. It don't seem reasonable that rain should come up from down there that way, but we couldn't see how the ground could ever get that wet from any ordinary rain from on top, and so we figgered it must of been a Reverse rain like that, that done it—or helped, anyway.

Paul thought he'd try to make up to Babe for the hay he was missin' by feedin' him Shredded Wheat Biscuit baled up with haywire, but Babe knowed that he wasn't gettin' nothin' but wind and turned it down flat, and I don't know as I blame him any; I know I would of done the same thing if I'd been him.

And all the time, of course, he was gettin' more and more vicious, and more and more crazy for them hotcakes, that he'd got such a habit for, and you couldn't hardly keep 'em away from him no more.

He got so ornery he just struck flat one day when Paul was plowin' down near Olympia.

Paul stopped and fuddled around a while to plant some oysters so's the governor would always have some fresh for his table when he was entertainin' governors from other states, and I guess maybe the Ox thought he was monkeyin' around too long. Anyway when Paul come back to go on and drive on further, Babe wouldn't move a step.

I guess you know Paul'd meant to connect up the Sound with the Columbia River and so make a complete job of it, but on account of that balky streak of Babe's that day it ain't never got done. Paul was about as mad as he ever was at Babe, but no sir, he couldn't make the Ox move an inch.

Anyway it was a pretty good Sound, Paul thought, and fulfilled all the specifications, except prob'ly it was a little rough and uneven around the edges where he'd tried to scratch around a little at first with that plow Carnegie'd made for him. He could of smoothed that out, I spose, and straightened it up, but what's the use? Seattle real estate men would have more frontage on the Sound to sell if he didn't, he figgered, and then besides he had a job at Bellingham too that he wanted to start in on as soon as he could.

The city council of Bellingham had wanted a Bay for Bellingham for a long time so's the ships could come closer up to the wharves and not have to sail up on dry land, and they sent down to Paul and asked him to dig a bay for 'em while he was at it, and they'd be willin' to pay him extra for his trouble, they said.

Well, Paul went up there, but right in the spot where he wanted to put the bay, an old homesteader by name of Baker had took up a homestead, and he wouldn't get out of the way or sell or do nothin'.

Paul tried for pretty near two weeks to get the old man to change his mind and he even hired one of them there lawyers that can talk backwards and forwards at the same time to talk to him for him, but he wouldn't budge, and then one day Paul got mad, and they had a real row.

About two weeks after that when old man Baker got out of the hospital, Bellingham Bay was all done.

Paul just happened to meet the old man on the street one day.

"There's your farm," he says to him. "I put the dirt all up there on the other side of the town for you. And you can name it for yourself if you want to."

And so that's how Mount Baker got its name.

Old Man Puget and his partners, Elliott, and Rainier, and Hood, as soon as they'd collected their money from the government, went up to settle with Paul, but they didn't like to part with the money they'd got very well, and they was goin' to try to jaw him down if they could.

Well, Paul he just stands there with one foot on either side of Deception Pass and lets 'em talk for a while, and then after a while he just calmly takes up his shovel and picks up a shovelful of dirt from the east side of the Sound and throws it out in the water, kind of as if he wasn't thinkin' about what he was doin'. Well, and then as they goes on talkin' and tryin' to explain to him that seein' it didn't take him as long as they'd expected it to take him, they'd rather pay him so much a day, and that would be fair, instead of payin' him for the whole job, and goes on that way, all of 'em together, Paul he just picks up another shovelful and another shovelful, and another shovelful, and without lookin' at 'em or payin' no attention to 'em, throws 'em into the Sound.

Well, when they seen all of a sudden what he was aimin' to do, and if they didn't pay him right away, he'd soon have the whole Sound filled up again, they run right for the moneysack and paid him quick, I can tell you.

You would think they would of learned their lesson the other time, when they sent him a carload of cheap tobacco—Paul just begun shovelin' dirt back in the Sound, till some clerk reported to 'em what he was doin' and they sent him a carload of good tobacco and an apology quick, I can tell you. But they didn't seem to've remembered that till next time.

Them shovelfuls of dirt that Paul throwed back in the Sound is the San Juan Islands now. Since they've got overgrown with trees and rocks and blackberry vines they've come to be mighty pretty to look at. But of course they're in the way of the ships a little bit, them that are goin' to Victoria.

Animals of the Short Grass Country

. . . The Short Grass is a region of superlatives, of extremes, of incredible excesses.

It grows the shortest grass—and the tallest; has the widest rivers—with the least water in them; the thickest dust and the deepest mud, the least rain and the heaviest downpours; the hottest days and the coolest nights; the brightest sunshine and the blackest clouds; the strongest winds, the most magnificent electrical storms, the longest summers, and the shortest winters, the biggest hail, the loudest thunder, and the brightest moonlight in the whole Mississippi Valley.

There the cattle had the longest horns and the shortest tempers. There the water makes you thirsty, the squirrels live underground, and

---

From *Short Grass Country*, by Stanley Vestal, pp. 184–185. American Folkways Series, edited by Erskine Caldwell. Copyright, 1941, by Stanley Vestal. New York: Duell, Sloan & Pearce.

the spiders have fur. There the riders have legs like a pulley-bone—they are so bowlegged they sit around a chair, not in it.

The native animals are all superlative in strength, toughness, stamina, or speed. The Plains buffalo is bigger than the woods buffalo, the antelope is swifter than anything that runs, with more curiosity than a goat—and hollow horns which it sheds like a deer. The jack-rabbit is speedier than any other hare, the centipedes have more legs, the scorpions sharper tails. Rattlesnakes are bigger and more venomous. Wolves are fiercer, coyotes more cunning than in other regions. And in addition to greater power and size, these creatures were more numerous than elsewhere.

Even imported animals soon acquired superior toughness on the Short Grass. The mustang, running wild, became swifter, hardier, warier than his ancestors. He hardly ever gave in, and almost never gave out. As that great Texan, Charles Goodnight, said of the Staked Plains, "It produces better cattle, why shouldn't it produce better men?"

The White Steed of the Prairies

. . . Every range had its own superb mustang, but supreme above the local superiors was the White Mustang of the Prairies. All men who rode horses in the mustang world knew of him, talked of him, wanted him.

This ubiquitous stallion went under many names: The Pacing White Stallion, the White Steed of the Prairies, the White Mustang, the White Sultan, the Ghost Horse of the Plains, the Phantom Wild Horse. Whatever his name, he answered to none. His fire, his grace, his beauty, his speed, his endurance, his intelligence were the attributes that men commonly admire most in horses, but in him they were supernal; his passion for liberty was the passion that his admirers and pursuers idealized most constantly, both in the abstract and in themselves. So, wherever spurs clicked or campfires burned over the unfenced world that stretched from the prickly pear flats of South Texas to the bad lands of Montana, the story of the Pacing White Stallion was told. Newspaper correspondents heard and repeated it; fiction makers elaborated it, and it was echoed in cities beyond the seas. A few old men yet recall snatches of it. From them and from scattered records I have pieced out the legend.

The earliest account of the Supreme Mustang, so far as I know, is found in Washington Irving's *A Tour on the Prairies.* On October the tenth, 1832, Irving set out from old Fort Gibson, in what is now eastern

---

From *Tales of the Mustang,* by J. Frank Dobie, pp. 32–41. Dallas: The Book Club of Texas.

Oklahoma, on his famous tour. Following up the north bank of the Arkansas River, which they crossed a short distance above its junction with the Cimarron,[1] his party proceeded in a westerly direction. At length they came into the range of the mustang, and in Irving's journal entry for October 21 are these words:

> We had been disappointed this day in our hopes of meeting with buffalo, but the sight of the wild horse had been a great novelty, and gave a turn to the conversation of the camp for the evening. There were several anecdotes told of a famous grey horse, which has ranged the prairies of this neighborhood for six or seven years, setting at naught every attempt of the hunters to capture him. They say he can pace . . . faster than the fleetest horse can run.

On through the 1830's, out in Santa Fé and along the Santa Fé Trail, both of which he described surpassingly well in his *Commerce of the Prairies,* printed in 1844, chatty Josiah Gregg heard "marvelous tales" of a "medium-sized stallion of perfect symmetry, milk-white, save a pair of black ears—a natural pacer." This mustang, continues Gregg, "the trapper celebrates in the northern Rocky Mountains; the hunter on the Arkansas; while others have him pacing on the borders of Texas." Among the "veracious memoranda" of Francois des Montaignes "taken during an expedition of exploration in the year 1845"[2] appears again "the celebrated snow-white pacer of the Canadian," capable of making himself "visible only to special and favorite individuals."

In 1841, nine years after Irving's tour, the Republic of Texas sent what is known as the Santa Fé Expedition to annex New Mexico. The picturesque and tragic fate of that expedition does not here concern us. Sharing in the fate was a brilliant newspaper correspondent from New Orleans, George W. Kendall, who kept a detailed journal. In an attempt to cross the Staked Plains, the Texans blundered almost as far north as Red River, and it was while they were in this region that Kendall heard stories of the Steed of the Prairies. His journals were originally published in the New Orleans *Picayune,* 1842; two years later they were incorporated in his two-volume book, *Narrative of the Texan Santa Fé Expedition.*

> Many were the stories [,recorded Kendall,] told by some of the old hunters of a large white horse that had often been seen in the vicinity of the Cross Timbers and near Red River. . . . As the camp stories ran, he has never been known to gallop or trot, but paces faster than any horse that has been sent out after him can run; and so game and untiring is the White Steed of the Prairies, for he is well known to trappers and hunters by that name, that he has tired down no less than three race-nags, sent expressly to catch him, with a Mexican rider well trained to the business of taking wild horses. . . .
>
> Some of the hunters go so far as to say that the White Steed has been

[1] For an account of Irving's crossing, see "Crossing the Arkansas River on a Buffalo Skin," below.

[2] An article entitled "The Plains," in *The Western Journal and Civilian,* St. Louis, 1853, Vol. X, p. 443.—J.F.D.

known to pace his mile in less than two minutes, and that he could keep up this pace until he had tired down everything in pursuit. Large sums have been offered for his capture, and the attempt has been frequently made. But he still roams his native prairies in freedom, solitary and alone. The fact of his being always found with no other horse in company was accounted for, by an old hunter, on the ground that he was too proud to be seen with those of his class, being an animal far superior in form and action to any of his brothers. This I put down as a rank embellishment, although it is a fact that the more beautiful and highly formed mustangs are frequently seen alone.

Kendall's *Narrative,* telling the world about the White Steed of the Prairies, went through seven editions between 1844 and 1856, and, according to good authority, had sold 40,000 copies within eight years after publication. It became the Baedeker of the Southwest. Travelers and other writers about any country usually note what they have been led to believe they should note. For years after the appearance of Kendall's work writers who put Texas in their books felt obliged to include the White Steed, sometimes referring to him as Kendall's. It is as easy for a writer to have "heard this tale" as it is for a social diplomat to have "heard" of some stranger to whom he is introduced.

Even before Kendall could get his newspaper articles into book form, Captain Marryat of *Mr. Midshipman Easy* fame plagiarized the story of the White Steed and clapped it into his rambling *Narrative of the Travels and Adventures of Monsieur Violet in California, Sonora, and Western Texas.* Meantime the account had inspired J. Barber to a ballad, "The White Steed of the Prairies."[3] . . . Then with the appearance of *Moby Dick,* in 1851, the White Mustang burst with thundering hoofbeats out of the "pastures of God" into the ranges of literary immortality. In that great chapter on "The Whiteness of the Whale," wherein Herman Melville reviews the white objects of the earth, ranging from the snowy Andes to the sacred elephants of India, he reaches his climax with a panegyric on the White Mustang. . . .

* * * * *

So far as the effect of whiteness on the imagination of Plains people is concerned, Melville might have adduced also the White Buffalo. Among many of the tribes it was sacred and there was a "White Buffalo Ceremony."[4] The value of the hide of a white buffalo came to be recognized by frontier hunters, and one skinned off by Prairie Dog Dave was sold to Robert M. Wright, a buffalo hunter and trader as well as author of *Dodge City, the Cowboy Capital,* for a thousand dollars.

---

[3] *The United States Magazine and Democratic Review,* New York, 1843, Vol. XII, pp. 367–368.—J.F.D.

[4] For a discussion of the albino buffalo and rituals connected with it, see Peabody Museum *Reports,* III, 260–275, Cambridge, 1887; also *The Omaha Tribe,* by Alice G. Fletcher and Francis La Flesche, in the 27th *Annual Report* of the Bureau of American Ethnology, Washington, 1911, pp. 275–309.—J.F.D.

But while white may be the color of mystery, the color that most profoundly stirs the imaginations of men, white horses have not in general been well thought of on the range. Flea-bitten grays and Mexican duns (sometimes with heavy yellow whiskers and yellow eyes) were looked on with favor; but white was too near the color of the albino, or *huero,* horse with "glass" eyes, a horse with tender skin and eyesight notoriously defective in bright sunlight, to be prized. The Mexicans, it is true, held palominos—now becoming very popular in the United States as saddle and polo horses—in high esteem. The *rancheros* of California during the mission days valued a "light cream-colored horse with silver mane and tail" (the *palomino*) higher than any other color,[5] and the carriages called *volantes* that the mission fathers rode in were drawn by white mules. "You'll never see a dead white mule," the old-timers used to say. Captain Flack, the *The Texan Ranger* (London, 1866), asserts that "it is upon record" that a rich Mexican widow whose son was returning to Mexico from Spain as a newly commissioned colonel presented his regiment with six hundred "pure white horses," the highest compliment she could pay. Referring probably to the same regiment of white horses, George W. Kendall says there were one thousand of them, all off one hacienda and "hardly a month's difference in their ages."[6]

In his noble chronicle, full of information and impregnated with humanity and understanding, *On the Border with Crook,* Captain John G. Bourke, commenting on the campaign against the Sioux in 1876, takes occasion to refute the popular prejudice among Anglo-Americans against white horses. "There may still be people," he says, "who give credence to the old superstitions about the relative endurance of horses of different colors, and believe that white is the weakest color. For their information I wish to say that the company of cavalry which had the smallest loss of horses during this exhausting march was the white horse troop of the Fifth; . . . not one of them was left behind." Charles W. Webber, who is reputed to have been a Texas Ranger and who is among the early writers on the Texas theme, while noting in his *Wild Scenes and Wild Hunters* (Philadelphia, 1852) that he had "often heard" of the White Steed of the Prairies "from the mustang hunters," observes that "all the white mustangs I have ever seen were natural pacers." How many white mustangs Webber had actually seen, nobody could swear. Nevertheless, that the horse most famous among plainsmen and frontiersmen should have been of a color against which they held a strong prejudice is remarkable.

---

[5] Guadalupe Vallejo, "Ranch and Mission Days in Alta California," *The Century Magazine,* Dec., 1890, Vol. XLI, pp. 183–192.—J.F.D.

[6] Kendall, George W., *Narrative of the Texan Santa Fe Expedition,* first published in New York, 1844; reference here is to the 1847 edition, New York, Vol. II, pp. 110–111. On their march as prisoners to Mexico City, the Texans whom Kendall accompanied—as a journalist prisoner—passed through the hacienda, in the state of Durango, off which the white horses had been taken. Kendall was told that the widow owning it had once possessed 300,000 head of horses.—J.F.D.

It is not only possible but entirely probable that mares in a state ot freedom would be strangely attracted to a white stallion. The *yegua madre* ("mother mare"), also called *madrina* or *caponera*—the bell mare picked to lead a train of mules or a remuda of young horses—was, in the days of pack trains and horse work on the open range, usually a gray or white mare. This color was selected to make the leader more conspicuous to the eyes of men, especially at night, but it also seemed to be a better cynosure for mules and horses themselves than any other color. Mules, vain by nature, will have nothing to do with a burro, unless to kick it, but they will follow a mare—above all, a gray or white mare—over a precipice, crowding each other to keep at her heels. The psychology and habits of ants, bees, and other creatures have been better studied than the psychology and habits of wild horses, and I am unable to cite experimental data, but I am ready to believe that a white animal, especially a white stallion, among them might have a psychological effect analogous to the effect of white that Melville found operating among men or that Alfred de Musset, by antithesis, pictured among the blackbirds.

The "Ghost" Horse

With the first touch of spring we broke camp and headed southwest across the big bend of the upper Columbia, toward the plateau between the Rockies and the Cascades. It was on this lofty plateau that the world's largest herd of wild horses had roamed during the last hundred and fifty years. Several hundred head of them are still there, where every summer efforts are being made to exterminate them by the provincial government of British Columbia. It was these horses that we were after, to replace the herd which the storm had driven away from our camp.

We struck the herd in the season of the year when it was weakest: early spring, after the horses had got their first good feed of green grass and their speed had been slowed by dysentery. Since these wild creatures can run to death any horse raised in captivity, it is doubly a hard job to try to ensnare them on foot. But, like wolves, wild horses are very curious animals; they will follow a person for miles out of mere curiosity. And, when chased, they will invariably turn back on their trails to see what it is all about; what their pursuers look like; what they are up to.

The big timber wolves would do the same, when we were traveling in the North Country. They would trot along behind us all day. When we would stop, they would stop, and stand motionless and look at us

---

From *Long Lance,* by Chief Buffalo Child Long Lance, Foreword by Irvin S. Cobb, pp. 189–208. Copyright, 1928, by Cosmopolitan Book Corporation. New York: Farrar & Rinehart, Inc.

with one foot raised; and when we would start again, they would continue to follow us. If we made a noise at them they would jump back and hide behind the nearest bush. From then on, they would keep out of sight, but whenever we looked back we would see them peeping at us from behind the farthest bush.

They used to scare us children, but our fathers told us not to be scared; the wolves would not hurt us; they were just curious about us—although, they said, if the wolves followed us all day they might try to snatch off our dogs when we camped that night. So they told us boys who were traveling in the rear to keep trying to "shoo" them away before we should make camp for the night. Wolves like dog meat better than any other, though male wolves will never harm a female dog.

But with the wild horses it was different. They always traveled ahead of us, but they had a way of turning back on their own trails and coming upon us from the side or the rear, to keep watch on us. It was this never-satisfied curiosity of the wild horse that enabled our braves to capture them on foot.

The method of our warriors was to locate a herd and then follow it unconcernedly for hours, and maybe for days, before making any attempt to round it up. This was to get the horses used to us and to show them that we would not harm them.

We had been trailing fresh manure for five days before we finally located our first herd away up on the expansive Couteau Plateau of central British Columbia. There they were: a herd of about five hundred animals grazing away over there on the side of a craggy little mountain on top of the plateau. Their quick, alert movements, more like those of a deer than those of a horse, showed they were high-strung beings that would dash off into space like a flock of wild birds on the slightest cause for excitement. There was one big, steel-dust stallion who grazed away from the rest and made frequent trips along the edge of the herd. It was obvious to our braves that this iron-colored fellow with the silver mane was the stallion who ruled the herd, and our warriors directed all of their attention to him, knowing that the movements of the entire herd depended on what he did.

When we had approached to within about five hundred yards of the herd, our braves began to make little noises, so that the horses could see us in the distance and would not be taken by surprise and frightened into a stampede at seeing us suddenly at closer range.

"Hoh! Hoh!" our braves grunted softly. The steel-dust stallion uttered a low whinny, and all the herd raised their heads high into the air and, standing perfectly still as though charmed, looked intently over at us with their big, nervous nostrils wide open. They stood that way for moments, without moving a muscle, looking hard at us. Then, as we came too near, the burly stallion tried to put fear into us by dashing straight at us with a deep, rasping roar.

Others followed him, and on they came like a yelling war party, their heads swinging wildly, their racing legs wide apart, and their long tails lashing the ground like faggots of steel wire. But before they reached us the speeding animals stiffened their legs and came to a sudden halt in a cloud of dust. While they were close they took one more good look at us, and then they turned and scampered away with the rest of the herd, which had already begun to retreat over the brow of the mountain.

But the big steel-dust stood his ground alone for a moment and openly defied us. He dug his front feet into the dirt far out in front of him, wagged his head furiously, and then stopped long enough to look and see what effect his mad antics were having upon us. Around and around he jumped gracefully into the air, swapping ends like a dog chasing its tail. Then again he raised his head as high as his superb stature would carry him, and with his long silver tail lying over his back, he blazed fire at us through the whites of his turbulent flint-colored eyes. Having displayed to us his courage, his defiance and his remarkable leadership, he now turned and pranced off, with heels flying so high and so lightly that one could almost imagine he was treading air.

Our braves laughed and said:

"Ah, *ponokamita,* vain elk-dog, you are a brave warrior. But trot along and have patience. We shall yet ride you against the Crows."

For five days we chased this huge herd of horses, traveling along leisurely behind them, knowing that they would not wander afar; that they would watch us like wolves as long as we were in their vicinity.

By the fifth day they had become so used to us that they merely moved along slowly when we approached them, nibbling the grass as they walked. All during this time our braves had been taming them by their subtle method. At first they just grunted at them. But now they were dancing and shouting at them. This was to let the horses know that although man could make a lot of noise and act fiercely, he would not harm them; that no injury could come to them through closer contact with man.

Nothing scares a horse quicker than a quiet thing that moves toward him and makes no noise. He will jump and break his neck at the noiseless movement of a rodent in the grass or a falling twig, while a roaring buffalo or a steaming train will pass him unnoticed. That is because he has the same kind of courage that man has: real courage; the courage to face any odds that he can see and hear and cope with, but a superstitious fear of anything ghostlike. The mountain-lion and most other animals of prey have courage of a different kind. A slight, unexplained noise will bring them to a low, crouching, waiting position, while a loud noise will send them scurrying for cover. They have more discretion and less valor than man or the horse.

On the tenth night of our chase our warriors made their final preparations to capture the herd. They had maneuvered the horses into the vicinity of a huge half-natural, half-artificial corral which they had built of logs against the two sides of a rock-bound gulch. From the entrance of this corral they had built two long fences, forming a runway, which gradually widened as it left the gate of the corral. This funnel-shaped entrance fanned out onto the plateau for more than a half-mile, and it was covered over with evergreens to disguise its artificiality. It was a replica of the old buffalo corral which we used to build to round up the buffaloes when they were plentiful on the plains.

The mouth at the outer end of this runway was about one hundred yards wide. From this point on, the runway was further extended and opened up by placing big tree tops, stones, and logs along the ground for several hundred yards. This was to direct the herd slowly into the mouth of the fenced part of the runway, where, once wedged inside, they could neither get out nor turn around and retrace their steps. They would be trapped; and the only thing left for them to do would be to keep on going toward the corral gate.

Subdued excitement reigned in our hidden camp on this tenth night of our chase; for it was the big night, the night that we were going to "blow in" the great, stubborn herd of wild horses. No one went to bed that night. Shortly before nightfall more than half of our braves, comprising all of our fastest-traveling scouts and young men, quietly slipped out of our camp and disappeared. According to prearranged directions, they fanned out to the right and left in a northerly route and crept noiselessly toward the place where the herd had disappeared that afternoon. All during the early night we heard wolves calling to one another; arctic owls, night hawks, and panthers crying out moanfully in the mystic darkness of the rugged plateau. They were the signals of our men, informing one another of their movements.

Then, about midnight, everything became deathly quiet. We knew that they had located the herd and surrounded it, and that they were now lying on their bellies, awaiting the first streaks of dawn and the signal to start the drive.

One of our subchiefs, Chief Mountain Elk, now went through our camp, quietly giving instructions for all hands to line themselves along the great runway to "beat in" the herd. Every woman, old person, and child in the camp was called up to take part in this particular phase of the drive. We children and the women crept over to the runway and sprawled ourselves along the outside of the fence, while the men went beyond the fenced part of the runway and concealed themselves behind the brush and logs—where it was a little more dangerous. Thus we crouched on the ground and shivered quietly for an hour or more before we heard a distant "Ho-h! . . . Ho-h!" It was the muffled driving cry of our warriors, the cry which for ten days they had been uttering to the horses to let them know that no harm could come to them from this sound. Thus, the horses did not stampede, as they would have done had they not recognized this noise in the darkness.

We youngsters lay breathless in expectancy. We had all picked out our favorite mounts in this beautiful herd of wild animals, and to us as we lay there, it was like the white boy lying in bed waiting for Santa Clause. Our fathers had all promised us that we could have the ponies that we had picked, and we could hardly wait to get our hands on them. My favorite was a beautiful calico pony, a roan, white, and red pinto—three different colors all splashed on his shoulders and flanks like a crazy-quilt of exquisite design. He had a red star on his forehead between his eyes, and I had already named him, *Naytukskie-Kukatos,* which in Blackfoot means One Star.

Presently we heard the distant rumble of horses' hoofs—a dull booming which shook the ground on which we lay. Then, "Yip-yip-yip, he-heeh-h-h," came the night call of the wolf from many different directions. It was our braves signaling to one another to keep the herd on the right path. From out of this medley of odd sounds we could hear the mares going "Wheeeeeh-hagh-hagh-hagh"—calling their little long-legged sons to their sides that they might not become lost in the darkness and confusion.

Our boyish hearts began to beat fast when we heard the first loud "*Yah! Yah! Yah!*" We knew that the herd had now entered the brush portion of the runway and that our warriors were jumping up from their hiding-place and showing themselves with fierce noises, in order to stampede the horses and send them racing headlong into our trap.

Immediately there was a loud thunder of pattering hoofs. Horses crying and yelling everywhere, like convulsive human beings in monster confusion. Above this din of bellowing throats and hammering feet we heard one loud, full, deep-chested roar which we all recognized, and it gave us boys a slight thrill of fear. It sounded like a cross between the roar of a lion and the bellow of an infuriated bull. It was the massive, steel-dust stallion, furious king of the herd. In our imagination we could see his long silver tail thrown over his back, his legs wide apart, and stark murder glistening from the whites of those terrible eyes. We wondered what he would do to us if he should call our bluff and crash through that fence into our midst.

But, now, here he came, leading his raging herd, and we had no further time to contemplate danger. Our job was to do as the others had done all along the line: to lie still and wait until the lead stallion had passed us, and then to jump to the top of the fence and yell and wave with all the ferocity that we could command. This was to keep the maddened herd from crashing the fence or trying to turn around, and to hasten their speed into our trap.

"*Therump, therump, therump.*" On came the storming herd. As we youngsters peeped through the brush-covered fence, we could see their sleek backs bobbing up and down in the starlit darkness like great billows of raging water. The turbulent steel-dust stallion was leading them with front feet wide apart and his forehead sweeping the ground like a pendulum. His death-dealing heels were swinging alternatingly to the right and left with each savage leap of his mighty frame.

Once he stopped and tried to breast the oncoming herd, but these erstwhile slaves of his whims struck and knocked him forward with terrific force. He rose from his knees, and like something that had gone insane, he shot his nostrils into the air and uttered a fearful bellow of defiance at any- and everything. He seemed to curse the very stars themselves. Never before had he tasted defeat, utter helplessness. The loyal herd that had watched his very ears for their commands was now running wildly over him.

I believe that, if at that moment there had been a solid iron wall in front of that stallion, he would have dashed his brains out against it. I remember looking backwards into the darkness for a convenient place to hop, if he should suddenly choose to rush headlong into the noise that was driving him wild with helpless rage. But even as I looked back, I heard a whistling noise, and my eyes were jerked back to the runway just in time to see the steel-dust king stretching himself past us like a huge greyhound. With each incredible leap he panted a breath that shrieked like a whistle.

No one will ever know what was in his brain; why he had so suddenly broken himself away from his herd. But on he went, leaving the other horses behind like a deer leaving a bunch of coyotes. A few seconds later the rest of the herd came booming past us. As we went over the fence, shouting and gesticulating, we looked into a blinding fog of sweat and breath, which fairly stung our nostrils with its pungency.

I thought that herd would never stop passing us. I had never seen so many horses before, it seemed. We stuck to our posts until it was nearly daylight, and still they came straggling along; now mostly colts limping and whining for their mothers.

When we climbed down from the fence and went down to the corral at daylight, the first thing we saw was four of our warriors lying on pallets, bleeding and unconscious. They were four of the best horsemen in our tribe; Circling Ghost, High Hunting Eagle, Wild Man, and Wolf Ribs. When our mothers asked what was the matter, some one pointed to the corral and said: "*Ponokomita–akai-mahkah-pay!*" ("That very bad horse!")

We looked and saw a dozen men trying to put leather on that wild steel-dust stallion, who, with his heavy moon-colored mane bristling belligerently over his bluish head and shoulders, looked now more like a lion than a horse. He was splotched here and there with his own blood, and his teeth were bared like a wolf's. Four men had tried to get down into the corral and throw rawhide around his neck. While the other wild horses had scurried away to the nethermost corners of the corral, this ferocious beast of a horse had plunged headlong into them and all but killed them before they could be dragged away.

He had proved to be one of the rarest specimens of horse known to man—a killer—a creature that kicked and bit and tore and crushed his victims until they were dead. One might live a hundred years among horses without ever seeing one of these hideous freaks of the horse world, so seldom are they produced. He had already killed two of his own herd, young stallions, right there in our corral. Little wonder, now, that he was the leader.

Our braves were taking no more chances with him. They were high up on top of the seven-foot corral fence, throwing their rawhide lariats in vain attempts to neck the murderous monstrosity. But this devil disguised as a horse had the reasoning of a human being. He would stand and watch the rawhide come twirling through the air, and then just as it was about to swirl over his head he would duck his shaggy neck and remain standing on the spot with his front feet spread apart, in devilish defiance of man and matter. None of our oldest men had ever seen anything like him.

It was finally decided to corner him with firebrands and throw a partition between him and the rest of the herd, so that our braves could get busy cutting out the best of the other animals, before turning the rest loose. This was done, and by nightfall we had captured and hobbled two hundred of the best bottoms anywhere in the Northwest.

The next day our braves began the arduous task of breaking the wild horses to the halter. They used the Indian method, which is very simple and methodical. While four men held on to a stout rawhide rope which was noosed around the animal's neck, another man would approach the horse's head gradually, "talking horse" to him and making many queer motions and sounds as he went nearer.

"Horse talk" is a low grunt which seems to charm a horse and make him stand perfectly still for a moment or so at a time. It sounds like "Hoh—Hoh," uttered deep down in one's chest. The horse will stop his rough antics and strain motionless on the rope for a few seconds; while he is doing this and looking straight at the approaching figure, the man will wave a blanket at him and hiss at him— "Shuh! Shuh!" It takes about fifteen minutes of this to make the horse realize that the man is harmless; that no motion which he makes, no sound that he utters, will harm him in any way.

It is a strange fact that a wild horse, of either the ranch or the open ranges, will not react to quiet kindliness at first. He must be treated gruffly—but not harshly—and then when he is on a touching acquaintance with man, kindness is the quickest way to win his affections.

When the man has reached the head of the horse his hardest job is to give him the first touch of man's hand, of which the horse seems to have a deathly fear. He maneuvers for several minutes before he gets a finger on the struggling nose, and rubs it and allows the horse to get his smell or scent. When this has been done, the brave loops a long, narrow string of rawhide around the horse's nose and then carries it up behind his ears and brings it down on the other side and slips it under the other side of the nose loop, making something like a loose-knotted halter, which will tighten up on the slightest pull from the horse.

This string is no stronger than a shoe-lace, yet, once the warrior has put it on the horse's head, he tells the other men to let go the strong rawhide thong, and from then on he alone handles the horse with the small piece of string held lightly in one hand. The secret of this is that whenever the horse makes a sudden pull on the string it grips certain nerves around the nose and back of the ears, and this either stuns him or hurts him so badly that he doesn't try to pull again.

With the horse held thus, the warrior now stands in front of him and strokes the front of his face and hisses at him at close range. It is the same noise that a person makes to drive away chickens—"shuh, shuh"—and perhaps the last sound an untrained person would venture to use in taming a wild, ferocious horse, yet it is the quickest way of gaining a horse's confidence and teaching him not to be afraid.

When the warrior has run his fingers over every inch of the horse's head and neck, he now starts to approach his shoulders and flanks with his fingers. The horse will start to jump about again at this, but a couple of sharp jerks on the string stop him, and as he stands trembling with fear, the warrior slowly runs his hand over his left side. When this is finished he stands back and takes a blanket and strikes all of the portions of his body that he has touched, and shouts "Shuh!" with each stiff stroke of the blanket.

When he has repeated these two operations on the other side of the horse, he now starts to do his legs. Each leg, beginning with his left front leg, must be gone over by his hand, with not an inch of its surface escaping his touch. This is the most ticklish part of the work; for his feet are the horse's deadly weapons. But two more jerks on the string quiet the horse's resentment, and within another fifteen minutes every square inch of the horse's body has been touched and rubbed, even down to his tail and the ticklish portions of his belly and between the legs.

Now, the job of breaking the horse is all but finished. There is just one other thing to do, and that is to accustom the horse to a man hopping on his back and riding him. This is done very simply, and within about five minutes.

The warrior takes the blanket and strikes the horse's back a number of blows. Then he lays the blanket on his back very gently. The horse will at first start to buck it off, but another jerk on the string, and he is quieted. The warrior picks the blanket up and lays it across his back again. The horse will jump out from under it perhaps twice before he will stand still. When he has been brought to this point, the man throws the blanket down and walks slowly to the side of the horse and places both hands on his back and presses down lightly. He keeps pressing a little harder and harder, until finally he places his elbows across his back and draws his body an inch off the ground, putting his full weight on the back of the animal. A horse might jump a little at the first experience of this weight, but he will stand still the next time it is tried.

After the warrior has hung on his back by his elbows for several periods of about thirty seconds each, he will now very gradually pull himself up, up, up, until he is ready to throw his right foot over to the other side. It is a strange fact that few horses broken in this manner ever try to buck. He will stand perfectly still, and the man will sit there and stroke him for a moment and then gently urge him to go; and the horse will awkwardly trot off in a mild, aimless amble, first this way and that—so bewildered and uncertain in his gait that one would think it was the first time he had ever tried to walk on his own feet.

The reason a horse can be broken in the above manner is that he is a remarkably intelligent being with rationality. A chicken has no reason; therefore it goes through its life running away from "shuhs" that never harm it. This keeps it from getting many extra crumbs that it could leisurely eat if it only had the reason to learn from experience as the horse does.

Four months later we were again back on our beloved plains in upper Montana. Our horses were the envy of every tribe who saw us that summer. They all wanted to know where we got them. Our chief told the story of this wild-horse hunt so many times that it has since become legend among the Indians of these prairies.

But at the end of the story our venerable leader would always look downcast, and in sadly measured words he would tell of the steel-dust stallion with the flowing moon-colored mane and tail, which he had picked out for himself. He would spend many minutes describing this superb horse, yet he would never finish the story, unless some one should ask him what became of the spectacular animal.

Then he would slowly tell how our band had worked all day trying to rope this beast, and how that night they had decided to leave him in the little fenced-off part of the corral, thinking that two or three days' contact with them might take some of the evil out of him. But the next morning when they visited the corral he had vanished. The horse had literally climbed over more than seven feet of corral fence, which separated him from the main corral, and there, with room for a running start, he had attacked the heavy log fence and rammed his body clear through it. Nothing was left to tell the tale but a few patches of blood and hair and a wrecked fence.

That should have ended the story of the steel-dust beast, but it did not. On our way out of the camp on the wild-horse plateau we had come across the bodies of seven wild stallions and a mare, which this fiend of the plateau had mutilated in his wake. He had turned killer through and through, even unto the destruction of his own kind. Our old people said that he had been crazed by the fact that he had lost control of his herd in that terrible dash down the runway. This blow to his prowess and pride of leadership had been too much for him; it had turned him into a destructive demon, a roaming maniac of the wilds.

This horse became famous throughout the Northwest as a lone traveler of the night. He went down on to the plains of Montana and Alberta, and in the darkest hours of the night he would turn up at the most unexpected points in the wilderness of the prairies. Never a sound from him; he had lost his mighty bellow. He haunted the plains by night, and was never seen by day. His sinister purpose in life was to destroy every horse he came across.

This silent, lone traveler of the night was often seen silhouetted against the moon on a butte, with his head erect, his tail thrown over his back like a statue, his long moon-colored mane and tail flowing like silver beneath the light of the stars. Owing to his peculiar nocturnal habits and to the fact that his remarkable tail and mane gave off in the moonlight something like a phosphorescent glow, he became known throughout the Northwest as the *Shunka-tonka-Wakan*—the Ghost Horse. The steel-blue color of his body melted so completely into the inky blueness of the night that his tail and mane stood out in the moonlight like shimmering threads of lighted silver, giving him a halo which had a truly ghostly aspect.

Running Buffalo

The country before us was now thronged with buffalo and a sketch of the manner of hunting them will not be out of place. There are two methods commonly practiced, "running" and "approaching." The chase on horseback, which goes by the name of "running," is the more violent and dashing mode of the two, that is to say, when the buffalo are in one of their wild moods; for otherwise it is tame enough. A practiced and skillful hunter, well mounted, will sometimes kill five or six cows in a single chase, loading his gun again and again as his horse rushes through the tumult. In attacking a small band of buffalo, or in separating a single animal from the herd and assailing it apart from the rest, there is less excitement and less danger. In fact, the animals are at times so stupid and lethargic that there is little sport in killing them. With a bold and well-trained horse the hunter may ride so close to the buffalo that as they gallop side by side he may touch him with his hand; nor is there much danger in this as long as the buffalo's strength and breath continue unabated; but when he becomes tired and can no longer run with ease, when his tongue lolls out and the foam flies from his jaws, then the hunter had better keep a more respectful distance;

From *The Oregon Trail,* Sketches of Prairie and Rocky-Mountain Life, by Francis Parkman, pp. 327–329, 331–336. Entered according to Act of Congress, in the year 1872, by Francis Parkman, in the Office of the Librarian of Congress, at Washington. Boston: Little, Brown, and Company, 1895.

the distressed brute may turn upon him at any instant; and especially at the moment when he fires his gun. The horse then leaps aside, and the hunter has need of a tenacious seat in the saddle, for if he is thrown to the ground there is no hope for him. When he sees his attack defeated, the buffalo resumes his flight, but if the shot is well directed he soon stops; for a few moments he stands still, then totters and falls heavily upon the prairie.

The chief difficulty in running buffalo, as it seems to me, is that of loading the gun or pistol at full gallop. Many hunters for convenience' sake carry three or four bullets in the mouth; the powder is poured down the muzzle of the piece, the bullet dropped in after it, the stock struck hard upon the pommel of the saddle, and the work is done. The danger of this is obvious. Should the blow on the pommel fail to send the bullet home, or should the bullet, in the act of aiming, start from its place and roll towards the muzzle, the gun would probably burst in discharge. Many a shattered hand and worse casualties besides have been the result of such an accident. To obviate it, some hunters make use of a ramrod, usually hung by a string from the neck, but this materially increases the difficulty of loading. The bows and arrows which the Indians use in running buffalo have many advantages over firearms, and even white men occasionally employ them.

The danger of the chase arises not so much from the onset of the wounded animal as from the nature of the ground which the hunter must ride over. The prairie does not always present a smooth, level, and uniform surface; very often it is broken with hills and hollows, intersected by ravines, and in the remoter parts studded by the stiff wild sage brushes. The most formidable obstructions, however, are the burrows of wild animals, wolves, badgers, and particularly prairie dogs, with whose holes the ground for a very great extent is frequently honeycombed. In the blindness of the chase the hunter rushes over it unconscious of danger; his horse, at full career, thrusts his leg deep into one of the burrows; the bone snaps, the rider is hurled forward to the ground and probably killed. Yet accidents in buffalo running happen less frequently than one would suppose; in the recklessness of the chase, the hunter enjoys all the impunity of a drunken man, and may ride in safety over gullies and declivities, where, should he attempt to pass in his sober senses, he would infallibly break his neck.

The method of "approaching," being practiced on foot, has many advantages over that of "running"; in the former, one neither breaks down his horse nor endangers his own life; he must be cool, collected, and watchful; must understand the buffalo, observe the features of the country and the course of the wind, and be well skilled in using the rifle. The buffalo are strange animals; sometimes they are so stupid and infatuated that a man may walk up to them in full sight on the open prairie, and even shoot several of their number before the rest will think it necessary to retreat. At another moment they will be so shy and wary that in order to approach them the utmost skill, experience, and judgment are necessary. Kit Carson, I believe, stands preëminent in running buffalo; in approaching, no man living can bear away the palm from Henry Chatillon.

* * * * *

We had gone scarcely a mile when we saw an imposing spectacle. From the river bank on the right, away over the swelling prairie on the left, and in front as far as the eye could reach, was one vast host of buffalo. The outskirts of the herd were within a quarter of a mile. In many parts they were crowded so densely together that in the distance their rounded backs presented a surface of uniform blackness; but elsewhere they were more scattered, and from amid the multitude rose little columns of dust where some of them were rolling on the ground. Here and there a battle was going forward among the bulls. We could distinctly see them rushing against each other, and hear the clattering of their horns and their hoarse bellowing. Shaw was riding at some distance in advance, with Henry Chatillon; I saw him stop and draw the leather covering from his gun. With such a sight before us, but one thing could be thought of. That morning I had used pistols in the chase. I had now a mind to try the virtue of a gun. Deslauriers had one, and I rode up to the side of the cart; there he sat under the white covering, biting his pipe between his teeth and grinning with excitement.

"Lend me your gun, Deslauriers."

"Oui, Monsieur, oui," said Deslauriers, tugging with might and main to stop the mule, which seemed obstinately bent on going forward. Then everything but his moccasins disappeared as he crawled into the cart and pulled at the gun to extricate it.

"Is it loaded?" I asked.

"Oui, bien chargé; you'll kill, mon bourgeois; yes, you'll kill—c'est un bon fusil."

I handed him my rifle and rode forward to Shaw.

"Are you ready?" he asked.

"Come on," said I.

"Keep down that hollow," said Henry, "and then they won't see you till you get close to them."

The hollow was a kind of wide ravine; it ran obliquely towards the buffalo, and we rode at a canter along the bottom until it became too shallow; then we bent close to our horses' necks, and, at last, finding that it could no longer conceal us, came out of it and rode directly towards the herd. It was within gunshot; before its outskirts, numerous grizzly old bulls were scattered, holding guard over their females. They glared at us in anger and astonishment, walked towards us a few yards, and then turning slowly round, retreated at a trot which afterwards broke into a clumsy gallop. In an instant the main body caught the alarm. The buffalo began to crowd away from the point towards which we were approaching, and a gap was opened in the side of the herd. We entered it, still restraining our excited horses. Every instant the tumult was thickening. The buffalo, pressing together in large bodies, crowded away from us on every hand. In front and on either side we could see dark columns and masses, half hidden by clouds of dust, rushing along in terror and confusion, and hear the tramp and clattering of ten thousand hoofs. That countless multitude of powerful brutes, ignorant of their own strength, were flying in a panic from the approach of two feeble horsemen. To remain quiet longer was impossible.

"Take that band on the left," said Shaw; "I'll take these in front."

He sprang off, and I saw no more of him. A heavy Indian whip was fastened by a band to my wrist; I swung it into the air and lashed my horse's flank with all the strength of my arm. Away she darted, stretching close to the ground. I could see nothing but a cloud of dust before me, but I knew that it concealed a band of many hundreds of buffalo. In a moment I was in the midst of the cloud, half suffocated by the dust and stunned by the trampling of the flying herd; but I was drunk with the chase and cared for nothing but the buffalo. Very soon a long dark mass became visible, looming through the dust; then I could distinguish each bulky carcass, the hoofs flying out beneath, the short tails held rigidly erect. In a moment I was so close that I could have touched them with my gun. Suddenly, to my amazement, the hoofs were jerked upwards, the tails flourished in the air, and amid a cloud of dust the buffalo seemed to sink into the earth before me. One vivid impression of that instant remains upon my mind. I remember looking down upon the backs of several buffalo dimly visible through the dust. We had run unawares upon a ravine. At that moment I was not the most accurate judge of depth and width, but when I passed it on my return, I found it about twelve feet deep and not quite twice as wide at the bottom. It was impossible to stop; I would have done so gladly if I could; so, half sliding, half plunging, down went the little mare. She came down on her knees in the loose sand at the bottom; I was pitched forward against her neck and nearly thrown over her head among the buffalo, who amid dust and confusion came tumbling in all around. The mare was on her feet in an instant and scrambling like a cat up the opposite side. I thought for a moment that she would have fallen back and crushed me, but with a violent effort she clambered out and gained the hard prairie above.

Glancing back, I saw the huge head of a bull clinging as it were by the forefeet at the edge of the dusty gulf. At length I was fairly among the buffalo. They were less densely crowded than before, and I could see nothing but bulls, who always run at the rear of a herd to protect their females. As I passed among them they would lower their heads, and turning as they ran, try to gore my horse; but as they were already at full speed there was no force in their onset, and as Pauline ran faster than they, they were always thrown behind her in the effort. I soon began to distinguish cows amid the throng. One just in front of me seemed to my liking, and I pushed close to her side. Dropping the reins, I fired, holding the muzzle of the gun within a foot of her shoulder. Quick as lightning she sprang at Pauline; the little mare dodged the attack, and I lost sight of the wounded animal amid the tumult. Immediately after, I selected another, and urging forward Pauline, shot into her both pistols in succession. For a while I kept her in view, but in attempting to load my gun, lost sight of her also in the confusion. Believing her to be mortally wounded and unable to keep up with the herd, I checked my horse. The crowd rushed onwards. The dust and tumult passed, and on the prairie, far behind the rest, I saw a solitary buffalo galloping heavily. In a moment I and my victim were running side by side. My firearms were all empty, and I had in my pouch nothing but rifle bullets, too large for the pistols and too small for the gun. I loaded the gun, however, but as often as I leveled it to fire, the bullets would roll out of the muzzle and the gun returned only a report like a squib, as the powder harmlessly exploded. I rode in front of the buffalo and tried to turn her back; but her eyes glared, her mane bristled, and, lowering her head, she rushed at me with the utmost fierceness and activity. Again and again I rode before her, and again and again she repeated her furious charge. But little Pauline was in her element. She dodged her enemy at every rush, until at length the buffalo stood still, exhausted with her own efforts, her tongue lolling from her jaws.

Riding to a little distance, I dismounted, thinking to gather a handful of dry grass to serve the purpose of wadding, and load the gun at my leisure. No sooner were my feet on the ground than the buffalo came bounding in such a rage towards me that I jumped back again into the saddle with all possible dispatch. After waiting a few minutes more, I made an attempt to ride up and stab her with my knife; but Pauline was near being gored in the attempt. At length, bethinking me of the fringes at the seams of my buckskin trousers, I jerked off a few of them, and, reloading the gun, forced them down the barrel to keep the bullet in its place; then approaching, I shot the wounded buffalo through the heart. Sinking to her knees, she rolled over lifeless on the prairie. To my astonishment, I found that, instead of a cow, I had been slaughtering a stout yearling bull. No longer wondering at his fierceness I opened his throat, and cutting out his tongue tied it at the back of my saddle. My mistake was one which a more experienced eye than mine might easily make in the dust and confusion of such a chase.

Then for the first time I had leisure to look at the scene around me. The prairie in front was darkened with the retreating multitude, and on either hand the buffalo came filing up in endless columns from the low plains upon the river. The Arkansas was three or four miles distant. I turned and moved slowly towards it. A long time passed before, far in the distance, I distinguished the white covering of the cart and the little black specks of horsemen before and behind it. Drawing near, I recognized Shaw's elegant tunic, the red flannel shirt, conspicuous far off. I overtook the party, and asked him what success he had had. He had assailed a fat cow, shot her with two bullets, and mortally wounded her. But neither of us was prepared for the chase that afternoon, and Shaw, like myself, had no spare bullets in his pouch; so he abandoned the disabled animal to Henry Chatillon, who followed, dispatched her with his rifle, and loaded his horse with the meat.

We encamped close to the river. The night was dark, and as we lay down we could hear, mingled with the howlings of wolves, the hoarse bellowing of the buffalo, like the ocean beating upon a distant coast.

The One-Eyed Buffalo

. . . The Arapaho hunter, Circle Runner . . . had a white horse, mighty fast, but the Arapaho didn't want him to run buffalo on it. Everybody knows that a white horse is bad medicine in a buffalo hunt. Buffalo don't like white horses, and anyway, they can see one miles away. So the chiefs wouldn't let Circle Runner hunt with the other hunters, unless he would ride a horse of a different color. It was time for the tribal hunt, up near the Big Horns, and it was agin the Injun law for a man to go off alone and hunt on his own hook. Fact is, the Injun soldiers—kind of camp police—had orders to soldier-whip any man caught hunting alone. And soldier-whipping is no joke, you bet.

But Circle Runner was a stubborn man, and needed meat, and he wouldn't give in. He made up his mind to ride his fast horse, soldiers or no soldiers. And so he told his old woman to slip out of camp with him, and away they went, hell-bent to kill meat. Each of them rode a pack-horse, and Circle Runner led his fast-running horse. It was summertime, when bulls are mean. Circle Runner had an old brassmounted pistol, and a horn full of powder.

He rode up the crick, trying to get the start of the other hunters, and told the old woman to hide in the brush. He left his pack-horse with her. Across the crick was a bunch of bulls.

"First thing, he picked out a fat bull, and banged away. Dropped it, too, and the others hung around, snuffing at the blood on the dead one. That give him time to reload, and he tried another shot. *Thit!* the bullet smacked into the bull. The herd began to move. So Circle Runner poured some powder into his pistol, stuck the muzzle to his mouth, and spit a ball into the barrel. Then he smacked the butt on his saddle-horn to sock her down tight. By that time the white horse war alongside the bull. But afore he could shoot, the bull whirled on him.

"The white horse war too quick for the bull, and stayed clear of his horns. The bull war facing him, and Circle Runner got a good look at it. First off, he thought the bull war blind. Thar warn't no eye on the

---

From *The Old Santa Fe Trail,* by Stanley Vestal, pp. 85–87. Copyright, 1930, by Walter Stanley Campbell. Boston: Houghton Mifflin Company.

off side—and when he looked at t'other side, he couldn't see no eye thar nuther. But that bull warn't blind—not a mite. And when that Injun saw how it war, he just about fell off his pony. He pretty near fainted. He war so scairt, he mighty near lost his heart out of his mouth.

"That bull had just *one* eye—and that war spang in the middle of his forehead! And when he turned that eye on Circle Runner, the Injun saw death in that eye.

"The horse must of seen it too. For that white horse whirled round and lit out, tight as he could go. And the bull right after him, with its horns in his tail, you might say. That horse war racin', and Circle Runner didn't try to stop him, you bet. It was the tightest race he ever run. No matter how he dodged and turned, the bull stuck to him. And every time the Injun looked back, he saw that big eye on him. He quit tryin' to shoot then, and just rode that horse, prayin' like mad.

"Lucky for the old woman, the horse didn't head for the crick. It went straight for the river. Circle Runner didn't know where it war headin', and didn't care. All he wanted war to git away from that One-eye. But he couldn't. The bull war always right thar, stickin' to him like a burr. Sometimes it come fast, and agin it slowed down a mite. But it never quit. And pretty soon that white horse begin to play out. And Circle Runner war too scairt to load his pistol. He thought he war gone, sartain. He let the horse go, and the horse went—lookin' for company.

"He got to the river, but that never stopped him. He went on acrost, as if it had been a puddle. He hardly even wet his feet, he went so fast. But the bull war faster. And then Circle Runner saw a bunch of men horseback—and he knowed they war the Injun soldiers! And he couldn't fool them that he warn't huntin', because he had brung the buffalo right along with him! He knowed they would beat him and kill his horse. He war scairt to death.

"But he war more scairt of the bull than he war of the soldiers. So he headed straight for 'em.

"When they saw him comin', and the buffalo after him, they unlimbered their bows and grabbed a handful of arrers, and come a high-tailin' for that bull. They aimed to kill the meat first, and knock the hindsights off of Circle Runner afterwards. And the bull never stopped. Afore you could say scat, arrers were flyin', stingin' that buffalo.

"'*Chit . . . chit . . . chit!*' they hit him—and that bull stopped suddent like, and stood thar groanin' and heavin', with the feathered ends of the arrers stickin' out of his ribs, movin' his head from side to side, lookin' at the cussed Injuns. And they set thar and looked at him, you bet, with their mouths wide open and their eyes bugged out. And thar he war, swayin' and gruntin' and weavin' from side to side, till all at oncet he lurched, and his knees buckled, and down he went, dead as a nail, and all four legs stiff as yore wipin'-stick. But that big *eye* war still open, and *watchin'*!

"Wal, you bet them soldiers never touched *that* buffalo! They stood around and looked at him. And then an old man spoke up, and they got out some paint, and some red cloth, and some white shells, and edged up and dropped 'em alongside that dead bull. Then they got on their horses and skipped, and clean forgot to go huntin' that day. That's a *fact*.

"Nope. They never whipped Circle Runner. He war big medicine after that. Maybeso they thought he'd been punished enough a'ready. . . ."

El Señor Coyote

The coyote, along with the cowboy and the rattlesnake, is an integral part of Western and Southwestern North America. Oren Arnold says he "probably is the one wild creature that is most associated with the West and the Southwest. He is part of our daily living here, an old timer likely to be seen or heard any day." Ernest Ingersoll calls him "a true Westerner," typifying the "independence, unrestrained gaiety, and brisk zeal which enter into the heart of him who sights the Rocky Mountains." Charles F. Lummis identifies him with the very landscape, and to John C. Van Dyke, he belongs to the desert country as essentially as the dry arroyos and washes along which he skulks. James W. Steele thinks that the representative animal of the West should not be the buffalo but the coyote, because he comes closer than the buffalo to being the figurehead of the great West. He should, therefore, adorn its escutcheons.

The word *coyote* is an *aztequismo,* having no counterpart in Castilian. It comes from the Nahuatl word *coyotl,* the radical meaning of which, according to scholars, is variable. Robelo, after explaining that the word *cocoyoctla* is plural, so made by the duplication of the first syllable, writes: "The name coyote can be a corruption of *cocoyoctla,* which is composed of *cocoyoctic,* hole or hollow thing, and of *tla,* a particle indicating abundance, and meaning 'Where there are many holes.'" This explanation gives rise, perhaps, to Brinton's view that the root of the word *coyote* meant *hole,* the animal being so named because of his habit of burrowing his den. . . .

. . . But whatever the root or its original meaning, or the reason for giving the name to this particular animal may be it is certain that both animal and name are indigenous to America.

Pronunciation of the word *coyote* varies with the locality. The correct Spanish pronunciation is given as ko-yo-ta, almost koi-o-ta, but in Western United States usage almost universally makes the first

---

From "The Coyote: Animal and Folk-Character," by Lillian Elizabeth Barclay, *Coyote Wisdom,* J. Frank Dobie, Mody C. Boatright, Harry H. Ransom, Editors, pp. 38–39, 40, 41–42, 45–47, 49–50, 56–58, 63–64. Texas Folk-Lore Society Publications, No. XIV, Copyright, 1938, by the Texas Folk-Lore Society. Austin: Texas Folk-Lore Society.

syllable ki, with the pronunciation either ki-o-te or ki-ot. A provincial pronunciation is ky-ute.

* * * * *

Besides having an untold number of nicknames, El Señor Coyote has more given names than a crown prince. The sur- or scientific names for the most generally known type (according to Lantz there are a dozen species, eight of which roam the United States) is *Canis latrans Say*. Indians, however, use no such generic term. Coyote was one of the Animal People, and as such had a very special and meaningful name. Among the tribes he is variously called Skinkoots, Mes-cha-cha-gan-is, Huk-sa-ra, Hatelwe, Cin-au-av, Song-tokepcha, Mee-yah-slay-cha-lah, and Sin-ke-lip, just to mention a few designations. What the farmers and the ranchers whose sheep he kills and whose chicken houses he raids call him is more pronounceable but scarcely as printable.

* * * * *

Like the Indians, authors of short stories with coyote as the central figure choose for him such special names as suit their intepretation of his character, some of the more interesting being Kiyi, Kiote, Gray Dusk, Bareribs, Skeezix, Tito, Kip, Señor Yip-yap, Romulus. Of the appellations bestowed upon him in the past half century by American writers, Ishmaelite seems to be most popular. Others are Desert Serenader, Scavenger of Sagebrush Land, Father Coyote, Hobo of the Hills, God's Dog, or the Medicine Dog, Desert Bohemian, Vagabond of the Desert, Mugwump of the Plains, Voice of the Night, Wingless Vulture of the Plains, Prowler of the Night, Pariah of the Skyline, Wild Dog of the Desert, the Charlie Chaplin of the Desert, Shaggy Fellow, Furry Gangster of the Desert, Desert Troubadour, Esau among the Tribes of the Desert, A Wanderer O' Nights and a Lier-by-Day, the Patti of the Plains, and Don Coyote.

It is odd how man acts when animal names are applied to him. If he be called a fox, he is a little flattered; if he be called a coyote, he is ready to fight. For years the appellation coyote, like that of rat or skunk, has gathered to itself an opprobrium, due, perhaps, to the animal's legendary traits of being a cowardly braggart, and his factual traits of liking carrion. But since each animal has at least a few bad traits and since coyote has no more than the average, it should follow that the name coyote should be no more resented as an epithet than the name of any other animal usually accepted with equanimity. Charles F. Lummis, indulging in a bit of cynicism at man's expense, remarks: "So far as concerns man and his one flatterer, the dog, the coyote shines brilliant by comparison. . . . Seeing the wild dog with so much wit, and the tame one so perennially witless (for the hounds never learn the joke), one might wonder at it—if one did not remember that the domestic *canis* is handicapped by long looking up to the least observant animal that goes on legs." Man does not like being called dog either. Yet, South Dakota accepts the nickname of Coyote proudly, and the Wichita Falls high school football team are the Coyotes.

* * * * *

As for his character, writers about the coyote, considered in the aggregate, have made him a super Dr. Jekyll and Mr. Hyde. T. Shoemaker catalogues him as crafty, alert, knowing, cunning, sly, watchful, wise, a marauder, a killer, hated by man and other animals. Pertinacity, zeal, sagacity, endurance, trickery, impudence, piracy, thievery, unmannerly deportment, strategy are some terms applied by other writers. "Every man's hand is against him, and with reason," states one. "He displays a cunning, exceeded only by his cowardice," declares another. "He has a lot of patience and a sense of humor," defends J. Frank Dobie. Lorene Squire argues that he is just a plain contradiction, a part of him the drift of the wind, part like a little dog Trixie, part a lone Gypsy always wandering, another part like a great gray wolf, and the rest of him just plain devil—a mean, sneaking, cowardly, low-down chicken stealer, but never a cringer or beggar, sometimes mocking, other times impudent, always independent, and airy, but ever loyal to his own. "A beautiful coyote hide wraps up more deviltry than any other hide of equal dimension stretched over an animated form," observes Enos A. Mills. "His successful cunning and his relentless ways of getting a living cause him to be cursed by those whom he plunders. But he is always interesting and appears to enjoy life even in the midst of lean times. He is the Clown of the Prairie. He is cynical, wise, and a good actor. He has a liking for action and adventure. He really is a happy fellow, something of a philosopher and full of wit."

Ingersoll sums him up thus: "He is the Ishmaelite of the desert; a consort of rattlesnakes and vultures; the tyrant of his inferiors; jackal to the puma; a bushwhacker upon the flanks of the buffalo ranges; the pariah of his own race, and despised of mankind. Withal, he maintains himself and his tribe increases; he outstrips animals fleeter than himself and foils those of far greater strength; and he excells all his rivals in cunning and intelligence."

Of all the indictments against the coyote, cowardice seems least justified by facts. It is not cowardice but judgment that causes the coyote to avoid making a target of himself, and his resourcefulness in this respect has caused disgruntled hunters, trappers, and property owners whose premises he has raided to proclaim him a coward. He has courage enough to go his way and make his raids in spite of the best efforts of all who would prevent him. No cowardly creature would persistently take chances in raiding melon patches closely guarded or in killing sheep inclosed near a house.

* * * * *

Indians say that coyote, unlike man, never kills wantonly, but only for food. As a matter of fact, given a chance, he may kill more kids out of a flock of goats than he can eat in a week—but then he is not particular about having his meat fresh. His business in life is not essentially different from that of man; namely, to find and get his daily meat. He looks for this with diligence and singleness of purpose, with skill and cunning and an animal patience which far excels the virtue known by that name in men and women. The qualities of skill and patience are particularly well shown in his killing, without coming to grief, a porcupine.

Often are yarns told of ferocious coyotes, as well as of wolves, attacking some human being. Vilhjalmur Stefansson, the explorer, has disposed of such reports in a book called *Adventures in Error*. . . .

Coyote is neither a pariah nor a hermit. Instead he is noted for being sociable and cooperative with his own kind. Mills reports seeing one or more coyotes staying near a crippled coyote as though taking care of him, and endeavoring to lure away any hunter who approached. Coyotes will assist each other by hunting in relays. They have a system of intercommunication, including signal stations, which may be a stone, a tree, a post, or an old buffalo skull, at which a coyote may leave a message, or learn by odor of the last comer. The whole country is marked by these intelligence depots. Coyote uses his voice to ask for information, to call for help, and to give warning. A leader may search out food, scout the lay of the land, and look out for traps or poison. When assured that all is quiet and clear, he will signal the pack to come. He may mount an eminence and broadcast his message, which will be picked up and relayed, so that within a few minutes the latest news or order or an urgent warning reaches all coyotes within a radius of many miles.

Many are the tales illustrating coyote's love of play, his penchant for teasing or joking, and his sense of humor. . . .

* * * * *

There have been many attempts to describe the "music" of the coyote. "A coyote's song is more conducive to sleep, more musical, more pleasing than the music from a neighbor's radio," remarked J. Frank Dobie in a lecture. In *On the Open Range* he writes, "I like to hear his lonely and eerie howl in the night. I like to ride along and know he is watching me from behind some prickly pear bush. Coyotes are good company." "A coyote," observes Oren Arnold, "has the most famous voice in the wilderness—a dog-like yelping, half bark and half growl. Two coyotes on opposite hills, calling each other, will sound like a dozen or more."

This multiplicity of sound is remarked by Jack O'Connor: "The coyote is among the noisiest of animals, giving at dusk a short, yipping bark that re-echoes through the cañons so that half a dozen coyotes seem like a hundred to the uninitiated. But in the serious business of running game he is silent except for little half-suppressed yelps of excitement."

C. F. Holder corroborates the impression of the one sounding as many: "Don Coyote yelped, becoming so enthusiastic over the melody of his song that notes fairly piled on one another, gathering volume until they became ventriloquistic and went echoing far and wide, conveying the impression to the one startled listener that a pack of particularly ferocious coyotes was surrounding the camp."

Enos Mills also describes coyote as a ventriloquist, saying: "He has a remarkable voice. It gives him a picturesque part. Usually his spoken effects are in the early evening; more rarely in the morning. Often a number, in a pack or widely separated, will engage in a concert. It is a concert of clowns; in it are varying and changing voices; all the breaks in the evening song are filled with startling ventriloquistic effects. The voice may be thrown in many directions, and the efforts of two or three coyotes seem like those of a numerous and scattered pack."

"One man in a million," says Charles F. Lummis, "can become a ventriloquist; every coyote is one at birth. He is the only breathing thing that has this unvarying birthright. . . . He can so 'place' his voice that you shall not know if it came from north, east, south, or west. As a multiplier—well, hearing one coyote, no newcomer will but swear it is a dozen. . . . That wail is the strangest, weirdest, most baffling sound known to any wilderness—a wild medley of bark, howl, shriek, and whine utterly confounding; and as to its articulation, glib as nothing else I know except the sound of irregular musketry. The swift patter of vocables is something almost indescribable. It is the voice which has earned him his scientific name—which is unscientifically applied. He is not a barker (*latrans*), but a bewailer, and should be ticketed *ululans*."

"His voice," asserts J. W. Steele, speaking of one certain coyote, "was the principal part of him. He threw back his head in an ecstasy of discord and gave it to the wind and the silence in a quick succession of staccato yelps that made two of him seem like two hundred. Nobody ever knew why he did it, the common opinion being that it was for amusement; not for others, but for himself, like a man practising upon a brass horn."

One must have spent an hour or two vainly trying to sleep before he is in a condition to appreciate fully those short, sharp barks, given in quick succession, growing faster and the pitch getting higher until they run into a long-drawn, lugubrious howl in the highest possible key. Rakes explains how this lugubrious "music" is made: "He opens his mouth rather widely, the more widely, the higher the pitch. Then the lower jaw is vibrated slightly up and down."

* * * * *

Among the beneficial habits credited to the coyote are these: He destroys rabbits, prairie dogs, rats, and other rodents and he is useful as a scavenger. His injurious habits include the killing of game and farm animals and fowls. Aside from advocating extermination as a cure for the coyote evil, the Biological Survey suggests that just as owners protect their fowls and live stock from coyotes and other prowling beasts (including dogs, for coyotes are often blamed for damage done by dogs) by proper housing and fencing.

To exterminate or not to exterminate has been and continues to be a moot question. Because the coyote's depredations on stock cost ranchmen and farmers some $500,000 a year, they asked state and federal aid in exterminating him. So in many states a bounty has been placed on Don Coyote, and the work of extermination goes merrily on. No fair play is accorded coyote. He is hounded for the bounty, for his pelt. Trappers have redoubled their efforts; forest rangers do their bit; poison is used; and dogs have been trained to go into dens to bring out the young, which are scalped for the bounty. In some vicinities farmers and ranchers have paid their taxes by means of bounty money; trappers and hunters have made a rather good living out of it.

* * * * *

The Coyote Hunt is gaining favor, supplanting the more formal and ceremonious Fox Hunt of the East because it is more exciting. Such hunts have always been popular in the West and the Southwest. . . .

The Outlaw Lobo

The sheepman was no friend of the lobo wolf . . . but he regarded him as an enemy a man could respect. The lobo, or loafer, as he was often called, was mean, no doubt about it, but his meanness had a quality in it that kept the sheepman endlessly fascinated, and it was he who put most of the dramatic incident into the sheepman's conflict with his animal enemies.

In earlier days, before the war upon them had depleted their ranks, the lobo wolves traveled, and often hunted, in packs. Hunters have watched them organize attacks upon antelopes and other herds of the Plains with all the sagacity, cunning and patience of a military council. The lobos station themselves in relays along the course they have planned for their victim and then send a couple of their members into the herd to cut out the fattest animal and drive him to the track they have laid out. Then the chase is on. The object is to run down the prey, then hamstring and devour it. When they hunt in pairs the same tactics are used; one wolf runs the game while the other rests.

With the extermination of buffalo and antelope the wolves transferred these tactics to sheep and cattle. Their depredations on flocks and herds were enormous, because they were fastidious and killed

---

From *The Golden Hoof,* The Story of the Sheep of the Southwest, by Winifred Kupper, pp. 122–129. Copyright, 1945, by Alfred A. Knopf, Inc. New York.

The lobo is the Western timber wolf.

many animals in one night in order to get just the tidbit they wanted from each. If it was a good season for game, they left the rest of their kill to any who wanted it. Often it was finished off by the coyotes, who had nothing against letting the other fellow do their killing for them.

But the lobo had the cattlemen as well as the sheepmen for enemies, and cattlemen were better equippd than the early sheepman to carry on the war against predators. Thus the wolf was killed in larger numbers than the coyote, and finally his pack was reduced to members of his own family. Now he had to do most of his hunting and killing by himself. He became a bandit with an interesting and unique personality, an individual to be reckoned with—a lone wolf. His personal characteristics were no longer lost in those of the pack. And that was why he became the arch villain in the sheepman's story. Every community in the sheep country has its own legend of one wily lobo that, by devices of his own, exacted toll from sheepmen and evaded capture for years.

That the wolf bandit was looked upon as an individual is attested by the circumstance that after his first year of depredation he was usually awarded that symbol of respect, a name, and thereby distinguished as an inhabitant of the community and a part of its history. The name was always preceded by the adjective "old," pronounced *ole*. More often than not it told the story of an escape from a trap. For when a wolf is caught in a trap he will chew himself out of it and limp away, leaving a claw, foot, or leg. His telltale tracks, after such an amputation, serve to christen him Old Club Foot, Old Crip, Old Stubby, Old Two Toes, Old Three Toes. The name Old Three Toes became the Smith or Jones of the lobo race. There was the Old Three Toes of Hall County, who forestalled capture for so long and murdered so many sheep that when he was finally caught he was stuffed and put in the First National Bank at Memphis, Texas. Nobody in Hall County wanted to forget him; he had given them too good a chase. He had a namesake in Montana, in Arkansas, in the Big Bend—all famous lobos.[1]

"There's one thing I never liked to hear when I went into a country to catch an outlaw wolf," one old trapper told me. "I never liked to hear that I was goin' out for Ole Crip, or Ole Club Foot, or Ole Three Toes. Them names meant the son-of-a-gun already knew about traps. Give me an Ole Shaggy or an Ole Whitey, any day. A feller had more of a chance with them. But if you wanted to feel real good about the job you'd got ahead of you, just let 'em tell you they was a lobo runnin' the country. Just lobo. That helped. If'n he hadn't been named yet, he hadn't been runnin' long, and they was always a good chance he wouldn't be an outlaw."

For a wolf didn't have to experience a trap to win a name. There was Old Black of the Big Bend, who had $30,000 worth of damage

[1] For the story of the South Dakota Three Toes, see Archer B. Gilfillan, *Sheep* (Boston, 1929), pp. 181–196.

chalked up against him and was alleged to have killed two Mexican herders. And there was Old Reddy of Hays County, who roamed the hills there for ten years, did $15,000 worth of damage, and was taken out of the trap and brought to the town square in San Marcos to be publicly executed for her crimes.

A lobo's fame was in direct ratio to the financial damage he had wrought. A smart wolf could last from three to six years, and in that time he could kill as much as fifty thousand dollars' worth of sheep in his territory. Unlike the coyote, he varied little from his meat diet. And he liked fresh meat and his own kill—fat yearling and juicy mutton. He was an epicure, and an extravagant one. Thirty sheep in one night might easily succumb to him. He has been known to carry a slaughtered sheep on his back to his pups. But he rarely took his kill right to the den. Too many bones lying around would be a giveaway. The young whelps listened, and when they heard his signal down around the bend they went to meet him.

Slipping into a pasture quietly, pursuing his game in a long easy lope, bringing it down just for the fun of it, scarcely touching it before beginning a new chase—such is the sport that the lobo glories in. His howl to the moon, to his mate, or to his confederates is the forthright expression of a creature that loves life and the chase. It lacks both the staccato *yip-yap* of the coyote and the ventriloquism whereby the single coyote pretends to be any number. With his howl the lobo dares any who will to come and catch him. In the early days he was so conscious of his prowess that he often failed to keep himself out of the sight of man.

"I was driving in for supplies one time," Robert Maudslay said, "and my dog was trailing behind the wagon. She was a little thing, but handy with sheep when we moved them. I had gone a long way when I noticed she's got uneasy about something. I looked around and saw a big gray shape slipping along behind a few greasewood bushes. Directly I saw another slinking along in the rear, and then another and another and another, showing their faces here and there among the greasewood. I, or the dog, was being trailed by a pack of wolves.

"I stopped the wagon and lifted my little friend inside, whereupon she scrambled to the back of the wagon, thrust her pointed nose outside, and began to bark very bravely. When the wagon stopped, the wolf in the lead stopped, too, and lay in the road not forty yards away. He was an old stager; one of his front paws was missing. I didn't like the gall of him lying there and just looking at me with a contemptuous grin on his face. I'd have given anything for a gun. I picked up a rock and threw it at him, but it didn't go within three feet of him; so he disdained to notice it. My second and third rocks made him get up and walk off, with dignity in every step. A fourth caught him in the hindquarters. He turned and snapped at it, and then trotted off to join his fellows. But I could tell perfectly well that he didn't have much of an opinion of me."

No doubt the lobo felt himself almost the equal of his two-legged adversary. Yet he never attacked men. At least, no real proof of such an attack has ever been given, though the possibility has often enough been debated. His brothers in Europe and Asia attacked men, and killed them. Why did the lobo wolf, so obviously akin to the man-killing wolves of Siberia, never avail himself of the same tactics? In Europe and Asia the poor peasants who were oftenest the victims were always unarmed and vulnerable, whereas in America the wolves had already learned that man carried a bite of his own. The Indians, much as they revered the wolf, were not to be slaughtered by him. Their arrows had taught the American wolf respect for man. When the white man came the wolf tranferred the same respect to him, and judiciously, for the white man rarely traveled the west unarmed. Yet there are anecdotes of attempts by Western wolves upon children, or upon lone women riding across country, or upon Mexican peons. Can the wolf have detected the helplessness of these creatures and been actuated by some obscure memory of the European and Asiatic peasants that stirred in him?

But, daring, independent, proud, and crafty as he might be, the outlaw lobo was always caught in the end. In the later days of the range, when sheepmen began to form into sheep-raising communities, and one lone wolf could become the common enemy of all, the wolf hunt became a perennial event of importance and excitement. Staged at night, with one or many of the most noted of the community's packs of strong, lean wolfhounds, and with the hunters on horseback and divided into groups, the hunt was an all-night affair in which sheepmen rode to hounds without benefit of pink coats, and with an objective that was starkly utilitarian. In one locality an outlaw wolf was hunted by the sheriff himself. He ruled that the lobo, having killed three hundred sheep, was a criminal, a murderer, and must answer as such to the law. He formed a posse of twenty-two hounds and their owners and went out to get him.

Sometimes the rancher set his own men on the job, and cowboys rode the range lassoing lobos instead of cows. Sheepherders went in for poisoning and trapping along with their herding. But this sort of hunting was done at the expense of the sheep and the cows. It was not long before the professional "wolfer" came to be the most important factor in the stockman's war with the lobo and the coyote. In the sheep country some of these wolfers became renowned and important characters. The lobo, educated as he had become to man's tactics, was not to be vanquished by a man of ordinary knowledge. His conqueror had to be more sagacious and cunning than he.

"And you can't catch every lobo by the same tricks," a wolfer will tell you. "A man had better go into a range he's going to work and study it out for a few days before he sets any traps. He had better study everything, even the lobo, while he figures on how to catch him. If you know lobos, you can study the lay of the range and figure how you'd work it yourself if you were a wolf going after sheep. If his tracks showed he'd been in a trap once, you had to hide every human sign and smell away from him. When you had figured by sign where he was going to be at a certain time of the night you had to fix your trap so he couldn't see it or smell it, or even guess you'd been along that way yourself earlier in the day. You had to rub out every sign you'd made yourself, and you had to be mighty sure you hadn't left any of your smell on the rabbit or whatever you used for bait. You had to figure he was just as smart as you were, only maybe he didn't know you were in his territory, and you'd better not let him know it. That way, maybe he wouldn't be suspicioning anything. If he got suspicious, you might just as well leave and come back after he'd forgot about you."

One old veteran outlaw with a six-year criminal record outwitted every attempt on his life until the wolfer hit upon a plan of capturing a female, taming her for six months, then staking her out, in heat, to lure the wily Samson to his ruin. A wolf bitch was more than once the cause of an outlaw's downfall. Maybe Old Three Toes of Hall County wouldn't be standing to-day in the Memphis bank, glassy-eyed and snarling, if he hadn't suffered a romantic lapse of precaution.

A good wolfer was well paid for all the pains he took to outwit the lobo. He could make as much as three thousand dollars a year—a lot more than the sheepherder or the cowboy could make tending the stock that were being protected. But, as in every other profession, there were some quacks and shysters. The bounties paid by the ranchmen and by the counties for wolf scalps attracted plenty of unscrupulous hunters who would carefully spare the lives of the females that would restock the range with more scalps for the next season, or who would round up wolves from one county and run them into another that paid higher bounties. Before the ranchman got wise the wolfer could show up in several counties and collect on the same scalps. "How about lettin' me have that scalp back?" one such wolfer asked. "I'm savin' 'em to take back home to show the kids." "Sure," said the rancher who had just paid the bounty; but he took out his knife and cut it into ribbons before he handed it over. "Shucks, man,' the wolfer told him with a grin. "Yuh don't know how handy I am with a needle. I could make that scalp look as good as new if I'd a mind to."

In the end there were too many of this sort among the wolf-trappers, and the ranchmen persuaded Washington to take a hand. To-day, in many counties of the Southwest, there are government-paid men whose business it is to destroy wolves and other predatory animals, and whose jobs depend on their success. The wild-animal enemies of stock are finding mutton and beef harder and harder to get.

To-day, too, the lobo and the coyote, along with the Golden Eagle, are hunted in some parts of the Southwest in a thoroughly modern manner, by airplane and with machine gun. Coyotes and wolves are flushed by a line of riders across a given territory; the airplane spots and swoops down upon the running prey, and the hunter shoots them from above. With the same weapon he attacks the eagles in the air. The clawed enemies of sheep are faced with a new adjustment, to devise a new method of combat with their two-legged adversary. No doubt their sagacity and cunning will find some way to circumvent even this mode of attack. The rivalry for the hoofed meat of the Plains will go on.

Snowshoe Thompson and the Wolves

I was never frightened but once during all my travels in the mountains. That was in the winter of 1857. I was crossing Hope Valley, when I came to a place where six great wolves—big timber wolves—were at work in the snow, digging out the carcass of some animal. Now, in my childhood in Norway, I had heard so many stories about the ferocity of wolves that I feared them more than any other wild animal. To my eyes, those before me looked to have hair on them a foot long. They were great, gaunt, shaggy fellows. My course lay near them. I knew I must show a bold front. All my life I had heard that the wolf—savage and cruel as he is—seldom has the courage to attack anything that does not run at his approach. I might easily run away from bears, but these were customers of a different kind. There was nothing of them but bones, sinews, and hair. They could skim over the snow like birds.

As I approached, the wolves left the carcass, and in single file came out a distance of about twenty-five yards toward my line of march. The leader of the pack then wheeled about and sat down on his haunches. When the next one came up he did the same, and so on, until all were seated in a line. They acted just like trained soldiers. I pledge you my word, I thought the devil was in them! There they sat, every eye and every sharp nose turned toward me as I approached. In the old country, I had heard of 'man-wolves,' and these acted as if of that supernatural kind. To look at them gave me cold chills, and I had a queer feeling about the roots of my hair. What most frightened me was the confidence they displayed, and the regular order in which they moved. But I dared not show the least sign of fear, so on I went.

Just when I was opposite them, and but twenty-five or thirty yards away, the leader of the pack threw back his head and uttered a long and prolonged howl. All the others of the pack did the same. "Ya-hoo-oo! Ya-OO, woo-oo!" cried all together. A more doleful and terrific sound I never heard. I thought it meant my death. The awful cry rang across the silent valley, was echoed by the hills, and re-echoed far away among the surrounding mountains.

Every moment I expected to see the whole pack dash at me. I would

---

From "Snowshoe Thompson," by Dan De Quille, *The Overland Monthly*, Devoted to the Development of the Country, Vol. VIII (Second Series, October, 1886), No. 46, pp. 428–429. Copyright, 1886, by Overland Monthly Co. San Francisco.

just then have given all I possessed to have had my revolver in my hand. However, I did not alter my gait nor change my line of march. I passed the file of wolves as a general moves along in front of his soldiers. The ugly brutes uttered but their first fearful howl. When they saw that their war-cry did not cause me to alter my course nor make me run, they feared to come after me; so they let me pass.

They sat still and watched me hungrily for some time, but when I was far away, I saw them all turn about and go back to the carcass. Had I turned back or tried to run away when they marched out to meet me, I am confident the whole pack would have been upon me in a moment. They all looked it. My *show* of courage intimidated them and kept them back.

Hugh Glass and the Grizzly

After the Leavenworth campaign was over, Andrew Henry set out for the Yellowstone River and Glass was one of the party.[1] Their route lay up Grand River through a country interspersed with thickets of brushwood, dwarf plum trees and other shrubs indigenous to this barren soil. As these nomadic parties usually drew their food, and to a large extent their raiment, from the country through which they were passing, it was necessary to keep one or two hunters ahead of the main party in search of game. Glass, having a high reputation as a hunter and a good shot, was often detailed upon this important duty. On the present occasion he was a short distance in advance of the party, forcing his way through a thicket, when he suddenly came upon a grizzly bear that had lain

From *The American Fur Trade of the Far West,* A History of the Pioneer Trading Posts and Early Fur Companies of the Missouri Valley and the Rocky Mountains and of the Overland Commerce with Santa Fe, by Hiram Martin Chittenden, Volume II, pp. 699–705. Copyright, 1901, by Francis P. Harper. New York. 1902.

Among the anecdotes that have come down to us of wild life on the plains, none is better authenticated than that of the escape of Hugh Glass from the very portal of death at the hands of a grizzly bear. The story has survived in oral tradition and is well known by the older men of the mountains and plains who still live. It has thrice been embodied in written description [*Missouri Intelligencer,* June 18, 1825; *Scenes in the Rocky Mountains* (Sage), p. 117; *Scenes and Adventures in the United States Army* (Cooke), p. 135]. The following account is taken from the *Missouri Intelligencer,* which in turn borrowed it from the *Portfolio.* It is in all respects the most circumstantial narrative extant and is evidently the most correct in its details. The incident is one of those which were so frequent in those early days, although it must have been considerably more noteworthy than the average or it would not have survived so long. Hugh Glass was born in Pennsylvania—the only scrap of his early history that has come down to us. He was called an "old man" as early as 1824. Our first real knowledge of him is in 1823, when he is discovered to be one of Ashley and Henry's men. He received a wound in Ashley's fight before the Aricara towns.—H.M.C., *ibid.,* p. 698.

[1] According to Cooke, Henry had eighty men bound for the headwaters of the Yellowstone. The incident with the bear occurred on the fifth day out, near evening.—H.M.C.

down in the sand. Before he could "set his triggers"[2] or even turn to fly, the bear seized him by the throat and lifted him off the ground. Then flinging him down, the ferocious animal tore off a mouthful of his flesh and turned and gave it to her cubs, which were near by. Glass now endeavored to escape, but the bear, followed by her cubs, pounced upon him again. She seized him by the shoulder and inflicted dangerous wounds in his hands and arms. His companion had by this time come up and was making war upon the cubs, but one of them drove him into the river, where, standing waist deep in the water, he killed his pursuer with a shot from his rifle. The main body now arrived, having heard cries for succor, and after several shots from close at hand, slew the bear as she was standing over the prostrate body of her victim.

Although still alive, the condition of the unfortunate hunter seemed well-nigh hopeless. His whole body was in a mangled condition. He was utterly unable to stand, and was suffering excruciating torment. There was no surgical aid to be had and it was impossible to move him. Delay of the party might bring disaster upon all, yet it was repugnant to the feelings of the men to leave the sufferer alone. In this predicament Major Henry succeeded, by offer of a reward,[3] in inducing two men to remain with Glass until he should expire, or until he should so far recover as to bear removal to some of the trading houses in that country. These men remained with Glass five days, when, despairing of his recovery, and at the same time seeing no prospects of immediate death, they cruelly abandoned him, taking with them his rifle and all his accoutrements, so that he was left without means of defense, subsistence, or shelter. The faithless wretches then set out on the trail of their employer, and when they overtook him, reported that Glass had died of his wounds and that they had buried him in the best manner possible. They produced his effects in confirmation and their story was readily accepted.

But Glass was *not* dead, and although the dread messenger had hovered for many days so near, yet the stricken sufferer would not receive him, but persistently motioned him away. When Glass realized the treachery of his companions, far from despairing on account of it, he felt a new determination to live, if for nothing else than to search out his base betrayers and call them to account. There was a spring near by and hither Glass drew himself. Over it hung a few bushes with wild cherries and near by were some buffalo berries that he could reach.

---

2 Cooke's account is quite different, the essential particulars being that Glass was caught too suddenly to retreat and staked his all upon a single deliberate shot; which, although it was ultimately fatal, was not immediately so. The bear rushed upon Glass with such speed and ferocity that escape was impossible. She overtook him, crushed him to the earth, and mangled him so terribly that it seemed as if he must have been killed. She then started after the other hunters, who barely escaped with their lives before the bear succumbed to the effects of Glass' shot.—H.M.C.

3 Cooke says that a purse of eighty dollars was made up by the men as a present to any two who would stay with Glass.—H.M.C.

Here he remained day after day, gradually nursing back his strength, until he felt that he could undertake to leave his lonesome and unhappy camping ground. He resolved to strike out for Fort Kiowa, a post on the Missouri River, a hundred miles away [South Dakota]. It required magnificent fortitude to set out on a journey like that, still unable to stand, and with hardly strength to drag one limb after the other; with no provisions nor means of securing any, and in a hostile country where he was at the absolute mercy of the most worthless renegade that might cross his path. But the deep purpose of revenge held him up, and a stroke of fortune came to his rescue.

He happened one day upon a spot where a pack of wolves had surrounded a buffalo calf and were harrying it to death. Glass lay low until the calf was dead, when he appeared upon the scene, put the wolves to flight, and took possession of the calf. Without knife or fire, it was not an easy thing to turn to account his good fortune, but hunger is not fastidious and Glass most likely took counsel of the wolves as to ways and means of devouring what he required. Taking what he could with him he pursued his way, with inconceivable hardship and distress, and at last reached Fort Kiowa.[4]

After an experience like that through which he had just passed, it might be supposed that Glass would have been inclined to rest at the Fort, at least until his wounds could get well. But he had not long been there when a party of trappers came along in a boat bound for the Yellowstone River. This was just the opportunity that he wanted, and he promptly joined them, bidding adieu to the protection of the fort.

When the party were nearing the Mandan villages, Glass thought to save a little time by going overland across a bend in the river to Tilton's Fort, a trading establishment in that vicinity. It proved to be a lucky move for on the following day all of his companions were massacred by the Aricara Indians.[5] Those always treacherous savages had but lately taken up their abode near the Mandan villages, and the travelers were wholly ignorant of the snare into which they were running. As Glass was approaching the fort he saw two squaws whom he at once recognized as Aricaras.[6] Alarmed at his danger he sought to conceal himself,

---

4 Cooke says that Glass' razor was left; that in the incident of the wolves and the buffalo calf he waited until the wolves had eaten enough to satisfy their hunger before he drove them off lest they should attack him. He further says that Glass went first to the Aricara villages, which he found deserted except by some dogs, and that he spent two days taming these before they would come near enough for him to get hold of them. This is, however, not probable, for Glass would not have gone deliberately back into the hands of those Indians while there was any other chance of life. Cooke also says that Glass then went to a trading post at the mouth of the Teton river.—H.M.C.

5 This event is confirmed by an entry in the *Missouri Intelligencer* of February 25, 1824.—H.M.C.

6 Cooke's account of this affair is very much colored, too much so to be true, and was probably the result of the natural growth which such stories undergo through many repetitions.—H.M.C.

but too late, for the squaws at once notified the warriors, who immediately began pursuit. Glass, still feeble from his wounds, made an ineffectual effort at flight. His enemies were almost within gun shot when two mounted Mandans rushed forward and seized him. Great was his surprise and joy at this unexpected deliverance, and it gave him increased faith that he should yet live to accomplish his mission of revenge.

The Indians carried Glass to Tilton's Fort, and the same night he left the fort alone and set out up the river. After traveling alone for thirty-eight days, all the way through hostile country, he had at length arrived at Henry's Fort, near the mouth of the Big Horn River. Here he was received as one risen from the dead, for no one had doubted the story of his companions. Glass was chagrined to find that his companions had gone to Fort Atkinson.[7] Still intent on his purpose of revenge, he promptly accepted an offer of service as a messenger to carry a dispatch to Fort Atkinson. Four men accompanied him and they left Henry's Fort on the 28th of February, 1824.

The route of the party lay eastward into the valley of Powder River, thence southward to the sources of that stream, and across into the valley of the Platte. Here they made some skin boats and floated down the river until they were out of the foothills, when, to their infinite dismay, they came upon a band of Arikaras, a part of Grey Eye's band, the chief who had been killed the previous summer by a shot from Leavenworth's artillery. The new chief's name was Elk Tongue. The warriors came down to the river and by many protestations of friendship induced the travelers to believe that they were sincere. Glass had at one time spent a whole winter with the chief, had joined him in the chase, had smoked his pipe, and had quaffed many a cup with him in the wigwam. When he alighted from his canoe the old chief embraced him as a brother. The whites were thrown off their guard and accepted an invitation to visit the chief's lodge. While partaking of the hospitable pipe a child was heard to utter a scream and on looking around, Glass perceived some squaws carrying away their effects. The little party well understood what this meant, and springing at once to their feet, fled with the utmost precipitation. Two of them were overtaken and put to death, one within a few yards of Glass, who had found concealment behind a point of rocks. Glass was thoroughly versed in the arts of Indian life and he succeeded in baffling their search until finally they abandoned it altogether. He had lost all of his property except a knife

[7] Cooke says that the younger of the two men was found at Henry fort; that he was petrified with fear when he saw Glass; but that Glass had compassion on him, and let him go on account of his youth, his penitence, and, more likely, because he considered Fitzgerald, who was the older, the real culprit.

Cooke has no account of Glass' adventures beyond his arrival at Henry's fort.—H.M.C.

and flint, and thus equipped he set out in a northeast direction to find Fort Kiowa.[8]

The buffalo calves at this season were very young, and as the country abounded in buffalo, Glass had no difficulty in getting what meat he desired, while his flint enabled him to build a fire. He was fifteen days in reaching Fort Kiowa, and at the first opportunity went down the river to Fort Atkinson, where he arrived in June, 1824. Here he found his faithless companion (for he now cherished revenge only against one of the party), who had enlisted in the army. Thus, under protection of the law, Glass did not feel disposed to resort to extreme measures. The commanding officer ordered his property to be given up and provided him with a new equipment. Thus appeased, he relinquished his scheme of revenge and contented himself with entertaining the people of the garrison with stories of his marvelous experiences.

In weighing the two principal authorities for this story we are inclined to think that Glass' sudden relinquishment of his purpose of revenge may have been due to new light obtained from the two men who deserted him. It was asking a great deal for those two men to expose themselves to destruction for one whose life they doubtless believed was already as good as lost, and whatever may have been the considerations of humanity, it was only heroic indifference to personal safety that could have induced them to stay. They should have stayed, of course, but their failure to do so, is not without its justification.

In Colonel Cooke's account, the name of one of the men left with Glass was Fitzgerald; the name of the other is not given, but he is said to have been a mere youth of seventeen and doubtless on his first trip to the mountains. Glass does not seem to have cherished revenge against him, but to have blamed Fitzgerald alone. Who the young man was is not known, but the late Captain La Barge, who remembers the tradition well, says that it was James Bridger. Bridger is supposed to have been born in 1804 and this would indicate 1821 or 1822 as the year of the occurrence. The discrepancy is not great enough to preclude the possibility of its being Bridger, but there is no other proof of it than this intangible tradition.

Glass turns up occasionally in the correspondence of those early days and we know that he was at Fort Union about 1830. He was at one time employed as hunter for the fort and used to hunt for bighorns on the bluffs opposite the post. These bluffs are still known as Glass' Bluffs.

Glass finally succumbed to his old enemies, the Aricaras, in the winter of 1832–3. The circumstances of his death were related[9] to Maximilian,

---

[8] "Although I had lost my rifle and all my plunder, I felt quite rich when I found my knife and steel in my shot pouch. These little fixens make a man feel right peart when he is three or four hundred miles away from anybody or anywhere—all alone among the painters [panthers] and the wild varmints." From article in *Missouri Intelligencer*.—H.M.C.

[9] By Johnson Gardner, the well-known free trapper.—H.M.C.

Prince of Wied, who has thus recorded them: "Old Glass, with two companions, had gone from Fort Cass [winter of 1832–3] to hunt bears on the Yellowstone, and as they were crossing the river on the ice farther down, they were all three shot, scalped, and plundered by a war party of thirty Aricaras who were concealed on the opposite bank. . . ."

Rattlesnake Lore

There are dozens of legends about the rattlesnake among the cow hands and farmers of the West. One fellow said to me, "There ain't nothin' on the livin' earth as fast as a rattler. You know why you always hits a rattler in the haid whin you shoots 'im?"

"No," I said. "Why is it?"

"Well, I'll tell you what's the fact," he replied. "The rattler sees the bullet a-comin' an he strikes it. He hits the bullet. The bullet don't hit him."

There's a crazy, farfetched tale of an old cattleman who bought a new pair of boots. On his way home from town he got off his horse for some reason or other and was bitten by a rattlesnake. He died. Some time later his son, seeing the old man's boots in a corner, put them on and went to work. That night he got sick, swelled up, and died. There was a scratch on one of his legs. Nobody knew why he died. A little later another member of the family put on the boots, which were still new. He died also with a scratch on his leg. I've forgotten how many people died from wearing the boots, but the tale has it that the mystery was finally solved by discovering a couple of rattlesnake fangs in the boots. They had broken off there when the old man had been bitten and had continued to bite all those who wore the boots later!

They say that rookie brakemen going to work on the plains' railroads are given those whirligig rattler toys which are used for noisemaking at carnivals and fairs. They are told to whirl them before they approach a switch because a rattlesnake might be coiled up there. The new brakeman is led to believe that when he sounds his toy loudly the rattlesnake in the switch will think a bigger snake is near and will evacuate his post.

A generally prevalent story about rattlesnakes says that when they are close to death they will strike themselves. I don't suppose there is any real basis for believing that a snake in extremity will commit suicide, but of the dozen or more rattlers I have seen killed most of them actually did bite themselves. They may simply have mistaken their own bodies in a mad rage of pain for the stick or stone that hit them, but they appeared to be deliberately putting an end to themselves.

From *An Artist in America,* by Thomas Hart Benton, pp. 210–211. Copyright, 1937, by Thomas Benton. New York: Robert M. McBride & Company.

The Road Runner Corrals a Rattlesnake

Now if thar's anythin' in Arizona for whose jedgement I don't have respect nacheral, it's birds. Arizona for sech folks as you an' me, an' coyotes an' jack-rabbits, is a good range. Sech as we-alls sorter fits into the general play an' gets action for our stacks. But whatever a bird can find entrancin' in some of them Southwestern deserts is allers too many for me.

As I su'gests, I former holds fowls, who of free choice continues a residence in Arizona, as imbeciles. Yet now an' then I observes things that makes me oncertain if I'm onto a bird's system; an' if after all Arizona is sech a dead kyard for birds. It's possible a gent might be 'way off on birds an' the views they holds of life. He might watch the play an' esteem 'em loser, when from a bird's p'int of view they's makin' a killin', an' even callin' the turn every deal.

What he'ps to open my eyes a lot on birds is two Road Runners Doc Peets an' me meets up with one afternoon comin' down from Lordsburg. These yere Road Runners is a lanky kind of prop'sition, jest a shade off from spring chickens for size. Which their arrangements as to neck an' laigs is onrestricted an' liberal, an their long suit is runnin' up an' down the sun-baked trails of Arizona with no object. Where he's partic'lar strong, this yere Road Runner, is in waitin' ontil some gent comes along, same as Doc Peets an' me that time, an' then attachin' of himse'f to said cavalcade an' racin' along ahead. A Road Runner keeps up this exercise for miles, an' be 'bout the length of a lariat ahead of your pony's nose all the time. When you-all lets out a link or two an' stiffens your pony with the spur, the Road Runner onbuckles sim'lar an' exults tharat. You ain't goin' to run up on him while he can wave a laig, you can gamble your last chip, an' you confers favors on him by sendin' your pony at him, Thar he stays, rackin' along ahead of you ontil satiated. Usual thar's two Road Runners, an' they clips it along side by side as if thar's somethin' in it for 'em; an' I reckons, rightly saveyed, thar is. However, the profits to Road Runners of them excursions ain't obvious, none whatever; so I won' try to set 'em forth. Them journeys they makes up an' down the trail shorely seems aimless to me.

But about Doc Peets an' me pullin' out from Lordsburg for Wolfville that evenin': Our ponies is puttin' the landscape behind 'em at a good road-gait when we notes a brace of them Road Runners with wings half lifted, pacin' to match our speed along the trail in front. As Road Runners is frequent with us, our minds don't bother with 'em none.

From *Wolfville,* by Alfred Henry Lewis (Dan Quin), pp. 295–301. Copyright, 1897, by Frederick A. Stokes Company. New York.

For the corral of thorns, see J. Frank Dobie, "The Roadrunner in Fact and Folklore," *In the Shadow of History* (Austin, 1939), pp. 162–168.

Now an' then Doc an' me can see they converses as they goes speedin' along a level or down a slope. It's as if one says to t'other, somethin' like this yere:

"How's your wind, Bill? Is it comin' easy?"

"Shore," it would seem like Bill answers. "Valves never is in sech shape. I'm on velvet; how's your laigs standin' the pace, Jim?"

"Laigs is workin' like they's new oiled," Jim replies back; "it's a plumb easy game. I reckons, Bill, me an' you could keep ahead of them mavericks a year if we-alls feels like it."

"Bet a blue stack on it," Bill answers. "I deems these yere gents soft. Before I'd ride sech ponies as them, I'd go projectin' round some night an' steal one."

"Them ponies is shorely a heap slothful," Jim answers.

At this mebby them Road Runners ruffles their feathers an' runs on swifter, jest to show what a slow racket keepin' ahead of me an' Peets is. An' these yere locoed birds keeps up sech conversations for hours.

Mind I ain't sayin' that what I tells you is what them Road Runners really remarks; but I turns it over to you-all the way it strikes me an' Doc at the time. What I aims to relate, however, is an incident as sheds light on how wise an' foxy Road Runners be.

Doc Peets an' me, as I states, ain't lavishin' no onreasonable notice on these yere birds, an' they've been scatterin' along the trail for mebby an hour, when one of 'em comes to a plumb halt, sharp. The other stops likewise an' rounds up ag'inst his mate; an' bein' cur'ous to note what's pesterin' 'em, Peets an' me curbs to a standstill. The Road Runner who stops first—the same bein' Bill—is lookin' sharp an' interested-like over across the plains.

"Rattlesnake," he imparts to his side partner.

"Where's he at?" says the side partner, which is Jim. "Where's this yere snake at, Bill? I don't note no rattlesnake."

"Come round yere by me," Bill says. "Now on a line with the top of yonder mesa an' a leetle to the left of that soap-weed; don't you-all see him quiled up thar asleep?"

"Which I shorely does," says Jim, locatin' the rattlesnake with his beady eye, "an' he's some sunk in slumber. Bill, that serpent is our meat."

"Move your moccasins easy," says Bill, "so's not to turn him out. Let's rustle up some flat cactuses an' corral him."

Tharupon these yere Road Runners turns in mighty diligent; an' not makin' no more noise than shadows, they goes pokin' out on the plains ontil they finds a flat cactus which is dead; so they can tear off the leaves with their bills. Doc Peets an' me sets in our saddles surveyin' their play; an' the way them Road Runners goes about the labors of their snake killin' impresses us it ain't the first bootchery of the kind they appears in. They shorely don't need no soopervisin'.

One after the other, Jim an' Bill teeters up, all silent, with a flat cactus leaf in their beaks, an' starts to fence in the rattlesnake with 'em.

They builds a corral of cactus all about him, which the same is mebby six-foot across. Them engineerin' feats takes Jim an' Bill twenty minutes. But they completes 'em; an' thar's the rattlesnake, plumb surrounded.

These yere cactuses, as you most likely saveys, is thorny no limit; an' the spikes is that sharp, needles is futile to 'em. Jim an' Bill knows the rattlesnake can't cross this thorny corral.

He don't look it none, but from the way he plays his hand, I takes it a rattlesnake is sensitive an' easy hurt onder the chin.

An' it's plain to me an' Peets them Road Runners is aware of said weaknesses of rattlesnakes, an' is bankin' their play tharon. We-alls figgers, lookin' on, that Jim an' Bill aims to put the rattlesnake in prison; leave him captive that-a-way in a cactus calaboose. But we don't size up Jim an' Bill accurate at all. Them two fowls is shorely profound.

No sooner is the corral made than Jim an' Bill, without a word of warnin', opens up a war-jig round the outside, flappin' their pinions an' screechin' like squaws. Nacherally the rattlesnake wakes up. The sight of them two Road Runners, Jim an' Bill, cussin' an swearin' at him, an' carryin' on that-a-way scares him.

It's trooth to say Bill an' Jim certainly conducts themse'fs scand'lous. The epithets they heaps on that pore ignorant rattlesnake, the taunts they flings at him, would have done Apaches proud.

The rattlesnakes buzzes an' quiles up, an' onsheaths his fangs, an' makes bluffs to strike Bill an' Jim, but they only hops an' dances about, thinkin' up more ornery things to say. Every time the rattlesnake goes to crawl away—which he does frequent—he strikes the cactus thorns an' pulls back. By an' by he sees he's elected, an' he gets that enraged he swells up till he's big as two snakes; Bill an' Jim maintainin' their sass. Them Road Runners is abreast of the play every minute, you can see that.

At last comes the finish, an' matters gets dealt down to the turn. The rattlesnake suddenly crooks his neck, he's so plumb locoed with rage an' fear, an' socks his fangs into hims'f. That's the fact; bites himse'f, an' never lets up till he's dead.

It don't seem to astound Jim an' Bill none when the rattlesnake 'sassinates himse'f that-a-way, an' I reckons they has this yere sooicide in view. They keeps pesterin' an' projectin' about ontil the rattlesnake is plumb defunct, an' then they emits a whirlwind of new whoops, an' goes over to one side an' pulls off a skelp dance. Jim an' Bill is shorely cel'bratin' a vict'ry.

After the skelp dance is over, Bill an' Jim tiptoes over mighty quiet an' sedate, an' Jim takes their prey by the tail an' yanks it. After the rattlesnake's drug out straight, him an' Bill runs their eyes along him like they's sizin' him up. With this yere last, however, it's cl'ar the Road Runners regards the deal as closed. They sa'nters off down the trail, arm in arm like, conversin' in low tones so Peets an' me never does hear what they says. When they's in what they takes to be the c'rrect p'sition, they stops an' looks back at me an' Peets. Bill turns to Jim like he's sayin':

"Thar's them two short-horns ag'in. I wonders if they ever aims to pull their freight, or do they reckon they'll pitch camp right yere?"

Prairie Dogs

In 1869, when swimming the Platte with a herd—a wide river in icy flood—[Charles Goodnight] found the stream full of prairie dogs headed for its south bank. He lifted one from the water and placed it on his horse's back, behind the saddle. It stayed on until he reached the north bank where he put it in the chuck-wagon, carried it on up the trail, and kept it until the outfit got back to the Pecos. At night the cowboys took it from the wagon and turned it out to graze, and as the animals make most interesting pets, the boss claimed the boys "had a hell of a time playing with it."

"There is an old myth," he continued, "that the prairie dog, rattlers, rabbits, and little owls live together in the same hole. Owls and rabbits do use the holes, separately, after the prairie dog has abandoned them. When the rattler enters, his intention is to swallow the dog, which he does, and my observation is that a dog will not enter his hole when there is a rattler in it, which he probably knows by scent. I have put dead rattlers in holes, and later found them thoroughly covered up by the dogs. They evidently attempt to cover the holes when there is a live snake in them, and it appears the rattler is aware of this, too. If you slowly pour dirt in on a rattler, he will make his appearance promptly."

Jim Bridger, the Wolves, and the Beaver

One day when hunting for fur-bearing animals along a certain river, [Jim Bridger] was suddenly taken upon by a pack of wolves. The incident caught him rather unawares, so he ran for the nearest tree and climbed out of reach. The wolves waited at its base for about two hours, when finally all departed except one and that one remained on guard. In about half an hour the pack returned with a beaver to chew down the tree.

From *Charles Goodnight, Cowman and Plainsman,* by J. Evetts Haley, pp. 427–428. Copyright, 1936, by J. Evetts Haley; 1949, by the University of Oklahoma Press, Publishing Division of the University. Norman, Oklahoma.

From *Foolish Questions, Yellowstone National Park,* by Jack Chaney, p. 55. Copyright, 1924, by Jack Chaney. [Lincoln, Nebraska.]

. . . It is alleged that he [Jim Bridger] once told the following.—J.C.

The Well-Trained Beaver

"Ah! Jones, that is a whopper."

"Sure as I live, but the beaver slept every night with the trapper, and in the day time, if he left the tent, the beaver would fall to work and make a dam across the floor of the tent, using the chist, skins, arms and everything."

"Oh! Jones!"

"But, I tell you it is true. Tame a beaver once, and you'll find I'se tellin' a plain statement as true as ever a Padre made."

"Padre! who'd believe a Mexican priest? Mr. Jones, that tame beaver of your'n must have been born in the States, where he hadn't trees and mud to build dams with, and had to resort to furnitur."

"That beaver," responded Jones, "was as near like a human bein' as any man present."

"How do you make that out, Mr. Jones?"

"Why, one day his master died. Well, they tried all they could to console the beaver, but it 'twant no use. He wouldn't be consoled. All he did was to git an ole shoe belongin' to his master, an' if he didn't haul that ere shoe around day after day wherever he went. Well, the beaver 'gan to grow thin, and one night they found he was a-dyin', jest from starvin' himself to death and a-huggin' the ole shoe."

"Oh! Jones," said the greenhorn, "you don't expect I'll swallow all that yarn?'

But Mr. Jones and all the other trappers present preserved an imperturbable dignity of mien, as if the very reference to the animal mentioned demanded from them all due reverence.

"Well, but that was not doing as a human being would do. I never seen a man carry an old shoe around till he died from starvin'."

"That is neither here nor there," continued Mr. Jones. "It was when the trapper first made the beaver's acquaintance that he showed he knew as much as a human critter. At that time he had one wife and lived with her all alone in a hole, side o' the dam. They had two sons and a darter. The darter the old beaver had married to a fine lookin' young beaver who lived t'other side the dam."

The whistle which the neophyte here gave seemed to give great dissatisfaction to all of the trappers present. One of them quietly asked him—

"Is that the way, youngster, you'se bin eddicated in perliteniss of manners? If it is, I know a beaver who kin larn you sumthin'. In the

---

From *The Life and Adventures of Kit Carson,* the Nestor of the Rocky Mountains, from Facts Narrated by Himself, by DeWitt C. Peters, p. 77. Entered according to Act of Congress, in the year 1858, by W. R. C. Clark & Co., in the Clerk's Office of United States District Court for the Southern District of New York. New York.

fust place, if a young beaver ever kums inter the presence of the ole uns, especially if she's, that is the ole uns, a female beaver, the young un 'mediately fetches his right fore paw up to his forehead, jest 'hind the right eyebrow, an' makes a reverintial bow of cerimony in salute. I'se seen that ar' oftener than you've put one leg ahead of t'other yit, young un."

The trappers present all confirmed the truth of this statement by a solemn nod of assent to the query, "Ain't that true, gentlemen?" which, at least, served to prevent unceremonious whistling.

It is thus that we might go on and fill page after page with this picture-talk of the trappers. Some of their yarns are pretty tightly strained, but most of them contain a capital hit and are usually founded on the facts. It is a well authenticated fact that the beaver has but one mate; and, that they live together a loving couple, as if husband and wife. As to their *liaisons*, coquetry, flirting and so forth, doubtless the society in some parts of the human family will bear a faithful resemblance in these respects also. As an example of industry the world will look in vain for a better one than is afforded by the little beaver of the Western Rivers. Look at them patiently felling the tallest trees; and so nicely adjusting their fall and calculating their height that they strike the opposite bank of their stream gaining a fixed and permanent lodgment. It is thus that these wonderful little creatures will often erect dams across wide rivers and effectually stop the rushing torrents.

The Canteen Fish

George McCarthy, owner of a guest ranch near Victorville, has entranced many visitors with his story of the canteen fish. . . .

* * * * *

George and a partner had been prospecting in the desert till they were far from any road or any other human habitation—or any water. They had built a little shack and were working toward the mouth of a canyon opening out of the mountains, on the theory that the rains and snows of many generations had washed gold down from the mountains. They knew torrents had come out of that canyon mouth at some time, because there was a deep sink in the desert which undoubtedly had been cut by those streams of long ago. But the two prospectors were miles from the nearest water hole, and all the "liquid silver" they had was in a barrel. (In the desert, "liquid silver" means water.) That barrel was their most carefully guarded treasure, for the water hole from which they had brought the water was drying up.

They knew they should turn back, but they had found traces of gold and could not till they were down to their last two canteens of water. They were about to give up and return to their shack when they found a little nugget in some gravel. Then they became feverish with excite-

From *It's An Old California Custom,* by Lee Shippey, pp. 195–200. Copyright, 1948, by Lee Shippey. New York: The Vanguard Press, Inc.

ment. They went on and found some coarse gold in the sand, and then on and on, lured by small but shining pockets of promise.

They had used up all the water in their canteens, and the sun was sinking behind the encircling mountains, before they realized that they were far from their shack and very close to dangerous thirst, and that if darkness caught them they might get lost.

They built a marker of such stones, greasewood, and cactus as they could gather in a hurry and turned back. Then one of the sudden storms which occasionally burst in the mountains blotted out the canyon above them. Realizing that a cloudburst up there might mean a flood in the broad sink in which they had been panning, they hurried. But they were still in the middle of the sink when the flash flood was on them. A wall of water higher than their heads roared down on them and hurled them ahead of it, swimming for their lives. Their situation was desperate, but they were hardy men. Their effort was to keep afloat and let the flood carry them till its force diminished.

They were swimming so when George's outstretched hand closed on something slippery and wriggly. Fearing it might be a rattlesnake, he flung it from him so violently that it landed on the bank, which was dry, as all the rain had fallen in the mountains above them. But as he flung it he saw it was not a snake but a fish. Then both men found themselves in the midst of a veritable school of fish, which apparently were even more helpless in the flood than they were.

The fish swarmed about them, climbing on them. By that time the men had managed to drift toward the side of the sink on which they had made camp and found they were in shallower water. Though the flood was still rushing down the sink, they could touch bottom and could see the way to safety.

Still the fish eddied around them, as purposeful as swarming bees. Thinking a fine fish fry would be good for supper, they began grasping them with both hands and hurling them out on to the bank.

The situation had been so dramatic George hadn't stopped to wonder at the miracle of a school of fish in the desert, but at last, almost exhausted, he called:

"We got more'n we can eat in a week. Let's get out. I've heard of it rainin' fish, but darned if this ain't the first time I ever believed it."

"These didn't come from the sky," said his partner. "These are canteen fish."

"What are canteen fish?"

"You don't find 'em anywhere except in the Mojave," said the other. "They live in the little water holes scattered through the desert, and they're sort of queer shaped. Each one has a hump on its back like a camel, which it can fill with water. That's its canteen, and they always carry a reserve supply. They have some strange way of knowin' when a water hole is goin' to dry up and before it does they all fill their canteens and start off across the desert to some bigger water hole. Guess they can smell water twenty miles away. They march in a regular column, flippin' along on their tails. These poor fish musta been crossin' the sink when the flood hit 'em. They're not used to anything but shallow water, like you'd find around some desert spring, and if it hadn't been for us they'd have all been drowned."

So George and his partner, full of pity, kept on throwing the fish out onto the bank until they had tossed out hundreds. By that time George had noticed that each one did have a queer hump or tank on its back. The fish kept struggling toward the two men instead of striving to elude them, but many were swept away by the turgid waters, and George could not help feeling full of sympathy for them as he saw the despair in their eyes as they were carried out of reach.

When at last the two men climbed out of the sink their sympathy for the creatures whose lives they had saved made it impossible to kill and eat any of them. By that time the water was receding rapidly, and soon the desert, they knew, would swallow it up. So they ran to the sink, filled their canteens, and ran with them to their shack. They emptied them into the barrel and ran back for more water. If they could only get enough water in that barrel to wash out some of the gold, they believed their fortunes would be made. But by that time the water was being blotted up by the sand so rapidly that it was only a forlorn hope.

As they carried back their refilled canteens, and a bucket they had had in the shack, with another load of water, they realized they were leading a procession. All the canteen fish, flipping along on their tails, were following them. The men exchanged ejaculations of surprise but hurried on, having no time to do more than vaguely wonder. But as they emptied their canteens into the barrel the riddle solved itself. The leaders of the fish parade flipped up on top of things piled beside the shack till they reached the level of the barrel-top and emptied their canteens into it. All the other fish followed suit, after which they happily flipped away to the vanishing stream to refill their canteens and bring back more.

"They'd caught on to the fact that we wanted that water mighty bad," George says, "and were so darned grateful to us for savin' their lives they wanted to show their appreciation."

II. WESTWARD JOURNEY

Just that long and terrible journey from the Mississippi to the ocean is an epic in itself. . . . The prairie schooner is as large a figure in the legends as the black ship that bore Ulysses homeward from Troy.—FRANK NORRIS

"The old prairie schooners," says Lindsay, "blundered forward on the western way, day after day, season after season, sometimes for years, for the pioneers often worked their way to the Virgin Land, which they had taken for goal. Often, indeed, they died on the way, they broke down on the way. Each yearned to the West even as they failed and threw their spirits westward. . . . The primitive instinct for moving was awakened by the road and many a pioneer found happiness in the going as much as in the attainment."—STEPHEN GRAHAM

Crossing the Arkansas River on a Buffalo Skin

October 15th, 1832

Fair day. All slept sound and arose at the sound of the bugle. After breakfast we traveled about four miles and came to the Arkansaw at the mouth of Red Fork. The stream of Arkansaw was swift and high. The Captain proposed to cross here. After some reflection I proposed to him to go up the river and try to find a better ford, for it was certain that several horses would be lost by swimming the stream at this place. The Government, of course, would be the ultimate sufferers, as the horses would die in the service of the country. The Captain and Mr. Irving acceded to my proposal, and followed up the Arkansaw a short distance, where we found that the abrupt hills would compel us to go

From *Washington Irving on the Prairie,* or A Narrative of a Tour of the Southwest in the Year 1832, by Henry Leavitt Ellsworth, edited by Stanley T. Williams and Barbara D. Simison, pp. 39–42. Copyright, 1937, by American Book Company. New York.

far into the interior to get around them. We looked again for a ford. Billet said he would examine. He threw off a few of his outer garments, and waded in. The water soon rose to his shoulders and he was wafted down the current and swam towards the opposite shore. About half-way across the river, he was able to touch bottom and, with occasional swimming over some deep holes, forded to the shore. He returned in a different place, but with the like success. The determination now was formed to build rafts, and axes were plied on every side. It was at this moment that our eyes were turned to the buffalo skin, bought by Mr. Pourteles of the Osage Indians. We took it off from the horse and speculated one time whether it would be sufficient to carry over our plunder, much less ourselves.

In the meantime while Mr. Irving and the rest of us were doubting, we saw Tonish and Billet preparing to tie up the corners and risk the experiment. They were confident; It was only the gentleman that doubted. Tho buffalo skin was of common size only. The corners were drawn together, so as to leave the bottom when filled in the shape of an oblong boat. Plunder or baggage (which words are synonymous here) was then put into the skin to fill it quite to the top. Mr. Irving said it would certainly sink. When the boat was loaded Tonish and Billet stripped themselves, and we aided to launch the boat into the river. It floated, and was so buoyant that more plunder was still added. Then Billet tied a string to the fore part and plunged in with an Indian yell, taking the string in his mouth and drawing the boat from the shore. Tonish followed behind with a similar yell, shoving the boat with one hand. Both swam with hand over hand like dogs. At times I feared they would perish and the little bark go down stream. Not only were our eyes intent upon them, but the ferry boat was new to the whole army, who flocked around to witness the scene.

The Arkansaw river was about as wide and swift as Connecticut river at Hartford, when the freshet is up to Mr. Buck's store. You will of course perceive the difficulty of crossing with a buffalo skin. While Tonish and Billet were crossing our plunder, Captain Beans and Doctor Holt were just by collecting the dry timber to form a raft. A few rangers went farther up, and happily found a place where the river could be forded with little swimming. Yet the plunder, saddle, and lower parts would certainly get wet.

Tonish and Billet crossed over a second load in same manner as the first, and until the ford was discovered above, we all calculated to cross in the buffalo skin. Mr. Latrobe, Pourteles, and Baily went up to the ford. Mr. Irving was going also. I proposed to him to try the buffalo skin. Our servants were almost exhausted, but we cheered their spirits by giving them a dollar each for the ferriage. I offered to go first, but Irving desired the opportunity and I consented. His boat was filled nearly full and launched regularly into the river. He was then taken in the arms of Billet and Tonish and placed with great care in the center of the tottering craft, and requested to sit perfectly still. The swimmers plunged in with their hideous yells, and Mr. Irving sat motionless, proud enough to be borne across the deep in a buffalo skin! When the swimmers had passed more than half the distance, and become able to touch the bottom, Mr. Irving was more careless as to his perpendicular stillness, and seizing one of the guns which lay beside him, he fired a salute to those who were behind. He soon reached the shore, and strided the sand along the beach on the opposite side as one who had just discovered and was taking possession of a new country! He was a short time left alone, in the Pawnee country.

The ferrymen soon came for me, hoping to carry myself and all the remaining plunder the next load. I told them it was impossible. They thought not. They accordingly collected all the scattered effects and when I saw the quantity and estimated the weight, I became suspicious I should get into the river, and without undressing entirely, I prepared to disencumber myself of some things, if the dangers should be great. Travelers tell great stories; and speak at random. I have an exact inventory of the baggage that was put in before I was placed upon the top of it by the arms of Tonish and Billet—

3 full saddle bags
4 guns
holsters and pistols; powder horns and shot pouches
½ a bushel of corn, besides all the fresh provisions of our mess
8 blankets
3 buckskin dresses
4 surcingles
axe, frying pan, tin kettle, coffee pot, and eating bowls
ropes and 1 bridle
2 great coats

On the top of these with several other small articles I was placed, with my double-barreled gun in my hands loaded for a salute if circumstances should be favorable. The swimmers plunged in. I never felt placed in so ticklish a situation. We descended rapidly with the current and yet gained fast upon the other shore. When the servants touched bottom, I was exceedingly glad and felt tolerably safe, and fired my salute, and curled down again as the water grew deeper fast. I reached the shore safely, and was greeted by my friend Mr. Irving, who was busily filling his little sketch book with the interesting events of the day.

Soon Mr. Latrobe and Pourteles joined us. They were dripping wet from about the middle. While we were packing our horses, we saw Captain Beans and Doctor Holt paddling along their rough made raft. Both were in the water two and a half feet. The current carried them much below us, and although they reached the shore in safety, a considerable part of their effects got wet, and especially their flour; to save which they were forced to bake it immediately. Some of the rangers who could not swim, and whose horses could not carry them over, threw in a dry log and clung to that, stemming the current as well as they could.

Missouri River Steamboat Tales

I[1]

. . . The captain was by no means the most important individual on the ante-bellum steamboat. In point of authority, of prestige and of general indispensability, he loomed exceedingly small beside that truly despotic lord of the old-time river, the pilot. Upon the pilot depended absolutely the safety of vessel, passengers and cargo, and when the boat was under way, his word was a law before which every one bowed. His profession was a very difficult one to learn, requiring years of apprenticeship, and as the pilots themselves were the only ones who could train new men for places in their ranks, they took good care that their numbers were kept down to small and select proportions in order that neither their power nor the princely salaries which they commanded should be diminished. Every pilot was, as he is to-day, licensed by the government and no boat could move without him, but as the profits of steamboating were great then, he could demand almost any wages he chose, and Captain Marsh relates several amusing anecdotes in this connection of pilots whom he knew and worked with.

One of these was Joe Oldham, a man famous in his time for three things; his skill as a pilot, his independence and his extravagance in personal adornment. His was the distinction of possessing the largest, heaviest, and most expensive gold watch on the river. Its stem contained a diamond worth five hundred dollars, and he wore it suspended about his neck by a massive gold chain. In the winter he wore huge fur mittens reaching to his elbows, and in the summer kid gloves of the most delicate hue.

One day a small, side-wheel packet, the *Moses Greenwood,* on her way up from the Ohio bound for Weston, Mo., came into St. Louis looking for a Missouri River pilot. It happened that Oldham was the only one in town and when the captain came to him, he blandly stated that he would take the *Moses Greenwood* to Weston and back, about a week's trip, for one thousand dollars. The captain demurred, but after several days during which no other pilots appeared, and being in a hurry, he went to Oldham and said that he would pay the price.

"Well, I can't accept now, Captain," answered the pilot, nonchalantly. "I'm going to a picnic this afternoon."

Pleadings were of no avail, and to the picnic he went.

On another occasion the steamer *Post Boy,* Captain Rider, came into St. Louis on her way to Leavenworth. Captain Rider sent for Oldham, who was again the only member of the craft in town, and he came to the levee, bedecked with diamonds as usual, wearing a silk hat and

[1] From *The Conquest of the Missouri,* Being the Story of the Life and Exploits of Captain Grant Marsh, by Joseph Mills Hanson, pp. 18–22. Copyright, 1909, by A. A. McClurg & Company; 1937, renewed; 1946, by Rinehart & Company, Inc. New York and Toronto: Murray Hill Books, Inc.

patent-leather shoes, and shielding himself from the summer sun with a gold-handled, silk umbrella.

"How much will you charge to take my boat to Leavenworth and back, Mr. Oldham?" asked the captain.

"Fifteen hundred dollars," answered the pilot, gently.

"What?" shouted Captain Rider. "Man, that's more than the boat will make."

Oldham shrugged his shoulders.

"Well, talk fast, Captain," he said. "I won't stand here in the hot sun fifteen minutes for fifteen hundred dollars."

The captain ground his teeth, but there was nothing to be done save pay the price or lie in port. So at length he said:

"All right, I'll consent to be robbed this time. We're all ready to start. Come aboard."

"But I'm not ready," quoth the pilot. "Just call a carriage and send me up to my rooms for my baggage."

Neverthelesss, once aboard he did his work well, making the round trip in the excellent time of nine days and with no mishaps from the pitfalls of the treacherous Big Muddy. Despite all the money he earned during the years of the river's prosperity, when it was over, poor improvident Oldham found himself penniless, and when he died, years after, it was in abject poverty, in a wretched hovel near the river bank at Yankton, South Dakota.

It was fortunate for Captain Rider in his transaction with Oldham, that the latter was not of as sensitive a disposition as was the pilot in another similar case. This man's name was Bob Burton and one day when the steamer *Aleonia,* Captain Miller, appeared in St. Louis, Bob demanded one thousand dollars for taking her to Weston, with the result that Captain Miller called him a robber and ordered him off the boat. As usual, the captain could secure no one else, and after several days, sent for Bob and told him that he would pay the thousand dollars.

"I won't go for less than fifteen hundred," replied Bob.

"What?" growled the captain. "You said you'd go for a thousand."

"Yes," said Bob, "but you insulted me, sir, and I charge you five hundred dollars for that."

Whatever the wages they could command, the pilots were not always entirely successful in navigating the difficult Missouri, but they seldom permitted themselves to be criticized or to appear disconcerted even in the face of repeated mishaps for which they were responsible. This was aptly demonstrated in the case of a certain member of the craft who once, in steering a boat up from St. Louis, met with so many accidents such as running aground, breaking the wheel and otherwise mutilating the vessel, that at last the captain came to him angrily and demanded:

"Look here, how many times have you been up the Missouri River, anyway?"

"Twice," responded the navigator unabashed. "Once in a skiff and once on horseback."

II[2]

Old rivermen are fond of tales that emphasize their skill in navigating the Missouri—tales at the expense of pilots on milder streams. There is the yarn about the steamboat pilot who went blind. He could no longer take a boat up the Big Muddy. But he was not downhearted. Said he, "They say the Missouri is nothing but mud—too thick to drink, too thin to cultivate—and claim that the Missouri *pollutes* the clear Mississippi. But the fact is that the Mississippi is the sinner. The Missouri is full of honest grit until it meets the Mississippi. Then it is the Mississippi which pollutes the Missouri, turning that honest grit to stinking slime. It is a plain case of Samson meeting Delilah.

"You think I am through because I am blind. No such thing. I'll be a pilot on the Mississippi. I can smell my way up that stream."

And then there is the story of the rootin', tootin' Missouri pilot who saw the channel ahead blocked by one of those big Mississippi steamboats and could find no water deep enough to carry him around. He was in a hurry; he could not wait on the slow progress of that cautious Mississippi pilot. So he just got out his spars and "grasshoppered"[3] over the bluffs for two or three miles until he had passed him!

III[4]

. . . A steamer . . . was attempting to grasshopper its way over a sandbar. . . . Her engines were straining, her paddlewheels churning madly, and every member of the crew was holding his breath as the vessel

---

[2] From *The Missouri,* by Stanley Vestal, pp. 48–49. Rivers of America, edited by Hervey Allen. Copyright, 1945, by Walter Stanley Campbell. New York and Toronto: Farrar & Rinehart, Inc.

[3] The practice . . . of sparring a boat over an obstructing shoal was a common one in the old steamboating days on the Missouri. The spars were long, heavy timbers resembling telegraph poles, and a set of them, two in number, were always carried on the sides of the boat near the bow ready for use. When she became lodged on a bar, the spars were raised and set in the river bottom, like posts, their tops inclined somewhat toward the bow. Above the line of the deck each was rigged with a tackle-block over which a manila cable was passed, one end being fastened to the gunwale of the boat and the other end wound around the capstan. As the capstan was turned and the paddlewheel revolved, the boat was thus lifted and pushed forward. Then the spars were re-set farther ahead and the process repeated until the boat was at last literally lifted over the bar. From the grotesque resemblance to a grasshopper which the craft bore when her spars were set, and from the fact that she might be said to move forward in a series of hops, the practice came to be called "grasshoppering."—Joseph Mills Hanson, *The Conquest of the Missouri* (Chicago, 1909), pp. 86–87.

[4] From *Land of the Dacotahs,* by Bruce Nelson, p. 101. Copyright, 1946, by the University of Minnesota. Minneapolis: University of Minnesota Press.

crept inch by inch over the bar. A "woodhawk"[5] living in a solitary cabin on the riverbank chose this moment to come down to the stream's edge for a pail of water. As he turned away with a brimming pail, his action caught the captain's eye.

"Hey," roared the fuming skipper, "you put that water back!"

Mule Teams

Owing to the delays of organizing and other preparations, we did not leave the Council Grove camp till May 27th. Although the usual hour of starting with the Prairie caravans is after an early breakfast, yet, on this occasion, we were hindered till in the afternoon. The familiar note of preparation, "Catch up! catch up!" was now sounded from the captain's camp, and re-echoed from every division and scattered group along the valley. On such occasions, a scene of confusion ensues, which must be seen to be appreciated. The woods and dales resound with the gleeful yells of the light-hearted wagoners, who, weary of inaction, and filled with joy at the prospect of getting under way, become clamorous in the extreme. Scarcely does the jockey on the race-course ply his whip more promptly at that magic word "Go," than do these emulous wagoners fly to harnessing their mules at the spirit-stirring sound of "Catch up." Each teamster vies with his fellows who shall be soonest ready; and it is a matter of boastful pride to be the first to cry out—"All's set!"

The uproarious bustle which follows—the hallooing of those in pursuit of animals—the exclamations which the unruly brutes call forth from their wrathful drivers; together with the clatter of bells—the rattle of yokes and harness—the jingle of chains—all conspire to produce a clamorous confusion, which would be altogether incomprehensible without the assistance of the eyes; while these alone would hardly suffice to unravel the labyrinthian maneuvers and hurly-burly of this precipitate breaking up. It is sometimes amusing to observe the athletic wagoner hurrying an animal to its post—to see him "heave upon" the halter of a stubborn mule, while the brute as obstinately "sets back," determined not to "move a peg" till his own good pleasure thinks it proper to do so—his whole manner seeming to say, "Wait till your hurry's over!" I have more than once seen a driver hitch a

[5] One of the nomadic woodchoppers who braved the perils of the Indians for the sake of selling cordwood to steamboats at eight dollars per cord. Cf. Joseph Mills Hanson, *The Conquest of the Missouri,* pp. 115–116.

From *Commerce of the Prairies,* the Journal of a Santa Fe Trader during Eight Expeditions across the Great Western Prairies and a Residence of Nearly Nine Years in Northern Mexico, by Josiah Gregg, pp. 50–52. Entered according to Act of Congress in the year 1844, by Henry G. Langley, in the Clerk's Office for the District Court for the Southern District of New York.

harnessed animal to the halter, and by that process haul "his mulishness" forward, while each of his four projected feet would leave a furrow behind; until at last the perplexed master would wrathfully exclaim, "A mule will be a mule any way you can fix it!"

"All's set!" is finally heard from some teamster—"All's set," is directly responded from every quarter. "Stretch out!" immediately vociferates the captain. Then, the "heps!" of drivers—the cracking of whips—the trampling of feet—the occasional creak of wheels—the rumbling of wagons—form a new scene of exquisite confusion, which I shall not attempt further to describe. "Fall in!" is heard from headquarters, and the wagons are forthwith strung out upon the long inclined plain, which stretches to the heights beyond Council Grove.

Grab a Root

When a teamster gets stuck at a crossing, his companions give him but one bit of advice. They tell him to "grab a root." The idea pictured, I suppose, is that of a drowning man catching at a shrub or root on the bank. Freely translated, it means, Make the best of your resources. If a man's horse ran away with him, a teamster would advise him to grab a root. If a railroad train ran off the track, or a boiler explosion took place, the teamster would advise everybody to grab a root. If a man fell desperately in love or were going to be hung, he would tell him to grab a root; and if he could not do it in this world, to seize the first chance in the other one.

Windwagon Thomas

As every one knows, the trade with Santa Fe began in 1821. At first, Franklin, Missouri, was the jumping-off place. Then steamboats began to go up the river as far as Fort Osage, Blue Mills and Wayne City (then Ducker's Ferry), a point within four miles of Independence, which then became the prairie port. But canny pioneers soon discovered that there was a better steamboat landing above, which they dubbed Westport Landing, and which has since become Kansas City. Westport had a good spring, groves for campers, ample grass for their animals, a landing above the Blue River (then often difficult to cross) and good stone for building. Sandbars in the river soon made Inde-

---

From "The Northwest Mule and His Driver," by S. J. Barrow, the *Atlantic Monthly,* Vol. XXXV (May, 1875), No. 211, p. 557.

From "Sailing the Prairies," by Stanley Vestal, *Southwest Review,* Vol. XXIII (July, 1938), No. 4, pp. 432–435. Copyright, 1938, by the Southwest Review. Dallas, Texas: Southern Methodist University.

pendence unapproachable. By 1840 Westport had most of the trade; it had become the recognized outfitting port, and maintained its place until the first locomotive reached Santa Fe, New Mexico, on February 9, 1880.

In 1853 an ex-sailor by the name of Thomas arrived in Westport. He had a Yankee scheme for navigating the prairies by wind-power. More, he had a small wagon mounted with a sail, and he lost no time in demonstrating his ability to travel in it, making the round trip from Westport to Council Grove (a distance of close upon three hundred miles) without the aid of man or beast. Then he proceeded to talk turkey to a group of prosperous citizens of Westport, urging the formation of a company to build and operate a fleet of such vehicles for the Santa Fe trade. Though the arguments he used have not been recorded, it is easy to imagine what they must have been: speed, economy (since no animals would be required) and complete freedom from the routine of the trail, since his "wind-wagon" required no water, wood or grass for its navigation.

Duly impressed, a group of backers chipped in and financed the building of a super-windwagon. The Overland Navigation Company included among its directors Dr. J. W. Parker, a leading physician; Henry Sager; Benjamin Newson, the Indian Agent; a young student of the law, J. J. Mastin; Thomas M. Adams, and the inventor, "Windwagon Thomas."

There was no difficulty in getting wagons built at Westport, for the outfitting of caravans was the principal business there. Apparently, the inventor was enough of a sailor to manufacture the nautical appurtenances.

The result was a mammoth wagon, built after the fashion of a Conestoga prairie schooner, like a crude boat. It was twenty-five feet long, seven feet in beam, with huge wheels, each twelve feet in diameter, with hubs as big as barrels. The sides of the wagonbox reached to the top of the wheels, making the interior six feet high, and above that was the deck. The wagon was rigged like a cat-boat, with the mast stepped well forward, and carried only a mainsail. The mast and sail towered twenty feet above deck. The vehicle, though made like a wagon, was intended to move backwards; that is, the tailgate of the wagon was the prow of the "ship," and the tongue was somehow brought up and over the stern to serve as a helm.

When the windwagon was completed, the company assembled one fine day to witness a demonstration. Two yoke of oxen hauled the huge contrivance out upon the open plain, and the directors—with one exception—climbed aboard. Thomas took his place on deck, made sail and grasped the helm. Before embarking, he had fortified himself with a number of potations.

Away went the ship over the prairies, scooting over hills and gullies, tacking and veering over the plain. Dr. Parker, who knew what broken bones meant, followed on his saddle mule. The speed made by the windwagon was so great as to amaze the passengers, accustomed as they were to nothing faster than a horse-drawn carriage.

Intoxicated by the success of his plan—and perhaps by the stimulants he had imbibed—Windwagon Thomas shouted to his passengers below deck, "Watch me run her against the wind." He put the helm over, and the craft came round grandly. But then the wind caught her, and in spite of his endeavors, the windwagon went into reverse. Nothing he could do availed. Dr. Parker had to get himself and his mule out of the way *pronto.* The other passengers became frightened, but dared not jump out, high as they were above ground. Something had locked the steering gear, and the craft went sailing round and round in a mile wide circle.

This diminished the speed somewhat, and one by one the directors of the Overland Navigation Company abandoned ship. The Captain was evidently determined to go down with colors flying. He remained on deck, until the mammoth vehicle brought up against a stake-and-rider fence on Turkey Creek.

Nothing the inventor could say would induce the Company to invest in the rest of the fleet. They had had enough of prairie seafaring. But the inventor was not downhearted. He got into his small model windwagon, and sailed away forever.

So far the white man's records. Now for the hearsay of the Indian.

Somewhere north of the Santa Fe Trail (the Arkansas River) a white man travelling in such a vehicle encountered a camp of Arapahoes. The flag the Indians mentioned was evidently the sail, though the red men had no notion that it had anything to do with the movement of the craft. In that camp was a visiting Sioux, or perhaps a Cheyenne, from whom our cloudy story comes. Apparently, the Indians found Thomas stalled, or should we say becalmed? That would account for their boast that they did not run. But the windwagon did run later, after they had made friends with its navigator. Whither he sailed, or what became of him, my informant could not tell.

A Day with a Wagon Train in 1843

It is four o'clock A.M.: the sentinels on duty have discharged their rifles—the signal that the hours of sleep are over—and every wagon and tent is pouring forth its night tenants, and slow-kindling smokes begin largely to rise and float away in the morning air. Sixty men start from the corral, spreading as they make through the vast herd of cattle and horses that make a semicircle around the encampment, the most distant perhaps two miles away.

From "A Day with the Cow Column in 1843," by Hon. Jessie Applegate, *Transactions of the Fourth Annual Reunion of the Oregon Pioneer Association for 1876 . . .*, pp. 58–59, 61–63. Salem, Oregon: E. M. Waite, Steam Printer and Bookbinder. 1877.

The herders pass the extreme verge and carefully examine for trails beyond, to see that none of the animals have strayed or been stolen during the night. This morning no trails lead beyond the outside animals in sight, and by five o'clock the herders begin to contract the great moving circle, and the well-trained animals move slowly towards camp, clipping here and there a thistle or a tempting bunch of grass on the way. In about an hour five thousand animals are close up to the encampment, and the teamsters are busy selecting their teams and driving them inside the corral to be yoked. The corral is a circle one hundred yards deep, formed with wagons connected strongly with each other; the wagon in the rear being connected with the wagon in front by its tongue and ox chains. It is a strong barrier that the most vicious ox cannot break and in case of attack from the Sioux would be no contemptible intrenchment.

From six to seven o'clock is a busy time; breakfast is to be eaten, the tents struck, the wagons loaded, and the teams yoked and brought up in readiness to be attached to their respective wagons. All know when, at seven o'clock, the signal to march sounds, that those not ready to take their proper places in the line of march must fall into the dusty rear for the day.

There are sixty wagons. They have been divided into fifteen divisions or platoons of four wagons each, and each platoon is entitled to lead in its turn. The leading platoon to-day will be the rear one to-morrow, and will bring up the rear unless some teamster, through indolence or negligence, has lost his place in the line, and is condemned to that uncomfortable post. It is within ten minutes of seven; the corral but now a strong barricade is everywhere broken, the teams being attached to the wagons. The women and children have taken their places in them. The pilot (a borderer who has passed his life on the verge of civilization and has been chosen to his post of leader from his knowledge of the savage and his experience in travel through roadless wastes) stands ready, in the midst of his pioneers and aids, to mount and lead the way. Ten or fifteen young men, not to-day on duty, form another cluster. They are ready to start on a buffalo hunt, are well mounted and well armed, as they need be, for the unfriendly Sioux have driven the buffalo out of the Platte, and the hunters must ride fifteen or twenty miles to find them. The cow drivers are hastening, as they get ready, to the rear of their charge to collect and prepare them for the day's march.

It is on the stroke of seven; the rushing to and fro, the cracking of whips, the loud command to oxen, and what seems to be the inextricable confusion of the last ten minutes has ceased. Fortunately every one had been found and every teamster is at his post. The clear notes of a trumpet sound in the front; the pilot and his guards mount their horses; the leading division of the wagons moves out of the encampment, and takes up the line of march; the rest fall into their places with the precision of clockwork, until the spot so lately full of life sinks back into that solitude that seems to reign over the broad plain and rushing river as the caravan draws its lazy length towards the distant El Dorado. . . .

* * * * *

The pilot, by measuring the ground and timing the speed of the horses, has determined the rate of each, so as to enable him to select the nooning place as nearly as the requisite grass and water can be had at the end of five hours' travel of the wagons. To-day, the ground being favorable, little time has been lost in preparing the road, so that he and his pioneers are at the nooning place an hour in advance of the wagons, which time is spent in preparing convenient watering places for the animals and digging little wells near the bank of the Platte. As the teams are not unyoked, but simply turned loose from the wagons, a corral is not formed at noon, but the wagons are drawn up in columns, four abreast, the leading wagon of each platoon on the left—the platoons being formed with that view. This brings friends together at noon as well as at night.

To-day an extra session of the Council is being held, to settle a dispute that does not admit of delay, between a proprietor and a young man who has undertaken to do a man's service on the journey for bed and board. Many such engagements exist, and much interest is taken in the manner in which this high court, from which there is no appeal, will define the rights of each party in such engagements. The Council was a high court in the most exalted sense. It was a Senate composed of the ablest and most respected fathers of the emigration. It exercised both legislative and judicial powers, and its laws and decisions proved it equal [to] and worthy [of] the high trust reposed in it. . . .

It is now one o'clock, the bugle has sounded, and the caravan has resumed its westward journey. It is in the same order, but the evening is far less animated than the morning march. A drowsiness has fallen apparently on man and beast; teamsters drop asleep on their perches, and even when walking by their teams; and the words of command are now addressed to the slowly creeping oxen in the softened tenor of women or the piping treble of children, while the snores of the teamsters make a droning accompaniment. . . .

* * * * *

. . . The sun is now getting low in the west, and at length the painstaking pilot is standing ready to conduct the train in the circle which he previously measured and marked out, which is to form the invariable fortification for the night. The leading wagons follow him so nearly around the circle that but a wagon length separates them. Each wagon follows in its track, the rear closing on the front, until its tongue and ox chains will perfectly reach from one to the other; and so accurate the measure and perfect the practice that the hindmost wagon of the train always precisely closes the gateway. As each wagon is brought into position it is dropped from its team (the teams being inside the circle), the team unyoked, and the yokes and chains are used to connect the wagon strongly with that in its front. Within ten minutes from the time the leading wagon halted, the barricade is formed, the teams unyoked and driven out to pasture. Every one is busy preparing fires of buffalo chips to cook the evening meal, pitching tents, and otherwise preparing for the night. . . .

The "Forlorn Hope" of the Donner Party

Although we were so meagerly informed, it is well that my readers should, at this point, become familiar with the experiences of the expedition know as the Forlorn Hope,[1] and also the various measures taken for our relief when our precarious condition was made known to the good people of California. It will be remembered that the Forlorn Hope was the party of fifteen which, as John Baptiste reported to us, made the last unaided attempt to cross the [Sierra Nevada] mountains.

Words cannot picture, nor mind conceive, more torturing hardships and privations than were endured by that little band on its way to the settlement. It left the camp on the sixteenth of December [,1846,] with scant rations for six days, hoping in that time to force its way to Bear Valley and there find game. But the storms which had been so pitiless

---

From *The Expedition of the Donner Party and Its Tragic Fate,* by Eliza P. Donner Houghton, pp. 77–90. Copyright, 1920, by Grafton Publishing Corporation. Los Angeles.

. . . In 1846 . . . a party attempted a new route from Fort Bridger, round the southern end of Great Salt Lake, and through the Truckee pass of the Sierra Nevada. The company was composed of George Donner, wife, and five children; Jacob Donner, wife and seven children; J. F. Reed, wife, and four children; W. H. Eddy, Breen, Pike, Foster, and others, with women and children; in all about eighty souls. . . . On the 29th of October they reached the eastern base of the Sierra, which loomed before them high into the heavens, a white wall glistening with frosted pines. Climbing upward as far as they could go, they found the top of Truckee pass five feet under snow. Returning to a cabin near their camp of the preceding night, they rested next day, and on the 31st the whole party again attempted to cross the mountains. They ascended to within three miles of the summit, where they now found ten feet of snow, each moment thickened by the clouds. It was very cold. The wind howled round the crags, and the whirling snow blinded, and every moment threatened to engulf them. They saw how impossible it was to proceed farther, so returning to the cabin, they made preparations to winter there, near what is now called Donner Lake.—*The Works of Hubert Howe Bancroft,* Vol. XXXV, *California Inter Pocula* (San Francisco, 1888), pp. 93, 99.

[1] The experiences of the Donner Party, to which he refers in a footnote, suggested to Bret Harte the opening chapters of "Gabriel Conroy"; but he has followed the sensational accounts circulated by the newspapers, and the survivors find his work a mere travesty of the facts. The narrative, however, does not purport to set forth the truth, but is confessedly imaginative.—E.P.D.H.

at the mountain camps followed the unprotected refugees with seemingly fiendish fury. After the first day from camp, its members could no longer keep together on their marches. The stronger broke the trail, and the rest followed to nightcamp as best they could.

On the third day, Stanton's sight failed, and he begged piteously to be led; but, soon realizing the heart-rending plight of his companions, he uncomplainingly submitted to his fate. Three successive nights, he staggered into camp long after the others had finished their stinted meal. Always he was shivering from cold, sometimes wet with sleet and rain.

It is recorded that at no time had the party allowed more than an ounce of food per meal to the individual, yet the rations gave out on the night of the twenty-second, while they were still in a wilderness of snowpeaks. Mr. Eddy only was better provided. In looking over his pack that morning for the purpose of throwing away any useless article, he unexpectedly found a small bag containing about a half-pound of dried bear-meat.[2] Fastened to the meat was a pencilled note from his wife, begging him to save the hidden treasure until his hour of direst need, since it might then be the means of saving his life. The note was signed, "Your own dear Elinor." With tenderest emotion, he slipped the food back, resolving to do the dear one's bidding, trusting that she and their children might live until he should return for them. The following morning, while the others were preparing to leave camp, Stanton sat beside the smoldering fire smoking his pipe. When ready to go forth, they asked him if he was coming, and he replied, "Yes, I am coming soon." Those were his parting words to his friends, and his greeting to the Angel of Death.[3] He never left that fireside, and his companions were too feeble to return for him when they found he did not come into camp.

Twenty-four hours later, the members of that hapless little band threw themselves upon the desolate waste of snow to ponder the problems of life and death; to search each other's face for answer to the question their lips durst not frame. Fathers who had left their families, and mothers who had left their babes, wanted to go back and die with them, if die they must; but Mr. Eddy and the Indians—those who had crossed the range with Stanton—declared that they would push on to the settlement. Then Mary Graves, in whose young heart were still whisperings of hope, courageously said:

"I, too, will go on, for to go back and hear the cries of hunger from my little brothers and sisters is more than I can stand. I shall go as far as I can, let the consequences be what they may."

W. F. Graves, her father, would not let his daughter proceed alone, and finally all decided to make a final, supreme effort. Yet—think of it—they were without one morsel of food!

---

[2] Mr. Eddy had killed the bear and dried the meat early in the winter.—E.P.D.H.

[3] His body was found there later by the First Relief Party.—E.P.D.H.

Even the wind seemed to hold its breath as the suggestion was made that, "were one to die, the rest might live." Then the suggestion was made that lots be cast and whoever drew the longest slip should be the sacrifice. Mr. Eddy endorsed the plan. Despite opposition from Mr. Foster and others, the slips of paper were prepared, and great-hearted Patrick Dolan drew the fatal slip. Patrick Dolan, who had come away from camp that his famishing friends might prolong their lives by means of the small stock of food which he had to leave! Harm a hair of that good man's head? Not a soul of that starving band would do it.

Mr. Eddy then proposed that they resume their journey as best they could until death should claim a victim. All acquiesced. Slowly rising to their feet, they managed to stagger and to crawl forward about three miles to a tree which furnished fuel for their Christmas fire. It was kindled with great difficulty, for in cutting the boughs, the hatchet blade flew off the handle and for a time was lost in deep snow.

Meanwhile, every puff of wind was laden with killing frost, and in sight of that glowing fire, Antonio froze to death. Mr. Graves, who was also breathing heavily, when told by Mr. Eddy that he was dying, replied that he did not care. He, however, called his daughters, Mrs. Fosdick and Mary Graves, to him, and by his parting injunctions, showed that he was still able to realize keenly the dangers that beset them. Remembering how their faces had paled at the suggestion of using human flesh for food, he admonished them to put aside the natural repugnance which stood between them and the possibility of life. He commanded them to banish sentiment and instinctive loathing, and think only of their starving mother, brothers, and sisters whom they had left in camp, and avail themselves of every means in their power to rescue them. He begged that his body be used to sustain the famishing, and bidding each farewell, his spirit left its bruised and worn tenement before half the troubles of the night were passed.

About ten o'clock, pelting hail, followed by snow on the wings of a tornado, swept every spark of fire from those shivering mortals, whose voices now mingled with the shrieking wind, calling to heaven for relief. Mr. Eddy, knowing that all would freeze to death in the darkness if allowed to remain exposed, succeeded after many efforts in getting them close together between their blankets where the snow covered them.

With the early morning, Patrick Dolan became delirious and left camp. He was brought back with difficulty and forcibly kept under cover until late in the day, when he sank into a stupor, whence he passed quietly into that sleep which knows no waking.

The crucial hour had come. Food lay before the starving, yet every eye turned from it and every hand dropped irresolute.

Another night of agony passed, during which Lemuel Murphy became delirious and called long and loud for food; but the cold was so intense that it kept all under their blankets until four o'clock in the afternoon, when Mr. Eddy succeeded in getting a fire in the trunk of a large pine tree. Whereupon, his companions, instead of seeking food, crept forth and broke off low branches, put them down before the fire and laid their attenuated forms upon them. The flames leaped up the trunk, and burned off dead boughs so that they dropped on the snow about them, but the unfortunates were too weak and too indifferent to fear the burning brands.

Mr. Eddy now fed his waning strength on shreds of his concealed bear meat, hoping that he might survive to save the giver. The rest in camp could scarcely walk, by the twenty-eighth, and their sensations of hunger were diminishing. This condition forebode delirium and death, unless stayed by the only means at hand. It was in very truth a pitiful alternative offered to the sufferers.

With sickening anguish the first morsels were prepared and given to Lemuel Murphy, but for him they were too late. Not one touched flesh of kindred body. Nor was there need of restraining hand, or warning voice to gauge the small quantity which safety prescribed to break the fast of the starving. Death would have been preferable to that awful meal, had relentless fate not said: "Take, eat that ye may live. Eat, lest ye go mad and leave your work undone!"

All but the Indians obeyed the mandate, and were strengthened and reconciled to prepare the remaining flesh to sustain them a few days longer on their journey.

Hitherto, the wanderers had been guided partly by the fitful sun, partly by Lewis and Salvador, the Indians who had come with Stanton from Sutter's Fort. In the morning, however, when they were ready to leave that spot, which was thereafter known as the "Camp of Death," Salvador, who could speak a little English, insisted that he and Lewis were lost, and, therefore, unable to guide them farther.

Nevertheless, the party at once set out and travelled instinctively until evening. The following morning they wrapped pieces of blanket around their cracked and swollen feet and again struggled onward until late in the afternoon, when they encamped upon a high ridge. There they saw beyond, in the distance, a wide plain which they believed to be the Sacramento Valley.

This imaginary glimpse of distant lowland gave them a peaceful sleep. The entire day of December 31 was spent in crossing a cañon, and every footstep left its trace of blood in the snow.

When they next encamped, Mr. Eddy saw that poor Jay Fosdick was failing, and he begged him to summon up all his courage and energy in order to reach the promised land, now so near. They were again without food; and William Foster, whose mind had become unbalanced by the long fast, was ready to kill Mrs. McCutchen or Miss Graves. Mr. Eddy confronted and intimidated the crazed sufferer, who next threatened the Indian guides, and would have carried out his threat then, had Mr. Eddy not secretly warned them against danger and urged them to flee. But nothing could save the Indians from Foster's insane passion later, when he found them on the trail in an unconscious and dying condition.

January 1, 1847, was, to the little band of eight, a day of less distressing trials; its members resumed travel early, braced by unswerving will-power. They stopped at midday and revived strength by eating the toasted strings of their snowshoes. Mr. Eddy also ate his worn out moccasins, and all felt a renewal of hope upon seeing before them an easier grade which led to night-camp where the snow was only six feet in depth. Soothed by a milder temperature, they resumed their march earlier next morning and descended to where the snow was but three feet deep. There they built their camp-fire and slightly crisped the leather of a pair of old boots and a pair of shoes which constituted their evening meal, and was the last of their effects available as food.

An extraordinary effort on the third day of the new year brought them to bare ground between patches of snow. They were still astray among the western foothills of the Sierras, and sat by a fire, under an oak tree all night, enduring hunger that was almost maddening.

Jay Fosdick was sinking rapidly, and Mr. Eddy resolved to take the gun and steal away from camp at dawn. But his conscience smote him, and he finally gave the others a hint of his intention of going in search of game, and of not returning unless successful. Not a moving creature nor a creeping thing had crossed the trail on their journey thither; but the open country before them, and minor marks well known to hunters, had caught Mr. Eddy's eye and strengthened his determination. Mrs. Pike, in dread and fear of the result, threw her arms about Mr. Eddy's neck and implored him not to leave them, and the others mingled their entreaties and protestations with hers. In silence he took his gun to go alone. Then Mary Graves declared that she would keep up with him, and without heeding further opposition the two set out. A short distance from camp they stopped at a place where a deer had recently lain.

With a thrill of emotion too intense for words, with a prayer in his heart too fervent for utterance, Mr. Eddy turned his tearful eyes toward Mary and saw her weeping like a child. A moment later, that man and that woman who had once said that they knew not how to pray, were kneeling beside that newly found track pleading in broken accents to the Giver of all life, for a manifestation of His power to save their starving band. Long restrained tears were still streaming down the cheeks of both, and soothing their anxious hearts as they rose to go in pursuit of the deer. J. Q. Thornton says:

> They had not proceeded far before they saw a large buck about eighty yards distant. Mr. Eddy raised his rifle and for some time tried to bring it to bear upon the deer, but such was his extreme weakness that he could not. He breathed a little, changed his manner of holding the gun, and made another

effort. Again his weakness prevented him from being able to hold upon it. He heard a low, suppressed sobbing behind him, and, turning around, saw Mary Graves weeping in great agitation, her head bowed, and her hands upon her face. Alarmed lest she should cause the deer to run, Mr. Eddy begged her to be quiet, which she was, after exclaiming, "Oh, I am afraid you will not kill it."

He brought the gun to his face the third time, and elevated the muzzle above the deer, let it descend until he saw the animal through the sight, when the rifle cracked. Mary immediately wept aloud, exclaiming, "Oh, merciful God, you have missed it!" Mr. Eddy assured her that he had not; that the rifle was upon it the moment of firing; and that, in addition to this, the animal had dropped its tail between its legs, which this animal always does when wounded.

His belief was speedily confirmed. The deer ran a short distance, then fell, and the two eager watchers hastened to it as fast as their weakened condition would allow. Mr. Eddy cut the throat of the expiring beast with his pocket-knife, and he and his companion knelt down and drank the warm blood that flowed from the wound.

The excitement of getting that blessed food, and the strength it imparted, produced a helpful reaction, and enabled them to sit down in peace to rest a while, before attempting to roll their treasure to the tree nearby, where they built a fire and prepared the entrails.

Mr. Eddy fired several shots after dark, so that the others might know that he had not abandoned them. Meanwhile, Mr. and Mrs. Foster, Mrs. McCutchen, and Mrs. Pike had moved forward and made their camp half-way between Mr. Eddy's new one and that of the previous night. Mr. Fosdick, however, being too weak to rise, remained at the first camp. His devoted wife pillowed his head upon her lap, and prayed that death would call them away together. Mr. Thornton continues:

The sufferer had heard the crack of Mr. Eddy's rifle at the time he killed the deer, and said, feebly, "There! Eddy has killed a deer! Now, if I can only get to him I shall live!"

But in the stillness of that cold, dark night, Jay Fosdick's spirit fled alone. His wife wrapped their only blanket about his body, and lay down beside him, hoping to freeze to death. The morning dawned bright, the sun came out, and the lone widow rose, kissed the face of her dead, and, with a small bundle in her hand, started to join Mr. Eddy. She passed a hunger-crazed man on the way from the middle camp, going to hers, and her heart grew sick, for she knew that her loved one's body would not be spared for burial rites.

She found Mr. Eddy drying his deer meat before the fire, and later saw him divide it so that each of his companions in the camps should have an equal share.

The seven survivors, each with his portion of venison, resumed travel on the sixth and continued in the foothills a number of days, crawling up the ascents, sliding down the steeps; often harassed by fears of becoming lost near the goal, yet unaware that they were astray.

The venison had been consumed. Hope had almost died in the heart of the bravest, when at the close of day on the tenth of January, twenty-five days from the date of leaving Donner Lake, they saw an Indian village at the edge of a thicket they were approaching. As the sufferers staggered forward, the Indians were overwhelmed at sight of their misery. The warriors gazed in stolid silence. The squaws wrung their hands and wept aloud. The larger children hid themselves, and the little ones clung to their mothers in fear. The first sense of horror having passed, those dusky mothers fed the unfortunates. Some brought them unground acorns to eat, while others mixed the meal into cakes and offered them as fast as they could cook them on heated stones. All except Mr. Eddy were strengthened by the food. It sickened him, and he resorted to green grass boiled in water.

The following morning the chief sent his runners to other *rancherias, en route* to the settlement, telling his people of the distress of the pale-faces who were coming toward them, and who would need food. When the Forlorn Hope was ready to move on, the chief led the way, and an Indian walked on either side of each sufferer supporting and helping the unsteady feet. At each *rancheria* the party was put in charge of a new leader and fresh supporters.

On the seventeenth, the chief with much difficulty procured, for Mr. Eddy, a gill of pine nuts which the latter found so nutritious that the following morning, on resuming travel, he was able to walk without support. They had proceeded less than a mile when his companions sank to the ground completely unnerved. They had suddenly given up and were willing to die. The Indians appeared greatly perplexed, and Mr. Eddy shook with sickening fear. Was his great effort come to naught! Should his wife and babes die while he stood guard over those who would no longer help themselves? No, he would push ahead and see what he yet could do!

The old chief sent an Indian with him as a guide and support. Relieved of the sight and personal responsibility of his enfeebled companions, Mr. Eddy felt a renewal of strength and determination. He pressed onward, scarcely heeding his dusky guide. At the end of five miles they met another Indian, and Mr. Eddy, now conscious that his feet were giving out, promised the stranger tobacco, if he would go with them and help to lead him to the "white man's house."

And so that long, desperate struggle for life, and for the sake of loved ones, ended an hour before sunset, when Mr. Eddy, leaning heavily upon the Indians, halted before the door of Colonel M. D. Richey's home, thirty-five miles from Sutter's Fort.

The first to meet him was the daughter of the house, whom he asked for bread. Thornton says:

She looked at him, burst out crying, and took hold of him to assist him into the room. He was immediately placed in bed, in which he lay unable to turn his body during four days. In a very short time he had food brought to him by

Mrs. Richey, who sobbed as she fed the miserable and frightful being before her. Shortly, Harriet, the daughter, had carried the news from house to house in the neighborhood, and horses were running at full speed from place to place until all preparations were made for taking relief to those whom Mr. Eddy had left in the morning.

William Johnson, John Howell, John Rhodes, Mr. Keiser, Mr. Sagur, Racine Tucker, and Joseph Varro assembled at Mr. Richey's immediately. The females collected the bread they had, with tea, sugar, and coffee, amounting to as much as four men could carry. Howell, Rhodes, Sagur and Tucker started at once, on foot, with the Indians as guides, and arrived at camp, between fifteen and eighteen miles distant, at midnight.

Mr. Eddy had warned the outgoing party against giving the sufferers as much food as they might want, but, on seeing them, the tender-hearted men could not deny their tearful begging for "more." One of the relief was kept busy until dawn preparing food which the rest gave to the enfeebled emigrants. This overdose of kindness made its victims temporarily very ill, but caused no lasting harm.

Early on the morning of January 18, Messrs. Richey, Johnson, Varro, and Keiser, equipped with horses and other necessaries, hurried away to bring in the refugees, together with their comrades who had gone on before. By ten o'clock that night the whole of the Forlorn Hope was safe in the homes of their benefactors. Mr. Richey declared that he and his party had retraced Mr. Eddy's track six miles, by the blood from his feet; and they could not have believed that he had traveled that eighteen miles, if they themselves had not passed over the ground in going to his discouraged companions.

Emigrants and Indians on the Plains in 1850

There were four hundred and eighty-six men and ninety women in the train, and they had one hundred and forty-eight wagons. Everything moved smoothly, until we were near the head of the North Platte river. We were now in the Sioux country, and I began to see a plenty of Indian sign. Jim [Bridger] and I had arranged that a certain signal meant for him to corral the wagons at once. As I was crossing the divide at the head of Sweet Water I discovered quite a band of Indians coming directly towards the train, but I did not think they had seen it yet. I rode back as fast as my horse could carry me. When I saw the train, I signaled to Jim to corral, and I never saw such a number of wagons corraled so quickly before or since, as they were. Jim told the women and children to leave the wagon and go inside the corral, and he told the men to stand outside with their guns, ready for

From *Capt. W. F. Drannan, Chief of Scouts,* as Pilot to Emigrant and Government Trains, Across the Plains of the Wild West of Fifty Years Ago, as told by Himself, pp. 59–63, 131–133, 135–137. Copyright, 1910, by the Rhodes & McClure Publishing Company. Chicago: Thos. W. Jackson Publishing Company.

action, but to hold their fire until he gave the word, and he said, "When you shoot, shoot to kill; and do your duty as brave men should."

In a moment, the Indians were in sight, coming over the hill at full speed. When they saw the wagons, they gave the war whoop. This scared the women, and they began to cry and scream and cling to their children. Jim jumped up on a wagon tongue and shouted at the top of his voice, "For God's sake, women, keep still, or you will all be killed."

This had the effect that he desired, and there was not a word or sound out of them. When the Indians were within a hundred yards from us their yelling was terrible to hear.

Jim now said, "Now, boys, give it to them, and let the red devils have something to yell about." And I never saw men stand up and fight better than these emigrants. They were fighting for their mothers and wives and children's lives, and they did it bravely. In a few minutes the fight was over, and what was left of the Indians got away in short order. We did not lose a man, and only one was slightly wounded. There were sixty-three dead warriors left on the field, and we captured twenty horses.

It was six miles from here to the nearest water, so we had to drive that distance to find a place to camp. We reached the camping ground a little before sunset. After attending to the teams and stationing the guards for the night Captain Davis came to Jim and me and said, "The ladies want to give you a reception tonight."

Jim said, "What for?"

Davis replied, "Saving our lives from those horrible savages."

Jim answered, "Why, durn it all, ain't that what you are paying us for? We just done our duty and no more, as we intend to do all the way to California."

By this time there was a dozen women around us. With the others was a middle-aged woman. She said, "Now, you men with the buckskin clothes, come and take supper with us. It is now all ready."

Jim said, "Come, Willie, let's go eat, for I am hungry and tired too."

While we were eating supper, three or four young ladies came up to us, and asked me if I didn't want to dance.

"The boys are cleaning off the ground now, and I want you for my first pardner," she said with a smile and a blush.

Jim said, "Will can't dance anything but the scalp dance."

One of the girls said, "What kind of a dance is that?"

Jim replied, "If the Indians had got some of your scalps this afternoon you would have known something about it by this time."

Jim told them that when the Indians scalped a young girl, they took the scalp to their wigwam and then gave a dance to show the young squaws what a brave deed they had done. "And all you girls had better watch out that they don't have some of your scalps to dance around before you get to California; but if you wish us to, Will and I will dance the scalp dance to-night, so you can see how it is done."

When they had the ground all fixed for the dance Jim and I took our handkerchiefs and put them on a couple of sticks, stuck the sticks into the ground, and went through the Indian scalp dance, making all the hideous motions with jumps and screams, loud enough to start the hair from its roots, after which Jim explained to them this strange custom telling them that if any of them was unfortunate enough to fall into the Indians' hands this was the performance that would be had around their scalps.

The girls said with a shudder they had seen enough of that kind of dancing without the Indians showing them. The lady who had invited us to supper said, "Now, girls, you see what these men have done for us, they have saved our lives, and do you realize the obligation we are under to them? Now, let us do everything we can for their comfort until we reach California."

And I must say that I never saw more kind-hearted people than these men and women were to us all the way, on this long and dangerous journey.

* * * * *

The next morning we pulled out of this place by the way of Landers. That afternoon about two o'clock I saw a small band of Indians coming directly towards us. They were about a mile away when I first saw them. I rode to the foot of a little hill which was close to me at the time I saw them. I dismounted from my horse and tied him to a sage brush and then I crept to the top of the hill to see how many there were of them. I watched until they were within a half a mile of my hiding place; I then counted thirty. I took them to be a hunting party by the way they were traveling. I signaled to my scouts to come to me at once. When they reached me the Indians were less than a quarter of a mile from me. I told them what was coming down the ravine, and told them to see that their guns and pistols were in order, "for as soon as they round that little point yonder, we will charge on them, and we will kill everyone we can. Now, don't shoot until we get within thirty yards of them. I will say, 'fire,' then I want every man to get an Indian. Now don't get rattled but shoot to kill and shout as loud as you can. It don't make any difference what you say, only make as big a noise as you can, and as soon as you empty your guns, pull your pistols and go after them."

In a moment more the time had come to act, and when I said, "Charge," every man responded and did his duty. I had been in several Indian fights before, but I never saw Indians so taken by surprise as this band was. They did not draw their arrows or run, until we had fired into them, and after they turned to run, they had gone at least two hundred yards before I saw them try to shoot an arrow.

We got fourteen of them in the first charge, and inside of three hundred yards, we got six more. The remainder had reached the thick brush, so we let them go.

We now commenced catching the horses. We caught sixteen horses, and they all had good hair ropes around their necks. We tied them all together and I left them in charge of two men, and the rest of us went to take the scalps of the Indians, and I was surprised to find when I said, "We will take the scalps of these Indians," that the men did not know what I meant. I showed them how to take the scalps off, and then they asked what I was going to do with them. I told them I was going to give them to Jim Bridger, and he would make guards out of them. Jim wouldn't take the biggest hundred dollar bill you could offer him for these scalps when he gets his hands on them.

One of the men said, "What will Bridger do with them horrid bloody things?"

I told him to just wait until night and then Jim would explain the use they would be to him. I tied the scalps to my saddle, left two men to care for the horses we had captured and bidding the others to follow me I struck out for the place where we were to camp that night.

Jim told me that night how surprised the emigrants were when the train came to the men who had charge of the horses, and saw the bodies of the dead Indians.

He said, "I had to let them stop the train a few minutes so they could all look at them." He said, "Some of the women wanted to know what had become of the hair off the top of their heads. I told them that I reckoned Will had taken them to give to me."

"And what are you going to do with those horrid Indians' hair?" one woman inquired.

"I am going to protect you and the rest of the train with them," he answered her.

Jim had cut long sticks, and had hung the scalps on the wagons, so they could be seen quite a distance away. After he had them all fixed he and I were standing together talking, he telling me the effect the sight of the dead Indians had on the emigrants and especially when they saw that their scalps had been taken off.

Two of the women came to us and invited us to eat supper with them at their tent. I will here explain to the reader that every family in the train had their own separate tent and cooked at their own fire. Jim and I accepted the invitations as we always did of the first that invited us to each meal.

As we finished eating it seemed as though all the women of the train gathered around us. There was one old lady in the crowd who seemed to be the one selected to do the talking. She said, "Mr. Bridger, I want you to tell me truly don't you think it was awfully wicked to cut those scalps off those Indians' heads and then hang the dreadful bloody things up on the wagons for us to look at?" And the tears were in her eyes as she finished her question.

Jim replied, "The best thing that has been done since we started on this trip is killing those Indians and better still taking their scalps. I did not hang those scalps up on your wagons for you to look at. I hung them up for the Indians that are alive to look at, and I will tell you this, the Indians will never attack the train as long as they see those same bloody things hanging there, for they will think they will lose their own scalps, if they do. I would rather have these Indians scalps to protect you with than a hundred of the best soldiers in the United States Army. The Indian does not fear death, but he dreads the thought of having his scalp taken off his head, for it is the Indian's belief that he cannot enter the happy hunting grounds after death if his scalp has been taken off his head, and I want to impress on your minds that if this train should be attacked, everyone of you that fell into the hands of the Indians, it would not matter whether they be men or women, would have their scalps torn off, and the same scalps would be hanging up on the Indians' wigwams for the squaws to dance around and I want all you ladies to distinctly understand that Will Drannan or myself will do nothing while we have charge of this train but what will be of benefit to you all, and will bear the strictest investigation."

Mormon Handcart Pioneers

When we [Swiss Mormon immigrants] reached Florence, Nebraska, near present Omaha, we were forced to stop for a while because there were not teams enough to take us across the plains to Salt Lake City. The men set to work making handcarts and my father, being a carpenter, helped to make thirty-three of them. Ours was a small two wheeled vehicle with two shafts and a cover on top. The carts were very much like those the street sweepers use in the cities to-day, except that ours were made entirely of wood without even an iron rim.

* * * * *

. . . Our company was the tenth and last to cross the Plains in handcarts. . . .

Our company was organized with Oscar O. Stoddard as captain. It contained 126 persons with twenty-two handcarts and three provision wagons drawn by oxen. We set out from Florence on July 6, 1860, for our thousand-mile trip. There were six to our cart. Father and Mother pulled it; Rosie (two years old) and Christian (six months old) rode; John (nine) and I (six) walked. Sometimes, when it was down hill, they let me ride too.

The first night out the mosquitoes gave us a hearty welcome. Father

---

From *Recollections of a Handcart Pioneer of 1860*, with Some Account of Frontier Life in Utah and Nevada, by Mary Ann Hafen, pp. 21, 22–26. Copyright, 1938, by LeRoy R. Hafen. Denver, Colorado: Privately Printed for Her Descendants.

had bought a cow to take along, so we could have milk on the way. At first he tied her to the back of the cart, but she would sometimes hang back, so he thought he would make a harness and have her pull the cart while he led her. By this time Mother's feet were so swollen that she could not wear shoes, but had to wrap her feet with cloth. Father thought that by having the cow pull the cart Mother might ride. This worked well for some time.

One day a group of Indians came riding up on horses. Their jingling trinkets, dragging poles, and strange appearance frightened the cow and sent her chasing off with the cart and children. We were afraid that the children might be killed, but the cow fell into a deep gully and the cart turned upside down. Although the children were under the trunk and bedding, they were unhurt, but after that Father did not hitch the cow to the cart again. He let three Danish boys take her to hitch to their cart. Then the Danish boys, each in turn, would help Father pull our cart.

Of course, we had many other difficulties. One was that it was hard for the carts to keep up with the three provision wagons drawn by ox teams. Often the men pulling the carts would try to take shortcuts through the brush and sand in order to keep up.

After about three weeks my Mother's feet became better so she could wear shoes again. She would get so discouraged and downhearted; but Father never lost courage. He would always cheer her up by telling her that we were going to Zion, that the Lord would take care of us, and that better times were coming.

Even when it rained the company did not stop traveling. A cover on the handcart shielded the two younger children. The rest of us found it more comfortable moving than standing still in the drizzle. In fording streams the men often carried the children and weaker women across on their backs. The company stopped over on Sundays for rest, and meetings were held for spiritual comfort and guidance. At night, when the handcarts were drawn up in a circle and the fires were lighted, the camp looked quite happy. Singing, music, and speeches by the leaders cheered every one. I remember that we stopped one night at an old Indian camp ground. There were many bright-colored beads in the ant hills.

At times we met or were passed by the overland stage coach with its passengers and mail bags and drawn by four fine horses. When the Pony Express dashed past it seemed almost like the wind racing over the prairie.

Our provisions began to get low. One day a herd of buffalo ran past and the men of our company shot two of them. Such a feast as we had when they were dressed! Each family was given a piece of meat to take along. My brother John, who pushed at the back of the cart, used to tell how hungry he was all the time and how tired he got from pushing. He said he felt that if he could just sit down for a few minutes he would feel so much better. But instead, Father would ask if he couldn't push a little harder. Mother was nursing the baby and could not help much, especially when the food ran short and she grew weak. When rations were reduced Father gave Mother a part of his share of the food, so he was not so strong either.

When we got that chunk of buffalo meat Father put it in the handcart. My brother John remembered that it was the fore part of the week and that father said he would save it for Sunday dinner. John said, "I was so very hungry and the meat smelled so good to me while pushing at the handcart that I could not resist. I had a little pocket knife and with it I cut off a piece or two each half day. Although I expected a severe whipping when Father found it out, I cut off little pieces each day. I would chew them so long that they got white and perfectly tasteless. When Father came to get the meat he asked me if I had been cutting off some of it. I said, 'Yes, I was so hungry I could not let it alone.' Instead of giving me a scolding or whipping, Father turned away and wiped tears from his eyes."

Even when we were on short rations, if we met a band of Indians, the Captain of our Company would give them some of the provisions so the Indians would let us go by in safety. Food finally became so low that word was sent to Salt Lake City and in about two weeks fresh supplies arrived.

At last, when we reached the top of Emigration Canyon, overlooking Salt Lake, on that September day, 1860, the whole company stopped to look down through the valley. Some yelled and tossed their hats in the air. A shout of joy arose at the thought that our long trip was over. that we had at last reached Zion, the place of rest. We all gave thanks to God for helping us safely over the Plains and mountains to our destination.

Joe Meek's Mule

[Joe Meek] said he once took a party of volunteers out in the Burnt River country, in Eastern Oregon, to protect incoming emigrants, and that his soldiers suddenly met a body of Indians. They had just crossed a river, but they decided to cross again, and they did so without any orders. His mount was a bucking mule that would budge for neither whip nor spur, and in consequence he was left alone while his comrades were making off down the river for a ford. He called out to them lustily, "Come back and fight the Indians, there's not more than a dozen of 'em, we can whip 'em." But they proceeded to go up the

From *Early Oregon*, Jottings of Personal Recollections of a Pioneer of 1850, by George E. Cole, pp. 44–45. Entered according to Act of Congress in the year 1905, by Geo. E. Cole, in the office of the Librarian of Congress at Washington. [No publisher or place.]

opposite river bank in full retreat. Suddenly an arrow struck his mule, which forthwith plunged down the river bank, forded the stream, and struck the trail far ahead of his companions, who were looking back to find him. Shouting, "Come on, boys, you can't whip 'em; there's more than a thousand of 'em," he led the way to the rear.

The Bullwhacker of the Plains

A curious character of overland life, when the plains were covered with teams, and long trains of freight-wagons, was the bullwhacker. He is in size and shape usually of very large proportions; very strong, long, unkempt hair, and face covered with the stiffest of beards. Eight or ten yoke of oxen were usually attached to each wagon, and often two wagons were doubled up; i.e., the tongue of the second wagon passed under the body of the wagon just before it, and then securely fastened. By the side of his wagon hung his trusty axe and ready rifle, and on the tops of the wagons were spread the red blankets used for their cover at night. Of the bullwhacker, it is said that his *oath* and his *whip* are both the longest ever known. The handle of the ordinary whip is not more than three feet in length, but the lash, which is of braided rawhide, is seldom less than twenty feet long. From the wooden handle, the lash swells gradually out for about six feet, where it is nearly ten inches in circumference (the point called the "belly"); from here it tapers to within a foot of the end, which terminates in the form of a ribbon-shaped thong. This is called by some facetiously a "persuader," and under its influence it will make the ox-team progress at the magic rate of twenty miles per day. The effect on a refractory ox is quite forcible. The lazy ox occasionally receives a reminder in the shape of a whack in the flank, that causes him to double up as if seared with a red-hot iron.

The bullwhacker is universally regarded as the champion swearer of America. He is more profane than the mate of a Mississippi River packet, and his own word is good to the effect that he "kin drink more whisky." The writer who heard this says that "accompanying this statement were *some of the most outstanding oaths that ever fell on the ear.*"

General Sherman humorously tells a story in defence of the extremely profane mule-driver who kept his trains so well closed up during the long marches of the army under his command. It is to this effect: "One of the members of a freighting firm in St. Louis desired to

---

From *The Pacific Tourist,* J. R. Bowman's Illustrated Trans-Continental Guide of Travel, from the Atlantic to the Pacific Ocean . . ., Frederick E. Shearer, Editor, with Special Contributions by Prof. F. V. Hayden, Clarence King, Capt. Dutton, A. C. Peale, Joaquin Miller, and J. B. Davis . . ., pp. 56–57. New York: J. R. Bowman, Publisher. 1882–1883.

discourage the continual blasphemy of the bullwhackers in their employ. Orders were accordingly issued to their train-masters to discharge any man that should curse the cattle. The wagon-masters were selected more for their piety than for any extensive knowledge of their duties in the handling of trains. The outfit had not proceeded more than a hundred and fifty miles before it was stuck fast. A messenger was dispatched to the firm with the information that the cattle would not pull a pound unless they were *cursed as usual.* Permission to do this was requested and granted, after which the train proceeded to Salt Lake, to which place good time was made."

The bullwhacker is astonishingly accurate with his lash. One of his favorite pastimes is to cut a coin from the top of a stick stuck loosely into the earth. If the coin is knocked off without disturbing the stake, it is his; if the stake is disturbed, the thrower loses the value of the coin. A curious incident is told of a bullwhacker, noted for the accuracy with which he throws his lash. He bet a comrade a pint of whisky that he could cut the cloth on the back of his pantaloons without touching the skin beneath. The bet was accepted. The individual put himself in position, stooping over to give fair chance. The blow was delivered carefully but in earnest, and thereon ensued the tallest jump ever put on record. The owner being minus a portion of his skin, as well as a large fragment of his breeches, and the bullwhacker's sorrowful cry, "Thunder, I've lost the whisky."

Rules of the Road

. . . When the road was narrow, as it always was in the hill country, or restricted to two passable muddy ruts, as it often was even in the Plains country, and when one outfit met another, which should get out of the way? Ethically, it was up to the lighter one to make the circuit; actually, there was often a dispute. Old Jim once met a teamster; they came nose to nose in the fairway. "Well," said the stranger, "reckon we'll camp right here." Old Jim agreed, not too pleasantly. He climbed off his horse and began pulling camp stuff off his wagon. The stranger gave a brief look at Old Jim's mules, and then at Old Jim himself. "Oh, hell," he decided, "I ain't got time to stay here all week." He pulled out to one side and drove on.

From *The Golden Hoof,* The Story of the Sheep of the Southwest, by Winifred Kupper, p. 171. Copyright, 1945, by Alfred A. Knopf, Inc. New York.

Western Travel Talk

Infantry soldiers are called by the Indians "heap walk men."

Indians call Major Powell's boats "water ponies."

Long trains of cars are called by the Indians "heap wagon, no hoss," ["bad medicine wagon"].

"Hash houses"—roadside restaurants. Waiters are called "hash slingers."

Telegraph operators are called "lightning shovers."

On the plains bacon is called "sowbelly"; Indian tents, "wigwams," "lodges," "tepees," "wickeeups."

Teamsters on the plains call a meal a "grub pile."

The Indians call the telegraph the "whispering spirit."

Old settlers on the Plains call Emigrants "Pilgrims"; . . . Ox drivers, "bull-whackers"; mule drivers, "mule skinners"; Utah whisky, "Valley Tan." To be out of money is "in the Cap"; "on the bed rock," etc.

The Pony Express

I. Cody Outwits the Road Agents

. . . It had become known in some mysterious manner, past finding out, that there was to be a large sum of money sent through by Pony Express, and that was what the road agents were after.

After [their] killing the other rider, and failing to get the treasure, Cody very naturally thought that they would make another effort to secure it; so when he reached the next relay station he walked about a while longer than was his wont.

This was to perfect a little plan he had decided upon, which was to take a second pair of saddle-pouches and put something in them and leave them in sight, while those that held the valuable express packages

---

From *Crofutt's Trans-Continental Tourist's Guide,* Containing a Full and Authentic Description of over Five Hundred Cities, Towns, Villages, Stations, Government Forts and Camps, Mountains, Lakes, Rivers, Sulphur, Soda and Hot Springs, Scenery, Watering Places, Summer Resorts; where to look for and hunt the Buffalo, Antelope, Deer, and other game; Trout Fishing, etc., etc., in fact, to tell you what is worth seeing—where to see it—where to go—how to go—and whom to stop with while passing over the Union Pacific Railroad, Central Pacific Railroad of Cal., Their Branches and Connections by Stage and Water, from the Atlantic to the Pacific Ocean, Third Vol., Second Annual Revise, pp. 141, 142, 183, 204. Entered according to Act of Congress, in the year 1871, by Geo. A. Crofutt, in the office of the Librarian of Congress, at Washington.

From *The Great Salt Lake Trail,* by Colonel Henry Inman and Colonel William F. Cody, pp. 193–198. Copyright, 1898, by The Macmillan Company. New York and London.

As told by a "friend who was once a station agent."

he folded up in his saddle-blanket in such a way that they could not be seen unless a search was made for them. The truth was, Cody knew that he carried the valuable package, and it was his duty to protect it with his life.

So with the clever scheme to outwit the road agents, if held up, he started once more upon his flying trip. He carried his revolver ready for instant use and flew along the trail with every nerve strung to meet any danger which might confront him. He had an idea where he would be halted, if halted at all, and it was a lonesome spot in a valley, the very place for a deed of crime.

As he drew near the spot, he was on the alert, and yet when two men suddenly stepped out from among the shrubs and confronted him, it gave him a start in spite of his nerve. They had him covered with rifles and brought him to a halt with the words: "Hold! Hands up, Pony Express Bill, for we know yer, my boy, and what yer carries."

"I carry the express; and it's hanging for you two if you interfere with me," was the plucky response.

"Ah, we don't want you, Billy, unless you force us to call in your checks; but it's what you carry we want."

"It won't do you any good to get the pouch, for there is nothing valuable in it."

"We are to be the judges of that, so throw us the valuables or catch a bullet. Which shall it be, Billy?"

The two men stood directly in front of the pony-rider, each one covering him with a rifle, and to resist was certain death. So Cody began to unfasten his pouches slowly, while he said, "Mark my words, men, you'll hang for this."

"We'll take chances on that, Bill."

The pouches being unfastened now, Cody raised them with one hand, while he said in an angry tone, "If you will have them, take them." With this he hurled the pouches at the head of one of them, who quickly dodged and turned to pick them up, just as Cody fired upon the other with the revolver in his left hand.

The bullet shattered the man's arm, while, driving the spurs into the flanks of his mare, Cody rode directly over the man who was stooping to pick up the pouches, his back turned to the pony-rider.

The horse struck him a hard blow that knocked him down, while he half fell on top of him, but was recovered by a touch of the spurs and bounded on, while the daring pony-rider gave a wild triumphant yell as he sped on like the wind.

The fallen man, though hurt, scrambled to his feet as soon as he could, picked up his rifle, and fired after the retreating youth, but without effect, and young Cody rode on, arriving at the station on time, and reported what had happened.

He had, however, no time to rest, for he was compelled to start back with his express pouches. He thus made the remarkable ride of three hundred and twenty-four miles without sleep, and stopping only to eat his meals, and resting then but a few moments. For saving the express pouches he was highly complimented by all, and years afterward he had the satisfaction of seeing his prophecy regarding the two road agents verified, for they were both captured and hanged by vigilantes for their many crimes.

II. Cody Is Chased by Indians

"There's Injun signs about, so keep your eyes open." So said the station-boss of the Pony Express, addressing young Cody, who had dashed up to the cabin, his horse panting like a hound, and the rider ready for the fifteen-mile flight to the next relay. "I'll be on the watch, boss, you bet," said the pony-rider, and with a yell to his fresh pony he was off like an arrow from a bow.

Down the trail ran the fleet pony like the wind, leaving the station quickly out of sight, and dashing at once into the solitude and dangers of the vast wilderness. Mountains were upon either side, towering cliffs here and there overhung the trail, and the wind sighed through the forest of pines like the mourning of departed spirits. Gazing ahead, the piercing eyes of the young rider saw every tree, bush, and rock, for he knew but too well that a deadly foe, lurking in ambush, might send an arrow or a bullet to his heart at any moment. Gradually, far down the valley, his quick glance fell upon a dark object above the boulder directly in his trail.

He saw the object move and disappear from sight down behind the rock. Without appearing to notice it, or checking his speed in the slightest, he held steadily upon his way. But he took in the situation at a glance, and saw that on each side of the boulder the valley inclined. Upon one side was a fringe of heavy timber, upon the other, a precipice, at the base of which were massive rocks.

"There is an Indian behind that rock, for I saw his head," muttered the young rider, as his horse flew on. Did he intend to take his chances, and dash along the trail directly by his ambushed foe? It would seem so, for he still stuck to the trail.

A moment more and he would be within range of a bullet, when, suddenly dashing his spurs into the pony's sides, Bill Cody wheeled to the right, and in an oblique course headed for the cliff. This proved to the foe in ambush that he was suspected, if not known, and at once there came the crack of a rifle, the puff of smoke rising above the rock where he was concealed. At the same moment a yell went up from a score of throats, and out of the timber on the other side of the valley darted a number of Indians, and these rode to head off the rider.

Did he turn back and seek safety in a retreat to the station? No! he was made of sterner stuff, and would run the gauntlet.

Out from behind the boulder, where they had been lying in ambush, sprang two braves in all the glory of their war-paint. Their horses were in the timber with their comrades, and, having failed to get a close shot at the pony-rider, they sought to bring him down at long range with their rifles. The bullets pattered under the hoofs of the flying pony, but he was unhurt, and his rider pressed him to his full speed.

With set teeth, flashing eyes, and determined to do or die, Will Cody rode on in the race for life, the Indians on foot running swiftly toward him, and the mounted braves sweeping down the valley at full speed.

The shots of the dismounted Indians failing to bring down the flying pony or their human game, the mounted redskins saw that their only chance was to overtake their prey by their speed. One of the number, whose war-bonnet showed that he was a chief, rode a horse that was much faster than the others, and he drew quickly ahead. Below the valley narrowed to a pass not a hundred yards in width, and if the pony rider could get to this wall ahead of his pursuers, he would be able to hold his own along the trail in the ten-mile run to the next relay station.

But, though he saw that there was no more fear from the two dismounted redskins, and that he would come out well in advance of the band on horseback, there was one who was most dangerous. That one was the chief, whose fleet horse was bringing him on at a terrible pace, and threatening to reach there at the same time with the pony-rider.

Nearer and nearer the two drew toward the path, the horse of Cody slightly ahead, and the young rider knew that a death-struggle was at hand. He did not check his horse, but kept his eyes alternately upon the pass and the chief. The other Indians he did not then take into consideration. At length that happened for which he had been looking.

When the chief saw that he would come out of the race some thirty yards behind his foe, he seized his bow and quick as a flash had fitted an arrow for its deadly flight. But in that instant Cody has also acted, and a revolver had sprung from his belt and a report followed the touching of the trigger. A wild yell burst from the lips of the chief, and he clutched madly at the air, reeled, and fell from his saddle, rolling over like a ball as he struck the ground.

The death-cry of the chief was echoed by the braves coming on down the valley, and a shower of arrows was sent after the fugitive pony-rider. An arrow slightly wounded his horse, but the others did no damage, and in another second Cody had dashed into the pass well ahead of his foes. It was a hot chase from then on until the pony-rider came within sight of the next station, when the Indians drew off and Cody dashed in on time, and in another minute was away on his next run.

Following the Buffalo Trails

. . . Fortunately we had the well-worn buffalo-trails that there run almost due north and south—the old paths over which they formerly went to and from the Platte for water—and following up one of these, after an hour or two, we found ourselves in sight of the river again. These trails are no wider than ordinary cow-paths, but they are worn deep into the soil, and show by their great number and depth what countless herds of buffalo must have roamed here in other days. They are a sure guide up and down the bluffs, many of which are so precipitous that safe ascent and descent elsewhere seems impossible. But the buffalo, by a wise instinct, seems to have hit just the right point, and deserves credit for such skilful engineering.

The Overland Stage

I. Stage Driver's Yell

While making my first trip to Denver, I must own up that I was somewhat frightened the second night out from Atchison. I did not know, when I first started out, that it was the custom of the drivers, when approaching a station at night, to most always send up a terrible yell. This was done to awaken the stock tender, so he might have the team harnessed, and also that the driver might be ready who was to succeed the incoming one on the next drive. We were going up the Little Blue valley. While asleep down in the front boot, under the driver's feet, I was suddenly awakened by what seemed to me one of the most unearthly yells I had ever heard from any human being. It appeared like the horrible yell of an Indian on the war-path. I felt quite sure that the savages were after somebody's scalp, but said nothing to the driver, a stranger. Soon I was agreeably disappointed when I discovered that I had only heard the yell of the driver. What he was making such a terrible yelling for was to me a puzzle at the time. I soon learned, however; and before I had made many trips could imi-

---

From *Across America; or, the Great West and the Pacific Coast,* by James F. Rusling, p. 52. Entered according to Act of Congress, in the year 1874, by James F. Rusling, in the office of the Librarian of Congress at Washington. New York: Sheldon & Company. 1875.

From *The Overland Stage to California,* Personal Reminiscences and Authentic History of the Great Overland Stage Line and Pony Express from the Missouri River to the Pacific Ocean, by Frank A. Root, Messenger in Charge of the Express, and Agent of the Post-Office Department to Look after the Transportation of the Mails over the Great Stage Line across the Plains and Mountains to California, . . . and William Elsey Connelley, . . . pp. 88–89, 91–92, 97. Copyright, 1901, by Frank A. Root and William Elsey Connelley. Topeka, Kansas. Reprinted, 1950, by Long's College Book Co., Columbus, Ohio.

tate the yell and make a screech as horrible-sounding as any driver. The spelling and pronouncing of the yell might be something like "Ah-whooh-wah," but only those who have heard it from one of the "Overland" boys can have the remotest idea of the shrill and hideous-sounding noise. There was another yell that some of the drivers, not being possessed of the soundest lungs, used. It was "Yep, yep, yep," but there was nothing specially hideous about it.

II. Detained by a "Hot Box"

Now and then some rather strange things occurred on the "Overland." It was imperative that the stage-coach axles be greased (or rather "doped," as the boys used to call it) at every "home" station, and these were from twenty-five to fifty miles apart. This duty had time and again been impressed upon drivers by the division agents, but occasionally one of them would forget the important work. As a natural consequence the result would be a "hot box."

One afternoon early in the summer of 1863, while we were on the rolling prairies near the Little Blue river, one of the front wheels of the stage was suddenly clogged and would not turn. On examination it was found to be sizzling hot. The stage had to stop and wait until the axle cooled off. As soon as practicable, the driver took off the wheel and made an inspection, the passengers and messenger holding up the axle. On further examination, it was found that the spindle had begun to "cut," and there was no alternative but to "dope" it before we could go any farther. But we were stumped; there was no "dope" on the stage.

The driver, an old-timer at staging, suggested, since "necessity is the mother of invention," that as a last resort he would bind a few blades of grass around the spindle, which he was certain would run us part way to the station, and we could stop and repeat the experiment. But one of the passengers chanced to have a piece of cheese in his grip sack, and a little of it was sliced off and applied; and it worked admirably, and was sufficient to run the coach safely to the next station, where the difficulty was quickly remedied by application of the proper "dope."

III. "Help Yourself to the Mustard"

A great many of the stock tenders out on the frontier who lived between "home" stations kept "bachelor's hall" and lived by themselves. At one of the stations on the eastern slope of the Rockies northwest of Latham was one; and at the hour for dinner one day in the summer of 1864 a weary pilgrim from the East, making his way overland, chanced to stop for a drink of water and to rest. He was invited by the host to dine. "I don't care if I do," quickly responded the anxious footman, and he took a seat at the table. The host cut off a slice of fat pork and the guest was asked to pass his plate. "Thank you," said he, "but I never eat it." "Very well," said the host; "just help yourself to the mustard"; and the host proceeded with his meal. It happened that fat pork and mustard comprised the entire list of edible articles then in the stock tender's house; and he offered his guest the best he had. For a long time it was a regular standing joke of the stage boys along the line, when any one refused anything at the table, to say, "Help yourself to the mustard."

Hank Monk, Stage Driver

. . . Who that has ever traveled over the Sierra Nevadas, on the Pioneer line of stages, but has encountered Hank Monk, who has achieved a celebrity on the *stage* almost rivaling that of Charles Kean, . . . and fully equal to that of "Mike Fink, the last of the Boatmen," in the days of Mississippi broad-horn-dom. Ada Clare and Lisle Lester have alike chaunted the praises of this bold whip of the snow-capped Sierras. Hank, besides being a dashing driver, always up to schedule time, as like the most of his class, from old Uncle Charley Sackrider—who for a long time drove on the Pioneer from Folsom to Placerville—down to the Schermerhorn's Boys, with the whip and neophytes in handling the ribbons—a bit of a wag withal.

On one trip, a nervous old gentleman in spectacles, unused to mountain travel, crossing the Sierras on his way to Washoe, by some means happening to be placed alongside our hero, and everything being new to him, for it was first appearance on *any stage* in California, was curious to know the why and wherefore of everything, wanting detailed explanations, and distracting the attention of the "Governor" of the vehicle from his fiery team; and, by the way, if steamboats parade the placard, "NO TALKING TO THE MAN AT THE WHEEL!" does it not behoove stage proprietors to put up a similar warning, not to annoy with trifling questions the man who has charge of the *four*—which, with the *fore* and hind ones, make eight—*wheels* of a coach filled with passengers. Looking over his gold-rimmed specs, and casting his eyes down among the mail-bags in the "boot," at their feet, he spied a hatchet; a horrid suspicion flashed across the nervous man's mind, and he tremblingly enquired the use of this indispensable accompaniment which his imagination distorted into the tomahawk of the "ruthless savage," of whose murderous deeds he had read in the "yaller kivered" rawhead and bloody bones stories familiar to his youthful days.

Knowing his man, and wishing to put a stop to his inquisitorial, leading and cross-questioning, he gravely replied: "Well, sir, I don't

---

From "A Chapter on Stage Travelling and Stage Drivers," from the Special Correspondent of the *Alta California*, "Traviata," Away up the North Fork of the American, Placer County, October 30, 1864, *Daily Alta California*, San Francisco, November 18, 1864.

often tell the use I make of that hatchet; but as you seem to be a sensible man, and one whom I can trust with the secret, I'll tell *you*. The fact is, there have a good many accidents occurred on this line; limbs been broken, and other injuries from the overturning of coaches, for which the Company have had to pay heavy damages; now, in order to avoid any such after-claps, when an upset occurs, and passengers have legs or arms broken, or are otherwise seriously injured, we end the matter by knocking them in the head with a hatchet and putting them out of their misery at once."

The old gentleman looked horrified, but remained speechless—for the remainder of Hank's "trick"; the story of the "Hatchet of Horror," immortalized alike by Dickens and Hank Monk, was too much for him. He swallowed it all, but the digestion interfered with that of the dinner he got at Strawberry, at which point he gladly exchanged for an inside seat with a young man who wished to ride outside and smoke; to whom, in consideration of the "Principe" handed over to the driver, the latter "norated" the story of *smoking* "the ancient marinere" over the mountains past Lake Bigler. When "mine ancient" returned to San Francisco, he lost no time in laying the matter before Louis McLane, the President of the Pioneer Company, who, while listening to the story, could scarcely control his risibles—and upon informing the old 'un that he had been sold by one of the best drivers and maddest wags on any of the stage lines in existence, could not see it, but went his way marveling at the wickedness of corporations in general, and the atrocities of a "perverse generation" of stage drivers in particular.

On one occasion, a Judge not unknown to Bulkhead fame, on his way to Humboldt, was driven over the Summit by our hero; it so fell out that he was the only passenger and had the coach solitary and alone to himself. It likewise happened that owing to some unavoidable delay the driver, who was always up and ahead, was on this occasion considerably behind time. Knowing the mettle and temper of his team, he let them out, and, as the phrase goes, the stage "went kitin" down the mountain, the fore wheels of the coach alternately rearing, and the hind wheels kicking up, while the body of the vehicle would spin around with all the velocity and buzz of a humming top. The ex-judicial bounded up and down like an India rubber ball; his face and figure assuming all the wriggling and extortions of a gutta-percha toy in the hands of Young America, he roared, he bellowed, cried "Stop driver and let me out; d—n you let me out;" but he might as well have called to the wind sweeping down the gorge, along whose rugged and precipitious edges he was waltzing to most fearful music. He bethought him of his sins of Bulkhead "bribery and corruption." It is even surmised that he prayed, *preying* being as familiar to him as household words.

Stopping a moment to wet the mouths of his team, the aforesaid, with a wrathful countenance and threatening gesture, remarked

"Young man, I am Judge—, and I'll report you to headquarters when I get back to San Francisco."

"You can report and be d—d," was the reply of the respondent in case, perhaps more emphatic than polite, but he had no fear of any arrest for "contempt of Court" before his eyes. "I am Hank Monk, driver of the Pioneer Company's stage. From no fault of mine I'm late, but I'll make my time if I kill every d—d one-horse Judge in California."

The solitary stage passenger not James, the novelist's, "horseman," finding out his man, held his peace, did not report him to headquarters, and we got our version from one of the fraternity.

Horace Greeley's Ride to Placerville

When Mr. Greeley was in California, ovations awaited him at every town. He had written powerful leaders in the *Tribune* in favour of the Pacific Railroad, which had greatly endeared him to the citizens of the Golden State. And therefore they made much of him when he went to see them.

At one town the enthusiastic populace tore his celebrated white coat to pieces, and carried the pieces home to remember him.

The citizens of Placerville prepared to fête the great journalist, and an extra coach, with extra relays of horses, was chartered of the California Stage Company to carry him from Folsom to Placerville—distance, forty miles. The extra was in some way delayed, and did not leave Folsom until late in the afternoon. Mr. Greeley was to be fêted at seven o'clock that evening by the citizens of Placerville, and it was altogether necessary that he should be there by that hour. So the Stage Company said to Henry Monk, the driver of the extra, "Henry, this great man must be there by seven to-night." And Henry answered, "The great man shall be there."

The roads were in an awful state, and during the first few miles out of Folsom slow progress was made.

"Sir," said Mr. Greeley, "are you aware that I *must* be at Placerville at seven o'clock to-night?"

"I've got my orders!" laconically returned Henry Monk.

Still the coach dragged slowly forward.

"Sir," said Mr. Greeley, "this is not a trifling matter. I *must* be there at seven!"

Again came the answer, "I've got my orders!"

But the speed was not increased, and Mr. Greeley chafed away an-

---

From *The Complete Works* of Charles E. Browne, Better Known as "Artemus Ward," pp. 206–210. London: John Camden Hotten. [1865]

Cf. Mark Twain's "A Bald-Headed Anecdote," *Roughing It* (New York and London, 1903), Vol. I, pp. 161–167: ". . . The adventure . . . *never occurred.*"

other half-hour; when, as he was again about to remonstrate with the driver, the horses suddenly started into a furious run, and all sorts of encouraging yells filled the air from the throat of Henry Monk.

"That is right, my good fellow!" cried Mr. Greeley. "I'll give you ten dollars when we get to Placerville. Now we *are* going!"

They were indeed, and at a terrible speed.

Crack! crack! went the whip, and again "that voice" split the air. "Git up! Hi yi! G'long! Yip—yip!"

And on they tore, over stones and ruts, up hill and down, at a rate of speed never before achieved by stage horses.

Mr. Greeley, who had been bouncing from one end of the coach to the other like an india-rubber ball, managed to get his head out of the window, when he said:

"Do-on't-on't you-u-u think we-e-e-e shall get there by seven even if we do-on't-on't go so fast?"

"I've got my orders!" That was all Henry Monk said. And on tore the coach.

It was becoming serious. Already the journalist was extremely sore from the terrible jolting, and again his head "might have been seen" at the window.

"Sir," he said, "I don't care—care—*air* if we *don't* get there at seven!"

"I have got my orders!" Fresh horses. Forward again, faster than before. Over rocks and stumps, on one of which the coach narrowly escaped turning a summerset.

"See here!" shrieked Mr. Greeley, "I don't care if we don't get there at all!"

"I've got my orders! I work for the Californy Stage Company, *I* do. That's wot I *work* for. They said, 'Git this man through by seving.' An' this man's goin through. You bet! Gerlong! Whoo-ep!"

Another frightful jolt, and Mr. Greeley's bald head suddenly found its way through the roof of the coach, amidst the crash of small timbers and the ripping of strong canvas.

"Stop, you—maniac!" he roared.

Again answered Henry Monk.

"I've got my orders! *Keep your seat, Horace!*"

At Mud Springs, a village a few miles from Placerville, they met a large delegation of the citizens of Placerville, who had come out to meet the celebrated editor, and escort him into town. There were a military company, a brass band, and a six-horse wagon-load of beautiful damsels in milk-white dresses, representing all the States in the Union. It was nearly dark now, but the delegation was amply provided with torches, and bonfires blazed all along the road to Placerville.

The citizens met the coach in the outskirts of Mud Springs, and Mr. Monk reined in his foam-covered steeds.

"Is Mr. Greeley on board?" asked the chairman of the committee.

"He was a few miles back!" said Mr. Monk: "yes," he added, after looking down through the hole which the fearful jolting had made in the coach-roof—"yes, I can see him! He is there!"

"Mr. Greeley," said the chairman of the committee, presenting himself at the window of the coach, "Mr. Greeley, sir! We are come to most cordially welcome you, sir—why, God bless me, sir, you are bleeding at the nose!"

"I've got my orders!" cried Mr. Monk. "My orders is as follers: Git him there by seving! It wants a quarter to seving. Stand out of the way!"

"But, sir," exclaimed the committee-man, seizing the off leader by the reins—"Mr. Monk, we are come to escort him into town! Look at the procession, sir, and the brass band, and the people, and the young women, sir!"

"I've got my orders!" screamed Mr. Monk. "My orders don't say nothin' about no brass bands and young women. My orders says, 'Git him there by seving!' Let go them lines! Clear the way there! Whoo-ep! *Keep your seat, Horace!"* and the coach dashed wildly through the procession, upsetting a portion of the brass band, and violently grazing the wagon which contained the beautiful young women in white.

Years hence gray-haired men, who were little boys in this procession, will tell their grandchildren how this stage tore through Mud Springs, and how Horace Greeley's bald head ever and anon showed itself, like a wild apparition, above the coach-roof.

Mr. Monk was in time. There is a tradition that Mr. Greeley was very indignant for a while; then he laughed, and finally presented Mr. Monk with a bran-new suit of clothes.

Mr. Monk himself is still in the employ of the California Stage Company, and is rather fond of relating a story that has made him famous all over the Pacific coast. But he says he yields to no man in his admiration for Horace Greeley.

Charlie McConnell's Story

. . . There are two fellows in the State prison yet, who were taken by one man a year or two ago . . . . Well . . ., the stage was going along all right when a fellow ran to the horses' heads, and two others covered the driver with their guns in the regular way. He told the driver to drop the reins, and made the passengers throw up their hands. Then he told the passengers to get down and stand in a row by the roadside,

---

From *Oregon: There and Back in 1877,* by Wallis Nash, pp. 92–94. London: Macmillan & Co. 1878.

As told by Charlie McConnell, "prince of drivers," to the author en route by stage from Redding, California, to Oregon.

and made the driver throw down the Wells Fargo box, which was what they were after.

Then they robbed the passengers all comfortable. When they came to one man, he asked them to give him back his watch, which was of no great account to them but had belonged to his grandfather. Instead of being civil, the rascal up with his hand and gave him a great smack on the face and told him to hold his tongue. So they took his watch, and the rest of the watches, and all their money and then told them to get up again and be off. So they all mounted again and drove off glad enough to be free.

As soon as they had gone about a quarter of a mile or so, the passenger told the driver to stop. "What for?" says he. "I am not going to have my face slapped for nothing," says the passenger. So he got out of the luggage a nice little repeating Henry rifle and got down off the coach and back he went.

Presently he saw, as he expected, a light in the bushes near the road. So he crept up through the trees, and saw the three rascals all round the Wells Fargo box, which they were trying to break open; they had put their guns down, never dreaming of danger. The passenger got up within a safe distance till he could cover them well; then he let fly, and the first shot dropped one of them dead, the next winged one of the others, and the third screamed out for mercy. So he went up and made the unhurt one help his wounded fellow back into the road and then he drove them in front of him till he came up to the coach and took the two nicely. And they are both in State prison now. . . . When the driver asked the man why he did such a risky thing as go back alone after three, all he said was, "I was not going to have my face slapped for nothing."

How Buffalo Bill Won His Sobriquet

The Western end of the Kansas Pacific was at this time in the heart of the buffalo country. Twelve hundred men were employed in the construction of the road. The Indians were very troublesome, and it was difficult to obtain fresh meat for the hands. The company therefore concluded to engage expert hunters to kill buffaloes.

Having heard of my experience and success as a buffalo hunter, Goddard Brothers, who had the contract for feeding the men, made me a good offer to become their hunter. They said they would require about twelve buffaloes a day—twenty-four hams and twelve humps, as only

---

From *An Autobiography of Buffalo Bill* (Colonel W. F. Cody), pp. 117–118. Copyright, 1920, by Cosmopolitan Book Corporation. New York.

For other "Buffalo By-Names," Cf. *Pony Express Courier,* Vol. I (January, 1935), No. 8, p. 31.

the hump and hindquarters of each animal were utilized. The work was dangerous. Indians were riding all over that section of the country, and my duties would require me to journey from five to ten miles from the railroad every day in order to secure the game, accompanied by only one man with a light wagon to haul the meat back to camp. I demanded a large salary, which they could well afford to pay, as the meat itself would cost them nothing. Under the terms of the contract which I signed with them, I was to receive five hundred dollars a month, agreeing on my part to supply them with all the meat they wanted.

Leaving Rose to complete our grading contract, I at once began my career as a buffalo hunter for the Kansas Pacific. It was not long before I acquired a considerable reputation, and it was at this time that the title "Buffalo Bill" was conferred upon me by the railroad hands. Of this title, which has stuck to me through life, I have never been ashamed.

During my engagement as hunter for the company, which covered a period of eighteen months, I killed 4,280 buffaloes and had many exciting adventures with the Indians, including a number of hair-breadth escapes.

Blasting

Talk about blastin'! The boy's yarn about blowin' up a mountain 's nothin' but a squib to what we did when we blasted the Ryo Grand railroad through the Royal Gorge.

One day the boss sez to me, sez he, "Hyar, you, do you know how to handle gunpowder?"

Sez I, "You bet!"

Sez he, "Do you see that ere ledge a thousand feet above us, stickin' out like a hat-brim?" Sez I, "You bet I do."

"Wall," sez he, "that 'll smash a train into a grease-spot some day, ef we don't blast it off."

"Jess so," sez I.

Wall, we went up a gulch, and clum the mountain an' come to the prissipass, and got down on all fours, an' looked down straight three thousand feet. The river down there looked like a lariat a-runnin' after a bronco. I began to feel like a kite a-sailin' in the air like. Forty church steeples in one war'n't nowhar to that ere pinnacle in the clouds. An' after a while it begun rainin' an' snowin' an' hailin' an'

From *The Crest of the Continent:* A Record of a Summer's Ramble in the Rocky Mountains and Beyond, by Ernest Ingersoll, pp. 196–200. Copyright, 1885, by S. K. Hooper. Chicago: R. R. Donnelly & Sons, Publishers.

If anybody doubts the full veracity of this tale, he is referred to Colonel Nat. Babcock, of Gunnison City.—E.I.

thund'rin' an' doin' a reglar tornado biznis down thar, an' a reglar summer day whar we wuz on top. Wall, there wuz a crevice from where we wuz, an' we sorter slid down into it, to within fifty feet o' the ledge, an' then they let me down on the ledge with a rope an' drill. When I got down thar, I looked up an' sez to the boss, "Boss, how are ye goin' to get that 'cussion powder down?" Yer see, we used this ere powder as 'll burn like a pine-knot 'thout explodin', but if yer happen to drop it, it 'll blow yer into next week 'fore ye kin wink yer eye.

"Wall," sez the boss, sez he, "hyar's fifty pound an' yer must ketch it."

"Ketch it," sez I, "Hain't ye gettin' a little keerless—s'pose I miss it?" I sez.

"But ye must n't miss it," sez he. " 'T seems to me yer gettin' mighty keerful of yourself all to wunst."

Sez I, "Boss, haul me up. I'm a fool, but not an idgit. Haul me up. I'm not so much afeared of the blowin' up ez of the comin' down. If I should miss comin' onto this ledge, thar's nobody a thousan' feet below thar to ketch me, an' I might get drowned in the Arkansaw, for I kain't swim."

So they hauled me up, an' let three other fellers down, an' the boss discharged me, an' I sot down sorter behind a rock, an' tole 'em they'd soon have a fust-class funeral, and might need me for pallbearer.

Wall, them fellers ketched the dynamite all right, and put 'er in, an' lit their fuse, but afore they could haul 'em up she went off. Great guns! 't was wuss 'n forty thousan' Fourth o' Julys. A million coyotes an' tin pans an' horns an' gongs ain't a sarcumstance. The' hull gorge fur ten mile bellered, an' bellered, an' kep' on bellerin' wuss 'n a corral o' Texas bulls. I foun' myself on my back a-lookin' up, an' th' las' thing I seed wuz two o' them fellers a-whirlin' clean over the mountain, two thousan' feet above. One of 'em had my jackknife an' tobacker, but 't was no use cryin'. 'T was a good jackknife, though; I don't keer so much fur the tobacker. He slung suthin' at me as he went over, but it did n't come nowhar near, 'n' I don't know yet what it was. When we all kinder come to, the boss looked at his watch, 'n' tole us all to witness that the fellers was blown up just at noon, an' was only entitled to half a day's wages,[1] an' quit 'thout notice. When we got courage to peep over an' look down, we found that the hat-brim was n't busted off at all; the hull thing was only a squib. But we noticed that a rock ez big ez a good-sized cabin, hed loosened, an' hed rolled down on top of it. While we sat lookin' at it, boss sez, sez he,

"Did you fellers see mor'n two go up?"

"No," sez we, an' pretty soon we heern t' other feller a' hollerin', "Come down 'n git me out!"

---

1 Cf. Levette J. Davidson and Forrester Blake, *Rocky Mountain Tales* (Norman, 1947), pp. 118–119; also the song, "Drill, Ye Tarriers, Drill."

Gents, you may have what's left of my old shoe, if the ledge had n't split open a leetle, 'n' that chap fell into the crack, 'n' the big rock rolled onto the ledge an' sorter gently held him thar. He war n't hurt a har. We weren't slow about gettin' down thar. We jist tied a rope to a pint o' rock an' slid. But you may hang me for a chipmunk ef we could git any whar near him, an' it was skeery business a-foolin' roun' on that ere verandy. 'T war n't much bigger 'n a hay-rack, an' a thousan' feet up. We hed some crowbars, but boss got a leetle excited, an' perty soon bent every one on 'em tryin' to prize off that bowlder that 'd weigh a hundred ton like. Then agin we wuz all on it, fer it kivered th' hull ledge, 'n' whar 'd we ben ef he 'd prized it off? All the while the chap kep' a-hollerin', "Hurry up; pass me some tobacker!" Oh, it was the pitterfulest cry you ever heern, an' we didn't know what to do till he yelled, "I'm a-losin' time; hain't you goin' to git me out?" Sez boss, "I 've bent all the crowbars, an' we can't git you out."

"Got any dynamite powder?" sez the feller.

"Yes."

"Well, then, why 'n' the name of the Denver 'n' Ryo Grand don't you blast me out?" sez he.

"We can't blast you out," sez boss, "for dynamite busts down, an' it 'll blow you down the canyon."

"Well, then," sez he, "one o' ye swing down under the ledge, an' put a shot in whar it's cracked below."

"You're wiser 'n' a woman," sez boss. "I'd never thought o' that."

So the boss took a rope, 'n' we swung him down, 'n' he put in a shot, 'n' was goin' to light the fuse, when the feller inside smelt the match.

"Hev ye tumbled to my racket?" sez he.

"You bet we have, feller priz'ner!" sez the boss.

"Touch 'er off!" sez the feller.

"All right," sez boss.

"Hold on!" yells the feller as wuz inside.

"What's the racket now?" sez the boss.

"You hain't got the sense of a blind mule," sez he. "Do you s'pose I want to drop down the canyon when the shot busts? Pass in a rope through the crack, 'n' I'll tie it roun' me, 'n' then you can touch 'er off kind o' easy like."

Wall, that struck us all as a pious idea. That feller knowed more 'n' a dozen blind mules—sed mules were n't fer off, neither. Wall, we passed in the rope, 'n' when we pulled boss up, he guv me 'tother end 'n' tole me to hole on tighter 'n' a puppy to a root. I tuck the rope, wrapped it round me 'n' climb up fifty feet to a pint o' rock right under 'nuther pint 'bout a hundred feet higher, that kinder hung over the pint whar I wuz. Boss 'n' t'other fellers skedaddled up the crevice 'n' hid.

Purty soon suthin' happened. I can't describe it, gents. The hull canyon wuz full o' blue blazes, flyin' rocks 'n' loose volcanoes. Both sides o' the gorge, two thousan' feet straight up, seemed to touch tops 'n' then swing open. I wuz sort o' dazed 'n' blinded, 'n' felt ez if the prissipasses 'n' the mountains wuz all on a tangle-foot drunk, staggerin' like. The rope tightened round my stummick, 'n' I seized onto it tight, 'n' yelled:

"Hole on, pard, I'll draw you up! Cheer up, my hearty," sez I, "cheer up! Jes az soon 'z I git my footin', I'll bring ye to terry firmy!"

Ye see, I wuz sort of confused 'n' blinded by the smoke 'n' dust, 'n' hed a queer feelin', like a spider a-swingin' an' a-whirlin' on a har. At last I got so'z I could see, 'n' looked down to see if the feller wuz a-swingin' clar of the rocks, but I couldn't see him. The ledge wuz blown clean off, 'n' the canyon seemed 'bout three thousan' feet deep. My stummick began to hurt me dreadful, 'n' I squirmed round 'n' looked up, 'n' durn my breeches, gents, ef I was n't within ten foot of the top of the gorge, 'n' the feller ez wuz blasted out wuz a-haulin' on me up.

Sez I when he got me to the top, sez I, "Which eend of this rope wuz *you* on, my friend?"

"I dunno," sez he. "Which eend wuz *you* on?"

"I dunno," sez I.

An', gents, to this day we can't tell ef it was which or 'tother ez was blasted out.

The Lost Train of the Moffat Road

. . . During a very severe winter blizzard, No. 3 westbound, seven hours late out of Denver, crept out of the Fraser Canyon, whistled for the Granby crossing, and picked up speed to cross the Granby Flats. Running out of sand a half hour later, they tied down the cab curtains and waited for daylight. In the morning, they found the train parked "plumb center" in Granby's main street ("right in front of Payne's Cafe," according to one version)! During the night, No. 2, eastbound, two days late out of Craig, reached Corona without passing No. 3. Subsequent investigation showed that No. 3 left the rails just east of the Granby crossing, and traveled almost a mile over the frozen highway before running out of sand. The engineer reported, during the hearing, that he suspected something wrong, for "the going was too good west of Fraser Canyon." The next day, a Chinook came up, melting the

---

From "Folklore of Eastern Middle Park, Colorado," by Ronald L. Ives, *The Journal of American Folklore,* Vol. 54 (January–June, 1941), Nos. 211–212, p. 34. Philadelphia: The American Folklore Society.

The Denver and Salt Lake Railroad, connecting Denver with Middle Park and points west, is almost entirely the work of David H. Moffat, upon whose spectacular and pathetic career many mountain legends are based.—R.L.I., *ibid.,* p. 33.

frozen soil, and the train sank to its axles in mud. Building of 1500 feet of special track was necessary before No. 3 could be salvaged. . . .

An Advance on His Wages

. . . A number of years ago, the N.P.R.R. Co. was forming a party of surveyors &c. to survey a pass in the mountains. The leader was very anxious to secure [Old Uncle Billy] Packerwood's services, so he went to see him and urged him very hard to go, offering wages that Mr. P. admitted to be very satisfactory. Still he acted as if he was hesitating whether or not to accept their offer. Finally he told the leader of the party that before he could accept, he must have an advance on his wages, with which he could procure an outfit. At this, they hesitated a moment and told him they were never in the habit of paying in advance, but as they needed his services so very badly they would advance him any sum he might name. Well, he replied, he guessed a dollar would do, as all the supplies he stood in need of for an outfit was a pound of tobacco and a cheap jackknife to cut it with. They passed over the dollar and the outfit was soon complete.

Morley's Ride

Around him [my father] there unfolded one of the most colorful sagas of the pioneer West. These are the historical facts of his most famous exploit, which came to be known as "Morley's ride."

A frenzied mining boom was in progress in the new town of Leadville, Colorado. The only possible route from Cañon City to Leadville was through the Royal Gorge, a breath-takingly beautiful crevasse which the Arkansas River has eaten three thousand feet down through the tightened rock barriers of western Colorado. Both the Santa Fé and the Denver and Rio Grande coveted a chance to serve this great new area of potential wealth, and sought to control the one approach, through which thousands were already flocking toilsomely.

Rights of way at that time rested upon the principle that possession is nine points of the law. The Denver and Rio Grande controlled the already existing rail approaches and telegraph lines into Cañon City, situated practically in the mouth of the gorge. Denver and Rio Grande officials planned the surprise move of taking a force of one hundred

---

From *Notes of the History and Resources of Washington Territory,* Furnished H. H. Bancroft of San Francisco, Cal., by Eldridge Morse of Snohomish City, Snohomish County. Wash[ington] Ter[ritory], Book I, pp. 102–103. Pacific Mss. The Bancroft Library, University of California, Berkeley.

From *No Life for a Lady,* by Agnes Morley Cleaveland, pp. 12–14. Copyright, 1941, by Agnes Morley Cleaveland. Boston: Houghton Mifflin Company.

men, gathered in the neighboring towns of Pueblo and La Junta, into Cañon City by train in order to be first in the actual process of building a railroad through the gorge.

Santa Fé officials learned of the plan only when it seemed too late to forestall it. One thin shred of hope was all they could muster. If a man could get through ahead of the train and draft a corps of Cañon City people to begin actual construction, the day might be saved. The citizenry of Cañon City was known to sympathize with the Santa Fé.

The man to execute the coup must, of course, be one who could not only make the heart-breaking ride himself, but at the end of it explain his mission to an excited populace, and galvanize it into effective, well-organized, and, above all, instant action. My father was able to do both.

The ride itself was a negligible incident in comparison to getting a town's entire population out with picks and shovels on a moment's notice. That was the real achievement. But it was the ride which became the legend. Even Helen Hunt Jackson wrote a poem about it, a parody of the "Charge of the Light Brigade," in which it was Morley who "volleyed and thundered."

Bradley's *Story of the Santa Fé* has possibly the most dramatic account of the episode. "Morley at once secured a good horse and started out at full gallop. It was a race of flesh and blood against a railroad and a desperate ride. Urging the animal to the limit of its endurance, Morley had arrived almost within sight of Cañon City when the animal fell dead from exhaustion. Leaping to his feet, the rider ran the rest of the way alone and safely reached the offices of the Cañon City and San Juan Company before the train of the Rio Grande laborers arrived."

Another account, that of Cy Warman in his *Story of the Railroad,* has it that this historic ride was made with a team and buckboard.

Actually, it was made on King William, a well-bred coal-black horse with a white star in his forehead. And, for the sake of my father's memory and the family honor, I want to testify that with a forty-mile ride ahead of him my father did not start out at "full gallop." (It always enrages me to see that done in the movies.) He eased his horse along at a brisk trot until the animal warmed up, and then alternately trotted and galloped him as the character of the mountainous country permitted.

But he did beat the train!

The horse did not drop dead, either: on the contrary, King William lived to a ripe old age and died long after the untimely death of his master. Loyal friends of both horse and master saw to it that he was never ridden again, but spent his venerable years in the best horse heaven which devotion could provide—open pasture in summer, shelter and food in winter. All agree that he carried himself to the end with an air of conscious pride, as though he understood his part in an adventure which has been the theme for many story-tellers, both accurate and inaccurate.

Some people may think that these details are too trifling to be insisted upon. But good horsemanship is not a trifle: my father's dramatic ride was all the more notable because he finished a forty-mile trip in record time without injury to his mount.

Tousle-headed, dust-caked, he rode into Cañon City, shouting, "The Santa Fé is here!"

Hardware stores swung their doors open and issued implements to all able-bodied men, who fell into line under my father's generalship.

Months of litigation and some physical violence, known as the "Grand Cañon War," ensued. The dispute was finally settled by the purchase of the Santa Fé's rights by the Denver and Rio Grande. . . .

The Line of the Road

The Arkansas River runs eastward through Colorado. Pike's Peak, which is one of the grandest mountain sights in all the world, stands forty miles north of the Arkansas River. The Cripple Creek gold camp (the greatest gold camp, please remember, on the western hemisphere), lies about seventeen miles southwest of Pike's Peak. It ought to be, therefore, you would naturally think, only about twenty-three miles from the river north to the Cripple Creek camp, and that is about what it actually is in a straight geographical line. But, bless your innocent, unsophisticated heart, a straight line has only a remote and thereby theoretical relation to this little railroad of ours.

If you were to go to the top of Pike's Peak and ravel your stocking (or your sock, as the case may chance to be), and throw the raveled thread down to the Arkansas River, forty miles to the south, and almost exactly two miles below the level of your feet, it would fall in a line that would look straight compared with the line of our modest but most interesting and useful little road.

Other railroads brag about their loops and their "horseshoe bends," and their surprising grades, and all that sort of thing. Well, we don't brag about anything, but we can take you over our little forty-mile line from Florence or Canyon City, on the Arkansas, up to Cripple Creek camp and show you grades and curves and loops till you can't stand—loops that would actually make the old loops and horseshoe bends they brag about look like straight lines by comparison.

And this isn't bragging either. We are sorry to have to say it, but the

---

From *Past and Present, Illustrative and Descriptive of the Cripple Creek Gold Mining District and the Gold Belt Line,* pp. 10–13. Compliments of the Traffic Department, the Florence and Cripple Creek Railroad, the Cañon City and Cripple Creek Railroad, the Golden Circle Railroad, C. F. Elliott, Traffic Manager. Denver: Printed and bound by the Merchants Publishing Company.

truth should not be concealed. We'd rather have a level road and a straight line, but if we talk at all, we're bound to tell the truth—and the plain, unvarnished truth is this: We've got more grades, more curves, more loops and more wonderful scenery than any other seventeen railroads in the United States can show on the same length of line. We are sorry to say it, but it's the truth—and the photographs we print herewith will show that it's nothing but the plain, haggard truth.

Now, if we wanted to brag—but we don't want to brag. It makes us feel more like weeping, and only a sense of duty compels us to confess to the world that there isn't a thing about our modest little line that is level; not a thing but what's crooked, except the management, and that's as straight as a loon's leg.

There have been stories circulated—not that we told them or even encouraged belief in them—that the curves on our line are so sharp that our engines have to be provided with curved or knuckle-jointed piston rods in order to traverse them.

Now it's a duty we owe to a confiding public to nail such lies as that. We don't want to encourage poor mechanics to spend their honest earnings traveling from the four quarters of the globe to see how we make a curved or jointed piston rod work. The story probably emanated from the brain of some newspaper writer, whose harmless purpose was to indicate to the imagination how very crooked our line is, but we don't encourage that sort of exaggeration, and we say, once for all, that it is false—the piston rods on our engines are straight and not jointed.

Our line, we confess, is so crooked and so steep that it will make you dizzy to look at a tracing of it on paper, but we have all the business we can do and have no need to bid for travel or traffic by any exaggeration of the scenic or mechanical interests of our road.

The Driving of the Last Spike at Promontory Point

American history, in its triumph of skill, labor, and genius, knows no event of greater thrilling interest, than the scene which attended

---

From *The Pacific Tourist,* J. R. Bowman's Illustrated Trans-Continental Guide of Travel, from the Atlantic to the Pacific Ocean . . ., Frederic E. Shearer, Editor, with Special Contributions by Prof. F. V. Hayden, Clarence King, Capt. Dutton, A. C. Peale, Joaquin Miller, and J. V. Davis . . ., pp. 181–184. New York: J. R. Bowman, Publisher. 1882–1883.

[Promontory, Utah,] is about nine miles from Blue Creek, and in the first seven miles we ascend over five hundred feet. While the road was under construction, this little place was quite lively, but its glory has departed, and its importance at this time is chiefly historic. . . . It is located between two peaks or ridges of the Promontory Range. . . .

This place is well known as the meeting of the two railroads [Central Pacific and Union Pacific].—F.E.S.

the driving of the last spike, which united the East and West with the bands of iron. First of great enterprises since the world's known history began—that gigantic task of joining the two great oceans with bands of steel, over which thousands of iron monsters are destined to labor for unnumbered years, bearing to this young country continued wealth and prosperity. The completion of a project so grand in conception, so successful in execution, and likely to prove so fruitful and rich in promise, was worthy of world-wide celebrity.

Upon the 10th of May, 1869, the rival roads approached each other, and two lengths of rails were left for the day's work. At 8 A.M., spectators began to arrive; at quarter to 9 A.M., the whistle of the Central Pacific Railroad is heard, and the first train arrives, bringing a large number of passengers. Then two additional trains arrive on the Union Pacific Railroad, from the East. At a quarter of 11 A.M., the Chinese workmen commenced leveling the bed of the road with picks and shovels, preparatory to placing the ties. At a quarter past eleven the Governor's (Governor Stanford's) train arrived. The engine was gaily decorated with little flags and ribbons—the red, white, and blue. The last tie is put in place—eight feet long, eight inches wide, and six inches thick. It was made of California laurel, finely polished, and ornamented with a silver escutcheon, bearing the following inscription:

THE LAST TIE LAID ON THE PACIFIC RAILROAD, MAY 10, 1869.

Then follow the names of the directors and officers of the Central Pacific Company and of the presenter of the tie.

The exact point of contact of the road was 1,085.8 miles west from Omaha, which allowed 690 miles to the Central Pacific Railroad, for Sacramento, for their portion of the work. The engine Jupiter, of the Central Pacific Railroad, and the engine 119 of the Union Pacific Railroad, moved up to within thirty feet of each other.

Just before noon the announcement was sent to Washington that the driving of the *last spike* of the railroad which connected the Atlantic and Pacific would be communicated to all the telegraph offices in the country the instant the work was done, and instantly a large crowd gathered around the offices of the Western Union Telegraph Company to receive the welcome news.

The manager of the company placed a magnetic ball in a conspicuous position, where all present could witness the performance, and connected the same with the main lines, notifying the various offices of the country that he was ready. New Orleans, New York, and Boston instantly answered "Ready."

In San Francisco, the wires were connected with the fire-alarm in the tower, where the heavy ring of the bell might spread the news immediately over the city, as quick as the event was completed.

Waiting for some time in impatience, at last came this message from Promontory Point, at 2:27 P.M.

Almost ready. Hats off, prayer is being offered.

A silence for the prayer ensued; at 2:40 P.M., the bell tapped again, and the officer at Promontory said:

We have got done praying, the spike is about to be presented.

Chicago replied:

We understand, all are ready in the East.

From Promontory Point:

All ready now; the spike will soon be driven. The signal will be three dots for the commencement of the blows.

For a moment the instrument was silent, and then the hammer of the magnet tapped the bell, *one, two, three,* the signal. Another pause of a few seconds, and the lightning came flashing eastward, 2,400 miles to Washington; and the blows of the hammer on the spike were repeated instantly in telegraphic accents upon the bell of the Capitol.[1] At 2:47 P.M., Promontory Point gave the signal, *"Done"*; and the great American Continent was successfully spanned.

Immediately thereafter, flashed over the line the following official announcement to the Associated Press:

> Promontory Summit, Utah, May 10.—THE LAST RAIL IS LAID! THE LAST SPIKE IS DRIVEN! THE PACIFIC RAILROAD IS COMPLETED! The point of junction is 1,086 miles west of the Missouri River, and 690 miles east of Sacramento City.
>
> LELAND STANFORD,
> Central Pacific Railroad
>
> T. C. DURANT,
> SIDNEY DILLON,
> JOHN DUFF,
> Union Pacific Railroad.

Such were the telegraphic incidents that attended the completion of the greatest work of the age—but during these few expectant moments the scene itself at Promontory Point was very impressive.

After the rival engines had moved up toward each other, a call was made for the people to stand back, in order that all might have a chance to see. Prayer was offered by Rev. Dr. Todd of Massachusetts. Brief remarks were then made by General Dodge and Governor Stanford. Three cheers were given for the Government of the United

[1] According to Oscar Lewis (*The Big Four,* New York, 1938, p. 99), "The silver hammer missed the spike, but the telegrapher, prepared for the contingency, simulated the blow with his key."

States, for the Railroad, for the Presidents, for the Star Spangled Banner, for the Laborers, and for those, respectively, who furnished the means. Four spikes were then furnished—two gold and two silver—by Montana, Idaho, California, and Nevada. They were each about seven inches long, and a little larger than the iron spike.

Dr. Harkness, of Sacramento, in presenting to Governor Stanford a spike of pure gold, delivered a short and appropriate speech.

The Hon. F. A. Tritle, of Nevada, presented Dr. Durant with a spike of silver, saying:

To the iron of the East, and the gold of the West, Nevada adds her link of silver to span the Continent and weld the oceans.

Governor Safford, of Arizona, presenting another spike, said:

Ribbed in iron, clad in silver, and crowned with gold, Arizona presents her offering to the enterprise that has banded the Continent and welded the oceans.

Dr. Durant stood on the north side of the tie, and Governor Stanford on the south side. At a given signal, these gentlemen struck the spikes, and at the same instant the electric spark was sent through the wires, east and west. The two locomotives moved up until they touched each other, and a bottle of wine was poured, as a libation, on the last rail.

A number of ladies graced the ceremonies with their presence, and at 1 P.M., under an almost cloudless sky, and in the presence of about 1,100 people, the greatest railroad on earth was completed.

A sumptuous repast was given to all the guests and railroad officers, and toward evening the trains each moved away and darkness fell upon the scene of joy and triumph.

Immediately after the ceremonies, the laurel tie was removed for preservation, and in its place an ordinary one substituted. Scarcely had it been put in its place before a grand advance was made upon it by the curiosity seekers and relic hunters and divided into numberless mementoes, and as fast as each tie was demolished and a new one substituted, this, too, shared the same fate, and probably within the first six months there were used as many new ties. It is said that even one of the rails did not escape the grand battery of knife and hack, and the first one had soon to be removed to give place to another.

A curious incident, connected with the laying of the last rails, has been little noticed hitherto. Two lengths of rails, 56 feet, had been omitted. The Union Pacific people brought up their pair of rails, and the work of placing them was done by Europeans. The Central Pacific people then laid their pair of rails, the labor being performed by Mongolians. The foremen, in both cases, were Americans. Here, near the center of the great American Continent, were representatives of Asia, Europe, and America—America directing and controlling.

Okies and Jalopies

Thus they changed their social life—changed as in the whole universe only man can change. They were not farm men any more, but migrant men. And the thought, the planning, the long staring silence that had gone out to the fields, went now to the roads, to the distance, to the West. That man whose mind had been bound with acres lived with narrow concrete miles. And his thought and his worry were not any more with rainfall, with wind and dust, with the thrust of the crops. Eyes watched the tires, ears listened to the clattering motors, and minds struggled with oil, with gasoline, with the thinning rubber between air and road. Then a broken gear was tragedy. Then water in the evening was the yearning, and food over the fire. Then health to go on was the need and strength to go on, and spirit to go on. The wills thrust westward ahead of them, and fears that had once apprehended drought or flood now lingered with anything that might stop the westward crawling.

The camps became fixed—each a short day's journey from the last.

And on the road the panic overcame some of the families, so that they drove night and day, stopped to sleep in the cars, and drove on to the West, flying from the road, flying from movement. And these lusted so greatly to be settled that they set their faces into the West and drove toward it, forcing the clashing engines over the roads.

But most of the families changed and grew quickly into the new life. And when the sun went down—

Time to look out for a place to stop.

And—there's some tents ahead.

The car pulled off the road and stopped, and because others were there first, certain courtesies were necessary. And the man, the leader of the family, leaned from the car.

Can we pull up here an' sleep?

Why, sure, be proud to have you. What State you from?

Come all the way from Arkansas.

They's Arkansas people down that fourth tent.

That so?

And the great question, How's the water?

Well, she don't taste so good, but they's plenty.

Well, thank ya.

No thanks to me.

But the courtesies had to be. The car lumbered over the ground to the end tent, and stopped. Then down from the car the weary people climbed, and stretched stiff bodies. Then the new tent sprang up; the children went for water and the older boys cut brush or wood. The

---

From *The Grapes of Wrath,* by John Steinbeck, pp. 267–269, 272–273. Copyright, 1939, by John Steinbeck. New York: The Viking Press.

fires started and supper was put on to boil or fry. Early comers moved over, and States were exchanged, and friends and sometimes relatives discovered.

Oklahoma, huh? What county?

Cherokee.

Why, I got folks there. Know the Allens? They's Allens all over Cherokee. Know the Willises?

Why, sure.

And a new unit was formed. The dusk came, but before the dark was down the new family was of the camp. A word had been passed with every family. They were known people—good people.

* * * * *

And perhaps a man brought out his guitar to the front of his tent. And he sat on a box to play, and every one in the camp moved slowly in toward him, drawn in toward him. Many men can chord a guitar, but perhaps this man was a picker. There you have something—the deep chords beating, beating, while the melody runs on the strings like little footsteps. Heavy hard fingers marching on the frets. The man played and the people moved slowly in on him until the circle was closed and tight, and then he sang "Ten-Cent Cotton and Forty-Cent Meat." And the circle sang softly with him. And he sang "Why Do You Cut Your Hair, Girls?" And the circle sang. He wailed the song, "I'm Leaving Old Texas," that eerie song that was sung before the Spaniards came, only the words were Indian then.

And now the group was welded to one thing, one unit, so that in the dark the eyes of the people were inward, and their minds played in other times, and their sadness was like rest, like sleep. He sang the "McAlester Blues" and then, to make up for it to the older people, he sang "Jesus Calls Me to His Side." The children drowsed with the music and went into the tents to sleep, and the singing came into their dreams.

And after a while the man with the guitar stood up and yawned. Good night, folks, he said.

And they murmured, Good night to you.

And each wished he could pick a guitar, because it is a gracious thing. Then the people went to their beds, and the camp was quiet. And the owls coasted overhead, and the coyotes gabbled in the distance, and into the camp skunks walked, looking for bits of food—waddling, arrogant skunks, afraid of nothing.

The night passed, and with the first streak of dawn the women came out of the tents, built up the fires, and put the coffee to boil. And the men came out and talked softly in the dawn.

When you cross the Colorado river, there's the desert, they say. Look out for the desert. See you don't get hung up. Take plenty water, case you get hung up.

I'm gonna take her at night.

Me too. She'll cut the living Jesus outa you.

The families ate quickly, and the dishes were dipped and wiped. The tents came down. There was a rush to go. And when the sun arose, the camping place was vacant, only a little litter left by the people. And the camping place was ready for a new world in a new night.

But along the highway the cars of the migrant people crawled out like bugs, and the narrow concrete miles stretched ahead.

PART THREE

Taming the West

. . . We have come to believe that our West, our epic, was an affair of Indians, road-agents, and desperadoes, and have taken no account of the brave men who stood for law and justice and liberty, and for those great ideas died by the hundreds, unknown and unsung—died that the West might be subdued.

—FRANK NORRIS

Western men were good men, but they were cruel. They killed off the Indians and buffaloes, too often "just for the fun of killing." Sometimes even the good men would get drunk and kill off one another. They made "Wild Bill" Hickok marshal "because he was a good killer."

—RALPH CHAPLIN

Introduction

WITH the struggle for law and order, blood-and-thunder came to the West, giving Americans their most heroic symbol next to the cowboy—the killer with his six-gun. As a border line between "savage and civilized life," the frontier provided the unsettled conditions and the transiency that attracted, fostered, and harbored the lawless and the reckless, the nomadic and the predatory, the unfit and the unadjusted. The thrill and glamor of the rip-roaring West first created and then was recreated and heightened by the Wild West show and the dime novel. As a result of the "cultural lag" the "Wild West" entered into literature and entertainment about the time it was passing out of life—in the post-Civil War generation, when Custer, the "glory-hunter," made his last stand and the last territories were being boomed and opened for settlement.[1]

The conflict between frontier Heroism and frontier Heroics—between the Common Man, "incurably addicted to civilization," and the Indian-imitating, glamor- and publicity-seeking Frontiersman—is responsible not only for the sharp cleavage between the law-abiding and lawless phases of the Wild West but also for the attempts at compromise in the stereotype of the "Good Bad Man" and in the inconsistencies and makeshifts of frontier legal machinery.

> I wouldn't let any lawyer interfere with law and order [, declared "Ranicky Bill",] just because they objected to this and that testimony by selecting a big word from Webster's under-the-bridge dictionary, and sayin', "Your Honor, I object on the grounds that hit's immeterial, irrevelent, and uncomprehensive." By godlins, I'd enforce the law. The way the law is now, sometimes hit's with order and sometimes hit's against order.[2]

Frontier justice ran the gamut of the Councils that settled disputes in the westward-journeying wagon trains, the Texas Rangers of the Republic days, the Lynch Law and mining law of the Gold Rush, the Vigilance Committees of San Francisco in 1851 and of the Kansas-Missouri border in 1854, the Vigilantes of Montana ten years later, and the grim bizarreries of a "Hanging Judge" Parker at Fort Smith and a "Fining Judge" Bean at Langtry, Texas. Frontier lawlessness similarly ranged from the "Cow-boys" of the Texas-Mexican border

---

[1] Cf. Percy H. Boynton, *The Rediscovery of the Frontier* (Chicago, 1931); E. Douglas Branch, *The Cowboy and His Interpreters* (New York, 1926); Bernard DeVoto, *Mark Twain's America* (Boston, 1932); James D. Hart, *The Popular Book* (New York, 1950); Albert Johanssen, *The House of Beadle and Adams and Its Dime and Nickel Novels* (Norman, 1950); Henry Nash Smith, *Virgin Land* (Cambridge, 1950); Richard J. Walsh and Milton S. Salsbury, *The Making of Buffalo Bill* (Indianapolis, 1928).

[2] Evan G. Barnard, *A Rider of the Cherokee Strip* (Boston and New York, 1936), pp. 166–167.

to the Lincoln County Cattle War of New Mexico and the Johnson County Cattle War of Wyoming, from the "bloody border" of Kansas-Missouri guerrilla warfare to "Arizona's dark and bloody ground" of the Graham-Tewksbury feud.

All this was not without its incongruously assorted humor and sentiment, mordant irony and macabre drama. In a California mining camp, according to Bret Harte, the ring leader of a lynch mob, impatient for the jury's verdict in a horse-stealing case, stuck his head through the door and said, on learning that the verdict had not yet been reached: "Well, take your own time, gentlemen; only remember that we're waitin' for this yer room to lay out the corpse in!" In California, too, William Hynson unwittingly assisted in the preparations for what was to prove his own hanging; and a polite Mexican prisoner made up for the Court's deficiencies in Spanish by translating his own sentence. Dry Diggings changed its name to Hangtown, for obvious reasons, and then, for equally obvious reasons, to Placerville. In Sacramento, a ruffian named Jim, brought to sudden justice by lynch law, impatiently tied the noose about his neck, slipped it up, and briefly addressed the mob. "He cursed the man he shot; he then cursed the world; and last of all he cursed himself; and with a terrible oath, he jumped into the air, and with a jerk that shook the tree, swung backwards and forwards over the heads of the crowd."[3] At Hell Gate Store, Montana, George Shears, lieutenant of Cyrus Skinner, one of the leaders of Henry Plummer's notorious gang of road agents, while in the process of being hanged by a posse, was asked to walk up a ladder to save them the trouble of preparing a drop for him. " 'Gentlemen,' he said, 'I am not used to this business. Shall I jump off or slide off?' He was told to jump."[4]

If whisky was not what Mark Twain cynically called the "van leader of civilization," it was the indispensable companion and agent of the frontier fur trade.

> . . . You take one barrel of Missouri River water, and two gallons of alcohol. Then you add two ounces of strychnine to make them crazy—because strychnine is the greatest stimulant in the world—and three plugs of tobacco to make them sick—because an Indian wouldn't figure it was whisky unless it made him sick—and five bars of soap to give it a bead, and half a pound of red pepper, and then you put in some sagebrush and boil it until it's brown. Strain this into a barrel and you've got your Indian whisky; that one bottle calls for one buffalo robe, and when the Indian got drunk it was two robes. And that's how some of the traders made their fortune.[5]

---

[3] *The Works of Hubert Howe Bancroft,* Vol. XXXVI, *Popular Tribunals,* Vol. I (San Francisco, 1887), p. 150.

[4] *Montana* (New York, 1939), p. 213.

[5] E. C. Abbott and Helena Huntington Smith, *We Pointed Them North* (New York, 1939), pp. 145–147.

The larger trading companies generally supported the government officers and tried to suppress the liquor trade, for they soon noted its degenerating effect upon the Indians. But the competition of unscrupulous traffickers often forced the higher

In the mountain man's lexicon the San Fernando de Taos variety of *aguardiente* was dubbed "Taos lightning."[6] Other nicknames for bad whisky were pizen, popskull, forty rod, panther milk or juice, tarantula juice, and tanglefoot or tangleleg. And the cowboy's sayings about their potency were as pointed and picturesque as their names: "One drink of it tempts you to steal your own clothes, two drinks makes you bite off your own ears, while three will actually make you save your drowning mother-in-law"—the cowboy being generally safe on all three counts, since, as one camp-cook added, "our clothes ain't worth stealing, our ears are too big and too tough, and our outfit ain't got no mother-in-law about it."[7]

More commonly, the effect of the cowboy's spree at the end of the trail was to "cut his wolf loose," so that he rode through town (any of the Kansas "terminus towns," say, like Abilene, Dodge City, or Ellsworth), yelling his head off and shooting into the air, proclaiming, to any one who cared to listen:

> I'm wild and woolly
> And full of fleas;
> Ain't never been curried
> Below the knees.
> I'm a wild she wolf
> From Bitter Creek,
> And it's my time
> To h-o-w-l, whoop-i-e-e ee.[8]

Without bad whisky it is difficult to conceive of the Western "bad man," or would-be "bad man," on whom fell the mantle of the ring-tailed-roarer. For the noisy braggart and bully, if "a mean hombre when drunk," was too often a silent coward when sober. At the same time a genuine gunfighter like Clay Allison was a "whale of a fellow" when sober, "and considerate of his companions"—"but throw a drink into him, and he was hell turned loose, rearin' for a chance to shoot—in self-defense." The close connection between whisky and crime no doubt suggested to Judge Roy Bean the unique possibilities of administering justice in a saloon.

The saying, "There is no Sunday west of Newton and no God west

---

class traders to employ liquor also.—LeRoy R. Hafen, editor, *Life in the Far West,* by George Frederick Ruxton (Norman, 1951), p. 99n.

Tabeau adds an interesting note on the Indian's rebellion against the liquor trade, the Ricaras being unwilling to drink unless paid: "Since you wish to laugh at my expense," they say to that one who offers them liquor, "you ought at least to pay me." (Pierre Antoine Tabeau, *Tabeau's Narrative of Loisel's Expedition to the Upper Missouri,* edited by Annie Heloise Abel, Norman, 1939, p. 171.)

[6] Levette Jay Davidson, "Old Trapper Talk," *American Speech,* Vol. XIII (April, 1938), No. 2, pp. 83–91.

[7] William A. Baillie-Grohman, *Camps in the Rockies* (New York, 1882), pp. 6–7.

[8] *A Treasury of American Folklore* (New York, 1944), p. 62.

of Pueblo," was supplemented with "and no law west of the Pecos." The exigencies of self-protection and the safeguarding of property, if not of life and limb, soon resulted in the crude, rough-hewn "law west of the Pecos." This was "law and order limited," which, more often than not, was "common sense if not common law."

According to O. Henry, "We only had two or three laws, such as against murder before witnesses and being caught stealing horses, and voting the Republican ticket."[9] Of the three offenses, horse stealing was the most heinous. A man's horse was his means of livelihood and life itself.

> . . . In those days horse-stealing was the crime of crimes. If two men got into trouble and one killed the other in a fight, there was very little said about it; but if a man was caught stealing a horse or a mule, his days were short or else he got whipped and banished from the diggings, sometimes branded.[10]

Frontier justice placed the responsibility upon the individual. The bad man considered himself "judge, jury, and executioner" in one. The fining "judge" or justice of the peace was a one-man court. And all put the emphasis on self-preservation, which had its science and its code of ethics: "Shoot first, think and ask questions afterward." "Shoot before the other fellow gets a chance, then talk." "Shoot first and never miss." "Draw quick and shoot straight"—but "Take your time" and "Never try to run a bluff with a six-gun."[11] To kill an unarmed man or to shoot a man in the back or unawares was murder. To take a man's life in self-defense, in support of the law, or in punishment for a crime was justifiable homicide.

The frontier code also distinguished between the gunman, or the professional or sneak killer, and the gunfighter (usually a peace officer), who fought fair and killed in self-defense or in line of duty. Hero-worship also placed the halo of the "good bad man," the Robin Hood or the Rob Roy, on the head of the chivalrous killer—driven to a life of crime to avenge a wrong, a good boy gone wrong, or generous to the weak and the poor, women and children. In the democratic West, even more than elsewhere, popular sympathy was with the outlaw who combined courage and expert marksmanship with wit and cunning and, perhaps, defiance of the rich and powerful.

The only place where the requirements of sportsmanship and fair play were not observed or enforced was in the exploitation and extermination of the Indian. On the frontier, where men were often "cheaper than horses" (as indicated by the severe penalties for horse-

---

[9] "Law and Order," *Sixes and Sevens* (New York, 1920), p. 229.

[10] John Carr, *Pioneer Days in California* (Eureka, 1891), pp. 120–121.

[11] B. A. Botkin, *The Pocket Treasury of American Folklore* (New York, 1950), pp. 13–14. For a comprehensive study of Western law and order, cf. Wayne Gard, *Frontier Justice* (Norman, 1949).

stealing), an Indian's life was held cheapest of all, with the possible exception of the Mexican in early Texas and the Chinese in early California. Billy the Kid boasted of having killed twenty-one men, "not including Indians, which, he said, don't count as human beings." In depriving (or cheating) the Indian of his land, furs, game, or life, the frontiersman acquired the glory of "a hero fighting a fire even though he had set it himself," as Carl Van Doren once put it.

The fire that was set was the fire of race hatred and greed. It was spread (according to the Report of the Joint Special Committee on the *Condition of the Indian Tribes*) by the "aggressions of lawless white men always to be found upon the frontier"; by the "steady and resistless encroachment of the white emigration toward the West, which is every day confining the Indians to narrower limits and driving off or killing the game, their only means of subsisting"; by the "unwise policy of the government" or "inhumane and dishonest administration of that policy"; and by "long and expensive wars brought on by the blunders and want of discretion of inexperienced officers in command."[12]

The Sheridan criterion of a good Indian as a dead Indian was reinforced by the stereotype of the blood-thirsty Red Devil, which replaced the earlier stereotype of the Noble Savage,[13] and the dime-novel formula of "Crack! Crack! Three more redskins bit the dust!" If the Indian survived both extermination and caricature, it was because, as General Howard told Cochise, "there were two parties in the United States—one friendly to the Indians, and the other hostile to them"; and it was to the credit of men like Howard that they served to swing the balance in favor of the former.

In more ways than one the Indian "turned the tables" and wreaked a subtle vengeance on his conquerors. Kit Carson believed that the "Indians in their outrages were only imitating or improving on the white man's bad example. . . . 'And ye call *these* civilized men Christians; and the Injuns savages, du ye?' "[14] At the same time, the frontiersman achieved glory and prestige by imitating the Indian—his dress, his ways of hunting and fighting. And by one of the ironies of history—matching the Indian's own ironic sense of humor—the Indian outlived his imitator.

> The Indian is the one figure on the Frontier who has not lost caste because of the civilizing of the region. He still stands for something; he is the genuine article. . . . The trappers and the explorers, the fur barons and the scouts, the soldiers and the showmen, the bandits and the cowmen, all have taken their turn upon the Indian's stage and performed the old Indian

---

[12] J. R. Doolittle (Washington, D.C., 1867), pp. 3–10.

[13] Cf. W. S. Campbell, "The Plains Indian in Literature—and in Life," *The Trans-Mississippi West* (Boulder, 1930), pp. 175–194.

[14] Stanley Vestal, *Kit Carson* (Boston, 1928), p. 290.

trick to satiety. They are gone. But the Red Man, master of ceremonies, remains. . . .[15]

In the fighting West two streams of chivalry met and merged. One was the Southern code of the duello and the feud. The other was the Indian warrior's (and, by imitation, the frontiersman's) code of fighting for sport and personal glory (symbolized by "counting coups"), which depended upon "freedom of action."[16] With the passing of this freedom and the introduction of modern firearms, chivalry had a hard time of it. The indisputable authority of "Colt on Revolvers" ("You can't argue with a gun") tended to displace moral responsibility, until today the deadly six-shooter has become the real hero of the "Western."

For the Western . . . merely simplifies reality so that you can handle it. Although on the surface most everything seems to be divided into either good or bad, beneath this primer of ethical neatness the Western acts out the same complex pattern of danger, threats, crises, and disasters with which the modern world is rife. With a difference. The psychological frontier defined by headlines, wars, economic insecurity, etc., is turned into an actual physical frontier abounding in just as many menacing elements, with the one saving grace: you are given a gun and allowed to defend yourself. An improvement over real life. You are also told whom to shoot.[17]

B. A. B.

---

[15] Stanley Vestal, "The Histrionic West," *Space,* edited by B. A. Botkin, Vol. I (June, 1934), No. 2, p. 16.

Cf. Robert Gessner, *Massacre* (New York, 1931); Helen Hunt Jackson, *A Century of Dishonor* (Cambridge, 1881); Stanley Vestal, *Sitting Bull* (Boston, 1932), *Warpath* (Boston, 1934), *New Sources of Indian History* (Norman, 1934), *Warpath and Council Fire* (New York, 1948); Paul I. Wellman, *Death on Horseback* (New York, 1947).

[16] Stanley Vestal, "Imitating the Indian," *Southwest Review,* Vol. XV (July, 1930), No. 4, pp. 444–445.

[17] Alfred Towne, "The Myth of the Western Hero," *Neurotica* 7 (Autumn, 1950), p. 3.

I. RED MEN AND WHITE

Some day they will take white man's road. I know this; but now they are Indians. They do not know what they want, my people. My mind is troubled about this thing. Some young men try to talk like white man; they try to act like white man. But they talk like white man who talks like crow, and they act like white man who acts bad, I believe. It is not good for young men to talk like white man who talks like crow. They send our young men off to school and there they learn to talk like white man who knows how to talk, I believe. I believe that is good. But at this school they make our young men do things like white man; but he is Indian. At this school they make things of iron, and they make things of wood. This is not good, I believe. I am troubled in my mind about this thing. I do not know if it is good for Indian to learn from white man. Indian knows many things, but white man says that these things are not good. I believe white man does not know many things that Indian knows.—BIG CHIEF, quoted by JOHN JOSEPH MATHEWS

Major Powell Makes Friends with the Indians

This evening, the *Shi'-vwits,* for whom we have sent, come in, and, after supper, we hold a long council. A blazing fire is built, and around this we sit—the Indians living there, the *Shi'-vwits,* Jacob Hamblin, and myself. This man, Hamblin, speaks their language well and has a great influence over all the Indians in the region round about. He is a silent, reserved man, and when he speaks, it is in a slow, quiet way that inspires great awe. His talk is so low that they must listen attentively to

From *First through the Grand Canyon,* Being the Record of the Pioneer Exploration of the Colorado River in 1869–70, by Major John Wesley Powell, edited by Horace Kephart, pp. 312–318. Copyright, 1915, by the Outing Publishing Company. New York.

hear, and they sit around him in deathlike silence. When he finishes a measured sentence, the chief repeats it, and they all give a solemn grunt. But, first, I fill my pipe, light it, and take a few whiffs, then pass it to Hamblin; he smokes, and gives it to the man next, and so it goes around. When it has passed the chief, he takes out his own pipe, fills and lights it, and passes it around after mine. I can smoke my own pipe in turn, but, when the Indian pipe comes around, I am nonplussed. It has a large stem, which has, at some time, been broken, and now there is a buckskin rag wound around it, and tied with sinew, so that the end of the stem is a huge mouthful, and looks like the burying ground of old dead spittle, venerable for a century. To gain time, I refill it, then engage in very earnest conversation, and, all unawares I pass it to my neighbor unlighted.

I tell the Indians that I wish to spend some months in their country during the coming year, and that I would like them to treat me as a friend. I do not wish to trade; do not want their lands. Heretofore I have found it very difficult to make the natives understand my object, but the gravity of the Mormon missionary helps me much. I tell them that all the great and good white men are anxious to know very many things; that they spend much time in learning, and that the greatest man is he who knows the most. They want to know all about the mountains and the valleys, the rivers and the cañons, the beasts, and birds, and snakes. Then I tell them of many Indian tribes, and where they live; of the European nations, of the Chinese, of Africans, and all the strange things about them that come to my mind. I tell them of the ocean, of great rivers and high mountains, of strange beasts and birds. At last I tell them I wish to learn about their cañons and mountains, and about themselves, to tell other men at home; and that I want to take pictures of everything and show them to my friends. All this occupied much time and the matter and manner made a deep impression.

Then the chief replies: "Your talk is good, and we believe what you say. We believe in Jacob, and look upon you as a father. When you are hungry, you may have our game. You may gather our sweet fruits. We will give you food when you come to our land. We will show you the springs, and you may drink; the water is good. We will be friends, and when you come we will be glad. We will tell the Indians who live on the other side of the great river that we have seen *Ka'-pu-rats,* and he is the Indians' friend. We will tell them he is Jacob's friend. We are very poor. Look at our women and children; they are naked. We have no horses; we climb the rocks and our feet are sore. We live among rocks, and they yield little food and many thorns. When the cold moons come, our children are hungry. We have not much to give, you must not think us mean. You are wise; we have heard you tell strange things. We are ignorant. Last year we killed three white men. Bad men said they were our enemies. They told great lies. We thought them true. We were mad; it made us big fools. We are very sorry. Do not think of them: it is done; let us be friends. We are ignorant—like little children in understanding compared with you. When we do wrong, do not get mad and be like children too.

"When white men kill our people, we kill them. Then they kill more of us. It is not good. We hear that the white men are a great number. When they stop killing us, there will be no Indian left to bury the dead. We love our country; we know not other lands. We hear that other lands are better; we do not know. The pines sing, and we are glad. Our children play in the warm sand; we hear them sing, and are glad. The seeds ripen, and we have to eat, and we are glad. We do not want their good lands, we want our rocks, and the great mountains where our fathers lived. We are very poor; we are very ignorant, but we are very honest. You have horses and many things. You are very wise; you have a good heart. We will be friends. Nothing more have I to say."

Ka'-pu-rats is the name by which I am known among the Utes and Shoshones, meaning "arm off." There was much more repetition than I have given, and much emphasis. After this a few presents were given, we shook hands, and the council broke up.

* * * * *

That night I slept in peace, although these murderers of my men and their friends, the *U-in-ka-rets,* were sleeping not five hundred yards away. While we were gone to the cañon, the pack-train and supplies, enough to make an Indian rich beyond his wildest dreams, were all left in their charge, and were all safe; not even a lump of sugar was pilfered by the children.

Jacob Hamblin Prays for Rain

In the autumn of 1855, I returned to Tooele Valley, and removed my family to the Santa Clara. My brother Oscar, also Brother Dudley Leavitt and their families accompanied me.

In the winter of 1855–6, we were instructed to build a fort for our protection. There were at that time on the Santa Clara ten missionaries and four stone masons from Cedar City. We employed Indian help, and everything we put our hands to prospered, so that in less than ten days, we built a fort one hundred feet square, of hammer-faced rock, the wall two feet thick and twelve feet high. It was afterwards said by President [Brigham] Young to be the best fort then in the Territory.

We invited the Indians to assist us to construct a strong, high dam

From *Jacob Hamblin,* A Narrative of His Personal Experience, as a Frontiersman, Missionary to the Indians, and Explorer, Disclosing Interpositions of Providence, Severe Privations, Perilous Situations, and Remarkable Escapes [as told to James A. Little], pp. 36–38. Fifth Volume of the Faith-Promoting Series, by James A. Little, Designed for the Instruction and Encouragement of Young Latter-Day Saints. Salt Lake City: Juvenile Instructor Office. 1881.

to take the water out of the Santa Clara to a choice piece of land. For this purpose they gathered into the settlement to the number of about thirty lodges, but rather reluctantly, for they believed that the "Tonaquint," their name for Santa Clara, would dry up in the coming season, as there was but little snow in the mountains.

With much hard labor we completed our dam, and watered our crops once in the spring of 1856. The water then failed, and our growing crops began to wither. The Indians then came to me and said, "You promised us water if we would help build a dam and plant corn. What about the promise, now the creek is dry? What will we do for something to eat next winter?"

The chief saw that I was troubled in my mind over the matter and said, "We have one medicine man; I will send him to the great mountain to make rain medicine, and you do the best you can, and maybe the rain will come; but it will take strong medicine, as I never knew it to rain this moon." I went up the creek, and found it dry for twelve miles.

The following morning at daylight, I saw the smoke of the medicine man ascending from the side of the Big Mountain, as the Indians called what is now known as the Pine Valley Mountain. Being among some Indians, I went aside by myself, and prayed to the God of Abraham to forgive me if I had been unwise in promising the Indians water for their crops if they would plant; and that the heavens might give rain, that we might not lose the influence we had over them.

It was a clear, cloudless morning, but, while still on my knees, heavy drops of rain fell on my back for about three seconds. I knew it to be a sign that my prayers were answered. I told the Indians that the rain would come. When I returned to the settlement, I told the brethren that we would have all the water we wanted.

The next morning, a gentle rain commenced falling. The water rose to its ordinary stage in the creek, and, what was unusual, it was clear. We watered our crops all that we wished, and both whites and Indians acknowledged the event to be a special providence.

I think more corn and squash were grown that year by us, than I ever saw before or since, on the same number of acres. The Indians gathered and stored up a large amount of corn, beans, and dried squash.

From that time they began to look upon us as having great influence with the clouds. They also believed that we could cause sickness to come upon any of them if we wished. We labored to have them understand these things in their true light, but this was difficult on account of their ignorance and superstitions.

No One Pumpkin Man

At a very early date, probably in 1860, a farmer from Wisconsin settled near what is now Fort Collins [,Colorado]. Jesse Sherwood, being a hunter of the pioneer type, had met many Indians in his home state and understood them well. A band of Arapahoes objected to his settling near them on their hunting grounds, but granted his modest request that he be allowed to remain until the harvest season, so that he might have food for his squaw and papoose during the winter.

When the virgin fields were yellow with their rich crops, the Arapahoes returned to their camp across the Cache La Poudre from Sherwood's ranch, and the Indian chief sent his squaw to White Hawk, as they called Sherwood, to get a yellow pumpkin. But White Hawk sent her away empty-handed. He at once called his man to harness a wagon, put in the side boards, and fill it with yellow pumpkins for his red brother. The chief was so angry at the account his squaw gave of her reception that he was not appeased by the almost immediate appearance of the wagon load of pumpkins, but summoning Sherwood and calling an interpreter, he demanded an explanation. White Hawk slowly and with great solemnity and dignity, smoking his pipe of peace, although it was very distasteful to him, replied: "I ain't no one pumpkin man." He dwelt in safety near the Arapahoes, and his influence over them was destined to become very great.

Indian Justice

At the camp on Green River, a trader informed me of another emigrant near there, also out hunting no great distance from his camp, when he was beset by a party of Snake Indians, who took his rifle from him, tied him to a tree, and shot him in the back—and killed him.—His comrades missed him too long, went on a search, and found him fast to the tree, a corpse.—They then got on the Indian trail, and found their camp, and demanded redress. The chief held a council, detected the murderer, and had him tied to a tree; and then told the emigrants that he was at their disposal. The emigrants replied that he had taken the life of one of us all—friends, and that they, the Indians, must punish him, in such manner as should be decreed. The old chief then called the brother of the culprit, and ordered him to cut the offender's

---

As told to Mary S. Sabin by Judge E. T. Wells. From the Katherine L. Craig Scrapbooks, No. 3, p. 50. Colorado State Historical Society, Denver, Colorado.

From *Gold Rush*, the Journals, Drawings, and Other Papers of J. Goldsborough Bruff, Captain, Washington City and California Mining Association, April 2, 1849—July 20, 1851, edited by Georgia Willis Read and Ruth Gaines, with a Foreword by F. W. Hodge, Vol. I, p. 87. Copyright, 1944, by Columbia University Press. New York.

throat, which he instantly done; and the emigrants returned, satisfied with the old chief's justice.

Indian Chivalry

I[1]

The Sioux are quite different from the Crows. They, too, are a big fine-looking people, but lighter red on the whole than the Crows and squarer. More Manchu looking, perhaps, less nomad Mongolian. And graver, and more fierce. Inclined to be grim. A proud people, well aware of their departed greatness. A chivalric people in their own way, who made war and made treaties formally, . . . and kept the latter with a strictness the white man intended perhaps, but never was quite able to accomplish.

A young uncle of mine—subsequently he became an Arizona and California cattleman—in his undergraduate days was a member of a college geological expedition that had come to eastern Wyoming in search of fossils. The expedition, happily encamped among lonely coulees and foothills, was ignorant of the fact that there was unrest among the Sioux and that many of them were off their reservations in the Dakotas. One day my uncle, riding alone, came up over a rise straight into the arms of a young Sioux, naked and in war paint, his pinto pony painted and beribboned.

The young Sioux held up his arm and asked my uncle his business. My uncle told him.

"Go back," said the young Sioux, "and stay quiet and do not go too far away from your camp. This time we are fighting the white soldiers, not the white man."

And the oddest thing about it was that this young Lakota warrior not only spoke perfect English, but English with a university accent.

II[2]

. . . The Indians, who are everywhere a begging race, were in the habit of visiting the houses of the settlers and demanding food. On one occasion, one of them came to the house of a now prominent citizen of Oregon, as usual petitioning for something to eat. The lady of the house, and mother of several young children, replied that she

---

[1] From *Powder River, Let 'er Buck,* by Struthers Burt, pp. 34–35. Copyright, 1938, by Struthers Burt. New York and Toronto: Farrar & Rinehart, Inc.

[2] From *The River of the West,* Life and Adventure in the Rocky Mountains and Oregon, Embracing Events in the Life-time of a Mountain-Man and Pioneer [Joseph L. Meek] . . ., by Mrs. Frances Fuller Victor, p. 338. Entered according to Act of Congress in the year 1869 by R. W. Bliss & Co. in the Clerk's Office of the District Court of the United States for the District of Connecticut. Hartford, Connecticut: Columbian Book Co. 1871.

had nothing to give. Not liking to believe her, the Indian persisted in his demand, when the lady pointed to her little children and said, "Go away; I have nothing—not even for those." The savage turned on his heel and strode quickly away, as the lady thought, offended. In a short time he reappeared with a sack of dried venison, which he laid at her feet. "Take that," he said, "and give the *tenas tillicum* [little children] something to eat." From that day, as long as he lived, that humane savage was a "friend of the family."

Indian Whisky

A great deal of whisky was sold to the Indians in defiance of the United States laws. As there was profit in it, it could not be otherwise. There were no officers within several hundred miles to enforce the law, and as far as there was any public opinion, it sustained the whisky traffic. I say whisky, but it is only by a euphuism [sic] that the vile stuff on which the Indians got drunk can be called by that name. The recipe for its manufacture was something like this:

1 quart alcohol,
1 pound rank, black chewing tobacco,
1 handful red peppers,
1 bottle Jamaica ginger,
1 quart black molasses,
Water from the Missouri *ad libitum*.

Mix well and boil till all the strength is drawn from the tobacco and peppers.

The Indian who had consumed a bottle of this stuff must have sighed sadly for soda water next morning; but it is possible that it did not do as much harm after all as a stronger and purer article would have done.

Exterminating the Indian

I[1]

They reached their camp by noon the following day, and on their arrival, Jim Bridger met them, saying, "Well, boys, did yer kill 'em all or did yer leave some for seed?"

From "Life at Muscleshell in 1869 and 1870," by Peter Koch, *Contributions to the Historical Society of Montana . . .*, Vol. II, p. 298. Copyright, 1896, by the State Historical Society of Montana. Helena, Montana: State Publishing Company.

---

1 From *The Life of Jim Baker, 1818–1898, Trapper, Scout, Guide, and Indian Fighter,* by Nolie Mumey, p. 76. Copyright, 1931, by Nolie Mumey. Denver, Colorado: The World Press, Inc.

II[2]

. . . The Comanches roamed all over Texas, killing any white people they saw. It got so bad that [General] McKenzie was sent out with a large body of soldiers to end the raids. He told his boys, "Kill all the nits and you will have no lice." The soldiers knew what he meant, so when they had cornered the Comanches here, the soldiers mowed down women and children along with the men, fifteen hundred in all, it is said.

An Indian's "Certificate"

I[1]

. . . Now and then a chief wanders through the settlement, half-clad in the grotesque finery received as annuity goods, and with a medal on his breast to show that he had signed a treaty or done some other service to the Government, and perhaps a dirty scrap of paper to back up his assertion that he is "Good Osage—heap good Injun." His errand generally is for old clothes and "cold grub"; and if a little whisky be added, the donor can have a war dance improvised for his special benefit. Occasionally a begging Indian receives a "certificate" from some wag, which is not so favorable. One such, which the bearer proudly presented me, ran thus:

> TO WHOM IT MAY CONCERN:
> The name of this noble red man is Hunkydori. He is of poor but pious parents. What he wouldn't steal a hound pup wouldn't pull out of a tan-yard. Red-hot stoves are supposed to be safe in his presence. Give him some cold grub, or a three cent drink, if you have any about you.
>
> REV. ROBERT COLLYER
> GEN. O. O. HOWARD

II[2]

The ranches in those days were few and far between. Beyond the Grove were Peacock's ranch, at Cow Creek, Alison's ranch, at Walnut Creek, and also that of William Greiffenstein, with whom I afterward

---

[2] From *Cow by the Tail,* by Jesse James Benton, p. 63. Copyright, 1943, by Jesse James Benton. Boston: Houghton Mifflin Co.

---

[1] From *Western Wilds and the Men Who Redeem Them,* An Authentic Narrative, Embracing an Account of Seven Years Travel and Adventure in the Far West; Wild Life in Arizona; Perils of the Plains; Life in the Canon and Death on the Desert; Thrilling Scenes and Romantic Incidents in the Lives of Western Pioneers; Adventures among the Red and White Savages of the West; A Full Account of the Mountain Meadow Massacre; the Custer Defeat; Life and Death of Brigham Young, etc., by J. H. Beadle, p. 439. Copyright, 1877, by John T. Jones. Cincinnati, Philadelphia, Chicago: Jones Brothers & Co.

[2] From *Dodge City,* The Cowboy Capital and The Great Southwest in the Days of the Wild Indian, the Buffalo, the Cowboy, Dance Halls, Gambling Halls and Bad Men, by Robert M. Wright, pp. 48–49. [Copyright, 1913, by Robert M. Wright.]

had the pleasure to serve in the House of Representatives. The following is a true story of the fate of Peacock, as related to me a few years after his death. Peacock kept a whisky ranch on Cow Creek. He and Satank, the great war chief of the Kiowas, were great friends and chums, as Peacock knew the sign language well. He had quite a large ranch and traded with the Indians, and, of course, supplied them with whisky. In consequence, the soldiers were always after him. Satank was his confidential friend and lookout. He had to cache his whisky and hide it in every conceivable manner, so that the troops would not find it. In fact, he dreaded the incursions of the soldiers much more than he did the Indians. One day Satank said to him: "Peacock, write me a nice letter that I can show to the wagon bosses and get all the chuck I want. Tell them I am the great war chief of the Kiowas, and ask them to give me the very best in the shop."

Peacock said, "All right, Satank," and sat down and penned this epistle: "This is Satank, the biggest liar, beggar, and thief on the plains. What he can't beg of you he will steal. Kick him out of your camp, as he is a lazy, good-for-nothing Indian."

Satank presented his letter several times to passing trains, and, of course, got a very cool reception, or rather a warm one. One wagon boss blacksnaked him, after which indignity he sought a friend, and said to him: "Look here! Peacock promised to write me a good letter, but I don't understand it. Every time I present it, the wagon boss gives me the devil. Read it, and tell me just what it says." His friend did so, interpreting it literally. "All right," said Satank, and the next morning at daylight he took some of his braves and rode to Peacock's ranch. He called to Peacock, "Get up; the soldiers are coming." The summons was quickly obeyed. Seizing his field-glass, Peacock ran to the top of his lookout, and the instant he appeared, Satank shot him full of holes, exclaiming as he did so, "Good-by, Mr. Peacock; I guess you won't write any more letters."

Then they went into the building and killed every man present, except one, a sick individual, who was lying in one of the rooms, gored through the leg by a buffalo. All that saved him was that the Indians were very superstitious about entering apartments where sick men lay, for fear they might have the small pox, which disease they dreaded more than any other.

The Killing of Crazy Horse

There was much talk at the post concerning the surrender of some of the Indians who had been engaged with Sitting Bull the previous

---

From *McGillycuddy: Agent,* A Biography of Dr. Valentine T. McGillycuddy, by Julia B. McGillycuddy, pp. 74–87. Copyright, 1941, by the Board of Trustees of the Leland Stanford Junior University. Stanford University, California: Stanford University Press.

Cf. Mari Sandoz, *Crazy Horse,* The Strange Man of the Oglalas (New York, 1944).

summer. Many of them had been willing to exchange the life of hardship on the plains for a comfortable and well-fed existence at the agencies. Touch the Clouds, Roman Nose, and Red Bear, acting under the advice of Spotted Tail, had surrendered with one thousand of their bands and were located at the Spotted Tail Agency, while one hundred Cheyennes had surrendered at Fort Robinson.

Yet months of solicitation on the part of Crook had failed to induce Crazy Horse, the victorious warrior of the campaign, to come in. Spotted Tail, with two hundred of his head men, had been to Montana in the dead of winter to urge the advisability of surrender for the fugitives entrenched in the mountains; but Crazy Horse was still undecided, though he knew he could not remain long in his retreat. Only one of two courses lay open to him—surrender, or flight to British America.

Owing to the hardships of the winter, Crazy Horse's wife was seriously ill. The medicine men had practised all their arts; but neither the sweat tepee nor their smoke pyres had brought relief from the cough which racked her body. This swayed the balance in favor of surrender rather than flight, for at an Indian agency doctors might perform some magic on his sick wife. There was also the consideration that the buffalo herds in the northwest were decreasing; these were fast yielding their empire to civilization.

At last, in May, 1877, Crazy Horse, the young war lord, consented to come in. His arrival was anticipated with great interest, couriers daily reporting his approach. The prairies were covered with buffalo grass, dotted with innumerable spring flowers, when his band marched out of the serrated cliffs of the Rocky Mountains, and meadow larks burst into songs that did not ease the pain in the heart of the warrior as he pushed on to Fort Robinson with his thousand followers and surrendered. Yet the surrender was not made with submission; nor was it unconditional. It was with provisos, rather than petitions, that the war chief made terms with the white man. He had not been conquered; and even if his capture in the States had impended, there had been always the possibility of escape to British America. For the present he had chosen to come to Fort Robinson and was willing, for the time at least, to live on government beef instead of trusting to the precarious bounty of the plains and to relinquish his wornout skin lodges for handsome new duck tents.

Crazy Horse's first request was that an army doctor come to see his sick wife. McGillycuddy attended the ailing woman, his wife often accompanying him on his professional visits to the camp. Fanny aroused much curiosity on her visits to the Indian villages. The squaws hunched themselves from the ground and approached her, exclaiming with low, guttural grunts. She greeted them with a friendly smile, shook hands with the squaws, and patted a papoose slung in a beaded bag from its mother's back. But their attention was riveted on her long green riding skirt as she sat on her horse. At last the most venturesome of the women lifted her skirt a trifle and peeked under. She nodded to the others. Their suspicions were correct; the white woman had but one foot. They looked commiseratingly at her. When the Doctor came out from the lodge of his patient and helped Fanny off her horse, asking her to go inside, the commiserating looks turned to amused surprise. The white woman had two feet. They had not seen the leg under the third horn. Fanny was well known in the camps by the time Crazy Horse's wife was one of McGillycuddy's patients. Their daily calls became half social, and a friendship developed between the Doctor and the Indian war chief while Fanny chatted with the women and children.

But Crook, a past master in his dealings with the Indians, had a new problem in the victorious warrior of the Sitting Bull campaign. The young leader was neither a politician nor a diplomat. He was a fanatic, whose sole interest was the cause of his people. And, since his surrender, a new situation had arisen among the Sioux. The two chiefs, Spotted Tail and Red Cloud, had become jealous of the adored warrior. They had not anticipated the hero worship which invariably follows the return of a successful military leader. Victor in the Battle of the Rosebud, and eight days later in the great Custer Battle, Crazy Horse became the idol of the young fighting element of the Sioux and Cheyennes, numbering many thousands, and suffered from the jealousy of his old friends. He became restless.

To solve the problem, Crook contemplated the appointment of Crazy Horse as head chief of the Ogallalas, thereby supplanting Red Cloud. It was not long, however, before he realized that agency life palled on the young warrior, who asked no tolerance, sufferance, or protection from the white man. Though Crazy Horse had agreed to a treaty of peace, he retained the right of free life on his hunting grounds and the privilege of living on the game which those lands supplied—lands long possessed by his ancestors.

Unostentatious, unself-conscious, fanatical, Crazy Horse showed the sufferings of his people on his mystic face. With no ornaments symbolic of his chieftainship— no eagle feathers or warshirt, no paint or beadwork—his silent figure passed among the camps, invariably alone. Only his eye betokened the power of the leader. Indian youths rolling their hoops or engaged in a game of shinny stopped their sports as the silent warrior passed, apparently unconscious of their homage or even of their presence. The problems of his race engrossed him. He longed to be roving again with his people over the great prairies and mountain ranges, hunting buffalo and deer or fishing the streams. Agency life with its regulation of rations was no life for a warrior accustomed to the satisfaction of maintenance by effort. Even to return, empty-handed, from the chase and to feel the pangs of hunger while awaiting a more successful hunt was better than living the life of a squaw, sitting about a campfire. His restlessness was increased by messages continually brought him by runners from Sitting Bull, who had crossed the British American line in the month of his own surrender, urging him to escape and join Sitting Bull in the north. Always there were tales of the herds of buffalo, of venison cooked on campfires, and of trout leaping in the sunlight. The young warrior laid plans to be off, counting on a following of about two thousand Indians.

Crook, aware of Crazy Horse's restlessness, in a council held soon after his surrender promised the Indians a big buffalo hunt in the fall. The prospect had kept the chief more or less contented until the time for the expected hunt arrived and he saw no move toward the fulfillment of the promise. By that time the general had become doubtful of the advisability of allowing the Indians to indulge in their favorite sport. Also Spotted Tail opposed the plan. It was more than probable, he said, that many of the malcontents would leave the hunting party and escape into British America to join Sitting Bull. And the promise of the buffalo hunt, like many others made to the Indians, remained unfulfilled.

. .

Crazy Horse's wife steadily improved in health; and as the friendship between him and the Doctor grew, he was led at last to talk of Indian wars. Though he seemed unwilling to speak of the campaign on the Little Big Horn, he was finally induced to do so. He told his story with no sign of boasting.

"No one got away," he said, "but the officer who put spurs to his horse and galloped to the east, and the Crow scout." Several warriors pursued the officer, but his horse was powerful and fleet and they soon gave up the chase to return to the fight. Just after they turned their horses a shot rang out in the direction of the fleeing officer and, looking back they saw him fall from his horse. His foot caught in the stirrup, and the war-maddened animal plunged across the prairie dragging his rider behind him. If he hadn't shot himself, the chief said, he would probably have reached Terry's camp the next day.

Crazy Horse said there were two thousand women and children in the Little Big Horn Valley when Reno surprised them. He was reticent when asked concerning the mutilation of the bodies of Custer's command but finally said that all but three suffered mutilation. He had given strict orders that Custer's body should be untouched because he was the soldier-chief. There was some difficulty in deciding which was his body, since two other officers also dressed in buckskin. Besides, Custer no longer wore the long hair nor the red shirt which had distinguished him from the rest. He at length was identified when maps and papers were found in his pockets.

Captain Keogh's body escaped mutilation for two reasons—the Indians knew and liked him well, and they found around his neck, when he was stripped, a silver charm, the Agnus Dei, which they looked upon as a holy charm.

The third unmutilated body was that of the little trumpeter who had visited the camps on the Missouri River and had become friendly with the Sioux. The squaws, to whom the rite of mutilation belonged, spared his corpse.

McGillycuddy asked Crazy Horse what had determined the abandonment of the stronghold in the Little Big Horn Valley. The chief explained that they had heard of the nearness of Terry's army through their scouts and had known that, once his forces joined with those of Crook's, which they had lately encountered, they would be overpowered. When told that Reno's command had seen the dust of his retreating party from their entrenchment on the bluffs Tuesday morning, the war-chief said: "It was not the dust we raised in our retreat they saw. We left the valley as soon as darkness came on Monday night. It was the dust of *Wicanpi Yamini's* army."

When Crook realized the disappointment as well as resentment in the heart of the war chief at the abandonment of the plan for the buffalo hunt, he shrewdly evolved a scheme of enlisting his services against another tribe of Indians, with whom Crazy Horse was not on friendly terms. These were the Nez Perces under Chief Joseph, whose reservation was in the Wallula Valley in Washington. Until that year their treaty rights had been observed, but in 1877 the settlers living on the fringe of the reservation waxed greedy for the lands in the fertile valley, and a reduction of their territory resulted. This led to a revolt of the hitherto peaceable tribe, who attacked the settlers, resisted the soldiers, and fled across Idaho into the mountains of Montana, where they were entrenched at this time.

Some old grudge existed between the Nez Perces and the Crazy Horse band. Crook recognized the value of this antagonism and hoped to enlist Crazy Horse's services against the common enemy. It not only would aid the military in their invasion of the retreat but would keep the young warrior occupied; and the general went to Fort Robinson on September 2 to formulate plans for co-operation. On the following day he proceeded with his staff to Crazy Horse's camp taking the scout, Frank Grouard, as interpreter in the council which had been called.

There was unfriendliness between Crazy Horse and Grouard because of the latter's desertion of Sitting Bull, who had brought him up, early in the spring of 1876 when Sitting Bull went on the warpath. Grouard was despised by the Indians, who claimed that Sitting Bull had treated him as his own son. Grouard had doubly outraged them by taking service with Crook against them. It was unfortunate for Crazy Horse that this renegade scout acted as interpreter in the council, which broke up in misunderstanding and suspicion.

While the council was in session at the Indian village, McGillycuddy started for the camp on his usual professional visit. When halfway to the village, he saw an ambulance approaching at a rapid pace. General Crook leaned out as he neared the Doctor and ordered him to return at once to the post, saying it would not be safe for him to go on, since the Indians were in a hostile mood and were threatening to go on the warpath. McGillycuddy said he had seen the chiefs every day and they had shown no hostility. He pleaded for permission to go on; but it was refused.

Soon after dinner the Doctor was visited by Louis Bordeaux, who exclaimed, "There's goin' to be the devil to pay if this thing ain't straightened up." He went on to say that Grouard had misinterpreted Crazy Horse's words in the council. After the general had asked if Crazy Horse would go to Montana and fight for the government, Crazy Horse had risen and answered: "Myself and my people are tired of war. We have come in and surrendered to the Great Father and asked for peace. But now, if he wishes us to go to war again and asks our help, we will go north and fight till there is not a Nez Perce left." He had sat down amid a chorus of *"How, How,"* from the other chiefs. But Grouard had not interpreted the last part of the warrior's speech correctly, Bordeaux said. He had quoted Crazy Horse as saying: "We will go north and fight till there is not a white man left."

Bordeaux had wanted to tell the general the mistake, but as soon as Grouard had finished speaking Crook and his staff had got up and walked out of the council lodge. The chiefs had not understood: They had been asked to become allies of the Great Father and had agreed to do so. They wondered why the white chief did not remain and make plans for the campaign. Bordeaux said that Grouard was afraid the Indians would kill him because of his desertion of Sitting Bull and, for that reason, wished to engage them in trouble with the government.

When Bordeaux departed, McGillycuddy went to Crook's quarters to tell him what he had said. But Crook had confidence in Grouard who had served him as interpreter for a long time, and did not trust Crazy Horse. He departed the following morning for Fort Laramie, a distance of sixty-three miles to the west.

McGillycuddy asked permission to make his regular visit to the camp the next morning, hoping that in a private talk with Crazy Horse he might get at the truth of Bordeaux's statement, which he thoroughly believed. Colonel Bradley, in command, refused his request, saying it would be unsafe for him to go to the village. McGillycuddy said he would take his wife with him to prove his faith in the chief. Bradley said he was crazy.

The second evening after his departure Crook sent orders to Bradley to send troops to the hostile village the following morning, arrest Crazy Horse, and hold him prisoner until further orders. McGillycuddy was detailed as surgeon with the command, which consisted of eight troops of cavalry, four hundred friendly Indians, and one piece of field artillery under Lieutenant Philo Clark.

Dark clouds scuttled across the sky; the hooves of the cavalry horses clattered up the valley, accompanied by the rumble of cannon wheels as the troops marched toward Crazy Horse's village. At a narrow defile entering the camp they encountered a lone horseman whose war bonnet of eagle feathers towered above his head and extended to the end of the horse's tail. The animal stood across the road leading into the camp. As the troops advanced, the warrior raised his hand crying: "This is the village of Crazy Horse; it is his ground; no soldier comes here."

It was a futile gesture. He was pushed roughly aside, and the troops marched on to the village or rather to the spot where, on the previous evening, the village had stood. Now, instead of a camp alive with fifteen hundred bucks, squaws, and children, not an Indian nor a lodge was in sight: Crazy Horse had got wind of the movement and, in the dark hours of night, silently had vanished with his band.

Bradley ordered a search among the Indian camps, but Crazy Horse was not to be found. It seemed that this land which he had fought to save for his people had opened its arms and encompassed him.

Early the next morning a courier arrived from the Spotted Tail Agency, forty-three miles to the east, with a message from Major Daniel Burke, commanding the troops at that agency, saying that Crazy Horse had come to Spotted Tail's village. Bradley sent orders to arrest the chief and return him to Fort Robinson where he belonged. The courier reached the Agency at sundown. Burke summoned Spotted Tail and told him of the order. Spotted Tail replied that Crazy Horse was his guest: he was a chief, and he could not be taken prisoner; but if the soldier-chief wished to speak with him, they would come together and hold council. Burke asked that he bring Crazy Horse to his office at nine o'clock the next morning.

The two chiefs arrived according to agreement, and Crazy Horse was informed that General Bradley requested his return to Fort Robinson for a council. The warrior replied that he was willing to counsel. Burke asked Lieutenant Jesse M. Lee, Acting Agent at the Spotted Tail Agency, to accompany Crazy Horse to Fort Robinson, withholding from Lee the information that the chief was under arrest. Louis Bordeaux was sent as interpreter with the two, who left immediately for Fort Robinson in an ambulance accompanied by a mounted Indian escort.

Halfway to the post they lunched under the trees on Chadron Creek. After the meal was finished, Crazy Horse, sauntering along the stream, heard the tread of moccasined feet behind him. A look of surprise crossed the warrior's face as he said: "I see I am a prisoner." Without a word of protest he retraced his steps to the ambulance.

At Fort Robinson, Lee, Crazy Horse, and Bordeaux went to the adjutant's office, and were received by Captain Kennington, officer of the day, to whom Lee reported that he had brought Crazy Horse to counsel with General Bradley. Kennington said he knew nothing of a council; his orders were to put Crazy Horse in the guardhouse. Bordeaux whispered to Lee that they had better get away. If they tried to put Crazy Horse in the guardhouse, the Indians would blame them for bringing him there. Lee suggested they go to see the Colonel; and they struck across the parade ground to his quarters, leaving the warrior with Kennington.

McGillycuddy was crossing the parade ground from his quarters on his way to the adjutant's office when he met Lee and Bordeaux, who seemed greatly disturbed. Lee remarked to the Doctor: "I'm not going to be made a goat of in this affair." As McGillycuddy approached the office he noticed a number of officers standing near. Before he reached the door it opened, and Kennington, Crazy Horse, and Little Big Man, who was serving as scout, came outside and turned toward the guardhouse. As Crazy Horse passed the Doctor, he greeted him with the friendly salutation, *"How kola."* The guardhouse door opened, the three entered, and the door was quickly closed. One of the officers said to the Doctor that the arrest had gone off smoothly enough; he guessed there would be no trouble after all.

Hardly had he spoken when the door flew open and Crazy Horse dashed out brandishing a knife in either hand. Captain Kennington grasped his left arm, Little Big Man his right, as Kennington cried: "Call out the guard!"

The officers scattered to company quarters, while the double guard of twenty men who had been stationed near the guardhouse drew in. Kennington loosed his hold on Crazy Horse and jumped to one side, while the guard immediately surrounded him. The chief lunged from side to side in his effort to escape through the circle. McGillycuddy saw one of the guard, a private of the Ninth Infantry, make a pass at him, and the chief fell to the ground writhing and struggling. The Doctor pushed his way through the guard and knelt by the warrior. Blood trickled from a wound above his right hip where the guard's bayonet had entered to traverse his abdomen. Froth oozed from his mouth; his pulse dropped rapidly, he was evidently mortally wounded.

McGillycuddy worked his way out of the crowd and explained to Kennington Crazy Horse's condition. Kennington replied that his orders had been to put the chief in the guardhouse and into the guardhouse he would go—the Doctor should take one leg, he'd take the other, a guard would take his head, and they'd put him in.

Several hundred Indians, mounted or on foot, were closing in on them, menacing in their attitude. The Doctor saw Grouard peering around the corner of the commissary building and beckoned him to come; but the interpreter shook his head and disappeared. McGillycuddy then saw his own interpreter, Johnny Provost, not far off, who answered his summons.

During the commotion Colonel Bradley had been pacing up and down the porch of his quarters several hundred feet across the parade ground. As Kennington and the Doctor started to raise the wounded chief, one of his warriors placed a hand on McGillycuddy's shoulder and motioned him to desist. At the same time the hostiles began loading their carbines and drawing toward them. Kennington accepted the Doctor's offer to report conditions to Bradley, who, after the situation was explained, answered that his orders were to be carried out. McGillycuddy returned and delivered his message.

Not far away, American Horse, one of the friendly Indians, sat mounted on his pony. The Doctor repeated the Colonel's message to him with the assurance that if the chiefs would consent to their taking Crazy Horse into the guardhouse he would care for him personally and give him every attention. American Horse replied that Crazy Horse was a chief and must not be put in prison.

Again McGillycuddy crossed to Bradley's quarters and reported the refusal of the friendly as well as the hostile Indians to allow the chief to be imprisoned. He suggested that, owing to the friendliness of the Indians toward him, he might be able to bring about a compromise and put the dying chief in the adjutant's office. He would not last the night, he said. Bradley consented to the compromise.

McGillycuddy then rejoined American Horse, who, when he heard of the change of plan, jumped off his pony and spread his blanket on the ground beside Crazy Horse; and, motioning some of the young bucks to come forward, he helped them lift him gently on the blanket and carry him into the adjutant's office.

"It was one of the knives on the soldiers' guns that wounded me," the warrior said, writhing in agony. "It passed across my body. I shall die before sunup." Morphine relieved his pain for a time.

On account of the general disturbance among the fifteen thousand Sioux surrounding the post, the entire garrison of eight hundred men was kept on picket all night. Attempts at reprisal were feared.

Until sundown the Indians were allowed in the post; they came continually to the office to inquire Crazy Horse's condition. After retreat, only his father, an old chief of eighty years, and his mother's uncle, Touch the Cloud, a chief of the Minnecoujou Sioux, whose name was inspired by his great height of nearly seven feet, were allowed to remain.

On a pile of blankets in a corner of the office the young chief lay dying. His father stood near, his face drawn. "We were not agency Indians," he said. "We belonged in the North on the buffalo ranges. We did not want the white man's beef; we asked only to live by hunting and fishing. But during the winter the Gray Fox[1] continually sent runners to us, saying, 'Come in, come in.' We have come in, and hard times are upon us. My son was a brave man; only thirty-six winters have passed over him. Red Cloud was jealous of him. We were getting tired of his jealousy and would not have remained here long." The

[1] General Crook.—J. B. McG.

old man stood with arms folded across his breast, his eyes fastened on his son's face.

The long evening wore on. The office, dimly lighted by an ill-smelling kerosene lamp, was dismal. The monotony of the watch was broken occasionally by the entrance of the officer of the day and the officer of the guard. The Doctor scarcely left the side of the patient.

As the effect of the morphine wore off, a look of recognition appeared in Crazy Horse's fast-dimming eyes. A half-stifled groan passed his lips as he said feebly, *"How kola."* Another hypodermic eased his pain. It was no use to let him suffer, the Doctor said to the two old chiefs, who sat on the floor at the far end of the room; he would die soon. The old men grunted approval.

Outside the office could be heard the rhythmic march of the sentry, his measured tread mocking the stertorous breathing of the dying warrior. At last through the chill night air taps sounded from the sentry before the guardhouse. Now Crazy Horse roused from his lethargy. The significance of the notes he was beyond understanding. A bugle call now meant one thing to the half-conscious warrior—the summons of the white soldier against his people. Perhaps in his dimming eye he saw the fair-haired general with his army charging on their stronghold in the valley of the Little Big Horn. On his failing brain may have been pictured the tragedy of his race, whose God-given lands and herds were being stolen from them, leaving them paupers in the hands of their conquerors. He raised his hand a trifle as his rallying cry to his braves on the banks of the Little Big Horn was repeated feebly, this time from pale lips: *"Okici ze anpetu waste. . . . "* His head dropped. The Doctor thought he would not speak again; but after a few seconds the words came faintly: *"Cante wasaka . . .,"* and once more leading his soldiers against the intruders, the greatest of the Sioux warriors rode into the happy hunting ground in search of the white buffalo.

McGillycuddy gave the Indian sign announcing to the watchers that Crazy Horse was dead. Touch the Cloud strode across the room to the corner where the body lay and drew the blanket over the head of the slain chief; then, drawing himself to his full height, he pointed to the slim figure outlined beneath the cover and said: "That is the lodge of Crazy Horse." Then, seeming to grow taller in the dim light as he pointed upward, he added: "The chief has gone above.

At midnight the adjutant's office was closed. McGillycuddy crossed the parade ground to his quarters. Touch the Cloud followed silently, rolled himself in his blanket, and lay down outside McGillycuddy's door, on guard lest any harm come to the man who, in after years, was known as *Tasunka Witko Kola,* Crazy Horse's friend, while he slept. In some mysterious manner word of the death of the war chief spread in an incredibly short time into the surrounding camps of the Indians, and from miles about rose the death wail, hideously gloomy in the darkness. In the early morning Crazy Horse's body was given to a delegation of Indians from his own band to prepare for burial. It was embalmed by a process of drying and placed on a platform on selected ground at the Spotted Tail Agency near Fort Sheridan. For three days his parents sat without food, beside his resting place; then Lieutenant Lee discovered them and sent food to them. The great warrior who by his loyalty to his people in fighting for their rights had become *persona non grata* to the white man did not know that a detail had been ordered to take him that night to the Dry Tortugas in Florida, the St. Helena of the Indian; death had spared him the ultimate humiliation.

Cochise

I. Why Cochise Went on the Warpath[1]

. . . Cochise, the most celebrated and cruel warrior who terrorized the Southwest two generations ago . . . was born in a canyon of the Chiricahua Mountains early in the nineteenth century. For almost twelve years—from 1861 to 1872—Cochise and his warriors ravaged a wide area of country extending from the Gila River far into Old Mexico, and eastward in New Mexico as far as the Mimbres River. He held impregnable strongholds far back and up amid the canyons and pinnacles of the rugged Dragoon and Chiricahua Mountains, and from these lurking places he would dispatch far and wide small bands of his picked warriors to plunder wagon trains, stampede cattle and horses, and murder unprotected settlers. He rarely attacked in the open, seldom risked an encounter with soldiers on the march or companies of well-armed men. His scouts, concealed in some lofty lookout, would scan the valleys and mesas for small companies of careless travelers or unguarded wagon trains of immigrants, and then at some favorable ford or pass, would ambush them—slay, burn, and loot with little loss on their part. Or they would creep up to some isolated ranch, kill the men, murder or carry into captivity women and children, plunder the household, destroy the crops, and drive the cattle before them into the mountain fastnesses. They were ever on the alert for surveying parties, mine inspectors, mail stages, and solitary travelers. Pursuit was vain, since they knew every trail, crevice, and canyon for a hundred miles in every direction, could travel on foot from fifty to seventy-five miles a day over the roughest country, had a secret code of smoke signals by which they could communicate over wide reaches of country, could conceal themselves behind rocks, cactus, and tufts of bear grass and pick off at will either soldier or settler who was so unwise as to risk

[1] From *Pioneer Days in Arizona,* from the Spanish Occupation to Statehood, by Frank C. Lockwood, pp. 160–163. Copyright, 1932, by The Macmillan Company. New York.

himself in their retreats—in vain because Cochise was incomparable as a commander and a strategist.

Up to 1860, Cochise had been on friendly terms with the Americans. Just previous to the incident I am about to relate, he had been encamped near Bowie, supplying wood to the station of the Overland Stage Company at that point. On more than one occasion when he had learned that other tribes were about to attack parties of immigrants, he had sent members of his own band to prevent such attacks. This situation was all suddenly changed by the unfortunate act of a young lieutenant of the United States Army, George N. Bascom, who had recently been assigned to duty in Arizona.

In October, 1860, a band of Apaches plundered the home of Johnny Ward, an Irishman, on the Sonoita River, and carried off the son of a Mexican woman with whom he was living. The boy was born while his mother was in captivity, his father being an Apache Indian. When Ward learned that the child had been taken he went to Fort Buchanan, about twelve miles distant, reported the fact to the commanding officer, and requested that an effort be made to restore the boy to his mother. It was known that the stage station at Apache Pass was frequented by Indians, and that Cochise and his band were then encamped nearby; so it was thought that information about the boy might there be secured. A platoon of the Seventh Infantry under command of Second Lieutenant George N. Bascom was, therefore, dispatched on this duty.

When Bascom arrived at the pass, he invited Cochise and a number of other chiefs to confer with him. He demanded that Cochise return the captured boy and the cattle that had been stolen from Ward's ranch. Cochise said that they did not have the boy and that they knew nothing about the affair, but that he would do his best to find out where the boy and the booty were and, if possible, have them returned. Bascom refused to take him at his word and placed him under arrest with other Indians who had been invited to this friendly conference. The Indians were imprisoned in a tent and a detail of soldiers was set to guard them. Cochise suddenly reached down into his geestring, drew a knife, and slashing open the rear of the tent, said to Bascom with an American oath and the basest of American epithets:

"I'm no prisoner of yours!"

Though wounded as he made his exit, and pursued by the soldiers, he made his way through the grass and rocks up the little hill where the Fort Bowie graveyard now is and escaped to the mountains. He captured two Americans, Jordan and Lyons, and offered to exchange them for his imprisoned companions. Bascom refused to make the exchange. A little later Wallace, the station keeper, who spoke Apache pretty well, feeling sure of the friendliness of the Indians toward him, visited the camp of Cochise to try to mediate. But he, too, was seized and held with the other captives. Cochise now brought his prisoners to a point within sight and hearing distance of the station, where they pleaded most earnestly with Bascom that terms be made, as the Indians were in war paint and had already tortured them. Bascom ignored these desperate appeals, even though Sergeant Reuben Bernard did his best to bring him to reason. The Sergeant was afterwards court-martialed on the charge of disobeying orders but was exonerated. Cochise, infuriated, at last put Wallace to the torture, and in full sight of the troops dragged him to death over the sharp rocks behind his galloping horse. The next day, when the detachment began to retreat toward Fort Buchanan, Bascom came upon two other Americans who had been put to the torture and hanged. He now retaliated by hanging his Indian prisoners, some of them Cochise's own relatives, to an oak tree that grew a hundred yards from the trail. From that hour Cochise vowed a war of extermination upon all whites in the Territory. During the next eleven years hundreds of American lives and hundreds of thousands of dollars of destroyed property were required to wipe out young Bascom's error.

II. General Howard Makes Peace with Cochise[2]

My several efforts to complete this most important part of my mission had been thus far unavailing, but I was not ready to give up the chase. I determined to seek for some one of Cochise's various trails to the east and follow that back till I could uncover his hiding-place. We had a glimmer of light to aid us—some vague stories from the wife of a half-breed living near Camp Apache. She was a Chiricahuan. She was sure the old chief would not let us go directly to any of his strongholds, but she knew that he occasionally went eastward, crossing New Mexico as far as the Rio Grande.

I resolved to go first to a camp of soldiers and Apaches in New Mexico which my instructions required me to visit. These Apaches were kindred to the Chiricahuas. The camp was at Tulerosa, in the western part of New Mexico. On my arrival I found there Victorio's Apache band, which had been recently brought from the Rio Grande. The home they came from bore the musical name of Cañada Alamosa. All were full of discontent at the transfer, and the officers of the garrison said that these Apaches had been sorely ill-used. At the first interview they pleaded: "Oh, take us back home to Agua Caliente on the Rio Grande! we are dying here. At Cañada Alamosa there is good land, good water, and good food." Patiently I heard the Indian's complaints and promised a visit to that salubrious Cañada, i.e., if Victorio would send with me a proper delegation; and, further, I would carry this petition for the Indian's return to the Rio Grande directly to the President.

---

[2] From *My Life and Personal Experiences among Our Hostile Indians,* A Record of Personal Observations, Adventures, and Campaigns among the Indians of the Great West . . ., by Major-General O. O. Howard, pp. 186–189, 203–209, 213, 219–222. Entered, according to Act of Congress, in the year 1907, by A. D. Worthington & Company, in the Office of the Librarian of Congress at Washington, D. C. Hartford, Connecticut.

While I was interviewing the Indians and the officers of the garrison, a returning troop of cavalry that had been chasing some wild Apaches brought in as its guide a singular character of whom I had frequently heard but had never seen. Everybody called him "Tom Jeffords." I may say that frontiersmen, though this was not much to his discredit, gave him a bad reputation. "Tom Jeffords! He's a bad egg; he trades with Indians, sells them whisky, powder and shot. They don't kill him 'cause he's bought 'em up."

At one period while the stage was running regularly on the Tucson road, Jeffords, living in that neighborhood, had managed to keep the good will of the Apaches. On one occasion, when the driver and other passengers were killed, Jeffords, who was on the stage, was spared. Whenever after that he had fallen into their hands he had always escaped. Major Pope told me that he had once managed to reach the Chiricahua chief through Jeffords, and that he was confident that the man had dealt honestly with him. I believed it a good providence which now threw him in my way.

Learning that the cavalry troops had actually arrived, I went to their camp to find Jeffords. The first tent I entered a tall, spare man, with reddish hair and whiskers of considerable length rose to meet me. He was pleasant and affable, and I was in the outset prepossessed in his favor. Giving my name I asked:

"Is this Mr. Jeffords?"

"Yes, sir, that is my name."

"Can you take me to the camp of the Indian Cochise?"

He looked steadily and inquiringly into my eyes and then asked:

"Will you go there with me, General, without soldiers?"

"Yes," I answered, "if necessary."

"Then I will take you to him." Something in his brave face and decided manner made me believe that he could and would do as he said.

With those Tulerosa Indians was a young chief called "Chie," the son of Magnus Colorado, Cochise's brother, a notorious chief captured and killed by our people in 1863. Jeffords said: "Chie must go with us as a guide and friendly witness." By giving a horse to him and another to his young wife, who was to stay behind, after some delay he was induced to go. The officers of the garrison trusted Chie and spoke well of him. He had often been a hunter for them.

Jeffords seemed in no haste. He favored our making the expedition, which I had promised, back to the Rio Grande. He declared that he must find Ponce, another young chief, who with a roving band had recently fled from Fort Stanton and was somewhere near Cañada Alamosa depredating on the country. Ponce's Apache father had been in his lifetime Cochise's friend. Ponce knew Spanish and would be a true interpreter. Of course, like a good general, Jeffords planned to have everything possible in our favor. "Ponce is a favorite friend of the old man," he averred. "He and Chie will make us welcome to Cochise's stronghold."

We made the expedition to Cañada Alamosa and attended to all Victorio's wants, and enabled him to renew his petition for a return to that favorite land. We then began a diligent search first for Ponce's band.

This was the make-up of my party which left Cañada Alamosa the 20th of September: Captain Jeffords, Jake May, an Anglo-Spanish interpreter, two packers leading their pack-horses, Chie, Captain Sladen, and myself. We were all well mounted. I had besides our pack-horses a good four-wheeled ambulance, and a driver who was also a passable cook. The ambulance was to keep on wagon roads, but the rest of us could follow the trail at will and so shorten the distances in each day's march. It was only at long halts that we had the ambulance with us at all.

* * * * *

We made our bivouac near the creek under a tree, amid a throng of those wild people who, in the outset, appeared curious and happy, not hostile. That evening Tygee, a sub-chief, paid us a visit, courteous enough, it is true, but he himself was gloomy and reserved, and had no word from Cochise. Even Ponce and Chie were troubled and silent.

"Will it be peace?" I asked.

Ponce shook his head and answered demurely: *"Quien sabe?"* i.e., "Who knows?"

When I had spread out my blanket and placed my saddle for a pillow, and was lying down for much-needed rest, the children came and nestled at my feet, laying their little heads upon my blanket. I turned to Captain Sladen and said: "This does not mean war"; so without particular apprehension I slept comfortably till morning. The Apache band had made their bivouac under the small trees at a distance near the debris of the great walls.

After our breakfast the following day we began to be uncertain as to our next step. I asked: "What shall we do now, Jeffords?"

"Pack up as if we could go where we please," he replied. Therefore, to show our independence, not very real, we were packing up and making ready, when suddenly the sound of many voices arose and echoed through the canyon. Ponce said: "It is he; he is coming!"

Immediately preparations were made by the Indians to receive their chief. The circle of sitters was enlarged on the higher bank of the creek, and a folded blanket placed for his seat.

First there appeared in advance, riding rapidly down the ravine, a single horseman, short, thick-set, and much painted with stripes of black and vermilion. He had a fierce look and carried a long lance in his hand. He dismounted and embraced Jeffords, while I asked: "Is that the man?"

"No," said Jeffords, "this is Juan, his brother." The Indians never say Cochise, but in Apache *"Shi-ca-she,"* and in Spanish *"Mi Hermano,"* meaning my brother.

We had hardly been made acquainted with the warlike Juan, who was diligently inspecting our personal possessions, when a mounted party appeared. It consisted of a fine-looking horseman, a younger Indian, and two women. The party proved to be the old Chief Cochise, his son Natchez, his sister, and his young wife. His elder son was absent.

Having ridden up to us Cochise dismounted and saluted Jeffords in Spanish as an old friend. He then turned to me as Jeffords was saying: "This is the man." The chief was fully six feet in height, well proportioned, with large eyes; his face was slightly colored with vermilion, hair straight and black, with a few silver threads. He warmly grasped my hand and said pleasantly: *"Buenos dias, Señor!"*

Having returned his salute I began to study his face. His countenance was pleasant, and made me feel how strange it is that such a man can be a notorious robber and cold-blooded murderer. In after interviews I observed that upon ordinary occasions he showed courtesy and simplicity, but, as the Chiricahua chief, when in council or mounted, leading his tribe, if Apache wrongs were touched upon, he was terribly severe in aspect.

As soon as Cochise's sister met Ponce he said something evidently very afflicting to her, for she sat down, and for some minutes uttered a loud and continuous Indian wail. Everybody stood still till she had finished, then Cochise and I passed up to where the blanket was placed and took seats. Already the Indians—men, women, and children—had arranged themselves about us in a large semicircle, giving due form and interest to the proceedings. Cochise now turned to Ponce and Chie, who were seated upon his right, and proceeded to gather from them what he could of my history and designs. Both Ponce and Chie were now my strong friends and their story evidently created a favorable impression.

Next Cochise turned to me and said something in Apache. Jeffords gave the substance in English: "Will the General explain the object of his visit?"

"The President sent me to make peace between you and the white people."

"Nobody wants peace more than I do," he replied.

"Then," I answered, "as I have full power we can make peace."

He then continued: "I have done no mischief since I came from Cañada Alamosa, but I am poor, my horses poor and few. I might have brought in more by raiding the Tucson road, but I did not do it."

Cochise, however, acknowledged later that he had recently sent out twelve captains in different directions in Mexico and Arizona to get their living. He next recited at some length his own story of the Apache wrongs.

I answered that I knew of these things; that there were two parties in the United States—one friendly to the Indians, and the other hostile to them; that the friends of the Indians were now in power, with General Grant at the head. I then broached my plan of making, on the Rio Grande, a common reservation for the different bands of Apaches, including his own.

"I have been there," Cochise replied, "and I like the country. Rather than not have peace I will go and take such of my people as I can, but that move will break up my tribe." Then he asked suddenly: "Why not give me Apache Pass? Give me that and I will protect the roads. I will see that nobody's property is taken by Indians." As he said this his eyes flashed and he lifted his chin proudly.

I answered: "Perhaps we could do that, but it would be vastly to the interest of the Chiricahuas to go to Alamosa. Five rivers are near there: the Rio Grande, the Alamosa, the Negro, the Palomas, and the Puerco; in their valleys are fine planting grounds and good grazing for thousands of cattle; plenty of mescal plants are there, and there is good hunting in the mountains."

He quickly turned the subject. "How long, General, will you stay? Will you wait for my captains to come in and have a talk?

These were startling questions, considering that our lives were at his disposal, but I answered promptly: "I came from Washington to meet your people and make peace, and will stay as long as necessary."

"It will take ten days," Cochise said. He appeared to be pleased at my answer and ordered his messengers to the captains to get ready; then his whole manner changed and he went into a complaining and sometimes fierce recital of the bloody history of the Apaches.

"We were once a large people covering these mountains; we lived well; we were at peace. One day my best friend was seized by an officer of the white men and treacherously killed. . . . The worst place of all is Apache Pass. There, five Indians, one my brother, were murdered. Their bodies were hung up and kept there till they were skeletons. . . . Now Americans and Mexicans kill an Apache on sight. I have retaliated with all my might. My people have killed Americans and Mexicans and taken their property. Their losses have been greater than mine. I have killed ten white men for every Indian slain, but I know that the whites are many and the Indians are few. Apaches are growing less and less every day. . . . Why shut me up on a reservation? We will make peace. We will keep it faithfully. But let us go around free as Americans do. Let us go wherever we please."

I answered that all this country did not properly belong to the Indians; that all God's children had an interest in it, and therefore to keep the peace we must fix metes and bounds; that such a peace as Cochise proposed would not last a week. "Suppose," I said, "some rough prospectors should fire upon and kill a portion of your band, or suppose some of your wild young men should take the life of a citizen, the peace would then be hopelessly broken."

After considerably more plaintive pleading he said: "You Americans began the fight." I replied, as before: "I know that. A large number of your friends fully believe what you state and they wish to see war, murder, and robbery cease."

He smiled and in a different tone added: "I am glad you have come, but will not the soldiers fire upon my Apaches as they come in?" To this I answered that I would send Captain Sladen to Camp Bowie to notify that garrison and to telegraph to other posts. Cochise shook his head doubtfully. "The soldiers may not obey Captain Sladen. They will obey you. I want you to go. Jeffords and Captain Sladen can stay here."

Looking around upon the people with a smile he added: "Our young women will look after the young captain." Thereupon shouting and laughter, with clapping of hands, came from all the women in response. I hardly think Sladen enjoyed the alternative, even though he had evidence of such popularity.

I decided to go back over the Dragoon mountain fifty miles or more to Camp Bowie, and therefore asked for a guide. None of Cochise's people dared to go. They answered the chief as he spoke to them: "There is no peace yet. We might be killed." At last Chie stepped forward and said: "I will go, if Jeffords will give me his mule."

Then, the mule being given, Chie and I prepared to make the journey. We mounted and rode westward to the mouth of the canyon. Our friends, accompanied by Cochise and several Indians, went with us that far. Stopping on high ground and leaning against a large smooth-faced stone we gazed around. Before us was a magnificent landscape. As Cochise raised his eyes and took in the view he exclaimed: *"Shi-cowah!"* i.e., "My Home!"

* * * * *

I was now to live with the Indians for some time. The new camping ground to which Cochise took us was north of the entrance to his stronghold, well up on the foothills where were clusters of oaks and several acres of grass land. Six miles off stood a globular height, springing three hundred feet from the plain, with the San Pedro River at its foot. On this hill, at the request of Cochise, Jeffords and Sladen had planted a white flag. Sladen told me how the Indian women and children clapped their hands when they first saw this emblem of peace. Jeffords had understood them when in one compound word in Apache they cried: "The-flag-of-peace-I-love!"

* * * * *

Other Apaches continued to come in until nearly all were in camp. Many of the newcomers were rough and very troublesome, and an adjustment of all vexed questions was hard to bring about. I was forced to abandon the Alamosa scheme, and to give them as Cochise had suggested, a reservation embracing a part of the Chiricahua mountains and of the valley adjoining on the west, which included the Big Sulphur Spring and Rodgers' ranch.

The evening after the council a strange ceremony for consulting the spirits was observed by the Indians. It took place on a separate plateau near my bivouac. I was not to be present at the beginning of the performance. I could, however, hear the muffled sound of voices of a multitude of women apparently imitating the low moaning of the wind. Then all—men and women—sang with ever increasing volume of sound, and the women's voices rose higher and higher. It was a wild, weird performance.

In due time the roughest-appearing Apache that I had ever seen, tall and muscular, his long hair hanging in braids down his back, ran toward me. His manner was not as fierce as his appearance would indicate, for he now spoke gently and invited me and all our white men to join the band on the plateau. Arriving there we sat outside the women's circle—the male Indians being seated within it. As soon as the singing ceased the men kept on talking, but without rising. An authoritative voice now silenced all the others. It was Cochise speaking in a mournful recitative. More than once I heard him use Jeffords' sobriquet, *"Stag-li-to,"* meaning Redbeard. Our whole case was evidently being discussed at the meeting. Those were solemn moments to us, for we could not determine on which side of the Styx their superstitions might land us.

Fortunately, the spirits were on our side. Their answer to the Indian incantation was rendered through Cochise, who said: "Hereafter the white man and the Indian are to drink of the same water, eat of the same bread, and be at peace." I felt that the object of my mission was now accomplished.

The day following the spirits' favorable declaration we all set out to meet, by appointment, the officers from Camp Bowie. We were to assemble at Dragoon Springs. During the journey I rode a stout mule, carrying double; Cochise's Indian interpreter, with his supple arms encircling my waist, was my companion. Cochise, with his face freshly and hideously painted with vermilion up to his hair, had a fierce and repellent aspect. The wild yells of his mounted warriors seemed to excite him almost as much as the *tizwin* had done. On the way they made several wild charges at imaginary foes, and I could see how wagon trains of mules could easily be frightened and stampeded almost beyond recall.

Arriving at Dragoon Springs Cochise located his men with such skill that every one of them could in two minutes have been safely under the cover of a ravine, and in three minutes more have escaped behind a protecting hill, and so have passed to the mountains without the least hindrance.

Cochise now said to Jeffords: "I know your party and I trust you, but those people from Apache Pass (Camp Bowie) I do not know. How long have you known them?"

"I never saw them," said Jeffords. That was all the conversation that occurred between the Indians and ourselves before our arrival and their quick formation near the Dragoon Springs.

Major Sumner, with several officers and a few civilians, came out to meet us. We immediately entered into a council with the Indians which lasted four hours. It was substantially a repetition of those which I have already described. The metes and bounds of the reservation were fixed, the agency at Sulphur Springs established, and Jeffords was appointed as the agent of the Indian department. It was arranged that all Apaches when off from a road were to show a white flag, and all on a road were to meet people, as white men do, without any manifestation of fear.

One day while in Cochise's camp I noticed a beautiful rifle, a breech-loader that had been the property of Lieutenant Stewart whom the Indians had killed in battle. As I was thoughtfully looking it over, the old chief, who was intently watching my face, suddenly said: *"No trieste,* General!" I was thinking of the young officer's sudden death and how he was mourned at home. Cochise interpreted my thought and said in Spanish: "You know, General, that we do things in war that we do not do in peace." It was hard to comply with the old chief's admonition and not keep a sad countenance, but I did my best and told him that as I had been in war myself for many years I knew that what he said was true, but I longed for the time to come when all people would make peace and there would be no more war.

Cochise had said in the spirit council to his fellow Indians: "Hereafter the white man and the Indian are to drink of the same water and eat of the same bread."

The Ghost Dance Trouble

. . . Suddenly great excitement came into our midst. It broke so suddenly over us that a great many of the Indians did not know which way to turn. It was the craze of a new religion called the "Ghost Dance." This was in 1890. At that time very few of the Indians had any education, but they were very superstitious and their feelings were easily aroused and played upon.

One day I was called into the agent's office. There I saw an Indian called Short Bull and a young man known as Ce-re-aka-ruga-pi, or

---

From *My People, the Sioux,* by Luther Standing Bear, Hereditary Chief of the Oglala Tribe of the Sioux Nation, edited by E. A. Brininstool, pp. 217–230. Copyright, 1928, by Luther Standing Bear. Boston and New York: Houghton Mifflin Company.

Cf. James Mooney, *The Ghost Dance Religion and the Sioux Outbreak of 1890,* Fourteenth Annual Report, Bureau of American Ethnology, Part II.

Breaks-the-Pot-on-Him. The agent started to question them in front of me, and I shall never forget what Short Bull said. The agent asked him to tell about the new religion which they were all getting so excited about, and why he believed in it. Said Short Bull:

"We heard there was a wonderful man in the Far West. He was a Messiah, so several tribes gathered together to go and see him. We went to the place where the sun sets, and there we saw this man. He told us we were to have a new earth; that the old earth would be covered up, and while it was being covered we were to keep dancing so that we could remain on top of the dirt.

"This man told us that all the white people would be covered up, because they did not believe; even the Indians who did not believe would also be covered. He showed us visions of the olden times when the buffalo were plenty; when the big camps were on the plains. All our people were dancing and having a big feast.

"This man hit the ground and he made fire. He spoke to all of us at once, and all the different tribes understood him. He said that all the white people would be destroyed. He taught us a song to sing during this dance. He showed us where the sun dropped into the ocean, and it boiled up and became hot."

At this point I spoke up and said to Short Bull, "That is not so; the ocean does not boil up with the setting of the sun."

Short Bull looked straight at me, but he had nothing further to say about the sun.

The agent spoke to both these men politely, and asked them not to stir up the Indians at Rosebud Agency. They both promised, and then left for home.

The first thing we knew, the majority of the Rosebud Indians had joined the ghost dancers. We could see the dust flying skyward from the dancing, and hear the beat of the tom-toms. They would keep up the dancing until they fell from exhaustion.

The ghost dance was being held about eight miles west of the agency on a flat, on the west side of Little Flat River. We could plainly locate the dancers from the dust they raised. The Indians were really serious about it, and had full faith in what they were doing. They felt that this new religion was going to rid them of the hated pale-faces who had antagonized them so long.

My father's band had not joined the dancers yet. Two of his brothers-in-law were in charge of them. High Pipe . . . was one of the men, and Black Horn was the other. Father had already moved over to Pine Ridge with his family, but had left his two brothers-in-law in charge of the balance of the Indians.

The dust was flying high in the sky every day from the dancing. As the enthusiasm grew, more Indians joined. Then George Wright, the agent, sent for me to see if I would go to my father's band with a message from him. This band was located about five miles west of the agency on the east side of Little White River, so they were only about three miles from the dancers across the river. They could both hear and see the dancers easier than ourselves.

I agreed to go, and Mr. Wright furnished me with a team and driver. He was a white man, and when we reached the camp I instructed him to drive into the center of it before he stopped. The tipis were all in a circle. It was quite a camp—about a quarter of a mile across it. When the wagon stopped, the Indians came out and stood around to listen to what I had to say. There was no excitement, but every one was curious as to the cause of my visit.

I told my people that I wanted to help them, and that was the reason I had come. I said it would not be right for them to join the ghost dancers as the Government was going to stop it, and it would not be best for them to be found there. I told them the Government would use soldiers to enforce the order if it became necessary.

The thought that the soldiers were coming disturbed them, but I told them if they felt afraid they could move their tipis in and put them up around my house and camp there. My house was only about a half-mile from the agency. They all agreed to come there the following morning. This pleased me immensely to think that my visit and talk had been a success. When I returned and told the agent, he, too, was very happy.

Just after I left the camp, my plans were all "knocked into a cocked hat," as you might say. One of my uncles, Hard Heart, entered the camp from Pine Ridge. When he saw that the Indians were all getting ready to break camp and go somewhere, he inquired the reason of the sudden move. When they told him they were getting ready to come in and camp by my house, he told them not to go. He said that a new world was coming to roll on top of the present one, and they must either join the ghost dancers or perish with those who did not believe. Still, that would not have deterred them from coming to me had not some one come into the camp that night and told them the soldiers were coming. That frightened them to such an extent that they were all packed up and gone long before daylight.

When I awoke the next morning and looked out of my window in expectation of seeing their tipis pitched about my house, I was greatly disappointed. There was no sign of their camp. I looked up the road in the direction they would have come, but there was no one in sight. Then I knew something had frightened them from keeping their promise.

The Indians who had decided to remain at the agency held a council so they could discuss the dance. Like all religious beliefs there were those who believed and there were the skeptics as well.

* * * * *

. . . After I had observed several of the leading chiefs going, I decided to go down and find out what they intended doing.

When I arrived, my brother-in-law, Chief Hollow Horn Bear, was speaking, and I stood at the door to listen. He was not a believer in the ghost dance, and was talking very strongly against it. All who were in favor of it exclaimed "Hauh!" every once in a while. Suddenly we who were standing near the door saw an Indian riding a white horse coming toward the house as fast as he could urge his pony. He had come from the agency and was headed straight for the council. As he dashed up, he leaped from his pony and rushed into the council hall. Hollow Horn Bear was still speaking, but this man, Brave Eagle, interrupted him, exclaiming, "Hey, hey! What are all you men doing here? Don't you know that the soldiers have taken all our women and children away from Cut Meat Creek? Why do you all sit here doing nothing?"

This caused considerable excitement as many of these men had relatives at Cut Meat Creek. The council broke up, and several of the Indians rushed to the agency. . . .

When we arrived at the agency, the agent was greatly excited. He was walking the floor, rubbing his head. "I can't understand what has happened," he said to me. "If there is anything wrong, I should have been sent a telegram." He had sent for his Indian Police, who were now arriving. The Indians who had gathered were all ready to start for Cut Meat Creek, and the police were likewise impatient to be off. Everybody was on horseback, and I stood and watched them start on their journey of twenty-five miles, none of them knowing what they would find after they got there. I was to remain at the agency until Mr. Wright returned.

Bad news travels fast. None of the Government employees at the reservation cared to work that day. Everybody was just standing around, wondering what was to happen next. Toward evening we saw the men all returning. Their horses were all fagged out from hard riding, and the men were tired, but the news they brought was good for us to hear.

The agent told us that when they reached the camp nothing had been disturbed; that the man who had brought the news had not told the truth. . . .

* * * * *

The following morning the news arrived of the terrible slaughter of Big Foot's whole band. Men, women, and children—even babies were killed in their mothers' arms! This was done by the soldiers. According to the white man's history this was known as the "battle" of Wounded Knee, but it was not a battle—it was a slaughter, a massacre. Those soldiers had been sent to protect these men, women, and children who had not joined the ghost dancers, but they had shot them down without even a chance to defend themselves.

When I heard of this, it made my blood boil. I was ready myself to go and fight them. There I was, doing my best to teach my people to follow in the white man's road—even trying to get them to believe in their religion—and this was my reward for it all! The very people I was following—and getting my people to follow—had no respect for motherhood, old age, or babyhood. Where was all their civilized training?

More of the Indians joined the dancers after the Wounded Knee affair. They felt that they could not meet with any worse fate than that which had been meted out to their friends and relatives.

Always after a trouble of this sort, rumors were apt to be flying thick and fast. As we had no telephones in those days, we had no way to determine the truth about the fate of our friends and relatives. All we received were rumors—and they were not of the best. One of the Indians came running into the agency with the report that he had overheard a remark that "they were going to kill all the Indians, regardless of education, because the only good Indians were the dead ones." That sounded pretty bad, but soon came another rumor: "All the Indians who stay with the white people and work with them will be regarded as white people and are not going to be killed."

It was about two days after the Wounded Knee affair that these rumors began to sift in at the agency. Orders were given that no Indian was to leave his or her house. Everybody's nerves were on edge. My own house was completely surrounded by the soldiers. I did not know whether my own family were alive or dead. My wife and children had gone to her father's before the trouble started.

I talked the situation over with my two friends, Julian Whistler and Frank Janis. We decided to fight if we had to, but agreed that we would not start trouble ourselves. As my brother-in-law had taken my rifle, I was left without any arms. My two friends had no guns. So we went out and each bought a gun and plenty of ammunition, and were ready to fight if it came to a "show-down." While we three were Carlisle graduates, we determined to stick by our race.

After getting these guns we felt much easier about going to bed nights. We kept the weapons fully loaded, waiting and fully expecting an attack.

* * * * *

Three or four days later I started over to find out how bad the reports were which we had heard about the fight. My father and mother and their family were at Pine Ridge at this time and I had heard nothing from them. It had snowed in the meantime, and the weather was very cold. It meant a ride of thirty miles on horseback, but I had a good horse, plenty of warm clothing, and I did not mind the jaunt.

When I arrived at the place where the fight had occurred between the Indians and the soldiers, all the bodies had been removed. Here and there lay the body of a horse. The tipi poles were broken and lay scattered about in heaps. Cooking utensils were strewed around in confusion; old wagons were overturned, with the tongues broken off.

Everything was confusion. It was early in the morning when I reached this place, and the silence was oppressive and terrible.

There were many little pools of water here and there, some with clear water and others red with the blood of my people. I was enraged enough at this sight to shoot any one, but nobody was to be seen. The place of death was forsaken and forbidding. I stood there in silence for several minutes, in reverence for the dead, and then turned and rode toward the agency.

On the way I met some Indians. My first question was for my father, his wives and my sisters and brothers. They told me that Father and his wives were all right, and that my two brothers, Ellis and Willard, were safe. So I returned to Rosebud Agency without seeing them.

All the Indians who believed in the ghost dance had now rushed into what was known as the "Bad Lands." It was located in the northern part of our reservation, and was a hard place to enter. The entrance was only large enough for one wagon at a time to pass in. It was an excellent place to stand off an enemy.

Those who had not at first believed in the ghost dance ran away with these Indians who were bound for the Bad Lands. After they had seen what the soldiers did to their friends and relatives, they were not taking any more chances. The few who had escaped the terrible slaughter at Wounded Knee also fled into the fastnesses of the Bad Lands, although they had no guns nor anything with which to put up a fight. The soldiers had taken everything away from them before shooting them down. But the other Indians had all brought firearms and plenty of ammunition.

These they divided. They felt sure that now they would have to fight to protect themselves against the white man. *Who could blame them?*

In the Bad Lands they had plenty of wood and water, but they needed meat. Some of the braves sneaked out in the night and rounded up all the cattle they could find and drove them into their place of retreat. There was no high chief left at the agency now, because Red Cloud, who had always called Pine Ridge his agency, was one of the Indians to run with his whole family into the Bad Lands.

Everybody in the camp now felt safe, as they had plenty of everything to supply their needs. They could dance when they pleased, and they had no agent from whom to ask permission. They were not under obligations to the Government for supplies, as they now had all they wanted. They kept two scouts posted at the entrance to the Bad Lands day and night, so there was no chance of interference without being seen. The soldiers did not even try to come near them. They knew better!

The troops realized that the Indians who had guns knew how to use them. Those who had bows and arrows were expert in their use. The Indians were really better armed than at the time they wiped out

Custer, fourteen years previously. Had the soldiers tried at the time to enter the Bad Lands, there would have been many deaths on both sides.

General Miles realized all this, so he thought up a plan toward a reconciliation. He called on a few of the chiefs who had remained at the agency, and asked them if they would not go to their people and try to make peace for them. This was a most dangerous mission to attempt to perform as the Indians had declared they would kill any one who came to them, regardless of color. The white man had started the fight, and now he wanted the Indian to act as mediator!

My father, who was now the head chief, said he would carry the peace pipe to these Indians if any one else would accompany him. Nine others volunteered to accompany him. These ten chiefs started off on horseback, not knowing whether they would ever return alive. My father carried the pipe, which all the Indians respected at that time.

When they arrived at the entrance to the Bad Lands, they were recognized by the scouts on duty, who allowed them to enter unmolested. They rode their horses in through the gateway in plain sight of all the Indians. Here they dismounted, my father still holding the peace pipe in both hands, straight out before him. Not a word was spoken. The Indians arranged themselves in a circle and sat down. They were making an appeal to their friends to come and accept the pipe of peace. Everything was as quiet as the grave. Among the Indians at that time, there was a strong superstition that if the pipe of peace was brought and not accepted, great harm would come to them or to their relatives.

The sight of this peace pipe made the fighting Indians wild! They were on horseback, and they rode right toward my father and the other chiefs. Not one of the latter moved, but sat perfectly still. One of these Indians had a loaded gun. His name was Ten Fingers. As he came near my father he said, "The white people have killed our people without mercy, and we want to fight them. Why have you brought us this pipe of peace?"

As he finished speaking, bang! went his rifle, the bullets striking the ground between my father's knees and spattering dirt in his face. Father never flinched or said a word of rebuke. He had faith in what he was doing in bringing the peace pipe to these enraged Indians.

You who are Christians—have you ever been in a high temper at a time when some one may have asked you to kiss the Bible? Then you will understand just how these Indians felt toward accepting the peace pipe offered them. However, after a time these wild Indians calmed down, and strange as it may seem, those ten chiefs brought all those hostiles into the agency without a shot being fired! There a peace was effected.

After the affair was over, somebody mentioned to my brother Ellis the incident in which Ten Fingers had fired his rifle between my father's knees while he was holding the peace pipe. This so enraged my brother that after dark he covered his head with a sheet, carried his rifle underneath it, and started out to locate Ten Fingers. He went from tipi to tipi, but could not find him—and it was probably lucky for Ten Fingers that he was not located.

Now that peace was finally restored, who was given the credit for it? Did the Indian who had brought the peace pipe receive any honor for the part he played? No, indeed! All the credit went to General Miles, who was proclaimed the "great peacemaker." Perhaps his salary was raised, or possibly he received a few more stripes to his sleeves. The Indians came to my father about it, and my father, who was the head chief throughout these ceremonies, went to General Miles for an explanation.

He told the General that the Indians thought they (who had remained loyal and at the agency) should have something from the Government to indicate that they belonged to the Progressives—something to show that they had not run away; some sort of emblem for them to wear to commemorate this great peace and the part they had in it.

The General said he would accede to this request of my father's. He secured the names of all the chiefs who had accompanied my father. He must have submitted their names to the officials at Washington, because in a short time some buttons arrived—one for each man. They were about an inch and a half in diameter, and were worn fastened to the coat lapel, much the same as a lodge emblem. On the face of these buttons was emblazoned a rising sun, and in the clear sky above were the words "Peace, Good Will." Below were two clasped hands, on each side of which was a shock of corn; at the extreme bottom was a plough. They were made of some cheap metal, silver-plated.

When these buttons arrived, General Miles sent for my father and gave him the buttons to distribute. The chiefs were greatly pleased to wear them, showing that they belonged to the Progressives. It was a mark of the Progressives. It was a mark of distinction and honor. But I often look back to this incident and wonder if the general public knows that the men who really settled the greatest trouble between the whites and Indians at Pine Ridge each received a dinky button worth about fifty cents!

Their Own Gods

When the first Spanish colony settled in New Mexico in the year 1598, their governor chose as his first capital a place now called

From *Indian Stories from the Pueblos,* by Frank G. Applegate, pp. 45–48. Copyright, 1929, by J. B. Lippincott Company. Philadelphia and London.

Chamita, about thirty-five miles north of Santa Fe, the present capital. The Spanish governor called his capital San Gabriel.

The site chosen for the colony lay in the beautiful valley of the Rio Grande River, just above the point where it is joined by the Chama River, so the colony had water on either side. Beyond the valley to the east towered a high range of the Rocky Mountains called by the Spaniards "Sierras Grandes," and on the west rose a somewhat lower range called "Jemez."

Chamita was chosen by the Spanish governor for his capital because of a large, well-built Indian town or pueblo there, whose inhabitants were most friendly. These Indians were so well disposed toward the newcomers that they gave up their well-built adobe houses to them and moved across the Rio Grande and built themselves new houses in a new town. These Indians also showed the Spaniards how to lead the water from the river in ditches to irrigate their cornfields. The Spaniards were so impressed with the gentleness, kindness, and generosity of these Indians that they called this Indian town by the name of "San Juan de los Caballeros," or "Saint John of the Gentlemen," which name it still bears.

The San Juan Indians being so well disposed, the padres who accompanied the colonists found little difficulty in converting them to Christianity, and taught them to pray to the images of Mary and Jesus for help in time of need, in place of appealing to the old tribal gods.

Soon there arose desperate need for the Indians to call on the new gods for help, for a terrible drought descended on that part of New Mexico. The growing corn of the Indians began to turn yellow and dry, and the water in the river became too low to be led by the irrigation ditches to the new fields which the Indians had made on the higher bank across the river when they gave up their old fields to the Spaniards. Formerly, had such a situation as this arisen, these Indians would have had a great rain-making ceremonial dance and called on their old gods to send them rain. Now, with implicit faith in the magic of the powerful gods of their new friends, the chiefs of the clans went to the padre at the mission church and asked him to lend them the blessed image of the child Jesus. The padre inquired of them why they wished the image, and the chief of the corn clan answered: "We wish to carry the child Jesus around the cornfields, so that he can see in what bad condition they now are, and maybe he will have pity on us and send the rain."

The padre agreed that the Christ child might go, and the Indians carried it with ceremony over all their fields, chanting and pleading with the little image for rain. Then they returned it to the padre at the mission and went home to await results.

Now as sometimes happens in New Mexico in summer, a great cloudburst rose over the Jemez Mountains and swept up the Rio

Grande valley. It deluged the Indian fields and beat the corn to the ground, and worse still, hail followed the rain and completed utterly the destruction of the crops.

When the Indians saw what had happened they were very much cast down, for corn was their main staple of diet. That evening the chiefs held a council and early the next morning they again presented themselves before the padre and this time asked that he lend them the image of Mother Mary. The padre was surprised and inquired the reason for the request. The chiefs hesitated, but on his refusing to lend them the image without explanation, one chief said: "Padre, we wish to carry the Mother Mary around the fields this morning, so that she can see for herself what a mess her naughty little boy has made of our cornfields."

The Indians of San Juan say to this day that if you will look at the image of Saint Mary in the old mission church there, you can still see on her cheeks traces of the tears she shed from pity when she saw their ruined cornfields.

Ever since that time the San Juan Indians have had respect for the Christian gods, but they appeal to their own tribal nature gods when they want rain for their growing corn. Then they dress in the ceremonial costumes as in ancient times and paint themselves with ceremonial colors and carrying sprigs of green spruce they form in long lines and shake gourd rattles filled with seeds, to simulate the rain falling to the green corn leaves. So they dance from sunrise to sunset, to bring down the rain, while nearby a large drum made of a hollowed cottonwood log, covered with rawhide, is beaten to imitate the thunder, and a chorus sings the ancient incantations.

The Portrait of San José

While law in the abstract may deserve its reputation as one of the driest of subjects, the history of its development, provisions, and applications contains much that is curious and interesting. There have been, among different nations and in different ages, laws remarkable for eccentricity; and as for the astonishing causes in which the aid of justice has been invoked, a mere catalogue of them would be of appalling length. Nor are these legal curiosities confined to bygone ages and half-civilized nations. Our own country has furnished laws and lawsuits perhaps as remarkable as any.

Among these suits, none is more interesting than one of the few legal contests in which the Pueblo Indians have ever figured. With these quiet, decorous, kind, and simple-hearted children of the Sun,

---

From *Some Strange Corners of Our Country,* The Wonderland of the Southwest, by Charles F. Lummis, pp. 262–270. Copyright, 1891, 1892, by the Century Co. New York.

quarrels of any sort are extremely rare, and legal controversies still rarer; but there was one lawsuit between two of the principal Pueblo towns which excited great interest among all the Indians and Mexicans of the territory, and the few Saxon-Americans who were then here; which nearly made a war—a lawsuit for a saint! It was finally adjudicated by the Supreme Court of New Mexico in January, 1857. It figures in the printed reports of that high tribunal, under the title, "The Pueblo of Laguna *vs.* the Pueblo of Acoma"—being an appeal in the case of Acoma *vs.* Laguna.

Of all the nineteen pueblos of New Mexico, Acoma is by far the most wonderful. Indeed, it is probably the most remarkable city in the world. Perched upon the level summit of a great "box" of rock whose perpendicular sides are nearly four hundred feet high, and reached by some of the dizziest paths ever trodden by human feet, the prehistoric town looks far across the wilderness. Its quaint terraced houses of gray adobe, its huge church—hardly less wonderful than the pyramids of Egypt as a monument of patient toil—its great reservoir in the solid rock, its superb scenery, its romantic history, and the strange customs of its six hundred people, all are rife with interest to the few Americans who visit the isolated city. Neither history nor tradition tells us when Acoma was founded. The pueblo was once situated on top of the Mesa Encantada (Enchanted Tableland), which rises seven hundred feet in air near the mesa now occupied. Four hundred years ago or so, a frightful storm swept away the enormous leaning rock which served as a ladder, and the patient people—who were away at the time—had to build a new city. The present Acoma was an old town when the first European—Coronado, the famous Spanish explorer—saw it in 1540. With that its authentic history begins—a strange, weird history, in scattered fragments, for which we must delve among the curious "memorials" of the Spanish conquerors and the scant records of the heroic priests.

Laguna lies about twenty miles northeast of Acoma, and is now a familiar sight to travelers on the A. & P. R.R., which skirts the base of the sloping rock on which the town is built. It is a much younger town than Acoma, of which it is a daughter colony, but has a half more people. It was founded in 1699.

One of the notable things about the venerable Catholic churches of New Mexico is the number of ancient paintings and statues of the saints which they contain. Some are the rude daubs on wood made by devout Indians, and some are the canvases of prominent artists of Mexico and Spain. It was concerning one of the latter that the curious lawsuit between Laguna and Acoma arose.

There is considerable mystery concerning this picture, arising from the lack of written history. The painting of San José (St. Joseph) was probably the one presented by Charles II of Spain. Entregas, in his "Visits," enumerates the pictures which he found in the Laguna church in 1773, and mentions among them "a canvas of a yard and a half, with the most holy likeness of St. Joseph with his blue mark, the which was presented by Our Lord the King." The Acomas, however, claim that the king gave the picture to them originally, and there is no doubt that it was in their possession over a hundred years ago.

When brave Fray Ramirez founded his lonely mission in Acoma in 1629, he dedicated the little adobe chapel "To God, to the Holy Catholic Church, and to St. Joseph." San José was the patron saint of the pueblo, and when the fine Spanish painting of him was hung on the dull walls of a later church, it became an object of peculiar veneration to the simple natives. Their faith in it was touching. Whether it was that the attacks of the merciless Apache might be averted, or that a pestilence might be checked, or that their crops might be abundant, it was to San José that they went with prayers and votive offerings. And as generation after generation was born, lived its quaint life, and was at last laid to rest in the wonderful graveyard, the veneration of the painting grew stronger and more clear, while oil and canvas were growing dim and moldy.

Many years ago—we do not know the date—the people of Laguna found themselves in a very bad way. Several successive crops had failed them, winter storms had wrought havoc to house and farm, and a terrible epidemic had carried off scores of children. And all this time Acoma was prospering wonderfully. Acoma believed it was because of San José; and Laguna began to believe so too. At last the governor and principal men of Laguna, after solemn council, mounted their silver-trapped ponies, wrapped their costliest blankets about them, and rode over valley and mesa to "the City in the Sky." A runner had announced their coming, and they were formally received by the *principales* of Acoma, and escorted to the dark estufa. After a propitiatory smoke the Laguna spokesman began the speech. They all knew how his pueblo had suffered, while Laguna had no saint on whom they could rely. It was now the first of March. Holy Week was almost here, and Laguna desired to celebrate it with unusual ceremonies, hoping thereby to secure divine favor. Would Acoma kindly lend San José to her sister pueblo for a season, that he might bring his blessing to the afflicted town?

A white-headed Acoma replied for his people. They knew how angry *Tata Dios* had been with Laguna, and wished to help appease him if possible. Acoma needed San José's presence in Holy Week; but she was prosperous and would do without him. She would lend him to Laguna for a month, but then he must be returned without fail.

So next day, when the Laguna delegation started homeward, two strong men carried the precious canvas carefully between them, and that night it hung upon the rudely decorated walls of the Laguna church, while hundreds of solemn Indians knelt before it. And in the procession of Holy Week it was borne in a little shrine about the town while its escort fired their rusty flint-locks in reiterant salute.

Old men tell me that there was a change in the fortunes of Laguna from that day forth. At all events, when the month was up the Lagunas did not return the borrowed painting, and the Acoma messengers who came next day to demand it were informed that it would stay where it was unless Acoma could take it by force of arms. The Acomas then appealed to their priest, Fray Mariano de Jesus Lopez, the last of the Franciscans here. He cited the *principales* of both pueblos to appear before him in Acoma on a certain day, bringing the saint.

When they were all assembled there, the priest ordered a season of prayer that God and San José would see justice done in the matter at issue, and after this held mass. He then suggested that they draw lots for the saint, to which both pueblos cordially agreed, believing that God would direct the result. It was a solemn and impressive sight when all were gathered in the great, gloomy church. Near the altar was a *tinaja* (earthen jar) covered with a white cloth. At each side stood a wee Acoma girl dressed in spotless white, from the paño over her shoulders to the queer, boot-like buckskin leggings. Beside one of them was the old priest, who acted for Acoma; and beside the other were Luis Saraceno and Margarita Hernandez, on behalf of Laguna. Twelve ballots were put in the *tinaja* and well shaken; eleven were blank, the twelfth had a picture of the saint rudely drawn upon it.

"Draw," said Fray Mariano, when all was ready; and Maria thrust her little arm into the jar and drew out a ballot, which she handed to the priest. "Acoma, blank! Draw, Lolita, for Laguna," Lolita dived down and drew a blank also. Maria drew the third ballot, and Lolita the fourth—both blanks. And then a devout murmur ran through the gathered Acomas as Maria drew forth the fifth paper, which bore the little picture of San José.

"God has decided in favor of Acoma," said the priest, "and San José stays in his old home." The crowd poured out of the church, the Acomas hugging each other and thanking God, the Lagunas walking surlily away.

Such a feast had never been in Acoma as the grateful people began to prepare; but their rejoicing was short-lived. That very evening a strong armed force of Lagunas came quietly up the great stone "ladder" to the lofty town, and appeared suddenly in front of the church. "Open the door," they said to the frightened sacristan, "or we will break it down. We have come for the saint." The news ran through the little town like wildfire. All Acoma was wild with grief and rage; and hopeless as a war with Laguna would have been, it would have commenced then and there but for the counsel of the priest. He exhorted his flock to avoid bloodshed and give the saint up to the Lagunas, leaving a final decision of the dispute to the courts. His advice prevailed; and after a few hours of excitement the Lagunas departed with their precious booty.

As soon thereafter as the machinery of the law could be set in motion, the Pueblo of Acoma filed in the District Court of the Second Judicial District of New Mexico a bill of Chancery *vs.* the Pueblo of Laguna, setting forth the above facts in detail.

They also asked that a receiver be appointed to take charge of San José till the matter should be decided. The Lagunas promptly filed an answer setting forth that they knew nothing of Acoma's claim that the picture was originally given to Acoma; that by their own traditions it was clearly the property of Laguna, and that Acoma stole it; that they went peaceably to reclaim it, and Acoma refused to give it up; that Acoma proposed to draw lots for it, but they refused and took it home.

Judge Kirby Benedict, sitting as chancellor, heard this extraordinary case, and the evidence being overwhelmingly in favor of Acoma, decided accordingly. The Lagunas appealed to the Supreme Court, which after most careful investigation affirmed the decision of the chancellor. In rendering his decision the judge said:

> Having disposed of all the points, . . . the court deems it not improper to indulge in some reflections on this interesting case. The history of this painting, its obscure origin, its age, and the fierce contest which these two Indian pueblos have carried on, bespeak the inappreciable value which is placed upon it. The intrinsic value of the oil, paint, and cloth by which San José is represented to the senses, it has been admitted in argument, probably would not exceed twenty-five cents; but this seemingly worthless painting has well-nigh cost these two pueblos a bloody and cruel struggle, and had it not been for weakness on the part of one of the pueblos, its history might have been written in blood. . . . One witness swore that unless San José is in Acoma, the people cannot prevail with God. All these supposed virtues and attributes pertaining to this saint, and the belief that the throne of God can be successfully approached only through him, have contributed to make this a case of deep interest, involving a portraiture of the feelings, passions, and character of these peculiar people. Let the decree below be affirmed.

This settled the matter, and Acoma sent a delegation to take the saint to his home. Halfway to Laguna they found the painting resting against a tree, beside the road, the face toward Acoma. To this day the simple people believe that San José knew he was now free, and was in such haste to get back to Acoma that he started out by himself. The dim and tattered canvas hangs beside the altar in the great church at Acoma still, and will so long as a shred is left.

Fray Mariano, who thus averted a destructive war, met a tragic end in 1848. He went out one morning to shoot a chicken for dinner. His venerable pistol would not work till he looked into it to see what was the matter. Then it went off and blew out his brains.

Wohaw

Indians did not try to steal oxen as they did horses and mules. They were the first cattle the Plains Indians saw. These Indians, hearing the bullwhackers shouting "Whoa," "Haw," and "Gee," called the oxen, and later all other cattle, "wohaws." In crossing the Indian territory, Texas drovers were generally met with demands for "wohaw," and many a stray was cut out of the herds to satisfy the demand. "Wohaw" was one of the few Indian words that passed into the vocabulary of the range.

The Indian on the White Man's Guns

In the days of the muzzle-loading rifles and revolvers, the Indian had the advantage. First he would draw the fire of his enemy, then rush in with bow or lance and try to finish the kill before the white man could reload. Breech-loading rifles and cartridges ended that kind of attack, and long-range guns like the old Sharps carbine added to the red man's fighting problems. After seeing one of his braves killed from a distance of nearly a mile by one of these rifles, one old chief is said to have exclaimed. "Damn white man's guns! Shoot to-day, kill to-morrow!"

Indians and Telegraph Wires

When the first locomotive was seen passing over the plains, an Indian guide in the employ of the United States exclaimed with inexpressible surprise. "Good medicine, *good medicine*. Look, look, at the tu-te [toot]." As he passed under the telegraph wires, which then were stretching along the Platte, through which the wind as it swept made the whirr and singing sound of a prairie harp, this guide heard the sound, and directly declared that they were talking *"medicines."* This was

---

From *The Longhorns,* by J. Frank Dobie, p. 251. Copyright, 1941, by J. Frank Dobie. Boston: Little, Brown and Company.

From *Longhorn Cowboy,* by James H. Cook, edited and with an introduction by Howard R. Driggs, pp. 93–94. Copyright, 1942, by James H. Cook and Howard R. Driggs; 1942, by World Book Company, Publishers. Yonkers.

From *The Pacific Tourist,* J. R. Bowman's Illustrated Trans-Continental Guide of Travel, from the Atlantic to the Pacific Ocean . . ., Frederick E. Shearer, Editor, with Special Contributions by Prof. F. V. Hayden, Clarence King, Capt. Dutton, A. C. Peale, Joaquin Miller, and J. B. Davis. . . ., p. 63. New York: J. R. Bowman, Publisher. 1882–1883.

supposed to be the creation of the *Great Spirit,* and everything of supernatural nature was *"medicine."*

The Indians have rarely ever molested the telegraph wires which span the continent. Shortly after the wires were erected, the attachés of the telegraph company invited a number of Indian chiefs to meet them at a given point, and from thence to travel, one party East and the other West.

When they had reached a distance of 100 miles apart, each party was invited to dictate a message to the other, which was sent over the wires. Then turning backward, they rode rapidly toward each other, and two days later met and compared notes. They were greatly astonished, and expressed themselves convinced that the *"Great Spirit"* had talked to them with the wires. They decided from that time it would be well to avoid meddling with the wires.

Soon after a young Sioux Indian was determined to show that he had no faith in the Great Spirit's connection with the wires, so he set to work with his hatchet to cut down one of the telegraph poles. A severe thunderstorm was going on at a distance; a charge of electricity being taken up by the wires, was passed to the pole which the Indian was cutting, and resulted in his instant death. After that the tribe never molested the telegraph again.

The Pigeon's Egg Head Goes to Washington

. . . I was called upon to proceed at once with the Story of *Wi-Jun-Jon* (the Pigeon's Egg Head); and I recited it as I first told it to poor Ba'tiste, on a former occasion, which was as follows:—

"Well, Ba'tiste, I promised last night, as you were going to sleep, that I would tell you a story this morning—did I not?

" 'Oui, Monsieur, oui—de "Pigeon's Head." '

"No, Ba'tiste, the 'Pigeon's Egg Head.'

" 'Well, den Monsieur Cataline, de "Pigeon Egg's Head." '

"No, Ba'tiste, you have it wrong yet. The Pigeon's Egg Head.

"'Sacré—well, *"Pe-jonse-ec-head."* '

"Right, Ba'tiste. Now you shall hear the 'Story of the Pigeon's Egg Head.'

"The Indian name of this man (being its literal translation into the Assinneboin language) was *Wi-jun-jon.*

" 'Wat! comment! by Gar (pardón); not *Wi-jun-jon,* le frère de ma

---

From *The Manners, Customs, and Conditions of the North American Indians,* by George Catlin, Written during Eight Years' Travel amongst the Wildest Tribes of Indians in North America, 1832–39, with Four Hundred Illustrations, Carefully Engraved from the Original Paintings, and Colored after Nature, in Two Volumes, Volume the Second, pp. 195–201. London: Published by the Author, at the Egyptian Hall, Piccadilly. 1841.

Wee-ne-on-ka, fils du chef Assinneboin? But excusez; go on, s'il vous plait.'

"*Wi-jun-jon* (the Pigeon's Egg Head) was a brave and a warrior of the Assinneboins—young—proud—handsome—valiant, and graceful. He had fought many a battle, and won many a laurel. The numerous scalps from his enemies' heads adorned his dress, and his claims were fair and just for the highest honors that his country could bestow upon his; for his father was chief of the nation.

"'Le même! de same—mon frère—mon ami! Bien, I am composé; go on, Monsieur.'

"Well, this young Assinneboin, the 'Pigeon's Egg Head,' was selected by Major Sanford, the Indian Agent, to represent his tribe in a delegation which visited Washington City under his charge in the winter of 1832. With this gentleman, the Assinneboin, together with representatives from several others of the Northwestern tribes, descended the Missouri river, several thousand miles, on their way to Washington.

"While descending the river in a Mackinaw boat, from the mouth of Yellow Stone, *Wi-jun-jon* and another of his tribe who was with him, at the first approach to the civilized settlements, commenced a register of the white men's houses (or cabins), by cutting a notch for each on the side of a pipe-stem, in order to be able to show when they got home how many white men's houses they saw on their journey. At first the cabins were scarce; but continually as they advanced down the river, more and more rapidly increased in numbers; and they soon found their pipe-stem filled with marks, and they determined to put the rest of them on the handle of a war club, which they soon got marked all over likewise; at length, while the boat was moored at the shore for the purpose of cooking the dinner of the party, *Wi-jun-jon* and his companion stepped into the bushes, and cut a long stick, from which they peeled the bark; and when the boat was again underweigh, they sat down, and with much labor, copied the notches on to it from the pipe-stem and club; and also kept adding a notch for every house they passed. This stick was soon filled; and in a day or two several others; when, at last, they seemed much at a loss to know what to do with their troublesome records, until they came in sight of St. Louis, which is a town of 15,000 inhabitants; upon which, after consulting a little, they pitched their sticks overboard into the river!

"I was in St. Louis at the time of their arrival, and painted their portraits while they rested in that place. *Wi-jun-jon* was the first, who reluctantly yielded to the solicitations of the Indian agent and myself, and appeared as sullen as death in my painting-room—with eyes fixed like those of a statue upon me, though his pride had plumed and tinted him in all the freshness and brilliancy of an Indian's toilet. In his nature's uncowering pride he stood a perfect model; but superstition had hung a lingering curve upon his lip, and pride had stiffened it into contempt. He had been urged into a measure against which his fears had pleaded; yet he stood unmoved and unflinching amid the struggles of mysteries that were hovering about him, foreboding ills of every kind, and misfortunes that were to happen to him in consequence of this operation.

"He was dressed in his native costume, which was classic and exceedingly beautiful;[1] his leggings and shirt were of the mountain-goat skin, richly garnished with quills of porcupine, and fringed with locks of scalps, taken from his enemies' heads. Over these floated his long hair in plaits, that fell nearly to the ground; his head was decked with the war-eagle's plumes—his robe was of the skin of the young buffalo bull, richly garnished and emblazoned with the battles of his life; his quiver and bow were slung, and his shield, of the skin of the bull's neck.

"I painted him in this beautiful dress, and so also the others who were with him; and after I had done, Major Sanford went on to Washington with them, where they spent the winter.

"*Wi-jun-jon* was the foremost on all occasions—the first to enter the levee—the first to shake the President's hand, and make his speech to him—the last to extend the hand to them, but the first to catch the smiles and admiration of the gentler sex. He traveled the giddy maze, and beheld, amid the buzzing din of civil life, their tricks of art, their handiworks, and their finery; he visited their principal cities—he saw their forts, their ships, their great guns, steamboats, balloons, &c., &c.; and in the spring returned to St. Louis, where I joined him and his companions on their way back to their own country.

"Through the politeness of Mr. Chouteau, of the American Fur Company, I was admitted (the only passenger except Major Sanford and his Indians) to a passage in their steamboat, on her first trip to the Yellowstone; and when I had embarked, and the boat was about to depart, *Wi-jun-jon* made his appearance on deck, in a full suit of regimentals! He had in Washington exchanged his beautifully garnished and classic costume for a full dress 'en militaire.'[2] It was perhaps presented to him by the President. It was broadcloth, of the finest blue, trimmed with lace of gold; on his shoulders were mounted two immense epaulettes; his neck was strangled with a shining black stock, and his feet were pinioned in a pair of water-proof boots, with high heels, which made him 'step like a yoked hog.'

" 'Ha-ha-hagh (pardón, Monsieur Cataline, for I almost laugh)—well, he was a fine gentleman, ha?'

"On his head was a high-crowned beaver hat, with a broad silver lace band, surmounted by a huge red feather, some two feet high; his coat collar, stiff with lace, came higher up than his ears, and over it flowed, down towards his haunches—his long Indian locks, stuck up in rolls and plaits, with red paint.

---

1 See Plate 271 in Catlin. 2 See Plate 272 in Catlin.

" 'Ha-ha-hagh-agh-ah.'

"Hold your tongue, Ba'tiste."

" 'Well, go on—go on.'

"A large silver medal was suspended from his neck by a blue ribbon —and across his right shoulder passed a wide belt, supporting by his side a broad sword.

" 'Diable!'

"On his hands he had drawn a pair of white kid gloves, and in them held a blue umbrella in one and a large fan in the other. In this fashion was poor *Wi-jun-jon* metamorphosed, on his return from Washington; and in this plight was he strutting and whistling Yankee Doodle, about the deck of the steamer that was wending its way up the mighty Missouri, and taking him to his native land again; where he was soon to light his pipe, and cheer the wigwam fireside, with tales of novelty and wonder.

"Well, Ba'tiste, I traveled with this newfangled gentleman until he reached his home, two thousand miles above St. Louis, and I could never look upon him for a moment without excessive laughter, at the ridiculous figure he cut—the strides, the angles, the stiffness of this traveling beau! Oh, Ba'tiste, if you could have seen him, you would have split your sides with laughter; he was—'puss in boots,' precisely!

" 'By gar, he is good compare! Ha-ha, Monsieur; (pardón) I am laugh; I am see him wen he is arrive in Yellowstone; you know I was dere. I am laugh much wen he is got off de boat, and all de Assinneboins was dere to look. Oh diable! I am laugh almost to die, I am split! —súppose he was pretty stiff, ha? "cob on spindle," ha? Oh, by gar, he is coot pour laugh—pour rire?'

"After *Wi-jun-jon* had got home, and passed the usual salutations among his friends, he commenced the simple narration of scenes he had passed through, and of things he had beheld among the whites; which appeared to them so much like fiction, that it was impossible to believe them, and they set him down as an impostor. 'He has been, (they said,) among the whites, who are great liars, and all he has learned is to come home and tell lies.' He sank rapidly into disgrace in his tribe; his high claims to political eminence all vanished; he was reputed worthless—the greatest liar of his nation; the chiefs shunned him and passed him by as one of the tribe who was lost; yet the ears of the gossiping portion of the tribe were open, and the campfire circle and the wigwam fireside gave silent audience to the whispered narratives of the 'traveled Indian.'

"The next day after he had arrived among his friends, the superfluous part of his coat (which was a laced frock) was converted into a pair of leggings for his wife; and his hat-band of silver lace furnished her a magnificent pair of garters. The remainder of the coat, curtailed of its original length, was seen buttoned upon the shoulders of his brother, over and above a pair of leggings of buckskin; and *Wi-jun-jon* was parading about among his gaping friends with a bow and quiver slung over his shoulders, which, *sans coat,* exhibited a fine linen shirt with studs and sleeve buttons. His broad-sword kept its place, but about noon, his boots gave way to a pair of garnished moccasins; and in such plight he gossiped away the day among his friends, while his heart spoke so freely and so effectually from the bung-hole of a little keg of whisky, which he had brought the whole way (as one of the choicest presents made him at Washington), that his tongue became silent.

"One of his little fair inamoratas, or 'catch crumbs,' such as live in the halo of all great men, fixed her eyes and her affections upon his beautiful silk braces, and the next day, while the keg was yet dealing out its kindnesses, he was seen paying visits to the lodges of his old acquaintance, swaggering about, with his keg under his arm, whistling Yankee Doodle, and Washington's Grand March; his white shirt, or that part of it that had been *flapping* in the wind, had been shockingly tithed—his pantaloons of blue, laced with gold, were razed into a pair of comfortable leggings—his bow and quiver were slung, and his broad-sword which trailed on the ground, had sought the center of gravity, and taken a position between his legs, and dragging behind him, served as a rudder to steer him over the 'earth's troubled surface.'

" 'Ha-ha-hagh——ah——o——oo——k, eh bien.'

"Two days' revel of this kind had drawn from his keg all its charms; and in the mellowness of his heart, all his finery had vanished, and all of its appendages, except his umbrella, to which his heart's strongest affections still clung, and with it, and under it, in rude dress of buckskin, he was afterwards to be seen, in all sorts of weather, acting the fop and the beau as well as he could, with his limited means. In this plight, and in this dress, with his umbrella always in his hand (as the only remaining evidence of his *quondam* greatness) he began in his sober moments to entertain and instruct his people by honest and simple narratives of things and scenes he had beheld during his tour to the East; but which (unfortunately for him) were to them too marvelous and improbable to be believed. He told the gaping multitude that were constantly gathering about him of the distance he had traveled—of the astonishing number of houses he had seen—of the towns and cities, with all their wealth and splendor—of traveling in steamboats, in stages, and on railroads. He described our forts, and seventy-four gun ships he had visited—their big guns—our great bridges—our great council-house at Washington and its doings—the curious and wonderful machines in the patent office (which he pronounced the *greatest medicine place* he had seen); he described the great war parade, which he saw in the city of New York—the ascent of the balloon from Castle Garden—the numbers of the white people, the beauty of the white squaws; their red cheeks, and many thousands of other things, all of which were so much beyond their comprehension that they 'could not be true' and 'he must be the very greatest liar in the whole world.'[3]

"But he was beginning to acquire a reputation of a different kind. He was denominated a *medicine-man,* and one too of the most extraordinary character; for they deemed him far above the ordinary sort of human beings, whose mind could *invent* and *conjure* up for their amusement such an ingenious *fabrication* of novelty and wonder. He steadily and unostentatiously persisted, however, in this way of entertaining his friends and his people, though he knew his standing was affected by it. He had an exhaustless theme to descant upon through the remainder of his life; and he seemed satisfied to lecture all his life, for the pleasure which it gave him.

"So great was his *medicine,* however, that they began, chiefs and all, to look upon him as a most extraordinary being, and the customary honors and forms began to be applied to him, and the respect shown him that belongs to all men in the Indian country, who are distinguished for their *medicine* or *mysteries.* In short, when all became familiar with the astonishing representations that he made, and with the wonderful alacrity with which 'he *created* them,' he was denominated the very greatest of *medicine;* and not only that, but the *'lying medicine.'* That he should be the greatest of *medicine,* and that for *lying, merely,* rendered him a prodigy in mysteries that commanded not only respect, but at length (when he was more maturely heard and listened to) admiration, awe, and at last dread and terror; which altogether must needs conspire to rid the world of a monster, whose more than human talents must be cut down to less than human measurement.

" 'Wat! Monsieur Cataline, dey av not try to kill him?'

"Yes, Ba'tiste, in this way the poor fellow had lived, and been for three years past continually relating the scenes he had beheld in his tour to the *'Far East';* until his medicine became so alarmingly great that they were unwilling he should live; they were disposed to kill him for a wizard. One of the young men of the tribe took the duty upon himself, and after much perplexity, hit upon the following plan, to wit:—he had fully resolved, in conjunction with others who were in the conspiracy, that the medicine of *Wi-jun-jon* was too great for the ordinary mode, and that he was so great a liar that a rifle bullet would not kill him; while the young man was in this distressing dilemma, which lasted for some weeks, he had a dream one night, which solved all his difficulties; and in consequence of which, he loitered about the store in the Fort, at the mouth of the Yellowstone, until he could procure, *by stealth,* (according to the injunction of his dream) the handle of an iron pot, which he supposed to possess the requisite virtue, and

[3] Most unfortunately for this poor fellow, the other one of his tribe, who traveled with him, and could have borne testimony to the truth of his statements, died of the quinsy on his way home.—G.C.

taking it into the woods, he there spent a whole day in straightening and filing it, to fit it into the barrel of his gun; after which, he made his appearance again in the Fort, with his gun under his robe, charged with the pot handle, and getting behind poor *Wi-jun-jon,* whilst he was talking with the Trader, placed the muzzle behind his head and blew out his brains!

" 'Sacré vengeance! oh, mon dieu! let me cry—I shall cry always, for evare—Oh he is not true, I hope? no Monsieur, no!'

"Yes, Ba'tiste, it is a fact: thus ended the days and the greatness and all the pride and hopes of *Wi-jun-jon,* the *'Pigeon's Egg Head'*—a warrior and a brave of the valiant Assinneboins, who traveled eight thousand miles to see the President, and all the great cities of the civilized world; and who for telling the *truth,* and *nothing but the truth,* was, after he got home, disgraced and killed for a wizard.

" 'Oh, Monsieur Cataline—I am distress—I am sick—I was hope he is not true—oh I am mortify. *Wi-jun-jon* was coot Ingin—he was my bruddare—eh bien—eh bien.'

"Now, my friend Ba'tiste, I see you are distressed, and I regret exceedingly that it must be so; he was your friend and relative, and I myself feel sad at the poor fellow's unhappy and luckless fate; for he was a handsome, an honest, and a noble Indian.

" 'C'est vrai, Monsieur, c'est vrai.'

"This man's death, Ba'tiste, has been a loss to himself, to his friends, and to the world; but you and I may profit by it, neverthless, if we bear it in mind—

" 'Oui, yes, Monsr. mais, súppose, 'tis bad wind dat blows nary way, ha?'

"Yes, Ba'tiste, we may profit by his misfortune, if we choose. We may call it a 'caution'; for instance, when I come to write your book, as you have proposed, the fate of this poor fellow, who was relating no more than what he actually saw, will *caution* you against the *imprudence of telling all that you actually know,* and narrating all that you have *seen,* lest like him you sink into disgrace for telling the truth. You know, Ba'tiste, that there are many things to be seen in the kind of life that you and I have been living for some years past, which it would be more prudent for us to suppress than to tell.

" 'Oui, Monsieur. Well, súppose, perhaps I am discourage about de book. Mais, we shall see, ha?' "

A House with a Hole in the Back Wall

There is one Indian belief which has maintained itself despite the change of diet. It has lived stubbornly through half a century of white

From *Here's Death Valley,* by C. B. Glasscock, pp. 64–66. Copyright, 1940, by C. B. Glasscock. Indianapolis and New York: The Bobbs-Merrill Company, Publishers.

influence while the legends of a hundred centuries have been largely forgotten. It was discovered, alive and insistent, when the National Park Service decided to replace the flimsy wickiups and hogans of the Indians in the mesquite-dotted sand hills adjoining Furnace Creek Ranch, with substantial and appropriate and even artistic homes of adobe brick with palm-thatched porches.

The first attractive little house faced north. When it was completed by the CCC boys and proudly turned over to the Park Service for presentation to an Indian family, not a single family would move into it. The Indians were stubborn about it. They wouldn't move in, and they wouldn't explain why. It was very discouraging to the Service. But Ray Goodwin, superintendent of Death Valley National Monument, is an executive and diplomatist of parts. He caught an Indian in an unguarded moment, and learned that all Indian houses must face east. He accepted that without pressing for reasons.

He directed the boys to build another house facing east. The Indians wouldn't move into that either. Now what was the matter? Here he had built a handsome house facing east, and the Indians shunned it as they had the one facing north. He urged the Indian who had told him of the east-facing necessity to move in. After long and stubborn refusal the Indian finally consented, but on one condition. He would like very much to accommodate Mr. Goodwin by moving into the house, but he must make one small alteration.

And what was that?

He must knock the back wall out of the house.

A slight alteration. Goodwin's eyebrows lifted. But he was game. He had built two houses, and if he couldn't induce an Indian to move into the one facing east without knocking out the back wall; well, he'd let him knock it out. But he also named one condition. He must be told why.

So the Indian told him that if one of his family happened to die in that house as it stood, the spirit would return through the familiar opening by which the body was removed. It would plead that it was lonely in the great outer world, and would induce some other member of the family to join it. Then there would be another death, and perhaps even more. If, on the other hand, the back wall of the house were knocked out, and the adobe bricks loosely replaced, a body could be removed through that hole as soon as the spirit had fled. The hole could be quickly refilled, and the lonely spirit could not find its way back to tempt others to join it.

It was quite logical. It also demonstrated the Indians' growing powers of reason under the white man's rule. They did not have to think up anything like that in the old days. With the old folks cheerfully remaining behind the regular migrations to starve to death, there had been no such problem. If a younger person happened to die in one of the flimsy wickiups, the returning lonely spirit could be foiled quite easily by burning the wickiup as soon as the body was removed. But the nice 'dobe houses would not burn, so the Indians evolved the improved scheme. Who says they are not smart?

And Superintendent Goodwin is smart too. He permitted the Indian to knock enough bricks out of the back wall to remove a body. The Indian moved in. After that the Park Service and the CCC boys built all the houses facing east, and with a large hole in the back wall filled with uncemented bricks. The Indians moved in as fast as the houses were finished. Now the village is a credit to its architects, appropriate to its setting, and an interesting addition to the scenic attractions of Death Valley.

An Indian in Trouble

. . . A trader's wife, well versed in Navajo modes of thought, sat behind the counter of her trading-post in the remotest part of the Reservation, and knitted, waiting for any chance customer.

The door opens and a silent figure slips in and stands motionless. Versed in the Indian code of manners, she takes no notice of his presence but knits on in silence until he is ready to speak. Ultimately he does so.

"Big trouble," he says.

She waits an appropriate length of time before she replies, "Can I help?"

No sound but the click of knitting needles until finally he speaks again.

"My aunt kill her husband with axe. Chop his head."

Again no sound but of knitting needles.

Finally: "What do you want me to do?"

This time the pause is longer. Then: "I want you to tell me if I must tell white police?"

The trader's wife had known the dead husband well.

"He needed killing, didn't he?"

The young brave nods violent assent.

"No tell white police," comes the voice of judgment to the accompaniment of clicking needles.

A moment later she is alone, still knitting.

The *Indito* and the Banker

The Mexicans, as you know, are quite fond of using the diminutive. Some say that it's because of the preponderance of Andalusians that

From *No Life for a Lady,* by Agnes Morley Cleaveland, pp. 306–307. Copyright, 1941, by Agnes Morley Cleaveland. Boston: Houghton Mifflin Company.

Told by Arthur L. Campa, University of Denver, Denver, July 23, 1950. Recorded by B. A. Botkin.

came to Mexico. The fact of the matter is that the Mexicans use the *ito* or a diminutive for almost anything. Always: Wait—*un ratito*—a little while. And they eat a *bocarito*—a mouthful. Everything is *ito.* And whenever they wish to refer to any foreigner whom they particularly like and for whom they also have some sort of a nickname, like they used to have for the Americans in the days of lesser relations (they refer to them as *gringos*)—today it's typical to see a couple of Mexicans standing on a corner watching a good-looking American girl who probably is taller than they are, and they refer to her as *una gringita.*

And they do the same thing with the Indians. If they tell a story about an Indian, it's not just *un Indio,* because *un Indio* would be the type of Indian that you would find in a story about war and massacre and so on. Usually it's *un Indito*—you know that then the story is going to be about a friendly Indian. These *Indito* stories are all over the Southwest and particularly in northern Mexico.

In New Mexico, where they follow this same practice in Spanish, they tell a story about *un Indito* on the reservation . . . that is sometimes attributed to the former chief of the Navajos—Chee Dodge—and a number of others. It's pretty widespread now. It seems that this *Indito* went to borrow some money from one of the local banks. And when he got there, they told him, Yes, that was the right place. He could borrow money. (He'd heard that you could go to the bank and get money.) "But one of the things you need to do," the clerk says, "is put up a little collateral."

That was a new thing for him.

"Collateral? What's that?" he says.

"Well," the clerk says, "you take some property that you own and you put it over here, and then we give you this money, and then in case you can't pay this money, this collateral here answers for the money you borrowed."

Well, that made sense to the *Indito.* So he says, "All right."

"What kind of property do you have?" the clerk said.

"Well," he says, "I've got horses."

"Well, how many horses have you got?"

"Well," he says, "I got five hundred, six hundred."

"Well, that's good. Supposing we say—oh, let's say ten dollars a horse. Eh? We'll put aside so many horses."

So he did. And he put the necessary number of horses to borrow the money. So they gave him some money, which he wanted in silver. And he went away.

Good as his word, a year later he came back. And he had two bags of money. In one he had counted out the money he had borrowed from the bank. He counted it out. Sure enough, everything was there, including the interest.

"Well, that's fine," the clerk says. "Very fine. Glad to do business with such an honest man."

Well, the *Indito* never said anything. He started out, picked up his other bag.

The man said, "Well, now, what do you have in that other bag there?"

"Well, I've got some more money. I sold the wool of my sheep," he said.

"Well, look," the clerk says. "Why don't you leave the money here? You don't have to be carrying it around. You might lose it. Somebody might steal it. Then when you need it you can come out and take out a little at a time. It will be safe, and it will be much more convenient for you."

Well, that again sounded very logical to him. So he took his bag and put it on the counter. And before the man could reach over to grab it, he said, "You got horses too?"

Oil-Rich Indians

Oklahomans love to recall the exploits of the oil-rich Indian. "He used to buy a bright-yellow high-powered motor car," they say. "On Saturday nights he would get drunk and crash into the bridge abutment. Monday morning he would buy another brand new car, explaining to the salesman: 'Bridge no get out of my way.' He used to wreck three or four cars a month." Just who this Indian was nobody seems to remember, but he is a symbol of the fabulous spending of an era that is dead, the early days of the oil industry when the parched acres from which a patched-pants farmer had scratched out a miserable living suddenly made him wealthy over night. Men who had had to wear borrowed cardboard to cover holes in their shoes found themselves in a position to buy $100,000 homes. And they did. The oil strike in Osage County in the 1920's made the Osage Indian tribe there the richest people on earth on a per capita basis—until the gadget salesman moved in to part the unwary from their money. When the oil wells played out, many a splurger had to leave town "scratching a broke backside"—as they say in forthright Oklahoman.

From the Lansing *State Journal,* June 6, 1947, cited in *Western Folklore,* Vol. VII (January, 1948), No. I, p. 71. Copyright, 1948, by the California Folklore Society. Berkeley and Los Angeles: Published for the California Folklore Society by the University of California Press.

How the Navajo Does Business

Harry Goulding's job for the last ten years might easily have reduced another storekeeper to laughing, sobbing, gibbering insanity inside of the first ten minutes. Harry thrives on it.

In addition to serving as guide and managing a tourist camp, he runs a trading post in Monument Valley, Utah, two hundred miles from the nearest railroad station. His customers are drawn from the fifty thousand Navajo Indians who live in the valley.

One summer, while Harry was talking with a white visitor, a Navajo wandered into the post. The white visitor stepped away from the counter to let the Navajo make his purchases. After all, the Navajos have first claim on Harry Goulding's attention.

"Yah-teh!" grunted the Navajo. "Greetings!"

"Yah-teh!" murmured Harry.

"Yah-teh!" grunted the Navajo again.

"Yah-teh!" Harry replied very solemnly.

"Yah-teh!" grunted the Indian a third time.

"Yah-teh!" answered Harry, his expression unchanged.

The Navajo leaned across the counter. Formalities were now over. For three long minutes silence ticked away. The Indian said nothing. The storekeeper gazed dreamily out the window where Monument Valley danced in the blazing sun.

The white visitor, ignored by both, shifted uneasily in the background and began to get embarrassed. But he kept his mouth shut.

Finally the Indian sighed, pulled himself away from the counter, and sat down on a box. More minutes went by. Suddenly the Navajo sighed again, slowly got to his feet, and muttered: "Bottle of pop!"

Harry Goulding opened a warm bottle of pop and gave it to the Indian, who paid Harry a dime and drank the pop.

An hour went by. The white visitor was fascinated now. He jumped a bit when the Indian suddenly said, "Want five dollars!" He watched Navajo and trader go into the back part of the post and remove a turquoise-studded belt, heavily mounted with ornate silver, from among hundreds of pieces of jewelry suspended from the rafters.

There was a tag on the belt. It bore the Navajo's name, his mother's tribe's name, his English name, and his government serial number. It bore also the extent of his indebtedness to Harry Goulding.

Gravely Harry erased the previous figure, added the five dollars to it, and re-entered it on the tag. They both returned to the front part

---

By James C. G. Conniff. From *Rocky Mountain Empire,* Revealing glimpses of the West in transition from old to new, from the pages of the *Rocky Mountain Empire Magazine* of *The Denver Post,* edited by Elvon L. Howe, pp. 21–23. Garden City, New York: Doubleday & Company, Inc.

of the trading post. Harry handed the Navajo five one-dollar bills. The Navajo, sighing deeply, sat down again.

For no apparent reason, his eyes looking off into the desert distances, the Navajo began a long and indirect story, full of "they sat" and "it is heard" and "the tale goes round that." It ran on, singsong, for twenty minutes. Right in the middle of it he broke off, went up to the counter, pointed at something that cost three dollars, and paid for it.

He resumed his seat. The story was never completed. It was forgotten.

An hour later the Navajo rose, handed the trader a dollar without pointing at anything, and walked out of the post. Goulding went back to where the jewelry hung, reduced the figure on the belt by one dollar, and returned to his white visitor.

"That's the way they like to do business," Harry explained. "Why should I try to rush them? I'm not going any place."

Just then the Navajo reappeared in the doorway. He walked up to the counter, pulled a rug from under his coat, and flopped it down in front of Harry. Neither said anything. Then Harry laid a five-dollar bill on the rug.

The Indian looked at it and yawned. He sat down with a sigh. Harry added another dollar to the five. The Indian just looked at it. By seven o'clock that night, when Harry closed up the post the Indian was still looking at it. He spent the night in a hut provided by Harry for customers unable to make up their minds.

Next morning he was back when the post opened. All morning he looked at the rug and the six dollars. At a quarter of twelve he picked up the money and pocketed it. That was the signal that the deal was closed. Harry put the rug under the counter. Without another word the Navajo sighed and departed.

"That'd drive me crazy," the white visitor shrilled at Harry. "How can you put up with it?"

"Oh, that guy was in a hurry," grinned Harry Goulding. "You should come around sometime when one of them really has trouble making up his mind. After the third day of it I almost forget myself. Once I nearly asked a chief if there was something I could do for him. That would've been fatal!"

Navajo Rug Designs

Some persons like to imagine that Navajo rug designs are of some religious or mystical significance. This is hardly the case, since the traders who handle their products often suggest the patterns to be followed. Also, any chance pattern which catches the Navajo weaver's

---

From *Shepherd's Empire,* by Charles Wayland Towne and Edward Norris Wentworth, pp. 158–159. Copyright, 1945, by the University of Oklahoma Press. Norman.

eye is often transferred to her leisurely loom. On an iron entrance gate at Ganado, Arizona, for instance, appeared the owner's name, J. L. HUBBELL. What was the trader's surprise when one day, with obvious pride, the weaver offered him a large and magnificent rug bearing a full replica of the lettering on his gate. But the "L" was woven backward! Of course, Hubbell had to buy—and keep—it.

To the Indian weaver letters mean absolutely nothing but design. Another talented squaw boasted of a fine rug she was weaving. She said it was to be a big one and would take a lot of time. The trader knew she was a fine worker and hoped for the best. Finally, after months of toil, she showed up with a huge rug, the pattern of which was a faithful duplicate of an Ivory Soap wrapper, letters and all!

The Elks' Club of Phoenix, Arizona, contracted for an enormous rug to cover their lodge-room floor. The Navajo was given the appropriate Elks symbol and lettering and told to go to work. A year or more passed. Then, one day, the proud and happy weaver came to town to display his masterpiece and collect his fee. The brothers stood around as the Indian unrolled the rug. Pop-eyed, they gazed at what should have been an elk's head and the familiar B.P.O.E. Instead they saw: ARBUCKLE'S COFFEE.

Asked why he hadn't woven the pattern that had been given him, the Indian replied: "Lost paper; found another. All the same, plenty letters, heap pretty!"

A Hopi Visit to California

My Dear Friend and Mr.

I wish to tell you about a travel I take to see a lady woman in the California when some of us Hopi mens go to see her at that place. We go in a train of cars and first thing we do when we get there, which is

---

By Frank G. Applegate, in *Folk-Say, A Regional Miscellany: 1930*, edited by B. A. Botkin, pp. 85–87. Copyright, 1930, by B. A. Botkin. Norman: The University of Oklahoma Press.

In the summer of 1923 I was living in the little village of Polacca, which is situated at the foot of the high mesa on which stands the old Hopi pueblo of Walpi. It was the year when the snake dance takes place at Walpi, and a great many white people had come to Hopi-land to see this unique and picturesque ceremony. Among these people there was a very wealthy woman from California who lingered on a while after the dance to visit with the Hopis. This woman showed that she was in sympathy with Hopi culture and customs, so the Indians came to like her quite well; and nearly every evening some of the older men would come down to her camp and sing Hopi songs for her. She in turn liked the Indians and their songs and considered what she might do to show them her appreciation of their friendship and music. Finally, since she was in a position to gratify any whim, she decided that it would be a gracious and at the same time an interesting thing to invite a number of the older and more intelligent men among the Indians who had never been away from the mesas of Hopi-land to visit her on her large Califar, is go to lady woman house and she is glad she see us and say, 'how are we.' We stay that first night at the lady woman house and sing and eat there too and the next day she show us thing she have and do it is very many and nice and we are glad to see it, for she got many things and automobile and oranges. We stay one night more at house of lady woman like before and next day we go to another place and see some kind of things I do not know what are, but we are glad to see anyway. Next day we go to another place and sleep there and next day we go to another place and sleep there too. Next day we go to a ocean and it is big too and got some water in it and we go on a kind of sheeps and can see through bottom of it which is glass many kinds of things and some nice fish which I like to see also. Next day we go on other big kind of sheeps all night on a ocean and I am feeling very bad for much water is every place and is no ground and sheeps go different kind of ways I do not like. I think that time I going to die from sick and never see you again my dear friend, but next day we are in San Frisco and I am glad also and see kind of mens from China and some other kind of things too and big houses. Then we go in automobile and see some big trees and I am glad are not so big the Hopi trees so we can chop them for wood more easy. Next day we go to another place and see prunes and oranges and some more houses and we sleep there that night. In the morning we go to a mountain and we look at a moon and some stars in a kind of long glasses, but I do not know how they make so big the stars in the California. Then we go to another ocean where are many white people who ride on funny kind of things. We sit down

---

fornia estate and while they were there to send them in the care of a guide to see all the sights of California.

At the time I heard some people say that this wealthy woman was doing this thing simply as a patronizing gesture to the Indians. Others said she was doing it through curiosity to see how these old Hopis who had always lived isolated in the desert would react when confronted by opulent California; and some of the more malicious said she was doing it through vanity to show off to the Indians and to let them see what a great and important person she was in her own setting; but the Indians themselves, who are very keen in reading the motives of others, never doubted that she did it through kindness of heart only.

Before she left for California she made all the necessary arrangements. One morning taxis came from Winslow, Arizona, a hundred miles to the south on the Santa Fe railroad, to fetch the Indians and transport them the first part of the journey. At the hotel in Winslow rooms with baths were ready for the Indians on their arrival and there was a guide to look after them and see that they arrived safely in California. Also in their rooms at the hotel there were awaiting each Indian a neat black suit of clothes, white shirts, ties, shoes, a hat, a suitcase and everything else that goes to make up a suitable outfit for traveling.

Now I have never known all the places that these intelligent old Hopis, most of whom could speak not a word of English, visited while in California, for I left the Hopi country before they returned; but afterwards I received a very good account of their visit, from the Indian point of view, in the form of a long letter from one of these Indians who is a very good friend of mine. He had dictated this letter to his son-in-law, who had gone to school, and the son-in-law had rendered the Hopi verbatim, as nearly as he was able, into English.—F. G. A., *ibid.*, pp. 84–85.

in a kind of wagon with little wheels on little railroad track and we go very fast up and down and around corners and we go through very strange places and I am very afraid and sit still, but Ko-kup-ti who sit with me is mad and he stand up and say in Hopi, "The lady woman is very bad woman and send us Hopi chiefs here to be kill so she can get all the Hopi land because it is much better than the California." Then I pull Ko-kup-ti back down on the seat quick before he fall and say to him, "no, lady woman is good and wish to show us everything white people have and funny things they do in California, and she do not wish Hopi land for she have it much better and all she wish and oranges too." But Ko-kup-ti believe it not, but he is all right once more when we go away from that place.

We go away from that place then and we go to another place and we sleep in that place where we go then and next day we go to another place and then we go to house of lady woman where she live again and she buy for us some new teeth who have not got plenty. We sleep there too and eat and sing some more and the lady woman have some friends to hear the sing. Soon we come back to our homes again and the lady woman do not take from us the nice clothes she give to us and we wear them when we come to our home and when I come to my house my family not know your dear friend because I look so nice and fat and have gold tooth and clothes.

Now dear friend I think many times of things I see when I go to see lady woman in the California and I am happy to see them too. When I come my daughter have little baby very soon and we name it Anita the same like nice lady woman. This is all dear friend and be happy and good bye. Your Hopi friend, Lolomi.

Indian Irony

I[1]

The Indians were much more penetrating and intelligent than we often give them credit for being. Take, for instance, Spotted Tail's little joke. The commission had proposed to lease the Black Hills for mining purposes for a hundred years, paying only a nominal rental. One day the commissioners had been driven out to the treaty tent in a government ambulance drawn by six mules. Most of the Indians were gone, but just as the ambulance was starting back, Spotted Tail rode up to it on his horse. The driver stopped and Senator Allison put out

[1] From *Rekindling Camp Fires,* the Exploits of Ben Arnold (Connor) (Wa-si-cu Tam-a-he-ca), An Authentic Narrative of Sixty Years in the Old West as Indian Fighter, Gold Miner, Cowboy, Hunter, and Army Scout, by Lewis F. Crawford, pp. 213–214. Copyright, 1926, by Lewis F. Crawford. Bismarck, North Dakota: Capital Book Company.

his head and asked what was wanted. Spotted Tail answered, "I want those mules."

"But you can't have them," protested the senator. "They don't belong to us and we can't sell them."

"I don't want to buy them," returned Spotted Tail, "I want to borrow them."

"For how long?"

"A hundred years."

"Why, you're crazy. There wouldn't be anything left of them in a hundred years. And besides they belong to the Great Father, to the whole nation. We couldn't let you have them."

"That is what I expected you to say," said Spotted Tail. "The Black Hills don't belong to the chiefs, either. They belong to all of us. We can't loan them or give them away."

II[2]

Not long ago a young churchman, who was over zealous and somewhat flip in his manner, went to Washakie [Chief of the Shoshones] and asked him if he could not work among his people and teach them about God. Washakie eyed the young man from head to foot, and then asked him, "Young man, are you sure you know God yourself?"

III[3]

While visiting an Indian village in one of the Dakotas many years ago, I rode up to the head chief's lodge, where I was expected to remain for the night. The chief came out and received me, while, at the same time, his squaw unsaddled my horse and placed the equipment alongside their teepee. I asked the chief if they would be safe there, whereupon he observed, "Yes, there isn't a white man within two days ride of here."

IV[4]

The government inspector at the Indian reservation was telling the tribal chieftain that it was a violation of the law to have more than one wife.

"Now, I want you to tell all of your wives except one that they can no longer look upon you as a husband," he warned.

"You tell um," suggested the chief.

---

[2] From "Washakie, Chief of the Shoshones," by Joseph A. Breckons, *Collections of the Wyoming Historical Society,* Volume I, edited by Robert C. Morris, p. 90. Cheyenne, Wyoming: The Wyoming Historical Society. 1879.

[3] As told by Bishop Whipple. From *The Frontier Trail,* or from Cowboy to Colonel, An Authentic Narrative of Forty-three years in the old West as Cattleman, Indian Fighter and Army Officer, by Colonel Homer W. Wheeler, p. 303. Copyright, 1923, by Times-Mirror Press. Los Angeles, California.

[4] From *Rocky Mountain Life,* Vol. 2 (December, 1948), No. 10, p. 45.

Black Horse and Teddy Roosevelt

. . . Black Horse, an Arapahoe Indian policeman, who, incidentally, did not know the ex-President except by the name of "Teddy," and who had been trained at a government school to be an expert accountant (extremely useful knowledge for a reservation; almost as useful as being taught to be a pearl-diver), was once sent to Washington on a mission. He was granted an interview with the President and found himself one morning in a long room with a man "with teeth" sitting at the other end of the room behind a desk. A grave prelate of the Roman Catholic Church was just leaving, and Black Horse paused at the door. And then, suddenly, "the man with teeth" looked up and seeing the waiting Indian in the distance, raised his hands and made motions with his fingers. He was talking sign-language.

Chief Seattle's Oration

Yonder sky that has wept tears of compassion upon my people for centuries untold, and which to us appears changeless and eternal, may change. Today is fair. Tomorrow it may be overcast with clouds. My words are like the stars that never change. Whatever Seattle says the great chief at Washington can rely upon with as much certainty as he can upon the return of the sun or the seasons. The White Chief says that Big Chief at Washington sends us greetings of friendship and goodwill. That is kind of him for we know he has little need of our friendship in return. His people are many. They are like the grass that covers vast prairies. My people are few. They resemble the scattering trees of a storm-swept plain. The great, and I presume—good, White Chief sends us word that he wishes to buy our lands but is willing to allow us enough to live comfortably. This indeed appears just, even generous, for the Red Man no longer has rights that he need respect, and the offer may be wise also, as we are no longer in need of an extensive country. . . . I will not dwell on, nor mourn over, our untimely decay, nor reproach our paleface brothers with hastening it, as we too may have been somewhat to blame.

Youth is impulsive. When our young men grow angry at some real or imaginary wrong, and disfigure their faces with black paint, it denotes that their hearts are black, and then they are often cruel and relentless, and our old men and old women are unable to restrain

---

From *The Diary of a Dude-Wrangler*, by Struthers Burt, pp. 31–32. Copyright, 1924, by Charles Scribner's Sons. New York and London.

From *Northwest Gateway*, The Story of the Port of Seattle, by Archie Binns, pp. 100–104. Copyright, 1941, by Archie Binns. Garden City, New York: Doubleday, Doran & Company, Inc.

them. Thus it has ever been. Thus it was when the white men first began to push our forefathers further westward. But let us hope that the hostilities between us may never return. We would have everything to lose and nothing to gain. Revenge by young men is considered gain, even at the cost of their own lives, but old men who stay at home in times of war, and mothers who have sons to lose, know better.

Our good father at Washington—for I presume he is now our father as well as yours, since King George has moved his boundaries further north—our great good father, I say, sends us word that if we do as he desires he will protect us. His brave warriors will be to us a bristling wall of strength, and his wonderful ships of war will fill our harbors so that our ancient enemies far to the northward—the Hydas and Tsimpsians—will cease to frighten our women, children and old men. Then in reality will he be our father and we his children. But can that ever be? Your God is not our God! Your God loves your people and hates mine. He folds his strong and protecting arms lovingly about the paleface and leads him by the hand as a father leads his infant son —but He has forsaken His red children—if they really are His. Our God, the Great Spirit, seems also to have forsaken us. Your God makes your people wax strong every day. Soon they will fill the land. Our people are ebbing away like a rapidly receding tide that will never return. The white man's God cannot love our people or He would protect them. They seem to be orphans who can look nowhere for help. How then can we be brothers? How can your God become our God and renew our prosperity and awaken in us dreams of returning greatness? If we have a common heavenly father He must be partial—for He came to his paleface children. We never saw Him. He gave you laws but He had no word for His red children whose teeming multitudes once filled this vast continent as stars fill the firmament. No; we are two distinct races with separate origins and separate destinies. There is little in common between us.

To us the ashes of our ancestors are sacred and their resting place is hallowed ground. You wander far from the graves of your ancestors and seemingly without regret. Your religion was written upon tables of stone by the iron finger of your God so that you could not forget. The Red Man could never comprehend nor remember it. Our religion is the traditions of our ancestors—the dreams of our old men, given them in solemn hours of night by the Great Spirit; and the visions of our sachems; and it is written in the hearts of our people.

Your dead cease to love you and the land of their nativity as soon as they pass the portals of the tomb and wander way beyond the stars. They are soon forgotten and never return. Our dead never forget the beautiful world that gave them being.

Day and night cannot dwell together. The Red Man has ever fled the approach of the White Man, as the morning mist flees before the morning sun. However, your proposition seems fair and I think that my people will accept it and will retire to the reservation you offer them. Then we will dwell apart in peace, for the words of the Great White Chief seem to be the words of nature speaking to my people out of dense darkness.

It matters little where we pass the remnant of our days. They will not be many. A few more moons; a few more winters—and not one of the descendants of the mighty hosts that once moved over this broad land or lived in happy homes, protected by the Great Spirit, will remain to mourn over the graves of a people once more powerful and hopeful than yours. But why should I mourn at the untimely fate of my people? Tribe follows tribe, and nation follows nation, like the waves of the sea. It is the order of nature, and regret is useless. Your time of decay may be distant, but it will surely come, for even the White Man whose God walked and talked with him as friend with friend, cannot be exempt from the common destiny. We may be brothers after all. We will see.

We will ponder your proposition, and when we decide we will let you know. But should we accept it, I here and now make this condition that we will not be denied the privilege without molestation of visiting at any time the tombs of our ancestors, friends and children. Every part of this soil is sacred in the estimation of my people. Every hillside, every valley, every plain and grove, has been hallowed by some sad or happy event in days long vanished. . . . The very dust upon which you now stand responds more lovingly to their footsteps than to yours, because it is rich with the blood of our ancestors and our bare feet are conscious of the sympathetic touch. . . . Even the little children who lived here and rejoiced here for a brief season will love these somber solitudes and at eventide they greet shadowy returning spirits. And when the last Red Man shall have perished, and the memory of my tribe shall have become a myth among the White Men, these shores will swarm with the invisible dead of my tribe, and when your children's children think themselves alone in the field, the store, the shop, upon the highway, or in the silence of the pathless woods, they will not be alone. . . . At night when the streets of your cities and villages are silent and you think them deserted, they will throng with the returning hosts that once filled and still love this beautiful land. The White Man will never be alone.

Let him be just and deal kindly with my people, for the dead are not powerless. Dead, did I say? There is no death, only a change of worlds.

II. "LAW AND ORDER, LTD."

Colonel Colt made all men equal.—FRONTIER SAYING

Gunmen and Gunfighters

. . . In the Old West there was an important distinction between . . . two types of the quick-shooting gentry of the frontier. The generic term was perhaps "killer," but between the two kinds of killers there was implied a certain degree of difference. The gunman was sneaking, murderous, and was always inclined to take every possible advantage of an enemy. He got the drop when his adversary was unarmed, or he killed from some safe covert, or he managed in some other way to evade the code of honorable shooting that existed in the days when "the six-shooter was the law of the land and every man stood his part."

* * * * *

The gunfighter, on the other hand, was chivalrous, and always generous and sportsmanlike toward an opponent. Frequently he was compelled to kill by force of circumstance and altogether against his will, as when he might have to shoot himself out of some saloon imbroglio among men who, drunk on "tanglefoot" whisky, had lost control of themselves. If the antagonist in a quarrel was not armed the gunfighter was willing to allow his opponent time to procure the requisite shooting-iron. Sometimes indeed the gunfighter, realizing that his opponent was not so good at the game as himself, would contrive to allow some sort of odds in the fight. Admiration for fair play and a sportsmanlike spirit accounts for our being stirred by tales of these members of the hard-riding, quick-shooting chivalry of the plains. Though they may have left trails of blood in their wake, we stoutly refuse to classify them as murderers and perhaps feel resentment if the law eventually grips them and vindicates itself by sending them to the penitentiary or to the scaffold.

From "Clay Allison," by Maurice G. Fulton, *Southwest Review,* Vol. XV (Winter, 1930), No. 2, pp. 192–194. Copyright, 1930, by the Southwest Review. Dallas, Texas: Southern Methodist University.

Joaquin Murieta: The Terror of the Stanislaus

The unsettled condition of society in California, the abundance of money, the amount of travel, mostly by treasure-laden miners, on the lonely roads of the mountains and plains, the herds of fine horses grazing everywhere within easy reach of the robber, and finally, the soft and genial climate of the country, rendered possible, developed, and conduced to the prosperity of the guild of the highwaymen, who had for their field of operations a territory quite as extensive, and as rich in booty and stirring hazard, as was the Spanish Main to the dreaded buccaneers, self-styled the Brotherhood of the Coast.

. . . I will now proceed to relate some of the exploits of him who deservedly stood head and shoulders over all other knights of the road in California, if not, indeed, superior to the most famous leaders of highwaymen recorded in the annals of other countries.

Joaquin Murieta, the terror of the Stanislaus, has a history, which, though crimson with murder, abounds in dramatic interest. He was a Mexican of good blood . . . , born in the department of Sonora, and received an ordinary education in the schools of his native country. In his youth he is said to have been mild, affectionate, and genial in disposition, the pet of the maestro, and a favorite among his fellows of the playground. Yet, while acknowledging the pulpy sweetness of his boyhood, it is safe to presume that there was a dash of bandit blood in the veins of Joaquin, which was eventually to fire his heart with the madness for an outlaw life. As Joaquin and his Rosita reached the new El Dorado, the first flash of the great gold fever was then spreading over its wild ranges. In the memorable spring of 1850 we find him engaged as an honest miner among the Stanislaus placers, where he had a rich claim, and was fast amassing a competency, when, one evening, a party of some half dozen American desperadoes swaggered into his little cabin where with Rosita he was resting after a hard day's work.

"You don't know, I suppose, that greasers are not allowed to take gold from American ground," began the leader insolently.

"If you mean that I have no right to my claim, in obtaining which I have conformed to all the laws of the district, I certainly did not know it," answered Joaquin with quiet dignity.

"Well, you may know it now. And you have got to go; so vamoose, git, and that instanter, and take that trumpery with you," jerking his thumb toward Rosita. "The women if anything are worse than the men."

From *The Works of Hubert Howe Bancroft,* Vol. XXXIV, *California Pastoral, 1769–1848,* pp. 654–670. Entered according to Act of Congress in the year 1888 by Hubert H. Bancroft, in the Office of the Librarian of Congress, at Washington. San Francisco: The History Company, Publishers.

Cf. Joseph Henry Jackson, *Bad Company* (New York, 1949), pp. 3–40.

Joaquin stepped forward with clinched hand, while the hot blood mantled his face: "I will leave these parts if such be your wish, but speak one word against that woman, and though you were ten times an American, you shall rue it."

Scarcely were these words uttered when another of the party reached over and struck Joaquin a severe blow in the face. The latter sprang for his bowie-knife, which he had thrown upon the bed on returning from his work, when Rosita, instinct with the danger such rashness threatened, threw herself before him, and seizing him in her arms, frantically held him. For the intruders to thrust aside the woman and strike the unarmed man senseless was the work of a moment. When Joaquin awoke to consciousness, it was to find Rosita prostrate, her face buried in her clothes, sobbing hysterically. Then he knew the worst.

Fleeing from his outraged home on the Stanislaus, Joaquin and his devoted companion sought refuge on a modest little rancho, hid away in the rugged seclusion of the Calaveras mountains. His dream of peace was soon broken, however, by the sudden apparition of two bearded missionaries, whose monosyllabic warning, "Git!" threw down his hopes and household gods once more into the dust. The hapless twain were driven out from the shadows of Calaveras, and once more became fugitives in the land. We next find Joaquin working as a miner at Murphy Diggings; but luck was against him in the placers, and he finally assumed the gay and remunerative occupation of monte-dealer, a department of industry at the time deemed respectable, even for Americans, not a few of them being thorough adepts in the art of "lay-outs," and both swift and relentless in catching their customers "in the door."

The new vocation was well-suited to the suave young Sonorense, and fortune for a while seemed to befriend him, the uncoined gold of the miners rolling into his ever thickening purse. But his pathway was destined to blush with redder hues than rosy fortune wears. While riding into town a horse that he had borrowed from a half-brother of his who lived on a rancho nearby, he was accosted by an American claiming the animal to have been stolen from him. Murieta pleaded that it was not his, but borrowed. This, however, availed him not. Indeed, it seems that the claim was a well-founded one, and Murieta was charged with the theft, the penalty whereof was death. A half-drunken crowd soon gathered around, and Murieta's protestations of innocence, and offers of money for a respite until witnesses could be forthcoming to prove the truth of his statement, were disregarded. He was pulled down from the saddle, and amid cries of "Kill the thief! Hang the greaser!" they hurriedly carried him to the rancho of his brother, whom they summarily launched into eternity from the branch of a neighboring tree. Joaquin was stripped, bound to the same tree, and flogged. While the heavy lash was lacerating his back, a demoniac expression appeared upon his face; he looked around and stamped the features of each of his persecutors on the tablets of his memory. When the executioners had finished their work, they departed, leaving him with his dead. It was then that Joaquin Murieta registered his oath of vengeance which he so relentlessly kept, rarely sparing even the innocent. From that hour he was the implacable foe of every American, and even of every being that bore the resemblance of a gringo. Lucifer had him now for his own.

Words have been put in Murieta's lips to the effect that he had at one time felt a great admiration for Americans and their institutions; and only after experiencing unjust persecution and brutality at their hands, had the scales fallen from his eyes, and a deadly hatred seized him. To avenge the wrongs inflicted on himself and his countrymen, who were constantly kicked, and cuffed, and robbed, was now the purpose of his life. To kill, destroy, marking his swift trail with blood, was now his dream; for every stripe that had been laid upon his yet unhealed back ten Yankee lives should be forfeited, and these ruffianly Anglo-Saxons be made to understand that the free citizens of the sister republic had not wholly sunk their origin, nor lost their manhood. Letting all this pass, however, the fact stands that not long after the infliction of the flogging, an American was found dead near Murphy Diggings, literally hacked to pieces with a knife. The body turned out to be that of one of those who had flogged Joaquin, and hanged his brother. Suspicion was not long at fault reaching the author of the bloody act. Other murders followed in swift succession, robbing being one of the incidents of each case. It then began to be whispered that the young victim of Yankee brutality was wreaking his vengeance. Joaquin's bloody deeds were in everybody's mind, and his name became a terror.

Within a few months the dashing boy was at the head of an organized band of highwaymen, which ravaged the country in every direction. This band consisted sometimes of twenty, and at other times of as many as eighty. The boy leader gave proof every day of possessing a peculiar genius controlling the most accomplished scoundrels that had ever congregated in Christendom. He was their master; his word was their law, and woe betide him who dared to disobey, while to break faith with a fellow-robber was quick death. A member of the band, perforated by four bullets, was captured in February, 1853, at Los Muertos, near Los Angeles, brought to San Andreas, tried, and hanged by the people. He was but an humble member of the profession, and when he saw that death was certain, he was induced to talk a little. He said that no member of the fraternity was much respected who had not killed his man, and each ranked in importance according to the number that he had slain. This was something as it is in the army. Every member was bound under most solemn oaths, first, to obey his superiors. Disobedience was punished with death. There was hardly one chance in a hundred that a traitor could escape; for it was the duty and pleasure of the betrayed whose lives were jeopardized by the treachery to hunt and slay the informer. It was well understood by all, even the stupidest of them, that good faith unto one another, union and discipline, were essential as well to their personal safety as to pecuniary success.

This completeness of organization, coupled with the awful power wielded by the leader, enabled the band during nearly three years to carry on its operations, and its boyish chief to flit between towns and country, flipping his fingers in the face of police and people, while throughout the length and breadth of the Californian valley, from Shasta to Tulare, and along the coast line of missions the country was wailing its dead and ringing with rewards. The modus operandi to accomplish the purposes of the organization was as follows: Each subaltern was restricted to certain limits beyond which he dare not step. He had to be at all times ready to receive an order from any captain or lieutenant of the band. His eyes and ears were to be always open, and his mouth closed; passing events were to be narrowly observed, such as the yield of the various mining claims, the drift of the gold dust, where a company kept their money, or certain Chinamen had hidden theirs. It was, moreover, his duty to shelter and protect any of the brotherhood needing his assistance; to warn them of danger, and provide horses and aid to escape; and generally, to assist them in all their undertakings.

Joaquin was always splendidly mounted; in fact much of his success depended on his horses. It was the special business of a certain portion of the brotherhood to keep the company well supplied with the best horses in the country. There were, also, members living in towns, and among the peaceable inhabitants, pursuing honest occupations, who were spies, and kept the officers of the band advised of matters they were desirous of knowing.

To relate the hundreds of incidents in which Joaquin and his chief captains and lieutenants personally displayed their skill and courage, would occupy more space than I can devote to the matter. I will, however, narrate some of the most daring deeds of the young leader.

In 1851 while sojourning in a secluded part of San José, he attended a fandango, where he became involved in a fracas, for which he was arrested and fined $12 by the magistrate. Being in charge of Deputy Sheriff Clark, who was not aware of his being the robber chief, he invited the latter to go with him to his house for the money. Clark had become obnoxious to Murieta for his vigorous pursuit of the band. On reaching an unfrequented place the robber suddenly turned upon the officer, and with a smile said, "Accept the compliments of Joaquin," and drove his jeweled poignard to the hilt in his breast. In the autumn of the same year Murieta and his band were at the Sonoran camp near Marysville, where they committed a number of robberies, and five murders, every one of the murdered men bearing on his neck the fatal mark of the flying noose. All had been lassoed, and dragged at the saddle bow by the lariat. In the wild region west of the white pyramid of Shasta, the band roamed many months engaged in horse-stealing, with now and then a murder. Once while two of the band were galloping near the town of Hamilton, an elk rushed past them hotly pursued by a beautiful girl mounted on a fine steed. She hurled her lasso at the animal and secured it, only to find herself in turn held fast by the lariats of the two banditti. Her terror was distracting. She implored them not to harm her, but little did they care for her entreaties. There was only one voice on earth which they would heed, and that came unexpectedly as if from another world. "Restore that girl to her horse instantly." It was Joaquin who spoke.

One evening not long afterward, Joaquin was sitting at a monte table in a small town on the Feather River, when an American boastfully offered to bet $500 that he would kill the scoundrel Joaquin the first time he met him. Carried away by one of his dare-devil impulses, Joaquin sprang upon the table, and thrusting his pistol in the man's face cried, "I take the bet; Joaquin is before you"; then tossing the corner of his serape over his shoulder, he jumped down, strode out of the room, mounted his horse and rode away with some of his henchmen at his heels.

In the spring of 1852 Murieta drove 300 stolen horses through Southern California into Sonora. On his return after a few weeks, he was quartered at the Arroyo de Cantúa, situated between the Coast Range and the Tulare lake. It is possible that it was just previous to this that they sojourned for a while in Los Angeles and vicinity. Riding with some of his men toward San Luis Gonzaga, and his purse being light, Murieta, after the manner of Robin Hood, resolved to rob the first man that came along. The victim happened to be a young fellow named Albert Ruddle, who was driving a wagon loaded with groceries. Joaquin requested the loan of what money he had, promising to return it at an early opportunity. Ruddle made a movement as if to draw a weapon. He was told to keep quiet or he would be killed, but as he persisted, Joaquin with a muttered imprecation, slashed him across the neck with his knife, almost severing the head from the body. After rifling the dead man's pockets, the robbers rode off.

While in Los Angeles for a few days, he heard that Deputy Sheriff Wilson of Santa Bárbara was on his trail, with the avowed intention of taking him dead or alive. He got up a sham fight between two Indians in front of the hotel where Wilson was staying. The latter came out to see the fight, when Joaquin rode swiftly to him, and hissing his own terrible name in his ear, drove a bullet through his head and drove away.

Riding one day alone toward the town of Los Hornitos, the chief met young Joe Lake, a playmate of his boyhood. In the course of their conversation Joaquin revealed his present mode of living, and said,

"Joe, you are the only American whose good opinion I crave. Believe me my friend, I was driven to this by hellish wrongs." "Why don't you leave the country, and abandon your criminal life?" answered Joe. "Too late, Joe, I must die now as I live, pistol in hand. Do not betray me; do not divulge having met me here. If you do, I shall be very sorry," significantly tapping the stock of his revolver. Lake deemed it his duty to apprise the authorities of Murieta's presence, and the usual persecution began. The next morning a portly ranchero came up to Lake, and saying, "You betrayed me, Joe!" plunged a knife into his breast, and rode away unharmed.

One evening, Joaquin rode into a camp where about 25 miners were at supper, and sitting sideways on his horse entered into conversation with them. It so happened that a man who knew him by sight soon after came from the creek, and on seeing him called out, "That is Joaquin; why, in the name of God don't you kill him?" Putting spurs to his horse with one bound he cleared the camp and dashed down the cañon. Finding his way blocked there he returned toward the camp, to avail himself of a narrow coyote trail around the brow of a precipice that overhung the awful depths of the cañon below. A shower of bullets greeted his reappearance, but none touched him, as he dashed up and along that dizzy path, waving his dagger and shouting defiance.

In the early part of March, 1853, Joaquin, unattended, visited a large Mexican camp on Burns creek, about twenty miles from the town of Mariposa. He presented the appearance of a dashing cavalier, with plumed sombrero, gold laced cloak, and gayly caparisoned steed, as he slowly rode down the principal thoroughfare of the camp, tinkling his spurs to the measures of some lively fandango, and was the cynosure of many admiring glances from the eyes of the señoritas. Passing in front of a saloon he called for a drink, and was just lifting it to his lips, when an American, one of two who were standing together and had recognized him, drew his revolver and fired a shot that cut the plume of the brigand's hat. The drink was never taken, but Joaquin, after having wounded one of the Americans in the arm and the other in the abdomen, galloped away without a scratch.

Later in the same month, Murieta and three or four of his men robbed a Chinese camp at Rich gulch, not far from San Andreas, of about $10,000, leaving three dead and five wounded. The next morning they entered another Chinese camp at the foot of the mountains, gashed the throats of three of the Chinamen, mortally wounded five others, and carried off some $3,000 in gold. They next visited several other Chinese camps, all of which they desolated, the cries of their victims being heard at long distances. Finding themselves pursued by a party of Americans, they calmly continued their devastation, until the pursuers were within half a mile of them, when they mounted their steeds, and rode away with the speed of the wind.

On one occasion, Murieta riding leisurely in disguise through Stockton, he saw the hand-bills offering $1,000 for his capture. Taking from his pocket a pencil, he wrote on the margin beneath one of them, "I will give $5,000. Joaquin," and quietly rode away.

One night a cattle-dealer, whose name was Cocariouris, was camping with one companion on the San Joaquin, when they were visited by several Mexicans, splendidly mounted and gaily attired, who asked for supper and a place to sleep. Their occupation being quite evident, they were treated with much politeness, and their requests promptly complied with. In the morning the robber was cordially greeted by the cattle dealer:

"And how does Señor Joaquin this morning?"

"You know me, then," replied the robber.

"I knew you the moment I saw you," said Cocariouris.

"And why did you not kill me last night when I slept, and secure the reward?" demanded Joaquin.

"I do not like to kill men; I do not care for the reward," replied the host. "Besides, you never injured me; you asked for food; if every man deserving to be hanged went supperless, there would be an empty chair at more tables than mine."

"True," replied Joaquin, meditatively, "and I will see that you lose nothing by your broad philosophy."

Cocariouris was often on the road with large herds of stock, not one head of which was ever, to his knowledge, touched by any of Murieta's band.

The audacity of this chief, united to his celerity of movement, at a time when the country had no communication by railway or telegraph, enabled him and his men to effect the most remarkable escapes, as we have seen. He would show himself now here, now there, like an impish apparition which vanished at the approach of danger.

In February, 1853, Joaquin and his band swept through Calaveras, robbing and slaughtering as they went. Again was a reward of $1,000 offered by the governor for his capture. The people of Mokelumne Hill and elsewhere were indignant at the smallness of the amount, when they themselves had spent many thousands in their fruitless attempts. The scourge continued, and gloom overspread the foothills.

One evening in April, 1853, shortly before Joaquin's death, three men rode up to the house of a rancho on the Salinas plains and demanded refreshments for themselves and their horses, which were readily and politely served. After supper they informed their host that they were from the upper country on their way to Sonora to buy cattle. Their spokesman being asked if they had seen or heard of the famous Joaquin, he replied, "I am that Joaquin, and no man shall take me alive." He then gave his oft-repeated narrative of the wrongs which had been inflicted on him and his. In the morning, after paying for the night's lodging and refreshments, Joaquin and his companions departed southward, as he had said, but only went as far as the region of

San Luis Obispo and Santa Barbara, and the cattle they took they seldom paid for. Murieta's movements were now very closely watched, and it was thought that his destination was Lower California.

I have merely referred to a few of the doings of this famous band of marauders, or a portion of it under the immediate direction of Murieta in person. But it should be borne in mind that the excellently organized fraternity was often divided, and under his several lieutenants, García, Claudio, Ruiz, and others, bore the terror of their chief's name simultaneously in widely different directions. Their operations became so repeated and destructive, extending meanwhile over such a great extent of country, that no community felt safe.

At last, the people throughout the state were aroused to the imporance of suppressing this overwhelming evil. For three years this bloody work had been going on—a long time in that rushing epoch—and it was a reflection on the manhood of California that the robbers should go so long uncaught. At length, on the 17th of May, 1853, the legislature of California passed an act authorizing Harry Love to bring his mountaineer's experience, bravery, and tested nerve into action, with a well-organized and equipped body of twenty mounted rangers, to hunt the marauders down. Love was soon in the field, and lost no time in getting upon the track of the brigands.

Poor Joaquin! Love encompassed him without and within. For his girl, Antonia la Molinera, who went about with him dressed in men's clothes, proved false, having run away with a traitorous member of the band, Pancho Daniel. Murieta swore he would kill both of them; and Antonia when she heard of it, and knowing him so well, and realizing that her life was not safe for a moment as long as he was at liberty, resolved to betray him into the hands of justice.

Murieta sent first Vergara to kill her, but Vergara proved false, and let the girl live, abandoning the banditti, and going to work on the rancho of Palos Verdes, where was later Wilmington. Murieta sent another member of his band to bring back Vergara, but a few days thereafter the messenger was found murdered in the street in Los Angeles. Likewise, others of Joaquin's girls were giving him trouble. Thus discord was in the camp, men proving traitorous and women false, which shows that the life of a robber is not always a happy one.

Stealthily enough Harry Love, with his fierce eyes and flowing hair, followed upon the trail of Joaquin, spying upon him by night, and keeping under close cover by day, thirsting for the blood-money, thirsting both for the blood and the money, eager to slay the slayer and rob the robber.

Thus the toils which must inevitably sooner or later end such a career were closing round Joaquin. In the latter part of July, with eight of his rangers, Love came upon a party of Mexicans in camp near the Tejon pass. Six of them were seated round a small fire, where preparations for breakfast were going forward, while the seventh, he of the slender figure, and graceful limbs, and large black eyes, and long black hair, a perfect Apollo, richly dressed, blooming in the pride of health and manly beauty, was washing down a superb bay horse, at a little distance from the fire, with some water which he held in a pan. Joaquin was unknown to the rangers, who dashed into the camp before they were discovered, and succeeded in cutting the robbers off from their horses. Captain Love rode up to the one standing by his horse, and enquired whither they were going.

"To Los Angeles," the chief replied.

Turning to one of the others, the captain put the same question when an entirely different answer was returned. Joaquin bit his lip and spoke angrily, "I command here; address yourself to me." He then moved a few steps toward the fire, around which lay the saddles, blankets, and arms of the party. He was ordered to stop, and when he did not heed, Love cocked his revolver upon him and told him to stand or he would shoot. The chief tossed his hair back scornfully while his eyes blazed with the lightnings of his wrath, and stepping backward, he stood again by the side of his handsome steed, his jeweled hand resting lightly on its mane. Three-Fingered Jack stood a little distance away, fully armed and waiting for his chief. At this critical moment Lieutenant Byrnes, with whom Joaquin was well acquainted, moved up, and Joaquin, realizing that the game was up, called out to his followers to save themselves the best they could, and threw himself upon the back of his charger without saddle or bridle, and sped down the mountain like a tempest. He leaped his horse over a precipice, when he fell, but was on his feet again in a moment, and remounting, the daring rider dashed on. Close at his heels came the rangers, firing as they rode, and soon the gallant steed, struck in the side, fell to the earth, and Joaquin ran on afoot. Three balls had pierced his body, when he turned with a lifted hand toward his pursuers, and called out: "It is enough; the work is done,"—reeled, fell upon his right arm, and, sinking slowly down before his pursuers, gave up the ghost without a groan.

Three-Fingered Jack, cornered, fought like a tiger, but the end was at hand. And so with others of the company. Claudio had fallen some time before. The bandits, now left without an efficient leader, and admonished by the swift and sorrowful fate of Joaquin, broke up the organization, and stole away from the theatre of their crimes. For purposes of identification, the head of Joaquin, and the mutilated hand of Three-Fingered Jack, were severed from the bodies, and, preserved in spirits, were brought to San Francisco in August, 1853, by Black and Nuttall, two of Harry Love's rangers. The head was placed on exhibition, as the following notice, which appeared in the papers of the city on the 18th of August, and for several days following, will show: "Joaquin's Head! is to be seen at King's, corner of Halleck and

Sansome streets. Admission one dollar." Then followed certificates of persons who had known Joaquin, as to the identity of the head. No money was recovered, though one of the prisoners declared that Jack had thrown away a heavy purse of gold during the chase. It is probable that others did the same, as the heavy operations of the band must have kept them well supplied with dust and coin. The growth, after death, of the hair on the head of Joaquin, and the fingernails of Jack's hand, caused quite a sensation among those not accustomed to such phenomena.

The number of murders committed by Joaquin and his men during the comparatively brief period in which they were abroad is truly astonishing. They were particularly hard on the Chinamen, literally strewing the highways with their carcasses, like slaughtered pigs, and robbing them at every turn. Several renegade Americans were among the robbers who won the respect of the bandit chief by deeds as bloody and heartless as ever stained the annals of human wrong.

Claudio . . . met his fate some time before the tragic scene at the Tejon pass. In the early part of 1853, attended by six of his men, Claudio was ravaging the country between Salinas and Monterey, robbing and slaying with a reckless hand. One Cocks, a justice of the peace at Salinas, and, withal a fearless man, summoned a party of eight and started in pursuit of the brigands. On the Salinas river, near Cooper's crossing, stood the adobe cabin of a man named Balder, whose reputation was very bad. Cocks and his party surrounded this house at night, and there, as they expected, found the robbers. A watch dog gave the alarm; but the Americans had already dismounted, and taking off their spurs, rushed in close to the walls. There was but one thing to do, for Claudio was not the kind of villain tamely to die in a kennel; bidding his men to follow, he threw the door open, and boldly led the way into the darkness, firing as he went. Unfortunately for the bandit he ran into the arms of Squire Cocks, who, being a powerful and determined man, held him with a grip of steel, until the robber dropping his revolver, exclaimed, "Estoy dado, señor; no tengo armas." "I surrender, sir: I have no arms." The lie was scarcely spoken when something was seen to glitter in the hand of Claudio. It was a murderous dirk which he had drawn from his legging; but a bullet from the pistol of an American stretched him lifeless before he could use it. With a single exception the brigands were all shot dead in the fight that ensued; the one making his escape being wounded, and was captured next day. He was sent to San Quentin for a term of years and afterward hanged.

Black Bart, Po8

. . . Robbery, you know, it's like most any other line of work. If you want to make a success of it you have to go at it business-like. You must plan all your moves beforehand so as to take just as few chances as you can. If you have the other fellow figured out and know just what you're going to do, you can keep just that one jump ahead—until finally, sooner or later, something happens that you hadn't counted on and you get caught.

Take Black Bart, now. He was the most successful road agent that ever operated on the Mother Lode. He followed the business for over eight years before he was caught, and pulled off more than thirty robberies without ever firing a shot. The reason was, he always laid careful plans, he worked alone, never struck near home, and always kept his business to himself.

His career got started in a curious way, more or less by accident; for he was a high-class, educated, middle-aged man—a wiry, dapper little fellow with sharp blue eyes and a gray mustache and imperial. His true name was Charles E. Boles. He had been a Union officer in the Civil War, and along in the early seventies was teaching school in the Northern Mines. But he loved a practical joke, you see, and it's only one step from that to crime.

One day, towards nightfall, he was riding along the road after school when he heard the stage come pelting down the grade. He knew the stage-driver, and thought that just for fun he'd give him a scare. So he hitched his horse in the bushes, tied a handkerchief over his face, and broke a stick off a manzanita bush about the size and shape of a pistol. Then when the stage came along, he stepped out into the road and told the driver to hold up. Well, they was no shotgun messenger aboard and the driver looked pretty scared, so Boles thought he'd see how far the joke would go.

"Throw out the box!" he says.

The driver pulled the old-style wooden Wells Fargo treasure-box from under the seat and tossed it out. It happened to land on a rock and broke open with such a crash that Boles, he jumped back off the road. The driver then thought this was his chance. He laid the whip to his horses and the stage went whirling on. So there was Professor Boles with his manzanita pistol in his hand and the treasure at his feet.

From *Ghost Town,* Wherein Is Told Much That Is Wonderful, Laughable, and Tragic, and Some That Is Hard to Believe about Life during the Gold Rush and Later in the Town of Columbia on California's Mother Lode, as Remembered by the Oldest Inhabitants and Here for the First Time Set Down by G. Ezra Dane, in collaboration with Beatrice J. Dane, pp. 139–149. Copyright, 1941, by G. Ezra Dane. New York: Alfred A. Knopf.

Cf. Joseph Henry Jackson, *Bad Company* (New York, 1949), 119–214.

They was no joke about that treasure. It was the real thing—a couple of thousand dollars in bullion bars and coin and sacks of gold dust scattered in the road. Boles, he commenced to gather it up and to heft it, and to think, "If I can get as much in two minutes by playing a little joke like this," he thought, "as I can in two years teaching school, maybe I had better quit teaching and stick to practical joking." So he put the treasure in his saddle-bags and struck out for down below.

Well, he went to San Francisco and banked his haul, and then he put up at a little genteel hotel. He took the name of C. E. Bolton and give out that he was a mining man and had to go off every so often to visit his mines. But really, of course, each time he'd be planning and putting over one of his little jokes on Wells Fargo, prospecting for bullion in their treasure-boxes. He'd mosey around one of the mining towns, you know, till he'd find out when a good-sized shipment of bullion would be going down. Then, miles away, he'd lay for the stage and hold it up. He always had the thing planned so it would go through without a hitch, and he'd make his get-away. He carried a real gun then, a double-barreled shotgun, but it was never loaded. Anyway, he never fired a shot, and he'd never rob a passenger. He'd only take Wells Fargo treasure, and always, after he emptied the box, he'd leave a piece of paper in it with some verses, that he'd sign *Black Bart,* and after that the letters *P o* and the figure *8—Po8;* that was his pun for poet.

Now, I'll give you a sample of Black Bart's poetry. His best one went like this:

Here I lay me down to sleep
To wait the coming morrow,
Perhaps success, perhaps defeat
And everlasting sorrow.

Let come what will, I'll try it on,
My condition can't be worse,
And if there's money in that box
'Tis money in my purse.

And here's another:

This is my way to get money and bread,
When I have a chance why should I refuse it.
I'll not need either when I'm dead,
And I only tax those who are able to lose it.

So blame me not for what I've done,
I don't deserve your curses;
And if for some cause I must be hung,
Let it be for my verses.

Well, it went on for years. This lone robber would hold up a stage, say, in Mendocino County, near the coast, and the broken box would be brought in with a new poem to Wells Fargo in it. The next time he might strike the Oregon State in Siskiyou County, above Yreka. Then maybe he would show up in Sierra County, on the Downieville road;

and then in the Southern Mines, near Jackson, or on the road to Copperopolis.

Every time, of course, the Wells Fargo detectives, Jim Hume and Thacker, and the local officers too, they'd set out to trail him. But he was always that one jump ahead. He was a wonderful hiker, Bart was. He'd often walk from twenty-five to fifty miles through the mountains after a robbery, by the trails he had picked out beforehand. That way, you see, he'd come out at some place where no one was looking for him, and he could take the stage or train for San Francisco. Sometimes, to cover his tracks still better, he'd even take the train in the opposite direction first, over to Reno; and then after a day or two he'd come back to San Francisco and be C. E. Bolton again, returned from a visit to his mines with the news that he had struck another pocket. And he was such a quiet, respectable old gent, with his neat gray mustache and imperial, and his derby hat, and cane, and his Prince Albert Coat, that nobody ever had the least suspicion of him.

He used to eat quite often at a restaurant near the Hall of Justice. There he got well acquainted with several of the police detectives, and my, how these San Francisco policemen used to laugh with their friend Bolton, the mining man, about the stupid country sheriffs that never could catch this joking road agent Black Bart, who had become so notorious by his stage robberies and his po8try.

The best joke of all was yet to come, though, when a fifteen-year-old country boy done what none of the sheriffs and stagedrivers and detectives had been able to do for seven years or more. That was when Black Bart held up the Sonora-Milton stage beyond Reynold's Ferry in November of '83.

He laid for the stage, you see, on the other side of the Stanislaus River, where the road wound up the Funk Hill grade, because he knew the stage would be going slow and couldn't make a run of it. Well, he jumped out of the bushes there, in a long linen duster to cover his clothes, and with a flour-sack over his face. His trick was to crouch under the heads of the lead horses, to shield himself till he could get the driver disarmed. So this driver—it was Reason McConnell—Bart made him get out and unhitch the horses and drive them on ahead. Then Bart, he tackled the box.

Wells Fargo, by this time, to make it harder for these road agents, they had their boxes made of iron and bolted right into the stages. But Bart had improved his methods, to keep up with them; he had a sledge and a gad and a drill, and he worked fast. He smashed the side of the stage out with his sledge so as he could get at the box, and soon had it pried open. Then he found he hadn't misfigured, for they was over four thousand in gold bullion there—a shipment from the Patterson Mine that he'd been waiting for—and about seven hundred in coin for good measure.

But while Bart thought his plans was working out so well, you see, Jimmy Rolleri—he was the boy that was running the ferry—he had come on with the stage up to Funk's Hill to hunt squirrels with his old rifle, and he'd jumped off just before the stage got in sight of Black Bart. Well, while Jimmy was strolling along and hunting along there, he heard Bart pounding on the box and he thought Reason McConnell must of had a breakdown. So he followed on up the road and on, and when he come in sight of the place, Bart was so busy he didn't notice him. But Reason made a sign to him to skirt around through the bushes up to where Reason was. So Jimmy did, and by the time he got there Bart had just put the treasure in his sack and was running down the road.

Reason, he grabbed Jimmy's old gun and took a couple of shots at Bart. But Bart just run all the faster, and Jimmy says: "Oh, Reason," he says, "let me have just one shot!" So Reason handed back the gun and Jimmy dropped to one knee there and drew a good bead and fired just before Bart got out of sight. They saw Bart drop the tools and things he had in one hand and snap his wrist, like this, as though he'd been hit, you know. But he held on to the treasure-sack with the other hand and kept right on running, so it looked as though he'd made another clean get-away.

Well, Reason and Jimmy, they tracked along where Bart had gone, and they found these tools he'd dropped, and his derby hat, and a starched cuff with blood on it that he must of flipped off when the bullet stung his hand. Then in the box they found Bart's latest poem, that went like this:

I'll start out to-morrow
With another empty sack.
From Wells Fargo I will borrow
But I'll never pay it back.

And it was signed, of course: *Black Bart, Po8.*

Reason and Jimmy, they hitched up again and drove pell-mell to Copperopolis and sent word of the hold-up to Ben Thorne, the famous Sheriff. He was the law in Calaveras County, for nearly fifty years, Ben was.

So old Ben, he rode over from San Andreas and he heard the story and looked over the evidence. And it was on the cuff he found his clue —a laundry mark, FXO7. Now, in them days no laundry up here used marks like that, and Ben figured it must of come from down below. So he took this cuff to San Francisco and showed it to Jim Hume, the Wells Fargo chief detective, and Hume give it to Harry Morse of the Morse Patrol to make the rounds of the laundry agencies. Pretty soon he come to one that said this mark was theirs, and they looked it up, and told Morse the cuff belonged to Mr. C. E. Bolton at the Webb House. Morse then hung around the place till Bart come in, and had the agent introduce him.

"I understand you're a mining man, Mr. Bolton," says Morse, and Bart says: "Yes." So then Morse told him: "I've been doing some prospecting," he says, "and I have some samples that I wish you'd take a look at."

Well, Bart was agreeable and started out with Morse for the office where Morse said he had these samples; and Morse walked him right through the side door of the Wells Fargo Building, and into Jim Hume's private office.

"Jim," he says, "this is Mr. C. E. Bolton, the mining man. I brought him in to see them samples," he says.

"Well," says Hume, "Mr. Bolton, I've been looking forward to the pleasure of meeting you for a long time—for about seven years, in fact," he says, "and I'll be very glad to hear what you have to say about these samples." And with that he spread out the evidence that Jimmy and Reason had picked up at Funk Hill—the cuff and the hat and the other stuff, you know. Bart, he must of known the game was up, but he just looked at these things in a casual sort of way, and then he took the hat and tried it on.

"Why," he says, "this fits me so well I'm tempted to buy it from you."

He had a fresh scar on his hand, too, where Jimmy's bullet had grazed him, so they put him in the San Francisco jail—you can imagine the surprise of his detective friends—and then Thorne took him to San Andreas. He showed Thorne where he had the four thousand in bullion and his gun in a hollow log on Funk Hill, and he pleaded guilty to his last robbery, so the judge only give him six years in San Quentin.

After he got settled down there at the prison he wrote a letter to Reason McConnell. It went about like this:

> Mr. McConnell:
>
> Dear Sir—You will please pardon me for this long delay in acknowledging your kind compliments so hastily sent me on the 3d of November last, but rest fully assured, my dear sir, that you are remembered, and with nothing but the most kindly feelings, as a man having done your whole duty to your employer, yourself, and to the community at large. I have often admired your fine qualities as a driver and only regret that I am unable to say as much for your marksmanship, though I wish you would convey my compliments to Jimmy Rolleri for his. I would like to hear from you, if consistent with your desires, and, my dear sir, you have my best wishes for an unmolested, prosperous, and happy drive through life.
>
> I am, dear sir, yours in haste,
>
> B.B.
>
> P.S.—But not in quite so much of a hurry as on a former occasion.

He was still joking when he come out of prison, too. The warden says to him: "Well, Bart," he says, "I hope you have learned your lesson and won't commit any more crimes."

"Oh, no, Warden," Bart says, "I'm through with all that now."

"What are you going to do, then, Bart?" the warden asked him. "Are you going to write poetry for a living?"

"Warden," says he, "didn't I tell you I wasn't going to commit any more crimes?"

Now I'm going to tell you what he did. If you don't believe me, I can't help that, but if you ask anybody else around these parts, he'll tell you the very same thing.

No sooner had they let the old boy out of San Quentin than a lone robber begun popping up again, in Mendocino County, Sierra County, Siskiyou, helping himself to the Wells Fargo boxes just when they was the heaviest. He didn't leave verses or sign his name to his work like Bart had used to do, and he was so well disguised that nobody could identify him, but the Wells Fargo detectives knew the style from long experience. So they got a hold of Bart and called him in.

"See here," they says, "we're willing to make a deal and call it quits if you are."

Bart said, well, he was getting pretty old and would like to retire from the road-agency business anyway, if only he had a little regular income. And finally the company agreed to put him on their pension list at two hundred dollars a month, providing he would report every week where he was and wouldn't rob them any more. So Black Bart, the Po8, had the last laugh on Wells Fargo after all.

Jesse James Uses His Wits

An amusing story is told of Jesse, who on a memorable occasion played the part of a rustic innocent abroad to perfection. It was the second day after the bank robbery at Corydon, Iowa. The whole region was up in arms in hot pursuit after the robbers. Jesse was riding along a way not much frequented, when he became suddenly aware of two men riding in hot fury not far distant. Confident that they had neither seen nor heard him, his ready wit suggested a speedy course of action. Jesse was dressed in the rough attire of a granger, and assumed a most uncouth simplicity both of dialect and manners. When he came within reasonable distance of the two well-armed, well-mounted horsemen, he, with a wary eye on their pistols and his hand not far from his own, accosted them:

"Well, gentleman, have you met anybody up the road ridin 'a hoss an' leadin' ov another one, 'cause you see as how I lives down on the Nodaway, an' some infernal thief has gone off with my two best hosses. I hearn about two miles furder down at the blacksmith shop that a man passed there about a hour an' a half ago with two hosses, an' they fits the descripshun of mine to a T. Have you seen sich?"

From *The James Boys,* A Complete and Accurate Recital of the Dare-Devil Criminal Career of the Famous Bandit Brothers, Frank and Jesse James, and Their Noted Band of Bank Plunderers, Train Robbers and Murderers, Specially Compiled for the Publishers, [by J. W. Buel,] pp. 243–246. Chicago: M. A. Donohue & Co. [N.d.]

Cf. *A Treasury of American Folklore* (New York, 1944), pp. 71–72, 107–112.

"No. Where are you traveling from?"

"Why, Lord, I've come all the way from the Nodaway. The infernal thieves are using us up awful. I wish I'd come on the infernal son of a seacook whose taken my hosses. I do, you bet, I'd go for him with these 'ere irons. I would that!" And Jesse revealed his "weapons" as he called them.

"Did you see anybody on the road ahead?" asked the tallest of the two horsemen.

"Not for some miles. I met four ugly-looking customers this mornin'. They looked like they might a' been hoss-thieves theirselves. D—n the hoss-thieves, say I!" said the rustic Jesse.

"Thieves are plenty now-a-days. They come into towns and break banks in open daylight. How far did you say the four men were ahead?"

"Well, I didn't say; but it must be more'n two hours since I met 'em, an' they were a ridin' purty fast, an' I've rid my hoss almost down, as you can see," answered Jesse.

"What kind of looking men were they?" asked the robber-hunters.

"Well, one was a sizable man, with a long, red beard, and a flopped black hat on, a ridin' on a big chestnut sorrel hoss, an' one more was a smallish man, with very black hair and beard, and sharp black eyes, an' he was a ridin' on a roan hoss, an' another was an oldish man, with some gray among his beard, an' he wore a blue huntin' shirt coat, an' he was a ridin' a gray hoss, and the last feller was a little weazle-faced chap, with tallowy complexion, who didn't ware no beard, an' he rode on a dark-brown hoss," said with rustic simplicity.

The two robber-hunters then consulted together.

"That's their description," said one. "Precisely," said the other. "Shall we follow?" asked one. 'I would like to," replied the other. "But there are four of them," was the remark in rejoinder. "Yes, that is bad. If Ed, Dick and Will would just hurry up. Those fellows are no doubt very dangerous men," was the comment of one. "You bet they are," was the response.

All this time Jesse had listened as an interested party. Now he thought he was privileged to make an inquiry.

"What's up, strangers, anyhow?" Jesse asked.

"You blow it! Don't you know that the Corydon bank, up in Iowa, was robbed yesterday?"

Jesse opened his eyes in well-feigned surprise.

"You don't say so!" he ejaculated.

"Yes, in broad daylight, and the men you met are the robbers, no doubt. There's a big reward offered to catch them."

"What's this country comin' to anyhow? Hoss thieves down on the Nodaway, an' bank rogues up to Iowa. 'Pears like hard-workin' honest folks can't get along much more," grumbled Jesse.

"Could you go back with us?"

"I'd like to, but the cussed hoss thieves will get away. Besides, you see, my horse is mighty nigh played out hisself. Howsumever, I might ride with you as fur as I can. D—n all thieves, say I, don't you?"

And Jesse actually turned with the two pursuers of the robbers, in pursuit of another posse of pursuers which Jesse had been enabled accurately to describe by having seen them pass him while lying snug in a dense thicket.

They might catch the robbers, and as he'd "have a sheer ov the reward, it would be better'n nothing at all fur his stolen hosses."

For miles Jesse rode with them, till, coming near a railway station, he begged to be excused on the ground that his horse was becoming lame. His excuse was accepted and he left the pursuers to their vain and hopeless pursuit.

A thousand similar stories might be related illustrating the coolness and bravery of Frank and Jesse James in the midst of danger.

Clay Allison: "A Whale of a Fellow" with a Gun

I. Why He Left Texas

What keeps the name of Clay Allison alive among these oldtimers . . . is not so much the large number of his killings, as the boisterous dare-deviltry, the grim diablerie, with which the man seemed possessed even when he was taking some one's life. Allison sober was an exceedingly pleasant and kind man, but Allison drunk was quite a different being—he became a man dangerous to cross. "He was a whale of a fellow," said a contemporary of Allison, "and considerate of his companions; but throw a drink into him, and he was hell turned loose, rearin' for a chance to shoot—in self defense."

In physical appearance Clay Allison was a striking, not to say magnificent figure. I have searched hard for a photograph of him, but have never been able to acquire one. Thus for details of his appearance, I have to fall back on word-portraits. He was about six feet two inches in height and weighed between 180 and 190 pounds. He is said to have had the blue eye that seems to have been quite the distinguishing characteristic of the killer, although one who knew him well insists that his eyes were black. His face is described as large, with all its features prominent. Usually there was a serious cast to his countenance; some even speak of it as having a "melancholy look." His hair was worn down to the shoulders, and his mustache was long and formidable, after the fashion of the times. For a man of such large physique, he was remarkably active and quick in his movements. Another reason why this particular characteristic has fixed itself strongly in the memories

---

From "Clay Allison," by Maurice G. Fulton, *Southwest Review,* Vol. XV (Winter, 1930), No. 2, pp. 194–195, 196, 197–204, 214–215. Copyright, 1930, by the Southwest Review. Dallas, Texas: Southern Methodist University.

of those who knew Clay Allison is that for the greater part of his life he was somewhat crippled from having accidentally shot himself in the instep.

Clay Allison was born in Tennessee about 1840, although some set 1835 as the date. At the beginning of the Civil War he left his father's farm and joined the Confederate Army. Little is known of his life as a soldier, but at the conclusion of the war he became one of the malcontents, like the James boys, who embarked on a guerrilla warfare against the detachments of Federal soldiers left behind to keep order in the South. Clay Allison's intense Southern sympathies led him to cherish an active hatred for Yankees. . . .

* * * * *

Shortly after the Civil War Allison drifted into the West. He spent some time in what was then called the Indian Territory.

In the course of time Allison drifted from the Indian Territory into Texas. He seems to have worked for a while as a cowpuncher at some ranch, probably on the headwaters of the Brazos, but about 1871 he appears in Colfax County, New Mexico, engaged in the cattle business. Tradition offers two ways of accounting for this change of base, one of them grim and bloody, the other natural and businesslike.

The bloody story runs as follows. While Allison was working in the Brazos section and apparently was on the road to becoming in the course of time one of the cattle kings of that section, he became involved in a serious difficulty with a friend and neighbor. Allison himself never told the cause of the difficulty, but the trouble was so grave it was impossible to settle it amicably. The two men therefore agreed to fight it out.

Allison's grim originality showed itself in the details under which the duel was to take place. It was agreed that a grave should be prepared, of the usual length and width, but with the exceptional depth of seven or eight feet. The two men were to strip themselves to the waist and then seat themselves inside the grave at the two ends, each grasping in his right hand a bowie knife of a stated size. At a given signal, they were to arise and start fighting. This they were to keep up until one or the other was dead. A final stipulation required the survivor then and there to cover the dead one with the earth removed in digging the grave. The story gives Allison the victory, but it also attributes to him such a high degree of remorse that it was impossible for him to remain in that vicinity. Therefore he sold out his interests and moved to Colfax County in New Mexico.

II. Making a Name for Himself in New Mexico

There are some who contend that Allison's move across the state line into Colorado was not altogether voluntary. They hold that by that time he had killed several men in New Mexico, and was in danger of being apprehended for his crimes. However that may be, it is certain that Allison had succeeded in making a name for himself in New Mexico for quick and fully effective shooting. His famous encounter with Bill Chunk [in 1873] was enough in itself to give him a niche in the gunfighter's hall of fame.

Bill Chunk happened to be a nephew of . . . Frank Tolbert. . . . The cause of the encounter seems to have been Chunk's consummate envy and jealousy of Allison's growing fame as a gunfighter. Chunk belonged rather to the other class—the gunmen; he usually shot for the fun of seeing his victims fall. He claimed at that time that his tally was fourteen, and he announced publicly that he would round it out to fifteen by getting Clay Allison next. It was in this mood and temper that he came into Allison's vicinity.

When Allison heard of Chunk's boast, he tacitly accepted the challenge by continuing to go about his business without trying in the least to keep out of Chunk's way. In those days the Clifton House, a large, two-story adobe building near the present site of Raton, New Mexico, was a famous hostelry, and the general gathering place for persons, good and bad, who might be traveling through Colfax County. It was there that Bill Chunk and Clay Allison, naturally enough in the course of events, happened to meet. No one would have suspected that one was a deadly foe of the other, or that the other man knew his life had been threatened. For a day and a night, they drank and caroused together, apparently in the utmost good fellowship, neither one being willing to take the initiative in bringing on the affray that was bound to come.

The next day Chunk commented on the fine-looking horse Allison was riding and proposed a horse race to see which had the better animal. Allison accepted the challenge, for his confidence in his horse was unbounded, and they repaired to a race track somewhere in the vicinity of the Clifton House. Of the race itself, all that is known is that Chunk's horse beat Allison's, to Allison's great chagrin. Violent words followed, and Allison completely lost his temper. The upshot was that he slapped Chunk in the face for some remark, and there was imminent danger that hostilities were to commence immediately. But for some cause, never satisfactorily explained, Chunk and Allison both delayed the onset and held a discussion of the terms of the fight after they went back to the Clifton House. Allison, with his flair for the unusual, contended for an agreement to mount their horses and face each other at a distance of one hundred yards; then, at a signal, they were to run their horses toward each other, firing at will until one or both dropped to the ground.

They were engrossed in this discussion when the dinner bell rang. Chunk suggested that they eat first, and fight afterwards, clenching his proposal with the remark, "We ought to see that the dead one goes to hell with a full stomach." Into the dining room the two went, taking their places at opposite ends of the dinner table, but with their drawn six-shooters resting on their laps under the table. During the meal Chunk casually dropped one hand below the table, as if to get his napkin, but in reality he seized his pistol and tried to lift it so as to fire at Allison. The barrel of the revolver, however, happened to strike the edge of the table, so that Chunk's aim was untrue. Allison fired immediately after. A red spot just above Chunk's eye showed where the bullet had struck. The dead man's head dropped sluggishly forward and fell face downward into the plate from which he had been eating.

Clay Allison coolly replaced his pistol in its holster and went on with his meal, requiring all the others at the table likewise to go on with their eating as though nothing unusual had taken place. When he had taken all the time needful for a complete meal, he arose, and taking the dinner bell from a shelf, he went to the window and began to ring it vigorously, announcing to those present inside and outside the building, "Gentlemen, the proposed fight is now off, owing to an accident to one of the principals."

III. His Career at Las Animas

It was with a reputation based on such exploits that Clay Allison came to Las Animas, Colorado. The Santa Fe was building west, and Las Animas was one of the succession of towns that for a few months were the terminals of the line. These towns were crude frontier settlements, filled not only with railroad employees of all sorts and others who might be said to have legitimate business, but also with the derelict population of both men and women that always collected in such towns. In the rough-and-tumble life of such a town Clay Allison became a conspicuous figure.

His career at Las Animas seems to have been inaugurated by a fist fight with a certain LeFevre, a rival stock buyer. The record is that Allison got the best of this fight, but there was later a clash with the town marshal, Charlie Faber, in which Allison did not fare so well. Charlie Faber knew Allison's reputation for making trouble when in his cups, and he had moreover a strong hatred for Allison mingled unquestionably with considerable fear. He had openly stated that if Allison created any disturbance which would justify getting the drop on him, he would not hesitate to shoot to kill unless Allison immediately gave himself over to the marshal with lamblike docility.

On this particular occasion Clay Allison and his brother John dropped into one of the Las Animas dance halls. They had both been drinking, but had not imbibed enough to reach the point where they wanted to make a disturbance. The marshal, Charlie Faber, happened to come into the hall, and seeing that the Allisons were violating the local ordinance by appearing on the floor of the dance hall with their pistols on their hips, he ordered them to remove their weapons. Clay Allison let his eyes rove around the room, and noticing that others among the men present were still wearing their pistols, he came to the conclusion that the marshal was attempting an invidious distinction. So he turned to Faber and said, "You see the rest of the boys have their guns on. Why don't you order them to take off theirs, if you are going to make us take off ours?"

This attitude seemed to presage trouble, and Charlie Faber slipped away to procure a weapon that might be certain and deadly when the expected trouble arose. In a short time he returned with a double-barrelled shotgun loaded with buckshot, and, standing in the doorway, took aim at the first one of the Allisons he saw, which happened to be John. Clay was on the alert. Seeing the move, he shouted across the room a warning to his brother. Hardly had he called, "Look out, John" when all three—Charlie Faber, John Allison, and Clay Allison—fired simultaneously, the report of their separate shots blending into one. The aim of both Clay and his brother had been unerring, and Charlie Faber fell to the floor with two bullets in his heart. Some of Faber's buckshot had splintered the right arm and penetrated the right side of John Allison, but Clay Allison was entirely unhurt.

In those times the killing of a town marshal was an offense which, if not thought rank enough to smell to heaven, was nevertheless such a grave affront to the nascent spirit of respect for law that the community could not ignore it. An attempt to arrest Clay Allison was in order, but he refused to surrender himself into custody before he was assured that his wounded brother would receive proper medical attention at once. John Allison was thereupon sent to the nearby army-post hospital at Fort Lyon. But before Clay Allison would allow himself to be arrested, he made one more stipulation. This was that no handcuffs or chains were to be employed. Those making the arrest gave such a promise and then blandly ignored it. When they had disarmed him, they subjected him to the indignity of being chained to the wall of his cell. It was easy enough for the two Allisons to come clear at their trial. All the dance-hall habitués who might have become witnesses had mysteriously decamped. Moreover, public opinion held that Charlie Faber's actions clearly indicated he was seeking to create friction, and that he had been caught in the trap of his own intentions.

For several years the two brothers were in constant association. If one was in a shooting scrape, the other was likely to be a participant also. Of course that part of the country compared and appraised the two as fighters, the consensus of opinion being that John Allison was in reality the better man in a fight, on account of his coolness and better judgment, as well as because of his staying qualities. But John Allison has been completely eclipsed by Clay Allison, whose affrays were more numerous and as a rule more spectacular.

The escapades of the Allison brothers in Las Animas were sometimes in lighter vein than the encounter with Charlie Faber in the dance hall. A whisky salesman by the name of Riggs long remembered a certain afternoon in Las Animas spent in the company of Clay

Allison. Clay and his brother had been drinking so much that the saloon keepers in their wisdom had closed their doors to them as a means of keeping them in bounds. As Riggs was proceeding from the train to the hotel, valise in hand, he happened to meet Clay Allison, riding the black horse he prized so highly. Riggs greeted him pleasantly, and remarked, "That's a mighty fine horse you're riding." "Yes," replied Allison, "you can bet your life this horse is a fine one. If I say the word, he will kick your hat off. Come over and see."

At this point Riggs realized how drunk Allison was, and he began to think fast as to how to get rid of him without causing trouble. As he knew the custom among the saloon keepers of closing their bars to Clay Allison when he was on a spree, Riggs reasoned that, such, more than likely, was the situation, and that Allison was probably very desirous of a drink. So Riggs turned aside the invitation to submit to equestrian calcitration by saying, "Clay, I'll just take your word about the horse kicking off my hat, but I know a better stunt than that. Come and join me in a good drink."

Realizing the lockout then in force against him, Allison said incredulously, "Riggs, you are not going to break into one of the saloons and commit burglary, are you? You can't get into a saloon any other way with me."

"I know a better way than that," answered Riggs. "You tie up your horse and come with me. I'll leave my valise in the drug store until we come back." Allison agreed, and Riggs took him over to the back door of a saloon belonging to one of Riggs' regular customers. There was no response to Riggs' knock, although the clink of glasses could be heard inside. Riggs called the proprietor by name, and said, "Hey, let me in. It's Riggs, the whisky man." Whereupon the proprietor opened the door, and in walked Riggs escorting Clay Allison. Consternation gripped everybody in the place, for no one ever knew what excitement might occur when Clay was on a spree.

"I just met my friend Allison," said Riggs, in a placative tone, "and have invited him to have a drink with me. It's my treat, boys; so let every man in the room take a drink with me to the health, happiness, and long life of Clay Allison." Then Riggs handed the bartender a five-dollar bill, saying as he did so, "You can hand me the change when I come back with my valise, which I left at the drug store on the corner. Excuse me, gentlemen, while I go and get it." With that he slipped out of the door, secured his valise, and made a mad rush for the station, reaching it just in time to board a freight train going in a direction opposite to that of his usual itinerary.

His ruse had saved him from trouble with Clay Allison, but it had exposed several of the citizenry of Las Animas to whatever might be the sequel. History does not record whether the men in the saloon suffered more than cold chills up and down their spines, but it is likely that Riggs' popularity suffered a decided slump in the community.

IV. Death in the Pecos Valley

Allison's end was different from that of most men who had made records similar to his. Usually those who took the lives of others made so many enemies among the friends of the latter that death in return was only a matter of time. But Clay Allison's death was of an altogether unorthodox kind. He died with his boots on, it is true, but hardly in the usual sense. In his case death came by accident, and that through the rather commonplace means of a fall from a freighter's wagon.

Of the exact circumstances there are two versions. One has it that while he was on a trip from Pecos to his ranch he fell from his wagon and was killed, intoxication perhaps being a contributing cause. The other account has more relish to it. One day Clay Allison got word from his cow camp that one of the cowboys had or had not done something, and the news put Allison into a terrible rage. Arming himself, he started for the place where the offender was supposed to be. On the way Allison stopped at the home of a friend, and naturally confided to him the nature of the mission he was on. This friend, scenting trouble, endeavored without success to dissuade the irate Allison from his purpose. Allison would not swerve a jot. In the hope that a delay might bring a change of mind, this friend induced Allison to stay for dinner. While waiting for the meal the two had several drinks, with the result that Allison felt creeping upon him the old urge of madcap behavior.

Seeing a freighter's wagon in the yard, loaded and with its two teams in harness, he became possessed of the idea that he must display his prowess in driving. Paying no heed to the protests of his friend, who owned the wagon, he perched himself on the driver's seat, gave the customary "yip" accompanied by a yell or two, and began his exhibition of fancy driving. During the performance, the wagon struck a deep chug-hole, and Allison fell from his insecure seat. One of the rear wheels of the heavily loaded wagon passed over his back, breaking it near the neck and killing him instantly.

Thus passed Clay Allison, of whom the survivors of those days are wont to say, perhaps with a great degree of truth, "Clay Allison was by far the most fearless man in his part of the West at any time in its history, barring none."

On His Own Terms

Allison was notoriously averse to "being arrested," but had always responded to "requests" to appear to answer to charges made against him. He claimed that he had never killed a man except in self defense and boasted that he would never fear trial for anything he had ever done. The deputy entrusted with the serving of the warrant in this particular case knew the desperado's peculiarities, and so when he found his man next day he said quietly: "Clay, the judge wants you about killing that Mexican." "All right," responded Allison cheerfully, "I'll go with you. Come along. But look here, Mr. Officer, don't ask me to give up my weapons." (He carried a Winchester and two six-shooting forty-fives.)

The deputy assented readily, for he knew that he could not, or felt that he would not, take the prisoner against his will. On the way to court, each on horseback, they chatted pleasantly enough. After a brief pause in the conversation, Clay remarked abruptly: "That's a pretty good hat you're wearing, Marshal. Let's see it."

The marshal took his sombrero from his head and passed it to Allison, who folded it into a wad, threw it into the air, and put two holes through it before it touched the ground. Dismounting, Allison picked up the sieve-like headgear, restored it to its astonished owner, and remarked, with what the marshal was pleased to think was a humorous smile, "Now, Marshal, you can tell 'em you've been under fire."

When the court house was reached, it was found that an important case was on trial, and the room was filled with lawyers, bailiffs, and witnesses. The judge, however, immediately declared the case on trial postponed and said that Allison should be heard immediately. Clay walked across the room and sat down with the utmost sang froid. His two big revolvers adorned his belt and his Winchester lay handily across his knees.

The clerk began to read the warrant, but, before he had finished, the judge looked down from his high seat and noticed the prisoner's rifle and revolvers.

Rap, rap, rap, sounded the judicial gavel upon the pine boards which composed the desk, and the court shouted in stentorian tones: "Marshal, disarm the prisoner."

From the Raton *Daily Independent,* November 12, 1886. Cited in "Cowboy Lore in Colorado," by Honora DeBusk Smith, in *Southwestern Lore,* Publications of the Texas Folklore Society, Number IX, 1931, edited J. Frank Dobie, pp. 29–31. Copyright by the Texas Folk-Lore Society, 1931. Dallas, Texas: The Southwest Press.

Another story regarding Allison that has as many versions as there are tellers serves to show his reputation. According to this tale, Allison killed a Mexican, named Alvarez, who had made an attempt upon his life. A court that happened to be in session somewhere in the vicinity issued a warrant for his arrest.—H.D.S.

"Clay," said the deputy apologetically, "you'd better let me have those weapons. I'll take good care of 'em."

"Look here now, pard," replied Allison, "you don't get my guns. "I've come here quietly and I am willing to stand trial, but I'll—"

The tattoo of the gavel on the bench interrupted Allison's response, and in an impatient voice the court asked: "Well, have you disarmed the prisoner?"

"Your honor," said Allison, rising to his feet, "I've got the biggest kind of respect for this court, but I want to say right here that no man can disarm me without a fight. I haven't got any friends here, and the crowd is armed; so I'm going to be ready to protect myself."

"Bailiff," fairly yelled the court, "once more I tell you to disarm that prisoner. The dignity of this court must and shall be preserved."

The bailiffs held a short consultation among themselves and started in a body toward the prisoner. The latter turned quickly in his chair and placed his Winchester in readiness for instant action.

The deputy marshal who had arrested Allison contemplated the display of firearms and then with an apologetic cough said to the court: "Your honor, the prisoner refuses to be disarmed."

"But I say that he must give up his arms," thundered the judge. "I won't hear the case unless he does."

"Then if you want the prisoner disarmed," replied the deputy angrily, "you can disarm him yourself; for I'll be d—d if I'll try to do it."

Rap, rap, rap, went the gavel again, and the voice of the judge, husky with pent-up rage, sounded over the room: "This court stands adjourned until 10 o'clock tomorrow morning!"

Allison jumped to his feet, said he'd be blankety blanked if he was going to fool around three or four days waiting for his trial, strode out of the room, and rode away. No one attempted to molest him, and although he remained in the neighborhood for several weeks thereafter he was not re-arrested.

Billy the Kid: Dime-Novel Hero

After quitting the hotel in Lincoln, the Kid mounted his horse and galloped away to the Staked Plain, where old John Chisum had a ranch. Chisum was there at the time, and Billy demanded a thousand dollars for services he had rendered him.

Niggardliness was added to the other evils of old John Chisum, and he refused the moderate sum.

From *The True Life of Billy the Kid,* by Don Jernado, *The Five Cent Wide Awake Library,* Vol. I (August 29, 1881), No. 451, pp. 14–15. Entered according to Act of Congress, in the year 1881, by Frank Tousey, in the office of the Librarian of Congress, at Washington, D.C. New York.

Cf. *A Treasury of American Folklore* (New York, 1944), pp. 69–71, 93–107.

A quarrel ensued in which the Kid came very near taking the old reprobate's life, but was finally induced, partly through fear, and partly through influence of friends, to quit the ranch.

He was riding along the road in an aimless manner, when he again came upon his friend and partner, Tom O'Fallaher.

"Well, Billy, what now?" asked Tom.

"Old Chisum an' I have had a row," replied the Kid.

"What, you and he split?"

"We have."

"What about?"

"He owes me, and won't pay."

"Why, blast his mug, take cattle enough to pay you."

The idea had never struck the Kid before. It was capital, and just the thing.

"I'll do it," he said. "We will organize the old band again, and prey upon his cattle. The old scoundrel, after all we have done for him, to be thrown aside for some new favorite."

"The old band and the good old times. The dashing down on ranches, and moonlight raids again; hip, hurrah for the jolly old band!"

The two rode along together.

"Do you know where the boys have scattered?" asked the Kid.

"The most of them are prowling about Lincoln and Fort Stanley."

"I will lay about Staked Plains, and do you make your way to Lincoln and Fort Stanley. Tell the boys of our rallying place. As soon as we have a dozen we will commence business."

Tom went as directed, and the Kid slept that night on the ground. The next day Tom returned with ten desperadoes of the old band.

The greeting was warm, and they at once swore allegiance to the new organization. That very night they swept down on the herds of Chisum, and drove away three hundred fat cattle. They had half the night to travel, and made good time. When dawn came they looked back and saw twenty or thirty horsemen in pursuit.

The Kid determined to give them battle, and hurrying the drove a mile or two further on, they came to a halt in a low piece of ground. Dismounting, they placed their horses in front of them, and with cocked rifles awaited the approach of the pursuers.

"The chaps was once our friends, Billy," said Tom.

"What care we for that?" replied the Kid. "They are all a set of —— scoundrels, and ought to be killed."

The pursuers saw the herd ahead, and with wild shouts came on at full speed.

Coolly the Kid's men awaited their approach.

A volley of keen rifle shots rang out upon the air, and half a dozen of the pursuers plunged headlong from their horses.

The outlaws were armed with repeating-rifles and double-barreled shot guns. The pursuers halted and fired a volley, which swept over the Kid's brigands on account of their being on low grounds.

Again a sharp volley from the outlaws rang out, this time bringing both men and horses to the earth.

The pursuers bolted.

Billy took advantage of the momentary check and cried:

"Mount quick!"

Instantly every man was in the saddle.

"Charge!"

With the rein in their teeth and a pistol in each hand, they swept down like an avalanche on the discomfited pursuers.

"Crack, crack, crack!" rang out the revolvers, sharp and keen, each bearing a death shriek with it.

The herdsmen of Chisum turned and fled, leaving half their original number dead or wounded on the plain.

The wounded were put to death.

An incident here will show the heartless cruelty of the Kid.

Among the wounded was George Dye, a former friend and acquaintance, who had remained true to the interest of John Chisum. His thigh was broken and his horse killed. The horse, in falling, fell on the sound leg of Dye, thus pinning him to the earth.

In this condition he was found by the Kid.

In vain Dye implored the desperado to spare his life, and called to his recollection the many days they had spent together, and their former friendship.

"It's no use to talk of that, George," said the Kid, with his murderous smile; "you make too good a mark where you lie." He cocked his pistol as he spoke, and aimed at his head.

"Oh! Billy, Billy," cried the terrified wretch, "for God's sake, don't shoot me!"

"Hold your head still, George, so I will not disfigure your face much, and give you but very little pain."

The words were spoken in that cool, determined, bloodthirsty manner, as only the Kid could speak.

Billy's men, knowing the former good friendship that had existed between Billy and George, supposed he was only having some sport at his friend's expense; George evidently thought so, too, for he ceased to struggle and avoid the aim, but with a fixed smile on his face gazed the Kid in the eye.

A moment the revolver was held with a breathless silence.

"Crack!" rang the shot. George Dye's head fell upon the grass alongside his dead horse. The fatal bullet had pierced his forehead.

The Kid's force increased to twenty-five men, and he embarked on a career of lawlessness never before known in the annals of crime. How many murders he committed, how many cattle he stole, how many daring deeds of deviltry he performed, will never be known, until the dark deeds of cowboys, congressmen, governors, thieves, lawmakers, and law-breakers, are laid bare to the world.

Bill Tilghman and the Doolin Gang

The Daltons, from the time Grat and Emmett returned from California and began their gang career, lasted only fifteen months. The Doolin gang, which followed, carried on for four years. Bill Doolin, it is said, was kept from the flaming guns of Coffeyville by the lameness of his horse. Emmett Dalton, in his memoirs, says they had found the gang too numerous, profits too small when divided among so many, and had told Doolin, Red Buck, and others to shift for themselves.

At any rate, Doolin became leader of a new outlaw gang, and made a record for the longest outlaw career, eight years from the time he joined the "wild bunch."

O. D. Halsell, Texas cattleman, in 1880 established his H X Bar ranch on the Cimarron, thirteen miles northeast of the future site of Guthrie. To build corrals and get out logs for cabins, he hired a youth from Arkansas, Bill Doolin, a lanky illiterate fellow; but he could use an ax, which Halsell's cowboys couldn't. In a few years, the backwoods boy had learned to ride and rope and shoot, was a top-hand cow-puncher. And he could read a newspaper and write a letter. Mr. Halsell entrusted him with much of his ranch business at Caldwell, Kansas, their nearest town.

Doolin was slender, six-feet-two, with fair hair and blue eyes, and a winning personality. With all this, there was a streak of wildness in him. He never made any pretense of wrongs to avenge or persecution that "drove him to a life of crime," the favorite outlaw sob-story. He knew work, hard, heavy work with his hands and in the saddle. When the change came, he made his choice.

The gang of which he was leader included Bill Dalton, a brother who had not been with the others in their outlaw career; "Little Bill" Raidler, who stood next to the leader, a man of good education, from Pennsylvania; George Weightman, known as Red Buck; George Newcomb, "Bitter Creek," handsome as a movie star; Charles Pierce; and Dick West, "Little Dick," who, as the last survivor, joined the later Jennings gang. Red Buck was known as a killer. He had served a term in prison for horse stealing. Within thirty days after his release, he had stolen seven good horses and, thus equipped, joined Doolin. Other members were Tulsa Jack, Dynamite Dick, and Arkansas Tom.

The gang knew every mile of the two territories, and they had con-

---

From *Marshal of the Last Frontier*, Life and Stories of William Matthew (Bill) Tilghman, for 50 years one of the greatest peace officers of the West, by his wife, Zoe A. Tilghman, pp. 205–230. Copyright, 1949, by the Arthur H. Clark Company. Cleveland.

venient hold-outs, [including] a cave, a place known as the Rock Fort, of stone walls and dugout. It belonged to a member of the Dunn family, five brothers and cousins whose homes were stopping places for the gang. At one of these, with much unsettled land about it, they often stayed and here Bill [Tilghman] saw a large post-oak tree riddled with bullets. They had used it as a target, shooting from a galloping horse. They trained themselves also in "dodging a bullet," a quick duck sideways and down, at the same time shooting at the pretended adversary.

The small town of Ingalls, ten miles east of Stillwater, was known as their holdout. Here they came openly. There was always some one to give warning if a marshal were approaching. Only a few miles distant were wild and unsettled parts of the Pawnee country, hills and timber along the Cimarron, where escape was easy.

Doolin had been with the Daltons in the first train robbery at Redrock, in June, 1891, and presumably in various other crimes. In November, 1892, a few weeks after the others were killed at Coffeyville, he, with Bitter Creek and Ol Yountis, robbed the bank at Spearville, Kansas, west of Dodge City. Bill's old friend, Chalk Beeson, was sheriff of Ford County, and followed them. Chris Madsen was at Fort Supply, and warned by telegraph, almost caught them with a squad of soldiers as they fled through western Oklahoma. In a running fight, Doolin was wounded in the foot. Madsen and Beeson traced Yountis to his sister's home at Orlando, near Guthrie. He chose to shoot it out with them and was killed. Doolin and Bitter Creek had disappeared.

But in all these affairs, no definite identification of Doolin had been made, and no warrant specifically issued against him. So it chanced that in the next summer when Bill dropped in one day to see his friend Fred Sutton at the Turf Exchange in Guthrie, Doolin and Bitter Creek came in. They were known in Guthrie as cowboys, and Bill met Doolin with his former employee, Oscar Halsell.

"Mr. Tilghman," said Doolin, "we're in kind of hard luck. Couldn't you set us up?"

"Why sure!" returned Bill; and to the bartender—"Give them what they want."

The drinks were quickly set out, and Bill started to pay when Doolin said: "Wait. We can pay for ourselves. I was just fooling."

He drew from his pocket a roll of bills and paid grandly. The two then proceeded to the gambling tables and more drinks.

On the street Bill met Mr. Halsell, who at the opening [of Oklahoma] had established a wholesale grocery business in Guthrie.

"I just saw your old cowboy, Doolin. What's he doing now?"

"Why, not anything that I know of," returned Mr. Halsell. "He made a trip to New Mexico a while back, looking for cattle work, he said."

Many months later, Bill learned that Doolin, Bill Dalton, Bitter

Creek, and Tulsa Jack had robbed a train at Cimarron, Kansas, on May 28. The roll which Doolin flashed was part of the proceeds of that robbery.

But there were John Doe warrants, and some personal, for members of the gang. And on September 1, 1893, a posse of deputy marshals drove into the town of Ingalls, hidden in the back of a covered wagon. A pitched battle ensued, in which marshals Houston, Speed, and Shadley were killed, Bitter Creek badly wounded, but carried off by his companions, and Arkansas Tom, ill, and trapped in the upper story of the little hotel, was captured.

Bill was laid up at this time from an accident, he and his horse having plunged off a broken bridge into a swollen creek, one night in the rain. Bill went on crutches for several weeks.

Now, with Chris Madsen, and Heck Thomas, he was assigned the duty of running down the Doolin gang. . . .

* * * * *

On a bitter January day of 1895, snow on the ground, Bill, with Neal Brown, drove to the Rock Fort dugout. But he was not looking for the Doolin gang just then. They had not been heard of for some weeks, and in fact had been off in Texas. He wanted to see Bill Dunn. Leaving his rifle in the spring wagon, he went to the dugout, which was entered by a short flight of steps, with a sloping door over the top now open, and an ordinary door below.

A gruff voice called, "Come in." Bill's eyes, dazzled by the snow, adjusted to the gloom. On either side were double bunks, screened by quilts hung up as curtains. In the far end, beside a little fireplace, sat a bearded man, smoking, a rifle across his knees. Bill recognized him as a cousin of the man he sought. Moving to the fire, he greeted him, and the man responded surlily.

"No, Bill Dunn wasn't around."

"A cold day."

A grunt.

"I just happened to be passing this way and stopped to see if I could match my fighting dog with his," the marshal explained. "He told me a while back he thought he had one that could whip mine."

Dunn made no answer. His hands a little warmed, Bill turned around with his back to the fire. He could see now—death! The muzzles of half a dozen Winchesters, trained on him, were sticking out from the curtained bunks.

Every nerve in his body tensed; but not by the flicker of an eyelash did he betray his knowledge. He waited. An eternity of seconds. Then, in a casual voice,

"I guess I better be going on." A pause. "How does a fellow get out of here?"

Dunn growled an answer: "The same damned way you got in."

"Well, tell him about the dog then."

Slowly, easily, Bill forced himself to walk to the door, to lift the latch. It was open. He was through, closing it—not too quickly. Make it natural.

"I could feel the bullets in my back at every step," he confessed later. As the latch fell, he flashed into action; threw his overcoat open, his revolver to his hand, even as he sprang up the steps. Whirling, he closed the sloping outer door; ran backward to the wagon, with his gun pointed, ready for the slightest lifting of that door. But it did not move. He sprang into the seat, seized his rifle, and aimed it.

"Drive like the devil," he said to Brown. "The dugout is full of outlaws!"

Not till months later was the full story of his adventure told. Doolin, Red Buck, Dynamite Dick, Tulsa Jack, Pierce, and Raidler had just come back from Texas, glad to find shelter at the Rock Fort after their long ride in the storm. Every one of them knew Bill Tilghman. They recognized him when he drove up, and since they could not leave the dugout without meeting him face to face, they hurriedly hung up the quilts and hid. They trained their guns on him, waiting for some move. But they saw no sign of discovery, no sign of fear. They waited.

When Bill passed the door, Red Buck leaped out in a fury to shoot him. Bill Doolin and Dunn seized and held him, with a lively tussle.

"Tilghman's too good a man to shoot in the back," said Doolin.

"We don't want any killing here," protested Dunn.

"If you kill Bill Tilghman there'll be a hundred men here before morning, and they'd dynamite this place off the earth."

Bill by this time was safely away. Red Buck scored by reminding them that he would likely be back with a posse, and they'd better move. It was no pleasant prospect setting out in weather for another long, cold ride. But they went.

* * * * *

The capture of Raidler made five of the gang killed or in prison. But Doolin, the leader, had seemingly disappeared. Bill had found a trail and lost it. Then learned that a man of Doolin's description, in the summer, came to the little town of Burden, Kansas, to buy supplies. He drove a poor team and wagon, and seemed to be just a tenant farmer. Bill found the house, a lonely place, with a ravine and trees, so that he could approach unseen. At night, he could slip up to the window and see Doolin's wife putting her baby to bed. For six weeks he watched the place, waiting for the outlaw to come in. Then, Mrs. Doolin left, buying a ticket for Perry, Oklahoma. She was bound, it appeared, for her father's home, and Bill wired to have her watched there.

He himself took another line. As a federal officer, he had called on the postmaster at Burden to watch her mail. No letters passed to or from her husband. Her chief correspondent seemed to be Mrs. Pierce, keeper of the hotel at Ingalls. She was not forwarding letters between them. Nevertheless, she was a friend and she might know something. Bill drove to Ingalls. He had stopped there before.

Mr. Pierce kept the livery stable, and his wife, a handsome, energetic woman, ran the small hotel. She was affable and liked to talk. Bill did justice to her biscuits and home-made preserves, and sat through a long evening in her parlor. But when he tried to bring the conversation around to the outlaws and Doolin, the landlady shied off. At last he went to bed.

Next morning he sat on the little porch, cleaning his rifle. Mrs. Pierce was sweeping. Bill carelessly remarked on the report of a train robbery in Texas. "It looked like Doolin's work." Mrs. Pierce flared.

"Everything they lay onto Doolin! He's not even in Texas. He's been two months at a springs for rheumatism."

She patted a letter in her apron pocket. Bill reached out his hand. "Let me see that."

"No, no. It's none of your business! It's just . . ."

Reluctantly, she yielded the letter. It seemed harmless, anyway. Edith Doolin wrote her to get a ring which she had let a girl friend wear, and send it to her. Her husband was better, the springs seemed to help him. Where would that be?

"Hot Springs and the baths are sure good," Bill remarked. "I've known lots of people that went there."

But his eyes, veiled, were on Mrs. Pierce's face, and the quick gleam of satisfaction told him that his guess was wrong. Eureka Springs, not quite so famous, would be a quieter place to hide, and nearer. Bill finished cleaning his gun, and was soon on his way to Guthrie.

To John Hale, chief deputy, he said that he had a tip on Doolin and would be going after him. E. D. Nix, the marshal, came in. How many men did he want?

"Not any. I think I can take him, if he's there." They both protested. "But Doolin's sworn not to be taken alive. He's a desperate man! He'd shoot you on sight."

"Not if he don't know me," returned Bill, with his quiet smile. "I'm going as a real detective—in disguise. That preacher coat of yours . . ."

In a moment he had slipped on the long-skirted Prince Albert which Marshall Nix, as a well-dressed dignitary, wore. It fitted well. He added the derby hat of Mr. Hale. The two stared at him. Though he had his clothes made by the best tailor in town, he had never worn hat or coat of these styles.

"It does make a difference. I'd hardly know you on the street."

January 12, 1896, Bill reached Eureka Springs, Arkansas. Houses clung to the rocky, tree-clad hills. The stream from the larger springs flowed through the town, with bridges here and there. Where a spring gushed from a hillside, a half-circle of stone wall had been built, and steps leading down. A man bent over, filling a bottle to carry home.

He came up the steps; a tall man, slightly stooped, wearing a neat suit, though in need of pressing; the pants down over the boot tops; a wide cowboy hat; and golden, drooping mustache—Doolin himself. He walked with a cane, but not showing lameness. A bulge under his left arm told of the forty-five in a shoulder holster.

Bill dodged into the nearest shop, presently following his man at a safe distance. The outlaw crossed a small park with big trees, where a foot-bridge spanned a little stream. Beyond, and up a foot path, to a house perched on the hillside; a long flight of steps going up, and a sign, "Rooms."

Bill turned back, tracing his course thoughtfully. To take the man alive he must get the drop on him quickly, by surprise. With watchful glances lest Doolin return, he studied the ground. When Doolin crossed the foot-bridge, if he could step out from behind that big tree with his shotgun— But the sight of a man with a shotgun would warn the outlaw, and he could see it a block away.

Going back to his hotel, Bill took his shotgun apart, wrapped it in papers, and sought a carpenter shop. He explained what he wanted; a light wooden box, with a hinged lid that could be instantly opened, and long enough to contain the gun. It would be painted black and have the appearance of a case for a musical instrument. With that, he could walk across the park, visible under the leafless trees, but not an object of suspicion. He would meet Doolin as he came toward town. An instant's concealment behind the large tree trunk and he could step out, with his gun on the outlaw as he crossed the foot-bridge. The carpenter promised to have the box ready that evening. Tomorrow, then.

Bill ate a noon dinner, studied again the park and the route that Doolin must travel, till he knew every detail. It was only two o'clock, and he had the afternoon to pass. Why not take a bath? There was the Basin bath house, which was reached from the main street by a short, wide bridge over the stream. A pleasant-faced, bald little man rose up and asked, "What can we do for you, sir?"

Bill's eye scanned the lobby. There were several loungers smoking and reading. At one side, a corner space was cut off for a cashier's stall; at the back a door marked "Baths"; near it a huge round-bellied stove, as tall as a man. There were bare, painted walls, scrubbed floor; a few wooden chairs, a bench in the corner back of the cashier's stall, partly screened by the large stove.

And on that bench sat Bill Doolin! The last man Bill wished to meet just then. Doolin held a newspaper before his face, reading. But hearing the proprietor's greeting he moved it to one side, peering with the wariness of the hunted outlaw upon the customer. Bill saw the movement from the corner of his eye, saw Doolin's face. Swifter than conscious thought, he acted.

"I want a bath," he said, easily, and stepping past the proprietor, opened the door marked "Baths." He stood in a little corridor, and even as he closed the door he flung his coat open, his six-shooter flashed into his hand. Had Doolin recognized him?

For a breathless instant he watched the door-knob, expecting it to turn. It did not move. Softly he grasped it, pushed the door open. Doolin still sat upon the bench, intent on his paper, no longer suspicious. Half crouching, his gun ready, keeping the big stove between himself and his quarry, Bill moved with noiseless feet. Then, with a leap, he was around the stove, facing the outlaw. His voice rang steel. "Bill, put up your hands!"

But quick as a striking snake, Doolin was on his feet, reaching for the gun in his shoulder holster. Bill's left hand grabbed for his wrist, but only caught the coat sleeve. Doolin strained to reach the gun.

With a panicked scramble, the other customers fled while the dismayed proprietor hovered near the door.

"Bill, you know me. Put up your hands!"

Doolin's eyes burned. He half nodded. But he still strained to get his gun. His sleeve ripped, and Bill felt it give. Doolin's fingers moved nearer . . . an inch . . . another. . . .

"Bill, don't make me kill you!"

Their eyes met. In the marshal's was power, purpose, an invincible spirit; in the outlaw's the fury and desperation of the trapped wild beast. Two strong men; but one was stronger. Doolin's gaze faltered. His straining body relaxed, his arms moved upwards. Bill kept the gun steady.

"Come here," he commanded the proprietor. Nervously the little man approached. "Get his gun! His gun . . . under his arm," Bill urged.

Now the man understood. He pulled back Doolin's coat, reached for the six-shooter, let go of it, and at the third grab, pulled it out. He tendered it to the officer.

"Take it away! I've got all the guns I need!" cried Bill. And to Doolin, "Turn around."

The outlaw turned facing the wall, and Bill, with his gun against his back, ran his hands over him in search of other weapons.

"You can put your hands down now, Bill," he said. The handcuffs clicked. "Do you want to come along quietly? It's no use to start anything. I've got four men around here."

Bill missed his bath. Five minutes from the time he entered the bath-house he walked out with his prisoner. As he left the door, the proprietor rushed forward and held out Doolin's gun, a pearl-handled, silver-plated forty-five. Bill took it and stuck it down inside the front of his pants. A dozen or two men and boys came running up to see the excitement, but Bill had no time for explanations.

A train would be leaving at four o'clock. Doolin was ready to go. "Get me out of this lynching country," he said. Eureka Springs was not so far from Southwest City, and he feared Missouri officers might claim him. Bill took him to the bank, where he had a hundred dollars, then to his room. He made him stand in the corner, while he himself gathered up Doolin's few belongings. On the dresser was a little silver cup.

"Is it yours?"

Doolin swallowed, nodding. "I bought it for my baby boy," he said.

"Are you thinking of your baby now?" Wonder, a strange respect, sympathy, were in the marshal's voice.

"Yes," said Doolin. Bill turned and laid the little cup gently in the suitcase.

"I'll see that he gets it, Bill," he said.

On the way to the station, Bill got his own bag, which he had not unpacked, and sent a boy with a message to the carpenter. He would not need that gun-box now. Doolin asked that the shackles be taken off.

"I give you my word that I will make no trouble. You can go to sleep on the train if you want to. And you know my word is good."

"Well, you know that I am no sucker, Doolin; and a single false move on your part will end you right there."

He took off the handcuffs, and seated Doolin next the window, himself next the aisle, with his right side and his gun away from the prisoner. Doolin looked about the platform, scanned the passengers coming into the car, keenly. At last he asked, "Where are your men?"

Bill settled himself in the seat with a slight relief of tension. A smile glimmered in his eyes.

"Doolin, I was just fooling you a little about that. There isn't anybody but me."

All his life he remembered the look the outlaw gave him; the savage, helpless rage of a trapped lobo; a man's heartbreak as he faced his doom.

The train pulled out.

It was Bill's second night on the train, with scarcely any sleep. He fought to keep awake as the train pounded across the corner of Missouri and southern Kansas. At Arkansas City they changed to the Santa Fe, to reach Guthrie a little after ten o'clock. Bill sent a telegram.

At Perry, a young man walked down the aisle. "Hello, Bill," he greeted the marshal. He sat down in the seat facing them. Doolin, not knowing he was a reporter for the *State Capital,* talked freely; told of his ill-health, and of his capture.

"The next I knew, he was standing four feet away from me and I was looking straight into his gun. I knew then that it was Bill Tilghman. If it had been anyone else I would have pulled my gun. I saw that if I made a move, he would kill me, so I put up my hands. . . ."[1]

The perennial rumor which bobbed up whenever an important cap-

---

[1] Guthrie, *Oklahoma State Capital,* January, 1896.—Z.A.T.

ture was made, that the outlaw had surrendered for the promise of a share in the reward money, had been whispered as soon as the news broke. The reporter asked Doolin, "Is it true?"

"They got me charged with the killing of three marshals at Ingalls," he said, grimly. "Does a man stick his neck in the rope for a few hundred dollars?"

At Lawrie, a switch stop north of Guthrie, Deputy Ed Kelly got on the train. "Great work, Bill!" he said with a warm handclasp.

* * * * *

Doolin was to be tried at Stillwater, on the Ingalls killings. He agreed with Bill and Mr. Hale to plead guilty when arraigned, with the promise from the U.S. attorney of a fifty-year sentence, the same as had been given Arkansas Tom, member of the gang who was captured in that fight. But in the court room Doolin answered, "Not guilty." There was nothing to do but bind him over for trial and take him back to jail. Bill, riding beside him in the back seat of the spring wagon, asked: "Doolin, why did you go back on your word that way? You're likely to hang if you go to trial."

The outlaw spoke softly. "I'll tell you, Mr. Tilghman, fifty years is a long time; and I believe there's a chance to beat that federal jail."

The federal jail at Guthrie was a long, plain two-story building of stone, fitted inside with the usual steel-barred entrance and front office. In the jail proper, the cells were steel cages set in the big room, and not reaching to the ceiling. The rest of the space was the "run-around" where prisoners were allowed to exercise, and many of them slept; for there were always more than the cells would hold. Those regarded as most dangerous were locked in the cells at night. The second floor had similar arrangements, save that the entrance was at the side, reached by a narrow outside stair.

Doolin had been a well-behaved prisoner, and having lately had an attack of his rheumatic fever, was not put in a cell. Bill, however, had warned the head jailer to watch him. There was in the jail a large, powerful Negro, held on a minor charge. To him Doolin said confidentially:

"Did you see those two white men talking to the jailer out in front? They're officers from Mississippi, and they're waiting for papers to take you back there on a charge of assaulting a white woman."

"But I neveh done it!" protested the other.

"That's no difference—if they say you did."

Too well the Negro knew the terror of his people, the tales of lynchings and tortures. A Negro accused of such a crime was already held guilty. By skilful words dropped in the next few days Doolin had him reduced to a state of terrified desperation, ready to do anything.

Lock-up time was nine o'clock. On the night of July 5, as usual, one guard, leaving his gun, entered to lock the cages, while the other stood with his gun at the door. Doolin approached the door, and the Negro, as he had told him, also came to the bars, reaching through to get a drink of water from the pail. Doolin suddenly threw his weight against the unlocked door, which flew open, knocking back the guard behind it; and the big Negro sprang through and upon him. Doolin snatched his gun. Both guards were quickly marched into cells, bound and gagged, Doolin, in command, gave orders, sternly kept all quiet, and unlocked the door. Thirty-seven prisoners slipped out and off into the darkness. A few, who had short sentences to serve, saw no advantage in escape.

Weak from illness, Doolin halted a young couple returning from a visit at the neighboring town of Marshall, just on the outskirts of Guthrie. With apologies to the young lady, he took their rig, telling his name and that he had just escaped. The officers found the rig a few days later. But Doolin had vanished.

More than forty years later, the life story of Eugene Manlove Rhodes was published, written by his wife. It solved the mystery. Doolin, perhaps getting aid from friends, and perhaps going part way on the train, had reached the New Mexico ranch of Rhodes. Here he stayed for several weeks, recuperating, making plans to bring his wife and baby here and start a new life. One day, as Mrs. Rhodes records, his quickness with a rope saved his host from being killed by a vicious horse. Very soon after this he left, "going straight to his death."

Mrs. Doolin, back at her father's home in Oklahoma, was closely watched. One day she brought a team to the blacksmith shop of Tom and Charlie Noble, to have them shod. That meant a journey. In that country most horses went unshod. A horseman rode through the night. Heck Thomas at Guthrie received the word, rode to Bee Dunn's place near Ingalls the next day, and the day after, with a posse, went on to Lawson, about fifteen miles northeast. They waited on the road near the Ellsworth home that night. There was a barking of dogs. Presently, a man leading a saddled horse came walking down the road in the moonlight, a Winchester in his hands.

"Throw up your hands, Doolin!" cried Heck Thomas. Then, a roar of guns, and a limp body lying in the road. He had fired one shot; but had received a charge of buckshot in his body and died almost instantly. Doolin's career was ended. Heck Thomas received six hundred dollars which he divided with members of the posse and his informants. The main rewards offered for arrest *and conviction* were never to be paid.

The same envious story bobbed up again, slightly altered, and was now and again repeated for many years. Doolin, they said, had died of consumption, and his father-in-law had made a deal with the officers for a share in the reward to be given to his daughter. Doolin's body was then set up and the charge of shot fired into it.

The record of the coroner's inquest and the necessity they would have to "fix" that official and a number of others, as well as the financial records of the governmental agencies and the firms which offered rewards, show the falsity of this story, which pretends to trace to the authority of an uncle of Mrs. Doolin.

Holding Up a Train

Most people would say, if their opinion was asked for, that holding up a train would be a hard job. Well, it isn't; it's easy. I have contributed some to the uneasiness of railroads and the insomnia of express companies, and the most trouble I ever had about a hold-up was in being swindled by unscrupulous people while spending the money I got. The danger wasn't anything to speak of, and we didn't mind the trouble.

One man has come pretty near robbing a train by himself; two have succeeded a few times; three can do it if they are hustlers, but five is about the right number. The time to do it and the place depend upon several things.

The first "stick-up" I was ever in happened in 1890. Maybe the way I got into it will explain how most train robbers start in the business. Five out of six Western outlaws are just cowboys out of a job and gone wrong. The sixth is a tough from the East who dresses up like a bad man and plays some low-down trick that gives the boys a bad name. Wire fences and "nesters" made five of them; a bad heart made the sixth.

Jim S—— and I were working on the 101 Ranch in Colorado. The nesters had the cowman on the go. They had taken up the land and elected officers who were hard to get along with. Jim and I rode into La Junta one day, going south from a round-up. We were having a little fun without malice toward anybody when a farmer administra-

---

From *Sixes and Sevens,* by O. Henry (William Sydney Porter), pp. 46–63. Copyright, 1904, 1911, by Doubleday, Page & Co. Garden City, New York. 1920.

The man who told me these things was for several years an outlaw in the Southwest and a follower of the pursuit he so frankly describes. His description of the *modus operandi* should prove interesting, his counsel of value to the potential passenger in some future "hold-up," while his estimate of the pleasures of train robbing will hardly induce any one to adopt it as a profession. I give the story in almost exactly his own words.—O.H.

Years later, when I was in the Ohio penitentiary and O. Henry had been released and was struggling for success in New York, I wrote him the details of this holdup and added a lot of incidents from other jobs. I wanted to write a short story about it.

* * * * *

In answer to my letter he sent me detailed instructions. He told me just how to write the "Holdup." I did the best I could and sent the manuscript to him. He waved the O. Henry wand over it, turned it into a real story, and sold it to *Everybody's.* It was one of his first successes. We went 50-50 on the profits.—Al Jennings, *Through the Shadows with O. Henry* (New York, 1921), p. 51.

tion cut in and tried to harvest us. Jim shot a deputy marshal, and I kind of corroborated his side of the argument. We skirmished up and down the main street, the boomers having bad luck all the time. After a while we leaned forward and shoved for the ranch down on the Ceriso. We were riding a couple of horses that couldn't fly, but they could catch birds.

A few days after that, a gang of the La Junta boomers came to the ranch and wanted us to go back with them. Naturally, we declined. We had the house on them, and before we were done refusing, that old 'dobe was plumb full of lead. When dark came we fagged 'em a batch of bullets and shoved out the back door for the rocks. They sure smoked us as we went. We had to drift, which we did, and rounded up down in Oklahoma.

Well, there wasn't anything we could get there, and, being mighty hard up, we decided to transact a little business with the railroads. Jim and I joined forces with Tom and Ike Moore—two brothers who had plenty of sand they were willing to convert into dust. I can call their names, for both of them are dead. Tom was shot while robbing a bank in Arkansas; Ike was killed during the more dangerous pastime of attending a dance in the Creek Nation.

We selected a place on the Santa Fe where there was a bridge across a deep creek surrounded by heavy timber. All passenger trains took water at the tank close to one end of the bridge. It was a quiet place, the nearest house being five miles away. The day before it happened, we rested our horses and "made medicine" as to how we should get about it. Our plans were not at all elaborate, as none of us had ever engaged in a hold-up before.

The Santa Fe flyer was due at the tank at 11:15 P.M. At eleven, Tom and I lay down on one side of the track, and Jim and Ike took the other. As the train rolled up, the headlight flashing far down the track and the steam hissing from the engine, I turned weak all over. I would have worked a whole year on the ranch for nothing to have been out of that affair right then. Some of the nerviest men in the business have told me that they felt the same way the first time.

The engine had hardly stopped when I jumped on the running-board on one side, while Jim mounted the other. As soon as the engineer and fireman saw our guns they threw up their hands without being told, and begged us not to shoot, saying they would do anything we wanted them to.

"Hit the ground," I ordered, and they both jumped off. We drove them before us down the side of the train. While this was happening, Tom and Ike had been blazing away, one on each side of the train, yelling like Apaches, so as to keep the passengers herded in the cars. Some fellow stuck a little twenty-two calibre out one of the coach windows and fired straight up in the air. I let drive and smashed the glass just over his head. That settled everything like resistance from that direction.

By this time all my nervousness was gone. I felt a kind of pleasant excitement as if I were at a dance or a frolic of some sort. The lights were all out in the coaches and, as Tom and Ike gradually quit firing and yelling, it got to be almost as still as a graveyard. I remember hearing a little bird chirping in a bush at the side of the track, as if it were complaining at being waked up.

I made the fireman get a lantern, and then I went to the express car and yelled to the messenger to open up or get perforated. He slid the door open and stood in it with his hands up. "Jump overboard, son," I said, and he hit the dirt like a lump of lead. There were two safes in the car—a big one and a little one. By the way, I first located the messenger's arsenal—a double-barrelled shot-gun with buckshot cartridges and a thirty-eight in a drawer. I drew the cartridges from the shot-gun, pocketed the pistol, and called the messenger inside. I shoved my gun against his nose and put him to work. He couldn't open the big one, but he did the little one. There was only nine hundred dollars in it. That was mighty small winnings for our trouble, so we decided to go through the passengers. We took our prisoners to the smoking car, and from there sent the engineer through the train to light up the coaches. Beginning with the first one, we placed a man at each door and ordered the passengers to stand between the seats with their hands up.

If you want to find out what cowards the majority of men are, all you have to do is rob a passenger train. I don't mean because they don't resist—I'll tell you later on why they can't do that—but it makes a man feel sorry for them the way they lose their heads. Big, burly drummers and farmers and ex-soldiers and high-collared dudes and sports that, a few minutes before, were filling the car with noise and bragging, get so scared that their ears flop.

There are very few people in the day coaches at that time of night, so we made a slim haul until we got to the sleeper. The Pullman conductor met me at one door while Jim was going round to the other one. He very politely informed me that I could not go into that car, as it did not belong to the railroad company, and, besides, the passengers had already been greatly disturbed by the shouting and firing. Never in all my life have I met with a finer instance of official dignity and reliance upon the power of Mr. Pullman's great name. I jabbed my six-shooter so hard against Mr. Conductor's front that I afterward found one of his vest buttons so firmly wedged in the end of the barrel that I had to shoot it out. He just shut up like a weak-springed knife and rolled down the car steps.

I opened the door of the sleeper and stepped inside. A big, fat old man came wabbling up to me, puffing and blowing. He had one coat-sleeve on and was trying to put his vest on over that. I don't know who he thought I was.

"Young man, young man," says he, "you must keep cool and not get excited. Above everything, keep cool."

"I can't," says I. "Excitement's just eating me up." And then I let out a yell and turned loose my forty-five through the skylight.

That old man tried to dive into one of the lower berths, but a screech came out of it and a bare foot that took him in the bread-basket and landed him on the floor. I saw Jim coming in the other door, and I hollered for everybody to climb out and line up.

They commenced to scramble down, and for a while we had a three-ringed circus. The men looked as frightened and tame as a lot of rabbits in a deep snow. They had on, on an average, about a quarter of a suit of clothes and one shoe apiece. One chap was sitting on the floor of the aisle, looking as if he were working a hard sum in arithmetic. He was trying, very solemn, to pull a lady's number two shoe on his number nine foot.

The ladies didn't stop to dress. They were so curious to see a real, live train robber, bless 'em, that they just wrapped blankets and sheets around themselves and came out, squeaky and fidgety looking. They always show more curiosity and sand than men do.

We got them all lined up and pretty quiet, and I went through the bunch. I found very little on them—I mean in the way of valuables. One man in the line was a sight. He was one of those big, overgrown, solemn snoozers that sit on the platform at lectures and look wise. Before crawling out he had managed to put on his long, frocktailed coat and his high silk hat. The rest of him was nothing but pajamas and bunions. When I dug into that Prince Albert, I expected to drag out at least a block of gold mine stock or an armful of Government bonds, but all I found was a little boy's French harp about four inches long. What it was there for, I don't know. I felt a little mad because he had fooled me so. I stuck the harp up against his mouth.

"If you can't play—play," I says.

"I can't play," says he.

"Then learn right off quick," says I, letting him smell the end of my gun-barrel.

He caught hold of the harp, turned red as a beet, and commenced to blow. He blew a dinky little tune I remembered hearing when I was a kid:

> Prettiest little gal in the country—oh!
> Mammy and Daddy told me so.

I made him keep on playing it all the time we were in the car. Now and then he'd get weak and off the key, and I'd turn my gun on him and ask what was the matter with that little gal, and whether he had any intention of going back to her, which would make him start up again like sixty. I think that old boy standing there in his silk hat and bare feet, playing his little French harp, was the funniest sight I ever saw. One little red-headed woman in the line broke out laughing at him. You could have heard her in the next car.

Then Jim held them steady while I searched the berths. I grappled around in those beds and filled a pillow-case with the strangest assortment of stuff you ever saw. Now and then I'd come across a little popgun pistol, just about right for plugging teeth with, which I'd throw out the window. When I finished with the collection, I dumped the pillow-case load in the middle of the aisle. There were a good many watches, bracelets, rings, and pocket-books, with a sprinkling of false teeth, whisky flasks, face-powder boxes, chocolate caramels, and heads of hair of various colours and lengths. There were also about a dozen ladies' stockings into which jewelry, watches, and rolls of bills had been stuffed and then wadded up tight and stuck under the mattresses. I offered to return what I called the "scalps," saying that we were not Indians on the warpath, but none of the ladies seemed to know to whom the hair belonged.

One of the women—and a good-looker she was—wrapped in a striped blanket, saw me pick up one of the stockings that was pretty chunky and heavy about the toe, and she snapped out:

"That's mine, sir. You're not in the business of robbing women, are you?"

Now, as this was our first hold-up, we hadn't agreed upon any code of ethics, so I hardly knew what to answer. But, anyway, I replied: "Well, not as a specialty. If this contains your personal property you can have it back."

"It just does," she declared eagerly, and reached out her hand for it.

"You'll excuse my taking a look at the contents," I said, holding the stocking up by the toe. Out dumped a big gent's gold watch, worth two hundred, a gent's leather pocket-book that we afterward found to contain six hundred dollars, a 32-calibre revolver; and the only thing of the lot that could have been a lady's personal property was a silver bracelet worth about fifty cents.

I said: "Madame, here's your property," and handed her the bracelet. "Now," I went on, "how can you expect us to act square with you when you try to deceive us in this manner? I'm surprised at such conduct."

The young woman flushed up as if she had been caught doing something dishonest. Some other woman down the line called out: "The mean thing!" I never knew whether she meant the other lady or me.

When we finished our job we ordered everybody back to bed, told 'em good night very politely at the door, and left. We rode forty miles before daylight and divided the stuff. Each one of us got $1,752.85 in money. We lumped the jewelry around. Then we scattered, each man for himself.

That was my first train robbery, and it was about as easily done as any of the ones that followed. But that was the last and only time I ever went through the passengers. I don't like that part of the business. Afterward I stuck strictly to the express car. During the next eight years I handled a good deal of money.

The best haul I made was just seven years after the first one. We found out about a train that was going to bring out a lot of money to pay off the soldiers at a Government post. We stuck that train up in broad daylight. Five of us lay in the sand hills near a little station. Ten soldiers were guarding the money on the train, but they might just as well have been at home on a furlough. We didn't even allow them to stick their heads out the windows to see the fun. We had no trouble at all in getting the money, which was all in gold. Of course, a big howl was raised at the time about the robbery. It was Government stuff, and the Government got sarcastic and wanted to know what the convoy of soldiers went along for. The only excuse given was that nobody was expecting an attack among those bare sand hills in daytime. I don't know what the Government thought about the excuse, but I know that it was a good one. The surprise—that is the keynote of the train-robbing business. The papers published all kinds of stories about the loss, finally agreeing that it was between nine thousand and ten thousand dollars. The Government sawed wood. Here are the correct figures, printed for the first time—forty-eight thousand dollars. If anybody will take the trouble to look over Uncle Sam's private accounts for that little debit to profit and loss, he will find that I am right to a cent.

By that time we were expert enough to know what to do. We rode due west twenty miles, making a trail that a Broadway policeman could have followed, and then we doubled back, hiding our tracks. On the second night after the hold-up, while posses were scouring the country in every direction, Jim and I were eating supper in the second story of a friend's house in the town where the alarm started from. Our friend pointed out to us, in an office across the street, a printing press at work striking off handbills offering a reward for our capture.

I have been asked what we do with the money we get. Well, I never could account for a tenth part of it after it was spent. It goes fast and freely. An outlaw has to have a good many friends. A highly respected citizen may, and often does, get along with very few, but a man on the dodge has got to have "sidekickers." With angry posses and reward-hungry officers cutting out a hot trail for him, he must have a few places scattered about the country where he can stop and feed himself and his horse and get a few hours' sleep without having to keep both eyes open. When he makes a haul he feels like dropping some of the coin with these friends, and he does it liberally. Sometimes I have, at the end of a hasty visit at one of these havens of refuge, flung a handful of gold and bills into the laps of the kids playing on the floor, without knowing whether my contribution was a hundred dollars or a thousand.

When old-timers make a big haul they generally go far away to one of the big cities to spend their money. Green hands, however successful a hold-up they make, nearly always give themselves away by showing too much money near the place where they got it.

I was in a job in '94 where we got twenty thousand dollars. We followed our favorite plan for a get-away—that is, doubled on our trail—and laid low for a time near the scene of the train's bad luck. One morning I picked up a newspaper and read an article with big headlines stating that the marshal, with eight deputies and a posse of thirty armed citizens, had the train robbers surrounded in a mesquite thicket on the Cimarron, and that it was a question of only a few hours when they would be dead men or prisoners. While I was reading that article I was sitting at breakfast in one of the most elegant private residences in Washington City, with a flunky in knee pants standing behind my chair. Jim was sitting across the table talking to his half-uncle, a retired naval officer, whose name you have often seen in the accounts of doings in the capital. We had gone there and bought rattling outfits of good clothes, and were resting from our labours among the nabobs. We must have been killed in that mesquite thicket, for I can make an affidavit that we didn't surrender.

Now I propose to tell why it is easy to hold up a train, and, then, why no one should ever do it.

In the first place, the attacking party has all the advantage. That is, of course, supposing that they are old-timers with the necessary experience and courage. They have the outside and are protected by the darkness, while the others are in the light, hemmed into a small space, and exposed, the moment they show a head at a window or door, to the aim of a man who is a dead shot and who won't hesitate to shoot.

But, in my opinion, the main condition that makes train robbing easy is the element of surprise in connection with the imagination of the passengers. If you have ever seen a horse that has eaten loco weed you will understand what I mean when I say that the passengers get locoed. That horse gets the awfulest imagination on him in the world. You can't coax him to cross a little branch stream two feet wide. It looks as big to him as the Mississippi River. That's just the way with the passenger. He thinks there are a hundred men yelling and shooting outside, when maybe there are only two or three. And the muzzle of a forty-five looks like the entrance to a tunnel. The passenger is all right, although he may do mean little tricks, like hiding a wad of money in his shoe and forgetting to dig up until you jostle his ribs some with the end of your six-shooter; but there's no harm in him.

As to the train crew, we never had any more trouble with them than if they had been so many sheep. I don't mean that they are cowards; I mean that they have got sense. They know they're not up against a bluff. It's the same way with the officers. I've seen secret service men, marshals, and railroad detectives fork over their change as meek as Moses. I saw one of the bravest marshals I ever knew hide his gun under his seat and dig up along with the rest while I was taking toll. He wasn't afraid; he simply knew that we had the drop on the whole outfit. Besides, many of those officers have families and they feel that they oughtn't to take chances; whereas death has no terrors for the man who holds up a train. He expects to get killed some day, and he generally does. My advice to you, if you should ever be in a hold-up, is to line up with the cowards and save your bravery for an occasion when it may be of some benefit to you. Another reason why officers are backward about mixing things with a train robber is a financial one. Every time there is a scrimmage and somebody gets killed, the officers lose money. If the train robber gets away they swear out a warrant against John Doe et al. and travel hundreds of miles and sign vouchers for thousands on the trail of the fugitives, and the Government foots the bills. So with them, it is a question of mileage rather than courage.

* * * * *

I don't think I ought to close without giving some deductions from my experience of eight years "on the dodge." It doesn't pay to rob trains. Leaving out the question of right and morals, which I don't think I ought to tackle, there is very little to envy in the life of an outlaw. After a while money ceases to have any value in his eyes. He gets to looking upon the railroads and express companies as his bankers, and his six-shooters as a cheque book for any amount. He throws away money right and left. Most of the time he is on the jump, riding day and night, and he lives so hard between times that he doesn't enjoy the taste of high life when he gets it. He knows that his time is bound to come to lose his life or liberty, and that the accuracy of his aim, the speed of his horse, and the fidelity of his "sider," are all that postpone the inevitable.

It isn't that he loses any sleep over danger from the officers of the law. In all my experience I never knew officers to attack a band of outlaws unless they outnumbered them at least three to one.

But the outlaw carries one thought constantly in his mind—and that is what makes him so sore against life, more than anything else—he knows where the marshals get their recruits of deputies. He knows that the majority of these upholders of the law were once lawbreakers, horse thieves, rustlers, highwaymen, and outlaws like himself, and that they gained their position and immunity by turning state's evidence, by turning traitor and delivering up their comrades to imprisonment and death. He knows that some day—unless he is shot first

—his Judas will set to work, the trap will be laid, and he will be the surprised instead of a surpriser at a stick-up.

That is why the man who holds up trains picks his company with a thousand times the care with which a careful girl chooses a sweetheart. That is why he raises himself from his blanket of nights and listens to the tread of every horse's hoofs on the distant road. That is why he broods suspiciously for days upon a jesting remark or an unusual movement of a tried comrade, or the broken mutterings of his closest friend, sleeping by his side.

And it is one of the reasons why the train-robbing profession is not so pleasant a one as either of its collateral branches—politics or cornering the market.

The Hanging of Tom Horn

Horn was a professional murderer. He operated in Wyoming in the '90's and in Colorado in 1900, then again in Wyoming in 1901. He was employed by a group of cattle ranchers to liquidate rustlers and sheepowners whose flocks intruded in "cattle country." His fees for murder ranged from $500 to $700. He "dry-gulched"[1] his victims. His trade mark was a rock placed beneath the head of a victim for the purpose of proving to his employers that the "dirty work" had been his. He was hanged for ambushing a 13-year-old boy whom he mistook for the

By John Charles Thompson. From *1945 Brand Book,* Containing Twelve Original Papers Relating to Western and Rocky Mountain History, edited by Herbert O. Brayer, pp. 111–116, 117–121, 123–129. Copyright, 1946, by the Westerners, Denver Posse. Denver.

For more than forty years there has endured in the minds of a numerous company a suspicion, which has acquired now the tenaciousness of tradition, that Tom Horn did not die at the end of a rope in the Laramie County jail at Cheyenne on November 20, 1903. This fantastic tradition is that the hanging of Horn was a mock execution; that he was cut down alive, revived, spirited away; that the cadaver carried from the jail was that of an unidentified tramp; that it was the body of this tramp which was taken to Boulder, Colorado, and there buried as that of Horn. I can testify otherwise—I saw Horn hanged and I saw his dead body on a mortuary slab. I knew him personally; there was no mistaking the identity of that body.

* * * * *

This piece is not a biography of Horn or history in detail of his homicidal accomplishments. It is designed only to allay the myth that he did not pay the supreme penalty prescribed for murder. There is incidental sketching of dramatic events of which I have personal knowledge. I may err concerning some facets of these gems of criminality; if so, the error is not intentional; more than forty years is a long period for recollection to bridge and I have not had time to document my tale.—J.C.T.

Cf. Jay Monaghan, *Last of the Bad Men* (Indianapolis, 1946).

[1] "'Dry-gulching' was a favorite method of disposing of troublesome nesters," as well as rustlers, their bodies being "found later in some dry gulch, food for ravens." See Charles Kelly, *Outlaw Trail* (Salt Lake City, 1938), p. 67.

lad's father. No other murder was proved against him but there was general belief that he committed at least four others. He was hanged not because the murder of the boy was fastened upon him "beyond peradventure of a reasonable doubt," but on "general principle" that he "had it coming."

* * * * *

Before he appeared on the Wyoming scene, Horn had a notable career as a scout in Indian warfare and as a stock detective in Arizona and New Mexico. There is not much time to sketch this here. His Wyoming advent was during a troublous era there. The famous and infamous "Johnson County invasion" was little more than three years past; the lynching of Jim Averell and "Cattle Kate" had been perpetrated only five or six years previously; there had been numerous other dark crimes to avenge alleged cattle stealing. There was "blood on the moon" and Horn was to add to it.

As the mid-nineties approached, the Wyoming Stock Growers Association, a powerful society of cattle-raisers, appointed a secret committee to employ a stock detective to obtain evidence against rustlers. United States Senator Joseph M. Carey of the firm of J. M. Carey & Bro., the far-flung range of which in Laramie, Converse, and Natrona counties was being raided by thieves, was chairman of this committee. The committee dug up Horn, whose real name was said to be Horner, and brought him to Wyoming. Soon after his employment, John C. Coble of the Iron Mountain Ranch Company, which also was suffering heavy losses to rustlers, is said to have broached a proposition that Horn was ready to kill cattle thieves for a fee of $500 a head. Carey, horrified by this proposal, demanded and obtained the discharge of Horn. Thereafter Horn was employed independently by a group of big cattlemen, reputed to have included Coble, Ora Haley, and several others.

Forthwith things began to happen. A small-time rancher named Lewis was shot in the back while working in the corral of his ranch about thirty-five miles northwest of Cheyenne. This was in 1895. A brief period later, a neighbor of Lewis, Levi Powell, was murdered from ambush as he worked in his meadow, accompanied by his six-year-old son. Seeing Horn in the court-house at Cheyenne, this boy identified him as the slayer of his father. There was no other evidence and Horn was not arrested. Interestingly, the Powell lad, grown to manhood, was shot to death by a step-son at the ranch on which his father had been killed.

The finger of public suspicion pointed so accusingly at Horn that there was a lull in assassination. In 1898 Horn enlisted for the war with Spain, went to Cuba as a packer, made a commendable record. He was back the following year, headquartered at the Coble ranch. In 1900 he went to Brown's Park, Colorado. Soon two ranchers under suspicion of rustling, Matt Rash and Isham Dart, the latter a Negro, were assassinated there. Riding out of Colorado after the murder of Rash, Horn met a posse which was seeking the murderer at Dixon, a hamlet on the Colorado-Wyoming line. He and a posseman became embroiled, fought with knives. Horn severely slashed his antagonist; himself suffered a terrific wound in the neck. Only a man of his robust physique could have survived this injury.

On July 18, 1901, Willie Nickell, thirteen-year-old son of Kels P. Nickell, a small rancher who had committed the error of introducing sheep in the Iron Mountain section over the protest of cattlemen, was shot to death by an unseen assassin. The killing occurred in the dimness of dawn. The boy was wearing his father's hat and coat, riding the elder Nickell's horse. A rock the size of a man's fist was placed under his head. Supposition was that he had been mistaken for his father; killed because of this error. Suspicion leveled on Horn but there was no evidence.

A week after Willie was slain, his father, while working in his garden, was twice shot by an unknown marksman; suffered severe wounds in an arm and hip. A few days later some of his sheep were clubbed to death by a person or persons unknown.

The Nickells had been feuding with the family of a neighbor, James E. Miller. Suspicion pointed also to the Millers and he and his two sons, in their mid-'teens, were arrested. At their preliminary hearing, a diminutive school-teacher who boarded at the Miller home, Gwendoline Kimmell, provided them a convincing alibi and they were discharged from custody. Horn also testified in behalf of the Millers. He was reported to have been attentive to Miss Kimmell.

Months passed without further developments. During this period suspicion of Horn grew darker and darker in the public mind. He decided to move to Canada, got as far as Omaha, changed his mind and returned. But for this change of mind he might have lived to a ripe old age.

On January 10, 1902, Joe LeFors, a deputy United States marshal and former stock detective, and Horn engaged in a drinking bout in a Cheyenne saloon. Horn became very drunk. LeFors invited him to go to the marshal's office. There, while Horn continued drinking, LeFors led him into a discussion of the Nickell killing. Egged on by leading questions, Horn became maudlinly boastful. Shrewdly interrogated by LeFors, he said things about the killing which were to be construed as a confession. Listening in an adjoining room, at a partly open door, were Deputy Marshal Les E. Snow and Court Stenographer Charles J. Ohnhaus. Ohnhaus made a stenographic record of the conversation.

Two days later Horn was arrested in the bar of the Inter Ocean Hotel. While Undersheriff Dick Proctor stood a few feet behind him, gun in hand, Sheriff Ed J. Smalley tapped him on the shoulder, told him he was under arrest. Horn, who could see Proctor reflected in the bar mirror, submitted quietly. At a preliminary hearing a few days later, the so-called confession was introduced. Horn was astounded. He was bound over without bail for the murder of Willie Nickell.

He went on trial October 10, 1902. Before a shred of testimony was offered he was a doomed man; public opinion had convicted him and intended to have him hanged. The trial lasted two weeks. Horn didn't have a dollar to his name, but an imposing array of counsel presented his defense—counsel whose fees probably ran to $5,000 or more. The State's case, presented by Prosecuting Attorney Walter R. Stoll, was circumstantial other than for the testimony of LeFors and the Ohnhaus notes of the alleged confession. On October 24, the jury returned the verdict, "Guilty of murder in the first degree," despite the testimony of a physician who performed an autopsy on the Nickell boy that the bullet which killed him was of much greater calibre than those of Horn's gun, a .30-.30.

Appeal was taken; the supreme court affirmed the verdict. One expedient after another delayed punishment more than a year. As the day set for the hanging drew near, pressure on Governor Chatterton for a reprieve was intensified. New evidence laid before the governor by the defense was quickly rebutted by Stoll. Gwendoline Kimmell came to the fore again with a retraction of her alibi evidence for the Millers; asserted she had overheard Miller and one of his sons plotting to kill Nickell. Perjury had a large place in the new evidence, but Gwendoline was the only witness against whom a perjury charge was lodged. She was arrested but not brought to trial. Governor Chatterton was not convinced by the new evidence, and refused to intervene to prevent the execution on November 20, 1903.

During his long imprisonment Horn became increasingly apprehensive that he would be unable to avoid the gallows. He constantly plotted to escape.

* * * * *

[After the exposure of a plot for his delivery,] Horn's liberty within the jail was curtailed, and vigilance against escape redoubled.

These precautions notwithstanding, Horn did escape eight months later. He enjoyed (perhaps it better would be said, survived) a few minutes of liberty. On the morning of August 9, 1903, he and Jim McCloud, a common garden variety of thief, attacked and overpowered Undersheriff Proctor in the cell block, took his keys, unlocked the door to the sheriff's office, and dragged him in, beaten almost into unconsciousness. They were searching the office for arms when Snow, the self-same deputy who had heard Horn's "confession," walked in. Instantly comprehending the situation, Snow bolted back through the door, ran along the court-house corridor to the open, firing his gun to give the alarm.

Horn and McCloud fled from the court-house in opposite directions. McCloud ran to the sheriff's barn, commandeered the only horse there.

He was endeavoring to mount the skittish animal when Smalley, who had been at breakfast in the sheriff's quarters in the court-house building, and had surmised correctly the significance of Snow's shooting, appeared in the alley on which the barn fronted, revolver in hand. Smalley fired twice at the fugitive, "creasing" him with each bullet. McCloud abandoned the horse, threw up his hands, and submitted to seizure by citizens who had been summoned by Snow's shots. In due time he was sent to the penitentiary for post-office robbery.

Horn ran out of the main door of the court-house. He had "materialized" an automatic pistol. He ran eastward along Nineteenth Street a block, turned north on Capitol, then east on Twentieth. Across Nineteenth from the court-house was an itinerant merry-go-round outfit. The proprietor, middle-aged O. M. Eldrich, pursued the fugitive, armed with a cheap nickel-plated revolver. At Eldrich's heels went a growing pack of citizenry who had just emerged from Sunday morning devotions at a nearby church.

As Horn turned into Twentieth, Eldrich began firing at him. As two bullets smacked into a building he was passing, Horn stopped, threw down his pistol, threw up his hands. Eldrich confidently kept him covered, unaware that he had exhausted the cartridges in his nickel-plated gun. Horn had not fired a shot; the "safety" of his pistol had not been released. Citizens and a police patrolman, Lou Stone, seized Horn, and began to march back toward the jail. As they approached the building, Snow appeared with a rifle. Seeing Horn, he quickly reversed the weapon and attempted to club the helpless prisoner. Stone threw up an arm to shield Horn, and thereupon suffered a fracture of the limb.

The popular and published explanation given at the time of Horn's failure to use his pistol was that he was unfamiliar with the weapon's "safety" and was unable to fire it. He had obtained the supposedly Belgian-made automatic while escaping from the sheriff's office. The truth, doubtless, was that Horn was familiar with the operation of the "safety," but was too shrewd to fire at Eldrich and other pursuers, realizing that another killing would surely seal his fate. He still had hope that legal action might enable him to avoid the noose.

Testimony by Dr. George P. Johnston, prominent physician, many, many years later, is illuminating concerning this part of the story. Johnston was the first man to go to Eldrich's aid as the merry-go-round operator held Horn at bay with an empty gun. Horn's pistol lay at the fugitive's feet. Johnston stooped to pick it up, changed his mind, let it lie, and went away as unobtrusively as was possible. His explanation, withheld for three decades or longer, was, in substance, as follows:

The automatic pistol, later known as a "Colt," had been but recently perfected in Horn's day. It then was known as a "Browning," the name of its inventor. Among the earliest of these weapons to arrive in Cheyenne was one owned by Johnston. He kept it in his desk in his office. Some months before Horn arrived at the end of his trail, Johnston related, John Coble walked into the office, requested that he be permitted to examine the novel firearm. Having had its operation explained to him, said Johnston, Coble drew a six-shooter, laid it on the desk, announced that he would take the automatic with him, exchange it for the six-shooter later, and walked out without awaiting an "aye" or "nay" by the physician. The next time he saw the automatic, Johnston continued, it lay at Horn's feet in the street—that was why he did not pick it up, and later discreetly refrained from putting in a claim to it. The fact that Horn had obtained an automatic in the sheriff's office and Johnston's story are reconcilable—Horn may have been equipped with the Johnston pistol and have discarded the Belgian pistol because he was familiar with the operation of the Johnston weapon.

During the 106 days remaining to Horn after his return to jail extreme precautions against further escape or delivery were observed. Special deputies kept guard at the court-house. As the day of the condemned man's doom neared, precautions became almost fantastic. On November 18, three days before the execution, two companies of militia went on guard. There was apprehension bordering on hysteria that Horn's employers, fearing that at the eleventh hour he would break and reveal their identity, would attempt a rescue with armed force. During those last three days only persons of known unimpeachable integrity were permitted to go to the courthouse unchallenged; all others attempting to approach were stopped by bayonets, allowed to proceed only if they could produce an official pass. Cheyenne was in the grip of an attack of "jitters" not equaled during the thirty years following 1873, when it suffered its last "Indian scare."

Throughout the night immediately preceding dawn of the day of execution a solid cordon of soldiers surrounded the court-house. Approaches to the building were declared "out of bounds" and roped off. Only the reckless among the population went near the "dead line"; others, heeding the counsel of common sense that a nervous militiaman might shoot first and inquire afterward, avoided the vicinity. Meanwhile, Horn slept placidly.

Before he slept, an eccentric preacher and several sistern of his congregation were permitted to enter the jail to sing hymns to the condemned man. The preacher emerged to assert that Horn had "confessed" to him while under the influence of sweet song. Concerning that, more presently. . . .

Word had gone out that the hanging would take place at 7 A.M. At crisp dawn of the 20th crowds began collecting outside the rope barriers. They soon numbered several thousand persons. There was naught to be seen other than the grim walls of the ugly court-house, but imagination morbidly pictured what was going on inside. Business virtually was suspended; the "Roman Holiday" spirit was in the air.

Persons accorded the privilege of observing Horn's "last mile" were admitted to the court-house at 7 o'clock. Guards with rifles at ready herded them into the county clerk's offices, two rooms across a corridor from the sheriff's office and entrance to the jail. These included about eight newspaper reporters, and a dozen visiting sheriffs and other peace officers; also the Irwin brothers, Big Charlie and Little Frank, close friends of Horn who had disdained enmity aroused by their efforts in his behalf. . . .

* * * * *

. . . With only a canvas curtain masking it from Horn's view, the gallows had been assembled two days previously; its mechanism had been tested repeatedly—the last time only thirty minutes before the hanging. Horn could hear every movement; a more barbaric ordeal for the condemned man could hardly have been arranged.

I, myself, had been accorded a demonstration of how the gallows worked. Morning before the day of execution, Proctor had slipped me through a side door into the jail; operated the mechanism with a 200-pound sack of sand as a "stand-in" for Horn.

"Notice, Charley," said the undersheriff, "that when the sack stops it will make only a half-turn. I've arranged it that way so Horn's back will be to the spectators as he hangs."

Sure enough, the sandbag made only a half-turn, then hung motionless save for a slight swinging.

Calmly from behind the curtain came Horn's voice.

"Did she work all right this time, Dick?" he asked.

"Sure, slick as a whistle," replied Proctor.

"That's good," commented Horn; "I don't want any slips.

* * * * *

Now back to Horn's "last mile." We newspapermen were crammed into a little space at the end of the platform adjoining Horn's cell; the visiting sheriffs were marshaled on the first-tier level below. The Irwin brothers, flanked by guards, stood beside them. The executioners and a venerable Episcopal clergyman, Dr. George C. Rafter, an acquaintance of Horn, were on the gangway at the opposite edge of the platform. Beside the Irwins stood two physicians, Dr. George P. Johnston and Dr. John H. Conway. They were gentlemen of the highest integrity whom nothing could have induced to contribute to a criminal conspiracy.

Horn, his back against the cell grill, was half-reclining on his narrow bed, puffing a cigar. He was perfectly composed. His soft shirt was unbuttoned at the collar, thus exposing the scar of the wound he had suffered in the fight at Dixon.

"Ready, Tom," said Proctor.

Horn arose, carefully placed his cigar on a cross-reinforcement of the grill, strode firmly the few steps required to take him to the side of the gallows platform.

He nodded to the Irwins; sardonically scanned the peace officers below.

"Ed," he commented to Smalley, "that's the sickest looking lot of damned sheriffs I ever seen."

"Would you like us to sing, Tom?" said Charlie Irwin.

"Yes, I'd like that," responded Horn.

So, while Proctor buckled straps that bound Horn's arms and legs, the Irwins, each in a rich tenor, sang a rather lugubrious song popular on the range, "Life Is Like a Mountain Railroad."

The clergyman read his church's prayer for the dying. Horn, standing relaxed, listened without a tremor.

"Would you like to say anything?" asked Smalley.

"No," replied Horn.

"Tom," spoke up Charlie Irwin, "did you confess to the preacher?"

"No," was the reply.

Proctor adjusted the noose, formed with the conventional knot of 13 wraps, to Horn's neck; drew a black hood over his head. Smalley on one side and a friend of Horn, T. Joe Cahill, on the other, lifted the doomed man onto the trap.

Instantly the sibilant sound of running water permeated the breathless stillness; the instrument of death had begun to operate. To the straining ears of the listeners that little sound had the magnitude of that of a rushing torrent.

Smalley, his face buried in the crook of an arm resting against the gallows, was trembling.

"What's the matter," came in a calm tone through the black cap, "getting nervous I might tip over?"

Seemingly interminable, the sound of escaping water ran on.

"Joe," said Horn, addressing Cahill, "they tell me you're married now. I hope you're doing well. Treat her right."

Indubitably, he was the best composed man in that chamber of death.

Still the sinister sound of running water; then mercifully, the leaves of the trap parted with a crash and Horn's body dropped through the opening.

Thirty-one seconds had elapsed since he had been lifted onto the trap!

He fell only four and one-half feet; his head and shoulders projected above the gallows floor. This drop was not sufficient; his neck was not broken. Proctor had feared to arrange a longer drop, apprehensive that stoppage of the fall of a body so heavy as Horn's might tear the head off. The slam of the massive hangman's knot against the side of Horn's skull shocked him into unconsciousness, however, and he did not suffer. For 17 minutes the physicians, with fingers on his pulse, felt impulses as a mighty heart labored on; then the pulse ceased.

Tom Horn was dead—unconfessed!

I did not see him die. Immediately upon his plunge through the trap the witnesses were required to leave. I hesitated sufficiently to watch the dangling body turn. It made precisely one-half turn—stopped. Proctor's reckoning in this respect had been accurate.

I was the first man to get out of the court-house. I emerged at a high lope, was intercepted in the middle of the street by Kels Nickell, who had contrived to get through the police line.

"Is the son-of-a-bitch dead?" he demanded.

"Yes," I replied, and loped on—I had an extra to get out.

An hour later I saw the Horn cadaver on a slab at the Gleason Mortuary. There was no mistaking the body—it was that of Horn.

Take it from me, gentlemen, Tom Horn is dead, the myth of a fake execution notwithstanding.

The Apache Kid: Bad Indian

Well, those Apaches were not as bad as most of the white people were here in those days. You see, there were a lot of white people came into this section all at once, miners and such, and some of them were pretty bad, and others were nearly as green as some of the tourists that come around these parts in winter now. All of 'em had heard of Geronimo and how bad he was, and they thought every Apache was just the same way, but for every Apache that was bad there were a hundred harmless ones. But that didn't make no difference with the whites, though, and no peaceful Apache could go about without some white fool taking a shot at him, and that made more bad Indians than anything else.

I had quite a little dealing with them and they didn't give me any trouble. Of course, there was the Apache Kid. He was a bad one, but he wasn't bad at first. He was brought up as a scout or something over on the reservation, and some other Indian killed his father, and instead of letting the white man's law settle things for him, he just settled it the Indian way and killed the feller himself. Just as soon as he done it he knew the agent was through with him and would be after him for what he done, so he took to the mountains and went "bad Indian," and when he did go bad he turned vicious all over.

He knew the best Indian scouts would always be on his trail, so he turned bad toward the Apaches as well as the whites. He had a little

As told by Jack Frazer, Mesa, Arizona. From "The Apache Kid," by Frank G. Applegate, *Folk-Say, A Regional Miscellany: 1931*, edited by B. A. Botkin, pp. 331–337. Copyright, 1931, by B. A. Botkin. Norman: University of Oklahoma Press.

the best of the Apache scouts, though, for besides being the cunningest Indian scout himself, he had also learned a lot of the white man's smartness as well. The other Apaches were all just as scared of him as the whites were, for he didn't treat them much better than anybody else. A bunch of Apaches would be sitting peacefully on their part of the reservation, wondering when the next blundering, green army captain, with a gang of scared soldiers, would come along and shoot them up, when the Apache Kid would come sneaking into their camp and paralyze the lot of them more than a whole regiment of soldiers would. The Kid would eat his fill, catch the best horse of the tribe, grab anything else he wanted, and then, cutting out the best-looking young squaw in the camp, ride off with the lot, leaving every Indian too scared to lift a hand. He didn't trust one of these squaws any too much either and kept her tied to him at night so she couldn't give him the slip, and if he had to leave her for a little bit during the day he tied her up good to a tree. When one of these squaws got too worn out with that hard sort of life, going with him everywhere through the mountains, he just turned her loose to find her way back to her people the best she could, while he went on his way and after a while got him another one the same way he got her.

At that time I had a ranch out about eighteen miles from Globe and about forty-five northeast of Mesa. I also had a nice little mine down near Globe where I was drilling rock, but things weren't going so good prospecting by then, and a good many of the boys were clearing out. There was a feller who had been keeping a store there and had been doing pretty well, but he was having to go too, with most of the miners gone, so when he was leaving he called me into the store and gave me a fine lap-robe with big red roses all over it. He said I had been a good customer and he was making me a gift of it. He also had a fine stand of buggy whips that he'd had ever since he'd started the store and never sold, that not being a horse and buggy country like Illinois where he'd come from, and he gave these whips, which had nice red and yellow tassels on them, to the other boys who had traded with him.

I took my buggy robe out to the ranch, where I was staying about half the time then, and used it for a bed cover, and it made a pretty one. I had staying with me at the ranch then a young lad about fourteen or fifteen years old named Charlie Dobie. He was born in Texas, I think, but had gone out to California with his folks. He didn't like it there and had come to Arizona. He was a nice, bright lad and not afraid of anything, and when I had to be away from the ranch he stayed there alone to look after things. I had a ranchhouse fourteen by sixteen feet which me and another fellow had made of logs which we had whip-sawed into thick slabs, and we had also built a lean-to the same size against one side of the house. There was a door in the middle of the front side of the house and another opposite it into the lean-to, and straight in front of that there was one going from the lean-to into the corral, so that one could look from the front of the house straight through into the corral when the doors were all open. There was a bunk built into each end of the house, and in one end of the lean-to there was a stove where we cooked and at the other end there was a table where we ate. I didn't like leaving Charlie alone there when I was away, but he laughed at me and said he wasn't afraid. The other Indians never bothered us, and the Apache Kid never had been in just them parts. Besides, Charlie had a good rifle and knew how to use it, and I tried never to be away from the ranch house more than one night at a time.

Things went on that way all right for quite a good while, and then one morning when I come to the ranch everything was very quiet and when I hollered Charlie didn't answer. Looking at the house, I saw all the doors were open straight through and I wondered what had made Charlie leave them that way, so I got off my horse and walked in the front door, and things were in a terrible mess there. Everything scattered all over the floor and some things missing and Charlie's rifle, which he always kept standing between his bunk and the front door, was gone too. Then I walked through into the lean-to, and things were just as bad there. Provisions all over the floor and a lot gone. I didn't stop long there but hurried to the back door and looked out and there was poor Charlie lying about twenty steps out in the corral. When I went up to him he was a terrible sight. He had been shot through the side and his head had been all smashed in by a big bloody stone which laid there by him. There were moccasin tracks all around in the dust, so I knew Indians had done it, and from the looks of things they hadn't been gone long. Well, it wasn't the first man I had seen who had been killed, though not many by Indians, and most of the others had it coming to them, but Charlie was a good lad and had never done any one, white or Indian, any harm that I knew of, and it nearly broke me up to have that happen to him.

I rounded up some of the boys and we gave Charlie as good a funeral as we could, and then I went over to Florence and told the sheriff what had happened. He said he would do all he could to find the murderers, but he was sure it was the Apache Kid's work. The next day he took a couple of deputies and went over into the Indian country. The sheriff was a good hand at his work, but nobody could have found the Kid, for he always saw every one long before they saw him. The sheriff went around to the different Indian camps, but the Apaches were all afraid to even mention the Kid's name because they were afraid he would kill them out of revenge. At last in one of the Indian camps the sheriff found the fancy lap-robe that the storekeeper had given me for a present, and he also found a young squaw, much the worse for wear, who the other Indians said owned it. Pinned down with this evidence, the squaw then told her story. She said the

Kid had taken her from that camp a couple of months before and kept her right with him every minute since then. One morning very early they had gone to the ranch where the robe had come from and the Kid, with her by his side, had sneaked up to the front door and looked in and, seeing the rifle, had picked it up. Just then the other door opened and a white boy looked in, but when he saw the Apache Kid he ran back to go out of another door into the corral. As he went through this door the Kid shot him and he fell, running, about fifty feet from the house. When they reached him he wasn't dead, so the Kid made her take a stone and crush the boy's head in. They then went through the house, and, taking what they wanted, slipped back to the mountains. Two days afterwards the Kid turned her loose because the scouts were close on his trail again, and he let her take the robe with her.

Well, there was nothing the sheriff could do to the squaw, for she had been forced to do what she did, so he took the lap-robe, and went back to Florence and I never got it back either, for the sheriff had a buggy and a girl there, but I guess it afterwards got him into enough trouble for he married the girl.

The Apache Kid was never seen for sure after Charlie Dobie was killed. A little while after that a couple of the boys, who had a ranch up on the San Pedro and worked it in between drilling holes in the rock around Globe, were at their ranch one night when one of them heard a noise at the corral, which stood in a little ravine below the house. So taking his rifle he slipped out to see if any one was bothering the horses. As he crept up to the corral, he saw two ghostly figures walking single file up the ravine with the hindmost leading his favorite horse. He fired twice at the two figures, the second shot following the first almost instantly. The person leading the horse gave a terrible scream and dropped to the ground while the other one disappeared in the brush which lined the ravine. When the two ranchers examined the one who had been shot, they found it was a pretty young squaw and that she was stone dead. The next morning they found a trail of blood leading away from where the other one had been shot at, and they followed it a long way until they finally lost the trail in the mountains.

The Apache Kid was never seen after that, and it has always been supposed that the rancher shot him that night and he crawled away to a secret hiding-place in the mountains to die alone, for his body was never found. That was a long time ago, forty years or more, I guess. There's not so many of the old boys left. Well, so long. Here's one that's got to be stirring or he'll be in the poorhouse yet.

Cherokee Bill and Judge Parker

One of the most fiendishly cruel criminals I ever knew was the Indian outlaw, Cherokee Bill. He had murdered thirteen men, one of them his own brother-in-law. Bill was leader of a bandit gang composed of "Chicken," "Skeeter," Long Gordon, Curtis Dason, Verdigris Kid, and Dooley Benge. Bill was a large man and a Samson in strength. He and his band won several pitched battles with posses that went to catch him, and when he was finally taken, by strategy, his strength was so great he snapped the handcuffs that linked his wrists together.

He was convicted of murder and Judge Parker sentenced him to death. This was in the latter years of Judge Parker's term, after Congress had given convicted ones the right of appeal from that court. Cherokee Bill had taken an appeal, and, while in jail, awaiting a decision, he became morose and obstinate. There were fifty-nine men in that jail under sentence of death at the time, and all had the freedom of the floor and mingled with one another in the daytime but were locked in their cells at night. It was a desperate gang, and Bill was the worst of all. Some one smuggled a six-shooter in to Bill and with it he held up the guards and killed one. Other guards came running up and as they came Bill began a sniping match with them. Every time he fired he gobbled. This gobble was peculiarly Indian, an unearthly sound something like the howl of a coyote and the gobble of a turkey cock merged. It was a death cry among the Territory Indians. A defendant before Parker once pleaded that he had killed another Indian because the latter gobbled at him. The prosecutor was aghast at the flippancy of the excuse, but the defendant introduced several witnesses who testified that when an Indian gobbled he meant sudden death to any or all in his path.

Henry Starr, a bandit under sentence of death, and himself part Cherokee, offered to help quiet Bill and the guards told him to go ahead.

"Bill, the guards have promised that if you will give up your gun and surrender they will not harm you. You can't get anywhere by killing a lot of people. You can't get out now, stop it and give up your gun," urged Starr.

"I'm going to kill every white man in sight, and if you don't hike out of range I'll kill you, too," Bill growled.

Starr had noticed that on several occasions when Cherokee's old mother came to see him, Bill had sat all the time with his arm around her. He loved his mother and she was probably the only person on

---

From *Hands Up!* Stories of the Six-Gun Fighters of the Old Wild West, as told by Fred E. Sutton and written down by A. B. McDonald, pp. 161–166. Copyright, 1927, by the Bobbs-Merrill Company. Indianapolis and New York.

earth he had any regard for. There is a soft spot in every man's heart, somewhere, if you only know where to find it, and Bill's soft spot was his love for his mother.

"Bill," called Starr, "you know your mother wouldn't want you to kill any more men than you've already killed. Don't make it any harder for her."

Bill handed his six-shooter to Starr and surrendered to him. Bill was tried at once for the murder of the guard, and was convicted. I was in court when Judge Parker sentenced Cherokee Bill a second time to be hanged. It was a hair-raising denouncement, and I could almost repeat it from memory but it would be too lengthy to reproduce here. Among the things Judge Parker said, as I recall them, were:

"You are a double-dyed monster. Behind you lies a long red wake of human gore. Your hands are steeped in it and your heart reeks with infamy. With hideous mien you stood at bay and fired shot after shot at the brave officers who gathered to control you, and now you come here, with this long list of murders behind you, that should cause even the imps of hell to shudder, and ask mercy from this court. Mercy! Mercy! You most ferocious of monsters, you plead for mercy, you, a creature whose very existence is a disgrace upon nature, a grievous burden to the atmosphere from which you draw breath! Away with you, you most fiendish of all monsters. Life is to you but a hollow mockery. Why should you plead for life? Away with creatures of your ilk, not fit to exist upon this fair land. It is too bad that you have only one life the law can take, otherwise you would be hanged thirteen times, once for each of the murders you have done.

"May the Good Giver of all forbid that ever another such creature as you should be given the breath of life. Better that you should have been strangled at birth than that you should ever have arrived at the age we call manhood, which you have desecrated until all nature points the finger of scorn toward those responsible for your having been born."

Bill's mother sat beside him in the court room and heard it all, and she followed him to the scaffold. She was not permitted to accompany him in his death walk from cell to gallows, but as he stood on the trap, with Maledon strapping his ankles together, he looked out and saw his mother in the crowd.

"Mother, you shouldn't have come here," he called to her.

"I can go wherever you go, Billy," she called back.

"Do you want to say anything to the crowd?" asked the hangman.

"No, I didn't come here to windjam; I come to die," was the answer.

When they cut down his body they found under his blouse a photograph of his mother, lying over his heart, and upon the back he had scrawled a verse of his own composition:

MY DREAM

I drempt I was in heaven, among the angels fair,
I'd near seen none so hansome, that twine in golden hair.
They look so neat and sang so sweet,
And playd the golden harp; I was about to pick an angel out,
And take her to my heart.
But the moment I begun to plea, I thought of you my love,
There was none Id seen so beautiful, on earth or heaven above,
Forgive me, mother, mother dear, I hope my dream comes true,
And we will meet on golden street and happy be with you.

The photograph, with the verse on the back, was given to Cherokee Bill's mother. She called at the jail to see Henry Starr and showed it to him. The bandit read it, returned it to her and said earnestly, "Bury it with him. When God sees it maybe He'll take him in."

Belle Starr, the Outlaw Queen

. . . [Belle Starr] rode the ranges of northwest Texas, the Oklahoma and Texas Panhandles with as thoroughgoing a group of desperadoes and cut-throats as ever missed a deserved national celebrity. Jim French, the Blue Duck, and Jack Spaniard were their leaders, but fugitives from border justice, highwaymen whose gangs had been decimated by prison sentences, temperamental half-breeds from the reservations, dangerously Americanized Mexicans from New Mexico and cowboys gone wrong through rustling often swelled their numbers to nearly fifty. They picked up mavericks in the Atascosa territory, rustled stampeded cattle from the trail drivers on their way to the Kansas shipping points, plied [her late husband] Jim Reed's old specialty of stealing horses from the Indians, held up cow-town banks occasionally, and did a little road agentry on the stage routes. In general they lived by villainy and, so far as the circumstances of the frontier would permit, lived well. They seem to have maintained some contact, or at least an hospitable acquaintance, with what was left of the Younger and Sam Bass gangs of train robbers.

From *Calamity Jane and the Lady Wildcats,* by Duncan Aikman, pp. 194–206. Copyright, 1927, by Duncan Aikman. New York: Henry Holt and Company.

Cf. Burton Rascoe (Deputy Sheriff of Pottawatomie County, Shawnee, Oklahoma), *Belle Starr,* "The Bandit Queen," The True Story of the Romantic and Exciting Career of the Daring and Glamorous Lady Famed in Legend and Story throughout the West as the Beautiful Girl Who Would Never Have Went Wrong if Things Hadn't Gone Wrong, The True Facts about the Dastardly Deeds and the Come-Uppence of Such Dick Turpins, Robin Hoods, and Rini Rinaldos as the Youngers, the Jameses, the Daltons, the Starrs, the Doolins, and the Jenningses, The Real Story with Court Records and Contemporary Newspaper Accounts and Testimony of Old Nesters, Here and There, in the Southwest, A Veritable Exposee of Badmen and Marshals and Why Crime Does Not Pay! (New York, 1941).

Belle's own activities with such a remote and secretive troupe are necessarily somewhat apocryphal. She dominated them a good deal by the force of her will and her proud, increasingly harsh personality. Her reserve made the boisterous keep their distance, and if any of the gang enjoyed her favors, it was by her wish, not theirs. Her commanding airs and her great lady's pose made them rustle to do the hard work of the camp for her so that when she did her share occasionally and with a certain suffering ostentation, she gained credit for immense condescensions. Her shrewdness and her astonishing literacy got her standing, if not as a leader of active operations, at least as the outfit's brains.

She knew, too, how to use her sophistication with frontier harshness sparingly enough to make it effective. Weeks would go by without her indulgence in a word or action unworthy of the first lady of Carthage. But when her hat blew off on a cross country gallop with the Blue Duck and that scorner of empty mannerisms failed to repair the mishap, he found himself looking down the widow Reed's revolver. "Now, damn your greasy hide," she threatened him. "You pick up that hat, and let this be a lesson in how to treat a lady that you won't forget!" By the gang's traditions, the Blue Duck never failed in courtesy afterward.

He had reason not to, for Belle shortly paid him more than handsomely for his condescension. The Blue Duck, on one of their Indian Territory expeditions, borrowed $2,000.00 from the outfit's temporarily flush treasury and lost it in a poker game at Fort Dodge. Belle sympathized with his suspicion that such an expert could not have been deprived of a fortune honestly. Next day, with a gun in each hand, she strolled into the gambling house and raided the pot for $7,000.00 "There's a little change due one of my friends, gentlemen," she informed them with a flash of her most charming irony. "If you want it back, come down to the territory and get it."

To this period, too, belongs the legend of her descent on a prosperous cow country seat in the character of a genteel Southern widow seeking investment opportunities. She charmed all with her accomplishments and cultivated manners. At the end of the week she had removed from the hotel and taken up her quarters as the guest of the banker's wife.

Then one afternoon the banker himself, sitting in his office in conference with her on the business outlook, was alarmed to observe that he was covered by her pistol. Still covered, he obligingly unlocked the safe, handed over its contents and submitted to binding and gagging. Mrs. Reed rode off into the safe prairie darkness. By next morning, when the banker returned to his home and was still trying to convince a suspicious wife that it was after all not so bad as an elopement, the assets were safe in the gang's treasury.

But the law, having settled with Sam Bass and the James family, was ready to close in on the Blue Duck and Jack Spaniard. With her usual shrewdness, Belle saw the portents and retired for a vacation to her late husband's recreation ground at the Starr ranch in the Cherokee country. Even here danger threatened, or perhaps the charming Sam Starr opened her eyes to the pleasing opportunities for rustling near the thriving new cow town of Ogallala, Nebraska. Here they went early in 1880. When they came back a year and a half later, urged, it is said, by neighborhood suspicions that their herds were increasing by more means than breeding and purchase, they were married.

In a remote spot on the Canadian river, eight miles from the post-office of Eufaula, the Starrs located a thousand-acre claim and settled down to a life of what, for the Indian country, passed as social leadership. They brought Pearl there with her exciting vestiges of stage child's coquetry. The hostess, prospering from her years with the Blue Duck in Nebraska, ordered sumptuous wardrobes from the St. Louis department stores. From somewhere, too, she acquired the last symbol of frontier cultivation, a piano.

The cabin was plain, with puncheon floor and calico print nailed over its log partitions for wall paper. Buffalo horns and deer antlers did duty for its interior decorations, instead of old masters, more creditably still, instead of Indian Territory store chromos. But chance visitors, always easily impressed in the '80s, marveled at the tastily chosen bric-a-brac on the rustic mantel. And if we are to believe a lady's most plausible biographer, the intellectual tastes of John Shirley, the first gentleman of Carthage, were represented by rows of books "of a sort as are seen in the best libraries."

Now and then, the chatelaine left her half-breed husband and her rustically charming daughter to visit, it was represented, the popular eastern watering places; likewise, as the biographer puts it, to "spend money lavishly and mingle freely with the wealth and culture of the nation." Once, at White Sulphur Springs, it is insisted that her playing of doleful ante-bellum popular airs on the piano charmed a circle of old Confederate ladies from Richmond into tears.

Did she really? Or was it simply that Indian Territory admiration could not contemplate the occasional mysterious absence of such splendor without explaining it in folklore?

The best authenticated Eastern visit, however, was not to a fashionable watering place or so mysteriously overlaid with tradition. "Now, Pearl," Belle wrote to her daughter in 1883 in one of the most genteelly persuasive explanations of a sentence to a reformatory yet penned west of the Mississippi, "there is a vast difference in that place and a penitentiary; you must bear that in mind and not think of mama being shut up in a gloomy prison."

It is said to be one of the finest institutions in the United States, surrounded by beautiful grounds, with fountains and everything nice. There I can have my education renewed, and I stand greatly in need of it. Sam will have to attend school and I think it will be the best thing that ever happened for him. And now you must not be unhappy and brood over our absence. It won't take the time long to glide by and as we come home we will get you, and then we will have such a nice time.

The institution thus eulogized was the Detroit House of Correction. Belle and Sam were sentenced to it, as often ironically happens to famous desperadoes, for a mere peccadillo. The heroine of bank raids, rustling by the herd, and at least one possible killing of a sheriff, fell before the federal courts at last for stealing a lone colt.

It was not, they insisted, even their theft. A plotting enemy, a former federal marshal, had publicly advised them to steal it, so the alibi ran, to avenge themselves on a neighbor who had killed their best stallion. Then, having shrewdly pointed suspicion, the wretch stole it himself and only turned the animal loose in the Starr pasture when his own guilt was about to come out. The court, however, either held that possession of a stolen article was nine points of a conviction, or that the Starrs deserved some punishment for their reputation. They went north with the spring batch of prisoners.

Belle took the blow with her usual nobleness. She was pale and gently proud with the court, haughtily contemptuous of newspaper reporters. At the House of Correction her dignified pathos was all but ravishing.

The warden, preparing to instruct her in her duties in the prison factory, invited her to "Take a chair, please." His meaning was for the new inmate to pick up a chair frame and follow him into the work-room where women prisoners were putting the cane seats in place. But Belle replied with a weary sadness: "No, in this place, I think I should stand, thanks." When her social error was tactfully explained to her, she smiled tenderly and reproached herself for her thoughtlessness.

At such graceful tactics the warden melted and placed her on the lightest work available. The matron wept over the charming wardrobe from the St. Louis department stores when it was replaced by the prison uniforms, talked current literature with her charge in off hours, and urged her to write a book about "the pleasant sides of work house life." Belle returned after nine months with a justifiable sense of having secured a new social triumph.

Unfortunately, she took out her expanded assurance on the luckless Pearl, now, by Territory standards, of marriageable age. With her accomplishments, distinguished ancestry and gentle breeding, Pearl, it was decided, must have nothing less than a "$25,000.00 man" and Belle adopted the methods of all aggressive dowagers in seeing to it that she got him.

A youth of otherwise eligible qualifications appeared without the required minimum and was haughtily sent packing. But he hung around the neighborhood and Belle, resorting to maternal stratagem, thoughtfully sent him a note, signed Pearl, announcing that a $25,-000.00 suitor (as yet wholly fictitious) had arrived and been accepted. The spurned youth took his dismissal philosophically and departed to marry as best he could on the rebound.

But unfortunately for Cherokee Strip social advancements, the territory was given to gigantic neighborhood picnics. At one of these a year afterward the suitor appeared and was horrified to discover Pearl without the $25,000.00 husband. Explanations followed, mutual condolences, and also seduction. Belle promptly chased the guilty bridegroom out of the country with a flourish of six-shooters. By almost equally ferocious tactics she secured Pearl's consent to a marriage with an infatuated livery stable proprietor worth considerably less than $25,000.00.

But her poise was weakening. Sam's position in the criminal records grew seriously embarrassing. He had to spend most of 1885 in New Mexico dodging warrants for a postoffice robbery. When he came back he was first shot up by a posse and then, after he had been arrested and his bond comfortably arranged, shot again in a quarrel over the ownership of his horse at a dance in Whitefield.

The neighborhood, too, was filling up with white settlers bringing with them the conventions which had punished her at Dallas. What with the family's disorderly notoriety and Pearl's public disgrace, he glamor was becoming every month less and less that of a wilderne social arbitress and more that of a common hell cat's. An acquitta on a horse-stealing charge in 1886, on no better alibi than she hac had three years previously, was received by the neighborhood with more signs of annoyance than of sympathy. Even when, in the roughriding exhibition at the Sebastian County fair in 1887, she picked up the editor of the local newspaper with a wild swoop from the saddle, the crowd which once had feared and paid homage, merely jeered.

She was getting fat, dowdy, shrewish-tempered, and, worst of all, she was losing her discretion. In 1888 a sinisterly genteel person named Edgar Watson came in vaguely from the southeast with his wife to become the Starrs' tenant. In womanly confidences, Belle wormed it out of the woman that Watson was wanted on a murder charge in Florida.

In the days of her skill at man management the mere possession of this secret would have enabled her to attach Watson to her enterprises as long as she had use of him. She used it now merely to inflame a silly quarrel. Watson took a letter for her at the Eufaula postoffice and forgot to deliver it. When it turned up a few weeks later she refused his explanations and treated him as a wilful mail robber. His natural retort was to taunt her with Sam's still-pending embarrassment over the postoffice burglary.

"I don't suppose the federal officers would trouble you," she crushed him, "but the Florida officers might."

For the terrorized Mr. Watson the threat was too much. Alone, so that no effective witnesses could be summoned against him, he ambushed her near his house while she was returning from the trial of one of Sam's cousins for the family vice—horse stealing. He knocked her off her saddle with a charge of turkey-shot. When she was safely on the ground, unconscious, he removed her own weapons and shot her again in the neck and breast until she died.

It was on her forty-third birthday. But one suspects that she had already learned all that she cared to know of what a woman may get by taking life with the high hand.

"I'm Calamity Jane"

. . . One finds her crowning legend of 1872 entirely unplausible. The cavalry, by this lurid piece of "autobiography," were attacking a Nez Perce village. Jane in her scout's trappings joined in the charge with Captain "Pat" Egan's company. The charge had wheeled back, with the captain, as became a military leader posing for the steel engraving artists, turning last.

At this crucial moment, his horse fell dead with a dozen bullet wounds and the captain lay pinned under its flank with a hundred war-painted braves rushing forward to make him prisoner. Jane whirled her horse, beat them to him, helped the captain free himself and mount behind her. Together they galloped away in a haze of Nez Perce missiles with the captain orating gratefully: "Jane, you're a wonderful little woman to have around in times of calamity. From now on your name's Calamity Jane."

Unfortunately, this epic has fatal discrepancies. Not a single old soldier that I have been able to find who served in the Indian armies with Egan ever heard of it until years afterward. The captain himself, a fighting Celt who pronounced his name with the accent on the last syllable and was given to indulging all emotions explosively, including gratitude, is never quoted as referring to it in all the scores of pages which eye-witness chroniclers of the Indian campaigns devoted to his colorful personality. There is no record of a charge attack by his troop on an Indian village in 1872. When Captain Egan did charge a Sioux camp in the dead of winter several years later, two authors of Indian war books riding with him, one of them bridle to bridle, did not observe that he was even for an instant put out of the combat or required a rescuer.

In fact, the only traceable relation between Calamity and the captain

---

Ibid., pp. 64–69.

occurred nearly four years later when Jane and a rare girl friend after her own heart borrowed cavalry uniforms for a few weeks at Fort Laramie and went about enjoying the novelties of barrack life and performing the necessary military courtesies. But the explosive Captain "Pat" was so far from feeling gratitude that he was overwhelmed with a profane chagrin to discover that he had spent a week returning the scandalous salutes of "a couple of God-damned chippies." He enthusiastically issued orders to have his "rescuer" chased off the reservation and not a single growl was heard in the barracks, by the best surviving recollections, that he owed her better treatment. The simple fact begins to appear that Jane, despite her talents and her amiabilities, was more the celebrity than the historian.

Yet in these years she acquired her name somehow. There are almost as many explanations as there are old-timers. Calamity was associated with her because she carried guns ostentatiously and was given to inviting it; because she suffered several successive buggy-smashing accidents in Cheyenne and was considered unlucky; because she bashed the heads of various insufficiently ardent lovers and a peace officer or two and therefore might be considered to bring it with her; because of her bedraggled and notoriously down-at-the-heels appearance when returning from her trail expeditions or in liquor; because in the cow towns she had found the charming epithet on an inconspicuous dance-house girl, otherwise named Grace or Polly or Annie, and had basely appropriated it; because her lovers, sometimes miscalled husbands, developed habits of dying violently.

At any rate, she seems to have secured public consent to her acquisition by the time she discouraged Darling Bob's pornographic allusions in Dodge City,[1] within a year after she had been merely Allegheny Dick's charming daughter and the prairie queen. Self-invented or however bestowed, she was shrewd enough to grasp the name's merit. Pickhandle Nan, Madame Moustache, Kitty the Schemer, Rowdy Kate —in an era of grotesque nomenclature these were amusing enough. But Calamity Jane had a macabre splendor all its own and beyond them, undertones of violence and defiance, of gunplay and delirium tremens, of prairie thunder, mountain whisky, hell, high water, and sudden death, that the best of the others lacked.

She rolled it on her tongue, she screeched it, tumbled it out with a mouthful of oaths in melodramatic contralto, and obviously loved it. "I'm Calamity Jane and this drink's on the house," she howled at hesitating Wyoming bartenders. "I'm Calamity Jane. Get to hell out of here and let me alone," were her first proud words when awakened

---

[1] In Dodge City about 1872, in the presence of reputable and sober witnesses, a cowboy ballad singer, with the insinuating name of Darling Bob Mackay, presumed on his talents for the risqué and asked her an intimate question concerning her lower lingerie. She filled the air with shrill and slightly obscene rebukes for his bawdiness, and his sombrero with warning bullets.—D.A., *ibid.*, p. 63.

from a somewhat unlady-like stupor in a Cheyenne woodshed. "I'm Calamity Jane and I sleep when and where I damn please," she informed a conventional young man from the East who returned to his quarters in an impeccable Cheyenne rooming house one Sunday afternoon in 1873 to find her stretched out in full bullwhacker's toggery on his otherwise inviolate couch. "Calam's here," the crowd roared in the Cheyenne dance house and the intermission gayeties of McDaniel's Theater. "You bet Calam's here," would come back the squaw-like war-whoop coupled with invocations to the sons of all the indignities. "Now let her rip."

Such a name itself conferred privileges, lustre. Celebrity, flamboyance, notoriety would grow up around it even if she did not trouble to invent legends herself. If one was to pose as the feminine divinity of Western wildness, there was nothing like beginning as a walking slogan.

The Hunting of Harry Tracy

Through the chilly gray dawn, the column of prisoners in striped uniforms lockstepped their way across the yard of the Salem, Oregon, penitentiary. It was June 9, 1902. At the entrance to the prison foundry building, the men were lined up against the wall and counted by Guards Ferrell and Girard.

"All accounted for," Girard called out. Ferrell nodded and began to walk to the head of the column. Suddenly one of the prisoners jumped out of the line and yanked a sawed-off Winchester rifle from beneath his jacket. Girard shouted a warning and Ferrell whirled around. The rifle barked and Ferrell fell, a bullet through his brain.

Harry Tracy, the Hole in the Wall rider who defied the posse in the windy pass nearly five years before, fired a second shot at Girard, but missed. David Merrill, who teamed up with Tracy after David Lant left for Wyoming, jumped to his side, also armed with a sawed-off Winchester. A lifer grabbed Tracy's weapon but was shot down by Merrill.

The prisoners began shouting and milling about the yard, and in the confusion both convicts scaled the wall by means of a convenient ladder. Once over they engaged the guards on the top of the wooden

---

From *Desperate Men,* Revelations from the Sealed Pinkerton Files, by James D. Horan, pp. 260–269. Copyright, 1949, 1951, by James D. Horan. New York: G. P. Putnam's Sons.

My source for the hunting of Harry Tracy was the dispatches published in the *New York Morning World* from its anonymous correspondent. But it was impossible to pass up without reading "The Hunting of Harry Tracy," written by that old master of the Western story, William MacLeod Raine, and published in *Wide World* magazine about the turn of the century.—J.D.H., *ibid.,* p. xiv.

stockade. Tracy selected one in the northeast corner. The man was dead before he reached the ground. Another fell, wounded in the right lung and stomach. He died a few minutes later. A third began firing but was shot in the shoulder and toppled from the wall. Tracy dragged him to his feet, and using him as a human shield broke through the outer gate. At the edge of the nearby forest Merrill pointed to the wounded guard.

"What about him?"

"This," Tracy replied and killed the helpless man. A few minutes later the fugitives vanished in the thick underbrush.

Back at the Salem penitentiary the prison population was in an uproar with armed guards herding the convicts back into their cells.

The sirens were wailing and telegraph and telephone lines humming with news of the break. America's greatest manhunt had begun.

The first day of their escape, Tracy and Merrill lay in the woods not far from the penitentiary. At dawn the following day, June 10, they entered the outskirts of Salem, robbed two men of their clothes, horses, and six-shooters, and headed for Portland. Bloodhounds sent from Washington State Penitentiary picked up their trail and a posse started in pursuit. Two law officers in a buggy who were far ahead of the baying hounds were waylaid on a lonely road by the convicts "who relieved them of their buggy and bade them a cheery good morning."

A few hours later they drove down the main street of the little town of Gervais in the stolen carriage with Tracy nodding and bowing to the flustered ladies who wondered who the stranger in the baggy blue suit might be.

On June 11, Tracy and Merrill abandoned the buggy a few miles from Gervais and disappeared in the forest. They were surrounded by a fifty-man posse but blasted their way free. A cordon was thrown about the countryside and "every man within a radius of ten miles who owns a gun" was ordered to join the posse.

But during the night Tracy and Merrill escaped after first holding up two more deputies and stealing their revolvers. The governor of Oregon ordered the state militia to join the manhunt, and two hundred and fifty soldiers arrived on the scene to reinforce the line.

Pulitzer's *New York Morning World* in a special dispatch declared: "A spokesman for the man hunters predicted tonight that Tracy is so hemmed in he will be caught within a few hours."

The announcement was premature.

By the morning it was discovered that Tracy and Merrill had broken through the cordon.

On June 14, they reached the outskirts of Portland, stole two horses, and forced a farmer's wife to cook them breakfast. Then they galloped along the countryside to the Columbia River. There they found a man painting a boat and forced him to drop his paintbrush and row them across the river to Washington. They dined at another farmhouse and bound and gagged their host. The bloodhounds were soon baying in the distance and Tracy ordered a stand made, the two men fighting off a force of nearly a hundred men and again escaping uninjured.

After the fight the pair swam the river and worked through the fields to Ridgefield, where they stole horses and forced other farmers and their wives to feed them.

On the evening of June 29, Tracy and Merrill again shot their way past a roadblock near Chehalis, Oregon. The next day they were seen on the Northern Pacific Railroad at Tenino, about forty miles from Tacoma. That was the last sight of David Merrill alive.

The entire Northwest was now in a state of alarm. Oregon's governor ordered the reward raised to eight thousand dollars, and the posses were told, "Shoot to kill on sight."

On July 2, Tracy swaggered onto the stage alone. The sun was breaking through the mist which hung over South Bay near Olympia, the state capital, when a haggard-looking man in a stained blue suit, unshaven and red-eyed, walked into the headquarters of an oyster fishing company. He forced the eight men in the building to line up against the wall and selected two to fix him some breakfast.

"I'm Tracy," he said. "Be quiet and you won't be harmed."

After a leisurely breakfast he tied the two impromptu cooks to chairs and gagged them. He herded the six others down the dock and pointed to a large gasoline launch.

"Who is the captain?" he asked.

"Captain Clark," he was told.

"Get him here and no monkey business."

In a few minutes Captain Clark and his son appeared. Tracy nodded to the launch.

"Get in."

One look into the granite-hard eyes was enough to convince Captain Clark. He climbed into the cabin, followed by his son and the six other men.

"Where to?" Clark asked.

Tracy grinned. "Seattle."

The outlaw took a seat in the corner of the tiny cabin, the rifle across his knees and the butts of two revolvers sticking out of his belt. During the twelve-hour journey he joked with the frightened men sitting in a semi-circle before him and commented on the weather. Once some one inquired, "Where is Merrill, Tracy?"

Tracy's face set. "I killed him."

After a brief interval of silence the outlaw added: "He had no nerve. During my trial he testified against me. He was scared to death most of the time. When I called him a coward, he became huffy, so we decided on a duel. We were to start back to back and walk ten paces. I knew he was going to cheat, so after eight paces I turned and fired. The first shot didn't do the job, so I shot him again."

There were no more questions.

Once when the launch was in sight of McNeil's Island, Tracy gestured with the rifle in the direction of the military prison. "Run the boat over there."

"For God's sake, why?" Captain Clark asked.

"I want to pick off a few guards from the walls," Tracy replied calmly.

Captain Clark quickly pointed out that they would surely be fired upon, and the outlaw reluctantly changed his mind.

At Meadow Point, near Seattle, Tracy ordered the launch docked. He tied and gagged Captain Clark and the crew, but forced one of the men to act as his guide. Late that night he released him. The fugitive made his way to the outskirts of Bothell and lay hidden under some logs in a driving downpour until morning. Later that day he encountered a twenty-two man posse and fought them to a standstill, killing one, a deputy sheriff, and wounding three others. He narrowly missed killing a newspaper man, Louie B. Sefrit of the *Seattle Times*.

The gun battle took place in a weed-choked yard before two small cabins. Three deputies scaled the rusty barbed-wire fence and began beating their way through the high grass and tree stumps. Tracy suddenly rose from behind a stump. He fired twice and two deputies fell. Reporter Sefrit pegged a shot with his Colt and Tracy turned to him. Bullets whistled overhead and the newsman wisely fell, feigning a mortal wound. From where he lay he could see Tracy peering at him through the rain. After a few minutes the fugitive began to back away. Another posse-man, scaling the fence, saw him and yelled. The Winchester roared again and the man fell dead in the grass. Still firing, the outlaw scurried through the thick underbrush and vanished.

A mile outside of Bothell, Tracy relieved a rancher of his horse, telling him he "needed it in a hurry." The owner tried to stop him and Tracy, probably to save ammunition, bashed out his brains with a gun butt. On the way to Seattle he stopped another farmer, Louis Johnson, in a wagon, and made him drive to Woodland Park, a suburb of Seattle. By this time Tracy was hungry and ordered the team tied outside the farmhouse of Mrs. R. H. Van Horn.

The farm woman answered his knock.

"I'm Tracy," the outlaw said, introducing himself. "I would like some food. Be quiet and no harm will come to you."

The frightened woman ushered him and Johnson into the kitchen. "This is hard work, dodging those posses," Tracy said calmly. He took off his coat and slumped in a chair. "You know," he added as Mrs. Van Horn began preparing the meal, "this is the first time I ever held up a woman. I don't like to tie or gag you so will you please promise not to say anything about my being here?"

"For to-night I will—but not tomorrow," the plucky woman replied.

The outlaw nodded. "Agreed. By to-morrow I will be so far away it won't make any difference."

As he ate, Tracy described his "yachting trip" as "very nice," but said that he was "disappointed" that he didn't have an opportunity of "knocking a few of the guards from the walls" at McNeil's Island.

A neighbor dropped by with a pail of milk and Tracy took his dry clothing. At about eight o'clock that evening there was a knock on the door. Tracy jumped to his feet. With a revolver he motioned to Johnson and the neighbor.

"Say anything and I will kill you."

Mrs. Van Horn nodded and went to the door. It was the butcher boy. As she paid her bill she managed to mouth the word "Tracy." The startled boy understood and ran down the road. The farm woman returned to the kitchen, sat at a table, and nonchalantly added her bill. Tracy watched her through narrowed eyes. Satisfied, he returned to his chair to joke with his two prisoners.

The butcher boy, meanwhile, had sounded the alarm, and a posse surrounded the house. Three men wormed their way through the bushes and lay in wait less than six feet from Johnson's wagon.

At about ten o'clock, Tracy yawned, and, thanking Mrs. Van Horn "most courteously" for the meal, stepped down the path using the two men as a shield. The rifles of the posse covered him every inch of the way, but at an order from the sheriff held their fire until Tracy climbed into the wagon alone.

Three members of the posse sprang to their feet and ran toward Tracy. Suddenly one shouted, "Throw down your arms, Tracy."

The outlaw spun around and fired several shots in rapid succession at the moving shadows. His incredible marksmanship was effective.

In its account of the shooting, the *New York Morning World* correspondent wrote:

> One of the dead men was shot in the face, in the shoulder, and in the breast. His left arm was also shattered. His body bore eloquent evidence of Tracy's magnificent marksmanship. After he had killed Policeman Breece he dropped on one knee and taking deliberate aim in the darkness put a bullet through the heart of Game Warden Rawley. Deputy Sheriff John Williams was Tracy's next victim. The bullet struck his rifle and, passing through his breast, killed him.

The posse fired several rounds at Tracy, but the outlaw scaled a fence and disappeared into the night.

For days Tracy roamed the countryside. He held up another farmhouse and forced a hired hand by the name of Anderson to become his pack horse. He next appeared at a logging camp "more dead than alive," as the *World* reporter declared, and ordered the men in the camp "to cook him a meal and supply him with provisions." Later that night he vanished in the darkness with Anderson carrying the supplies—after warning the loggers not to sound an alarm "for an hour or two."

The next heard of Tracy was at Renton where he compelled a family to shelter him and his human pack horse for the evening and to cook him a meal.

"I'm Tracy," he told the farm woman. "I suppose you heard of me. But don't be afraid. I never harmed a woman in my life."

That evening, rifle in hand, he went down to the spring and filled a bucket. He came back grinning. He told the family he had spotted the special train coming down the tracks loaded with possemen.

"I reckon there were some men on that train looking for me," he said in mock surprise.

While the small army of law officers crawled cautiously through the brush surrounding the farmhouse, Tracy insisted that the afternoon meal be served. He was completely at ease, telling jokes and describing the highlights of his escape. Once he rose and looked out the window.

"It's a shame that my trousers are unironed with so many ladies here," he said when he returned to the dinner table. "Perhaps I had better go out and capture a deputy."

When one of the ladies in the house said that she was frightened to go home alone, Tracy chivalrously volunteered to accompany her, pointing out that any man could call himself lucky if he had a chance to escort a charming lady home in the moonlight.

It was late afternoon when Tracy decided that he must leave. Again and again he thanked his unwilling hostess, wished every one happiness and luck, and then opened the front door. At that moment the unfortunate Anderson was discovered tied like a mule to a tree and the posse broke their lines and began running toward the spot. Tracy walked through the woods and, when he was grabbed by two deputies in the gathering gloom, escaped by informing them, "I'm a newspaper reporter." He was released with a warning to "be on the lookout."

Bloodhounds were again put on his trail, as the *World* correspondent reports, but he threw them off by scattering red pepper behind him and made his way into Seattle where he spent a night of revelry with two crooks who were also fugitives from the law.

The following week he entered a country store and called a nearby sheriff on the telephone.

"This is Tracy," he said. "I just wanted you to know I'm still around." When the law officer began sputtering, the outlaw told him, "Don't feel too bad. You've done much better than the other sheriffs. At least you spoke to the man you were after. Good-by."

Weeks later he showed up in eastern Washington headed for Hole in the Wall. He came upon A. B. Shruer, who was hunting deer, and ordered him to throw up his hands. Shruer, believing it was a joke, refused, and Tracy, not in a joking mood, fired a warning shot. The powder blast burned the hunter's hands.

"I'm sorry I hurt you," he said, "but when I say throw up your hands, I mean it."

The desperado walked over to the fire and examined the food cooking in a small pot. "I'm hungry," he said, and squatting down, began picking out bits of meat. "Come on," he invited Shruer, "have some supper."

After he had finished eating, the fugitive scanned the sky. "I guess it's going to rain." After he had disarmed Shruer, he said "goodnight" and disappeared into the woods.

The *New York World,* which told the story explained unnecessarily: "Mr. Shruer did not attempt to detain him."

For days there was no news of Tracy. Then he was sighted in a small sloop riding the treacherous waters off Deception Pass in Puget Sound. Again the manhunt was in full swing. Instead of horses, bloodhounds, and carriages, the posse took to revenue cutters, gasoline launches, and steamers.

"The war against Tracy, the outlaw, is now a naval war," the *New York World* correspondent declared. "Two steamers, the revenue cutter *Grant* and the *Scout,* are on the sound with three posses embracing some of the most noted manhunters in the entire West. All the towns are ready for him with posses trying to head him from the Olympia mountain country. 'If he gets there,' one deputy said, 'his leave on liberty will be a long one.' The mountainous country in that section is densely wooded and terribly precipitous."

After a twenty-four hour search covering one hundred and twenty-five miles of the sound and its adjacent area, the weary posse returned to Seattle. Tracy had again made good his escape.

The cutters patrolled the sound and the bloodhounds bayed helplessly. Tracy vanished. It was thought that he had made his way to Hole in the Wall, but he suddenly appeared in a running gun battle with a farmer and his son. He was wounded in the right hip and took refuge in a dense swamp. How long this incredible man stayed there is not known. It must have been a terrifying ordeal splashing through the scummy water, eaten alive by the clouds of mosquitoes, hungry and thirsty and the wound in his hip like a white-hot coal.

He emerged at last to find food and slept one night in a barn. He was discovered and had to shoot his way through a sheriff's posse. That same afternoon he "exchanged shots" with another band of manhunters and escaped by jumping aboard a passing freight train.

A few days later, according to the *New York World,* "he met a man on a road and told him that his wound was bothering him a great deal."

In August, Tracy reached the country south of the Colville Indian Reservation. He was exhausted and vicious as a wounded wolf. He was spotted on a ranch a few miles from Creston, Oregon, and the telephone summoned a posse of Lincoln County citizens.

He broke out of a trap and began to move down a broad valley, pausing now and then to exchange shots with his pursuers. The duel lasted most of the afternoon and, as the purple twilight closed in, the exhausted fugitive made a stand behind a large boulder. He fired several times at the deputies who dodged from rock to rock but, owing to the gathering darkness and his exhausted condition, missed each time. The posse began a flanking movement and Tracy made a dash for a nearby wheat field. Several rifles barked almost in unison. The outlaw stumbled and fell but dragged himself foot by foot into the field as the bullets thudded in the ground on all sides.

A second posse arrived and the field was completely surrounded. In the silence a shot rang out. The manhunters waited all that night, peering anxiously through the tense blackness. When the sun came up, the wave of men moved across the field foot by foot. Tracy was found with a bullet hole in his right temple, the revolver still clutched in his hand. The most famous manhunt in America's criminal history had ended.

Mustang Gray

The tenacious-memoried Dolph Quinn, of Beeville, Texas, whose father was such an ardent Mustang Gray man that he named his first-born son Mabry Gray, says that, according to his father, . . . "Mustang Gray asked no questions of any Mexican, made no distinction. That a man was a Mexican was enough to arouse his venom; if he had property, so much the worse for him."

For instance, one time Mustang Gray, Pat Quinn, and another "Mustanger" named Andy Walker were in Corpus Christi, when some Mexicans came in with a *caballada* from the Rio Grande. They camped near a mud flat, about where Portland is now. Gray and his companions wanted the horses—and, of course, considered them legitimate prey. They rode to the mud flat, dismounted, pulled off all their clothes, wallowed in the mud, tied *cabestros* (hair ropes) around their foreheads, all to give themselves the appearance of wild Indians, and charged into camp. The Mexicans stampeded in one direction and

---

From "Mustang Gray: Fact, Tradition, and Song," by J. Frank Dobie, *Tone the Bell Easy,* Publications of the Texas Folk-Lore Society, No. X, edited by J. Frank Dobie, pp. 115–121. Copyright, 1932 by the Texas Folk-Lore Society. Austin.

Maberry B. ("Mustang") Gray, came to Texas from South Carolina in 1835 at the age of twenty-one; fought in the battle of San Jacinto; was a leader, for a decade, of the border raiders known as "Cow-boys"; during the Mexican War, served as a lieutenant in a company of Texas Mounted Volunteers, called Rangers; in 1846–47 commanded a company of "Mustangers" or the "Mustang Grays"; and died a year or two after the Mexican War. For the ballad, "Mustang Gray," see Part Six, below.

their horses in another, all except one *viejo* too old to run, who stood his ground and picked up an *escopeta* (blunderbuss). Mustang Gray was in the lead, the loose end of the *cabestro* around his forehead dragging the ground. At the edge of the camp Andy Walker's horse stepped on the rope, jerking Mustang from his mount just as the old Mexican fired. His gun did no damage. Mustang finished him while the other two men scurried after the runaway horses.

Another time Mustang Gray and Walker met two Mexicans at a lake. One of them had a knife that Mustang fancied. He offered to trade a pistol for it. The owner refused. Mustang pulled his pistol—one of the new Colt's. "Here," he said, "try it. Shoot that bird." The Mexican made a motion. Mustang shot him dead. At this the Mexicans' horses scared and ran. Yelling for Walker to secure them, Gray lunged upon the remaining Mexican. When Walker returned, he found the Mexican smothered in mud and water at the edge of the lake.

As long as the *mesteños,* or mustang horses, that used to roam all over the Southwest, but nowhere else in such numbers as between the Nueces and the Rio Grande, are remembered, the story of how Mabry Gray won his name will, I think, be told. The story has been printed more than once.[1] I have heard several men, all scant of detail, tell it.

Soon after coming to Texas, young Gray with some other men went far out from the settlements to hunt buffaloes. In a chase after a bunch of them that scattered and ran Gray became separated from his companions. His horse fell, throwing him to the ground. Gray was uninjured, but when he jumped to his feet he saw the horse, excited by the chase and frightened by the buffaloes, racing rapidly out of sight. For hours Gray wandered about afoot, hoping to catch sight of one of the other hunters. Darkness found him still alone and afoot in the vast solitude.

After a restless night of thirst and anxiety he arose with the dawn to try to retrace his steps. Before long he spied a wounded buffalo in a small thicket. He still had his gun and ammunition, and he quickly killed the animal. Then, having cut off a portion of meat, he turned to look for water. A clump of green guided him to a pond. There he drank, made a fire, cooked the meat, and after he had eaten it, felt fortified. He had wandered about the preceding day so much that he was completely lost; but now he could calmly plan. Around the pond he saw horse tracks—mustangs. He must capture one and ride it to the settlements. But he had no rope or saddle. He could do without the saddle.

About this time he saw a band of mustangs galloping towards the pond. He climbed a tree and watched them pass beneath, paw about,

[1] Jeremiah Clemens, *Mustang Gray,* has a version of it; it is to be found in *Rangers and Pioneers of Texas,* by A. J. Sowell, San Antonio, 1884, pp. 71–76. Using the Sowell version as a basis, I myself included the story, which with a few changes is here reproduced, in *On the Open Range,* Dallas, 1931, pp. 86–88.—J.F.D.

drink, and leave. His plans were made. Of course he carried the customary Bowie knife of the frontier. He returned to the carcass of the buffalo he had killed, skinned it, brought the hide back to the pond, and spent the remainder of the day carving it into a strong reata. All animals have regular hours for watering, and when, next morning, the time approached for the mustangs to come again, Gray tied one end of his reata to a strong limb of the tree over the trail, with the other end of it in hand climbed up, and, loop open, took a position that would give him a clear space in which to swing and cast it. He knew that he would have but one cast, or throw, at the mustangs. He must not miss. He did not miss.

The animal he had selected was a stout stallion. It ran on the rope, threw itself, and still the reata held. It reared, kicked, plunged, but all to no purpose. It was held fast. For a long time Gray worked with the stallion, somewhat accustoming him to the sight and smell and feel of a man. He had made a hackamore (halter) and reins out of some of the buffalo hide, and this he finally adjusted on the mustang's head. Then he managed to get astride. The stallion tore away, but he did not run far until he hit the end of the rope, which was still fastened to the tree, jerking himself down and throwing his rider. After this Gray petted the animal and worked with him some more. At last he felt confident of being able to keep his seat and direct the course of the mustang.

Now he fastened his gun to his own back, untied the reata from the tree, again mounted, headed the mustang towards the settlements, and let him go. The prairie was open without bush or bluff. The wild horse ran for many miles until he was completely exhausted. That night Gray staked him out. A wild horse learns very rapidly to fear a rope; the stallion grazed. The quickest way in the world to tame a wild horse is to ride him off his range into solitude, where he soon comes to depend upon as well as fear his master. On the second morning Gray had little trouble in mounting the mustang and controlling him.

Thus riding bareback, he traveled for several days. Then, quite by accident, he came to the camp of his companion hunters, who had given him up for lost. They at once dubbed him Mustang Gray, and by that name he went until he died.

There are various tales illustrative of how well-trained Mustang's horses were. After the capture of Monterrey, as Pat Quinn used to tell the story, General Worth, acting under orders from Taylor, ordered the city cleared of soldiers—particularly of Texans. When the order was announced, Mustang Gray and other rangers were on the plaza mounted. The plaza was spread with tables used for serving *tamales, enchiladas,* and other food upon. Turning to one of the riders named Thompson, Mustang shouted, "Will your horse take that row of tables?" "Yes." Both rangers started leaping their horses from one table to another. Thompson's crashed through a table, but Mustang rode clear across the plaza—and then, obedient to military orders, out of town. In Clemens' novel, Mustang Gray rides his horse into a gambling hall and makes him place a hoof on a certain card lying upon a deal table. At Goliad, Corpus Christi, or some other place he, as a common story goes, rode his charger up a flight of stairs and into a barroom.

An old Mexican woman living at Goliad, whose ancestors were there long before Moses Austin secured permission to bring English-speaking colonists to Texas, tells this tale.[2] After the Texas Revolution the outlaws were worse around Goliad and Victoria than anywhere else. One day while a good old Mexican priest was saying mass in the mission church of La Bahia, a band of these terrible men from Goliad, across the San Antonio River, entered, and with sombreros on their heads, pistols in their belts, spurs on their heels, and quirts in their hands, strode down the aisle towards the padre, cursing and theatening as they came. Mustang Gray was at their head. The padre paused in his prayers, and, turning to them, requested them to leave the house of God in peace. Perhaps it was the reserve and dignity of the old padre that halted the bandits. Anyhow, they left.

An hour later, all worshipers having withdrawn, the padre closed the church door and set out walking for his home in Goliad. He had not gone far when Mustang Gray and some other bandits stepped out of the brush in which they had been awaiting him and seized him roughly. "Now you are in our house," they taunted, "and must do as we say." They roped him and bound his hands and made him dance to what they called "pistol music." The padre was still dancing to this music and some of the bandits had begun to enliven his jumps with sharp blows of their quirts, when a party of responsible citizens came along. These men quickly overpowered the bandits and freed the priest.

"Now, Father," they said, "these vile wretches are in your power. They deserve to swing from the stoutest live oak tree in Goliad County, and we will do with them whatever you say. You name the punishment and we'll give it."

"Then release them," simply replied the old padre. "Let their consciences be both their accusers and their punishers."

The padre paused, swept his arms toward Goliad, and concluded, "From this day forth may God's curse be upon that town."

And, to conclude with the words of the old Mexican woman of La Bahia, "that is why Goliad, since the time of the padre and Mustang Gray, never has amounted to anything and never will amount to anything."

Of course any man who plundered as often and successfully as Mustang Gray must have accumulated a lot of loot, and of course there is a legend about it. This story of Mustang Gray's morral of gold

[2] Through Kate Stoner O'Connor, of Victoria.—J.F.D.

was told to me by Walter Billingsley, of San Antonio. He heard it, he says, repeated several times by Billy Richards, who lived to be over a hundred years old and died at Rio Grande City about 1920.

Away back yonder during the time of the Texas Republic, Billy Richards and Mustang Gray were riding from the Rio Grande towards Goliad. At Moore Lake, six miles west of San Patricio, they met a band of Mexicans, with whom they got into a row. The result was several dead Mexicans—all in the party—and the transfer of their property to Gray and Richards. The property consisted of horses, saddles, and a morral (fibre bag) containing $16,000 in gold.

They knew where they could trade off the horses, but they did not have any immediate use for the gold. There was no bank to put it in. It would not be safe or convenient, or sensible either, to lug it around. They decided to bury it. A good place for such hiding was the Paso Piedra (Rock Crossing) on the Nueces River, about three miles below San Patricio. They went to Paso Piedra and on the west side of the river dug a shallow hole at the root of a mesquite tree, and buried the morral with the gold in it. They traded off the horses and then the Mexican War came on.

After it was over Billy Richards and Mustang Gray went *pasearing* down to Monterrey—where Mustang Gray had been rescued by a Spanish señorita who loved him. There he took the cholera and died. His body was brought back to Rio Grande City and buried.

Why Richards did not go immediately to Paso Piedra and dig up the money will never be known. Those were troublous times. Perhaps Richards had no immediate use for the money. It was safe in the morral under the ground. Also he was "a peculiar old Texan." However, after a good many years he undertook to find the morral. He could not locate it. He took in old man John Timon, who ranched near San Patricio, to help him hunt. They hunted a lot. Other people have hunted since, among them Walter Billingsley. The gold is still near the old Paso Piedra unless someone has dug it up, or the mesquite tree under which it was buried has caved into the river. There are many, many mesquite trees west of the Nueces.

Sam Bass and the Texas Rangers

After the fight on Salt Creek only Sam Bass, Sebe Barnes, and Frank Jackson were left of the once formidable gang. These men had gained nothing from their three train robberies in northern Texas, and were so hard pressed by the officers of the law on all sides that Bass re-

---

From *Six Years with the Texas Rangers, 1875 to 1881,* by James B. Gillett, edited, with an introduction, by M. M. Quaife, pp. 116–128.

Cf. *A Treasury of American Folklore* (New York, 1944), pp. 114–122.

luctantly decided to leave the country and try to make his way to Mexico. Through some pretended friends of Bass General Jones learned of the contemplated move. He, with Captain Peak and other officers, approached Jim Murphy, one of Bass's gang captured about the time of the Salt Creek fight, who was awaiting trial by the federal authorities for train robbery, and promised they would secure his release if he would betray Bass. Murphy hesitated and said his former chief had been kind to his family, had given them money and provisions, and that it would be ungrateful to betray his friend. The general declared he understood Murphy's position fully, but Bass was an outlaw, a pest to the country, who was preparing to leave the state and so could no longer help him. General Jones warned Murphy that the evidence against him was overwhelming and was certain to send him to federal prison—probably for life—and exhorted him to remember his wife and children. Murphy finally yielded and agreed to betray Bass and his gang at the first opportunity.

According to the plan agreed upon, Murphy was to give bond and when the federal court convened at Tyler, Texas, a few weeks later he was not to show up. It would then be published all over the country that Murphy had skipped bond and rejoined Bass. This was carried out to the letter. Murphy joined Bass in the elm bottoms of Denton County and agreed to rob a train or bank and get out of the country. Some of Bass's friends, suspicious of Murphy's actions, wrote Sam that he was playing a double game and advised him to kill the traitor at once. Bass immediately confronted Murphy with these reports and reminded him how freely he had handed out his gold to Murphy's family. Bass declared he had never advised or solicited Jim to join him, and said it was a low-down, mean, and ungrateful trick to betray him. He told Murphy plainly if he had anything to say to say it quickly. Barnes agreed with his chief and urged Murphy's death.

The plotter denied any intention of betraying Bass and offered to take the lead in any robbery he should plan and be the first to enter the express car or climb over the bank railing. Bass was mad and so was Barnes. They determined to kill the liar at once. Frank Jackson had taken no part in the conversation, but he now declared he had known Murphy since he was a little boy (they were, in fact, cousins), and he was sure Murphy was sincere and meant to stand by them through thick and thin. Bass was not satisfied, and insisted that Murphy be killed then and there. Jackson finally told Bass and Barnes that they could not kill Murphy without first killing him. Although the youngest of the party—he was only twenty-two years old—Jackson had great influence over his chief. He was brave and daring, and Bass at that time could not very well get along without him, so his counsel prevailed and Murphy was spared. The bandits then determined to quit the country. Their plan was to rob a small bank somewhere en route to Mexico and thus secure the funds needed to facilitate their escape, for they were all broke.

Bass, Sebe Barnes, Frank Jackson, and Jim Murphy left Denton County early in July, 1878. With his usual boldness, Bass, after he had passed Dallas County, made no attempt at concealment, but traveled the public highway in broad daylight. Bass and Barnes were still suspicious of Murphy, and never let him out of their sight, though they refused to talk to him or to associate with him in any way. When Bass reached Waco, the party camped on the outskirts of the town and remained there two or three days. They visited the town each day, looked over the situation, and in one bank saw much gold and currency. Jackson was enthusiastic and wanted to rob it at once. Bass, being more careful and experienced, thought it too hazardous an undertaking, for the run through crowded streets to the outskirts of the city was too far, and so vetoed the attempt.

While in Waco the gang stepped into a saloon to get a drink. Bass laid a $20 gold piece on the bar and remarked, "There goes the last twenty of the Union Pacific money, and damned little good it has done me." On leaving Waco the robbers stole a fine mare from a farmer named Billy Mounds and traveled the main road to Belton. They were now out of money and planned to rob the bank at Round Rock, Williamson County.

General Jones was now getting anxious over the gang. Not a word had been heard from Jim Murphy since he had rejoined the band, for he had been so closely watched that he had had no opportunity to communicate with the authorities, and it seemed as if he would be forced to participate in the next robbery in spite of himself.

At Belton, Sam sold an extra pony his party had after stealing the mare at Waco. The purchaser demanded a bill of sale, as the vendors were strangers in the country. While Bass and Barnes were in a store writing out the required document, Murphy seized the opportunity to write a short note to General Jones, saying "We are on our way to Round Rock to rob the bank. For God's sake be there to prevent it." As the postoffice adjoined the store, the traitor succeeded in mailing his letter of betrayal a moment before Bass came out on the street again. The gang continued their way to Round Rock and camped near the old town, which is situated about one mile north of new Round Rock. The bandits concluded to rest and feed their horses for three or four days before attempting their robbery. This delay was providential, for it gave General Jones time to assemble his rangers to repel the attack.

After Major Jones was made adjutant general of Texas he caused a small detachment of four or five rangers to camp on the Capitol grounds at Austin. He drew his units from different companies along the line. Each unit would be detailed to camp in Austin, and about every six weeks or two months the detail would be relieved by a squad from another company. It will readily be seen that this was a wise policy, as the detail was always on hand and could be sent in any direction by rail or on horseback at short notice. Besides, General Jones was devoted to his rangers and liked to have them around where he could see them daily. At the time of which I write four men from Company E—Corporal Vernon Wilson and privates Dick Ware, Chris Connor, and Geo. Harold—were camped at Austin. The corporal, who was a nephew of Governor Coke and a well-educated man, helped General Jones as a clerk in his office, but was in charge of the squad on the Capitol grounds, slept in camp, and had his meals with them.

When General Jones received Murphy's letter he was astonished at Bass's audacity in approaching within fifteen or twenty miles of the state capital, the very headquarters of the Frontier Battalion, to rob a bank. The letter was written at Belton, Texas, and received at the adjutant general's office on the last mail in the afternoon. The company of rangers nearest Round Rock was Lieutenant Reynolds' Company E, stationed at San Saba, one hundred and fifteen miles distant. There was no telegraph to San Saba then. General Jones reflected a few minutes after receipt of the letter and then arranged his plan rapidly.

He turned to Corporal Wilson and told him that Sam Bass and his gang were, or soon would be, at Round Rock, to rob the bank there. "I want you to leave at once to carry an order to Lieutenant Reynolds. It is sixty-five miles to Lampasas and you can make that place early enough in the morning to catch the Lampasas and San Saba stage. You must make that stage at all hazards. Save neither yourself nor your horse, but get these orders to Lieutenant Reynolds as quickly as possible," he ordered.

Corporal Wilson hurried to the livery stable, saddled his horse, and got away from Austin on his wild ride just at nightfall. His horse was fresh and fat and in no condition to make such a run. However, Wilson reached Lampasas at daylight next morning and made the outgoing stage to San Saba, but killed his gallant little gray horse in doing it. From Lampasas to San Saba was fifty miles, and it took the stage, which was a small, two-horse outfit, all day to make the trip. As soon as he landed in town Wilson hired a horse and galloped three miles down to Lieutenant Reynolds' camp and delivered his orders.

After dispatching Corporal Wilson to Lieutenant Reynolds, General Jones hurried over to the ranger camp on the Capitol grounds and ordered the three rangers, Ware, Connor, and Harold, to proceed to Round Rock, put their horses in Highsmith's livery stable, and keep themselves concealed until he himself could reach them by train next morning. The following morning General Jones went to Round Rock accompanied by Morris Moore, an ex-ranger now serving as deputy sheriff of Travis County. On reaching his destination the general called on Deputy Sheriff Grimes of Williamson County and told him Bass was expected in town to rob the bank, and that a scout of rangers would be in town as soon as possible. Jones advised Grimes to keep a sharp lookout for strangers, but on no account to attempt an arrest until the rangers could arrive.

I well remember the hot July evening when Corporal Wilson arrived in our camp with his orders. The company had just had supper, and the horses had been fed and tied up for the night. We knew the sudden appearance of the corporal meant something of unusual importance. Soon Sergeant Nevill came hurrying to us with orders to detail a party for an immediate scout. Lieutenant Reynolds' orders had been brief, but to the point: "Bass at Round Rock. We must be there as early as possible tomorrow. Make a detail of eight men and select those that have the horses best able to make a fast run. And you, with them, report to me here at my tent ready to ride in thirty minutes."

First Sergeant C. L. Nevill, Second Sergeant Henry McGee, Second Corporal J. B. Gillett, Privates Abe Anglin, Dave Ligon, Bill Derrick, and John R. and W. L. Banister were selected for the detail. Lieutenant Reynolds ordered two of our best little pack-mules hitched to a light spring hack, for he had been sick and was not in condition to make the journey horseback. In thirty minutes from the time Corporal Wilson reached camp we were mounted, armed, and ready to go. Lieutenant Reynolds took his seat in the hack, threw some blankets in, and Corporal Wilson, who had not had a minute's sleep for over thirty-six hours, lay down to get a little rest as we moved along. We left our camp on the San Saba River just at sunset and traveled in a fast trot and sometimes in a lope the entire night.

Our old friend and comrade, Jack Martin, then in the mercantile business at the little town of Senterfitt, heard us pass by in the night, and next morning said to some of his customers that hell was to pay somewhere as the rangers had passed his store during the night on a dead run.

The first rays of the rising sun shone on us at the crossing of North Gabriel, fifteen miles south of Lampasas. We had ridden sixty-five miles that short summer night—we had forty-five miles yet to go before reaching Round Rock. We halted on the Gabriel for a breakfast of bread, broiled bacon, and black coffee. The horses had a bundle of oats each. Lieutenant Reynolds held his watch on us and it took us just thirty minutes to breakfast and be off again. We were now facing a hot July sun and our horses were beginning to show the effects of the hard ride of the night before and slowed down perceptibly. We did not halt again until we reached the vicinity of old Round Rock between one and two o'clock in the afternoon of Friday, July nineteenth. The lieutenant camped us on the banks of Brushy Creek and drove into new Round Creek to report his arrival to General Jones.

Bass had decided to rob the bank on Saturday, the twentieth. After his gang had eaten dinner in camp Friday evening they saddled their ponies and started over to town to take a last look at the bank and select a route to follow in leaving the place after the robbery. As they left camp Jim Murphy, knowing that the bandits might be set upon at any time, suggested that he stop at May's store in old Round Rock and get a bushel of corn, as they were out of feed for their horses. Bass, Barnes, and Jackson rode on into town, hitched their horses in an alley just back of the bank, passed that building, and made a mental note of its situation. They then went up the main street of the town and entered Copprel's store to buy some tobacco. As the three bandits passed into the store, Deputy Sheriff Moore, who was standing on the sidewalk with Deputy Sheriff Grimes, said he thought one of the newcomers had a pistol.

"I will go in and see," replied Grimes.

"I believe you have a pistol," remarked Grimes, approaching Bass and trying to search him.

"Yes, of course I have a pistol," said Bass. At the words the robbers pulled their guns and killed Grimes as he backed away to the door. He fell dead on the sidewalk. They then turned on Moore and shot him through the lungs as he attempted to draw his weapon.

At the crack of the first pistol Dick Ware, who was seated in a barber shop only a few steps away waiting his turn for a shave, rushed into the street and encountered the three bandits just as they were leaving the store. Seeing Ware rapidly advancing on them, Bass and his men fired on him at close range, one of their bullets striking a hitching post within six inches of his head and knocking splinters into his face. This assault never halted Ware for an instant. He was as brave as courage itself and never hesitated to take the most desperate chance when the occasion demanded it. For a few minutes he fought the robbers single-handed. General Jones, returning from the telegraph office, ran into the fight. He was armed with only a small Colt's double-action pistol, but threw himself into the fray. Connor and Harold had now come up and joined in the fusilade. The general, seeing the robbers on foot and almost within his grasp, drew in close and urged his men to strain every nerve to capture or exterminate them. By this time every man in the town who could secure a gun had joined in the fight.

The bandits had now reached their horses, and realizing their situation was critical they fought with the energy of despair. If ever a train robber could be called a hero, Frank Jackson proved himself one. Barnes was shot down and killed at his feet and Bass was mortally wounded and unable to defend himself or even mount his horse, while the bullets continued to pour in like hail from every quarter. With heroic courage, Jackson held the rangers back with his pistol in his right hand while with his left he unhitched Bass's horse and assisted him into the saddle. Then, mounting his own horse, Jackson and his chief galloped out of the very jaws of hell itself. In their flight they passed through old Round Rock, and Jim Murphy, standing in the door of May's store, saw them go by on the dead run. The betrayer noticed Jackson was holding Bass, pale and bleeding, in the saddle.

Lieutenant Reynolds, entering Round Rock, came within five minutes of meeting Bass and Jackson in the road. Before he reached town he met posses of citizens and rangers in pursuit of the robbers. When the fugitives reached the cemetery they halted long enough for Jackson to secure a Winchester they had hidden in the grass there; then they left the road and were lost for a time. The battle was now over and the play spoiled by two overzealous deputies bringing on a premature fight, after they had been warned to be careful. Naturally, Moore and Grimes should have known that the three strangers were the Sam Bass gang.

Lieutenant Reynolds started Sergeant Nevill and his rangers early next morning in search of the flying bandits. After traveling some distance in the direction the robbers had last been seen we came upon a man lying under a large oak tree. Seeing we were armed, as we advanced upon him he called out to us not to shoot, saying he was Sam Bass, the man we were hunting.

After entering the woods the evening before, Bass had become so sick and faint from loss of blood that he could go no farther. Jackson had dismounted and wanted to stay with his chief, declaring he was a match for all their pursuers.

"No, Frank," replied Bass. "I am done for."

The wounded leader told his companion to tie his horse near at hand so he could get away if he should feel better during the night. Jackson was finally prevailed upon to leave Bass and make his own escape.

When daylight came Saturday morning Bass got up and walked to a near-by house. As he approached the place a lady, seeing him approaching covered with blood, left the house and started to run off, as she was alone with a small servant girl. Bass saw she was frightened and called her to stop, saying he was perishing for a drink of water and would return to a tree not far away and lie down if she would only send him a drink. She sent him a quart cup of water, but the poor fellow was too far gone to drink it. We found him under this tree an hour later. He had a wound through the center of his left hand, the bullet having pierced the middle finger.

Bass's death wound was given him by Dick Ware, who used a .45 caliber Colt's long-barreled six-shooter. The ball from Ware's pistol struck Bass's belt, cutting two cartridges in pieces and entering his back just above the right hip bone. The bullet mushroomed badly, and made a fearful wound that tore the victim's right kidney all to pieces. From the moment he was shot until his death three days later Bass suffered untold agonies. As he lay on the ground Friday night where Jackson had left him the wounded man tore his undershirt into more than a hundred pieces and wiped the blood from his body.

Bass was taken to Round Rock and given the best of medical attention, but died the following day. While he was yet able to talk, General Jones appealed to him to reveal to the authorities the names of the confederates he had had that they might be apprehended.

"Sam, you have done much evil in this world and have only a few hours to live. Now, while you have a chance to do the state some good, please tell me who your associates were in those violations of the laws of your country."

Sam replied that he could not betray his friends, and that he might as well die with what he knew in him.

He was buried in the cemetery at old Round Rock, where a small monument was erected over his grave by a sister. Its simple inscription, defaced in recent years by relic-seekers, read:

SAMUEL BASS

Born July 21st, 1851
Died July 21st, 1878

A brave man reposes in death here. Why was he not true?

Frank Jackson made his way back to Denton County and hung around some time hoping to get an opportunity to murder the betrayer of his chief, an ingrate whose cause he himself had so ably championed. Jackson declared that if he could meet Jim Murphy he would kill him, cut off his head, and carry it away in a gunny sack.

Murphy returned to Denton, but learned that Jackson was hiding in the elm bottoms awaiting a chance to slay him. He thereupon asked permission of the sheriff to remain about the jail for protection. While skulking about the prison one of his eyes became infected. A physician gave him some medicine to drop into the diseased eye, at the same time cautioning him to be careful as the fluid was deadly poison. Murphy drank the entire contents of the bottle, and was dead in a few hours. Remorse, no doubt, caused him to end his life.

Of the four men who fought the Round Rock battle with Sam Bass and his gang all are dead. Of the ten men who made the long ride from San Saba to Round Rock, I, alone, am still among the living.

The Siege of Elfego Baca

The town of Frisco in Western Socorro County [,New Mexico,] was a tiny Mexican settlement with an Upper Plaza, Middle Plaza, and Lower Plaza. Now known as Reserve and County seat of Catron County and ninety miles from a railroad, it was then the happy romping ground of certain outfits of Texas cowpunchers who spent their Saturday evenings and holidays in taking pot shots at the populace who had been so unfortunate as to come within range of their limber six shooters. It was especially at the mercy of the hired employees of one Slaughter, who yearly drove his herds through from Texas to Western Socorro, picking up what stray native cattle happened to be in the way and finally arriving at his ranch near Frisco with considerable new wealth.

There had been remonstrance about this, but no action, for the Slaughter outfit was well heeled and a bit rough and quick on the trigger. There was even less remonstrance among the terror-stricken inhabitants of Frisco. Should the Justice of the Peace seek so far to retain his legal dignity as to incarcerate one of the offenders, it would be simply an excuse for the jolly Slaughter boys to come down and practice target shooting at his fleeing form and to kick open the jail and take out their little pal. The Slaughter outfit, in short, was a law unto itself.

It was into this atmosphere that young Elfego Baca strayed one day in the fall of 1884, with no intent in mind other than to look things over and visit friends.

It is as well to quote now directly from Mr. J. H. Cook's book, *Fifty Years on the Old Frontier,* published in 1923 by the Yale University Press. Mr. Cook took part in the occurrence, the facts of which have been substantiated numerous times, especially in the testimony of the several murder trials arising out of the fracas.

Mr. Cook says:

> It appeared that on the previous day a cowboy named McCarty, employed by Mr. Slaughter, a cattleman holding some stock a few miles from the Plaza, had ridden into the Upper Plaza. Securing a few drinks of liquor at a store kept by a man named Milligan, he had proceeded to shoot up the place. Riding back and forth in the street, he shot at everything, animate and inanimate, which met his gaze. While the drunken cowboy was thus engaged, a young Mexican named Elfego Baca rode into the Plaza. He was a special deputy sheriff from the County Seat of Socorro County, and he was out on an electioneering trip, making speeches in the various Mexican settlements of the county.

From *Law and Order, Ltd.,* The Rousing Life of Elfego Baca of New Mexico, by Kyle S. Crichton, pp. 27–48. Copyright, 1929, by Kyle S. Crichton and Elfego Baca. Santa Fe: New Mexican Publishing Corporation.

McCarty, the drunken cowboy, did not notice Baca's arrival, but Baca had noticed him. Meeting the Justice of Peace and some of the other residents of the Plaza, Baca asked them why they allowed the cowboy to jeopardize their lives and property in such manner. The reply was that, if they arrested or harmed McCarty, his friends would come and do a lot of harm to the settlement. Baca told them that when such things were tolerated it only made the cowboys bolder, and that it should be stopped at once. He insisted that they should not let the Americans living among them get the impression that the Mexicans were afraid of them. He further informed them that he was a peace officer, that it was his duty to stop McCarty from endangering the lives of the citizens of the place, and that he would show McCarty there was at least one Mexican in the country who was not afraid of an American cowboy.

We must interrupt Mr. Cook at this point to clear up a few things as we go along. Young Baca, with the ever present urge for law enforcement, was a deputy sheriff self appointed. He was aged nineteen at the time, and his badge was one of the sort now ladled out by detective correspondence schools. It was not the badge of a deputy sheriff of Socorro or any other County, but it was enough of a badge to convince Frisco amid the excitement. It was the fact of his assumption of office that he did not possess that brought him within the toils of the law when the affair was concluded. But to go on with Mr. Cook's excellent narrative:

Baca went out at once and arrested and disarmed McCarty with but little trouble; for he was really not a bad man—merely a little too playful at times. Taking his prisoner before the Justice of Peace in the Plaza, Baca was informed by his Honor that he did not care to hear the case, as there would surely be an aftermath which could result badly for the Plaza. Baca replied that, in such a case, where the Justice seemed intimidated, he considered it his own duty to take his prisoner to the County Seat, where the case could be tried.

As it was too late for Baca to start at once for the town of Socorro, he decided to remain with the prisoner in the Mexican settlement overnight. He took McCarty down to the Middle Plaza, where there was more suitable accommodations for himself and his prisoner. By some means word of McCarty's arrest had gone out from the Plaza. A number of Mr. Slaughter's cowboys, headed by Mr. Perham, their foreman, rode down at once to the place where Baca was holding McCarty and demanded his release. When Baca was informed that the prisoner would be taken from him right then and there, he told them that he would give them the time it would take to count three to get out of town. Baca counted "one, two, three," and opened fire on the Americans with his pistol. The Slaughter cowboys started to get out of harm's way very suddenly. By some chance, Mr. Perham's horse fell and killed its rider. One of the Americans, Allen by name, was shot by Baca through the knee. Baca held to his prisoner.

By this time, if we may be allowed to stop Mr. Cook again, things in Upper, Middle, and Lower Frisco were churned to a pretty stage. The shock received by the Slaughter representatives in coming to relieve young Elfego of the responsibility of his prisoner and getting his curt order to depart before he had completed his arithmetic to the extent of "three" was almost more of a stunner than the fact of Perham's unfortunate crushing by his falling horse. It was enough to start couriers in all directions to round up the "Americanos" to the defense of their heaven-sent rights. It was such a courier who dashed up to the ranch house of Mr. Cook at a furious gait and called hurriedly that the Mexicans had gone on the warpath at Frisco and that they were trying to wipe out all the Americans living near the settlement. He rushed on to carry the news to others, much like Paul Revere of old, though in not so worthy a cause. Cook arrived at the Plaza to find the Mexicans as docile and cowed as ever and the source of all the "uprising" and the massacre of the Americans to lie in the person of young Baca, who clung steadfastly to his prisoner and his determination. The Mexicans at all times kept well out of range of trouble, being greatly outnumbered by the cowboys and helpless before them. They left Elfego to fight his own battles. But to get back to Cook again:

> We held a council and decided to select one or two of our number to go to the Plaza, see the Justice of the Peace and Mr. Baca, and try to arrange for the trial of McCarty at the Plaza; for the charge against him was not a desperately serious one, and we all realized that considerable trouble might be started. Our committee waited upon the Justice and Mr. Baca, and they agreed to our suggestion. Mr. Baca stated that he would have the prisoner at the Justice's office at the stated hour. The crowd which I was with, and which, the evidence showed later, was composed of eighty men, then rode down to the Upper Plaza at the time appointed for the trial. Baca had McCarty at the Justice's office. After taking his prisoner inside, he came out and greeted us, saying, "Good morning, Gentlemen."

We must depart with Mr. Cook here definitely, for things were about to happen at a pace not to be taken at the leisurely gait of reminiscence forty years later. The Slaughter outfit, with the death of Perham fresh in its mind, was in no mood for either fair play or polite words. Despite the efforts of Cook, Clement Hightower, and Jerome Martin—all known to Baca—who had arranged for the truce and bringing of McCarty for trial, the Slaughter cavalcade was not to be soothed. As Baca brought up McCarty to the Justice of the Peace's office, he was met by the horde of Slaughter—eighty in number, as later testified to at the trial—who swung up from the arroyo by the office, and swept down upon young Baca standing by the corner of the building. It was then that he addressed the crowd, as related by Cook.

"Good morning, Mr. Wilson," said Baca affably.

"Good morning, you dirty Mexican blankety blank," replied Wilson in turn, following it up by words of like purport. It was then also that a shot was fired by one of the Slaughter crowd.

It was then, also, that Baca drew out his guns, covered the closest of the Slaughter outfit, and backed hastily through an alleyway to the protection of a tiny *jacal* that stood in a clearing at the end of the lane. He found there a woman and her two boys.

"Vamos!" yelled Baca. "Get out before you're killed!"

Close on Elfego's heels had come the Slaughter outfit, headed by Jim Herne, a Texan with a bounty over his head and disdain for Mexicans in his heart. He got off his horse, dragged his rifle from its position on the saddle, and advanced toward the *jacal* inhabited by Baca.

"I'll get this dirty little Mexican out of here," he said. "Come on, you," he bellowed. "Come out of there, and come damned quick!"

Baca's answer was two revolver shots, both of which hit vital spots. Either of them was enough to kill Herne, and one did. Friends bore the body away hastily and the siege was on.

It was nine o'clock in the morning, and young Elfego Baca was at bay, with eighty of the roughest, sharpest shooting Texas cowboys in history facing him from easy shooting distance. A *jacal* is a building made by hammering long stakes into the ground—much like a corral—and plastering them over both inside and outside in semblance of an adobe house. It is positively not an adobe house, and not much of a house of any kind when bullets start whistling through. For the stakes are set at least two inches apart and wet mud is after all only wet mud which eventually dries and makes no sort of resistance to the product of Mr. Remington operating in the firearms of Mr. Colt.

Any likelihood of the Spanish-American population of the Upper, Middle, or Lower Plaza doing anything in behalf of young Mr. Baca was spoiled by the fact that the greater part of the populace was suffering from that malignant affliction known as yellow jaundice.

Included in the number so affected were the male members of the community who had in the past enjoyed considerable Indian war experience and might have been willing to relieve the pressure on Baca by stray pot shots in the direction of the invading Texans.

It was the practice of the invaders to do their artillery work in volume. It was not a question of one shot following another at intervals, but of one concerted volley directed full into the *jacal*—pronounced hack-awl. In the circumstances young Baca was resigned to fate. He did what he could in protection, which was practically nothing at all, and sat down in a corner of the hut to await the end. He retained interest in the proceedings, however, to the point of watching carefully through the cracks in the weary structure for possible views of a Texas head that might be started on its way to eternity. All told in the battle, he made way with four more or less prominent Texas citizens, and wounded others, who did not boast about it when it was all over.

The day dragged slowly for young Elfego. In the *jacal* he found a plaster paris reproduction of a saint, known as *Mi Señora Santa Ana.*

Upon the head of the worthy saint young Baca was wont to rest his Stetson hat in such a position as to be evident through the tiny windows of the hut to the impatient Texans. His own position would be in another part of the fort. Attempts to take Baca by surprise were met by well aimed shots that discouraged them. To make things more difficult for the imprisoned young man, the cowboys stretched blankets between the houses where they were located. It gave Baca nothing to fire at, and it gave the Slaughter troupe a splendid vantage point for attack.

The concerted firing was kept up and the *jacal* was becoming more riddled by the minute. Along about six o'clock of the first day, a barrage of shots cut away the stakes that make up the construction of the *jacal* and deposited a section of the building upon the form of young Baca. He was pinned by the falling debris, pushed over on his face with his legs firmly held from behind by heaps of mortar and falling stakes. He lay in this position for a period of two hours without attempting to free himself and quite content to listen to the "Swoosh!" of the bullets over his head. Upon arrival of darkness, he pulled himself from his crouching position and took stock of his chances. He decided upon due deliberation that it mattered very little what he did. Since life was to remain but little longer within his sturdy frame, he decided that it was as well to act at home in his refuge. The hot stove —left by the departing owner—was still alive. He put on additional sticks of cottonwood, and brought it to a fine blaze. He made coffee; he heated meat; and he made—last but by far not least—he made tortillas! But . . . he was not hungry in the least, and his mastication was only perfunctory—a sort of culinary defiance of the fates. He was not hungry then and he was not hungry in the morning twenty-four hours after his confinement when he employed the stove again for preparation of breakfast.

Near midnight of the first night, Baca from his place of hiding saw a tiny light creeping along the ground in his direction. He was not aware of it—having no knowledge of mining—but what was approaching him was a lighted fuse attached to a stick of dynamite which had been secured from the Cooney mining camp by sundry of Slaughter's cowboys who had galloped off in that direction when it was once evident that young Elfego was not to be dislodged from his refuge without the demise of many.

"I saw the light . . . but thought it was a cigarette butt thrown by one of the cowboys and being blown in my direction by the wind. I watched it curiously. It would be still for a moment and then it would come on again. I thought it was funny that a cigarette should keep lit that long, but I didn't know any other explanation of it. I didn't know what dynamite or a fuse was. . . . The light kept coming, and I kept watching and the next thing I knew: BLOOEY! ! !"

Plaster fell in all directions and half of the *jacal* collapsed in ruins.

With the luck that remained with him always, the half that collapsed was not the half that held Elfego. What remained of the *jacal* after the previous shower of bullets and now the shattering of the dynamite was one protected corner where Baca stood.

Dynamite or no dynamite, the followers of Slaughter by this time had such an opinion of the charmed existence of young Baca that they refrained from investigating the result of their night's work until morning.

At the first bright peeps of dawn, they looked anxiously in the direction of the temporary abode of Mr. Baca. What their astonished eyes beheld was a tiny trickle of smoke coming from the chimney in the lone remaining section of the house. Mr. Baca was having breakfast! And the fervent Texas curses threatened to dry up the Frisco with their vehemence. There was simply no dealing with a fellow as lucky as that! They took out their wrath in successive and vindictive volleys that hit every last remaining individual thing in the *jacal* except the form of one Baca. At the trial was exhibited a broom with eight bullet holes in the handle. The door of the hut—about half the size of an ordinary door of these days—contained 367 bullet holes and had all the appearance of a first-class sieve. It was testified that over 4,000 bullets penetrated the *jacal* when the fusillade finally ceased at 6 o'clock on the evening of the second day. In other words, Elfego Baca held off the eighty Texans from 9 o'clock of one morning until 6 o'clock of the next evening—a total of thirty-three hours.

But on the morning of the second day, the Slaughter outfit was far from calling a truce. They concentrated steady fire on the lone corner of the *jacal* still remaining until it seemed impossible for human form to keep alive in the hurricane. Everything was hit but Elfego Baca. Spoons and knives and forks—all came in for their individual attention by the pistol adeptness of the Texans, but Elfego was untouched.

About ten o'clock, Baca saw a form start across the open space between the blankets of the Slaughter outfit and the hut wherein he stood. It was a cowboy sheltered behind the cast-iron front of what had once been a stove. He kept well covered and he approached slowly with care. Nothing showed above the cast-iron surface. The figure had all the appearance of a knight of old accoutred for the joust but minus the horse. The armor was home-made but highly effective. Elfego wasted no shots. He watched with a hawk-like eye for the first slip-up of the armored Texan. He watched for the first mistake in the slow business-like crawl; he watched for the first errored appearance of the cowboy's head over the top of the rejuvenated stove. With patience his chance came. There *was* a fleeting second when the cowboy's discretion was not equal to his valor. He ventured a peek at his goal. It was his last peek of the day. The bullet from Elfego's gun entered his scalp and journeyed across the top of his pate and skimmed off into space. It was as lovely a shot as ever made by Annie Oakley in her palmy days. It was a perfect shot. It put an end to progress toward the present residence of Elfego Baca by way of cast-iron aid. The cowboy was not dead—indeed, very far from dead, but he had enough for the day. He bore his bleeding scalp hastily back to the protection of his fellows.

With four dead and many more wounded, the Slaughter outfit took pause to consider the matter. Mr. Cook goes on from here to say that "Excitement ran high. Baca must be killed or captured. Just how either was to be effected was a question. Many plans were suggested. By this time every one was convinced that Baca would sell his life as dearly as possible. He was at bay and thoroughly aroused. A number of my English friends were with me in the Plaza. I told them that I considered the Americans gathered at the Plaza neither more nor less than a mob. Baca, I was informed, was a county officer, and the law was on his side. I felt that although he may have overdone his duty, the best thing possible for all concerned was not to kill him, but to secure him and get him to the County Seat at Socorro."

It was very good of Mr. Cook to be so considerate of Elfego Baca, who had so far done rather well in defending himself. It would seem, offhand, that sympathy was rather due the Texas cowboys who had been most unconscionably handled by the lone Baca in a ruined hut. It was also true, however, and must be admitted, that there would be a time when Baca would have to surrender. Cook's effort at compromise was something that Baca had cause to be thankful for.

Mr. Cook writes further: "An American deputy sheriff named Ross put in an appearance about this time; but he did not care to take a chance by showing himself to Baca in order to talk to him and persuade him to come out of the fort."

Mr. Ross may have subsequently amounted to very little in an historical way, but he should at least have mention here as a gentleman of rare good sense. He did later go into the Plaza toward the *jacal* with intent at mollification and compromise with the doughty young Baca, but he went in company with Cook and a Spanish-American friend of Baca's named Francisquito Naranjo. "A very brave man," [said] Mr. Baca, . . . speaking of Mr. Naranjo, "and my good friend."

It was Cook who took it upon himself to recruit Naranjo from the group of Spanish-Americans who were now gathered in numbers about the Plaza on the hills that skirted the river valley. Cook went up to address the Spanish-Americans, making them the proposition that he and Ross should go unarmed into the space in the Plaza before the *jacal* with some one whose voice Baca would recognize and listen to—provided he was still alive. "The evidence showed," writes Cook, "that four thousand shots had been fired into the *jacal* in which Baca had been hiding since he had killed Herne." Cook, as has been said, had conversed with the Spanish-American friends of Baca. "I told the Mexicans," writes Cook further, "that if Baca were alive and would give himself up, I would be responsible to them for his life until he could be taken to the county seat. To my surprise, my offer was agreed to."

Mr. Cook surely had little need for surprise. Naranjo, as a mean manipulator of a gun himself and as a close friend of Elfego Baca, was fully aware of the slim chance his pal would have for life the longer the battle went on. He was more than anxious to risk a shot from Elfego for the chance of getting him out of the *jacal* alive and to the protection of the county jail at Socorro. He came down into the Plaza with Cook and Ross, and once within hailing distance of the hut, called to Baca: "Are you alive? Come on out; you're well protected!"

Baca was startled out of his wits, both by the nearness of the voice that had approached that close without his knowing it and by the fact that it was the voice of his friend, Naranjo.

"Naranjo!" he yelled, "is it you?"

"*Si,*" bellowed Naranjo in return. "It's all right. Come on out!"

Suddenly, according to the report of Cook, Baca sprang out of the *jacal* through a small window opening. He had, says Cook, a six shooter in each hand, and was clad only in his underclothes. This is a quaint touch which Elfego, forty years later, denies vehemently. It is a matter of small moment. It is enough to know that Baca descended suddenly into the sunlight of the Plaza by way of a small window opening in the hut.

From where he had been in the fort, he could not see the party of which Naranjo was one, and when he alighted and saw Cook and Ross he felt immediately that he had been double crossed by his friend. He was still afire with the certainty that he was going to stay alive as long as the fates were willing.

"Line up!" he yelled sharply to Cook and Ross, flourishing the two guns menacingly, and maneuvering the Americans between himself and the cowboys across the Plaza. Cook and Ross, remembering the incident of the "one, two, three, BANG!" wasted no time in obeying orders. Ross and Cook were in a perilous position, for they knew that a false move would bring the Baca guns into action. Baca was also in a bad fix, for his friends from the hillside, in the excess of their enthusiasm at seeing him alive, yelled for him to make a run for it. Plain suicide could not compare in certainty with a run then with rifles in the hands of the best shots in New Mexico trained upon him from the first break.

As it was, things were again getting dark for Baca. The Texans were crowding in on him from their hiding places on three sides of the Plaza, and there was insistence that the dirty Mexican be hanged *pronto*. Cook, as the arranger of the compromise and with the gun of

Baca aimed at his breast, made a very hasty and creditable speech to the effect that they all knew how Baca had been induced to surrender, and that it would mean death to him (Cook), either immediately or later, if Baca were not given safe escort to Socorro.

"Immediately," said Baca, to reassure him.

Cook's talk, as he reports it, did not seem to satisfy either his Texas friends or his new acquaintance, Mr. Baca. He concludes forty years later that his death then would not have interfered greatly with the happiness of the Slaughter Cohorts, so he talked to them in a different vein. He told them that they were a mob in the eyes of the law; that Baca had done things for which he could not escape being hanged; and that the laws of the land, not a mob, should attend to his case. He also reminded them—which was more effective—that any double dealing with Baca would result in a pretty little race war indulged in by half the State of New Mexico and which would end in the eventual decease of all of them—if they remained to do business in the vicinity. They considered that carefully and agreed that the escort would be afforded Mr. Baca upon his complete surrender. All he had to do was to give up his guns and place himself in the hands of the jolly Slaughter boys for the trip to Socorro.

Would Mr. Baca give up his guns! Mr. Baca would as soon leap off the rim of the Grand Canyon on the back of a giraffe. Mr. Baca's guns would leave his hands only after life had grown cold within him. Mr. Baca would go to Socorro on one condition only. That was that he was to retain full use of his two guns, and that he was to be allowed to sit on the rear seat of a buck board wagon with the Slaughter troop entire before him. Ross, the deputy, was to sit in the front seat of the buck board with the driver, and Baca was to be in the rear of all of them during the trip to Socorro.

The cavalcade started the long ride to Socorro that took all of the night and the better part of the next day. Baca arrived in Socorro a hero, but also a captive. He was locked up in the new county jail. The new jail sat almost exactly upon the precise spot where Elfego Baca was born. The jail was barely finished in time to receive Baca, the first prisoner. The first case tried in the new court house was of the same Elfego Baca, arising out of the Frisco riot. It was only one of the small coincidences that make life so interesting.

In concluding the Frisco incident, Mr. Cook writes:

I left New Mexico a short time after the trouble at the San Francisco Plaza, and never knew the outcome of Baca's trial until within the last few years, when I learned that he was not hanged for the shooting of those men in the Plaza. On the contrary he had become one of the most prominent attorneys in the State of New Mexico. Should Mr. Baca read about this incident, the part which I played in it, and my point of view about the affair, I think he will readily understand why I have reason to be very glad that no greater loss of life was caused by Cowboy McCarty's efforts to work off a little surplus energy in an attempt to terrorize a peaceful Mexican settlement.

Elfego Baca was tried twice for the Frisco killings, and acquitted on both charges. They are among the famous trials of New Mexico. Prosecuting Baca were H. B. Ferguson, district attorney and later representative to Congress from New Mexico; Colonel Brethen and Neill B. Field. He was defended by Attorney Shaw, Judge Warrant, and B. S. Rodey, later federal judge in both Porto Rico and Alaska and representative to Congress.

Not the least interesting part of the testimony was that of a cowboy who testified solemnly and with utmost seriousness that if he took a .45 Colt pistol, aimed it directly at Baca's chest from a distance of a foot away, and fired—there would be absolutely no effect. He gave it as his deliberate opinion that Elfego was possessed of something from God or the devil, and that he would not be surprised if it were a great deal more from the latter than from the former.

It is this same legend of a "charmed existence" that made the little plaster saint of St. Anna so cherished a possession of the Spanish-American family who rescued it from the ruins of the *jacal* and, though very poor and needy, refused subsequently to part with it. Proper ceremonies are celebrated every Saint Anna's day in the section about Magdalena where the plaster saint now resides.

It is worshipped as a good luck emblem, and Elfego's own offer of ten cows for the plaster image was respectfully turned down. There can be no price for a saint that was responsible for the miracle of the Middle Plaza at the village of San Francisco.

Wild Bill Hickok Cleans Up Abilene

When [Joseph G.] McCoy decided on Abilene as the future shipping point for cattle, it consisted of about a dozen log huts. The town had been laid out some years before but had made no progress. Four-fifths of these low, rude huts were covered with dirt roofs. But one shingle roof was to be found in the place. There were two business houses—general stores—each in their one-room log cabin. So poor had appeared the prospect that even the saloons had passed the place by, only one, quartered in a squalid log house, being found there. McCoy bought the entire town-site for the sum of five dollars an acre. He erected a hotel which he named "Drover's Cottage." There was no one in Abilene capable of managing this tavern; so he sent to St. Louis for one Gore, and his wife Lou. These two became famed among the cattlemen.

By 1867, Abilene was a growing frontier town, wicked and restless. Buildings sprang up, stores were stocked with merchandise, saloons were promptly and plentifully installed. The bad men of the border

From *Wild Bill and His Era,* The Life and Adventures of James Butler Hickok, by William Elsey Connelley, pp. 152–154, 155, 160. Copyright, 1933, by Rufus Rockwell Wilson. New York: The Press of the Pioneers.

Cf. *A Treasury of American Folklore* (New York, 1944), pp. 67–69, 72–93.

flocked to the new town. T. C. Henry was elected mayor. He appointed Tom Smith marshal. Smith was fearless, and he established a degree of law and order. But, unfortunately, he was murdered at a critical time in the campaign for law enforcement, and the town relapsed.

In 1871 the people elected McCoy for mayor. He knew of Wild Bill's effective campaign in Hays [City] and it occurred to him that here was the right man for marshal of Abilene. Hickok had often stopped there, and it is likely that he and McCoy had met more than once. McCoy wanted Hickok for marshal of Abilene, the city council confirmed the appointment, and came to an agreement by which Hickok was to have one hundred and fifty dollars a month, and half the fines collected in Police Court. Under these conditions Wild Bill became the marshal, April 15, 1871.

The record of his administration was but poorly kept. The newspaper of the town was hostile to the Texas cattle business and gave it scant mention. A search of the files fails to reveal any extended account of the cattle shipments or of the administration of the town's affairs. This failure of record makes it difficult properly to treat the administration of Wild Bill as marshal of Abilene. McCoy in later years said that Wild Bill had killed forty-three men up to the time of his appointment. These had been killed in the line of duty as a peace-officer, and did not include those he had slain in his service in the Civil War nor Indians killed in scouting on the Plains. He also asserted that Wild Bill's administration was satisfactory to him and continued: "Talk about a rule of iron. We had it in Abilene. We had to rule that way. There was no fooling with courts of law. When we decided that such a thing was to be done we did it. Wild Bill cleaned up the town and kept it clean, but we had to kill a few roughs to do it." How many men may be included in the term, "a few roughs," we have now no means of knowing. Abilene admits but two; but there were undoubtedly more.

There are here and there in the record some glimpses of Wild Bill in the performance of his duties at Abilene. There was always a heavy bowie knife with a razor edge concealed in his sash. He was armed with a sawed-off shotgun and in addition he sometimes carried a repeating rifle. He patrolled the streets walking in the center. He knew that he was liable to be assassinated at any minute. When he entered a building he always kicked the door back against the wall so that no one could be concealed there. Once inside, he stood where he could face the entire crowd. He talked little. But what he did say was to the point. The people—the good man and the bad man—quickly learned that he stood solely for order. The business man felt secure with him on guard. The bad man knew that a single break meant death. It was a situation which never before existed in any town in America. It was the iron will of one man holding at bay the malice, crime, and recklessness of the wickedest town on the frontier. A man who passed through this period says, "We were used to seeing men killed because some one disliked their looks, the color of their eyes, cut of their clothes, or the refusal to take a drink, or because they danced too much with one girl." After the arrival of Wild Bill those killings became a thing of the past.

About the first service required of Wild Bill as marshal was to maintain a quorum of the city council. Business was booming and the councilmen could scarcely find time to attend their meetings. One of the councilmen was particularly remiss in this duty. At an important meeting the council was one member short of a quorum. Wild Bill was ordered to produce a quorum. The first councilman he found was this tardy member. He demurred, but Bill marched him to the meeting at the point of his revolver. There, unobserved, the reluctant member slipped away. Bill was immediately directed to produce a quorum. A second time he sought the elusive councilman, who protested volubly. Bill picked him up, threw him across one shoulder and carried him again to the council chamber. There, he sat during the ensuing meeting, pistol in hand. The too-busy councilman also remained.

* * * * *

Here is an incident of Wild Bill's discharge of duty at Abilene. One night he roughly handled some troublesome cowboys. They decided to ride into Abilene and hang Bill. Next morning a number of cowboys met and started to town. Some say that there were a hundred cowboys in the mob. There was no real leader, and no plan of action. It was their belief that Bill would be found in a saloon. They would seize him and hang him to a telegraph pole. To them it was a perfectly feasible plan. But Wild Bill knew what was going on. He went out to the Last Chance Saloon, for there was the road by which the cowboys would pass. As they approached, Bill stepped out of the saloon with his Winchester leveled, and a brace of six-shooters in his belt. It was a cruelly unexpected appearance. Bill called, "Hide out, you sons of guns!"

The leader, in telling of the event later, said, "Every fellow in our crowd thought Bill meant him, and they all proceeded to 'hide out.' There was confusion for a minute; the leaders wheeled their horses; and in the mix-up, each tried to get the lead going the other way. To them it seemed a long time before they got strung out. There was no thought of resistance to Bill's order, and soon every member of the band was hitting the trail for his own camp as fast as his horse could carry him. So ended the attempt to hang Wild Bill."

It is the proud boast of Abilene that in the days of its Texas cattle-trade it was the wickedest city in the world. This may or may not be true, but it was wicked enough. Certainly there was never another town in Kansas to compare with—not even Dodge City, in its cowboy glory. Its saloons grew gorgeous with mirrors and cut glass. Mahogany bars became common. The town acquired sophistication. Its crudities were interspersed with tawdry and expensive trappings. The latest devices for lighting were imported and installed, and great reflectors behind the oil lamps threw light far into the streets. Expensive gambling paraphernalia filled the gaming-rooms. Nothing was spared which would produce a dazzling appearance. The dance-houses never closed and their scarlet women gave color to the streets.

Some of its saloons were so famous (or infamous) that memory of them still lives. There was the Alamo where the Italian and his wife made music on a piano and violin. The very name was a lure to the cowboy from Texas. The Bull's Head was owned and operated by Ben Thompson, a Texan with a long list of murders to his credit, and Phil Coe, a professional gambler of huge proportions and magnificent appearance. It was splendidly equipped, and its faro bank was said to be the best that money could buy. Within the space of two blocks about these were thirty others, many of them as extravagantly furnished. All of the better places had pianos. Some of them boasted horns; and bull-fiddles roared and thundered in the chorus. There was the Novelty Theatre. Its bills were long and gripping. "Six Buckets of Blood, or Who Stabbed the Captain" is said to have been the title of a play presented there and shown in other cattle towns.

It is estimated that in the summer of 1871 there were more than five thousand cowboys in and around Abilene. The streets of the town were congested day and night. People were there from every quarter. Five thousand visitors were in town at one time, and twenty-five hundred were counted in the saloons of one block in an afternoon. And it was this seething horde that Wild Bill and his one deputy held in subjection to order!

The century-old conflict of the man with the hoe against the stockman had been fought out at Abilene by the end of the season of 1871. The man with the hoe had won. The town held an agricultural fair as a demonstration of faith in the possibilities of the soil. In February a published notice was spread broadcast in which the future drovers were practically forbidden to bring cattle to Abilene.

> We, the undersigned, members of the Farmers' Protective Association, and officers and citizens of Dickinson County, Kansas, most respectfully request all who had contemplated driving Texas cattle to Abilene the coming season, to seek some other point for shipment, as the inhabitants of Dickinson County will no longer submit to the evils of the trade.

Texas cattle had made Abilene, had lifted it from a bunch of squalid huts to a thriving city. It was an ungracious dismissal.

But the drovers accepted this deposal with good grace. The end of the sale season had always been celebrated with a round-up—a general gathering in the town to show good will, have a good time, and say good-bye. The round-up this year was to be the greatest of all these post-season gatherings. Wild Bill made the rules and as they were fair and reasonable they were accepted without question. The principal restriction was that there was to be no shooting. There was to be no reckless riding in the streets.

The deposition of the drovers carried with it as a matter of course the exit of the Texas-owned saloons and kindred institutions. The

Bull's Head had a standing feud with Wild Bill. He had stood by, pistol in hand, and compelled the repainting of an obscene sign displayed by the management and had at the instance of the City Council forced Coe to bring the faro bank from a back room to the front in the barroom. And there were other matters of friction, one of which was that with the square deal, the cowboys had broken the faro bank after it had been brought into the light of day. Bill had ruled with an iron hand and lawless institutions are always in secret rebellion against repression of their practices. It was said that an inner circle of Texans, engaged in the saloon business and gambling hells, had conspired to kill Bill on the night of the round-up, and that in selecting the man to carry out the decree the lot had fallen on Coe. Whether this was true or false, or whether the tragedy of the night grew out of the temper of the occasion, will never be known. But bad feeling existed. Coe was the aggressor and brought on the train of events which cost him his life.

It devolved on Pat McGonigal and his brother to give the word to go. They rode up to the Drover's Cottage at sunset, tied their bronchos to the hitching rack, then walked leisurely down Texas Street and met their friends. Their appearance was the signal, and the round-up was on. Jake Karatosky was a Jew and a principal merchant of the town. He was seized and carried to the Applejack saloon and made to treat the crowd. Other citizens shared the same fate. It was all in fun of a rough kind, and no one resented it. All seemed to enjoy this strenuous frolic and roistering merry-making. The bars were crowded and excitement increased.

The revellers sought Wild Bill. It was the intention to carry him to a bar and have a drink with him. He was found at supper in a popular restaurant, but refused in any way to take part in the night's capers, knowing that fun might suddenly change and end in disaster. But he invited them to drink at his expense at the bar of the Novelty Theatre and admonished them that shooting was in violation of their pledged word and the city ordinance. The danger-point was reached about ten o'clock. A great mob surged through the town. Texas Street was crowded. The tide was rising and Wild Bill feared it might break beyond control. People sought cover and put out lights. Wild Bill and his deputy, Mike Williams, stood at the Novelty, for trouble was likely to break there if anywhere.

Phil Coe left his own saloon and appeared in front of the Alamo, which was packed with excited men. The air was charged with expectancy. Coe did not enter the Alamo, but stopped in the street and fired his pistol, claiming to have shot at a dog, which was clearly an excuse, for in that crowd there was little room for a dog. Any shot at a dog would have killed or wounded some man. Hearing this shot, Wild Bill ordered Williams to remain on guard at the Novelty, and ran swiftly across to the rear door of the Alamo, which he entered. He demanded the particulars of the shooting, denouncing the bad faith of the cowboys and saloon men.

There was a well just outside the Alamo, and Coe was standing at the curb. When Bill inquired the second time Coe said he had fired the shot; then he fired another, and the ball grazed Bill's side. Bill's action was so swift that his motions could not be followed by the eye. In a flash a pistol was in each hand. The two fired simultaneously—there was but one report. Two balls struck Coe in the abdomen, and Bill exclaimed, "I've shot too low." He was at the door when he said this. Instantly he fired two shots at another man just emerging from the darkness and coming swiftly up with two pistols in hand. Coe fired another shot at Bill and missed, then fell across the well-curb. A hundred pistols were drawn and cocked as Wild Bill fired his first shot. By the time he fired the second time the room was cleared and Coe's friends were gone.

The second man shot dropped his pistols, threw his hands above his head, and fell forward dead. It was then that Bill recognized in the stranger, Williams—his deputy whom he had left at the Novelty with orders to remain there. He cried out that he had shot his best friend. He lifted Williams from the floor and laid him on a poker table. He was horror-stricken and grief-stricken.

Now Wild Bill's wrath broke against the Texan. He stalked forth and declared an end to the festivities. He ordered the cowboys from the streets. He was the sword of vengeance—"the blue-eyed Son of the Border had gone wild again." "That night," said Colonel Little, "the desperate heroes of border strife hid in cellars and sunflower patches, or on swift ponies found their way to their cattle camps."

Wild Bill's friends liked to remember him as they saw him that night. Alone, he cleared the town. Plunging into crowds of angry and excited men who he knew wished to take his life, he dispersed and forced them to leave town. He ignored the peril in which he walked. As he strode from street to street—from gambling-house to saloon—lights went out and the town sank to silence.

The town reduced to repose, Bill asked for Coe. Two men had supported him to his rooms. There his clothing was torn apart to find his wounds. When told that there were two bullets in his body he exclaimed: "My father received similar wounds and lived. And I will live." But he was mortally wounded. Hickok sought a clergyman and led him to Coe's bedside. Coe never weakened. He knew soon that he could not recover, but this did not daunt him. He died as other Texans had died, without fear. And among those who felt regret for his death was Wild Bill.

Wyatt Earp on Gunplay

I was a fair hand with pistol, rifle, or shotgun, but I learned more about gun-fighting from Tom Speers's cronies during the summer of '71

From *Wyatt Earp, Frontier Marshal,* by Stuart N. Lake, pp. 37–41. Boston and New York: Houghton Mifflin Company.

than I had dreamed was in the book. Those old-timers took their gunplay seriously, which was natural under conditions in which they lived. Shooting, to them, was considerably more than aiming at a mark and pulling a trigger. Models of weapons, methods of wearing them, means of getting them into action and of operating them, all to the one end of combining high speed with absolute accuracy, contributed to the frontiersman's shooting skill. The sought-after degree of proficiency was that which could turn to most effective account the split-second between life and death. Hours upon hours of practice, and wide experience in actualities supported their arguments over style.

The most important lesson I learned from those proficient gunfighters was that the winner of a gunplay usually was the man who took his time. The second was that, if I hoped to live long on the frontier, I would shun flashy trick-shooting—grandstand play—as I would poison. Later, as a peace officer, I was to fight some desperate battles against notorious gunmen of the Old West, and wonder has been expressed that I came through them all unscathed. Certain outlaws and their friends have said I wore a steel vest under my shirt. There have been times when I'd have welcomed such a garment, but I never saw one in my life outside of a museum, and I very much doubt that any other frontiersman has either. Luck was with me in my gunfights, of course; so were the lessons learned in Market Square during the summer of '71.

Jack Gallagher's advice summed up what others had to say, to wear weapons in the handiest position—in my case, as far as pistols were concerned, in open holsters, one on each hip if I was carrying two, hung rather low as my arms were long, and with the muzzles a little forward on my thighs. Some men wore their guns belted high on the waist; a few, butts forward, army style, for a cross-draw; others carried one gun directly in front of the stomach, either inside or outside the waistband, and another gun in a holster slung below the left armpit; still others wore two of these shoulder holsters. Style was a matter of individual preference.

When mounted on a horse and, "armed to the teeth," as the saying goes, a man's rifle was slung in a boot just ahead of his right stirrup, his shotgun carried on the left by a thong looped over the saddle-horn. With the adoption of breech-loading weapons, a rider equipped with two pistols, rifle, and shotgun customarily had one of the belts to which his pistol-holsters were attached filled with pistol ammunition, the other with rifle cartridges, while a heavier, wider belt filled with shotgun shells was looped around the saddle-horn underneath the thong which held that weapon. He was a riding arsenal, but there might well be times when he would need the munitions. Bowie knives were worn largely for utility's sake in a belt sheath back of the hip; when I came on the scene their popularity for purposes of offense was on the wane, although I have seen old-timers who carried them slung about their necks and who preferred them above all other weapons in the settlement of purely personal quarrels.

When I say that I learned to take my time in a gunfight, I do not wish to be misunderstood, for the time to be taken was only that split-fraction of a second that means the difference between deadly accuracy with a six-gun and a miss. It is hard to make this clear to a man who has never been in a gunfight. Perhaps I can best describe such time-taking as going into action with the greatest speed of which a man's muscles are capable, but mentally unflustered by an urge to hurry or the need for complicated nervous and muscular actions which trick-shooting involves. Mentally deliberate, but muscularly faster than thought, is what I mean.

In all my life as a frontier peace officer, I did not know a really proficient gun-fighter who had anything but contempt for the gun-fanner, or the man who literally shot from the hip. In later years I read a great deal about this type of gunplay, supposedly employed by men noted for skill with a forty-five.

From personal experience and from numerous six-gun battles which I witnessed, I can only support the opinion advanced by the men who gave me most valuable instruction in fast and accurate shooting, which was that the gun-fanner and the hip-shooter stood small chance to live against a man who, as old Jack Gallagher always put it, took his time and pulled the trigger once.

Cocking and firing mechanisms on new revolvers were almost invariably altered by their purchasers in the interests of smoother, effortless handling, usually by filing the dog which controlled the hammer, some going so far as to remove triggers entirely or lash them against the guard, in which cases the guns were fired by thumbing the hammer. This is not to be confused with fanning, in which the triggerless gun was held in one hand while the other was brushed rapidly across the hammer fanwise to cock the gun, and firing it by the weight of the hammer itself. A skilful gun-fanner could fire five shots from a forty-five so rapidly that the individual reports were indistinguishable, but what could happen to him in a gunfight was pretty close to murder.

I saw Jack Gallagher's theory borne out so many times in deadly operation that I was never tempted to forsake the principles of gun-fighting as I had them from him and his associates.

There was no man in the Kansas City group who was Wild Bill's equal with a six-gun. Bill's correct name, by the way, was James B. Hickok. Legend and the imaginations of certain people have exaggerated the number of men he killed in gunfights and have misrepresented the manner in which he did his killing. At that, they could not very well overdo his skill with pistols.

Hickok knew all the fancy tricks and was as good as the best at that sort of gunplay, but when he had serious business in hand, a man to get, the acid test of marksmanship, I doubt if he employed them. At least, he told me that he did not. I have seen him in action and I never saw him fan a gun, shoot from the hip, or try to fire two pistols simultaneously. Neither have I ever heard a reliable old-timer tell of any trick-shooting employed by Hickok when fast straight-shooting meant life or death.

That two-gun business is another matter that can stand some truth before the last of the old-time gun-fighters has gone on. They wore two guns, most of the six-gun-toters did, and when the time came for action went after them with both hands. But they didn't shoot them that way.

Primarily, two guns made the threat of something in reserve; they were useful as a display of force when a lone man stacked up against a crowd. Some men could shoot equally well with either hand, and in a gunplay might alternate their fire; others exhausted the loads from the gun in the right hand, or left, as the case might be, then shifted the reserve weapon to the natural shooting hand if that was necessary and possible. Such a move—the border-shift—could be made faster than the eye could follow a topnotch gun-thrower, but if the man was as good as that, the shift seldom would be required.

Whenever you see a picture of some two-gun man in action with both weapons held closely against his hips and both spitting smoke together, you can put it down that you are looking at the picture of a fool, or at a fake. I remember quite a few of those so-called two-gun men who tried to operate everything at once, but like the fanners, they didn't last long in proficient company.

In the days of which I am talking, among men whom I have in mind, when a man went after his guns, he did so with a single, serious purpose. There was no such thing as a bluff; when a gun-fighter reached for his forty-five, every faculty he owned was keyed to shooting as speedily and as accurately as possible, to making his first shot the last of the fight. He just had to think of his gun solely as something with which to kill another before he himself could be killed. The possibility of intimidating an antagonist was remote, although the "drop" was thoroughly respected, and few men in the West would draw against it. I have seen men so fast and so sure of themselves that they did go after their guns while men who intended to kill them had them covered, and what is more win out in the play. They were rare. It is safe to say, for all general purposes, that anything in gun-fighting which smacked of show-off or bluff was left to braggarts who were ignorant or careless of their lives.

Bat Masterson's Gun

. . . I never knew a man who amounted to anything to notch his guns with "credits," as they were called, for men he had killed. Outlaws, gunmen of the wild crew who killed for the sake of brag, followed this

Ibid., pp. 41–42.
As told by Wyatt Earp.

custom. I have worked with most of the noted peace officers—Hickok, Billy Tilghman, Pat Sughrue, Bat Masterson, Charlie. Bassett, and others of like caliber—have handled their weapons many times, but never knew one of them to carry a notched gun.

Strange how such wild tales become current. I know the start of one, about Bat Masterson's "favorite six-gun with twenty-two notches in the butt." Bat's sense of humor was responsible, and he didn't dream of the consequences.

Some rapacious collector of souvenirs pestered Bat half to death with demands for a six-gun that Bat had used on the frontier. This collector called on Bat in his New York office and so insistently that Bat decided to give him a gun to get rid of him. Bat did not want to part with one he had used, so he went to a pawnshop and bought an old Colt's forty-five which he took to his office in anticipation of the collector's return. With the gun lying on the desk, Bat was struck with the idea that while he was providing a souvenir, he might as well give one worth the trouble it had caused, so he took out his penknife and then and there cut twenty-two "credits" in the pawnshop gun. When the collector called for his souvenir and Bat handed it to him, he managed to gasp a question as to whether Bat had killed twenty-two men with it.

"I didn't tell him yes, and I didn't tell him no," Bat said, "and I didn't exactly lie to him. I simply said I hadn't counted either Mexicans or Indians, and he went away tickled to death."

It wasn't long, however, before tales of the Old West with stories about Bat Masterson's notched gun and the twenty-two men he had killed began to creep into print. The case may offer a fair example of how other yarns started.

William Hynson and the Hanging

"Necktie sociable," "strangulation jig," and many such euphonious names the people of Montana had for hanging.

* * * * *

One day in August, 1868, as William Hynson was standing in the street near the post-office in Benton he was accosted by one of the citizens of the place:

"There is a man to be hanged, Bill, and we want you to help us."

"What's his name? what is he to be hanged for?" asked Hynson.

From *The Works of Hubert Howe Bancroft,* Vol. XXXVI, *Popular Tribunals,* Vol. I, pp. 705–706. Entered according to Act of Congress in the Year 1887, by Hubert H. Bancroft in the Office of the Librarian of Congress, at Washington. San Francisco: The History Company, Publishers.

"Never mind that, I have no time to talk; get a good strong rope and help me rig it, while the Committee brings the fellow out."

Hynson obeyed. As long as he was not chief actor in the tragedy, it was a pleasure rather than otherwise to be of service to the noble men who were exercising so healthful an influence upon society. The rope was brought. Soon a rude scaffold was ready, in the erection of which Hynson assisted with alacrity.

"Can't you tell me who the man is?" he asked again.

"No, no; fasten that end of the rope strong. You will know all about it presently."

Coming up by twos and threes, a crowd soon gathered, when Hynson was ordered to take his place beneath the gallows which he had helped to erect, for he was the man for whom it was erected. He had stolen a rifle from Mr. Clagett; he had murdered a Chinawoman, valued by her owners at six hundred dollars; he had knocked down and robbed a freighter; he was a bad man, and he must die. Hynson did not like it at all; but forced to comply, he took his position and was soon dangling.

The Millionaire and the Miners

. . . In 1877 a wealthy Detroiter went home from his mines in Leadville and told some very large stories. His exaggerated and bragging accounts led several hundred poor men to return with him to Leadville, where he glibly promised them employment. They got there only to find the camp already crowded with unemployed men dependent on the charity of the miners. Most of them were without means, and soon starvation stared them in the face. When the miners learned the situation, they made the braggart millionaire a frontier call. An impolite rope was stretched over a cedar branch, and one end discommoded his neck. "Now," said the visitors, "you fooled these men out here to starve, by your blowing. They've got no work and no way to get home. Give them fifty dollars apiece to take them back to Detroit, or you'll dance on nothing in less'n two minutes."

The millionaire was mulish and they swung him up once, twice, three times. At the third elevation he gasped surrender, and signed a check for the required amount. A trustyman galloped off toward distant Denver, and in a few days was back with the money to send the befooled Detroiters home.

From *A Tramp Across the Continent*, by Charles F. Lummis, pp. 54–55. Copyright, 1892, by Charles Scribner's Sons. New York.

A Square Deal in Gambling

. . . Many of the superstitions which are still religiously observed by dyed-in-the-wool Poker players originated in the games which were always in progress in the frontier saloons—Western Poker addicts were the first to convince themselves that it was bad luck to count chips or to play with a kibitzer looking over the shoulder, that the player who drew a pat hand of jacks full on red sevens would not leave the game alive, and that luck could be improved by walking around a chair. Perhaps the commonest belief in the West, however, was that bad luck would forever dog the footsteps of a man who played Poker with a one-eyed gambler, a superstition which gave rise to the expression, "There's a one-eyed man in the game," meaning "Look out for a cheat." The bad repute of the one-eyed player is said to have come about in this fashion:

A little game of draw was in progress in Omaha, and among its participants was a one-eyed man. He was playing in rather remarkable luck, but no one could very well find fault with that. Presently, however, there came a jackpot, and it was the one-eyed man's deal. He opened the pot, and while he was giving himself cards a certain bellicose gentleman named Jones thought he detected the one-eyed man in the act of palming a card. Quick as a flash, Jones whipped out a revolver and placed it on the table in front of him.

"Gentlemen," he said decisively, "we will have a fresh deal; this one doesn't go."

The players were surprised, but as none of them had bettered his hand save the opener, who made no sign of disapproval, they willingly consented.

"And now that we start on a new deal," pursued Mr. Jones, carelessly toying with the revolver, "let me announce that we are going to have nothing but square deals. I am not making any insinuations or bringing any charges, and I will say only this, that if I catch any son-of-a-gun cheating I will shoot his other eye out."

From *Jack Pots,* Stories of the Great American Game, by Eugene Edwards (Chicago, 1900), p. 321. Cited in *Sucker's Progress,* An Informal History of Gambling in America from the Colonies to Canfield, by Herbert Asbury, pp. 352–353. Copyright, 1938, by Dodd, Mead and Company, Inc. New York.

The Looloo

Luck favored the stranger from the start, and he won steadily. Finally, he drew four aces, and after the stakes had been run up to a comfortable figure, he magnanimously refused to bet further.

"This is downright robbery," he exclaimed, "and I don't want to end the game here by bankrupting you. So here goes." He threw down four aces and reached for the money.

"Hold on!" cried his antagonist. "I'll take care of the dust, if you please."

"But I held four aces—see?"

"Well, what of it. I've got a looloo."

The stranger was dazed, "A looloo?" he repeated. "What is a looloo, anyway?"

"Three clubs and two diamonds," coolly replied the miner, raking in the stakes. "I guess you ain't accustomed to our Poker rules out here. See there?"

He jerked his thumb toward a pasteboard sign which ornamented the wall of the saloon. It read:

A LOOLOO

BEATS FOUR ACES

The game proceeded, but it was plainly evident that the unsophisticated tiger hunter had something on his mind. Within five minutes he suddenly braced up, his face was wreathed in smiles, and he began betting once more with his former vigor and recklessness. . . .

The stranger threw down his cards with an exultant whoop. "It's my time to howl just about now!" he cried, as he reached for the money. "There's a looloo for you—three clubs and two diamonds."

"Tut! Tut!" exclaimed the miner. "Really this is too bad. You evidently don't understand our rules at all. You certainly don't mean to tell me that you play Poker in such a fast-and-loose, slipshod way down East, do you? Why, look at that rule over there."

He pointed directly over the head of the busy bartender. The bit of pasteboard bore this legend:

THE LOOLOO CAN BE PLAYED

BUT ONCE IN A NIGHT.

From *Poker Stories,* as Told by Statesmen, Soldiers, Lawyers, Commercial Travelers, Bankers, Actors, Editors, Millionaires, Members of the Ananias Club, and the Talent, Embracing the Most Remarkable Games, 1894–95, collected and edited by John F. B. Lillard, New York, 1896. Cited in *Sucker's Progress,* An Informal History of Gambling in America from the Colonies to Canfield, by Herbert Asbury, pp. 30–31. Copyright, 1938, by Dodd, Mead and Company, Inc. New York.

The most famous of all eccentric hands, the Looloo, is said to have been invented in a saloon in Butte, Montana, during the 1870's in a game between a stranger and a Butte miner. —Herbert Asbury, *Sucker's Progress* (New York, 1938), p. 30.

Collateral in Denver

One morning the janitor of a Denver bank opened the door and was surprised to observe three rather tired-looking citizens seated on the steps, the center one of whom held a sealed envelope carefully in sight of his companions.

"Want to make a deposit, gentlemen?" asked the cashier, who shortly arrived. "Step inside."

"No, I want to negotiate a loan," said the man with the envelope, "and there ain't a minute to lose. I want $5,000 quicker than hell can scorch a feather."

"What collaterals have you—Government?" inquired the bank official.

"Government nothin'. I've got something that beats four per cents all hollow. You see I've been sitting in a poker game across the street, and there's over $4,000 in the pot. There are three or four pretty strong hands out, and as I've every cent in the center the boys have given me thirty minutes to raise a stake on my hand. It's in this envelope. Just look at it, but don't give it away to these gentlemen. They're in the game, and came along to see I don't monkey with the cards."

"But, my dear sir," said the cashier, who had quietly opened the envelope and found it to contain four kings and an ace. "This is certainly irregular—we don't lend money on cards."

"But you ain't going to see me raised out on a hand like that?" whispered the pokerist. "These fellows think I'm bluffing and I can just clean out the whole gang. I've got 'em right in the door."

"Can't help it, sir. Never heard of such a thing," said the cashier, and the disappointed applicant and friends drifted sadly out. On the corner they met the bank's president, who was himself just from a quiet little all-night game. They explained the case again, and the next moment the superior officer darted into the bank, seized a bag of twenties and followed the trio. In about ten minutes he returned with the bag and an extra handful of twenties, which he flung on the counter.

"Here, credit five hundred to interest account," he said to the cashier. "Why, I thought you had more business snap. Ever play poker?"

"No, sir."

"Ah, thought not—thought not. If you did you'd know what good collateral was. Remember that in future four kings and an ace are always good in this institution for our entire assets, sir—our entire assets."

From *Poker Stories,* collected and edited by John F. B. Lillard (New York, 1896), pp. 88–90. Cited in *Sucker's Progress,* An Informal History of Gambling in America from the Colonies to Canfield, by Herbert Asbury, pp. 28–29. Copyright, 1938, by Dodd, Mead and Company, Inc. New York.

Justice in Nevada

The administration of Justice in Nevada was formerly conducted in a manner deemed essential to the necessities of the case at the time, rather than on the fixed principles of law that now prevail. In 1860, Judge A——, just having been appointed justice for Stouckee township, had before him a case originating in a dispute for the possession of a wood-claim, which terminated by one of the parties shooting the other's head off. The want of any mitigating circumstances, and the fact that a person had shortly before been executed for a similar offense near by, caused the friends of the prisoner to make unusual preparations for his defense, and the best counsel in the state, including Governor Low, appeared as his counsel.

Judge A—— listened closely to the evidence, promptly overruled all attempts to exclude any portion of it, and waving down with the utmost dignity the prosecuting attorney, who was about to address the court, delivered himself as follows to the prisoner:

"Young man, seeing as this is your first offense, I shall let you off *this* time; but you must be *very careful* how you go shootin' round this way in future, for they hung a man over in Carson the other day *just for doing the very same thing*!"

Judge Roy Bean: "Law West of the Pecos"

I[1]

When the Southern Pacific Railroad was built from El Paso to San Antonio, a certain station near the Río Grande, which is the border line between the United States and Mexico, was named Langtry. It was just west of the Río Pecos. Roy Bean opened a saloon there and called it "The Jersey Lily." This saloon and its keeper made the station of Langtry, Texas, almost as famous as the Jersey Lily herself, the beautiful Lily Langtry. It was here that the dashing youth of yesteryear became Justice of the Peace, an office which he has held continuously down to the time I am now writing, with one brief ex-

From *Bench and Bar,* A Complete Digest of the Wit, Humor, Asperities and Amenities of the Law, by L. J. Bigelow, pp. 445–446. New Edition, Greatly Enlarged. Entered according to Act of Congress, in the year 1871, by Harper & Brothers in the Office of the Librarian of Congress, at Washington. New York.

[1] From *On the Old West Coast,* Being Further Reminiscences of a Ranger, Major Horace Bell, edited by Lanier Bartlett, pp. 228–233. Copyright, 1930, by William Morrow & Co., Inc. New York.

Cf. *A Treasury of American Folklore* (New York, 1944), pp. 131–132, 134–150.

ception. One time as an election approached, some boosters for another settlement that had sprung up down nearer the river put up a rival candidate to Roy. The latter, feeling so sure that his re-election was automatically assured, gave little attention to the rival claimant, with the surprising result that the upstart was actually elected and the judicial seat moved down to the river bank.

"But I am the only man that could ever make anything out of the office," said Justice Bean to me when he was laughing about that political slipup, "and in a little while the Río Grande judge came up to propose to me that I buy him out. He brought his commission along with him, his docket, and all his papers, and dickered with me. He was sick of the job. So I gave him a demijohn of whisky, two bear skins, and a pet coon for the right, title, honor, and emoluments of the office. I've run the thing ever since without opposition."

Roy's court is held in the bar-room of "The Jersey Lily" saloon. The bar, or counter, is the judicial bench, and whisky barrels set up on end in front of it constitute the legal bar. The opposing lawyers, if there are any, use the heads of the barrels as desks. From this courtroom in the desert have issued decisions that have carried the fame of Justice Bean the world round. Judge Bean and Coroner Bean, for he also occupied the latter distinguished office.

While the railroad was under construction beyond Langtry, a section boss killed a Chinese laborer. He was arrested and brought before Judge Bean. The boss was a popular man in that section and valuable to the railroad authorities, so the latter exerted strong pressure on the court to get him acquitted. Judge Bean proved very patient in his examination of the case. He examined a great many witnesses very solemnly. He consulted his book of law often. This book, the only one he ever consulted in running his court, was a compilation of the laws of the State of California published in 1856.

"They send me the Texas statutes, codes, and so forth every year," Judge Bean once explained to me, "but I never read them. All the law I want I take from the compiled laws of the State of California. They are good enough for my state, they are good enough for anybody, they are good enough for me. I administer the law upon the authority of that book and don't need any other."

After the testimony in the trial of the section boss was all in, which showed conclusively that the accused had murdered the Chinaman, the Court opened the compiled laws of the State of California, spread the volume before him with great ceremony, and delivered this opinion:

"The Court has been very patient in inquiring into this case. It is true that the defendant shot the Chinaman and killed him. It seems as if there ought to be some sort of punishment meted out, but there doesn't seem to be any provided for. What they don't know about Chinamen in California they don't know anywheres, yet I've looked this book through and can't find any place where it is named as an offense for a white man to kill a Chinaman. So far as the feelings of this Court goes it would be the greatest pleasure to hold the defendant for murder, but the situation is not the fault of this Court. Therefore the judgment of the Court is that the defendant be discharged."

A case that came before "The Jersey Lily" bar, with the proprietor acting this time both as judge and coroner, was that of a man accidentally killed by one of the Southern Pacific trains. On the body at the time were found forty dollars and a revolver. The judgment of Coroner Bean was that no fault attached to the railroad company for the unfortunate occurrence. The judgment of Justice of the Peace Bean followed, and was this: "Yet the Court must take into consideration another feature of this case. That is to say, a concealed weapon was found on this person. He was therefore violating the law at the time of his death and the Court is driven to the disagreeable necessity of imposing on the deceased a fine of forty dollars. The weapon will be confiscate to the Court."

A wiry cowpuncher rode in one day escorting a buxom prairie lass and applied to Judge Bean for a marriage license. It was issued and the ceremony performed on the spot. After paying over a liberal fee, the cowboy and his bride dashed away into the wilds on their mustangs to enjoy the delights of matrimony.

About a year later the pair came back and complained to His Honor that they couldn't get along together and wanted a divorce. The Judge told them that divorces were very expensive. The cowpuncher thought he could stand a pretty good pull on his resources to get relief, so the Judge named his price, received it, pronounced the pair divorced, and they rode away, each in a separate direction.

The judge of the District Court in El Paso had heard tales of queer decisions issuing from the Justice of the Peace at Langtry but paid no attention to them until he got wind of this divorce proceedings. Then he thought he would go down and have a talk with the Langtry justice. Said the District Judge to Justice of the Peace Bean over the bar—the social bar—of "The Jersey Lily": "Justice Bean, the question of separating a man and wife by divorce assumes a degree of gravity that precludes hasty treatment. I have come down to talk to you about this matter. What have you to say in regard to your jurisdiction to grant divorces?"

"Why," answered Justice Bean, "I'm the only jurisdiction west of the Pecos—if I can't grant a married couple relief from each other, who can? And besides, I'd like to ask you this: When you commit an error in your court and it is brought to your attention, what do you do about it?"

"Do you mean to ask me, do I correct an error in some case that has been before my court?"

"That's what I mean, Judge."

"Why, certainly, if I commit an error I correct it if it is called to my attention in the proper way."

"All right, that's just what I did when I divorced that cowpuncher and his woman. I had issued the license and I had married them. They brought to my attention the fact that I had made an error in those matters and I corrected that error."

The District Judge allowed that Justice Bean had the better of the argument, and it is to be presumed that the two judicial wiseacres thereupon turned their attentions exclusively to decisions concerning the choice of liquors.

I last heard of Roy Bean through an Associated Press dispatch in a newspaper. The dispatch was dated Langtry, May 27, 1901, and read as follows:

> Judge Roy Bean, notorious throughout western Texas and many times the subject of magazine articles, also known as "The Law West of the Pecos," again distinguished himself last night by going through a Pullman car while the westbound Southern Pacific train was stopping at Langtry and, with a .45-caliber Colt in his hand, collecting from an eastern tourist thirty-five cents due for a bottle of beer. The tourist had bought the beer at the Judge's saloon but had rushed off without paying for it. Going through the car, Bean peered into each passenger's face until he found his man when he said, "Thirty-five cents or I press the button." He was handed a dollar bill and returned the correct change.
>
> As the Judge left the car, he turned in the aisle and said to the frightened passengers, "If you don't know what kind of hombre I am, I'll tell you. I'm the law west of the Pecos." The passengers thought it was a holdup.

At the time of this "holdup" Roy Bean was over seventy years old.

II[2]

When a beer salesman would visit a bar in those days, he was expected to stand treat for the crowd—maybe several rounds; and then the empty bottles were counted and he settled. Judge Bean on such occasions would manage to work off all the old empties he had accumulated. One salesman mustered up sufficient courage to complain that one bottle didn't look freshly emptied. Bean said, with an innocent air, "It does look fairly dry, but it's the way of drinkin' that some of the boys has. They don't often get good beer and, when they do, they not only drink the bottle dry but they sop it out. Purty good vouch for yore beer, son."

* * * * *

Trains stopped long enough for thirsty customers to buy a bottle of beer at Bean's bar. The Judge, who also acted as bartender, hated to give change and he would delay until the engine had given a

---

2 From *Cowtown Columnist,* by Boyce House, pp. 32–34, 36–38. Copyright, 1946, by the Naylor Company. San Antonio, Texas,

warning toot and if the passenger was displeased by the high price, he didn't linger to argue for fear he would miss the train.

There was one exception—an Eastern dude who bought a bottle of beer and laid down a twenty-dollar gold piece. Bean slowly counted out $19 in change.

"What!" the customer shouted, "a dollar for a bottle of beer!" and then he began to cuss.

Bean yanked his six-shooter from under the counter and announced, "Court will come to order! I fine you $6.66⅔ for public profanity; $6.66⅔ for disturbin' the peace; $6.66⅔ for contempt of court." This, of course, accounted for the entire $20. Then, with a grand gesture, Bean concluded, "The beer's on me."

* * * * *

For marriage ceremonies, old Roy had a formula; "By the authority of the Constitution of the United States, the great State of Texas, and the Law West of the Pecos, I hereby pronounce you man and wife. May God have mercy on your souls!"

He varied this on one occasion when there was to be a marriage between members of two prominent Langtry families. The license was issued at the county seat, Del Rio, and was sent on the train, but the train was late, very late. The wedding feast had been in readiness a good while, and Judge Bean was hungry, so at last he proceeded with the ceremony, concluding somewhat like this: "By virtue of the authority vested in me by the State of Texas and the marriage license coming in on the No. 10, I now pronounce you man and wife."

* * * * *

There is no end to the stories about Bean. An old burro of his was killed by a train and he sent in a claim to the railroad for $1,500 for his "prize Kentucky jack"; however, he received considerably less!

At his bar, he had a lump of glass which he would drop into a cocktail as he was stirring it and there would be a tinkle as of a piece of ice. Later, he would fish out the lump for future use.

When the scaffolding of the high bridge over the Pecos collapsed, ten men fell 300 feet to the rocks. Seven were killed instantly and the others so badly hurt that there was no chance of recovery. Judge Bean arrived on a mule to find the ten laid out in a row. Over them, one by one, he pronounced, "This man seems to have come to his death by them big timbers falling on him." When a member of the coroner's jury objected that not all of the men were dead, Bean rejoined, "Well, they're gonna die and I'm not gonna make another thirty-mile ride on a soreback mule to hold another inquest. Legally and officially, them fellers is dead." One lingered for three days after he was "dead" in the eyes of the law.

Then there was the time that Judge Bean went into the hog business with a partner. There were no profits and Bean wanted to dissolve the partnership, but the other was not willing. So at last Judge Bean brought suit in his own court, had the partner summoned, then Bean testified, made a speech and rendered a decision in favor of himself for one-half the hogs and further decreed that the other half be sold to pay the costs of court!

A California Variant of Judge Bean's Famous Sentence

An intermountain court faced the duty of sentencing a culprit to death. His Honor braced himself for the responsibility by freely sampling liquor on hand in his room. After going through the legal formalities, he addressed the prisoner thus:

"Don Juan Valjean Vigilanti Karranzas [*hic*], stand up and listen to me. It is usually [*hic*] considered a privilege to come from foreign shores to be Americanized [*hic*] and live under the protection of our flag. When a man does so and commits a crime [*hic*], he knows full well that he must pay the penalty.

"Don Juan Valjean Vigilanti Karranzas, you took the life of a fellow man [*hic*]. You have had a fair and impartial trial by a jury of twelve men and they have found you guilty, and it now becomes my duty to sentence you.

"Soon the blast of a cold and cruel winter will be but a memory. The warm spring sunshine will melt the snows [*hic*] on yonder mountain peak, and little silvery rivulets will trickle down the mountain to this fertile valley below and will moisten the crust of this mother earth. The little posies [*hic*] will poke their heads up through the ground and will bloom in all their springtime beauty and will discharge [*hic*] their fragrance throughout the land.

"The warm spring air will kiss the buds and they will unfold [*hic*] and cast their shadows over the greensward below them. The gentle spring zephyrs [*hic*] will tickle the tassels of the tall grasses, and they will wave [*hic*] to and fro in perfect rhythm with the pussy willows and the columbines.

"The little birds will return from their havens of refuge in the southland where they went to avoid the [*hic*] blizzardly blasts of a cold and cruel winter. They will build their nests [*hic*] and rear their young, and their little voices will find this fertile valley with their melodies.

"All nature will be in tune in one grand and [*hic*] glorious symposium of springtime beauty and joy, and the world will be happy. But

---

From *Gold, Guns, and Ghost Towns,* by W. A. Chalfant, pp. 121–122. Copyright, 1947, by the Board of Trustees of the Leland Stanford Junior University. Stanford, California: Stanford University Press.

you, Don Juan Valjean Karranzas, you scum of the earth, you won't be here to see it. For two weeks from today [*hic*], at high noon, within the confines of the four walls of the county jail [*hic*], you are going to be hanged by your neck until dead."

The outcome of this case of Don Juan, etc., was that he escaped from prison, and remained at liberty to enjoy the pleasures the court had set forth in such flowery fashion.

The Mexican Prisoner Translates His Own Sentence

The bench and bar of San José from the first numbered as many able jurists as might be found in any thriving town of equal size in America. To the more refined gravity of sedate societies their manner might seem a little coarse, and their expletives irreverent, but their law, and the practical application of it, could not be questioned. The court of sessions of San José, in 1850, as then organized, exercised jurisdiction in criminal cases of the highest degree. Judge Rogers was a large, broad-featured, big-mouthed, Johnsonian sort of man, able, profane, and almost brutal in his vulgarity, yet withal, below the superficial asperities of his nature, genial and sympathetic.

One day it became his painful duty to sentence a Mexican who had been tried before him to death. The prisoner did not speak English, and the judge deemed it proper that the sentence, as delivered, should be done into Spanish. The clerk of the court being competent was asked to act as interpreter, but as he was a man of shrinking sensibilities, he expressed abhorrence at the thought of being the medium of communicating the death intelligence to a human being. There are moods in the temper of strong men in which impediment only excites determination. All early Californians had a smattering of Spanish. When the clerk declined the office of translator, with a big round oath Judge Rogers swore he would make the man understand.

"You, sir, get up! *levantate*! *arriba*! *Sabe*? You been tried; tried by jury! damn you! *sabe*? You have been found—what the devil's the Spanish for guilty? Never mind—*sabe*? You have been found guilty, and you are going to be hanged; *sabe*? Hanged? *Entiende*?"

The Mexican was as courageous as the judge was coarse. Evidently he did understand, for with the characteristic nonchalance of his race, he replied, illustrating by signs and gurglings the hanging and choking process:

"*Si, señor, debo ser colgado con chicote; aborcado así; no es nada; gracias á Vd.* (Yes, sir, I am to be hanged at a rope's end; strangled, so; it is nothing; thank you.)"

From *The Works of Hubert Howe Bancroft, California Inter Pocula,* pp. 656–657. Entered according to Act of Congress in the Year 1888 by Hubert H. Bancroft, in the Office of the Librarian of Congress, at Washington. San Francisco: The History Company. Publishers.

The Chinese and the Mule

It was in 1855, at Auburn Ravine, in Placer County, not far from the then flourishing mining camp of Ophirville. A teamster by the name of Chute had turned out his fourteen mule-team for the winter to pick up for themselves an honest living by eating grass in the neighboring gulches and foothills. A Chinese mining party were scratching the auriferous ground of the neighborhood, when one day an adventurous mule invaded the camp in search of a dinner among the tents, bunks, and cooking utensils of what he regarded as an inferior race. Mules have no respect for the Chinese, no regard for the Burlingame Treaty, and look upon the burden-bearing barbarians as usurping outsiders, who are their rivals in packing. The cook assaulted the mule with his long-handled frying-pan. The mule resented the indignity with his heels. The result—a dead Chinaman. The Chinese are a peaceful, non-resistant, and law-abiding people. They will stand killing by the superior race; but there is a point where even resignation ceases to be a virtue. The mule is that point. A meeting of the Chinese miners was promptly convened, the mule was arrested—imitating the white miners—a court was organized, a judge and jury appointed. In a spirit of fair play the mule was accorded counsel. The facts were proven, and the mule, after a fair and impartial trial of his peers, was found guilty and sentenced to death by the halter. He listened to the evidence with perfect indifference; looked upon all the proceedings with unconcern. He was led to execution with the coolness of a fatalist, and only kicked when the rope, thrown over the branch of a stout oak, lifted him and left him dancing upon nothing. The news of his execution was conveyed to his owner, who, hastening to the spot, found his faithful servant suspended by the neck—dead.

Upon expostulating with the Chinese, he was met by the unanswerable logic of the times.

"Chinaman kill 'Melican man, 'Melican man hang Chinaman. Mule kill Chinaman, Chinaman allee same hang mule. What you want?"

A compromise was made, the Chinese paid for the mule, and eat him, and thus to us it seems that substantial justice was done.

No Verdict Needed

Early in the fifties, on a still, hot summer's afternoon, a certain man, in a camp of the northern mines which shall be nameless, having

---

By "Rochester." From *The Argonaut,* San Francisco, California, Saturday, November 24, 1877, Vol. I, No. 36, p. 5.

From *Mountaineering in the Sierra Nevada,* by Clarence King, pp. 300–302. Entered according to Act of Congress, in the year 1871, by James R. Osgood & Co., in the Office of the Librarian of Congress, at Washington. Boston. 1882.

tracked his two donkeys and one horse a half mile, and discovering that a man's track with spur-marks followed them, came back to town and told "the boys," who loitered about a popular saloon, that in his opinion "some Mexican had stole the animals."

Such news as this naturally demanded drinks all round. "Do you know, gentlemen," said one who assumed leadership, "that just naturally to shoot these Greasers ain't the best way. Give 'em a fair trial, and rope 'em with all the majesty of law. That's the cure."

Such words of moderation were well received, and they drank again to "here's hoping we ketch that Greaser."

As they loafed back to the veranda a Mexican walked over the hill brow, jingling his spurs pleasantly in accord with a whistled waltz.

The advocate for law said in undertone, "That's the cuss."

A rush, a struggle, and the Mexican, bound hand and foot, lay on his back in the bar-room. The camp turned out to a man.

Happily such cries as "String him up!" "Burn the doggoned 'lubricator!' " and other equally pleasant phrases fell unheeded upon his Spanish ear.

A jury, upon which they forced my friend, was quickly gathered in the street, and despite refusals to serve, the crowd hurried them in behind the bar.

A brief statement of the case was made by the *ci devant* advocate, and they shoved the jury into a commodious poker-room, where were seats grouped about neat, green tables. The noise outside in the bar-room by and by died away into complete silence, but from afar down the cañon came confused sounds as of disorderly cheering.

They came nearer, and again the light-hearted noise of human laughter mingled with clinking glasses around the bar.

A low knock at the jury door; the lock burst in, and a dozen smiling fellows asked the verdict.

A foreman promptly answered "*Not guilty.*"

With volleyed oaths, and ominous laying of hands on pistol hilts, the boys slammed the door with, "You'll have to do better than that!"

In half an hour the advocate gently opened the door again.

"Your *opinion,* gentlemen?"

"Guilty!"

"Correct! You can come out. We hung him an hour ago."

The jury took theirs "neat"; and when, after a few minutes, the pleasant village returned to its former tranquility, it was "allowed" at more than one saloon that "Mexicans 'll know enough to let white men's stock alone after this." One and another exchanged the belief that this sort of thing was more sensible than " 'nipping' 'em on sight."

When, before sunset, the bar-keeper concluded to sweep some dust out of his poker-room back-door, he felt a momentary surprise at finding the missing horse dozing under the shadow of an oak, and the two lost donkeys serenely masticating playing-cards, of which many bushels lay in a dusty pile.

He was reminded then that the animals had been there all day.

Judge Lynch Comes to Cheyenne

. . . When Cheyenne was only six months old, so frequent were the murders and robberies, and the city authorities so powerless, that a vigilance committee was organized. The first knowledge of its existence happened thus: Three men were arrested on the 10th day of January, 1868, charged with having stolen $900. They were put under bonds to appear before the court on the 14th of the same month. On the morning of the day after they were arrested, they were found on Eddy Street, tied together, walking abreast, with a large piece of canvas attached to them, on which the following words were conspicuous:

$900 stole; $500 returned; thieves—F. St. Clair, W. Grier, E. D. Brownville. City authorities, please not interfere until 10 o'clock A.M. Next case goes up a tree. Beware of Vigilance Committee.

"Fining Judge" Burnett

There were many justices, however, who flagrantly abused their judicial authority for personal gain—those who arbitrarily imposed upon the citizenry through intimidation and violence.

Charleston, on the San Pedro River in Arizona, about eight miles from Tombstone, the location of the Corbin Mill where ore from the celebrated "Toughnut Mine" was treated, was undoubtedly even more lawless, tougher and rougher than the famous city of Tombstone,

---

From *The Pacific Tourist*, J. R. Bowman's Illustrated Trans-Continental Guide of Travel, from the Atlantic to the Pacific Ocean, containing Full Descriptions of Railroad Routes across the Continent, All Pleasure Resorts and Places of Most Noted Scenery in the Far West, also of All Cities, Towns, Villages, U.S. Forts, Springs, Lakes, Mountains, Routes of Summer Travel, Best Localities for Hunting, Fishing, Sporting, and Enjoyment, with all Needful Information for the Pleasure Traveler, Miner, Settler, or Business Man; a Complete Traveler's Guide of The Union and Central Pacific Railroads, and All Points of Business or Pleasure Travel to California, Colorado, Nebraska, Wyoming, Utah, Nevada, Montana, the Mines and Mining of the Territories, the Lands of the Pacific Coast, the Wonders of the Rocky Mountains, the Scenery of the Sierra Nevadas, the Colorado Mountains, the Big Trees, the Geysers, the Yosemite, and the Yellowstone, by Frederick E. Shearer, Editor, with Special Contributions by Prof. F. V. Hayden, Clarence King, Capt. Dutton, A. C. Peale, Joaquin Miller, and J. B. Davis. . . ., p. 66. New York: J. R. Bowman, Publisher. 1882–1883.

From "Vagaries of Frontier Justice," by Charles T. Connell, *Touring Topics*, Vol. 25 (June, 1933), No. 7, Part I, pp. 21, 34. Copyright, 1933, by The Automobile Club of Southern California. Los Angeles.

where most of the epitaphs in Boot Hill cemetery read, "Died with his boots on."

Charleston also had about the toughest justice of the peace in the West, not excepting the notorious Roy Bean, of Pecos. The honorable judge, after his first three months in office, is reported to have submitted a demand on county officials for hundreds of dollars in fees, and, when the account had been trimmed downward, he notified the county officers that "Hereafter the justice's court of Charleston precinct will look after itself."

And it is recorded, the justice ran an independent court of justice. In the course of routine daily doings a saloon-keeper shot and killed a foreman in the Corbin mill. The alert judge placed a fine of $1000 against the killer in a hurry-up trial, which was paid in cash. However, the killer protested, and sought the advice of a prominent attorney, with a view to appealing his case, but the wise attorney advised his client he was getting off easy. The slayer soon realized his predicament, just in time to escape for parts unknown, for the sheriff was after him with a warrant charging him with murder.

On another occasion the avaricious judge with plenty of nerve, walked up to a prosperous cattleman (a desperate character, crazed with drink, who was shooting up the town), pulled him off his horse, took his gun from him; held court on the spot, found him guilty of discharging firearms within the town's limits, thereby endangering the lives of law-abiding citizens, and fined him twenty head of three-year-old steers. The steers were forthwith delivered on the judge's private range, and turned loose among his extensive herd.

Through his arbitrary methods, and he worked fast, Jim Burnett, the thrifty magistrate, accumulated quite a competency, and it is told that as a side line he held the contract for furnishing cordwood to the Corbin mill. Hundreds of Mexican woodchoppers were engaged in bringing cordwood, which was sold to Burnett for delivery at the mill. Whenever the Mexican woodchoppers got drunk and hilarious, which was quite often, they were arrested by a cooperating constable, and the accommodating judge fined them from two to five cords of wood delivered at the mill.

The Gambler and the Judge

One of our foremost gambling characters [on the Comstock lode] was Doughnut Bill, otherwise Sweetcake William. This sagebrush flower toiled not, and was wont to spin only from one faro table to

From *An Editor on the Comstock Lode,* by Wells Drury, Foreword by Ella Bishop Drury, pp. 129–131. Copyright, 1936, by Audrey Drury. New York and Toronto: Farrar & Rinehart, Inc.

another. Bill never did a day's work in his life, and it was tiring him out. He had a languid air when he was called to answer one day in the court of Judge Cox of Virginia City.

"You are charged with assault and battery," said his Honor, "in having belted a man over the head at the Diamond Grotto Saloon last night."

"Jesso," calmly replied William, stroking a dyed mustache with a hand burdened with rings. "Ye see, Judge, I walked back to the game an' took out a twenty in two-bit chips. I bet five on the four an' six to win an' coppered the queen to take the eight with two an' a half. Then I put down two on the ace straight, fur I was bound to make a scratch, bein' down to my seams, as it were, with the hash-man an' the lan'lady. The five on the four an' six was raked in. I got away with my bet on the queen an' eight an' looked aroun' to see how the ace was gittin' along, when I see a stiff walkin' away with it fur a sleeper. I didn't say nuthin' but took it outen his fist all in good natur, an' win a ten by copperin' the jack. By this time the deal was nearly out, an' the deuce, trey, nine, seven, eight, an' ten-spot was cases. 'Copper the odd an' take the even,' sez I, layin' down all I had—jest twenty-eight big dollars. Well, yer Honor—"

"My good fellow," interrupted the Judge, "you are talking Greek to me. I know nothing of this jargon."

"What's that, Jedge?" asked William, slightly puzzled.

"I say, my good fellow, that this hasn't anything to do with your case of assault and battery. You gamblers are becoming too turbulent altogether. I have a good mind to make an example of you, sir. It would be well for men of your class to remember that you are allowed to carry on your immoral trade merely upon sufferance. When civilization, sir, advances somewhat in these Western outposts, the country will not be mortified by the spectacles of legalized vice which now disgrace the State of Nevada and render it so difficult a task to keep the rising generation from following the evil examples which are constantly rising before their eyes. Proceed, sir, but drop your professional slang and remember that this Court knows nothing about the game of faro or any other gambling device."

"Oh, ye don't?" said William. "P'r'aps ye don't call to mind the night you an' me snatched a fifteen-dollar sleeper when a drunk didn't sabe enough to pick up a split on a bet o' thirty. P'r'aps ye don't remember when I staked you at three this mornin' over in the Dew Drop Inn? P'r'aps you and Jake Small ain't snacks in ropin' in snoozers? P'r'aps—"

"Silence!" roared the Court, glaring at the grinning crowd of hangers-on, outside the rail. "There seems to be nothing in this case, William. You leave the Court to infer that you were being cheated and you lifted the stiff under the ear. You're discharged."

Was Wes Hardin Shot in the Back of the Head?

That night [John Wesley Hardin] walked into the virtually empty Acme Saloon [in El Paso, Texas,] raised his left foot in familiar posture on the rail, dropped his chin in his left palm, supported by his elbow bent on the bar, and began rolling dice with the tender, Henry Brown, for a quarter a throw. Hardin shook first and tossed the ivories out.

"Four sixes to beat," he said, as Brown picked up the dice.

Just then the carefully elusive figure of Old John Selman eased in at the swinging doors behind him and cut loose with his .45. Hardin slid to the floor while Selman still pumped in the lead. Captain Frank Carr, of the police force, was there in a few minutes "after the shooting and he found two guns. Colts forty-ones, but . . . no sign of the mail shirt" Hardin was rumored to wear. And the writer for the *Times,* aware that the hardened Selman was still alive, gave him that partisan portrayal now known as "a good press," saying, "The first shot did the work. It entered the eye and came out at the back of the head."

Justice W. D. Howe was called for the inquest. Jeff [Milton] went down for a last look at Hardin, who, with forty-odd notches on his guns, was now comfortably dead in the middle of the Acme floor. His ready eye saw where the bullet had hit. At a table near by sat Selman, wearing a comical little hat, sweating like an Alabama Negro on election day and receiving the acclaim of the mob. Extending a nervous paw to Jeff, he said, "Shake hands with me, Cap, I've killed the son-of-a-bitch. I shot him right in the eye."

"I don't mix with a murderer," said Milton with contempt. "You shot that feller right in the back of the head. You can't shake hands with me, certain!"

Next day the *Times* revised its original report. Selman was arrested, but his attorney, Charlie de Pat, got him out on $10,000 bond, while the preliminary hearing was full of ghastly humor resulting from release of the tension.

The police force breathed a sigh of relief, and the *Times* editorialized on the "climate," claiming that the reputation of the town "as a health resort is already firmly established."

But when George H. Higgins, an Episcopal minister transmogrified into a homeopathic surgeon, was put on the stand after examining the corpse, to determine if it was really murder, if Hardin was really shot in the back of the head or in the eye, he sounded the humorous good sense of the whole town.

"If he was shot in the eye," came his conditional answer, "I'd say it

---

From *Jeff Milton, A Good Man with a Gun,* by J. Evetts Haley, pp. 247–248.

was excellent marksmanship. If he was shot in the back of the head, then I'd say it was excellent judgment."

The Lone Ranger

They rode slowly, saving their strength and the strength of the two big stallions, the snow-white one called Silver and the slightly smaller paint horse that Tonto had named Scout. Yet, despite the easy manner of both the Lone Ranger and his faithful Indian companion, Tonto, they were alert and watchful. They had to be. There were many people who would have liked nothing more than to put bullets through the hearts of these two men. People who had sworn to kill the Lone Ranger because he had served justice by sending their friends to jail or to the hangman's noose.

He was an astonishing man, this Lone Ranger. He had become an almost legendary character throughout the length and breadth of seven states in the early West. Some folks regarded him as a myth, but countless others who had seen him in thrilling action told astounding stories of his skill with rope or gun, his hard riding, and uncanny judgment.

"Look ahead," the Lone Ranger told Tonto, speaking from behind a mask. "The moon is rising and we can see the top of the hill now."

"That right," agreed the Indian. "There plenty cottonwood on top of hill. Maybe we hide horse there. Go to Snake River on foot."

"We'll see," promised the Lone Ranger. He had not yet told Tonto his purpose in heading toward the town of Snake River which bordered on the stream of water for which it was named. He had not told Tonto that he intended to leave him behind when he made his entry into the town itself. There was time enough for that later.

The Lone Ranger had his own peculiar way of serving justice. There were frequent times when sheriffs and other officers of the law disagreed with his methods, but the results of those methods generally found the lawless in jail and the people they oppressed happier for the Lone Ranger's appearance. For several minutes, the two rode toward the distant cottonwoods in silence.

Tonto glanced across the small space that separated the two horsemen, and pride showed in his dark eyes as he studied the fine profile of the masked man. Tonto felt that he had done much to bring this heroic figure to the West. And it was true. It was Tonto who had rescued the one remaining member of the small band of Texas Rangers who had engaged in a fierce battle with an outlaw army. Of the entire band, only one lived, and even this man was more nearly dead than alive.

From *The Lone Ranger and Tonto,* written by Fran Striker, and based on the famous *Lone Ranger* adventures created by Geo. W. Trendle, pp. 1–4, 6. Copyright, 1940, by the Lone Ranger, Inc. New York: Grosset & Dunlap, Publishers.

Tonto remembered vividly how he had carried the still form to his cave, and there applied all the instinctive knowledge of his people in a tireless fight to fan the feeble spark of life to a new flame. For days the Texas Ranger tossed in fever on a crude pallet of straw in the cave. Then, slowly, he regained his health, to learn from Tonto the fate of his friends. He swore then that he would not rest until the last of that marauding band had been made to pay for the massacre. Tonto remembered the steely expression of grim determination that had shown in the Texas Ranger's face when he said, "The last one living—the *Lone Ranger*." He remembered how the white man had unpinned his Texas Ranger's badge, and put it into his pocket; and how he had masked himself, so that none of the outlaws would know that he still lived. Then he had ridden out, masked, sometimes looked upon as an outlaw, while he brought one after another of the killers into the hands of the law.

"We can't stop now," the Lone Ranger had told Tonto when the last of the murderers was finally jailed. "There is too great a need for some one who can at times take the law into his own hands. The people of the West need help, and we're going to try to give it to them."

And that was just the beginning. The Lone Ranger and Tonto became inseparable. Each was the counterpart of the other. Where the Lone Ranger excelled in shooting and roping, Tonto was the superior in following a trail, in healing the sick, and in treating the wounded. When decisive action was required to secure information upon which to plan their actions, the Lone Ranger acted; when quiet stolid waiting in the hope of overhearing certain facts would accomplish the best results, then Tonto took charge.

* * * * *

. . . He made certain his two holsters were well tied to his thighs, and that his brace of heavy six-guns was fully loaded, and in smooth working order. Those guns held bullets that had become a symbol of the Lone Ranger—bullets of solid silver! The gleaming weapons had barked many times in self-defense and in the defense of others, but they had yet to take a life. When the Lone Ranger shot, he shot to disarm or to wound, but he never shot to kill.

Boot Hill

Boot Hill! Back in the wild old days you found one on the new town's outskirts and one where the cattle trail came down to the ford, and one was at the summit of the pass. There was another on the mesa

---

From *When the West Was Young*, by Frederick R. Bechdolt, pp. 277–278. Copyright, 1922, by the Century Company. New York.

overlooking the water-hole where the wagon outfits halted after the long dry drive. The cowboys read the faded writing on the wooden headboards and from the stories made long ballads which they sang to the herds on the bedding grounds. The herds have long since vanished, the cowboys have ridden away over the skyline, the plaintive songs are slipping from the memories of a few old men, and we go riding by the places where those headboards stood, oblivious.

Of the frontier cemeteries whose dead came to their ends, shod in accordance with the grim phrase of their times, there remains one just outside the town of Tombstone to the north. Here straggling mesquite bushes grow on the summit of the ridge; cacti and ocatilla sprawl over the sun-baked earth hiding between their thorny stems the headboards and the long narrow heaps of stones which no man could mistake. Some of these headboards still bear traces of black-lettered epitaphs which tell how death came to strong men in the full flush of youth. But the vast majority of the boulder heaps are marked by cedar slabs whose penciled legends the elements have long since washed away.

The sun shines hot here on the summit of the ridge. Across the wide mesquite flat the granite ramparts of the Dragoons frown all the long day, and the bleak hill graveyard frowns back at them. Thus the men who came to this last resting-place frowned back at Death.

There was a day when very mining camp and cowtown from the Rio Grande to the Yellowstone owned its boot hill; a day when lone graves marked the trails and solitary headboards rotted slowly in the unpeopled wilderness. Many of these isolated wooden monuments fell before the long assaults of the elements; the low mounds vanished and the grass billowed in the wind hiding the last vestiges of the leveled sepulchers. Sometimes the spot was favorable; outfits rested there; new headboards rose about the first one; for the road was long and weary, the fords were perilous from quicksands; thirst lurked in the desert, and the Indians were always waiting. The camp became a settlement, and in the days of its infancy, when there was no law save that of might, the graveyard spread over a larger area. There came an era when a member of that stern straight-shooting breed who blazed the trails for the coming of the statutes wielded the powers of high justice, the middle, and the low. Outlaw and rustler opposed the dominion of this peace officer. Then the cemetery boomed like the young town. Finally things settled down to jury trials and men let lawyers do most of the fighting with forensics instead of forty-fives. Churches were built and school-houses; a new graveyard was established; brush and weeds hid the old one's leaning headboards. Time passed; a city grew; the boot hill was forgotten.

PART FOUR

The Changing West

In such localities where soil or climate or altitude permit, the West in its more obvious phases has become a broader sort of East, but in localities where the soil or climate or altitude do not permit, the West is much as it has always been. In short, the "old West" is spotted; but the spots are large and many of them bid fair to be permanent.

—STRUTHERS BURT

Look for native festivals, look for signs on garages and shops, signs of the stepped horizon, the altar-line of the mesas, signs of the four great winds of the world, of the fructifying cloud—at San Felipe you will find it on the baptismal font—signs of the plumed serpent, Guardian of the Water Sources, acceptable local symbols of widespread service and increase. Look for a Thunderbird Tourist Service. What more competent embodiment of the spirit of service, in a land where for ten thousand years it has been looked for from the corn rows, augury of a fruitful season, the dark-bodied, dun-feathered cloud of the summer rain, wing stretched from mountain to mountain, with arrows of the lightning in its claws.

—MARY AUSTIN

Introduction

CHANGE has been the law in the West—the kinds of change that, first, made a Westerner out of the Easterner and, next, made the Old West into the New, or a "broader sort of East." But the spirit of the Old West still survives, in the way that history "begins with the fact and ends with the symbol." And it is still a fact, as Westerners like to remind Easterners, that some parts of the West—the desert, for example—can never be completely conquered; that as a physical entity the Old West cannot die as long as there are vast stretches of wilderness still to be explored.

The changes that the Easterner underwent in the process of becoming a Westerner were incidental to the changes wrought in the West itself by successive waves of migration and settlement. From the start of the westward journey, the wagon emigrant suffered a land-change, which consisted chiefly in learning to make do with available materials or do without, for shelter, fuel, clothing, and food. The pioneer's ingenuity in adapting himself to his environment has left a trail of stories of soddies, cow chips, and flour-sack garments, of rawhide harness and buckskin pants. The flour-sack tradition is by no means dead: in George Milburn's story of "Imogene Caraway" the "Pride of Texas" has become "Bar-None."[1]

Among the less widely advertised benefits of cow chips are two that Charles C. Lowther praises:

> We have got a lawyer in this here town that claims that whenever he sets down to write his speeches he always likes to be close to a chip fire on account it sort o' fetches him closer to the common people out on the claims a-provin' up on government land. . . .
>
> . . . Up in Hodgeman County a feller come out there so sickly looking you would be almost scared to look at him. He couldn' eat nor sleep to do any good at all. But he got himself a sack and started out to rustle fuel on the prairie. At first he was terrible weak, but he kept at it day after day. By Thanksgiving time he was lookin' better and at Christmas he had a pile of chips as big as a cabin. I shot an antelope and invited this sickly lookin' tenderfoot over and he was able to eat like a bull snake and sleep like a bear. Burnin' cow chips to keep warm by had cured him.[2]

There are innumerable variants on the rawhide theme, all the way from sayings that Texas (the "Rawhide State") was "bound together with rawhide" in the days before barbed wire, and that "what a Texan can't mend with rawhide ain't worth mending,"[3] to the legend of the "Rawhide Railroad." The latter, the first railroad in the "Inland Empire," was a narrow-gauge short line from Wallula to Walla

---

1 *Oklahoma Town* (New York, 1931), pp. 22–26.

2 *Dodge City, Kansas* (Philadelphia, 1940), pp. 24–25.

3 J. Frank Dobie, *The Longhorns* (Boston, 1941), p. 225.

Walla built by Dr. Dorsey Syng Baker in the early Seventies. With pioneer ingenuity Dr. Baker hit upon the idea of covering the wooden rails with strap iron to reduce the wear and tear. Because "strap" was thought of as a strip of leather or rawhide and because the strap iron developed the annoying habit of curling up at the ends and puncturing or derailing cars, some wag, equally ingenious, started the jest that the coyotes must have eaten the rawhide covering off the rails and "there would be no train until the conductor and brakeman could rope a steer, kill him and skin him, and replace the rawhide on the track."[4]

According to one story, the origin of barbed wire was as simple as this: One day a rancher noticed a staple clinched around the smooth wire of his drift fence, which had been torn loose from its posts by drifting cattle, and so he got the idea that a wire with staples on it would render a fence, if not hog-tight and horse-high, at least steer-proof.[5] It was barbed wire that broke the plains for the dry farmer no less truly than the plow—barbed wire and the windmill, which "could be made of old wagon axles, Four X coffee boxes, and scrap iron at a cost as low as $1.50."[6]

If you ask a Southwesterner why there are several windmills standing around a water-tank in a pasture, he will reply: "Well, you see, there is too much wind for one mill to handle!"[7] On the other hand, there is the saying, "In this country we climb for water and dig for wood"; (that is, "climb the windmill tower to turn the wheel by hand and dig mesquite roots"), or "No woman should live in this country who cannot climb a windmill or shoot a gun."[8]

When the small rancher found his stock cut off from grass and water by the cattle barons' fences, hogging the big pastures that once were open range, fence-cutting wars resulted, with signs like the following scrawled on a fence post: "If your bull you hunt for, call at the first ranch this side of Hell and brand him when you get him."[9]

"You better roll up this snag of fence you got strung around here or it won't be healthy for you," a ranch hand threatened Old Jules on the Running Water in Western Nebraska in the Eighties. ". . . You grangers'll never have no money. It don't never rain in this damned

---

[4] Fred Lockley, *Oregon Journal*, January 4, 1924. Cf. W. W. Baker, "The Building of the Walla Walla and Columbia River Railroad," *Washington Historical Quarterly*, Vol. XIV (January, 1923), pp. 3–13. For extracts from the *Rawhide Railroad*, by George Estes (Canby, Oregon, 1916), see *A Treasury of American Folklore* (New York, 1944), pp. 520–524.

[5] Stanley Vestal, *Short Grass Country* (New York, 1941), p. 51.

[6] Walter Prescott Webb, "The Great Plains and the Industrial Revolution," *The Trans-Mississippi West*, edited by James F. Willard and Colin B. Goodykoontz (Boulder, 1930), p. 332. See this and Webb's *The Great Plains* (Boston, 1931) for the six-shooter, barbed wire, the well drill and windmill, and big farm machinery.

[7] Stanley Vestal, *op. cit.*, p. 50.

[8] For these and other sayings quoted from W. P. Webb's *The Great Plains*, see *A Treasury of American Folklore* (New York, 1944), p. 332.

[9] *Galveston News*, December 19, 1883, cited by E. D. Holt, "The Saga of Barbed Wire in the Tom Green Country," *West Texas Historical Association Year Book*, Vol. II, June, 1928, p. 39.

country and you'll stop lead or stretch rope if you keeps shootin' cattle."[10] As he spoke, the "horsebacker" laid his hand caressingly on his Colt, the ideal weapon for the man on horseback which Samuel Colt perfected and began to manufacture in 1836. The six-shooter not only made "all men equal" but "multiplied every soldier by six," thus revolutionizing Plains warfare and replacing the rifle as the weapon of Western folklore and especially the lore of the bad man. It brought in its train a whole new vocabulary of guns and gunplay: peacemaker, equalizer, persuader; thumber, gun-tipper; fanning, slip and hip shooting, single and double roll, border shift, etc.[11]

The war between the rancher and the nester was part of a rivalry between two orders of society that goes back to the days of Cain and Abel. It was a war between the nomadic and the settled way of life, between a man's country and a woman's country. The conflict ended in a fusion of the two, a compromise between the frontier, with its urge to keep moving, and the section, with its need of taking root. The coming of the dry farmer sharpened the conflict between two classes of stockmen, the cattleman and the sheepman, and revealed the homesteader as their common foe. In the long run all three buried the hatchet. Nowadays the Texas sheepherder rides instead of walks, wears chaps in the brush, a cowboy hat and high boots. "It is rumored of one important sheepman of West Texas that he had a special pair of patent leather high-heeled boots made to wear with his tuxedo, simply because he cannot dance in anything but good cowboy boots."[12] For that matter, even the plowman rides today—his saddle horse, riding plow, or tractor—and his sons play cowboy. The cowboy continues to steal the show, and the bronc-buster on a bucking bronco remains the arch-symbol of the region.

To complete the conquest of the open range and its conversion into fence and homestead country, the settler had as his tools and allies big farm machinery and the social institutions of the "home, the school, the church, and the Sunday School to compete with the camp, saloon, dance hall, and gaming table."[13] All this was made possible by the railroad, which brought hordes of new settlers to the Western farm lands, brought the East and West closer together, and brought the farmer to town. To many an old timer, be he cattleman or farmer, the railroad spelled the passing of the old order and the coming of the new. Barbed wire rendered the long cattle drive obsolete and the railroad indispensable. Many a town war was fought over the location of the railroad as well as of the county seat. Many a boom town became a ghost town when it lost the railroad. In the Cherokee strip the town of Enid was divided by the curious Railroad War.

The railroad would not stop trains at South Town. People had to get off at North Town. They were told that they were in Enid, the place they were

---

[10] Mari Sandoz, *Old Jules* (Boston, 1935), pp. 36–38.

[11] Cf. Ramon F. Adams, *Cowboy Lingo* (Boston, 1936) and *Western Words* (Norman, 1944).

[12] Winifred Kupper, *The Golden Hoof* (New York, 1945), p. 117.

[13] Edward Everett Dale, *Cow Country* (Norman, 1945), p. 220.

looking for. If they insisted on going on to South Town they would have to get a rig, and no rigs could be hired for that purpose in North Town. When South Town people went to get the travelers, North Towners would try to upset the rigs and cut the harness. . . . For a while it looked as if South Town was a goner. Then the people decided that passengers and freight left at North Town should reach South Town whether or no. Every mule-freight was furnished with an armed guard, and a regular stage was sent to meet the passenger trains. Mr. Howell drove the stage, and he carried the Winchester in a holster beside his high seat. . . .

Still, Rock Island trains whistled through South Town without stopping. Red lanterns and dynamite caps on the track failed to stop them. Bullets failed to stop them: conductors would draw the window blinds and tell passengers to scrooch down away from the glass. One night some one sawed the pilings of the trestle and a freight train went into the south branch of Boggy. That was the first train to stop in South Town. If you know the right parties in Enid you can see the saw that was responsible. Some day it may go to the Oklahoma Historical Society.[14]

On May 10th, 1869, the last spike was driven and the last tie laid at Promontory Point, linking the East and West with "bands of iron." The writer in *The Pacific Tourist* noted a curious incident in connection with the laying of the last rails. "The Union Pacific people brought up their pair of rails and the work of placing them was done by Europeans. The Central Pacific people then laid their pair of rails, the labor being performed by Mongolians. The foremen, in both cases, were Americans. Here, near the center of the great American Continent, were representatives of Asia, Europe, and America—America directing and controlling."[15] The incident symbolizes the joining of both Easts and Wests, but, as time proved only too well, Eastern capital was directing and controlling.

In 1893 the Cherokee Strip was opened to settlement. An old-timer who made the run from Caldwell, Kansas, recalls how he left his horse and buggy at a livery stable and made the race on a Rock Island freight train with two big locomotives and twenty-seven cattle cars. When at 12 o'clock noon the soldiers fired their guns in the air

the engines began to chug-chug and the old freight started, everybody on it yelling and shouting. . . . People were racing in every known vehicle. They were on horseback, on bicycles and foot. . . . It was reported afterwards that the train carried 5,000 people that day. The train wouldn't stop at South Enid where the land office was, so a crowd of us got off at Waukomis and walked back. The name was appropriate. We had to "Walk-home. . . .

The first Sunday after the opening a Congregationalist minister stood on a dry goods box in the center of the town and preached the first sermon ever preached in Enid. His text was, "And what shall it profit a man, if he gain the whole world and lose his own soul." "No Bible text could have been more appropriate, for people seem to have gone wild with greed. It was every man for himself."[16]

---

[14] Marquis James, *The Cherokee Strip* (New York, 1945), pp. 13–14.

[15] See "The Driving of the Last Spike at Promontory Point," Part Two, above.

[16] *Southwestern Folk History* (Oklahoma City, 1939), pp. 77–79.

The railroad (soon followed by the highway and the airway) completed the invasion of the West by the East and the conquest of the Wild West and of time and space, which had begun with the introduction of the horse by the Spanish and continued with the development of Western transportation through the days of ox and mule team, pony express, and stagecoach. The railroad not only made history but created legend in the West. Legends involving the men who built empires as well as railroads—Jim Hill and the "Big Four," Stanford, Crocker, Huntington, and Hopkins,[17] and fabulous characters like Lucky Baldwin, who threatened to tear up the Santa Fe tracks through his Santa Anita ranch when a train refused to stop for him, and Death Valley Scotty, who made the headlines when he hired a special train to take him from Barstow to Los Angeles and then to Chicago in an unbeaten record of forty-five hours.

The steam engine came to the West in other forms—the steam thresher (along with the McCormick reaper, the combine, the tractor); the donkey engine of the logger and the oil driller. When finally steam heat came to the bunkhouse, something went out of the logging camp that steam and improved living and working conditions can never bring back—the "old-time life and fun," the yarns and the songs of the bunkhouse bard, the shanty boy, and fiddler. Today the lumberjacks' Saturday night in town is a tame affair. "No," the hotel night clerk told Stewart Holbrook, "they don't kick out windows any more. But one'll kick hell out of more timber than the two of his grandpappies could. They're highball these days." Even if they do wear rayon underwear, smoke cigarets, and use talcum powder after shaving.[18] Today, too, when the cowboy goes to town on his day off, he gets his hair cut, sees a movie (preferably a horse opera) and buys a Western story magazine and a comic book (his favorite reading matter) and maybe a new rope. He seldom gets into trouble because he is "more discreet, somewhat better educated" and has a "wider range of tastes" than his prototype.[19]

In the new West the oil boom has replaced the gold rush as the symbol of sudden wealth and its equally sudden loss, of the mad gamble and scramble of speculation and exploitation. The prospector who went to heaven and started a rumor of a gold strike in hell, then fell for it himself, has been transferred to an oilfield setting. But now that land's end has been reached and the frontier has passed, a sour note enters into the stories of overnight rags-to-riches. "Damn the oil!" roared the cattle baron on whose range oil had been found, "I need water for my cattle."[20] "I'm a-goin' to buy myself a new ax," said the old farm wife; "that old ax I been a-choppin' wood for the cookstove with is so dull it's about to drive me crazy."[21] Another old

---

[17] Cf. Stewart H. Holbrook, *The Story of American Railroads* (New York, 1947), and Oscar Lewis, *The Big Four* (New York, 1941).

[18] *Little Annie Oakley and Other Rugged People* (New York, 1948), pp. 214–215.

[19] Donald Wayne, "Texas Cattleman," *Holiday*, Vol. 4 (December, 1948), No. 6, pp. 100, 121.

[20] Curtis Bishop and Bascom Giles, *Lots of Land* (Austin, 1949), p. 283.

[21] John William Rogers, *The Lusty Texans of Dallas* (New York, 1951), p. 274.

woman, told that now she could give her laundry out or at least buy a washing machine, said grimly, without straightening up from her washboard: "I don't know about this oil business. It's here to-day and gone to-morrow. But I do know that I can get these clothes clean. I've been doing that all my life."[22] On the other hand, sudden riches may go to a poor rancher's head and give him delusions of cultural as well as social grandeur, so that he not only buys himself a mansion but "endows an institute of animal husbandry and spends his declining years telling the state university how to educate the youth of the land."[23]

With the coming of "Culture," along with the machine age and big business, the West has become self-conscious about its past, the Western tradition, and the spirit of the Old West. When a culture becomes moribund and nostalgic, it becomes a cult. From the beginning of the "histrionic West," Western stuff has been good business and it has now become big business. E. C. Abbott recalls the time that Buffalo Bill came into a saloon at North Platte and took off his hat. His long hair, which he kept rolled under his hat, fell down on his shoulders. As he rolled it back under his hat, the saloon man said, "Say, Bill, why the hell don't you cut the damn stuff off?" And Cody replied, "If I did, I'd starve to death."[24]

Now that the "young man's country" of the West has become an old man's country, with more and more middle-aged and aged Easterners and Middle Westerners retiring to California, and more and more young Westerners going East, the old-timer has his day, every day and not just at old-timers' association picnics and banquets and Frontier Days' celebrations. Although a lot of nonsense has been written and talked about the good old days, the old-timer who has lived to see the country grow up and pass through all the stages of Western development right under his eyes has learned to take change in his stride and has earned the right to be skeptical about much so-called "progress." He well may say with Will Rogers, "An ax handle wrapped up with cowhide I believe would have fit and felt better in my hand than a niblick. I wish I could have lived my whole life and drank out of a gourd instead of a paper envelope."[25] Or with Charlie Russell: "Those were good old days. For we were kids then the buffalo went long ago the wild cows we knew and the cow hosses have joined them and most of the cow punchers of our time have crossed the big devide we usto know every body but time has made us strangers but we got no licence to kick we got the cream let these comlatlys have the skim milk."[26]

B.A.B.

---

[22] Donald Day, *Big Country: Texas* (New York, 1947), p. 278.

[23] Green Peyton, *America's Heartland: The Southwest* (Norman, 1948), p. 95.

[24] *We Pointed Them North* (New York, 1939), pp. 60–61.

[25] Speech to Texas Old Time Trail Drivers Association, cited by Boyce House, *City of Flaming Adventure* (San Antonio, 1949), p. 140.

[26] Letter to Pat T. Tucker, October 27, 1921, *The Frontier,* Vol. IX (March, 1929), No. 3, p. 226.

I. MINERS

"Ho! for gold! We're a-goin'! Wagons making. Clothes preparing. Our business abandoning. Selling our houses. Putting off our wives and children upon their relations, or leaving them alone by themselves. Going to be rich, all round. No use being poor. No use to plod along, for your mere living, with your nose and belly in the dust, and your heels in the air. O no! Here we go to Pike's Peak. Times are hard—we go to Pike's Peak. Will be better no doubt, at Pike's Peak." So say many of our city people, and away goes their property, their homes and firesides, and happy prospective of their families, and their own personal comforts.

—ALTON DEMOCRAT, 1859

First News of the Gold Discovery

In the newly made raceway of the sawmill recently erected by Captain Sutter on the American Fork, gold has been found in considerable quantities. One person brought thirty dollars' worth to New Helvetia, gathered there in a short time. California, no doubt, is rich in mineral wealth; great chances here for scientific capitalists. Gold has been found in almost every part of the country.

Marshall's Own Story of the Discovery of Gold

In May,[1] 1847, with my rifle, blanket, and a few crackers to eat with the venison (for the deer then were awful plenty) I ascended the Ameri-

---

From the *Californian,* March 15, 1848, cited by Ralph P. Bieber in *Southern Trails to California in 1849,* the Southwest Historical Series, edited by Ralph P. Bieber, Vol. V, p. 65. Copyright, 1937, by the Arthur H. Clark Company. Glendale, California.

This item, which was the first printed account of the gold discovery, was not copied by the press in the eastern part of the United States.—R.P.B.

From "Marshall's Own Account of the Gold Discovery," as told to Charles B. Gillespie, *The Century Illustrated Monthly Magazine,* Vol. XLI (February, 1891), No. 4, pp. 537–538. Copyright, 1891, by the Century Company, New York.

[1] Documents show this to be March.—Mannel Hahn

Annotations from "The Discovery of Gold in California," by Mannel Hahn, *The*

can River, according to Mr. Sutter's wish,[2] as he wanted to find a good site for a saw-mill, where we could have plenty of timber, and where wagons would be able to ascend and descend the river hills. Many fellows had been out before me, but they could not find any place to suit; so when I left I told Mr. Sutter I would go along the river to its very head and find the place, if such a place existed anywhere upon the river or any of its forks. I traveled along the river the whole way. Many a place would suit very well for the erection of the mill, with plenty of timber everywhere, but then nothing but a mule could climb the hills; and when I would find a spot where the hills were not steep, there was no timber to be had; and so it was not until I had been out several days and reached this place, which, after first sight, looked like the exact spot we were hunting.

I passed a couple of days examining the hills, and found a place where wagons could ascend and descend with all ease. On my return to the fort I went out through the country examining the cañons and gulches and picking out the easiest places for crossing them with loaded wagons.

You may be sure Mr. Sutter was pleased when I reported my success. We entered into partnership; I was to build the mill, and he was to find provisions, teams, tools, and to pay a portion of the men's wages. I be-

---

Westerners Brand Book, Vol. V (May, 1948), No. 3, pp. 15–16. Chicago, Illinois: Issued monthly as the official publication of the Chicago Corral of Westerners.

For other articles on the gold discovery and California backgrounds, in the *Century,* Vol. XLI, the index to that volume should be consulted. For the gold rush, see also *The Works of Hubert Howe Bancroft,* Vol. XXIII, *History of California,* Vol. VI, 1848–1859 (San Francisco, 1888) and Vol. XXXV, *California Inter Pocula* (San Francisco, 1888), pp. 63–67.

2 [John A.] Sutter wanted to build a flour mill on his land. To do so, he needed a sawmill—the hand sawing of timbers was too slow. Finding that James W. Marshall was a worthy millwright, he sent him up the wooded valley to build a sawmill. The Coloma valley, 45 miles from the fort, was selected because wagons could get there without trouble and there was plenty of yellow pine available. Furthermore, the stream was convenient for a dam and race without much digging, and flooding was not a danger. On March 27, 1847, Sutter and Marshall signed articles of agreement for a partnership—Sutter to furnish men, money and materials, and Marshall to furnish the know-how and to manage the sawmill enterprise.

By August, Marshall had six Mormons, three Gentiles, and twelve or more Indians at work; and the little self-contained mill settlement was busied at constructing the mill, damming the stream, digging the race, and hanging the wheel. In January of 1848, the gates were opened to flush some of the muck out of the race. After a while, the gates were closed. They worked perfectly.

One morning, Marshall—but here [above] is his own story as related to a pioneer miner in 1859, sitting on the bank of the race above the spot where history was made.

* * * * *

This narrative was written down by Charles B. Gillespie, a "49er" who was making a sketch of Sutter's Mill on Sunday and met Marshall, who then sat above the race with him and dictated this yarn. The internal evidence—which is all we have beside Gillespie's word for it—is strong, and I am inclined to believe it is the "pure quill," for it agrees at every point with other known facts. . . .—M.H., *ibid.,* pp. 14–15, 16.

lieve I was at the time the only millwright in the whole country. In August, everything being ready, we freighted two wagons with tools and provisions, and accompanied by six men, I left the fort, and after a good deal of difficulty reached this place one beautiful afternoon and formed our camp on yon little rise of ground right above the town.

Our first business was to put up log houses, as we intended remaining here all winter. This was done in less than no time, for my men were great with the axe. We then cut timber and fell to work hewing it for the framework of the mill. The Indians gathered about us in great numbers. I employed about forty of them to assist us with the dam, which we put up in a kind of way in about four weeks. In digging the foundation of the mill we cut some distance into the soft granite; we opened the forebay and then I left for the fort, giving orders to Mr. Weimar to have a ditch cut through the bar in the rear of the mill, and after quitting work in the evening to raise the gate and let the water run all night, as it would assist us very much in deepening and widening the tail-race.

I returned in a few days and found everything favorable, all the men being at work in the ditch. When the channel was opened it was my custom every evening to raise the gate, and let the water wash out as much sand and gravel through the night as possible; and in the morning, while the men were getting breakfast, I would walk down, and, shutting off the water, look along the race and see what was to be done, so that I might tell Mr. Weimar, who had charge of the Indians, at what particular point to set them to work for the day. As I was the only millwright present, all of my time was employed upon the framework and machinery.

One morning in January—it was a clear, cold morning: I shall never forget that morning—as I was taking my usual walk along the race after shutting off the water, my eye was caught with the glimpse of something shining in the bottom of the ditch. There was about a foot of water running then. I reached my hand down and picked it up; it made my heart thump, for I was certain it was gold. The piece was about half the size and of the shape of a pea. Then I saw another piece in the water. After taking it out I sat down and began to think right hard. I thought it was gold, and yet it did not seem to be of the right color; all the gold coin I had seen was of a reddish tinge; this looked more like brass. I recalled to mind all the metals I had ever seen or heard of, but could find none that resembled this. Suddenly the idea flashed across my mind that it might be iron pyrites. I trembled to think of it! The question could soon be determined. Putting one of the pieces on a hard river stone, I took another and commenced hammering it. It was soft, and didn't break; it therefore must be gold, but largely mixed with some other metal, very likely silver; for pure gold, I thought, would certainly have a brighter color.

When I returned to our cabin for breakfast, I showed the two pieces to my men. They were all a good deal excited, and had they not thought that the gold only existed in small quantities they would have abandoned everything and left me to finish my job alone. However, to satisfy them, I told them that as soon as we had the mill finished we would devote a week to gold hunting and see what we could make out of it.

While we were working in the race after this discovery we always kept a sharp lookout, and in the course of three or four days we had picked up about three ounces—our work still progressing as lively as ever, for none of us imagined at that time that the whole country was sowed with gold.

In about a week's time after the discovery I had to make another trip to the fort; and, to gain what information I could respecting the real value of the metal, took all that we had collected with me and showed it to Mr. Sutter, who at once declared it was gold, but thought with me that it was greatly mixed with some other metal. It puzzled us a good deal to hit upon the means of telling the exact quantity of gold contained in the alloy; however, we at last stumbled on an old American cyclopedia, where we saw the specific gravity of all the metals, and rules given to find the quantity of each in a given bulk. After hunting over the whole fort and borrowing from some of the men, we got three dollars and a half in silver, and with a small pair of scales we soon ciphered it out that there was no silver nor copper in the gold, but that it was entirely pure.

This fact being ascertained, we thought it our best policy to keep it as quiet as possible till we should have finished our mill. But there was a great number of disbanded Mormon soldiers in and about the fort, and when they came to hear of it, why it just spread like wildfire, and soon the whole country was in a bustle. I had scarcely arrived at the mill again till several persons appeared with pans, shovels, and hoes, and those that had not iron picks had wooden ones, all anxious to fall to work and dig up our mill; but this we would not permit. As fast as one party disappeared another would arrive, and sometimes I had the greatest kind of trouble to get rid of them. I sent them all off in different directions, telling them about such and such places where I was certain there was plenty of gold if they would only take the trouble of looking for it. At that time I never imagined that the gold was so abundant. I told them to go to such and such places, because it appeared that they would dig nowhere but in such places as I pointed out, and I believe that such was their confidence in me that they would have dug on the very top of yon mountain if I had told them to do so.

The second place where gold was discovered was in a gulch near the Mountaineer House, on the road to Sacramento. The third place was on a bar on the South Fork of the American River a little above the junction of the Middle and South forks. The diggings at Hangtown [now Placerville] were discovered next by myself, for we all went out for a while as soon as our job was finished. The Indians next discovered the diggings at Kelsey's, and thus in a very short time we discovered that the whole country was but one bed of gold. So there, stranger, is the entire history of the gold discovery in California—a discovery that hasn't as yet been of much benefit to me.[3]

Prospecting

. . . We have spent the day in *prospecting*. The term, as it designates a very important part of the business of mining, requires explanation. I should first, however, give some description of the bar upon which we are to labor. This lies on both sides of the river, and is covered with smooth, brassy-looking rocks, some of which weigh many tons. It is a

---

[3] The results of the gold rush are known. From San Francisco in March, the word spread to the East and by 1849 huge parties totaling some 75,000 in a year came out to reap the golden harvest. Although the discovery of gold was made in a Mexican province, eleven days later Alta California was ceded to the United States. The promise made to the early settlers that their claims would be validated by the government were only partly fulfilled. Sutter lost his larger claim—the votes of several thousand gold-hungry prospectors offered more lure to the officials than Sutter's lone German-accented vote! The immigrants who tasted Sutter's bounty were unwilling to share fortune with him. Mismanagement—at which he was adept—sapped his means, and he was soon penniless. Yet such was his popularity that the state legislature voted him a pension of $3,000 a year, which it paid until he left California to go to Lititz, Pennsylvania, and petition Congress for repayment for the losses he had suffered, In 1880, he died, his claim still unsettled. He was buried in Lititz and a hotel there is named in his honor. Sutter County in California also perpetuates his name.

Poor Marshall fared no better. His lumber brought him plenty of money—it sold as high as $500 per M board feet. But the stand of timber was soon depleted. Money flowed from him when he had it. Turning to mining, he found rich deposits, and abandoned them. He refused friendship. That Sutter should be proclaimed the discoverer of gold irked him. That men he had purposely misdirected made good finds soured him. When Sutter went broke and was accorded a pension, he snarled out an autobiography and finally received a pension of $100 a month—later raised—and for six years had enough for comfort. Then the legislature failed to renew the grant, and Marshall holed up with another indigent miner in a solitary cabin. For eight years he lived and snarled in sight of his first and historic find. He died in 1885, 73 years old, a perfect misanthrope. He was buried at Coloma, and four years later the Society of the Native Sons covered his mean grave with a monument topped by a bronze figure of the Discoverer of Gold—for which they paid enough to have eased the last eight years of penury and want he suffered!

None of those who were on the ground-floor collected big dividends. Though none rose as high as Sutter, none fell as deep as he and Marshall. They lived out comfortable, uninspired lives. The Mormons, who fared best, settled in Utah.—M.H., *ibid.*, p. 17.

From *Sixteen Months at the Gold Diggings*, by Daniel B. Woods, pp. 50–52. Entered, according to Act of Congress, in the year 1851, by Leonard Woods, in the Office of the Clerk of the District Court of New York. New York: Harper & Brothers, Publishers. 1852.

For an account of California gold mining methods and processes, see "Dame Shirley (Louise Amelia Knapp Smith Klappe), *The Shirley Letters from the California Mines, 1851–1852,* edited by Carl I. Wheat (New York, 1949), pp. 130–137. For Nevada prospecting and mining terminology, see *Nevada* (Portland, 1940), pp. 58–63.

little higher than the water level; but we find, as we dig down, that the water soon begins to flow in, and must be "baled out." This bar, or rather succession of bars, extends a distance of some miles up and down the river, over which the water runs with surprising rapidity in the freshets, which are common during the rainy season, and break up and reduce the gold-bearing quartz, tearing it away from its primitive bed, robbing it, in its course, of its virgin gold, and attriting it till it is at length deposited, in greater or less abundance, within some crevice or some water-worn hollow, or beneath some rock so formed as to receive it. These bars vary from a few feet to several hundred yards in width.

In order to find the deposits, the ground must be "prospected." A spot is first selected, in the choice of which science has little and chance everything to do. The stones and loose upper soil, as also the subsoil, almost down to the primitive rock, are removed. Upon or near this rock most of the gold is found; and it is the object, in every mining operation, to reach this, however great the labor, and even if it lies forty, eighty, or a hundred feet beneath the surface. If, when this stratabelt of rock is obtained, it is found to present a smooth surface, it may as well be abandoned at once; if soft and pliable, or if seamed with crevices running at angles with the river, the prospect of the mine is favorable.

Some of the dirt is then put into a pan, and taken to the water, and washed out with great care. The miner stoops down by the stream, choosing a place where there is the least current, and, dipping a quantity of water into the pan with the dirt, stirs it about with his hands, washing and throwing out the large pebbles till the dirt is thoroughly wet, and the water is then taken into the pan, and the whole mass is well stirred and shaken, and the top gravel thrown off with the fingers, while the gold, being heavier, sinks deeper in the pan. It is then shaken about, more water being continually added, and thrown off with a sideway motion, which carries with it the dirt at the top, while the gold settles yet lower down. It must be often stirred with the hands to prevent "baking," as the hardening of the sand at the bottom is called. When the dirt is nearly washed out, great care is requisite to prevent the lighter scales of gold from being washed out with the magnetic sand, which is best done by pushing back the gold, and clearing the sand from the edge of the pan with the thumb. At length a ridge of gold scales, mixed with a little sand, remains in the pan, from the quantity of which some estimate may be formed of the richness of the place. If there are five to eight grains, it is considered that "it will pay." If less gold is found, the miner digs or opens a new hole, till he finds a place affording a good prospect. When this is done, he sets his cradle by the side of the stream, in some convenient place, and proceeds to work all the dirt. This is aptly named prospecting and is the hardest part of a miner's business. Thus have we employed the whole of this day, digging one hole after another—washing out many testpans—hoping, at every new attempt, to find that which would reward our toil, and we have made *ten cents* each.

Jumping Claims

If a miner has not complied with all the requirements of law, his claim (or mine) can, on the second New Year's day following the date of location, be re-located by himself or others, who may be on the ground before him. . . .

A person stuck up notices on a claim near a cabin in which three men were sleeping, awaiting early morning to locate it. The locater, after securing the claim, thoughtfully woke the boys to tell them they needn't get up so early, as the claim was located.

One party on a location, who owned it until 12 o'clock, stood two others off until that hour on his rights as owner. At exactly 12, he put his notice in the split-stakes, and sang 12 o'clock before the others, who had no watch, knew what time it was, and then drove off.

A prospector started out with his notice written and in his pocket. He lost it on the way, seven miles from town, had no pencil or paper, and returned home, while another man located the claim.

There was a little episode in Quigley's Gulch, wherein three bad partners had made it up to relocate themselves in a claim and leave out the fourth partner. The latter had previously been warned against coming upon the claim that night, and was told by a friend that his partners were going to relocate it all to themselves; so he secured a rifle, and after the three bad partners had gone up to the mine, he crawled up on the shady side of the gulch to a cabin below the claim about 100 yards and there watched. At 11:45 his partners started up to stake the ground, whereupon, with a fearful yell, he turned loose with his gun, and could see the crusted snow fly, at every pop just over his partners' heads. They heard the bullets humming so near their ears that a panic seized them and they fled for town. As soon as they were out of sight he quietly walked up and located it all to himself, and left his bad partners out in the cold.

John Curtin, with his partner, went to re-locate a claim up on Sugar Loaf Peak, the highest range or divide between Deer Creek and Bullion. In trying to step too long a pace to set his end stake to the top of the peak at some croppings, his big-soled boots slipped upon the snow crust which, by constant exposure to the sun in the daytime, melted and again froze in the shade until it was a sheet of ice down the mountain side and very precipitous. John went head first, following his hat to the bottom, 500 feet, and lit on a big snow-drift. His clothes were torn and his finger nails worn off by clutching at the crust. Getting up to see if

---

From the *Tombstone* (Arizona) *Epitaph*, Vol. IX, No. 1, August 6, 1887, p. 4, col. 4. The Salt Lake *Tribune* notes several incidents, more or less ludicrous, of the kind indicated.—Ed.

For tricks of miners and "bogus" miners, see Dan De Quille, *The Big Bonanza* (New York, 1947), pp. 331–339.

he was all there, he heard his partner calling, and hallowing back. His partner shouted:

"What yer doing down there?" and John was so mad he answered: "Was getting so cold, I came down after wood." In fifteen minutes he lit a fire in the grove he arrived at so suddenly, and was joined by his partner thirty minutes later, who was exhausted. John concluded that the joke was on his partner after all.

A well-known Bullion miner named Mike Hynes had told all the town he had several rich locations to jump between the noted mines. Before Christmas day he had a draughtsman and expert to draw off his notices and put each one in a box on the claims he intended jumping. Being a little behind time on New Year's eve, he was coming up the gulch to tack up his boxes, and the first square view he got of his intended claims was one calculated to make his hair stand on end as sitting on each end of the seven claims and upon each of the seven boxes was a man, and each man had a Winchester repeating rifle pointed at Mike, who was so amazed that he passed by each one! merely remarking "Good evening, Happy New Year!" And he didn't feel very well until he got to a saloon at Bullion, where he braced up and remarked that he guessed he hadn't lost any mines, and he wouldn't give $5 for all he had come to jump.

The Lucky Louse, or, Blood Will Tell

It was one day in the rainy winter of '54 and '55, and too wet to work in the mines, so the boys begun to wander in early down at the Long Tom. By noon all the tables was full and the gambling got more exciting as the day wore on. Some of the boys set right there at the tables from morning through all the day and on into the evening, without stopping except to take on a drink or to make room for more.

If you once get the gambling fever, you know, in a place like that, the longer you keep at it, the higher the fever gets. That fever's catching and it'll spread through a crowd like any other fever. So monte, faro, seven-up, and the different brands of poker got too slow for some,

---

From *Ghost Town,* Wherein Is Told Much That Is Wonderful, Laughable, and Tragic, and Some That Is Hard to Believe, about Life during the Gold Rush and Later in the Town of Columbia on California's Mother Lode, as Remembered by the Oldest Inhabitants and Here for the First Time Set Down by G. Ezra Dane in collaboration with Beatrice J. Dane, pp. 13–18. Copyright, 1941, by G. Ezra Dane. New York: Alfred A. Knopf.

Frank A. Morgan, born in Columbia in 1871, died at Sonora in 1934. He was the son of George Morgan, who went as a British soldier to Australia, there married an Irish girl, Margaret Reilly, came with her to California in '52, and became the proprietor of Columbia's City Hotel. Frank Morgan's many years "on the road" through the Mother Lode country made him a practised raconteur, and to him we owe the basic patterns for . . . the Lucky Louse. . . .—G.E.D. and B.J.D., *ibid.,* p. 305.

The Danes' *Ghost Town* and Dan De Quille's *The Big Bonanza* are two indispensable volumes of mining lore and humor that belong beside Twain's *Roughing It.*

and they begun laying bets on any chance that offered. At some of the tables they was betting on the turn of a card, and they was one crowd having a spitting tournament at the stove. Then they was some fellows betting which of two flies on the wall would move first, and others at the door laying bets whether or not the next man to come in would be Irish. But the greatest bet in betting history was laid that night by young Ad Pence. An inspiration it was, no less.

"Boys," says Ad, pounding on the bar to get the attention of the crowd, "boys," says he, "luck's been agin me so far, but I've got five hundred here that says I've a louse that can beat, in a fair race, any louse that ever cut his teeth on any miner's hide."

He'd caught a good lively one and held him up for all the boys to see.

"I say this louse is the champeen," says Ad, "for I've been chasing him around my carcass for a week and I've only just caught up with him. Five hundred backs him against all comers."

Well, at that all the games stopped short, and everybody crowded up to the bar where Ad was showing off this champeen louse. But none of the boys would admit that he kept this kind of stock and it begun to look as though nobody was going to take the bet. Then a stranger, a big Irishman with a red beard, come elbowing his way through the crowd and up to the bar where Ad was standing.

"Will ye let me have a look at that louse?" he says.

So Ad held it out and the stranger squinted at it from one side and then from the other. "A dainty crayther indade he is," says he, "but I think he's no racer. His belly's too low and his legs are too short by a long ways. Now wait just a bit and I'll have something to show ye."

So the stranger put his hand inside his shirt, and scrabbled around in there for a minute, and when he pulled it out again, between his thumb and finger he held a struggling louse.

"Me boy," he says, "your five hundred is as good as gone. But before I take it from ye, I want ye to have a good look at *this* louse. Ye'll never see the likes of him again. Ye say yours is the champeen, but ye've only had him a wake, and he has not so much as a name. I say he's but a mongrel. Now *this* one is the greatest racing louse in all the world, and he has the most distinguished pedigray that ever a louse did boast. And I don't want to be taking your money under any false pretenses, so I'm going to tell ye his history, and when ye've heard it, if ye want to withdraw, I'll freely let ye do so.

"Just before me old grandfather died, back in Ireland, he called me to his bedside and he said to me: 'Grandson,' says he, 'I'm a pore man. I've no money to lave ye, nor any property. But there's wan threasure I have, Grandson,' says the old man, 'Katie, the finest little seam squirrel in all of Ireland, and a direct discindent of one that fed on Saint Patrick.

" 'Take her, Grandson,' says he, 'kape good care of her and fade her well, and she'll surely bring ye luck.'

"Now, me boy, this louse ye see here is Larry, Katie's great-great-great-grandson, and the blood of Saint Patrick himself runs in his veins, so he's bound to bring me luck. And to show the faith I have in him and in Holy Saint Patrick, bejayziz, I'll lay a thousand to that five hundred ye bet on yer mongrel louse! Now, do ye still want to make the bet?"

"I do," says Ad. "Your louse may be good, but I know what mine can do from long chasing of him, and my bet on him still stands."

So Ad and the stranger placed their stakes with Doc Johns, and side betting begun in the crowd.

"There can be no race without a racetrack," says the stranger, and he calls to the bar-tender. "Bring us a plate," he says. "Now, boys, the middle's the start, the edge is the goal, and the first little pants rabbit over the rim is the winner."

So the bar-tender brought the plate, and the stranger felt of it. "No louse," says he, "would ever set a good pace on this cold plate. Let's hate it up a bit, and then you'll see them kick up their heels and run."

So they heated the plate piping hot over the stove and set it on a table where all could see. And when Doc Johns counted off: "One, two, three, go!" each man dropped his louse in the middle of the plate, and they were off, a-scrambling and a-jumping because it was so hot, you know. The boys was cheering and yelling and standing on chairs to see, and laying bets right and left.

Well, neck and neck it was at the start acrost the bottom of the plate, but Ad's louse pulled ahead a bit and he was the first to reach the rise of the rim. Then come the last hard pull for the edge. He started up the rise, but when he got about half-way up he lost his footing on the slippery rim and slid down again. So he backed up and he took another run for it, and got up a little further, but again he slid back. He was a game one, that louse was. He tried it again and again, but he couldn't quite make it. No, sir, it was on that last hard pull up the rim of the plate that the blood of Saint Patrick began to tell, for Larry, the stranger's lucky louse, he started up slow and careful, and he kept on a-pulling and a-scrambling and up and up he went and *over* the edge to victory and into his master's hand. A hero he was, for sure!

The fellows jumped down from the tables then and Jack White, he says: "Three cheers for Larry and the blood of Saint Patrick!" So the boys roared out the three cheers. And they *was* cheers too, for them young fellows didn't have no colds, nor consumption neither.

Well, then Doc Johns paid over the fifteen hundred dollars to the stranger, and Ad went up to shake his hand. "Stranger," he says, "it was a fair race, and the best louse won. The money's yours and I don't begrudge it to you. But I've one request to make of you, stranger, and if you'll grant it, I'll be forever grateful."

"And what may that be?" says the stranger.

"Just let me borrow Larry till tomorrow," says Ad.

"But what for?" says the stranger. "Why might ye be wanting to borry me pet?"

"Why, man!" says Ad, "I want to improve my breed!"

Ant Race

. . . Traveling along on the mountain [toward Georgetown] we came to a level place, where we saw two men sitting under a big oak tree. They had no shirts on, and seemed to be busily engaged. We wanted a rest, and went to them. In those days men needed no introduction—all was free and easy. We did not stand on ceremony, but went to see what they were doing and found them engaged in a very interesting game. Their shirts were spread out near a large ant-hill, and each man had several Mexican dollars in front of him and was betting on the ants. Their shirts were pretty well covered with vermin, and each ant running over the shirts would seize a "grayback" and make for the ant-hill with it. The betting was as to which ant would get to the ant-hill first with his "grayback." They wanted us to join the game, but we respectfully declined, not being expert in the racing qualities of California ants. But the experience we gained proved very useful to us in after days. The ant-hill was often resorted to when "graybacks" became too plentiful in camp.

How Mark Twain Got a Clear Title to Jim Gillis's "Jumping Frog" Story

. . . Jim Gillis was a prosperous "pocket-miner" on the Mother Lode, a region which still yields, to the industrious and the knowing, "pockets" of placer gold. Jim was a gentleman of the old school, a prince of good fellows, charming in personality and manner, and known as the boss story-teller in all the region of the Southern Mines. He received Mark with open arms and made him welcome to the best in the land. If ever hospitality dwelt in the hearts of men it was and is

---

From *Pioneer Days in California,* by John Carr, pp. 74–75. Copyright, 1891, by John Carr. Eureka, California: Times Publishing Company, Book and Job Printers.

From *An Editor on the Comstock Lode,* by Wells Drury, pp. 225–226, 228–231. Copyright, 1936, by Audrey Drury. New York and Toronto: Farrar & Rinehart, Incorporated.

For "The Celebrated Jumping Frog of Calaveras County" and the earliest known printed version of the anecdote, in the Sonora *Herald,* June 11, 1853, see *A Treasury of American Folklore,* pp. 494–499. The origin and history of the story are discussed by Bernard DeVoto, in *Mark Twain's America* (Boston, 1932), and Oscar Lewis, in *The Origin of the Celebrated Jumping Frog of Calaveras County* (San Francisco, 1931).

For Mark Twain on the Comstock, see also Ivan Benson, *Mark Twain's Western Years* (Stanford, 1938); William R. Gillis, *Gold Rush Days with Mark Twain* (New York, 1930); George D. Lyman, *The Saga of the Comstock Lode* (New York, 1934); and Effie Mona Mack, *Mark Twain in Nevada* (New York, 1947).

manifested most generously among the mountaineer miners of California and Nevada.

Jim not only entertained Mark for several months, but told him all his best stories. He took Mark to Angels Camp and on his native heath had Ross Coon, one of the characters of the camp, give him the story of the "Jumping Frog of Calaveras," besides myriads of other yarns, which later proved rich material for Mark's writings. You may read of that sojourn on the Mother Lode in *Roughing It*.

Mark got permission to publish the Jumping Frog story as his own in consideration of the fact that his feelings were badly hurt by an occurrence in the Gillis mansion, and the tale of the saltatory amphibian was accepted as settlement in full for the shock sustained by his sensitive nature.

* * * * *

. . . The way in which Jim Gillis' pet hog, John Henry, helped him in his business was by rooting up the ground on the hillsides, thus giving the rain a chance to wash out the gold and carry it to the crevices.

Jim spent a month training his pig. The way he got the pig interested in pocket-mining was decidedly clever. He took a lot of his big homemade biscuits, of which John Henry, Mark Twain and all the other visitors to the cabin were extremely fond, and buried them in the side of a hill. Then with his poll-pick he began to scratch up the gravel and toled the pig up to the biscuits one after another. After that whenever John Henry saw Jim start out with his pick he thought he was sure of a biscuit feast, and with squeals of pleasurable anticipation he would make for the hillside, where he would tear up the ground like a Panama Canal dredger.

John Henry had a companion, a bull-dog named Towser, that grew up with him. Towser was more ornamental than useful, but this did not lower him in John Henry's esteem.

The only time they disagreed was at night, and then they quarreled about the possession of the empty bunk which was located directly under Jim Gillis' bed. They had been "raised pets" and always slept in the house. You see, Jim's house had bunks in it, one above another, like almost all early California cabins. Jim's two partners, Tom Kelty and Sam Dinsmore, occupied bunks on the other side of the cabin.

Jim would wait until bedtime before he let the hog and dog in, and would enjoy the circus of watching them by the light from the big fireplace as they would struggle for possession of the bunk. The contest would usually end by both getting tired out, and finally they would settle down and sleep fondly locked in each other's embrace.

Jim said that lots of times it made the tears come to his eyes to watch how tenderly they regarded each other after the scrimmage for priority of right was over.

After starving around the San Francisco newspaper offices for a long time, when Mark Twain paid a visit to Jim's country home he knew he would be welcome, for his fund of anecdotes always assured him a reception wherever he went.

Along in the evening Mark began to think about his lodgings, and seeing that three of the four bunks were filled with the bedding of Jim and his partners he drawled out:

"Where are you a-goin' to stow me away tonight? You don't seem to have any extra beds."

Jim winked at his companions and said:

"I guess we'll make some kind of a shakedown for you in the bottom bunk under my bed, and tomorrow I'll go over to town and get a mattress for you."

That suited Mark well enough, and it was soon arranged that way. The supper of beans, bacon, flapjacks and molasses was soon over, and after the usual games of seven-up all went to bed.

Mark's couch was the hardest of all, but he was soon asleep. The others were awake, waiting to see something happen. The night was cold; the wind whistled shrilly along the foothills, coming from the snow-line above. John Henry and Towser were outside clamoring for admission. They felt that the winter of their discontent had arrived and they had been forgotten.

Jim could reach the latch-string from where he lay. Putting out his hand he pulled it and the door flew open.

Towser and John Henry rushed for the bunk. They did not sense that it was already occupied. On top of the sleeping Mark they clambered, the dog first and the hog close following. Then began such a battle royal as was never before seen in the Gillis cabin.

First it was John Henry on top and then it was Towser.

Mark was entangled among the bed-clothing and could not get up. He could only yell and swear. He was thoroughly terrorized by the suddenness of the onslaught, coming as it did to startle him from his peaceful dreams of piloting on the Mississippi.

The men in the other bunks roared with laughter and held their sides to keep them from splitting.

"Go it, Towser!"

"Give it to 'im, John Henry!"

"Hold 'em level, Mark," they roared.

Jim in his eagerness to see what was going on under him narrowly escaped falling down into the struggling mass of hog, dog and Twain.

When the topmost contestants were exhausted Mark managed to escape. He was not much hurt, but was pretty well scared and unutterably disgusted. He swore vengeance on Towser, John Henry, Jim Gillis, and everybody else he could think of. He damned the golden earth by sections and quartersections, up-hill, and down-hill, crosswise and lengthwise, but the more he sputtered and swore the more the others laughed.

At last Jim took compassion on Mark and took him in the upper bunk. It was a little narrow, but it was a great deal better than running the risk of another visit from the pets.

Next morning Mark packed up his collar-box and was about to leave, but Jim persuaded him to stay, and by giving him a clear title to the story of "The Jumping Frog of Calaveras," assuaged his anger. That tale was the beginning of Mark's fortune. John Henry did the business.

They all agreed not to say a word about the matter, and it was years later that Steve Gillis [Jim's brother] told me the story.

Jim Gillis and Bret Harte

Bret Harte also passed by Jackass Hill. Moreover, he stopped there and enjoyed the Gillis hospitality. And there is a well-founded story about his visit which is worth repeating here, for the light it casts on Harte's character. The Gillis boys didn't care for Bret Harte; that's the nub of the tale. And apparently they had good reason for their views.

It was Jim Gillis, really, who had the best reason for disliking Harte. As the story goes, Harte, with a roll of blankets on his back, walked down through Calaveras County looking for a job teaching school. He crossed the Stanislaus River at Robinson's Ferry, plodded southward on the old Slumgullion Road, and reached Jackass Hill just in time to see Gillis and his friend Dick Stoker take out a rich pocket of gold. Harte was hungry and tired and didn't seem very enthusiastic about the find. That may have been the first thing the partners didn't like about him. A man does want a fellow-mortal—almost any fellow-mortal—to rejoice with him at a piece of good fortune. Worse, Harte was wearing patent-leather shoes. That alone was enough to stamp him as a "dude." Miners did not care much for "Dudes." The Gillises seem to have formed their opinion of Harte then and there.

But they were decent to him. They put him up for the night, fed him, and sent him on down to San Francisco. Jim also lent Harte twenty dollars.

Then Jim met Harte again, some years later in San Francisco. He was not thinking of the twenty dollars, which wasn't so very much in those days. But he remembered Harte and went over to him with outstretched hand. "Hello, Bret," he said. "How are you?"

But now Bret Harte was the author of "The Luck of Roaring Camp." He was famous. He was admired and made much of everywhere, though Jim did not realize that. Jim was surprised when Harte adjusted his eye-glass and looked him up and down. "Ah, really, my dear fellow," said Harte. "You're mistaken, I'm sure!"

Perhaps Jim was taken aback, but he was too cool a hand to show it.

From *Anybody's Gold,* The Story of California's Mining Towns, by Joseph Henry Jackson, pp. 333–334.

He merely looked Harte over. "Maybe I am," he replied, "but I'll tell you. If you fork over the twenty dollars I gave you on Jackass Hill I'll be plenty glad to forget you, too!" Harte, they say, paid.

Equality in the Mining Camp

The mines put all men for once upon a level. Clothes, money, manners, family connections, letters of introduction, never before counted for so little. The whole community was substantially given an even start in the race. Gold was so abundant, and its sources seemed for a time so inexhaustible, that the aggrandizing power of wealth was momentarily annihilated. Social and financial inequalities between man and man were together swept out of sight. Each stranger was welcomed, told to take a pan and pick and go to work for himself. The richest miner in the camp was seldom able to hire a servant; those who had formerly been glad to serve others were digging in their own claims. The veriest greenhorn was as likely to uncover the richest mine on the gulch as was the wisest of ex-professors of geology; and, on the other hand, the best claim on the river might suddenly "give out" and never again yield a dollar. The poorest man in camp could have a handful of gold-dust for the asking from a more successful neighbor, to give him another start, and help him "hunt for better luck." No one was ever allowed to suffer: the treasure-vaults of the Sierra were too near, and seemingly too exhaustless.

To a little camp of 1848 (so an old miner writes me) a lad of sixteen came one day, footsore, weary, hungry, and penniless. There were thirty robust and cheerful miners at work in the ravine; and the lad sat on the bank, watching them a while in silence, his face telling the sad story of his fortunes. At last one stalwart miner spoke to his fellows, saying:

"Boys, I'll work an hour for that chap if you will."

At the end of the hour a hundred dollars' worth of gold-dust was laid in the youth's handkerchief. The miners made out a list of tools and necessaries.

"You go," they said, "and buy these, and come back. We'll have a good claim staked out for you. Then you've got to paddle for yourself." Thus genuine and unconventional was the hospitality of the mining camp.

From *Mining Camps,* A Study in American Frontier Government, by Charles Howard Shinn, Introduction by Joseph Henry Jackson, pp. 104–105. Copyright, 1947, by Alfred A. Knopf, Inc. New York.

Striking It Rich

I[1]

At another time a young man about eighteen years old, tall and broad-shouldered, with heavy black hair hanging shaggily about his face and head, and wearing a big, floppy hat, well pulled down over his head, came trudging into camp carrying his roll of blankets over his shoulders. He had walked up from Sutter's Fort, taking several days to make the trip. The first thing he asked after he had dropped his roll, removed his hat and brushed the wet hair out of his eyes was, "Howdy folks! This here is a mining camp, isn't it?" One of the miners sitting on the porch replied, "You bet it is! Where'd you come from?" The youth threw back his broad shoulders and said, "Wal, I come from old Missoura, I did, to dig fer gold. I told Mam I would dig until I was a rich man, by Gor! and then I'd take the money back to her. Can any of you folks tell me whar is the gold you dig fer?"

One of the men thought he would have a little sport over the "green" young fellow. He said, "Come with me and I'll find something for you." He located an old, battered, discarded rocker and a leaky bucket and told him to go about one hundred yards up the side of the steep hill, back of the hotel, and stake his claim, beginning with a certain large pine tree. The young lawyer stepped up and said, "I'll go along with you and show you how." The lad said, "Wal, say, mister, that's fair kind of you. I'll give you the first fifty dollars that I dig up if you will help me and see that my claim is registered." He was a wiser young man than he looked to be, and said, "I want to be sure that what I git no one can take away from me. I want what's mine to be mine."

The next morning the young Missourian was out before any one in camp was up and was excitedly digging and scraping the dirt near the old pine tree. This he carried, bucketful, after bucketful, down to the rocker by the side of the creek. Then he poured water into the old rocker with the leaky bucket, losing about half of each bucketful. He "rocked the cradle" and poured water and picked out rocks all morning. After a few hours of the hardest kind of toil, carrying, rocking, and separating the large rocks, he had the contents of the rocker down to a fine dirt on the bottom of the rocker. Then he dropped on his knees by the side of the rocker, to examine the dirt carefully. With a big yell, he jumped to his feet. "By Gor!" he cried, "I've struck it. Hurrah for Mam!"

The miners working along the creek side could not believe what they heard. When they saw the boy jumping up and down, waving his old

[1] From *Prairie to Pacific,* A narrative of a trip across the plains of a family from Illinois with a covered wagon and oxen in Eighteen Hundred Fifty Three, by Aunt Kate [Kate McDaniel Furniss] in her eighty-sixth year, edited by Mai Luman Hill, (unpaged), Chapter XIX. Typescript in the California State Library, Sacramento. An incident in Grass Valley, California.

hat and yelling "I've got it! By Gor!" they all came rushing over to the boy's rocker. Sure enough! There was so much coarse and fine gold that there was no doubt that the young Missourian had "struck it rich." Then everyone got excited. They had him take the dirt from different places over the claim, thinking that perhaps some one had played a joke on the boy and had "planted" the gold around the tree. There was not a bucketful that did not go from one to five dollars. That night he paid the young lawyer what he had promised him. At the end of five days he sold his claim to four miners for ten thousand dollars in gold. As he started for Sacramento where he expected to get a boat for San Francisco he said, "Now, by Gor! I'm going back to Mam!" The whole hillside was soon staked off in claims. No one had thought of going so far up as the hillside away from the creek to look for gold.

II[2]

In a state rich in minerals, freaks of fortune are inevitable. Many mines have been discovered by pure chance. Good-luck stories, some authentic, some legendary, are part of the atmosphere of Nevada. A prospector shot at a snake and split a rock of high-grade ore. Three drunken men rolled a boulder down a hill; it chipped off rock and exposed a vein of rich ore. It is said that Henry Comstock found the famous Virginia City lode when he saw queer-looking stuff in a gopher hole. In Searchlight a shaft sunk 225 feet for water struck valuable deposits of silver, gold, and copper. Men digging an outdoor toilet in Tonopah uncovered a "pockety pay shoot" of rich ore. Two young miners' sons panned a badger mound at Weepah; two feet down they discovered gold ore worth $78,000 a ton. Guy Pritchard, after failing for years as a prospector, gave up and got a job repairing the old road between Hawthorne and Bodie. After lunch one day he sat down to rest, reached lazily for a rock to throw, and discovered silver and galena worth $90 a ton.

Above all, lost pack animals get the honor of bringing about discoveries, a theme that popular fiction like Dane Coolidge's *Trail of Gold* and Mark Requa's *Grubstake* have exploited until it is growing stale. From the Spanish conquest of South America to the arrival of the first Stanley Steamer in Goldfield, the lost burro, mule, or horse had his chance, at least in legend, to lead the course of empire.

The classic example in Nevada lore is Jim Butler's discovery of Tonopah. According to Butler's early version of the discovery, in May, 1900, he and his wife set out from Belmont to go to the Southern Klondyke Mining District. On the night of the eighteenth they camped at a spring in a desolate spot at the foot of a hill. Next morning they found that their pack burros had strayed. Butler set out uphill to find them, cornered them, and headed them toward camp. To speed their return

---

[2] From *Desert Challenge,* An Interpretation of Nevada, by Richard G. Lillard, pp. 180–182. Copyright, 1942, by Richard G. Lillard. New York: Alfred A. Knopf.

trip, he picked up a rock and was about to hurl it at their rumps when he noticed it was mineralized quartz. Near by was the outcropping. The Butlers gathered specimens and went on the remaining ten miles to Southern Klondyke. They showed their samples to the camp assayer, who expressed the opinion that the rock was worthless and demanded an assaying fee that they could not pay. On their return trip to Belmont they picked up more specimens.

Butler gave them to young Tasker Oddie, district attorney of Nye County, offering him a half interest if he would get an assay made. Oddie was equally poor in cash, and in turn he gave the specimens to Walter Gayheart for one-half of his interest. Gayheart, an Austin engineer, made the assay and found values of $80 to $600 a ton in gold and silver. After Butler had leisurely harvested the hay on his ranch in Monitor Valley, he led his partners to the spot, and there on August 25 they located the Desert Queen, the Burro, the Mizpah, the Buckboard, and many other claims. They staked off every foot of ground anywhere near the richest outcrop, that on Mizpah Hill. Their very location monuments were made of highgrade ore. From one fifteen-foot shaft they filled two wagons with ore. They hauled the loads to Austin. The net proceeds were $600. The Tonopah rush began; and during the next twenty years Tonopah produced metal valued at $125,000,000, almost half of it from the original mine.

III[3]

The discovery of ore-bearing bodies of rock is the chief task of the prospector. Much of this work today is done by men trained in geology, but there are still many men "up in the hills" hunting for a precious "ledge" who have only the most rudimentary knowledge of geology, if any at all. These men usually rely only on the thoroughness with which they comb a region and on their luck. Experienced miners can regale one with tales by the hour of prospectors who "stuck it out" until they came across an ore body. One of the best tales of this kind in Utah concerns the prospector of the old Shoebridge Bonanza Mine. After numerous unsuccessful trips he threw away his pick in despair. As it struck the ground it exposed to view a rich vein of silver. Many are the tales of such accidental discoveries. A well known one concerns a lucky teamster named Allen, whose government mule accidentally kicked up a piece of rock that revealed the presence of gold. The founding of the Mercur Camp traditionally dates from this discovery. Another such story concerns the accidental finding of a ledge near the Fish Springs in Juab County by a sheepherder. As he was riding through a narrow pass the stirrup of his saddle chanced to break off some rock which glistened in the sun. Miners are reported to have passed through this same defile many times, but none had ever noticed the outcropping.

---

[3] From "Folklore from Utah's Silver Mining Camps," by Wayland D. Hand, *The Journal of American Folklore,* Vol. 54 (July–December, 1941), Nos. 213–214, pp. 135–137. Philadelphia: The American Folklore Society.

The more successful prospectors are often referred to as being able to "smell the ore." Down in the mine this term is also applied to miners with keen judgment in picking up trails of ore that have "pinched out." In mines of consequence, of course, the workings are determined by mining engineers and geologists, but even their success is often humorously explained in terms of their "smell for the ore."

Old time miners recall the use of divining rods of various kinds and even the use of the compass in locating ore bodies. I can form no idea of how widespread the use of these contraptions was in early days. Today one encounters an occasional divining rod operator. These practioneers employ everything from the traditional forked stick, usually the willow, to mechanical contraptions of one kind and another. The term "doodlebug" is often applied to the latter gadgets.

From olden times there have survived certain popular notions and practices in the locating of ore bodies by non-geological surface indications. Some miners believe, for example, that ore-bearing ground will not hold snow. This notion may be a borrowing from the more widely current belief that snow will not overlie oil-bearing shale. The most unusual surface indicator of this nature that I have heard about in Utah is the socalled "lead flower," which is supposed to betray the presence of lead bodies below. This account I obtained from an old German miner in Highland Boy, who in turn heard it from a countryman. The flower in question, I think, is the common sego lily, Utah's state flower. Inquiries elsewhere brought no corroboration that this flower or, for that matter, any other plant is believed to indicate the presence of mineral wealth below, although it is quite generally known that experienced prospectors watch the stands of timber in various areas as indicators of mineralization.

Well known among mining folk, of course, is the help afforded by burrowing animals, particularly ground hogs and gophers, in turning up ore. Their "dumps" are carefully examined for traces of mineral. Horn silver, valued at a dollar a pound, was taken from gopher mounds on the Eureka Mining Company property in 1870 and there are numerous less well known instances. The tradition of housewives' watching the craws of domestic fowls, so widespread in California, is little known in Utah.

IV[4]

The day was hot at Frisco, Utah, and the three drank beer and talked. It appeared from their conversation that they had all more or less experience in prospecting. One said:

"The biggest thing I ever struck was once when me and Newt Bowden was prospectin'. One day we felt the earth kinder tremblin', an' we saw a smoke on the top of a mountain. We climbed up to the top—'twas

[4] From the *Colorado Miner,* January 24, 1880, p. 1, col. 9. Reprinted from the *Salt Lake City Tribune.* Clipping files of the Western History Collection, Denver Public Library, Denver, Colorado.

a long pull. When we got there we found it was a volcano. 'Twas all bilin' in the crater. One place in the crater was lower than t'other parts, and a cliff struck right down from this low place; it went 'bout 700 feet. The earth kept tremblin'. An' a stream 'bout twenty feet wide by five feet deep run outen the crater or gap, an' made a clear jump 700 feet down."

"Water?" interrupted one of the listeners; "pooty hot, wasn't it?"

"Water! 'twas quicksilver."

"Quicksilver?'

"You bet. We went down to the foot of the fall. The stream of quicksilver from this fall run a few hundred yards an' sunk. It kept tremblin'."

"What made the tremblin'?"

"The quicksilver striking below—heavy you know. Me and Newt both got sick; he sicker than me. He kep' gittin' worse, and died before I could get him to camp. I got to the camp and was sick for months—was salervated. My teeth all came out. I hain't no teeth now, nor toe nails, nuther."

"Why didn't you go back to the quicksilver?"

" 'Fraid er gettin' salervated again. Killed Newt, you know."

No. 2 said: "Well, the richest discovery I ever made was one time when I was by myself. I saw a bluff 'bout three miles off; it had a queer look. I went to it; 'twas more'n a thousand feet high, an' nearly every bit of it was solid native silver. You could walk 'long and look at it for a mile 'thout seein' anything but pure silver. Some places silver had oozed out while the cliff was hot, an' had made things look like big icicles; some of 'em was hangin' down 500 feet long. I located 'bout three miles of the ledge an' left."

"How came you so poor?" asked one.

"Well, I'd got back in a day's ride of camp, an' was packin' up one mornin' after breakfast; as I came to my fryin'-pan my mule had one foot in it, an' I tapped him on the leg to make him step outen it, an' he up an' kicked me in the head."

"But he didn't break your head."

"No; but I can't remember directions since."

The third one began: "I was by myself, too, when I struck it big. One day I was prospectin' through an open country an' traveled on until after night tryin' to find water. At last I rode over a ridge, and noticed that my mule's shoes kept clinkin' against somethin'. I had a fine young mule. There was a valley at the bottom of the ridge, and water. I went to sleep, an' waked up when day begin to break, but rolled over an' slept till after the sun was up, but I couldn't hold my eyes open until I tried a long time, there was such a glitter."

"Mica?" one of the party suggested.

"Gold, sir! Gold everywhere! I'd thrown part of my blanket over a chunk to make a piller; the chunk was solid gold! The ridge I'd come over was solid gold. On t'other side of the valley was mountains of gold risin' up an' glitterin' in the sunshine. One high mountain had snow on the top, but was gold up to the snow. Fellers, that mountain looked like a picter. I'd jest began to think my bacon eatin' days were over, when three men came up to me, two young men an' one old man. Judgin' from their actions—I couldn't understand their talk—the young fellers wanted to kill me, but the old chap persuaded them not ter. They all had gold buttons on their clothes an' heel taps an' tap soles of gold. The old man was smokin' a gold pipe with a long stem. They blin'-folded me an' led me away." The narrator stopped and seemed to be retrospecting.

"Well, did they lead you far?" he was asked.

"Seems to me I listened to the clink of them tap soles for nearly 10,000 miles."

"Was they long about it?"

"When I laid down in that gold valley that night, though I say it myself, I was young an' good lookin', my beard was as black as a crow, an' hair thick as a dog's; but when they lef' me, an' got out of hearin' an' I uncovered my eyes, my beard was gray."

"An' your head?"

"Like it is now, not a hair on it?"

"What became of your fine young mule?"

"The old man rode it on the trip till it fell dead of old age."

The Lazy Miner

Why, even a lazy man could do pretty well in diggins as rich as that. You take, for instance, one of these first comers, he was even too lazy to wash his drawers. To save himself the work of scrubbing them, he just tied them to a limb that overhung a little stream and let them dangle in the water. He figured, you see, that the current would wash them for him overnight. And the next morning when he come to fish them out, lo and b'God! he found his drawers gold-plated.

A Cemetery Find

The only religious service I ever saw undertaken in the mines in 1848 was at a miner's funeral on the South Fork. Amongst the miners was

---

From *Ghost Town,* Wherein Is Told Much That Is Wonderful, Laughable, and Tragic, and Some That Is Hard to Believe, about Life during the Gold Rush and Later in the Town of Columbia on California's Mother Lode, as Remembered by the Oldest Inhabitants and Here for the First Time Set Down by G. Ezra Dane, in collaboration with Beatrice J. Dane, p. 2. Copyright, 1941, by G. Ezra Dane. New York: Alfred A. Knopf.

From "Anecdotes and Sketches Illustrative of California and Miners' Life," in *Life in California,* together with a Description of the Great Tulare Valley, by James H. Carson, Esq., the Discoverer of Carson's Creek and one of the Early Pioneers of the West, pp. 22–23. Stockton, California: Printed and published at the office of the "San Joaquin Republican." 1852.

one known as "the Parson." Those who were acquainted with him asserted that the Parson had "onst" been a "powerful preacher" in the Eastern States, but digging for gold had gradually tarnished his Gospel habiliments; in short, he had become carnal, and would take a big drink with any of his friends he met. A miner had died who was much liked, and we determined to give him as respectable a funeral as circumstances would permit. The parson was requested to officiate and minister on the occasion, which he readily assented to, and soon made his appearance at the camp of the deceased—where a goodly number were collected, amongst whom the cups passed swiftly round, and many a drink went down to the repose of the soul departed. The Parson never missed a "round," and by the time we got the corpse in the grave, he had become somewhat "muddled." The grave had been dug in a flat some hundred yards from the camps. After the body had been placed in the grave, the miners gathered around it, and the Parson read a long chapter from the Bible, after which he said it was necessary to sing a Psalm. No hymn book could be procured—and no one had ever committed a hymn to memory, with the exception of the Parson, who soon started one to the tune of "Old Hundred." He got through the first verse, and the first line of the second, and there *stuck*. After several ineffectual and comical attempts to "start her" again, he coolly informed us that the Lord had obliterated from his memory the whole of that solemn Psalm but we would go to prayer. At the order of prayer some remained standing—numbers knelt around the grave—and one old case sat down, remarking at the time, that he "knew when the old Parson had his steam up he was h—l on prayer; and he was going to take it easy." The Parson had been praying some ten minutes when some of those kneeling around the grave commenced examining the dirt that had been thrown up and found it to be (as they expressed it) "lousy with gold." This discovery necessarily created an excitement in the assembly. The Parson had become "warmed up" and his supplications for the soul of the departed could be heard "Echoing through mountain, hill, and dell," when he suddenly stopped, opened one eye—and looked down to see what was disturbing his hearers, and very coolly enquired, "Boys, what's that?" and continued, "Gold! by g–d! and the richest kind of diggins!—the very dirt we have been looking for!" The truth flowed across his mind —then he raised his hand and with a comic expression of countenance informed us that the "congregation are dismissed," and it was highly necessary that that dirt should be well tried before we proceeded any farther, and away he "scud" for his pick and pan.

Suffice it to say, that poor George B— was not buried there, but taken from his *rich hole,* and a grave made for him "high up the mountain's side."

Gold in Gizzards and Paunches

Chickens were persistent gatherers of small nuggets in these mining towns, and their gizzards were regularly searched by the cooks who prepared them for the oven. At Diamond Springs in 1856 one was killed for a Sunday dinner whose gizzard panned out $12.80.

* * * * *

Goats and cattle have a penchant for "chewing the rag," and any piece of buckskin that falls across their way. It is perhaps due to the salty taste these substances have that stimulates the liking. A butcher in Calaveras County found in the paunch of a steer he slaughtered several $5 pieces and a few nuggets. They had probably been swallowed in a buckskin purse dropped by some one crossing the grazing grounds of the animal.

* * * * *

Near Yreka, Siskiyou County, in 1855, a miner felled a tree near his cabin to obtain his supply of firewood. One afternoon he took off his coat and tossed it upon a stump and proceeded to chop a quantity of sticks from the tree. Out of the pocket of the coat stuck the end of a buckskin sack containing over $500 worth of gold dust. An old milch cow, pastured in the vicinity, finally grazed up to where the coat was lying and the miner glanced at the cow just in time to see his sack of gold disappear in the cow's mouth. As a bovine swallows and ruminates afterward, there was no chance for him to prevent the animal gulping it down. He drove her over to her owner's corral and there found that she was the dearest old animal in the world, and, on account of her being such a prolific milk producer, she had not an equal in the State. Of course, he had to buy her so as to keep possession of his gold and it is said that she cost him $150. He kept her corralled for ten days, during which time he tried in every possible way to effect a gold cure without success and then he had to kill her. The gold was found in her paunch undamaged but the buckskin sack had been digested.

Gopher Gold

Among the miners at Carson Creek, near the Stanislaus River, was an old man who had been there some months—it was generally believed

---

From *The Good Luck Era* in *The Autobiography of Charles Peters; (and) The Good Luck Era,* the Pioneer Mining Days of the '50's, pp. 181, 220–221. Sacramento, California: The LaGrave Co., Publishers. [N.d.]

From *The Works of Hubert Howe Bancroft,* Vol. XXXV, *California Inter Pocula,* pp. 794–795. Entered according to Act of Congress in the Year 1888, by Hubert H. Bancroft in the Office of the Librarian of Congress at Washington. San Francisco: The History Company, Publishers.

that he had been successful—no one knew what he did with his gold, for he was a man of economical habits, and free from the vice of gambling. People believed that he buried his gold. One day the old man threw the whole camp into excitement by frantically rushing about and declaring that he had been robbed of his gold. He was rather liked and most of the miners sympathized with him, and offered to assist him in finding the gold, and in catching and punishing the robber.

After numerous inquiries of the old man, it was ascertained that he had been in the habit of burying his treasures in different places; and that the amount of which he had been robbed was concealed in a leathern bag at the foot of a certain tree—which particular bag was filled with lump gold, specimens, etc. He took several persons to the spot and showed them the hole cornered by a flat stone.

Upon examining the place carefully, a large gopher's hole was discovered in the side of the cavity in which the bag had been deposited. One of the party suggested to search the gopher's hole. A shovel was brought and the side drift carefully followed. After tracing it about ten or twelve feet, there was found a little ante-room or chamber of about six inches deep, made in the side of the main road or hole, with a neatly paved floor of lumps of gold, and in the rear of this extravagantly furnished apartment was found a portion of the old man's leathern bag.

The den of the robbers had evidently been found, but only a small portion of the gold—where was the rest? Following the trail of the robber a little farther, they came upon a succession of apartments or niches, and found each one as regularly and beautifully paved with gold as if done by the hand of man, while in each was found a small portion of the leathern bag, as if used as a lounge or mattress. Not a single particle of gold was found along the line of the main road; all had been carefully carried into and deposited in the side rooms. The whole amount was weighed, and found to be exactly equal to the gold the old man had buried in the bag. The gopher succeeded in escaping unharmed. Such is the gopher story of the Stanislaus.

We have another gopher story. "Last Monday our usually quiet burgh was awakened by the intelligence that new diggings had been discovered within a few hundred yards of the town, paying twelve dollars to the pan. Hundreds immediately flocked with picks and spades to the place, and in a short time had staked off the whole hillside. They worked very diligently until evening, when the discoverers let some of their friends into the secret. They had buried bags of gold dust there last spring, and in digging for it found that the gophers had eaten the buckskin bags, obliging them to wash the surrounding earth. Ten minutes after this announcement there was not a miner or tool to be seen about the new diggings."

Lost Mine Stories

I. Their Pattern[1]

"The palpable sense of mystery in the desert air," which, as Mary Austin once wrote, "breeds fables, chiefly of lost treasures," bred a batch of tales in early Nevada. Where Butler and Humphrey discovered mines that founded towns, Hardin and "Alkali" Jones glimpsed mines, only to lose them, and the world has yet to know just where they are. Like the Southwest, Nevada is specked with lost mines and treasures, and some of Coronado's children are ever on the hunt. J. Frank Dobie points out that there are no legends about the gold at Fort Knox or the silver at West Point. It is the gold not yet found that draws and lifts the human spirit. Stories of unfound gold and silver are based on facts or on "mere hope, imagination, hallucination, aye, plain fertility, in lying—who can say?" Professional mining men smile. Rule-of-thumb prospectors admit their skepticism. But if enough realistic details are piled in, even the cynic will have a moment's thrill: "If only the story is true and I can find that mine!"

The stories follow a fairly regular pattern, be they about the Three Little Lakes of Gold, the Whiteman Lost Cement Mine, the Lost Golden Eagle, or the Lost Chicken Craw. The outcropping or rich float is found under some emergency (thus the discoverer has no time accurately to find his bearings). Some rich samples are exhibited (which prove there is ore at the place described). For one of several reasons, return for rediscovery and location is delayed, or else the mine simply cannot be found again. Indian hostilities keep whites out of the region. Indians cover up the outcropping to keep whites from stampeding in and scaring away wild game. Years elapse and the finder's memory fails him. The area is topographically too regular, and the specific spot eludes identification. Cloudbursts cover the lost ledge with debris. Or, necessity and circumstance keep the finder distracted elsewhere for years, and when he finally does organize a party he is blind or feeble or about to die. He draws a map, which is so vague that followers cannot make sense of it. If he is still healthy he may be killed accidentally before the party sets out. Some times the sole evidence of a fabulously rich mine is in ore fragments that an Indian brings to a trading post. But however the story may manipulate man's destiny to leave Nature her secret, it always provides charts and circumstantial descriptions, and witnesses who saw either the discoverer or the ore he brought in.

---

[1] From *Desert Challenge,* An Interpretation of Nevada, by Richard G. Lillard, pp. 182–183. Copyright, 1942, by Richard G. Lillard. New York: Alfred A. Knopf.

See also Oren Arnold, *Superstitions' Gold* (Phoenix, 1934); Philip A. Bailey, *Golden Mirages* (New York, 1940); J. Frank Dobie, *Coronado's Children* (Dallas, 1931) and *Apache Gold and Yaqui Silver* (Boston, 1939); as well as articles in *The Desert Magazine,* El Centro, California, and *Westways* (formerly *Touring Topics*), Los Angeles.

II. The Lost Hardin Mine[2]

. . . In 1849 a party of fourteen emigrant wagons was crossing northwestern Nevada on the Lassen cutoff, which cut west from the Humboldt River route near Winnemucca. They camped at Double Hot Springs to rest and to give their cattle time to graze in the tall grass. When they started westward again, three hunters went out, including a man named Hardin. The three planned to cross a near-lying mountain and rejoin the wagons on the other side. They found no game and, what was worse, they got lost. They saw a team on a road in the distance. As they wandered toward it they got into a burned, black igneous country, part of the Black Rock Range. In one place they floundered through soft, gray, sifted ashes. The ashy place was near the margin of a shallow gulch. Along the gulch and in the ashes were chunks of whitish metal, some the size of beans, some forty or fifty pounds in bulk. Everywhere there protruded pieces the size of bricks. Metal lay around by the wagonload, as if Aladdin's cave had been blown open. One of the hunters had been in the Mexican War and had later worked on pack trains in the Sierra Madre before returning to the United States. He identified the slabs as silver. They gathered up all they could and clambered down to the valley floor, where they found an emigrant with all but one yoke of oxen dead. He was at work with hammer and saw cutting down his wagon from a four wheeler to a cart, so that his famished cattle could pull it and wife and child to California alive. The hunters tried to get him to pull the silver to California. He said he wouldn't pack it, even if it were pure gold. Hardin threw down the largest piece by the road, the three divided the smaller pieces, and went on to Mud Meadows. They found their party and showed samples of their find. Steve Bass saw the silver and watched Hardin melt it into buttons in a gouge in his ax handle covered with hot coals. The emigrants left some fragments at the meadows and took others on to California.

The men told their story in the mining towns around Mount Shasta, but no one was particularly excited, because gold was more valuable and more accessible. One of Hardin's companions wandered to Oregon, where a Rogue River man, A. B. Jennison, heard of the silver. Later he heard the same account from Hardin himself, who became a blacksmith in a wagon shop in Petaluma, California. In 1852 a doctor crossed the same desert area and found the big piece of silver Hardin had thrown down by the road. He did not take it but realized later it was pure silver. He planned to return, but just before his trip was to start he fell mortally sick. Before he died he gave all particulars to Tom Harvey and George Lathrop. A party of emigrants camped near Mud Meadows in the same year and found small pieces of silver left by the Hardin party. These they took to Shasta City and sold to a jeweler named

[2] *Ibid.*, pp. 183–185.

Lewis. He displayed the silver in his window, where it was seen by L. D. Vary and Isaac Roop.

Indian hostilities in the Black Rock area kept searchers away till 1858. In that year Jennison was there with a party and Hardin himself returned. He searched for three years. There were dozens of men hunting for the marvelous silver deposit, but they found nothing. The face of the mountains had been changed. Perhaps the original silver chunks had been uncovered by a cloudburst, and after Hardin saw them water spouts cut new deep gullies and sent down avalanches of broken rock and totally buried the silver again. Hardin left during the Indian War of 1860. Later he helped the settlers during the Honey Lake border war, but his search was over. In 1865 an Albert E. Jamison discovered rich prospects in the area and in 1866 the camp of Hardinville was established, but no mines there ever uncovered the bricks of virgin silver.

III. The Silver Gunsight[3]

Sixty-two men on their way to the goldfields of California. Sixty-two men who knew nothing of the country, resting at Salt Lake City, listening to all advice, wondering if there weren't a pass through the Sierras that they might find if they went the southern route through the Colorado desert. Sixty-two men traveling to certain death.

Death awaited in that valley which bears its name. But it grew impatient, and went ahead to meet some of the party. They were glad of that, we may be sure, after their troubled wanderings through unknown country, hungry, thirsty, weary. They were surely ready to die. And by the time Death Valley had been reached, all but four of the sixty-two had lost their lives.

Somewhere in Inyo county the forlorn four men wandered on. They had come thus far, and they must reach wealth before they, too, died.

George Dennis took up his gun, and sighted along the barrel. Now, that was a pretty howdy-do! The sight had come off. It was lost somewhere on the backtrail, and needles in haystacks would be easy to find compared with that gunsight. What could he do now? He needed that little aid to aiming.

There was grayish metal of some sort in the ledge at his side. Perhaps it would be soft enough to cut. He tried; he managed to whittle out a crude sight, and to attach it to the gun. Well, that was better. They needed that gun if they expected to eat until they came across gold.

The next day, after a night spent in the shelter of the friendly ledge, the four weary men stumbled on. Two of them died. George Dennis and one other man kept going. At last they reached San Bernardino.

---

3 From "Golden Phantoms, Fascinating Tales of Lost Mines," by Editha L. Watson, in the *Steamboat Pilot,* Steamboat Springs, Colorado, July 8, 1937.

Clipping files of the Western History Collection, Denver Public Library, Denver, Colorado.

If Dennis had not met the old prospector when he did, he might never have known that hideous nightmare which haunted him ever afterward. But the experienced miner saw that gun—saw the gunsight—saw, too, that it was made of almost pure silver.

Where did it come from? Oh, from a ledge back there in the Death Valley region somewhere—why?

He found out why! They counted the days since he had made that gunsight, guessed at the miles, hoped for the direction. They went back, as well as they could, toward the ledge of silver. But the Southwest is a large place, and even a square mile can conceal many things beyond finding.

IV. The Lost Dutchman Mine[4]

One day, while the boys were out riding, an American with a brand-new pack outfit came in and began to ask about the Lost Dutchman Mine. That is a favorite form of insanity in Arizona to this day, and Johnny and the rest of them had just about decided it was on the other side of the river. But they had all served their time trying to trail old Jake Miller and locate his fabulous gold mine, and when this stranger came in with his Apache guide I knew what was on his mind.

He did not ask, straight out, for information about the mine but inquired for mysterious landmarks which would guide him in his quest. So I told him that, being a stranger, I did not know the range; but Johnny Jones knew every canyon in the Four Peaks country and he could ask him when he came in. So, after supper, he came over and began to work his auger on Juanito.

"Mr. Jones," he said, "do you know a hidden spring in this country where the skull of a man was found?"

"Oh yes," smiled Johnny. "It is right down the canyon a few miles. My brother-in-law over here is the one that found the skull."

He pointed to Gomez, sitting over by the fire, and the stranger glanced at his guide. This had evidently been peddled out to him as something extra-special but the first man he asked knew all about it.

"That was the skull of Jerry Miller," went on Johnny, "the Dutchman's nephew, that he killed when he was running away. People claim he did the shooting over at Mormon Flat, but his skull had a bullet-hole right through his forehead and Gomez found it at Hidden Water."

"So!" exclaimed the treasure hunter, raising his eyebrows at his sullen guide. "Oh—do you know a trail this side of the Four Peaks where there is a human face painted on a rock?"

"Sure," returned Johnny. "Been by there, lots of times. It was made by this crazy Mormon that lives down on Bulldog Cliffs. You go right up this second canyon—"

And he described, with great particularity, just how to reach the spot.

---

[4] From *Arizona Cowboys*, by Dane Coolidge, pp. 110–121. Copyright, 1938, by Dane Coolidge. New York: E. P. Dutton and Co., Inc.

"I wonder," said the prospector at last, "if you've ever seen a cave with a big armchair in it, at the base of an overhanging cliff."

"Well," shrugged Johnny, as a crowd gathered round to hear these innermost secrets, "that sounds like this Opeshaw's work. He's the crazy Mormon that lives up Bulldog Canyon. He steals everything he can get his hands on, hides it out in the mountains and then forgets where he put it. Why, he spent months taking his brother's wagon to pieces, packing it up the cliff and putting it together again— away up there on the peaks, where a mountain sheep could hardly navigate. He takes gunny-sacks, clothes, harness, tools—"

"This chair that I speak of," interrupted the stranger, "had a horse's hoof on the right side, where he—"

"Oh! Why didn't you say so?" beamed Johnny. "That belonged to Henry Brown, over in Asher's Basin. He lived in a big cave under the cliff and all he did was sit over the fire and smoke cigarettes until his face was the color of leather. And do you know what that horse's foot was for? He put his cigarette in the frog of it, whenever he wanted to spit."

The stranger never knew that Johnny was kidding him, and he went on with such tall stories about the Lost Dutchman Mine that he had us all goggle-eyed. Johnny had spent more time than he liked to admit in the pursuit of this will-o'-the-wisp and he was in that low mood when he took grim pleasure in blasting other people's fond hopes. Every time the prospector asked about some rusty musket, or even about the Dutchman himself, he would lay the goods on the line; and at last he told the whole story.

"This Dutchman," he said, "went by the name of Jake Miller, though some folks said it was Walz. He and his nephew, Jerry, that got killed down the wash here, were Germans that had served in the Confederate Army; but after Lee surrendered they were afraid the Union soldiers would kill them and skipped across the Line into Mexico.

"They came to the big ranch of the Peralta brothers, probably somewhere down in Sonora, and found them assembling about eighty armed peons and a whale of a big pack-train, to boot. That was a long time ago, when Arizona was just a county of New Mexico and nobody lived here anyhow, but these brothers told him this country was full of gold and they were going to get some.

"When Jake saw some of the rock—which was the pure quill, believe me—he told them they were foolish to take along so many cowardly peons. It would just attract the attention of the Apaches without doing them any real good. But if they would give him half the gold he would go along and protect them, as he and Jerry were both sure shots. Well, the Peralta brothers agreed to leave the peons behind and they came up into this country, going through Tucson and the mountains around Pinal until they got to this gold mine, which was rich.

"They loaded up the mules and went back to their hacienda, giving the Dutchman and Jerry sixty thousand dollars for their half. Then they went up against some big gambling game and in two days' time they were broke. So they came to the Dutchman and asked them to go back to the mine, although they were deathly afraid of the Apaches; and old Jake, taking advantage of their fear, turned around and *bought* the mine. He gave them back the sixty thousand dollars, and all he asked was the use of their pack-train to carry in a lot of supplies.

"Back at the mine they unloaded the mules, dismissed the packers and settled down to dig out the ore, which was easy half gold. But within a month or so Jake and Jerry had a quarrel. Jerry wanted to go to Santa Fe, at that time the Territorial Capitol, and record their claim; but Jake was afraid the Union soldiers would kill them, or start a rush of Northern men that would take the mine away from them.

"But Jerry was bull-headed, and one night he started for Santa Fe. Jake trailed him to Hidden Water and, right there by the spring, he shot him through the head and buried him. Then he went back and kept on digging, but the murder kind of preyed on his mind and when Phoenix was started he finally went down there and hired an old colored woman to take care of him. He sold what gold he had with him to the Valley Bank for $18,800, as you can see by looking at their books, and took in a young Mexican named Rodriguez to help him have a good time.

"This Mexican was a bad one, drunk and gambling all the time, but whenever he ran out of money the Dutchman woulld bring in more gold. The ore was so rich it got everybody excited and, every time he started out, half the town was trying to trail him. That's why he always came up through this country—on the north side of the river; but when he got up here he lost his trail in the rocks and crossed over down by Mormon Flat.

"In a few days Jake would come in with all the ore he could carry; but one time when he went back he found two soldiers, working his mine. They had been going up over the trail from Fort Huachuca to Camp McDowell and all we know is he killed both of them and buried them near the mine. After that he was afraid to go back any more. He went kind of crazy and, knowing he was going to die, he made a map of the country for Rodriguez.

"Sure, here's where the map comes in—like you read about in all these lost treasure stories; but there's a man named Dick Holmes down in Phoenix that could go right to that mine. He was one of the first to trail old Jake when he would sneak away out of town, and when he heard that the Dutchman was sick and delirious he slipped in and passed himself off for Rodriguez. Well, Jake told him the whole story of the mine, just like I'm telling it to you; but he couldn't give him the map, because Rodriguez had it hid.

"So the old Dutchman died and Dick went to work on the Mexican. Got him drunk and stole the map off him, but after that he was afraid to leave town because he knew Rodriguez would kill him. The Apaches were bad then but Rodriguez made up his mind he would find that mine, anyhow, so he went back to Mexico to hunt up the brothers Peralta, but both of them were dead.

"But there were some old packers who remembered the trail, and they got together about fifty men and led him right to the mine. It had been worked in the old Spanish way, by digging a round hole thirty or forty feet across—and a tunnel, over at one side. They got out enough ore to fill their leather pack-boxes and started on the trail home, but there was a Mojave Apache watching them and he ran back to the Verde, got the rest of the Indians, and they killed every one of those Mexicans—including Rodriguez, of course.

"But here's the joke on the Indians. They didn't know gold when they saw it, so they dumped all that ore in the sand-wash in order to get the leather sacks. It's stray rocks from this float that start all the gold rushes in that big canyon north of Superstition Mountain. There ain't a bit of doubt that mine is up there somewhere, but Dick Holmes has got a *map*. He knows right where it is, but he's afraid to go after it. Afraid my brothers-in-law—or me, maybe—will follow him up and kill him to get the mine. Or the map—it would be just as good.

"I remember a couple of Danes that came down from Colorado to work on the Apache Trail road. They had a map, and explored the country east of Superstition for several years in all their spare time. One of them had a horse he thought a lot of and when a flood came down the canyon, cutting them off from supplies, he went over to the road camp to buy some grain.

"But they were short of feed too and his money was bogus—until at last he pulled out a chunk of gold and left it for security. I was just a boy then but I happened to be over there and I asked one of these Danes if this gold was from the Lost Dutchman mine.

" 'Yes kid,' he says, real sarcastic; and of course that shut me up. Old Arizona Jim is still hunting around for it and claims in a couple of months he's going to find it. He's always inquiring for an old *arrastra* at the head of Pine Canyon, but everybody knows that was built by ore-thieves when they were high-grading the Silver King. But I think, myself, it will be found by some Indian."

Johnny stopped abruptly, lit a cigarette and blew out a cloud of smoke while the stranger waited on his words.

"Why?" he asked at last; and Johnny glanced at the guide.

"Well," he says, "it was the Mojave Apaches and Tontos that killed Rodriguez; and after they robbed the pack-train they went back to the hole to see what the Mexicans were after. They rolled some big boulders into the pit and filled up the tunnel into the hill; and now, of course, they're the only ones that know where the mine used to be. But, not being citizens, of course they can't locate it and the white men would take it away from them; so they're keeping it a secret. I don't know of but one Indian that is game to tell where it is, and unfortunately he is in prison."

"What for?" asked the prospector; and Johnny took him into his confidence.

"For cutting his wife's head off," he said. "He made me an offer to take me to the spot if I'd get him a pardon from the Governor. But he's such a bad Indian I can't work it. It seems these Indians have got a superstition against showing any man the mine, and this squaw was going to do that. So he cut off her head to keep her from talking and the Judge sent him up for life."

He rolled his eyes at the stranger and his guide and rose up to go to bed, and the next morning our prospector was gone. He had probably got to thinking what might happen to him if he found the Lost Dutchman Mine. He was on the wrong side of the river anyway, because neither Indians nor Mexicans would venture into that haunted country which lies behind the Superstitions. The story is that a big war-party of Pimas had pursued some raiding Apaches into that country and not one of them had come back. As they could not believe that even the bloodthirsty Apaches could wipe out the whole band, the Pimas had come to the conclusion that some devil ruled over the land. Certain it is that, even to this day, there are prowlers up in those cliffs who waylay and kill intruders; and it is an off year when some hardy prospector fails to find another skeleton with a bullet-hole through the skull.

But the original discoverer of that mine of gold now known as the Lost Dutchman is believed by many to be Captain Weaver, after whom Weaver's Needle is named. He was stationed at Picket Post, near Pinal, and as the Apaches were wary of the white man's shooting they carefully kept away. Bored at last by months of idleness Weaver began to ride out with an escort while he explored the surrounding peaks; until at last, venturing out alone, he was taken prisoner by the Indians.

Now it was the custom of the Apaches to torture their captives by all sorts of devices, but so stoical and calm was this white man that they spared him while they thought up something worse. At last an Indian who had been made a prisoner and had had a chance to observe their madness over gold went out and brought in a few nuggets, at which the Captain went wild.

This was what they were looking for—something to make him fight for his life and not die too easy or too soon; so they took him out to where the gold lay everywhere, led him back and bound him fast. They were having a big council to devise new means of torture when, that very same night, he dug the earth away from a sharp stone, sawed his rawhide thongs against its point and made his escape—taking the gold.

But when the great chief Cochise heard about it he sent back word that the White Eye would be back. All they had to do was wait and he would return to where he had seen the gold. So they kept watch on Picket Post until the Captain rode out, and this time they put him to death. But in his desk at the Post, other soldiers found a map, with a sketch showing the peak now called Weaver's Needle, almost on a line with the Four Peaks—and the gold. One after the other they disappeared into the wilderness until, as none came back, they went forth in force and drove all the Indians out of the country. But they never found the gold.

Even today the more enlightened of the gold-seekers still look for the mine south of Salt River, on a line between the Needle and the Peaks. It lies just behind the Superstition Mountains, and oldtimers, seeing its blue against the sky, still think of the brave Captain who had used it as a landmark to guide him back to the gold. From the canyon where the Apaches had kept him he had seen that sharp peak through a gap and sketched it out when he got home. But now no one knows about Weaver and his Needle, and perhaps it is just as well.

Tall Finds

Sitting in a bar-room one night, three prospectors were recounting some of their famous "strikes."

"The best ore I ever found," said Jack Fisher, "was over in Western Nevada. It was the most peculiar formation I ever saw—pink quartz filled with spheres of gold, and we called it the Birdshot Mine. None of the spheres were bigger than number six shot, and none smaller than number eights. The proportion of quartz to gold was uniform, too. It was so perfect that the ore became a standard currency for that part of the country."

"Yeah, I know all about that," replied Mel Foster. "But you never heard all the facts about a strike I made on the other side of that same range. I never told a living soul about it until I finished cleanin' up. It was in the same formation you mentioned, except that a deep canyon cut back through the vein. The lower end of this canyon was pinched together, just above a waterfall. At the foot of the waterfall was a hollow place in the rock the size of a bathtub. For hundreds of centuries gold had collected in that trap—gold that was the size of wheat grains—and the falling water cleaned out all the gravel, leaving only the pure stuff. I took out more than two tons of it!"

Shorty Harris, dean of prospectors, stifled a yawn.

"Sure, sure, I've heard both of those stories before," he said. "But I never told you about the mine I found in Mexico. It was the hardest quartz I ever saw—and the smoothest. There was a narrow crack in that quartz, and the gold had been melted by volcanic heat and run down into it, just like a mold. I dug it out in sheets, and them sheets were exactly the right thickness so that I sent 'em to the mint and had 'em cut and stamped into twenties!"

From "Tall Tales of the Desert," by Philip Johnston, *Westways*, Vol. 33 (November, 1941), No. 11, Part I, p. 21. Copyright, 1941, by the Automobile Club of Southern California.

Tall Tales from the Colorado Gold Fields

I[1]

A man living in Clear Creek canyon killed a cow which had been reduced to a skeleton supposed to be [on account] of drinking the water from Clear Creek. In the paunch of the cow was found more than eight pounds of mineral sediment—a blanket deposit—which, on being assayed, returned a value of $10,253 per ton in gold, a trifle more than $5 per pound. A boom is intimated in that section.

II[2]

An old fifty-niner was recently bragging that in the early days he once packed two sixteen-foot sluice-boxes, weighing over two tons, a distance of two miles. A bystander hinted that the load was rather heavy, when a second fifty-niner came to the rescue of the first by saying that he knew his story to be true, as he was on the same bar at the time and "tracked his friend half a mile across a piece of bare bed-rock, into which he sank over five inches at every step he took."

III[3]

The Colorado Springs *Mail* vouches for the truth of the following interesting tale: A story illustrative of the richness of Cripple Creek is going the rounds of the camp and has reached this city. It is, in effect, that last Monday night a burglar entered a tent where a miner was asleep. The thief took the miner's limited amount of cash, $6.25, and was just departing when the sleeper awoke. He started after the burglar, chased him several blocks and being unable to catch him returned to his tent. The miner was barefoot and on his return his feet hurt him badly. Sitting down on his cot he took his candle and with his penknife picked out $6.80 worth of gold out of the soles of his feet.

The Tenderfoot at Cripple Creek

When the tenderfoot strikes the Cripple Creek district he generally puts himself on exhibition, and if the whole town does not know he has arrived it is not because he hasn't tried to let the people know all

---

1 From the Boulder (Colorado) *Herald*. Cited in the *Rocky Mountain News*, Denver, April 21, 1883, p. 3. col. 2.

2 From the Rocky Mountain *Herald*, Denver, Colorado, February 26, 1876, p. 2, col. 3.

3 From the Creede (Colorado) *Candle*, February 18, 1892. p. 2.

From the clipping files of the Western History Collection, Denver Public Library, Denver, Colorado.

From the clipping files of the Western History Collection. [No source.]

about it. He is surprised that he does not see men leisurely chipping gold out of the rocks when they need a little spare cash. Usually he is burdened with a curiosity that nearly causes his head to split. He must see the camp—he must know all about it. He hires a rig and a driver, and starts out after the manner of a man thirsting for knowledge—burning up with a desire to acquire information and add to his stock of gray matter. Usually he runs up against some one who seems to have been looking for him, and bites. But this particular tenderfoot did not have time to bite—he swallowed everything in sight.

He was terribly inquisitive. He might know the difference between a pail full of lard and a coal shed in Vermont, but he cannot, not for his life, tell the difference between a mine and an ashpit when he reaches Cripple Creek. The yellow stuff lying on the dumps of some of the mines he sizes up as gold at a glance, and all the argument of the wise men cannot convince him that he is mistaken—not in a thousand years.

The winding roads attracted his attention first, and the narrow cañons amaze him, and he remarks that it must be with great difficulty that wagons pass through some of the gulches.

"Yaas," drawled the driver. "Circus cum here last summer. Had a terrible time—couldn't get the elephant through one of them narrow gulches."

"You don't say so—"

"Course I say so. Didn't you jest hear me say so? I did say so, an' it's so. See?"

"Aw—beg—pardon—but what, aw, did they do—with the elephant, I mean?"

"Had to back him all the way down to Florence, stranger!"

Then the tenderfoot suffered a relapse.

Coming around the road into Mound City the creek takes on a decidedly yellow appearance, after its waters have passed through the chlorination mill there, and of course he tries to keep silent. But he can't. His head would burst if he didn't speak.

"Curious color—the water, I mean."

"Yaas. Assays $40 a ton in gold."

"Aw—all staked off, I presume."

"Sure thing—clean down to Galveston."

"An' another thing. Pardon the suggestion, stranger, but if you is a drinking man, wot can't dam hisself up agin th' likker habit, all yu has ter do is ter drink outern this yer stream an' it's all same gold cure."

"You don't say so," he gasps.

"Who don't say so? I tell—"

"Beg your pardon. Aw—so cures have been effected?"

"Hundreds on 'em, stranger."

"I would like to meet some of the men who have been cured. Where are they?"

"Dead."

"You don't—I mean—what was the cause, effect of the cure?"

"Now you're shoutin'. They cum up here an' swill down this here watter, an' while it stops th' likker habit, it are certain death—no mistake erbout it."

"How?"

"Well, I tell yer, seein' as how yu is a stranger in these 'er parts. They drinks this stuff an' it settles in their systims, an' they becums regular topers of the stuff, an' they keeps on, an' by-an-by they gets so full of th' blamed stuff that the temptation is too great fer mortal man—or enny other man, to stand it, an'—"

"Why, I declare. You mean—"

"That's it. Yes, siree. They is jest waylaid an' shot down, filled full of lead by men wot is poor an' can't help it. Then they is all ready fer the smelter, has th' proper amount o' lead in 'em fer flux, an' they goes th' way uv all ore. Many a otherwise decent and desarving man in this here destreect got their start in that-a-way."

And the tenderfoot marveled until his head ached.

* * * * *

The Independence mine excited him. He had read about it and he is not slow to tell the driver all he knows about it, and then he commences to ply him with questions.

"Does Mr. Stratton get much gold out of it? How rich is the gold he gets?"

"Rich? Why, man alive, Stratton gets gold outern that er mine so rich that he has to break up rock with it to get a assay."

"Aw."

"Has a tough time gettin' th' rock sometimes, too."

Salting a Mine

The Pacific coast mine operators are discussing with considerable interest the latest reported "salt" operation in connection with the sale of an Arizona mine. It was a nefarious success, and the victim was "Diamond Joe" Reynolds, a well-known character residing east of the Rocky mountains, who had acquired a fortune by various successful speculations. Somehow or other Joe caught the mine fever and had it bad. He felt that he couldn't die happy unless he owned a gold-mine that he might leave as a legacy to his family. Its yearly dividends should keep the wolf away from their door when he would be dancing with the angels in the spirit land. The fever has left him now, but his experience has cost him nearly $100,000, which is a pretty round doctor's bill even when a radical cure is effected. "Diamond Joe" heard a great

---

By "Verdenal," in the *San Francisco Chronicle*. Reprinted in the *Tombstone* (Arizona) *Epitaph,* Vol. IX, No. 6, September 10, 1887, p. 1, col. 3.

deal about Arizona mines in general, and particularly, but in a quiet way, about a mine that was located within easy enough reaching distance of Prescott, which I shall call the "Annie Moore" for short. The "Annie" was closely held by three adventurous miners who, taking their lives in their hands during an Apache raid, continued their prospecting until a shaft had attained goodly depth and an adit level had proved beyond reasonable doubt sufficient ore "in sight" to justify value. The ledge was gold-bearing, not very wide, but yielded $40 to the ton, good, bad and indifferent, and that was not to be sneezed at. They "proved" their mine by the aid of a jerk-water two-stamp mill, and report credited them with periodical visits to Prescott where they disposed of the product. That was the kind of a mine Joe wanted and he went for it. The upset price was $60,000 for the plant, but one of the parties, holding a one-third interest, was averse to selling and had to be coaxed into consenting to the "give away" of the property as he called it. Joe took an "expert" down with him, and it was agreed that if the assays were satisfactory the bargain was a "go."

The samples were taken, sealed, and carried by Joe and two of the partners to Prescott. Lo! and behold! the assayer could only find $4.32 in gold per ton, with a trace of silver! That was a set-back, and the partners were dumb with amazement. They gradually found speech, and convinced Joe that their reluctant partner had "fixed" the samples. "Tell you what we'll do," said the honest partners; "we are sure that something is wrong. You go back with your expert to the mine, take out ten, twenty, thirty or fifty tons and make a working test; run the ore through the mill; we will stay here; if the ore doesn't go what we say, we'll pay all of your expenses; if the mill returns are satisfactory, then you pay us $75,000." Joe hankered after a mine, and answered, "It's a whack." The papers were duly signed, money deposited in the Prescott National Bank, and Joe went back to the mine. The run kept the mill busy for two weeks; the amalgam was retorted, and the product of twenty tons yielded an average of $41.70 per ton! Joe bought the mine without more ado; the partners divided according to their respective interests and left for the "states" to have a good time. Joe monopolized the Prescott office wire, telegraphing Chambers & Frazer for a new ten-stamp mill to be sent out instanter. Then he sent for a force of men to take out ore and keep the baby mill running. He had to send a new engineer, because the old one (who had run through the twenty tons, by the way) quit on short notice. How many dividend dreams affected Joe's slumbers is not known. He went back on pressing advices from his foreman that something was wrong. The "clean up" showed very hungry ore, only about $3 per ton. Another mill man was sent for, but he declared upon seeing the ore that you might as well try to squeeze blood out of a turnip as to make that stuff pay. A run proved the fact that Joe had been cleverly salted. If he had had his own engineer to run the mill, it couldn't possibly have happened. The order for the new mill was countermanded. Joe made a bonfire of everything combustible on the place, and has sworn off being a mine owner. Moral: always be sure of your engineer.

Unwatering a Mining Shaft

There are lots of stories in the mining regions of Colorado about the early days when, of course, metal mining was the best occupation to follow. There were a number of local characters concerning whom stories were told. One of them was Gassy Thompson up around Empire, and he also was known in Central City and Black Hawk and over at Georgetown. One of the stories I like best about Gassy is the one telling how he unwatered a mine. If a mining shaft is left unworked for a while, very likely water will accumulate for maybe several hundred feet. And if the mine is to be operated again, then it has to be pumped out. And if done by hand, this, of course, takes quite a long time and means a lot of back-breaking work. Gassy took a contract to unwater this particular mining shaft and then regretted that he had signed up for so much work. He went up to look over the place and found that there was a lot of water in the mine. So he sat down to think. He noticed a stray dog running along, he hurled a rock at it, knocked it over, went over and killed the dog. Then with a brilliant idea back of his actions he dragged it to the mouth of the shaft, found an old hat and coat that had been abandoned nearby, dabbed it over with some of the dog's blood. Then he tied a rock around the dog's neck and dropped it in and heard it hit the water and splash and go to the bottom. His next step was to go down to Central City and sort of circulate through the bars, spreading the word that he suspected foul play up at that mine, that there was evidence that there had been a struggle, and blood was around there. He didn't know just what had happened but it looked bad to him. Before long the boys went up to investigate and they found sure enough evidences that aroused their suspicions. So they went back down town and got the sherriff. He in turn organized a posse and they borrowed some pumps from the county commissioners and they went up to that mine. The boys set to with a will and before long they had pumped the shaft dry. Sure enough, they found the body, but it was of the dog. In the meantime, Gassy, of course, had skipped the country. He did come back a little later to collect the wages from the owners of the shaft for the quickest and most efficient job of unwatering a mine that had been done for some time.

Told by Levette J. Davidson, University of Denver, Denver, Colorado, July 24, 1950. Recorded by B. A. Botkin.

Smart Burros

I[1]

. . . The burro, in his native habitat, is a noble beast—not in appearance, not in disposition, not in speed or energy, but in heart, stamina and adaptability. Like the prospector who commands him, the burro may lie and steal, but he persists. He gets there, regardless of all obstacles, as gaunt and hungry and thirsty as his master, but still on his feet.

The true prospector gives him credit not only for a devilish ingenuity in evading work and obtaining food, but for an uncanny intelligence. The old-timer who has lived with and leaned upon the beast for a third of a century can tell a hundred tales of burro wisdom. Charley Higgins, who has made a study of burros over a thousand miles of desert wastes, and in scores of desert camps, tells one of the best.

"It was at the old camp of Tuscarora, back twenty-five or thirty years ago," says Charley. "Tuscarora was what the magazine writers like to call a 'ghost town.' It was sort of ghostly at that. There were a number of old abandoned shacks and cabins, with the doors and windows fallen in. But there was a little excitement there at this time I'm speaking about, and a number of men were working, and prospectors doing location work on new claims. Down in the flat there must have been fifty or sixty burros roaming around, picking up what they could.

"I needed three or four good burros for a trip I was planning and I went to a prospector I knew and offered to buy his string. He was working then, and didn't need 'em. He said all right, and when he finished his shift he went with me down to the flat and we walked around and he pointed out his burros to me. We made a deal, and next morning I went down to cut out these burros. They weren't there. All the rest of the herd was there, calm as usual, but these four were gone.

"So I went back to my friend and told him. He said I must be mistaken. But I knew I wasn't. I knew burros, and I'd have been able to pick out these four in four hundred after he had pointed them out to me, just as you'd be able to pick out a friend in any crowd. Well, finally he went down with me to see about it, and sure enough the other fifty or sixty burros were scattered down in the flat below the old abandoned cabins, but his burros weren't there. We looked at every animal. At last we gave it up, and started back to camp, figuring I'd have to buy some others.

"But just as I passed one of the old abandoned cabins, I caught a

[1] From *Gold in Them Hills,* The Story of the West's Last Wild Mining Days, by C. B. Glasscock, pp. 186–190. Copyright, 1932, by C. B. Glasscock. Indianapolis: The Bobbs-Merrill Company.

See also "Rocky Mountain Canary," Part Five, below.

glimpse of a grey nose sticking out through a window. I went in, and what do you suppose? Hiding there in that cabin were those four burros I'd bought. And some folks say a burro is dumb."

Perhaps Charley would not want to be put on record as believing that those four burros knew his plan to put them to work, but you are welcome to your conclusions. On the heels of this story he tells another, with a twinkle in his eye.

One prospector meeting another in a small temporary camp, asked his friend if he were going to the new strike in the Skull Mountains. It was in the early evening when the burros had come into camp for water, and were standing within ear-shot.

"No," said the second prospector, "I don't reckon I'll go." Half an hour later, however, when the burros had strayed away about their business, he drew the newcomer aside. "Sure, I'll jine ye. I was figgerin' on gettin' an early start in the mornin', an' I didn't want them damn burros to know."

Burros are not only essential to the old prospector's livelihood, but are a reliable source of entertainment and speculation. Slim Ludwick, prospecting in southern Nevada, had stopped temporarily at the camp of Gold Circle, when Jerry O'Rourke, one of the notables of the Greenwater district, came in with a string of eight burros.

"Lend me fifty dollars, Slim," said O'Rourke.

"I'll lend nothing to an eight-burro man. I'll buy that big jack, Jerry, there. Give you thirty dollars for him."

Slim was a judge of burros and, as it transpired, of men. The big jack had a reputation on the desert based upon a report that he had ridden from Gold Circle to Battle Mountain, sixty miles in ten hours. Jerry O'Rourke's pride in the beast was insulted by Slim's offered price.

"Go to hell," said O'Rourke. "That's the best ridin' and the best fightin' burro in Nevada."

"Well," said Slim, "if you think so much of him, and you need fifty dollars, I'll tell you what I'll do. I'll pay you fifty for him, and bet it right back with you that I can round up another burro in half an hour that'll lick him."

"Sold," said O'Rourke.

II[2]

The smartest boorow I ever had, . . . was Maria. Mebbe next to the smartest. Maria always led my string. The other boorows would do whatever she told 'em. Once I got too heavy a pack on her. It was high-grade from my claims down by the old Confidence. When I unloaded her that night she just give me a look and walked away. Next mornin' I couldn't find her. Of course I couldn't go on without Maria. I spent four days lookin' for her. Then when I'd give up and come back to

[2] From *Here's Death Valley*, by C. B. Glasscock, pp. 153–154. Copyright, 1940, by C. B. Glasscock. Indianapolis and New York: The Bobbs-Merrill Company.

camp ahead of time, I seen another boorow carryin' a pail of water with the bail in his teeth. Another one was carryin' a block of hay with a wire around it. I follered careful where they couldn't see me, and I seen 'em go into a narrow cave behind a greasewood bush, off a barranca. And there was Maria, livin' fat and easy. I apologized to her. I had to. I told her I wouldn't never overload her again. After that Maria worked for me long and faithful.

But another boorow I had was even smarter. I noticed one night he seemed kind of sick. When I give him a bucket of water, nice and cold out of the spring, he jest took a sip and let out a moan like a squaw with a bellyache, and give me a dirty look. I tried to make it up to him by givin' him a hot flapjack off my stack, and I noticed he held it in his mouth for two-three minutes before he swallowed it. Later on I noticed him drinkin' some warm water I'd set aside to wash up with. And all of a sudden I ree-lized that boorow had a toothache. I held out another hot flapjack and when he opened his mouth for it I saw a hole in the tooth. Well, next mornin' he was gone. He didn't come into camp for water like the others. But I was prospectin' around there some, so I didn't bother. It must of been about four days later when he showed up again jest as full of ginger as a boorow can get. No toothache no more. He walked right up to me, and opened his mouth and let out a terrific bray. And do you know what? . . .

They was a solid gold fillin' in that holler tooth. I spent months lookin' for the ledge he'd got it off of. I never did find it.

III[3]

As we finished our maps and our meal, Florence Piver, Mrs. Reid's daughter, said something about using the leftover batter for a couple of outsize hotcakes for the burros. It appeared they'd stick their heads right in the kitchen window if encouraged.

"Plenty burros round here." Charlie Walker shook his own sandy mane.

"Too many," Agnes Reid added. "Twenty-seven of them right up there in the canyon."

"Effete," said Charlie. "That's what they are."

"Effete burros?"

"Exactly. Too damn civilized for their own good. And tricky."

Those burros—Charlie said—even expect their drinks to be brought to them. They're so lazy they won't go a couple of miles to the waterhole as their ancestors did. Their new-fangled notions certainly raise hob with the water system.

How come? I asked.

A two-inch iron pipe leads from a spring to the mine, where Charlie occupies himself, mostly laid along the top of the ground. The burros

[3] From *Death Valley and Its Country,* by George Palmer Putnam, pp. 184–185. Copyright, 1946, by George Palmer Putnam. New York: Duell, Sloan and Pearce.

are so spoiled by modern conveniences they want their refreshment delivered right where they are.

"They kick hell out of the pipe," Charlie explained. "It's old pipe and busts easy. You'll see a burro with his mug up against one of those leaks he's made, guzzling."

Charlie assured me one story I'd heard about the burros and the pipes was dubious. That more elaborate creation alleged that the burros would *unscrew* the pipes. One would hold a length of pipe in his iron jaws so that it would not turn, the way a human does with a monkey-wrench, while his partner twisted the adjoining pipe until the coupling came apart.

"That," declared Charlie, "sounds like an exaggeration. I never saw the burros unscrew two pieces of pipe. But," he added judiciously, "I wouldn't be surprised it's been done."

"And," he chuckled at the memory, "one time I saw a burro get mighty surprised. That pipe line lies right on top of the ground. The day I'm thinkin' of the thermometer was about a hundred and twenty degrees. Well, the burro knocked a hole in the old pipe, all right, but when he put his mouth down to drink, it damn near scalded him. *Steam,* that's what came out."

The Magnetized Mule

When Scotty finishes the story of Verbena, he is apt to remind his audience what a hard country his country used to be.

"Cruel. That's what it was. An' full of the damndest surprises," he'd add meditatively, which meant that another story was coming up.

The time I have in mind the yarn was about that mule Scotty had to leave standing in his tracks, all because of an odd freak of some highly mineralized rock.

As our historian states it, he was riding along the top of a narrow ridge. He stopped for a moment to have a look around, but when he was ready to move on, the mule couldn't budge.

"Beatin' him didn't do no good. Seemed like he couldn't lift his feet no matter how hard he tried. That's the first time ever I saw a mule who *looked scared.*" Scotty indicated that phenomenon made *him* a bit uneasy, too.

"So, I got off to see what was wrong. I stepped around to the mule's head thinking I might try a blindfold to get him started. An' would you believe it, once my two feet were on that ledge, *I* couldn't move either. They was clamped down tight. After a bit I figured out the trouble. That rock was *magnetized.* The magnetic pull was holding the mule's shoes, an' it had caught hold of the hobnails in my boots, too. So I worked out of my boots. By the time I got back over that trail my stockings were plumb wore out."

Ibid., pp. 116–117.

"What about the mule?" someone asked.

Scotty showed he felt badly about that.

"The poor critter," he said sadly. "I had to leave him right there. He died, I reckon."

The Self-Rising Donkey

The miners all did their own cooking, but this was no great task, as when you had mentioned slapjacks, beans, bacon, and coffee, you were at the bottom of the bill of fare. A few men in every camp, however, developed a decided genius in the art culinary and concocted some wonderful dishes, the raw material at hand considered.

About three fourths of the prospecting miners who came over [to Nevada] from California packed their traps on the backs of donkeys, and driving these before them, boldly, if not swiftly, scaled the Sierras. These donkeys became a great nuisance about the several camps. All became thieves of the most accomplished type. They would steal flour, sugar, bacon, beans, and everything eatable about the camp. They would even devour gunny-sacks in which bacon had been packed, old woolen shirts, and almost everything but the picks and shovels. The donkeys would be seen demurely grazing on the flats and on the hillsides when the miners left camp in the morning to go out prospecting, but all the time they had one eye upon every movement that was made. Hardly were the miners out of sight ere the donkeys were in the camp, with heads in the tents devouring all within reach. When the miners returned, the donkeys were all out picking about on the hillsides, as calmly as though nothing had happened, but the swearing heard in camp as the work of the cunning beasts came to light would have furnished any ordinary bull-driver a stock of oaths that he could not exhaust in six months.

One of these donkeys—too confiding—was caught in the act. Many of the miners used a kind of flour called "self-rising." There was mixed with it when it was ground all of the ingredients used in the manufacture of yeast powders. All the miner had to do in making bread from this flour was to add the proper quantity of water and mix it, when it "came up" beautifully. The donkey in question had struck a sack of this flour and had eaten all he could hold of it. He then went down to a spring near the camp and drank a quantity of water. When we came home that evening, Mr. Donkey was still at the spring. The self-rising principle in the flour had done its work. The beast was round as an

---

From *History of the Big Bonanza,* An Authentic Account of the Discovery, History, and Working of the World Renowned Comstock Silver Lode of Nevada . . ., by Dan De Quille (William Wright), pp. 113–114. Entered According to Act of Congress in the year 1876, by American Publishing Company, in the office of the Librarian of Congress at Washington. Hartford, Connecticut: American Publishing Company; San Francisco, California: A. L. Bancroft & Company.

apple, and his legs stood out like those of a carpenter's bench. He was very dead. Here was one of the thieves. Cunning as he had been, he was caught at last, and with "wool in his teeth."

An Expert Witness

Friend of mine was testifyin' for the defense in a case before Judge Stratton at Buckhorn once. The lawyer for the defense was tryin' to qualify him as an expert witness, an' asked him how long he'd been a prospector. "Thirty years," he says. Well, pretty soon the prosecutin' attorney gets to cross-examine him.

"How many years have you prospected?" he asks.

" 'Bout five years," says the witness.

"Ah ha!" says the prosecutor, lookin' mean an' successful. "Your Honor, I'd like to have you note that the witness under oath has already said he has been a prospector for thirty years, an' now he says he's prospected five years."

"Wait a minute, wait a minute," says the witness. "I said I'd been a prospector for thirty years, an' I have. I said I'd prospected five years, an' I have. Both statements is facts, your Honor. Five years I prospected and the other twenty-five I spent lookin' for my burros. You know how it is, your Honor."

"The witness qualifies as an expert," says the j.p., thereby qualifyin' himself as a judge.

The Fatal Shirt

About seven o'clock last evening the pistol was again used with fatal effect on Allen street, resulting in the death of T. J. Waters from gunshot wounds from a weapon in the hands of E. L. Bradshaw. The causes which led to this unfortunate tragedy are brief. Waters was what is considered a sporting man, and has been in Tombstone several months. He was about forty years of age, powerful built, stood over six feet in height and weighed about 190 pounds. When sober he was a clever sort of man but quite the opposite when under the influence of liquor. Yesterday he won considerable money and had been drinking a great deal, hence was in a mood to be easily irritated. Bradshaw was an intimate friend of Waters but a very different character, being a man

---

From *Gold in Them Hills,* The Story of the West's Last Wild Mining Days, by C. B. Glasscock, pp. 19–20. Copyright, 1932, by C. B. Glasscock. Indianapolis and New York: The Bobbs-Merrill Company.

From the *Tombstone Epitaph,* July 25, 1880, cited in *Tombstone's Epitaph,* by Douglas D. Martin, pp. 60–61. Copyright, 1951, by the University of New Mexico Press. Albuquerque.

of medium size, over fifty years of age and very reserved and peaceable in his disposition. We understand that these two men had prospected together and when Waters first came to Tombstone he lived in Bradshaw's cabin. Yesterday morning Waters purchased a blue and black plaid shirt, little dreaming that the fated garment would hurl his soul into eternity before the sun had set.

It so happened that several good-natured remarks were made about the new shirt during the day until Waters had taken sufficient liquor to make the joking obnoxious to him, and he began to show an ugly resentment and was very abusive with, "Now, if anyone don't like what I've said let him get up, G—d d—n him. I'm chief. I'm boss. I'll knock the first s— of a b— down that says anything about my shirt again."

This happened in the back room at Corrigan's saloon and as Waters stepped into the front room Bradshaw happened in, and seeing the new shirt his friend was wearing made some pleasant remark about it, whereupon Waters, without a word, struck Bradshaw a powerful blow over the left eye which sent him senseless to the floor. Waters then walked over to Vogan & Flynn's, to see, as he said, "if any s— of a b— there don't like this shirt." He had just entered the street when Ed. Ferris made some remark about the new shirt, which Waters promptly resented in his pugilistic style. After some more rowing Waters went back to Corrigan's saloon.

As soon as Bradshaw recovered from the knockdown he went into the back room, washed off the blood, went down to his cabin, put a bandage on his eye and his pistol in his pocket. He then came up to Allen street and took his seat in front of Vogan & Flynn's saloon. Seeing Waters in Corrigan's door, Bradshaw crossed towards the Eagle Brewery, and walking down the sidewalk until within a few feet of Waters, said, "Why did you do that?" Waters said something whereupon Bradshaw drew his pistol and fired four shots, all taking effect, one under the left arm probably pierced the heart, two entered about the center of the back between the shoulders and one in the top of the head ranged downward toward the neck, any one of which would probably have resulted fatally. Waters fell at the second shot and soon expired. Bradshaw was promptly arrested and an examination will be had in the morning before Justice Gray.

Mean Business

There are occasions on which, among small communities, an overwhelming emotion, common to all, may obliterate all feeling of relative superiority; but the history of the world can show no such picture of human nature upon the same scale as was to be seen in the mines,

---

From *Three Years in California,* by J. D. Borthwick, pp. 371–372. Edinburgh and London: William Blackwood and Sons. 1857.

where, among a population of hundreds of thousands of men, from all parts of the world, and from every order of society, no individual or class was accounted superior to another.

The cause of such a state of things was one which would tend to produce the same results elsewhere. It consisted in this, that each man enjoyed the capability of making as much money as his neighbor; for hard labor, which any man could accomplish with legs and arms, without much assistance from his head, was as remunerative as any other occupation—consequently, all men indiscriminately were found so employing themselves, and mining or any other kind of labor was considered as dignified and as honorable a pursuit as any other.

In fact, so paramount was this idea, that in some men it created an impression that not to labor was degrading—that those who did not live by actual physical toil were men who did not come up to the scratch—who rather shirked the common lot of all, "man's original inheritance, that he should sweat for his poor pittance." I recollect once arriving in the middle of the night in San Francisco, when it was not by any means the place it now is, and finding all the hotels full, I was compelled to take refuge in an establishment which offered no other accommodation to the public than a lot of beds—half-a-dozen in a room. When I was paying my dollar in the morning for having enjoyed the privilege of sleeping on one of these concerns, an old miner was doing the same. He had no coin, but weighed out an ounce of dust, and while getting his change he seemed to be studying the keeper of the house, as a novel and interesting specimen of human nature. The result showed itself in an expression of supreme contempt on his worn and sunburnt features, as he addressed the object of his contemplation: "Say now, stranger, do you do nothin' else but just sit thar and take a dollar from every man that sleeps on them beds?"

"Yes, that's my business," replied the man.

"Well, then," said the miner after a little further reflection, "it's a d——d mean way of making your living, that's all I can say."

Pat Casey, Bonanza King

It is related of a prospector from the Emerald Isle, whom we will designate as Pat, that while attending a funeral, he picked up some dirt that was thrown from the new grave, and just from force of habit examined it. He suddenly arose from his knees and commenced staking off a claim. The minister observed this, and concluded his prayer in this

---

From "'Gassy' Thompson—and Others: Stories of Local Characters," by Levette J. Davidson, *California Folklore Quarterly,* Vol. V (October, 1946), No. 4, pp. 344–348, *passim.* Copyright, 1946, by the California Folklore Society. Berkeley and Los Angeles: Published for the California Folklore Society by the University of California Press.

manner: "Stake me off a claim, Pat, this we ask for Christ's sake—Amen."

Pat afterward became one of the bonanza kings of the period; exchanged his suit labeled "Superfine Flour" for broadcloth, and went to New York to cut a swell. He stopped at the largest and most fashionable hotel, and was assigned a room on the fifth floor. When he left his room that evening for a saunter in the city, thinking the halls and stairways rather bewildering, *he blazed a way,* in order to be able to retrace his steps. It cost him $2,000 for repairs.[1]

Casey always carried, conspicuously displayed, a memorandum book, with a number of pencils. Notwithstanding the fact that he could neither read nor write, he made bold dashes at writing things in that memorandum book. Pat was singularly susceptible to flattery, extravagantly fond of telling how much business he had to do every day. It was his common boast that he "used up ten lead pencils a day and then didn't half do his business."[2]

* * * * *

On one occasion he went up to the mines with a bottle of whisky intending to treat his men. Looking down in the shaft, he called out, "How many of yez are down there?" "Five," came back the answer. "The half of yez come up and drink."[3]

* * * * *

Many people resented Pat's popularity with the Goddess of Fortune; they took a somewhat malicious pleasure in circulating stories that illustrated his lack of learning. For example, he is said to have been asked to contribute to the purchase of a fine chandelier for the new Catholic church in Central. Reaching for his well-filled purse, Pat said, "Sure. But, begorry, I wonder who you can git up here that can play it after ye git it."

Some of the citizens, desiring to give tone to a park to be laid out on the shore of a nearby lake, proposed to buy half a dozen gondolas. When Pat was asked for a subscription, he is said to have replied: "Why buy so many gondolas? Why not get just one male and one female and let nature take its course?"

---

1 Alice Polk Hill, *Tales of the Colorado Pioneers* (Denver, 1884), pp. 103–104.—L.J.D.

2 *Glimpses of Golden Gilpin,* issued by Gilpin County Chamber of Commerce, Central City, Colorado, "50th Anniversary of the Discovery of Gold in the Borders" (ca. 1908 or 1909.)—L.J.D.

3 "To Pike's Peak in Search of Gold in 1859," *The Trail,* Denver, Vol. IV (November, 1911), No. 6, pp. 8–9.—L.J.D.

The Despondent Prospector

They also tell in Kerbyville [,Oregon,] of the despondent prospector who came into town and tried to buy two sticks of dynamite. The storekeeper haggled, not desiring to break a box of explosives. The despondent prospector finally plunged. He bought the whole box. And he took it back to his claim, seated himself comfortably on it, and touched off the wholesale lot. They still estimate that the despondent prospector could have used the dynamite to clear his land and turn it into the agricultural mine it now is.

The Rise and Fall of a Mining Magnate

The rise and fall of a mining magnate was relentlessly reflected in the salutations of the community, according to Patrick Quinn. From poor prospector he gradually became rich mine-owner, and when his gold ledge near Devil's Gate petered out he fell accordingly in public estimation. The summary of his life and fortune was contained in the way general reference was made to him. This is as he gave it to me:

Quinn
Pat Quinn
C. Patrick Quinn
Col. Cornelius Patrick Quinn
Col. C. P. Quinn
Patrick Quinn
Pat Quinn
Old Quinn

Ghost Gold

. . . In the old days . . . every mineral-bearing locality was filled with men whose claim to fame existed in the fact that they might be poor to-day and rich to-morrow; children of fortune whose assertions could not be denied for the simple reason that to do so would neces-

---

From *Oregon Sketches,* by Wallace Smith, p. 126. Copyright, 1924, 1925, by the New York Times Company; 1925, by Wallace Smith. New York and London: G. P. Putnam's Sons.

From *An Editor on the Comstock Lode,* by Wells Drury, pp. 31–32. Copyright, 1936, by Audrey Drury. New York and Toronto: Farrar and Rinehart, Inc.

From *High Country,* The Rockies Yesterday and To-day, by Courtney Riley Cooper, pp. 187–192. Copyright, 1925, 1926, by Courtney Riley Cooper. Boston: Little, Brown, and Company.

sitate the gift of prophecy. The remainder of that army still wanders the hills, old now, gray now, stooped and bent now. But the lure, the passion, is still as fierce as ever.

One night at sunset, my pack outfit dipped over a hill of sage and down into the remains of what was once a teeming town. A big mine had been there, and a smelter and a mill—but desertion has done its work. Where had stood the usual dance halls and the usual saloons, and the usual by-products of mining, which seemed to run greatly to drinking and gambling and women, judging from the customary remains of a defunct mining camp, now were only so many buildings in various stages of decay, the mud roofs of the log cabins broken away in yawning patches, windows gaping, doors standing open. House hunters of the day, we rode the various lines of cabins and selected our abode for the night. Then, as the pack horses one by one gave up their burdens and moved forth to the grassy streets to roll, we halted for a moment in our labors, to observe that we were not alone.

An old man was approaching from far at the other end of the squalid, deserted village. A gaunt man, a bent man, leaning upon a lengthy home-made staff of aspen; a man who moved slowly, laboriously, and when he approached within hailing distance displayed himself as ghastly pale except for his lips, and these were blue, as though he had used theatrical grease paint on them. He grunted and sighed as he walked, his watery eyes peering at us as though they saw only through a film. At last he sank on an adjacent doorstep.

"I'm Old Man Brown," he announced. "Been prospeckin' a little around here. Goin' to camp here tonight?"

We nodded to our dismantled equipment in obvious answer. A thin, shaking hand rose to the blue lips and rubbed them in quivering fashion.

"Mighty glad o' that," he said. "You wouldn't mind me grubbin' with you? A feller said he'd bring me some grub a week or so ago, but he never done it. Last Thursday I got pretty hungry, so I dug some worms an' walked four miles over to Beaver Creek an' stayed all night there. Caught eleven fish. Been livin' on 'em ever since—" the lean hand shook at the blue lips again—"but they're all gone now."

"Poor devil!" I muttered, as I helped Charlie lift the last pannier from the back of his beloved Big Major. But Charlie only grunted.

"Wait till he gets th' wrinkles out of his belly!" he prophesied.

An hour later, a different Mr. Brown pushed back his chair from the commandeered table of a commandeered, deserted log cabin, and with the air of a connoisseur raised a gift cigar between two very stiff fingers. He lighted it and puffed slowly, as though testing the grade of the tobacco. He blew a billow of smoke toward the newspaper-decorated ceiling, then turned upon us his weak blue eyes.

"Tell you right now," he said, " 'twouldn't take much to bring this country back around here. No sirree. 'Course, it's shet down now, but then, that wouldn't mean nothin'. Why, do you know, I've seen th' time when these hills around here was just black with prospectors, grubbin' in the sage for surface indications. Good ore too—if they'd only known where to look for it." He waved a hand to indicate the whole sagebrushed, mesa land, lying gray and glowering about us in the blackness of an approaching storm, the black outlines of a fire-gutted mill upon the hill, the slanting building which housed the disused smelter. "An' everything'll come right back too, the minute there's the slightest start. There's a couple of School of Mines boys goin' to retimber that old shaft up there, and if they do, just you watch this district!"

I looked out the grimy window, at the slatternly cabins, the careening buildings, the ancient dance halls and saloons.

"Suppose it does come back?" I asked. "What of it?"

"What of it?" The eminent Mr. Brown pounded his staff upon the ancient floor. "Why, this here was one of the best little towns of its size in Colorado. We had dance halls here an' everything. An' this districk was one of th' best too, an' don't you let anybody fool you. I've got a dozen or more claims staked out around here an' there ain't one of 'em, if it was worked right, that wouldn't make a man independent rich!"

Shortly afterward, he left us flat, stumbling along with the aid of his staff, and mumbling to himself through those theatrical blue lips. Charlie winked a knowing eye.

"Didn't I tell you?" he asked. "Iron th' wrinkles out o' their bellies an' they all sing different. Wouldn't sell you none of them claims, either, for less 'n a million. Don't I know?"

Again I looked out the window, at a decrepit little wreck of a town, huddled now, it seemed, in its attempt to escape the fury of slashing wind and driving rain; a miserable, piteous excuse for a town, where men at best could only exist until they gained the money to hurry elsewhere, a town without home possibilities, without comforts, without anything save the rudest of frontier equipment.

"But why should anybody be thrilled at the idea of bringing a place like this to life—"

Charlie grunted—he who had been reared in the companionship of such men as Old Man Brown, and had lived in a log cabin town himself.

"Say, it ain't the town," he announced. "He don't even know it's here. Most of 'em—" then Charlie made a motion toward his forehead—"most of 'em's touched a bit. From bein' alone so much an' in the high country. An' from lookin' for gold so long that by now it's stickin' out of every rock. An' from holdin' on to it."

Jack, busy with the dishes, looked up.

"Funny about 'em that way, isn't it," he asked. "Crazy to get somebody to take hold of their property—until somebody wants it."

"Then nobody can have it," announced Charlie. "Say, there was the Dutchman, over by Lake Pass. You know, that last cabin we passed before we hit the willows? Where that mine dump was? Well, that was the Dutchman's. Used to pretty near starve to death there, grubbin' around in his tunnel and gettin' something to eat when he could—an' not eatin' half the time. Then along comes a man from Denver an' stays all night with him, an' looked at his ore an' got all fed up on how rich the mine was an' everything. An' just as a favor to the Dutchman, he said he'd take some of the stuff down to Denver an' see if he couldn't get somebody interested in it. Well, he did—just as a favor, understand. He wasn't gettin' anything out of it himself—but he just felt sorry for the old man. So, finally, they made a deal where these people paid the old man five thousand dollars and were going to pay him the rest of fifty thousand dollars in installments.

"Fifty thousand dollars!" repeated Charlie, drawing out the amount as though he liked the taste of it. "An' here he was, 'way over sixty years old; it'd been enough to keep him like a millionaire for the rest of his days. But you know what? The Leadville papers run a story about it all, sayin' what a fine mine it was an' all that. An' the old man seen it. 'Humph!' he says. 'If it's worth that to them, it's worth that to me' So he give 'em back the money an' wouldn't have anything more to do with 'em, an' a couple o' months later, somebody came along by the cabin an' found him sittin' there on the mine dump—dead. A rock or something 'd fallen on him while he was countin' up his millions!"

Nor was Charlie's illustration of the old-time prospector and miner an unusual one. I've met a great many of the old fellows in the years I have been wandering the high country of the Rockies, stuck away in cabins at timber line, roaming the hills, living on the bounty of the community. I've never met one who wasn't feverish for a partner, or for somebody to "take a-hold of the property." And I've never met one who, at the final drawing up of the papers, wouldn't become as skittish as a mule deer, and think better about going through with the deal!

Because, after all, it isn't the money. There are times when I believe it never was the money. It was the thrill of discovery; the romance of being a prospector, the obedience to the wandering instinct, and gold was merely a wonderful excuse. As far as making a stake for life was concerned, that was largely on the surface. The history of mining communities shows few instances of prospectors who ever quit, once they had located pay ore. Off again—just as soon as they could sell their claim—off again to new country; over the hill and away to where the mountains beckoned and the will-o'-the-wisp lured them on anew. That was the zest. That the thing which carried them on—the gold which meant adventure; and of all western characters, the prospector is the only one who cannot be overdrawn. His past is fiction, his life is fiction, and his present is fiction—and he a fiction character living it!

II. COWBOYS

Oh, I am a Texas cowboy, right off the Texas plains.
My trade is cinchin' saddles and pullin' of bridle reins,
And I can throw a lasso with the greatest of ease;
I can rope and ride a bronco any damn way I please.

—COWBOY SONG

The Cowboy's Life

. . . It was a land of scattered ranches, of herds of long-horned cattle, and of reckless riders who unmoved looked in the eyes of life or of death. In that land we led a free and hardy life, with horse and with rifle. We worked under the scorching midsummer sun, when the wide plains simmered and wavered in the heat; and we knew the freezing misery of riding night guard round the cattle in the late fall round-up. In the soft springtime the stars were glorious in our eyes each night before we fell asleep; and in the winter we rode through blinding blizzards, when the driven snow-dust burnt our faces. There were monotonous days, as we guided the trail cattle or the beef herds, hour after hour, at the slowest of walks; and minutes or hours teeming with excitement as we stopped stampedes or swam the herds across rivers treacherous with quicksands or brimmed with running ice. We knew toil and hardship and hunger and thirst; and we saw men die violent deaths as they worked among the horses and cattle, or fought in evil feuds with one another; but we felt the beat of hardy life in our veins, and ours was the glory of work and the joy of living.

The Genesis of the Cowboy

I. IN REVOLUTIONARY DAYS[1]

During the Revolution a band of marauders, consisting mostly of Tory refugees who adhered to the British interests, infested the neutral ground in Westchester county, N. Y., between the American and British

From *Theodore Roosevelt, An Autobiography,* pp. 93–94. Copyright, 1913, by Charles Scribner's Sons; 1913, by the Outlook Company; 1941, by Edith K. Carow Roosevelt. New York: Charles Scribner's Sons.

[1] From *Harper's Encyclopaedia of United States History,* from 458 A.D. to 1909, based upon the plan of Benson John Lossing, LL.D., Vol. II, p. 407. Copyright, 1901 and 1905, by Harper & Brothers. New York and London.

lines, and because they stole many cattle, were called Cowboys. They generally plundered the Whigs, or adherents of the Continental Congress; but, like their opponents, the Skinners, they were not always scrupulous in the choice of their victims. In recent years the phrase has been applied to the men employed on the great cattle-ranches of the West and Southwest. They are a fearless set of fellows and expert horsemen. Many modern "cowboys" were mustered into the two volunteer cavalry regiments for service in the war with Spain (1898), popularly known as the "Rough Riders."[2]

II. Cameron's Cowboys[3]

In the days when Texas was a nation, when farmer boys along the Trinity and Brazos were carrying rifles to their evening chores for fear of lurking Indians, and the men of the Southwestern settlements were constantly under arms against invading Mexicans, a number of young fellows drifted down into the country between the lower Nueces and the Rio Grande. The most of them had lost their fathers at the Alamo and in the massacre of Fannin's men at Goliad. They came hither to seek adventure and to make their livings, two projects which were at that time compatible.

The land was wild: great grass-grown pampas intersected by wide river bottoms where dense thickets of mesquite and cat's-claw grew. Here in former years there had been enormous ranches, but the Mexican owners had migrated beyond the Rio Grande with the unsettled conditions of the Texan revolution; the Indians had burned their homes; nothing remained of that pastoral civilization save a few crumbling adobe walls and the bands of cattle, which had lapsed to wildness like the land. These roved the prairies and browsed in the timber, shy as the antelope which wandered in the hills, lean-bodied, swift as mustangs.

The youths hunted them down. They knew nothing of the reata's uses; such few of them as had seen the rawhide ropes scorned them as they scorned everything Mexican. But all of them were expert horsemen. They made their expeditions during the periods of the full moon. By day and night they chased the wild longhorns across the open plateaus and through the timbered bottoms, relaying their ponies when they got the chance, outwearing the fear-maddened herds until, through sheer exhaustion, the brutes became half-tractable. Then they corraled them in stout pens and drove them eastward to the markets.

They dressed in smoke-tanned buckskin, for in this land where there were neither women nor looms a man must get his raiment as he got his meat, with his long-barreled rifle. A few wore boots, but most of them were shod in moccasins. They were among the first in Texas to use the slouching wide-brimmed hat which afterward became universal

---

[2] Cf. *Theodore Roosevelt, An Autobiography* (New York, 1943), pp. 120, 123.

[3] From *Tales of the Old-Timers,* by Frederick R. Bechdolt, pp. 185–187. Copyright, 1924, by the Century Co. New York and London.

throughout the cattle country. Some of them had built cabins . . . near the streams, but they seldom saw their habitations. Save when the snow was on the ground, they spent their days and nights in the open.

It was a period of Indian raids, and Santa Ana's troops were constantly crossing the Rio Grande to make brief forays against the isolated border towns. Scarcely a month went by which did not witness the galloping of horsemen who brought to ranch and village and budding frontier metropolis the call to arms. Every district had its ranger company, commanded by some local veteran, whose members were ready to seize their rifles and sling on their long powder-horns at a moment's notice. The young fellows from the Nueces were well known among the other bands for their iron endurance in the saddle, their faultless marksmanship, the boldness of their fighting.

So it came that they received a name from those with whom they rode pursuing Indians or Mexicans. And the term by which men called them stuck to them through the years. It fell to them quite naturally because of their vocation. They were known as the "Cowboys."

It was the first time that the word was used west of the Mississippi, and always thereafter it retained its peculiar significance; it was handed down by these riders of the latter thirties to the booted herders who succeeded them, and so it spread all over the West.

"Cameron's Cowboys" was the way that most men put it. For as his men stood out among the Texans, the leader whom they had chosen stood out among them—Ewen Cameron.

III. Caballeros[4]

. . . *Cavalier* means "horseman." The Texan had behind him the horse-riding tradition of the more literal than figurative "cavalier South." In the lower part of Texas he met the herd-owning Spanish *caballero*—which word also means "horseman." He met the Spaniard's vaquero, the mounted worker with cows. He met the ranching industry of the open range, appropriated it, and shortly thereafter began extending it beyond the limits of the wildest initial dream. The coming together, not in blood but in place and occupation, of this Anglo-American, this Spanish owner, and this Mexican vaquero produced the Texas cowboy—a blend, a type, new to the world. The cow that called forth both him and the industry he represented was the mother of the Texas Longhorn.

The same cow was in California. The Anglo-Americans that towards the high noon of the last century suddenly rushed into that land and took it over were all gold-mad. They went to eating up the cow. With gold to buy with and the cow almost consumed, the price of meat rose to such heights that early in the 1850's Texas cowboys ready to fight Comanche or Apache began driving herds to California. Geology, geography, and the character of Texas cows, cowboys, and cowmen,

[4] From *The Longhorns,* by J. Frank Dobie, p. xiv. Copyright, 1941, by J. Frank Dobie. Boston: Little, Brown and Company.

together with movements of population and with economic conditions, conspired to put the Texas stamp upon the range industry of all Western America.

IV. Vaquero and Cowpuncher[5]

In Southwest Texas, where six years ago and more I was "running cattle," cowboys were—and still are—generally referred to as "vaqueros" (often pronounced *bakeros*), "hands," or "cowhands." The word "cowboy" was sometimes used, but not nearly so commonly as now. *Vaquero* —from *vaca* (cow)—was originally applied only to Spanish or Mexican cowboys. But from an early day, Texans, especially those near the border, have used the word without reference to race. . . .

As for "cowpuncher" and "puncher," I do not recall having heard the terms in the old days, and the use of them, however common in the Northwest, is still limited, among men of the older generation at least, on the ranges of South and West Texas. I remember distinctly the first time I heard the word "cowpuncher" used. It was in the spring of 1879 and I was loading a train of cattle for the Cimarron Cattle Company at Las Animas, Colorado, for Kansas City. We had a man to go in charge of the cattle, but in those days the railroads gave a pass for every car or two of stock. Several boys around Las Animas who had run away from home to taste the Wild West wanted to go back East. They applied to me for passes, which I secured for them as far as Kansas City. When I handed the passes over I gave one of the boys a prodpole with instructions to help our regular man punch up the cattle if they got down in the cars. The boys were a rollicky bunch and they called themselves "cowpunchers," which they literally were, though I doubt if any one of them knew the difference between a jingle-bob and an offstrap. Originally, then, the word "cowpuncher" applied only to the chaperon of a shipment of cattle. The cowpuncher might be the best all around cowman in the country or he might be a sailor who had never saddled a horse. The prodpole was the symbol of his office. Clearly, "cowpuncher" is a misnomer for the cowboy. I have never liked the word. I have done my share of punching cattle on the cars, but even there I was a vaquero.

Tough Cowboys

. . . An Indian chief once asked Sheridan for a cannon.

"What! Do you want to kill my soldiers with it?" asked the general.

"No," replied the chief, "want to kill cowboy. Kill soldier with a club."

[5] From *A Vaquero of the Brush Country,* by J. Frank Dobie, Partly from the Reminiscences of John Young, pp. 1–2. Copyright, 1929, by the Southwest Press. Dallas.

From *Dodge City,* The Cowboy Capital and the Great Southwest in the Days of the Wild Indian, the Buffalo, the Cowboy, Dance Halls, Gambling Halls, and Bad Men, by Robert M. Wright, p. 283. [Copyright, 1913, by Robert M. Wright.]

Cowboy on a Spree

I was never really bad. I never had a reputation as a bad man, only when I was a kid—oh, I was just stinking to kill somebody when I was a kid, because most all the men I associated with had shot somebody, but as I told you, a kid's the most dangerous thing alive. I never got into any crooked stuff, like so many of them—rustling cattle or robbing trains or anything like that. And whatever I may have done that I have reasons to regret, I can say that I was always on the side of the law.

I carried a chip on my shoulder for years, and I got into my share of fights. But I never got into a fight when I was drinking, only when I was sober and knew what I was doing. Because I was always so happy when I was drinking, I loved everybody and everybody seemed to love me.

You see after I got over that early foolishness I wasn't looking for fights, I was looking for fun, and that I believe was the case with nine-tenths of them. They were wild and reckless, it's true, and to understand that you would have to know the kind of life they led. They were not like these city fellows with a saloon on every corner. They didn't get to drink very often. They were out there for months on end, on the trail or living in some cow camp, eating bad food, sleeping in wet clothes, going without everything that means life to a man—though that was all they ever talked or thought about—and when they hit the bright lights of some little cow town that looked like gay Paree to them, they just went crazy.

Not that they done much damage, usually. They just shot up in the air and shot out a few lights, and as often as not the boss would pay for it all in the morning. Like one time in Douglas, Wyoming, in '86, when Bill Deaton was bringing a trail herd up here to Montana for T. C. Power, the boys started tearing things to pieces in this little saloon, and they roped the bar and drug it out on the prairie. And Bill gave the fellow $250 next day.

Talking about food, do you know what was the first things a cowpuncher ordered to eat when he got to town? Oysters and celery. And eggs. Those things were what he didn't get and what he was crazy for.

A lot of this shooting you hear about was just crazy high spirits. You'd be standing up to the bar with a pipe in your mouth, and bang! the pieces would fall on the floor. Somebody took a shot at it, but it was all in fun. There was a fellow that used to be around Miles City, by the name of Tom Irvine, who was the best shot I ever saw. One night when they were all in the saloon, Louis King, that deputy I was telling you about, was standing there with a cigar in his mouth, and Tom pulled his six-gun out and shot the end off. Louis never budged. He

---

From *We Pointed Them North,* Recollections of a Cowpuncher, by E. C. Abbott ("Teddy Blue") and Helena Huntington Smith, pp. 256–258. Copyright, 1939, by Farrar & Rinehart, Inc. New York and Toronto.

just stuck his face out a little further and Tom clipped another half inch off the cigar so it was down to a little stub. Still Louis never moved, but only stood there with it held out between his lips as though he was daring Tom to come on and shoot again.

Tom said: "You go to hell," and shoved his gun back in the scabbard.

A lot of the saloon men didn't care much for all the shooting. And in later years it got to be the custom for the fellows to take off their artillery when they came in town. They would leave it at the livery barn with their horse and outfit. But that was after things were getting civilized. In the early days nobody did much about it. Only that fellow Marsh, who run a saloon at Rocky Point, was one who knew how to handle cowpunchers. He used to tell them: "Anything goes, boys, but me and the mirror." And he'd put a wineglass out on the end of the bar and say: "I'll bet you the drinks you can't hit it." Of course that took all the fun out of it, and there was never much shooting in his place. The other fellow at Rocky Point would flutter his hands and say: "Don't shoot in here, boys. Please don't shoot." And they made his place a pepperbox.

Singing Cowboy

A feller asked me once why old time cowboys always sung to the cattle while riding around a herd at night. Wal, there has been a heap of versions and many answers to that question, but from my own experience this here so-called singin' was done to let the sleepin' cattle know someone was around lookin' after their safety.

You know, out on the range, or on the trail, things is mighty quiet. An unusual or sudden noise will wake cattle up sudden and scare 'em. They are liable to jump and run. If they ain't stopped pretty quick, it will be a "stampede." A night man rides round and round the cattle as they sleep. If the rider is movin' around slow, and ain't makin' any noise, and happens to step up against one of the critters that might be lyin' out a little ways from the main bunch, it will wake up startled and jump into the herd and frighten all of them that are close. This often causes a big stampede. Now, as the cow-hand is ridin' around singin' or whistlin' in a sorta low voice he wakes them cattle nearest to him in a sorta lazy way and they go back to sleep when he passes on. All this may not be very clear to the uninitiated, but old trail or roundup hands can figger out what I'm tryin' to say.

No particular sort of singin' is required. A heap of them old hands couldn't carry a tune in a hand basket, but they could sorta croon, or some would whistle. I just read an Eastern magazine story where a

---

From *Longhorn Trail Drivers,* Being a True Story of the Cattle Drives of Long Ago, by Frank M. King, pp. 49–50. Copyright, 1940, by Frank M. King. "The first edition privately published for his friends by the Author."

writer was tellin' about them singin' cowboys. He was sayin' that the only way to stop a stampeded herd was to sing to 'em. Here is a part of one paragraph that writer had in his story: "The human voice seemed the most powerful influence that could be used to affect the brutes, force being entirely out of the question."

Now I been on night herd, on the trail, and have rode herd and "cut" during roundup. I've mixed up with a few stampedes and I want to tell the cockeyed world that when them cattle start to run in earnest, it was sho 'nough too dadburned late to sing. You just naturally had to outrun and outguess 'em.

Roosevelt on the Round-Up

The spring and early summer round-ups were especially for the branding of calves. There was much hard work and some risk on a round-up, but also much fun. The meeting-place was appointed weeks beforehand, and all the ranchmen of the territory to be covered by the round-up sent their representatives. There were no fences in the West that I knew, and their place was taken by the cowboy and the branding-iron. The cattle wandered free. Each calf was branded with the brand of the cow it was following. Sometimes in winter there was what we called line riding; that is, camps were established and the line riders traveled a definite beat across the desolate waste of snow, to and fro from one camp to another, to prevent the cattle from drifting. But as a rule nothing was done to keep the cattle in any one place. In the spring there was a general round-up in each locality. Each outfit took part in its own round-up and all the outfits of a given region combined to send representatives to the two or three round-ups that covered the neighborhoods near by into which their cattle might drift. For example, our Little Missouri round-up generally worked down the river from a distance of some fifty or sixty miles above my ranch towards the Kildeer Mountains, about the same distance below. In addition we would usually send representatives to the Yellowstone round-up, and to the round-up along the upper Little Missouri, and, moreover, if we heard that cattle had drifted, perhaps towards the Indian reservation south-east of us, we would send a wagon and rider after them.

At the meeting-point, which might be in the valley of a half-dry stream, or in some broad bottom of the river itself, or perchance by a couple of ponds under some queerly shaped butte that was a landmark for the region round about, we would all gather on the appointed day. The chuck-wagons, containing the bedding and food, each drawn by four horses and driven by the teamster cook, would come jolting and

---

From *Theodore Roosevelt,* An Autobiography, pp. 98–102. Copyright, 1913, by The Outlook Company; 1913, by Charles Scribner's Sons; 1941, by Edith K. Carow Roosevelt. New York: Charles Scribner's Sons.

rattling over the uneven sward. Accompanying each wagon were eight or ten riders, the cowpunchers, while their horses, a band of a hundred or so, were driven by the two herders, one of whom was known as the day wrangler and one as the night wrangler. The men were lean, sinewy fellows, accustomed to riding half-broken horses at any speed over any country by day or by night. They wore flannel shirts, with loose handkerchiefs knotted round their necks, broad hats, high-heeled boots with jingling spurs, and sometimes leather shaps, although often they merely had their trousers tucked into the tops of their high boots. There was a good deal of rough horseplay, and, as with any other gathering of men or boys of high animal spirits, the horseplay sometimes became very rough indeed; and as the men usually carried revolvers, and as there were occasionally one or two noted gun-fighters among them, there was now and then a shooting affray. A man who was a coward or who shirked his work had a bad time, of course; a man could not afford to let himself be bullied or treated as a butt; and, on the other hand, if he was "looking for a fight," he was certain to find it. But my own experience was that if a man did not talk until his associates knew him well and liked him, and if he did his work, he never had any difficulty in getting on. In my own round-up district I speedily grew to be friends with most of the men. When I went among strangers I always had to spend twenty-four hours in living down the fact that I wore spectacles, remaining as long as I could judiciously deaf to any side remarks about "four eyes," unless it became evident that my being quiet was misconstrued and that it was better to bring matters to a head at once.

If, for instance, I was sent off to represent the Little Missouri brands on some neighboring round-up, such as the Yellowstone, I usually showed that kind of diplomacy which consists in not uttering one word that can be avoided. I would probably have a couple of days' solitary ride, mounted on one horse and driving eight or ten others before me, one of them carrying my bedding. Loose horses drive best at a trot, or canter, and if a man is traveling alone in this fashion it is a good thing to have them reach the camp ground sufficiently late to make them desire to feed and sleep where they are until morning. In consequence I never spent more than two days on the journey from whatever the point was at which I left the Little Missouri, sleeping the one night for as limited a number of hours as possible.

As soon as I reached the meeting-place I would find out the wagon to which I was assigned. Riding to it, I turned my horses into the saddle-band and reported to the wagon boss, or, in his absence, to the cook—always a privileged character, who was allowed and expected to order men around. He would usually grumble savagely and profanely about my having been put with his wagon, but this was merely conventional on his part; and if I sat down and said nothing he would probably soon ask me if I wanted anything to eat, to which the correct answer was that I was not hungry and would wait until mealtime. The bedding rolls of the riders would be strewn around the grass, and I would put mine down a little outside the ring, where I would not be in any one's way, with my six or eight branding-irons beside it. The men would ride in, laughing and talking with one another, and perhaps nodding to me. One of their number, usually the wagon foreman, might put some question to me as to what brands I represented, but no other word would be addressed to me, nor would I be expected to volunteer any conversation. Supper would consist of bacon, Dutch oven bread, and possibly beef; once I won the good graces of my companions at the outset by appearing with two antelope which I had shot. After supper I would roll up in my bedding as soon as possible, and the others would follow suit at their pleasure.

At three in the morning or thereabouts, at a yell from the cook, all hands would turn hurriedly out. Dressing was a simple affair. Then each man rolled and corded his bedding—if he did not, the cook would leave it behind and he would go without any for the rest of the trip—and came to the fire, where he picked out a tin cup, tin plate, and knife and fork, helped himself to coffee and to whatever food there was, and ate it standing or squatting as best suited him. Dawn was probably breaking by this time, and the trampling of unshod hoofs showed that the night wrangler was bringing in the pony herd. Two of the men would then run ropes from the wagon at right angles to one another, and into this as a corral the horses would be driven. Each man might rope one of his own horses, or more often point it out to the most skillful roper of the outfit, who would rope it for him—for if the man was an unskillful roper and roped the wrong horse or roped the horse in the wrong place there was a chance of the whole herd stampeding. Each man then saddled and bridled his horse. This was usually followed by some resolute bucking on the part of two or three of the horses, especially in the early days of each round-up. The bucking was always a source of amusement to all the men whose horses did not buck, and these fortunate ones would gather round giving ironical advice, and especially adjuring the rider not to "go to leather"—that is, not to steady himself in the saddle by catching hold of the saddle-horn.

As soon as the men had mounted, the whole outfit started on the long circle, the morning circle. Usually the ranch foreman who bossed a given wagon was put in charge of the men of one group by the round-up foreman; he might keep his men together until they had gone some ten or fifteen miles from camp, and then drop them in couples at different points. Each couple made its way toward the wagon, gathering all the cattle it could find. The morning's ride might last six or eight hours, and it was still longer before some of the men got in. Singly and in twos and threes they appeared from every quarter of the horizon, the dust rising from the hoofs of the steers and bulls, the cows and calves, they had collected. Two or three of the men were left to take care of the herd while the others changed horses, ate a hasty dinner, and then came out to the afternoon work. This consisted of each man in succession being sent into the herd, usually with a companion, to cut out the cows of his brand or brands which were followed by unbranded calves, and also to cut out any mavericks or unbranded yearlings. We worked each animal gently out to the edge of the herd, and then with a sudden dash took it off at a run. It was always desperately anxious to break back and rejoin the herd. There was much breakneck galloping and twisting and turning before its desire was thwarted and it was driven to join the rest of the cut—that is, the other animals which had been cut out, and which were being held by one or two other men. Cattle hate being alone, and it was no easy matter to hold the first one or two that were cut out; but soon they got a little herd of their own, and then they were contented. When the cutting out had all been done, the calves were branded, and all misadventures of the "calf wrestlers," the men who seized, threw, and held each calf when roped by the mounted roper, were hailed with yelling laughter. Then the animals which for one reason or another it was desired to drive along with the round-up were put into one herd and left in charge of a couple of night guards, and the rest of us would loaf back to the wagon for supper and bed.

Round-Up Cook

Cooks were paid from fifteen to twenty-five dollars a month more than riders. Long before the wagon crew was gathered for the spring work, the wagon boss had his cook hired, frequently paying him wages for a month or two before he was needed, just to hold him.

The cook was monarch of all he surveyed. Everybody paid him homage, and the wise "stray man" with the outfit or casual drifter dropping in for a meal or two always grabbed one of the flour-sack towels and helped him get his dirty dishes out of the way. Nor has this situation changed with the passing years. Four or five years ago, at the headquarters ranch of a big cow outfit in the Black Hills of South Dakota, the kitchen was decorated with large plainly read signs, such as:

IF YOU CAN'T WASH DISHES, DON'T EAT.

WE USE WOOD IN THE COOKSTOVE CUT 16 INCHES
LONG, BUT *No Longer.*

A BUSY COOK LOVES A FULL WOOD BOX.

A FULL WATER BUCKET MAKES A HAPPY COOK.

STRAY MEN ARE NOT EXEMPT FROM HELPING WASH
DISHES, BRINGING WOOD OR WATER.

THE WELL IS JUST 110 STEPS FROM THE KITCHEN,
MOSTLY DOWNHILL BOTH WAYS.

From *Cattle,* by William MacLeod Raine and Will C. Barnes, pp. 297–298. Copyright, 1930, by William MacLeod Raine and Will C. Barnes. Garden City, New York: Doubleday, Doran & Company, Inc.

Just why a round-up cook had to be cranky was never clear, but all of them were more or less constructed along those lines, generally more.

With an outfit of twenty men out on a round-up which was to last for two or three months, and away from town the whole time, much depended on the cook's loyalty to his job. Consequently he was coddled in every possible way to keep him good-natured and at work. A puncher could quarrel with or "josh" the horse wrangler, or any of the men he wanted to, and the boss seldom interfered, but let him start something with the cook, and if that personage himself didn't take up the challenge forthwith the boss would quietly tell the offender either to "roll his tail for home" or let the cook alone. No wagon boss cared to have a cook quit him fifty or seventy miles from town with a crew of hungry men on his hands. Horse wranglers and punchers there were in plenty, but of good round-up cooks the supply was terribly low and the demand awfully keen.

Therefore it was always "Hats off to the cook."

The Cowboy's Recipe for Coffee

The cowboy's recipe for making coffee: Take one pound of coffee; wet it good with water; boil it over a hot fire for thirty minutes; pitch a horse shoe in and, if it sinks, put in some more coffee.

The Locoed Horse

Some plants are dangerous to cattle and not to sheep. Loco (a Spanish word meaning *crazy*) is an example of this. Although sheep are poisoned by it, they are under the care of a herder and can be kept away from those parts of the range where it grows in large quantities. To become locoed an animal must eat a large amount of the weed and keep it up for some time, the effect of the poison being cumulative.

Of all animals, horses are the most easily affected by the plant. As far as the open range industry goes, horse production is now a very small item. Here and there wild horses are still to be found. They are fast disappearing, however, and will eventually be a thing of the past—another bit of range romance gone into history. But in the days when every rider had at least fifteen horses in his string, and every cattleman ran a small herd of range mares from which to raise his own saddle animals, the losses from loco were serious.

Loco is found generally throughout the entire Rocky Mountain re-

---

From *A Corral Full of Stories,* rounded up by Joe M. Evans, p. 22. Copyright, 1939, by Joe M. Evans. El Paso, Texas: Printed by the McMath Company, Inc.

From *Cattle,* by William MacLeod Raine and Will C. Barnes, pp. 323–324. Copyright, 1930, by William MacLeod Raine and Will C. Barnes. Garden City, New York: Doubleday, Doran & Company, Inc.

gion, but is unusually prevalent in the country south of Denver, covering southern Colorado, Arizona, New Mexico, western Oklahoma, and western Texas. Over the open prairies one may often see great bodies of it. In full bloom, with lovely purple flowers, it might well be taken for a field of alfalfa.

Not every year is a loco year. It seems to come along about every seventh or eighth spring. Let the winter be a wet one, with early and heavy rains, and the Southwestern range men will shake their heads and prophesy a bad loco year. On such occasions the lovely green bunches seem to come up on the barren ranges almost overnight. By the middle of April in the Southwest, when all other vegetation is still dead and brown, the loco plants show up green and enticing everywhere. Naturally the stock eat it hungrily, for if appearance means anything it is dainty food.

The effect of loco on horses is singular. They seem to lose all sense of proportion. Their eyesight is apparently affected, and they have some brain trouble that makes them stagger around like drunks. A locoed cowpony will shy at a small stick and will not step over a rope lying on the ground. While being ridden on the range he will sometimes jump three feet into the air to avoid a shallow crack in the ground that looks dangerous to him.

As Smart as a Cutting Horse

I[1]

In the language of the range, to say that somebody is "as smart as a cutting horse" is to say that he is smarter than a Philadelphia lawyer, smarter than a steel trap, smarter than a coyote, smarter than a Harvard graduate—all combined. There just can't be anything smarter than a smart cutting horse. He can do everything but talk Meskin—and he understands that. . . .

Cutting chutes, small pastures as compared with large pastures and the open range, the inactivity of heavy modern cattle as compared with the agility and running powers of the old-time Longhorn breed, and the easy way in which cattle are now generally worked in contrast to the old-cut-and slash chousing have all combined to diminish the work of cutting horses and make them scarcer. But cutting horses are still used, are still the objects of pride and of talk. Sometimes, to show his horse's ability, a rider, after selecting an animal in a herd to be cut out, will remove his horse's bridle and allow the horse to exercise his own judgment. Wonderful tales that grew up about cutting horses are still a part of the living lore of the range.

* * * * *

[1] From "As Smart as a Cutting Horse," by J. Frank Dobie, *Mustangs and Cow Horses*, edited by J. Frank Dobie, Mody C. Boatright, Harry H. Ransom, pp. 403–405, 407–408. Publications No. XVI of the Texas Folk-Lore Society. Copyright, 1940, by the Texas Folk-Lore Society, Austin.

One morning right after a good rain a Mexican vaquero reported to Jack Maltsberger that he had found where some cow thief had roped an animal out in the pasture. He'd seen the fresh tracks. Jack went with him to make examination. Plainly a horse had followed a cow and the cow had been thrown. But no track of a dismounted man was visible. Jack rode on. Soon the cow tracks and the horse tracks separated. Following those of the horse, Jack found an extra good roping and cutting horse that had been turned out to get over some lameness. The horse was well. Wanting some exercise, he had evidently run the cow and knocked her down.

* * * * *

In addition to being smarter than most folks and being always on his toes, the cutting horse is so well reined and is so agile that he can be brought to a stop on a quarter of a dollar and give you back fifteen cents in change. "This little gray pony was named Toro," Frank M. King remembers in *Wranglin' the Past*. "He was a neck-reined wonder, a flash as a cut horse, a corral and prairie rope-hoss, a demon of determination in his work, but lovely as a baby when at ease. It was often said by the cowboys that Toro could cut the baking powder out of a biscuit without breaking the crust."

II[2]

A man had a cutting horse so good that he could actually read brands. If you had a herd of mixed branded cattle and you wanted them separated, putting all those that were branded, say, T Cross in one group, all branded Horseshoe in another group, etc., all you had to do was to let this horse know what brand you wanted and he would go in and get them. One spring after the work was done this horse was turned out on the range. And one morning he didn't come up for water. And the rancher noticed that he hadn't come up and wondered what was the matter with him. He rode out, looked down in the pasture, and saw the horse going through all sorts of intricate maneuvers. But he couldn't tell from that distance what he was doing. He rode on further, and found that the horse was on top of an ant bed. He was cutting the bull ants out of the herd, separating them from the others.

Old Blue, the Lead Steer

Old Blue was born in a sunny clime, beneath the lacy shade of the mesquite in southern Texas. With a herd of thousands of other flinty-

[2] Told by Mody C. Boatright, University of Texas, at Denver, Colorado, July 15, 1950. Recorded by B. A. Botkin.

From *Charles Goodnight,* Cowman & Plainsman, by J. Evetts Haley, pp. 431–436.

hoofed brutes, he marched north one spring in the middle seventies. He crossed the rocky hills of the Edwards Plateau, felt the burning thirsts of the Staked Plains drive, and then swelled his paunch to bursting with the brackish Pecos water. Each morning his long, steady stride carried him to the lead, and his fine blue head swung in rhythm with his tireless legs as he marched between the pointers along the Goodnight Trail, up the desolate valley of the Pecos, "graveyard of the cowman's hopes." The wild-looking, soft-voiced men, who handled that herd with matchless ease, fought Indians on the way, it is said, and lost cattle by the hundreds, but Old Blue led on until the salt grass of the valley gave way to the black grama of the high plateaus. And he was as slick as a *grulla* colt by the time he topped Trinchera Pass and felt the cool wind in his face as he looked down on the fresh world beyond. He, too, was a trail blazer, young and adventurous, and when he raked off the flies in the shinnery as he headed down the Colorado slope, he forever renounced the ties of his lazy birthland, and pointed the way to Goodnight's ranch on the Arkansas.

His owner had received him from Chisum at Bosque Grande, but when the herd went on as Indian beef, Blue, then a three-year-old, was kept behind and broken to the yoke. Southern Colorado was his home until he was brought to the Quitaque in 1877, after which he again fell into the hands of Goodnight, who realized right well that he was no ordinary ox, and who promised him then and there: "Blue, you work no more. You'll be a leader of our herd."

The beef was fat and the JA punchers, like the balance of the cattle kingdom, were pointing toward Dodge City, "cowboy capital of the world." Goodnight swung a brass bell around Old Blue's neck and as that bell rang off the miles in tune to his stride Blue was the proudest animal that ever switched his tail at flies. At night a cowboy pitched his rope around Blue's neck, for he was as gentle as could be, slipped a leather strap around the clapper or crammed the bell full of grass, and the herd bedded in peace. Soon the beeves learned to follow the bell, and if perchance, the clapper came undone at night, the herd would be on its feet, ready to trail, in no time.

Beyond the Beaver the outfit passed the only settler on the trail, and beside his sod house was a little field with pumpkins, squash, and melons. Cow-chips made good fuel, and the owner implored them to camp nearby, as he was twenty miles from wood. They trailed on to Seven Mile Hill, and at last looked down the slope to Dodge City. In the evening they camped on the south side of the river, while McAnulty and Cresswell had herds nearby. The JA boss turned his weather eye to the sky that night, and called to his boys: "All saddle and tie up. We'll have hell before day." About midnight it commenced sleeting and snowing, but all hands struck for the herd and managed to hold it, though the two neighboring ones were lost in the storm. At daylight the boss yelled: "Loose the bell and take the river." Old Blue broke the ice along the edge of the Arkansas, swam the stream in the middle, and headed straight for the railroad corrals as two thousand JA's crowded on his fetlocks. Soon he was at a run, and the frozen ground was shaking to the beat of eight thousand hoofs. Inside the gate he prudently jumped aside and rested while the herd swarmed and milled against the far side of the corral. The cowpunchers jammed the steers up the chute and into the cars, and as the train pulled out for Kansas City, they, and the saddle horses, and Old Blue stretched their necks over the top rail of the corral and watched them go.

With shelled corn in the wagon for him and the mounts, the outfit headed south across the cold baldies for the ranch, Blue stretching his legs, sometimes thirty miles a day, to keep up with the saddle horses. A party of Kiowas tried to get him while the outfit was camped on Wolf Creek, but by that time he was eating out of the skillets, and the JA cowboys would have fought the whole of Indian Nation or kept him. His name was made, and for eight years he pointed herds to Dodge, sometimes making two trips a year. He was a philosophical old steer that did not care for stampedes, but attended strictly to business, leaving others to slip their horns and hip themselves on such foolishness as running over corrals and stampeding at night. In stampede he habitually stepped aside to bawl, and if the boys "had them milling," he was often the cause of bringing the herd back into control.

When Mann drove one of the beef herds in 1880, he had Old Blue along. Club-Footed Jack looked after the steer, hobbled him out with the horses at night, and unhobbled and drove him in with the horses of a morning. Old Blue prowled around the pots and pans looking for stray pieces of meat, biscuits, and prunes, while the outfit broke camp, and Mann yelled at the hands: "Let 'em graze."

When they began to get dry, Club-Footed Jack unleashed the clapper and drove Old Blue directly through the herd to the point. The scattered beeves looked for him and the bell, bawled their heads off and fell in behind. This herd had been buggering and running from everything, but as they hesitated in the wings of the railroad corral, Blue stopped and lured them on by bawling while the JA hands were busy behind, and the snaky ones were soon inside.

Some cowpunchers watched the JA outfit pen the herd, remarking: "Those steers must be from the bull-chip ranch."

"What do you mean?" asked Frank Mitchell.

"They must have been roped in the open, branded at a bull-chip fire, and never saw a corral before."

"You're right," he chimed, as he broke for town.

Occasionally at home Old Blue had work to do, as when they necked him to an outlaw steer down in the cañon, and turned him loose. He was big and stout—weighed around fourteen hundred pounds—and as he thought of the corn in the trough at the ranch, he dragged his unwilling yoke-mate directly into the corral. Mainly, however, he lived a life of pampered ease until the boys gathered the beef in the fall.

His last days were spent in retirement on the Palo Duro, petted, honored, and admired. After twenty years of adventure such as few men and no other steer experienced, he died of age and idleness, and his cowboy friends chopped off his horns and reverently nailed them above the ranch office door. Emerson Hough's Old Alamo, marching *North of Thirty-Six,* and Andy Adam's Poker Steer, changing hands on the turn of a card, may bask in the reflected glory of the most representative animal of the cow country, king of all the longhorns—Old Blue.

Getting the Best of a Cattle Count

Shanghai Pierce was the most widely known cowman in the Southwest. This was partly due to his immense size and a peculiar piping quality of voice, but mostly to certain shrewd and humorous characteristics which gave rise to many good-natured stories about him. These he seemed to enjoy as much as anybody. Andy Adams, himself a cowboy in the old times and author of *The Log of a Cowboy,* relates how Old Shanghai got the best of a count on a running cut once while delivering some cattle to some greenhorn army men. He says he heard Old Shanghai tell it while gassing with some other herd owners in the bar at Wright House in Dodge.

"I was selling a thousand beef steers to these army fellers," said he. "I got the idea that they weren't up to snuff in receiving cattle out on the prairie and I got them to agree to a running cut. Me and my foreman were to count the cattle as they came through between us and the army men were to count for themselves. The steers were wild and ran past us like greased lightning. I lost the count myself several times and started over at a guess, and when I thought about so many had passed, I cut them off and sang out, 'Just an even thousand, what do you boys make it?'

" 'Just an even thousand,' replied my foreman. The army greenhorns didn't like to admit that they couldn't count a thousand cattle as well as anybody else could, so they didn't ask for a recount, but accepted the cattle into carload lots and shipped them. They found they were a hundred and eighteen head short. They wanted to come back on me to make good, but shucks! I told 'em they were too late. How did I know but what their Jim Crow outfit let some of the critters get away overnight?"

From *Glamorous Days,* by Frank H. Bushick, pp. 116–117. Copyright, 1934, by the Naylor Co. San Antonio, Texas.

Cowman's Code regarding Horses and the Trail

Property in the West consists of horses and cattle. There is no such thing as petty thievery. As Charlie Russell once said, "I've known many old-timers who would hold up a stage or steal a slick-ear, but they was not camp robbers." Locks on doors were unknown until the nester came, and in the old trail days bags of silver and gold lay around camp unnoticed with never a thought of theft. There was horse and cattle stealing to be sure, and the code of the West made a strange distinction between the two. To set a man afoot by stealing his horse carried a penalty of death, for depriving a man of his horse could mean life itself on the plains. Public opinion regarded the cow as just property and its theft a case for the courts.

The cowman also has a code regarding his horses. No matter how hungry he may be himself, he takes care of his horse before looking after his own comfort. When climbing mountains on horseback, he picks the easiest way; when riding along a hard-surfaced road he rides at the side where it is soft.

When meeting another person on a trail, etiquette requires that a man approach within speaking distance and pass a word before changing his course unless, for a very good reason, he is justified in such a change. The West holds that every person has the right to ascertain the intent of all other persons about him. Unwarranted violation of this is usually interpreted as a confession of guilt, or as a deliberate and flagrant insult.

When two men meet, speak, and pass on, it is a violation of the West's code for either to look back over his shoulder. Such an act is interpreted as an expression of distrust, as though one feared a shot in the dark. If he stops to talk along the trail he dismounts and loosens the cinches to give his horse's back some air. When greeting a stranger on the trail one is careful not to lift his hand if he rides a skittish horse. Some critters bolt if a man lifts a hand near them. He merely nods and says "Howdy." If the stranger lights to "cool his saddle," the other does not remain ahorse while carrying on a conversation. The polite thing to do is to dismount and talk with him face to face. This shows one is not looking for any advantage over the other.

If he meets a rider on a grade, he gives him the inside. Thus he can always dismount without stepping down in front of, behind, or against the other's horse. This rule does not hold good if the dust-drift blows his way. In that case, he rides downwind.

From "The Cowman's Code of Ethics," by Ramon F. Adams, *1949 Brand Book,* A Baker's Dozen of Essays on the West: Its History, Places, and People, written by Members and Guests of the Denver Posse of the Westerners, edited by Don Bloch, Registrar of Marks and Brands, pp. 152–154. Copyright, 1950, by the Westerners, Denver Posse. Denver, Colorado.

Cf. Philip Ashton Rollins, *The Cowboy* (New York, 1922), pp. 67–68.

When a new man signs with an outfit the boss points out to him the horses he is to ride, giving him no information concerning them. Information is often taken as an offense; telling him nothing is a compliment and a good way to start a new man. He then feels that you have confidence in his ability. Each rider is responsible for the condition of his "string"; and, while the boss never interferes, the rider whose horses show signs of abuse is apt to be looking for a new job. The man who leaves his mount in good flesh with sound back is worth much more than the man who would be afoot after a two-weeks' roundup.

A man's "string" of horses is rarely broken. If it is, or the foreman takes a fellow's pet horse away from him, it is a sure sign he is asking him to quit before he has to be fired.

No buster hired to break horses abuses them. No outfit wants spoiled horses. If the breaker is thrown, and not crippled in the fall, he is certain to crawl back upon the animal. It never does a horse any good to let him think he has won the argument. A good hand never gives a horse too much work; nor does he jump his horse into a run if he has a long way to travel.

A cowman saddles and unsaddles his own horse and an offer to help is unwelcome. Only in a serious emergency will he lend his horse to another. He knows a horse is easily spoiled or crippled by the wrong person riding him. One of the worst possible breaches of range etiquette is for a man to ride another's "company" horse without first asking permission, even from his best pal, for no two cowboys train a horse alike, and one spoils it for the other. To mount without leave another's "private" or "individual" horse, his own personal property—well, slapping a man's face could scarcely be more insulting.

The Cowpuncher and His Outfit

"Speakin' of cowpunchers," says Rawhide Rawlins, "I'm glad to see in the last few years that them that know the business have been writin' about 'em. It begin to look like they'd be wiped out without a history. Up to a few years ago there's mighty little known about cows and cow

---

From *Trails Plowed Under,* by Charles M. Russell, pp. 1–3. Copyright, 1927, by Doubleday, Page & Company. Garden City, New York.

For the cowboy's boots and spurs, see Will James, *All in the Day's Riding* (New York and London, 1936), pp. 27–30, 52–56; Jo Mora, *Trail Dust and Saddle Leather* (New York, 1946), pp. 43–46, 110–117; Philip Ashton Rollins, *The Cowboy* (New York, 1922), pp. 113–116. For the boots as an "insignia of a calling," see E. Hough, *The Story of the Cowboy* (New York and London, 1930), pp. 52–53. The "Lone Star" emblem on boots, chaps, saddles, and bridles is thus explained by Rollins (p. 107): "The Texans, with their intense State pride, asked for this adornment, and the manufacturers, putting it on the Texans' accoutrements, standardized output, and starred the equipment of almost everybody who did not object." For "Chaps," see Mora, *op. cit.,* pp. 86–90.

people. It was sure amusin' to read some of them old stories about cowpunchin'. You'd think a puncher growed horns an' was haired over.

"It put me in mind of the Eastern girl that asks her mother: 'Ma,' says she, 'do cowboys eat grass?' 'No, dear,' says the old lady, 'they're part human,' an' I don't know but the old gal had 'em sized up right. If they are human, they're a separate species. I'm talkin' about the old-times ones, before the country's strung with wire an' nesters had grabbed all the water, an' a cowpuncher's home was big. He ranged from Mexico to the Big Bow River of the north, an' from where the trees get scarce in the East to the old Pacific. He don't need no iron hoss, but covers his country on one that eats grass an' wears hair. All the tools he needed was saddle, bridle, quirt, hackamore, an' rawhide riatta or seagrass rope; that covered his hoss.

"The puncher himself was rigged, startin' at the top, with a good hat—not one of the floppy kind you see in pictures, with the rim turned up in front. The top-cover he wears holds its shape an' was made to protect his face from the weather; maybe to hold it on, he wore a buckskin string under the chin or back of the head. Round his neck a big silk handkerchief, tied loose, an' in the drag of a trail herd it was drawn over the face to the eyes, hold-up fashion, to protect the nose an' throat from dust. In old times, a leather blab or mask was used the same. Coat, vest, an' shirt suits his own taste. Maybe he'd wear California pants, light buckskin in color, with large brown plaid, sometimes foxed, or what you'd call reinforced with buck or antelope skin. Over these came his chaparejos or leggins. His feet were covered with good high-heeled boots, finished off with steel spurs of Spanish pattern. His weapon's usually a forty-five Colt's six-gun, which is packed in a belt, swingin' a little below his right hip. Sometimes a Winchester in a scabbard, slung to his saddle under his stirrup-leather, either right or left side, but generally left, stock forward, lock down, as his rope hangs at his saddle-fork on the right.

"By all I can find out from old, gray-headed punchers, the cow business started in California, an' the Spaniards were the first to burn marks on their cattle an' hosses, an' use the rope. Then men from the States drifted west to Texas, pickin' up the brandin' iron an' lass-rope, an' the business spread north, east, an' west, till the spotted long-horns walked in every trail marked out by their brown cousins, the buffalo.

"Texas an' California, bein' the startin' places, made two species of cowpunchers; those west of the Rockies rangin' north, usin' centerfire or single-cinch saddles, with high fork an' cantle; packed a sixty or sixty-five foot rawhide rope, an' swung a big loop. These cow people were generally strong on pretty, usin' plenty of hoss jewelry, silver-mounted spurs, bits, an' conchas; instead of a quirt, used a romal, or quirt braided to the end of the reins. Their saddles were full stamped, with from twenty-four to twenty-eight-inch eagle-bill tapederos. Their chaparejos were made of fur or hair, either bear, angora goat, or hair sealskin. These fellows were sure fancy, an' called themselves buccaroos, coming from the Spanish word, *vaquero*.

"The cowpuncher east of the Rockies originated in Texas an' ranged north to the Big Bow. He wasn't so much for pretty; his saddle was low horn, rimfire, or double-cinch; sometimes 'macheer.' Their rope was seldom over forty feet, for being a good deal in a brush country, they were forced to swing a small loop. These men generally tied, instead of taking their dallie-welts, or wrapping their rope around the saddle horn. Their chaparejos were made of heavy bullhide, to protect the leg from brush an' thorns, with hog-snout tapederos.

"Cowpunchers were mighty particular about their rig, an' in all the camps you'd find a fashion leader. From a cowpuncher's idea, these fellers was sure good to look at, an' I tell you right now, there ain't no prettier sight for my eyes than one of those good-lookin', long-backed cowpunchers, sittin' up on a high-forked full-stamped California saddle with a live hoss between his legs."

The Bandana

Modern cowboys seem to be giving up the bandana handkerchief. Perhaps the moving pictures have made it tawdry. Yet there was a time when this article was almost as necessary to a cowboy's equipment as a rope, and it served for purposes almost as varied. The prevailing color of the bandana was red, but blues and blacks were common, and of course silk bandanas were prized above those made of cotton.

When the cowboy got up in the morning and went down to the water hole to wash his face he used his bandana for a towel. Then he tied it around his neck, letting the fold hang down in front, thus appearing rather nattily dressed for breakfast. After he had roped out his bronc and tried to bridle him he probably found that the horse had to be blindfolded before he could do anything with him. The bandana was what he used to blindfold the horse with. Mounted, the cowboy removed the blind from the horse and put it again around his own neck. Perhaps he rode only a short distance before he spied a big calf that should be branded. He roped the calf; then if he did not have a "piggin string"—a short rope used for tying down animals—he tied the calf's legs together with the bandana and thus kept the calf fast while he branded it. In the summer time the cowboy adjusted the bandana to protect his neck from the sun. He often wore gloves too, for he liked to present neat hands and neck. If the hot sun was in his face, he adjusted the bandana in front of him, tying it so that the fold would hang over his cheeks, nose, and mouth like a mask. If his business was

From *A Vaquero of the Brush Country*, by J. Frank Dobie, Partly from the Reminiscences of John Young, pp. 263–265. Copyright, 1929, by the Southwest Press. Dallas, Texas.

with a dust-raising herd of cattle, the bandana adjusted in the same way made a respirator; in blizzardly weather it likewise protected his face and ears. In the swift, unhalting work required in pen the cowboy could, without losing time, grab a fold of the bandana loosely hung about his neck and wipe away the blinding sweat. In the pen, too, the bandana served as a rag for holding the hot handles of branding irons.

Many a cowboy has spread his bandana, perhaps none too clean itself, over dirty, muddy water and used it as a strainer to drink through; sometimes he used it as a cup towel, which he called a "drying rag." If the bandana was dirty, it was probably not so dirty as the other apparel of the cowboy, for when he came to a hole of water, he was wont to dismount and wash out his handkerchief, letting it dry while he rode along, holding it in his hand or spread over his hat. Often he wore it under his hat in order to help keep his head cool. At other times, in the face of a fierce gale, he used it to tie down his hat. The bandana made a good sling for a broken arm; it made a good bandage for a blood wound. Early Irish settlers on the Nueces River used to believe that a bandana handkerchief that had been worn by a drowned man would, if cast into a stream above the sunken body, float until it came over the body and then sink, thus locating it. Many a cowboy out on the lonely plains has been buried with a clean bandana spread over his face to keep the dirt, or the coarse blanket on which the dirt was poured, from touching it. The bandana has been used to hang men with. Rustlers used to "wave" strangers around with it, as a warning against nearer approach, though the hat was more commonly used for signaling. Like the Mexican sombrero or the four-gallon Stetson, the bandana could not be made too large. When the cowboys of the West make their final parade on the grassy shores of Paradise, the guidon that leads them should be a bandana handkerchief. It deserves to be called the flag of the range country.

The Cowboy's Rope

I[1]

An essential part of the cowpuncher's outfit is his "rope." This is carried in a coil at the left side of the saddle-horn, fastened by one of the many thongs which are scattered over the saddle. The rope in the Spanish country is called *reata* (*la reata*),[2] and even to-day is often made of rawhide, with an eye reinforced with that durable material.

---

[1] From *The Story of the Cowboy,* by E. Hough, p. 62. Copyright, 1897, by D. Appleton and Co.; 1924, by Charlotte Amelia Hough. New York and London. 1930.

For more on ropes and roping, see Jo Mora, *Trail Dust and Saddle Leather* (New York, 1946), pp. 52–66. See also "The Passing of the Old-Time Cowboy," below.

[2] From *reatar,* to retie or re-bind, hence the word *reata* in Spain means a cord with which to tie horses together so that they will travel in a line. It also means a line of horses thus tied. In America *reata* signifies a cord or rope made of woven or braided

Such a hide rope is called a "lariat" in the South. The *reata* was softened and made pliable by dragging it for some days behind the ranch wagon or at the saddle, the trailing on the ground performing this function perfectly. The modern rope is merely a well-made three-quarter-inch hemp rope, about thirty feet in length, with a leather eye admitting a free play of the noose, the eye being sometimes well soaped to make the rope run freely. This implement is universally called on the range a "rope." The term "lasso" [from the Spanish *lazo*], which we read about in books, is never heard, unless in California, nor is the common term of the Mexican, *reata*. The "lariat" is in the North used sometimes as another term, more especially to describe the picket rope by which the horse is tied out. In Texas this would be called a "stake rope." The common name gives the verb form, and the cowpuncher never speaks of "lassoing" an animal, but of "roping" it.

II[3]

Without a rope the old time vaquero felt as lost as a hunter without a gun. The rope was so much a part of him that the Mexican ranch people when wishing to describe an all-around good hand said simply, though figuratively, that he was *un buen reata* (literally, "a good rope"). A big game hunter likes to recall the various kinds of animals he has killed; the old time cowboy frequently took pride in the variety of creatures he had lassoed, and there were many varieties, ranging from elks to polecats, for him to "count coup" on. At a time when his lariat was in constant use it was almost second nature for him to "hang" it on anything he saw. In his excellent book, *Tales from the X-Bar Horse Camp,* Will C. Barnes tells how a waddie out in Arizona lost a fifty-dollar saddle by roping one of the camels that had been imported by Jefferson Davis, while Secretary of War, for government transportation across the American desert and that were later turned loose to shift for themselves. The tried and true prescription for sobering up a

leather or rawhide strands; a hard-twisted rope of any kind used for lassoing purposes. *Reata,* the Spanish form of the word, is used about as often by English-speaking cowboys and others along the border as *lariat*. Grammatically, of course, it is more correct to say "This is my *reata*" than to say "This is my *lariat*." The latter when translated is literally "This is my *the* rope"; *lariat* being nothing more than an adaptation of *la reata,* "the rope." It is true that *lariat* has been extended to include any rope used for lassoing, much more generally than has *reata,* and both terms are used loosely for *mecate,* the proper name for a rope made of horsehair, and for *pita,* the lasso rope made of hemp (*cañamo*). The early use of *lariat* by Americans who visited or lived in the frontier country indicates that it was taken by them to signify a rope for picketing animals while they fed either at noontime or at other resting periods. This restricted usage was not long current. Properly, it applies, in the border regions at least, to the particular rope made of braided leather or rawhide. Other names are assigned to other kinds of rope.—Harold W. Bentley, *A Dictionary of Spanish Terms in English, with Special Reference to the American Southwest* (New York, 1932), p. 194.

3 From *A Vaquero of the Brush Country,* by J. Frank Dobie, Partly from the Reminiscences of John Young, pp. 255–257. Copyright, 1929, by the Southwest Press. Dallas, Texas.

drunken cowboy was to rope him and jerk him off his horse.

The wildest thing, however, that a cowboy ever roped—wilder than camel or another cowboy—was probably the smokestack of an engine. . . . Nearly every old time cow town has its memory and its yarn of the cowboy who "roped a train." One time at Cotulla, on the Nueces River, a vaquero who was a little the braver for liquor roped the smokestack of an engine that was moving towards Laredo at the rate of twenty miles per hour. The rope was strong and so was the engine. After the engineer stopped the train and the cowboy got himself and his horse separated from the property belonging to the I. & G. N. Railroad Company, he was thoroughly sober.

Then there was Peckerwood Pete. Peckerwood Pete had never been within sight of a railroad; so when he learned that the Texas and Pacific was actually running trains through Colorado City, Texas, he saddled Straightedge and set out. Straightedge was a wonderful roping horse; he would squat and brace himself for a hard jerk every time Pete cast a loop from his back. The jerk was inevitable when Pete "throwed," for Pete never missed. He was the prize roper on Sulphur Draw.

After he had ridden east for two days he met, coming from Colorado City, three of the boys who lived a little farther up the draw than he lived. They told him that the train was some sight. What interested them particularly was that it had a cow-catcher; they did not know exactly what the business of the cow-catcher was, but they knew that one was employed by the train. Peckerwood Pete tarried not. Like a true Westerner, he was for progress, and he made up his mind at once to leave ranch jobs behind him forever and become an up-to-date cow-catcher for the T. and P. Certainly Straightedge could fill the bill as a horse, and as for himself he had caught more cows than any other hand between the Colorado and the Pecos.

Some such recommendation as this, in modest manner, he conveyed to the conductor of the train when it pulled into Colorado City. The conductor told him that a try-out would be necessary before he was engaged as official cow-catcher.

"Ride up the track about a quarter of a mile," said the conductor, "and wait for us. Then when the engine comes by, show us how well you can rope. Rope it around the smokestack."

Peckerwood Pete rode up the track. By the time the engine got to him it was hitting a pretty good lick. Straightedge was as shy as a rabbit, but Peckerwood finally got him to lay in after the clanging, smoking object. Then, when at the right distance and the right angle, the cowboy who would be cow-catcher whirled his rope. The loop shot true, Straightedge squatted, the cinches broke—and really that's about the end of the story. If anybody wishes the fictitious details, he can get them out of an odd little pamphlet entitled *Forty-Nine States Story Book* that was written and published by Hill and Smith in Dallas shortly before the advent of the automobile.

Will Turner Tells How to Make a Rawhide Reata

A good rawhide reata is the pride of a cowman. While they use it at hard work on the range and in the branding corrals, they'll fondle it lovingly when at ease, or in camp.

I select the hide of an old cow if possible that died in poverty. Skinny poor, you know. No fat on that kind of hide, but it's full of glue. And then, I stretch that old hide out flat, and cut off the legs and neck. I cut one strip right down lengthwise over the backbone. This is two inches wide. I work this up into latigos, and now I have the two sides with no brands on them. Brands spoil a hide for ropes. I soak the hide in cold water for a while. And then I begin on one side and cut a narrow strip from the outer edge, circle like, toward the center, until I run out of hide. Then I do the same to the other side, and get two strips from each side, each sixty or seventy feet long. You know, it takes four strips to make a rope, and I get 'em from the one hide. And then these strips are again soaked in water until they get soft. Then I stretch 'em out as long and tight as possible and let 'em dry that way. Then I take a sharp knife and careful-like, scrape off the hair.

The four strips must be even in thickness and width. Then set a sharp knife on a board just as high above it as the thong is to be thick, and just pull this thong through the blade of the knife. It'll be just right. Even thickness. Then for width just set two razor sharp knives just as wide apart as the thong is to be wide, and pull it through. Now you got it. Four thongs as exactly alike as peas in a pod. Then all you got to do is braid it and braid it tight. Stretch again. Make a hondo, slip through, and coil the finished reata. Grease it with tallow.

The Cowboy's Saddle

I[1]

The saddle of the cowboy is the first, last, and most important part of his outfit. It is a curious thing, this saddle developed by the cattle trade, and the world has no other like it. It is not the production of fad or fancy, but of necessity. Its great weight—a regular cow saddle

From *The Valley of Tall Grass,* by Adelaide Hawes, pp. 142–143. Copyright, 1950, by Adelaide Hawes. Bruneau, Idaho.

The making of both the rawhide reata and the mecate, or hair rope, is described in detail by William MacLeod Raine and Will C. Barnes, in *Cattle* (Garden City, 1930), pp. 310–315.

[1] From *The Story of the Cowboy,* by E. Hough, pp. 64–67. Copyright, 1897, by D. Appleton and Co.; 1924, by Charlotte Amelia Hough. New York and London. 1930.

For more on the saddle and stirrups, see Jo Mora, *Trail Dust and Saddle Leather* (New York, 1946), pp. 91–110.

weighs from thirty to forty pounds—is readily excusable when one remembers that it is not only seat but workbench for the cowman. A light saddle would be torn to pieces at the first rush of a maddened steer, but the sturdy frame of a cow saddle will throw the heaviest bull on the range. The saddle is made for riding upon a country essentially flat, and it is not intended for jumping—indeed, can not be used for high jumping, with its high cantle and pommel. Yet it is exactly right for the use for which it is designed. The high cantle gives a firmness to the seat of the cowboy when he snubs a steer with a sternness sufficient to send it rolling heels over head. The high pommel, or "horn," steel forged and covered with cross braids of honest leather, serves as anchor post for this same steer, a turn of the rope about it accomplishing that purpose at once. The tree of the saddle forks low down over the back of the pony, so that the saddle sits firmly and can not readily be pulled off. The great broad cinches—especially the hind cinch so much detested by the pony, and a frequent incentive to steady bucking—bind the big saddle fast to the pony until they are practically one fabric. The long and heavy wooden stirrups seem ungraceful till one has ridden in them, and then he would use no other sort. The strong wooden house of the stirrup protects the foot from being crushed when riding through timber or among cattle or other horses. The pony can not bite the foot—as he sometimes has a fashion of doing viciously—through the wood and the long cover of leather that sometimes further protects it, neither can the thorns scratch the foot or the limbs of trees drag the foot from its place.

The shape of the tree of the cow saddle is the best that can be made for its use, though it or any other tree is hard upon the pony's back, for the saddle is heavy of itself, and the rider is no mere stripling. The deep seat is a good chair for a man who is in it nearly all year. In the saddle, the cowpuncher stands nearly upright, his legs in a line from his shoulders and hips down. He rides partly with the balancing seat, and does not grip with his knees so much as one must in sitting a pad saddle, but his saddle is suited to his calling, and it is a bad horse and a big steer that shall shake him, no matter what the theories of it be. The question of the cowpuncher's saddle and his use of it can be covered with a little conversation once heard on the trail of a cow outfit. A gentleman of foreign birth, but of observing habits, was telling a cowpuncher what he thought about his riding and his saddle. "I say, you couldn't jump a fence in that thing, you know," said he.

"Stranger," said the cowpuncher, "this yer is God's country, an' they ain't no fences, but I shore think I could jump more fences than you could rope steers if you rid in that postage stamp thing of yourn."

* * * * *

In the early days of the "Texas saddle," or the first type of the cow saddles, these articles were made in the shops of the Southwest. Before long, however, after the drive got into the Northern country, the saddles of Cheyenne became the favorites of the range, North and South, they being made of better leather. The "California tree" was sometimes used. There was some local variety in manufacture, but the saddle of the cowman remained constant in the main points above mentioned. The old Spaniard who designed it put forth many models which have endured practically without change.

A good saddle would cost the cowboy from forty to one hundred dollars. In his boyish notions of economy, to want a thing was to have it if he had the money, and a saddle once seen and coveted was apt to be bought. The embossing and ornamentation of the saddle had most to do with its cost. The Spanish saddles of the Southwest were often heavily decorated with silver, as were the bits, spurs, and bridle reins, as well as the clothing of the rider; but this sort of foppery never prevailed to any extent among American cowpunchers. There was one rude and wild sort of decoration sometimes in practice by the younger cowboys on the range. They often took the skins of rattlesnakes, of which there were very many seen nearly every day, and spread them while yet wet upon the leather of their saddles. The natural glue of the skin would hold it firmly in place when it dried. Some saddles have been seen fairly covered with these lines of diamond-marked skins. It was not uncommon to see the skins of these snakes also used as hat bands.

II[2]

Each saddle best fitted its special owner, for it gradually acquired tiny humps and hollows that registered with his anatomy, and induced both comfort and security of seat. These little moldings, which suited well the owner, would often fight the contour of a stranger's legs. Wherefore each man swore by his own saddle and at all others. Texas Ike, in good faith and with generous impulse, said: "Jim, don't bother to get your saddle. Ride mine. It's the best that ever came out of Cheyenne. It's as comfortable as a trundle-bed." Jim mounted, squirmed, grunted, and in equally good faith remarked: "Tex, where in hell did you ever find this Spanish Inquisition chamber anyhow? You must be using it like the priests wore hair shirts."

A cowboy so valued his saddle, particularly after it had been broken in, that he almost never would part with it. He has gone so far as, in a poker game, to lose his money, guns, chaps, horse, and even shirt, and then, with saddle on his back, to "strike out" for the ranch still thoroughly cheerful and with "his tail up." Even such punchers as upon completion of the Texas Drive returned to Texas by rail instead of on horseback carried their saddles with them.

Moreover, it was a bit disgraceful to sell one's saddle. It was akin to disposing of the ancestral plate and family jewels. The phrase, "He's

---

2 From *The Cowboy,* His Characteristics, His Equipment, and His Part in the Development of the West, by Philip Ashton Rollins, pp. 133–134. Copyright, 1922, by Charles Scribner's Sons. New York.

sold his saddle," became of general usage, and was employed in a figurative way to denote that anybody in any calling had become financially or morally insolvent. Years ago in a little school at Gardiner, Montana, a small, tow-headed youth, when asked by the teacher as to who Benedict Arnold was and what he had done, replied: "He was one of our generals and he sold his saddle."

He Was Attached to His Rig

A man named Murchison was boss of our outfit, and working with it was a younger brother of his, Joe Murchison. Joe always carried two six-shooters, a rifle in a scabbard, a dirk, and wore, of course, the usual leggins, boots, and spurs that went to make up a peeler's rig. He could not swim a lick, but when we had to cross a swimming stream he always refused to take off a single pound of his hardware and he made fun of anybody who did lighten up. Most of the hands would pull off the heavy parts of their equipment and tie them to the saddle horn.

Once when we got to the Cimarron it was up big swimming. Joe plunged in, spurs, leggins, "hog-legs," and all. His horse made it out into the deepest water and then sank. Joe went under with him and neither reappeared. We scattered downstream, throwing in ropes, chunks of drift, everything we could find, hoping that Joe would bob up and grab something. About two hundred feet below our crossing place the water was shallower and some willows leaned over into the stream. After a while Joe's head appeared under the willows and he reached up and pulled himself out. He swore that he had walked on the bottom of the river bed out of the deep water.

"Well, I guess you'll pull off some of that luggin' the next time you go into deep water," somebody said.

"Hell, no," Joe replied. "I can't swim and if I hadn't had all this weight on I'd never in the world been able to keep myself down to the bottom so that I could walk out. Weight's what saved my life."

The King Ranch

Texans have a way of saying that the Santa Gertrudis' front gate is a hundred miles from the doorstep and the owner is thinking of moving

---

From *A Vaquero of the Brush Country,* Partly from the Reminiscences of John Young, by J. Frank Dobie, pp. 127–128. Copyright, 1929, by the Southwest Press. Dallas.

One of the seven hundred wonders of the world has always been to me the recklessness in water of cowboys who could not swim at all. A yarn told by O. E. Brewster, ramrod of the Cherokee Strip Cowpunchers' Association of Oklahoma, illustrates the recklessness admirably.—J.F.D.

From "The Greatest Ranch in the World," by Joseph Martin Dawson, *The Texas Monthly,* Vol. III (April, 1929), No. 4, p. 463.

further back to avoid the dust. "If I should be sent out to bring the cows home from the upper pasture to milk," laughed Miss Sarah Kleberg, the owner's daughter, "I'd have to take a camp outfit and a week's grub with a couple of pack horses, for it would require that before I could get back home."

The Origin of the 101 Brand

Gid Guthrie was Miller's trail boss that year [1878]. They'd made their buy in South Texas, and on the way north, they laid over at San Antonio one night to let the hands romp and stomp and paw up a little sand before taking the long trail into Kansas. The hands didn't need any urging; they made up as tough a trail crew as ever looked a cow brute in the rump. They'd located a honkytonk downtown called "The Hundred and One," which made a brag of having the wildest women, the rawest whisky, and the worst gamblers in that old Mexican town. The boys wanted to investigate; this outfit might be bluffing.

They sampled the whisky. They tried out the women. They matched wits with the gamblers and then fist-whipped them for cheats and swindlers. Before daylight, they were prizing up hell and propping it with a chunk. Some were down and the rest were staggering. It took four trips and half the town police for Miller to get the crew out of the wrecked place and back out to where the cattle were bedded down.

Miller knew trail hands; he knew they had to whoop it up fast while they were at it and squeeze a lot of town-going into a mighty short time. For months to come, day and night, all they'd know would be bawling steers, pitching horses, stampedes, hot suns, and shivery nights. So he said nothing.

But the next year when they started trimming up another South Texas trail herd and Gid Guthrie wanted to know what sort of road brand to put on the steers, G. W. Miller was ready.

"We'll forget the Lee Kokernut brand we've been using," he told Guthrie. "I've bought out that iron. We'll brand 101 this time. Before I'm done, I aim to make this tough crew so sick of the sight of them figures they'll ride a ten-mile circle around town to keep from reading that honkytonk signboard. Too many of 'em got burnt last year; it hinders their work."

From *Fabulous Empire,* Colonel Zack Miller's Story, by Fred Gipson, pp. 1–3. Copyright, 1946, by Donald Day, Fred Gipson, Zack T. Miller. Boston: Houghton Mifflin Company.

Other explanations are that the 101 brand signifies the 101,000 acres supposedly contained in the ranch; and that it was an adaptation of the brand of the Bar-O-Bar ranch, which Miller bought, with the bars turned upright so that they could be more easily seen at a distance. See Ellsworth Collings and Alma Miller England, *The 101 Ranch* (Norman, 1937), pp. 15–17.

For the technique and lore of cattle brands and branding, see Oren Arnold and John P. Hale, *Hot Irons* (New York, 1940).

John Hiatt, G.W.'s nephew of Hunnewell, Kansas, laid claim to building the brand fire that burnt the first 101 on a cow. G.W. had had some irons made to horn-brand and some to hide-brand on the left hip. He bobbed the tails of his steels and dewlapped every head, cutting the dewlap from the top down so that when it dried, it stuck straight out. Time he was done, a man couldn't mistake a Miller steer as far as he could see it. And time the hands grazed those steers into Kansas, there wasn't a one of them who ever mentioned the San Antonio honkytonk as a good place for a little general hell-raising.

The XIT Brand

While Farwell was developing syndicate procedures in London, there was real action that summer of 1885 in Texas. Drought still burned the southwestern section of the state, the range was badly overstocked, and the ranchers from whom Campbell had contracted to buy cattle were anxious to get rid of the hungry, thirsty stock. Sending their own drivers or hiring independent trail outfits, they got the 22,000 cattle under way at almost the same time. A dozen scattering herds plodded in hot, wavering lines toward Buffalo Springs.

One herd of 2,500 cattle from near San Angelo was in charge of Ab Blocker, who was known on the Texas range and the long, long cattle trails as "the man with hell in his neck." A dark six-footer, his face shadowed by a thick brush of mustache and a devilish goatee, Blocker was then only twenty-nine, but by reputation he was already king of the trail drivers. Ranchers often said of him: "That's Blocker—he's sighted the North Star down the backs of more longhorn steers than any man, dead or alive." . . .

* * * * *

Now Blocker liked to strut a bit at the end of a drive, and he felt especially cocky this time because he had been first to arrive at the new ranch. Swaggering up to Campbell, he said: "Here's your damn cows."

Campbell slowly took a long, black cigar from his mouth. "I'm Colonel Campbell."

There was a glint in Blocker's eyes. "What's your brand, Colonel?"

"We haven't decided on a brand," Campbell replied firmly, but without anger.

Blocker snorted. "Hell, man, you ain't got no ranch. May have three million acres o' dry ground, an' a lot of poor cow stuff, but you ain't got a ranch till you got a brand and got it burned in the hides of your cows. Biggest ranch in the world and no brand. That's crazy as hell."

From *Cattle Empire,* The Fabulous Story of the 3,000,000 Acre XIT, by Lewis Nordyke, pp. 78–79, 82–85. Copyright, 1949, by Lewis Nordyke. New York: William Morrow and Company.

Puffing on his cigar, Campbell eyed the big-mouthed trail boss. "Would you suggest a brand?"

"Hell, yes," Blocker said, proving once again that no mustache could strain the color from his language. "I'll figure one out. Us git some tallyin' done here, an' then we'll see 'bout the brand business."

While the cattle were being counted and driven into the corrals, another herd, the one Blocker's outfit had passed in the night, arrived. Blocker had guessed right: Joe Collins was the trail boss.

Soon every man in both outfits except those occupied with the cattle was busy with fingers or sticks on bare patches of ground or with stubs of pencils on the backs of old letters. A cowboy's favorite pastime was trying to work out brand designs.

Blocker, squatting on his heels, started marking with a forefinger on a sandy spot as Campbell and some of the punchers watched. Blocker knew he was the star of this little show. "You know," he said with enjoyment, "there's three things 'bout a brand. First, you want it to look good an' sound good. Second, you want it to be easy to put on. Third, you want one that no damn brand-runner can change."

He continued to make marks in the sand, mumbling almost to himself. "An 'X' is always good. So 's a bar or a diamond or any good-soundin' letter." He marked and smoothed the sand several times; then he got up. "Here's your brand," he said. With the heel of his boot he drew three enormous letters in the dirt. "Here she is. The XIT."[1]

The men crowded in closer. Campbell studied the design and admitted that it looked good.

"*Is* good." Blocker was emphatic. "Looks good, easy to put on an' hard to change. Jus' five socks with one bar of iron, an' there you are."

Campbell liked the XIT. He drew it in the sand and tried to change it by adding marks. For he knew that a clever, good-sounding design was not sufficient. A crafty rustler could take a hot running iron and alter some brands into new designs, completely obscuring the original one.

Then and there Campbell adopted the XIT brand. And the cowboys quickly shifted from designing brands to trying to change this new one.

---

[1] Mrs. H. G. Norton of Wichita, Kansas, a daughter, of Barbecue Campbell, wrote the author that she believed her father and Ab Blocker designed the brand to mean "Ten in Texas." This interpretation of the meaning of the brand was very popular and was based on the widespread notion that the ranch lay in ten counties. It actually lay in only nine counties, however. On the other hand, Mrs. R. L. Duke of Dalhart, Texas, wife of the last manager of the XIT, has been under the impression that the brand was originated in Chicago and sent to Barbecue Campbell. But when the author accompanied Ab Blocker to Buffalo Springs, the latter squatted on his boot heels on the very spot where he had marked the first XIT brand in 1885 and demonstrated how he had designed it. Dick Pincham was also with Blocker on this return visit to the Springs—the first time the men had seen each other since the day Blocker arrived with the first cattle. Pincham's version of the brand designing tallied with that of Blocker. Both of them also told the author many things about trail driving, ranching, cowboys, and the start of the XIT. They were grand old men and great story tellers.—L.N.

Campbell, the patient gentleman, invited Blocker to be the first to brand an XIT cow. "I'd like to see just how you Texas boys handle it," he said.

Using some of the wood Mabry had piled up in readiness for branding, Blocker's men kindled a fire. Goat searched a cowhide pouch lashed under his chuckwagon, and found a branding iron with a simple bar design—that is, a bar about five inches long welded crosswise on the end of an iron wagon-rod—and stuck it in the fire. Blocker mounted his horse and fed out a long loop from his lariat. When the iron was hot, Blocker motioned to Goat. The cook opened the corral gate and a longhorn cow shot out with her head down. Blocker twirled his loop overhead, snaked the rope through the air, and yanked it up on the cow's front feet—a throw known as forefooting. A quick movement of Blocker's horse, and the cow crashed to the ground. Cowboys piled on her.

Blocker crawled off his horse, grabbed the iron, and socked it five times to the cow's side. Then the punchers jumped aside and the wild-eyed cow leaped up, the first of hundreds of thousands to cringe under the XIT brand.

Blocker handed the rope to Goat. As one by one the cows were let out, the cook jerked them down and Blocker burned in the brand, the only pause being the time necessary to reheat the iron. About twenty cows had been branded when Campbell stepped up to the sweating, grinning Blocker.

"You're damned good, Mr. Blocker," he said. "But I think that's enough for right now. It's just that we don't treat our cattle that rough. We're branding in chutes; branding 'em standing up. Have a cigar."

Blocker dropped the iron. "All right with me, but now you know how we do it in Texas. Well, I got to git my stuff together an' git rollin'." He strutted off to his wagon.

John Chisum's Jingle-Bob and the Stampede

Uncle John Chisum was not more widely known than his famous brand of the Long Rail and Jingle-Bob. No other brand in history ever decorated so many cows at one time. It once identified one hundred thousand cattle as his own. It is gone from the ranges now; only a few old-timers know what it was. To those who never saw it, it is a riddle. The Long Rail is easy to guess. It was just a long bar on the side of a cow, running almost from stem to stern. But what was the Jingle-Bob? Sounding like a nonsense name, it was one of the wisest brands [or earmarks] ever invented. Many people to-day, including a few cattlemen, think of it as a bit of knifework on the dewlap. But it was the re-

---

As told by Sallie Chisum (Mrs. Roberts), Roswell, New Mexico, 1924.

sult of a deep slit in both ears so that one part of the ear flapped down and the other part stood up in its natural way. Not every cowboy could cut the ears correctly. A botch job either left both parts of the bifurcated ear standing erect or both hanging down. It took no little skill to cut the ear so that one part hung down and the other stood upright. Uncle John assigned the work only to a few trusted cowhands, who were adept in Jingle-Bob craftsmanship.

It was easy to identify Chisum cattle singly or in small bunches by the Long Rail. You could read that brand a mile. But it was in the work of identifying cattle in a big herd that the Jingle-Bob demonstrated its right to be classed among the fine arts. After a stampede, for instance. Night stampedes were common on the trail. Any unusual sound might cause them—a peal of thunder, the report of a gun, the howl of a wolf, the galloping of a horse. Once panic had seized the senseless, half-wild brutes, they went blundering and thundering away in the darkness. It was sometimes possible, but not often, for the cowboys to turn them and get them milling in a circle and so bring them to a halt. But they usually ran until they tired themselves out, and many a stampede has carried a terror-stricken herd twenty or thirty miles from its bedding ground.

Often a herd on a rampage ran into another herd, and stampeded it, and next day, when both herds had quieted down, it was a big job, sometimes lasting several days, to separate the cattle. Cowboys could not see the body brands on cows lost among several thousand others. They had to ride into the herd and thread their way laboriously among the animals to pick out their own brands. But no matter where a Jingle-Bob steer happened to be, whether at the center of the herd or away across a thousand backs at the far end, there was no mistaking him. He had but to show his head to be instantly identified.

I may say that once you had seen the Jingle-Bob you never forgot it. It had a strangely transfiguring effect on bovine beauty. A lean, long-legged steer of the old range breed, with his absurdly long horns, his half-scared, half-truculent, and wholly stupid physiognomy, was a weird beast at best; but the Jingle-Bob, which seemed to crown his gargoyle head with four ears, two pricked up and two flopping down, added the last ridiculous touch and made him, in fact, look like the devil.

How the Cattle Rustler Alters Brands

The first use of the word "rustler" was as a synonym for "hustler," becoming an established term for any person who was active, pushing,

---

From *Cowboy Lingo,* by Ramon F. Adams, pp. 157–161. Copyright, 1936, by Ramon F. Adams. Boston: Houghton Mifflin Company.

and bustling in any enterprise; again it was used as the name for the "wrangler," and, used as a verb, meant to herd horses. "To rustle the horses" meant to herd them to the desired place. Later, the word became almost exclusively used with reference to cattle thieves, starting from the days of the "maverick," when cowboys were paid by their employers to "get out and rustle a few mavericks," just as one spoke of "rustling some wood" for the fire. These same cowboys soon became interested in putting their own brand upon these ownerless calves to get a start in the cattle business, and this soon became looked upon as thievery. Thus the word became evolved into the meaning of a thief, and is so recognized over the entire West, though Texans preferred the blunter word of "cow thief."

An old saying of the early range was that all a man needed to start a brand of his own was "a rope, a runnin'-iron, and the nerve to use it." The struggle for existence on a fierce frontier developed nerve; ropes and running-irons were cheap, and so cow thieves were developed until "rustling" became quite an industry.

An early name for the genuine rustler, one faithful to his illegal art, was a "waddy";[1] later this term was also applied to any cowpuncher. He was a "pure" when he was a thoroughbred and loyal to his fellows. He was also spoken of by such names as "brand-burner," "brand-blotter," "brand-blotcher," "brand-artist," "long-rope," or "rope and ring man," and he was said to "swing a wide loop." It was often said of one suspected of stealing that he was "careless with his brandin'-iron," or, "his calves don't suck the right cows."

Telling any honest cattleman that his cows have twins was fighting talk. A cow with twins generally meant that a "critter" of another brand was bawling for its "rustled" calf. When the rustler worked overtime it was said that he "kept his brandin'-iron smooth." A branding-iron must be smooth and free from rust and scale to give satisfaction.

The practice of "burning" cattle, of altering brands so that the old part and the new would form a perfect and quite different brand, was raised to the dignity of an art by the rustler. He had to do the work skilfully enough to deceive, not only the average range stockman, but the shrewdest and most expert cowman among them. The bungling of a "worked-over" brand was called "botching," and a botched job was an acute mortification to most rustlers.

He might "blot" the old brand entirely out with a hot flat iron and run a new one on, but this was a crude method. More likely he would change the old brand into a new and entirely different one by adding lines, numerals, curves or symbols with a piece of hot telegraph wire,

---

[1] In the spring and fall, when some ranches are short-handed, they take on any one who is able to ride a horse and use him for a week or so; hence the word *waddy*, derived from *wadding*—anything to fill in.—Ramon F. Adams, *Western Words* (Norman, Oklahoma, 1944), p. 173.

or a "cinch-ring," or "runnin'-iron."[2] Or again he might use the "wet blanket" process whereby a scrap of wet woolen blanket was laid over the old brand and a hot iron applied to it, through the blanket.

He might make use of the "picked brand" or the "hair brand"[3] . . . or he might "sleeper" the animal. A "sleeper" was a calf which had been earmarked with the proper mark of the owner by the cattle thief who intended to come back later and steal the animal. The ear-mark was used by the cowpuncher as a quick means of identification; thus, during round-up, should the ranch hands come upon such an animal, they would likely take it for granted that it had been branded at the time it was marked and leave it to roam, the thief returning later and putting his own brand upon it or driving it away.

Another method of the cattle thief was the use of the "slow brand." It was against the law, of course, to mutilate any brand, and it further required that every brand should be recorded in the county of its origin. A man who blotted out a brand and put another in its place was naturally chary of putting this new brand on record. He simply ran it, trusting to get the cattle out of the country at the first opportunity, and such a brand was said to be a "slow brand."

When a man killed an animal that belonged to some one else for food or for sale to butcher shops, he was said to "slow-elk" it, and such an animal was called a "slow elk" or "big antelope."

Mother cows and their calves, upon becoming separated, back-track for miles to reach the spot at which each last saw the other. Because of this instinct, the rustler was forced to wean the calves he stole before he applied his brand, or have them so secured that they could not return to their mothers. In doing this he used many different methods. He might "sand" the calves—that is, put sand in their eyes so that they could not see to follow the mother. The calf was then driven off to a distance, and by the time he reached his destination he would be thoroughly weaned.

Another method employed by the rustler was to "hot-foot" the calf—that is, burn it between the toes with a hot iron, making its feet too sore to walk. Often the rustler would cut the muscles which supported the calf's eyelids so that they would drop closed. Thus separated from his

---

[2] A "running-iron" was a branding-iron made in the form of a straight poker or rod curved at one end, and was used much after the free and fluent style in which shipping clerks mark boxes. Texas, in the seventies, passed a law against the use of this "iron" in branding. This was a blow aimed at the "rustler," whose innocent single iron would tell no tales if he were caught riding across the range. After this law it became the custom to use branding-irons made of a fixed stamp or pattern.—R.F.A., *Cowboy Lingo*, p. 121.

[3] A "picked brand" was accomplished by picking out tufts of hair in the lines desired by the aid of a jackknife. It was seldom used except by dishonest men until they could get the animal out of the country, as it was only temporary. A "hair brand" was one whereby the branding-iron was held against the animal just long enough to burn the hair, not the hide. The hair grew out, effacing the signs of the brand, and the rustler could then put his own brand on the animal.—R.F.A., *ibid.*, p. 130.

mother, he would "bawl his head off" for a few days, but, getting no response and not being able to see to return to his maternal milk, he became hungry, groped around for food, and was soon weaned. The muscles healed, but the lids always drooped slightly, and these calves were referred to as "droop-eyes."

Occasionally some rustler followed the even more brutal practice of splitting the calf's tongue so he could not nurse. When the calf was weaned, these "tongue-splitters" placed their own brand upon them. Very often the man following this dangerous industry made genuine orphans of the calves by killing the mother. He was then said, in cowboy language, to "pin crape on the kid." If he was caught, it was said that he "ran a butcher shop an' got his cattle mixed," and he later perhaps spent his time "makin' hair bridles," which was synonymous with being sent to the penitentiary. More than one rustler was said to have "lost his voice explainin' to so many judges how he come to have his brand on somebody' else's cows."

As one cowboy said, in speaking of an acquaintance suspected of rustling: "Bill's good-hearted an' hates to see calves wanderin' round wearin' no brand. They look so homeless that he's always willin' to stake 'em to a brand with his own iron."

Corrals of some friendly small rancher, or those of the larger ranches placed at a distance from headquarters and used infrequently except in round-up season, were often used by the rustlers for a temporary holding of stolen cattle until they could be pushed out of the country. These were called "road houses."

If the rustler while at his fire "workin' over" a brand, or "runnin' a brand" on an animal, was approached by a rider in the distance, he "waved him round." In cowboy language this meant that he waved a hat or other object in a semicircle from left to right, and in the sign language of the plains, it meant that the one approaching was not wanted and had better stay away if he didn't want to stop "hot lead."

A Twist in Horse Stealing

. . . A ranchman in South Texas went broke in the cow game and had nothing but twelve head of good horses left when he closed out. By selling these horses in the usual way, he figured that he would have little more than eating money, so he thought up something different. Throwing in with a feller named McLaughlin, he turned over eleven of the twelve horses to him, keeping just one big blue roan for himself. McLaughlin then pulled out with the eleven horses, selling one here and another there whenever he got the chance. The real owner, fol-

From *Pardner of the Wind,* by N. Howard ("Jack") Thorp, in collaboration with Neil M. Clark, pp. 141–142. Copyright, 1945, by the Caxton Printers, Ltd. Caldwell, Idaho.

lowing on his trail a week or so later, claimed that the horses had been stolen from him, proved his ownership of the brand by showing a certificate of registration, and the unlucky buyers had to let the salt go in the gravy and give him back the horses McLaughlin had sold. The partners in crime met every now and then to divide the proceeds, and to place the recovered horses in McLaughlin's hands, so he could sell them again. Starting way down near San Saba, Texas, those slick *hombres* worked north, selling the same horses a dozen times and never taking less than forty dollars for any horse and sometimes getting as much as seventy. In a couple of months they cleaned up several thousand dollars. However, they were caught up with and landed in the penitentiary.

Roping a Fence Post

The opposition to the old time drift fence often reached the stage of positive action of some kind. In the early days a drift fence was erected in what is now the northern part of Schleicher County, and as this fence controlled much land not owned by the fence owners there was considerable dislike to the fence. The "old-timers" would often take it down and leave it down when it obstructed their path. It became common sport for the boys living near by to meet and practise roping the posts of this fence. With their ponies at a dead run, they would cast their loops and then see how far they could drag the posts and fence. The crowd once prevailed upon a newcomer—a long, tall, rough lad—to try his hand at it. He was new at the game but was more than anxious to show that he was a jolly good fellow. Accordingly, he chose the largest fence post that he could find so as to better demonstrate his skill. The post he chose was a corner post and had been placed there to stay. The cowboy made a perfect throw. The loop settled neatly over the top of the post and came to rest on the top wire. The onlookers were thrilled. All went well until the slack in the rope was taken up by the running pony and then "business picked up" in a hurry. The saddle girth snapped and the saddle and the cowboy came to a sudden and unexpected stop. The onlookers doubled up with mirth, but the ungainly cowboy got up with the remark that they could fence up all West Texas if they wanted to, he'd be damned if he cared.

From "The Saga of Barbed Wire in the Tom Green Country," by R. D. Holt, *West Texas Historical Association Year Book,* Volume IV, June, 1928, pp. 47–48.

These barbed wire drift fences often spelled disaster and death to cattle drifting before a "norther." They would strike the fence and there die by the hundreds.—R. D. H., *ibid.,* p. 46.

Nerve versus Bluff

A cowboy came in off the range one day to one of the small Arizona towns and proceeded to celebrate at the one saloon of the place. As the rot-gut began to get in its work he started shooting out the lights, making people drink with him, and generally rendering life unpleasant for everybody. And no one seemed to have the nerve to try and stop him. Now there happened to be a shoe drummer in the town that night and he sauntered into the saloon to while away the time. He observed the cowpuncher for some time with evident disfavor. Finally, as the fellow pulled an extra rough stunt, he walked quietly up to him and said: "Look here; I'll give you five minutes to get out of town." And the cowboy put up his gun, walked out of the saloon to where his horse was hitched and rode out of town. After he was gone, someone went up to the drummer and asked him: "What would you have done if that fellow hadn't got out when you told him to?" And the drummer considered a moment and said: "Well, I'd have extended the time."

The Passing of the Old-Time Cowboy

The change in the character of the cowboy did not come suddenly but was a matter of evolution. The "bob" wire fence was one of the chief agents of the economic forces which modified him and made him adapt himself to his new environment. The old-timer with high-heeled boots not built for hard work on the ground, with spurs which he hated to remove even to attend the dances in the schoolhouse, found himself sadly hampered and really outclassed at post-holed digging, haymaking, and such "degrading" labor. His place was taken by a new type of cowboy, who, when engaged in such work, wore flat-heeled shoes instead of boots, who cast aside the chaps for blue denim [jeans] —"Levis," they called them, from the name of the first manufacturer, old Levi Straus, of San Francisco, a pioneer in the overall business in the Far West. The old-timers grew up on the ranges and rode from infancy. The new cowboys were recruited from among the farmer boys who, during the branding season, worked on the range and between times helped irrigate the crops and put up the hay for winter feeding.

From *Cattle, Horses, & Men of the Western Range,* by John H. (Jack) Culley, p. 30. Copyright, 1940, by John H. Culley. Los Angeles: The Ward Ritchie Press.

From *Cattle,* by William MacLeod Raine and Will C. Barnes, pp. 282–287. Copyright, 1930, by William MacLeod Raine and Will C. Barnes. Garden City, New York: Doubleday, Doran & Company, Inc.

For the present-day cowboy, see C. L. Sonnichsen, *Cowboys and Cattle Kings* (Norman, 1950). Frank C. Goodwyn, in *Life on the King Ranch* (New York, 1951), gives a picture of changing ranch ways.

Of the old-time type of cowboy, those who were in their prime in the years between 1870 and 1890, few are left.

It used to be a saying that when a cowboy reached the age at which he could no longer flank a calf or ride a bucker and stick to the saddle, he became either a "chambermaid" in some livery stable or a bartender. The march of progress robbed him of both these lines of industry. When you do find one of the old-timers, he has generally exchanged the bucking bronc for a "Tin Lizzie." If he had the good fortune to save his wages—and few did—he is running a motor outfit of his own. The old sign "Livery Stable, Hay and Grain for Sale" has been painted out, and the words "Garage, Gas and Oil" tell the story of the downfall of the cowboy.

"These here now present-day cow persons, they make me good an' tired," remarked an old-time New Mexico cowman not long ago. "They want all quiet hosses to ride, and I cain't git nobody to bust broncs no more. They can take the carbureter off my car and clean it, but ding bust 'em, they couldn't forefoot a bronc and saddle him in two weeks. Waugh!" How he did snort!

Texas, once the very breeding place of top waddies, has more cattle then ever, but the old ranges have been cut up into fenced pastures, and the line rider carries a couple of pounds of wire fence staples in his saddle pockets, with a pair of fence pliers and a wire stretcher tied to his saddle. He does not have to be able to rope and tie down a steer in fifty seconds—unless he wants to be a rodeo performer.

In Arizona, New Mexico, southern Utah, Nevada, Montana, and eastern Oregon there are still many good-sized range cow outfits using the public domain exclusively, and there you may find cowboys that run fairly true to type. But there are many changes. Instead of using a buckboard pulled by a couple of old cow ponies, the owner now drives out to the round-up in his high-powered car from which he watches the boys cut out the steers from the herd.

Roping bids fair to become a lost art, except among rodeo performers. When cows were worth about $5 each, the owners did not particularly object to having their men practice on the stock, for without constant practice no man could hope to keep up his skill. But with rising prices, and cows worth $50 and up, roping became an expensive affair for the owners. They raised serious demurrer to training expert ropers at such costs, since practice was to be had only with range stock, which meant heavy losses in broken legs, horns, ribs, and often necks.

In the old days half a dozen punchers might be riding along a road toward the headquarters ranch. Across the road a string of cattle might come trailing out from water. A high-headed steer would stop for a moment, shake his head, sniff at the men, and race madly across the flat. Fourth of July was close at hand, with roping matches in every little cow town in the country. Away went a man after him, untying his rope from the saddle horn and forming a loop as he rode. Not far behind him trailed one or two more, eager to take their turn should the first boy "waste a loop."

There were two distinct ways of throwing a steer (busting 'em). The first and most skillful was by "going over their withers." To do this the roper lay as close as he could crowd his pony alongside the steer on his left side. With an overhand reverse swing of the loop he threw it over the steer's withers so that it hung on the right side almost to the ground. He held fast to it until the rapidly moving animal stepped into the loop with both front feet. With a quick jerk it was pulled up around the front legs against the longhorn's brisket. The pony was then swung directly away from the steer. With the rope tied to the saddle horn, the jerk that came when the end of the rope was reached dragged the feet of the brute from under him. He was turned completely over, front feet high in the air, held fast by the rope and so stunned by the fearful bump that there was little fight left in him. If the pony knew his business, he held the rope taut while the rider leaped from the saddle, ran to the steer, and with his hogging rope quickly tied the fore feet and one hind foot closely together. The job was done. This was a clever trick and took lots of practice.

The ordinary "sure-fire" method was to rope the steer by the horns, give the slack of the rope a sudden flip around the animal's rump just above the hocks, and then, spurring the pony for a supreme effort, "go yonderly" ahead and to the left. This pulled the steer's head away from the rider and back against his body and jerked the hind legs from under him. He landed all in a heap, generally with his head under his body in such a way that it was almost impossible for him to get up. With the two hind feet pulled well forward toward the front feet, hog-tying was a matter of seconds only.

But such practice was surely rough on stock and cost the owners many a range animal.

To forbid the men their roping was out of the question. The outfits got around the situation by getting state legislatures to pass laws forbidding roping exhibitions. Generally the laws were fostered by the various societies for the prevention of cruelty to animals, which relieved the bosses from all responsibility for starting the thing. No one ever knew such a bill to fail of passage. There was too much quiet pressure behind it from stock owners.

With the law in effect, the incentive for gaining skill was taken away, and there was, of course, far less of such work on the open ranges.

In nearly every range state the cowpunchers' wings were clipped by taking from him his ready six-shooter, the "hog leg" he had carried for years. Heavy penalties were enforced against the wearing of such ornaments in town or on the ranges. So the weapon was hidden away in the bed roll, for a genuine old-timer couldn't imagine himself without his six-gun somewhere near. His happiness was further curtailed by the passage of laws against open gambling. When the wave of prohibition swept across the range country from Canada to Mexico and the saloons were turned into ice-cream parlors and soft-drink emporiums, he had to content himself with lemonade—"sassyparilla" as he contemptuously called all soft drinks. He thought the world was coming to an end for sure.

With these waddies have gone the longhorn cattle, the maverick, and the rustler. In the place of the longhorns are great herds of range cattle with blood in their veins the equal of any in the corn-belt regions. The boys who now herd cattle frequently ride, not the bucking broncs of early times, but saddle horses whose ancestors have won Derbys. At the saddle horn, instead of the six-shooter, the riders carry a pair of fence pliers, and in the saddle pockets, instead of a pint flask of "red licker" is tucked a tobacco sack full of fence staples.

The rustler disappeared, or at least became a *rara avis,* with the breaking up of the big outfits. A thousand small ranchers, many of whom raise cattle, live on the range where one great syndicate ran its immense herds. Time was when the little fellow was friendly toward the brand blotter. He was despoiling the common enemy. But when the syndicates went out of business and left the country to the small fry, the waddy with a long loop for other men's calves found nothing but hostility. Those who had tolerated him would have none of his brand blotting now. They sicked the law on him and locked him up in a penitentiary.

The old-time cowboy was more picturesque and adventurous, but his successor is a better all-round worker and a better citizen. The longhorn too was picturesque, but his descendants on the open ranges weigh twice as much, make better feeders, and produce more high-priced meat. The open trackless range was mysterious and romantic, but the wire fence saves money for herders. It reduces losses in strays and depletion from winter storms, and it allows a much better use of the range.

From Bucking Contest to Rodeo

But a few years ago, every camp and hamlet in the cow country had its bucking contest. As the range began to disappear before the wire fence, the cultivated fields and the railroads, so did the cattle and the cowboy and the bucking contests. But his is a tenacious clan and dies hard, as do all inherent potential elements of a nation or a civilization. Many a remote ranch or hamlet still "pulls off" its old time bucking contest, though they are more centralized now in certain local points.

From *Let 'Er Buck,* A Story of the Passing of the Old West, by Charles Wellington Furlong, pp. 12–13. Copyright, 1921, by Charles Wellington Furlong. New York and London: G. P. Putnam's Sons.

Cf. Winifred Johnston, "Cow Country Theatre," *Southwest Review,* Vol. XVIII (October, 1932), No. 1, pp. 10–27; C. P. Westermeier, *Man, Beast, Dust* (World Press, 1947).

The contestants come in from greater distances to compete, and give to many the character of great range shows or carnivals.

Such carnivals are held in certain centers of the West; to each is given its name. Cheyenne has its "Frontier Days"; Fort Worth, Texas, the "Cattle Men's Carnival"; Denver has its "Festival of Mountain and Plain"; Winnipeg, has its "Stampede"; Grangeville, Idaho, its "Border Days"; Kearney, Nebraska, its "Frontier Round-Up"; Salinas, California its "Rodeo"; Ukiah, Oregon, its "Cowboys' Convention"; and Walla Walla, Washington, has its "Frontier Days"; a civic show in which there is more real competition than in any other outside of Pendleton [,Oregon, with its "Round-Up"]. Then there are minor and more sporadic contests held in Belle Fouche, South Dakota; Billings and Bozeman, Montana; Bovina, Texas; Sioux City, Iowa; Battle Ground, Tacoma, and Seattle in Washington, with others in Arizona and New Mexico, as well as a thousand less known little ones.

To Cheyenne must be given the credit of presenting what was probably the first big contest, Frontier Days, staged as a show. . . .

Each show has a slogan, as indispensable as that of clan or college, expressed in terms of the cow-camp. A few of the words of that terse and expressive phraseology are arbitrary and carry no special significance of their origin or of themselves, but those in common usage are wonderfully to the point to one who knows chaparral and sage brush and loves the smell of leather. At Walla Walla the slogan is "Let 'er kick"; at Grangeville, "Hook 'em cow," a term of encouragement to a roped or "bulldogged" steer. At Pendleton it is "Let 'er buck," a phrase which, briefly interpreted, means "get busy," but is primarily applied to a cowboy about to mount the hurricane deck of a "bucking" broncho; and when you hear that cowboy yell, whether in the arena at Pendleton or on the range, it is a safe bet that something startling is about to begin.

Pitching Horses and Panthers

I[1]

. . . The difference between bucking and pitching is merely geographic: the farther south you sweat, the higher they pitch and the farther north you freeze, the harder they buck. As one old peeler remarked, "Wherever there's broncs, there's likely to be promptitude." A special diction pertaining to the subject is as extensive as it is vivid and vigorous. This diction popped out of a big, free, fresh, lusty country where cries like "Sock the spurs to him, "Bathe his butt with yer

---

[1] From "Pitching Horses and Panthers," by J. Frank Dobie, *Mustangs and Cow Horses,* edited by J. Frank Dobie, Mody C. Boatright, Harry H. Ransom, Publication No. XVI of the Texas Folk-Lore Society, p. 291. Copyright, 1940, by the Texas Folk-Lore Society, Austin.

quirt," and "Let 'er buck" vivified the air around camp and corral. It expressed the nature of men who called any horse that had been saddled a time or two "broke," and who had no use for a horse "without a little life to him. . . ."

II[2]

When the horse "hid his head an' kicked the lid off," or "warped his backbone an' hallelujahed all over the lot," the comments upon his ability were such as "he's a beast with a bellyful of bed springs," "frolicsome little beast," "real hunk o' death," "cutey, little grave-digger," "he's tryin' to chin the moon"; and perhaps the rider was warned that the horse would "buck his whiskers off," or "he'll throw y'u so high the birds'll build nests in yo' hair 'fore y'u light," or "he'll stomp y'u in the ground so deep y'u'll take roots an' sprout."

If the horse was a bucker of ability, he was a "gut-twister," and it was "like ridin' a cyclone with the bridle off," and it "took a man with whiskers to ride 'im." Of the man making a good ride it was said that "he sets that bronc as easy as a hoss-fly on a mule's ear," that he was "stickin' like a tick makin' a gotch-ear," or it was "jes like buckin' off a porous plaster," and you "couldn't have chopped him loose from that hoss with an ax." About the man who had little riding ability it was said he "couldn't ride a covered wagon," or "couldn't ride nuthin' wilder than a wheel chair."

III[3]

. . . It is said that horses do not pitch—or buck—in Europe or Asia. . . . Pitching is supposed to be an equine institution of the Americas, and plenty of theories have been advanced to explain its origin. The commonest theory is that the Spanish horses of the Americas were preyed on by panthers—which is a fact—and learned how to "unwind" while trying to pitch off panthers that had leaped on their backs. Then the colts of these panther-throwers inherited the peculiar calisthenics generated by their ancestors and practised them to unseat men. This folk idea is a contradiction to the law that acquired characteristics or habits are not hereditary. Yet if an animal never acquired anything new, how could evolution proceed? . . .

Dudes and Dude-Wranglers

Howard Eaton started the dude business and invented the word dude. That was about thirty-five years ago. The word has none of the

---

2 From *Cowboy Lingo*, by Ramon F. Adams, pp. 103-104. Copyright, 1936, by Ramon F. Adams. Boston: Houghton Mifflin Company.

3 J. Frank Dobie, *op. cit.*, pp. 291, 293.

From *The Diary of a Dude Wrangler*, by Struthers Burt, pp. 60–61, 50. Copyright, 1924, by Charles Scribner's Sons. New York and London.

slurring connotations attached to the term tenderfoot. It does not imply ignorance or softness, it simply means some one, usually a person not resident in the country, who hires some one else to guide him or cook for him, or who pays money to stay on a ranch. The governor of Wyoming can be a dude if he hires guides when he goes hunting, so can the oldest and toughest cattleman in the world. I know a Cherokee Indian who for several years was a dude. His homestead in Oklahoma contained oil and he used to come into our country after elk. Amusingly enough, his guides told me that he was a poor hunter, too easily lost, and what we describe as "an ornery dude"—hard to please. And often nowadays I, a dude-wrangler, am a dude by deliberate choice—that is, I take guides and cooks with me into the hills. It's splendid fun to do all the work in camp, until—for many years—you've done it. Then it's the grimmest kind of hard work, unless there are no more than two, or, at the outside, three persons. To be a dude is a perfectly honest avocation.

Howard Eaton, if I have not heard the story incorrectly, became, like most of his followers, a dude-wrangler by chance. He was an extremely popular man, originally from Pittsburgh, and with his two brothers had a horse ranch in South Dakota. Like most popular men who have a ranch, he was overwhelmed with guests, and after a while discovered that what he was making on his horses he was losing on entertaining. At first his idea was to make his friends pay merely their share of the expenses, but as they continued to come in increasing numbers, he saw a business opportunity and took it. Eventually he moved his outfit to Wolf, Wyoming, and there it is to-day, a most interesting village, already historic.

* * * * *

The dude-wrangler knows a dude ranch is not a cow ranch; he knows that when Eastern damsels put on overalls and wear egregious scarfs they don't look in the least like cowgirls, but he encourages them to do these things because it is good for their souls and because it adds color to a business that is not imitative but just as autochthonous as the cattle business itself.

Will Rogers Gets Started

I. Roping a Wild Steer

One night [in the old Madison Square Garden in New York City in 1905] one of the steers used in the roping act [of Zack Mulhall's Wild West Show] ran wild and jumped over the railing of the arena into the crowd. As the frightened spectators dashed up the stairs, the steer

From *Will Rogers,* Ambassador of Good Will, Prince of Wit and Wisdom, by P. J. O'Brien, pp. 52, 53–55. Copyright, 1935, by P. J. O'Brien. Philadelphia: The John C. Winston Company.

was about to charge into them. [Twenty-six-year-old Will] Rogers, who had seen the animal start its mad dash, coiled up his lariat as he ran across the tanbark. Swish! The snaky coil of manila flew through the air and settled over the head of the enraged animal. Will dug the high heels of his cowboy boots into the tanbark and leaned back on the rope. He choked all the fight out of the steer and then led him back to the temporary corral in the Garden. The next day Will Rogers found himself proclaimed a hero on the front pages of all the New York newspapers. . . .

II. They Liked His Cowboy Drawl

. . . Will was seized with a new ambition and that was to stay in New York. . . .

. . . He trouped on the Klaw & Erlanger circuit, opening and closing the shows. His was strictly a "dumb" act. He had yet to find that his greatest talent was in the ready wit with which he amused stagehands and fellow players.

. . . Will Rogers was inherently a showman. In his vaudeville days he used to put on his act and then stand in the "entrance" to the stage studying the other acts that were put on. He was in love with the theater and wanted to excel in it. It did not take him long to realize that laughs—not physical skill—produce the most money in the show business. Rogers was not long in realizing that what he needed in his bit was a few wisecracks. . . . He was, however, modest and shy to an extreme and that may have held him back for a time, but eventually he added more and more talking to the act. It did not catch on with audiences at the start and sometimes he was content just to present his roping act.

In his early act, Rogers used a lariat, a white horse, and his rider as properties. As the orchestra played "Cheyenne," Will would shuffle down to the center of the stage with a rope in each hand. The horse and rider would come galloping out of the wings across the stage and in the twinkling of an eye, Rogers would throw the rope in his right hand around the horse and the one in his left hand around the rider. It was a difficult trick, but it was executed so swiftly that the spectators could not appreciate what had happened. A fellow actor told Rogers that if he would stop the music and make a brief explanation of what he intended to do, the stunt would appeal more to the audience.

At the next show Will walked out and held up his hand. "Stop that noise," he said. The audience roared with delight. Will Rogers had made his first wisecrack from the stage.

"Folks," the cowboy continued, "you can see I got one of these ropes in each hand. When the hoss and rider come out, I'm going to try to throw one of 'em over the hoss and the other over the rider."

Again the audience burst into laughter. Will was angry. He had not meant to say anything comic.

"They laughed at me," he declared as other players assured him he had made a hit.

"Sure, they laughed," the actors replied. "You were funny."

Horse Opera

HOPALONG CASSIDY[1]

Among all the U.S. enterprisers who devote themselves to titillating the unripened mind, none has succeeded as Hoppy [William "Hopalong Cassidy" Boyd] has, both with his under-age customers and the thousands of manufacturers, retailers, and advertising men who hawk his wares. Last week [November 20, 1950] 63 television stations were pumping out his old movies, 152 radio stations were carrying his voice, 155 newspapers were printing his new Hopalong Cassidy comic strip, and 108 licensed manufacturers were turning out Hopalong Cassidy products at the rate of $70,000,000 a year.

* * * * *

Earlier generations of U.S. children had been exposed to this sort of thing, of course. More than one house was burned to the ground in the '90s by small boys reading Nick Carter in the attic by candlelight. Buffalo Bill and his Wild West show set hordes of amateur buckaroos to lassoing gate posts and hapless cats. As early as 1907, the *Youth's Companion* promised boys who sent in a new subscription and $1.15 a "No. 3 striking bag . . . new pear shape, very popular, particularly adapted for quick work. . . ." Girls could earn "artistic wood-burning outfits" by selling gold-eye needles.

In the 1920s, a kid with 25¢ and any sort of buyer's instinct at all could have his blood genuinely curdled once a week at the movies—if he was lucky he could watch Bill Hart galloping noiselessly across the prairie, and shudder at the sight of Pearl White lashed to the railroad tracks. But when radio invaded the U.S. home, children began to absorb this kind of nerve-jangling opiate every day and, when it was refused them, to complain as bitterly as if they were denied nourishment.

When the fevered radio advertisers of the 1930s tried to discover just how much dough could be squeezed out of Junior—a process approached in much the same spirit as that with which the Texas Rangers squeezed information out of Mexican bandits—it seemed improbable that the growing nervous system could stand much more stimulation or

[1] From "Kiddies in the Old Corral," *Time, The Weekly News Magazine,* Vol. LVI (November 27, 1950), No. 22, pp. 18–20. Copyright, 1950, by Time, Inc. New York.

Cf. Collie Small, "Hopalong Can't Miss," *The Saturday Evening Post,* Vol. 219 (June 14, 1947), No. 50, pp. 20–21, 164, 166–167. "The price of Indians is way up," Boyd says, "I used to get a whole tribe for practically nothing. Now they have a union."—p. 167.

that the tender, childish gullet could gulp down more bread, breakfast food, candy, or soft drinks.

This turned out to be a naive underestimate of Junior's appetites: he pined for more and more entertainment and he got it—almost always with the encouragement of his parents, who discovered that blood and thunder would pacify him almost as effectively as Seconal, and that cutting off his comic books would reduce him to obedience faster than the old-fashioned razor strop.

Before World War II, the networks, it is true, did reform themselves up to a point. Advertising tactics which smacked faintly of blackmail (General Mills once suggested that a character in one of its shows would die for lack of medical attention unless more Wheaties were sold) were reluctantly abandoned.

But to the untrained ear the change was virtually undetectable. The Green Hornet, The Lone Ranger ("Hi-yo, Silver—awa-a-a-a-a-y!"), Soo-oo-per-ma-a-an, The Shadow, and an ear-shattering collection of other thrillers kept on blasting through millions of loudspeakers; the announcer's thrilling command—"Ask mother NOW!"—echoed louder than ever. Fancier and more complicated box-top premiums (Planetary Maps, Atomic Bomb Rings, Magni-glow Writing Rings, Detective Badges, Compass-Magnifying Glasses, Explorer's Sun Watches) came flooding through the mails by the ton.

And on top of all this came television, which not only assaulted the childish ear, but (in the words of Fred Allen) threatened to change Americans into creatures with eyeballs as big as cantaloupes and no brain at all. Last week countless hordes of U.S. children not only went to the movies once a week, listened to their radio favorites among twenty-seven children's network programs (often reading comic books and blowing bubble gum at the same time), but spent millions of kiddie-hours squinting hypnotically at the thirty-five shows offered them on flickering television screens.

The kiddies exhibited a leaping enthusiasm for the new and massive doses of entertainment offered by video. Overnight, almost every little boy and girl in the nation had become a cowboy; in those carefully metered periods which they spent outdoors between programs, they saw cattle rustlers around every corner. They were not the first U.S. children to indulge in make-believe about the Old West. But they were the first to catch the fever simultaneously from coast to coast and to demand such splendid arms and accouterments.

Children with impressively styled cap guns and bejeweled double holsters (many tied to their thighs to facilitate a fast draw) were so commonplace that those without them seemed a little underdressed, and those who still carried such outmoded armament as X-Ray Guns or Atomic Disintegrators, hopelessly old-fashioned. When firing, they sometimes seemed a little confused by their multi-programmed backgrounds; instead of just crying "Bang!" like the older generations, they imitated rockets and/or ricocheting bullets ("Ptche-e-e-e-e-w"), enormous steel springs ("Boing-oing-oing!"), or machine guns ("Ha-ha-ha-ha-ha-ha!").

But in all else—even to the horselike galloping which had become as *de rigueur* among seven-year-old girls (who also whinnied occasionally) as the slouch among debutantes of the '20s—they were faithful to their hero, the clear-eyed Hopalong. Black Hopalong Cassidy shirts and Hopalong Cassidy pants were simple necessities; the more fashionable put on Hopalong Cassidy pajamas to sleep in a Hopalong Cassidy bed, had Hopalong Cassidy wallpaper (which outsold every design in the U.S. this year), ate Hopalong Cassidy cookies and peanut butter and rode a Hopalong Cassidy bicycle (which has handle bars shaped like steer horns).

The man who touched off this twin epidemic of hero-worship and product-hunger had not only done so with Howdy-Doody to left of him and Kukla, Fran, and Ollie to right of him, but with little of the background which might be deemed necessary for hog-tying a whole generation. He shudders at Western music (particularly when sung by his principal rivals, Roy Rogers and Gene Autry), has never branded a cow or mended a fence, cannot bulldog a steer. Though he has learned to ride competently enough, he would rather see his Nielsen rating drop (last week's: 34.8) than climb aboard a rodeo bronc.

* * * * *

In Author Clarence Mulford's original pulp-paper stories, Hoppy had been a ragged, tobacco-chewing, whiskery cowpoke who walked with a bad limp. But Boyd made him a veritable Galahad of the range —a soft-spoken paragon who did not smoke, drink, or kiss girls, who tried to capture the rustlers instead of shooting them, and who always let the villain draw first if gunplay was inevitable.

* * * * *

Last week Hoppy's public, by and large, was still wildly loyal to him. But here and there, kiddie-dissension reared its innocent-looking head. A few children seemed in an uneasy state of transition from cowboys to interplanetary travel as depicted in such programs as *Tom Corbett, Space Cadet,* and *Space Patrol.* Others just seemed to think Hoppy was too darned good for this world.

Said nine-year-old Tim Leffler, of San Francisco: "Hopalong's dull—if he'd only just die once in a while!" Carl Bleiken, a seven-year-old televiewer of Hingham, Mass., complained: "I like Bobby Benson of B-Bar-B Ranch better. He's more truer. Hopalong never gets wounded, Bobby Benson does. There's a whole bunch in Bobby Benson, and they have good teamwork, not like Hopalong Cassidy." But the deadliest arrow was launched by little Jack Clough of Rye, N.Y. Jeered he: "Slipalong Catastrophe!"

A cowboy never knew when the herd would tromp him down.

Gene Autry[2]

Like Thomas Edison and David Sarnoff, business man Gene Autry's early days were spent tapping out messages on a telegraph key.

"Being a telegraph operator in a little place like Chelsea, Oklahoma, can be a mighty lonesome job. Round sundown one evening in October, a long time ago, an ordinary-looking feller I hadn't seen before came up to my window in the railroad station and asked me to send a message. There wasn't any fire out in the waiting room, so I invited this stranger to come back into my office and sit down.

"After he got through writing out his message—a long one—he pointed to my guitar leaning against the wall and asked if I could play. I told him sure I could, and sang him a song—I was only about eighteen, and in those days I'd sing at the drop of a hat. Then he joined in, and we sang a couple together.

" 'Young feller,' he said to me, 'you're good. Why don't you go East and get yourself a job singing on the radio?'

"Well, anybody who could sing at all was always being told by somebody in that little town—'You ought to get on the radio.' So I laughed and said sure, and didn't pay much attention to what the stranger said . . . until after he handed me his message and left.

"The message was a newspaper column, and the feller who sent it was Will Rogers."

He took Rogers' advice and headed for New York, soon found he could get a lot farther by chucking his business suit out the window and donning a cowboy outfit. "Couldn't get a job in a business suit, never wore one since."

Not the slightest bit bowlegged, Autry sauntered through radio, movies, and finally records—where he's made 25,000,000 of them for Columbia, second only to Bing Crosby. Nobody fenced Autry in; his range of comic books, flying schools, movie theaters, children's cowboy outfits and rodeos is more far-flung than even the great King Ranch in Texas. . . .

* * * * *

Like any sound business man, he keeps a sharp eye on the tastes of his public. "Been getting a lot of letters lately from teen-age girls who'd like some romance in the pictures—I think the girl in Westerns is in for a big build-up. It's okay with me. I think Champion is a

[2] From "New York Close-Up," by Tex McCrary and Jinx Falkenburg, *New York Herald Tribune,* November 8, 1950, p. 33. Copyright, 1950, by N.Y. Herald Tribune, Inc.

The caption under Gene Autry's photograph reads: "Son of a successful horse trader, Gene Autry has rustled up a fortune by combining clear singing and straight shooting, and shrewdly avoids the usual Western corn. 'I'd shoot dead the first man in my movies who hollered, "They went thataway." ' "

Cf. Don Ross, "Knight in Million-Dollar Armor," *New York Herald Tribune,* October 15, 1950, Section 5, pp. 1–2.

fine animal, but"—here he grinned—"I'm getting mighty tired of kissing my horse!"

Roy Rogers[3]

Republic Pictures and some other studios have been making "Westerns" for decades to satisfy this interest in cowboys and Indians. John Wayne, Bill Boyd, Gene Autry, Gabby Hayes, Wild Bill Elliott, Johnny Mack Brown, and I have been capturing bad men for almost as long as we can remember.[4]

Now, because of intense interest in the Old West, many of the big-city slicker stars, such as Gregory Peck, William Holden, Alan Ladd, have been getting in on the act. As one critic put it: "There's more Westerin' in Hollywood today than there ever was on the old Chisholm Trail."

It is probably natural that millions of American youngsters make idols of their favorite Western stars. A child psychologist told me once that hero worship is a normal phase all kids go through. I'm flattered to think that quite a few have chosen me.

When I was a kid I remember that I was a fervent Hoot Gibson fan. Then suddenly I found I had ditched Hoot for Tom Mix. My conversion occurred mainly, I believe, because I fell in love with Tom's horse, Tony.

Today I suspect that an awful lot of my fans are really fans of my palomino horse, Trigger. And I think that's a good thing, too, because it is fine for youngsters to love animals. I often sneak into theaters to see my own movies. One thing I've noticed is that the real roof-

---

[3] From "Don't Shoot, Ma!," by Rog Rogers, *The American Magazine,* Vol. CXLVIII (August, 1949), No. 2, pp. 29, 131–132. Copyright, 1949, by the Crowell-Collier Publishing Company. New York.

[4] Beginning in 1910 the Essanay Company released a weekly one-reel film featuring "Broncho Billy," the first movie cowboy hero and popular idol. According to E. Douglas Branch (*The Cowboy and His Interpreters,* New York, 1926, p. 229): "In the summer of 1913 newspapers gravely printed the story of a certain little Dorothy who suffered from pneumonia; Dorothy, 'peaked and anemic,' was condemned to a second operation. The child resisted desperately, until her mother cried, inspired, 'Remember, Broncho Billy! You know Broncho Billy is brave and never breaks his word.' And Dorothy sweetly submitted."

Alfred Towne (*Neurotica 7,* New York, Autumn, 1950, p. 4) thus psychoanalyzes the several stages in the development of the hero of Horse Opera: "William S. Hart (*The Squaw Man*) was a simple, raw-boned individual who was endowed with nothing but a granite face and a courage bolstered by his conception of right and wrong. Like Owen Wister's *Virginian,* his code was simple: 'When you call me that, *smile!*' But as the Western proceeded to higher points of refinement . . . his world became one of sartorial and idiosyncratic details: silk shirts, chaps studded with glittering stones, colorful bandanas around his neck; his guns magnificent objets d'art. Very often his horse became more a personality than he. Tom Mix and Tony are typical of this adolescent period of the Western. The singing cowboy represented by Roy Rogers and Gene Autry developed a hero as efficient with a guitar and ballad as with a six-shooter. . . . In Hopalong Cassidy we have the father-surrogate, the silver-haired paternal figure loved by a whole new generation."

raising shrieks of joy occur when Trigger charges onto the scene, whether I'm on him or not!

The plot typically involves little more than the triumph of law and order, decency and clean living. We Western "heroes" never cuss, spit, gamble, shoot pool, or step into a saloon except to have it out with bad men. We never hit a little man . . . we refuse all rewards . . . we give villains more than an even break, even on the draw.

Most important of all, in my pictures, at least, I usually get whipped pretty badly somewhere in the show. We try to demonstrate that in real life everyone suffers reverses once in a while. But we also show that by sticking to it and working together, the forces of law and decency will always triumph in the end. We also try to work into our scripts and scenarios a few little lectures to the kids on kindness to animals, sportsmanship, game conservation, and so on.

As for morality, our Westerns are rampantly pure. The hero is always gallant, but never makes love. I am permitted to kiss Trigger, but never the heroine. At the end of a picture I doff my hat to the girl whose ranch I have just saved, pat Trigger, and ride off into the sunset.

My fans, especially the small fry, love it that way. They don't care for mushy stuff and think that smooching in the Great Outdoors is not only boring but indecent. . . .

* * * * *

Before the final sunset fade-out scene we always have a wild chase, with a lot of shooting. The chief villain tries to make a getaway, Trigger and I catch up with him, I pull him off his horse, and we go wrestling down the rocky hillside. I naturally get in the last poke on the screen. Actually, I've been knocked cold in three of those tussles.

* * * * *

Most of my young fans like to think I'm a hard-bitten cowboy from way back, and occasionally my more extravagant promotors have encouraged the notion. I've read reports that I was reared on ranches in such places as Montana, Cody, Wyo., Texas, and Arizona.

The fact is that I was raised on a farm in a hollow up back of Duck Run, Ohio—and my great ambition until I was in my teens was to be a dentist. My name then was Leonard Slye.

I didn't become a dentist (and thus a symbol of pain to youngsters), because my family was poor. I had to drop out of high school to run the farm, and later work beside Dad at a shoe factory. Then I came West to try my luck. I picked peaches with the migrant Oakies, dug ditches, drove gravel trucks, and picked up dimes pushing cars out of mudholes.

Most of the time I was hungry. Some other hungry young friends and I organized a singing group. We first called ourselves the Rocky Mountaineers. (I also played guitar.) We toured the Southwest under various titles, but had the same miserable luck. The Depression was on. We slept three in a bed. To eat we often had to go out and shoot rabbit or hawks. (Today we joke about our "hawk sandwich" days.)

For several months we were stuck in Roswell, N. Mex., because we were really flat broke. To help raise carfare back to California, I took a job on a ranch and was put to work hustling wild horses for a couple of months.

One day, in Los Angeles, I overheard a man in a hat store mention that Republic Pictures was looking for a new singing cowboy. I raced out and nailed the job. It was just dumb luck.

III. HERDERS

A sheepman ain't got no friends.—OLD SAYING

The Kind-Hearted Sheepman

I[1]

This fellow, Bert Weaver, [from Missouri] was a plucky chap, but one of the kind that seems just naturally unlucky. He was a good enough worker, but somehow he was always out of work.

One summer he'd been down through the Cimarron country [in Colorado] looking for a job among the sheep men there. He couldn't seem to make a deal, though, so he started back. One night he camped at a little empty shack on the prairie. He slept on the dirt floor inside right under a window. It was wide open, of course, and so was the door, for it was terrible hot weather.

In the night he woke all of a sudden with a queer feeling he wasn't alone. He lay still, but pulled out his knife. Pretty soon he saw something white coming. It jumped right over him out of the window, startling him something awful.

"It can't be a nightmare, for I'm broad awake," says Bert to himself. "It's ridiculous to think of ghosts, but what else can it be? If I see the thing again, I'll knife it."

---

1 From "Cowboy Lore in Colorado," by Honora DeBusk Smith, *Southwestern Lore*, edited by J. Frank Dobie, Publications of the Texas Folk-Lore Society, No. IX, 1931, p. 44. Copyright, 1931, by the Texas Folk-Lore Society. Dallas: The Southwest Press.

In half a minute another white thing jumped over him. He shut his eyes, and jabbed at it hard. He felt the knife go in and make a deep wound, but before he could say Jack Robinson, on came another and another. By this time he was pretty badly scared, but he kept right on slashing and stabbing. Finally, there was a lull, and Bert crept out of doors, tired and shaky, and fell asleep out there on the buffalo grass.

Next morning he found he had slaughtered eighteen or nineteen sheep that belonged to Old Man Luning. Bert felt pretty cheap about it, but he was an honest fellow; so he went and explained matters to the old man and offered to work it out. Luning was the kind of fellow that loved a joke, and he was so tickled by Bert's story that he declared the fun was well worth the loss of the sheep. What's more, he gave Bert a job, and I reckon he worked for the old man as long as he lived.

II[2]

We all agreed there was some difference in sheepmen, and that Rambolet Bill and Cottswool Canvasback certainly belonged to the better class, and we all fell to telling stories of the generous, open-handed things that sheepmen of our acquaintance had done.

Packsaddle Jack said he knowed a sheepman once by the name of Black Face, who was so good hearted that he paid twenty dollars towards one of his herders' doctor bill when he lost both feet by being frozen in the great Wyoming blizzard in '94. The herder stayed with the sheep for seventy-two hours in the Bad Lands and saved all the three thousand sheep except seven that got over the bank of the creek into ice and water and drowned. The herder having got all but these seven head out and getting his feet wet they froze so hard that Black Face said his feet was rattling together like rocks when he found him still herding the sheep. Of course, the sheep might have all perished in the storm if the herder didn't stay with them, and of course, the herder didn't have anything to eat the entire three days in the storm, as he was miles from any habitation, and that way saved Black Face thirty cents in grub. But we all agreed that while Black Face would feel the greatest anguish at the loss of the seven sheep and giving up the twenty dollars, yet the satisfaction of doing a generous deed and the pride he would experience when it was mentioned in the item column of the local county paper would partially alleviate that anguish.

Eatumup Jake said he knew a sheepman by the name of Hatchet Face from Connecticut, who had sheep ranches out there in Utah, and he was so kind-hearted that when one of his herders kept his sheep in a widow neighbor's field till they ate everything in sight, even her lawn and flower garden, he apologized to the widow when she returned from

---

2 From *Cowboy Life on the Sidetrack,* being an extremely humorous and sarcastic story of the trials and tribulations endured by a party of stockmen making a shipment from the West to the East, by Frank Benton, Cheyenne, Wyoming, pp. 70–75. Copyright, 1903, by Frank Benton. Denver, Colorado: The Western Stories Syndicate.

nursing a poor family through a spell of sickness, and told her he would pay her something, and while he never did pay her anything, yet he always seemed sorry, while a lot of sheepmen would have laid awake nights to have studied a way how to eat out the widow again. Eatumup Jake said Old Hatchet Face, when he prayed in church Sundays (he being a strict Presbyterian), he always prayed for the poor and widows and orphans, and that showed he had a good heart, to use what influence he had with God Almighty and get Him to do something for widows and orphans and poor people.

Dillberry Ike said he knew a sheepman by the name of Shearclose, and while he never gave his hired help any meat to eat except old broken-mouthed ewes in the winter and dead lambs in the spring and summer, and herded his sheep around homesteader's little ranches till their milk cows mighty near starved to death, yet old Shearclose gave five dollars for a ticket to a charity ball once when a list of names of all the people who bought tickets was printed in the county paper.

After we summed all these things up, our hearts got so warm thinking of these acts of generosity by sheepmen that we concluded to make a hunt for Rambolet Bill, Cottswool Canvasback and Jackdo. We now discussed a great many plans how to rescue them. While we were arguing the stock train came, and when we told the conductor, he immediately had the agent wire General Freight Agent C. J. Lane, at Omaha, the following message:

> Two prominent sheepmen swept away by freshet while camping ahead of special train No. 79531. Please wire instructions how to find them.

Lane immediately wired back not to find them, and if there was any trace of them to obliterate it at once.

The Herder and His Boss

. . . Many a herder has wandered around a little when he first got out in the morning, praying that he might find his sheep before the boss found them, or him. It was probably some such accident that lay behind the story of the herder who suddenly presented himself before the boss at the ranch buildings one morning and asked if he wished to have him keep on herding. "Why, yes!" said the surprised boss. "I have no kick on your work." "All right, then," said the relieved herder, "you'd better give me another bunch of sheep. I lost those."

* * * * *

There was the sheepman . . . out in Montana who was putting his sheep on land to which his title was so clouded that it could not be

---

From *Sheep*, by Archer B. Gilfillan, pp. 42, 94–95. Copyright, 1928, 1929, by Archer B. Gilfillan. Boston: Little, Brown and Company.

seen at all. He expected trouble and warned his herder, old Andy Swanson.

"Now I'm going to give you a 30-30 and a lot of ammunition, and if anybody comes bothering you just let him have it."

"Well," replied old Andy, who did not relish being made a cat's paw, "I'm getting forty-five dollars a month, and I guess that's not fighting wages."

The question of food furnished to the wagon has probably caused more friction between sheepman and herder than any other one thing. The herder is absolutely at the mercy of his boss in this respect as long as he works for him. Obviously he can't eat what he doesn't have. A farm hand eats with the family, faring just as well as they do, and he could hardly ask anything better; but all that the herder eats must be packed and brought out to him.

There was the sheepman, for example, who furnished his herder a can of coffee, a sack of flour, and a slab of fat pork, and told him to cook anything he wanted. On the other hand there was the new herder who was told to look the wagon over and make out an order for the things he needed. The list he sent in looked like a mail-order grocery catalogue copied out with very few omissions. The boss, looking it over carefully, added one item not down, namely, "a new herder."

Then there was the sheepman who was tactfully approached by his herder on the subject of a little meat for the wagon. The sheepman, although a meat eater, was a vegetarian when it came to furnishing the wagon.

"You've got a gun, haven't you?" he asked the herder.

"Yes."

"And ammunition?"

"Yes."

"And there are plenty of rabbits on the prairie, aren't there?"

"Yes."

"Well, there's your meat."

A few days later the sheepman on one of his visits to the wagon found a fine ewe dead on her back. He questioned the herder.

"Did you know that ewe was dead there?"

"No."

"Where were you?"

"I was out hunting jack rabbits."

The Sheepman and the Skunk

Cattlemen, who hated the smell of sheep, were fond of ascribing a sheepy odor as well as a disreputable appearance to the men who tended sheep. The only sheepman legend that cowmen ever tell in

---

From *The Golden Hoof,* The Story of the Sheep of the Southwest, by Winifred Kupper, p. 77. Copyright, 1945, by Alfred A. Knopf, Inc. New York.

mixed company has to do with a cowman, a farmer, and a sheepman who visited a carnival show. One tent bore the sign "Five Dollars if you can stay in this tent five minutes." The cowman swaggered in with assurance. In two seconds he was out, sputtering and coughing and urging the next man to try it. The farmer went in, and in half a minute he came hurrying out in discomfiture. Then the sheepman ambled in. The other two waited. One minute went by—two, three, four. Just as the cowman and the farmer had made up their minds to go to the rescue, the tent's exhibit, a large, virile, and highly disgusted skunk, ran out from under the tent flap and made for the creek.

The Sheepman Calls the Cowman's Bluff

The [range] war in West Texas was carried on largely in the form of threats, bluffs, and curses delivered by the cattlemen, often through his henchman the cowboy. The sheepman's defense was usually diplomacy or strategy. It had to be. The sheepman was always outnumbered, often on foot, and sometimes unarmed. The classic threat was a rope and a tree, and, considering the scarcity of trees on the Plains, it must have been largely rhetorical. "If you don't get to hell out of here with those damn sheep before they get to my waterhole and stink it up," a cowman near San Angelo told a sheepman once, "I'll have a rope and a tree ready for you by sundown." In this instance the sheepman resorted to strategy. "Now see here, it's this way," he began. And he kept on. He argued at length. A sheepman was never at a loss for words. And while he argued, his Mexican herders slipped the sheep down to the precious waterhole, watered them, and got them well on their way before he ran out of words or the cowman knew what was happening.

Sometimes it was necessary to call a cowman's bluff and stand on one's rights. One sheepman in the South Concho country, ordered off the range by a swaggering cowman, was given his choice between three days to move and death at the end of a rope. The sheepman drew a map of the territory around his sheep camp and sent it off to Austin to find out to whom the land belonged. The answer was that, with the exception of four hundred acres some miles away from his camp, it belonged to the State of Texas. The infinitesimal tract excepted belonged to the cowman, and it was all that did belong to him. The next time he came around for a settlement the sheepman told him what he had found out. He added that if there were any more trouble he would arrange to have fifty thousand sheep brought in within three months. There was no more trouble.[1]

* * * * *

Ibid., pp. 110–111, 114–115.

[1] Roy Holt, "C. C. Doty, West Texas Pioneer," *Sheep and Goat Raiser,* San Angelo, Texas, November, 1941, p. 21.—W.K.

"This range ain't no good for sheep," the cowmen of the Texas Pecos country once told a sheepman when they found him driving a bunch of sheep in. "There's not enough water—your sheep'll shorely die."

The sheepman looked at the healthy cattle all around. "Don't see anything wrong with the cows around here," he said. "Looks like they're in might good shape, anyhow."

"Oh, yeah, sure, cattle do all right here," the cowmen admitted. "But sheep, now—sheep's different. Sheep need more water'n cows. You shorely know that?"

The sheepman knew that they needed less. He moved in and bought a ranch. Being a sheepman and therefore thrifty, he dug some good deep wells. With them scattered about the range, the sheepman need not drive his sheep so far to his one or two waterholes. Moreover, there was no danger that thousands of sheep would trample the range around a single waterhole, ruining the grass.

Soon a terrible drought hit the country. Every waterhole was dried to a clay bone. The cattleman saw their gaunt cattle walking hopelessly about, stretching out their necks, opening their parched mouths in dry, soundless bellows, and they did the only thing they could. They drove their herds to the sheepman's wells. There have been droughts on the Plains when men have guarded their waterholes with guns; but this sheepman, meeting the cattlemen and their herds, had no gun in his hands.

There was, however, a look of serious concern on his face. "Good Lord, men," he warned, "don't you know that these sheep have poisoned the range around these wells? Your cattle are bound to die if you bring 'em on it. You shorely know that?" The cattlemen grinned sheepishly and watered their animals.

Crazy as a Sheepherder

. . . The western phrase "crazy as a sheepherder" embodies this idea that the loneliness of his life actually drove him insane. . . .

* * * * *

In 1887 a sheepman took a bunch of sheep to the Big Bend country. In that region was a cattleman who had sworn to kill anybody who ever came in there with sheep, and though the sheepman had a lease and a right to be there, they weren't going to avail him much against the cowman's guns. After he had located his sheep at Rosillo Springs a delegation of three cowpunchers rode up and wanted to know what the hell he was doing there with sheep. Outnumbered, he resorted to stratagem. He had been reading about Jules Verne's trip to the moon, and he began to paraphrase it for the cowboys. He and his partner, he

Ibid., pp. 73, 74.

told the cowboys, had constructed a machine for a trip to the moon and got it loaded with ballast, water, and supplies, and since they couldn't leave the faithful old sheep dog they had put him inside, too. They had risen to about five thousand feet and were traveling at a fair speed when they discovered at midnight that they were losing altitude. They began throwing out ballast, but they kept on losing altitude. They threw out other things; and finally, in desperation, they threw out the old sheep dog. They traveled without difficulty after that, and at daylight they looked out to discover that the dog, faithful to his trust, was traveling right alongside 'em in the air. When the sheepman got to this point the leader of the cowboys got up in a hurry and said to the others: "This damned fool is crazy! Let's get out of here."[1] And from then on that bit of range belonged to the sheepman.

The Dissipating Lead Goat

A sheep is better than a goat for leading, inasmuch as the flock will follow him more willingly. But a goat can work harder at it—particularly the old type of Spanish goat, with his lean, tireless body and his light coat of mottled brown, tan, and white. He can work longer at the job than his Angora brother, who is apt to be a little too highbred for menial tasks. And a job it is, this leading bunch after bunch of stupid sheep to fill cars on the railroad track. Sometimes the sheep will follow him in a steady stream; sometimes he has to return again and again for small groups that hang back.

It's hard work, but it has its compensations. The lead goat starts life as a pet around the house, a *sancho*. He is given milk out of a bottle; he is petted and pampered and given the run of the place. When he begins work, say at the stockyards, he gets to be quite a personage. Every stockman round about knows him and calls him by name, and the railroad officials themselves look upon him as an important part of their outfit.

"Sure these lead goats have names," the man at the San Angelo stockyards explained. "That one over there is Bill, and this one here is Sancho. Bill's just learning the trade, Sancho's teaching him. He'll likely be better than Sancho. Got less temperament. But after he's hung around these stockmen as long as Sancho has, there's no telling what sort of character he'll develop. Trouble is, we're having to leave his education up to Sancho. Used to have a Mexican here to train 'em. Nobody can train a lead goat like a Mexican can. A lead goat can be

---

[1] Told by Florence Fenley, in *Old Timers* (Uvalde, Texas, Hornby Press, 1939), p. 22.

Ibid., pp. 148–151.

as ornery as a mule sometimes. We call 'em Bill and Sancho between working times, but while they're working they've got the same name as all lead goats have—Son-of-a-bitch."

The lead goat or sheep, with his usefulness and his orneriness, is the one member of a characterless group to be recognized as an individual. "Back in the early days," reminisces Jack Potter of Clayton, New Mexico, "when the Colorado & Southern Railroad built through this country and established shipping points up and down their line, oldtime pioneer sheep and cowmen could hardly get used to this modern way of handling livestock—shipping, not driving. When it came time for the first big shipment to be loaded out, the wild range sheep were not used to corrals or shipping pens. Even their lead goats failed to function when they were supposed to lead the sheep into stock cars, especially the second deck, to which the leading chute was much higher than the lower. By doing a little research work, the C. & S. soon found a gentle goat that would lead up and through both decks for hours at a time, and he became so prominent that the boys insisted on naming him for some big sheepman or boss.

" 'Most everyone had selected a name for the lead goat. At first it was suggested naming him Bob Dean; next, Jim Cater; third, Sol Floersheim; and last of all Horace Abbot. The name Horace Abbot fitted in because Abbot was the only one in the group that had chin whiskers that matched the goat's.

"At this time there was a tramp or handyman named Timbuck doing odd jobs around town and sleeping in a stall in the livery stable. He and Horace Abbot had adjoining stalls and became great pals. In the busy shipping season Timbuck would be employed to help load out, and many a day you could see Timbuck and Horace Abbot start for the yards early and return late. Timbuck, after a day's work, would take home a pint of whisky, which he called his wake-up tonic. He had taught Horace Abbot to drink out of a bottle. The goat learned how to chew tobacco and kept on dissipating. Many a night he would hang around the back door of the saloon, waiting for Timbuck, and they would start home in the darkness, both of them pretty well stewed. Finally the shipping increased, and Timbuck and Horace Abbot fixed up an old box car on the stockyards siding and ate and slept in it. After a hard day's work they would come downtown to the Favorite Saloon, Timbuck never taking a drink without taking one out to Horace Abbot. They would leave late in the evening, with Timbuck leaning on Abbot, for their home in the box car.

"One day an order came down the line from the dispatcher's office at Trinidad, giving orders for Number 19 to pick up all empties on the siding at Clayton. Well, that night the car that was used as a home by Timbuck and Horace Abbot was attached to Number 19, very likely unbeknown to the loving friends inside. No doubt after this nocturnal ride they awakened in some greener field. When it was discovered that they were really gone, one old wise hombre out of a group said: 'Clayton has lost a fine citizen and a good lead goat.'

"Later many rumors came in. One was that they had arrived at Pueblo, and that Timbuck went into the mountains to prospect and that the C. & S. had given Horace Abbot the Keeley treatment and was using him as a leader in stockyards and packing houses."[1]

The Ghost Sheep Dog

"Instinct and training—what's the difference? Instinct in an animal needs no training. You can train some dogs to be good shepherds, but the best shepherd dog I ever heard anything about had absolutely nothing to do with men and men had absolutely nothing to do with him. Instinct is what comes into a creature either through ancestral blood or through food. They say, you know—these *pastor* people—that the milk any female gives any suckling carries the instincts of her kind."

I nodded. The man seemed to be a philosopher and not a mere watcher of sheep. His features and tones of voice expressed an incredulity not conveyed in the printed word. He went on.

"They—these Mexican sheep-herder people—used to tell about a dog over in the country between Devil's River and the Conchos that managed a flock of ghost sheep, grazing them on the prairie at night and bedding them by day in the breaks. He knew how to protect them against bad weather. He was a little black-and-white dog, not of the shepherd strain at all, a little dog scarcely bigger than a large gopher, a little gopher-built dog that seemed to run on his belly. Various *pastores* got a fleeting glimpse of him in moonlight, though no one ever laid hand on him. Nobody could see his sheep, however.

"Like the extraordinary offspring of some of the gods in old tales, this extraordinary dog, so the story went, was born out in the fields. No sooner was he born than his mother left him, frightened away by something strange, maybe a dog-repelling man, something. Anyhow, the puppy, its eyes still closed, was left to fare alone. Understand now, I am just telling you the story—not what I know."

The shepherd philosopher looked for encouragement; then he went on, while my thoughts turned for the moment to those English herders of olden days said to be dreamers very different from hilarious cow hands.

"It so happened that an old solitary ewe came along smelling the

---

[1] Jack Potter, *Union County Leader,* Clayton, New Mexico.

By Merrill Bishop. From *In the Shadow of History,* Texas Folk-Lore Society Publications No. XV, J. Frank Dobie, Mody C. Boatright, Harry H. Ransom, editors, pp. 119–121.

ground. Catching the dog scent, she naturally bristled up a bit as ewes will do. Then, seeing the pup did not move, she nosed it to investigate. Then the pup did the smelling. He was hungry. He had never suckled his own mother, but instinct guided him to the ewe's udder. I don't know where her lambs were. That makes no difference. She had milk.

"She responded to the suckling and lay down. Soon she got up, expecting that the lamb she had found would get up also, but it didn't. It just lay there and whimpered. Not knowing what else to do now, the ewe pushed it into some grass and hid it as she must have hidden many a lamb of her own. She grazed a little and then came back and lay down by the pup and fed it. Night came, and she and the pup stayed together. The attachment between sheep and dog had begun. In the end she brought up the pup.

"Before a year had passed, the *pastor* people knew that a strange pup was wandering through the herds. The next thing they knew, this maturing pup, which was never to get big, was cutting out whatever sheep he wanted. Nobody saw him cutting out sheep, but the most careful and reliable *pastores* were losing sheep from their flocks. At the same time not a shepherd dog, not even the best trained and dependable dog, would attack the thief any more than a man would attack a ghost.

"The ghost dog, which wasn't exactly a ghost either, could be glimpsed occasionally, but, as I have said, the sheep he kept couldn't be seen. The *pastor* people decided that the ewe-dog had changed the nature of his sheep so that they would feed at night like deer and stay asleep in some hidden place during the day. The ewe-dog had his flock established. That fact could not be doubted. Through the milk that had nurtured him the dog had an instinct that made him know the needs of his sheep; at the same time his proper blood made him a guard against coyotes.

"But no matter how many instincts there are, whether real or ghostly, it is the primal instinct that has always made the smartest of men and animals step aside. So the *pastor* people decided to use a female of his species to catch the dog that was stealing their sheep and turning them into ghosts. They had a bitch in heat and they put her out in a glade which, signs told them, the ghost herd was using. They told her to stay there. She obeyed.

"She stayed until the ewe-dog came along. The men who set the trap forgot that she might be interested in the male as the male was in her. She followed him. In time she came back—alone. The ewe-dog about the same time quit stealing more sheep for his herd, though whether he quit guiding his ghost flock is not known.

"The female shepherd dog came back and had her litter of pups. They grew up squatty, with that gopher-like build, black-and-white. They became the most remarkable sheep dogs the country has ever known. Their sire transmitted into them the combined sheep and dog instincts that made him the master herder. To this day a man with a sheep dog to sell can get more for it, maybe, if he alleges that it descended from the ewe-dog.

"Men are worse than animals in lots of ways. They believe what they want to believe."

Pastors and Snakes

Jesus was peculiar in that he never stopped moving his feet. He never let his feet rest for a moment, even though his body was still. At last this incessant shuffling got on my nerves and I asked why he was never still.

"Señor, it is the habit I have acquired by long years of herding sheep. You are probably aware that the rattlesnake is often about on the warpath. The rattlesnake is harmless when he is making love or looking for food or water, but, señor, he is seldom harmless. A bite is sure death to a lone *pastor*. I keep my feet and legs constantly moving so that if I come across one he will not bite me. For a rattlesnake will not bite a moving object. Ah, señor, rattlesnakes remove their fangs when they are courting so that if they quarrel they cannot hurt each other, and when they go forth hunting food or drink, they leave their poison sacs in their den, so as not to poison their food."

Apolinario Orrites and I had been busy all day gathering "strays" out of an adjoining ranch with the help of the neighboring ranchman. We had made an early start, and were coming home tired after a long hot summer day. Just about dark we stirred up a rattlesnake. I held "Poly's" horse while he killed the snake. When he returned to his horse, he remarked that he believed the snake had taken out his poison sacs. I explained to him, in a tired, half-hearted sort of a way, that a snake could not remove his poison glands at will. He contradicted me, and I will do my best to give a translation of what he had to say:

"Señor, I know that you have studied much, and of many things you know much more than I. I have lived in the open all my life, and I have had much talk with *pastores* who, as you know, are very lonesome and spend much time studying all forms of life. They tell me that

---

From "The Mexican *Pastor*," by Edgar B. Kincaid, *Southwestern Lore*, edited by J. Frank Dobie, Publications of the Texas Folk-Lore Society, No. IX, 1931, pp. 66–68. Copyright, 1931, by the Texas Folk-Lore Society. Dallas: The Southwest Press.

. . . [The sheep and goat] *pastor* is still a familiar figure along the Texas border, on the unfenced government lands of New Mexico, and elsewhere in the Southwest. Solitary, superstitious, patient, and seldom "brainy," he has strongly marked individual characteristics, and when he has a chance to talk is apt to dispense a lore peculiar to his kind.—E.B.K., *ibid.*, p. 63.

when a rattlesnake gets ready to eat or drink he removes his poison sacs, leaving them on a clean rock. I have never seen these poison sacs, after they were removed, but I have talked to many who have, and I owe my life to this very fact.

"You know goats are sometimes *muy diablo,* and this day they had given me much trouble. I was so tired and thirsty that I was not cautious as I usually am. When I got to a spring, I had no eyes for anything but the water. I threw myself on the ground and put my mouth to the water, but I did not drink. Just beside me was a very large rattlesnake, and I heard him rattle as he moved. This snake did not offer to bite me but began to run. There were plenty of rocks and I killed him very quickly, and then I drank. After I had time to rest, I was very sorry that I had been so quick to kill the snake, for was not this snake on his way to get his poison sacs? I would have had the chance to see what very few ever see. The snake had evidently just eaten, and, being thirsty, had gone to the spring to get some water. No, señor, I could not find the poison sacs, but I know that if he had had them, I should have been bitten."

One Nickel

Cristobal Nuñez and Transito Baca are two venerable residents of Llanito, brothers-in-law, and equally addicted to legitimately obtained hiccoughs. Having amassed a few round *pesos* by labor at a sheep-shearing, they formed a partnership, bought ten gallons of whiskey in Santa Fe, and started over mountainous roads to retail it in outlying *plazas* from a small cart. Each knowing the other's failing, they swore a solemn oath that neither would give the other a drop during the trip; and thus forearmed, they set out. They had spent every cent, save a nickel which Cristobal had accidentally retained.

"Valgame Dios!" groaned Cristobal, after they had gone a few miles, "but it is very long without to drink. For the love of the Virgin, *cuñado,* give me a little to me."

"But how! That thou not rememberest our compromise?" asked the virtuous Transito.

Cristobal groaned again, and rode a few miles in silence. Then an idea percolated through his shaggy locks—the nickel in his pocket.

"It is truth, *compadre,* that we compromised not to give us not one drop. But of the *to sell* was nothing said. See! That I have *cinco centavos!* Sell me a drinklet to me."

"'Sta bueno!" said Transito, pocketing the nickel and pouring his

---

From *The Land of Poco Tiempo,* by Charles F. Lummis, pp. 13–15. Copyright, 1893, by Charles Scribner's Sons; 1921, by Charles F. Lummis. New York: Charles Scribner's Sons. 1928.

Cf. "Cheap," *A Treasury of Jewish Folklore* (New York, 1948), pp. 11–12.

companion a small dose. "The saints are witnesses that I kept my oath. I give not, but sell."

Everything takes its time in New Mexico; but in half an hour the inspiration got across the wagon to Transito.

"Carrambas! How buy not *I* a drinklet *también?* I have *cinco centavos* now. Sell-me a little to me, *compadre."* And Cristobal did so, thereby regaining his nickel.

"But wait-me a so-little, and I will buy a drinklet from thee also, that we may drink joined."

Back went the nickel to Transito; and in a moment the two old men were clinking glasses mutually *"á la vuestra salud, compadre."* This seemed more social, till a disturbing thought occurred to Transito.

"Pero hombre! Thou hast had two drinks, and I only one. Go, sell-me to me another, that we are equals."

This logic was not to be gainsaid; and Cristobal doled out the whiskey and resumed the nimble coin. Just then a trace broke.

"Ill-said horses! And of ill-said fathers and mothers! That now we have to go to camp here. Tomorrow we will fix the harness."

But they did not fix it to-morrow, nor the next day, nor the next. They just stayed in camp and attended strictly to business—which was remarkably good. Now Cristobal was merchant, and Transito customer; and now *al contrario.* No one else came along to disturb the routine of trade, until the third day, when a sheep-herder found two white-headed men sleeping beside an empty ten-gallon keg. A much-worn nickel lay in one half-closed fist, and the wool-propeller took it along for luck.

"And how to you went the journey?" people asked in Llanito.

"Mala suerte," sighed Cristobal, sadly. "We sold all our whiskey; by some *ladrón* robbed to us asleep of all we had taken in."

New Mexico Sheepherder's Lore

"And why do you call your burros *almanaques?"* I asked, as Basilico Garduño was fixing a pallet for me near the fire. "Oh, they are the almanac of the *pastor.* I can tell of sudden changes in the weather by watching their actions and hearing their braying at unusual hours of the day or night." That was new to me. I had heard burros called many things, some of them unprintable, but never almanacs.

My bed consisted of three woolly sheepskins next to the ground, a blanket over these, and another with which to cover myself. Additional warmth, if needed, would have to be supplied by the "poor man's blanket," the fire, wood for which stood neatly stacked close enough so that I could throw an occasional stick on it without getting up.

By Lorin W. Brown. From "Men at Work." Manuscripts of the Federal Writers' Project of the Works Progress Administration for the State of New Mexico.

My friend . . . lay on a pallet . . . on the opposite side of the fire. Both of us had lighted cigarettes, and I talked to him about the stars. He had interesting names for some of the more familiar constellations. The Pleiades, he called *Las Cabrillas* (herd of little goats), the Great Dipper was *La Carreta* (the cart), and he pointed out to me what seemed to be one star, but which were, he said, in reality two, if your eyesight was good enough. He said the Indians used this phenomenon to test the eyes of their young men. I had to take his word for this; all I could see was one star. *La Estrella del Pastor,* as the morning star was called, received its name, according to him, from the fact that the shepherd is supposed to be up when it appears. He added drily that all the stars might also be called Shepherd's Stars since a *pastor* sees them all nearly every night, sleeping as he does with one eye open, especially when on the summer range in the high mountains.

The moon appeared over the top of El Cerro Redondo. Basilico said it promised wet weather because its points were tilted so that it would not hold water. He told me he could figure in advance the different phases of the moon for months ahead. This knowledge he found very useful in caring for his flock. For instance, a full moon was of great advantage at lambing time. He therefore figured out the exact day to turn the rams (*carneros mesos*) in with the ewes so that the lambs would begin to drop while there was a full moon to light the *pastor's* labors. A full moon was also to be desired when the sheep were driven from summer to winter range or back again.

* * * * *

As we crossed a small stream, Basilico stopped to pluck a green feathery plant which grew under the overhanging bank, close by some violets. "What is that?" I asked, as he thrust the fernlike wisps into his mouth. "It is *plumajillo;* very good for the stomach. Try some?" It was bitter to the taste and should have rated very high in the locality, where the efficacy of any medicine is measured by the strength of its flavor. Basilico asked if I would bring him some *hediondilla* from the vicinity of Socorro the next time I was down there. I confessed that I did not know what that was, but from the name, which means "stinking," it could not be anything pleasant. I learned later that it was the creosote bush, a popular remedy for kidney ailments.

"You know much about herbs, no?"

"Yes, every *pastor* knows about *yerbas del campo* (wild herbs). It is well that he does, he is so much alone. Only a broken leg holds any terror for a sheepherder. I can name you a great number of herbs, and the particular benefits of each, but that would take a long time. Some other time I will give you some of each and directions for using them."

After the sheep had bedded down, as we sat smoking our after-supper cigarette, Basilico talked about herbs. He recited a list that would put an herbalist's catalogue to shame. The most prominent was *osha,* which is so highly regarded by native New Mexicans that it is considered virtually a cure-all. Others were *altamisa, Chimaja, chamiso, orteguilla, poleo, yerba buena, amole, canaigra.*[1] The only way one could fix this list of names in mind would be, he suggested, to get a sample of each and record its properties in detail. While on the subject, Basilico also mentioned *pingue* (Colorado rubber plant) and loco weed, from which the pastor must guard his sheep. *Pingue* is especially destructive in the month of October, or after the first frosts. It is more resistant to frost than grass, and stays green and tender after the latter has begun to dry up. For this reason the sheep turn to the *pingue* and great losses result, unless the *pastor* is careful to keep his flock away from infested regions during that critical period. Loco weed causes losses in the months of February and March. Stock that feed on it go "crazy"; it affects them like a drug; having once tasted it they cannot leave it alone. Eating nothing else, they stagger along, their actions extremely erratic, and finally die from lack of nourishment.

Sheep Shearing

In the morning the shearing crew arrived amid a cloud of dust in a small truck piled high with bedding rolls and other equipment. They were a noisy band of itinerants, shearing sheep on a commission basis all over the State and into Colorado. Basilico would have nothing to do with them, except for handling his sheep so as to keep the shearers constantly supplied. To prepare the sheep for shearing, he would drive about a hundred of them at a time into a small adobe room with but one opening. Here, closely confined, the warmth of their bodies caused "sweating," which makes shearing easier. To get them into the room, he used the patriarch of the small herd of goats he kept with his sheep. It was amusing to see how well the bearded old rogue knew his business. He no sooner entered the door with the sheep close on his heels, then he stepped aside near the exit. He knew that he must get out again and be ready for the next bunch. His whole demeanor showed his supreme contempt for the victims of his guile and his wish to escape close confinement with such idiots.

The sheared sheep, looking more foolish than ever in their nakedness, were held by the dogs in a corner of the hills, while Basilico took care of doling out the others to the shed, as required. I watched the shearers deftly turn their victims, the wool clip rolling off in a soft mat. As each was finished, a cry of *"Uno!"* (one) brought the boss, who acted as inspector. His *"Bueno!"* (good) permitted the shearer to re-

[1] Cf. L. S. M. Curtin, *By the Prophet of the Earth* (Santa Fe, 1949).

Ibid.

lease the animal as properly sheared. A metal disk was handed the worker, to be used at the end of the day in computing his pay.

The crew of shearers would be in the neighborhood for several days, since other owners had requested the use of the sheds for shearing their flocks. I knew Basilico hated to remain in their company any longer than was necessary. He would lose his temper under the bantering of the shearers, who treated all *pastores* with contempt. The crowning insult was that they persisted in calling him Basil Loco. I left that evening, atop a load of the huge sacks into which the wool was packed after shearing.

A Deal in Wool

Through the door walks a newcomer bearing a sack stuffed with wool. Placing it upon the scales, the trader notes an unwonted heaviness—a soggy weight that bespeaks a contents not wholly from ovine backs. Without a word, he retires to the store room and empties the bag on a large pile of wool. Then he walks to the cash drawer, extracts several small coins, and lays upon the counter eighty cents.

Quickly the customer's genial countenance is transformed by an expression of mingled amazement and indignation. A string of slithering, guttural words flow from his lips, which the white man's practised ears interpret as follows:

"You cheated me! You're a stingy *Pelakana!* You know that wool was worth a dollar and four bits!"

Unruffled by this outburst, the merchant regards his patron with a faint smile of amusement while a torrent of invective and censure is heaped upon him. At last it is his turn to speak:

"The wool in that sack came from the backs of two sheep; but the water in the wool came from my spring. I saw you dipping it out a little while ago. Now, if you had brought your own water, I might have paid you ten or twenty cents more; but do you think I am foolish enough to pay for water that already belongs to *me*?"

There is a loud guffaw from all present. It is *touché* for the trader, and Navajo sense of humor is keen. The seller at first looks downcast and sheepish, but soon joins the merriment—and all is well.

From "Tales of a Navajo Trading-Post," by Philip Johnston, *Touring Topics,* Vol. 25 (June, 1933), No. 7, Part I, pp. 16–17. Copyright, 1933, by the Automobile Club of Southern California. Los Angeles.

IV. SETTLERS

It was a frontier saying that homesteading was a gamble: "Yeah, the United States Government is betting you 160 acres of land that you can't live on it eight months."—EDITH EUDORA KOHL

"Clodhoppers versus Grasshoppers"

Heavy freight trains were delayed for hours by their gathering on the track in large numbers, the wheels crushing their bodies and forming an oily, soapy substance, which caused the wheels to spin around and around, with no power to go forward. The engineer would stand in the cab looking as humiliated as a dethroned monarch, and all hands would proceed to sand the track. "All aboard!" the conductor would shout, the train would proceed a little distance, and again be brought to a standstill. The same process would be repeated, except that our engineer did sometimes use language not the most euphonious.

They were unwelcome customers in the dry-goods stores; they ate into the lace curtains and attacked everything that had any starch into it. Whether they were working in the interest of the manufacturers or consumers is not well defined. The proprietors and clerks shooed and brushed and shook the goods, hustled the intruders from shelf and counter. The locusts whizzed and whirred about and probably wondered why they were interfered with, as dry goods were mighty poor living anyway.

The pests, continually moving in every direction, made their way into the houses; indignant housekeepers swept them up in dustpans full, and then in larger quantities. They invaded the pantry, hopped into pans of milk, or helped themselves to the best in the larder. They annoyed the cook beyond measure. One lady was busy making plum-butter, when into the boiling mass lit a big grasshopper; it was no sooner removed than another and another unfortunately lost their lives in this tragic manner. Through the whole afternoon the fight was kept up, and the lady declares to this day that she fears more than one hopper was boiled in that plum-butter.

Another said: "One day they were so thick about my house I could not raise the cover of the kettle to see if the meat was cooked enough

---

From *A Kansas Farm, or the Promised Land,* by Fannie McCormick, pp. 81–86. Copyright, 1891, by Fannie McCormick. New York: John B. Alden, Publisher.

without a lot of grasshoppers going in, and I did not know what to do. They even crawled down the nose of the tea-kettles; at least four or five of them would be found swimming about on the water in them, and there was no other possible mode of entrance. They crept into the sleeping-rooms, wardrobes, trunks, and boxes, doing great damage unless a continual warfare was made against them."

One lady took down a nice cashmere dress to put on and found the whole front width eaten to shreds, and a linen lawn hanging near it was also destroyed. When putting on a dress it was no uncommon thing for two or three grasshoppers to go buzzing out of the lower end of the sleeves.

The kitchen water-bucket was dispensed with, as it only contained a lot of struggling grasshoppers, and everybody went to the pump to get a drink or fill the kettles. . . .

The few plants and shrubs that consented to take root in the hard, wild soil, and were growing under the windows and in the yards, were very precious to the women here in those times, and when the grasshoppers came one lady pinned sheets closely around the vines under the windows, little dreaming that the pests would destroy both.

One source of revenue in a new country is the poultry-yard, which is usually looked after by the women, and is quite profitable, often yielding sufficient income to pay all grocery bills, and frequently to purchase everything needed for the house. When the grasshoppers came the chickens feasted upon them as if they intended to eat up the whole swarm, and one person jokingly remarked that there was *one* good thing about the coming of the grasshoppers—"we don't have to feed our chickens any more." Nor was she ever troubled with feeding that flock again, for every one died. Eating such quantities of grasshoppers seemed to poison the fowls, and out of three or four hundred not one would survive.

The grasshoppers were an unmitigated scourge, without one redeeming feature, and how Pharaoh could have resisted the plague of locusts will always remain a mystery to those who suffered by their depredations in modern times. They remained in each place about a week, and when the wind blew from a favorable quarter arose and departed. In 1874 they troubled the whole country, more or less, from the Rocky Mountains to the Missouri River. They left behind them a scene of desolation; even the trees had been stripped of leaves, and the tender twigs of fruit-trees had been eaten off. Many orchards were entirely destroyed.

Our people were for the time being paralyzed and helpless; but did they sit down and repine over the calamity? Not a bit of it. With true Kansas grit they bestirred themselves to make the most of a bad job. A plain statement of the case was given to the public; some counties appointed special committees to go East for supplies, and other counties voted "relief bonds" to help themselves.

Cyclone Yarns

I. The Brush Man

Near the end of a sultry afternoon on August 16, 1910, a tornado passed near Hartwell, Nebraska. An agent for a patented scrub brush was demonstrating a sample of his wares at the door of a farm home when the storm struck, whirling him in the air, and removing with the exception of the house, every stock and straw from the premises. The last gust of the storm dropped the agent once more at the farm house door. "As I was saying," he began, "this brush is a regular cyclone. It sweeps clean and does a thorough job."

II. Western Economy

On June 6, 1912, a cyclone passed over Stillwell, Oklahoma. One of the early settlers in the community had dug a wide deep well and had curbed the walls with pieces of native rock. Misfortune dogged the steps of the pioneer until the point was reached where the mortgage was due and he was about to be dispossessed when the cyclone crossed his place; the "twister" pulled up the old well as a derrick would lift a straw and carried it several hundred feet where it was left firmly planted but upside down near the farmer's barn. He plastered it inside and out and has used it ever since as a silo; from the old well gushed a geyser of oil. The farmer now has a summer home in the Adirondacks, and a winter home in Palm Beach.

III. Ladies Aid

On July 13, 1913, a cyclone passed near Sweetwater, Nebraska. .One of the members of the Ladies Aid Society was filling an ice cream freezer with the unfrozen constituents of that delicacy in preparation for the ice cream social at the church in town that evening. She had just clamped the lid down when the storm struck, whisking the freezer

---

From *Nebraska Folklore Pamphlets, Number Thirteen, Tall Tales,* reproduced from material gathered for a book on the folklore of the State, issued irregularly, at least once each month, by the Federal Writers' Project in Nebraska, prepared in co-operation with the State Superintendent of Public Instruction, pp. 6–8.

By George L. Jackson. Lincoln, Nebraska. July, 1938.

People of the effete east do not, as a rule, understand the tornadoes of the "States of the Plains." When New Englanders or New Yorkers read newspaper accounts of a western tornado in which straws are alleged to have been driven through trees, or the feathers plucked from a flock of chickens, they are inclined to raise their eyebrows and sniff contemptuously, thus manifesting their doubts as to the reporter's veracity.

Natives of the prairie states are numerous indeed who can vouch for the truthfulness of all the reported "freaks of the storm." Scientists have painstakingly investigated much meteorological data that tend to show conclusively that the "fishy" sounding newspaper stories are not the figments of disordered minds but rather are true incidents and of fairly common occurrence.—G.L.J., *ibid.,* pp. 5–6.

from her hands and hurling it aloft. The freezer was found on the church steps, filled with hailstones, and the cream frozen to a turn.

IV. The Lord Provides

On the 18th of May in 1916, a man near Scotland, South Dakota, had just put the finishing touches on a garage in preparation for a new Ford that he intended purchasing when one of the typical midwest cyclones appeared on the horizon. After the passage of the storm he emerged from his cyclone cellar and was surprised to find in his garage a brand new Buick bearing a Kansas license tag.

V. A "Honey"

One afternoon a whirlwind swept into our yard, struck the bee hives and played swing your partners right and left with the bees. Then it spun the windlass of the well around like a crank and it followed the bucket and rope right down into the well. When the whirlwind reached the bottom it shot the bucket sky high and blew the water out with a roar. The water fell a second later like a mighty cloudburst.

Pa found the old windlass blowed chuckful of bee stingers drove porcupine-fashion right into the wood. The well was bone dry and has never freshened since. The bucket was standing by the overturned bee hive and was full of clear strained honey.[1]

[1] Told by Mrs. J. A. Milliken, Aurora.

Dugout and Sod House

. . . When the hardy settler began the conquest of the prairie, he found at hand material for shelter and fuel. The dugout and the sod house provided shelter, and buffalo chips and prairie grass served for fuel. Where timber was available it was natural for the people to make the conventional log house. Even in the eastern part of the trans-Missouri-Red River territories, however, dugouts and makeshift, hay-covered, sod structures were used at first for shelter. As settlement crept westward and timber became more scarce, the homesteader came to depend more and more on soil and grass for homes. The typical prairie home was made of sod or was dug out of the side of a hill or ravine.

It was customary for the emigrant upon locating his homestead to arrange a temporary shelter until the permanent dwelling was ready for occupancy. When the wagon halted, the head of the family took out a spade and began to construct the dwelling. The dugout was more easily made than the sod house and hence many pioneers, anxious to

From *The Sod-House Frontier, 1854–1890,* A Social History of the Northern Plains from the Creation of Kansas & Nebraska to the Admission of the Dakotas, by Everett Dick, pp. 110–111, 112, 113–115.

get settled and to plant crops, made this type of dwelling their first home. In a few days excavation for the dugout was complete. The family meanwhile lived in the covered wagon box while the father used the running gears to haul the logs, poles, brush, and grass needed for the roof and front of the dugout. The mother of the family cooked the meals by a camp-fire and the group slept in the wagon or other temporary abode. Sometimes a hole dug in the ground and covered with canvas or sheets supplied the necessary shelter. Mr. and Mrs. M. E. Babcock of Fillmore County, Nebraska, made their first home by sewing four sheets together for a tent. Within a few days a windstorm blew down their shelter at night and wrecked their covering irreparably. The first residence in Antelope County, Nebraska, was a shack made of poles and grass.

The dugout was a room dug in the side of a hill or ravine. A few rails or posts were used to make a door frame and possibly a window. The door, of course, opened out into the ravine. The front wall was made of square cut turf, or logs if they were obtainable. A roof sloping back onto the hill was made of poles or logs covered over with brush, a layer of prairie grass thick enough to hold dirt, and finally a layer of dirt over the grass. It was by no means ideal, however, for after a rain the high water often drove the occupants from their home. It was necessary to dig a trench from the house to the drainage level to carry water off the floor. Then, too, a frog pond for a front yard meant mosquitoes in summer and a very unhealthful environment. Even in dry weather the place was dirty.

* * * * *

Not infrequently a combination sod house and dugout was made. The sod house, although a little harder to build, was much more satisfactory and lasted some years. It was widely used even in the eastern portion of the prairie states. . . .

* * * * *

A spade was used to cut the sod into bricks about three feet long. These bricks were then carried to the building site by wagon or by a float made of planks or the forks of a tree. J. Clarence Norton of La Harpe, Kansas, related that in building the house on the homestead, the line for the wall was drawn after dark so that it could be located by the north star. For the first layer of the wall the three foot bricks were placed side by side around the foundation except where the door was to be made. The cracks were then filled with dirt and two more layers were placed on these. The joints were broken as in brick laying. Every third course was laid crosswise of the others to bind them together. This process was continued until the wall was high enough to put a roof on the structure. A door frame and two window frames were set in the wall and the sod built around them at the proper time. Sometimes the builder drove hickory withes down into the wall as a sort of reinforcement. The gables were built up of sod or frame according to the means of the settler. The poorer settler built a roof in the crudest manner. A forked post set in each end of the cabin furnished a support for the ridge pole. The rafters were made of poles and the sheeting of brush; a layer of prairie grass covered this, and over all sod was placed. The settler who could afford it put a frame roof on his sod house. In that event sheeting was nailed on the rafters and tar paper spread over the sheeting boards. This was then covered with sods thinner than those used to cover the side walls, and laid with grass side down; the cracks were filled with fine clay. From time to time this dirt filling had to be renewed as the rains carried it away. In a short time great growths of sunflowers and grass appeared on the roofs. If the house were to be plastered, a mixture of clay and ashes was used. If it were to be a smooth finish, the builder took a spade and hewed the wall to a smooth finish and symmetrical proportions. The whole thing, as one pioneer said, was "made without mortar, square, plumb, or greenbacks." All that was needed was a pair of willing hands, and many home seekers came to the plains with no assets other than a wagon cover. The little sod cabin was frequently divided into two rooms by a piece of rag carpet or quilt. The windows and door were closed with buffalo robes or other blankets. The house was crudely furnished. A nail keg and a soap box did duty as chairs. A dry goods box made a table and a rude bed of boards was fashioned in the corner. When the migration immediately following the Civil War broke in its fury, the demand for doors, sashes, and blinds was so great that even small towns ordered in carload lots. The dealer at the little town of Milford, Nebraska, advertised in March, 1871, that he had three carloads of this type of merchandise on the way.

The ordinary sod house had grave faults. Its few windows permitted little light and air for ventilation. The immaculate housekeeper abominated them because they were so hard to keep clean. The dirt and straw kept dropping on everything in the house. The most disagreeable feature of these houses was the leaky roof. Few of the sod-covered houses really turned water. A heavy rain came, soaked into the dirt roof, and soon little rivulets of muddy water were running through the sleepers' hair. The sod-house dweller had to learn to migrate when it rained. If the rain came from the north, the north side of the house leaked, and it was necessary to move everything to the south side, if from the south, a move had to be made again. When the roof was saturated it dripped for three days after the sky was bright without. Dishes, pots, pans, and kettles were placed about the house to catch the continual dripping. One pioneer woman remembered frying pancakes with someone holding an umbrella over her and the stove. A visitor at the home of a Dakota woman said that when great clouds rolled up in the afternoon the lady of the homestead began gathering up all the old dishes in the house and placing them here and there on the floor, on the stove, and on the bed. The visitor remarked that the prairie woman seemed to understand her business for when the rain came down in torrents a few minutes later every drop that came through the numerous holes in the roof of the shack went straight into those vessels. After a heavy rain it was necessary to hang all the bed clothing and wearing apparel on the line to dry. One old settler mentioned keeping the clothes in the covered wagon to keep them dry.

When the roof was well soaked its weight was immense. The heavy rafters sank deeper and deeper into the soggy walls until occasionally the roof caved in or the walls collapsed, burying people underneath the ruins. To prevent this kind of accident, heavy posts were placed in the house to support the roof; these were a great nuisance because they took up so much room. Frequently the cabin was covered with long coarse prairie grass. This type of roof also had the fault of dripping water after a heavy rain.

There were, however, some striking advantages of the sod house. It was cool in summer and warm in winter. There was no fear of the wind blowing it over and no danger of destruction by prairie fires. Neither was there danger of fire from a faulty fireplace. A fireplace was safely built of sod. The average life of a sod house was six or seven years.

Flour-Sack Days

The older woman remembers well the flour-sack days of Texas, and she doesn't have to be so old, either. The sheets, the pillowcases, the tablecloths, the dishtowels, the children's underwear, the doilies and antimacassars and center-table covers, the jelly-strainers, milk-strainers, pudding bags, and overnight cases! Miles of Mexican drawn work went into the flour-sack cloth, miles of hemstitching and tiny tucks, millions of fine, painstaking stitches. The flour sack played a major role in the Texas woman's household economy and art of living.

"I married John," a little lady, now a sprightly seventy-five, often tells, "and I came to Texas to take what might befall. I had been brought up in Philadelphia and been trained for a musical career, so I'd hardly washed a dish or mended a stocking before I came to Texas. But it was all such fun! After two years in our camp my trousseau clothes began to wear out. My dresses were of good, strong material, and I had mended them here and there where the brush had torn them, so that they did very nicely. But my underwear had got quite beyond mending. So one day I asked John about it. 'John,' I said, 'do you think you could get me a few yards of white material at the store the next time you go to town?' 'Honey,' he said, 'I wish I could, but we've barely enough for some things I need for the sheep, and I don't want to ask Schreiner for another dollar till I've paid something back. Could you

---

From *The Golden Hoof,* The Story of the Southwest, by Winifred Kupper, pp. 174–175.

possibly wait till the wool is sold this fall?' I give you my word that I hadn't heard of flour-sack underwear at the time. I had seen very little of women in those two years. So I thought my idea was quite original. I took two flour sacks and fashioned a pair of drawers. Such work as went into them! I always did like pretty underwear; so I stitched ruffles and tucks, very fine tucks, and then added featherstitching. I was very, very proud of them, and I could hardly wait to see John. He came in at last, and as soon as I could I danced out in front of him. 'How do you like my handiwork?' I asked him, and I lifted my skirts and twirled around. He burst out laughing, and he laughed until he had to hold his sides. I was surprised and even a little hurt. I'd spent *hours* on those drawers. But still he laughed. And finally, when he could talk, I found out why. You see, nobody had ever told me how to bleach out the lettering that was on every sack. I had tried boiling, but it had only turned the red letters to a delicate pink. 'Oh, well,' I had told myself, 'the letters will all be lost in the folds.' But they hadn't been; and on the side of me, in back, was plainly printed in large pink letters 'THE PRIDE' and on the other side 'OF TEXAS.' "

Tough Buckskin

Everybody knows that the early pioneers and plainsmen wore clothes of buckskin. They did it not only because cloth was hard to get, but because buckskin, although soft and comfortable, will stand great wear and tear. One may be pardoned, however, if he doubts the story of the strength of buckskin told by a group of old settlers, who were discussing the degeneracy of the present age.

"I was breaking sod in Northern Texas," he said, "with four yoke of oxen. Something frightened them, and we started on a dead run straight for a large sycamore stump, which was at least three feet in diameter.

"The plow struck it about in the center and split it wide open. I was still clinging to the handles of the plow, which went clean through the stump, dragging me after. The stump flew together again and caught me by the seat of my buckskin pants."

"What happened then?" asked one of the listeners.

"Well, sir, would you believe it? We pulled that stump out by the roots."

From the *Youth's Companion*, cited in the Denver Times, July 8, 1902. Clipping files of the Western History Collection, Denver Public Library, Denver, Colorado.

The Rawhide Harness

If, considering technique as well as interpretation of life, I were asked to pick out the best short story dealing with any theme of the Southwest, I should choose Stewart Edward White's "Rawhide." Yet it is but a writing man's utilization of a tradition that, in popular anecdotes of reality and in more popular folk yarns, has for generations been massing itself into a cycle both grim and rollicky. Longhorn hides and men who rode "rawhide horses," swung rawhide ropes and slept on rawhide beds gave the tradition its body and zest. This was during times in a parched land when thirst was supposed to be allayed by keeping either a bullet or a bit of rawhide in the mouth. Rawhide, lead and thirst seem to go together.

One blazing summer day, long ago now, Print Olive rode up on a rustler burning out the brand on one of his cows, in the San Gabriel country. He killed the cow, made the thief help skin her, wrapped him up in the hide, and left him in the sun.

The salient qualities of rawhide are durability and toughness, flexibility and power to stretch when wet, and a corresponding power to contract when dry and remain as stiff as an ax-handle.

Over and over, with multiplied variations, the story has been told of the settler who one summer day hitched a horse with rawhide traces to a "lizard" and went down to the creek a half mile away to drag a barrel of water to his house. Just after he got the barrel filled, a rain came up. With head down, walking close beside the horse so as to use its body as a shield against the driving rain, he drove back up the hill. About the time he stopped beside the kitchen door, the rain ceased and the sun came out. He looked and he saw that he had no sled or barrel of water. All he could see was a thin, long-stretched-out pair of rawhide traces.

The settler was neither startled nor perplexed. He unhitched, threw the hames—to which the forward ends of traces are attached—over a stump, sat down under the shed at the front of his house, and while he slowly chewed tobacco and fanned the gnats away, watched the road. The sun was scorching now and the earth was steaming. After a while he saw the barrel on the sled snailing homeward. The dependable laws of heat and dryness and of rawhide were contracting the traces. Finally the sled stopped right at the stump.

One time a freighter with two wagons of eight oxen each got bogged in the black waxy San Miguel country, in the bottom of a creek. He took the oxen out of his second wagon and hitched them to the first, but still the sixteen oxen couldn't budge the wagon. They would pull, pull, all of them together, laying all their weight against the yoke, not

From *The Longhorns*, by J. Frank Dobie, pp. 221–224, 236. Boston: Little, Brown and Company.

lunging like horses or mules, but steady. Yet the wheels would not move. They seemed vised with steel in the deep, tight mud.

Then the freighter had an idea. He told his helpers to unyoke the oxen and let them graze. He had heard a range bull bellowing down in a thicket. He got the wind, crawled up, and shot him. The bull was an old-timer with hide as thick as an elephant's—almost. The men skinned him. Then the freighter cut a broad band, around and around, out of the thick hide. It was damp and pliable from animal moisture, but he let it soak an hour in the creek water. Then he tied one end of it to the wagon tongue, pulled with all his forces on the other end until the thong was taut, and tied it around a mesquite tree well up on the bank.

The sun was shining. The freighter filled his pipe, smoked, took a nap, chunked up the coals around the coffeepot, drained it, and then, after filling his pipe again, began watching the spokes of his wheels. At last he saw a minute movement. The hot sun was at work. The freighter shifted himself into better shade. Every now and then he could note a fraction of a revolution in the wheels, as slow but as inevitable as the late afternoon prolongation of the shadow of a high mountain across a valley floor.

At the end of the day the wagon was perceptibly forward. That night the freighter let the rawhide soak again. The next morning he fastened it once more to the tongue and stretched it to the mesquite. The sun shone. The rawhide pulled—pulled like raw bacon drawing a boil to a head. The freighter almost got tired of resting, smoking his pipe, and napping in the shade. His oxen were getting a fine rest and fill of grass. He wasn't an impatient man. If he had been, he would not have chosen oxen. Again the rawhide was soaked over night. On the third day it drew the wagon clean out of the mud and up on to the hard bank.

Horse-High, Bull-Strong, and Hog-Tight

The scarcity of timber through this [prairie] section had stimulated the invention of substitutes [for fences]. The chief novelty was wire fence, usually made by fastening three wires on a row of posts with slip cleats. This was only to turn cattle; but a fancy article was made with six strands, which rendered it in local parlance, "horse-high, bull-strong, and pig-tight."

Most of the counties thought it cheaper to forbid pigs running at large. In Missouri and the timbered portions of the border States, I heard this statute denounced in much the same terms as the prohibitory

From *Western Wilds and the Men Who Redeem Them,* An Authentic Narrative, . . . by J. H. Beadle, p. 21. Copyright, 1877, by John T. Jones. Cincinnati, Philadelphia, and Chicago: Jones Brothers & Co.

Cf. Mamie Meredith, "The Nomenclature of American Pioneer Fences," *Southern Folklore Quarterly,* Vol. XV (June, 1951), No. 2, pp. 109–151.

liquor law—"an invasion of our liberties, sir!" Further north popular sentiment was expressed in the pithy saying: "A man's a hog that'll let a hog run."

Toughing It Through with the Weather

People from everywhere settled Northwestern Oklahoma. They brought with them their customs and ideas from North, West, East, and South; and, except that of the Cheyenne Indian, whatever is distinctive in the folklore of that section results from the blending of the imported lore which by adoption became the common property of the country. A small part of it may have developed locally, but it is generally possible to trace the lore to a source outside the state. Conditions have not favored the development of a distinctively local lore. Since about 1900, when the influx of settlers came, the time has been short for such a development; and very brief indeed has been the period from settlement to the development of modern means of transportation and communication that broke down any isolation which might have fostered the formation of a distinct folk. Short, too, seems the time for the blending of the imported lore—so short that in some cases there has been no blend and diametrically opposed views exist side by side. Some contend that a wet new moon is one which stands on its point ready to pour out water, while others as stoutly insist that such a moon is a dry one, because it has been drained of its moisture. Many, long, and heated are the debates I have heard on this question by those who had closely observed the infallibility of their view over long periods of years—but I do not recall having seen an opinion changed by such a discussion.

Among the old timers of Northwest Oklahoma it is very generally believed that the weather does not now reach the severe extremes it formerly did. While it may be due to the vividness of childhood memory, it seems to me that winter weather especially does not show the severity it did twenty-five years ago. History has recorded the rigors of the weather in 1867 when Custer left the newly established Camp Supply and made his way southward through a blizzard to begin his operations against the Indians on the Washita, and the oldest old timer who still lives at Supply tells of the great extremes in weather at Old Fort Supply in the days following her arrival in 1872.

"The storms were worse then than they are now," she says. "I remember when the snow covered everything so deep we had to rap on the inside of our dugout door to attract the attention of the soldiers on the outside so that they would dig the snow away and let us out. One hail-

---

From "You Can't Tell about the Weather," by Walter R. Smith, *Folk-Say, A Regional Miscellany: 1930,* edited by B. A. Botkin, pp. 173–175. Norman: University of Oklahoma Press.

storm broke every window in the fort. The window openings had to be boarded up until other windows could be got, and these had to be requisitioned for and freighted from Leavenworth. It was a month before the windows came, for freighting was slow in them days. And the summers could be as hot and dry as the winters was cold. I've seen hot winds blow for days and days and the whole country withered up dry enough to burn in July. We don't have blizzards like we used to. We still have little old northers, but people would freeze to death in them old-time blizzards. The weather has sure changed."

It would look as if the isolated life she lived at the old army post would have bred faith in weather signs, but such is not the case. Once, when we needed rain badly, I asked her if she didn't think it looked as if it would rain. "I don't know," she replied. "You can't tell about the weather. It may rain to-night, or it may stay dry for a long spell yet. Some say we'll have a hard winter this time, but I don't know. You can't tell."

Such an expression of the hopelessness of all attempts to read weather signs is rare indeed. Every one knows the saying that only fools and newcomers prophesy weather in Oklahoma; but although it is readily enough quoted for the benefit of the newly arrived, it is quite as readily disregarded as soon as he is out of earshot. Those who have lived longest in the country are most likely to make observations about the weather and venture the opinion that the dry weather won't last much longer or that we can't hope for an "open" winter this time.

It seems to me that the chief element of faith in weather lore is optimism. I may be basing my conclusion too much upon my knowledge of the settlement of Northwestern Oklahoma. I remember the flood of settlers which came in about 1900, many of them to leave again in a short time when they could no longer look upon their situation with enough hopefulness to make the struggle bearable. Most of those who "starved out" were not the type to win a country which objected to being won, and they gave up the struggle and left the country in all its stubbornness to those of a hardier nature. To-day, as in the days of settlement, those who "toughed it through" try to see beyond a "streak of bad weather," beyond a dry "spell," to better days ahead—real or hoped for. This optimism, it seems to me, is the chief reason for their faith in weather lore. It is a striking fact that few of the original settlers are not believers in weather lore to a greater or less extent. . . .

The *Chisera* Deals in Rain

A *Chisera,* you must know, is a witch, in this instance a rain-maker. In a dry year the General put the Indians to turning the creek into an irrigating ditch to water the barley. Said they:—

From *The Flock,* by Mary Austin, pp. 231–233. Copyright, 1906, by Mary Austin. Boston and New York: Houghton, Mifflin & Co.

"Why so much bending of backs and breaking of shovel handles? There is a woman at Whiskey Flat who will bring rain abundantly for the price of a fat steer."

"Let her be proven," said the General, like Elijah to the prophets of Baal.

The *Chisera* wanted more than a steer,—beads, calico, the material for a considerable feast, all of which was furnished her. First the Indians fed and then the *Chisera* danced. She leaped before the gods of Rain as David before the Ark of the Lord when it came up from Kirjath-jearim; she stamped and shuffled and swung to the roll of the hollow skins and rattles of rams' horns; three days she danced, and the Indians sat about her singing with their eyes upon the ground. Day and night they sustained her with the whisper and beat of their moaning voices. Is there in fact a vibration in nature which struck into rhythm precipitates rain, as a random chord on the organ brings a rush of tears? At any rate it rained, *and* it rained, and it *rained*! The barley quickened in the field, a thousand acres of mesa flung up suddenly a million sprouting things. Rain fell three weeks. The barley and the wheat lay over heavily, the cattle left off feeding, the budding mesa was too wet to bloom.

"For another steer," said the *Chisera,* "I will make it stop."

So the toll of food, and cloth, and beads was paid again, and in three days the sun broke gloriously on a succulent green world. It is a pity, I think, that the *Chisera* is dead.

The Squatter's Farewell

One time, a squatter on a section of [Texas] state land to the west built a shack on his squat, settled his growing family in the shack, lived there the three years required for "proving up" his claim, and then sold out. Unable to afford a well and a windmill, he had, all during the three years, hauled water in barrels from another man's well several miles away. After delivering his estate to the purchaser, he drove away in a rickety wagon containing all the worldly goods the family owned. A hundred yards off, he stopped his team, got down, and walked back to the shack. The new owner was leaning in the front door watching. The squatter picked up the bucket beside the water barrel, dipped it in, pulled it out full, and then deliberately threw the contents over the roof.

"Wait a minute there. What are you wasting all that water for?" the new owner cried out.

"I've always had a hankering to know if the roof would leak."

From "Texas," by J. Frank Dobie, *Holiday,* Vol. 4 (October, 1948), No. 4, pp. 94–95.

The Plow That Broke the Plains

One day in the spring of 1883 as a Scandinavian farmer, John Christiansen, plowed his fields in . . . North Dakota, he looked up to find that he was being watched . . . by an old and solemn Sioux Indian.

Silently the old Indian watched as the dark soil curled up and the prairie grass was turned under. Christiansen stopped, leaned against the plow handle, pushed his black Stetson back on his head, rolled a cigarette. He watched amusedly as the old Indian knelt, thrust his fingers into the plow furrow, measured its depth, fingered the sod and the buried grass.

Then the old Indian straightened up, looked at the farmer.

"Wrong side up," he said, and went away.

For a number of years that was regarded as a very amusing story indeed, betraying the ignorance of the poor Indian. Now there's a marker on Highway No. 10 in North Dakota on the spot where the words were spoken—a little reminder to the white man that his red brother was not so dumb.

What Made San Ysidro Stop Plowing

No people are closer to or more familiar with their saints than the descendants of the Spanish *conquistadores* of New Mexico. Living as they have in isolation for so long a period, they have come gradually to localize the stories of many of their most popular saints and to assign to them provincial attributes in keeping with the New Mexico environment. The following localization of such a story, coupled with one of the ancient folk-sayings of the Spanish Colonials, concerns San Ysidro, the farmers' saint, and comes from Quemado, a little plaza situated in one of the foothill valleys north of Santa Fe. This story is set down just as it was told by one of the older inhabitants of Quemado, except that the Spanish of the version has been rendered freely into English.

San Ysidro was a small bean- and chili-rancher and lived near the Rio Grande, on one side of which stood his house, while his fields lay on the other.

From *Montana: High, Wide, and Handsome,* by Joseph Kinsey Howard, p. 14. Copyright, 1943, by Yale University Press. New Haven.

From "New Mexico Legends," by Frank G. Applegate, *Southwest Review,* Vol. 17 (January, 1932), No. 2, pp. 199–201. Copyright, 1932, by the Southwest Review. Dallas, Texas: Southern Methodist University.

Santa Rita was his wife and she was a very good woman, for every day she would cook a fine dinner and take it to her husband where he worked in the fields. When she came to the river and was about to cross over to the fields, the water, out of respect for her holiness, would separate, part of it flowing upstream and part of it downstream, so that she might cross over without getting wet. For this reason we always pray to Santa Rita for help in times of floods and high waters.

One spring, on the fifteenth of May, which is San Ysidro's fiesta day, San Ysidro crossed the river and began plowing his fields. But an angel soon appeared before him and said, "San Ysidro, God has sent me to tell you that you must not plow today, for it is your fiesta day and holy, and He will not like it if you plow on a saint's day." San Ysidro, however, did not stop his oxen and only shouted to the angel, "I'm sorry, angel, but you tell God I can't stop plowing now, for the season is very late this year. It is now already the fifteenth of May and my beans and chili should have been planted long before this." The angel, who was now following along in the furrow which San Ysidro continued calmly to plow, again called to San Ysidro: "God told me to tell you that if you didn't stop plowing He would send a hail-storm to ruin your beans and chili when they come up." "Well," San Ysidro called back over his shoulder, but without slowing down, "you can just tell God I'm going to plow this field today, saint's day or no saint's day, and that I'll make the best of His hail-storm when it comes and save all the plants I can."

The angel, instead of returning an answer to this, simply vanished, and San Ysidro continued with his work. But it was not long before a second angel appeared in the field, and this one also commanded San Ysidro to stop his plowing. But instead of stopping, San Ysidro only whacked his oxen the harder and as he set his plow a little deeper in the ground, replied to the angel somewhat testily: "There is no use for you to talk to me. Whatever happens, I'm going to plow this field today; I don't care if it is my fiesta. And I can tell you further, it would be just the same to me if it were the fiesta of all the saints combined, instead of just my own." "Well," said the angel meekly, "I can only tell you what God told me to tell you. He said to tell you that if you didn't stop plowing this time He would send cutworms and grasshoppers to eat all the beans and chili that the hail didn't destroy."

San Ysidro was a little vexed by this time, but he remained as calm as possible as he replied to the angel: "You can just tell God to send on His cutworms and His grasshoppers, or any kind of bugs He has, and I'll kill all of them I can. And while you are about it, you can also tell Him I'm going to plow this field today, whatever happens, and that I'd be pleased if He wouldn't annoy me further by sending you young angels down here. There must be something more useful He could have you doing."

At this retort the second angel vanished suddenly, but before San Ysidro had plowed even one more furrow, a third angel made his appearance and said: "San Ysidro, God says that if you don't mind Him and stop plowing this minute, He will get really angry and send a bad neighbor to live right next door to you."

Upon hearing these words, San Ysidro dropped his goad and shouted "Whoa!" to his oxen. When they had stopped he drew his plow out of the ground as quickly as possible and then, turning toward the angel, said: "Tell God He wins. I give up. I would try to make the best of His hail-storms and cutworms and grasshoppers, or anything else of the sort He could send me, but to have a bad neighbor is too much of a trial for even a saint."

The Piñon

Our most important contribution to the horticulture of the West . . . is the piñon tree. A species of pine, it is too scrubby to be used as lumber, but it does furnish fuel of a quality unsurpassed and unsurpassable. I stand on that statement, defying all challengers. The piñon is as resinous as pitch pine, but is a denser wood and burns longer. A rich piñon knot, too heavy to lift, can be set afire with a single match (if you're skillful about it). When it gets to burning, stand back or scorch.

Aside from having warmed the Southwest for a countless number of generations, the piñon tree bears a crop that has furnished food for the same generations, and is today one of considerable commercial value. The piñon nut is known to the trade as the pine nut, possibly because there is no letter *ñ* in the English alphabet and the pronunciation of "pinyon," were it so spelled, would be pinion instead of pin-*yówn* as it should be. I feel personally affronted when I am offered at a candy store a small cellophane bag of "pine nuts,"[1] price ten cents, and am told they came from the "pinion" tree.

I'm accustomed to piñons in carload lots or even warehouse lots! I believe it was fifty carloads that went out of Magdalena in our best piñon year. The wholesale house who shipped them told me they'd drawn a single check for thirty-five thousand dollars and Magdalena is only one of a dozen shipping points in New Mexico alone. There is also Arizona, Colorado and Utah. Eastern candymakers and more particularly New York's pushcart trade furnish the market, and there has been a steadily increasing foreign demand. The nut's oil content is as rich as its food value is high.

But, alas, the piñon is a rugged individualist and bears its crop not with any regularity, but when it gets ready. Whatever the natural conditions which determine when it bears and when it doesn't, they have

From *No Life for a Lady,* by Agnes Morley Cleaveland, pp. 293–297. Copyright, 1941, by Agnes Morley Cleaveland. Boston: Houghton Mifflin Company.

[1] Known as Indian nuts in the East.

not yet been established. Possibly they will be. Meantime, it pleases me to think that the piñon tree is doing as it pleases when it pleases.

Certainly good piñon years are unpredictable until it is too late for adequate planning. This may explain why no attempt has been made to cultivate piñons. It is only in recent years that owners of land with heavy stands of piñon have made any effort to prevent all and sundry from coming on to their property to harvest the crop.

When the season is good and the market reasonable, pickers will receive up to ten cents per pound. A good wood rat's nest will yield as high as fifty pounds for about three minutes' work in destroying the nest and shoveling out the nuts. But wood rats' nests are the nuggets in the run-of-the-mill mining for piñons. The far greater yield is from the fallen nuts under the trees, after the first hard frost has burst open the cones and sent the nuts showering down.

The technic of picking piñons is to sit oneself under a tree and begin to pick. It's tedious but strains no muscles other than those used in shifting position, a hardship which can be mitigated by the use of a Chinese fanlike split-bamboo rake, a labor-saving device which I claim credit for introducing.

When the field surrounding the particular tree under which you are sitting and laboring has been fairly well cleaned up, you spread a wagon sheet under the tree and shake down more nuts and half-opened cones and twigs and debris generally, which may or may not be worth while. It's always a question, for there are so many more trees at hand where the reaping may be better without this hullabaloo.

There are those, especially the very young, who gather piñons flat on their stomachs, inching their way along like ponderous lizards in a sandy wash.

An entire family gathering piñon nuts at ten cents a pound can have done very well at the end of a season! The piñon crop has tided many a homesteader over a hard winter.

If one makes a serious business of it, of course one goes into camp and stays. In piñon years, the night campfires of piñon pickers glow on the landscape near and far.

Indians flock from the reservation and the unemployed, white, black, and brown, from the towns. In every sort of vehicle, so long as its wheels will turn, they overflow into the piñon country, on a sort of combination picnic and working for a living hegira. There are no rent, light, telephone, water, or heat bills to torment, and the piñons can be eaten, if worse comes, so it is little wonder the piñon pickers become something of a problem to the permanent residents of the community. In fact, many owners of patented land have been forced to forbid entry to this increasing horde, who scare away the cattle even if they don't butcher them (which they sometimes do), and who clean out the fuel which the rightful owner had reserved for his own use. In countless other ways they constitute themselves a nuisance if not a menace.

A large sheep-owner recently posted his range against piñon pickers, on the ground that he wanted to fatten his sheep on the nuts. Sheep, hogs, and turkey will on a good piñon diet put on fat at a miraculous rate. Every Southwest housewife and schoolteacher has occasion to dread a good piñon year. Piñons are little globules of fat encased in brittle brown shells, and when stepped on leave a grease spot that has been well ground into the rug. This is the housewife's plaint. The schoolteachers object to the sharp crack, crack all over the schoolroom as the nut shells split in two between skillful young teeth. There is an especial skill in eating piñons which makes detection difficult, or would, but for the crack. The experienced piñon-eater slips a nut into his mouth, works it into position with lips and tongue, and bites down on its one angular edge. The shell falls away in two halves, which may be adroitly spat out without the fingers having gone near the mouth after the nut has once been delivered.

The invention of a piñon silencer would be a boon to the schoolchildren of the southwest. Teacher could never catch them at it. There are countless inventions for shelling them. Rolling between two boards isn't bad.

One young man teacher of adequate height, whose rural log schoolhouse stood in a piñon grove, was driven to the use of drastic measures. When school reconvened after each recess he lined up the student body. Each boy he grasped by the ankles and held aloft and shook vigorously until all the piñons secreted in pockets rattled down. The girls he put on their honor. Moreover, they had fewer pockets. He reported that the method was only partially successful. The youngsters enjoyed the game. It delayed the pursuit of knowledge.

On the long winter evenings when we first came to the Datils our favorite recreation was to play mumble peg in a shallow box of packed dirt and eat piñons, spitting the shells half across the room into the open fireplace.

And a long solitary ride can be made far more tolerable by a pint or so of piñon nuts in the chaps pocket. Passing the jar of piñons is a gesture of hospitality for the ranch hostess, but the uninitiated may suffer as much embarrassment on first being offered a piñon as do those who have an artichoke set before them for the first time. If I were trying to unmask a pretender, one claiming to be a Westerner, I'd hand him a piñon nut. He might successfully imitate our dress, our speech, and our manners, but unless he'd had long practice eating piñons he'd give himself plumb away.

Frijoles, Tortillas, Enchiladas, Tamales

What we call Spanish food here is actually Indian. I am not familiar with Spanish cooking on its native hearth. I therefore cannot say

---

From *The Valley Below,* by Alice Marriott, pp. 190–194, 195, 197–198.

exactly what food habits the conquistadors brought to the New World with them, beyond eating early and often. I do know that the recipes I have collected from Indian and Spanish women are basic for this region and for parts of Old Mexico.

North America has made several notable contributions to the food economy of the world. Among the agricultural Indian tribes at the time of the Conquest, certain vegetable foods were so universally found that they have come to be known to ethnologists as the "American agricultural triad." The three are corn, beans, and squashes. They were unknown to Europeans before their settlement of North America. With them, in the Southwestern states, go chile peppers.

At first glance, corn, beans, squashes, and chiles, with occasional meat dishes, seem to provide a limited diet. What the food may lack in variety it makes up for in vitamins. According to tests conducted by the United States Indian Service and the Department of Agriculture, the diet is almost perfectly balanced. Chile is a rich source of vitamin C, an important factor in an area where citrus fruits and green vegetables are hard for the average family to keep on hand.

The great Spanish contributions to Southwestern cookery were onions and garlic. They join in happy union with the American triad and its cousin, the tomato. They, with basil, thyme, rosemary, and the local wild mint called oregano, are the great sources of seasoning, aside from the omnipresent chile.

I know I am sticking my neck out in giving recipes for Southwestern dishes. There are as many variations of each as there are cooks, as many battles over the fine points of seasoning as there are over sugar or no sugar in corn bread in the East. But you can't write about any part of the country without eventually mentioning food, and that is even more true than usual here, where the food is a part of the local color. So with due apologies to the proponents of other versions, I present my recipes.

From day to day, the average Southwestern family outside the big towns lives on beans, as the average English family lives on potatoes. Beans here are called *frijoles,* with the "j" pronounced as "h" and the "e" sounded. Old-time Anglos in the region, who have learned to eat Spanish foods without bothering too much about the finer points of pronunciation, call them "free-hole beans." However they are pronounced, they are the staple, three times a day, of regional cooking.

You can do a lot of things with *frijoles.* It depends on the kind of beans you start with to some extent. The best for all around use, and true *frijoles,* are *pinto* (painted) beans—small, cream colored, and speckled with red. When cooked, they turn an even, uniform tan. The trick in cooking pinto beans is to clean them thoroughly first. If they have been dried and thrashed at home on the sand and gravel of the front yard, fragments of the earth from which they came are likely to adhere to them.

Having sweated the larger boulders out of your beans, you soak the beans overnight. In the morning you throw away the first water and add a piece of meat—whatever is handy—some salt, a pod of chile, an onion cut fine, and plenty of fresh water. Then boil the mixture slowly in an iron kettle until the *frijoles* are soft. This takes from two to four hours, so it is just as well to start early in the day. Just before the beans are done, you can add a fresh tomato, also cut small. The salt with which they are cooked will cause some of the beans to disintegrate, and this thickens the rest of the dish. Eat your beans hot or cold, with chile sauce and *tortillas* on the side.

If there are beans left over from dinner, and there sometimes are, you can have *frijoles refritos,* or refried beans, for another meal. Crush the beans to a pulp, then put them into a frying pan with a little fat and some salt, and turn them frequently. They thus acquire quite a different taste from that with which they began. *Frijoles refritos* are a wonderful accompaniment for all the spicy made-dishes of the region, for the blandness of the beans helps to take the sting out of chile.

Almost everything else starts with *tortillas,* which are the standard local bread. A *tortilla* is made by mixing hand-ground corn meal—and it should be the hand-ground kind if you can possibly get it—with salt and boiling water to make a dough. Then you pat the dough into a thin sheet between your palms, and slap it down on a hot stove or griddle to brown quickly on either side. It takes a great deal of skill and training to become a good *tortilla*-slapper. When the skill has been acquired, together with the time-sense requisite for turning the *tortillas,* you can make enough for a meal in nothing flat. Well, anyway, in less time than it takes to make hot biscuits.

For those who lack the training or the inclination to make their own *tortillas,* there are ready-made ones to be bought from the grocer, either fresh or canned. I have even heard that one of the quick-freezing companies markets frozen *tortillas,* although I have never encountered them myself.

When it is first made, a *tortilla* has the texture of a sheet of damp blotting paper. It is limp and flabby, and, especially if it is made of blue corn meal, highly uninviting to the eye. The initiated love it for itself alone; they eat it and rejoice. For the sissy newcomer who wants something pretty to look at, there is the *tostado* (toasted one), made by plunging the *tortilla* into hot fat until it is as crisp as a potato chip. Marketed under several trade names, small tostados are a standard Southwestern accompaniment for beer.

* * * * *

Chile sauce is as basic to Southwestern cooking as the *tortilla.* This sauce is not to be confused with the relish that passes under the same name in the South and Middle West. No mild compound of hashed vegetables, sugar, and imported spices is the Southwestern chile sauce.

You start with three or four whole, dried, red chile peppers. They go in a pan, preferably enamel or earthenware, with a clove of garlic and a quart of water. When the mixture has boiled until the chiles are pulpy, put it through a sieve to remove the seeds and membranes of the peppers. The sauce can be thickened a little with flour, and it can be salted, but purists object to this tampering with Nature's experiment in spontaneous combustion. They eat it as is, and they eat it on everything. Often chile seems to replace salt in the Southwestern diet.

Commercial chile powder is a poor substitute for the real, hand-ground article. It lacks the authentic tang, for it is tempered with flour or cornstarch and further reduced in potency by the addition of other spices. The best chile in the world grows near us, from Pojoaque to Chimayo. Most of the local groceries grind their own chile and market it in bulk.

Starting with tortillas and chile sauce, you can proceed in several directions. By stacking the *tortillas* with alternate layers of meat or cheese, like pancakes, and then covering the stack with grated cheese, chopped raw onions, and chile sauce, you can make *enchiladas*. If you care to be extra fancy, you can put a poached or fried egg on top of the heap. It is then an *enchilada con huevo* (with egg), and a dish for feast days.

In some kitchens the *tortilla* is rolled around the filling, and the *enchilada* looks more like a sausage than a short stack. The two schools of *enchilada*-making are at daggers drawn most of the time. Proponents of either method will eat the dish as prepared by the other school, but with bitter comments and muttered complaints.

* * * * *

Tamales must be included with the other festive dishes. *Tamales* are something really lush. The best ones are those you buy from a street peddler and eat drippily, sitting on the curb or in your car. No other *tamales* have the fine, free tang of those obtained and eaten in this way.

If you want to be reasonably germfree, though, you can make your *tamales* at home. You start with a thick mush of hand-ground meal, and for *tamales* white corn meal is better than blue. Spread the cooled mush liberally on corn shucks, the thin ones that grow next to the ears. Yes, you can use parchment paper, but the *tamales* won't taste the same.

Over the mush you spread the filling. I like to use chopped beef, with minced onion and a little garlic, a pinch of *oregano,* and a pinch of chile. Toss the meat lightly in a frying pan, with a little fat, until it browns. Don't be seduced by hamburger or ground round. The best tamales are made with chopped leftovers.

You put another layer of mush over the filling. Then you roll the *tamal.* This is where the trick comes in. You should take the corn shuck firmly between thumb and fingers at either end, and roll it with a single twist. Then twist the ends of the shucks together, or, to make them doubly secure, tie them with string. *Tamales* can be baked in a covered pan in a slow oven, if you are the cautious type. If you are reckless and willing to go native, you plunge them in a kettle of boiling water and cook them like dumplings.

* * * * *

The beverages served with a Spanish meal should be planned to take the sting out of the chile. Water is not a good drink for this purpose. The average tender-tongue takes his first bite of a chile-seasoned dish and reaches automatically for his water glass. Unless an old-timer is there to restrain him, he spends the next twenty-four hours bitterly regretting his action, for water "sets" the bite of the chile. So does tea, and, to some extent, coffee.

The best thing to drink with any dish seasoned with chile is milk. It is so soothing that the second—and the last—bite tastes like the first. A bite of chile, a sip of milk, and a mouthful of beans or *tortillas,* is the approved formula. Next best to milk is beer. Taken in the same order as milk, it is almost as effective, and those who like it maintain that it makes the food taste better. Certainly it has an affinity for Southwestern foods that table wines seem to lack. The acid of the wine serves only to prolong the agony. I once knew a woman who had lived in France for many years, who insisted on serving Burgundy with chile. She said she liked it, but she was an exceptional woman in many ways.

The question arises, "Why eat chile at all, if each bite produces mortal agony?" There is a variety of answers. In the first place, as has been pointed out, chile is the best locally available source of vitamin C, which explains the frank craving for it that some Southwesterners develop. In the second place, chile provides the eater with a mild stimulation, comparable to that derived from the lightest wines. And, in the third place, chile-eaters don't need a reason. They like chile, and the pain of eating it only tickles their masochistic palates.

As is the case with many peoples who lack facilities for canning or for storing canned foods, the Spanish Americans sun-dry many of their crops. Meat is sun-dried as are vegetables and fruits. The first time I saw strips of meat cut tissue-thin and hung over a clothesline for wind, flies, and dust to season, I doubted whether any good could come of the method. Since then I have learned to eat dried meat and like it. I do prefer it when the cook follows the directions given in the Department of Agriculture bulletin on the subject, and wraps the clothesline and its pendant burden in a piece of cheesecloth. I have been known to eat meat dried by the aboriginal method, but Martha still resists it.

The drying of corn and of chiles *colorados* is a beautiful thing to see. The long strings of vegetables are hung against the house walls in autumn and are as much a part of the landscape as the yellowing cottonwoods and aspens. People write poems and paint pictures of drying corn and chiles. In fact, they come to New Mexico for those express purposes and do nothing else when they get there. Reputations have been built on the painting or prosodizing of corn and chiles in autumn.

Indians and Mormon Cookery

Nowhere is Mormon culture more distinctive than in its cookery. Not only did Mormons absorb dishes from every European culture, but they borrowed what they could from the Indians. I do not suppose you would be interested in the annual Squaw Harvest of grass seeds, oose apples, rat heads, and long green worms to be dried and rolled up. Nor even perhaps in the squaw's winter's flour from powdered mesquite and mescrew beans. But take her *piñon bread,* the recipe for which was carried over from samples found in ancient cliff dwellings: Grind an equal amount of corn and pinenuts (you can add modern touches such as baking powder if you wish), wrap securely in a wet cornhusk, and bake in coal. Pulverized jerky can be substituted for the pinenuts. This bread should be eaten hot, with molasses.

Even today you can find Moromon houswives making *jerky:* Cut strips of freshly killed beef thin and about a foot long, immerse quickly in boiling water, salt and pepper liberally, cover with cheesecloth, and hang on a clothesline in the hot sun, or over the smoke of a campfire. Indian fashion, which gives the jerky a wild, smoky flavor. There is nothing so delicious as jerky, and one chew will last a hungry boy all day.

Fruit Packers

The packing shed is a large, almost square building constructed of rough one-by-twelve boards with large cracks between them. The floor is smooth so that the hand trucks can be rolled easily over it, and the roof is made of tin, which serves to increase the heat. It has only two walls: one side is open for unloading wagons from the orchard; the other side opens onto a spur track where freight cars are loaded with packed pears.

Old Man Blake's son, the packing shed foreman, knows I have worked here before and gives me no orders. The Japanese or Hindu crews started work yesterday, so the shed is partially filled with lug boxes of green pears in piles of six boxes each, placed on the right side of the machine. Young Blake turns on the power, and the machine begins the humming, whirring sound that will be dinned into the brain of every man and woman there. The machine takes the place of a whistle or a time-clock. When it starts, everybody goes to work. When it stops, everybody quits working.

From *This Is the Place: Utah:* by Maurine Whipple, p. 178. Copyright, 1945, by Maurine Whipple. New York: Alfred A. Knopf.

By John Delgado. From "Men at Work." Manuscripts of the Federal Writers' Project of the Works Progress Administration for Northern California.

It is the heart and nerve center of the fifty-man plant. It is an uncomplicated mechanism, so simple as to be almost childish, yet were it to falter, some four hundred men and women—packers and pickers, sorters and truckers, teamsters, waterboys and foremen—would be idle. It consists of an endless canvas belt which carries the pears under three sets of brushes. The brushes turn counter-wise to the movement of the belt, so that the fruit is twirled about. As the pears pass under the brushes, they are cleansed of the poisonous spray covering which protects them from parasitic growths.

There are about two hundred pickers on the ranch—white, Japanese and Hindu. Countless times each day they climb their ladders with empty buckets, which they fill as they work down the trees, and sink ankle-deep into the soft soil as they empty the buckets into lug boxes. They must be careful to pull the pear against the grain of the limb to break the whole stem cleanly; they must not drop the fruit too hard or it will be bruised. Sometimes it is so hot they cannot work in the middle of the afternoon and must put in their nine hours early in the morning and late in the evening. They are given two ten-minute "smoke times" during which they can relax in the shade of a tree and enjoy a cigarette.

A score of teamsters scatter throughout the ranch to gather the lug boxes from the field. They rise at daybreak and, before breakfast, prepare the horses for the hard day's work. In the field they have to load the wagons alone. Through the day, from all corners of the ranch, they converge upon the packing shed, man and animal covered with perspiration and dust. At the shed a swamper helps unload the forty boxes carried each trip. Truckers carry the fruit to the machine.

A half-dozen young men—holding the coveted "waterboy" jobs—race around the ranch in light two-wheel sulkies, carrying five-gallon cans of water to the pickers. Foremen walk from row to row behind the pickers, scanning the trees to see that no desirable fruit is left behind, for by the next picking it will be too ripe.

At the other end of the machine from me are eight girls—the sorters—lined four on each side of the endless canvas belt. The cleaned fruit passes before them on review; they pick from the moving belt fruit that is bruised or too small. They work steadily, keeping up with the flow of fruit, their eyes intent upon the belt, their fingers flitting here and there to remove the spoiled pears.

Beyond them are two lines of packers—Japanese of both sexes. Endless cables carry the fruit to them. The cables are narrow at first but widen gradually, so that the small fruit drops through into the first bin and the largest into the last bin. Thus the pears are graded so that those dropping into each bin are of nearly uniform size.

The packers face the machine, with their right hands nearest the bins. Directly in front of them is a packing box. To their left is a sheaf of tissue-thin paper with the Blake brand. Their movements are so fast they can scarcely be followed. Both hands move at the same time. The right grabs a pear, the left a single sheet of paper. With lightning speed they wrap the pear and slap it into the box, tier on tier to get the maximum number into each box. Rapidly the box fills, even with the side at each end but forming a heap in the center. Packers are paid on a piece-work basis and are the fastest and highest-paid workers on the ranch.

As each box is filled, the packer lifts it to a set of rollers inclined downward. A slight push moves them to the "topper," who nails the lids on. The topper slides the box under a machine with a concave steel hood. A lever operated by foot forces the hood neatly down over the heaping box, leaving only the ends of the lids exposed so that the nails can be driven in. The topper piles the boxes in shaky stacks beside him and they are quickly trucked away to the waiting box cars. As soon as the cars are filled, an engine hooks onto them and rolls them to Marysville, where they will become part of a 99-car refrigerated train for the East.

The machine is the outstanding unit in this interdependent series of operations that takes a green, dusty, spray-covered pear from the Sacramento Valley and transforms it into a delicacy for the best New York hotels. Here in this rural area it is the symbol of the mechanization of work done by human hands for centuries.

V. TIMBER

Look out, Chokertown, here we come! We're the blue-eyed, bandy-legged, hump-backed old mackinaw hodags from Dosewallips! Look out, Chokertown, here we come! Eight feet to the nearest limb and six foot through at the butt.

—STEWART H. HOLBROOK

"Loggin' Is Half Farmin'"

A grizzled old logger who had sacrificed two fingers to a rotary saw looked up from the bowl of mulligatawny in which he had practically immersed his face. "Not much difference 'tween loggin' and farmin',"

From *Our Promised Land,* by Richard L. Neuberger, p. 253. Copyright, 1938, by Richard L. Neuberger. New York: The Macmillan Company.

he vouchsafed. "You cut down trees in one and pull up radishes in the other. You just have t' wait a little longer for the trees to grow—that's all." He put his face back into the bowl and began eating again.

From Timber Beast to Timber Mechanic

[It was] a February night in a sandhouse at The Dalles. Hoboes huddled miserably about a fire. Too bitterly cold for sleep. Complaints, denunciations, life defiled and cursed. There we were, used in the working seasons to dig the ditches, build the railroads, harvest the crops; and when winter closed up seasonal work we were made outcasts, jailed, or harried from town to town like criminals. Well, the working stiffs of the Northwest were learning something. In that sandhouse our miserable gang was told of Direct Action and the Red Card. I signed up with the others. We could pay our dues when we got a job.

Then the talk had changed. A dream emerged. It was in such circumstances that American folklore, the art of the plain man, flourished. The eternal force behind all creations of art, noble and lowly, is the desire to escape from reality. And there in the sandhouse I heard again the story of the Hoboes' Heaven. I had heard it before, but Singer Larkin told it with genuine intensity of feeling. Briefly, his tale was about a Heaven in which every house was a saloon, every road a race track, and the only jobs poker playing and crap shooting. Liquor and warmth and play. The saloon was the nearest thing to beauty and comfort that the Western workingman knew in those days. Small wonder that he idealized it in his bitterest hours, that he turned to it when the cold politics of industrial revolt failed to inspire him with hope.

* * * * *

Before the summer was over I was to reach a clearer understanding of the reason for Ericsen's, and for Fritz's, Blazier's, Our House, Billy the Mug's, the Horseshoe, and other famous skidroad saloons of the Pacific Northwest's lumber centers. They were, in fact, the only refuge of the "timber beast," the only places where he was welcomed as a man, where he could find solace and comfort after a hard and mean existence in the woods. In that summer I lost much of my own youth, and forgot about fairy tales. It was to be many years before I recovered my boyish perception of the fact that the fanciful tales of Western workingmen were as truly art creations out of their own life as are the formal works of educated story-tellers.

The saloon, a famous political leader informs us, is a defunct in-

From "The Passing of the Timber Beast," by James Stevens, *The Frontier,* A Magazine of the Northwest, Vol. IX (January, 1929), No. 2, pp. 93–98. Copyright, 1928, by H. G. Merriam. Missoula, Montana: State University of Montana.

stitution. No one dares to defend it. The place of the saloon in the social life of the time in which it flourished has, however, never been intelligently and fairly studied. It is isolated from the life of its time, attacked alone, and never considered in its relations to the greater evils of its day. For example, the timber beast. The timber beast was the great evil of the Northwest twenty years ago; and he will always remain a black blot on the history of that time and on the record of the society which was responsible for him.

As I discovered, soon after shipping from Portland to a Columbia River logging camp, the man who joined the tribe of loggers made himself a pariah among the nice folk of the farms and towns. To these gentry—all of whom were in some way dependent on the lumber industry and consequently on the labor of the men of the woods—the man who appeared with a blanket roll on his back, stagged overalls on his legs, and calked boots on his feet, was simply a strayed animal. He was permitted to stay in town only until his wool was clipped. Then he was herded back to the corral. "Timber beast" he was called, and so he was treated. In those days few loggers attempted to dress up when they came to town, and they never thought of seeking acquaintance among decent girls. Ah, no! Loggers must keep below the Deadline in Seattle and to the North End in Portland. There saloons and red lights were provided and also sundry gambling games, so that there was no chance of a timber beast returning to camp unplucked. The virtuous police protected the good citizens. The skidroad cops had an uncanny instinct for discovering when a logger's last dime was gone. Then and only then was the timber beast herded back to camp.

If the saloon was an evil the logging camp of its time was incomparably more so. The men of the woods were herded into dirty, lousy and unventilated bunkhouses. They were forced to carry their own blankets. There were no facilities for bathing. There were no dry rooms, and after ten or twelve hours of labor in the rain every bunkhouse was pungent with the fumes of drying wool. Grub was plentiful, but it was coarse and badly cooked; the boss of the cookhouse in those days was invariably referred to as "the belly-burglar." On the job ground-lead logging was still the rule, and every camp had a high monthly toll of injury and death. Industrial hospitalization was hardly thought of; any seriously injured man was certain to get the "black bottle" in a county hospital or in the hell-holes conducted by medical murderers who fattened on "hospital fees" collected from lumber companies. Workmen's compensation laws were then in the class of "radical and fantastic legislation." Two dollars per ten hours was the common labor wage, and half of that went for board. In short, every condition of existence in the logging camp of that era was brutalizing and degrading, and the man who could stand it perhaps earned the name of "timber beast."

Yet, out of such conditions came the Paul Bunyan stories and many other tales that survive because of the beauty of the fancies woven into them by forgotten bards. No doubt it was the misery of life which made imaginative loggers create the stories of Paul Bunyan's camp, with its incomparable cookhouse, delightful bunkhouse life, and interesting labors. Certainly it is true that the bunkhouse bard passed with the timber beast and the miserable conditions of existence in the logging camps.

At any rate, my own experiences in my first year of logging survive in my mind as two tremendous contrasts. One is black with the misery and grief of life and labor in the logging camp of that time; the other shines and rings with the glamor of the moments of escape, when I foregathered with the despised timber beasts in saloons like Ericsen's and escaped reality. There we became heroes. There, over the glasses and under the lights, our labors seemed Herculean, and we boasted that none but bullies like ourselves could stand them. In Ericsen's we swaggered to the bar and bawled our defiance. Timber beasts, and proud of it! We repeated tales about mighty men of the woods to justify our kind. We sang old ballads. We were outcasts, but we had a tribal life. In Ericsen's was glory, and there we found pride. . . . The aftermath, of course, was a sick and bitter awakening in a foul-smelling bunkhouse, to be high-balled to work by an iron-fisted bull of the woods . . . but a little of the glamor always remained, to make us feel some hope in our existence. There was always a blow-in ahead. . . .

The timber beasts, the saloon, and all of the old life that belonged to them passed in the war. Many different groups claim the credit for making the logger's trade a respectable and profitable one. The I. W. W., once the most vociferous and violent of Western labor organizations, claims the credit for sheets and showers in the camps and for the eight-hour day. The lumbermen insist that they themselves inaugurated the social and economic changes. Politicians horn in and shout for recognition. The fact is, however, that no organization or individual was more than an agent for the inevitable change. The real cause was the sweep of the tide of Eastern urban civilization over the West.

Transportation and finance had at last bound the West to the East. Small lumbering and logging operations were being bought up by the big companies. The manufacture and marketing of lumber were reorganized along Eastern industrial lines. Vast mechanical developments occurred in both the mills and the woods. The degree of Logging Engineer was conferred on graduates of forestry schools. The bull of the woods who ruled by brawn gave way to the logging superintendent who was technically skilled. Logging railroads, new types of bull donkeys, high lead and skyline logging methods brought mechanics to the woods. The logger became a skilled laborer, and as such he demanded the wages and living conditions enjoyed by skilled laborers in the cities. All of the changes were coming into effect when America entered the war. The economic condition of the logger had improved tremendously, but he was still a timber beast in the eyes of farm and town folks. War conditions, however, elevated his social status and made his trade respected, even admired.

This resulted from the entry of the government into spruce production. Col. Bruce Disque was sent out from Washington to organize the lumber industry for wartime needs. The Spruce Division was formed, the government eight-hour day established in the logging camps. Loggers became soldiers, and soldiers were popular. When the erstwhile timber beasts came to town he no longer wore the old regalia of stagged pants and calked boots; instead, he was shiny and neat in a tailored uniform. He was no longer kept to the North End and below the Deadline. Now he was one of Uncle Sam's boys, a fit companion for decent girls, a man honored by all. He learned the pleasures of the theater, the automobile and the dance palace. He discovered that with this broadening of his social life the necessity for the saloon was diminished and his appetite for its beverages fell away. He was no longer a timber beast; at last he was a man.

And he was more of a man in the woods. Production per man far exceeded the figures of the old era. The lumberman learned that better food, cleaner living conditions, shorter hours, respectable treatment meant more logs and lumber. After the war, some of the old-time lumbermen fought for a return to the old conditions, but the younger and more progressive men among them held to the once revolutionary idea that it was better in every sense to regard workers in the woods as men rather than as beasts.

So the logger of today is a man with a highly respectable and profitable trade; he is no longer a drudging and despised timber beast but a skilled mechanic of the timber. His bunkhouse is orderly, clean and comfortable. He sits at a table loaded with savory, well-prepared food. There is a camp garage for his automobile. He enjoys the radio and the graphophone. He is protected by company insurance, workmen's compensation laws, and first-class hospital service. When he drives to town he goes to his tailor's, where his hundred-dollar suit has been kept for him, dresses up in an elegant style, and stops at one of the best hotels. He has friends among smart and pretty business girls. His only concern with liquor is to be socially acceptable; that is, he must never be without a full pocket flask.

Certainly for this logger the saloon is a defunct institution, but only because other institutions that once made his life wretched and bitter are also defunct. The romance of his life is also gone, for that romance was made by the contrast in his life, the high vivid spot among the darkest of shadows. He no longer suffers miserably in a life of bleak toil, and he no longer riots in a tumultuous blow-in, or dreams purple fancies of a logger's heaven ruled by a beneficent god such as the good and great Paul Bunyan. He is no longer the outcast, the timber beast; he is the everyday skilled American workman, prosperous and proud. Romance passed with his old life. I for one often look back with regret on "the good old days," but I know that is because I forget the long months of labor in the woods and only remember vividly the few nights in Ericsen's. So I cheer the passing of the timber beast and salute the timber mechanic, that fat and sassy plutocrat of the modern logging camp.

Skidroad

The early loggers saw at once there could be no quick yanking and twitching around, with a team of horses, such big stuff as grew in the coast fir country. What was needed was a lot of power and a strong, steady pull. So the boys reverted to the loggers' ancient beast of burden, the ox. Only here, they called oxen "the bulls," and for half a century bulls did most of the logging west of the Cascade Range.

Sleighs wouldn't do to handle these big logs, and there was seldom

---

From *Holy Old Mackinaw,* A Natural History of the American Lumberjack, by Stewart H. Holbrook, pp. 163–165, 193. Copyright, 1938, by The Macmillan Company. New York. 1944.

I've never lost an opportunity to tell about skidroad since they've corrupted the word into skidrow—r-o-w—which is one of the curses of contemporary English in the United States. For a great many years skidroad was the designation of what you might call the Bowery district of the Western towns. It began in Seattle with Henry Yesler's sawmill skidroad, which went right down through the present-day Seattle to his sawmill. Along the skidroad in the early days grew up the saloons and the bawdy houses and one thing and another to entertain loggers. Naturally, when Seattle grew up and the skidroad was done away with, they still called it skidroad, wherever the boys from the timber met when they came to town. Portland's Burnside Street, which was the same thing, was called the Skidroad.

And skidroad it was from perhaps 1874 until around 1938 when a quickie writer for a large national magazine came to Seattle. He was going to do a piece about Seattle, and therefore there would have to be something about the Skidroad. He overindulged, and in the morning his hearing wasn't very clear, and he was talking with the boys there, and they mentioned the Skidroad. "Why, you must see the Skidroad, which is Yesler Way and Occidental, First Avenue South and Pioneer Square." And he wrote it down skidrow. Immediately, as is the way with things, through some mysterious manner, skidrow became the word that was getting into the newspapers. Now James Stevens of Seattle, myself, and a lot of other decent men for years have fought this apparently losing battle against the use of the word skidrow, which is used only by people who don't know what they're talking about.

We have the Skidrow on Madison Street in Chicago, and they have a Skidrow in Ogden. I spoke to the United Press and the Associated Press about it, and they've done wonders in trying to defeat it. And finally I've got *Time* magazine through harassing them so that three times in the last month they've used skidroad, and I claim we're getting somewhere. But it still calls for the work of every man of good will in the United States to prevent the use of skidrow—r-o-w. There isn't such a thing!—Stewart H. Holbrook, Portland, Oregon, July 30, 1950. Recorded by B. A. Botkin.

much snow, anyway. The ground was too rough and too soft to think of using the Big Wheels of Michigan. And only here and there was a stream deep and powerful enough to do much river driving. Faced with such new conditions the boys quickly adapted themselves. They built skidroads.

The skidroad was the Western loggers' first and greatest contribution to the science of moving timber. They first cleared a path in the forest. At suitable intervals they felled trees across this path, cut them free of limbs, then buried them half-deep in the soft ground. These were the skids that made a skidroad, a sort of track that would keep moving logs from hanging up on rocks or miring in mud. The completed job looked not unlike ties laid for a gargantuan railroad.

It was crude, but it worked beautifully. They hitched the bulls to the logs—five, six, even ten yokes of them, in charge of the bull-whacker, the teamster, undoubtedly the master of all profane men, and they pulled long turns of the big sticks, held together by hooks, over the skids.

It was something to see, this skidroad logging on the West Shore. First, you heard the loud, clear call of the bullwhacker's voice echoing down the forest road that was more like a deep green canyon, so tall and thick stood the fir; and the clank of chains and the wailing of oxbows as the heavy animals got into the pull and "leaned on her." And then the powerful line of red and black and spotted white would swing by with measured tread, the teamster, sacred goadstick over his shoulder, walking beside the team, petting and cursing them to high heaven by turns, the huge logs coming along behind with a dignified roll. Back of the oxen, but ahead of the logs, walked the skid greaser, daubing thick oil on the skid poles that smoked from friction.

Gray old men, sitting around bunkhouse stoves, still cackle in their high voices that it was the noblest sight they ever saw; and they curse the steam that relegated the bull teams to the murals of Western hotels and barrooms.

Ground-Lead and High-Lead

While John Dolbeer was puttering with the successful logging donkey engine that took his name, other men were experimenting with steam in the fir forests. They appear to have been vague men who left no clear record, but there is no doubt that they devised a steam donkey with an upright capstan. This engine they called a gypsy, or spool, donkey. By the mid-nineties both gypsies and Dolbeers had brought "ground-lead" logging into style; by means of a line pulled

Ibid., pp. 180–186.

by a turning wheel or capstan, the logs were yarded, or *led* along the ground.

* * * * *

Ground-lead logging speeded production in the woods. It was necessary—if the boys were going to keep up with what was going on in the sawmills. All through the nineties and well into the century bigger and better and faster mills were being built in Washington, Oregon, and California by boss lumbermen from the Lake States. Lumber cities like Bellingham, Everett, Hoquiam, Aberdeen, and Tacoma had come into being. Seattle had long outgrown the settlement around Henry Yesler's mill and now had half a dozen big plants. Even Olympia, Washington's capital, was making a lot of boards. Portland was still the metropolis of the Northwest and its biggest sawmill town as well. Down in California sizable towns were growing up at Crescent City, Eureka, Scotia, Fort Bragg, Westwood, McCloud, and Weed. By 1900 the rush of Eastern lumbermen to the West Coast was in full swing and would last almost exactly twenty-five years more. If the loggers were going to keep the mill ponds of these fast new plants filled with roundstuff, they'd have to speed things up—to *highball,* they called it.

The *high-lead* tree was the answer. It was nothing more than the idea expounded by Horace Butters in his "Butters' Patent Log Skidding Machine," back in Michigan of the eighties. It had gone South to log the swamps and bayous of their cypress and pine. It emerged in the Pacific Northwest as something "new."

The high lead[1] was simply the old ground lead with an aerial twist to it. A block, or pulley, was hung high in the big tree. Through this ran the line from the donkey engine. Thus a log could be hauled in with one end in the air, riding free of stumps and underbrush.

It proved to be the genuine McCoy, and it brought into being a new job, that of the high climber or high rigger, probably the most spectacular fellow in all American industry. With sharp steel spurs strapped to his legs, a safety belt around his waist, and an ax and saw dangling beneath him, this steeplejack of the woods hitches himself with a rope up a tall fir,[2] limbing it as he goes. Anywhere from one hundred and fifty to two hundred feet from the ground, he straps himself loosely to the tree and saws off its top.[3] Hanging there against the sky, he must work carefully, lest he cut his safety belt, for death on the stumps and ground far below yawns at him from all sides.

And when, after highly skilled work in a cramped position, the great top of the tree starts to lean, then to fall, the high climber must brace

---

[1] The high lead is in use in 1938 but is on the way out.—S.H.H.

[2] Some camps use steel towers, called "skidders," instead of trees.—S.H.H.

[3] Sometimes dynamite is used. The climber straps the powder sticks around the tree, hangs a long fuse, lights it, and gets out of there. The resulting explosion is worth seeing, but the topping job isn't so "pretty" as a sawed one.—S.H.H.

himself well. The trunk vibrates wickedly in wide arcs, and top and man for an instant are little more than a blur. Down, down goes the treetop, crashing its tons of weight on the forest floor to send echoes up the canyon and over the hump to the next camp.[4]

The tree is now a spar and it is first guyed all around with steel cables. At its top by an elaborate process is hung a pulley block such as you are not likely to see elsewhere. High-lead blocks weigh up to a ton and a quarter each, few of them less than eighteen hundred pounds. Once in a while one of them falls, and none in its path has ever needed first-aid attention.

From the donkey engine a monstrous steel cable—the main line—is run up through this block, then out into the woods. Logs, around which a steel choker has been wrapped, are attached to the main line and yarded to the foot of the spar. Horses aren't used to return the main line to the woods; a second drum on the donkey carries a haul-back line to do this job. The high lead almost doubled production.

High-lead logging also brought a noticeable increase in the accident rate; with stuff flying through the air, rather than moving over the ground, there was considerable more opportunity for a man to get hit. Added to this natural hazard was the "yarding bonus" offered by many operators. The boss would set a footage mark, usually rather high, for a crew. If the crew managed to yard more than this figure, every man got a dollar or so added to his wages for that day. But worst of all, perhaps, were the wilder hook tenders who seemed to think that setting a "world's record" for a day's logging would give them everlasting fame as highball loggers.

A high-lead yarding crew has about the same occupational names as did a ground-lead crew, with additions. The *rigging slinger* hooks the chokers to the main line; the *chaser* unhooks them at the spar tree. The flagman of ground-lead days has given way to the *whistle punk,* the lad, who, with a jerk line or an electric device, blows the starting, stopping, and backing-up signals for the *donkey puncher* at the engine's levers. It isn't exactly an assembly line, but it's all routine. Over and over again, it is the same process. The chokerman puts a choker around the log, the rigging slinger attaches it to the main line, the hooker yells "Hi!" to the punk, the punk jerks the whistle, and some two thousand feet away, and often out of sight, the whistle on the donkey toots once. The donkey puncher opens up. There is a great singing of taut cables as the powerful machine goes into the pull, while the log, thick as a man is high, churns and groans in an upheaval that could be likened to a whale thrashing about in shallow

---

[4] Some high climbers are good showmen. When they have topped a tree, they take a r'ar of snuff, or roll a cigarette, and stand on their head at the top of the spar. Some low-minded climbers mark the completed job by attempting one of Gargantua's tricks on the loggers watching below.—S.H.H.

water. Once in motion, it is a veritable juggernaut's car, crushing all before it, including only too often a man who isn't "in the clear."

Pulled to the foot of the spar tree, the logs are slapped onto railroad cars by a McLean loading boom[5] or other tackle so quickly that one hardly realizes what is happening. The long train of big sticks—twenty, fifty, even a hundred cars, is made up, and away they go down the mountain, around curves, and over high, dizzy trestles, so rough is the terrain, to the waiting log pond.

Sober men marveled at the ruthless power and great speed of high-lead logging. They said it was and would be the last word. But it wasn't. Somebody topped and rigged *two* spar trees, and the "flying machine" or skyline system was born. A taut cable runs between the two spars, a hundred and fifty feet above the ground, and over this cable, on a device called a bicycle, the logs come zinging in to the landing, traveling swiftly through the air and never once touching ground, stumps, or snags. Logs are moved thus upmountain, down-mountain, and across wide canyons, with a speed that is amazing.

The donkey engines that run these prodigious rigs have outgrown the name. They are great hulks of steam, or diesel, or electric operation, many of them sixty feet long. Imaginative loggers tell of their power, that they could straighten out the Temperate Zone, just as Babe, the Big Blue Ox, did for Paul Bunyan, time of the Winter of the Blue Snow when the temperature went to twenty-four feet below zero.

The whole effect on the eye of a modern logging operation is a somewhat disconcerting maze of large and small cables running through the air in every direction, and the ground covered with stationary engines, pumps, woodbucking power saw, steel rails, switches, locomotives, cars, telephones, humidity gauges, movable power plants, and traveling machine shops. It is, in short, a gigantic factory without a roof.

A Day in Shingletown

Before I was dry behind the ears I was well in the way of becoming a "timber beast." Left an orphan at the age of ten I had been spewed from the fifth grade of school onto the skidroad with my neck fur yet to grow. By the time I was a fuzz-face I had gone through the many stages of waterboy, whistle-punk, bull-cook, and swamper in a logging camp; a mule-twister on a railroad and a gandy-dancer; a bundler and

[5] The invention of C. C. McLean, one-time white-water man of the Michigan woods, long-time logging superintendent and still at it, in 1938, at Valsetz, Oregon.—S.H.H.

By Verne Bright. From "Men at Work." Manuscripts of the Federal Writers' Project of the Works Progress Administration for the State of Oregon.

sawyer in a box-shook factory; a lathe-saw operator, planerman, lumber-piler; and tackled many another job in and out of the woods. Gradually I had grown from gaycat to timber-kitten. But in all the hullabaloo of jobs I had never worked a shingle mill.

And then one night in Erickson's I met a rounder who said: "In the empire of lumber the shingle-weavers are the untouchables, the aristocrats." He leaned his elbow on the bar and took a long quaff from his schooner of Heidelberg. "Yes, sir," he went on, "the shingle-weavers are the house of lords in this man's parliament. A lumber mill, now, or a logging camp! There's a dog's life. But a shingle mill—ah! by the holy old mackinaw, that's the only place for a real man of the forest." So I decided to become a shingle-weaver.

With this idea in mind one night at dusk I swung off a string of empty log trucks in the little seacoast village of Shingletown. Along the steep shore of the bay sprawled the settlement, and up a street that rose almost perpendicularly into the darkness a neon sign flashed, BAYSIDE HOTEL. I climbed the hill, rented a room, and turned in for the night.

The new sun was gleaming on the distant breakers beyond the sand-pit that thrust a long finger of dunes between the bay and the sea as I came out of the gray weather-beaten house that clutched precariously at the steep forested hillside. The morning breeze from beyond the bay was sharp with the odor of clam flats while the white seagulls, perched on the salt-caked piling at the edge of the water, lifted raucous cries. Below me the village scattered, and beyond it columns of smoke and steam belched from the stacks of the shingle-mill among a cluster of houseboats, barges and drying fish-nets. Curving along the bayside stretched the one paved street, the landward side bordered with rain-silvered wooden buildings, interspersed here and there with modern brick or concrete structures. As I stood looking out over the town and the bay toward the sea I began humming a ballad of the camps:

> Oh they said you are a flunkie and I said, how come?
> If you think I'm just a gaycat you're pretty damn dumb.
> I'm a timber beast from Kokomo, I'm leavin' this damn land,
> I'm gonna be a weaver an' with the weavers stand.

And I grinned like the cat that licked the cream as I started down toward the mill. I had just turned twenty-one and here, I thought, is maybe the kind of job I could stick to and settle down permanent. It was time a fellow was thinking about the future.

Well, I decided to see the whole works before hitting the tyee for a job. Even before the early shift came on I was walking the booms at the mill pond. I looked the place over. It was new and strange to the eyes of an inland logger. A young squirt of a kid was on the booms, pike-pole in hand, waiting the beginning whistle. He was only about eighteen, slender, and tough as a pine knot. But he had the steady eye and the agile foot of an old time river-hog. His dress was that of a typical riverman: "tin" rain-hat of paraffined canvas; gray flannel shirt under a black slicker jacket; tin pants "stagged" or cut off six inches below the knees; and sixteen-inch Chippeway logger boots, with half-inch steel spikes or calks in the soles.

I walked over to the kid and gave him a bit of chin music, not wishing to appear too inquisitive, but wanting to find out all I could about his job.

"Well," drawled the kid as he nudged a big blue butt with his pike pole, "these here logs are all cedar. They're gathered at the regular loggin' camps up in the mountains and hauled to the river on trucks where they're dumped in and floated down in rafts. We run this here boom made by timber chained together around 'em to keep 'em from floating off down the bay. My job is to select the logs and herd 'em down to the slip yonder, and the slip man chases 'em into the jack-ladder, that inclined trough or slip that goes up into the mill. He stands on that little platform at the bottom of the jack-ladder and with his pike hauls 'em in reach of the bull-chain which pulls 'em up into the mill."

The kid jumped lightly from the boom to a floating log. It was small and bobbed beneath him, but in an instant he had leaped to firmer footing on a huge king-cedar that he rode like an expert performer riding a circus stallion. Jauntily he guided his mount toward the log-slip, then leaped to a smaller log about two feet in diameter and began to roll it. The log gained momentum until it was a whirling blur of water and foam. Suddenly the kid brought the log to a quick stop tipped his hat back careless-like and announced: "That's called birling."

I walked to the end of the boom and up the cat-walk beside the bull-chain. As I reached the top of the incline the mill whistle blew. The head sawyer in his cage by the huge circular cut-off gave a signal and a sharp short *toot! toot!* stabbed the morning air. Slowly at first, as if reluctant to rouse from the night's inertia, all the machinery in the mill began to take on life: each wheel and pulley and saw accelerated, the noise rising in a gradual crescendo until the whole mill was enveloped in a consuming roar.

The bull-chain began to move; the pikeman hazed a log into the slip. The hooked cleats on the log-haul caught the timber and pulled it into the trough. Up the jack-ladder it came dripping-wet to the saw platform. As it reached the head-rig the log was brought up sharp by a steel stop which determined the length of the block to be cut; the cut-off sawyer kicked a lever throwing the bull-chain out of gear and settling giant steel clamps that held the log firmly. A great circular saw ten feet in diameter hovered beside the log, buzzing like a huge angry wasp. The hairy hands of the sawyer gripped the levers; he was an old man with lined face and intent eyes. He tugged at a lever and the saw, a whirring blur of chained lightning, swiftly sliced off a block, round and yellow as a mammoth cheese. As the cut fell away the old sawyer calmly kicked the stop lever and the log moved forward—sixteen inches, precisely.

The splitter-man, a "skookum-charlie" with shoulders as wide as a door, grabbed the block and heaved it onto the power splitter. The powerful machine, fed by steam, quartered the block and requartered it ready for the saws. With a flip of his hookaroon the splitter slid the small blocks to the conveyor which bore them to the battery of shingle machines that stretched away into the depths of the mill.

I squeezed back against the wall as the blocks toppled from the head-rig and were shoved into the splitting machine. The sharp whines of the saws crashed on my ears, mingled with the heavy hum of the cyclone-fan blowing the refuse to the fuel house. The air was thick with sawdust and the incense smell of the cedar was heavy as perfume in a rooming-house.

Just then the big tyee came along.

"Hi-ya bub!" he grunted, "looking for someone?"

After hemming and hawing a bit I got my back up and answered him: "Yeah! I was sorta looking for the head push. You him?"

"That's right. Need a job?"

"Well, I thought I'd kinda like to work in a shingle mill. I've worked in box-factories, lathe-mills, logging camps and sawmills; but I'm a greenhorn about a shingle mill."

"I need a man out on the pond if you'd like the job. Maybe later I could use you in the mill."

"Gee, thanks, mister!"

* * * * *

. . . The first day on my new job proved to be my last.

The boom was filled with all shapes and sizes of cedar logs; big ones, little ones, rough barked ones, and some slipperier than hell. I didn't have any calked boots, either, but figured on getting them come pay-day. I thought I knew as much about bucking logs as the next one, but this job was different. I had to stand on the log I was bucking and saw straight up and down with the other end of my saw under the log in the water. When the tide was running as it was that day the pressure of the water against the saw made it buckle and bind and run plenty hard. But I was bound to make good so I sawed away with a will, pausing now and then to get my breath and smell the tang of salt-water and cedar. I had my first log about half sawed through when along came a tug-boat raising swells six feet high that rolled out behind her and spread from shore to shore of the bay.

I straightened up from my bucking and just stood there watching the tug-boat coming up the bay and enjoying the scenery and the tangy smells. The tug was running in close to the boom where I was standing. As she came closer she tooted her whistle and it echoed back and forth among the hills along the bay. She was whistling to warn me but I didn't know it at the time. I only stood there gawking. Just then I glanced toward the mill and saw the pond man waving friendly-like at me, so I waved back and went on staring at the tug-boat.

When the tug had passed, the big swells she had churned up began to roll out toward the boom, and before I knew it they hit the boom and things began to happen. Those sixty-foot cedar logs began jumping around like corks in a wash tub, and me standing right in the midst of them. There I was with slick-soled shoes; if I lost my footing and fell between those milling logs I would be ground to hamburger. I knew then what the boom man had been yelling and waving to me about. However, I didn't have much time to think things out. I had to do something pretty damned quick or I was a goner. About twenty feet away was a piling thrust ten or twelve feet in the air. With my heart in my mouth and my soul in the hands of the Lord I started for that piling, hopping from log to log, timing each jump so I wouldn't lose my balance. My timing must of been good. In a second or two that seemed like a year or two, I reached the piling. I couldn't climb it because it was slimy and spray-washed and slick as a peeled onion. From the top of it though, there was a piece of old cable dangling. My luck was good; just as I got on the blue butt that was scratching its side on the piling a big swell, a four-foot roller, lifted the log and me on top of it within reach of the rusty cable. I grabbed it and hung on, pulling my legs up under me.

When the logs quieted down again, I slid from the pole and walked shakily across the boom to where my saw still stuck half way through the log, the slippery handle waiting for me to grab a-hold and finish the cut. But as far as I know the saw is still waiting. I didn't have stomach for any more of that kind of logging. I pulled stakes and went away from there.

As I scrambled along the booms toward shore the boom man hollered: "Next time watch out for them tugs; this ain't no summer picnic!"

"There ain't going to be any next time," I yelled back. He grinned and watched me climb the bank. I looked back at the shingle mill belching smoke and steam. . . .

"Yi-ah! yi-ah! yi-ah!" screamed the gulls.

VI. OIL

A wildcatter is a person who drills for oil in a place where oil is not known to exist. . . . According to oil-field tradition, the original wildcatters drilled so far from town and all proven territory that they used hoot owls for chickens and wildcats for watch-dogs.—J. FRANK DOBIE

Oil Sayings

Always hang on to your mineral rights. Can't ever tell what they might be worth some day.

* * * * *

Wherever lightning strikes, you'll find oil.
Drill on a hilltop, never in a valley.
There's always oil under a graveyard.

* * * * *

Oil is where you find it.
More money has been put into the ground than was ever taken out of it. Put in by doodlebug suckers!
A geologist—a fellow with a pencil in one hand and an eraser in the other!

* * * * *

You spud in at the surface, sue at the oil sand.
A dry hole clears a title, a producer always clouds it.

Oil Is Where You Find It

I[1]

All kinds of tales are told about the ingenious devices which oilmen have used to hide—or uncover—news of an important strike. There

From *Big Country, Texas,* by Donald Day, pp. 233, 246, 257, 275. American Folkways Series, edited by Erskine Caldwell. Copyright, 1947, by Donald Day. New York: Duell, Sloan & Pearce.

[1] From *America's Heartland, The Southwest,* by Green Peyton, pp. 96–97. Copyright, 1948, by the University of Oklahoma Press. Norman.

The folklore of the oil business never has been adequately told. It can't be told here either, much as I would like to linger on it. The point of these anecdotes is that oil *does* have its own rich field of memoirs and mythology. The reason it has never been tapped may be the uneasy atmosphere of top secrecy in which the industry has wrapped itself; or it may be that the pursuit of oil is such a highly technical avocation that storytellers shy away from it.—G.P.

is the one about Tom Slick, who found the Cushing field in Oklahoma. He had leased all the land he could lay hands on around Cushing before he brought in the first well. To make doubly sure that he would have the field to himself, Slick hired all the livery rigs in town, locked them in the stables, and sent all the notaries off on a free vacation, so that no interloper could get a lease notarized.

On the other hand, Pete Frost of Houston, making his start in the oil business, heard of a hole that was being drilled in strictest secrecy out in the country. He put on old clothes, borrowed a brace of rabbit dogs from a farmer, and set off in the direction of the well. As he came out from behind some brush, near the guarded entrance to the enclosure, he fired his gun three times and shook his head with a dispirited air.

"Miss him?" said the guard sympathetically.

"Sure did," said Frost.

They struck up a conversation about the cussedness of jack rabbits. While the guard's head was turned, Frost flipped up the edge of the tarpaulin that covered the gauge on the well. A quick glance at the figure to which the needle pointed told him that the owner had struck oil. He took the dogs home, leased all the land he could get in the neighborhood, and started drilling his own well. A few months later he was a rich man.

There was the group of farmers near Ranger, Texas, a few miles west of Fort Worth, who made a deal with W. K. Gordon, a mining engineer, to drill a well for them. The first hole was abandoned at 3,400 feet when the bit broke. They tried again, and got down to 3,200 feet without a show of oil. Then a wire came from Gordon's office in New York, directing him to abandon the dry hole. Out of sheer stubbornness, Gordon let the crew drill 200 feet more. They were about to give up in disgust when the well blew in. Not only that: as the stream of oil gushed over the derrick, they heard a distant rumbling and looked around to find that the first well had come in, too.

II[2]

It was almost sunset as a tired teamster urged his plodding horses on, less than a mile from their destination. The terminus was a large new stake, where some men with a queer idea were planning to drill a well which they said was sure to find oil. The heavy load of rig

---

[2] From *Flush Production,* The Epic of Oil in the Gulf-Southwest, by Gerald Forbes, pp. 202–204, 213. Copyright, 1942, by the University of Oklahoma Press, Norman.

Certainly one oil-field story has become a legend. It may have occurred once, but the regularity with which it is retold throughout the Southwest casts doubt on its authenticity. Doubtless all the significant oil pools and many of the lesser ones, from Kansas to Mexico, and Louisiana to New Mexico, have served as the scene for this bit of lore. Thousands of persons in the Southwest tell it with sincere belief in its accuracy. Here it is retold once more.—G.F.

timbers twisted as one of the great horses hesitated before plunging into a puddle of mud with the weighty burden. The teamster went into action with his whip, as two of the wheels sank into the soft soil and the wagon stopped behind the lunging horses. The great team was unable to move the loaded wagon. The driver had a great deal of sympathy for his horses; they had pulled the load nearly twenty miles since sunrise.

Grumbling and muttering, the teamster dropped from his seat to the ground and glanced at the sinking sun. To free the wagon he must unload it. Then he must drive the empty vehicle to firm ground and reload. Only a short distance remained to be driven before the lumber would be deposited near the stake, where the tired man and his plodding team would turn back. Thoughtfully the teamster gritted his teeth and stacked the heavy timbers on the ground. The team easily took the empty wagon from the mud. The man then took a short-handled ax from his tool box and sharpened a large stake, which he drove firmly into the earth near the stack of heavy lumber. They wanted a stake, so he gave them a stake.

The next day the rig-builders came and erected a derrick around the teamster's stake. The rig-builders were followed by the drilling crew, who set up their machinery and had gone deep into the earth before the owners of the well discovered the change in location. The well was completed. It opened a great new pool. Then several months passed before a well at the original location proved to be an expensive dry hole.

That story has been told with many variations. Sometimes the teamster lost his directions, or the truck broke down, or the location could not be found, or the dark eye-socket of a bleached cow's skull attracted attention, but the conclusion is always the same: the new well was a good one and the old location was dry.

* * * * *

Among the many strange characters recurrently seen in the early days of the oil industry was the "man with the doodlebug."[3] He was always mysteriously marked from the crowd, generally by the uncommon nature of his garments. In a throng of booted men in overalls, one dressed in kid shoes, a frock coat, and a clean derby attracted attention. This man, who spoke softly, carried a shiny black box under his arm. His services were for sale, and when employed he prowled about the countryside muttering strange words and syllables until the magical black box, his doodlebug, stopped him. There, he told his employer, was the exact spot on which to drill for oil. A simpler form of the doodlebug was the forked stick, which allegedly signified the

[3] Cf. H. H. Adams, "Doodlebugs and Doodlebuggers," *California Folklore Quarterly,* Vol. III (January, 1944), No. 1, pp. 53–58; Mody C. Boatright, "Oil by Hook or Crook," *Southwest Review,* Vol. XXXI (Spring, 1946), No. 2, pp. 122–128; David Donoghue, "Myths in Oil Finding," *Southwestern Lore* (Dallas, 1931), pp. 45–47.

presence of oil by a downward pull when carried under tension over the "oil stream." This was the old water witch idea. In one case a farmer owned land that a large oil company wanted to lease, but he refused to sign a contract until the firm had agreed to make the first hole at the spot selected by an "oil smeller," a term now used by oil men for all such media. The well that was drilled produced about five hundred barrels of petroleum daily. The strange thing about that well was that surrounding holes in every direction were dry, which of course confirmed the farmer's faith in legerdemain.

Lease Hounds

The lobbies of the Metropolitan and the Westbrook in Fort Worth were the scenes of intensive "drilling" as men bent eagerly over maps and bought and sold leases without ever having seen them or ever having been closer than one hundred miles of the oil field.

A story was told of a man arrested in Fort Worth for vagrancy. "Don't you have any business or profession?" the judge inquired. The prisoner's response was, "I was an oil man but some so-and-so stole my map."

At the head of the newly-created companies, in many instances, were men completely lacking in oil field experience. Some were more concerned about getting a tract that could be made the basis for brilliant promotional literature than they were about striking oil. For that reason they paid fantastic figures for small leases, disrupting the price situation for the veteran operators.

Queer beliefs, which were by no means confined to the newcomers in the game, were held as to the desirability of leases. Although the oil had been stored in the earth, of course, for aeons before the coming of the Texas & Pacific Railroad, there was a wide feeling that the railway constituted the boundary of the Ranger-Eastland district proper and leases south of the railroad were not in demand until an intrepid soul ignored the dividing line and brought in a well.

Pretty much the same view was held with reference to creeks and even public roads as though Nature had said to the sea of oil far below the earth's surface, "Thus far shalt thou come but on the south side of this country lane thy proud waves shall be stayed."

Because of the success experienced by the Harmony Baptist Church wells at Pleasant Grove and the Merriman school and church wells, there was an especially strong demand for school and church grounds and there seemed a well-defined belief that if one could lease a cemetery, a gusher was bound to result!

From *Were You in Ranger?* by Boyce House, pp. 117–119.

Oil Field Names

The names of companies active in the Ranger field were touched with glamor.

Some were christened with names famous in the development of the area and linked with the section in which the investors lived. There were the Hog Creek Central, Wyandotte Hog Creek, Ranger-Hog Creek, Hog Creek Junior, Desdemona Hogg Creek, and Hogg Town Oil and Gas—the spelling of the last two, perhaps, being occasioned by the confusion of Hogtown and Hog Creek with the name of Hogg, the farmer whose land was the scene of a bevy of big wells.

The Duke farm, which witnessed the discovery of the Desdemona pool, was a favorite with name-seekers—the Grand Duke Producing Company, Heart of the Duke (in reference to location in the pool), Duke Extension, El Paso Duke, Italian Duke, Post-Duke, Duke-Burk-Ranger, Duke-Knowles Annex, Royal Duke, Duke Consolidated Royalty Syndicate, Erath Duke, Duke Dome, Alamo-Duke, Tex-Duke, Giant Duke, Duke of Dublin, Comanche-Duke, and Iowa-Duke.

There were the Ranger Big Pool, El Paso-Ranger, Okeh Ranger, Desdemona-Cisco, Desdemona Oil, Desdemona & Burkburnett, Desdemona Producers, Comanche Chief, Big Chief, Comanche Gusher, and Comanche Queen.

History, legend, and nature were ransacked for titles. Radium, Mother Pool, Eldorado, King Midas, Hercules, Magic, and Victory were a few. Others were Dixie, Kentucky River, Cotton States, Arizona, and Oklamania. There were the Rainbow, Texas Venture, Little Giant, All-American, Sammies, and Pocahontas.

In the procession of colorful names were Texas Eagle, Black Steer, Longhorn, and Black Diamond, besides Ocean, Ajax, Pacific, and Home. Still others were the Guaranty, Banker, and Integrity. Less pretentious cognomens were Lucky Boy, Home Boy, and Jones Boys.

These represented a wide variety not only in names but in other ways. Some were in existence long before the McCleskey was drilled; others sprang up during the Ranger boom. Some held extensive holdings in a number of fields; others had half an acre at Desdemona. But all were active in the drilling operations.

* * * * *

Long before the days of "They satisfy" and "What a whale of a difference a few cents makes," the author of an oil stock advertisement linked the aroma of tobacco with his appeal:

"Some prefer 'Duke's Mixture'; others like 'Bull'; but the smoke of King Midas makes 'em all sit up and take notice."

Ibid., pp. 115–117.

Paul Bunyan in the Oil Fields

Paul Bunyan appears in the oil fields as a jack of all trades who nevertheless is proficient in each far beyond the best of his rivals. He is regarded by the different groups of workers as having had a large part in developing the tools and methods of their trade. His own huge strength and uncanny skill, however, enable him often to discard the slow and cumbersome conventional practices. For instance, as a rigbuilder, as the oil-field carpenter is called, he demonstrated clearly that he was supreme. He could sight so accurately that no plumb line was necessary. The arduous and difficult job of "pulling," "running," and "sighting" a derrick, i.e., building it, took Paul only one day, thereby saving two days of the usual time, as well as the labor of two men. The customary hatchet was too light for him; his weighed eight pounds and drove any nail to the head at a single blow. He could build a pair of

---

By John Lee Brooks. From *Foller de Drinkin' Gou'd,* Publications of the Texas Folk-Lore Society, No. VII, edited by J. Frank Dobie, pp. 48–53. Copyright, 1928, by the Texas Folk-Lore Society. Austin: University of Texas Press.

With the development of the oil industry in the second half of the nineteenth century, it was quite natural that the heroic Paul Bunyan should be adopted into a trade which called for just as much strength as logging and even more courage, determination, and resource. Beginning in West Virginia, Paul became the embodiment of superhuman ability as an oil man, and he was known wherever there were American oil-workers.

My introduction to this legendary figure came during the summer of 1920 spent in the Hewitt field, near Ardmore, Oklahoma. I was learning the game as a "boll-weevil" and so was the victim of many "sells," such as being sent for a left-handed monkey-wrench or the pipe-stretchers. The old-timers particularly enjoyed making casual references to miraculous time and labor saving practices that the powerful and ingenious Paul Bunyan used on his rig. There was nothing, however, like a cycle of stories; there were no extended tales.

A year later, I returned to the oil field, this time near Breckenridge, Texas, where I worked for several months in a gasoline plant. At last I got a chance to go out as a tool-dresser, or helper, on a standard (cable tool) drilling rig. Both my driller and the one on the opposite tour [shift] were old heads, having started back in West Virginia twenty or thirty years earlier. Paul Bunyan was an old friend of theirs, and occasionally, in the lighter moods, they amused themselves and "kidded" me by calling to mind some of his exploits.

The coming of the casing crew, however, brought out the freest expressions of Bunyan stories. When the work was going on smoothly, there was a continual flow of profane banter, which involved always a good deal of "fancy lyin'." The presence of a rank "boll-weevil" furnished a perfect opportunity to try their memories and imaginations in telling of the famous Paul. Their yarns were addressed ostensibly to every one but me, yet even though I didn't say a word, there were huge laughs and elaborately casual glances at me that were unmistakably significant. They watched every move I made with keenly critical eyes, and offered the most ironical suggestions by way of help, mentioning Paul as an authority; or they told some time later, with apparently no reference to my work, of what Paul Bunyan once did to a "boll-weevil" who spliced a rope in a certain way (exactly my way, of course). Nothing I could say, not even a disgusted "Aw, Hell!" failed to call out roars of laughter and many slappings of shoulder and leg.

the great wooden "bull-wheels"[1] in half a day, hang the massive "walking-beam"[2] by himself, and "skid a rig" (the whole derrick) several yards over by hand. If any timbers, or even the crown block,[3] fell off the structure in the process of building, Paul, who worked below, caught them in his hands to save the lumber as well as the heads of those who might be underneath.

Bunyan was such a powerful and tireless worker, and so considerate of his men, that he used to let them sleep half the tour while he did alone the work of the crew of five. His childish pride in his own ability led him to perform many stunts. One day without help he built a rig and "spudded in"[4] the hole with a Ford motor. He boasted that he could dig faster with a "sharp-shooter"[5] than any crew could drill, but since he could never find any one to call his bet, he did not try this feat. It was not uncommon for him, whenever he grew impatient in building a rig, to drive a sixteen-pound hammer into the ground so deep that the oil

---

During a two years' absence from the field I learned to appreciate the Bunyan myth as folklore and went back not to work but to collect Bunyaniana. I drifted along the trail of the oil development through Ranger, Breckenridge, Eastland, Cisco, Big Lake, Best, and finally to McCamey, the latest frontier. I had been having the typical luck of the folklorist—picking up here and there a mannerism, an incident, or running across a grizzled driller who knew Paul Bunyan but just couldn't remember any stories right then. At McCamey, however, where things were doing, I hoped to find Paul Bunyan in action. . . .

My hopes were not justified by the results. Paul Bunyan did not reign here and revel. I loafed about, raking up speaking acquaintances with all who looked as if they might even have heard of Paul and buying drinks for half the idlers in McCamey, but I found no one who gave me more than a reminiscent smile and perhaps a slight incident or two. I went out to the camps, but I found no considerable body of narrative. Either I failed to discover an old-time tale-teller with the genuine creative fancy, or I lacked the key to unlock their word-hoards. My efforts resulted in a heterogeneous mass of incidents that spoke of Paul Bunyan more often as a rig-builder and driller, but also as a pipeliner, a tank-builder, and even as a constructor of telegraph lines.

These fragmentary incidents, I became convinced, were the shreds of a widespread and varied legend of Paul Bunyan as an oil field hero; yet the legend, new as it was in a comparatively new industry, seemed to be succumbing to the machinery of modern life so fatal to all folk creation. I have tried to give this disjected material a semblance of coherence.—J.L.B., *ibid.*, pp. 46–47, 48.

See also Acel Garland, "Pipeline Days and Paul Bunyan," and Wayne Martin and B. A. Botkin, "Paul Bunyan on the Water Pipeline," *A Treasury of American Folklore* (New York, 1944), pp. 222–227, 626–629.

For the life and tales of an earlier flesh-and-blood hero of the cable-tool drillers, see Mody C. Boatright, *Gib Morgan, Minstrel of the Oil Fields* (Texas Folk-Lore Society, 1945). See also Kemp Morgan in Frank Shay's *Here's Audacity!* (New York, 1930).

[1] The "bull-wheels" form the large reel on which the drilling cable is wound.—J.L.B.

[2] The "walking-beam" is a great wooden beam that is worked with a seesaw action by the engine, raising and lowering the tools in the hole for drilling.—J.L.B.

[3] The crown block is the wooden block on top of the derrick; it holds the pulley wheels over which the steel cables run.—J.L.B.

[4] "Spudded in"—i.e., started the hole. The first two or three hundred feet of hole is drilled in a special manner without the walking-beam.—J.L.B.

[5] A "sharp-shooter" is a long narrow spade.—J.L.B.

came to the surface without drilling. This practice was deplored by the operators because it called for the very inconvenient and wasteful task of dipping the oil out of the hole.

Sometimes Paul's fiery nature caused even greater losses. The visits of officious "high-powers"[6] often made him lose control of his hot temper. At these times the crew ran frantically for cover and left him to vent his rage in a wholesale smashing of derricks for a mile around. The most violent manifestation of this weakness brought him a fortune. One day while up in the derrick, he grew terribly angry at one of his crew who was below. Paul hurled his hatchet at the man with such force that, missing its aim, it penetrated the ground so far that oil gushed up. Quickly forgetting his anger, Paul and his crew set about casing and cementing the hole. The well brought him a million dollars, every cent of which he spent for Mail Pouch tobacco.[7] He had conceived the scheme of soaking his tobacco in corn-whisky and making a "clean-up" by selling it to the oil-field "bullies." His own appetite got the better of him, however, and he chewed it all himself.

Paul did not waste his time with derricks of the usual size. His structures towered far above their conventional neighbors and had telephone connections for each member of the crew. After drilling started, the derrick man was able to come down only twice a month, for payday. On one occasion Paul determined to break his record for height. He built the structure up, up, up until it became so tall that he and his crew moved to Heaven and lived there while they finished their work. Paul determined to drill a well worthy of his derrick. He penetrated to China before he stopped drilling.

While building another tall rig, at Bakersfield, California, Paul had a remarkable experience. He was up on the derrick at work when a terrific wind storm carried him out to sea. His first conscious moment found him alone in the Pacific 500 miles from land with his hatchet in his hand, astride a board. A whale appeared and attacked him. Paul fell into the water, killed the big fish with a single blow of his hatchet, and, mounting the dead whale, paddled with his plank back to California.

As a driller Paul Bunyan is quite as striking a figure. He was equally at home on a rotary or on a standard rig; in fact, he devised most of the implements and practices of the trade. His naive humor is seen in the names used by every driller, toolie, and roughneck: the "headache post"; "Maud," the heavy break-out tongs; "bull-wheel" and "calf-wheel"; the "lazy-bench," and many other names.[8] On his own rig,

[6] "High-powers" are officials of high rank in the company controlling the drilling.—J.L.B.

[7] Mail Pouch chewing tobacco is perhaps the favorite brand in the oil field; Beechnut is a close second.—J.L.B.

[8] For these standard or cable tool rig terms, see James W. Winfrey, "Oil Patch Talk," in *From Hell to Breakfast,* Texas Folk-Lore Society Publication No. XIX, Mody C. Boatright and Donald Day, editors (1944), p. 148: "The wire line drum,

when he was using a rotary, he did not unjoint the drill-stem in small sections, to be stacked in the derrick, but simply ran the 2,000 feet of steel pipe up into the air and held it in his hands until the bit was changed. For his own convenience, to allow him to leave the rig, he invented a way of winding the drill-pipe around a big drum. He thus saved many days of the time usually required to drill a well. His boilers were so big that any one who carelessly went near the injectors[9] was sucked up inside. If a boiler blew up, Paul jumped astride it and rode it back safely to earth; he would not be baffled by such annoyances as that.

His experiences on a standard tool rig were often bizarre and colorful. One time while drilling in a mountainous country, he ran on to a "granite-rock" and pounded for a week without making any apparent progress. He put on an extra set of jars[10] without any effect; a third and a fourth set of jars did not help materially, and he finally put on fifteen sets in a desperate effort to save the hole. The terrific pounding jarred the whole lease up fifty feet above the surrounding land before he broke through the rock. On another mountain-side location Paul drilled what seemed to be a very deep hole. Finally he ran into "soft diggin' "[11] and decided to set casing before going any farther. He started putting in the casing; it kept going down until it seemed that it wouldn't stop. At last one of the crew who had gone over to another location on an errand came running back to tell him that the pipe was coming out the other side of the mountain. Paul discovered that the "tough diggin' " had deflected the tools; he had drilled through the mountain; the casing had run out and made a pipeline for two miles down the valley. Another experience was more tragic. Paul was drilling in Mexico this time. There was a heavy flow of rubber that drenched the whole rig

---

drum pulley, and break wheel make up the 'bull wheel.' When 'sucker rods' (also called sucker poles) are pulled, the bull wheel is connected to the 'band wheel' in the 'belt house' by the 'bull rope,' a heavy manila rope or small wire line. The band wheel is belt driven by some kind of prime mover. While the standard rig is 'bobbin' ' (pumping), the pump down in the well is suspended from the end of the 'walking beam' by the sucker rods and 'beam hanger.' The walking beam rocks on the 'sampson post' riding the 'saddle bearing.' A post set under the walking beam to catch the weight of the sucker rods in case the pitman breaks on a standard rig is the 'headache post.' On more modern rigs a steel segment of a circle on the rod end of the walking beam is the 'horse-head.' The beam hanger is a 'bridle.' The oscillating motion is transmitted from the prime mover through a crank to the beam by a vertical member called a 'pitman.' " The "calf wheel" is auxiliary to the "bull wheel."

A chaise longue-looking affair is made by a fireman out of 2x12 boards for his personal use in front of the boiler and is called his "lazy bench."— James W. Winfrey, *ibid.*, p. 144.

[9] The injector sucks water, usually from a depression in the ground, forcing it into the boiler.—J.L.B.

[10] The jars are two heavy steel links attached above the drill stem, allowing several inches of play and therefore increasing the shock of the blow.—J.L.B.

[11] "Soft diggin' " and "tough diggin' " are common expressions for soft and hard rock.—J.L.B.

and cooled before it could be washed off The poor toolie, who was up in the derrick, could not keep his hold on the slippery boards and fell. He hit the rubber-covered floor and bounced for three days and nights. They finally had to shoot him to keep him from starving to death.[12]

Perhaps the strangest of all Paul's experiences came as the result of an accident. One day he carelessly allowed himself to be caught in the steel drilling cable while the bit was being lowered into the hole. Before he could be stopped he found himself at the bottom of the well in a large cavity in a very warm atmosphere. "It was hot as Hell down there," Paul described the atmosphere later. He soon found that he actually was in Hell. Walking on deeper into the mountain cave, he met the Devil, who greeted him warmly, as if the famous driller were perfectly known to him. The Devil took him all around the place, and at last showed him the harem. The beauties were so ravishing that Paul tried to carry one along, and the Devil in a rage chased him back up the well. Before Paul left, however, he settled a certain question that had been bothering him. Some time before, a "roustabout" who had a grudge against him had sneaked up behind him, cut off his leg, and thrown it down the well. Paul had never grown accustomed to his wooden leg; so while down in Hell he asked about his lost flesh-and-blood limb. The Devil told him it was already roasting on the coals and that he could not have it.

Paul Bunyan would never admit defeat until forced to do so, and then he always made the best of his losses. A particularly good example of his pertinacity and grit is seen in an exploit of his out on the California coast. He was shooting a well,[13] but the charge of five hundred quarts of nitro-glycerine exploded while going down the hole. A terrific flow of oil caught the crew altogether unprepared to take care of it. Before they could think, Paul jumped to the well and sat upon the pipe, stopping the flow. The incredible pressure of gas and oil thus restrained forced the casing out of the ground, carrying Paul up in the air so high that he stayed three days before a derrick could be built to rescue him. The well was capped and the oil saved.

Paul lost only two holes in his long drilling career. The first loss occurred in the Texas Panhandle. He drilled into an alum bed and the hole shrank up tight, catching the tools so firmly that they could not be released. The second misfortune was just a "piece of hard luck" that Paul could not help. He had been drilling for several months on the top of a very high hill. One night just before the "graveyard shift"[14] came on, a fearful windstorm struck the location, driving with such velocity that it blew all the dirt away from the hole. There was noth-

---

[12] Cf. the story of Pecos Bill's "bouncing bride," "The Saga of Pecos Hill," *The Century Magazine,* October, 1923 [*A Treasury of American Folklore,* p. 185].—J.L.B.

[13] "Shooting a well" is exploding a charge of nitro-glycerine, "soup," at the bottom of the hole to break up the sand and stimulate the flow of oil.—J.L.B.

[14] The "graveyard shift" works from twelve at night till twelve noon.—J.L.B.

ing for Paul to do but saw the well up and sell it for post-holes.[15] Another of the rare failures of Bunyan was his attempt to transplant "dry holes"[16] to Europe. They were of no use over here, and besides saving a lot of drilling over there, they might make wells. They were all warped, however, in the rough trip over the waves and had to be thrown away.

VII. LAST WESTS

The age of rugged individualism is over. . . . These giants of another day played their parts well. They were cast in the rôles of builders, and they built. They built for themselves first and the rest of the world second. . . . But the story would not be complete if it did not tell also about the part played by the men at the bottom—the men who sweated and struggled and worked for a pittance to build the West we know. . . .—GLENN CHESNEY QUIETT

Yuba Dam

Near Marysville we passed the little village of Yuba Dam, the scene of an early California story, which *Harper's Monthly* first made public. It avers that on a quiet Sunday morning a traveler reached the three little houses which comprise the town.

"My friend," he asked of a citizen, "what village is this?"

"Yuby Dam."

The stranger, shocked at such impoliteness and profanity, put spurs to his horse. At the door of the next cabin stood a decent housewife,

15 . . . One train load of post holes Paul shipped were exposed to a salt atmosphere and were so badly rusted as to be a dead loss when they arrived at the point of delivery. Since then he has been painting them and wrapping them in wax paper. —Margarete Carpenter, in *Coyote Wisdom,* Texas Folklore Society Publications No. XIV, J. Frank Dobie, Mody C. Boatright, and Harry H. Ransom, editors (1938), p. 264.

16 A "dry hole," a "duster," is one which did not produce oil.—J.L.B.

From *Beyond the Mississippi:* From the Great River to the Great Ocean, Life and Adventure on the Prairies, Mountains, and Pacific Coast . . . 1857–1867, by Albert D. Richardson, p. 394. Hartford, Connecticut: American Publishing Company.

broom in hand. He repeated the inquiry: "Madam, will you please tell me the name of this village?"

"Yuby Dam."

Still more scandalized, the interrogator rode on until he met a little boy playing in the street. Here at least he might obtain a proper answer: "My son, what is this place called?"

"Yuby Dam!"

"Heavens!" exclaimed the astounded stranger as he galloped out of the town. "What a place is this, where even the women and children swear—and on Sunday, too!"

How Hangtown Got Its Name

To Placerville belongs the honor of the first popular tribunal of the placer-mining epoch. Distant but nine miles from Coloma, where gold was first discovered, the spot where now stands the town was early occupied by diggers. Placerville, however, was not the original name of the camp. It was first called Dry Diggings; afterward, for the reason which we shall presently see, Hangtown.

It was not a pleasing spectacle, this first display of unchained justice among the miners; but what could they do? Five men, one night about the middle of January, 1849, had entered the sleeping-room of a Mexican gambler named Lopez, and had attempted to rob him. One of them had placed a pistol at the head of the gambler, while the others seized his effects. Before they could escape Lopez had succeeded in giving the alarm. Roused by his cries, the miners had rushed in and arrested the whole gang.

Again I ask, what could they do? Stand there holding the thieves until a jail was built, or until congress should send sheriff and judge? They must either turn them loose to further and instant crimes, their numbers quickly multiplied by the absence of punishment, or they must themselves do justice, God helping them, as best they might. So they selected from amongst their number twelve, who ordered the culprits to receive each thirty-nine lashes; which having been well laid on, with due energy and decorum, three of the five, Garcia and Bissi, Frenchmen, and Manuel, a Chileno, were further charged with robbery and attempted murder on the Stanislaus the autumn previous. The charge was easily enough proved; the men, lying exhausted from their late punishment, were unable to stand or speak during this second trial. "What shall be done with them?" the improvised judge asked of the two hundred assembled. "Hang them," said one. E. Gould

From *The Works of Hubert Howe Bancroft,* Vol. XXXVI, *Popular Tribunals,* Vol. I, pp. 144–145. Entered according to Act of Congress in the Year 1887, by Hubert H. Bancroft in the Office of the Librarian of Congress, at Washington. San Francisco: The History Company, Publishers.

Buffum was there, and mounting a stump begged them, in the name of God, humanity, and law, to desist from their meditated action. But the miners, now warmed with drink, would not listen to him. The prisoners were bad men, and this thing must be stopped at once. So with ropes round their necks, the three condemned were driven in a wagon under a tree, and there hanged; after which they were cut down and buried in their blankets. And thereupon the place which before this was known as Dry Diggings was for a time called Hangtown.

How Virginia City Was Named

. . . Virginia City took its name from the native state of "Old Virginny," James Finney, as he was known in Nevada—James Fenimore, as he was before an encounter in the Kern River, California, mining fields caused a change of his place of residence. He was credited with suggesting the camp's name when, in the course of one of his frequent grand drunks, he tumbled over and broke a loaded whisky bottle, and rather than waste the libation to Mother Earth he utilized the disaster by declaring: "I christen this ground Virginia." The designation was adopted by a miners' meeting in September, 1859.

The State of Deseret

In those years men sought Heaven-on-Earth, and the names preserved the record of that search. . . .

In Ontario County, New York, [Joseph Smith] saw visions. Near Manchester stood an ordinary hill, but young Joseph Smith knew it as the Hill Cumorah. The angel Moroni told him to dig there, and find certain gold plates. The Eight Witnesses testified that the plates had "the appearance of gold . . . for we have seen and hefted." A century later, when the Saints were rich and powerful, they returned and bought that land, so that now the Hill Cumorah is as surely named a part of the United States as any Baldy or Round Top.

Then the Book of Mormon came into being, and many people followed its words. The Gentiles murdered Joseph Smith in an Illinois jail, but of the remaining faithful Brigham Young forged a strong people. Like Moses, he led them through the wilderness; standing on a mountainside he looked out at last, and said: "This is the place!"

From *Outposts of Civilization,* by W. A. Chalfant, p. 84. Copyright, 1928, by the Christopher Publishing House, Boston.

From *Names on the Land,* A Historical Account of Place-Naming in the United States, by George R. Stewart, pp. 260–262, 285–286. Copyright, 1945, by George R. Stewart. New York: Random House.

They were Americans, and few of them were men of learning. Most often they gave simple American names in that new and desert land. Where they settled, the mountain men had already plainly named the Great Salt Lake. The Saints let it stand, but the stream which had been called Utah River, they renamed. Since they had come like Israelites to the Promised Land, they called it the Jordan.

Upon its banks they founded a city, four-square. Not when William Penn dreamed of Philadelphia or L'Enfant planned Washington was an American city set apart for a greater future. This was to be no mere earthly capital, but a sacred refuge. A great city should have a great name. That they did not call it Zion or Jerusalem seems strange. Perhaps they thought that such a name might help stir up hatred among the Gentiles, as had happened before at their towns called Adam-Ondi-Ahman and Nauvoo. In the end, like other Americans of the time, they took an established name of the country, not too short to lack dignity. First the quorum of the Twelve decided, and then the public assembly confirmed that it should be City of the Great Salt Lake.

The whole region had as yet no name. They often called it Zion, but that was by figure of speech, and for a name they borrowed from their own holy word. In the Book of Mormon, that part called the Book of Ether, you may read how Jared and his brother and their families migrated into the wilderness to a Promised Land, and in the Chapter 2, Verse 3:

> And they did also carry with them Deseret, which, by interpretation, is a honey bee; and thus they did carry with them swarms of bees.

Deseret was not the name of a place, but in the story it brought to mind a far-off valley, "which is choice above all other lands." Also it was like the word *desert*. So they called their new country and their government, Deseret.

As they spread about in it and planted colonies, they gave mostly American names, but differed in two ways. Since they felt themselves a chosen and separate people, they spoke to one another as "Brother Joseph," or "Sister Sarah." So they naturally called their towns by baptismal names—Abraham, Heber, Hyrum, Brigham City. Even when they named a county for the President of the United States, they called it Millard, not Fillmore. Also they called themselves the Latter-day Saints, and the word *saint* was common among them. From this custom sprang several towns, such as St. John and St. George, named not for any beloved apostle or any dragon-slayer, but for John Rowberry and George A. Smith, good Mormon church officials.

The Mormons gave no more Biblical names than other people, but they had a treasure-store in the Book of Mormons. Joseph Smith had recorded many names, some the same as those of the Bible, others like them but a little different. So, besides Deseret, towns sprang up for Moroni the angel, Alma and Nephi the prophets, and Lehi the king, and many others.

* * * * *

. . . But Deseret came from the Book of Mormon, a work regarded as infamous by the great majority of Americans. Politically also Brigham Young was suspected of wishing to establish an independent government, and many objected to recognizing him, and the name which he had presumptuously set up.

There was moreover an obvious substitute, which was in accordance with tradition. As early as 1720 the Spaniards had written down the name of a tribe as Yutta. The Americans spelled it Ute, Uta, or Utah; Frémont in his reports had favored the last. The name had been applied to a lake, and to its outflowing stream which the Mormons renamed the Jordan. A river bearing a tribal name was thus available, and in addition Senator Benton, Frémont's father-in-law, was largely concerned with western affairs

The Mormons, however, were strongly for Deseret, and for the first time local sentiment clashed with Congress. The religious question was kept politely out of public debate. Mr. Benton said that he opposed Deseret because it suggested *desert,* and was repulsive. The Mormons, on the other hand, passed a resolution: "Do they object to the name of our state? It is good enough for us who have to wear it." Always before, Congress had accepted the local preference, but this situation was unique. There were objections also to Utah—the Indians of that name, some branches of them at least, were notoriously dirty, lice-infested, and grasshopper-eating. Nevertheless, a section of the great body of legislation known as the Compromise of 1850 established: "a temporary government by the name of the Territory of Utah."

D. C. Oakes and the Pike's Peak Hoax

Many of the new arrivals were mere surface deposits, having come with Utopian ideas in regard to the wealth of the country, expecting to find great nuggets of yellow metal lying around loose, and streams burdened with liquid silver. These romantic fortune-seekers soon returned East, anathematizing the country and declaring Pike's Peak to be an unmitigated swindle, and under the inscription, "Pike's Peak or Bust," was written, in larger, blacker letters, "Busted, by Thunder." The plains for six hundred miles were the theatre of a restless, surging wave of humanity. D. C. Oakes had published a pamphlet, describing and lauding the country. It was the means of inducing many to emigrate. He had returned to the States, and was on his way back with a

From *Tales of the Colorado Pioneers,* by Alice Polk Hill, pp. 27–28. Denver: Pierson & Gardner. 1884.

saw-mill, when he met the stampeders. They said he had "sworn deceitfully"—in other words, had told outrageous falsehoods, which they spelled with three letters, and they threatened to hang him and burn his mill. He met them bravely, by stating the fact of his having invested every dollar he was worth in that mill, which ought to be proof conclusive of his faith in the country. They gave him his life, but had the satisfaction of pelting him with execrating epithets. A little farther on he came to a new-made grave, and on the headstone, which was the storm-polished shoulderblade of a buffalo, was written the following epitaph:

Here lies the body of D. C. Oakes,
Killed for aiding the Pike's Peak hoax.

The Naming of Silver Dollar

Early in January of the year 1890, [William Jennings] Bryan set forth from his home in Nebraska on a journey to Colorado to pursue the silver question to its source. The "Tiberius Gracchus of the West" knew of Tabor as the richest silver mine owner in the state, and he naturally supposed that Tabor knew all that was to be known about silver. He was to discover that Tabor's knowledge of money was confined to the fact that it would buy plug hats and plush.

The earnest young man with flashing brown eyes, broad mouth, and lofty brow won his way at once into the Tabor mansion. Tabor naturally tried to offer his guest a drink at the first shot. A puzzled look spread over Haw's face when the serious young man declared he had never tasted any beverage stronger than grape juice.

Well, an intimacy had to be struck somehow before they settled down to the tedious talk about metals, so Tabor took Bryan on a tour of his mansion. Baby Doe was weak and pale, for it was only two weeks since she had borne her second daughter, on January 5, 1890. Tabor and Bryan tiptoed into the nursery. Baby Doe stood at the head of the crib.

Young Demosthenes tickled the feet of the infant and she gurgled merrily.

Bryan stepped back and exclaimed exultantly: "Why, Senator, that baby's laughter has the ring of a silver dollar."

Tabor looked foolish. Then his face changed to a brown study. He and Baby Doe had been puzzled to find a name for their second born. Haw's face lighted up. Bryan, in one of his slippery verbal moments, had named the child. Silver Dollar Tabor!

But Baby Doe had liked Rosemary. Good, said Tabor. Then he

From *Silver Dollar,* The Story of the Tabors, by David Karsner, pp. 244–246. Copyright, 1932, by Covici-Friede, Inc. New York: Crown Publishers.

added Echo Honeymoon. And the infant was christened Rosemary Silver Dollar Echo Honeymoon Tabor. Her parents called her Silver. Tabor liked that. It had the ring of dollars.

It was time for Bryan and Tabor to get down to their talk. Tabor half listened. It might have done him a lot of good, had he given his undivided attention to what the Nebraskan was saying, but instead he sipped a string of highballs, plucked at the diamond in his cuffs, and was grateful to Bryan for naming his baby Silver Dollar.

New York-Alki

. . . In 1857 . . . the captain of a passing sailing vessel shouted to Lee Terry, standing in front of a little row of cabins near the water, "What town is this?"

Perhaps there was derision in his tone. At any rate, Terry was inspired to seize upon the proud name of his former home in the East, and he replied, "New York"

"Yes, sure," roared the skipper, as his ship disappeared round the point. "New York-Alki, I reckon"—Alki, pronounced by the pioneers with a short *i,* meaning, in the Chinook Indian jargon, "by and by." So New York-Alki it became. And thus baptized by the fire of civic aspiration, the city [of Seattle] that was by and by to become the New York of the Northeast had its auspicious beginning.

Asa Mercer's Cargoes of Maidens

. . . Since these were the days before matrimonial bureaus, Asa Mercer, a young man of Washington Territory, decided to set about personally solving the problem which so obviously existed in frontier country where girls were so scarce that when dances were given in some communities every man who brought a girl got in free, and anyone turning up with extra females received twenty-five cents a head for his benefaction. Essays had been appearing from the first in Northwest newspapers on such subjects as "Scarcity of White Women," "Need of Good Wives." Finally in 1860 the *Puget Sound Herald* of Steilacoom advertised an open meeting to which all bachelors were

---

From *They Built the West,* An Epic of Rails and Cities, by Glenn Chesney Quiett, p. 439. Copyright, 1934, by D. Appleton-Century Company, Inc. New York and London.

From *Westward the Women,* by Nancy Wilson Ross, pp. 113–119. Copyright, 1944, by Nancy Wilson Ross. New York: Alfred A. Knopf.

For A. S. Mercer's own account, see Clarence B. Bagley, "The Mercer Immigration: Two Cargoes of Maidens for the Sound Country," *The Quarterly of the Oregon Historical Society,* Vol. V. (March, 1904), No. 1, pp. 1–24.

invited in order to discuss their dilemma. Out of this first meeting came further meetings and at last Asa's bold plan to import eligible women from the Eastern states by way of a journey round the Horn.

> Attention, Bachelors: Believing that our only chance for a realization of the benefits and early attainments of matrimonial alliances depends upon the arrival in our midst of a number of the fair sex from the Atlantic states, and that, to bring about such an arrival a united effort and action are called for on our part, we respectfully request a full attendance of all eligible and sincerely desirous bachelors of this community to assemble on Tuesday evening next, February 28th, in Delin and Shorey's building to devise ways and means to secure this much-needed and desirable emigration to our shore.

Although there is no record that Asa Mercer knew it, there was actually an American precedent for his bold plan. In the seventeenth century several cargoes of girls from England, "agreeable persons, young and incorrupt," came to the Virginia colony and were eagerly bought up at the boat landing by lonely planters who paid one hundred and twenty pounds of tobacco—worth roughly eighty dollars—for a bride. In most respects the Far West traces its traditions of conduct to New England, but in this instance it breaks sharply with Puritan precedent, for the New England colonists headed their catalogue of desperately needed items from the old country—such as copper kettles, tame turkeys, peas, and beans—with "ministers." Virginia frankly headed its list: "wives."

So essential was Asa's plan considered in the Far West that funds would have been made available from the public treasury for his journey had the treasury not been empty. He had, however, the full backing of William Pickering, the Governor of Washington Territory, his own brother, Judge Thomas Mercer, and many another influential citizen.

Asa laid his plans carefully. He would not go into New England communities and crudely talk about matrimonial chances in the Pacific Northwest. He would present to the young women of New England a picture of the opportunities this developing country extended to schoolteachers, nurses, music teachers, dressmakers, and housekeepers.

He was able on his first trip to sell his idea to eleven young women of New England, who came seven thousand miles round the Horn in the spring of 1864, and were, for the most part, snapped up at once as brides. On the strength of this modest coup Asa Mercer was elected unanimously to the upper house of the Territorial Legislative Assembly.

Fired by this initial success, Asa decided to try again on a larger scale. Very soon he was signing contracts which read:

> I, Asa Mercer, of Seattle, Washington Territory, hereby agree to bring a suitable wife, of good moral character and reputation from the East to Seattle on or before September, 1865, for each of the parties whose signatures are

hereunto attached, they first paying to me or my agent the sum of three hundred dollars, with which to pay the passage of said ladies from the East and to compensate me for my trouble.

Asa was not interested in making a fortune on his venture, but he did want the event to become one of national significance. He decided to offer homes and employment to the wives and orphans of Civil War soldiers.

As a boy of five, back home in Illinois, he had been dandled on the knee of Abraham Lincoln and he felt sure that he would be granted an audience with the President. But unfortunately his arrival in the East coincided almost exactly with the assassination of Lincoln. Thus Asa had to turn elsewhere for help. He got it from the Governor of Massachusetts. John A. Andrews, "the most talked about and seemingly the most popular and influential man and politician in the country." Andrews thought Mercer's idea a sound one. He introduced the brisk young man from the Far West to Edward Everett Hale.

Asa was then passed along from one important man to another in the big cities, receiving verbal encouragement in some quarters, sharp attacks in others, and very little substantial help. In Washington, after weeks of the inevitable run-around, he finally got the ear of Ulysses S. Grant, who had served as a soldier in the unsettled stretches of the Far West and knew what Mercer was talking about. Grant was able, on his personal voucher, to get Mercer an order for a steamship to carry five hundred women from New York to Seattle. This order, however, the Quartermaster General refused to accept. He found it illegal, sharing perhaps the timidity of President Johnson and his Cabinet, who approved Asa's scheme but feared the moral responsibility involved. Eventually, under pressure, the Quartermaster General yielded enough to offer Mercer a 1,600-ton ship for eighty thousand dollars spot cash.

This was a sum far beyond the reach of Mercer's purse, but he found a man who had it in his hand and was ready to spend it on what seemed to him a good commercial venture—not because of a cargo of women, but because of the value of a ship on the West Coast. This man was Ben Holladay, the fabulous entrepreneur and high-liver of Portland, Oregon. Holladay offered to buy the boat and let Mercer ship his cargo of females at the nominal price.

Believing that his troubles were over, Mercer went about happily giving his scheme wider publicity. He inserted a card in the *New York Times* that set out to explain the conditions in the Pacific Northwest which made such a venture feasible. Using the past tense, he wrote: "Churches and schools there were, but the great elevating, refining and moralizing element—true woman—was wonderfully wanting. Not that the ladies of Washington Territory were less pure and high-minded than those of any other land, but the limited number of them left the good work greater than they could perform."

Asa, in bustling about New England, was not always received with open arms. What Connecticut and New Hampshire had to say is not recorded, but the *New York Times* reported that Massachusetts newspapers ridiculed the women who considered embarking on the venture and warned them not to allow themselves to "be lost among the Amarugens," as they called the inhabitants of Washington Territory. On the whole, the *New York Times* was kind to Mercer's scheme, headlining it warmly: "Brilliant Prospect for the Settlers and Miners of the Pacific Slope." But the *New York Herald* took another stand. Warning that the whole scheme was obviously intended to fill Western houses of ill-fame with the flower of New England womanhood, it managed to bring about a number of cancellations. In the end the boat set sail under the most chaotic conditions with one hundred passengers instead of the five hundred expected.

One of the women from Lowell, Massachusetts, who made the trip with her mother and became a resident of Whidby Island, in Washington, was able to recall the details of it many years later in an article for the *Washington Historical Quarterly.* Flora Engle found on boarding Holladay's bargain vessel that "nothing had been done to the steamer since it was last used for transporting soldiers, except, possibly a partial fumigation. Mr. Mercer, not so dashing as he was when he left the West coast, hid out in a coal bin until they were well out to sea.

The food on the trip, according to Mrs. Engle, was disgraceful—everywhere, that is, but at the captain's table. Mercer, upon his emergence from the hold, took his meals with the captain until the hungry and disgruntled passengers convinced him that his conduct was tactless to say the least. After that Asa shared with his charges the fried salt beef, the tea steeped in salt water, and—at one seventeen-day stretch—the slightly parboiled beans, the main dinner dish. At one point in the journey a distracted New England housewife obtained permission to go into the galley and bake some Massachusetts gingerbread. There was a can of strawberry preserves on board that was still tenderly remembered by one passenger at least fifty years later. Whenever the passengers threatened to make trouble over their fare, some timid soul, raised on New England sea stories, would always stop them with the whispered argument: "Hush, you might incite mutiny."

So they endured. And perhaps their limited rations were a blessing in disguise, said the lady who wrote down the chronicle for posterity. There was no seasickness among them, after the first day or two, on the whole 7,000-mile trip, and this might have been due to the fact that their stomachs had nothing to disgorge.

In spite of the rations, life on shipboard was pleasant and even exciting. There was constant diversion. A young reporter, Rod, of the *New York Times,* who had gone along to write up the expedition, diverted himself by paying court to one after another of the eligible young girls. In the end every one of them rejected him. What was the matter with Rod? The chronicler fails to state. Certainly Rod's dispatches to the *Times* are disappointing. He had little to say about his companions after a first description of their conduct during a squall. He was particularly unfeeling about the terrified young woman who begged the captain on her knees to put her ashore in a rowboat. Rod hints nothing of personal adventures aboard ship and saves all his impassioned phrasing for a description of the harbor of Rio de Janeiro. Were it not for Flora Engle we should never guess, in turning the thin, stained pages of the *New York Times* of eighty years ago, that this young man with a Baedeker mind had been both ardent and unlucky with Mercer's girls.

But though Rod was unlucky, the "sly young archer, Cupid," was not idle. Mercer himself fell under the spell of a Baltimore belle named Annie Stephens. Happily "his passion was reciprocated." There were four other bona fide romances resulting in marriage at the journey's end. Some young women, fearing that they might be accused of setting out on a deliberate matrimonial venture, were extremely careful to give no encouragement to the men on shipboard. One in particular awed the company at the outset by announcing that she intended to "clothe herself in her reserve, throw herself back upon her dignity, and remain so." They had reason to believe later, commented Mrs. Engle, that her prop had given way.

One young lady with more fire than prudence got into trouble with the captain. When he gave orders for all officers to remain in their quarters, "since he was disgusted with the daily doings of his engineers," the young miss made a chalk line on the deck near the saloon door and wrote above it: "Officers not allowed aft." For this piece of cheek she was confined to her room by the captain—locked in.

In California the party lost some of its members. "What inducements," says the loyal Mrs. Engle, "some of them found to remain in California I do not pretend to say."

That there were many inducements offered them to remain is clear from such a bit of evidence as a poem published in a San Francisco paper. Paraphrasing Tennyson's *Charge of the Light Brigade,* and exaggerating the number of females rather remarkably, the unknown poet of the Golden Gate published the following:

> Husbands to the right of them,
> Husbands to the left of them,
> Husbands behind them
> Now badgered and thundered.
> Stormed at with words so fell,
> What shall their feelings tell?
> There goes the steamer's bell,
> Back from the Golden Gate
> All that was left of them
> Went the 700.

Oh, when can their glory fade!
Oh, the wild charge they made!
All the town wondered.
Honor the charge they made,
Honor the bright brigade,
Sweet 700.

The majority of the party came up the coast to the Northwest in a new clean ship with good engines and a good cook. At Cape Flattery they met their first welcoming committee, a band of Indians in canoes, coming to gape, to sell fish, and incidentally to startle some of the more delicate ladies by the unconcerned scantiness of their attire.

It didn't take Mercer's girls long to settle into their new life. They taught school, they married, they raised children, they "grew up with the country." They had served to advertise the Pacific Northwest in a way no other enterprise could have done, and Asa Mercer—for all the personal attacks he had had to endure—must have been well satisfied with this part of his ambitious program.

Seattle versus Tacoma

Town rivalry was always one of the most entertaining features of Far Western development. It was not the states that were calling each other names and pushing each other out of the way, for in earlier days states were mere geographical and political entities. It was the rare cities that were self-conscious, ambitious, passionate. No man stopped to think, fifteen or twenty years ago, that he was a resident of Washington: his whole mind was occupied with being a citizen of Seattle or of Tacoma. Whichever he happened to be, he lay awake nights worrying about the other place. The Northwest of 1925 is very different from the Northwest of the Lewis and Clark Exposition year, when I first saw it. On Tacoma Day at the 1905 Exposition the good Tacomans covered the grounds, like confetti-laden wedding guests, with little handbills that said, "Watch Tacoma Grow." Seattle was greatly troubled until an anxious session of citizens created a new race of handbills reading "Seattle Grows Without Watching." They even quarreled about their respective totem poles. An honest resident of Tacoma—a minister of the Gospel—confessed to me in 1905 that the Tacoma totem pole was a modern copy; but he went on to say, "Anyhow, we came by it honestly. The Seattle business men went to Alaska and *stole* theirs." . . .

From *The Aristocratic West,* by Katharine Fullerton Gerould, pp. 70–71. Copyright, 1925, by Harper & Brothers. New York and London.

Mt. Rainier or Mt. Takhoma

. . . [The] rivalry [between Seattle and Tacoma] was the aftermath of a bitter fight over which of the two was to be the terminus of the Northern Pacific. Relations were not improved after "the big mountain" was officially named Rainier when as a matter of fact (to rake the coals of an old fire) it should have remained "Takhoma," as even the most casual reader of Theodore Winthrop's *The Canoe and the Saddle* might have ascertained. As things stand now, Easterners frequently and understandably accent it on the first syllable, believing it to be a comparative of [*rainy*]. Actually it is the name of an Englishman whose monument ought not to be so heroic and who was never within half a world of Puget Sound. "This mountain," writes Captain Vancouver with galling superiority in his Journals, "I *distinguished* with the name of my friend Rear Admiral Regnier." That the peak might already have been named by the natives occurred to Vancouver no more than did the possibility that it was the Rear Admiral who was thereby distinguished, and not the mountain.

Seattle's slogan was invented, fittingly enough, by Henry Broderick, one of its more prominent realtors. It was "WHEN SEATTLE HAS A MILLION—WHAT WILL YOU HAVE?" "Budweiser beer," the Tacoma wags used to reply. And while the retort was obvious, it was nonetheless double-edged, because Budweiser competed with a malt beverage made in Seattle under the hated name of "Rainier."

To Hell—and Dodge City

The story is told that, in those days, a "drunk" boarded a train and gave the conductor a handful of bills.

"Where to?" the conductor asked.

"To h–," said the passenger.

"The fare to Dodge City is $2.50," replied the conductor as he handed back the change.

From *Evergreen Land,* A Portrait of the State of Washington, by Nard Jones, pp. 183–184. Copyright, 1947, by Anne and Nard Jones. New York: Dodd, Mead & Company.

Cf. *Before the United States Geographic Board, In the Matter of the Proposal to Change the Name of Mount Rainier, Statement of Charles Tallmadge Conover, Representing Numerous Citizens of the State of Washington in Favor of Retaining the Present Name, and Oral Presentation by C. T. Conover and Victor J. Farrar; The Decision* [No place or publisher, 1917], 58p.

From *City of Flaming Adventure:* The Chronicle of San Antonio, by Boyce House, p. 138. Copyright, 1949, by the Naylor Company. San Antonio.

Azuza

. . . A famous syndicated columnist, traveling through California, once wrote that the name [Azuza] signified "from A to Z, the best in U.S.A." That is one of the things that make one wonder how many other incorrect statements made by famous columnists are treasured as truth in the minds of many persons. The fact is that the name is of Indian origin, long antedating the time when California was part of the United States. Roger Dalton, whose English grandfather became Don Enrique Dalton and the owner of Rancho Azuza Dalton, on a small part of which the present city of Azuza stands, testifies that the Mexican land grants issued after the secularization of the mission lands designated the region by the Indian name, and it is so recorded in the record books of the 1830's. Probably it was the poetic touch of a chamber-of-commerce booster that resulted in the "A to Z in U.S.A." legend, for the real meaning of that pretty name is not quite so alluring. The real meaning is "skunk hill."

How to Pronounce "Los Angeles"

. . . In the City of Angels . . . two thirds of the population butcher the name Los Angeles in twelve distinct and recorded varieties of blunder. The overwhelming slaughter . . . is in "jellifying the *g*." You can't say jelly, nor George nor even Jim in Spanish. But most of the population seem to take Our Lady of Angels to be one "Lost Angie Lees." Almost any pronunciation will do which recognizes the two vital points—for no English-speaking person can be expected to give the exact Spanish term. But even our lally-mouths should be able to get:

O, long, G, hard and rhyme with Yes.
And all about Loce Ang-el-ess.

From *It's an Old California Custom,* by Lee Shippey, pp. 227–228. Copyright, 1948, by Lee Shippey. New York: The Vanguard Press, Inc.

From *Flowers of Our Lost Romance,* by Charles F. Lummis, p. 194. Copyright, 1929, by Houghton Mifflin Company. Boston and New York.

For the beginning of the jingle, see Carey McWilliams, *Southern California Country* (New York, 1946), p. 116:

The Lady would remind you please,
Her name is not Los Angie Lees—
Nor Angie anything whatever,
She hopes her friends will be so clever
To share her fit historic pride
The G shall not be jellified.

The Boom in Los Angeles

Los Angeles was the largest town in California at the time of the American occupation. It was the native metropolis, on a small scale, to be sure, but still the metropolis. It took on growth from the time it became an incorporated American city in 1850, but for some years the gold excitement in the north held down the increase of population in the south to an insignificant figure. From 1850 to 1856 the old Mexican town was very loosely, very informally governed by its new masters, as may be inferred by accounts of the free and easy—or rather free and strenuous—conditions that existed there. This was due to an excessive expression of individualism rather than to organized political corruption. But from 1856 on to and through the great real estate boom which began in 1885 and lasted three years, the banner of organized rascality floated over the municipal hall of Los Angeles, and its rulers were banded together in a speculative conspiracy against all that was honest.

The city began to increase its rate of growth about 1875, but it was still a slow movement until the boom struck in '85. This boom was one of the crimes of the age. Only a few people profited by it while hundreds of thousands were trapped into insane purchase of property and crazy speculation, and finally ruined. The daily press of Los Angeles boomed the boom from the word go. The writer of these lines was the only person having access to printer's ink that published a word of warning to the credulous. I was publishing a weekly paper then and did all that was possible to save people from ruin.

At the height of the boom I printed a carefully written article calling attention to the great number of lots that had been cut by the boomers from orchards, vineyards, barleyfields, and vegetable gardens in and around Los Angeles—acres and acres of productive, income-paying land suddenly reduced to waste. A vineyard that was worth three or four hundred dollars an acre as a horticultural proposition they would figure would be worth ten thousand dollars an acre cut up into lots. This jump in value was entirely false, of course, just a speculative inflation that worked for the moment if people believed it. As the result of the uprooting of these productive plots, we had for years the unsightly waste places in and about the city, scars from the exploding boom that it will take years more to heal over. I showed in this article that in case all these lots were sold and a house built on each, as promised by the boomers, Los Angeles would then have a population greater than London. But mighty few of the investors seemed to think that this was a preposterous possibility at all.

From *On the Old West Coast,* Being Further Reminiscences of a Ranger, Major Horace Bell, edited by Lanier Bartlett, pp. 267–272. Copyright, 1930, by William Morrow & Co., Inc. New York.

I will give a few instances of the wildcatting during these memorable years. All the land from Redondo-by-the-Sea to Widneyville-by-the-Desert they cut up into town lots. They built cement sidewalks for miles into the desert fastness. They built railroad lines, where the main line did not run through, and took out train loads of crazy people with their pockets full of cash. Bands played gay music as they traveled. From the trains they herded them into wagons, tallyhos, or stages, and hauled them to the heart of the proposed new "city." Here a vast array of refreshment tables would be set up in serried ranks, covered with cold lunch, while barrels of beer, whisky, and wine would be tapped to the blare of the band. All free of course, and most stimulating when the hour arrived for bidding in lots. Lots selling on those feast days for thousands of dollars apiece were afterward assessed for taxation at two dollars a lot and many of them reverted to the tax collector. My goodness, the colleges they proposed and sometimes actually built! A college for at least every thousand acres. The college seemed to be a big selling point. And hotels! Magnificent structures were actually erected that never held a guest after opening day and were later dedicated to the insurance companies by the fire route.

"Widneyville-by-the-Desert" was a prize exhibit of those days. The promoters referred to it as "the modern Elysium," I believe, or some such high-toned Greek brag. A tremendous excursion was organized to conduct the speculative hordes to the site of the proposed ideal city on the opening day. A natural and to the Eastern tenderfoot a rather appalling growth of cactus and yucca palms, commonly called Joshua trees, covered the desert hereabouts. These spiny, writhing Joshua trees are really a horrific sight if you are not used to them, but the promoters of Widneyville had a bright idea that saved them the expense of clearing the growth off. They did a little judicious trimming on the cactus plants and yuccas, shaping them up into a certain uniformity, then shipped out a carload of cheap windfall oranges, and on the end of each bayonet-like spike on the yuccas and on each cactus spine they impaled an orange. Suddenly the desert fruited like the orange grove! Down the lines of the proposed streets staked out in the desert, and around the great square outlined by the surveyors, crowded innumerable orange trees loaded with their golden harvest. The Easterners stood agape at the Elysian sight, hardly listening to the salesmen as they described the college, the several churches, the great sanitarium, and the magnificent hotel—temperance hotel—that would so soon surround the central plaza of Widneyville.

"Here, you see, ladies and gentlemen, is the natural home of the orange," said the conductor of the excursion as he addressed the assembled multitude. "These beautiful trees, so prolific of fruit, are a natural growth. This is the only spot west of the Rocky Mountains where the orange is indigenous. In a little while we will have irrigation canals all over the tract and when these orange trees are irrigated their fruit will grow as big as pumpkins. There'll be a fortune in every block, ladies and gentlemen."

Blocks and blocks were sold from the plat of "Widneyville-by-the-Desert," at boom prices but no house was built on the actual site.

On the sea coast the boomers discovered some imaginary natural advantages in a bight or curve in the shoreline, laid out a city, and called it "Redondo-by-the-Sea." Redondo was advertised as the greatest and safest harbor in the world. The boosters hired engineers and got them to certify that it had limitless possibilities as a safe shipping point. As a matter of fact, Redondo is an open roadstead, to-day as it was then, a pocket that catches all the force of the northwest wind, bringing the rollers in with crushing violence when it blows. But on a calm day the water looks pretty smooth, and in such weather the eminent engineers and other eminences would say: "You see, there is a submarine oil well in the offing that spouts oil perpetually. This keeps the waters of Redondo as calm as a millpond. It will be the great harbor of the Pacific Coast."

The Redondo boomers organized several steamship lines, on paper; one to China, one to Australia, another to South America. Great cargo carriers from the ends of the earth were to cast their anchors in the oil pond of Redondo. There was a little old salt pond not far back from the beach, where the Mexicans and the American pioneers used to go and boil the water down into salt. This pond was about as big as a garden in the backyard of a Dutch tavern. Well, the promoters blazoned the news that this pond was to be dredged out, surrounded with docks, and connected with the ocean by a great canal. The canal was to have locks and all that sort of thing and by an astounding feat of engineering arrangements were to be made to let the water out of the basin when desired so that ships, while resting at their docks, could be standing high and dry, which would give a fine chance to scrape the barnacles off their bottoms. Lots of overland railroads, so it was claimed, were eagerly awaiting the opportunity to extend their railroads directly to the sides of these docks so that they would be in immediate touch with the whole United States. While a ship's bottom was being scraped, her cargo would be passing directly into the railroad cars alongside. Not a moment wasted.

Elaborate maps and sea charts were prepared showing that the Asiatic trade was bound to center at Redondo. Redondo was nearer China than any other spot on the American coast. It was nearer to every other place, including New York.

The daily press of Los Angeles blazoned the great future of Redondo-by-the-Sea. Every person investing there would be sure of a fortune even if he or she never wanted to live there. You could get a pretty good waterfront lot for from twenty thousand to fifty thousand dollars. Villa lots back in the bleak dunes could be had for from one thousand to ten thousand dollars each. People bought them, too, and a few foolhardy sea captains brought their ships to the wharf that was built into the open sea, and some of these vessels were dashed to pieces on the shore. But nothing came of the great commercial project which had furnished the basis for the ridiculous valuations on property there, and the place lapsed into the status of an indifferent bathing beach.

Lucky Baldwin and the Santa Anita Ranch

. . . Lucky Baldwin has not lacked eulogists. They have praised his brandy and wine, his Arab racers, the great mines he developed, or promoted, and explain that his nickname came from "that luck which attends foresight and application." But eulogies, as the Great Cham said of lapidary inscriptions, are not usually written under oath. Elias Jackson Baldwin was a gambler first, a plunger and high-roller, fond of the paddock and the roulette wheel. He had a talent for *réclame* of a lurid, theatrical sort, and one of his first exploits was to bring from Japan a juggling troupe that he exhibited in New York at Niblo's Gardens. He came to San Francisco twenty years after the Gold Rush, and speculated in land. He speculated in mining and in race tracks, usually with luck, and often his luck depended little on foresight.

What of the time, when after telling his brokers to sell off his Comstock shares, he left for Hawaii, without signing the certificates? In the vault they stayed, unsold. On his return he found they had increased in value a hundred times. And luck sometimes failed entirely. His mammoth hotel, The Baldwin, burned to ashes in three hours, at the loss of a million dollars each hour. He dropped a million and a half in land and mine speculation in the San Bernardinos. And this year, 1875, saw the debacle of the Comstock Lode, and the failure of the Bank of California, with Lucky Baldwin separated from his money by the closed door. He was one of the "Ralston gang," though a minor nabob and not one of the true bonanza kings. But he had his revenge, for he sat at the conference that forced Ralston to resign. Baldwin had always the knack of being in at the kill. In a few months he had recouped in a lift of the market, and departed south with a boxful of money in bank notes.

He had his eye on the large Santa Anita ranch, which began only twelve miles away from the small town of Los Angeles, and stretched for leagues along the foot of the Sierra Madre Mountains, and touched the community of San Gabriel. He had long known of this ranch, and the further end of it, L. J. Rose's Sunnyslope, the noblest farm, at the time, in southern California. Rose bred cattle and horses; he owned

---

From *Vines in the Sun,* A Journey through the California Vineyards, by Idwal Jones, pp. 228–231, 232–233, 234, 237–238. Copyright, 1949, by Idwal Jones. New York: William Morrow & Company.

Stamboul, a horse valued at $50,000; he had large citrus groves, a vineyard, and a winery that turned out eight thousand gallons of brandy a week.

Santa Anita ranch was handsomer than Cucamonga, greener, more opulent, with coverts of live oak, and of so clear a sweep that from the head of its flat valley Baldwin could look straight on to the ocean. It had an area of twelve square miles. It was densely green this springtime; bands of half-wild horses, glowing-eyed, lustrous of hide and mane, were racing over it as if on a pampa in Uruguay. And if Lucky Baldwin loved anything more than money, of which he had sufficient, and women (with whom his luck was unsure), it was horses. The scenery was inspiring; Baldwin had a delight in noble vistas, and that is a virtue not lightly to be set aside. He liked earth, and had been brought up as a farm boy. This would make an admirable estate for him. All the nabobs and bonanza kings—Mackay, Flood, Fair, Stanford—had vast estates. And possibly Santa Anita ranch could be bought, and at a depressed figure. Once it had belonged to Hugo Reid, a Scotchman who turned Mexican citizen, married an Indian girl, and acquired a grant of land. Then it was owned by Joseph Rowe, who brought the first circus to California, retired, and turned his horses loose here. It went through other hands, and was now owned by Harris Newmark, the Los Angeles merchant, upon whom Baldwin called, with a tin box under his arm, and asked if Santa Anita could be bought.

"It could be," said Newmark, "at a hundred and seventy-five thousand."

Baldwin, genuinely shocked, cried out in protest, then argued. But since Newmark was immovable, he left, to wait about town until the merchant should change his mind and send for him. He called again, but Newmark now informed him the price was two hundred thousand, and next week it would be higher. Baldwin, threatened by apoplexy, stamped out and went to his hotel, where he stayed until his lawyer should come. Colonel Kowalski arrived four days later, and to him Baldwin related his agonizing scene with Newmark. The Colonel listened, peeling a cucumber and stirring the yard-long peel into a bowl of brandy punch. He was not only an expert in land titles and Spanish grants, but celebrated as the inventor of punch with that demulcent, cucumber peel, and as such enjoyed much esteem in San Francisco.

"H'm," said the Colonel, tasting, as his eyes dwelt on the tin box, "I don't know how much you've got in that box, but it can't hold more than the ranch is worth. I'd close, if I were you."

Baldwin hurried out to the merchant's again, and agreed to take the ranch.

"It will be a quarter of a million now," said Newmark, smiling.

"Sir," rejoined Baldwin, "it isn't next week yet," and the merchant politely admitted a slight error.

Baldwin opened the box, and taking out twelve thousand dollars, made a deposit to be held until the deed of sale should be drawn up. It was done, speedily. In his memoirs, which he wrote several years later, Newmark said that when the box was opened, he had a glimpse of five million dollars in gold bank-notes.

Santa Anita was Baldwin's. Buying adjacent land, he expanded the holding to nearly sixty thousand acres. He established three villages, including Arcadia, where he built a mansion, tentatively Queen Anne, but loaded with fretwork and gingerbread; the grounds ornamented with bowers, fountain, and shady clumps of palms and elephants' ears. A racetrack was laid out, and a stable to shelter 1,500 horses. The land had the right pitch to drain it perfectly in the rainy season. He crossed it, length and breadth, with a series of double avenues, some seven miles long, each with its double colonnade of pepper trees and eucalypti.

Baldwin's luck had slumped again; revenues would have to come in fast. Foremen came in from San Gabriel Vineyard, from Sunnyslope, plowed two square miles in a tract of decomposed granite and quartz, a mixture adapted to growths for the brandy maker, and set them under vines.

The climate here is described as of a perpetual springtime, though a deluded visitor might in August regard it as sub-tropical. But the aridity was mitigated by water brought in from the hills by hundreds of miles of pipe, and from deep artesian wells, to flow in countless rivulets that turned Santa Anita as lushly green as Suffolk or Hampshire, the resemblance heightened by the knolls and tracts of live oak.

* * * * *

. . . Baldwin the Lucky was lucky indeed, for he had got settled just before the immense wave of pilgrims—all wealthy— swept over southern California in its first boom. They all drove to Santa Anita where, rapturous under parasols, they were conveyed by barouche, tally-ho, or basket-carriage, through this floral paradise, this demesne of Ceres and Bacchus, though a Bacchus sedate and trousered, to wind up for tea and scones in a sun-dappled arbor of bamboo and wisteria by the pool. Another Xanadu, one rhapsodist described it, and so it may have been —one ruled over by a Kubla Khan who had subdivided it into lots for sale. The best of them, with patches of oak forest, suitable for a gentleman's private park, were going at a ramping price. The pilgrims were largely of a High Victorian stamp, sprinkled with diplomats and sportsmen of the nobility. Baldwin was at ease only in the paddock and stables, or with his cronies at poker.

The vineyard played second fiddle to the stables, where Baldwin himself was dictator, but with the vineyard he did not interfere. It yielded 100,000 gallons of wine, and about half as much brandy: and the revenue was greatly needed, for too often the horses galloped to a deficit.

* * * * *

"To collect money from Baldwin, first get a court judgment," one of his associates used to remark. He preferred to pay his bills in raw brandy. His gimcrack mansion and the theatrical display he liked reflected his want of taste and knowledge, but he was perfectly aware of this lack, and he was shrewd enough to leave the vineyard and the winery to the care of the men he had imported from Livermore. . . .

* * * * *

Baldwin required more profits than the vineyard alone was likely to yield. He had park sites and vistas to sell, and the brush shelters of the Indians, with their packs of dogs, their weekly riots and stabbings, did not fit into the pattern of the estate, so decorous, landscaped, and soothingly English with its belvederes, ponds, monkey-puzzle trees and thatched Tudor cottages. Further, three railroads were now laid through Santa Anita, and the passenger trains moved through the demesne at slower pace, to prolong the delight of the travelers in the panorama. If they debarked to visit the farm, they would, naturally, be taken through the winery, which was to be a model of its kind. . . . Baldwin had given right-of-way to the railroads with the proviso that any and all trains were to stop on signal. His favorite was the Santa Fe, whose crack express was the precursor of the *Super Chief,* which stops only once on the stretch between San Bernardino and Los Angeles, and that at Pasadena. In 1900 he stopped at a desert station, on his way home from the mountains, and asked for a ticket to Santa Anita. The request, as customary, was not only discouraged but turned down. He was told the next train did not stop there, because it was a through express. Calling for a telegraph blank, Baldwin wrote an order to his ranch manager. "Put 200 men to work at once tearing up Santa Fe tracks through my ranch. E. J. Baldwin."

The nabob was incensed. That station on his estate was his pride, and he had built it, in the much admired though ugly style of the period, at his own cost. A ticket was thrust at him, and the agent, after soothing Baldwin, had next to quell the rage of the conductor.

The station has been deserted and forgotten now for years, but bedevilment lurks in the proviso that yet holds, and if a ghost on its platform should flag the *Super Chief,* that train is still bound to halt, or else the land covered by the deed shall revert to "granter or his heirs." Contracts that Baldwin's lawyer, the humorous Kowalski, drew up were no easier to rend than armor-plate.

Westways says:

> As there are heirs the railway still adheres to the contract, but this has an amusing angle. Because of the steep grade from Pasadena east, a long train stopping at Santa Anita would have to back up for a couple of miles in order to gain momentum to make the hump. So if you insist on a ticket to Santa Anita, and won't be put off by the agent telling you that the train does not stop there, he will offer to pay your taxi fare from Pasadena to your destination, provided it is within a five-mile radius of the Santa Anita station.

If you still hold out and insist that you want a ticket to, and want to get off at, Santa Anita, they'll stop the train—*Navajo* or *Super Chief*.

But everything considered, it might be wiser to take a philosophical view of the changing times. Besides, a lawsuit is expensive, even if you win.

Death Valley Scotty Makes the Headlines

In June, 1905, a man and a mule left a cabin in the northern reaches of Death Valley and headed south into the swirling, blistering haze shrouding the fathomless sink of an accursed and fearful desert basin. Fire demons and the dervishes of thirst danced around the man and the mule as they moved along secret trails to plunge into impenetrable deserts of burning sand and bitter salt. Above them blinding heat bounced from the glowing hot ranges of Death Valley, as the sturdy, sunburned man and his hardened beast bridged bottomless alkaline marshes, fought through quicksands and poison gas, climbed surely up the naked rock faces of unscalable mountains. Howling sandstorms buffeted them. Sidewinders and the larger rattlesnakes rushed them, disputing their right to tour Death Valley in the summertime. The rattling noise of the attacking snakes made a positive din. High overhead a convoy of buzzards formed patient and hungry escort to the man and the mule. The buzzards were wasting their time. The mule was sure-footed, faithful and blue; and the man was Walter Scott.

Scotty and his mule went steadily southward through the fevered days of June. Their passage through the horrors of Death Valley was quite without event. Apache Indians who had been making a life work of lying in ambush for Scotty had gone home to Arizona for more ammunition and some corn cakes. No white enemies sniped at Scotty or his mule and they both reached Barstow safely—and a little bored. Scotty parked the mule outside the railroad station and went in and asked the ticket agent for a special train. Scotty wanted to go to Chicago. But first, please, he would like a special train to Los Angeles. Requests for special trains were rare in Barstow in 1905. Barstow stood in a ring around Scotty and admired him.

There was public inquiry into the financial status of Mr. Scott and much telegraphing back and forth between Barstow and Los Angeles before the Santa Fe Railroad began to rummage in its roundhouses for a locomotive and a coach for this perfect stranger from Death Valley. The railroad men were very reluctant to rent one of their special trains to a desert man to whom they had never been prop-

---

From *Death Valley Men*, by Bourke Lee, pp. 2–5, 73–77. Copyright, 1932, by Bourke Lee. New York: The Macmillan Company.

Cf. C. B. Glasscock, *Here's Death Valley* (Indianapolis, 1940), and Clarence P. Milligan, *Death Valley and Scotty* (Los Angeles, 1942).

erly introduced, and their hesitancy cost Scotty considerable loss in time. He impatiently flourished the first of the great rolls of currency which were to become a Scotty tradition and restlessly awaited his special train. To gaping Barstow, Scotty spoke of vast wealth locked in the rocks of a secret mine. When his special train at last rolled into the station, Scotty climbed aboard and sped westward toward the very small town of Los Angeles. In some uncanny fashion, news of Scotty's approach and intentions had leaked from the offices of the railroad into the city rooms of the newspapers. Los Angeles was expecting Scotty, and as he rode most of the way from Barstow in the engine cab, it was a sooty and begrimed Scott who climbed down from the special train into the City of Angels. Dirty but happy, Scotty waved his big hat to the cheering crowd. Death Valley's gift to city editors took his first bow.

Talking to railroad officials in Los Angeles, Scotty said he wanted to go to Chicago faster than any one had ever gone there before. He was in a terrific hurry. He was in such a hurry that he could wait a couple of days for a special train provided the special made record time to Chicago. The leak in the railroad offices was still leaking and all the highly confidential discussions between Scotty and the railroad men were broadcast in the streets. People even found out how much Scotty was paying for the special train. Some five thousand dollars changed hands. Several days passed while preparations for the record run went forward, and the railroad men had the opportunity to explain at great length that they had never seen Mr. Scott of Death Valley before. No one had asked them; but then it was nice to know that the railroad was accommodating enough to rent a special train to a perfect stranger. Folks thought it was sporting of the railroad to let an unknown miner have a special train. Of course he said he wanted to go to Chicago but the railroad was taking the chance of his running off to Seattle or New Orleans instead.

Scotty spent a day in San Bernardino closeted in a hotel room in mysterious conference and then Scotty went away on his special train. The special made speeds as high as 106 miles per hour. Scotty reached Chicago and the front pages of all the newspapers in the land in a few minutes under forty-five hours. The record still stands.

Having nothing especial to do in Chicago, Scotty of Death Valley went on to New York. He bore the pitiless glare of publicity without blinking. The newspaper men were fine fellars. Scotty was colorful copy. The fascination was reciprocal. Scotty expanded in the bright white light. Scotty had his picture in the paper. Scotty liked it. He loved it. The huzzah! and the boom! boom! of the front page meant so much to Scotty that he has been trying to stay there ever since. Through twenty-five years he has done rather well.

"Where does all your money come from, Mr. Scott?"

"Well, now! if I was to tell you that, you'd know as much as I do. I got a mine. She's some mine way down in Death Valley. That's a wicked valley, but I know how to get around there. Me and my mules know the valley and my mine. Nobody else is likely to know that mine as long as I can keep it a secret."

* * * * *

In August, 1930, six months after Scotty's great wealth was swept away in the newspapers, I visited him at Death Valley Ranch. I had not seen him since the headlines screamed in February. I found him in the kitchen of the big house. "Hello!" he cried, "you're just in time for mulligan. I got a real mulligan here, and you'll like it."

It was good mulligan because Scotty is a good cook. After lunch we sat back. Scotty spread himself along the leather cushions of the built-in seat around the kitchen table. I said, "It's too bad, Scotty, and I want you to know I'm sorry—your being broke, I mean."

"Hah!" cried Scotty. "So many public schools in the country and still so much ignorance."

"Tell me about it," I said.

Scotty said, "I was sitting here in the kitchen one afternoon and two ladies came in to see my castle. They were all excited about it, and they went on about how wonderful it was. They never expected to find such a wonderful place in the desert. And I said, 'Why! didn't you know it was here? Didn't you ever hear about my castle?'

"They said, 'We heard about it in Tonopah and we came in.'

"I asked them: 'You never heard about it until you got to Tonopah?' I could hardly believe it.

" 'Why, no,' they says.

"So I asked them where they were from. I thought they must be from another world, but it turns out they're from Oregon or someplace real handy. And they had never heard of Death Valley Scotty's castle! . . . I showed them around and after they went away I came in here and sat down and did some real serious thinking. I knew I had to put on a show. I'd been putting on shows for years, but here was two ladies who had never heard of my castle until they got to Tonopah! I knew I had to put on a good show right away.

"I had twelve or fifteen thousand dollars in cash and after a lot of thought I decided to take a trip to Paris. I went to Los Angeles and told them I was going to Paris. The morning papers gave me about an inch saying that Death Valley Scotty was going to Paris. At the bank, the banker says he hears I'm going to Paris and tells me that one of the bank officials is going to Paris and if I can wait for him, why, he'll be company for me. The manager of the hotel says that a couple of his friends are going to Paris and would like to go with me. Every place I went some one was going to Paris, and everybody I talked to had a friend who was going to Paris, or they were packing to go themselves. This Paris idea of mine didn't seem to be so good and I was like a coyote dragging a trap—it worried me.

"When I got to Chicago I went down to the Board of Trade to see some old friends. They said they saw in the paper that I was going to Paris. It had been in the Chicago papers and it said just that, just one line: Death Valley Scotty going to Paris.

" 'Yes,' I said, 'I'm going to Paris, and it don't seem to be going over very good. We got to think of something better. What would be a good story?'

"We all had lunch in one of those Board of Trade dumps—you know, way over in a corner—and we all did a lot of figuring, and my friends were sorry for me but we couldn't think of a good story. And my friends said that if I really was going to Paris, why they knew some people who were going to Paris and we could all go together. . . .

"I hung around Chicago for a couple of days wondering what I could do to put on a show. There was no excitement in this Paris business, people were going to Paris faster than they went broke last fall and it wasn't news. One afternoon I went into a theater and sat there watching the show and thinking about my own troubles. The show was all about this man who once had a lot of money but had lost it somehow or other. I wasn't paying much attention to the show—all about this rich man who had gone broke. And then suddenly I sat right up in my seat. A rich man who went broke! Bang! There was my cue! I got right out of that theater. I knew what I was going to do.

"I got on a train for the Coast and I wired that I was returning. When Kansas City was several stops away, a newspaper man climbed on the train and located me. We talked. Yes, my Paris trip was off. I'd just found out I was broke—heard it in Chicago. Well, this fellow sat and listened to me and was sorry I was broke, but there didn't seem to be any excitement in the news. We talked along, back, and forth, and then I happened to say that I had lost the Death Valley Castle—Blooie! There she was! That was what the world wanted to know! . . . And the world sure heard about it."

"It was a grand story, Scotty," I said.

"Wasn't it? Boy! Why, in Los Angeles, the papers sold twenty-two thousand more copies than they did on Lindbergh's flight and seventeen thousand more than they did when Aimee disappeared. Sure, it made a sucker out of me, but what do I care? If I go to all the trouble of cooking up a good story and the papers don't play it up big, why, then I'd have some reason to be sore. Praise me or condemn me, but don't ignore me. I didn't watch Major Burke work for twelve years for nothing. . . . You know Major Burke? Major Burke of the Wild West Show?"

Others have already called Major Burke, of Buffalo Bill's Wild West Show, the first of the great American press agents. Scotty still considers Major Burke the greatest of them all.

"And at that," said Scotty, "P. T. Barnum had a circus, and Major Burke had a Wild West Show, while I'm just a one-man show, the greatest one-man show on earth. I'm a lobo wolf. I've fought them all for twenty-five years. I'll lead the pack and make the kills, but the pack can't claim me as one of them. I like people. If I didn't I wouldn't go to so much trouble to entertain them. But I keep to myself. I always have. I always will. I'll never commercialize myself. I'm not selling anything. I'm not taking up any collections. I don't ever intend to. That's why I say I'm a lobo wolf."

Orange Empire

Basically the orange tree itself provides the key to an understanding of the social life of the citrus belt. For the orange, as Charles Fletcher Lummis once pointed out, is not only a fruit but a romance. The orange tree is the living symbol of richness, luxury, and elegance. With its rich black-green shade, its evergreen foliage, and its romantic fragrance, it is the millionaire of all the trees of America, the "golden apple" of the fabled Gardens of the Hesperides. The aristocrat of the orchards, it has, by a natural affinity, drawn to it the rich and the well-born, creating a unique type of rural-urban aristocracy. There is no crop in the whole range of American agriculture the growing of which confers quite the same status that is associated with ownership of an orange grove. To own a large wheat farm in Washington unquestionably gives a sense of possession and proud dominion; to own a well-stocked corn-and-hog farm in the Middle West undeniably confers a sense of solid well-being and plenty; but to own an orange grove in Southern California is to live on the real gold coast of American agriculture. It is not by chance that millionaire row in Pasadena should be called Orange Grove Avenue.

* * * * *

. . . To pick an orange in Southern California, unless you are an employee working under the direction of a foreman, is a perilous undertaking. If performed surreptitiously, it is likely to invite a blast from a shotgun, a jolt from an electrically charged wire fence, or a sentence in jail. Many of the larger concerns employ armed guards to police the sacred trees. According to Charles Fletcher Lummis, ferocious bull-dogs were used, at an earlier time, to keep visitors out of the groves. Some years ago, a Mexican boy was killed in Los Angeles County by a blast from a shotgun which a grower, by an ingenious process, had attached to a tree in such a manner that the trigger would be pulled by a disturbance of the wire fence enclosing the grove. Almost every resident and visitor in Southern California has wanted to pick an orange; but few persons can claim the distinction of having done so.

* * * * *

From *Southern California Country,* An Island on the Land, by Carey McWilliams, pp. 207, 223, 224–226. American Folkways Series, edited by Erskine Caldwell. Copyright, 1946, by Carey McWilliams. New York: Duell, Sloan & Pearce.

Not only is it difficult to pick an orange in Southern California, but, as William Allen White once observed, it is almost impossible to get a glass of real orange juice in the region, particularly in the citrus belt. . . . Despite the absence of orange juice, however, the orange remains the dominant symbol of the region. Mountains of oranges, "the fairest fruit in the history of the human race," are exhibited at the National Orange Fair held, over a period of two weeks, in San Bernardino each February. Frequently a million oranges, lemons, and grapefruit are used in building the towering columns and curious structures of citrus fruit seen at the fair. Oranges are converted into caricatures of Donald Duck, Mickey Mouse, Minnie, Pluto, the Three Little Pigs, and the Big Bad Wolf. . . .

* * * * *

Once the groves were a major tourist attraction as thousands of tourists were whisked through them, a mile-a-minute, on the famous Kite-route of the Pacific Electric. . . . To-day oranges are raised, not as a tourist attraction, not to provide elegant backgrounds for suburban estates, not to inflate land values, not even to provide orange juice for local residents, but as slick standardized commodities produced on an assembly-line basis for sale, and only for sale.

"Sunny Cafeteria"

It is not by accident that the forty-eight state societies have, for so many years, held most of their meetings in the cafeterias of Los Angeles. I am convinced that the popularity of the cafeteria in Los Angeles is primarily due to the loneliness of the people. A cafeteria is a friendlier type of eating-place than a restaurant. The possibility of meeting some one—just *some one*—is much greater in a cafeteria than in a cafe or restaurant. Furthermore, the informality of the cafeteria has always appealed to the ex-farmer and rural townsman. Essentially, a cafeteria is a sort of indoor picnic, particularly in Los Angeles, where so many cafeterias are dressed up with artificial trees, water wheels, cascading fountains, palm leaves, and all the paraphernalia of a park. Many of the early cafeterias of Los Angeles were flooded with light from skylights, bore names like "The Fern Cafeteria," and were decorated with all sorts of potted plants, ferns, vines, and flowers.

In the curious Spanish that was spoken in Los Angeles "before the gringo came," a cafeteria was, in effect, a saloon that served food. The cafeteria, as we know it to-day, actually had its origin in Los Angeles, where, in 1912, Boos Brothers opened the first self-service restaurant (one year before the federation of state societies was organized). Even before Boos Brothers appeared on the scene, I am informed by Clifford Clinton, one of the most successful cafeteria operators in Los

---

Ibid., pp. 171–172.

Angeles, that "a little old woman had a hole-in-the-wall place on Broadway where you ran a tray along a railing and were served food." Cafeterias and state societies have always been intimately associated in Los Angeles. It may be that newcomers, unfamiliar with established eating places, are naturally drawn to cafeterias. In Los Angeles, cafeterias are quasi-public institutions around which a flourishing social life has always revolved. All sorts of groups, organizations, and associations hold their meetings in cafeterias. A cafeteria in Los Angeles is a place where you go to attend a meeting and, perhaps, to eat. Most of the larger cafeterias have numerous meeting rooms, rest rooms, chapels, alcoves, balconies, and sell a variety of gadgets from books to gardenias, from tourist scenes to curios. Harry Leon Wilson, in 1923, was the first writer to refer to Southern California as "Sunny Cafeteria."

Mushroom Towns in Southern California

One day I was driving my engine over the prairie at the rate of forty miles an hour, without a house in sight, and supposing the nearest town to be thirty miles distant. But as I glanced ahead I was astonished to see that I was approaching a large city. I rubbed my eyes, thinking it was a mirage.

"Jim," says I to the fireman, "what's this place?"

"Blamed if I know," says Jim, staring out of the cab. "I declare if there ain't a new town growed up here since we went over the line yesterday."

"I believe you are right, Jim. Ring the bell or we shall run over somebody."

So I slowed up and we pulled into a depot, where more'n five hundred people were waiting to see the first train come into the place. The conductor learned the name of the town, put it down on the schedule, and we went on.

"Jim," says I, as we pulled out, "keep your eyes open for new towns. First thing you know we'll be running by some strange place."

"That's so," says Jim. "An' hadn't we better git one of the brakemen to watch out on the rear platform for towns that spring up after the engine gets by?"

"Never Call It 'Frisco' "

. . . Back in the 1880's the whole town giggled about the Chinese cook named Ching Pon, who, upon seeing a Washington Street cable

From *Tombstone Daily Prospector,* March 29, 1888.

The following yarn related by an engineer on the S.P.R.R. in connection with the rapid growth of Southern California towns is too good to keep.—Editor.

From *Baghdad-by-the-Bay,* by Herb Caen, pp. 116, 118, 186, 229. Copyright, 1949, by Herb Caen. Garden City: Doubleday & Co.

car stalled at Polk, hurried over to the gripman and inquired: "Whatsa malla—sling bloke?" For a couple of decades after, delighted San Franciscans hurled that pidgin sentence whenever they spotted a cable car stalled in its tracks.

* * * * *

. . . Of course practically every San Franciscan has his own gag about the cables. For instance, if you're a tourist, don't walk up to a San Franscynic and ask him how the cars operate. A favorite, bored retort is: "Well, you see that gimmick there in the middle? It's got a gizmo on the end that hooks onto the dingbat in the slot—that's all there is to it."

* * * * *

While militant moralists were preaching that a wrathful God had shaken the wicked city and applied the torch, the irrepressible Charlie Field noticed that Hotaling's whisky warehouse still stood intact in the middle of an otherwise razed business district, and jingled gaily:

> If, as they say, God spanked the town
> For being over-frisky,
> Why did he burn the churches down
> And spare Hotaling's whisky?

* * * * *

Perhaps the best explanation for this well-slaked thirst was given back in 1853 by a visiting woman newspaper correspondent who enthused: "Hail to the San Franciscan—whose cool climate both fosters a desire for liquor and enables him to carry it!"

Emperor Norton

"Emperor Norton" was the noblest and best known of all of the strange characters of that earlier period [in San Francisco]. Joshua A. Norton was his real name. He was of Hebrew parentage, born February 4, 1819, either in Edinburg or London. Of his early life there is little known as he rarely spoke of it. Like many others who came to California at that time, he lived too actively in the present and the past was seldom mentioned. Before coming to California he had been for some time at Algoa Bay, Cape of Good Hope, and it is said that while there he had been a member of the Cape Mounted Riflemen. He finally reached San Francisco in December, 1849, having come from Rio de Janeiro on the Hamburg vessel *Franzika.*

Norton at once engaged in business. He was occupied in extensive transactions in real estate, and many tremendous operations in importation commissions. His native shrewdness was even unusual; his

---

From *Forgotten Characters of Old San Francisco, 1850–1870,* by Robert Ernest Cowan, pp. 41–59. Copyright, 1938, by Robert E. Cowan. Los Angeles: The Ward Ritchie Press.

intelligence was wonderfully clear, and his business judgment was remarkably accurate. To this acumen were added the rarer attributes of a sound and inflexible moral and financial integrity. Some of these commissions involved transactions to the extent of several hundreds of thousands of dollars weekly, and Joshua Norton rapidly became wealthy. He had brought with him to California $40,000 and towards the close of 1853, he had amassed a fortune of a quarter of a million dollars.

In 1853, in association with one Thorne and others he attempted to control the rice market. Earlier he had operated heavily, had been uniformly successful, and was applauded for his daring and foresight, cooperation was offered and accepted from other large firms, and an immense quantity of rice was secured and held. Everything was promising for yield of immense fortune as profit, as rice was thirty-six cents per pound in bulk unloaded. Almost the last pound of rice in this port had been purchased by the combination. The profits were being calculated when two unexpected cargoes of rice arrived, which the combination could not take up nor control. The market was drugged and prices fell much below cost. To add to the general disaster, in order to protect themselves, some of the associated firms sold out and Norton was financially ruined. He contended stoutly to his closing days that one well-known firm owed him $60,000.

Extensive litigation followed. The first of these cases was that of Ruiz Hermanos vs. Norton, et al. In this contention Norton was sustained in the lower court, but upon appeal this decision was reversed by the Supreme Court. This was in November, 1853. Other serious embarrassments followed, and the sacrifice of his extensive holdings of real estate, principally around North Beach, was the last chapter of his unfortunate disaster. The previous excitement of false expectations and shock of these disappointments, coupled with the legal troubles, constituted a severe blow to Norton's sanity. He retired into obscurity, and when he emerged in 1857, he gave palpable and distinct evidence of an overthrown mind.

His obsession took the form of a belief that he was the Emperor of the United States. He claimed that by an act of the Legislature of 1853, he had been made Emperor of California. With this he was dissatisfied, and not unreasonably so, for he argued that California was but one of a union of states, and as such could neither loyally nor logically create an emperor. Furthermore, he would not renounce what he styled the "national cause," so the act was accordingly suppressed.

The earliest printed proclamation of the self-created Emperor appeared in 1859.

At the peremptory request and desire of a large majority of the citizens of these United States, I, Joshua Norton, formerly of Algoa Bay, Cape of Good Hope, and now for the last 9 years and 10 months past of S.F., Cal., declare and proclaim myself Emperor of these U.S., and direct the representatives of the different States of the Union to assemble in Musical Hall, of this city, on the 1st day of Feb. next, then and there to make such alterations in the existing laws of the Union as may ameliorate the evils under which the country is laboring, and thereby cause confidence to exist, both at home and abroad, in our stability and integrity.

NORTON I
Emperor of the United States
17th September, 1859.

Having assumed the sword and the plume, Norton I actively entered upon the many duties that pertained to his royal station. It is of interest to note that the pretensions of Norton were early recognized by the public of San Francisco and as speedily humored. His name had temporarily disappeared from the city directory, but in Langley's issue for 1862, we find the following: "Norton, Joshua (Emperor), dwl. Metropolitan Hotel." His empire was established and Norton I, Emperor of the United States, had begun to reign.

One day at this period, some important news was received from Mexico, and in this as in all such matters, the Emperor was greatly interested. In a spirit of levity, some joker stated that Mexico needed a protector, and suggested that Norton was the logical choice. Thereupon "Protector of Mexico" was added to the official title and retained for almost a decade. It was dropped during the unhappy career of Maximilian, for, as Norton sanely and even prophetically observed: "It is impossible to protect such an unsettled nation."

The imperialistic duties were manifold, comprehending grave affairs both national and international. The Civil War gave him deep concern. On July 12, 1860, he declared the Union dissolved. Early in the war he declared a blockade, and in 1862 he issued a mandate to the Protestant and Catholic churches to ordain him publicly as Emperor, that he might more efficiently bring order out of the chaos into which the country had been plunged by the violent conflict and fierce dissensions of its rebellious people.

Some of the proclamations to be found in the contemporary journals were jokes which originated with the graceless wags and inspired idiots of the day. Others, of which one or two are extant, were the inspiration of Norton himself alone. They are couched in terms of sanity and composed in superior English. Most of them are national in purport and bear upon relations with Great Britain, Russia, Mexico, and other foreign countries. Others relate to the affairs of the Civil War. One has survived which is entirely personal. In February, 1860, the Emperor desired to visit Sacramento where the legislature was then in session. The Steam Navigation company denied him transportation. Norton issued an order to the commander of the revenue cutter to blockade the Sacramento river until the offending company could be brought to terms.

The proclamations appearing as jokes are easily recognized. Norton had no part in them as they were the work of the conscienceless wags and amiable villains of the times. One of these fictitious documents was issued in observance of the forty-sixth birthday of the Emperor:

Owing to unsettled questions between His Majesty Maximilian I, El Duque de Gwino, The Tycoon, the King of the Mosquitos, the King of the Cannibal Islands, &c., the usual display of bunting on foreign shipping and on public buildings, in commemoration of our 46th birthday, will be omitted.

Feb. 4, 1865.

Another proclamation was to the effect that the Emperor contemplated marriage, but to avoid arousing jealousy among the fairer sex, he played no favorites and they were to decide for themselves which one of them should be Empress.

Falsified telegraphic news was also a source of great amusement for the versatile wits. In 1864, Jefferson Davis telegraphed to inquire if it were true that Norton was in sympathy with Lincoln, also the request that $500 be sent, as Davis had but one pair of trousers, and even that was worn out. Another telegram was from Lincoln. The President thanked the Emperor for his support, and said he had a good story to tell but at present was too busy settling accounts with a seedy individual named Davis. Norton was instructed to proceed to Petaluma, there to remain until further notice. What the Emperor thought of these effusions will never be known. But inter-linear reading is not altogether difficult, for in many directions the mind of Norton was unusually clear, and at all times he was remarkably philosophic.

* * * * *

His most famous proclamation was issued August 18, 1869. Whether or not it was drafted by the Emperor is insignificant, but its contents are extraordinary and of the greatest prophetic importance. It was a command that bridges be constructed across the bay of San Francisco. The project at that time was looked upon as wildly visionary and entirely impracticable. It was received with no credulity and subjected to scornful derision. But a slight survey of the events of that time may disclose some pertinent facts. The overland railroad had just been completed on May 10, 1869, which was a far-reaching event. Stanford and his associates were already attempting to secure Yerba Buena to make it a great terminal depot. Norton's shrewdness and unusual business abilities had suffered no impairment, crazed as he was otherwise. And no man in San Francisco was better qualified to realize the enormous commercial and economic value of those shadowy bridges. Sixty-seven years have elapsed since that proclamation was issued, but the vision of the gentle old Emperor was not so fantastic after all.

In personal appearance the Emperor was always a picturesque and striking figure. He was of medium height, heavy-set, with brown hair that was inclined to curl, heavy eye-brows under a massive forehead, moustache and beard that became a royal personage, and clear and penetrating eyes. His garb was of navy blue cut in military style and profusely adorned with brass buttons. The shoulders were surmounted with massive gilt epaulettes, sometimes tarnished from exposure. In the earlier years of his reign he had worn a military cap embellished with red trimmings, which is quite familiar in the cartoons of the time. About 1865, one of his loyal subjects presented the Emperor with a tall beaver hat, which was thoughtfully decorated with a cockade of feathers and a rosette. The cap had outlived its usefulness and was laid aside forever. The hat, replaced from time to time, continued to be the royal headgear until the close of the Emperor's reign. In 1867, one of his subjects had sent from Oregon a large and unusual specimen of grapevine intended for a walking-stick. It was shod with a ferule and gold-mounted, and thereafter constituted his sceptre. He was never without it, but in inclement weather he carried also an umbrella, knowing wisely that royalty may be drenched and that his Kingly authority was no greater than that of his illustrious predecessor, Canute.

He bore a sort of resemblance to Napoleon III, which fact when commented upon brought forth the ridiculous rumor that Norton was the son of that ill-starred monarch. This misstatement, so obvious in its utter absurdity, was hatched in the scattered brains of some irresponsible contemporary whose living prototypes, loud with vacant volubilities and rich in historical misapplications, are yet in our midst.

The private life of the Emperor was simple. For seventeen years he had lived at the Eureka Lodging House, and the regal apartment was not palatial. It was a room of 6x10 feet in dimensions, with threadbare carpet and disabled furniture. The chief mural decorations were portraits of the foreign rulers and his collection of hats. His familiar form was seen and known everywhere. He was a constant attendant of churches, theatres, musical affairs, civic gatherings, and school commencements. He was deeply interested in higher education and in the earlier days of the University was a frequent visitor. He was fond of children and to them he was always gentle and courteous. There was at that time a Lyceum of Free Culture of which he was a member, and there he sustained many debates most intelligently and logically. It is said that he had some interest in spiritualism, but in which direction is not known. For sustenance he had the freedom of nearly every restaurant in the city, as also of every saloon. He was unusually abstemious, and if he frequently appeared in the popular saloons of Barry and Patten and "Frank's," or in the famous "Bank Exchange" and the "Pantheon," it was not in quest of liquor, but of "free lunch."

It was his custom to visit the markets and the docks, and to view buildings in progress of construction. This was not from idle curiosity but from genuine interest, for in all these and kindred matters he was keenly informed. From time to time visits were made to men of affairs, but the Emperor had that rare discretion that never permitted himself to be regarded as a nuisance. He was even welcomed, for his own business training had taught him to appear at a suitable time and to retire at a proper moment. He had never met with royalty but once, and the distinguished personage was Dom Pedro, Emperor of Brazil.

No sketch of Norton would be entirely complete without some reference to "Bummer" and "Lazarus," the two dogs that enjoyed the freedom of San Francisco in the sixties. Lazarus was a wretched beast of low degree, and Bummer was but little better. But in some of his long gone ancestors there must have been a strain of nobility, for it was Bummer who sniffed this in the Emperor, and thereafter associated himself with the royal presence, with the miserable Lazarus as humble retainer. This was not of Norton's choice, but—noblesse oblige.

* * * * *

The last hoax played upon him was also the crowning effort of the graceless, witty scamps of his realm. Norton was induced to believe that by marriage with Queen Victoria, he could bind closer the ties of the two great nations. Telegrams of congratulations upon the approaching happy event were found among his effects. These purported to be from Alexander of Russia, Beaconsfield, Grévy, former President Grant, and others.

The close of the Emperor's life and the end of his long reign came on January 8, 1880. Early in the evening while standing at the corner of California street and Grant avenue, he was observed to fall. Assistance was rendered immediately, but ten minutes later the Emperor was gone. Death had been caused by sanguineous apoplexy. An autopsy by Doctors Stivers and Douglass, made with special reference to the brain, disclosed the fact that the organ was quite normal, and the more unusual fact that it weighed 51 ounces. The costs of the funeral were provided by Joseph G. Eastland, R. E. Brewster, and the members of the Pacific Club. The final ceremonies were conducted at the Morgue, and the eulogy was delivered by Rev. N. L. Githens, Rector of the Church of the Advent. It is estimated that 10,000 people of all walks in life came to view that silent figure, which rested in a wilderness of flowers. A lady, well-known and of high social standing, with her own fingers pinned upon the lapel of the sleeping monarch a beautiful boutonniere of hyacinth and a spray of fern, remarking quietly that Norton had been kind to her when she was a child and he was in the heyday of his success. . . .

Death in Chinatown

Little Pete's real name was Fong Chong and when he was not working at his eminently respectable trade of selling shoes to the white

From *San Francisco, A Pageant,* by Charles Caldwell Dobie, pp. 204–205, 207–209.

retail trade he was directing the activities of a blackmailing society, which he had the honor of founding, called the Gi Sin Seer. This was an association of what was known in police circles as highbinders. Highbinders had another name—they were called hatchetmen, very much as the militant gangster of these prohibition days is called a gunman. He dressed in a black costume, made in loose Chinese fashion, topped by a black felt hat with a wide, stiff brim, and, when bent on swift action, he carried a pistol concealed in his long sleeves.

Little Pete's blackmailing clique was so successful that it unwittingly promoted competition just as any successful venture is sure to do. A rival organization called the Bo Sin Seer sprang up. Like Al Capone, Little Pete remained the powerful arbiter of criminal circles, but at a great expenditure of cash and forethought. So seriously did the Bo Sin Seer threaten his prestige and even his life that it became necessary for the estimable Fong Chong, otherwise known as Little Pete, to go forth daily protected by a bodyguard.

* * * * *

. . . But there comes a time in even a gangster's life when he relaxes his vigilance. This moment arrived on a bright and shining afternoon when Little Pete, impatient to hear the latest reports from the race-track that had been denied him, sent his bodyguard in search of an evening paper while he entered, unprotected, the apple-green interior of his favorite barber shop to have his forehead shaved and his queue rebraided.

It is not hard to reconstruct the picture if one has ever looked into a Chinese barber shop of the pre-queue era. This was before the natives of Far Cathay discovered that their beloved and highly prized pigtails were a badge of servitude wished upon them centuries before by their Manchu conquerors.

Even though Fong Chong, otherwise known as Little Pete, is not by his own estimate a respectable man, he would almost as soon lose his life as his pigtail and he takes great pride in its glossy length shot through with a thread of scarlet silk. When he enters the shop his pigtail is wrapped, braidlike, about his head. This the obsequious barber unwinds, while his assistant brings water in a porcelain basin of robin's egg blue etched with pink lotus blossoms. Setting the basin upon a lacquered table, the assistant proceeds to assemble the implements necessary for the rejuvenation of Celestial males. He lays out the razor, the scissors, the clean towels. And one thing more, unknown to Occidental shaving parlors—a long steel instrument shaped like a very narrow spoon for removing wax from the ears.

Little Pete opens his loose jacket of dark blue cloth at the throat, disclosing an undervest of pale lavender silk. He is in the mood for the relaxation that comes with steaming towels and a barber's deft touch upon his respectably shaved forehead. He closes his eyes. The barber turns his back for a moment to test the edge of his razor. Two figures as swift and black as crows dart from nowhere into the doorway. There is a crackle of sound like the sputtering of a string of firecrackers ushering in the New Year: Little Pete falls forward in a crimson pool. . . .

When the police arrive there will not be a soul in sight upon the streets. The barber will be honing his razor and his assistant polishing the bright instrument shaped like a very narrow spoon.

Three days later, Chinatown will witness the most gorgeous funeral of its career. An American band will escort the body to its brief resting place, there will be floral pieces by the score from admiring Occidentals, truckloads of roasted pigs and sweetmeats for the delectation of hungry spirits at the graveside. Even the hundred-footed dragon that is brought out only on great feast days will wind a sinuous way behind the funeral coach. For a man so powerful in life may also be powerful in death and it is well to pay his spirit tribute. In short, Little Pete will have a funeral that would have been the despair and envy of any Chicago gangster brought low by his enemies in the year nineteen hundred and thirty.

A few days later, a highbinder named Big John, who headed a rival tong, will fold his tent and silently depart for the comparative security of China.

Barbary Coast Picnic

Shanghai Kelly's saloon and boarding-house was a three-story frame structure at No. 33 Pacific Street, between Drum and Davis streets, under part of which tidewater flowed. Kelly preferred to handle *bona fide* sailors, partly because they were more docile and partly because there was seldom any danger of reprisal, no matter how they were treated. But, in common with his co-workers in the crimping field, he would, if necessary to fill out a crew, shanghai whoever fell into his hands. And for a price he would shanghai any man whose enemies wanted him out of the way. Kelly's runners and strong-arm men went into the streets or the dives of the Barbary Coast and blackjacked the men they wanted, or induced them to visit Kelly's saloon. There they were drugged, blackjacked, and dropped through trapdoors, of which there were three in the floor in front of the bar, into a boat which was

---

From *The Barbary Coast,* An Informal History of the San Francisco Underworld, by Herbert Asbury, pp. 216–218. Copyright, 1933, by Alfred A. Knopf, Inc. New York.

The dominant figure of the waterfront during the years in which Miss Piggott and Mother Bronson flourished, and perhaps the most successful and dangerous crimp who ever operated in San Francisco, was a short, thick-set Irishman, with flaming red hair, a bristling red beard, and an irascible disposition. Throughout the underworld, and wherever sailors gathered, he was known and feared as Shanghai Kelly.—H. A., *ibid.,* p. 215.

always tied up to a pillar of the house. In his drugging operations this prince of shanghaiers used the Miss Piggott Special[1] and also gave his victims a concoction of his own invention, compounded of schnapps and beer and seasoned with opium or laudanum. Besides these quieting doses he used a cigar heavily doped with opium, which was known as "the Shanghai smoke" and was manufactured especially for him by a Chinese cigar-maker.

Kelly's boarding-house was usually filled with sailors, many of whom put themselves in his power of their own accord and with full knowledge of what would undoubtedly happen to them, because he provided free women as well as free liquor and permitted any sort of debauchery a man might fancy—and sometimes men who had been several years at sea came ashore with very exotic ideas. Once during the middle eighteen-seventies, however, Shanghai Kelly found his place practically bare of seamen at a time when three ships anchored off the Heads, outside the Golden Gate, wanted crews immediately. One of these vessels was the *Reefer,* a notorious hell-ship out of New York, which was commanded by a captain with whom no sailor in his right mind would ship if he could avoid it. Confronted by the necessity of shanghaiing strangers in wholesale lots, Kelly performed the exploit which set the cap-stone to his fame and which is still talked about along the San Francisco waterfront as the most daring job of crimping in the history of the city. He chartered the *Goliah,* an old paddle-wheel steamer which had wheezed about the Bay for many years, and announced that he would celebrate his forthcoming birthday with a picnic, at which there would be free liquor and other attractions. He issued a blanket invitation to the Barbary Coast, and the riff-raff of that quarter answered in droves. As guests came aboard, however, Shanghai Kelly counted them, and when ninety men stood on deck, he cast off, and the *Goliah* chugged down the Bay and outside the Golden Gate into the broad Pacific. Barrels of beer and whisky were broached, and the picnickers began to drink Kelly's health with great enthusiasm. But the liquor was heavily drugged, and within two hours every man on board, excepting Kelly and his henchmen, was asleep. Thereupon the *Goliah* steamed alongside the *Reefer* and the two other ships, and a crew for each vessel was hoisted aboard, although there was scarcely a man among the ninety who knew one end of a ship from the other. On her way back to San Francisco the *Goliah* took off the survivors of the ship *Yankee Blade,* which had been wrecked on a rock off Point Conception, west of Santa Barbara. The landing of the rescued men at the Market Street wharf caused great excitement, and no one seemed to notice that Shanghai Kelly had returned without his picnic guests.

---

[1] Composed of equal parts of whisky, brandy, and gin, with a goodly lacing of laudanum or opium.—H. A., *ibid.,* p. 213.

San Diego Bottom-Scratcher

There was a club in San Diego known as the Bottom-Scratchers Club. The only way you could get into it was to bring up three abalones from the bottom of the ocean in thirty feet of water, and then bring in a live shark by the tail with your bare hands. I am willing to be quoted as standing rockbound and steadfast on a platform of to hell with being a Bottom-Scratcher. Only five men had been able to meet the club requirements. One of the five had had to retire because of busted eardrums; another was practically emeritus, because he turned blue in cold water.

The club's president had the title of Chief Walrus. The club was only about five years old, and the first incumbent was still Chief Walrus. His name was Glenn Orr. He was a friendly well-built man of thirty-one who ran a crane for the city of San Diego whenever the city wanted something built, which was all the time. He worked six days a week. On Sundays, summer and winter, regardless of wind, snow, sleet, or mail carriers, he was out in the water diving and crawling around the bottom of the ocean. His feet were cut up from walking on the bottom, his shoulders were scratched and scarred from scraping against barnacles on underwater ledges. And in the small of his back there was a big scar where a sea lion had bitten him; he was down on the bottom prying loose abalones when the sea lion came plunging down from above. He never even saw it coming. He had to go to the hospital for that one.

This bottom-scratching was done purely for sport. They didn't use diving helmets or anything; they just went down and held their breath. Not one of them but had been caught by some circumstance, and held his breath almost to the dying point, and come to the top roaring sick at his stomach. Each man always carried a long sharp knife when he dived to the bottom. Sometimes it was strapped around a wrist, sometimes stuck in a sheath inside his trunks. Once a sea lion bit Glenn Orr's underwater flashlight right out of his hand. He got to the top and wouldn't go back after the flashlight unless somebody went with him, and I don't blame him. Twice he got his knife caught in an underwater rock crevice. That wouldn't have been so bad, except that the knife was tied around his wrist, trapping him there. On each occasion he gave a big yank and broke the cord—a feat he probably couldn't accomplish if he was doing it just for fun.

The Bottom-Scratchers could hold their breath under water for three minutes. Glenn's chest had expanded four inches since he had been diving. Furthermore, he had taken on considerable weight. The

---

From *Home Country*, by Ernie Pyle, pp. 443–444.

cold water did it; he said nature was providing him with blubber against the cold, just as it does a walrus.

The Bottom-Scratchers did their diving just off the breakwater at La Jolla, a half hour's drive north of San Diego, where the water usually seemed to be clearer. Mainly they were after abalones. An abalone is a thing in a shell, sort of like a clam, only the shell is about as big as a plate. It has suction cups around its rim, and it glues itself to the rocks on the bottom. A man could no more pry one loose with his hands than he could fly, but if you slip a knife underneath, it comes off easily.

Glenn Orr had been swimming so long it was second nature to him. He was the first swimmer I'd met who didn't make fun of me because I couldn't swim. He said some people just naturally couldn't swim, the same as some people couldn't swallow swords.

He was not the least bit afraid of sharks; they were just a nuisance. They would dart around you and get in the way when you were trying to pry abalones loose. He wouldn't say that a shark would not attack a man, but he had never been attacked. Killing a shark was nothing at all in his life. He couldn't even estimate how many he had killed—sometimes three and four in one Sunday, and other mild things like octopuses and sting rays.

About those sharks they had to bring up by the tail for their initiation: these were little sharks, only three feet long. Little and harmless, you know, like small rattlesnakes.

Reno Humor

. . . [Reno] is the home of high-comedy localisms that sound witty but often enough suggest heartbreak or cynical disillusionment: taking the cure (putting in the six weeks' residence), Alimony Park (the city plaza opposite the county courthouse), Bridge of Sighs (the Virginia Street bridge over the Truckee River), pouring a divorcee on the train (seeing her off after the decree), wash day (Monday, sometimes Tuesday, too, when default cases come up), the Separator (the courthouse), divorcee (meaning either man or woman, from arrival in Nevada until actually divorced), Divorcee Special (the noon train from the East), Dresden (a relatively sexless woman who lives to be looked at), six weeks' sentence (the divorce business).

Reno is the victim of journalists and jokesmiths. "Renovate," says Walter Winchell, means to give unhappy marriage the quickest known treatment. *Life* and many myth peddlers tell of divorcees who kiss the courthouse pillars and throw their rings into the Truckee River. An *Esquire* cartoon shows a convertible coupe with the top down, a girl at the wheel roaring along a desert road. A road sign reads, "Reno: 50

From *Desert Challenge,* An Interpretation of Nevada, by Richard G. Lillard, pp. 341–342. Copyright, 1942, by Richard G. Lillard. New York: Alfred A. Knopf.

miles." Two wind-blown matrons sit in the rumble seat. One says to the other, "She's always going back to the scene of her divorce!" A drawing in *Pic* exhibits a sexy young woman, accompanied by a pudgy lawyer, as she leaves the Reno courthouse after the granting of a decree. "Boy," she exclaims, taking a deep breath that swells her breasts into her form-fitting suit, "I feel like a new man!" . . .

The Umatilla-Pendleton County Seat War

In the pioneer days when the long, tempestuous journey around the tip end of South America, where it was said men hung their consciences on the Horn, was the only way of bringing freight to Oregon: in those days before "Bill" Cody rounded up buffalo meat for the Kansas Pacific and the railroads were built, Umatilla, sixty miles down the river from Pendleton, was the head of navigation and the focal point of departure for pack-trains to the placer mines of Idaho, which were the great things in those days, as agriculture had not then developed. Anybody who lived anywhere at that time lived in Umatilla which had almost as large a floating population as its permanent one, for it was the center both for supplies and a "fling" to the far-flung population of the greater portion of three states.

The rest of Eastern Oregon contained only scattering settlements; for instance, Pendleton itself at that time consisted of the stage-stop hotel, the Pendleton, a general store and the few typical false fronts of a Western pioneer town. There were only two residences, the house of Judge Bailey and one other. Thus Umatilla became the county seat of Umatilla County, which at that time, 1863, included practically all of Oregon east of the John Day River, as it was the metropolis and great trade emporium of Eastern Oregon, which included most of Washington, Oregon and Idaho.

As the ends of those great ever-projecting probosces of civilization, the railroads, thrust their feelers further west, the Horn route fell into disuse and the overland routes from the East increased the development and population of Eastern Oregon. When in 1868 the Central Pacific pushed into Nevada, the bulk of the Idaho trade followed it. This killed Umatilla—which was "some town" in its day—and decreased its population; while that of Eastern Oregon especially between '66 and '68 increased, and Pendleton became a more natural and easily reached center for the inhabitants.

These were the reasons advanced for the transfer of the county seat to Pendleton, and this question was agitated. All the settlers of Eastern Oregon now demanded by a signed petition that the county seat be moved nearer their center of population. Pendleton considered

---

From *Let 'Er Buck*, by Charles Wellington Furlong, pp. 14–16. Copyright, 1921, by Charles Wellington Furlong. New York and London: G. P. Putnam's Sons.

itself the logical site and when the petition was granted by the legislature, though no definite place was decided upon, Judge Bailey in January, 1868, ordered the county officers to remove the records to Pendleton. This was done, but in lieu of a courthouse, Judge Bailey's cellar was the official repository. Judge Wilson of Umatilla declared this removal premature and the records had to be carted back over the old Oregon Trail again to the Umatilla courthouse.

While the question burned, Pendleton worked. The change and location of a seat for the county was not going to be delayed through any fault of theirs, besides, it was obvious that it should be at Pendleton, and now that they had made up their minds, they built a courthouse in short order before the question was settled. But the matter held fire too long for the "go get 'em" spirit of the little town. Anyway, what's the use of having a courthouse and nothing to put in it?

On a certain week-end [in 1869], a score of men, heavily armed, rode down "The Meadow," lying to the west of Pendleton along the river, across the desert, and under the cover of darkness that Saturday night entered Umatilla. Early the next morning at the hour when men and dogs sleep heaviest, in the very heart of Umatilla, they piled not only all the records of the county and the county seal, but the county officers themselves, in a commandeered wagon and under heavy mounted escort departed quickly, and deposited their official booty in the "courthouse" in Pendleton.

"Why didn't they recapture it?" Well, they *say* because it was Sunday.

Tombstone Finds Its *Epitaph*

Tombstone was dead, and its epitaph had been written beforehand. One evening, at the start of the boom, J. C. Clum, a newspaper man, and several of us were in a tent talking when Clum said. "I would start a newspaper if I had the capital." One of the men said, "How much would it take?" "Six hundred dollars." "I'll let you have it." Then one of the men said, "What shall we call it?" Another said, "What is a Tombstone without an Epitaph?" So the "Tombstone Epitaph" brought the news to the city's fourteen thousand inhabitants, and kept a record of its short but stormy life.

From "Experiences in Arizona in the '80's," by Alfred Robert Kirkwood, *The Pony Express Courier,* Vol. II (November, 1935), No. 6, p. 14. Official Publication for the Pony Express Route & Pioneer Trails Association, Inc. Placerville, California.

According to *Arizona* (New York, 1940, p. 248), the *Epitaph* was christened by Ed Schieffelin, who in 1877 named "Tombstone Ledge," after Al Sieber's warning that instead of a mine he would find a tombstone in the Apache-infested hills.

Joe Hill Becomes a Legend

Joe Hill [whose real name was Joseph Hillstrom] was twenty years old in 1902 when he arrived in this country. He had a common-school education and a fair knowledge of English which he had picked up at the Y.M.C.A. in his home town, Jevla, Westerjutland. Joe continued his education by reading while working as a seaman on freighters plying between Gothenburg and England. He left Sweden when his mother died.

In New York City, Joe Hill worked for a couple of weeks as a porter in a Bowery saloon, then at any kind of odd job he could find. At the end of a year he and his cousin shoved off for Chicago via the boxcar route. They wanted to go to the West Coast. Joe Hill remained in Chicago two months and managed to save up twenty dollars for a road stake. His cousin had gone on to California. The boys met at San Pedro, where they lived for three years, alternating their time between longshoring and working freight steamers on the Honolulu run. Association with migratory workers at sea and ashore attracted Joe Hill to the I.W.W. He joined the organization in San Pedro and never transferred.

He could play almost any kind of musical instrument and delighted in improvising satirical parodies of well-known songs. At the Mission Church, 331 Beacon Street, San Pedro, he struck up a friendship with Mrs. Macon, the director. There was a piano in the mission, where Joe Hill, between jobs, would sit by the hour picking out the words for his parodies line by line, to the amusement of his fellow maritime workers. He would polish up the verses at night and eventually assemble them into songs.

Everybody around the mission marveled at Joe Hill's untiring industry. He had the reputation of being a "harmless man" as well as notably unselfish. Frequently he would give away "his last rice." He never had a steady girl, always protesting that he was "too busy." His cousin, more typical of the maritime trade, urged him repeatedly, "Come on, Joe, and have a good time." Joe never went. John Holland would find him late at night scribbling verse, "twisting the hair on his forehead with his finger as he figured out the rhymes." Joe Hill never smoked or drank. He was fond of Chinese dishes, which he prepared with great skill. It was said of him that he could "eat with chopsticks like a native."

It was during the great strike on the Southern Pacific Railroad in 1910 that Joe Hill first gained fame as a rebel songwriter. "Casey Jones,

---

From *Wobbly,* The Rough-and-Tumble Story of an American Radical, by Ralph Chaplin, pp. 185–189, 193. Copyright, 1948, by the University of Chicago. Chicago: University of Chicago Press.

the Union Scab" was printed on cards and sold for strike relief in every West Coast city. Joe Hill could never understand why his parodies became so popular. He was greatly surprised to find himself in the limelight and his roughneck songs famous throughout the world. It was Joe Hill, more than any other songwriter, who made the I.W.W. a singing organization. He sang to hoboes on land or sea in their own language. The first I.W.W. songbook was written by him, illustrated by him, and published by him at his own expense.

Joe Hill also pioneered in making the I.W.W. a fighting organization. He participated in both the Fresno and the San Diego free-speech fights, and he is said to have been shot in the leg at the Battle of Mexicali. This, it will be remembered, was one of the first skirmishes of the Mexican revolution.

It was because of a neighbor from his native town of Jevlu that Joe Hill left San Pedro on the journey from which he was never to return. This friend was also a migratory worker and a Wobbly.[1] His name was Westergren. Joe was told that Westergren was in the hospital at Los Angeles. There is no record of what happened in that city, but Joe Hill next turned up near Salt Lake City working as a laborer in Bingham Canyon. The rest is one of the most tragic pages in labor history. The I.W.W. version of the story, current at the time, follows.

A strike was being promoted in Bingham Canyon, and Joe Hill was considered by the employers the chief agitator and organizer. Utah was treating Wobblies rough in those days. The jails were full of them. Chain gangs, composed of those convicted of carrying the "Red Card," were put to work repairing county and city roads under gun guards. A grocer named Morrison was killed in an attempted holdup. Joe Hill was tried and convicted, appealed and lost, all the while refusing steadfastly to permit I.W.W. defense funds to be used in his behalf. Elizabeth Gurley Flynn visited Joe Hill in prison and urged him to change his mind. Then followed a world-wide publicity drive paralleled only later on in the Sacco-Vanzetti case. The governor's mansion was swamped with letters and telegrams. Mass meetings were held in principal cities throughout our own and in other nations. The story broke into front-page headlines. Halftone cuts of Joe Hill in handcuffs were conspicuously displayed. The Swedish minister intervened,

---

[1] The I.W.W. were often called "Wobblies": they used the term for themselves, and it is said to have come from their integrity in financial matters. As an international organization, the I.W.W. organized working men in British Columbia, and they were strong in the lumber region of Vancouver Island. The loggers' favorite eating place in Victoria was a Chinese restaurant where the proprietor sometimes gave credit. Through trial and error, he learned that I.W.W. were a good risk. When a logger wanted credit, he would ask, "I Wobbly Wobbly?" and if the logger had a membership card, he was approved. The Chinaman's rough-and-tumble with the letter "W" resulted in the term "Wobbly."—Archie Binns, *The Roaring Land* (New York, 1942), pp. 87–88.

and President Wilson, appealing to the governor, obtained a two-week reprieve for Joe.

But the execution date was finally set for November 19, 1915. The laws of Utah permitted a condemned man to choose between hanging and a firing squad. Joe Hill insisted on the latter. He preferred a soldier's death. Big charts appeared in the newspapers depicting the march from death cell to execution yard.

* * * * *

Joe Hill from his death cell sent his last songs and poems. Among them was "Workers of the World, Awaken." I was deeply convinced of Joe's innocence. His kind are not killers. No man guilty of murder would have dared to discharge even incompetent counsel and attempt to defend himself in a hostile court before a hostile jury. Only an innocent man with nothing to fear from a fair verdict would have had the courage to declare, "I do not want a pardon or commutation of sentence. I want a new trial."

Joe Hill wrote a statement "To the People of Utah" shortly after the final verdict was returned. [It began:]

I never killed Morrison and do not know a thing about it.

He was, as the records plainly show, killed by some enemy for the sake of revenge, and I have not been in this city long enough to make an enemy. Shortly before my arrest I came down from Park City, where I was working in the mines. Owing to the prominence of Mr. Morrison, there had to be a "goat" and the undersigned being as they thought, a friendless tramp, a Swede and, worst of all, an I.W.W. had no right to live anyway, and was therefore duly selected to be the "goat."

[It ended:]

I have always worked hard for a living and paid for everything I got, and my spare time I spent painting pictures, writing songs and composing music.

Now if the people of the State of Utah want to shoot me without giving me half a chance to state my side of the case, then bring on your firing squads —I am ready for you.

I have lived like an artist and I shall die like an artist—Respectfully yours, Joseph Hillstrom.

I was in the general office when Bill Haywood received Joe Hill's farewell note. Bill read it without comment, then stared out of the window. I could only see the blind side of his face. He shoved the letter across the desk to Frank Little, who read it aloud, rather stumblingly, to the rest of us:

Goodbye, Bill: I die like a true rebel. Don't waste any time mourning—organize! It is a hundred miles from here to Wyoming. Could you arrange to have my body hauled to the state line to be buried? I don't want to be found dead in Utah.—Joe Hill.

Bill scribbled a brief answer:

Goodbye, Joe: You will live long in the hearts of the working class. Your songs will be sung wherever the workers toil, urging them to organize.—W. D. Haywood.

Joe Hill was shot to death on November 19, 1915. . . .

* * * * *

The following day the papers told how he had been strapped in a chair with a red cardboard heart pinned on his breast for a target and how he had refused to be blindfolded. The papers told also of Joe Hill shouting the orders to the firing squad for his own execution.

* * * * *

Joe Hill, in one of his most poignant death-cell poems, had indicated that he wanted his ashes scattered upon the earth so that flowers might be nourished by them. This was done, on a scale of which Joe Hill had never dreamed. In every state in the Union, in every country in South America, Europe, and Asia, in South Africa, New Zealand, and Australia, tiny envelopes of Joe Hill's ashes were scattered to the winds by I.W.W. members and sympathizers singing his songs and recounting the saga of his life and death. Joe Hill had touched the heart of the world.

Joe Hill's Last Will

My will is easy to decide,
For there is nothing to divide.
My kin don't need to fuss and moan—
Moss does not cling to rolling stone.
My body? Ah, if I could choose,
I would to ashes it reduce,
And let the merry breezes blow
My dust to where some flowers grow.
Perhaps some fading flower then
Would come to life and bloom again.
This is my last and final will,
Good luck to all of you—Joe Hill.

From *Holy Old Mackinaw,* A Natural History of the American Lumberjack, by Stewart H. Holbrook, pp. 240–241. Copyright, 1938, by The Macmillan Company. New York. 1944.

Wherever there was a Wobbly—in pine, fir, or redwood country—bunkhouse forums were sure to hear of Wobbly Joe Hill (Hillstrom), best known of the I.W.W. martyrs and a writer of "songs of discontent," who was convicted of murder and went down in front of a firing squad of the State of Utah, at Salt Lake City, on November 19, 1915. "Joe Hill's Last Will," reputedly written on the eve of his execution, was famous bunkhouse poetry.—S.H.H.

PART FIVE

Western Story-Tellers

A man in the States might have been a liar in a small way, but when he comes West he soon takes lessons from the prairies, where ranges a hundred miles away seem within touchin' distance, streams run uphill, and Nature appears to lie some herself.

—CHARLES M. RUSSELL

Uncle Dick Wooton told how once, when he, old Bill Williams, and many other trappers were lying around the campfire one night, the strange fellow, in a preaching style of delivery, related to them all how he was to be changed into a buck elk and intended to make his pasture in the very region where they then were. He described certain peculiarities which would distinguish him from the common run of elk, and was very careful to caution all those present never to shoot such an animal, should they ever run across him.

—HENRY INMAN

Introduction

THE world of Western story-telling is a frontier world, in which, as in other frontier situations, the story-teller has adapted his materials and means to his conditions and ends and taken from the land as much as he brings to it. If amidst this bewildering kaleidoscope of fact and fantasy, the truth sounds like a lie and a lie sounds like the truth, the reason may well be that in the clear, dry air of the West the far seems near, the near big, and the illusory real. In a land where the "rabbits have somehow gotten the body of the hare and the ears of the ass; the frogs, the body of the toad, the horns of the stag-beetle, and the tail of the lizard," it is not surprising to hear that a coyote chased a jackrabbit down the main street of Yuma one summer Saturday afternoon, "walking, both walking," or that an Arizona frog "will be seven years old next month and he hasn't learned to swim yet. If it does not rain soon we are afraid he will turn into a long horned toad."[1]

Or, as Will H. Robinson puts it, "if there can be scorpions, tarantulas, centipedes, collar-lizards, chuckawallas, horn toads, and Gila monsters all about, cluttering up the country, why shouldn't there be other unusual and fearsome things?" His Gilaopolis, for example, which belongs to the same general family as the Gila monster but often attains the size of a big calf. At spring roundup time it is attacked by a high fever, which nothing will cure except canned fruit juice. Raiding a chuck-wagon at night, it breaks open the case with its powerful claws, melts the solder on the cans with its feverish breath, and greedily drinks the juice. One spring Dick Bowersox's pet "Heely" broke into the cellar and imbibed three quarts of green paint and two gallons of home brew, then chewed up a week's wash on the line, half killed Dick's white-faced bull, pushed his flivver over the cliff, and ran for the hills. Among other curious desert creatures of the imagination Robinson names the Hellidid, the sneeze-duck, the whiffletit, the koohopper, the giant goober-bug, and the left-footed bee-chaser.[2]

---

[1] Dick Wick Hall, *A Treasury of American Folklore* (New York, 1944), p. 338.

[2] *Yarns of the Southwest* (Phoenix, 1921), pp. 31–35. Cf. *The Indoor Bird Watcher's Manual* (New York, 1950), in which Helen Ferril and Anne Folsom, with the help of professional watchers like Bernard DeVoto and Stewart Holbrook, study the habitat, habits, and calls of such rare ornithological specimens as the Culture Vulture, the Stool Pigeon, the Scarlet Teenager, and the Red-Eyed Bleerio.

Before bird-watching became a parlor game, there were satirical-mythical birds like the Kansas jayhawk and the mugwump. The former is the bird with bright yellow slippers and yellow beak that flies backward because he doesn't care where he's going "but sure wants to know where he's been!" (Kirke Mechem, *The Mythical Jayhawk,* cited by John Gunther, *Inside U.S.A.,* New York, 1947, p. 262). The latter is the bird with head and tail that look the same, whose name is derived from its habit of sitting on fences "with his mug on one side and his wump on the other. . . . The birds were often undecided themselves which end was which, and sometimes

Once a Hassayamper has drunk of the "lying waters" and become indifferent to fine shadings of truth and falsehood, he looks about for victims. His natural prey is the Easterner. The latter is already somewhat imposed upon by the country itself. To one who has "always associated clearness and nearness," rivers and water, Western distances and rivers are deceptive. As, for example, in the case of the stranger to the sheep country who was observed by a native in the act of stripping on the edge of a narrow trickle of a stream. Having started that morning for a butte, which had seemed near enough but was still several miles away, he explained that he wasn't "taking any chances" and was going to swim across.[3]

The Western story-teller comes up against two kinds of Easterners, both of whom affect him in much the same way. One is represented by the curious, "dumb" lady dude who told her Grand Canyon guide that the "only thing I can't understand is how the river got way down there at the bottom." "Lady," he replied, "that's one of th' funniest things about this here place. Th' river used to be up here on th' rim, but one day it just slipped off."[4] The other is the snobbish or "educated feller" who comes to scoff or heckle, like the young officer who said to Joe Meek at the fort at Vancouver:

"Mr. Meek . . . if you have been so long in the country and have witnessed such wonderful transformations, doubtless you may have observed equally great ones in nature; in the rivers and mountains, for instance?"

Meek gave a lightning glance at the speaker, who had so mistaken his respondent.

"I reckon I have," said he slowly.

Then, waving his hand gracefully toward the majestic Mt. Hood, towering thousands of feet above the summit of the Cascade range, and white with everlasting snows: "When *I* came to this country, Mount Hood was *a hole in the ground!*"[5]

The expansiveness of the Western liar is not unrelated to Western showmanship and sectional rivalry or local pride. So the same Joe Meek, resplendent in his trapper's regalia, on an official visit to Washington during his cousin President Polk's administration, announced to an astonished hotel clerk, whom he asked to sign the register for him on the pretense that he could not write: "I am Joseph L. Meek,

---

started to fly away in opposite directions. The resultant worry and strain is thought to have led to their disappearance." (Paul R. Beath, *Febold Feboldson,* Lincoln, 1948, p. 17).

For other mythical birds of the West, see *A Treasury of American Folklore* (New York, 1944), pp. 638–639, 646–647.

[3] Archer B. Gilfillan, *Sheep* (Boston, 1929), p. 19. See also above, pp. 102–103.

[4] Hoffman Birney, *Roads to Roam* (Philadelphia, 1930), p. 73.

[5] Frances Fuller Victor, *The River of the West* (Hartford, 1869), pp. 366–367.

Cf. Chauncey Thomas, Denver, Colorado, in a letter to the editor in 1930: "When Pike's Peak was a hole in the ground" is a common synonym in the Colorado Rockies for "a long time ago." "I'm the man who turned the water down in the Platte" is a Colorado saying to indicate long residence; i.e., as if the Platte were an irrigation ditch and he was the first man to turn the water into it. The fact is, I'm the man who did it.

Minister Plenipotentiary and Envoy Extraordinary from all Oregon to the United States of America."[6]

The Western liar is thus related to the frontier boaster and the local booster. As the Western paradise becomes the "paradise of puffers," the boaster becomes a booster when he begins to brag about the attractions and advantages of his community, state, or region instead of his personal exploits. Here again, fortunately, the resources and opportunities of the West have "just enough truth in them to make good story material and to incite the imagination to try to improve on actual happenings." Since one may boast about his liabilities as well as his assets and since the boast contains within itself the seed of its own travesty, boosting soon passes into boosting in reverse and mock boosting.[7] Both may be an improvement on the pure product. A good deal of Western humor, centering in fertile soil and healthful climate, revolves around boosting Texans and Californians, with other states falling in line, in self-defense; e.g.:

I asked an Idaho patriot why the potatoes were so big. Answer: "We fertilize 'em with cornmeal and irrigate with milk."[8]

The big Texan—big in body and talk—traces his legendary lineage to Davy Crockett of the Crockett almanacs,[9] while California boosting, dating from the gold rush, took a tremendous spurt with the Los Angeles boom of the Eighties.

. . . Our farmers raise crops of grain and vegetables *faster,* which they sell *fast,* at *faster* rates than any portion of the *fast* world we live in. We now have *fast* steamboats, *fast* horses, *fast* express lines, and some of the *fastest* "hombres" that can be met with. . . .[10]

They say it takes two Eastern men to believe a Californian, but it only takes one Eastern woman to tell true stories which do seem almost too big for belief. One man got lost in a mustard field, and he was on horseback too.[11]

The "fastest hombre" and the man who gets ahead fastest in a new

---

[6] George E. Cole, *Early Oregon* (1905), pp. 43–45.

[7] Cf. *A Treasury of American Folklore* (New York, 1944), pp. 3, 282, 318.

[8] John Gunther, *Inside U.S.A.* (New York, 1947), p. 114. According to H. Allen Smith (*We Went Thataway,* Garden City, 1949, pp. 62–63): "South Dakota is the only state in the Union that doesn't brag about itself. It is the antithesis of Texas. The people of South Dakota in fact apologize for their commonwealth, for themselves and the shape they are in, and for their domestic beasts. This attitude of humility and self-mortification on the part of the inhabitants helps to make South Dakota one of the most captivating communities in the Republic."

[9] Joseph Leach, "Crockett's Almanacs and the Typical Texan," *Southwest Review,* Spring, 1950, pp. 88–95. For typical Texas brags, see Boyce House, *I Give You Texas!* and *Texas—Proud and Loud* (San Antonio, 1943, 1945), and John Randolph, *Texas Brags* (Hufsmith, Texas, 1950). See also *A Treasury of American Folklore* (New York, 1944), pp. 276–356, for state and local boosting and knocking and related local rivalry and prejudice.

[10] James H. Carson, *Life in California* (Stockton, 1852), pp. 40–41.

[11] Kate Sanborn, *A Truthful Woman in Southern California* (New York, 1895), p. 128. For the "sociology of the boom" and kindred topics, see Carey McWilliams, *Southern California Country* (New York, 1946), a penetrating analysis of the "folklore of climatology," millenialism and utopianism, heterodoxy and paradox, in relation to the cultural landscape and migration.

country is apt to be the man who pulls a "fast one." Behind tall lying, boasting, and boosting lies the hoax. The excitement-charged, rumor-filled air of the mining regions bred hoaxes faster than fortunes were made and lost. There were not only the giant hoaxes of Pikes Peak, Gold Lake, and the Ralston Diamond Mine, and the small swindles of claim-jumping and mine-salting. There were also the humorous "Whizzers," or practical jokes, like Pike Sellers' tree-top mining or "jack-pine gold" whizzer at Downie Flats.[12] At Downieville, too, was founded the hoaxing, hell-bent-for-initiation fraternity of E. Clampsus Vitus (recently revived by G. Ezra Dane and others as E. Clampus Vitus), whose chief dignitary was called "Noble Grand Humbug" and whose constitution contained two articles: I. "All members are officers." II. "All offices are of Equal Indignity."[13]

The golden era was also the era of "literary men jokers." The first Far Western humorist, "John Phoenix," wrote much as his creator, George H. Derby, behaved. In the San Francisco of the Fifties and especially in the literary circle of Barry and Patten's saloon, Derby became a legend for his punning and burlesque hoaxes, one of the more tasteful being the time he stopped the Golden Eagle Bakery wagon and asked the driver for "three golden eagles, baked brown and crisp."[14] In their literary and practical "quaints" and "sells" wits and wags catered to the popular taste for japery and humbuggery, which were part of "seeing the Elephant."[15]

Bret Harte's poem, "To the Pliocene Skull," was inspired by the discovery of a skull at the bottom of a mining shaft at Cherokee Flat, which the experts declared to be Pliocene but which proved to be a skull stolen from a dentist's office at Angels Camp—possibly by Ross Coon,[16] Mark Twain's source for the "Jumping Frog." Jim Bridger's petrified forest yarns were rivaled by stories like Twain's "The Petrified Man" (directed at a Humboldt coroner) and Dan De Quille's "The Silver Man." "Stories about petrified things were highly entertaining to those who worked all day in hard-rock. They liked to laugh at the

---

[12] Robert Welles Ritchie, *A Treasury of American Folklore* (New York, 1944), pp. 390–391. See also his *The Hell-Roarin' Forty-Niners* (New York, 1928) and G. Ezra Dane and Beatrice J. Dane, *Ghost Town* (New York, 1941) for additional material on Mother Lode wags and "whizzers." Lucius Beebe and Charles M. Clegg discuss the "myth" of California and other hoaxes in their introduction to Hinton Helper's *Dreadful California* (Indianapolis, 1948).

[13] Cf. *E. Clampus Vitus, Ritual* (Downieville, Sierra Democrat, printer, n.d.) and *The Curious Book of Clampus* (Yerba Buena, 1935).

[14] For John Phoenix, see George R. Stewart, *John Phoenix, Esq., the Veritable Squibob* (New York, 1937).

[15] ". . . Its connotation seems to have been to the effect that one had experienced the ultimate possibilities of a situation, had passed through a most difficult experience, or had hit hard luck in a manner seemingly inevitable."—Carl I. Wheat, in *The Shirley Letters from the California Mines* (New York, 1949), p. 174.

[16] Idwal Jones, "Mother Lode Folk," in *The Sierra Nevada: The Range of Light,* edited by Roderick Peattie (New York, 1947), pp. 280–281. For tall tales in verse by Harte, see "Dow's Flat" and "The Stage-Driver's Story" (*The Poetical Works of Bret Harte,* Boston, 1887), pp. 38, 168.

force that often flouted them."[17] Many hoaxes boomeranged. Mark Twain's "last hoax" forced him to quit town and his job to avoid arrest for violating the state law against duelling.

Hoaxing and "literary men jokers" were not limited to the Mother Lode and the Comstock. In Denver at the beginning of the Eighties Eugene Field was remembered chiefly for his practical jokes. Once, when Oscar Wilde was coming to town, Field, in velvet coat and flaxen wig and curls, with a sunflower in his lapel, drove down to the station before the arrival of Wilde's train and was greeted and paraded as the British lecturer. More disastrous was the time he arranged for the demonstration of a friend's invention, a hand-grenade fire extinguisher, and replaced the chemicals with coal oil.

The hoaxing epidemic spread. An Arkansas Valley imitation of the Cardiff Giant, the "Solid Muldoon," inspired the name of Colorado's most picturesque and witty mining camp newspaper founded at Ouray in 1879 by the "verbal volcano," Dave Day.[18] In 1892 another "petrified man" turned up at Chadron, Nebraska; and a new species of mythical creature, the "lake monster," blossomed all over the lot, from Alkali (Walgren) Lake in Nebraska to Utah's Bear Lake.[19]

Other tasteless or cruel hoaxes were inspired by eccentrics like San Francisco's Emperor Norton and Oofty-Goofty. In still another direction, journalists like Fred Hart of the *Reese River Reveille,* Austin, Nevada, created liars' clubs to feed the public taste for burlesques on the news and whoppers. To dispel any notion that hoaxing is dead or dying in the West, one need only point to the antics of a Death Valley Scotty, the Northwest's "Rawhide Railroad" and more recent "Bundles for Congress" and "Society for the Preservation of Cigar Store Indians," and the countless fake "Jesse Jameses" that keep turning up.[20]

The main stream of hoaxing in Western migration and expansion is fed by the tributaries of occupational pranks and tricks. These include initiation tricks at the expense of the neophyte cowboy, such as the card game ending in a faked row and shooting scare; getting the best of a cattle count and otherwise "jobbing" the greenhorn cattle-

---

[17] George D. Lyman, *The Saga of the Comstock Lode* (New York, 1941), p. 280, *q.v.*, (pp. 293–304) for "Mark Twain's Last Hoax." Cf. C. Grant Loomis, "The Tall Tales of Dan De Quille," *California Folklore Quarterly,* Vol. V (January, 1946), No. 1, pp. 26–71.

[18] For the account of Field's impersonation of Wilde I am indebted to Levette J. Davidson, University of Denver. For the fire-extinguisher story and other Fieldiana, see Edwin A. Beamis, "Journalism in Colorado," in *Colorado and Its People,* edited by LeRoy R. Hafen (New York, 1948), Vol. II, pp. 268–270. The *Solid Muldoon's* origin is related in the *Great Divide* (Vol. III, pp. 73, 80).

[19] For the Nebraska legends, see *Nebraska Folklore Pamphlets,* No. 13, *Tall Tales* (Lincoln, 1937), pp. 1–5. For "The Bear Lake Monsters," see Austin E. Fife, *Utah Humanities Review,* Vol. II (April, 1948), No. 2, pp. 99–106.

[20] For George Estes' "The Rawhide Railroad," see *A Treasury of American Folklore* (New York, 1944), pp. 520–524; also Stewart H. Holbrook, "Lament for the Lost Art of Lying," *The New York Times Magazine,* February 5, 1950, pp. 18, 51–54, where two "Jesse James lads" are treated. For the Jesse James survival hoax, see also Homer Croy, *Jesse James Was My Neighbor* (New York, 1949). The Northwest hoaxes are discussed by Nard Jones, *Evergreen Land* (New York, 1947), pp. 105–106.

buyer; keeping a rival sheepherder from a choice pasture by such stratagems as stampeding the flock with a wind-blown newspaper or making a false trail leading to and around the meadow; and the ventriloquist tricks of ghost-playing miners. Sometimes the tenderfoot turns the tables, as when the Virginian trumps Trampas with his tall tale of frog ranching at Tulare, California, or when a greenhorn logger, after being cussed out by the bullpuncher for not being able to tell the difference between a peavy and a canthook, returns from an all-day search with an old muley (dehorned) cow: "You wanted a cant hook, and this is the only thing I can find that can't hook."[21]

The Western tall-tale teller's technical bag of tricks is modest. Although he uses exaggeration, he uses it with discretion, for, as Mark Twain's Mr. H. admonished a fellow liar in *Life on the Mississippi,* "always dress a fact in tights, never in an ulster." A yarn may stretch credulity but must not abuse it. Above all, the art of the yarn is the art of pace ("never hurried, never dragged") and skilful timing, pausing for emphasis and delaying the ending. For the effectiveness of the tall tale depends upon building it tall and then, with a final stroke, like the last block placed on top of the swaying pile, laying it low.[22] A good example of this technique is seen in Will H. Robinson's story of the growing salve, which is used to grow back a new tail on a tame coyote, after its tail had been caught in the pen door and cut off.

> "Then them boys had a fine idee, and rubbed some of the stuff on the cut place on the tail, and sure as I'm a truthful man, another coyote grew out of the tail, only," here Uncle Noah spat reminiscently, "he was a wild coyote and they had to kill him."[23]

Although the tall tale, like the cowboy, is not the whole show in the West, like him it has stolen the show. And some of its traits are shared with other types of Western story-telling. Allied to the trickiness of the tall tale—its baiting of the tenderfoot, its trick ending—is the popularity of the trickster-hero or rogue, from Coyote to Pedro de Urdemalas, from the wily prospector's burro and miner's mule to the bad man. All nature is tricky—from the mischief of the Washoe and Mojave Zephyrs and the sorcery of the chinook to the mystery and menace of the desert and the mountains. All of these—wind and sand and rock—are gods or devils—*genius loci* or *deus ex machina*—and in worshipping them man becomes like them. The animals, too, are clever or strong, gods or devils—not only the Coyote-creator-trickster and his Northwest counterpart, Raven, and the desert or Rocky Mountain

---

[21] For the sheepherders' tricks, see Mary Austin, *The Flock* (Boston, 1906), pp. 157–165. For the miners' tricks, see Wayland D. Hand, "The Folklore, Customs, and Traditions of the Butte Miner," *California Folklore Quarterly,* Vol. V (January, 1946), No. 1, pp. 7–8. The story of the canthook, as told to William C. Haight by Charles Imus, Portland, February 24, 1939, is from "Oregon Folklore Studies," Manuscripts of the Federal Writers' Project of Oregon, in the Folklore Section of the Library of Congress.

[22] Cf. Mody C. Boatright, *Folk Laughter on the American Frontier* (New York, 1949), p. 90.

[23] *Yarns of the Southwest* (Phoenix, 1921), p. 14.

"canary," but also the Longhorn that has become synonymous with Texan; the grizzly and the bronco—symbols of California and Wyoming, respectively; the Pacing White Mustang—symbol of the unattainable. From the animals as hunters and hunted the Southwest storyteller has derived the hunting pattern—"tracking out the movements of the prey, the creeping up of the hunter, the pounce, the attack and victory,"[24] which explains the appeal of all hunting stories of the West, whether one is hunting game, gold, water, or man. Even the small creatures—the beaver, the prairie dog, the packrat, the road runner, the owl, the rattlesnake, the frog, the lowly louse and flea—play their part among the tricksters and the tricked of Western legend and lore.

The Western story-teller takes his irony and violence as well as his themes and symbols from the land. The violence of California's earthquakes, historical upsets, booms and busts, migrations, and "cultural confusion." The irony of life and death on the desert, which man has never quite conquered, and which has never quite conquered man. As Bill Brophy told me in Albuquerque, desert folk believe in miracles. They have learned to get by as the sheep get by, when they have nibbled the last blade of grass and then it rains.

What Wally Boren and Harry Oliver have to say of the desert and desert tall tales applies equally well to the whole range of Western story-telling—picaresque or epic, pioneer recollections, old-timers' tales, lost mine and ghost town lore, legends of California missions and padres and New Mexico saints, realistic stories of Indian life, apocryphal biography and zoology, tenderfoot and "biter bit" tales, Western thrillers and historical legends, miracles and hoaxes:

> Over in the Southwest the desert heat an' the wind an' the dryness make it a hard, raw country. You have to have a sense of humor and be a sort of philosopher to like it, I guess. It's about the only place in the world where tall tales, atom-bomb stories, an' the plain truth sound exactly alike. . . .
>
> "There's enough in nature in these parts," Mister Oliver concludes, "to keep us modest. After all, thousands of years before man began trying to think, the desert tortoise already had a turret top, retractable landing gear and a portable house."[25]

Last September, in Taos, New Mexico, in "Doughbelly's Clip Joint," which is what the sign says on the window of his real estate office, an old-time cowpuncher and champion bronc rider, named Doughbelly Price, spoke his life story into my tape recorder, with his feet

---

[24] Mary Austin, "The Folk Story in America," *South Atlantic Quarterly,* Vol. XXXIII (January, 1934), No. 1, pp. 10–19.

For Western animals in fact and folklore, see J. Frank Dobie, *Tales of the Mustang* (Dallas, 1936), *The Longhorns* (Boston, 1941), *The Voice of the Coyote* (1949), *The Ben Lilly Legend* (1950), and the chapters on various animals in his *Guide to Life and Literature of the Southwest* (Austin, 1943).

[25] "Desert Tall Tales," in "Wally's Wagon," *This Week Magazine, New York Herald Tribune,* June 25, 1950, p. 19. Harry Oliver edits *Desert Rat Scrap Book,* at 1000 Palms, California, and is the author of *Desert Rough Cuts: A Haywire History of the Borego Desert* (Los Angeles, 1938) and *99 Days in the Desert with Sandy Walker* (Corona, n.d.).

propped up on his desk. His salty humor and racy idiom are in the true Western story-teller's tradition.

It was in the spring of Nineteen and Thirteen. I weighed 110 pounds over and all. And a man by the name of Brown—I believe was his name—he was at that time president of the Mohawk Oil Company—decided he wanted to go into the race horse business. So he bought forty-two head of potential race horses, and I was a-breakin' out the two and three year olds because I was light, learnin' 'em to score and breakin' 'em to the saddle, and so forth. Me and two other boys. We had a nice livin' quarters at Haslam, Texas, and a race track there that we was a-gettin' along fine. Till along come Thanksgiving and Brown brought up four or five of his "Jew" friends. Good men all of them, but they had to have goose. And he bought two great big geese up there and I had to do the cookin'. Well, we was a-drinkin' "nigger" gin in square quart bottles. Was pretty well organized there and I was a-gettin' along all right. I was a-makin' up sour-dough biscuits on a table that was too tall for me, and turned it off and the dough hit me right in the belly and filled both boots full. Well, I had a knife. I was a-scrapin' that dough offa my belly when the boss stepped in at the door and said, "Well, you doughbellied sonuvabitch!" Well, in about two weeks then I got a letter from him, "The Honorable Doughbelly Price." Well, it's been Doughbelly ever since.[26]

B. A. B.

---

[26] Recorded by B. A. Botkin, Taos, New Mexico, September 6, 1950. Mimeographed on one of Doughbelly Price's letterheads, under his picture, is the following handout entitled "This is Taos":

Taos is the only place that has no dimensions. it was laid out by Varas [*sic*] 6700 feet high And humped up in places. If ironed out flat, it would be twice the size, completely sunk in Rotten politics. Wonderful climate that sometimes turns Into a howling blizzard. Controlled only by the ports of Entry and that Controlled by politics.

TOURISTS—Yes, we Have them poor things. they plan the trip eleven months And get one month of Bitter disappointment. Get home Tired & constipated, broke car knocking tires gone. And a hand full of Indian jewelry (made in Massachusetts). beheld Taos in all Its glory been scalped not by Indians but by everybody.

INDIANS—Yes, a very valuable Asset, as he can do His own thinking. Gets two prices for a blanket and stays Out of politics. Can see you walk And say three words And tell you What state you are from and what is the best way to scalp You for the most. Crazy, oh yes!

COWBOYS—Very few. a Cowboy is A politician with his brains knocked out and can be found Most anywhere. He is not needed. Big hat run over boots and doesn't know for sure If cattle sleep in trees or On the ground. Treat kindly he is a species of the Lord's neglect.

ARTISTS—Yes, two kinds male And female. a species of Humanity that can stand for hours and oh and ah At a clump of aspen trees or a hump in the ground eat a dish of scenery with cream and sugar. Argue the last art Exhibit. and the beauty of a string of chili. a necessary evil.

But come to this land of sunshine And pinto beans. Get some of this Real Estate in your gizzard And grass burs between your toes where women are called "MUJERES" and corn "MICE."

TAOS

WELCOMES YOU BUT DON'T COME BROKE. We have plenty now in that condition.

I. TALL TALES AND YARNS

An Eastern visitor once wrote in a bread-and-butter letter to a Roundup newspaper editor: "Out there every prairie dog hole is a gold mine; every hill a mountain; every creek a river; and everybody you meet is a liar."

—MONTANA, A STATE GUIDE BOOK

The Tenderfoot and the Hassayamper

The impressions that greet the tenderfoot upon his arrival in the American Southwest crowd each other in rapid succession. One of the first convictions to sink into his mind, and perhaps one that never leaves it, is that its denizens are as friendly a people as are to be found upon the face of the earth. The true native will share almost anything with him—especially his climate, his dinner, his debts, and his favorite story.

Naturally the Southwest flaunts much that is strange and unfamilar. The newcomer asks many questions; the Arizonan, Texan, or New Mexican is more than glad to answer them. He answers some questions before they are asked. Usually after about the third day the tenderfoot's thoughts crystallize into some such formula as follows:

"If a native tells you anything, it's a lie."

A week later he changes it. "If the story sounds like the truth, it undoubtedly is a lie; but if it sounds like a lie, it may be true."

However, along toward the end of the month, the man from Elsewhere, if he is of the elect, begins to have his ears quickened by the real heart-beat of the West, and is ready to accept that article in the creed of the Hassayamper averring that sometimes the hyperbole of the raconteur may contain more truth, which after all is often only relative, than the exact numerals of the statistician.

But perhaps exactly what a Hassayamper may be needs explanation. Just as the gold-seekers of California were called "Forty-niners" and the pioneers of the Yukon are "Sourdoughs," so those hardy souls who came to the deserts and mountains of the Southwest when one still traveled in stage coaches, when flour and bacon and beans were brought overland in sixteen-mule freight wagons, when national banks

From *Yarns of the Desert,* by Will H. Robinson, pp. 5–7. Copyright, 1921, by William Henry Robinson. Phoenix, Arizona: The Berryhill Company.

were scarce and faro banks were plentiful, when springs of amber-colored fluid gushed perennially at such moist oases as the "Palace" or "Congress Hall"—these were the Hassayampers.

Now be it known that the Hassayampa is a river, sparkling, beautiful and picturesque in its upper reaches in the pine-covered mountains of Yavapai, but later losing both sparkle and character in flat, torrid sands of the desert southward where it joins the Gila.

In the early days painted savages fought many a battle along its bed, Spanish friars used its crystal drops in holy baptism, and miners drew from its depths water for their *arrastras;* and from then until now, along its banks, men have toiled and quarreled, gambled and loved.

In time legends were born about the mystical qualities of its waters. Some say that he who drinks above the ford can never tell a lie, while the antithesis of this is true of one who drinks below. Others turn the saying around—only no two will agree upon which is the proper ford!

The legend, though, that has the sound verification of time as well as the sanction of antiquity is that any one who drinks from any place along the river will never know either the extremes of poverty or riches, in thought will always be the most incorrigible of optimists, in speech the most graceful of romanticists, and should he ever be so unfortunate as to leave Arizona, he will always come back.

Jim Bridger's Lies

James Bridger, probably better than any other man, typified the western frontiersman, and faithfully personified the spirit of the old West. He emitted the redolent atmosphere of the trapper like the north pole glows with the aurora. Therefore his fame as an interesting frontiersman crept out of the official army exploration reports like a grass fire might escape from a fenced pastureland.

The flame of interest that was kindled in the stories of bygone trapper days at Raynolds' winter quarters on Deer Creek was slowly fanned into a national conflagration of entertainment. Unfortunately, however, Bridger's truthful narratives of experience, and his faithful descriptions of the natural phenomena of the Yellowstone Park and other regions, were to be twisted almost beyond recognition in the

From *James Bridger, Trapper, Frontiersman, Scout and Guide,* A Historical Narrative (Illustrated), by J. Cecil Alter, with which is incorporated a verbatim copy-annotated, of *James Bridger, A Biographical Sketch* (Illustrated), by Maj. Gen. Grenville M. Dodge, pp. 380–391. Copyright, 1925, by J. Cecil Alter. Salt Lake City, Utah: Shepard Book Co. Reprinted, 1951, by Long's College Book Co., Columbus, Ohio.

For "Old Jim Bridger" and another Western (Pikes Peak) prevaricator, Sergeant O'Keefe, see Levette J. Davidson and Forrester Blake, *Rocky Mountain Tales* (Norman, 1947), pp. 3–40, 227–256.

withering heat of ridicule and disbelief. This came about largely through second hand narrators, who still attributed the re-told story to Bridger.

Soon after arriving at the Westport farm in the late fall of 1860, Bridger was sought out by Ned Buntline, a prominent story writer of the day, and "Bridger gave him enough adventures to keep him writing the balance of his life," according to General Dodge. "Bridger took a liking to Buntline," Dodge continues, "and took him across the plains with him on a scouting trip. After a while Buntline returned to the East, and not long afterward the Jim Bridger stories commenced to be published. One of these was printed every week, and Bridger's companions used to save them up and read them to him. Buntline made Bridger famous, and carried him through more hairbreadth escapes than any man ever had."

Thus through the alchemy of the journalist the flame of Bridger's stories was transformed into chunks of pure gold for Buntline, and Bridger himself soon found that he was not so much of a frontiersman as a story-teller, the author of "Old Jim Bridger's Lies," to the unfortunate discredit of the truthful old scout. Bridger's stories were greedily seized upon by story-tellers everywhere, and tagged with Bridger's name, after countless metamorphoses.

Elbert Hubbard once used the word "kabojolism" as an antonym for plagiarism; that is, crediting sayings or writings to persons who did not make them. The kabojolist was, for instance, one who wanted to say something risky, and attributed it to another for his own safety. Thus were most of James Bridger's supposed stories, pure kabojolisms.

His glass mountain of the Yellowstone Park area (Obsidian Cliff), which became a celebrated neutral ground for Indians seeking choice arrowheads, and which is no less wonderful today than when Bridger first told the world about it, was made the vehicle or excuse for all the grotesque brood of "Glass Mountain" tales that a host of willing story-tellers could think of. All were, of course, attributed to Bridger.

His two-ocean river, which is today a wonder of geography, and ever will remain, became the forked tongue of the serpent, as a disbelieving and cynical public peddled the tale with its many absurd variations. His river that was hot at the bottom made such a good story that even after the discovery of the hot springs in the bed of the Fire Hole River, certain spirits persisted in keeping the circumstances separated, evidently to maintain the charm of the friction-heated river story, after it had been legally executed.

Bridger's original story of the use of the hot springs of the geyser basins as fireless cookers is an experience that may be repeated by the traveler today with as much adventure and success as of old; and the cooking of the fish as drawn from the water, where the hot spring water supposedly covers the cold shore waters of Yellowstone Lake, is but one of a large school of fish stories which have been kabojolized on a helpless Bridger.

Bridger found his way to the petrified standing tree in the park, when it was in a wilderness indeed; and even today with a good path, well signed, leading to it only about one in a thousand park visitors reaches it. And for telling a listening world about this stump, Bridger's story came back to him in the echo, with everything in existence petrified. The mammoth hot springs terraces, though they are today exactly as Bridger originally described them, having terraces and pools of varying temperatures to suit every need, became impossible creations of nature, which automatically separated the waters into different temperatures for fairy visitors who bathed at the imaginary fonts.

Little wonder then it is that the old scout, having a sense of humor and a knowledge gained at his own expense that the average person loves to be humbugged or entertained rather than enlightened, should at last toss the stories back again to a waiting world, with ears and mouth agape, embellished as only he could embellish them, with a knowledge of the facts as well as the fiction.

General Miles relates one such story of Bridger's, though like most careful writers, he admits getting the story at second hand. "The story is told that on some such [story-telling] occasion, one night after supper, a comrade who in his travels and explorations had gone as far south as the Zuni village, New Mexico, and had discovered the famous petrified forest of Arizona, inquired of Bridger:

" 'Jim, were you ever down to Zuni?'

" 'No, thar ain't any beaver down thar.'

" 'But, Jim, there are some things in this world besides beaver. I was down there last winter and saw great trees with limbs and bark and all turned into stone.'

" 'O,' returned Jim, 'that's peetrifaction. Come with me to the Yellowstone next summer, and I'll show you peetrified trees a-growing, with peetrified birds on 'em a-singing peetrified songs.'[1]

"Now it so happened that he had been to the Yellowstone," General Miles apologizes for him; "and had seen the 'peetrified' trees standing but not the 'peetrified' birds or the 'peetrified' songs. The geysers of the Yellowstone eject hot water, supersaturated with carbonate of lime and geyserite, to a height of from one hundred and fifty to two hundred feet. This water is carried laterally by the wind, sometimes two hundred or three hundred feet, saturating the trees, and gradually covering the nearest side with a crystal formation, while on the other side are living branches. So Jim Bridger's story was in part true."

Other petrification stories are given by Chittenden. "According to Bridger's account there exists in the Park country, a mountain which was once cursed by a great medicine man of the Crow nation. Everything upon the mountain at the time of this dire event became instantly petrified and has remained so ever since. All forms of life are standing

[1] Cf. "Black Harris and the Putrified Forest" and "Mushmouth Charlie's Lecture on the Petrified Forest," *A Treasury of American Folklore* (New York, 1944), pp. 557–560.

about in stone where they were suddenly caught by the petrifying influences, even as the inhabitants of ancient Pompeii were surprised by the ashes of Vesuvius. Sage brush, grass, prairie fowl, antelope, elk, and bears, may there be seen as perfect as in actual life. Dashing torrents and the spray mist from them stand forth in arrested motion as if carved from rock by a sculptor's chisel. Even flowers are blooming in colors of crystal, and birds soar with wings spread in motionless flight, while the air floats with music and perfumes siliceous, and the sun and the moon shine with petrified light!

"The author [General Chittenden] feels bound to defend even Bridger's reputation from any such extravaganza as the following which is clearly the work of some later interpolator. According to this anonymous authority, Bridger, one evening, after a long day's ride, was approaching a familiar camping place in this region of petrifications but from a direction not before taken. Quite unexpectedly he came upon a narrow, deep, precipitous chasm which completely blocked his way. Exhausted as both he and his horse were with their long march, he was completely disheartened at this obstacle, to pass which, might cause him several hours of strenuous exertion and carry him far into the night.

"Riding up to the brink to reconnoiter he found that he could not stop his horse, which kept moving right along as if by its own momentum, out over the edge of the precipice, straight on at a steady gait and on a level line, as if supported by an invisible bridge. Almost before he realized it he was safe on the other side, and in his desired camp. His utter amazement at this miracle soon abated when he remembered the strange character of the country he was in, and he concluded that this chasm was simply a place where the attraction of gravitation was petrified."

General Chittenden tells how Bridger discovered the glass mountain (Obsidian Cliff). "Coming one day in sight of a magnificent elk, he took careful aim at the unsuspecting animal and fired. To his great amazement, the elk not only was not wounded but seemed not even to have heard the report of the rifle. Bridger drew considerably nearer and gave the elk the benefit of his most deliberate aim; but with the same result as before. A third and a fourth effort met with a similar fate.

"Utterly exasperated, he seized his rifle by the barrel, resolved to use it as a club, since it had failed as a firearm. Rushing madly toward the elk, he suddenly crashed into an immovable vertical wall which proved to be a mountain of perfectly transparent glass, on the farther side of which, still in peaceful security, the elk was quietly grazing. Stranger still, the mountain was not only of pure glass, but was a perfect telescopic lens, and, whereas the elk seemed but a few hundred yards off, it was in reality twenty-five miles away."

Captain J. Lee Humfreville, speaking of the fact that Bridger was much sought after by the emigrants crossing the plains, since his reputation as a guide and Indian scout and fighter was well known, says:

"The pilgrims annoyed him with all sorts of questions, which often compelled the old man to beat a retreat, yet he had a streak of humor, and gave them a ghost story every now and then. Some of these stories were unique. He had a quick and surprisingly vivid imagination, and reeled off story after story with a spontaneity that was astonishing. He told these stories, too, with a solemn gravity that was intensely amusing. I know that I am largely indebted to him for keeping up my spirits when they were at a low ebb. I always knew something good was coming when he began to tell a story, but never dared to smile until the climax was reached, for that would have spoiled it all."

Captain Humfreville gives another version of the petrification story, as Bridger presumably told it to a tenderfoot, looking for adventure. " 'Is there anything remarkable to be seen about here?' an inquisitive pilgrim asked him one day.

" 'W-a-l-l,' he replied, in a peculiar drawling tone, which he generally assumed in telling stories, in order to gain time to give his imagination fuller play, 'there's a cur'ous mountain a few miles off'n the road to the north of here, but the doggon'd trouble is you can't see the blamed thing.'

" 'A mountain and can't see it—that's curious,' interrupted the pilgrim. 'How large is it?'

" 'Wall, I should say it's nigh onto three miles in circumference at the base but its height is unknown,' continued Bridger with imperturbable gravity.

" 'Is it so high you can't see the top of it?' inquired the puzzled traveler.

" 'That's what I say, stranger; you can't see the base of it either. Didn't you ever hear of the Crystal Mountain?'

" 'I never did.'

" 'Wall, I'll tell you what it is. It's a mountain of crystal rock, an' so clear that the most powerful field glasses can't see it, much less the naked eye. You'll wonder, p'r'aps, how a thing that can't be seen nohow wus ever discovered. It came about in this way. You see, a lot of bones and the carcasses of animals an' birds was found scattered all around the base. You see they ran or flew against this invisible rock and jest killed themselves dead. You kin feel the rock an' that's all. You can't see it. It's a good many miles high, for everlastin' quantities of bird's bones are jest piled up all around the base of it.' "

Bridger is said to have had a unique method for determining the altitude of a place, according to Chittenden. "At the point whose elevation is desired, bore down until salt water is reached, and then measure the distance."

Bridger's famous echo is described by Chittenden. "Opposite a certain camping ground where he frequently stopped there arose the bald, flat face of a mountain, but so distant that the echo from any sound which originated in camp did not return for the space of about six hours. Bridger converted this circumstance into an ideal alarm clock.

Upon retiring for the night he would call out lustily, 'Time to Get Up!' and true to his calculation, the alarm would roll back at the precise hour next morning when it was necessary for the camp to bestir itself."

Colonel Inman declared that Bridger told him "and also many others, at various times, that in the winter of 1830 it began to snow in the valley of the Great Salt Lake, and continued for seventy days without cessation. The whole country was covered to a depth of seventy feet, and all the vast herds of buffalo were caught in the storm and died, but their carcasses were perfectly preserved.

" 'When spring came, all I had to do,' declared he, 'was to tumble 'em into Salt Lake an' I had pickled buffalo enough for myself and the whole Ute nation for years!' He said that on account of that terrible storm which annihilated them, there have been no buffalo in that region since."

* * * * *

Captain Humfreville gives a short version of a popular and widely circulated tale of personal adventure credited to Bridger. "He had been suddenly surprised by a party of six Indians, and putting spurs to his horse sought to escape. The Indians, mounted on fleet ponies, quickly followed in pursuit. His only weapon was a six-shooter. The moment the leading Indian came within shooting distance, he turned in his saddle and gave him a shot. His shot always meant a dead Indian. In this way he picked off five of the Indians, but the last one kept up the pursuit relentlessly and refused to be shaken off.

" 'We wus nearin' the edge of a deep and wide gorge,' said Bridger. 'No horse could leap over that awful chasm, an' a fall to the bottom meant sartin death. (This has been said to be the Grand Canyon of the Colorado). I turned my horse suddint an' the Injun was upon me. We both fired to once, an' both horses was killed. We now engaged in a han'-to-han' conflict with butcher knives. He wus a powerful Injun—tallest I ever see. It wus a long and fierce struggle. One moment I hed the best of it, an' the next the odds wus again me. Finally——' "

"Here Bridger paused as if to get breath.

" 'How did it end?' at length asked one of his breathless listeners anxiously.

" '*The Injun killed me,*' he replied with slow deliberation."

John Hance, Grand Canyon Prevaricator

Said Bucky O'Neill, "God made the Canyon, John Hance the trails. Without the other, neither would be complete." A distinguished

From *More Arizona Characters,* by Frank C. Lockwood, pp. 41–47. University of Arizona Bulletin, Vol. XIII (July 1, 1942), No. 3, General Bulletin No. 6. Copyright, 1943, by the University of Arizona. Tucson.

traveler, Chester P. Dorland, wrote in the guest book in which visitors used to record their impressions after seeing the Canyon:

Captain John Hance—a genius, a philosopher, and a poet, the possessor of a fund of information, vastly important, if true. He laughs with the giddy, yarns to the gullible, talks sense to the sedate, and is a most excellent judge of scenery, human nature, and pie. To see the Canyon only, and not to see Captain Hance, is to miss half the show.

Early Arizonians asked no questions about a comrade's past. I have talked with many of Hance's old friends, but none of them can say with certainty what state Hance came from. If any one questioned him concerning his past, he would go straight up in the air and reply that he did not like ancient history. His own account of his advent into Arizona is simple enough and ought to satisfy anybody. He said he was in Texas and wanted to come to Arizona. At that time there were thousands of buffalo on the plains, and they were migrating—moving westward. He climbed into a tree and as an immense herd came by he dropped onto the back of a big buffalo bull and stayed on him for two weeks, when the herd reached Arizona.

"Well, what did you eat all that time?" some troublesome skeptic would ask.

"Why, I had plenty of meat; there was the hump of the buffalo right in front of me—the tastiest part of the animal."[1]

Very early, Hance went to the Grand Canyon. His friends asked him how he made a living.

"Oh," he would reply, "I made it farming. I had a nice little farm over there. But me and my wife couldn't get along together; so we separated. I kept the farm and gave her the road."

As a matter of fact, no one can assert that Hance ever was married. It is my own belief that, like so many other mysterious and lonely wanderers among the deserts of the West, he was the martyr of a broken heart, for after all, he was a man of sentiment, and his drollery was most likely built up as a protective coloring to hide an incurable wound. Fifty years ago to Eastern visitors the trip to the Grand Canyon was an overwhelming experience—wonderful and romantic beyond their dreams; and as a part of all this, here was John Hance, —robust and fascinating, as mysterious as the Canyon itself—guiding them down his dangerous trail.

One day two women in the party, unable to restrain their curiosity, asked:

"Mr. Hance, haven't you ever been married?"

"Yes," he replied, "and no one ever had a better woman. She was a lovely creature."

"Where is your wife?"

1 Cf. "Crockett's Great Ride on the Mammoth Buffalo," Verne Bright, "Davy Crockett Legend and Tales in the Oregon Country," *Oregon Historical Quarterly*, Vol. LI (September, 1950), No. 3, pp. 213–215.

"Oh, she's gone."

"Why, what happened?"

"Well," he said, "you see, my business is the Canyon here—and it's a tough job. You know, you can ride down the trail quite a little ways. While she was here, sometimes I would saddle a horse for her and one for myself, and we would ride down the trail together as far as we could and then walk the rest of the way. One day I was going down and didn't want her to go with me. But nothing would do but she must go. She seemed to sort of mourn for me when I left her alone. Well, when we got as far as that narrow ledge down there ahead of us, her horse stepped on a loose stone and fell. It was a terrible task for me to get down to her; and when I picked her up I found she had a broken leg. I couldn't get her out. It was an awful situation."

"Well, what did you do?" gasped the ladies.

"Hell! What could I do but shoot her and leave her there; that's what I did."

Fearing that the Hance tradition might not long survive in its purity unless some one wrote down the actual facts concerning him, so far as they could be ascertained, and at the same time recorded with meticulous veracity the best of his authentic tall tales, a few years ago I set about accomplishing that task. Fortunately, many of his intimate friends still survived. Several of these I interviewed. There were, too, among my associates eminent men of science who had met him at the Grand Canyon almost fifty years ago, had talked often with him, and were willing to repeat some of his most picturesque falsifications for me. Two of these gentlemen, Dr. D. T. MacDougal and Mr. Godfrey Sykes, are no less gifted as raconteurs than they are famous as scientists; so I count it a piece of rare good fortune to have received from them Hance classics just as they dropped from his own lips, more than a long generation ago.

Dr. MacDougal first went down the Grand Canyon Trail with Hance in 1891. He recalls vividly the guide's personal appearance and peculiarities at that time.

* * * * *

I heard him tell this soap story to the "guinea hens" (women tourists) at El Tovar. I knew the story in general and knew also that he had some such experience as he described, but had never heard him tell it till one day I listened to him as he was sitting at the head of a table next to ours. He began by saying that upon one occasion the snow became so heavy up at the rim of the Canyon that there were no longer any visitors, and he decided to go down to Flagstaff to spend the winter.

Said he, "It was a delicate job to know just when the winter was actually beginning. Each season I timed my departure with reference to two things: the lowness of my grub supply and the near approach of a heavy snowfall. One night when I was all set to get out, a terrible storm came. It lasted two or three days. I contrived a pair of snowshoes and started from camp. After a few hours' travel with these snowshoes, fashioned from split pine, I fell and hurt my ankle so bad that I could not go any further. However, I managed some way to work my way back to the cabin.

"When I got there, I found nothing left but half a jar of sorghum molasses and a box of Babbitt's Best Soap. I prepared a mixture of soap and molasses in a skillet, slicing the soap into flakes, adding a few shavings from an old boot leg to make the mixture as tasty as possible. Ladies and gentlemen, that was all I had to eat for a week, when the snow melted. I tell you frankly, and I expect you to believe me, I have never liked the taste of soap from that day to this."

Every morning he would tell that story at the breakfast table. There would be a dead silence after he had finished—the people not knowing whether to laugh or not.

Here is one of John's scientific gems. He was commenting on the water of the Colorado River. "It was so thick with the mud," he said, "that it was positively tough. One noon I kneeled down for a drink, and when I tried to stop I was almost [choked] before I could get my knife out of my pocket and cut it off."

When I saw John in 1898, he had sold one of his mining claims for $10,000. He was telling about it and was asserting that he still had a lot of valuable claims. He had taken the $10,000 and gone to San Francisco. His money lasted ten days. He said:

"We had a pretty good time; but I tell you that though I spent $1,000 a day each day I was there, thousands of people in San Francisco didn't even know there was such a person as John Hance. Sometime I'm going to get about $50,000 and wake that town up."

After his trip to San Francisco some one asserted that Hance had blown out the gas in his room at the hotel. He had been warned before he went to be careful—and to be sure to turn off the gas. "If you leave it on, it may suffocate you," was the warning. When he came back some one asked, "Did you blow out the gas?"

"No," he replied, "I was too slick for that—I just flicked it out with my hat."

Mr. Godfrey Sykes was on intimate terms with Hance when the trail was young; and he relates some excellent stories about the old guide, several of which I had never heard before. Said Sykes in our conversation, "Here is a botanical item. Hance was guiding a party down the trail one day, and there was a young lady in the company who was interested in botany. As she went along she was picking leaves from the various trees and plants and was examining them and talking about them. Finally she said:

" 'You know, Mr. Hance, the tree is a wonderful organism—it really breathes.'

"John thought a moment. 'Why, yes,' he said, 'it does.' Again he reflected. 'You know, that explains something that has puzzled me a long time; I used to make camp under a big mesquite tree, and night after night that thing would keep me awake with its snoring.' "

As Sykes was a scientist deeply interested in fact and nature's strange ways, the following story stuck in his memory. Said Hance: "A tourist person came up to the Canyon one morning and looked over the rim. The day was damp and he had on a pair of rubber boots. He leaned out a little too far and fell over. He was able to keep an upright position, so when he struck the bottom he bounced. Naturally he came up past the rim again. This experience was repeated several times, but he was never able to grab hold of the rim. In the end," said John, "we had to shoot him to keep him from starving to death."[2]

* * * * *

In July, 1933, the writer had the good fortune to interview at leisure Mr. Edgar Whipple, a very old man who has lived in Coconimo County for more than fifty years. During a whole generation he and Hance were intimate friends. . . .

Said Whipple, who knew every one of Hance's stories by heart and related them with gusto:

John had a splendid horse that would do anything for him. One day he decided that this steed could jump the Grand Canyon, and he determined to make him do it. He believed that the all-important thing was to get a good start before taking off. So he went back three miles and ran his horse full speed to the rim. The take-off was very successful.

"But," said Hance, "I wasn't halfway across before I saw that he couldn't make it. We hadn't taken a big enough start."

"Well, what happened?"

"Oh, I just turned around and went back."[3]

In the Captain's cabin hung a pair of snowshoes that his guests used to view with admiration. One day a heavy fog completely filled the gorge. A group of tourists were hanging about the rim trying to see down into the Canyon. Hance came along and took a look into and across the depths.

"Well," he remarked, "the Canyon's just about right to cross."

"What do you mean?" some one asked.

"Why, I can put on my snowshoes now and go right across on the fog."

He then told how one time he had gone over there and had stayed too long.

"The fog went out and left me on the other side without food or drink. I had been marooned three or four days when it returned, though not so thick as before. I had grown very light by this time and got across all right, though the fog was so thin in spots that several times I thought I was going to hit the bottom. I sure did fill up when I got back on this side."

Grand Canyon Guides and Dudes

The guides, of course, have quite a line of conversation that goes with the mule trip. One of the most common questions at the head of

[2] Cf. Edward O'Reilly, "The Saga of Pecos Bill," *A Treasury of American Folklore* (New York, 1944), pp. 180–185.

[3] Cf. *A Treasury of American Folklore* (New York, 1944), p. 617.

From "Grand Canyon's Long-Eared Taxi," by Lon Garrison, *Arizona Highways,* Vol. XXVI (June, 1950), No. 6, p. 7. Also reprinted for distribution by Fred Harvey.

the trail, John Bradley reports, is: "Have you a real gentle mule for me?" To this the guide is apt to reply solemnly, "No, ma'am, I'm right sorry, but we just sent the last gentle mule down with the last party. If you ain't ever rode before, why we'll just give you a mule that ain't ever been rode before either, an' you can start right out together."

The Augerino and the Ratchet Owl

Where irrigation is practised, ranchers are humorously angry about the activities of the "Augerino," a malevolent subterranean creature whose sole mission in life is to let the water out of irrigation ditches. This imaginary animal is described as an enormous corkscrew-shaped worm, which drills a helical burrow a few feet under the surface, and lines its hole with silica to prevent caveins. According to reports, the "Augerino" moves very slowly; is immune to all poisons and weapons; and cannot change its course. No person now living in Middle Park [,Colorado,] will admit having seen an "Augerino," but the creatures are still supposed to be living, for "Hell, the ditches still leak, don't they?"

* * * * *

In recent years, the apocryphal zoology of the mountain region has undergone numerous extensions and improvements, as the various accounts have been told and retold, with alterations to suit the imagination of the teller. At least a few of the nonexistent animals of this region were deliberately invented for the edification of "flatlanders," whose credulity, at times, appears limitless. Typical of these recent inventions is the "Ratchet Owl," a photophobic creature that always faces away from the sun. In early morning, the "ratchet owl" faces west, but as the sun follows its daily course, the bird must turn its head, and at sunset is facing due east. To prevent undue strain on its neck muscles, this owl is equipped with a ratchet, which permits easy clockwise rotation of its head, but inhibits counter-clockwise motion. At some time during the night, the owl, in preparation for the coming day, releases the ratchet, making a fearful noise, and allows its head to return to a west-facing position.. Actually, the sound of "a ratchet owl letting loose" is caused by tree limbs rubbing together.

From "Folklore of Eastern Park, Colorado," by Ronald L. Ives, *The Journal of American Folklore,* Vol. 54 (January–June, 1941), Nos. 211–212, pp. 29, 30. Philadelphia: The American Folklore Society.

For other fearsome critters of the West, see *A Treasury of American Folklore* (New York, 1944), pp. 638–650.

The Fur-Bearing Trout

I[1]

Old timers living along the Arkansas river near Salida have told tales for many years of the fur-bearing trout indigenous to the waters of the Arkansas near there.

Tourists and other tenderfeet in particular have been regaled with accounts of the unusual fish, and Salidans of good reputation have been wont to relate that the authenticity of their stories has never been questioned—in fact, they're willing to bet it's never even been suspected.

Then, last week, out of Pratt, Kan., where water in any quantities large enough to hold a trout—fur-bearing or otherwise—is a rarity, came an urgent request for proof of the existence of the furry fin-flippers.

Directed at the Salida Chamber of Commerce, the message read:

"Answer collect by Western Union if you have fur-bearing trout in Arkansas river there."

Upon the sturdy shoulders of Wilbur B. Foshay, secretary of the Chamber of Commerce, fell the delicate task of informing the credulous Kansan, without detracting from the obvious tourist-attracting qualities of the pelted piscatorial prizes.

With admirable diplomacy, and considerable aplomb, Foshay dispatched posthaste a photograph of the fish, obtained from a Salida photographer, and then told the Kansan to use his own judgment as to the authenticity of the species. The photograph sent has been available in Salida for some time.

Foshay's cautious letter accompanying the photograph left nothing to be desired, except maybe a little more evidence of the authenticity of the trout.

So a survey of real old-timers of the area was conducted, and the following corroborative evidence uncovered:

From Narrow-Gauge Ned of Poncha Pass came this report:

"Fur-bearing trout? We used to have 'em around here, but I haven't seen any lately. My pappy had some over at the hot springs, but the stream ruined all their fur in the course of several generations, and they finally left. We were mighty sorry to see them go, but it was a shame to see such valuable furs being spoiled, so we finally agreed. Last I heard, they'd settled up at Iceberg lake."

Texas Creek Tess, at one time impressario of the naughty can-can dance at the Owl-Ear Bar, recalled:

"The boys tell me that them pesky trout got to carrying on over

[1] From the Pueblo (Colorado) *Chieftain,* November 15, 1938. Clipping files of the Western History Collection, Denver Public Library, Denver, Colorado.

around the silver fox farms on moonlight nights, and the fox growers had to shoot 'em to protect their valuable fox strains."

Willy Axletree, the Hermit of Wet Mountain valley, had another explanation:

"Tess only told you one side of the story. The trout got to running about with the foxes, all right, but they weren't silver foxes until *afterwards*. It was that trout strain that accounted for the silver coloration to begin with, and as the silver foxes came in, the fur-bearing trout just naturally moved out, rather than play second fiddle to their own descendants."

Agate Creek Andy, however, insisted:

"You ain't heard the real tale of them fur-bearing trout yet. They left after they lost their race to the Spiral Mango-bats around Tenderfoot Mountain. The trout claimed a victory in the first two laps, but they got bested on the home stretch when the Mango-bats really got their sidehill leg-action going. There was just no beatin' 'em. That's where that 'S' up thar come from," he declared, lapsing into the vernacular. "Hit don' stand for Salida at all, like they tell ya."

But to Harrison Hickoryhead, the Gorgemore graybeard, went the official award for the most logical explanation. He said:

"Wa-a-al, it just like y'said, pardner. Them leetle trouts was fur-bearin', shore enuff. In fact, that wuz whut brought on their downfall, as y'mought say. They wuz just *too* fur-bearin', and folks got to imposin' on them t'beat anything, knowing the leetle trouts wouldn't retaliate. Things wuz bad fur a long time, but 'twan't till them eastern cappytalists got to settin' beaver traps for them that they got real discouraged. Then it just seemed like their leetle hearts bursted wide open.

"And after that they wan't near so fur-bearin' as they had been.

"There's still some of 'em around, if you know where to look, which I do, but I ain't tellin', but their fur is pretty few and fur between compared to whut it wuz. And they ain't near as fur-bearin' as they wuz. Not near!"

II[2]

Salidans caught muskrats and not fur-bearing trout when they went out to settle the long dispute over whether or not the Arkansas river is inhabited by pelted fish during the winter, the Alamosa *Courier* says. The three muskrats paid with their lives and their pelts.

Wilbur Foshay, secretary of the Salida Chamber of Commerce, had three fur-bearing fish under the glass of his office. They were splendid examples of taxidermy. The trout were clad in tight-fitting muskrat skins resembling ladies muffs.

Foshay wouldn't admit failure, however.

2 From the Lamar (Colorado) *Daily News,* February 6, 1939. Clipping files of the Western History Collection, Denver Public Library, Denver, Colorado.

"I've brought back fur-bearing trout, haven't I?" he grinned. Seeing's believing.

Foshay had been granted a special license by the state game and fish commission in an effort to settle the dispute over the existence of such fish. Many old-timers swear that trout collect a fungus like winter growth in winter which causes the fur-bearing appearance.

III[3]

The fur-bearing trout or beazel is known to the trout streams of Colorado, Michigan, Pennsylvania and Maine.

The origin of this unusual trout in the Arkansas river of Colorado is a story peculiar in itself and follows thusly:

The town of Leadville was incorporated as a mining town in the year 1878. It was during the winter of 1877 and 1878 that meat was supplied to the miners in the form of venison by professional game hunters. Now, during winter months they ate so much venison and fried potatoes that the venison tallow became caked in the roofs of their mouths to the extent that they were unable to taste their coffee and other beverages. This was indeed distressing, and often they eliminated this handicap by wiring a bundle of pitch splinters on top of their heads and setting fire to it. The result was that the tallow was melted and they again had the sense of taste, but the net result was that 97 per cent of the miners in the camp became baldheaded.

About the middle of the spring a gentleman from Kentucky who had been in the hair tonic business in that state reached camp. He was a Republican and had left that state to avoid trouble with the government tax agents who tried to collect the heavy tax on his product.

In time he started to manufacture his hair tonic from potatoes in a small creek south of Leadville and to sell his product to miners of the camp.

It was a rainy Sunday evening that he was coming to town with four jugs of the tonic, one in each hand and one under each arm. It was necessary for him to cross a trout stream which empties into the Arkansas river, on a footlog, and in so doing he slipped and had to drop two of the jugs to retain his balance. The result was that the falling jugs struck rocks in the stream and were broken, spilling hair tonic into the water.

Not long after that trout fishermen of that vicinity changed their methods. Instead of the usual rod and reel, they would go down the creek on Saturday afternoon, stick a red, white, and blue pole in the bank, put on a white coat, wave a copy of the Police Gazette in one hand and brandish a scissors in the other, and yell, "Next," until they had the limit of these fine fur-bearing trout with full beards, etc. The

[3] From the Elk Mountain (Colorado) *Pilot,* February 23, 1939. Clipping files of the Western History Collection, Denver Public Library, Denver, Colorado.

trout would leap up onto the bank after these tonsorial lures and were picked up by the fishermen.

This practice continued until mine-tailings from the mill riled the water so that the trout could no longer see the barber poles.

Then catches of fur-bearing trout ceased to be made in the Arkansas river until recently the fishermen of our neighboring city have taken advantage of the clear water in mid-winter and have discovered the snow worm as a successful lure.

The Feathered Rabbit

The tale of the fur-bearing trout at Salida, Colorado, prompted A. S. McIntyre, Walsenburg prospector, to come forward Saturday with a Bunyanesque yarn about the feathered jackrabbits thriving in Huerfano county.

"If those boys at Salida think a trout that grows fur to keep warm in winter is something to brag about, let 'em listen to this," McIntyre challenged.

"It all happened about ten years ago when a farmer on the Huerfano river was doing some early spring plowing and happened to dig up a nest of little jackrabbits," the prospector recounted.

"Well, sir, he was a kind old fellow and didn't want to see those little jackrabbits die right there, so he put them up in his chicken coop.

"When dry summer weather rolled around and feed got kinda scarce, the chickens ate all the fur off those rabbits, yes, sir!

"But even then the bunnies and the hens were real chummy and it wasn't anything to see those naked rabbits sleeping peaceful in a hen's nest," McIntyre spieled on.

"The big surprise came when winter started coming on.

"Those rabbits began to sprout feathers, yes sir!

"Now that bunch of rabbits has increased many times and all the offspring are feather-bearing.

"Why," expounded McIntyre, wagging a finger, "I've even seen a rabbit perched out on the woodpile flapping his ears and trying to squeeze out a cackle. Yes, sir!"

From an Associated Press dispatch, dated Walsenburg, Colorado, February 18, 1939, in the Denver (Colorado) *Post,* February 19, 1939, p. 10. Clipping files of the Western History Collection, Denver Public Library, Denver, Colorado.

"Rocky Mountain Canary"

The Rocky Mountain burro, or, as he is sometimes called because of his musical voice, "Rocky Mountain canary," was an essential feature of the early days in prospecting, also in working mines even after the mines had gone underground. Many stories are told of the burros that were stubborn or the burros that were faithful or the burros that were intelligent. One I like is concerning the well-trained burro called Old Tom that one prospector trusted implicitly. He used to ride along the gulches going from one good prospect hole to another to work. One day he went to sleep because it was a warm afternoon. It seemed the burro was dozing off too, although it kept on plodding along the path until it came to the edge of a great precipice, and without wakening, the burro went over, and of course, the prospector on top. As they fell, both came to, and the prospector was quick enough to realize that if they landed they'd both be dead! As they were falling—one hundred, two hundred, three hundred, four hundred feet—the prospector had a little chance to think it over. And so when they got about fifty feet from the ground, he called "whoa!" And Old Tom just through good training didn't do a thing but stop—short! And then the prospector just kind of eased himself off and lowered down, and finally he and Old Tom both were there unhurt on the bottom of the canyon. All he had to do then was to mount Old Tom and the two of them proceeded on their way—all because the prospector had properly trained his burro to obey.

Of course not all burros were that well trained. Some of them were stubborn. In one of the mines there was a trammer who found a new burro balking—wouldn't pull the ore car. So, wondering what he'd do next, he reached into his pocket and pulled out a package of chawin' terbacca. And after taking a chaw himself he noticed that his burro wrinkled up its nose and seemed interested. He reached out the package of Beechnut to his burro. The burro took about twenty cents' worth in one big chaw and with a smile on its face set off to work the rest of the day uncomplaining. Well, this trammer had to buy a lot of chawin' terbacca, but he never had any trouble getting work out of that burro.

One time, though, this trammer decided to change jobs, and he went over to a new mine, and was getting along fine when along came the boss from the old mine. He said: "Look here! You've got a right to change your job, if you want to. But you haven't got no right to take

---

Told by Levette J. Davidson, University of Denver, Denver, Colorado, July 24, 1950. Recorded by B. A. Botkin.

Cf. Levette J. Davidson, "Rocky Mountain Burro Tales," *The Brand Book,* Vol. 6 (Denver, July, 1950), pp. 1–14. For a variant of the burro's fall, see *A Treasury of American Folklore* (New York, 1944), p. 616. For tobacco-chewing and kindred traits of miners' mules, see *Copper Camp* (New York, 1943), pp. 198–202.

over your trammin' tricks. How on earth do you get that burro to work?"

And of course the trammer said: "Well, I'll tell you. 'Tain't no secret now. But I want to advise you. That burro will do anything you ask if you just give him chawin' terbacca. But be sure and get Beechnut! 'Tain't Horseshoe, nor 'tain't Star! It's Beechnut that does it!"

Packrats and Dynamite

"Solly," as friends were wont to tab him, was a renowned trade rat who operated out of a Leadville mine. According to the stories, the miners tell, Solly ate dynamite in lieu of wheaties to make himself big and tough. The men used to soften sticks of dynamite "up thar" by putting them inside their boots. One day a miner whose boots were somewhat eroded felt something tugging at his legs. Solomon intrepidly pulled and tugged at the dynamite stick until he had hauled it out, then carefully replaced it with a stone—an even-Steven swap as far as he was concerned. Then he began nibbling on the tallow-like blasting material, totally unconcerned.

This taste in rat food spread throughout Colorado and the mountain area with the growth of mining. And soon the packrats who believe in a fair exchange of commodities were trading on the open market for any succulent delicacies (such as dynamite) which they could find. Sometimes the rat currency proved to be a piece of high-grade ore which helped the miners locate a new source of the precious metal.

The Original "Petrified Man" Story

A petrified man was found some time ago in the mountains south of Gravelly Ford. Every limb and feature of the stony mummy was perfect, not even excepting the left leg, which had evidently been a wooden one during the lifetime of the owner—which lifetime, by the way, came

---

By Elsie Haynes. From *Rocky Mountain Life,* Vol. I (July, 1946), No. 4, pp. 24, 27. Denver, Colorado: Coloradoans, Inc.

From *The San Francisco Bulletin,* October 15, 1862, p. 1., col. 4, quoting from the Virginia City (Nevada) *Territorial Enterprise,* October 5, 1862.

For Mark Twain's own account of how he wrote "The Petrified Man" to show up a certain coroner and justice of the peace of Humboldt and at the same time take off the wild stories of petrifications and other natural marvels current in Nevada and California, see *Mark Twain's Sketches, New and Old* (Hartford, 1890). This and his other hoax, "My Bloody Massacre," also written for the Virginia City *Territorial Enterprise,* in 1863, and similar hoaxes by Dan De Quille ("The Silver Man" and "The Solar Armor") are reprinted by Duncan Emrich in *Comstock Bonanza* (New York, 1950). Hoaxing as a Western art is discussed in the same author's *It's an Old Western Custom* (New York, 1949).

to a close about a century ago, in the opinion of a savant who has examined the defunct. The body was in a sitting posture and leaning against a huge mass of croppings; the attitude was pensive, the right thumb resting against the side of the nose; the left thumb partially supported the chin, the forefinger pressing the inner corner of the left eye and drawing it partly open; the right eye was closed, and the fingers of the right hand spread apart. This strange freak of nature created a profound sensation in the vicinity, and our informant states that, by request, Justice Sewell or Sowell of Humboldt City at once proceeded to the spot and held an inquest on the body. The verdict of the jury was that "deceased came to his death from protracted exposure," etc. The people of the neighborhood volunteered to bury the poor unfortunate, and were even anxious to do so; but it was discovered, when they attempted to remove him, that the water which had dripped upon him for ages from the crag above, had coursed down his back and deposited a limestone sediment under him which had glued him to the bed rock upon which he sat, as with a cement of adamant, and Judge S. refused to allow the charitable citizens to blast him from his position. The opinion expressed by his Honor that such a course would be little less than sacrilege was eminently just and proper. Everybody goes to see the stone man, as many as 300 persons having visited the hardened creature during the past five or six weeks.

A Missourian's Brains

His name was John Shipton but in the Hood River country he was known as Happy Jack. He came to Boise Basin during the gold rush, bringing with him his fiddle and its three strings upon which he could make better music than other fiddlers on a full set. One day he left his mountain retreat to hold the farmers' harvest. Most of the ranchers on Silver Creek were Missourians, and Happy Jack was an Arkansan with a quaint drawl, and both Jack and his native State were held under sarcastic summary.

"They tell me the women in Arkansaw chaw terbacker and go barefoot and eat tree mice. Is that so, Jack?"

"Hey, Jack, and does the men go barefoot, too?"

"I guess so," said Jack. "And we made the shoes ourselves. Hey, I remember one time back in 1840, and pap, he sent me out huntin to git a hide for to make a pair of shoes. He counted the bullets and measured out the powder and I had to fetch a hide for every bullet or I got a tannun. Well, I hunted all day and didn't see nothin to shoot at except

From *Idaho, A Guide in Word and Picture,* prepared by the Federal Writers' Project of the Works Progress Administration, Vardis Fisher, State Director, pp. 395–396. Copyright, 1937, by Franklin Girard, Secretary of State of Idaho; Ira H. Masters, Secretary of State of Idaho. Sponsored by the Secretary of State. Caldwell, Idaho: The Caxton Printers, Ltd. Copyright, 1937, 1950, by Oxford University Press, Inc.

a few squirrels. So long about sundown I reckoned I'd kill a squirrel but every time I'd go to shoot at them dad-burned things they'd hide behind a tree and I couldn't see nothin but the head and I didn't want to shoot the head for pap warned me to bring the brains of anything I killed to tan the hide with. Well, I finally got mad and shot one in the head and I just about blowed all the brains out. That made me feel pretty bad. Well, I was in for a wallopun when I happened to remember there was a settlement of Missourians over the hill just about as far as I could see and twice as far as I could holler. Well, so I decided to go down there and shoot one them-there Missourians for some brains to tan that squirrel hide with."

"Oh, the heck you did," said one of the men.

"Yes, and I did," said Jack. "But that ain't the worst of it. Say, you know I had to kill nine of them-there Missourians to get enough brains to tan that hide?"

Fay Hubbard's Dog

Soon after the Oregon Short Line Railway was laid, Fay Hubbard went to Omaha with sheep, and after he had squandered all his money but five dollars he decided to buy a dog and ride the blinds back to his home. But the only thing he had ever ridden was a horse and he got by mistake on the observation platform, taking his hound with him, and was accosted by an angry conductor who told him he didn't mind a hobo but he hated a pooch. Hubbard said he would tie the dog behind and let him follow the train on a leash; and did so, and at the end of the first fifty miles the dog was hardly panting. Whereupon, more annoyed than ever, the conductor yelled for more steam, swearing that he would drag the beast to death; but at eighty miles an hour the dog trotted serenely, sometimes on three legs, sometimes on two, and with a philosophic eye on his master. At Grand Island the conductor ordered more speed, and from there to North Platte the train did a hundred miles an hour and the dog never tightened the rope, though the telephone poles alongside looked like the teeth of a fine comb. Seeing with what nimble ease the hound followed the conductor fell into a great fury and the train was whipped up to incredible speed; and though the dog now had to use four legs, he did so with grace and without perturbation, with the rope sagging like a clothesline between him and the train. At a hundred and eighty miles the conductor looked out and saw that the dog had vanished.

"And where is your gad-dinged pooch now?" he asked.

Ibid., pp. 393–394.

Cf. Jack Conroy, "The Boomer Fireman's Fast Sooner Hound," *A Treasury of American Folklore* (New York, 1944), pp. 533–536.

For the use of a dog as a "cow catcher" of a locomotive, see "The Rawhide Railroad," *ibid.*, p. 522.

Hubbard said to look ahead, and as he did so the train came to a crashing stop with the boxcars telescoping one another like a bunch of egg crates hit with a pile driver. For the dog had broken the rope, had taken the red flag from the cowcatcher, and had run ahead to flag the engineer for a washout. And from here the dog rode to Idaho, and dogs have been free passengers on Union Pacific trains through the State ever since.

The Smart Coon Dog

I remember it was along about 1855, and I set that dog on a coon track. Well, he tracked him for two or three miles through the woods until he came to a piece of ground that had just been plowed and he lost the scent because the coon went over that-there ground before the plowing. Well, the farmer raised a good crop that year. I waited and when he plowed the ground again, what do you think happened? Why, he turned that coon track up and that old dog, he just picked up the scent and caught that coon in no time. And that was the biggest coon I ever saw.

The Old Spotted Dog

While I didn't have anything else to do, I got to watching an old spotted dog. He was just an ordinary dog, but when I looked at him close, he was alert and friendly with every one. Got to inquiring around and found out he'd been bumped off a freight train and seemed to have no owner. He made himself at home and started right in business. When a crowd of cowboys would go into a saloon, he would follow 'em in and begin entertaining. He could do all kinds of tricks—turn somersaults, lay down and roll over, sit up on his hind feet, and such like.

He would always rush to the door and shake hands with all the newcomers. The boys would lay a coin on his nose, and he'd toss it high in the air and catch it in his mouth and pretend to swallow it. But you could bet your life he dident swallow it—he stuck it in one side of his lip and when he got a lip full of money, he'd dash out the back door and disappear for a few minutes. What he really done was

---

Ibid., p. 359.

From *The Autobiography of Will Rogers*, selected and edited by Donald Day, with a foreword by Bill and Jim Rogers, pp. 9–10.

hide his money. As soon as he worked one saloon, he would pull out and go to another place.

I got to thinking while watching this old dog, how much smarter he is than me. Here I am out of a job five hundred miles from home, and setting around and can't find a thing to do, and this old dog hops off a train and starts right in making money, hand over fist.

Me and some boys around town tried to locate his hidden treasure, but this old dog was too slick for us. He never fooled away no time on three or four of us boys that was looking for work. He seemed to know we was broke, but he was very friendly. As he was passing along by me, he'd wag his tail and kinda wink. I musta looked hungry and forlorn. I think he wanted to buy me a meal.

When times was dull and he got hungry, he would mysteriously disappear. Pretty soon he'd show up at a butcher shop with a dime in his mouth and lay it on the counter and the butcher would give him a piece of steak or a bone. He always paid for what he got in the line of grub. Pretty soon he seemed to get tired of the town, and one morning he was gone. A railroad man told us later that he seen this same dog in Trinidad, Colorado.

The Bear, the Corn, and the Hogs

You talk about bears! Why, when I first came to Rooshan River bears was plentier than cattle is now, and they was a little bit the smartest bears that I or anybody else ever seed. Why, do you know, there was a neighbor of mine had a fine field of corn, and he also had a fine lot of hogs. In the fall, when the corn began to get ripe, the bears would come into the field and make awful work among the corn; they were jest liter'ly cleanin' it out, and the hogs was a-disappearin' too, and the old fellow couldn't find where the bears had killed any of the hogs, and he was clean beat out. At last, when all of his hogs and a good deal of his corn had disappeared, he thought it was about time to investigate. So he started out. After huntin' around for some time he found a trail leadin' off from the corn field in the direction of a patch of timber about three miles away. He followed the trail, and when he got to the timber he discovered his hogs nicely inclosed in a pen, and the bears was a-packin' the corn out there, and feedin' it to the hogs, fattenin' them for their own eatin' for their winter meat!

From *Phinny's Calendar, or Western Almanac,* for the Year of Our Lord 1875 . . . , by George R. Perkins, LL.D., (n.p.). Buffalo, New York: Published by James M. Lent.

A correspondent of a California contemporary writes: "The following rather tough bear story was told in my hearing by an old settler in Russian River Valley. I give it as I got it."—G.R.P.

Bear George on Jakey's Fork

In the fall of '85, when the big cats were around, I went up along Jakey's Fork of the Big Wind River, just to look around, and it wasn't long till, sure enough, I got in with a bunch of bear. First I saw an old sow with two cubs. Had to kill the big one, but I took the cubs back to camp and kept them around for quite a spell till they grew up.

Them cubs was sure fun to watch. Used to play a lot together, slapping one another and chasing. They'd wrestle, and square off, too. But one of them got big awful quick, and when he was about a year old began to get mean. Used to sleep all day and hell around all night, busting boxes and cracking off branches. After a lot of that and no sleep, I got short on temper. Washed my odd shirt one day and spread it for drying, and then left camp for an armful of wood. When I got back, what do you think that damn bear'd done? He had my shirt ribboned and was nosing it into the dirt. He and I set to, and he came out dead.

That left one bear. He was a good deal more tractable, and easy to get along with. Right smart, too. Could learn most anything if you set about teaching him. Why, he was more help around the camp than an extra man. Used to pound tent stakes for me. I'd hold a stake up for him and spread some grease on the top. Pretty soon a fly would light on the grease. The bear would slam down on the fly—and the stake was set.

He and I was real pardners. Hunting bear is hard work, and when I found out how much help he was on the job, I was tickled. He knew where the big ones hid out and could take me right there—on his back. By this time that bear was a two-year-old, a fine-developed silver tip, big as a cow. I rode him all over the hills and we sure had some great shooting. All grizzlies, too. He could find bear where a dog would just drop his tail and say there wasn't no bear.

He used to get the meals. Took quite a while to teach him, but he soon got the idea. We'd pitch camp on a trout stream every night, and first thing, he'd build a fire. He'd get his wood together, always putting some fine, dry stuff on top. Then I'd take the Dutch oven lid and rub a little bacon fat along the edge. The bear would start licking the fat and chewing the iron. That bear had teeth! Say, would those sparks fly! Wouldn't be long before the fire was going and the frying pan was hot. Then the bear'd wade into the stream and look sharp. Sure

---

Manuscripts of the Federal Writers' Project of the Works Progress Administration for the State of Wyoming.

For another bear-riding hunter, see Theodore H. Hittell, *The Adventures of James Capen Adams, Mountaineer and Grizzly Bear Hunter* (Reprinted, Boston, 1911) and Dr. Frank Powell, *Old Grizzly Adams, the Bear Tamer,* Beadle's Boy's Library of Sport, Story, and Adventure, Vol. I, No. 11 (New York, 1882).

enough, down would splash that big paw and come out with a trout spinning on one claw. A few twists and a snap, and the cleaned trout was in the pan. Used to toss 'em up clear from the creek.

That bear hardly ever missed his throws and I came to expect a bull's eye every time. But one evening up in the real bear country, as I was saying, up along Jakey's Fork, the bear got nervous and began to miss his pan. Just couldn't get control. That was mighty disappointing, and it made me sore. I grabbed the Dutch oven lid and shied it at the bear's head. And my aim was better. The lid caught him alongside the mouth and knocked out a lot of teeth.

It didn't make him sore, but it didn't quiet him down much, either. He kept grunting around and looking off over the hill just north. And then I knew why he was nervous. There were bear over that ridge.

So we starts out, with me riding him up the slope a ways. Then I slips down off his back, and he takes right up the hill and out of sight through a little fringe of timber with me following up fast as I can, and when I gets to the top, here's my bear, mixing it with a couple of other big silver tips out on a sagebrush flat. Say, that was some fight, let me tell you. It was bright moonlight up there, and those grizzlies sure looked big, slashing at one another. I'm enjoying the scrap till all at once I remembers. My bear hasn't any teeth on one side of his mouth! And there he is, giving and taking, only it looks like he's taking more than he's giving. So I grabs me a piece of tree and wades in, cracking snoots and thumping skulls, trying to get the bear out of the mess he's in. But with them crowding in at one another and me ducking those roundhouse passes it's hard to get much done. Anyhow, I picks out this critter and starts shagging him down hill toward camp. Boys, he was really stubborn. Didn't seem to understand a thing I said. Wouldn't be driven a-tall. Just milled around like a steer that's been eating loco weed. I'd get him faced toward camp and start him going, and then he swaps ends and r'ars back on his hind legs, making passes at the air and me till I laid in with that club and give him a dusting. That brought him around, and off we started, me on his back.

We finally made it down to just outside camp, and I was sure in a sweat from hazing him along. But as for getting him into camp proper, that was something else. He'd come just so close to the tent, then sidle off into the woods and make a circle of camp, with me still riding and kicking his ribs. Back we'd come to the front of camp, then he'd wheel off through the trees again and it began to look like an all night trip, with me hauling on his head every time we came around, and him jerking away to the timber.

Riding on a bear's back all night ain't much like watching a ball game, but I allowed I'd wear him down. And I did. Daylight was just looking over the far ridge when we came out of the timber for another circling. He gave a long sigh and turned toward the tent. But he couldn't make it. His legs buckled under, and down he went, tuckered out, I guess.

I never saw such a tired bear. Not a hair stirring. And that worried me, seeing as I'd been so cussed that afternoon, throwing the oven lid and all. So I get down beside him to see if his mouth is still raw from being hit hard. I pulls his mouth open and looks in. His mouth is dry, but not raw. And he has a full batch of teeth. I had killed my pet bear and rode in one of the wild ones!

The Love Mad Lopez, the Pigs, and the Mission Bell

Now another piece of folk lore that has been forgotten are the tales about the Great Don Jose Lopez—The Love Mad Lopez who was the first man to grow the crying frijole in California. It was none other than he who trained the singing coyote. Most of his life was spent in riding around California Arizona & New Mexico on his flying palm tree hunting the sangua lima. What a sangua lima is nobody seems to know, but anyway the great Love Mad Lopez when he would have a yearning to go on an errand of love would call together the Order of Caballeros of the Love Mad Lopez, jump on his flying palm tree, & away he would ride ever ready to succor some poor lady in distress.

It was the great Lopez who first caused San Francisco Bay to form. He chased the evil spirit from Mt. Diablo & finally run him to earth. The earth then became sick & sunk out of sight & the evil being was drownded. This spirit was making the cattle sick & had been causing

---

By Frederick Morrison. From *California Folklore Quarterly,* Vol. I (October, 1942), No. 4, pp. 369–371. Berkeley and Los Angeles: Published for the California Folklore Society by the University of California Press.

The narrator of the following amazing bit of folklore is Mr. Frederick Morrison, an old resident of Los Angeles—the Pueblo, as he still calls it. Mr. Morrison is a folklore enthusiast who first came to the attention of the editors of the *Quarterly* through a letter in which he commented on some of the material we published and championed the principle of an ethnographic limitation of "California" to a roughly triangular territory bounded on the north by a line running from Santa Maria to Taos, New Mexico, on the east by a line from Taos to the lower end of Sonora, Mexico, and on the west by the Pacific Ocean. The editors replied to his letter and asked him to send in any stories he might have. We were rewarded by a number of tales, among which the Lopez cycle seemed unusually interesting.

Mr. Morrison modestly writes: "If you could rewrite this material you could make it the basis for a good story; these are partly true and partly folklore. I heard the one about the Love Mad Lopez from a fellow named Daniel Boone descended from Boone of Kentucky fame and the Lopez family of Arizona." We have, however, refrained from rewriting the tales, but have carefully preserved the original style and spelling. The style is typical of the folk narrator and as such deserves to be preserved.

Needless to say, we are hoping for additional Lopez stories from our readers and, eventually, for a study of the dissemination, parallels, and other details of the material.—The Editors.

much sorrow among the californians. Unlike Paul Bunyan the Great Lopez did not spend his time cutting down the trees & denuding the forests; making way for future erosion. He was the one who first planted the Redwoods, he made the painted desert red, cut the grand canyon, not Paul Bunyan, kindled Mt. Lassen, made Mt. Shasta, in fact erected most of California. He was greater than Paul Bunyan. For he was Bunyan, Barron Mauchesun & Don Quijote all rolled into one.

Anyway one story that stands out in my memory & it has appeared under many forms is the yarn about the first hog Ranch in California.

Once upon a time a Spanish Ship brought a boar and some sows to California. Well the Love Mad Lopez thought it would be a good idea to raise pigs to supply food for his Caballeros. So he bought the pigs & started raising them. They grew fat and healthy and multiplied exceedingly. Even the poor buzzards were out of luck for they ate up all the carcases left them nothing. These pigs were quite wild & just couldn't ever seem to get enough to eat. One old sow wandered off the home range into the mission garden ate up everything eatable & what she didn't eat she rooted up. Now this made the Padres very angry at the great Lopez for letting one of his swine steal from the Holy Church. So they sent one of their employees an Indian fellow to shoot the pig dead which he promptly did.

Now this was against the whole idea & principles of the order for the Caballeros did not believe in killing, being motivated only by love. They used the pigs only for food, but they didn't eat the pig flesh they only drunk the milk.

Apparently these Caballeros of the Order of Don Jose Lopez—the Love Mad Lopez—were the first to milk pigs, drink pigs milk & make pig cheese.

When Don Jose found that one of his pigs were dead he was heartbroken he called the Caballeros together & they laid plans on how to teach the Padres a lesson. Anyway late one night they crept up to the mission & stole the bell and carted it back to Ranch. You may guess there was a great hubbub at the mission in the morning when the indian whos duty it was to ring the bell found that it had been purloined away.

Well anyway the Caballeros took the Bell back to the ranch and would ring it at milking time every day. The pigs soon got used to its clang & they would stampede into the Caballeria (stable) to be milked at the very first bong. It mattered not how far an old sow had wandered when that bell sounded they would come rushing in squeeling like locomotives.

This bell became very handy for whenever a caballero wanted a little pig milk all he had to do was ring the Bell & he would immediately be surrounded by a horde of squeeling milk factories. Well this went on for a number of years and the whole ranch was over run by wild pigs, gray old tuskers, gay young squeelers & just plain pigs, fat sows, thin sows, & pleasingly plump sows. It soon became apparent to the great

Lopez and his Love Mad Caballeros that they would be forced to part with some of these beloved pigs. It was very sad indeed all the noble Caballero wept bitter tears. Anyway come spring round up the great Lopez got the whole Order together & they started to drive the pigs to town with the aid of the singing coyote. Anyway when they got to town & were passing the mission, the bell—a new one having been since acquired—started to ring calling the indians to mass. Well the pigs came charging and stampeding into the sacred edifice squeeling & oinking so that the devout thought they were being attacked by the devil and they ran to the priest for protection. The Padres were very much enraged & ordered the Pigs slaughtered immediately for this sacrelidge against the Holy Church. Now there was a yankee ship waiting to take on some pig meat & when the captain heard the great commotion on shore mingled with shots & so forth. He became very much alarmed thinking it was a revolution & fearing for the safety of his vessel, he ordered all sails set & the anchor weighed immediately. As the ship was drawing away from the coast a bell was sounded aboard here & the pigs hearing it rushed down into the Blue pacific & headed for China. Anyway when last seen they were approaching Hawaian Islands. This disheartened the Great Love Mad Lopez so much that he rode back to his ranch dug up the roots of the flying palm tree climbed aboard & flew away to return no more.

The Auto Race at Salton Sea

In the Mojave and Colorado deserts, which really are one, the lone prospector with his laden mule or burro may still be seen, for the mule or burro can go many places even a jeep cannot. Every little desert town has its "desert rats," who seem to have no other occupation besides prospecting and who somehow make a living at it. Mostly they are rather secretive and rarely volunteer much information except when more or less influenced by bottled conviviality, but anyone who asks them supercilious questions is likely to hear some marvelous tales of latest developments at Daggett or Ryolite or Calico or some other place, which once was rich with gold but has been robbed of everything except traditions. Most of the stories are not inspired by malice but are offered as entertainment. But if some dude-ranch guest from far away swallows them hook, line, and sinker it is a tribute to the raconteur's art, and a thing his fellow desert rats chuckle over, so that the aura of local fame sheds its glory on him.

That is only fair, for many of the guests who flee Chicago, New York, and Boston to spend the winter at desert resorts look on all the desert rats and other quaint characters as among the things provided

---

From *It's An Old California Custom,* by Lee Shippey, pp. 190–194. Copyright, 1948, by Lee Shippey. New York: The Vanguard Press, Inc.

for their amusement—which, quite frequently, they are—and if the natives can have fun at the expense of the visitors, they are only returning the compliment.

What is more, they return it with interest, proving that city slickers are more gullible than country bumpkins ever were. This, for example, is reported as authentic: A big car full of visitors and driven by a smug Angeleno—than whom no one can be smugger—drew up at Indio for a glass of grapefruit juice. Seeing a bewhiskered, innocent-looking desert rat, the driver questioned him for the entertainment of his guests:

"Grandpa, you look like you know this country. What's going on around here?"

The two women and the other men in the car were leaning forward, smiling to one another at this quaint and curious creature they were studying. Quite evidently they were tourists from the Middle West. The desert rat looked them over so mildly as to put them wholly off guard before he drawled:

"Ain't nothin' goin' on today. You shoulda been here yistiddy."

"What went on yesterday?"

"Auto races at Salton Sea. Some of the best auto racers from L.A."

"You don't say? Where could they find a place to race there?"

"Oh, they jist tore through cactus and greasewood when they had to. But mostly the sand was purty smooth."

"Who won?"

"That was the funny thing. Young feller from Mecca, in his old battered-up Ford, beat 'em all."

"You mean he beat the big professional racers from Los Angeles?" demanded the driver incredulously.

"Yep. He sure did."

"How did that happen?"

"He jist knowed the country better, I reckon."

"What happened?"

"It was so hot the light oil burnt right out of the bearin's of the city fellers' cars, but the Mecca boy got some of that dry ice they make over at Niland an' his car picked up jist like it would on a frosty mornin', once it got warmed up."

"You don't mean to tell me some of the country's greatest car racers didn't take everything into consideration?"

"Oh, they caught on pretty quick. But they never woulda got near the Mecca boy if it hadn't been for the cholla. He run over that cactus an' punctured all four tires."

"How could he win after that?"

"Well, he jist happened to see a nest o' rattlesnakes right ahead and he run smack into 'em. They bit all the tires an' they swelled up so fast you'd never of knowed anything had happened. So the Mecca boy won by a good ten feet."

The desert rat looked innocent and simpleminded. The two women and the other men murmured ejaculations but looked to the driver. He wasn't sure what to do and looked suspiciously at a package under the desert rat's right arm.

"What are you going to do with all that whisky, Grandpa?" he demanded.

"Do with it?" repeated the desert man mildly. "Why, what's one quart of whisky among one?"

Then one of the listening group near by snickered, and the interrogator drove on with his guests.

The Gooey Duck

. . . Men of the Evergreen Land, big and small, have never taken themselves too seriously, or their troubles either, and neither have they hesitated to take advantage of those strangers who do.

But sometimes the stranger is needlessly wary. I remember an afternoon at the Olympia Yacht Club when a nice young man from New York was being told of the fun in catching gweducs.

"What kind of ducks?" he inquired incredulously.

"G-w-e-d-u-c-s is the way Webster spells it," he was told. "But around here we call them gooey-ducks."

"I see. How are they caught?"

"Well, you hunt them with a shovel and a length of stovepipe. What a gooey-duck really is, is a very large kind of clam that is found only around Puget Sound. It's got a neck four or five feet long, and the shell is maybe six inches in diameter. They weigh up to eight or nine pounds sometimes."

The New Yorker tried to get into the spirit of the thing. "Tomorrow," he said, "I will get myself a small shovel, and also a length of stove-pipe. On that stove-pipe I shall have lettered the device: *A gooey-duck or bust!*"

"But this is the truth," he was told. "You see, the clam burrows into the sand at low water. It'll go down five feet if the neck is that long. When you get after him he pulls in his neck and hopes you won't spot him in that four or five feet of sand. That's where the stove-pipe comes in."

"And after you get this kind of duck, what do you do with it?" asked the man from Manhattan.

"His neck goes into chowder and the rest you can slice into steaks.

From *Evergreen Land,* A Portrait of the State of Washington, by Nard Jones, pp. 104–105. Copyright, 1947, by Anne and Nard Jones. New York: Dodd, Mead & Company.

For the geoduck, cf. Nancy Wilson Ross, *Farthest Reach* (New York, 1941), pp. 337–344.

It's good eating. The tide is out at five o'clock tomorrow morning. Want to meet us at the beach?"

"Sure," said the stranger amiably. "I said I'd be there."

But, alas, he was not. He was not, because he was determined not to be taken in by one of our broad practical jests of the kind he knew obtained in the farthest reach. However, his hosts were waiting for him at five o'clock the next morning—simply because everything they had told him was true!

The "Iron Man" of the Hoh

Fifteen years ago when the trails into the upper Hoh were being built, [John] Huelsdonk [the "Iron Man of the Hoh"] would strap 175 to 200 pounds of provisions on his back and pack them up to the trail crews. He did this not for bravado, but for two men's pay. And two men's pay during the short working season helped put his four daughters through the University.

Once a forest ranger met him on the trail between Forks and the Huelsdonk ranch. The barrel-chested settler had a cook stove on his back, and was trudging unconcernedly down the forest aisle [carrying the range from Forks, an Olympic outpost, to his homestead, a distance of twenty-two miles]. The ranger said: "That must be quite a load, eh John?"

"Well," Huelsdonk replied in all sincerity, "it isn't so bad, only there's a sack of flour in the oven that keeps shifting around and unsettling the load."

The Sissy from Anaconda

Several years ago I stopped off in the wonderful city of Butte, Montana, to see some friends and to investigate the reputation of Butte. I

From the Seattle *Times,* August 16, 1931, Pacific Northwest Collection, the University of Washington Library, Seattle, Washington.

Cf. Archie Binns, "People of the Washington Coast Range," in *The Pacific Coast Ranges,* edited by Roderick Peattie (New York, 1946), pp. 292–295.

Told by Stewart H. Holbrook, Portland, Oregon, July 30, 1950. Recorded by B. A. Botkin.

Cf. Jack Conroy, "The Sissy from the Hardscrabble County Rock Quarries," *A Treasury of American Folklore* (New York, 1944), pp. 529–531; E. E. Dale, *Cow Country* (Norman, 1945), pp. 140–141. The "Sissy" is a modern "Bad Man from Bodie."

For the name Anaconda, see *Copper Camp* (New York, 1943), pp. 18–19: One adventurous Irish miner, Michael Hickey, ex-soldier of the Union Army, [who discovered the great copper lead in 1882] had read an editorial by Horace Greeley in the New York *Tribune* stating that Grant's army was "encircling Lee's forces like a giant anaconda." "That word struck me as a mighty good one," said Hickey. "I always remembered it, and when I wanted a name for my mine, I remembered Greeley's editorial and called it the 'Anaconda.'"

was told that there was an old bartender down at the Exchange Saloon that probably could tell me more than anybody else about early Butte. So I went down to see him. "Well," he said, "if you'll come back tonight, after we've closed up, I'll tell you anything I know about Butte." He was one of the old school bartenders with the roached hair and the big waxed mustache, and he had a gold watch chain that would weigh a pound easily—the type of the old gentleman bartender.

I went down there and we sat on the Deacon's seat outside the saloon in the evening. And he said, "Well, mister, so you heard Butte is tough. I tell you Butte was not tough. But we had a tough town right near here. Did you ever hear of Anaconda?"

And I said, "Yes, I have."

"Well," he said, "mister, by God, there's where they're tough!"

"Well," I said, "tell me about it."

He said, "It was, oh, it was twenty-odd years ago, one hot jeezily day in August, and there was a bunch of us barflies sitting out on the porch here, and we see comin' down the trail a little old man. He was leadin' a great big cougar in one hand and a grizzly b'ar in the other. They were both on leashes. He come along until he got right in front of the saloon, and he stopped and reached over and he took that cougar by the ears and he *slammed* him down on his haunches and says, 'Sit there, you sonuvabitch!' Then he turned around and looked at the bear and the bear was whinin' and—pffft!—he spit in the bear's eye and said, 'Shut up, you bastard!' And he grabbed *him* and sat *him* down.

"Then this little old guy, he walked right down the path and right into the saloon, he never looked right nor left. So I went in and got around the bar and I said, 'Will you have a drink, mister?' He says, 'Yes, give me a bottle of your best drinkin' liquor.' So I set out a bottle on the counter and a tumbler. That's the way we did business here. He looked at the tumbler and looked up at me, took the tumbler—wham!—and threw it down to the floor, broke it all to pieces. Then he up with the liquor and he drank her right straight down. Gurgle, gurgle, gurgle! Thirty-two ounces! Down she went in the hatch in two big drinks! He put it back on the counter—the empty bottle—and he said, 'Well, mister, that was pretty good liquor. Now give me another glass of that wine.' And I put out another bottle. He up with it and was just going to start a-drinkin'—he stopped, he set it down on the counter. He began fumblin', reachin' into his shirt, and he felt all around in there. And then he pulled out, mister, the goddamnedest rattlesnake I ever see! There was fourteen rattles on it and they was all clackin' like castanets. And that snake's mouth was open and it was drippin' venom! His tongue was a-goin'. The little guy looked at him. 'Why,' he said, 'goddam you! Ugh!' And he bit the rattlesnake's head off and spit it out and he says, 'I'll learn you to bite me, you sonuvabitch!' And then he drank the liquor.

"I said, 'Say, mister, where do you come from?'

"The little guy says, 'Who? Me?' He had a little high-pitched voice.

"And I said, 'Yes, where do *you* come from?'

" 'Oh,' he says, 'I come from down the road a piece here. A town called Anaconda.'

" 'Oh,' I said, 'you come from Anaconda, do you.'

" 'Yeah!'

" 'Well,' I said, 'they must be pretty tough down there.'

" 'Tough!' he said. 'Goddam! They run all us sissies out of there yesterday!' "

Maritime Tall Tales of the Northwest Coast

There is a story about the CPR [Canadian Pacific Railroad] boats that may bear retelling. These vessels, which run on the Vancouver, Victoria and Seattle route, are notorious for keeping to their schedules, in spite of the heavy mists and fogs that frequent Puget Sound and the coast. It is rumored that so well do the masters know the courses that they handle their vessels with a stop-watch. For instance, in a fog, the skipper will give a course, hold it for so many seconds, and then change it for so many minutes or seconds more. They have things worked out pretty fine.

One time one of these glorified ferries ran into a pea-soup fog. She had a new mate on board and he was nervous. After four or five hours of pelting full speed the master sent the first officer for'ard and stopped the ship. "Jump!" he said. "We're there!" "But I can't see a damned thing!" protested the first officer. "Jump anyway!" roared the skipper. "There's the wharf right alongside!" So the first officer jumped blindly into the fog overside, and sure enough he hit the wharf. That's navigating! Split second stuff! The skipper put his stop-wach away and took a drink. They say he did not even look to see what had happened to the mate. He knew!

* * * * *

There was an engineer once who desired to have his best suit of clothes cleaned before going ashore, and while his ship was reaching for the coast he invented a sort of washing machine out of an oil drum, some gears, and so forth, connecting it to the winch. He placed his suit inside the contraption and, starting it, went away and forgot it. When he returned he discovered his suit to be in rags and tatters, but he merely did a simple and obvious thing. He reversed the winch and after a while drew the suit forth all whole again and cleaned and pressed.

* * * * *

There is, of course, also, the classic of the skipper and the chief engineer who desired to change places, each asserting the other had

---

By Albert Richard Wetjen, in a letter to the editor, 1929.

the easiest job, a job which he could run much better himself. So they changed over and proceeded on the voyage. After an hour or so the skipper whistled up to the bridge from the engine room. "You win," he said. "I've got this damned machinery tied into a knot." "All bets is off," declared the chief engineer on the bridge. "We've been stuck on a sandbank for the past half hour!"

Two Branding Tall Tales

I. The Cowboy and the Bear[1]

One of our cowboys was branding calves out on the range and jumped a bear. He took to him on his pony. He pulled his pistol to shoot and just as he did his horse jumped a log and instead of killing the bear he shot his boot heel off, dropped his pistol, and lost his hat. He jerked down his rope and caught the bear right around the neck. The bear rose up on his hind feet, caught the rope in his fore paws and here he came towards the pony. The cowboy jumped off his horse, and tore out down the mountain. He looked back after running a piece and saw the bear coming. He was sitting up in the saddle, had the cowboy's hat on, and was making a loop to try and rope him.

II. Tall Ear-Marking[2]

Years ago some cowboys were branding in the old Salero corral. The dust was so damn thick you couldn't tell a calf from a cowboy.

The branding and ear marking was going fast so that they could get into camp by dusk. After they were finished and the dust began to settle down a little, one cowboy lifted his hand to scratch his ear and to his surprise, he didn't have any!

The Musical Snake

Every one thought old Uncle Jerry was crazy. He had a little place out on Killdugan Creek [near Sweetwater, Texas,]—a quarter section

[1] From *A Corral Full of Stories,* rounded up by Joe M. Evans, p. 49. Copyright, 1939, by Joe M. Evans, El Paso, Texas: Printed by the McMath Company, Inc.

[2] From *Folk Tales from the Patagonia Area, Santa Cruz County, Arizona,* p. 37. University of Arizona Bulletin, General Bulletin No. 13, Vol. XIX (October 1948), No. 4. Copyright, 1949, by the University of Arizona Press. Tucson.

By Roy Scudday. From *Hell to Breakfast,* Mody C. Boatright and Donald Day, Editors, Texas Folk-Lore Society Publication No. XIX, J. Frank Dobie, General Editor, pp. 162–164. Copyright, 1944, by the Texas Folk-Lore Society. Austin and Dallas: Texas Folk-Lore Society and University Press in Dallas, Southern Methodist University.

Jim Bridger, the old frontier scout and trapper, used to spin some really tall tales about Indians, bears, and hair-raising adventures, but I believe he missed this one which an old uncle of mine used to tell me for a bedtime story.—R.S.

For a variant, see "The Migration of the Snakes and Frogs," Portland *Morning Oregonian,* September 21. November 3, 9, 19, 26, 1935.

of grazing land—and all he had on it was a few milk cows, some chickens, and two old hide-racks that passed as horses. Uncle Jerry had a rickety little cabin on his land, and he lived there by himself—he and his cows, horses, and chickens.

When the big drought hit, many of the little farmers and ranchers went under. They were either forced out by the drought or sold out to the big ranchers, who bought the land for a song. And all the folks really thought Uncle Jerry had lost his mind when he refused to sell out to Jess Bradford, who had one of the biggest spreads in the section. And Jess offered a fair price, too, considering the circumstances.

But Uncle Jerry just sat on his tumbledown front porch, playing his harmonica, shaking his head, and saying, "Nope, I ain't goin' to sell. This drought cain't last forever."

Now, old Uncle Jerry was a harmonica-playing fool. Nobody questioned his ability on the mouth organ. Whenever any of the folks gave a barn dance, Uncle Jerry was always asked to help provide the music. Hot or sweet, fast or slow, he could play any way you wanted.

Well, one hot afternoon in June, just before sundown, Uncle Jerry was sitting out on his porch serenading the chickens with his evening harmonica concert. He had just swung into "The Stars and Stripes Forever" when he happened to glance down at his feet—and there coiled up, with his big wicked head swaying to the music was the biggest, blackest diamond-back rattlesnake Uncle Jerry ever laid eyes on. He swore later that it was seven feet long if it was an inch.

Well, Uncle Jerry nearly swallowed his harmonica, but he had sense enough to keep on blowing. He played every piece he knew, from "Turkey in the Straw" to the "Wedding March," and when he ran out of pieces to play he started over again. But he noticed that the rattler kind of perked up, and swayed a little more when he played the "Stars and Stripes." Pretty soon Jerry ran completely out of breath, so he put down his harmonica, and said, "Go ahead and bite me, you durned varmint. Damned if I'll entertain you any more."

But the snake, just as if he was completely satisfied, shook his rattlers a little as if he were applauding, and crawled off.

After that, every afternoon when Uncle Jerry came out to play, that snake would appear just in time for the concert. The old boy became attached to the snake, and named him J. P. Sousa, after the composer of the snake's favorite tune. He enjoyed all the music, but he seemed to really get a kick out of the "Stars and Stripes." He even learned to "rattle his rattlers" in time to the music, and thereafter an enthusiastic duet was indulged in.

One afternoon J. P. Sousa failed to show up. Uncle Jerry tried to play, but his heart wasn't in it. It was just like an orchestra trying to play to an empty auditorium. Uncle Jerry hopefully kept an eye open for J. P., but finally gave him up for gone. After that, there were no more evening concerts.

The drought was finally broken with some good midsummer rains, just like Uncle Jerry said it would be. And the people began to wonder if he was quite as crazy as they thought he was. Killdugan Creek was full, and Jerry had one of the richest quarter sections of pasture land in the country.

One day Jess Bradford came out to look over Jerry's land. He offered a price that even Jerry himself hadn't dreamed of. But Jess had some new white-faced heifers that he wanted to put out to graze on the good grass of Jerry's land, and he didn't mind paying a big price for it. So Uncle Jerry hitched his two old crowbait horses to his rickety buckboard and drove Jess over the pasture, showing him the best grazing and watering spots.

They were bouncing along, and as they neared a little hill, the sound of martial music came to their ears. It sounded a little familiar to Jerry, so he jerked his team to a halt, and scrambled out of the wagon, and started up the rise, as fast as his arthritic joints would allow.

When he finally reached the top, a strange sight met his eyes. On top of the hill was a big, flat rock. And on this rock were twenty-eight big diamond-back rattlers, grouped in a circle. In the center, his head waving proudly, and his rattles beating out the time just a little louder than the rest, was old J. P. Sousa, leading his musicians in a loud but positive rendition of "The Stars and Stripes Forever."

Pecos Bill, Boss Cowman

I. Roping and Riding Fool

". . . He was the most famous and noted man in the whole cow country."

"It was him," said Hank, "that invented ropin'. He had a rope that reached from the Rio Grande to the Big Bow, and he shore did swing a mean loop. He used to amuse his self by throwin' a little *Julian*[1] up in the sky and fetchin' down the buzzards and eagles that flew over. He roped everything he ever seen: bears and wolves and panthers, elk and buffalo. The first time he seen a train, he thought it was some kind of varmint, and damn me if he didn't sling a loop over it and dang near wreck the thing.

"One time his ropin' shore did come in handy, for he saved the life of a very dear friend."

"How was that?" asked Lanky.

"Well, Bill had a hoss that he thought the world of, and he had a

---

From *Tall Tales from Texas*, by Mody C. Boatright, pp. 83–86, 89, 97–98. Copyright, 1934, by Southwest Press. Dallas, Texas.

[1] A type of loop. Pronounced *hoolián*.—M.C.B.

good reason to, too, for he had raised him from a colt, feedin' him on a special diet of nitro-glycerin and barbed wire, which made him very tough and also very ornery when anybody tried to handle him but Bill. The hoss thought the world of Bill, but when anybody else come around, it was all off. He had more ways of pitchin' than Carter had oats. Lots of men tried to ride him, but only one man besides Bill ever mounted that hoss and lived. That's the reason Bill named him Widow-Maker."

"Who was that man?" asked Lanky.

"That was Bill's friend that I was goin' to tell you about Bill savin' his life," said Hank. "You see this feller gits his heart set on ridin' Widow-Maker. Bill tried to talk him out of it, but he wouldn't listen. He said he could ride anything that had hair. It had been his ambition from youth, he said, to find a critter that could make him pull leather. So Bill, seein' the pore feller's heart was about to break, finally told him to go ahead.

"He gits on Widow-Maker, and that hoss begins to go through his gaits, doin' the end-to-end, the sunfish, and the back-throw; and about that time the rider goes up in the sky. Bill watches him through a spy-glass and sees him land on Pike's Peak. No doubt he would of starved to death up there, but Bill roped him by the neck and drug him down, thus savin' his life."

"Yeah," said Red, "Widow-Maker was jist the sort of hoss that suited Bill exactly. For one thing, it saved him a lot of shootin', because he didn't have no trouble keepin' other people off his mount; and as for Bill, he could ride anything that had hair and some things that didn't have. Once, jist for fun, he throwed a surcingle on a streak of lightnin' and rode it over Pike's Peak.

"Another time he bet a Stetson hat he could ride a cyclone. He went up on the Kansas line and simply eared that tornado down and got on it. Down he come across Oklahoma and the Panhandle a-settin' on that tornado, a-curlin' his mustache and a-spurrin' it in the withers. Seein' it couldn't throw him, it jist naturally rained out from under him, and that's the way Bill got the only spill he ever had."

II. Pecos Bill's Ranch

". . . He staked out New Mexico and fenced Arizona for a calf pasture. He built a big ranch-house and had a big yard around it. It was so far from the yard gate to the front door, that he used to keep a string of saddle hosses at stations along the way, for the convenience of visitors. Bill always was a hospitable sort of chap, and when company come, he always tried to persuade them to stay as long as he could git 'em to. Deputy sheriffs and brand inspectors he never would let leave a-tall.

"One time his outfit was so big that he would have his cooks jist dam up a draw to mix the biscuit dough in. They would dump in the flour and the salt and the bakin'-powder and mix it up with teams and fresnoes. You can still see places where the dough was left in the bottom of the draw when they moved on. Alkali lakes they call 'em. That's the bakin'-powder that stayed in the ground.

"One time when there was a big drought and water got scerce on Bill's range, he lit in and dug the Rio Grande and ditched water from the Gulf of Mexico. Old man Windy Williams was water boy on the job, and he said Bill shore drove his men hard for a few days till they got through, and it kept him busy carryin' water."

III. How Pecos Bill Died

". . . I heard that Bill went to Fort Worth one time, and there he seen a Boston man who had jist come to Texas with a mail-order cowboy outfit on; when Bill seen him, he jist naturally laid down and laughed his self to death."

"That may be so," said Joe, "but I doubt it. I heard one tale about the death of Pecos Bill that I believe is the real correct and true account."

"And what was that?" asked Lanky.

"Well, Bill happened to drift into Cheyenne jest as the first rodeo was bein' put on. Bein' a bit curious to know what it was all about, he went out to the grounds to look the thing over. When he seen the ropers and the riders, he begun to weep; the first tears he'd shed since the death of Slue-Foot Sue. Well, finally, when a country lawyer jest three years out of Mississippi got up to make a speech and referred to the men on horseback as cowboys, Bill turned white and begun to tremble. And then when the country lawyer went on to talk about 'keepin' inviolate the sacred traditions of the Old West,' Bill jest went out and crawled in a prairie-dog hole and died of solemncholy."

Southwesterners in Heaven

I[1]

An honest man died and soon was knocking on the Pearly Gates. Saint Peter opened his register: "Where are you from, my friend?"

"I'm a Southwesterner, Sir. Born and raised on the Mexican frontier."

"The sunny Southwest, eh?" The good saint was hesitant, but finally opened the gates. "Well, come on in. But you won't like it."

* * * * *

A Texan died and went to Heaven. Things were mighty nice. He found Sam Houston, Stephen F. Austin, James Bowie, Jim Hogg, Ma

1 From *Sun in Your Eyes,* New Light on the Southwest, by Oren Arnold, pp. 217, 218–219. Copyright, 1947, by the University of New Mexico Press. Albuquerque.

Ferguson, and many another, all now celestial and serene. Harps were in tune, ambrosia was plentiful. Yet he didn't seem content, and one day Saint Peter spoke to him, "Anything on your mind, son?"

The Texan lifted his halo respectfully and answered, "Well, Sir, it's nicer Up Here than I figured it could be, and we Texans appreciate it. But we hadn't ought to be selfish. Could you all make room maybe to let in a few Americans, too?"

II[2]

When one has lived long on the North Plains of Texas, he will always have a "honin' " for 'em.

An old story of a cowboy's dream will illustrate how an old hand feels about it.

This here cowboy, my old pal, Pink Robertson, dreamed he died and went to heaven. (This *is* a dream!) The arrival of a Texas cowboy was such an unusual event that Saint Peter took the day off to show the puncher around. Finally he showed the cowboy a half dozen men staked out like unbroken broncs. The cowboy faced Saint Peter inquiringly.

"Yes, we're still in heaven," replied the Saint.

"Then why in hell," exclaimed the old boy from the North Plains, "do you have these here men all staked out?"

"Well," said Saint Peter, with a slight attempt to restrain his impatience, "them are all cowboys from the Panhandle of Texas. If we turn 'em loose, the rascals will every last one go back."

III[3]

. . . Juan died, flew to heaven, and was greeted by Saint Peter with the usual question. "Where are you from?"

"Albuquerque, sir," Juan said.

"Say it again, please?"

"Albuquerque, New Mexico."

From here on, the versions differed. The first had Saint Peter saying, "Spell it!" Juan said, "I'd rather go to hell!" In the second version Saint Peter said, "Get out of here, liar! Albuquerque! There's no such place." But Juan, reminded of home by the heavenly air and hoping to stay, dumbfounded Saint Peter by calling for a map and proving that there really was such a place. "Forgive me, son," said the keeper of the keys. "You see, we never had anybody from there before."

---

[2] From *Wranglin' the Past, the Reminiscences of Frank M. King,* p. 60. Copyright, 1935 and 1946, by Frank M. King. First revised edition after limited edition, privately published in 1935 by the author for his friends.

[3] From "The Cities of America, Albuquerque," by Neil M. Clark, *The Saturday Evening Post,* Vol. 22 (April 8, 1950), No. 41, p. 139. Copyright, 1950, by the Curtis Publishing Co. Philadelphia.

II. FOLK TALES AND LEGENDS

What makes history, whether authenticated or legendary, live is that part of it that appeals to the imagination. . . . Yet it is the thing created and not the creator that the world remembers. Nothing could make a creator happier.—J. FRANK DOBIE

The Oregon Beeswax Legend

[Toward the end of the sixteenth century,] *Acapulco* galleons were carrying treasure from Manila to Mexico, and the eastward drift of weather brought tribute to the feet of the Oregon mountains. Thirty-odd miles below the mouth of the Columbia River, a large vessel drove ashore on the sandspit that shelters Nehalem Bay. According to the Indians, all the crew had light complexions except one, whose skin was black. There were twenty men, and when they found there was no hope of getting the ship off the beach, they accepted the Indians' hospitality and built huts on shore. One of the things they brought from the ship was a heavy chest, which they wished to bury; but they were not satisfied with the low, almost featureless Nehalem shore. Five miles to the north was a high, bare mountain, with the Pacific forever charging and bursting against its western base—an unforgettable landmark, visible for many leagues at sea. The sailors carried their chest to the southwest side, where the mountain rose from a little meadow. Elk were feeding on the grassy slopes that went up toward the sky, and when the castaways saw them they cried, "Carne!" which is Spanish for "meat." From then, according to the Indians, the mountain was called Neacarne, "the place of the meat," which has been corrupted into Neahkahnie.

Near the foot of the mountain the sailors dug a pit into which they lowered the chest, filled the pit, and went back to live with the Indians—but not for long.

One of the habits of the castaways was to ignore marital arrangements and take their pick of women. When they refused to learn the ways of civilization, their hosts surrounded the huts and exterminated them, and peace descended upon Nehalem. The castaways were buried

From "People of the Oregon Coast Range," by Archie Binns, *The Pacific Coast Ranges,* edited by Roderick Peattie, pp. 248–250. Copyright, 1946, by Vanguard Press, Inc. New York.

on the shore where they had been betrayed by their arrogance; the dead Negro slept on the mysterious chest at the foot of the mountain; the Indians, who feared places of burial, avoided the spot and in time forgot its location.

Long afterward, white settlers of Nehalem heard the Indian legends of the ship and the buried chest. The ship was still there, with its teakwood frames sticking out of the sand, and in the meadow at the foot of Neahkahnie Mountain they found a large rock carved with European symbols: crosses, the letter *W*, and *DE* followed by a row of dots above an arrow that pointed toward the mountain. Near by was a smaller rock with other symbols and an arrow pointing toward the larger rock. It took little imagination to deduce that the long-buried chest held treasure and that the carving on the larger rock was a code for locating it.

Few people can resist the idea of a treasure hunt, and enough have tried at Neahkahnie. None of them found the treasure, but old age found Pat Smith of Manzanita at the end of forty years' search. Lynn Wood, a Portland streetcar conductor, and his father drove a shaft into the side of the mountain, and they found death when it caved in on them. The chest is still concealed somewhere about Neahkahnie Mountain—if there ever was a chest—and the treasure rock is still there, in the tall grass behind a garage. Anyone so inclined may consider its obscure instructions and follow the direction of the arrow that points toward golden wealth, or old age, or sudden death.

Part of the treasure ship's cargo had been cakes of beeswax and candles. Occasionally the sea brought some of them to the surface. In 1813 Alexander Henry of the Northwest Company, visiting the site of Astoria, wrote in his *Journal*: "The old Clatsop chief arrived with salmon; with him a man with extraordinarily dark red hair, supposed to be an offspring of the ship wrecked within a few miles of the entrance of this river many years ago. Great quantities of beeswax continue to be dug out of the sand near this spot, and the Indians bring it to trade with us." The following year he observed: "They bring us frequently lumps of beeswax fresh out of the sand which they collect on the coast to the south, where the Spanish ship was cast away some years ago and the crew all murdered by natives." Late that century learned men proved to their own satisfaction that the wax was of mineral origin from a natural outcropping. Their declaration was so emphatic that no one seems to have commented on the cleverness of nature who had stamped trademarks on the cakes of wax and made some of it in the shape of candles supplied with wicks. Hopeful money was sunk into an oil well where the skeleton of a derrick is now being covered by sand dunes. Later, more learned men proved scientifically that the substance was beeswax, and their analysis proved that its source was the region from which the *Acapulco* galleons sailed.

The Line That Travis Drew

In 1873 the *Texas Almanac* published W. P. Zuber's narrative, "An Escape from the Alamo," to which was appended a statement from his mother verifying the account. It sets forth how a man named Rose appeared at the Zuber home in Grimes County some days after the fall of the Alamo. He was in a pitiable plight physically, starved, his legs full of thorns, his wallet clotted with blood. The Zubers were good Samaritans to him. He told them how in the Alamo on the night of March 3, 1836, Travis had made a remarkable speech to his men; how at the end of it he had drawn a line across the dirt floor with his sword, and invited all who would stay, fight, and die to cross over; how all went over, Bowie being carried on his cot, except Rose himself; how he climbed the wall, threw his wallet on the ground, where it soaked up Mexican blood, and how he then got through the cordon of Mexicans and made his way east afoot.

Up to the year 1873, the chronicles of Texas contained no mention of an escape from the Alamo, though the name of Rose had been set down, both in print and in stone, as one of the men who died in the Alamo. Up to this date also, the chronicles of Texas contained no intimation of the speech made by Travis or of the line drawn by his sword. The personal experiences of Rose on his fear-hounded walk across a wide land either uninhabited or now deserted by families who had joined in the Runaway Scrape still makes good reading—a kind of parallel to John C. Duval's *Early Times in Texas*—the story of his escape from Goliad. But this part of the Zuber—or Rose—narrative is minor compared to the speech of Travis, the drawing of the line, and the crossing of the men to his side, four of them bearing the cot on which the shrunken lion Jim Bowie lay.

Here was indeed something new, dramatic, and vital to inflame the imagination of the Texas people—a people who, though towers may rise higher than the Tower of Babel to mark the San Jacinto Battlefield and though monuments commemorating events and personalities of history may sprinkle the roadsides from Red River to the Rio Grande, cherish the Alamo as they cherish no other spot either in Texas or in the world beyond. The story seized not only the popular mind; it seized the imagination of story-tellers, poets, and historians.

* * * * *

The medium that gave the story its widest vogue was Mrs. Anna J. Hardwicke (Mrs. Percy V.) Pennybacker's *History of Texas for Schools*. No publisher would take the book and she and her husband issued it themselves, the first edition appearing in 1888. During the next twenty-

---

By J. Frank Dobie. From *In the Shadow of History,* Texas Folk-Lore Society Publications No. XV, J. Frank Dobie, Mody C. Boatright, Harry H. Ransom, editors, pp. 9–16. Copyright, 1939, by the Texas Folk-Lore Society. Austin.

five years, it went into six editions and "several hundred thousand copies were sold, chiefly for use in Texas schools."

To quote from the 1888 edition of this work, which for a quarter of a century gave the school children and also teachers attending the state normals their chief education in Texas history:

On March 4 [*sic*], the Mexicans kept up a terrible cannonade. Just before sunset, this suddenly ceased, and Santa Anna ordered his men to withdraw some distance from the Alamo. The weary Texans, who, for ten days and nights, had toiled like giants, sank down to snatch a few moments' rest. Travis seemed to know that this was the lull before the last fury of storm that was to destroy them all; he ordered his men to parade in single file. Then followed one of the grandest scenes history records. In a voice trembling with emotion, Travis told his men that death was inevitable, and showed that he had detained them thus long, hoping for reinforcements.

When Travis had finished, the silence of the grave reigned over all. Drawing his sword, he drew a line in front of his men and cried: "Those who wish to die like heroes and patriots come over to me." There was no hesitation. In a few minutes every soldier, save one, had crossed. Even the wounded dragged themselves across the fatal mark. Colonel Bowie was too ill to leave his couch, but he was not to be deterred by this. "Lads," he said, "I can't get over to you, but won't some of you be kind enough to lift my cot on the other side of the line?" In an instant it was done.

* * * * *

. . . What makes history, whether authenticated or legendary, live is that part of it that appeals to the imagination. Amid many imagination-rousing facts connected with the siege and fall of the Alamo—the superlatively moving letter written by Travis; the picture of Crockett playing his fiddle to cheer the boys up; Bowie on his cot with pistols and Bowie knife; Bonham dashing back from liberty to die with his comrades; the final charge of Santa Anna's men to the strains of the death-announcing *deguello;* the extermination of a hundred and eighty-odd Texans at the hands of an army numbering perhaps five thousand, of whom more than fifteen hundred were killed before the last free man in the walls of the old mission went down; the one sentence entitled to immortality that Texas can claim: "Thermopylae had her message of defeat, the Alamo had none"—amid these and other facts no circumstance has appealed more to popular imagination than the story of how Travis drew the line and invited individuals of the little group to choose between life and immortality. . . .

* * * * *

Could Rose, with his "broken English," no matter how good his memory, have transmitted the Travis speech as we have it from Zuber, who wrote it down thirty-five years after Rose had given it to Zuber's parents, who in turn repeated it to him? Zuber frankly said that he was transmitting only approximation. But it was the kind of speech that the inward-burning Travis might have made, the Travis who wrote "I shall never surrender or retreat," "I am determined to sustain myself as long as possible and die like a soldier," and whose rubric was "Victory or Death." And for Travis to have drawn the line would have been entirely natural, the more natural because of the fact that in both history and fiction Rubicon lines have repeatedly been drawn for fateful crossings. Because an act has precedent is no reason for denying it. History is sprinkled with momentous sentences spoken by military men at crucial hours. These men about to die in the Alamo must have been conscious of doing a fine and brave thing. Travis certainly thought that he was acting a part that the light of centuries to come would illumine. To have imagination is no reflection on integrity. A magnificent gesture does not abnegate sincerity. Not everything orally transmitted is *mere* legend; there is traditional history as well as traditional folk-lore.

For hundreds of thousands of Texans and others who could not cite a single authenticated word spoken in the Alamo or a single authenticated act performed by a single man of the besieged group—for these hundreds of thousands of human beings the gesture and the challenge made by William Barrett Travis are a living reality—almost the only personal reality of the Alamo. In a book of reminiscences written by an old cowpuncher of Montana I came only yesterday upon this passage: "The Alamo had fallen. Brave Bob Travis, that drew the dead line with his sword, lay cold in death at the gate."[1] In the "chronicles of wasted time" Travis's dead line belongs as inherently to Texas as William Tell's apple belongs to Switzerland, or as dying Sir Philip Sidney's generosity in refusing a drink of water so that a wounded soldier whose "necessity was greater" might sup it, belongs to England.

* * * * *

Yet it is the thing created and not the creator that the world remembers. Nothing could make a creator happier. Rose has been forgotten, will continue to be forgotten. That line that Travis drew cuts out and off everything else. To illustrate the forgetting and the remembering, too, I will quote from a book dealing with San Antonio, written by an informed newspaper man thirty years ago.

> In the Chapel, sick almost unto death, Bowie lay on a cot, prone and unable to rise. Travis with his sword drew a line across the space in front of where his forces had been assembled. . . . He said: "All who wish to leave, stand in their places. All who wish to remain and fight to the end cross over this line and come to me." All but one crossed over to him. Bowie had his cot lifted and brought over. Rose was the only man who did not cross that line. . . . During the night Crockett lifted Rose up and helped him out of one of the windows. Rose was never heard of after. Probably he perished miserably,

[1] E. C. Abbott and Helena Huntington Smith, *We Pointed Them North* (New York, 1939), p. 259.

butchered before he had gone many yards from the shadow of the structure in which his comrades remained. No one knows his fate, or, if so, it has never been told.[2]

One of Them

The stranger came to the corral gate just as Niels Nielson was finishing up the chores. He was an old man who looked like a tramp, and he was driving a ratty team.

"Howdy," he said.

Niels Nielson nodded, leaning on his manure fork. The stranger was travel worn. His rig was covered with dust, the wheels stuck with red clay.

"Wondered if you could put me and the team up to-night," the stranger said. He didn't ask it. He said it, and waited. Nielson tipped back his hat to scratch his head.

"Yeah," he said. "Sure, I guess so. I haven't got any hay for your team, though."

The man sat quietly on the wagon seat. "Come a long ways," he said. "From way down the valley. Eighty miles, must of been."

Nielson looked away to spit on the ground, his face perfectly straight, but he thought. Eighty miles in that old rig, with that team. In a pig's eye. He raised his head again. "You might get the Bishop to put the team up," he said.

"Where's he live?" The stranger remained slumped on the seat, the lines slack over the bony hips of the horses.

Nielson stuck the fork in the ground by the corral bars. "Just up the street," he said. "I'll go on down with you." He started walking, and the stranger flapped the lines and creaked after him.

---

[2] Charles M. Barnes, *Combats and Conquests, or Immortal Heroes* (San Antonio, 1910), pp. 33–34.—J.F.D.

From *Mormon Country*, by Wallace Stegner, pp. 158–165. American Folkways Series, edited by Erskine Caldwell. Copyright, 1942, by Wallace Stegner. New York: Duell, Sloan & Pearce.

I have fictionized the Nielson story somewhat and invented a few details, but the outline is exactly as the family told it to Mr. [Hector] Lee.—W.S.

According to the Book of Mormon, the Three Nephites were faithful disciples of Jesus who were given immortality so that they might continue to do His works. In the course of their wanderings, they appear, usually singly and mysteriously, at Mormon homes in the guise of poor travelers seeking hospitality, in return for which they give food, healing, spiritual message or uplift, or physical help. Their identity is not made known until they leave, and then by some sign of their supernatural being. The legend is similar to that of the Wandering Jew, Joseph of Arimathea, and St. John the Divine. For the Nephite tales and their background, see Austin E. Fife, "The Legend of the Three Nephites among the Mormons," *Journal of American Folklore* Vol. LIII (January-March, 1940), No. 207, pp. 1–49; Hector Lee, *The Three Nephites: The Substance and Significance of the Legend in Folklore* (Albuquerque, 1949).

The bishop was willing. "Sure," he said. "Turn 'em into my pasture. I'll feed 'em with mine in the morning."

"I thank you," the stranger said. "I'd appreciate it."

Nielson helped him unhitch and spank the weary horses through the pasture gate. Dust flew from under his hand when he slapped the off horse on the haunch. "Well, come on," he said. "Mother'll be having supper pretty soon. Got any baggage you want to bring along?"

"No," said the stranger. "If you could lend me the loan of a towel and some soap, I'd appreciate it."

"We ain't got much, but we got that much," Nielson said.

They walked together up the street, stepped across the ditch and around to the kitchen door. Mrs. Nielson was putting crocks of milk in the cellarway. "Mama," Nielson said, "can you find soap and a towel for this man? He's staying overnight."

Mrs. Nielson's eyes flicked from her husband to the stranger, and two little downward lines appeared at the corners of her mouth. "Yes," she said briefly. She went into the house and in a minute came back with a towel and a slab of homemade soap. "Basin's right there," she said. "Water's in the pump."

She and Niels Nielson went inside. "Where'd he come from?" she said.

"Just drove up. Said he'd come eighty mile. You should of seen his team. The Bishop's got 'em in his pasture." He chuckled a little, tonguing a cracked lip.

"Aren't you kind of liberal?"

The stranger was splashing in the basin outside. They could hear him snorting. Nielson met his wife's look. "Now, Mama," he said. "That's all right." He went into the other room.

In a few minutes the stranger came in, his shirt collar still rolled down and his hands and arms scrubbed to the elbow. Mrs. Nielson stood curiously in the kitchen, and he smiled at her. His teeth were good.

"It warms the heart to find hospitality," he said, with a little inclusive bow that took in even the twelve-year-old boy staring from the other side of the room. "I stopped at several places in this town, and not one of those families was willing to take in a tired traveler and his worn-out team." He rubbed his hands together and smiled at Mrs. Nielson again. His voice was deep and calm and a little oratorical. "But they will regret their selfishness," he said. "There will come a day when they will wish that they had not been so close they couldn't help a stranger in need." His hands rubbed harder, as if he relished the prospect. "Those people will see signs and wonders," he said. "I hate to think what is going to happen to those folks."

Over the stranger's shoulder Niels Nielson saw his wife's eyes open wide and the lines at the corners of her mouth deepen. He frowned at her, and she turned to set the table.

They ate in the kitchen—a bowl of bread and milk apiece, with a loaf and a crock ready for refills. Niels Nielson apologized for the fare. "We ain't got much," he said. "You're welcome to what we have, but it ain't much."

"Hospitality," said the stranger, "sweetens the meat."

Supper opened the gates of the stranger's talk. He expanded. He grew voluble. Sitting with the family after the meal, his caked and curling shoes stuck out comfortably in front of him, he spread himself. He told of places he had visited all over the world—Vienna, Budapest, Stockholm, London, New York. He had traveled the length and breadth of America hundreds of times. Niels Nielson sat and listened, and a little wrinkle of humorous disbelief grew between his eyes. From time to time he looked at his wife. What a blowhard, they said to each other silently.

"You ever been in Kansas?" Mrs. Nielson said suddenly.

The traveler turned and beamed upon her. "Oh, yes. All over the state. You know Kansas?"

"I come from there," she said. Her face took on a completely blank, stupid expression. "I was wondering how the folks back in Atchison were. You ever been through Atchison?"

"Know it very well," the stranger said promptly. "Know a good many people there, matter of fact. You ever know a family name of Birrell?"

Mrs. Nielson looked at her husband. "Birrell," she said, "I don't . . ."

"Lived just around the corner from the bank," said the stranger. "Very kind, very hospitable family. Two young daughters, must be about fourteen and sixteen now."

"Well," she said, "I . . ."

"Smith?" the stranger said. "Henry Smith? His wife has just passed away, poor man, leaving him with three young children. Very sad. Very sad case."

"How long since you been in Atchison?" Mrs. Nielson asked weakly.

"Let's see . . . year, year and a half. Say, you know the James family?"

"Walter James?"

"That's it!" he said, and slapped his leg. The dust rose thinly. "Walter James. How long since you've seen those folks?"

"Land," Mrs. Nielson said, flustered, "it must be fifteen years. Walter James' daughter Sue and I used to be best friends. What's happened to her?"

"Married," the stranger said. "Married and the mother of four sound young ones. Last I saw her she still looked like a girl, just as young as young."

"And still that long black hair?" she said. She was sitting a little farther forward. "I remember it used to come clear down below her waist. She could sit on it."

"Not a gray hair in it," the stranger said. "She coils it up on top of her head somehow. Beautiful hair, just like a young girl's."

Mrs. Nielson laughed a little jerkily. "Well, isn't that the *oddest!*"

she said. "Imagine meeting some one that knows Sue James. Who'd she marry?"

The stranger scratched his head. "Let's see. Butler, was it? Brown, Billings, Brewer . . .?"

"Not Bill Brewer?"

"The same. William Brewer."

Mrs. Nielson dissolved into a fit of weakening laughter.

"Imagine!" she said. "Why, Bill Brewer was about the rattiest, no-accountest, beatenest, timid little squirt of a boy. He must be four years younger than she is."

"Grew up into a fine man," said the stranger. "First-rate man. Prosperous, good family man. Well liked everywhere."

She shook her head, still laughing. Then she stopped laughing and looked at the traveler. She looked from him to Niels, and her forehead was knitted. "Well, I certainly have to apologize," she said. "Tell you the truth, I thought you were stringing us with all that talk about your travels. And here you know Sue James! Well . . ." Her forehead smoothed out, puckered again. "What threw me off right from the start," she said, "Niels told me you said you'd driven eighty miles today. How could you do that, with a scrawny team?"

The stranger had been smiling benignly upon her all through her apology. "That team," he said, "ain't *quite* as bad as it looks." He smiled more broadly, as if enjoying something secret and pleasant. Mrs. Nielson shook her head again and started to stand up.

Involuntarily the breath wheezed in her throat as the pain hit her, and her hand grabbed at her side. She staggered, threw a helpless look at Niels, and started out of the room, bent over, her hand still clutched in her side. Niels half rose, but the stranger's voice stopped him.

"Are you in pain?"

Mrs. Nielson turned and grimaced from the doorway into the kitchen. "I've had it for quite a while," she said apologetically. "They seem to think I have cancer."

The stranger sat still, looking up at her with the shadow of the benign smile still on his face. Then he stood up, and both Mrs. Nielson and her husband noticed the quiet dignity in his movement. "You will never have pain there any more," he said.

After a moment's staring, Mrs. Nielson went out back to the toilet, and in the toilet, as she told people later, "something passed her, it looked like cancer that they operate nowadays for," and her pain vanished. Still bewildered, but anxious now to do everything for the stranger, a little afraid of him and vastly puzzled, she went into the house and told her boy privately to go over to the neighbor's to sleep. The stranger would have to have his bed.

The boy scowled, kicked the floor, hung around. After a while he beckoned his father into the kitchen. "Do I have to give up my bed for that old tramp? Probably he'll leave crumbs in it and everything."

Niels looked at his son, thought a minute, and went back to consult with his wife. It wasn't quite fair to turn the kid out of his bed. Maybe they could make some other arrangement. But before he had a chance to catch his wife's eye the stranger, who could not possibly have overheard the conversation in the kitchen stood up. "You tell your boy he needn't be afraid of me leaving crumbs in his bed," he said. "I'm a clean man. Besides, I don't want his bed. I can make me a layout here on the floor."

Nielson, after a minute's baffled wonder, went after some quilts.

Early in the morning Mrs. Nielson, miraculously free from pain, rose and put herself out for the stranger's breakfast, but he seemed preoccupied and ate little. Eventually she gave up urging him and asked if he wouldn't like to take a lunch along.

"That might be all right," he said.

He took the lunch she fixed for him, smiled all around the family, and raised his hand in a gesture of blessing. The same dignity that they had noticed when he spoke about Mrs. Nielson's pain came upon them. "You will never want for bread," he said. "May God bless you."

They watched him start off down the road. Within a very few minutes some relatives came up the same road. "Did you notice the man with the scrawny team as you came up." Mrs. Nielson said. "He was the strangest man."

They looked at her blankly. "What team?" they said. "We didn't meet any man with a team."

Mrs. Nielson gasped, but not with pain this time. "Why, there wasn't any other way he *could* go!" she said. "He started out just a minute ago. You'd have had to meet him." She looked at them with her eyes widening and her mouth opening. The traveling, the prophecies of what would happen to the inhospitable families, the curing of her pain, the way he seemed to know everything that every one thought, the blessing when he left, the mysterious disappearance. . . .

"Oh, my goodness!" she said. "He must have been one of *them!*"

The Mormon Legend of the Gulls

The grain which had sprouted early had stooled well and had a rich color which promised a bounteous harvest. But before May had passed an unexpected pest put in its appearance in the guise of millions of

From *A Comprehensive History of the Church of Jesus Christ of Latter-Day Saints,* by B. H. Roberts (Salt Lake City, 1930), Vol. III, pp. 331–333.

It is of interest to note that a strikingly similar miraculous deliverance by sea gulls is told concerning Fathers Salvatierra and Ugarte at the time of the founding of the Comondú Mission in Lower California, in the first years of the eighteenth century. Reported in *The Journey of the Flame,* by Antonio de Fierro Blanco, translated by Walter de Steiguer (New York, Literary Guild, 1933), pp, 170–176. A monument to the gull, state bird of Utah, now stands on the Temple Square in Salt Lake City.—Austin E. Fife, "Popular Legends of the Mormons," *California Folklore Quarterly,* Vol. I (April, 1942), No. 2, pp. 114, 115n.

large black crickets which descended upon the new-made fields of grain. They devoured every blade of grain as they went, cutting day and night with unabated appetites that left the fields bare and brown behind them. The men, women, and children came and dug holes burying the pests bushels at a time but this didn't seem to affect their numbers. Then ditches were ploughed around the fields and an effort was made to drown the crickets but all to no purpose—even greater numbers descended from the hills. Fire was tried, but with no result. "Man's ingenuity was baffled. He might as well try to sweep back the rising tide of the ocean with a broom." Since the days of ancient Egypt's curse of locusts there had probably been nothing like it. And the failure to destroy this indestructible pest meant starvation not only to the first settlers of the Great Salt Lake valley, but to the thousands of men, women, and children then en route across the plains. "Small wonder if the hearts of the colonists failed them. They were beaten by the ceaseless gnawing of this horde of insatiable black invaders.

"Then the miraculous happened. I say it deliberately, the miraculous happened, as men commonly view the miraculous. There was heard the shrill, half scream, half plaintive cry of some sea gulls hovering over the wheat fields. Presently they light and begin devouring the crickets. Others come—thousands of them—from over the lake. The upper feathers of the gull's wings are tinted with a delicate gray, and some of the flight feathers, primaries, to be exact, are marked with black, but the prevailing color is white; and as they came upon the new wheat fields, stretched upward, and then gracefully folded their wings and began devouring the devourers, to the cricket-vexed colonists they seemed like white-winged angels of deliverance—these gulls. They were tireless in their destructive—nay, their *saving* work. It was noted that when they were glutted with crickets they would go to the streams, drink, vomit, and return again to the slaughter. And so it continued, day after day, until the plague was stayed, and the crops of the Pioneers saved.

"Is it matter for wonder that the lake sea gulls were held as sacred by the early Utah settlers, and that later they were protected by legislative enactments?"

The Swallows of San Juan Capistrano

Commonly heedless of the extraordinary architectural treasures so abundant at San Juan Capistrano, most people think of the mission as the scene of the mysterious migrations of the swallows. The gardens and ruins, in fact, are alive with birds of many types, as though they were still basking in the tender affection of Saint Francis and his

---

From *The Franciscan Missions of California,* by John A. Berger, pp. 154–155. Garden City: Doubleday & Co., Inc.

descendants. The cooing of dozens of fearless doves greets the visitor as he passes through the entrance gate. The gardens are filled with song. The ivy-covered ruins of the church are astir with fussy, crimson-headed linnets. But these birds only form the background for the famous flights of the swallows. With a regularity which has become legendary, a small squadron of scouts announce each spring the imminent approach of the main body of migrants. Punctually for more than a century and a half, so the legend relates, on Saint Joseph's Day, March 19, the main flock sweeps in from the ocean in such numbers that, like a cloud, they darken the whole patio. They lose no time in settling themselves for the summer in their mud nests scattered along the corners and arches. Then with equal regularity the visitors depart on Saint John's day, October 23. Their quaint, upside-down homes are not long deserted before a colony of white-throated swifts immediately take up the haunts from which they are driven each March by the arrival of the swallows. So dependable are the perennial arrival and departure that crowds of visitors witness the accompanying fiesta, special mass, concert by the children's choir, and other ceremonies, which to-day are allotted a nationwide radio broadcast. A colorful background is supplied by the natives of the mission village, who deck themselves out in the red and yellow costumes of the old Spanish days. The uninterrupted precision of this religious miracle has never been effectually explained.

The Bells of San Juan Capistrano

Of the Mission bells there are many traditions known to all the older people of San Juan Capistrano. One of these relates to the good old padre, Fray José Zalvidea. Of all the mission padres, he more than the others still survives in the living memory of the people and his name is the "open sesame" to the treasure caves of local tradition.

Adhering to the ancient custom of his brethren, he always traveled afoot on his journeys to other Missions or on calls to the sick. Once while returning from a visit to a rancheria in the north, the story runs, he was overtaken near El Toro, some twelve miles away, by the other padre of the Mission who rode in a carreta, drawn by oxen. On being invited to get in and ride, he refused and answered pleasantly—

"Never mind, my brother, I shall arrive at the Mission before you to ring the Angelus."

The other Father, respecting Padre José's desire to proceed afoot, did not urge him further, but continued on his way in the carreta.

Now, in those days, El Camino Real came into San Juan from the

---

From *Little Chapters about San Juan Capistrano* [,by St. John O'Sullivan, unpaged]. Copyright, 1912, by St. John O'Sullivan. San Juan Capistrano; California: Published by permission of authority.

north, not as it does now, along the level side of the Trabuco Valley, but some roads to the east, over the rolling breasts of the lomas. From the Mission patio one may still see the depression in the hill-top to the northwest of the Mission, where the roadway came over the swelling ground there, and gave the weary traveler from the north a first full view of the Mission. When the Father in the carreta reached this point on the King's Highway, it was just the hour for the Angelus, and promptly on the moment the bells rang out the three-fold call to prayer. Wondering who could have rung the Angelus in the absence of both Fathers, he hastened forward and found that Father Zalvidea, true to his word, had reached the Mission before him; but how he did so, to this day remains a mystery.

The Governor's Right Eye

Old Governor Hermenegildo Salvatierra, of Presidio, California, sported only one eye—the left—because the other had been shot out by an Indian arrow. With his sound one he was gazing into the fire, on a windy afternoon in the rainy season, when a chunky man in a sou'wester was ushered into his presence, and after announcing that he was no other than Captain Peleg Scudder, of the schooner General Court, from Salem, he was made welcome in a manner quite out of proportion in its warmth to the importance that such a disclosure would have for the every-day ciitzen.

He was hailed with wassail and even with wine. The joy of the commandant was so great that at the third bowl he sang a love ballad, in a voice somewhat cracked, and got on the table to teach the Yankee how to dance the cachuca. The law forbade any extended stay of Americans in Spanish waters, and the General Court took herself off that very night—for this, mind you, was in 1797, when the Spaniard ruled the farther coast.

Next day Salvatierra appeared before his astonished people with a right eye. The priests attached to the fort gave a special service of praise, and told the miracle to the red men of their neighborhood as an illustration of the effect of goodness, prayer, and faith. People came from far and near that they might go to church and see this marvel for themselves. But, alas, for the governor's repute for piety! It soon began to be whispered around that the new eye was an evil one; that it read the deepest thoughts of men with its inflexible, cold stare; that under its influence some of the fathers had been betrayed into confessing

---

From *Myths and Legends of Our Own Land,* by Charles M. Skinner, Vol. II, pp. 260–263. Copyright, 1896, by J. B. Lippincott Company. Philadelphia and London.

Cf. Mary Austin, "The Governor's Eye," *One-Smoke Stories* (Boston, 1934), pp. 30–33, and Bret Harte, "The Right Eye of the Commander," *The Writings of Bret Harte,* Standard Library Edition, (Boston, 1871), Vol. I, pp. 398–407.

things that the commandant had never supposed a clergyman to be guilty of. The people feared that eye, and ascribed such rogueries to the old man as had been entirely foreign to his nature hitherto.

This common fear and suspicion reacted, inevitably, and Salvatierra began, unconsciously, to exhibit some of the traits that his subjects said he possessed. He changed slowly from the indulgent parent to the stern and exacting law-giver. He did not know, however, what the people had been saying about him, and never suspected that his eye was likely to get him into trouble.

It was a warm night and he had gone to bed with his windows open—windows that opened from his garden, and were level, at the bottom, with the floor. A shadowy form stole along the gravel path and entered one of these windows. It was that of a mission Indian. He had gathered from the talk of the faithful that it would be a service to the deity as well as to men to destroy the power of that evil eye. He came beside the bed and looked attentively at the governor, sleeping there in the light of a candle. Then he howled with fright—howled so loudly that the old man sprang to his feet—for while the left eye had been fast asleep the evil one was broad awake and looking at him with a ghostly glare.

In another second the commandant was at the window whirling his trusty Toledo about his head, lopping ears and noses from the red renegades who had followed in the track of the first. In the scrimmage he received another jab in the right eye with a fist. When day dawned it was discovered, with joy, that the evil eye was darkened—and forever. The people trusted him once more. Finding that he was no longer an object of dread, his voice became kinder, his manner more gentle. A heavy and unusual rain, that had been falling, passed off that very day, so that the destruction from flood, which had been prophesied at the missions, was stayed and the clergy sang "Te Deum" in the church. The old commandant never, to his dying day, had the heart to confess that the evil eye was only a glass one.

The Best Saint That Ever Lived

In the little villages of the Rio Arriba country of Spanish-Colonial New Mexico, there are still current many tales of Padre Martinez and some of the cunning means he used in providing for himself a fat living in places where other, less worldly and less self-seeking priests had languished in emaciation.

There can be no doubt but that Padre Martinez regarded his parish and its *visitas* more in the light of sources of revenue than as spiritual

From *Native Tales of New Mexico*, by Frank G. Applegate, pp. 43–48. Copyright, 1932, by J. B. Lippincott Company. Philadelphia and London.

responsibilities, and, being himself a native of the land, he was exceedingly and intimately acquainted with all the little failings, prejudices, likes and dislikes of his charges and could turn them all to his own account.

However, there was one village, a *visita,* under his ministration that baffled all his efforts, as it had those of his predecessors, to wring from it a revenue commensurate with its manifest prosperity. In fact, San José was a problem to the rather covetous padre and seemingly an insoluble one. It was like a thorn in his side, for although this *placita* of San José was situated at the edge of Las Angosturas, the most fertile strip of land along the Rio Grande, and had just above it mesas covered with some of the richest pasturage in New Mexico for the large flocks of the villagers, yet with all his most diligent efforts, the padre could extract from the inhabitants of this village not one *centavo* beyond the absolutely lowest minimum fees for marriages and christenings and, for the dead, barely sufficient masses that they might but get one foot through the door leading from purgatory to paradise, the living leaving it to their heaven-bound relatives to push the balance of their way through.

Whenever the padre partook of a meal in the village, which happened whenever he made a visit there, he was served only the ordinary fare of the people, *frijoles,* chilli, *tortillas,* and stewed mutton, and never a single fowl in the whole *placita* lost even a feather because of his coming. There was never a question of freewill giving and even when the padre delivered one of his most eloquent and carefully prepared sermons, the people merely appeared uninterested, bored, and a little sullen.

Now, Padre Martinez didn't like this situation, for although he was full of energy and did not mind laboring in the vineyard of the Lord, yet he felt that since he labored so diligently, there should be at least a little harvest to gather in. However, he was not one to give up and call a field infertile merely because the methods he had employed heretofore had failed of results; yet try as he would, he could, by himself, discover no solution to his difficulty. Finally, in his perplexity, he sought out the sacristan of the church, who was also the village storekeeper, to see whether that one could give him any worth-while advice on how to loosen the pursestrings of his communicants. At the same time he laid his problem frankly and openly before the sacristan. The latter listened carefully to the priest's tale of frustration and then, considering seriously for a moment, said: "Padre, if you will allow me the privilege of speaking to you as one business man to another and not like a penitent to his confessor, I can tell you exactly what the trouble is. The people of San José don't like your sermons."

"They don't like my sermons!" exclaimed the padre excitedly. "Why, I preach the very best sermons I can think of to make them turn out their pockets."

"Perhaps so," returned the sacristan, "but you don't get any results, do you? Well, I'll you why you don't, and you can see for yourself if I'm not right. Now you stand up there in the pulpit with your back to San José, who stands there on the altar, and do you ever mention the name of San José? No, you don't. You stand up there and preach a lot of stuff about the Virgin and what she can do, and all about Jesus and what he can do, and talk about confessions and sin. Then you tell us that San Antonio let women alone and San Francisco preached to the birds and fish and God knows what other nonsense, because none of us ever listen to a bit of it. Now what about San José? He just stands there behind you neglected while you preach away and he is the only saint any one of us here knows well or cares about. He's our *santo* and he's the only one of them all who ever takes the least trouble to do anything for us. We think he is the best saint that ever lived, for he never even got mad when his wife had a child that wasn't his. All the other saints are just wasted, as far as we are concerned, and it only makes us angry to hear their names mentioned. We want to hear only about San José."

A hint was sufficient to a man with the perspicacity of Padre Martinez, and, since his next visit to the village of San José would coincide with the fiesta of San José, he took measures accordingly. On that day, as was always customary, all the people flocked to the church, but it could be plainly seen that they did so haltingly and reluctantly and from a sense of duty, rather than from any desire on their part to be there. Padre Martinez, however, was getting ready for a harvest and when the time for the sermon arrived, he made preparations accordingly. Taking the sacristan aside and giving him a box of ample size, he told him to circulate it through the congregation while the preaching was going on, so that if any felt touched by his sermon, they could give then and there, while in the mood. Then in place of mounting into the pulpit himself, he turned briskly, and seizing the image of San José, placed it there in his stead. At this action, his congregation began to appear interested for the first time since he had begun to minister to them. Standing beside the pulpit, Padre Martinez began to speak. "Perhaps all of you wonder why I have placed San José in the pulpit. It is because San José, without speaking, can preach a better sermon than I. This is the fiesta of that greatest of saints, San José. San José is the best saint of them all, for San José is ready to help every one. This San José here is the best San José in New Mexico to work miracles. San Antonio is not so good as San José. San Francisco is not so good as San José. San José didn't bother to preach to birds and fish. San José does things for you people. You men should pray to San José. San José will give you more sheep. You women should pray to San José. San José will keep your husband safe. You girls should pray to San José. San José will find you a good man. You boys should pray to San José. San José will give you a beautiful wife. San José will help you all through purgatory. San José will help you all into heaven. San José—" Just at this point the sacristan who, up to this time had been very much occupied, came running up to the padre and, pulling him by the sleeve, whispered in his ear: "For God's sake, padre, the box is full of money now, so don't say San José again or to-morrow there won't be a single cent left in the whole *placita,* and remember, I'm the storekeeper here."

New Mexican Trickster Tales

The Smart Indian[1]

Once there were a rich man, he too rich, and when he had a daughter he make a promise to God that when his daughter get married he invite only rich men to the fiesta, and no poor mens. So when she got married, all the rich mens came but no poor mens. He put some men outside, and they chase away all the poor mens in torn coats. So all the poor mens sit outside, and can't go in to the fiesta. Now there was a Indian, and he come up and he was very hungry. And he see all the poor mens sitting there and he says, "Where can I get something to eat?" and some of the poor mens say, "Go to the fiesta, there's a lot to eat." But some others say no, only rich mens go to that fiesta. So the Indian he stand and think awhile, and then say, "I go to the fiesta anyhow." So he went up and the mens say, "Where you going?" and he say, "I'm going to the fiesta." And they say, "You can't, only rich mens can come." So the Indian say, "I must speak to the rich man," and they say, "You can't speak to him," but he says, "I must speak to him." So they go in to the rich man and say, "There's an Indian here who say he want to come to the fiesta." So the rich man says, "Tell him to go way." So they go back and tell the Indian. "Go back, come tomorrow." So the Indian say, "I must speak to the rich man if only a few words." So the rich man come and the Indian say, "Do you want to buy some gold?" Now the rich mans always thinking of money, and he says, "Come in, come in," and he puts him down at a table, and gives him plenty to eat, because he think he get the gold cheap. When he finished he puts him at another table, and gives him plenty to drink, and then the Indian say, "I'm full." So then the rich man goes down to his store, and he says, "Have you gold to sell? where is the gold?" But the Indian say, "Oh no, I just wanted to know. Now if I find gold I know you will buy it. I bring it here." So the rich man is too mad, and he beat the Indian and throw him out, but the Indian don't care; his belly full.

From "A New Mexican Village [Hot Springs]," by Helen Zunser, *The Journal of American Folklore,* Vol. 48 (April–June, 1935), No. 188, pp. 176–178. New York: The American Folklore Society, G. E. Stechert & Co., Agents.

[1] Told by Antonio.—H.Z.

THE MEAN RICH MAN[2]

Once there were a rich man, very mean, and he think all the time how to fool the mens who work for him, and get them to work too hard for little money. So one day he goes to the town, and he sees a simple man standing in the street, not doing nothing, so (with his mouth open). He go up to him and say, "You want to work?" and the simple man says sure, and he say, "Come up to my place, and I give you fifty cents a day." And the simple man he says sure, and the rich man laugh to hisself, and think "Oh now I get this simple man to work hard."

So they get to this rich man's house, and it too late to work, so in the morning he wake him up and say, "Hey, you got to go to the fields to work." So the simple mans get up and he eat a good breakfast, the rich man's wife give it to him. And the rich man say, "You got to go far to work, over fields, too far to come home for lunch." So the simple man say, "You give me my lunch now. I want it now so no one have to come after me with my lunch." And the rich mans too glad, he give him the lunch so that no one has to stop work to go give the simple man eat. And when the simple man finished, the rich man say, "Oh why don't you eat your supper now so you don't have to come home early?" He think he can't eat much now, and then his wife don't have to give him to eat after.

So the simple mans said, "All right," and he eat his supper. Then the rich man say, "Now go to the field to work," and the simple man say, "Oh, no, all my life after supper I go right to sleep. All my life I have a habit, not change now." And he go to sleep, and the rich mans too mad.

THE APPLE TREE[3]

Once there was a fellow who go to California to look for work. He get a job with a farmer, picking apples. Now this farmer have a fine daughter, and the boy want to kiss her, but the father never go way, always around. She willing too. So he thinks him a way.

One day he way on top of the apple tree picking apples, throwing them down. Farmer and his daughter on bottom, they pick up the apples, put them in baskets. Now all of a sudden the boy runs down from the tree, very fast, very quick.

"What's the matter?" the farmer say.

"Oh, I quit, I no stay here any more."

"Why you quit? What the matter?"

The boy a good worker. Farmer don't want him to go way.

"Oh, I don't like to stay in a place where I see such things."

"What do you see?"

---

[2] Told by Antonio.—H.Z.

[3] Told by Fernan.—H.Z.

"I look down from the tree and see you kiss your daughter. I not like that."

The farmer say, "Oh, no, that not true."

"Well, if you don't believe me, go see yourself."

So the farmer climb on the top of the tree and look down. The boy and girl kissing. He holler down, "Yes, what you say is true." They two have a good time.

How Pedro Urdemalas Got into and out of Heaven

It seems that Pedro Urdemalas, swindling his bosses out of fabulous sums, had lived a long life on earth. When it was over, he climbed the clouds to heaven and knocked on the golden gate.

"Who is it?" asked Saint Peter, who was Pedro's *tocayo*. That is, they had the same name.

"This is your *tocayo,* Pedro Urdemalas. Let me in."

"Where is your passport? Where were you born?" To Nicolas [,who told the story], Saint Peter was a customs officer, the golden stairs were the bridge across the Rio Grande, and Pedro was himself trying to get home again.

"I was born in a valley between two hills." Imitating Pedro, Nicolas made his voice thin and plaintive as the baa of the freshly branded calves that had not yet found their mothers.

"What was the name of the valley?" Imitating Saint Peter, Nicolas made his voice heavy and demanding as the bawl of bulls plaguing the worried mothers of the calves.

"Oh, it had many names, *tocayo.*" Nicolas squinched his shoulders and stuck out his upward-turned palms in imitation of Pedro. "Different people gave it different names. I think it ran east and west. All kinds of good things grew there. Watermelons, beans, grass for the cows, corn for the hogs, oats for the horses. And a river ran through it, with water which went all the way from its head in the hills to its mouth in the sea. When there was rain, everything grew green, but when it was dry, the grass died and the cows and hogs and horses became thin."

Nicolas shook his fist and told me that Saint Peter's angry yelling shook the stars. "Stop wasting my time! What do I care for watermelons, beans, grass for the cows, corn for the hogs, and oats for the horses? Am I a cow or a hog or a horse? No! I am a saint! A spirit! And spirits do not eat, for there is no body to need eating. Only spirit, thin as the

---

From *Life on the King Ranch,* by Frank Goodwyn, pp. 122–128. Copyright, 1951, by Frank Goodwyn. New York: Thomas Y. Crowell Co.

For other picaresque, trickster stories of the successful rogue, Pedro de Urdemalas, see Riley Aiken, in *Puro Mexicano* (Austin, 1935), pp. 49–55; Aurelio M. Espinosa, *Cuentos populares españoles* (Stanford, 1923–1926); and José Manuel Espinosa, *Spanish Folk-Tales from New Mexico* (New York, 1937).

air. Nor do I care for your rivers or hills, nor for your green grass of rainy weather or your dead grass of dry times. I am here by command of Dios, to see that no man passes in without permission from the bosses. If you do not know the day and place of your being born, you cannot get a passport, and without a passport you cannot pass this gate. It is the law."

"But I was born a long time ago, *tocayo*. I cannot remember."

"That is your bad luck. Not mine."

"But please, *tocayo*. Have pity on a poor *pelado* who wants only to get a glimpse of your beautiful place, so that he may tell the others of his land what it is like. Nobody from Texas has ever seen inside heaven. Just one little peep is all I ask, *tocayo*."

Now Saint Peter, being a man of mercy, opened the gate just a little. Instead of looking, Pedro stuck his finger in. Quickly, Saint Peter tried to shut the gate, but Pedro cried, "Ouch! *Tocayo!* My finger got caught in the gate! Please do not cut it off! Open the gate a little more, so I can get it out."

Saint Peter, who could not bear to see a man suffer, opened the gate a little more. Instead of taking his finger out, Pedro stuck his whole hand in.

"Ouch! *Tocayo!* You will cut off my hand! Open the gate just enough for me to get it out."

This was not going as Saint Peter had intended, but his kindness of heart would not let him do otherwise than open the gate a bit more for Pedro to get his hand out. This time Pedro stuck his whole arm in.

"Ouch! *Tocayo!* Now you have caught my arm! You should not be so careless with your gate!"

Saint Peter, who would not think of cutting off a man's arm, opened the gate a little more. Instead of taking his arm out, Pedro took off his big straw hat and threw it into heaven. It went bouncing and rolling over the clouds behind Saint Peter.

"Oh, what a shame, *tocayo!*" Pedro lamented. "It seems that I can never have anything but bad luck. The wind has blown off my hat! It is the only one I have, and hell is such a hot place I am told. Almost as hot as Texas when the Texans are branding calves. You cannot send me away without a hat. Please let me come in and find it."

Now as all the world knows, Saint Peter has no hair himself. He could not bear to think of a man going bareheaded in hell, to say nothing of Texas. So he let Pedro in to find his hat. Pedro, very happy, went running over the clouds behind his hat. Saint Peter looked at the sun, which was his clock. Thirty minutes passed, then thirty hours, then thirty days, but still there was no sign of Pedro.

One day an angel came and knelt before the throne of Dios our Señor, saying, "Sir, I lost a feather from one of my wings. Do you think there could be a thief around here?"

"Hush!" whispered Dios. 'You must not mention thieves in this holy place! You will ruin my good reputation! Go back and play on your harp, and maybe you will find your feather. Here is a fresh cloud that I have just made. You may use it for a pillow." He tossed the new cloud to the angel, who took it and flew away pacified if not happy.

Next day a second angel came. "Our Sir, I lost a ring from my finger. Are you sure that no ——"

"Hush! Do not say that word. Go back and play on your harp and maybe you will find your ring. Here is a fresh cloud, one of the softest I have ever made. You may cushion your knees on it when you kneel before the cross." For even angels must kneel before the cross of Christ.

Next day a third angel came. "Our Sir! I lost ——"

"Hush!" said Dios. "I know what you are going to say. We will go and talk to Saint Peter. We must find out what kind of persons he has been letting in lately."

So they went to see Saint Peter, but he only shook his head. Then he thought a moment and said, "Now that I remember, a man from Texas named Pedro Urdemalas came in after his hat some time ago. He has not yet gone back out. I suppose he has not found it."

"Pedro Urdemalas!" gasped Dios, turning pale, for Pedro Urdemalas was known everywhere to be terrible for his deviltry.

"Pedro Urdemalas!" echoed the angels, also turning pale.

"Find him," commanded Dios, "and throw him out."

They hunted and they hunted but they never found Pedro. One by one the angels came back dragging their tired wings, bringing the bad news of failure.

Saint Peter scratched his bald head and tried to be helpful. "He may have slipped out through the cellar."

"My cellar!" screamed Dios, shaking his long beard with such thundering terror that the foundations of the sky almost came loose. "And I've got fifty gallons of good mescal down there! Go get him, you dead beats! Hurry! Don't stand there like idiots! Get him out of here!"

The angels scattered like a flock of frightened turkeys, rushing in every direction at once, lifting up big clouds and little clouds to look under them, sometimes stopping and panting a moment behind a half-formed star, temporarily hidden from the wrath of Dios. After a long time they came back, with sweat dripping from their wings. They had found nothing.

At last Dios, who knows all things, thought of a plan. He sent an angel to the earth after a Texan. Soon the angel returned, carrying a Texan by the collar.

"Bring him a chair," said Dios.

They brought the Texan a chair and he sat down beside the golden gate.

Dios asked, "Do you know a song called 'La Cucaracha'?"

"Oh, sure," said the Texan. "Everybody in Texas knows that song." He crossed his legs and used his hat to brush the stardust off his boots.

"Sing it," said Dios.

The Texan put his hat on one side of his head, tuned his guitar—

for, as you know, all good Texans have guitars—and began to sing: "The *cucaracha*, the *cucaracha*, he will pace along no more, because he lacks—because he has no marijuana to smoke."

The angels had never heard such a song before. They were very quiet.

"Again!" commanded Dios.

The Texan sang again. Nothing happened.

But the third time he sang, a straw hat went spinning into the sky beyond the faraway clouds. Dust began to rise in that direction, and the angels heard somebody yell, "Long live Mexico!"

Dios pointed his long, bony finger. "Yonder he is. I knew that he would not be able to stay quiet when he heard that song." Then Dios reached over the clouds, lifted Pedro by the back of his neck as a mother cat lifts kittens, held him out over the edges of heaven, and dropped him back down to the earth, where he still works cattle in the Texas sun.

The Devil in Texas

It was an abnormally hot day in Hell. The big devils and the little devils were all busy feeding the fires, making final preparations to give a warm reception to a barber, a student and a banker who had announced their arrival. A timid knock sounded on the door, and Satan, who was sitting on a throne of flames, sent one of his henchmen to see who the arrivals might be. In walked four men. One, razor in hand, gave away his profession; the second held on to a wallet like Judas Iscariot to his; the third exhibited a notebook devoid of notes. The three were abnormally terrified. The fourth did not appear a bit impressed by the fiery reception awarded them, but with the coolness and nonchalance of one accustomed to such things glanced about with a look of curiosity. He was an athletic sort of a man, wore a five gallon hat, *chivarras* and spurs, and played with a lariat he held in his hands. He seemed to be as much at home as the others were terrified. Before he was assigned any particular work, he walked to where a devil was shoveling coals, and, taking the shovel from his hands, began to work. Satan was so much impressed that he paid no attention to the others but went to where the stranger was. He did not like this man's attitude at all. He liked to watch the agony on the face of the condemned, but here was this man as cool as a September morn. He went through the flames, over the flames, into the flames and did not mind the heat at all. This was more than his Satanic Majesty could endure. Approaching the man, he commanded him to stop and listen to what he had to say. But the man would not stop and kept on working.

From "Tales and Songs of the Texas-Mexicans," by Jovitá Gonzalez, *Man, Bird and Beast*, Publications of the Texas Folk-Lore Society, Vol. VIII, 1930, edited by J. Frank Dobie, pp. 106–109. Copyright, 1930, by the Texas Folk-Lore Society. Austin.

"Oh, well," said Satan, "if that's the way you feel keep it up, but I really would like to know something about you and where you come from."

"If that's the case," the stranger replied, "then I feel I must satisfy your curiosity. I am Pedro de Urdemañas by name. I have lived through the ages deceiving people, living at the expense of women who are foolish enough to fall in love with me. Now as a beggar, now as a blind man I have earned my living. As a gypsy and a horse trader in Spain, then as a soldier of fortune in the new world, I have managed to live without working. I have lived through the equatorial heat of South America, through the cold of the Andes and the desert heat of the Southwest. I am immune to the heat and the cold, and really bask in the warmth of this place."

The Devil was more impressed than ever and wanted to know more of this strange personage.

"Where was your home before you came here?" he continued.

"Oh, in the most wonderful land of all. I am sure you would love it. Have you ever been in Texas?"

The devil shook his head.

"Well, that's where I come from. It is a marvelous country."

"Indeed?" said the Evil One, "and what is it like?"

Pedro described the land in such glowing terms that the Devil was getting interested in reality. "And what's more," continued Pedro, "there is plenty of work for you down there."

At this Satan cocked his ears, for if there was one thing he liked better than anything else it was to get more workers for his shops.

"But listen," he confided, "you say there are many cows there. Well, you see I have never seen one and would not know what to do were I to see one."

"You have nothing to fear about that. There is a marked similarity between you and a cow. Both have horns and a tail. I am sure you and the cows will become very good friends."

After this comparison, Satan was more anxious than ever to go to this strange land where cows lived.

So early the next day before the Hell fires were started, he set out earth-bound. Since his most productive work had been done in the cities and he knew nothing of ranch life, Satan left for Texas gaily appareled in the latest New York style. He knew how to dress, and as he strolled through the earth seeking for Texas, he left many broken hearts in his path.

Finally, on an August day he set foot on a little prairie surrounded by thorny brush, near the lower Rio Grande. It was a hot day indeed. The sand that flew in whirlwinds was hotter than the flames of the infernal region. It burned the Devil's face and scorched his throat. His tongue was swollen; his temples throbbed with the force of a hammer beat. As he staggered panting under the noonday heat, he saw something that gladdened his eyes. A muddy stream glided its way lazily across a sandy bed. His eyes caught sight of a small plant bearing red berries, and his heart gladdened at the sight of it. It was too good to be true. Here was what he most wished for—water and fresh berries to eat. He picked a handful of the ripest and freshest, and with the greediness of the starved put them all into his mouth. With a cry like the bellow of a bull he ducked his head in the stream. He was burning up. The fire that he was used to was nothing compared to the fire from chili peppers that now devoured him.

But he went on, more determined than ever to know all about the land that he had come to see. That afternoon he saw something that, had he not been a devil, would have reminded him of heaven. The ripest of purple figs were growing on a plant that was not a fig tree.

"Here," thought Satan, "is something I can eat without any fear. I remember seeing figs like these in the Garden of Eden." Hungrily he reached for one, but at the first bite he threw it away with a cry of pain. His mouth and tongue were full of thorns. With an oath and a groan he turned from the prickly pear and continued his journey.

Late that same day, just before sunset, he heard the barking of dogs. He continued in that direction from whence the sound came, and soon he came to a ranch house. A group of men, dressed like Pedro de Urdemañas—that new arrival in Hell who had sent him to Texas—ran here and there on horses gesticulating. The sight of them rather cheered Satan up.

And then he saw what Pedro told him he resembled—a cow. Here was a blow indeed. Could he, the king of Hell, look like one of those insipid creatures, devoid of all character and expression? Ah, he would get even with Pedro on his return and send him to the seventh hell, where the greatest sinners were and the fire burnt the hottest. His reflections were interrupted by something that filled him with wonder. One of the mounted men threw a cow down by merely touching its tail. "How marvelous!" thought Satan. "I'll learn the trick so I can have fun with the other devils when I go back home."

He approached one of the *vaqueros* and in the suavest of tones said, "My friend, will you tell me what you did to make the lady cow fall?"

The cowboy looked at the city man in surprise, and with a wink at those around him replied, "Sure, just squeeze its tail."

Satan approached the nearest cow—an old gentle milk cow—gingerly, and squeezed its tail with all his might.

Now, as all of you know, no decent cow will allow any one, even though it be the king of Devils, to take such familiarity with her. She ceased chewing her cud, and, gathering all her strength in her hind legs, shot out a kick that sent Satan whirling through the air.

Very much upset and chagrined, he got up. But what hurt more were the yells of derision that greeted him. Without even looking back, he ran hell-bound, and did not stop until he got home. The first thing he did on his arrival was to expel Pedro from the infernal region. He would have nothing to do with one who had been the cause of his humiliation. And since then Satan has never been in Texas, and Pedro de Urdemañas still wanders through the Texas ranches always in the shape of some fun-loving *vaquero.*

Repaying Good with Evil

One time a rattlesnake got caught under a rock so that he could not move. A duck came walking along, and the rattlesnake called out, "Brother Duck, please shove this rock so that I can free myself."

"With all pleasure," said the duck, and he shoved the rock with his strong breast.

As soon as the rattlesnake was free, he said: "I have been held prisoner a long time and am hungry. I will eat you." He was in front of the duck and ready to strike, and the duck was without power to run.

"No," said the duck, "that would not be just."

"Why not just?" asked the rattlesnake.

"I have done you a good deed, and like a Christian you should do as you would be done by," the duck said.

"But do you not know," responded the rattlesnake, "that a good deed is repaid with evil?"

"No, I do not know that," the duck said. "Let us find a judge."

"The truth is so well known that I agree to leave the matter to a judge," said the rattlesnake.

So the two started off, the rattlesnake keeping close to the duck. Before they had gone very far they came upon a venerable burro.

"Here is a sage being," the rattlesnake said. "Ask him if a good deed is not repaid with an evil one."

The duck put the question to the burro.

"Yes," replied the burro, "a good deed is always repaid with an evil one. Behold me. For a lifetime, I worked for my master. I worked when I had nothing to eat. I worked whether it was hot or cold, wet or dry. I worked without complaint, always steadily, even if not swiftly. With reason I was trusted. What is the result? Now that I am old and weak and my back is one great sore from packsaddles, my master has turned me out to starve. In the end, nothing but evil is paid for good."

From *The Voice of the Coyote,* by J. Frank Dobie, pp. 309–311. Copyright, 1947, 1949, by the Curtis Publishing Company; 1949, by J. Frank Dobie. Boston: Little, Brown and Company.

One August day in the year 1936 I was at a small ranch leased by my brother in the Brush Country about fifty miles north of the Rio Grande. There were two men besides myself: a coyote trapper working for the government, and a vaquero named Mariano. Mariano lived by himself but had an ancient Ford car, his *cucaracha,* in which he occasionally drove to town. On this particular morning his saddle horse came up missing; not a horse could be caught, and the "cockroach" did "not wish to go." As Mariano said, it was "Sunday with us." I watched the panting paisanos water at the tank; I pumped the trapper for all the coyote lore he knew; then I begged Mariano to tell me a coyote story. This is what he told.—J.F.D.

"One judge is not enough," said the duck. "Let us consult another."

"I accept," said the rattlesnake. "You will see."

The two went on. Soon they came upon an ox. He was lying down chewing his cud, but from the way his bones stuck out it was plain that he had little to eat.

"There is a calm and just judge," said the rattlesnake. "State the case to him."

The duck asked the ox the same question he had asked the burro.

"We judge by what we know," replied the ox. "Look at me. For many years I pulled my master's plow and his cart and the sled on which water was hauled to his cabin. It was work, work, work. I was tired at times, but I was always patient and I always pulled when the word was given. Now what is the result? I no longer have strength. My legs tremble with my own weight. So I have been turned out to graze, but not that I may have rest and be free. Oh, no. My master thinks that this skeleton will gain a little flesh. Then he will butcher me to make jerky out of my flesh and soup out of my bones. A good deed is repaid with an evil deed. That is my judgment."

"These judges are prejudiced," said the duck. "I appeal the case to that coyote I see coming yonder. Get between me and him and ask him the question."

"I am willing to give you the benefit of the wise," the rattlesnake replied. The coyote came near, and the rattlesnake stated the case to him.

The coyote scratched his ear. "Before I render a decision," he said, "I will have to be shown exactly in what position you were when the duck freed you."

This answer pleased the duck, and the rattlesnake was willing to demonstrate. So all three went back to the rock that had been on the rattlesnake's back.

"Now lie down and allow me to place the rock just as it was before the duck rolled it off you," the coyote said.

The rattlesnake placed himself in position and the coyote pushed the rock on top of him.

"Is that how you were?" asked the coyote.

"Exactly thus," responded the rattlesnake.

"Then stay that way," the coyote laughed. "If good is repaid with evil, this time the evil brings good to the duck."

The Devil and the Lord

One day when the sun was so hot that it seemed to shine through even the thickest leaves, our Lord Jesus, who is master of all that is good, and the Devil, who is master of all that is bad, walked side by

From *The Devil in Texas,* by Frank Goodwyn, pp. 11–13. Copyright, 1936, by Dealey and Lowe. Dallas, Texas.

side across hot sands that were shaded by the thin-leaved trees of this country. If any man had seen them, he could have easily known that they were arguing.

"Satan," our good Lord was saying, "you are very mischievous. Why don't you try to do good things sometimes?"

"My Lord," replied the Devil, "you ask too much of me. I cannot be good. I have been bad too long. I would not have the faith of mankind which is needed to make creatures act nobly. Even if I should do a good deed, I would still be branded as a wicked creature."

"You speak very foolishly," said our Lord.

"No," said the Devil, "I speak the truth. Let me prove it to you. Do you see that muddy lake among those drooping trees yonder?"

"Yes."

"And do you see that brindle cow which is wading out into that lake for a drink of water?"

"Yes."

"Very well, my Lord. Now, with your power, let me see you cause that cow to be bogged in that mud."

Our Lord Jesus raised his hand and called upon the Almighty One. At once, the cow sank to her belly in the soft mud and began to struggle and grunt helplessly.

"And now," said the Devil, "let us hide behind this prickly pear to see what will happen."

So they hid behind the prickly pear. Soon, a cowboy came riding by the lake and saw the poor cow which our Lord Jesus had caused to be bogged in the mud.

"For the sake of Heaven!" exclaimed the cowboy. "Look at that poor cow bogged to her belly in the soft mud. I shall go and bring my friends to help me get this poor helpless cow out. Surely, the Devil has been near this lake, for only the Devil himself could do such a bad deed as this."

"You see," whispered the Devil to our Lord, "I am blamed for all bad things even though you, my Lord, may ordain them. Now watch me, and I shall do a good deed. I shall get the cow out, and you may see what happens.

As soon as the cowboy had gone, the Devil ran out along the edge of the lake, flopped his tail, rattled his teeth, and blinked his eyes. At once, the cow was raised from the mud and walked easily from the lake.

Before long, the cowboy returned with three friends to help save the cow and the Devil hid again with our good Lord behind the prickly pear. When the cowboy and his friends found that the cow was now out of the mud, they threw up their hands and exclaimed: "For the sake of Heaven! How did that cow get out of the mud? Surely, our good Lord, Jesus, has been near this lake, for only He Himself could do such a good deed as this!"

"You see," whispered the Devil, "even if I should be good, it would help me none, for all good deeds are thrown at your feet and all the bad deeds are thrown at mine. When good deeds are done, you get the glory. When bad deeds are done, I get the blame, regardless of who does the deeds themselves. And so, I am punished for all the evils of men, while you are rewarded for all the virtues of men. This is what men call 'justice.' What would it avail me if I should try to be good?"

Tomacito and the Buffalo

Tomacito was never entirely happy unless he could be doing the same things that ordinary, normal-sized humans did. He disliked exceedingly to be left out of anything that was going on, for his dignity was as great as that of any one and he especially resented ever being reminded that he was too small to do the things that other men did easily.

Two men of the village admired Tomacito immensely because of his cleverness, but nevertheless they rather disliked having him go with them on arduous or dangerous undertakings for fear that on account of his small size an accident might befall him. Tomacito, however, had the greatest confidence in himself, tiny though he was, and felt perfectly capable of giving a good account of himself on all occasions and of taking care of himself in any emergency.

One time, some of the men of Tomacito's native village were going out on the great plains beyond Las Vegas to hunt buffalo in order to lay in a supply of meat and robes for their families, and Tomacito begged to be allowed to go along, but the hunters told him most decidedly that he could not go, that he was entirely too small for such work, and would only get in their way and be stepped on by the large, hairy animals. But Tomacito would listen to no refusal and pleaded so earnestly, declaring that he would cause no trouble to any one, that he finally won the hunters' consent and they allowed him to accompany them.

Finally, after a week's travel they arrived at the plains and in sight of a large herd of buffalo; whereupon every one was seized with uncontrollable excitement, and forgetting everything else, forthwith engaged in the chase. In the great commotion that then ensued, Tomacito was quite overlooked by his companions and it was only after many buffalo had been killed and the remainder of the herd had dispersed, that any one thought of him at all. Then he could be found nowhere. His comrades searched for him diligently, called his name repeatedly, and looked for him in prairie dog and badger holes, but all without success.

Finally, the hunters were compelled to give up the quest for Tomacito, and with hearts filled with sorrow at the loss of their little companion, they returned home to their families.

From *Native Tales of New Mexico,* by Frank G. Applegate, pp. 161–165. Copyright, 1932, by J. B. Lippincott Company. Philadelphia and London.

When the villagers, who remained at home, heard the sad news about Tomacito, they were saddened and all mourned for him as dead and each contributed a little money that a tiny mass might be said for him, for they all remembered his manful and happy disposition and great courage in spite of the handicap of his miniature body.

The second season the men of the village decided to go on another hunt, and as they wended their way toward the buffalo plains, they thought sadly of Tomacito and how he had made the last journey out seem short with his merry ways. But these sad thoughts could not keep them from the work in hand, and soon they killed a large buffalo and started to butcher it, when suddenly they heard a muffled little voice calling and cursing:

"Por Dios! Por Dios! Tontos, do you know what you are doing there? You are spoiling my house and my living." And suddenly out jumped Tomacito from inside the buffalo, valiantly flourishing his tiny knife.

But when he saw his former friends and fellow villagers, he became quite as overjoyed as they at their sudden reunion. Then he related to them his adventures since he had seen them last.

When the hunters had abandoned him to chase the buffalos the previous year, he himself had become too excited to remain out of danger and had run out among the herd to hunt also. With his spear he had attacked a large buffalo as high upon his front ankle as he could reach with his spear, and the huge beast, thinking that there was a fly biting him, had reached down and licked him into his mouth and swallowed him whole.

At first, Tomacito had been a little frightened and didn't at all like the situation in which he found himself, for he missed his companions dreadfully, but he finally became used to his new life and found at least one compensation in it. He could have fresh buffalo liver every day for dinner. When his *serape* became worn out, he made himself another of buffalo wool, which later became the despair of all the Chimayo weavers for he used a single thickness of wool for each thread of both warp and woof, so that the texture of the cloth was exceedingly fine.

When the hunters returned to the village with Tomacito, every one there was exceedingly happy to see the little fellow again and they made a grand fiesta for him, at which he drank nearly half a thimble of wine, after which he boasted gloriously of his prowess as a buffalo hunter, and never did he ask to go again to the plains with the hunters, but satisfied his longings for the chase in hunting and spearing cockroaches in his mother's kitchen.

High Horse's Courting

You know, in the old days, it was not so very easy to get a girl when you wanted to be married. Sometimes it was hard work for a young man and he had to stand a great deal. Say I am a young man and I have seen a young girl who looks so beautiful to me that I feel all sick when I think about her. I can not just go and tell her about it and then get married if she is willing. I have to be a very sneaky fellow to talk to her at all, and after I have managed to talk to her, that is only the beginning.

Probably for a long time I have been feeling sick about a certain girl because I love her so much, but she will not even look at me, and her parents keep a good watch over her. But I keep feeling worse and worse all the time; so maybe I sneak up to her tepee in the dark and wait until she comes out. Maybe I just wait there all night and don't get any sleep at all and she does not come out. Then I feel sicker than ever about her.

Maybe I hide in the brush by a spring where she sometimes goes to get water, and when she comes by, if nobody is looking, then I jump out and hold her and just make her listen to me. If she likes me too, I can tell that from the way she acts, for she is very bashful and maybe will not say a word or even look at me the first time. So I let her go, and then maybe I sneak around until I can see her father alone, and I tell him how many horses I can give him for his beautiful girl, and by now I am feeling so sick that maybe I would give him all the horses in the world if I had them.

Well, this young man I am telling about was called High Horse, and there was a girl in the village who looked so beautiful to him that he was just sick all over from thinking about her so much and he was getting sicker all the time. The girl was very shy, and her parents thought a great deal of her because they were not young any more and this was the only child they had. So they watched her all day long, and they fixed it so that she would be safe at night too when they were asleep. They thought so much of her that they had made a rawhide bed for her to sleep in, and after they knew that High Horse was sneaking around after her, they took rawhide thongs and tied the girl in bed at night so that nobody could steal her when they were asleep, for they were not sure but that their girl might really want to be stolen.

Well, after High Horse had been sneaking around a good while and hiding and waiting for the girl and getting sicker all the time, he finally caught her alone and made her talk to him. Then he found out that she liked him maybe a little. Of course this did not make him feel

---

From *Black Elk Speaks,* Being the Life Story of a Holy Man of the Ogalala Sioux, as told to John G. Neihardt (Flaming Rainbow) pp. 67–76. Copyright, 1932, by John G. Neihardt. New York: William Morrow & Co.

well. It made him sicker than ever, but now he felt as brave as a bison bull, and so he went right to her father and said he loved the girl so much that he would give two good horses for her—one of them young and the other one not so very old.

But the old man just waved his hand, meaning for High Horse to go away and quit talking foolishness like that.

High Horse was feeling sicker than ever about it; but there was another young fellow who said he would loan High Horse two ponies and when he got some more horses, why, he could just give them back for the ones he had borrowed.

Then High Horse went back to the old man and said he would give four horses for the girl—two of them young and the other two not hardly old at all. But the old man just waved his hand and would not say anything.

So High Horse sneaked around until he could talk to the girl again, and he asked her to run away with him. He told her he thought he would just fall over and die if she did not. But she said she would not do that; she wanted to be bought like a fine woman. You see she thought a great deal of herself too.

That made High Horse feel so very sick that he could not eat a bite, and he went around with his head hanging down as though he might just fall down and die any time.

Red Deer was another young fellow, and he and High Horse were great comrades, always doing things together. Red Deer saw how High Horse was acting, and he said: "Cousin, what is the matter? Are you sick in the belly? You look as though you were going to die."

Then High Horse told Red Deer how it was, and said he thought he could not stay alive much longer if he could not marry the girl pretty quick.

Red Deer thought awhile about it, and then he said: "Cousin, I have a plan, and if you are man enough to do as I tell you, then everything will be all right. She will not run away with you; her old man will not take four horses; and four horses are all you can get. You must steal her and run away with her. Then afterwhile you can come back and the old man cannot do anything because she will be your woman. Probably she wants you to steal her anyway."

So they planned what High Horse had to do, and he said he loved the girl so much that he was man enough to do anything Red Deer or anybody else could think up.

So this is what they did.

That night late they sneaked up to the girl's tepee and waited until it sounded inside as though the old man and the old woman and the girl were sound asleep. Then High Horse crawled under the tepee with a knife. He had to cut the rawhide thongs first, and then Red Deer, who was pulling up the stakes around that side of the tepee, was going to help drag the girl outside and gag her. After that, High Horse could put her across his pony in front of him and hurry out of there and be happy all the rest of his life.

When High Horse had crawled inside, he felt so nervous that he could hear his heart drumming, and it seemed so loud he felt sure it would waken the old folks. But it did not, and afterwhile he began cutting the thongs. Every time he cut one it made a pop and nearly scared him to death. But he was getting along all right and all the thongs were cut down as far as the girl's thighs, when he became so nervous that his knife slipped and stuck the girl. She gave a big, loud yell. Then the old folks jumped up and yelled too. By this time High Horse was outside, and he and Red Deer were running away like antelope. The old man and some other people chased the young men but they got away in the dark and nobody knew who it was.

Well, if you ever wanted a beautiful girl you will know how sick High Horse was now. It was very bad the way he felt, and it looked as though he would starve even if he did not drop over dead sometime.

Red Deer kept thinking about this, and after a few days he went to High Horse and said: "Cousin, take courage! I have another plan, and I am sure, if you are man enough, we can steal her this time." And High Horse said: "I am man enough to do anything anybody can think up, if I can only get that girl."

So this is what they did.

They went away from the village alone, and Red Deer made High Horse strip naked. Then he painted High Horse solid white all over, and after that he painted black stripes all over the white and put black rings around High Horse's eyes. High Horse looked terrible. He looked so terrible that when Red Deer was through painting and took a good look at what he had done, he said it scared even him a little.

"Now," Red Deer said, "if you get caught again, everybody will be so scared they will think you are a bad spirit and will be afraid to chase you."

So when the night was getting old and everybody was sound asleep, they sneaked back to the girl's tepee. High Horse crawled in with his knife, as before, and Red Deer waited outside, ready to drag the girl out and gag her when High Horse had all the thongs cut.

High Horse crept up by the girl's bed and began cutting at the thongs. But he kept thinking, "If they see me they will shoot me because I look so terrible." The girl was restless and kept squirming around in bed, and when a thong was cut, it popped. So High Horse worked very slowly and carefully.

But he must have made some noise, for suddenly the old woman awoke and said to her old man: "Old Man, wake up! There is somebody in this tepee!" But the old man was sleepy and didn't want to be bothered. He said: "Of course there is somebody in this tepee. Go to sleep and don't bother me." Then he snored some more.

But High Horse was so scared by now that he lay very still and as flat to the ground as he could. Now, you see, he had not been sleeping very well for a long time because he was so sick about the girl. And while he was lying there waiting for the old woman to snore, he just forgot everything, even how beautiful the girl was. Red Deer who was lying outside ready to do his part, wondered and wondered what had happened in there, but he did not dare call out to High Horse.

Afterwhile the day began to break and Red Deer had to leave with the two ponies he had staked there for his comrade and girl, or somebody would see him.

So he left.

Now when it was getting light in the tepee, the girl awoke and the first thing she saw was a terrible animal, all white with black stripes on it, lying asleep beside her bed. So she screamed, and then the old woman screamed and the old man yelled. High Horse jumped up, scared almost to death, and he nearly knocked the tepee down getting out of there.

People were coming running from all over the village with guns and bows and axes, and everybody was yelling.

By now High Horse was running so fast that he hardly touched the ground at all, and he looked so terrible that the people fled from him and let him run. Some braves wanted to shoot at him, but the others said he might be some sacred being and it would bring bad trouble to kill him.

High Horse made for the river that was near, and in among the brush he found a hollow tree and dived into it. Afterwhile some braves came there and he could hear them saying that it was some bad spirit that had come out of the water and gone back in again.

That morning the people were ordered to break camp and move away from there. So they did, while High Horse was hiding in his hollow tree.

Now Red Deer had been watching all this from his own tepee and trying to look as though he were as much surprised and scared as all the others. So when the camp moved, he sneaked back to where he had seen his comrade disappear. When he was down there in the brush, he called, and High Horse answered, because he knew his friend's voice. They washed off the paint from High Horse and sat down on the river bank to talk about their troubles.

High Horse said he never would go back to the village as long as he lived and he did not care what happened to him now. He said he was going to go on the war-path all by himself. Red Deer said: "No, cousin, you are not going on the war-path alone, because I am going with you."

So Red Deer got everything ready, and at night they started out on the war-path all alone. After several days they came to a Crow camp just about sundown, and when it was dark they sneaked up to where the Crow horses were grazing, killed the horse guard, who was not thinking about enemies because he thought all the Lakotas were far away, and drove off about a hundred horses.

They got a big start because all the Crow horses stampeded and it was probably morning before the Crow warriors could catch any horses to ride. Red Deer and High Horse fled with their herd three days and nights before they reached the village of their people. Then they drove the whole herd right into the village and up in front of the girl's tepee. The old man was there, and High Horse called out to him and asked if he thought maybe that would be enough horses for his girl. The old man did not wave him away that time. It was not the horses that he wanted. What he wanted was a son who was a real man and good for something.

So High Horse got his girl after all, and I think he deserved her.

Strong Medicine

Very long ago, before we obtained horses, when we used dogs to draw and to carry our belongings, there came a time when our Ka'ina (Blood) tribe made a peace agreement with the Crees. For several winters after that, members of the two tribes frequently visited one another.

Came to the Ka'ina camp, one day, a number of Cree visitors, and were welcomed in the lodges of their friends. One of the Crees, a big, fine-appearing man, visiting here and there in the camp, saw a very beautiful young woman, and wanted her, although back in the camp of his own people he had three women. He began following this young woman about, and at last, getting a chance to speak to her out of hearing of others, he asked her to go with him to his camp, become his woman. That made her very angry; she called him a dog face; told him to go away and never again speak to her. He laughed, told her that she would become his woman later on.

Some days after this, the young woman was out with others, picking berries, when the Cree suddenly ran in among them and seized her and made her run off with him, threatening to stab her with his big flint

---

From *The Sun God's Children,* by James Willard Schultz and Jessie Louise Donaldson, with portraits of Blackfeet Indians by Winold Reiss, pp. 237–243. Copyright, 1930, by James Willard Schultz and Winold Reiss. Boston and New York: Houghton Mifflin Company.

One evening in our Waterton Lakes Park camp, when a number of guests of the big hotel came to sit with us around our lodge fire and listen to our talk—interpreted to them, of course—I said to Old Ahko Mukstokigs (Many Big Ears, Blackfeet name for mules), "Old friend, it is now for you to tell of your fighting days."

"Tonight, why not something different?" he queried. "So far, all our talk here has been of war. Oh, I went against enemy tribes many times, counted *coups* on two Crees, two Kalispels, one Assiniboin, one Crow, that I killed on different raids; stole many horses, and one woman, a woman of the River People. But somehow I don't feel like talking of all that, to-night. It is this that has been in my thoughts all day, and I think that it will interest you. . . ."—J.W.S. and J.L.D.

knife if she held back. The other women hurried in to camp and told of her seizure by the Cree. Her man was out hunting; she had no near relatives; the visiting Crees said that the one who had stolen her was a very dangerous man, for he had a medicine that enabled him to kill people without striking them himself. So was it that none attempted to trail the stealer and rescue the woman.

The woman's man, Big Elk, did not return from his hunt until the following day. And upon learning that the Cree had stolen his woman he became very angry. Were all the men of his tribe cowards, that they did not run after the thief and kill him? he asked. Well, he himself was no coward. What if the thief did have a powerful medicine? He was going right to the Cree camp and take his woman. Yes, there were others who had a powerful medicine. He had one. He would soon learn which was the more powerful of the two.

Two days later, Big Elk entered the Cree camp, went to the chief of the tribe, and complained of the thief; asked for help in recovering his woman. The chief replied that the man had a medicine so powerful that none dared anger him.

"I will see how powerful he is. Which of these is his lodge?"

The chief pointed to it. Big Elk went quickly to it, entered, sat down just inside the doorway. On the women's side of the lodge was his woman. Upon his couch in the rear of the lodge, sat the thief.

"My woman, I have come for you," said Big Elk. His woman made no reply to that; she was crying; she held out her hands to him, but at once dropped them in her lap when the thief shouted to Big Elk:

"You can't have the woman. You go from my lodge at once."

"I will go from it with my woman. I have come for her. I shall have her," Big Elk replied.

"Never again will she be your woman. She is mine. I shall keep her. And now I tell you this: leave my lodge at once, return to your people, or you shall die right here. I have a powerful medicine; I shall cause it to kill you, right there where you sit, if you do not do as I say," shouted the Cree.

"Try it. I am not afraid of your medicine."

"Twice, now, I have told you to leave my lodge. Again I tell you, go, or suffer a terrible death."

Big Elk made no answer to that; just sat down and stared at the Cree. Said the Cree: "Again, and for the last time, I tell you to leave my lodge at once."

No reply.

That was the fourth time that he had been ordered to leave the lodge, and he knew, did Big Elk, that the Cree would now attempt to carry out his threat. But still he did not move, just sat there motionless staring straight into his enemy's eyes.

The Cree took from the head of his couch a quill-embroidered, red-painted sack, opened it, brought out a small image of a man, set it upright upon the ground, and said to Big Elk: "There he is, my powerful medicine. He will go over to you, kill you right there where you sit."

"Good. Tell him to come."

The Cree spoke to the image, and it started walking around the fireplace and toward Big Elk. And said the Cree: "Your end is near; when he reaches you, he will kill you."

"Never will he get me," said Big Elk, and brought out his own medicine, an image of a spider; made of soft deer leather, embroidered with quills of various colors. He prayed to it, a short little prayer, set it upon the ground, and it started running toward the man image; got near it, cast an end of its body thread around the neck of the image, then ran across the lodge and to a pole, and up it, trailing its body thread as it went. Then, when well up the pole, it began to draw in the thread, and soon the noosed image was pulled from the ground, slowly was drawn up, higher and higher, nearer to the drawer, the spider image.

The women cried out at this strange sight, and the Cree thief stared at his medicine image with eyes of fear.

Then said Big Elk to the thief: "Your medicine that you said was so powerful, it is worthless, a nothing-medicine. When my spider draws it all the way up, seizes and bites it into small pieces, then do you die, right there where you sit."

The thief stared at Big Elk with fear, his lips trembled; he held out trembling hands and cried: "Pity me. Do not let your spider seize my little man. I give you back your woman; take her and go."

Big Elk made no answer to that. He sat there smiling, singing very softly the song of his spider image. The man image rose higher and higher, twirling this way, that way, and when it was but a little way from the spider image, the Cree thief began to cry, and whimpered to Big Elk: "Do not let your spider draw my man any higher; I give not only your woman; I also give you my weasel-skin war shirt, my eagle-tail feathered war bonnet, my weapons, all else of mine that you may like. Pity me, great chief, allow me to live."

"Your medicine, then, is a useless medicine, without power?"

"Just that; powerless. Pity me. Let me live."

Big Elk laughed. Spoke to his spider image, and it let the man image drop to the ground, and there it lay, neither the Cree thief nor his women paying any attention to it. The spider descended the pole, walked over to Big Elk, and he took it up and put it back in his medicine sack. And then said to the Cree: "I want two of your dogs with the travois that they draw. Load upon the travois your war clothes, and the other things that you gave me; also some food, and several good robes. Do this; have your women do it quickly, if you want to live."

The thief spoke to his women; they hurried to get the dogs and travois, and loaded them with the valuable things. When that was done, Big Elk said to the Cree: "Well, we go, my woman and I. Come again to my camp and steal her. Come soon."

And with that, the two left the lodge, and, leading the dogs, went their homeward way.

Woman-Who-Lived-With-Wolves

Queer things happened around the "Fork"—where the Cheyenne River came in. Not far up the stream on Cherry Creek, a young Sioux matron had a violent quarrel with her man. It was wintertime, cold and snowing, but she was so angry that she left the camp, taking no food and only the clothes she wore, striking out blindly into the storm. All that day and night she kept on, hungry and cold, trying to get as far away as possible before the snow stopped falling; for then, she knew, her tracks would be visible and her relatives would be able to find her. She was bitterly determined never to go home again.

When the snow stopped falling, she halted, fearing to make tracks. Then she noticed that the wind had swept the slope of the hill above her partly bare. She thought she would go up there, away from the trail, where she could leave no tracks.

As she went on, tired, chilled through, and hungry, she stumbled on the mouth of a small cave. It appeared to be empty. She crawled in, pulled her blanket over her head, and fell into a shivering sleep.

After a bit she ceased to shiver, dimly feeling a glow of warmth on either side. Warm fur touched her cold hands. She relaxed and fell sound asleep.

When she woke in that narrow den, she looked up at the yellow eyes, white fangs, and lolling tongues of four big gray buffalo wolves. They sat on their haunches close about her, regarding her with fixed attention. Frightened, she caught her breath and sat up. The wolves got to their feet, seemed to smile, and whined a little, making friendly noises which she interpreted, in her Indian way, as human talk. Her fear melted. She spoke to them.

The wolves left her to hunt, and when they returned, the biggest came dragging in a chunk of raw meat. She was too hungry to mind that—she ate her fill. *Washtay!* That was good.

Having been thus accepted by the wolves, she set up housekeeping among them and every day prepared the meat which they brought in, making pemmican and clothing for herself from the hides of deer pulled down by her new furry brothers.

Indians on Cherry Creek who remember her say that she stayed one whole winter in the wolf den, but that no Sioux ever discovered her hideout. Chief White Bull, who knew her well, told me that she cooked her own meat, building a fire in a hole at night so that no one could see her smoke. Being a well-trained, competent young woman, she man-

---

From *The Missouri,* by Stanley Vestal, pp. 151–155. Rivers of America, edited by Hervey Allen. Copyright, 1945, by Walter Stanley Campbell. New York and Toronto: Farrar & Rinehart, Inc.

Cf. "The Wolf Boy," as told by Tsa-to-ke to B. A. Botkin, *Folk-Say,* edited by B. A. Botkin (Norman, 1929), pp. 32–36; L. D. Bertillion, "The Lobo Girl of Devil's River," *A Treasury of American Folklore* (New York, 1944), pp. 758–763.

aged to live quite comfortably, and quite as happily as ever did Mowgli or Romulus.

All things come to an end in time. And one day it seemed to her that the wolves told her she must go. She was not to live with them any more.

But Woman-Who-Lived-With-Wolves was in no mood to return to her family in the Sioux camp. She no longer felt any love for her relatives, and she knew that her marvelous experience had set her off from all other women in the tribe. She was now a medicine woman. Still, she was lonely without the wolves.

One spring morning a party of young men from the Sioux camp rode out looking for wild horses. They saw a cloud on the prairie—so much dust that it was hard to tell just what was causing it. But they slipped up the coulee toward the dust, they saw it was a band of mares closely guarded by a handsome spotted stallion. The young men uncoiled their lariats and quirted their ponies into a run. They hoped that they might capture some good horses, for the grass was not yet high and the animals were lean and might tire quickly. Charging in from three sides, the hunters gradually overtook the herd. The frightened mares would have scattered, but the stallion, racing from side to side of his galloping harem, nipped and pawed at every straggler and kept the mares in a compact bunch. He set a fast pace.

Finally, however, the Sioux closed in and separated the stallion from his mares. Then all the animals scattered over the prairie.

Soon after, one of the hunters dimly saw through the dust cloud some creature—not a horse—running among the animals. He could not tell what it was at first. Then he saw it was an Indian woman.

He called to her. But she did not stop; she ran on and on, sprinting over the prairie. All the riders took after her. One of them dropped a noose over her shoulders and stopped her in her tracks. Others rode up, jumped from their horses, caught her arms. She fought like a wild thing, snarling, biting, clawing, glaring wildly at them through her long flying hair; but she had no chance. They held her. They recognized her as the runaway wife.

Some of the young men thought she must have been running with the horses. But White Bull told me this seemed unlikely. Said he, "How could a person get meat while running with a herd of horses? She would starve—even if the animals had been willing to let her run with them."

It seems more likely that she just happened to be in the path of the wild horses as they fled from the hunters, and that they passed and left her in the dust to be taken by the young men.

The hunters took the wild woman back to camp.

There her relatives made her welcome, but she, wary as a wolf, sat still, making no sound. But the women of her family gentled her, combing her hair, painting her face, dressing her in new clothing, and so by slow degrees restored her to something like a normal state of mind.

At length she told her curious, pitiful relatives something of her strange adventures. Other people dared not question her. She was now a famous medicine woman, a person of supernatural powers—powers that were feared, envied, and sought after. For to the Indian, anything sufficiently unusual to seem unnatural was believed supernatural. Apparently she used her powers to help her people.

Other persons in the tribe who had been favored with gifts of mysterious power naturally wished to test the strength of this new rival, and a contest was arranged at which White Bull and Boat-Upper-Lip challenged Woman-Who-Lived-With-Wolves to compete with them.

This contest was held in public, and each contestant exerted his power to "kill" or overcome the power of his opponents. They stood some distance apart, and, holding missiles charged with power in their palms, "shot" these at their rivals to see whose power was strongest. Boat-Upper-Lip and Woman-Who-Lived-With-Wolves combined to overthrow White Bull. They shot bumblebees, grasshoppers, and rolled up buffalo hairs at him. But his power was strong and he withstood them, keeping his feet and his courage.

When his turn came, White Bull faced his two rivals. He was encouraged by the fact that they had not been able to make him pass out; but it remained to be seen whether his medicine was strong enough to bowl them over.

Staring fixedly at them, he held in his hand some of those small worms which come out of the forehead of an elk. Gesturing at them as though throwing these, he "hit" them both. They could not repel his medicine. First one and then the other fell unconscious. Victor, White Bull then magnanimously used his power to revive his defeated rivals. He drew the missile worms out of their bodies and brought them to. After that everyone in camp believed that the elk was a real helper to White Bull—his medicine was strong.

In spite of such a public setback, Woman-Who-Lived-With-Wolves was highly respected throughout the rest of her long life. Some of her relatives still live along the Missouri, and your Indian friends will, if you like, lead you to the cave where she kept house through that long winter for her brothers, the wolves.

The Enchanted Mesa

Among so warlike a people as the Indians it is not surprising to find legends of wholesale massacre. Indeed, it is alleged by the story-tellers of the Caddo tribe that a cannibal company in Oklahoma surrounded their neighbors—in the most literal meaning of that term—and that the neighbors revenged themselves by surrounding the cannibals in the more usual meaning and killed them, to the last one, not a babe being spared. But not all these deaths were ill deserved, and not all,

---

From *American Myths and Legends,* by Charles M. Skinner, Vol. II, pp. 139–142.

even among the fighters, came in war. Sad was the fate that befell the Acomas of New Mexico. Seventy-five miles southwest of Albuquerque stands their old home, the Mesa Encantada (the Enchanted Mesa) of Katzimo. This table of rock, covering forty acres, with a ground-plan like a figure 8, rises to a height of four hundred and fifty feet, with precipitous sides, and was never scaled, within the memory of living men, until 1897. Three hundred feet above the plain was a great opening like a cathedral arch, which was the entrance to a stair leading through a crevice in the rock to the summit, where was once a town of fifteen hundred people living in this manner, after the fashion of the pueblos of this day, because of security against the Apaches. From the plain to the arch was an outer stair of stone spiring up the sides of a great column, canted against the mesa; and down to the plain came the men, every day, to work in the maize-fields and berry-patches, to hunt, and to make pottery.

It was while they were so employed that the storm occurred which broke away the outer steps, tumbling them on the heads of twenty of the men who had gathered near for shelter, and leaving three hundred women and children in their houses on the summit, cut off, as on an island, without food. All attempts of theirs to descend, and those of the men to climb, were futile, while the best archers could not shoot far enough to send pieces of game up on their arrows. The men waited below in agony, looking up at the faces of their wives and little ones as they bent over the brink and strained their fading eyes on them. One woman, crazed by thirst, leaped off. Fewer were the faces, day by day, until at last there were none. Then the survivors gathered their few belongings and built another home on a mesa two miles distant—Acoma, city of the sky.

Before this time the Spaniards had reached this country, and in their greed for gold, which they believed to abound here, were abusing the people, although the monks who traveled with them preached a religion of love to the red men. Outraged beyond endurance, the Acomas attacked the Spaniards who had settled about the Mesa Encantada and slew every one of them, except a priest. This worthy father was in the town on the summit when the attack was made, and, believing himself pursued, he leaped from the edge; but to the marvel of none more than himself he descended through space in safety. This salvation he ascribed to his religion; but his big zarape, that opened like a parachute and buoyed him up, may have had something to do with it. The natives, believing that he possessed supernatural power, spared his life, on condition that he cease from preaching doctrines to them that were irrevocably associated in their minds with robbery and slaughter. Taking a squaw to wife, he lived among them in fair content thenceforward; and strangers think they discern traces of Spanish lineage in the faces of some of the Acomas. In 1897 a government exploring party, under Professor Hodge, reached the top of the

Enchanted Mesa and found proof of its ancient occupancy in chips and tools of stone, pottery, and relics of masonry, as well as a part of the old trail.

The Miracle of Sanctuario

. . . It was some years after the Chimayo Rebellion in 1837 that a priest came to the settlements on the upper Santa Cruz, which are known under the collective name of Chimayo. He ministered to the people who were without a church, and after a while asked them to build a chapel on a spot he had selected. But the people were too indifferent and refused to heed the admonition. One day the priest disappeared and the next morning, from a cottonwood tree that stood on the spot designated by the priest for a chapel, there protruded a foot. The people were so impressed with the miracle that they built the chapel and made it the most beautiful church in all of New Mexico. From the nearby mountains were brought the beams that formed the "vegas" of the ceiling. These rested on corbels that were cut into realistic shape and embellished with harmonious designs. They carved images of Santiago and San Rafael, they painted on wood a wonderful altar picture, and even the railing of the altar was hand-chiseled. Last of all, they carved out of wood the image of a Christ child. On its feet they put shoes. But lo and behold, the next morning the shoes of the Christ child were worn out. New sandals were fashioned, but each morning they had to be replaced. At the same time, sickness disappeared, the crops were abundant, the numbers of sheep multiplied, better markets were found for the Chimayo blankets woven in the homes, and the Chimayos prospered wonderfully. It was evident that the Christ child each night went up and down the valley to bless the people and its households. The story of the miracle spread abroad. The earth on which the chapel stood became holy ground and the clay that formed the floor of the tiny side chapel of San Rafael healed the pilgrims who came from far and near. The place was called "Sanctuario," and to this day pilgrims from as far away as Colorado, Texas, and Arizona come to the chapel to be cured of bodily ills and receive a spiritual blessing. Offerings of those who have been healed are placed upon the altar, and votive candles on the ground in front of the altar are kept constantly burning.

Stories are told of the cures effected by the holy clay from the little chapel of San Rafael, where a good sized well or kiva has been dug in the floor by believers removing the sanctified earth . . .

From "A New Mexico Lourdes," by Paul A. F. Walter, *El Palacio,* Journal of the Museum of New Mexico, Vol. III (January, 1916), No. 2, p. 3. Santa Fe: The Archaeological Society of New Mexico.

The Buried Treasure of Cochiti

Very long time ago—maybe three or four hundred year ago—when the Spaniards first come to this country they are trying to find some gold all the time and they ask from us Indians to tell to them where is gold. But we tell to them we do not know it what is gold. Then they show us a little which is gold and we see it is seed of the sun which we call it then, but we say to them we do not know where is any of it, for we do not wish them to get any of it, for it is sacred thing for us and only our cacique has some of it and use it for ceremonies to the sun and it would be bad thing for us if the Spaniards get any of it from us.

The Spaniards go away then that time but a little after they come back again to our pueblo with soldiers and padres and they say they wish to make all us savage Cochiti Indians to stop our own religion and be only Catholics. Our cacique do not like this and think the padre wish to make all us Indians to be witches and to take away from us our seed of the sun, so when the soldiers are go away we drive the padre away also and when the Spanish soldiers come to fight us for doing so we all run away from our pueblo and go to the Potrero Viejo towards the mountains above the Cañado de Cochiti where we used to live a long time ago at that time and we take with us all the seed of the sun which we have and also all the turquoise and some ceremonial things from the pueblo so that the Spanish cannot find them.

Soon after that we find the Spanish soldiers are coming to the potrero to fight with us because we have scare the padre away from our pueblo. Then the old men do not know what to do with the gold and other things because they are afraid the Spaniards will get them when they fight us. So we hold a council so we know what we will do. At council we think it is better to hide them and some of us want to bury them under a big rock and some of us want to hide them in a cave that is in the canyon, but the others think maybe the Spaniards or some of the Indians they have with them will find the things if we do that. Then the old cacique, who say nothing before, say it is better to bury them under the water of the rito which runs through the canyon,

---

From "The Buried Treasure of Cochiti," by Frank G. Applegate, *Folk-Say,* A Regional Miscellany: 1930, edited by B. A. Botkin, pp. 215-218. Copyright, 1930, by B. A. Botkin. Norman, Oklahoma: University of Oklahoma Press.

In one Indian pueblo, that of Cochiti, I have found very strong and persistent belief in buried Indian treasure. The story of this buried treasure was told me by an intelligent Indian of Cochiti who has been three times governor of that pueblo, and this Indian's convictions as to the truth of his story could be judged from his sincere and serious air when telling it.

This Indian had had the story from his father, also a leading man of the pueblo, and he from his father, and so on back to the time when the treasure had been buried. My Indian friend told me the story of the buried treasure as follows.—F.G.A.

for then the Spaniards cannot find it. So we decide that way is best and the old cacique and the one who will be cacique when the old one dies bury it that night under the water when no one can see where they are, for the cacique thinks that if we all know where the things are buried some of us might tell the Spanish if they capture us and hurt us to make us tell.

The next day we have a big fight with the Spanish soldiers who have guns, while we have only bows and arrows, so many of us are killed and our old cacique and the one who helped him were also killed and we do not know what place under the water they bury the gold and other things.

We make peace with the Spanish after that and come and make our pueblo where it is now and all the time since then we have hunt for those things that are buried. I hunt many times myself, for my father say it is there and he hunt too and all the other Cochitis from old time hunt also, but we never let the Spanish people see us hunt. One Cochiti one time tell some Spanish we hide things in a cave in the canyon and all the time the Mexicans look in caves in the canyons to find the gold and one time they break a big ceremonial mountain lion of stone which we have on another potrero from old time, for they think maybe the gold is buried under it, but they do not find it.

One time one Indian of Cochiti who is a very funny Indian tell some Mexicans who show him some gold that he knows where is much of such stuff in one place in the mountains. He say he see it many times when he is hunting but he do not know what is gold and just think it is some kind of yellow rock. He say he will with kindness show his friends the Mexicans where it is. So he take them up the canyon to the mountains by a very hard trail he knows. It is a very long way and the Mexicans get very tired and ask where is the gold and the Indian say, "Very soon now." After while night is coming and they are very high on a mountain. Then the Indian say he have lost the trail and for them to wait a minute while he hunt for it. But he do not hunt for it, but go to his home and leave the Mexicans. This Indian laugh very much for himself and tell us other Indians and we laugh much also.

The Mexicans wait a long time for him to come back to find the gold and they do not find the way to their home till the next night and they say to us that when they come down the canyon the next night they see woodpeckers, jays, owls, crows, and bats flying to the big cave near the place where all of our people are killed long time ago in the fight with the Spanish. They say they watch and all these birds make a big noise when they get into the cave and then they see the back of the cave open and it is all light behind it with big fires and all the birds go in there and the back shut up again.

Then they say they hear a big noise from behind the back of the cave like it was Indians singing and yelling and giving the war whoops and dancing and the Mexicans say the birds are all turn to the witch spirits of old time Indians who go in the cave at night and look like birds and then change to Indian witches and that these witches watch the gold and have it *encantada* so no one can get it again. The Mexicans run away from there that evening and do not go there any more at night. But we Indians know the gold and other things are not hid in a cave, but are buried under the water of the rito. But we have never find them because the cacique is killed before he can tell us where it is he bury them, so now our cacique has got only a little seed of the sun in a little deerskin bag that he use for medicine.

"Do you think there was much gold buried by the cacique under the water?" I asked my Indian friend, and he answered, "I do not know, but I do not think so very much. I think the most things the cacique bury are turquoise and wampum and ceremonial things for our religion. I think we never have much gold."

Plenty Coups' Story of Skeleton Cliff

Above the town of Billings, Montana, and overlooking all the beautiful valley of the Yellowstone with its houses clustered thick, its winding river, its wheat and bean and beet fields, towers a butte known as "Skeleton Cliff."

That shale-ribbed butte, tipped by its groves of pine trees, is a tome, each tree and rock a page upon which have been recorded the tragedies of a vanished race of Indian braves and the adventures of frontiersmen, many of whom followed the buffalo trail to their undoing.

On or near the butte, for the past two hundred years, have occurred repeatedly the momentous events that have made Montana history. Above it looms "Kelly Mountain," on whose topmost peak is the grave of Captain Kelly, "The Little Man with the Big Heart," who spent the daring young years of his life making of the valley a safe abode for coming generations. He knew this country when it was hideous with the war cry of Indians, and when its breast was dyed red by the blood of the hunted buffalo and by the blood of the whites and the reds who battled for supremacy over the contested land.

Farmers have supplanted hunters and warriors. Wheat fields cover the buffalo trail that Kelly followed so often on his jogging Indian pony. Automobile highways circle hills that but half a century ago served as ambush for lurking Blackfeet and Sioux, ready with bow and arrow. And Kelly sleeps his last sleep above that valley where, so he tells us, he spent the happiest years of his life as plainsman and scout, the valley he helped prepare for civilization.

On another butte above Skeleton Cliff, to the right of Kelly Mountain, stands the monument of another plainsman, still living, Bill

---

From *Blankets and Moccasins,* by Glendolin Damon Wagner and Dr. William A. Allen (White Eagle), pp. 200–211. Copyright, 1933, by The Caxton Printers, Ltd. Caldwell, Idaho.

Hart. Immortalized in bronze, he leans against his horse, Paint, and rolls a cigarette as he gazes out across the valley where his adventurous youth was spent.

Below Skeleton Cliff, just across the winding road that was once a buffalo trail leading from the plains over rimrocks and through Alkali Pass to the Yellowstone River, is "Boot Hill" Cemetery. The low hill is dotted with the graves of Dan Lahey, Bill Preston, Muggins Taylor, Dave Courier—all those hot-headed, quick-shooting, dare-devil man-children who challenged death with every breath they drew and loved the tonic sense of danger.

When Doctor Allen—young Doc Allen then—first came to the Yellowstone Valley and set up a dental-barber-blacksmith shop, Kelly was dashing gayly over the plains from Yellowstone River to Cañon Creek, hunting, scouting, and incidentally putting the fear of the law into the hearts of wild red men. There was no Billings. The town of Coulson on the south bank of the Yellowstone was in its infancy and its enterprising citizens were bemoaning the deplorable fact that their town could not boast a cemetery because, as yet, no one had died.

"And," they argued, sadly, "a town ain't a real town without a cemetery."

Their discontent, however, soon ceased to find cause upon which to thrive, for, in the midst of their grumbling, John Alderson killed Dave Courier in a quarrel concerning squatter rights. And those same men who had bemoaned the lack of a graveyard bore Dave very tenderly up to the low hill just below Skeleton Cliff and buried him there, with his boots on. A long line of mourners, roughly clad, heavily booted, stood with heads bared reverently, an expression of solemnity on their weather-beaten faces, while clods of dirt fell upon what had once been "Dave." Bill Hamilton was there and Ed and Charlie Newman, Muggins Taylor, Skookum Jo, Sam Alexander, and Bud McAdow, their boisterous high spirits hushed by this first visit of death.

The town of Coulson had its graveyard, and the famous "Boothill" cemetery its first victim.

At that time, just above the hill with its one lonely grave, was a clump of pine trees clinging to the shale ribs of Skeleton Cliff. Often, from the door of his shop in Coulson, Doc Allen had noticed hawks and crows hovering thick above that spot. And when there was a breeze, he saw long streamers of gaudy hue floating out from the pines. Finally, his curiosity sufficiently aroused, Allen crossed the river in his boat and climbed the rimrock to that particular clump of pine trees on Skeleton Cliff which held such attraction for the birds.

He peered up into the branches, to shrink back from the sight confronting him. It was a ghastly joke that while the town of Coulson had been lamenting its dearth of dead men these trees were drooping under the weight of their dead.

For each tree there was one skeleton or more, perhaps a hundred all told, seeming to grin with ghoulish mirth as they dipped and swayed and rattled their bones, dangling from branches in the breeze. Bright blankets had apparently been used as shrouds, swathing the bodies, and these blankets, rotted and torn to shreds by time and weather, floated like gay banners through the air.

The bodies, Allen perceived, had been bound to the trees with tough rawhide thongs, but the thongs too were beginning to rot, sometimes releasing a bleached skeleton so that it dangled from the branches as though it were dancing to the tune of the wind.

Scattered on the ground beneath the pines were brass and copper rings, polished elk-tooth necklaces, feathered head-pieces, beaded moccasins and belts, tomahawks—all the cherished trinkets of a people that had been childishly vain, royally proud, vitally alive.

Allen's interest was aroused. Often he had seen the bodies of Indians laid to rest in trees or on scaffolds or in crevices in rocks, but only one or two in a place. For so many in this spot he could not account. He was convinced that back of the mystery there must be a story. Persistently, after that, he plied everyone he met, both whites and reds, with questions. Though many palefaces had seen the skeletons in their aerial sepulcher none could explain their presence there. If the Indians knew they refused to tell.

It was not till some two years after his discovery that Allen's curiosity was satisfied. Then, one night as he and Plenty Coups lay stretched by a camp fire on the plains after a hard day's elk hunt, the young Indian told a tale of his people. In that tale or legend may lie the solution to the mystery that has made of Skeleton Cliff a point of historic interest.

"I tell White Eagle a story as my uncle told it to me," he said. "Many snows ago there was a branch of River Crows who were big men, heap tall, heap strong. It is said of them that they were all over six feet tall and that they had hair reaching the ground. They were very proud of their long hair. In battle or on the hunt they wore it braided and wrapped round their heads, but when idling about camp they let it hang loose. They were brave warriors. They were to our people what Custer's men were to the whites, always guarding us from enemies. They had no squaws. Their tepees were set at the foot of the cliff now known as Skeleton or Sacrifice Cliff. From there they could see all the wide plain below, could see enemies from far off. These Crow braves had six-foot bows made of mountain ash with tough sinews glued along the back to strengthen them. And their arrows were long and flint-pointed and very sharp.

"For many snows those big warriors lived their lives upon the peak close to the Blue and guarded the Crow villages down in the valley. They were young and strong and knew no fear, and their hearts sang all day long. At night their camp fires could be seen leaping up into the trees and their songs could be heard all over the valley. In their camps, and in the camps of all their people, were always many buffalo tongues and much dried elk meat and buffalo meat. Over their heads the pines sang to them. At their feet ran the waters of the Echeta Casha. And the stream of life flowed swift and warm in their veins.

"Though they had heard of a strange sickness that was taking Sioux and Blackfeet tribes as far down as the Missouri, yet they felt no fear, for the Great Spirit had been very kind to His Crow children. He would let no harm come to them. They were strong with the strength of youth; they were strong like the sapling that bends but does not break; they were strong like the bow that is stretched only to spring back into place.

"Then, after one sleep, so my uncle told me, there was a warrior who could not rise from his bed of buffalo hides. His limbs were heavy and tired and, when he tried to stand, were weak like the limbs of a sick squaw, so that he sank down again. His eyes were dimmed, his body ached, and his throat burned for water. When he called for water, and others hearing him went into his tepee, they saw that upon his face and his body were red spots. Those spots stung like the sting of a bee. In his heart and in the hearts of all who saw him was fear.

"Quickly they built a sweat lodge, and, heating stones to a white heat, poured water over them until the lodge was filled with steam. Then they carried the sick warrior into the lodge so that the evil spirits should all be sweated away. When he was wet with sweat they carried him down to the Echeta Casha and bathed him in the cold water. But nothing they did was good. Though they called loudly upon the Great Spirit He did not seem to hear them. For many sleeps the medicine men gathered in the tepee of the sick man and danced and sang and beat their tom-toms close to him, but even they could not drive out the evil spirits. In spite of all that was done for him the young brave left his earthly home and was taken across the Slippery Log to the Happy Hunting Ground. Then they wrapped him in a blanket and bound him to a tree on the side of the cliff. Near him they tied all the things he loved best, his war bonnet and tomahawk and war club. Beside him they also placed dried meat. And they killed his horse and left it on the ground below him, for he would need all those things on his journey.

"Soon another warrior was stricken, and another, and still another, until over the entire hunting village hung a great fear of the evil spirit that was painting the faces of the warriors with ugly red marks, as though they were preparing for battle, and was making them weak, with feet that stumbled, like one who had drunk of the white man's fire water. It seemed that neither their strong medicine nor the wise medicine men with their dances and yells and bag of charms, nor even the Great Spirit could help them. The sick warriors crept into the sweat lodges and took sweat baths, and then, while their blood flowed like streams of fire through their bodies, bathed in the icy waters of the river. To many of them came terrible visions, so that they talked strange talk. Many of them, unable longer to endure the suffering, plunged knives into their hearts. And with every sleep another brave died, and another.

"The sick ones begged the strong ones to leave before they also were stricken down. But Crows do not desert their sick brothers. And when the sick ones died the strong ones carried them out of their tepees, wrapped them in blankets, and bound them to trees, there to sleep their last sleep. Very soon, on the bodies of the strong would come those strange red marks, and the fire in the veins, and the aching head and burning thirst. Then they too took sweat baths and plunged into the cold river and staggered back to their beds in their tepees, never to rise again.

"We know now that they did the wrong thing, but they did not know then and there was no one to tell them. We know now that the palefaces call that strange sickness 'smallpox.' We have been told that many snows ago a paleface miner was drifting down the Echeta Casha where it enters into the Missouri at the Fort called 'Union.' Suddenly this strange sickness came upon him, out there alone. He paddled to shore and took off his clothes, for his body burned, and he longed for the touch of cold water. He bathed in the river and then he lay down under the trees. An Indian of the Blackfeet tribe found him there dead and took his clothes and put them on and rode into his village. Soon most of the Blackfeet were sick and many of them died, and then the Sioux, and finally the great Crow warriors.

"My uncle told me," Plenty Coups went on, "that while a few of the Crow braves were yet strong they erected a big mound of stones, four feet wide and sixteen feet long, so that as long as a stone should rest upon a stone, people of snows not yet fallen might see and know of the evil that had come into the camp of our people.

"And then," Plenty Coups said, "as to what follows, some tell one story and some another. It has been said that when there were only sixteen warriors left of the many, then, because they knew that in their veins ran the evil which had destroyed their brothers, and because they feared the evil spirit might soon destroy all the Crow tribe, they gathered around the camp fire one night in council. Their hearts were heavy. They smoked the medicine pipe and the wise ones spoke.

" 'We can never return to our people,' one of them said. 'The sickness which took our brothers is also in us. It is better that sixteen braves die than that the great nation of Crows be destroyed. I have spoken.'

" 'Our brother speaks well,' another said. 'His tongue is not crooked. We are weary. Our hearts have ceased to sing. Never again shall we find joy in the hunt nor in war dances nor in feast days. We are like old, old men. Let us seek peace in the Happy Hunting Ground.'

"And, so it is said, those sixteen braves rode their horses up onto the top of that butte which is highest in all the valley and drove them over and down onto the sharp rocks below. And there they died together, the young braves and their horses.

"But the story as my uncle told it is like this: When the great band of warriors had been taken until only sixteen were left, then all the happiness went out of their hearts. It seemed to them very still in the big camp where all had been laughter and shouts and dancing and songs. No longer did they feel joy in hunting the buffalo, for few were left to eat even the buffalo tongues, yellow with fat. When they walked, they walked like old, old men, nor were their feet light in the tribal dances. When they spoke to the Great Spirit their words did not reach up into the Blue. The song of the wind in the pine trees was a sad song now, sounding to them like the voices of their comrades who had been called away across the Log. And when the sun fell down behind the rimrocks it left a heavy, thick darkness that seemed filled with evil spirits, and they were afraid, so few in all the black, silent loneliness. Nothing could ever again be as it had been.

"One night as they sat around their camp fire, while the darkness, peopled with evil ones, crept closer and closer to them, the headman spoke: 'For some cause which we do not understand,' he said, 'the Great Spirit is angry with His children the Crows. When we pray to Him, He does not hear. Though we have danced and chanted our medicine songs and beat the tom-toms, yet we have not done enough. Something more is wanted of us by the Great Spirit. He demands a sacrifice, the greatest in our power to give. Let us say to Him that we will give our lives if He will grant once more to our people health and strength and happiness. But let us ask for a sign so that we may know our words have been heard. We will prepare for death. We will chant our death songs. Then, if our sacrifice seems good to the Great Spirit He will make the fire leap higher than the tallest tree. If not, then the fire shall die down. I have spoken.'

"So they gathered pine branches and built a great fire. Then they dressed in their war costumes and painted their faces and danced round the fire, singing their songs and watching the flames. The fire burned brighter and leaped higher until it reached far above the tallest tree.

"The headman pointed to the flames. 'The Great Spirit has heard our words,' he said. 'That is His promise that He will smile again upon our people.'

"Then the sixteen young warriors blindfolded their horses and mounted them and drove them along the buffalo trail until they came to a high point overlooking the river. The headman gave the sign. Together they struck their horses with quirts so that the animals went plunging and screaming over the edge and their hoofs clung to the stones and the soft shale gave way and they and their riders went down, many hundreds of feet, into the Echeta Casha.

"The braves had made their last journey along the dark trail. They had given their lives so that the Great Spirit should once more be kind to His children the Crows. And," Plenty Coups added, gravely, "White Eagle knows that He has been kind."

No Country like the Crow Country

The Crow country . . . is a good country. The Great Spirit has put it exactly in the right place; while you are in it, you fare well; whenever you go out of it, whichever way you travel, you fare worse.

If you go to the south, there you have to wander over great barren plains; the water is warm and bad, and you meet the fever and ague.

To the north it is cold; the winters are long and bitter, with no grass; you cannot keep horses there, but must travel with dogs. What is a country without horses!

On the Columbia they are poor and dirty, paddle about in canoes, and eat fish. Their teeth are worn out; they are always taking fish-bones out of their mouths. Fish is poor food.

To the east they dwell in villages; they live well; but they drink the muddy water of the Missouri—that is bad. A Crow's dog would not drink such water.

About the forks of the Missouri is a fine country; good water, good grass, plenty of buffalo. In summer it is almost as good as the Crow country; but in winter it is cold, the grass is gone, and there is no salt weed for the horses.

The Crow country is exactly in the right place. It has many mountains and sunny plains; all kinds of climate, and good things for every season. When the summer heats scorch the prairies, you can draw up under the mountains where the air is sweet and cool, the grass fresh, and the bright streams come tumbling out of the snow banks.

There you can hunt the elk, the deer, and the antelope, when their skins are fit for dressing; there you will find plenty of white bears and mountain sheep.

In the autumn when your horses are fit and strong from the mountain pastures, you can go down into the plains and hunt the buffalo, or trap beaver on the streams. And when winter comes on, you can take shelter in the woody bottoms, along the rivers; there you will find buffalo meat for yourselves and cottonwood bark for your horses; or you may winter in the Wind river valley, where there is salt weed in abundance.

The Crow country is exactly in the right place. Everything good is to be found there. There is no country like the Crow Country.

From *The Lost Trappers,* A Collection of Interesting Scenes and Events in the Rocky Mountains; together with a Short Description of California . . ., by David H. Coyner, pp. 97–99. Entered, according to Act of Congress, in the year 1847, by David H. Coyner, in the Clerk's Office of the District Court of the United States, in and for the Western District of Virginia. Cincinnati: Anderson, Gates & Wright. 1859.

I will take the privilege of giving a very interesting account of the Crow Country which is to be found in Captain Bonneville's notes, prepared for publication by Irving. It is a description of the Crow country, given by a Crow chief, Arapooish, to Mr. Robert Campbell, of the Rocky Mountain Fur Company.—D.H.C.

PART SIX

Western Songs and Ballads

He strove for the diapason, the great song that should embrace in itself a whole epoch, a complete era, the voice of an entire people, wherein all people should be included—they and their legends, their folklore, their fightings, their loves and their lusts, their blunt, grim humor, their stoicism under stress, their adventures, their treasures found in a day and gambled in a night, their direct, crude speech, their generosity and cruelty, their heroism and bestiality, their religion and profanity, their self-sacrifice and obscenity—a true and fearless setting forth of a passing phase of history, uncompromising, sincere; each group in its proper environment; the valley, the plain, and the mountain; the ranch, the range, and the mine—all this, all the traits and types of every community from the Dakotas to the Mexicos, from Winnipeg to Guadalupe, gathered together, swept together, welded and riven together in one single, mighty song, the Song of the West.

—Frank Norris

Introduction

The appeal of Western folk songs and ballads is quite independent of their musical interest and value, which on the whole would seem to be inferior to that of the folk music of older regions like the South. Their appeal is largely a matter of mood and tone, idiom and style—a freshness and vigor, a native tang and flavor, the heroic and democratic spirit of "a man's a man for a' that," unsurpassed by the songs of any other American region.

Western song excels in story-telling that combines heroic action with chivalrous sentiment. The sentiment is as important as the action, first, because "loyalty to comrades" and "respect for good women" are inseparable from the Western code; secondly, because men removed from civilization crave some of the "tenderer things" along with the raw stuff of life.[1] As "Teddy Blue" puts it, "Cowboys used to love to sing about people dying; I don't know why. I guess it was because they was so full of life themselves."[2]

Cowboys sang for many different reasons and in many different ways: to keep themselves and their cattle company; to entertain their comrades; to let off steam. On the one hand, they might sing anything that came into their heads, as in the "Ogallaly Song," which "was just made up as the trail went north by men singing on night guard, with a verse for every river on the trail." This sort of group improvisation, however refreshing in its spontaneity, cannot be expected to produce skilfully plotted narrative songs of the "Billy Venero" and "Utah Carroll" type. Under the influence of the Western poem and recitation, in and out of print, the cowboy sang songs that are closer in spirit and style to John A. Lomax's *Songs of the Cattle Trail and Cow Camp* than they are to his *Cowboy Songs.* N. Howard ("Jack") Thorp wrote "Little Joe the Wrangler," Badger Clark's "The Glory Trail," glorifying the cowboy that could not be thrown by a mount that could not be broken, became the cowboys' "High Chin Bob"—perhaps the most notable example of the making of a folk hero by a poet.

The hybrid eclecticism of Western folk song practice and the reciprocity of oral and written usage, characteristic of a region settled on the run, reached its height in the songs of the Forty-Niners, which drew heavily on minstrel tunes of the period.

---

[1] Cf. Charles J. Finger, *Frontier Songs* (Garden City, 1927), pp. 6, 23.

[2] E. C. Abbott ("Teddy Blue") and Helena Huntington Smith, *We Pointed Them North* (New York, 1939), p. 261. The sentiment of "The Cowboy's Lament" often struck him as incongruously funny: "Because first he is lying there dead, wrapped up in his blanket, and then he starts in telling this big long story of his life and how he met his downfall. 'I first took to drinking and then to card-playing'—and they'd all be drunk when they was singing it, most likely."

. . . Many songs were needed for the endless days, and the memories of the gold-seekers were ransacked back towards their youth. New words for old tunes; old words revised. Everybody on the Atlantic seaboard was singing Stephen Foster's "Oh, Susanna": the Forty-Niner fortune hunters quickly refurbished the tune with words relevant to their adventure.[3]

Another gold rush song, "Sacramento," to the tune of Stephen Foster's "Camptown Races" via the sailor's song-bag, points to another phase of the cultural dynamics of Western migration and settlement. The interaction of maritime and mining activities in the Gold Rush era led, on the one hand, to the inclusion of California references in sailors' songs, and, on the other hand, to the spreading of these songs to the diggings by men who had shipped or sailed around the Horn.[4] The reverse of the process is seen in the back-migration of "topical ballads illustrating California history" carried by returning Forty-Niners as far East as New England.[5]

The two-way flow still goes on, in one direction or another. Up Seattle way, Judge Francis D. Henry's "The Old Settler," or "Acres of Clams"—a favorite of old settlers' picnics—has recently been revived by Ivar Haglund as the theme song of his "Ivar's Acres of Clams" restaurant, while Haglund himself, on his radio program, has been writing and singing parodies of folk songs to sell fish dinners and to advertise his Aquarium! Farther down the Coast, George Sterling's "Abalone" and the literary-sounding, "I Catcha da Plenty of Feesh," are part of the sophisticated folk-song heritage of Bohemian San Franciscans, while Badger Clark's "A Border Affair" has become the semi-traditional "Spanish Is a Loving Tongue." The proportion of parody runs high in songs of social significance, from Nebraska Farmers' Alliance songs to Joe Hill's "Casey Jones," beginning:

Now the shopmen on the S.P. line to strike sent out a call,
But Casey Jones, the engineer, he wouldn't strike at all.
The boiler it was leakin' and the driver's on the bum,
And the bearings of the engine they were all out of plumb.

Chorus:
But Casey Jones kept that junk-pile runnin';
Casey Jones was workin' double time.
Casey Jones got a wooden medal
For being good and faithful on the S.P. line.[6]

---

[3] Cornel Lengyel, editor, *A San Francisco Songster* (San Francisco, 1939), mimeographed, p. 10.

[4] James Murray, "Sailors' Songs with California Significance," *California Folklore Quarterly,* Vol. V (April, 1946), No. 2, pp. 143–152. According to Charles Seeger, the voyage around the Horn, with its stopover at Valparaiso, was responsible also for the naming of the "Chile Town" section of San Francisco and the introduction into California of the national dance of Chile, *la Chilena.*

[5] Sidney Robertson Cowell, "The Recording of Folk Music in California," *California Folklore Quarterly,* Vol. I (January, 1942), No. 1, p. 7. This is an excellent survey of the regional and ethnic mixture of California's folk song heritage. See also her *Gold Rush Song Book* (San Francisco, 1940), for the checkered career of texts and tunes.

[6] From the singing of Harry ("Haywire Mac") McClintock, recorded by Sam Eskin.

In the latest phase of Western folk song diffusion and acculturation, migrants from the Dust Bowl have brought Southern folk music into California, especially via the Farm Security Administration camps, as in the last song in this section, "Fod," and in the "Okie" songs of the contemporary ballad writer and singer, Woody Guthrie. His "Gypsy Davy" shows the assimilation of the British ballad to the cowboy style. His "Dust Bowl Ballads" and his songs written for the Bonneville Power Administration prove that ballad-making is not a "closed account." As proof of his success in recapturing not only the folk spirit but the regional character of Western song, his "Roll On, Columbia" is fast becoming a regional song of the Pacific Northwest.

The cultural dynamics of Western folk song extends also to the present vogue of the imitation cowboy song and the Western style of dance music and hot swing (as in Oklahoma's Bob Wills), which rivals the vogue of "country" or "hillbilly" music on jukebox and radio. Today's process is complicated and accelerated by "city-billy" singers who not only write songs based on oral tradition but speed such songs on their way back into the public domain, as in the current "Hound Dog":

Rotten potatoes and a dirty tow sack,
Pain in my belly and a crick in my back.

Chorus:
Hound dog, bay at the moon,
Lift up your long head and bay at the moon.

My cornmeal is weevily, my sorghum's gone bad.
Kinfolks have ate up what little I had.

That God has forgot me has give me some pain,
But now he's forgot how to make it to rain.[7]

B. A. B.

Notes on the Music

Metronome marks have been indicated only when the tune was transcribed from a recording or when such marks are included in the original published sources.

When suitable to the song, chord letters have been placed above the staff line as an aid not only to players of traditional instruments like the guitar but also to pianists who may wish to make their own accompaniments. These chord letters, however, are intended only as suggestions and in many cases different chord patterns are possible.

For notes on transcribing, accompanying, and singing folk songs the reader is referred to the discussion of the subject by the music consultant, Ruth Crawford Seeger, in her *American Folk Songs for Children* (New York, 1948) and in the Lomaxes' *Our Singing Country* (New York, 1941).

---

[7] By Dub Smith. As sung by the Mechau Family, of Redstone, Colorado, at Denver, Colorado, July 22, 1950, recorded by Tom Harvey, and included in their album, *Mechau Ballads,* edited by Earl Robinson.

I. AROUND CAPE HORN

Rio[1] Grande

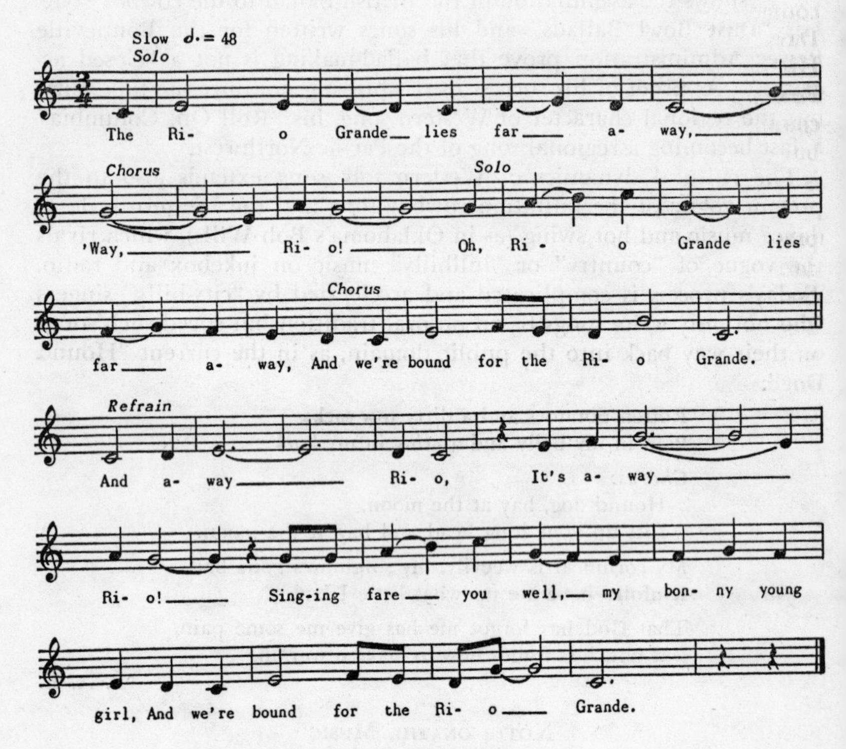

I thought I heard our old man say,
I thought I heard our old man say.

Two dollars a day is the sailor's pay.
So it's pack up your donkey and get under way.

I left my old woman a month's half pay.
So heave up our anchor, away we must go.

Sung by Captain Leighton Robinson, Alex Barr, Arthur Brodeur, and Leighton McKenzie, Belvedere, California, 1939. Recorded by Sidney Robertson. Archive of American Folk Song, Library of Congress, Washington, D.C. Record No. 4232 A. Transcribed by Ruth Crawford Seeger.

[1] Pronounced Rī-o.

The Girls around Cape Horn

When we arrived in Rio we lay there quite a while,
A-fixing up our rigging and bending our new sails.
From ship to ship they cheered us as we did sail along,
And they wished us pleasant weather while rounding of Cape Horn.

While rounding of Cape Horn, my boys, fair nights and pleasant days.
Next place we dropped our anchor was in Valparaiso Bay,
Where those Spanish girls they did roll down; I solemnly do swear
They far excel those Yankee girls with their dark and wavy hair.

They love a Yankee sailor when he goes on a spree.
He'll dance and sing and make things ring, and his money he will spend free,
And when his money it is all gone on him they won't impose;
They far excel those Liverpool girls who will pawn and steal his clothes.

Here's a health to Valparaiso along the Chile main,
Likewise to those Peruvian girls, they treated me so fine.
If ever I live to get paid off, I'll sit and drink till morn
A health to the dashing Spanish girls I met around Cape Horn.

From *Songs of American Sailormen*, by Joanna C. Colcord, pp. 177–178. Enlarged and revised edition. Copyright, 1938, by W. W. Norton & Company, Inc. New York.

Sacramento

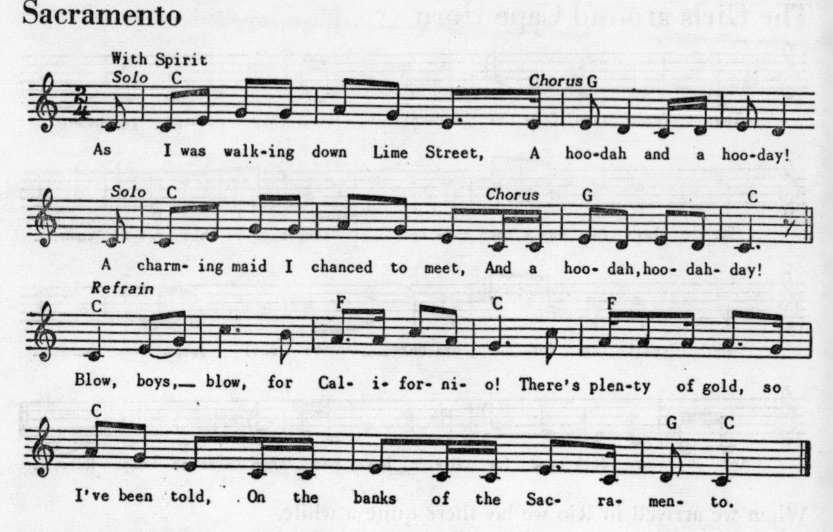

I asked her if she'd take a trip
Down to the wharf to see my ship.

She said, "I have a sweetheart true,
And I will not leave him now for you."

Shenandoah

Four long years, sir, I did court her,
Away, the rolling river,

Four long years, sir, I did court her,
And away, I'm bound away
'Cross the wide Missouri.

From *King's Book of Shanties,* by Stanton H. King, Official Government Chanty-Man, p. 15. Copyright, 1918, by Oliver Ditson Company. Philadelphia: Oliver Ditson Company, Theodore Dresser Co., Distributors.

Sung by Captain Leighton Robinson, Mill Valley, California, January 23, 1951. Recorded by Sam Eskin. Transcribed by Ruth Crawford Seeger.

II. MINERS

The Days of Forty-Nine

I had comrades then—a saucy set. They were rough, I must confess,
But staunch and brave, as true as steel, like hunters from the West.
But they like many another fish have now run out their line,
But like good old bricks they stood the kicks of the days of Forty-Nine.

There was Monte Pete—I'll ne'er forget the luck he always had.
He'd deal for you both night and day, or as long as you had a scad.
One night a pistol laid him out. 'Twas his last lay-out, in fine,
It caught Pete, sure, right bang in the door, in the days of Forty-Nine.

There was New York Jake, a butcher boy, so fond of getting tight.
Whenever Jake got full of gin he was looking for a fight.
One night he ran against a knife in the hands of old Bob Kline—
So over Jake we had a wake, in the days of Forty-Nine.

From *The Gold Rush Song Book,* Comprising a Group of Twenty-Five Authentic Ballads as They Were Sung by the Men Who Dug for Gold in California during the Period of the Great Gold Rush of 1849, compiled by Eleanora Black and Sidney Robertson, with music, pp. 53–55. Copyright, 1940, by the Colt Press. San Francisco, California.

Sung by Leon Ponce, Columbia, Tuolumne County, California, September, 1939. Recorded by Sidney Robertson for the Archive of California Folk Music at the University of California. Archive of American Folk Song, Library of Congress, Washington, D. C. Records No. 3363 A1, 3365 A2. Text from *Pioneers of '49,* by Nicholas Ball, Lee & Shepard, Boston, 1891.

For other gold rush songs, see *A Treasury of American Folklore* (New York, 1944), pp. 861–864.

There was another chap from New Orleans—Big Ruben was his name.
On the Plaza there, with a sardine box, he opened a Faro game.
He dealt so fair that a millionaire he became in course of time,
Till death stepped in and called the tune in the days of Forty-Nine.

There was Kentucky Bill, one of the boys who was always in for a game.
No matter whether he lost or won, to him 'twas all the same.
He'd ante a slug, he'd pass the buck, he'd go a hatful blind.
In a game of death Bill lost his breath, in the days of Forty-Nine.

There was North Caroline Jess, a hard old case, who never would repent.
Jess was never known to miss a meal, or ever pay a cent.
But poor old Jess, like all the rest, to Death did at last resign,
And in his bloom he went up the flume in the days of Forty-Nine.

There was Rackensack Jim, who could out-roar a buffalo bull, you bet!
He roared all night, he roared all day, he may be roaring yet.
One night he fell in a prospect hole—'twas a roaring bad design—
For in that hole Jim roared out his soul in the days of Forty-Nine.

Of all the comrades I had then, there's none left now but me;
And the only thing I'm fitting for is a senator to be.
The people cry, as I pass by, "There goes a traveling sign.
That's old Tom Moore, a bummer of the days of Forty-Nine."

* * * * *

Joe Bowers

Ibid., pp. 22–23.

Sung by Ben Strong, Cassville, Missouri, December, 1936. Recorded by Sidney Robertson for the Farm Security Administration. Text from *Johnson's Original Comic Songs,* D. Appleton, San Francisco, 1860.

I used to love a gal thar, they call'd her Sally Black.
I axed her for to marry me, she said it was a whack.
Says she to me, "Joe Bowers, before we hitch for life,
You'd orter have a little home to keep your little wife."

Says I, "My dearest Sally, oh Sally, for your sake,
I'll go to Californy, and try to raise a stake."
Says she to me, "Joe Bowers, oh, you're the chap to win,
Give me a buss to seal the bargain," and she threw a douzen in!

I shall ne'er forgit my feelin's when I bid adieu to all.
Sally cotched me round the neck, then I began to bawl.
When I sot in, they all commenced—you ne'er did hear the like,
How they all took on and cried, the day I left old Pike.

When I got to this 'ere country, I hadn't nary red.
I had such wolfish feelin's I wish'd myself 'most dead;
But the thoughts of my dear Sally soon made them feelin's git,
And whispered hopes to Bowers—Lord, I wish I had 'em yit!

At length I went to minin', put in my biggest licks,
Come down upon the boulders jist like a thousand bricks.
I worked both late and airly, in rain, and sun, and snow,
But I was working for my Sally, so 'twas all the same to Joe.

I made a very lucky strike, as the gold itself did tell,
And saved it for my Sally, the gal I loved so well.
I saved it for my Sally, that I might pour it at her feet,
That she might kiss and hug me, and call me something sweet.

But one day I got a letter from my dear, kind brother, Ike—
It come from old Missouri, sent all the way from Pike.
It brought me the gol-darn'dest news as ever you did hear—
My heart is almost bustin', so, pray, excuse this tear.

It said my Sal was fickle, that her love for me had fled;
That she'd married with a butcher, whose har was orful red!
It tole me more than that—oh! it's enough to make one swar,
It said Sally had a baby, and the baby had red har!

Now, I've told you all I could tell, about this sad affair,
'Bout Sally marryin' the butcher, and the butcher had red har.
Whether 'twas a boy or gal child, the letter never said,
It only said its cussed har was inclined to be a red!

Cousin Jack Song

You'll find them on the mountain top, you'll find them on the plains;
You'll find those boys where'er you go, and you'll find their mining claims.

They come from distant Tombstone and Virginia on the Hill.
You ne'er can beat a Cousin Jack for hammering on the drill.

Amongst you other Irishmen do justice if you can,
For there's none that can compete with the good old Cornishman.

From "Mining Songs," by Duncan Emrich, *Southern Folklore Quarterly,* Vol. 6 (June, 1942), No. 2, pp. 103–104.

Sung by Oakley Johns, Grass Valley, California, 1941. Recorded by Duncan Emrich.

Israel James of the same city believes that it was originally written by Charley Tregonning, who at one time worked in Grass Valley.—D. E.

For the name, character, mining lore, stories, customs, etc. of the "Cousin Jack" (feminine "Cousin Jennie," pronounced *Jinnie*)—the "world's racial miner" and "often unconsciously . . . the funniest of the whole mining breed," according to Joe Chisholm—see Caroline Bancroft, "Folklore of the Central City District, Colorado," *California Folklore Quarterly,* Vol. IV (October, 1945), No. 4, pp. 315–342; and "Cousin Jack Stories from Central City," *Colorado Magazine,* Vol. XXI (1944), No. 2, pp. 51–56; also, Joe Chisholm, *Brewery Gulch* (San Antonio, 1949), pp. 117–121.

A "Cousin Jack," of course, is a Cornishman. Now, here's the story as to why they got the name "Cousin Jacks." Whether there's anything to it, I don't know. These Cornishmen came over here and they'd go to work in the mine. And they'd go to the superintendent or the boss and say, "Have you got a job for my 'Cousin Jack' who lives in England?" . . . Well, it was just like you'd call a feller from Oklahoma an "Okie."—Louis Carter, Denver, Colorado, July 20, 1950, recorded by B. A. Botkin.

The Americans gave [the nickname] to the Cousin Jacks somewhat in derision. But the Cousin Jacks, who have this wonderful sense of humor, have always accepted it, and they call themselves "Cousin Jack." . . . "Any Cornishman who left

The Dreary Black Hills

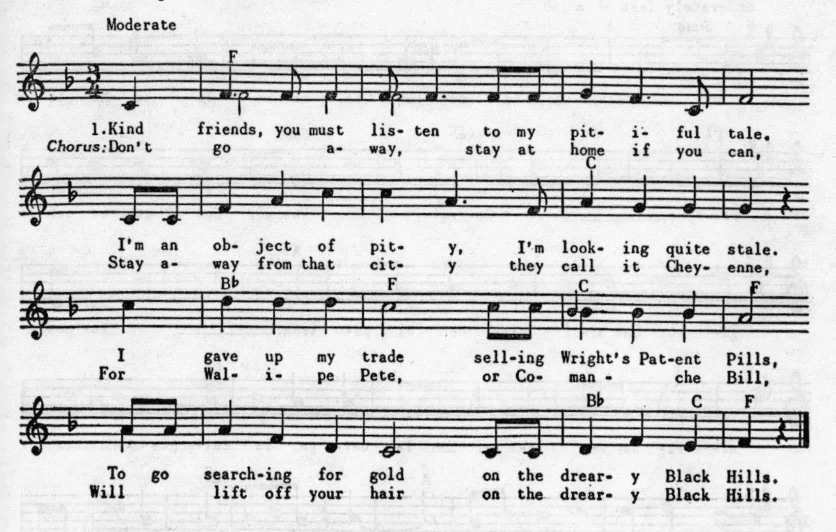

I got to Cheyenne, no gold could I find,
I thought of the lunch route I'd left far behind.
Through rain, cold, and snow, frozen clean to the gills,
They call me the orphan of the dreary Black Hills.

The round house in Cheyenne is filled every night,
With loafers and bummers of most every plight,
On their backs is no clothes, in their pockets no bills.
Each day they keep starting for the dreary Black Hills.

Kind friends, to conclude, my advice I'll unfold,
Don't go to the Black Hills a-searching for gold.
Railroad speculators their pockets you'll fill
If you go for gold to the dreary Black Hills.

Cornwall is a 'Cousin Jack.' Anybody who stayed there is Cornish."—Caroline Bancroft, *ibid*.

From *Singing Cowboy,* A Book of Western Songs, collected and edited by Margaret Larkin, arranged for the piano by Helen Black, pp. 87–90. Copyright, 1931, by Alfred A. Knopf, Inc. New York.

Mi Mulita

My little mule, my little mule, my little mule,
Do not let me down.
Let's get on with this little load
For here comes the boss.
Come, let's get on, little mule,

With this load, little load,
With this load of coal.
Here comes the boss.
Let's get along, mule,
The load of coal.

From *Coal Dust on the Fiddle,* Songs and Stories of the Bituminous Industry, by George Korson, pp. 192–193. Copyright, 1943, by the University of Pennsylvania Press. Philadelphia.

Sung by Eduardo Gallegos, of Albuquerque, New Mexico, at Washington, D. C., May 5, 1941. Recorded by George Korson.

Many years ago, a Spanish-American ranchero was plodding along a dusty road alongside his mule which was burdened with a heavy load of wood. A mine boss passing by was impressed by the strength of the mule and offered to buy it for use in a New Mexico coal mine. "Oh, no, I cannot part with my little mule," said the ranchero. "If I sell him I must go wherever he goes." The mine boss thereupon bought the mule and hired its master. The ranchero sang this song as he drove his mule in the mines.—Eduardo Gallegos.

"Oo-ra," above, possibly an anglicization of the *arre* which Spanish muleteers frequently call to their mules.—G. K.

III. INDIANS AND PIONEERS

In Kansas

Oh, they chew tobacco thin in the Kansas,
They chew tobacco thin in the Kansas.
They chew tobacco thin
And they let it go down their chin,
And they lick it up again in Kansas.

Oh, the chickens they grow tall in the Kansas,
The chickens they grow tall in the Kansas.
The chickens they grow tall,
They eat them guts and all
When they kill them in the fall in Kansas.

Sung with guitar by George Vinton Graham, San Jose, California, 1938. Recorded by Sidney Robertson. Archive of American Folk Song, Library of Congress, Washington, D. C. Record No. 3818 A3. Transcribed by Ruth Crawford Seeger.

The Little Old Sod Shanty

Yet I rather like the novelty of living in this way,
Though my bill of fare is always rather tame,
But I'm happy as a clam on the land of Uncle Sam
In the little old sod shanty on my claim.
But when I left my Eastern home, a bachelor so gay,
To try and win my way to wealth and fame,
I little thought I'd come down to burning twisted hay
In the little old sod shanty on my claim.

Sung with guitar by Clyde (Slim) Wilson, Springfield, Missouri, 1936. Recorded by Sidney Robertson. Archive of American Folk Song, Library of Congress, Washington, D. C. Record No. 3199 Bl. Transcribed by Ruth Crawford Seeger.

My clothes are plastered o'er with dough, I'm looking like a fright,
And everything is scattered round the room,
But I wouldn't give the freedom that I have out in the West
For the table of the Eastern man's old home.
Still I wish that some kindhearted girl would pity on me take,
And relieve me from the mess that I am in;
The angel how I'd bless her if this her home she'd make
In the little old sod shanty on my claim.

And we would make our fortunes on the prairies of the West,
Just as happy as two lovers we'd remain;
We'd forget the trials and troubles we endured at the first,
In the little old sod shanty on my claim.
And if fate should bless us with now and then an heir,
To cheer our hearts with honest pride of fame.
Oh, then we'd be contented for the toil that we had spent
In the little old sod shanty on our claim.

The Sioux Indians

We crossed the Missouri, a very wide stream,
Which bore us away to the deserts and plains—
Of hunting and fishing and looking for gold
And shooting free antelope and the wild buffalo.

Sung by Lannis Sutton, Doxie, Oklahoma, at Palo Alto, California, January 14, 1951. Recorded by Sam Eskin. Transcribed by Ruth Crawford Seeger.

The talk of Sioux Indians all over the plain,
Of killing some drivers and burning their train.
They shot those poor drivers with arrows and bows.
When captured by Indians, no mercy was shown.

We traveled three weeks till we came to the place,
Corralled all five wagons on the green, grassy place,
Stretched out all five tents on the green, grassy ground
While the mules and the horses was grazing all round.

While taking refreshments, we heard a loud yell.
'Twas a cry of Sioux Indians coming out on our trail.
We spring to our rifles, with a flash in each eye.
Our leader says, "Brave boys, let's fight till we die."

We mounted our horses, made ready for a fight.
All in a sudden they came to our sight.
Of our little band there was just twenty-four,
And of those Sioux Indians five hundred or more.

They came down upon us with a whoop and a yell,
At the crack of our rifles sixteen of them fell.
They saw their bold comrades lying dead on the ground.
They whooped and they yelled and they circled all round.

They made a bold rush coming into our train.
The arrows fell round us like hail and like rain.
But with our long rifles we fed them hot lead
Till many a Sioux Indian around us lie dead.

The talk of Sioux Indians all over the plain
Was enough to make the heart of any man pain.
We fought them with courage, we spoke not a word.
At the end of the battle that's all that was heard.

We killed the bold chief at the head of command.
He died like a warrior with a bow in his hand.
They saw their bold chief lying dead in his gore.
They whooped and they yelled and we saw them no more.

We hitched up our horses and started our train.
We had three more fights, our trip on the plains.
In our last battle just three brave boys fell.
We laid them to rest in the green shady dell.

'Way Out in Idyho

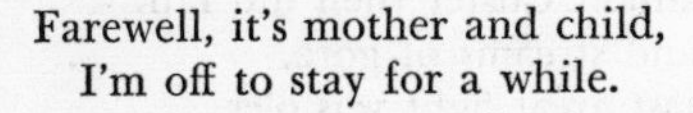
Farewell, it's mother and child,
I'm off to stay for a while.

So won't you kiss me before I go,
And call me your darling child?

Custer's Last Charge

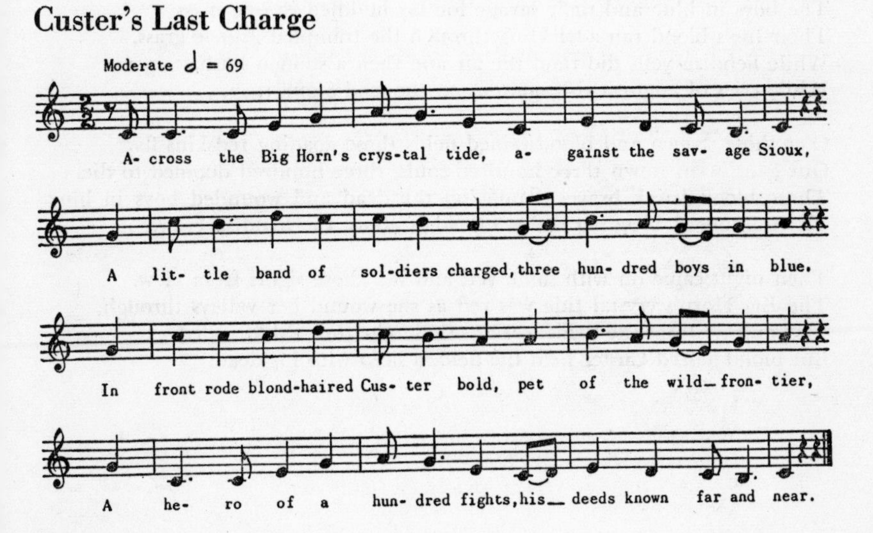

From *Cowboy Songs, Folk Songs and Ballads from "Green Grow the Lilacs," by Lynn Riggs,* as produced by the Theatre Guild, Inc., p. 11. Copyright, 1932, by Samuel French. New York.

Sung by Warde H. Ford, Central Valley, California, 1938. Recorded by Sidney Robertson. Archive of American Folk Song, Library of Congress, Washington, D. C. Record No. 4199 B. Transcribed by Ruth Crawford Seeger.

"Charge, comrades, charge! There's death ahead, disgrace lurks in our rear!
Drive rowels deep! Come on, come on!" came his yells with ringing cheer.
And on the foe those heroes charged. There rose an awful yell.
It seemed as though those soldiers stormed the lowest gates of hell.

Three hundred rifles rattled forth, and torn was human form.
The black smoke rose in rolling waves above the leaden storm.
The death groans of the dying braves, their wounded piercing cries,
The hurling of the arrows fleet did cloud the noonday skies.

The snorting steeds with shrieks of fright, the firearms' deafening roar;
The war song sung by the dying braves who fell to rise no more.
O'er hill and dale the war song waved round craggy mountain side.
Along down death's dark valley ran a cruel crimson tide.

Our blond-haired chief was everywhere 'mid showers of hurling lead.
The starry banner waved above the dying and the dead.
With bridle rein in firm-set teeth, revolver in each hand,
He hoped with his few gallant boys to quell the great Sioux band.

Again they charged. Three thousand guns poured forth their last-sent ball;
Three thousand war whoops rent the air. Gallant Custer then did fall.
And all around where Custer fell ran pools and streams of gore,
Heaped bodies of both red and white whose last great fight was o'er.

The boys in blue and their savage foe lay huddled in one mass,
Their life's blood ran a-trickling through the trampled prairie grass,
While fiendish yells did rend the air and then a sudden hush,
While cries of anguish rise again as on the mad Sioux rush.

O'er those strewn and bloodstained fields those goading redskins fly.
Our gang went down three hundred souls, three hundred doomed to die.
Those blood-drunk braves sprang on the dead and wounded boys in blue.
Three hundred bleeding scalps ran high above the fiendish crew.

Then night came on with sable veil and hid those sights from view.
The Big Horn's crystal tide was red as she wound her valleys through.
And quickly from the fields of slain those gloating redskins fled—
But blond-haired Custer held the field, a hero with his dead.

The Old Settler (Acres of Clams)

For one who gets riches by minin',
Perceivin' that others grow poor,
I made up my mind to try farmin'—
The only pursuit that is sure.

So rollin' my grub in a blanket
I left all my tools on the ground,
And started one morning to shank it
For a country they called Puget Sound.

Written by Judge Francis D. Henry. Sung by Michael Loring, Portland, Oregon, August 1, 1950. Recorded by B. A. Botkin. Transcribed by Ruth Crawford Seeger.

The refrain is formed by repeating the fourth and third lines of each stanza as in the refrain for Stanza 1.

This song has been revived by Ivar Haglund as the theme song of "Ivar's Acres of Clams" restaurant in Seattle, Washington.

Arrivin' flat broke in mid-winter
I found it enveloped in fog,
And covered all over with timber
Thick as hair on the back of a dog.

I staked out a claim in the forest,
And set myself down to hard toil;
For two years I chopped and I log-
gered,
But I never got down to the soil.

I tried to get out of the country,
But poverty forced me to stay
Until I became an Old Settler
Now you couldn't drive me away.

No longer the slave of ambition,
I laugh at the world and its shams
And think of my happy condition,
Surrounded by acres of clams.

The Regular Army, Oh!

From *"Sound Off!" Soldier Songs from the Revolution to World War II,* by Edward Arthur Dolph, pp. 6–9. Copyright, 1929, 1942, by Farrar & Rinehart, Inc. New York and Toronto.

We had our choice of going to the army or to jail,
Or it's up the Hudson River with a copper take a sail;
So we puckered up our courage and with bravery we did go,
And we cursed the day we marched away with the Regular Army, oh!

When we went out to Fort Hobo they run us in the mill,
And there they made us take a bath, 'twas sure against our will;
But with three full meals within our belts, each day, we had our fill,
And we sat upon the dump cart and watched the terriers drill.

The captain's name was Murphy, of "dacint Frinch descint,"
Sure he knew all the holy words in the Hebrew testament;
And when he said to Hogan, "Just move your feet a foot,"
Sure Hogan jumped a half a mile on Sergeant Riley's boot.

The best of all the officers is Second Lieutenant McDuff;
Of smoking cigarettes and sleep he never got enough.
Says the captain, "All we want of you is to go to Reveille,
And we'll let the first sergeant run the company."

There's corns upon me feet, me boy, and bunions on me toes,
And lugging a gun in the red-hot sun puts freckles on me nose,
And if you want a furlough to the captain you do go,
And he says, "Go to bed and wait till you're dead in the Regular Army, oh!"

We went to Arizona for to fight the Indians there;
We were nearly caught bald-headed but they didn't get our hair;
We lay among the ditches in the dirty yellow mud,
And we never saw an onion, a turnip, or a spud.

We were captured by the Indians and brought ferninst the chafe,
Says he, "We'll have an Irish stew," the dirty Indian thafe.
On the telegraphic wire we skipped to Mexico,
And we blessed the day we marched away from the Regular Army, oh!

In 1874 a version of it appeared in sheet-music form with words by Ed Harrigan and music adapted and arranged by Braham. But it has been sung in different forms, for the soldier on the frontier adopted it, changed it when he felt inclined, and made it his own. . . . An old war correspondent who was with General Miles in the Sioux campaigns of the Seventies tells of hearing the general sing this stanza:

We're marching off for Sitting Bull
And this is the way we go;
Forty miles a day on beans and hay
In the Regular Army, oh!

—E. A. D.

Root, Hog, or Die

I went out in the country, commenced to making hay,
The wages that I got was a dollar and a half a day.
Two suppers after night, and there's no use to cry,
There's no use of whining, it was root, hog, or die.

Oh, I went from there down to Bellew,
I met with a stranger who helped to put me through.
It was in a game of poker and he give the cards a sly.
And he soon got my money, then it's root, hog, or die.

Oh, I got mad and I begin to swear.
I forced down the corn juice till I got on a tear.
The marshal of the city who was standing nearby,
He took me to the calaboose to root, hog, or die.

Oh, he took me out to court next morning just at ten.
There set the judge and a dozen other men.
They fined me twenty dollars, and I found it rather high,
But there's no use of whining, it was root, hog, or die.

Oh, along about then I begin to repent.
They fined me twenty dollars and I didn't have a cent.
Good luck would have it, a friend was standing by,
And he paid off my fine, saying root, hog, or die.

Sung with guitar by R. R. Denoon, Springfield, Missouri, November 12, 1936. Recorded by Sidney Robertson. Archive of American Folk Song, Library of Congress, Washington, D. C. Record No. 3346 A1. Transcribed by Ruth Crawford Seeger.

Come, all you young men and take my advice,
To never play poker, go to throwing any dice,
For if you do, you'll get too much of rye,
And you'll land in the calaboose to root, hog, or die.

IV. MORMONS

On the Road to California (The Buffalo Bull Fight)

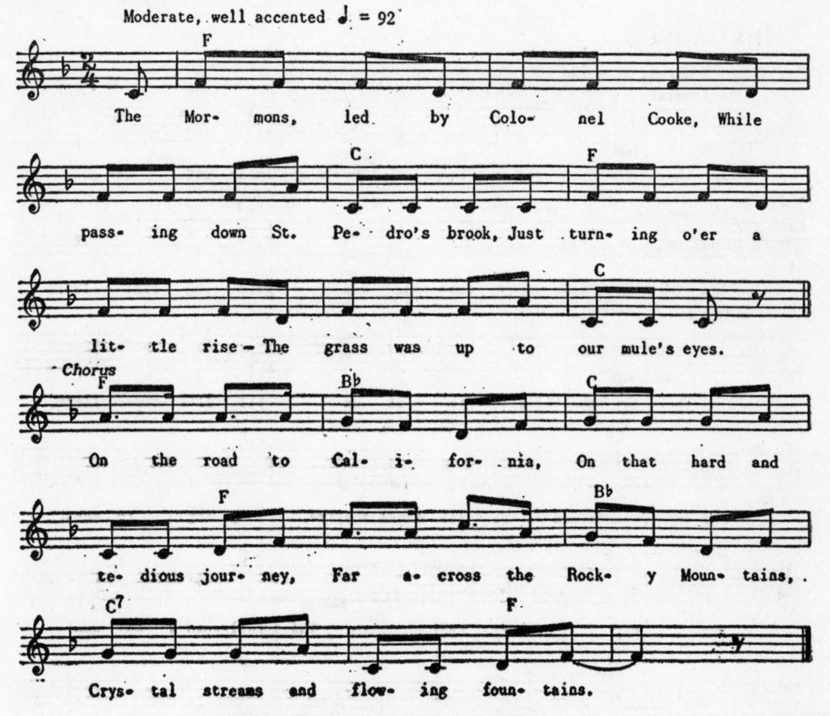

Just as our mules begun to pull,
Out from the grass there jumped a bull.
As soon as he appeared in sight,
He raised his head all ready for a fight.

Sung with piano by William T. Morris, St. George, Utah, 1947. Recorded by Austin E. Fife and Alta M. Fife. Archive of American Folk Song, Library of Congress, Washington, D. C. Transcribed by Ruth Crawford Seeger.

For another version, see Alfred M. Durham, *Pioneer Songs* (1932, 1940), pp. 192–193.

I saw a man as I passed by,
A bull had hooked him in that side;
And from that side the blood did pour,
Three inches deep it made a gore.

When this bull battle it was o'er
And sound of muskets heard no more,
We went next day and there found slain
Four mules, twelve bulls upon the plain.

Echo Canyon

Sung by L. M. Hilton, Ogden, Utah, 1946. Recorded by Austin E. Fife and Alta M. Fife. Archive of American Folk Song, Library of Congress, Washington, D. C. Record No. 9109 (F). Transcribed by Ruth Crawford Seeger.

Now there's Mister Reed, he's a gentleman too.
He knows very well what we Mormons can do.
He knows in our work we are faithful and true,
And if Mormon boys start it, it's bound to go through.

Our camp is united, we all labor hard,
And if we are faithful we'll gain our reward.
Our leader is wise and a great leader, too,
And all things he tells us, we're right glad to do.

The boys in our camp are light-hearted and gay.
We work on the railroad ten hours a day.
We're thinking of fine times we'll have in the fall
When we'll be with our ladies and go to the ball.

We surely must live in a very fast age.
We've traveled by ox team and then took the stage.
But when such conveyance is all done away,
We'll travel in steam cars upon the railway.

The great locomotive next season will come
To gather the saints from their far distant home,
And bring them to Utah in peace here to stay
While the judgments of God sweep the wicked away.

The Handcart Song

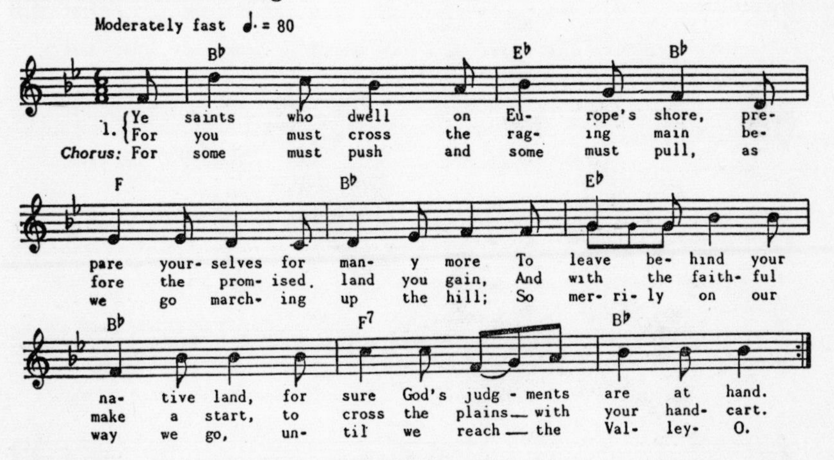

Mormon boys and men under the direction of Brigham Young who helped build the railroad into Utah in 1868 and '69 composed this song, and it has been sung in Utah ever since. My grandparents taught it to me when I was a small boy.—L. M. H.

Sung by L. M. Hilton, Ogden, Utah, August 26, 1946. Recorded by Austin E. and Alta M. Fife. Archive of American Folk Song, Library of Congress, Washington, D. C. Transcribed by Ruth Crawford Seeger.

The lands that boast of modern light, we know are all as dark as night,
Where poor men toil and want for bread, where peasant hosts are blindly led.
These lands that boast of liberty you ne'er again would wish to see,
When you from Europe make a start to cross the plains with your handcart.

As on the road the carts are pulled, 'twould very much surprise the world
To see the old and feeble dame thus lend a hand to pull the same;
And maidens fair will dance and sing, young men more happy than the king,
And children, too, will laugh and play, their strength increasing day by day.

But some will say, "It is too bad, the saints upon the foot to pad,
And more than that, to pull a load as they go marching o'er the road."
But then we say, "It is the plan to gather up the best of men,
And women, too, for none but they will ever travel in this way."

And long before the valley's gained, we will be met upon the plain
With music sweet and friends so dear, and fresh supplies our hearts to cheer;
And then with music and with song, how cheerfully we'll march along,
And thank the day we made a start to cross the plains with our handcarts.

When you get there among the rest, obedient be and you'll be blessed,
And in God's chambers be shut in, while judgments cleanse the earth from sin;
For we do know it will be so, God's servant spoke it long ago.
We say it is high time to start to cross the plains with our handcarts.

This song was sung by those who crossed the plains in handcarts, made up on the way. It's been a song that every one loved to sing in Utah ever since pioneer days. My grandmother sang it to me when I was a baby. I can't remember when I didn't sing it and know it and love it.—L. M. H.

Cf. Alfred M. Durham, *Pioneer Songs* (1932, 1940), p. 21.

V. COWBOYS

I Am a Texas Cowboy

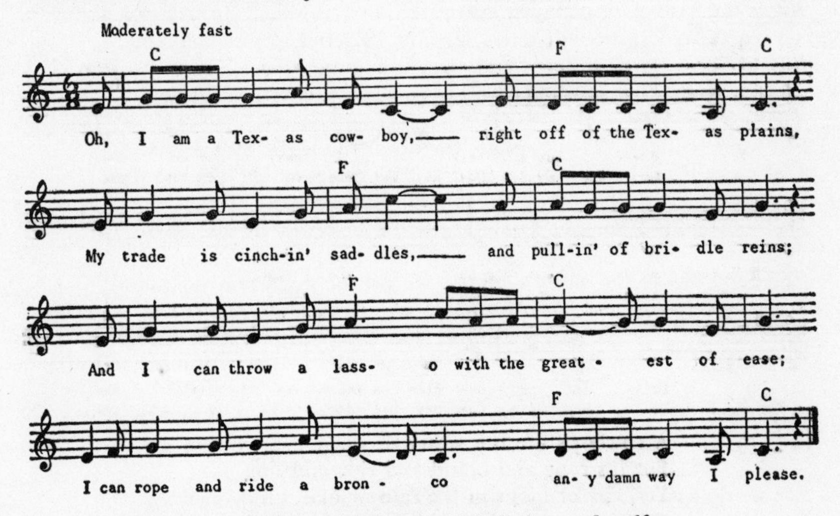

I love the rollin' prairies, with all their joy and strife.
Behind a herd of longhorns I've journeyed all my life.
And if I had a little wife, how happy I would be,
For the prettiest girl in all the world has fell in love with me.

And when we get 'em bedded down and settled for the night,
Some cayuse shakes his saddle and he gives the herd a fright.
And as they madly stampede and gallop fast away,
In the heat of the moment I can hear some cowboy say:

"Oh, I am a Texas cowboy, just off the stormy plains.
My trade is hosses, cinches, saddles, ropes, and bridle reins.
Oh, I can tip a lariat and with a graceful ease
I can rope a streak of lightnin' and I ride it where I please."

Again we got 'em bedded down; I'm feelin' most forlorn.
A fire in the west arises and with lightnin' on their horns.
The boss says, "Boys, yore pay is here, you'll get it all in gold."
Oh, I'm bound to follow the longhorns until I am too old.

From *Powder River Jack and Kitty Lee's Cowboy Song Book,* with Music; Cowboy Wails and Cattle Trails of the Wild West, compiled by Powder River Jack and Kitty Lee, p. 79. Copyright, 1938, by Powder River Jack Lee, Deer Lodge, Montana. Butte, Montana: Printed and Engraved by the McKee Printing Company.

For other cowboy songs, see *A Treasury of American Folklore* (New York, 1944), pp. 851–860.

Doney Gal

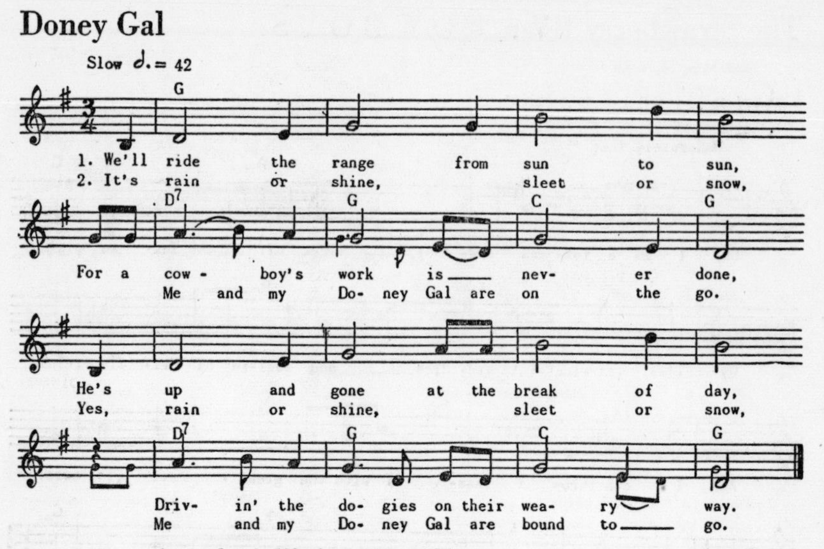

A cowboy's life is a weary thing,
For it's rope and brand and ride and sing.
Yes, day or night in the rain or hail,
He'll stay with his dogies out on the trail.

Rain or shine, sleet or snow,
Me and my Doney Gal are on the go.
We travel down that lonesome trail
Where a man and his horse seldom ever fail.

We whoop at the sun and yell through the hail,
But we drive the poor dogies down the trail;
And we'll laugh at the storms, the sleet and snow,
When we reach the little town of San Antonio.

From *Our Singing Country,* A Second Volume of American Ballads and Folk Songs, collected and compiled by John A. Lomax and Alan Lomax; Ruth Crawford Seeger, music editor, pp. 250–251. Copyright 1941, by John A. Lomax. New York: The Macmillan Company.

Sung by Mrs. Louise Henson, San Antonio, Texas, 1937. Recorded by John A. Lomax. Archive of American Folk Song, Library of Congress, Washington, D. C. Record No. 542.

Text rearranged.—J. A. L.

The Strawberry Roan

Sung with guitar by Pete Cantos, Altadena, California, at Cheyenne, Wyoming, July 25, 1959. Recorded by B. A. Botkin. Transcribed by Ruth Crawford Seeger.

Well, he said that this pony was a good one to buck,
And at throwin' top riders he sure had the luck.
And I asked what he'd pay if I were to stay
Just to ride that old pony around for a day.
Now he said, "It's worth ten," and I said, "I'm your man."
Oh, the pony wasn't livin' that I couldn't fan.
The pony wasn't livin' and he never drew breath
That I could not ride out till he plumb starved to death.

Chorus 1.

Well, bright in the morning and right after chuck,
I went to the corral to see that pony buck.
Now there in the corner, all standin' alone,
Was this pig-eyed old pony, that strawberry roan,
With the little pin ears, at the top they were split,
And a 44 brand was stamped on his left hip.
His legs were all spavined, and he had pigeon toes,
With a crick in his neck and a big Roman nose.

Chorus 1.

When I opened up the gate, then he threw up his head,
And he looked at me cross-eyed, with eyes that were red.
So I pulled down my hat and I shakes out my twine.
And I told that old stranger that ten bucks was mine.
First come the hobbles, and there was a fight
While I threw on my saddle and cinched her down tight.
And I got on the top just a-feelin' so fine,
And I said, "Let him go, boys, and let him unwind."

Chorus 2:

Oh, that strawberry roan!
Oh, that strawberry roan!
He bucks high in the east and comes low in the west.
Just to stay on that saddle I'm a-doin' my best.
Stay on that strawberry roan!
Stay on that strawberry roan!

Say, *that* little old pony, say, he sure unwound,
He never spent much of his time on the ground.
He bucked high in the east and sunfished in the west.
Just to stay on his middle I'm a-doin' my best.

Chorus 3:

Oh, that strawberry roan!
Oh, that strawberry roan!
Oh, that sunfishin' critter's well leavin' alone.
There is not a cowboy from Texas to Nome
That could ride that strawberry roan!
Stay off that strawberry roan!

Billy Venero

Cow Ranch, forty miles away, was a little spot that lay
  In a deep and shady valley of the mighty wilderness.
Half a score of homes were there, and in one a maiden fair
  Held the heart of Billy Venero, Venero's little Bess.

So no wonder he grew pale when he heard the cowboy's tale,
  Of the men that he'd seen murdered day before at Rocky Run.
"Sure as there's a God above, I will save the girl I love.
  By my love for little Bessie, I'll see that something's done."

Not a moment he delayed when his brave resolve was made.
  "Why, man," his comrades told him, when they heard his daring plan.
"You are riding straight to death." But he answered, "Save your breath.
  I may never reach the Cow Ranch, but I'll do the best I can."

As he crossed the alkali all his thoughts flew on ahead
  To the little band at Cow Ranch, thinking not of danger near.
With his quirt's unceasing whirl and the jingle of his spurs,
  Little Chapo bore the cowboy o'er the far away frontier.

Lower and lower sank the sun; he drew rein at Rocky Run.
  "Here those men met death, my Chapo," and he stroked the glossy mane.
"So shall those we go to warn ere the coming of the morn.
  If we fail—God help my Bessie." And he started on again.

From *The Cowboy Sings,* Traditional Songs of the Western Frontier Arranged for General Singing, edited by Kenneth S. Clark, pp. 60–61.

Sharp and clear, a rifle shot woke the echoes of that spot.
  "I am wounded," cried Venero, and he swayed from side to side.
"While there's life there's always hope. Slowly onward I will lope.
  If we fail to reach the Cow Ranch, Bessie Lee shall know I tried."

"I will save her yet," he cried. "Bessie Lee shall know I tried."
  And for her sake then he halted in the shadow of a hill.
From his chapareras he took with weak hands a little book,
  Tore a blank leaf from its pages, saying, "This shall be my will."

From a limb a twig he broke, and he dipped his pen of oak
  In the warm blood that was spurting from a wound above his heart.
"Rouse," he wrote, "before too late. Apache warriors lie in wait.
  Good-by, God bless you, darling." And he felt the cold tears start.

Then he made his message fast, love's first message and its last.
  To the saddle horn he tied it, and his lips were white with pain.
"Take this message, if not me, straight to little Bessie Lee."
  Then he tied himself to the saddle, and he gave his horse the rein.

Just at dusk a horse of brown wet with sweat came panting down
  The little lane at Cow Ranch, stopped in front of Bessie's door.
But the cowboy was asleep, and his slumbers were so deep
  Little Bess could never wake him though she tried for evermore.

You have heard the story told by the young and by the old,
  Away down yonder at the Cow Ranch, the night the Apaches came.
Of that sharp and bloody fight, how the chief fell in the fight,
  And the panic-stricken warriors when they heard Venero's name.

And the heavens and earth between keep a little flower so green,
That little Bess had planted ere they laid her by his side.

Utah Carroll

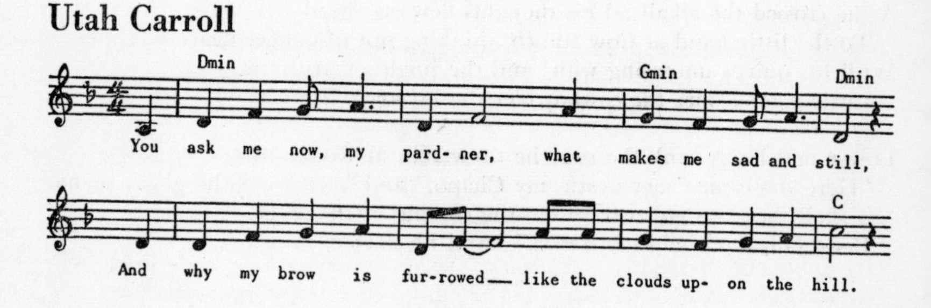

From *Powder River Jack and Kitty Lee's Cowboy Song Book,* with Music; Cowboy Wails and Cattle Trails of the Wild West, compiled by Powder River Jack and Kitty Lee, pp. 50–51. Copyright, 1938, by Powder River Jack Lee, Deer Lodge, Montana. Butte, Montana: Printed and Engraved by the McKee Printing Company.

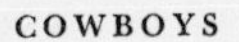

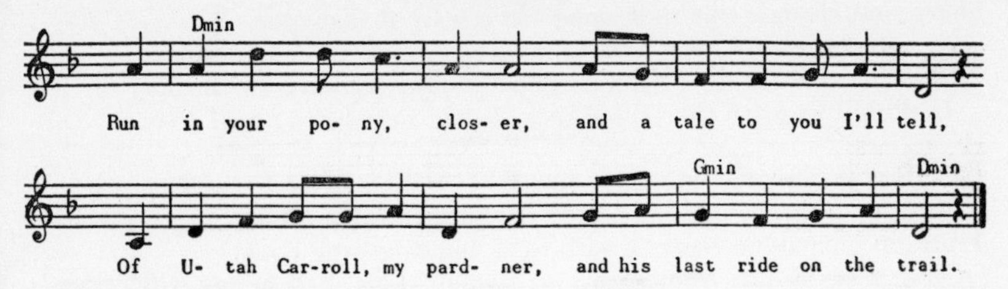

Mid the cactus and the thistle of Mexico's fair land,
Where the cattle roam in thousands, with many a mark and brand,
There's a grave with neither headstone, with neither mark nor name,
There lies my pardner sleeping, in the land from which I came.

We rode the range together, we rode it side by side,
I loved him like a brother. I wept when Utah died.
We were rounding up one morning, and the work was almost done
When on one side the cattle broke and started in to run.

The boss man's little daughter was running down a steer.
The cattle saw her blanket and charged with maddened fear.
Little Varro saw her danger and turned her pony a pace,
And, leaning in the saddle, tied the blanket in its place.

She leaned—and lost her balance, and fell before that tide.
Utah saw her danger. "Lay still," to her he cried.
His only hope was to catch her and raise her at full speed
As he had oft been known to catch the trail rope off his steed.

His pony reached the maiden, with firm and steady bound.
He swung out, leaning sideways to raise her from the ground.
He spurred his pony onward and we thought her safe from harm
As Utah firmly grasped her and held her on his arm.

But the cinches of his saddle made that a fatal ride,
For the back cinch snapped asunder and he fell by Varro's side.
But he picked up the blanket and swung it o'er her head,
And running toward the cattle, "Lay still, little Varro," he said.

Well, Utah turned the stampede and saved his little friend,
Then turned to face the cattle and meet his fatal end,
His six-gun from the pocket and scabbard quickly drew—
He was bound to die defending as all young cowboys do.

His six-shooter flashed like lightning, the reports rang loud and clear.
As the cattle rushed and killed him, he dropped the leading steer.
And when we broke the circle, where Utah's body lay,
All wounded, bruised, and bleeding, his young life ebbed away.

"On some bright future morning," I heard the preacher say,
"I hope we'll all meet Utah at the great roundup some day."
And we wrapped him in the blanket sent by his little friend.
It was the same red blanket that brought him to his end.

The Wyoming Nester

"You've homesteaded all of this country,
Where the slicks and the mavericks did roam;
You've driven me far from my country,
Far from my birthplace and home.

"The cattle are still getting thinner,
And the ranches are shorter on men,
But I've got me a full quart of whisky
And nearly a full quart of gin.

"You have taken up all of the water
And all of the land that's nearby—"
And he took a big drink from his bottle
Of good old '99 rye.

He rode far into the evening,
His limbs at last had grown tired.
He shifted himself in his saddle,
And he slowly hung down his head.

His saddle he used for a pillow;
His blanket he used for a bed,
As he lay himself down for a night's slumber
These words he to himself then said:

"I'm leaving this grand state forever,
This land and the home of my birth.
It fills my heart with sorrow,
But it fills your heart with mirth."

From "More Ballads and Songs of the Frontier Folk," by J. Frank Dobie, *Foller de Drinkin' Gou'd,* Publications of the Texas Folk-Lore Society, No. 7, edited by J. Frank Dobie, pp. 175–176. Copyright, 1928, by the Texas Folk-Lore Society. Austin.

As Jack Willis (the boss) and I nursed the footsore drag cattle down the long, long slopes of the Gila Range, I heard him singing this song, and before we parted he taught it to me. The first stanza may be used as a chorus. Willis, a Texan, who has handled cattle over half a dozen states, says the song is widely known among cowboys, particularly of the Rocky Mountain region.—J. F. D.

The Ogallaly Song

From *We Pointed Them North, Recollections of a Cowpuncher,* by E. C. Abbott ("Teddy Blue") and Helena Huntington Smith, pp. 262–267. Copyright, 1939, by Farrar and Rinehart, Inc. New York and Toronto.

. . . That was not really a song, but was just made up as the trail went north by men singing on night guard, with a verse for every river on the trail. That song starts out on the Nueces River, which is the furthest south of all the Texas rivers that flow into the Rio Grande, and from there it follows the trail clear on up to the Yellowstone. But when I first heard it it only went as far as Ogallaly on the South Platte, which is why I called it the Ogallaly song. I must have heard them singing it when I was on the trail in '79 with the Olive brothers herd, but the first time I remember was one night in '81, on the Cimarron. There were thirteen herds camped on the Cimarron that night and you could count their fires. A Blocker herd was bedded close to ours; it was bright starlight, and John Henry was riding around the herd singing the Ogallaly song. John Henry was the Blocker's top nigger. . . .

. . . Here is a part of the Ogallaly song as it was sung before I came along and put more to it.

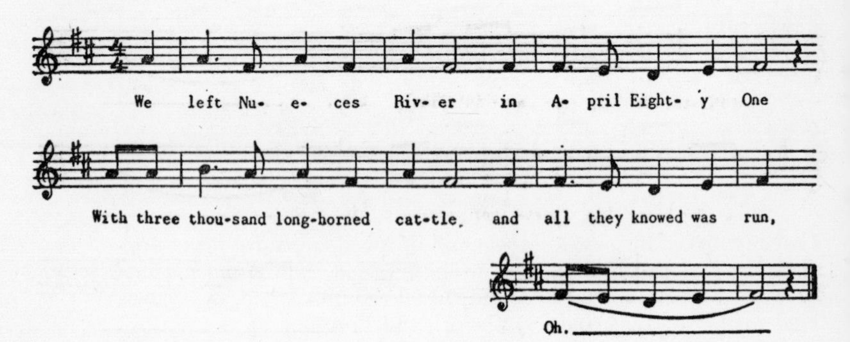

We got them through the brush all right, clear up to San Antone,
We got some grub and headed north, as slick as any bone.

We crossed the Colorado at Austin, a big town,
And headed north until we struck the store of high renown.[1]

The old Red River was on the prod and swum from bank to bank,
We busted him and got across, a good horse for to thank.

The Washita was running full, but we got them all across,
And counted out on the other bank, and never had a loss.

Then we got to old Dodge City on the Arkansaw,
Got a few drinks and some more grub and pulled out north once more.

On the Republican we got another storm,
The boss he says this is the damnedest country I've seen since I was born.

---

[1] Doan's store, on Red River, the "jumping off place" on the Western trail.—E. C. A. and H. H. S.

Away High Up in the Mogliones (High Chin Bob)

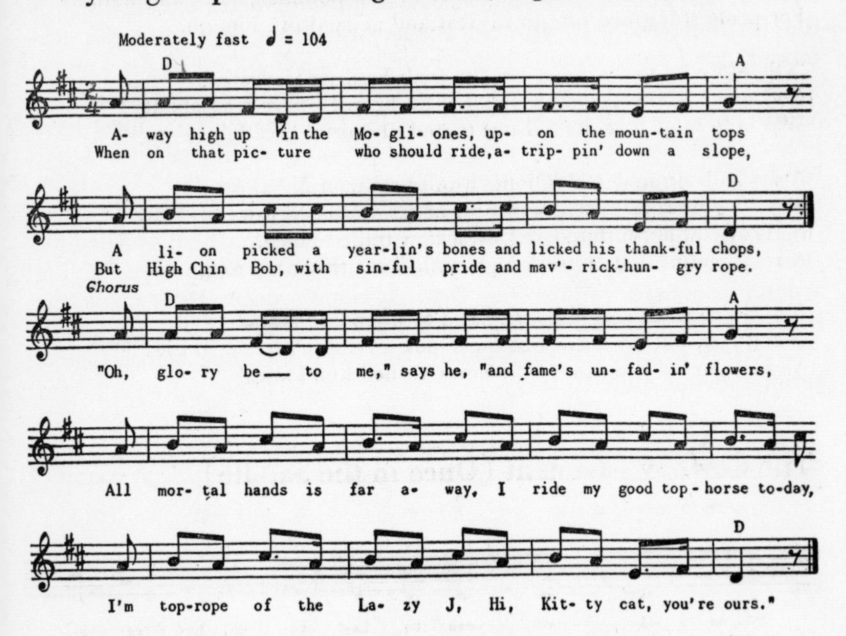

That lion licked his paw so brown and dreamed sweet dreams of veal—
And then that circlin' loop sung down and roped him round his meal.
He yowled quick fury to the world till all the hills yelled back.
That top-horse gave a snort and whirl, and Bob took up the slack.

"Oh, glory be to me," says he. "I've hit the glory trail.
No mortal man as I have read durst loop a ragin' lion's head,
Nor ever horse could drag one dead until we told the tale."

Away up high in the Mogliones, that top-horse done his best
Through whippin' brush and rattlin' stones, and canyon's floor to crest.
Yet ever when Bob turned and hoped the limp remains to find,
A red-eyed lion, belly roped but healthy, loped behind.

"Oh, glory be to me," says he, "this glory trail is rough.
But till the toot of Judgment Morn I'll keep this dally round the horn,
For never any hero born could stoop to holler ' 'Nuff!' "

As sung by Rudolf Bretz, Croton-on-Hudson, New York, August 26, 1951. Learned from Tony Kraber. Recorded by B. A. Botkin. Transcribed by Ruth Crawford Seeger.

For the origin of this song in Badger Clark's "The Glory Trail," see the Friends of the Middle Border's *Middle Border Bulletin*, Vol. VI (September, 1946), No. 1, p. 3. The "Mogliones" or "Mokiones" are the Mogollon Rim in eastern Arizona.

Three suns had rode their circles home beyond the desert's rim,
And turned their star herds loose to roam the ranges high and dim.
But up and down and round and 'cross Bob pounded, weak and wan,
For pride still glued him to his seat and glory drove him on.

"Oh, glory be to me," says he, "he can't be drug to death.
And now I know beyond a doubt them heroes I have read about
Was only fools that stuck it out to end of mortal breath."

Away high up in the Mogliones a prospect man did swear
That moonbeams melted down his bones and hoisted up his hair.
A ribby cow-horse thundered by, a lion trailed along,
A rider, gaunt, but chin on high, yelled out this crazy song:

"Oh, glory be to me," says he, "and to my noble noose!
O stranger, tell my friends below I took a rampin' dream in tow,
And if I never laid him low, I never turned him loose."

The Cowboy's Lament (Once in the Saddle)

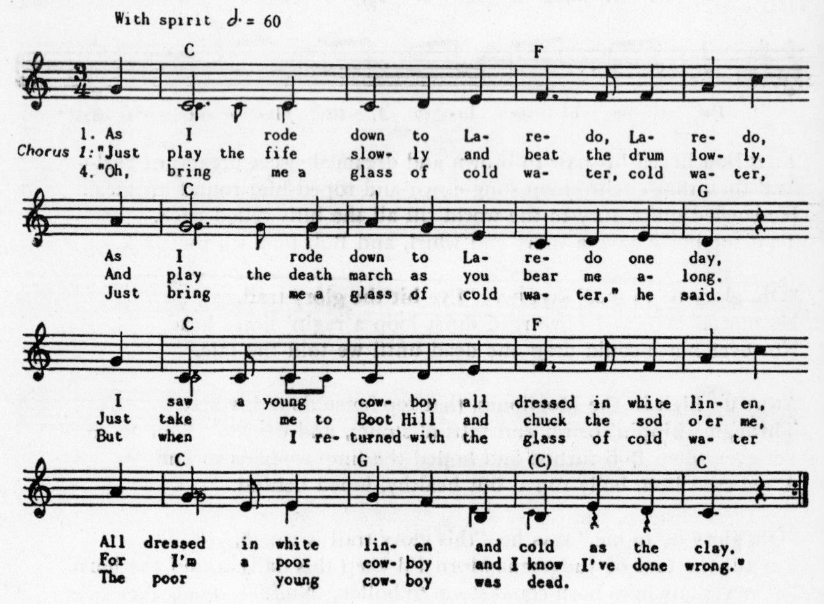

Sung by Verne Bright, Aloha, Oregon, at Portland, Oregon, July 31, 1950. Recorded by B. A. Botkin. Transcribed by Ruth Crawford Seeger.

As learned from my father, Leonard Bright, in Western Kansas and Oklahoma in the 'Seventies.—V. B.

2. "I see by your outfit that you are a cowboy."
   These words he spoke as I went strolling by.
"Come sit here beside me and hear my sad story,
   For I'm shot through the body and know I must die.

3. "Oh, once in the saddle I used to go dashing,
   Oh, once in my saddle I used to go gay.
I first took to drinking and then to card-playing,
   Got shot through the body and now here I lay."

Chorus 2:

Just play the fife slowly and beat the drum lowly,
   And play the death march as you bear him along,
Just take him to Boot Hill and chuck the sod o'er him,
   For he's a young cowboy and he knows he's done wrong.

VI. LOGGERS AND WORK STIFFS

Jim Porter's Shanty Song

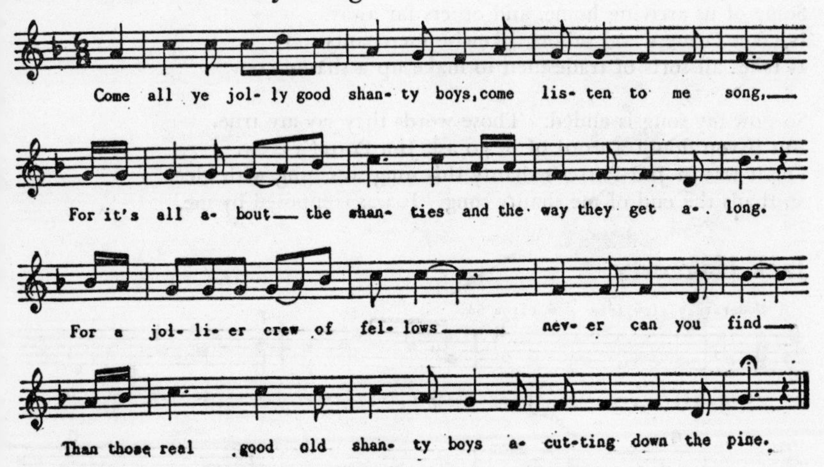

The choppers and the sawers they lay the timbers low,
The skidders and the swampers they holler to and fro.
Next comes the sassy loaders before the break of day.
"Come, load up your teams, me boys!" And to the woods they sway.

From *Ballads and Songs of the Shanty-Boy,* collected and edited by Franz Rickaby, pp. 69–71. Copyright, 1926, by Harvard University Press. Cambridge. Sung by Mrs. J. S. Murphy, Minto, North Dakota.

For the broken ice is floating, and our business is to try.
Three hundred able-bodied men are wanted on the drive.
With cant-hooks and with jam-pikes these noble men do go
And risk their sweet lives on some running stream, you know.

On a cold and frosty morning they shiver with the cold.
The ice upon their jam-pikes, which they can scarcely hold.
The axe and saw does loudly sing unto the sun goes down.
Hurrah, my boys! For the day is spent. For the shanty we are bound.

Arriving at the shanty with cold and with wet feet,
Pull off your boots, me boys, for supper you must eat.
Then supper being ready, to supper we must go,
For it's not the style of one of us to lose our hash, you know.

* * * * * *

At four o'clock in the morning our foreman he will say,
"Come, roll out, ye teamsters! It's just the break of day."
The teamsters they get up, and their things they cannot find.
They'll blame it on the swampers, and they'll curse them till they're blind.

But as springtime rolls on, how happy we will be,
Some of us arriving home, and others far away.
It takes farmers and sailors, likewise merchants too—
It takes all sorts of tradesmen to make up a shanty crew.

So now my song is ended. Those words they say are true.
But if you doubt a word of it, go ask Jim Porter's crew.
For it was in Jim Porter's shanty this song was sung with glee.
So that's the end of me shanty song. It was composed by me.

Jack Haggerty

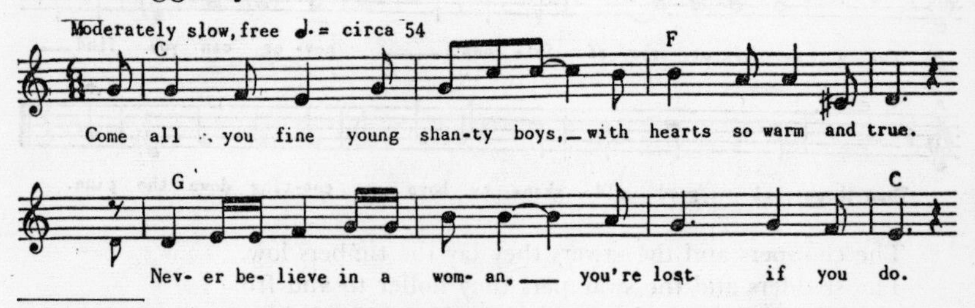

Sung by James Stevens, Seattle, Washington, August 4, 1950. Recorded by B. A. Botkin. Transcribed by Ruth Crawford Seeger.

This ballad that I am going to render in the way of the old-time lumberjack in the shanty camps was heard by me many years ago when I was working in the pine camps east of the mountains in Oregon and also in Northern California.

The ballad, "Jack Haggerty," originally was a very long one, and it was a great favorite of the old-time shanty camps. Stewart White makes reference to it in one of his novels. He liked it, his daddy liked it, and the jacks that worked for his daddy evidently were singing it very often. Just why, some people may wonder hearing it now. The version that I have to give is rather condensed, but it's mainly the old lines, and it's true in spirit.—J. S.

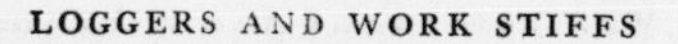

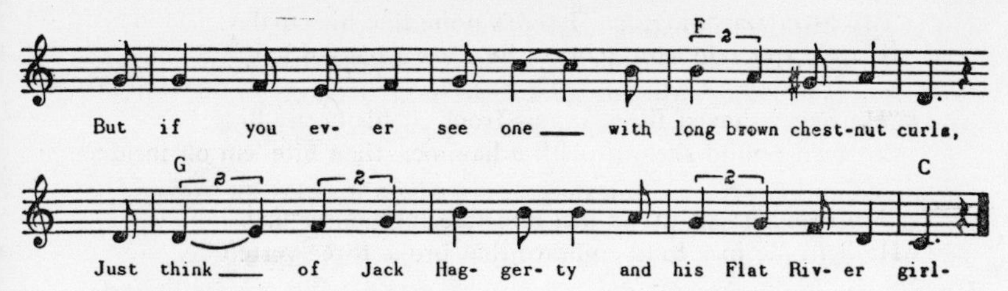

Her form was like the dove's, so handsome and so neat.
Her long brown chestnut curls hung to her tiny feet.
She was a blacksmith's daughter from the Flat River side,
And tenderly she promised that she would be my bride.

On her mother, Jane Tucker, I lay all the blame.
She turned my love agin me and blackened my fair name.
Now I'm a pinewoods rover, who'll never have a home.
Take warning, all you gallant jacks, leave the fickle sex alone.

Take warning, all you shanty boys, with hearts so warm and true,
And never believe in a woman, you're lost if you do.
But if you ever see one with long brown chestnut curls,
Just think of Jack Haggerty and his Flat River girl.

The Frozen Logger

"I see you are a logger and not a common bum,
For no one but a logger stirs his coffee with his thumb.

Ibid.

[In 1929] I was associated with Stewart Holbrook and H. L. Davis [on a] radio program of Paul Bunyan sketches. Holbrook supplied the ideas, I provided the lies, and Davis and I together composed the ballads for the program, trying to hold true to the creative spirit of the old-time bunk-shanty bards. One that is now being included in the stock of American folk songs by Burl Ives, Alan Lomax, and other authorities, is "The Frozen Logger."—James Stevens, "Bunk-Shanty Ballads and Tales," *Oregon Historical Quarterly*, Vol. L (December, 1949), No. 4, p. 241.

"My lover was a logger. There's none like him to-day.
If you'd sprinkle whisky on it, he'd eat a bale of hay.

"He never shaved the whiskers from off his horny hide;
But he'd pound them in with a hammer, then bite 'em off inside.

"My logger came to see me, one freezing winter day.
He held me in a fond embrace that broke three vertebrae.

"He kissed me when we parted—so hard he broke my jaw,
And I could not speak to tell him he'd forgot his mackinaw.

"I watched my logger lover going through the snow,
A-sa'ntering gaily homeward at forty-eight below.

"The weather tried to freeze him. It tried its level best.
At a hundred degrees below zero, he buttoned up his vest.

"It froze clean down to China. It froze to the stars above.
At one thousand degrees below zero, it froze my logger love.

"They tried in vain to thaw him. Then, if you'll believe me, sir,
They made him into ax blades to chop the Douglas fir.

"That's how I lost my lover. And in this cafe I come
And here I wait till some one stirs his coffee with his thumb.

"And then I tell my story of my love they could not thaw,
Who kissed me when we parted—so hard he broke my jaw."

Jackhammer Blues

Written and sung by Woody Guthrie, Bonneville Power Administration, Portland, Oregon, May, 1941. Recorded by Bonneville Power Administration. Transcribed by Ruth Crawford Seeger.

With another version of this, "Jackhammer John," in Woody Guthrie's *American Folksong* (New York, 1947), p. 26, the author notes: "From an old folk song 'Brown's Ferry Blues.'"

Well, I was born in Portland town.
I've built every port from Alaska down.
Lord, Lord, Lord, I got them jackhammer blues.
Built your bridges, dug your mines,
I've been in jail about a thousand times.
Hey, hey, hey, I got them jackhammer blues.

Jackhammer John, a-where've you been?
I've been out chasin' them gals again.
Lord, Lord, Lord, I got them jackhammer blues.
Jackhammer man, from a jackhammer town,
I can hammer on my hammer till the sun goes down.
Lord, I thought you knowed I got them jackhammer blues.

Well, I hammered on the Boulder, hammered on the Butte,
Columbia River, on a five-mile chute.
Lord, Lord, Lord, I got them jackhammer blues.
Workin' on the Bonneville, I hammered all night,
Tryin' to bring to those people some electric light.
Lord, Lord, well, I got them jackhammer blues.

Hammered on the Bonneville and the Coulee too,
Always broke when the job is through.
I thought you knowed I got them jackhammer blues.
Hammered on the river from sun to sun,
Fifteen million salmon run.
Lord, Lord, well, I guess I got them jackhammer blues.

Hammered in the rain, I hammered in the dust,
I hammered in the best, and I hammered in the worst,
Lord, Lord, Lord, I got them jackhammer blues.
Got a jackhammer gal, she's sweet as pie,
Gonna hammer on my hammer till the day I die,
I thought you knowed I got them jackhammer blues.

Roll On, Columbia

Now other great rivers add power to you,
Yakima, Snake, and the Klickitat too,
Sandy, Willamette, and Hood River too,
It's roll on, Columbia, roll on.

Tom Jefferson's vision would not let him rest.
An empire he saw, the Pacific Northwest.
Sent Lewis and Clark, and they did the rest.
It's roll on, Columbia, roll on.

At Bonneville Dam there are ships in the locks.
The waters have risen and covered the rocks.
Shiploads of plenty will steam past the docks.
So roll on, Columbia, roll on.

And far up the river is Grand Coulee Dam,
The mightiest thing ever built by a man,
To run the great factories and water the land,
It's roll on, Columbia, roll on.

Written by Woody Guthrie, Bonneville Power Administration, Portland, Oregon, May, 1941. Sung by Michael Loring, Portland, Oregon, August 1, 1950. Recorded by B. A. Botkin. Transcribed by Ruth Crawford Seeger.

The Dying Hobo

Moderately fast 𝅗𝅥 = 100

F Bb
1.At an old sta- tion_ wa- ter tank, one cold De- cem- ber
Chorus: "I'm a- leav- ing,"said the_ ho- bo, "for a land that's fair and

F
day, In- side an emp- ty box car, a_
bright, Where the weath-er it's warm e- nough to

C F
dy- ing ho- bo_ lay, His com-rades stood be- side him,with an
sleep out-doors all_ night. The hand- outs grows on_ bush- es, the

Bb F
ach- ing, bowed- down head, Pa- tient- ee- lie
men they wear no socks, The whis- ky comes a-

C F
list'- ning to what the dy- ing ho- bo said.
flow- ing through the clifts- es of the rocks."

F Bb
2."It's tell my girl in Chi- ca- go, the first face of
3." I see that en- gine_ com- ing, I'll catch her on the

F
view, That I'm on board on a east-bound train, and a
fly, It's hard to say good- by, old boy, but it

C F
com- ing right on through- Tell her not to
is- n't hard to die;" His head flew_ back, his

Bb F
wait for_ me, don't let her poor heart break. Tell her I'm
eyes were_ closed; he nev- er spoke a- gain. His

DC for Chorus
C F
com- ing to the coun- try where the ho- boes nev- er wake."
com- rades left him dy- ing, to catch that east-bound train.

Sung by Luvicie Beasley, from the Cherokee Nation, Oklahoma, at Somerton, Arizona, December 8, 1948. Recorded by Sam Eskin. Transcribed by Ruth Crawford Seeger.

"The first face of view" is evidently a corruption of "the fairest face I've viewed" or "whose face no more I'll view."

VII. BAD MEN

The Texas Rangers

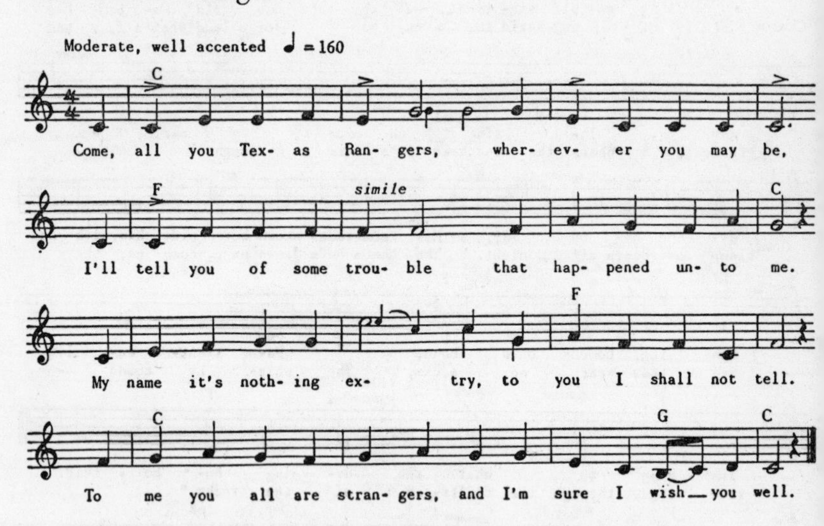

When at the age of seventeen, I begun to roam,
I marched from San Antonio unto the Rio Grande.
Our captain he informed us, perhaps he thought it right:
"Before you reach your station," he said, "boys, you'll have to fight."

I saw the Injuns coming, I heard them give their yell.
My feelings at that moment, no human tongue can tell.
I saw their glittering arrows, all around my head they hailed.
My heart sank low within, my courage almost failed.

They fought for nine long hours until the strife was o'er.
The like of dead and wounded I've never seen before.
As bold as Texas Rangers as ever reached the West
Lay there beneath their comrades. Sweet peace may be their rest!

Sung by Lloyd Fowler, Beaumont, Texas, March 12, 1948. Recorded by Sam Eskin. Transcribed by Ruth Crawford Seeger.

This song has been recorded by Sam Eskin in *Songs of All Times,* Cook Laboratories, Stamford, Connecticut, 1951, with slight variations in the text.

I thought of my old mother and what she had to say:
"To you they all are strangers, and with me you'd better stay."
I told her she was old and childish, and the best she did not know.
My mind was bent on rambling, and I was bound to go.

Now if you have a mother, likewise a sister too,
And maybe so a sweetheart, to weep and mourn for you,
If this be your condition, and you have a mind to roam,
I'll tell you by experience—you'd better stay at home.

Mustang Gray

From "Mustang Gray: Fact, Tradition, and Song," by J. Frank Dobie, *Tone the Bell Easy,* Publications of the Texas Folklore Society No. X, 1932, edited by J. Frank Dobie, pp. 122–123. Copyright, 1932, by the Texas Folklore Society. Austin.

. . . In 1884 . . . some verses of it were published by A. J. Sowell in his *Rangers and Pioneers of Texas.* To me it has a sweep, an economy, an energy that distinguish it from nearly all other frontier ballads. No tune, so far as I know, has ever been printed. The one here given was supplied to me by a veteran Texan and trail-driver named James Hatch, of San Antonio.

It is easy to find claimants to the authorship of pioneer folk songs as well as of other kinds of folk songs. I cannot prove absolutely, but I am convinced that James T. Lytle, who was a Texas Ranger during the Mexican War, who later became a lawyer, and who is the undisputed author of the once very popular "Texas Ranger's Song," beginning,

Mount! mount! and away o'er the green prairies wide,

and very likely the author of "The Maid of Monterrey," also composed "Mustang Gray."—J. F. D.

He ne'er would sleep within a tent, no comforts would he know;
But like a brave old Tex-i-an a-ranging he would go.
When Texas was invaded by a mighty tyrant foe,
He mounted his noble warhorse and a-ranging he did go.

Once he was taken prisoner, bound in chains upon the way.
He wore the yoke of bondage, through the streets of Monterrey.
A señorita loved him and followed by his side.
She opened the gates and gave to him her father's steed to ride.

God bless the señorita, the belle of Monterrey.
She opened wide the prison door and let him ride away.
And when this veteran's life was spent, it was his last command
To bury him on Texas soil on the banks of the Rio Grande.

And there the lonely traveler, when passing by his grave,
Will shed a farewell tear o'er the bravest of the brave.
Now he'll go no more a-ranging, the savage to affright.
He's heard his last war-whoop and fought his last fight.

Cole Younger

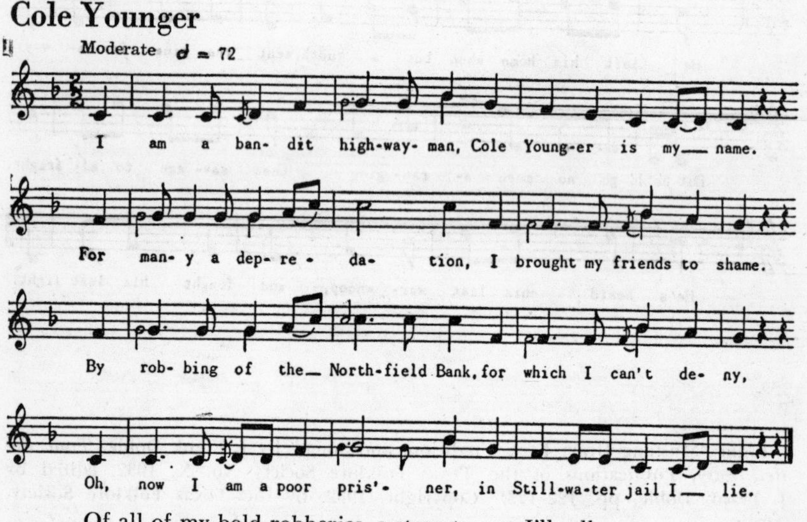

Of all of my bold robberies, a story to you I'll tell.
A Californy miner, upon him I fell.
I robbed him of his money, boys, and bid him go his way.
For which I will be sorry of until my dying day.

"Cole, now we'll buy fast horses," as Brother Bob did say.
"Cole, now we'll buy fast horses, on which to ride away.
We'll strive for our father's revenge, and seek to win the prize,
We'll fight those anti-guerrillas until the day we die."

Sung by Ben Rice, Springfield, Missouri, December, 1936. Recorded by Sidney Robertson. Archive of American Folk Song, Library of Congress, Washington, D.C. Record No. 3212 B1. Transcribed by Ruth Crawford Seeger.

We started out for Texas, that good old Lone Star state,
And on Nebraska's prairies the James boys we did meet.
With our guns, knives and pistols, we all sat down to play,
With a bottle of good old whisky, boys, to pass the time away.

The Union Pacific railways, on them we next surprised,
The fears of our bloody hands brought tears into their eyes.
The engineerman, fireman killed, conductor escaped his life.
Oh, now their bodies are lying beneath Nebraska's burning skies.

We saddled up our horses and northward we did go,
To the God-forsaken country, called Minnea-sot-e-o,
I had my eye on the Caddo bank, when Brother Bob did say:
"Cole, if you undertake this job, you'll always curse the day."

We then all took our stations, and to the bank did go,
'Twas as I crossed the counter I hit my fatal blow.
"It's hand us over your money, boys, and make no delay,
For we are the noted Younger boys, then spare no time to pray."

The Portland County Jail

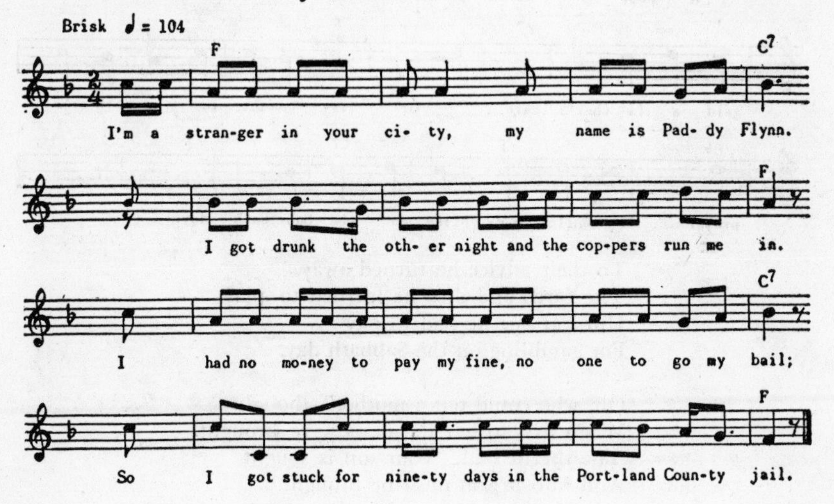

Sung by John Gross, Portland, Oregon, July 31, 1950. Recorded by B. A. Botkin. Transcribed by Ruth Crawford Seeger.

This version of "The Portland County Jail" was learned from Albert Richard Wetjen of Portland many years ago.—J. G.

Oh, the only friend that I had left was Happy Sailor Jack.
He told me all the lies he knew and all the safes he'd cracked.
He'd cracked them in Seattle, he'd robbed the Western Mail.
'Twould freeze the blood of an honest man in the Portland County jail.

Oh, such a bunch of devils no one ever saw—
Robbers, thieves, and highwaymen, breakers of the law.
They sang a song the whole night long, the curses fell like hail.
I'll bless the day that takes me away from the Portland County jail.

Oh, the finest friend I ever had was Officer McGurk.
He said I was a lazy bum, a no-good and a shirk.
One Saturday night when I got tight, he trun me in the can.
And now you see he's made of me an honest workingman.

Gambling on the Sabbath Day

Moderately fast 𝅗𝅥 = 100

F C F
A poor un - worth- y son who___ dared To dis- re -

C7 F
gard a fa- ther's care Or lis- ten___ to a moth-er's

To their advice he turned away.
The cards and dice he learned to play,
Until at last he had to pay
For gambling on the Sabbath day.

Oh, who could tell a mother's thought
When first to her the news were brought.
The sheriff said, "Your son is sought,
And into prison must be brought."

His weeping mother standing by
To hear them tell the reason why
So long in prison he must lie
And on the scaffold he must die.

Sung by Lannis Sutton, Doxie, Oklahoma, at Palo Alto, California, January 14, 1951. Recorded by Sam Eskin. Transcribed by Ruth Crawford Seeger.

His father, sixty years of age,
The best of counsel did engage,
To see if something could be done
To save their disobedient son.

But nothing could their counsel do.
Their tes-ti-mony was too true,
For he the deadly weapon drew
That pierced his comrade's body through.

Oh, hear him on the scaffold tell
His weeping mother farewell:
"My soul now fears a mortal hell,
And soon with the demons I must dwell.

"Oh, darling sister, do not weep,
For soon with the demons I shall sleep.
For on the scaffold I must pay
For gambling on the Sabbath day."

The sheriff cut the slender cord.
His soul went out to meet his Lord.
The doctor said, "This wretch is dead."
The spirit from his body fled.

His weeping mother cried aloud:
"Oh, God save this gazing crowd
That none will ever have to pay
For gambling on the Sabbath day."

VIII. DISASTER SONGS

The Santa Barbara Earthquake

But on one fatal morning the sun rose in the sky.
The people all were praying, "Oh, Lord, please hear our cry."

When daylight found the people with sad and aching heart,
They were searching for their families that the earthquake tore apart.

But some of them were sleeping beneath the fallen stone.
Their lips were closed forever, never more to cry and mourn.

Sung by Vester Whitworth, Farm Security Administration Camp, Arvin, California, 1940. Recorded by Charles Todd and Robert Sonkin. Archive of American Folk Song, Library of Congress, Washington, D. C. Record No. 4098 B1. Transcribed by Ruth Crawford Seeger.

It's just another warning from God up in the sky
To tell all you good people that He still remains on high.

We do not know the moment when He shall call us home,
But we should all be ready before our time has come.

The Sherman Cyclone

I[1]

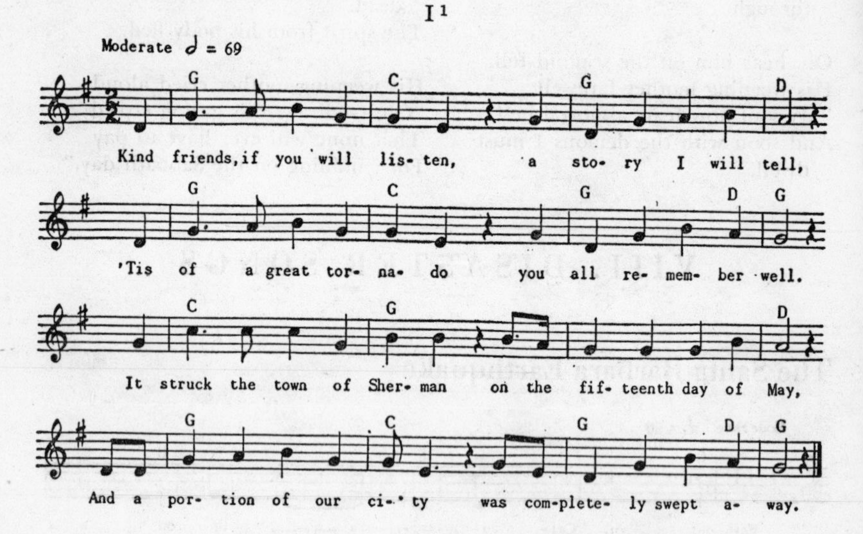

We saw the storm approaching, the clouds grew deathly black,
And through our little city it left an awful track.
The people fled in terror, their lives were swept away.
Now beneath the sod they're sleeping till the final judgment day.

II[2]

The people gay and happy in their cozy little rooms,
They little thought so shortly they'd be forced to meet their doom.
But, alas, their days were ended, their lives were snatched away—
Now beneath the sod they're sleeping to the final judgment day.

[1] Sung by Mrs. Hallie May Preece, Austin, Texas, 1937. Recorded by John A. Lomax. Archive of American Folk Song, Library of Congress, Washington, D. C. Record No. 926 A2. Transcribed by Ruth Crawford Seeger.

[2] From *Texas Folk Songs*, by William A. Owens, Musical Arrangements by Willa Mae Kelly Koehn, pp. 130–131. Publications of the Texas Folklore Society, No. XXIII, Mody C. Boatright, Editor. Austin and Dallas: The Texas Folklore Society and University Press in Dallas.

We saw the storm approaching, the clouds looked deathly black,
And through our little city it made its dreadful track.
We saw the lightning streaming, we heard the thunder roll.
It was but the shortest moment, and the story soon was told.

We heard the crash of timbers, of buildings tumbling down,
Distressing screams of victims—oh, what a dreadful sound.
It would melt the hardest hearted to hear them loudly cry,
"Oh, God, have mercy on me. Is this my time to die?"

Some sought for homes of refuge, their lives to rescue there,
While others were dashed to cinders, and whirled into despair.
The rain it fell in torrents, the storm was quickly o'er.
The like of dead and wounded was never here before.

The loss of life and ruins are hard to estimate.
The happiest of families there had to separate.
God helped the broken-hearted that yet are left behind,
To make their preparation, for soon may be their time.

Soon the storm was over, the people gathered round;
And there the dead and dying lay prostrate on the ground.
To render their assistance so quickly they begin
To remove them from their struggle, soon all were taken in.

By aid of kind physicians we dressed their ghastly wounds.
Our town has never witnessed such a horrid afternoon.
The good people of our city, you may safely be assured,
Will nurse the sad afflicted till health may be restored.

The Great Dust Storm

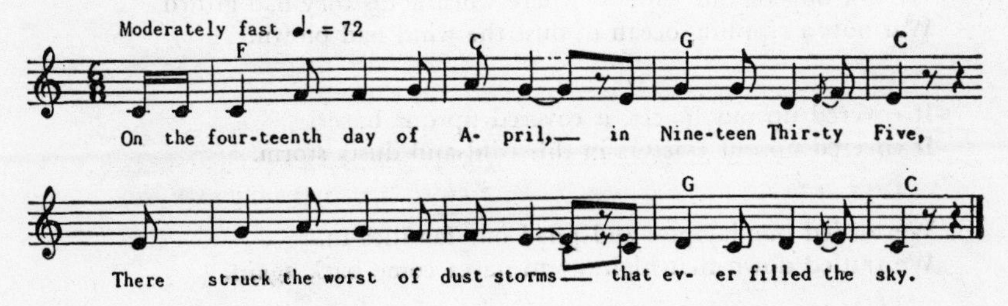

You could see that dust storm comin', the cloud was death-like black,
And through our mighty nation it left a dreadful track.

From *Dust Bowl Ballads,* Volume II, written and sung by Woody Guthrie, Victor Album P-28, Record No. 26622 A. Camden, New Jersey: RCA Victor Division, RCA Manufacturing Company, Inc. Transcribed by Ruth Crawford Seeger.

From Oklahoma City to the Arizona line,
The corner of Nebrasky to the lazy Rio Grande,

It fell across our city like a curtain of black rolled down.
We thought it was our judgment, we thought it was our doom.

The radio reported. We listened with alarm
To the wild and windy actions of this great mysterious storm.

From Albuquerq' and Clovis and all New Mexico,
They said it was the blackest that they had ever saw.

From old Dodge City, Kansas, the dust had rung their knell,
And a few more comrades sleeping on top of old Boot Hill.

From Denver, Colorado, they said it blew so strong.
They thought that they could hold out but they didn't know how long.

Our relatives were huddled into their oil-boom shacks,
And the children they was cryin' as it whistled through the cracks,

And the family it was crowded into their little room—
They thought the world had ended and they thought it was their doom.

The storm took place at sundown. It lasted through the night.
When we looked out next morning, we saw a terrible sight.

We saw outside our window where wheatfields they had grown
Was now a rippling ocean of dust the wind had blown.

It covered up our fences, it covered up our barns.
It covered up our tractors in this wild and dusty storm.

We loaded our jalopies and piled our families in.
We rattled down that highway to never come back again.

IX. "WHEN THEY GO TO COURTING"

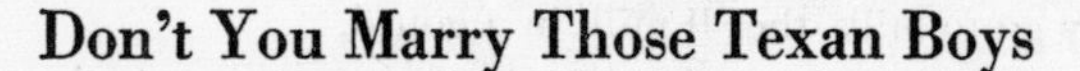

Don't You Marry Those Texan Boys

They'll lead you on blackjack hill,
They're so much against your will.
They'll leave you there for to starve on the place,
For this is the way with the Texas race,
For this is the way with the Texas race.

When they want to ride they'll go to the gang,
There they'll catch them a wild mustang.
They'll lead him up with a great long rope,
And on their journey they will lope.

When they get to their journey's end,
It's "Can't you loan me a rope, my friend?
For I am riding a wild mustang,
And I want to take him on the plain."

When they go to courting, what do you reckon they wear?
Their old leather coats all pitched with tar,
Their old straw hats, no rim, no crown,
Their old cotton socks that they wore the winter around.

Sung by Mary Newcomb, Washington, D. C. Recorded by Charles Seeger. Transcribed by Ruth Crawford Seeger.

When they come in you'll get them a chair.
The first thing they say is, "Daddy shot a bear."
The next thing they say when they sit down:
"Madam, your johnny-cake's baking too brown."

When they go to milk, they'll milk in a gourd,
Sit in the corner and cover it with a board.
Some gets little and some gets more,
For this is the way that the Texans run.

Up in the corner about as high as your head,
There they'll build you a scaffold for a bed,
You go to bed, but there ain't no use.
Your feet stick out for a chicken roost.

All Her Answers to Me Were No

"Madam, I have gold and silver,
  Madam, I have a house and land,
Madam, I have a world of pleasure.
  You can have it at your command."

"What care I for your gold and silver?
  What care I for your house and land?
What care I for your world of pleasure?
  All I want is a handsome man."

"Madam, you seem for to boast on beauty.
  Beauty is a thing that'll fade away.
Gather a red rose in the morning,
  Then by noon it'll fade away.

Sung by Lannis Sutton, Doxie, Oklahoma, at Palo Alto, California, January 14, 1951. Recorded by Sam Eskin. Transcribed by Ruth Crawford Seeger.

"The ripest apple soon gets rotten,
The warmest [glove?] soon gets cold.
Young man's promise soon forgotten,
Pray, little miss, don't be so bold.

"The Arkansas boys they ain't the fellers,
Don't know how to court the girls,
Turn their backs and hide their faces.
Pray, little miss, this ain't the way.

"The Texas boys they are the fellers,
They know how to court the girls,
Hug them a little and kiss them plenty.
Pray, little miss, this is the way.

"Madam, I have been to London.
Madam, I have been to France.
Many of a time my mammy's whipped me,
Oh, Lord, honey, how she made me dance!"

The Gypsy Davy

Sung with guitar by Woody Guthrie, Okemah, Oklahoma, at Washington, D. C., 1940. Recorded by Alan Lomax. Transcribed by Ruth Crawford Seeger.

From *Folk Music of the United States,* from records in the Archive of American Folk Song, Album 1, "Anglo-American Ballads," edited by Alan Lomax, Record No. AAFS 2 A. Washington, D. C.: Archive of American Folk Song, Library of Congress. 1942.

"Go saddle for me my buckskin horse
And a hundred dollar saddle.
Point out to me their wagon tracks,
And after them I'll travel,
After them I'll ride."

Well, he had not rode till the midnight moon
Till he saw the campfire gleamin',
And he heard the gypsy's big guitar
And the voice of the lady singin'
The song of the Gypsy Dave.

"Well, have you forsaken your house and home?
Have you forsaken your baby?
Have you forsaken your husband dear
To go with the Gypsy Davy,
And sing with the Gypsy Dave?"

"Yes, I've forsaken my house and home
To go with the Gypsy Davy,
And I'll forsake my husband dear
But not my blue-eyed baby,
Not my blue-eyed babe."

She laughed to leave her husband dear,
And her butlers and her ladies,
But the tears come a-trickelin' down her cheeks,
When she thought about her blue-eyed baby,
And thought of her blue-eyed babe.

"Take off, take off your buckskin gloves,
Made of Spanish leather,
And give to me your lily-white hand,
'N' we'll go back home together,
Go back home again."

"No, I won't take off my buckskin gloves,
Made of Spanish leather.
I'll go my way from day to day,
And sing with the Gypsy Davy,
'N' sing with the Gypsy Dave."

The original ballad comes out of seventeenth century England where it was called "Johnny Fa" or "The Raggle Taggle Gypsies." In America in the early part of the nineteenth century it was sufficiently well known to be parodied on the stage. Woody Guthrie, our best contemporary ballad composer, has edited this version to fit his Oklahoma upbringing. The "milk white steed" of the earlier ballad has become the "buckskin horse"; the "lily white gloves" have turned "buckskin," too. Then Woody has put in a stanza of his own, number 3, which makes the story over into a Western ballad, "big guitar" and all. The melody has been completely Americanized, and the guitar accompaniment is a recent development.—A. L.

¡Ay! Vienen Los Yankees (Here Come the Yankees)

Ah! here come the Yankees.
See! they're coming by.
Now let's all go easy
On formality.

Y las señoritas
Que hablan el inglés,
Los Yankees dicen, "Kiss me!"
Y ellas dicen, "Yes."

See how the young ladies
Rush English to learn.
"Kiss me," say the Yankees.
The ladies answer, "Yes."

X. "THEY DANCED AND THEY PLAYED"

Five Times Five Is Twenty-Five

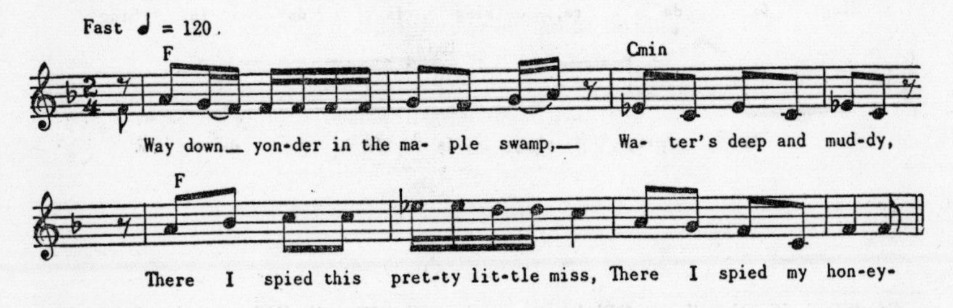

From *Spanish-American Folk-Songs,* as sung and played by Mrs. Francisca de la Guerra Dibblee, Miss Carlota Manuela Corella, Miss E. A. Seeger, Mrs. Geoffrey Hamer, Mrs. Theodore Barnes, Mrs. Karbe, Señorita Luz Gonzales Dosal, Mrs. Dane Coolidge, Señora Ramirez, Señora R. Fuentes, Mrs. L. Buhler, Miss I. Buhler, Señora Lobo, Mr. Walter C. Riotte, Mr. W. Findlay, Pedro Diaz, Maximilian Salinas, Father O'Sullivan, collected by Eleanor Hague, p. 109. *Memoirs of the American Folk-Lore Society,* Vol. X, 1917. Lancaster, Pa., and New York: Published by the American Folklore Society. G. E. Stechert & Co., New York, Agents.

From Southern California. Variant of tune of *Las Margaritas* as sung in Mexico. Words date from 1848 or about that time.—E. H.

Sung by Lannis Sutton, Doxie, Oklahoma, at Palo Alto, California, January 14, 1951. Recorded by Sam Eskin. Transcribed by Ruth Crawford Seeger.

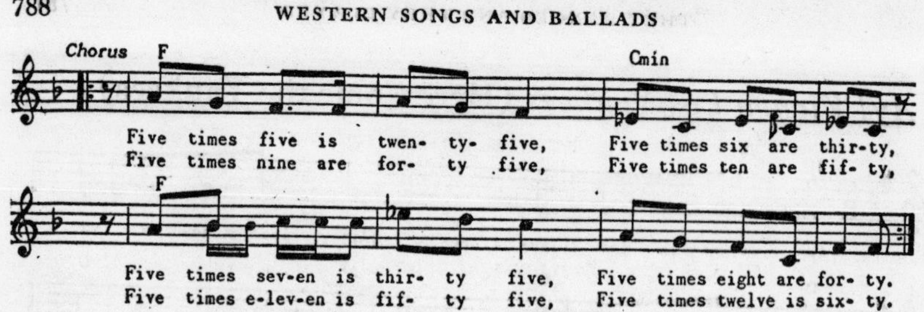

Raccoon's out a-choppin' wood,
  Possum he's a-haulin',
My old dog a-sittin' on a log,
  Splittin' his throat a-squallin'.

I'll take my little miss by her hand,
  Lead her like she's a pigeon.
Make her dance one more reel,
  Scatter her religion.

Little Fight in Mexico

Cf. "Twistification," an Oklahoma version of "Weevily Wheat," B. A. Botkin, *The American Play-Party Song* (Lincoln, 1937), pp. 349–350.

From *The American Play-Party Song,* with a Collection of Oklahoma Texts and Tunes, by B. A. Botkin, pp. 232–233. Copyright, 1937, by B. A. Botkin. University Studies of the University of Nebraska, Vol. XXXVII, Nos. 1–4. Lincoln, Nebraska.

Sung by O. B. Campbell, Medford, Grant County, Oklahoma, 1932. Tune from Professor Kenneth C. Kaufman, University of Oklahoma, Norman, from Eastern Custer County, Oklahoma.

Directions: Players in couples with odd boy. Promenade with partners. When "come to the place where the blood was shed," girls continue forward and boys step back so the partners are changed. If singer (odd boy) finds girl he wants for his partner, he takes her and song continues.—Cora Frances Starritt, Ada, Pontotoc County, Oklahoma.

Come to the place where the blood was shed,
The girls turned back and the boys went ahead.

When those girls and boys do meet,
They do hug and kiss so sweet.

You had better get up, you are mighty in the way.
Choose you a partner and come along and play.

La Viudita de Santa Isabel
(The Little Widow of Saint Isabel)

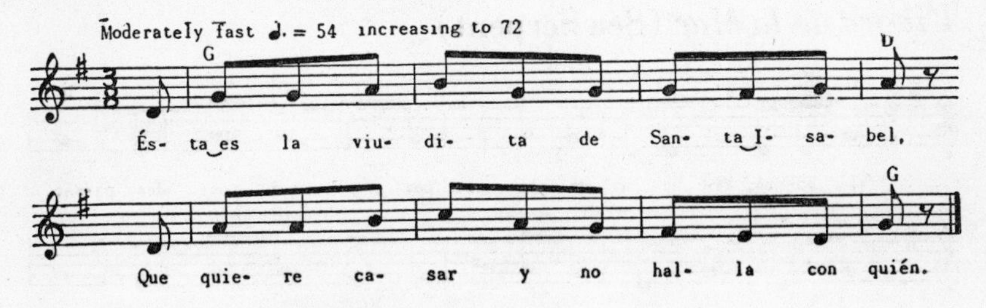

This is the poor widow
Of Saint Isabel.
She wishes to marry,
With whom she can't tell.

Sung by Josephine Gonzales, Aurora Gonzales, Pearl Menchaco, Adela Flores, and Belia Trujillo, San Antonio, Texas, 1934. Recorded by John A. and Alan Lomax.

From *Folk Music of the United States,* from records in the Archive of American Folk Song, Album V, Bahaman Songs, French Ballads and Dance Tunes, Spanish Religious Songs and Game Songs, edited by Alan Lomax, Record No. AAFS 25 B4. The Library of Congress, Division of Music, Recording Laboratory, Washington, D. C. Transcribed by Ruth Crawford Seeger.

Directions: Any number can play this game. First choose a girl for the little widow and a boy for the priest's servant. These two stand opposite each other, while the others form a line and sing the first stanzas of the song. The servant steps forward and sings the last two stanzas, and while he is singing the others pretend to be running, nearly falling, and giving their hearts to the little widow. They pretend to drink coffee and then tea. When the servant sings the last lines of the last stanza, they join hands and dance around the little widow and the priest's servant.—*The Spanish-American Song and Game Book* (New York, 1942), p. 41.

El mozo del cura
le mandó un papel
le mandó a decir
que secase con él.

The priest's servant wrote her,
It pleased her quite well.
She sent him a letter
From Saint Isabel.

Corriendo, corriendo,
me dí un tropezón;
por darle la mano,
le di el corazón.

Oh, I ran so swiftly
I 'most fell apart.
I held out my hand,
But I gave her my heart.

Me gusta la leche,
me gusta el café,
pero más me gustan
los ojos de usted.

Oh, I like my coffee
And I like my tea,
But you know I give all
My true love to thee.

Víbora de la Mar (Sea Serpent)

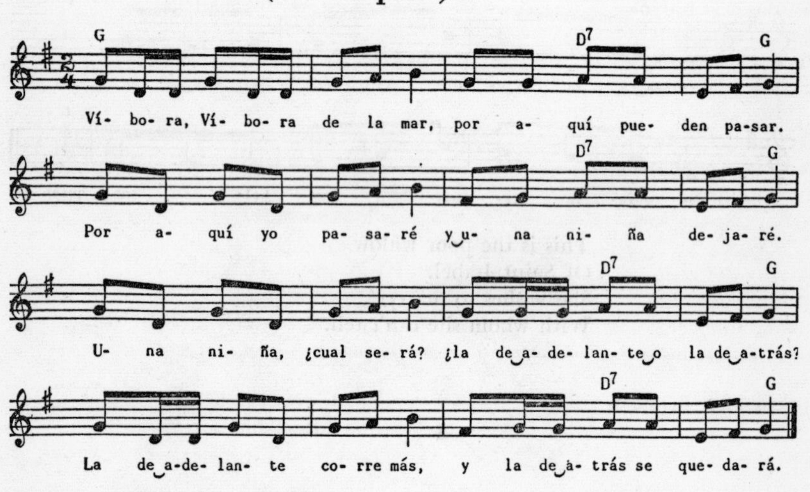

Serpent, serpent from the sea,
You must follow, follow me.
Under this archway we now must
glide
And we'll leave a girl inside.

One little girl—who can she be?
One ahead or back of me?
That one ahead—how she runs away,
So the last one has to stay.

From *The Spanish-American Song and Game Book,* Illustrated, compiled by Workers of the Writers' Program, Music Program, and Art Program of the Work Projects Administration in the State of New Mexico, pp. 18–19. Sponsored by the University of New Mexico and State Superintendent of Public Instruction of New Mexico. Copyright, 1942, by the Coronado Cuarto Centennial Commission of New Mexico. New York: A. S. Barnes and Company.

Directions: The two tallest ones in the group are chosen to be the arch of the bridge. They decide, without letting the others hear them, what they will ask them to choose—blue or red, bread or cake, or anything they please. Then they join hands and raise them to make an arch, and the others form a line and pass

Señora Santa Ana

Señora Santa Ana,
Why is the child crying?

He cries for an apple,
The apple he has lost. } 2

Vamos a la huerta
cortaremos dos;
una para el niño
y otra para Dios.

Let's go to the orchard.
We will pick two apples,
One for the little child,
The other one for God.

Arriba del cielo
hay una ventana
por donde se asoma
Señora Santa Ana.

Away up in heaven,
There is a window.
Señora Santa Ana
Is looking out of it.

Arriba del cielo
hay un bujerito
por donde se asoma
el Niño chiquito.

Away up in heaven,
There is a peephole,
Through which the Holy Child
Is peeping, peeping out.

La Virgen lavaba,
San José tendía,
el Niño lloraba
San Juan lo mecía.

The Virgin was washing,
Saint Joseph hung up clothes.
The Christ Child was crying,
Saint John was rocking him.

---

under, singing as they go. At the last words of the song the two who form the arch capture the one who happens to be passing under it. The one who is caught is asked, "Which would you rather have, something red or something blue?" If the ones forming the arch have agreed that red is the right answer, and if the one who is caught says, "Red," he returns to the line and the game continues. If his guess is wrong, he is told to hop on one foot and nod to each one in the line, or something like that. Then the game begins again until another one is caught.

Sung by girls of Blalock School, near Brownsville, Texas, 1939. Recorded by John A. and Ruby T. Lomax. Record No. 2613 B1.

From *14 Traditional Spanish Songs from Texas,* transcribed by Gustavo Duran, from recordings made in Texas, 1934–39, by John A., Ruby T., and Alan Lomax for the Archive of American Folk Song in the Music Division of the Library of Congress, p. 9. Washington, D. C.: Music Division. Pan American Union, Music Series, No. 4. 1942.

English by Quisqueya Díaz.

Fod

Well, I fell down upon the ground,
I shut both eyes and looked all around.

I set upon a stump to take my rest.
It looked like a woodchuck on his nest.

The woodchuck grinned a banjo song,
And up stepped a skunk with the britches on.

The woodchuck and skunk got into a fight.
The fume was so strong it put out the light.

They danced and they played till the chimney begin to rust.
It was hard to tell which smelt the wust.

Sung with guitar and mandolin by Henry King and family, Visalia, California, 1941. Recorded by Charles Todd and Robert Sonkin. Transcribed by Ruth Crawford Seeger.

From *Folk Music of the United States,* from records in the Archive of American Folk Song, Album II, "Anglo-American Shanties, Lyric Songs, Dance Tunes, and Spirituals," edited by Alan Lomax, Record No. AAFS 8 B1. Washington, D. C. Archive of American Folk Song, Library of Congress. 1942.

The King family came to California from Arkansas as migratory farm workers. They brought their instruments and their songs with them, and, as they have traveled from farm to farm, following the crops and entertaining their fellow "Okies," they have become a legend of fun and good cheer for their people.—A. L.

Index of Authors,[1] Titles, and First Lines of Songs

[1] Including names of singers and other informants and persons who recorded them.

Index of Subjects, Names, and Places